AF725176

## Individual Income Tax Formula

| | |
|---|---|
| Income (broadly conceived) | $XX,XXX |
| Less: Exclusions | (X,XXX) |
| Gross income | $XX,XXX |
| Less: Deductions for adjusted gross income | (X,XXX) |
| Adjusted gross income | $XX,XXX |
| Less: Deductions from adjusted gross income— | |
| The greater of— | |
| The total itemized deductions or standard deduction | (X,XXX) |
| Taxable income | $XX,XXX |

## Basic Standard Deduction Amounts

| Filing Status | Standard Deduction Amount 2021 |
|---|---|
| Single | $12,550 |
| Married, filing jointly | 25,100 |
| Surviving spouse | 25,100 |
| Head of household | 18,800 |
| Married, filing separately | 12,550 |

## Amount of Each Additional Standard Deduction for Age and Blindness

| Filing Status | Standard Deduction Amount 2021 |
|---|---|
| Single | $1,700 |
| Married, filing jointly | 1,350 |
| Surviving spouse | 1,350 |
| Head of household | 1,700 |
| Married, filing separately | 1,350 |

# ProConnect™ Tax

intuit. Accountants

## Work like a pro.

Get the #1 cloud-based professional tax software for free.[1, 2]

Go beyond the basics and connect with the modern tools you need to work efficiently.

- **Work with confidence.**
  Get returns done right the first time with access to all the forms you need, backed by industry-leading calculations and diagnostics.
- **Work smarter.**
  Save time with logical data-entry worksheets instead of traditional forms-based methods. Plus, get quick training resources so it's easy to stay up to speed.
- **Work from anywhere.**
  It's all online, so there's nothing to install or maintain. And whether you're on your mobile phone or laptop, PC or Mac – you're always good to go.

Visit TaxEducation.Intuit.com to get started.

*Only one sign-up per student. No special code required. If you have trouble accessing or using the software, reach out to us at taxeducation_support@intuit.com anytime for help.*

[1] Based on Intuit internal data of the number of paid users of ProConnect Tax for Tax Year 2019 compared to publicly available statements from competitors for the same time period.

[2] If you sign-up for the free version of ProConnect Tax for students and educators, you will not have access to certain features, including functionality such as Electronic Filing Services and Intuit Link.

 ISBN: 9780357141519

ISBN-13: 978-0-357-51111-4 • ISBN-10: 0-357-51111-5

2022 EDITION

# Concepts in Federal Taxation

Kevin E. Murphy
Oklahoma State University

Mark Higgins
Saint Louis University

Randall K. Skalberg
University of Minnesota Duluth

CENGAGE

Australia • Brazil • Canada • Mexico • Singapore • United Kingdom • United States

CENGAGE

***Concepts in Federal Taxation*, 2022 Edition**

**Kevin E. Murphy, Mark Higgins, Randall K. Skalberg**

Senior Vice President, Higher Ed Product, Content, and Market Development: Erin Joyner

Product Director: Joe Sabatino

Associate Product Manager: Jonathan Gross

Senior Content Manager: Tricia Hempel

Senior Digital Project Manager: Tim Richison

Marketing Manager: Chris Walz

Production Service: MPS Limited

Designer: Chris Doughman

Text/Cover Designer: Ke Design

Cover Image: marcnorman/iStock/Getty Images

Intellectual Property
Analyst: Ashley Maynard
Project Manager: Kellianne Besse



For product information and technology assistance, contact us at **Cengage Customer & Sales Support, 1-800-354-9706 or support.cengage.com**.

For permission to use material from this text or product, submit all requests online at **www.cengage.com/permissions**.

Tax forms reproduced courtesy of the Internal Revenue Service (www.irs.gov).

Library of Congress Control Number: 2021901063

Package
Student Edition + Tax Prep Software + RIA Checkpoint ISBN: 9780357515785

Package:
Loose-leaf Edition + Tax Prep Software + RIA Checkpoint ISBN: 9780357515808

**Cengage**
200 Pier 4 Boulevard
Boston, MA 02210
USA

Cengage is a leading provider of customized learning solutions with employees residing in nearly 40 different countries and sales in more than 125 countries around the world. Find your local representative at **www.cengage.com**.

To learn more about Cengage platforms and services, register or access your online learning solution, or purchase materials for your course, visit **www.cengage.com.**

Printed in Mexico
Print Number: 01 Print Year: 2021

# BRIEF CONTENTS

# CONTENTS

# Part 5

## Income Tax Entities 13-1

# Part 6

# PREFACE

Many students view the introductory tax course as an impossible task of learning the Internal Revenue Code. The Code, which is the statutory basis of the federal income tax system, is complex and can be intimidating to students and tax professionals. However, we feel strongly that tax education can be interesting and, with the straightforward yet complete coverage in *Concepts in Federal Taxation*, offer a refreshing, thought-provoking textbook. Designed specifically for the introductory tax course, this book is rigorous enough for students specializing in taxation, but it will not intimidate those who plan to pursue other areas of accounting and business.

## FUNDAMENTAL STRUCTURE

### Conceptual Approach

There are two ways to look at the rules that govern federal taxation: the technical approach and the conceptual approach. The traditional "technical approach" looks at the reams of tax authority as thousands of specific and distinct code sections, regulations, exceptions, and qualifications. This approach treats income tax in such great depth that the first-time tax student has difficulty understanding the myriad rules, exceptions to those general rules, and exceptions to the exceptions. As a result, students tend to view the first tax course as a long string of unrelated topics that they must memorize to pass the course.

The "conceptual approach" presents taxation as a small number of unifying concepts—principles that apply in the application of specific tax rules and authorities. These concepts define taxation. An analogy can be made to mathematical operations: by understanding how multiplication works and memorizing the nine times tables, people learn to multiply any number by any other number. One can multiply 23 by 25 correctly without having memorized a times table that includes that pair of numbers. Likewise, knowing the underlying concepts that shape tax law allows students to understand a wide range of tax law without committing every line of the Internal Revenue Code to memory.

### Organization

Instead of focusing on the individual aspects of taxation, this textbook emphasizes transactions that are common to all tax entities. This allows the text to focus more on the overall scheme of taxation (What is income? What is a deduction? and so on) with individual tax return preparation a secondary issue. As a result, Chapter 1 introduces the individual tax formula and briefly discusses the "for" versus "from" adjusted gross income distinction that is unique to individuals, but the mechanics of the individual tax calculation are not discussed in detail until Chapter 8. Furthermore, itemized deductions are not accorded the traditional in-depth treatment. Again, the focus is on the more common itemized deductions, and elaborate technical detail is omitted for the more unusual items.

The text is organized into the following six parts:

- **Part I: Conceptual Foundations of the Tax Law**
  - **Chapter 1** provides an overview of the tax system, briefly discusses other types of taxes, outlines the general income tax calculation, discusses the nature of tax planning, and introduces ethical considerations of tax practice.
  - **Chapter 2** develops the conceptual framework and uses it to explain the operation of the tax system in general. Each subsequent chapter begins with a brief review of the concepts discussed in this chapter.

- **Part II: Gross Income**
  - **Chapter 3** classifies various sources of income and explains the common problems encountered within each income classification. Its overview of property transactions differentiates the taxation of capital gains and losses from other sources of income. The chapter concludes with an introduction to the accounting methods that affect the recognition of income.
  - **Chapter 4** classifies allowable exclusions from income according to the purpose of the exclusion and discusses the problems commonly encountered with exclusions in each category.
- **Part III: Deductions**
  - **Chapter 5** provides an overview of the general criteria necessary to obtain a tax deduction and concludes with a discussion of the effect of a taxpayer's accounting method on the timing of deductions.
  - **Chapter 6** addresses specific business expense deductions that are subject to special rules and limitations.
  - **Chapter 7** covers deductions for losses. The chapter distinguishes annual losses from transaction losses, and discusses the limitations on the deductibility of the two types of losses. This discussion includes the treatment of net operating losses, the at-risk rules, passive losses, capital losses, and casualty losses.
  - **Chapter 8** discusses the unique features of the individual income tax calculation, itemized deductions, and tax credits available to individuals.
- **Part IV: Property Transactions**
  - **Chapter 9** introduces the property investment cycle and discusses common acquisition problems.
  - **Chapter 10** provides the allowable deductions for property expenditures. This includes the MACRS depreciation system, depletion deductions, and allowable amortization deductions.
  - **Chapter 11** discusses dispositions of property and explains the classification and calculation of the gain or loss from a disposition of property.
  - **Chapter 12** covers the common nonrecognition situations related to property dispositions, including exchanges, involuntary conversions, and sales of a principal residence.
- **Part V: Income Tax Entities**
  - **Chapter 13** discusses the nontax characteristics that should be considered in choosing a business entity and the incidence of taxation of each entity and presents the comparative differences at formation of a business.
  - **Chapter 14** compares the differences in tax treatments during the operation of an entity and concludes with an overview of the effect of distributions on an entity and its owners.
  - **Chapter 15** finishes the life-cycle discussion with coverage of deferred compensation, tax credits, the alternative minimum tax, and international tax aspects of entities.
- **Part VI: Tax Research**
  - **Chapter 16** provides the mechanics of tax research. Problems that require the student to find particular types of authorities using print, CD-ROM, and Internet tax services, and research cases for all chapters in the text are provided in this chapter. Instructors wishing to introduce students to tax research may want to cover this chapter early in the course.

## HALLMARK FEATURES

The most important objective at the introductory level is to gain a conceptual view of income tax law and then relate those concepts to basic aspects of everyday economic life. Through continual reinforcement, the concepts quickly become the backbone of understanding. The 2022 edition of *Concepts in Federal Taxation* has a lineup of outstanding features that will help students improve their skills and understanding while learning the concepts.

## Learning Objectives

Each chapter opens with a set of learning objectives to guide students through mastering the chapter's material. Learning objectives are shown in the margins near the relevant chapter content and are also identified in the end of chapter materials to reinforce these key learning objectives and help students learn more efficiently.

## Concept Review

To solidify and expound upon the conceptual foundation presented in Chapter 2, the subsequent chapters begin with a review of the general concepts, accounting concepts, income concepts, and deduction concepts that have been covered in previous chapters. Page references for each concept allow students to easily locate material and refresh their memory.

### concept review

GENERAL CONCEPTS

**Ability to pay** A tax should be based on the amount that the taxpayer can afford to pay, relative to other taxpayers. pg. 2-2

**Administrative convenience** Those items for which the cost of compliance would exceed the revenue generated are not taxed. pg. 2-3

**Arm's-length transaction** A transaction in which all parties have bargained in good faith and for their individual benefit, not for the benefit of the transaction group. pg. 2-4

**Related party** Family members, corporations that are owned by family members, and certain other relationships between entities in which the power to control the substance of a transaction is evidenced through majority ownership. pg. 2-4

ACCOUNTING CONCEPTS

**Annual accounting period** All entities must report the results of their operations on an annual basis (the tax year). Each tax year stands on its own, apart from other tax years. pg. 2-9

**Assignment of income** The tax entity that owns the income produced is responsible for the tax on the income, regardless of which entity actually receives the income. pg. 2-8

**Conduit entity** An entity for which the tax attributes flow through to its owners for tax purposes. pg. 2-6

**Substance over form** Transactions are to be taxed according to their true intention rather than some form that may have been contrived. pg. 2-11

**Tax benefit rule** Any deduction taken in a prior year that is recovered in a subsequent year is income in the year of recovery, to the extent that a tax benefit was received from the deduction. pg. 2-10

INCOME CONCEPTS

**All-inclusive income** All income received is taxable unless a specific provision in the tax law either excludes the income from taxation or defers its recognition to a future tax year. pg. 2-12

**Capital recovery** No income is realized until the taxpayer receives more than the amount invested to produce the income. The amount invested in an asset represents the maximum amount recoverable. pg. 2-13

**Claim of right** A realization occurs whenever an amount is received without any restriction as to its disposition. pg. 2-14

**Constructive receipt** Income is deemed to be received when it is made unconditionally available to the taxpayer. pg. 2-15

**Legislative grace** Any tax relief provided is the result of a specific act of Congress that must be strictly applied and interpreted. All income received is taxable unless a specific provision in the tax law excludes the income from taxation. Deductions must be approached with the philosophy that nothing is deductible unless a provision in the tax law allows the deduction. pg. 2-12

**Realization** No income or loss is recognized until it has been realized. A realization involves a change in the form and/or substance of a taxpayer's property rights that results from an arm's-length transaction. pg. 2-14

**Wherewithal to pay** Income is recognized in the period in which the taxpayer has the means to pay the tax on the income. pg. 2-16

## Examples

Continually rated as this textbook's biggest strength, each chapter includes numerous student-friendly examples. The examples present familiar situations in a question-and-discussion format that offers detailed explanations.

**Example 24** Jorge receives 200 shares of MNO Corporation common stock as a gift from his grandfather. At the date of the gift, the shares have a fair market value of $20,000. During the current year, Jorge receives dividends totaling $2,000 on the stock. Recall that the tax law excludes the value of a gift from the gross income of the recipient. What are the tax effects for Jorge of the gift from his grandfather?

**Discussion: The receipt of the stock as a gift from the grandfather is specifically excluded from Jorge's income by the tax law. However, the exclusion applies only to the value of the gift received and does not exclude from tax any subsequent income Jorge receives on the gift property.[12] Therefore, Jorge is taxed on the $2,000 in dividends received on the stock.**

## Concept Check

Concept Checks appear throughout each chapter to keep students on track by reinforcing the critical tax concepts illustrated.

**concept check**

The *capital recovery concept* allows the recovery of capital invested in an asset. The amount invested in an asset is the maximum amount recoverable under this concept. *Adjusted basis* represents a taxpayer's unrecovered investment in an asset. Therefore, the maximum loss that can be recognized from a casualty or theft is the asset's adjusted basis. An *arm's-length* transaction is one in which all parties to the transaction have bargained in good faith and for their individual benefit, not for the benefit of the transaction group. *Related party* transactions are usually subject to scrutiny by the IRS because the tax law assumes that related parties do not transact at arm's length. The substance-over-form doctrine taxes transactions according to their true intent rather than some (possibly) contrived form of the transaction. This concept prevents a taxpayer from recognizing a loss on the sale of stock if it is replaced within 30 days of (either before or after) the date of sale.

# END-OF-CHAPTER MATERIALS

Ensure that students master chapter concepts with a wide array of end-of-chapter assignments designed to do everything from testing basic chapter comprehension to applying concepts and procedures to complex tax situations.

## Chapter Summary

Students can verify their understanding of the key concepts illustrated in the chapter by reviewing the succinct Chapter Summary, which appears at the end of every chapter.

## Key Terms

Part of the difficulty of this course can be traced to its specialized vocabulary. As learning the terminology serves as a basis for learning how to apply the concepts, each chapter includes a list of key terms with page references.

## Primary Tax Sources

Rather than interrupting the text with extensive footnoting of specific subsections of the Internal Revenue Code, the primary tax law sources appear at the end of each chapter with explanatory notations. This approach uses more references to Treasury regulations, revenue rulings, and court cases than may appear in other introductory tax textbooks.

## Discussion Questions and Problems

Many of the approximately 1,300 end-of-chapter problems do not call for mathematical solutions. Rather, they require an explanation of the appropriate treatment, based on the concepts. These problems are valuable learning tools, which encourage students to apply the concepts and formulate a solution.

Traditional problems that can be solved by reference to the examples in the chapter are also provided, and they address every topic in the chapter. In most cases, two or more problems exist for each topic. A number of problems exist for each learning objective. Problems that require client communication are designated with a Communication Skills icon.

Communication Skills

## Issue Identification Problems

These problems ask students to identify the tax issues inherent in a factual situation and determine the possible tax treatments.

## Technology Applications

A complete end-of-chapter section containing problems on Research Skills and Spreadsheet Skills enhance students' familiarity with the technology tools needed for problem solving.

Tax Simulation

- **Tax Simulations** in Chapters 3–12 teach database searching and writing skills that are important requirements for understanding tax concepts. These cases can be solved using only the Code and Regulations, giving students hands-on practice with the research and writing skills required to complete the tax simulations featured on the CPA Examination.

Research Skills

- **Research Skills Exercises** require students to research relevant tax topics.
- **RIA Research Exercises** require students to use the Checkpoint® tax research database to complete the assignment.

the answer company™ THOMSON REUTERS®

Tax Form Skills

- **Tax Form Problems** containing expanded client information allow students to complete tax forms obtained from the IRS website without additional instruction. These problems may be also worked using tax preparation software such as Intuit ProConnect Tax Software.

Spreadsheet Skills

- **Spreadsheet Skills Problems** are designed to make students aware that spreadsheets are useful tax planning tools.

## Comprehensive Problems

These problems cover several issues discussed within a chapter, requiring students to develop an advanced understanding by combining and applying multiple concepts.

## Integrative Problems

These problems require students to fuse together material learned in previous chapters, combining it with information found within the current chapter. This approach allows students to complete a complex tax return in two stages, spreading the work out over the semester rather than preparing it for a single due date.

## Tax Return Problem (Appendix A)

This problem is presented in three phases, which correspond to the organization of the text. Each phase presents some information in actual tax documents that a taxpayer might receive from common third-party sources. This approach makes it easier to become familiar with tax reporting and tax compliance forms as the material is covered, rather than in one burst at the end of the semester. The problem can be worked manually or with tax preparation software such as ProConnect Tax Software.

## Discussion Cases

These cases stimulate thinking about issues raised in the chapter. All case material can be used to emphasize communication in the tax curriculum.

## Tax Planning Cases

These cases require students to use the concepts in the chapter to devise an optimal tax plan for the facts given.

## Ethics Discussion Cases

These cases provide ethical dilemmas related to the chapter material that must be resolved according to the Statements on Standards for Tax Services of the American Institute of Certified Public Accountants (AICPA). A link to the complete AICPA statements on standards is provided.

# RECENT REVISIONS

## Fine-Tuned End of Chapter Material

All end of chapter content has been thoroughly updated with respect to tax law changes. This material has also been carefully revised to enhance the readability of the question parts.

## Updates Reflect the Latest Tax Laws

This annual edition reflects the latest tax laws and changes to tax codes and regulations to keep your course current—including the new tax rate schedules and amounts.

# INSTRUCTOR RESOURCES

*Concepts in Federal Taxation* has been adopted by a wide range of schools and by instructors who have unique philosophies and approaches in their courses. Our supplemental materials have been developed to have a positive impact on all aspects of the course.

## Instructor Companion Website

www.cengage.com/login

Easily download the instructor resources you need from the password-protected, instructor-only website. If you are a new instructor, you will need to register with Cengage by creating a new instructor account. Instructors will be directed to the Cengage dashboard after logging in. Here, instructors may add any Cengage book to the "bookshelf," including the 2022 edition of *Concepts in Federal Taxation* simply by searching by the author, title, or ISBN (9780357515785). After adding the book to your "bookshelf," you will be able to access the links to the Instructor Companion website and accompanying resources.

## Instructor's Manual

Simplify class preparation with the wealth of teaching tips and advanced assignment ideas provided in the Instructor's Manual. A concise overview and detailed lecture outline (including references to relevant problems in the textbook) are provided for each chapter, along with invaluable teaching ideas—including those for incorporating writing assignments, class/group exercises, and research projects. This rich array of resources is further enhanced with the inclusion of useful planning documents on designing a course, grading and developing team activities, and sample syllabi that outline the incorporation of technology, communication, and group assignments in the tax curriculum. Available on the instructor website.

## Solutions Manual

Carefully verified to ensure accuracy, the Solutions Manual reproduces all end-of-chapter materials from the textbook and provides in-depth discussions of the answers to help instructors efficiently grade assignments. Charts that detail all problems by topic have been included to simplify planning and assignment selection. In addition, problems requiring key skills like critical thinking and communication, as well as comprehensive and integrative problems, have been labeled. Available on the instructor website.

## Test Bank

The Test Bank helps instructors efficiently assess your students' understanding with problems and questions that reflect the textbook's conceptual approach. The Test Bank offers a variety of question types—including true/false, matching, multiple choice, short answer, and comprehensive problems. Test Bank questions are also identified by level of difficulty for easy selection and have been tagged to Accredited Business Program and AICPA standards. This is particularly valuable during the accreditation process or when your school wants to standardize assessment. Available through Cognero, a full-featured, online assessment system.

## Cengage Testing Powered by Cognero

This is a flexible, online system that allows you to: author, edit, and manage test bank content, create multiple test versions in an instant, and deliver tests from your LMS, your classroom or wherever you want.

# STUDENT RESOURCES

## Checkpoint Student Edition from Thomson Reuters®

Students are introduced to tax research with access to Checkpoint®, the leading online tax research database. Its intuitive, Web-based design makes it fast and simple to navigate and its comprehensive collection of primary tax law, cases, and rulings is unmatched. Each new copy of this textbook has been automatically bundled with access to Checkpoint® for six months.

## ProConnect Tax™

Each new copy of this textbook has been automatically bundled with ProConnect Tax™ access.

## Contact the Murphy-Higgins Team with Suggestions and Comments

We encourage all adopters to participate in the continuing development of this book by providing comments and suggestions for improving the textbook and supplementary materials. Please address these comments to:

Randall K. Skalberg at the University of Minnesota Duluth: rskalber@d.umn.edu
Mark Higgins at Saint Louis University: markhiggins@slu.edu

You may also contact a member of the taxation team:

Associate Product Manager Jonathan Gross at jonathan.gross@cengage.com
Marketing Manager Chris Walz at christopher.walz@cengage.com

Thank you again for your support.

Kevin E. Murphy
Mark Higgins
Randall K. Skalberg

# INTRODUCTION

## WHY STUDY FEDERAL INCOME TAXATION?

If you are beginning the study of the federal income tax law and plan to become a tax attorney or accountant, why you are taking this course is obvious. But if you want to become a management accountant or auditor, why should you study federal income taxation? Don't accountants rely on tax specialists to do tax research and prepare tax returns? Better yet, why should a business executive, an attorney, a physician, or a farmer take a tax course? Each of them also can, and often does, have professional tax advisers to take care of his or her tax problems. The heart of the answer lies in the fact that most economic transactions have an income tax effect.

The income tax law influences personal decisions of individuals. The decision to buy a house instead of renting one may depend on the after-tax cost of the alternatives. Although the payment of rent reimburses the owner of the dwelling for mortgage interest and property tax, a tenant cannot deduct the cost of renting a home. However, a homeowner can save income tax by deducting home mortgage interest and property tax and perhaps reduce the after-tax cost of buying relative to renting.

**Example 1** Zola lives in an apartment she rents for $700 per month. She is considering purchasing a house, which will require an initial cash outlay of $5,000 and monthly payments of $850. Although none of the $5,000 initial down payment is deductible, $800 of the monthly payment is deductible as interest expense. Assuming that Zola earns 6% on her investments and is in the 24% tax rate bracket, what is the after-tax monthly cost of purchasing the house?

**Discussion: Assuming that Zola itemizes her deductions, the $800 interest payment will be deductible. Her taxable income will be reduced by $800 per month, resulting in tax savings of $192 ($800 × 24%). This leaves her with a net after-tax house payment of $608. However, she will lose interest income on the $5,000 investment of $25 per month [($5,000 × 6%) = $300 ÷ 12 = $25]. She will not have to pay any tax on the lost interest, resulting in an after-tax interest loss of $19 [$25 − ($25 × 24%)]. Her net after-tax monthly cost of purchasing the house is $627 ($608 + $19). Because this is less than her rent of $700, Zola will come out ahead by $73 per month by purchasing the house.**

**This analysis of Zola's investment in a house considers only the tax aspects of the investment. Clearly, other factors influence the decision to purchase a house—potential appreciation in value, the intangible value of owning your own home, and so on. The point is that the tax consequences are one objective factor to consider when making various decisions, but they are rarely the sole or controlling factor.**

Other personal decisions are often influenced by tax savings. For example, a taxpayer may decide to accelerate or defer charitable donations or elective medical treatment to claim the deductions in the year that results in the most significant tax savings. Even child-care decisions may be based on the availability of tax savings in the form of a child-care tax credit.

**Example 2** On January 1 of each year, Steve gives $2,000 to his church. For 2020, his income is more than double its usual amount because of a one-time bonus he receives from his employer. In a typical year, Steve is in the 24% tax rate bracket. Because of his increased income in 2020, Steve estimates that he will be in the 32% tax rate bracket, but his income will return to normal in 2021. What steps might Steve take to reduce his tax bill?

**Discussion: Instead of waiting until January 1, 2021, to make his regular $2,000 donation, which will reduce his tax by $480 ($2,000 × 24%), Steve could pay the contribution in 2020. By taking the deduction in 2020 when he is in the 32% tax**

**rate bracket, Steve saves $640 ($2,000 × 32%) in tax. By accelerating his $2,000 charitable contribution by a few days, he saves an extra $160 in tax ($640 − $480).**

From these examples, you can see that income taxes can and do have an influence on routine decisions. However, the cost of the income tax is more than just the outlay for the tax liability. A knowledge of the income tax laws enables taxpayers to make decisions that can reduce these other costs. By being familiar with the tax laws, an individual can enter into transactions that will provide the best tax result for both the taxpayer and the taxpayer's family. By minimizing the income tax burden, taxpayers conserve wealth that can be put to other uses. Last, taxpayers are responsible for reporting their correct taxable income to the government. Knowing the tax laws protects against audits by the IRS that could result in additional tax owed and penalties for improper reporting of the tax liability.

## Significance of Tax Costs

Keeping records and filling out forms to comply with the tax law can consume a substantial amount of time. Table I-1 presents the IRS's estimates of the time involved in record keeping, learning about tax law, preparing a return, and assembling the various commonly filed tax forms. As you can see, the IRS estimates that completing and filing the basic tax return form (Form 1040) requires more than 22 hours on average. When you consider that many taxpayers file a multitude of forms and schedules to detail their tax affairs, the time involved in complying with the tax law is quite substantial.

Tax compliance may also cost a taxpayer money. Taxpayers must weigh the cost of the time and investment needed to prepare their own tax returns, the out-of-pocket cost of hiring a tax preparer to prepare the return, and the risk of additional time and monetary costs for any errors. Thus, taxpayers need to choose whether to save money and spend the time to prepare their own tax returns or to pay to have someone else help determine the proper amount of income tax.

When deciding whether to prepare their own returns, taxpayers should be aware that the amount of income tax shown on the return may contain errors or differences of opinion that may be found in an IRS audit. These differences of opinion can result from a taxpayer's or the tax preparer's lack of familiarity with the tax law and how it applies to the taxpayer. Similarly, the IRS agent performing the audit may not fully understand the law as it applies to a particular situation. In addition to clerical mistakes, tax return errors can result from inadequate communication between a taxpayer and tax preparer. A tax audit may reveal that the taxpayer either is entitled to a refund or owes more tax. If you are entitled to a refund, you have lost the use of the money while it was held by the U.S. Treasury. If you have to pay more tax, you may have to pay extra costs in the form of penalties and interest on the tax

*Table I-1*

**Estimated Average Taxpayer Burden for Individuals by Activity**

| Type of Taxpayer | Percentage of Returns | Average Burden: Average Time (Hours): Total Time* | Record Keeping | Tax Planning | Form Completion and Submission | All Other | Average Cost (Dollars)** |
|---|---|---|---|---|---|---|---|
| All taxpayers | 100 | 11 | 5 | 2 | 4 | 1 | $210 |
| Type of taxpayer | | | | | | | |
| Nonbusiness*** | 70 | 7 | 2 | 1 | 3 | 1 | 130 |
| Business*** | 30 | 19 | 10 | 3 | 5 | 1 | 410 |

*Detail may not add to total time due to rounding.
**Dollars rounded to the nearest $10.
***You are considered a "business" filer if you file one or more of the following with Form 1040 or 1040-SR: Schedule C, E, or F or Form 2106. You are considered a "nonbusiness" filer if you don't file any of those schedules or forms with Form 1040 or 1040-SR.

you owe. An audit of your return will require an additional investment of your personal time and, quite likely, additional out-of-pocket costs for professional tax advice. In addition, many taxpayers are intimidated when facing an income tax audit.

As your involvement in professional activities increases, taxes and the costs of compliance grow in importance. If you are like most taxpayers, you will want to pay the least tax required by the law. You will also want to spend as little time and money as possible to satisfy the compliance requirements. As Table I-2 shows, in 2000, an average taxpayer worked May 1 to pay federal, state, and local taxes and a taxpayer worked almost one-third (33.00 percent) of the year to pay taxes. Major federal income tax cuts enacted from 2001 through 2009 decreased tax freedom day to April 9 in 2010. However by 2019, tax freedom day has increased to April 16 which represents 29% of the tax year pay federal, state, and local taxes. As Table I-2 demonstrates, the amounts paid for taxes represent major expenditures for the typical taxpayer.

## Conservation of Wealth

An understanding of basic tax concepts and planning can often help conserve wealth by reducing taxes. To reduce taxes, you need to be able to recognize potential planning situations and problems. Because you know your financial affairs better than anyone else, you are in the best position to spot potential tax-saving opportunities. You should never wait for your tax adviser to find new ways to save you taxes. Although a competent tax adviser will know about tax-planning techniques and current tax developments, you will be more familiar than an adviser is with your financial affairs and objectives. A tax adviser is best used in the same way you use other professionals. When you visit your physician, you usually describe the symptom that brought you to the office to help the doctor identify the proper treatment. When you visit your attorney for a legal problem, you

*Table I-2*

**Tax Freedom Days in the U.S.**

| Year | Tax Freedom Day | % of Year |
|---|---|---|
| 1960 | April 11 | 27.70% |
| 1970 | April 19 | 29.60% |
| 1980 | April 21 | 30.40% |
| 1990 | April 21 | 30.40% |
| 2000 | May 1 | 33.00% |
| 2010 | April 9 | 26.90% |
| 2011 | April12 | 27.70% |
| 2012 | April 13 | 29.20% |
| 2013 | April 18 | 29.40% |
| 2014 | April 21 | 30.20% |
| 2015 | April 24 | 31.20% |
| 2016 | April 22 | 30.90% |
| 2017 | April 23 | 30.90% |
| 2018 | April 19 | 29.70% |
| 2019 | April 16 | 29.00% |

take along the information necessary to help the lawyer identify the legal issues. In both instances, you evaluate information and decide when you need professional assistance. Likewise, you will need to evaluate information, based on your understanding of the tax laws, to determine when you need to consult a professional tax adviser.

**Example 3** Gwen, 19, is a full-time student at State University. Her parents pay all her expenses, which total $12,000 a year. Gwen does not have any other source of support, and she does not pay any income tax. Gwen's father, Marty, owns a substantial portfolio of bonds that earns $12,000 in income each year. Marty is in the 32% tax rate bracket.

**Discussion: A tax plan could save Marty money by transferring ownership of the bond portfolio to Gwen, who is in a lower tax bracket. Marty pays $3,840 ($12,000 × 32%) in tax on the investment income. The amount of income left after paying tax is $8,160 ($12,000 − $3,840).**

**If Marty gave the bond portfolio to Gwen as a gift (which is not subject to income tax), she would be taxed on the income at a lower tax rate than her father. Assuming that Gwen has no other income, her tax on the income would be $1,124. The family could save $2,716 ($3,840 − $1,124) in tax by shifting the income to Gwen. The amount of income left after paying tax is increased to $10,876 ($12,000 − $1,124).**

## Taxes Influence Routine Decisions

An auditor, management accountant, attorney, physician, or farmer may never prepare a business tax return. Yet, they need a general understanding of the tax effects of their daily business decisions. For example, an auditor might find that an improperly recorded transaction results in an undisclosed tax liability or refund. A managerial accountant may need to consider the tax effects of buying or selling plant assets or acquiring a new business. To provide reliable advice to clients, lawyers often need a general understanding of how the tax laws apply to different types of entities. A doctor may need a general understanding of fringe-benefit plans that can be set up to keep highly qualified nurses and medical technicians as employees. A farmer can benefit from familiarity with the complex rules that govern reporting of income from farm production and the deduction of farm expenses. Individuals can also benefit from a knowledge of the tax laws in their everyday decisions.

**Example 4** Isaac wants to remodel his house. During a special promotion, his bank will finance the purchase with a 7% unsecured personal loan. Isaac knows that he can obtain a home equity loan from his bank at 8% interest. If Isaac is in the 24% tax bracket, which loan should he use to finance his remodeling?

**Discussion: Interest paid on personal loans is not deductible. However, interest paid on a home equity loan is deductible and treated as acquisition indebtedness if the funds are used to substantially improve the taxpayer's home. If Isaac itemizes his deductions, the interest on the home equity loan is deductible. This makes the real after-tax cost of the home equity loan 6.08% [8% − (8% × 24%)]. Therefore, the home equity loan actually offers a lower after-tax cost than the personal loan.**

**However, note that if Isaac does not itemize deductions (i.e., he uses the standard deduction), he receives no benefit from the deduction for home equity loan interest. In this case, the personal loan would have a lower after-tax cost, because neither loan would produce deductible interest.**

## Self-Protection

Another reason for being aware of the federal income tax law is self-protection. Perhaps you have heard others say that all they have to do is give a list of income and deduction items to their tax return preparer. When they get the completed tax return back and pay the tax due, their responsibility for complying with the tax law is finished. If any mistakes are made, it is the preparer's problem. This assumption is erroneous and can lead to disaster.

Taxpayers are fully liable for additional tax, interest, and penalties due because of an error on their tax return. If a person paid to prepare a return misinterprets the information and/or makes a mistake that results in an underpayment of tax, the taxpayer will have to pay any additional amounts owed to the government. Whether the preparer will reimburse the taxpayer for the penalties and interest depends on the agreement with the preparer. Legal recourse against the preparer is available in certain circumstances, but the cost of obtaining reimbursement (e.g., legal fees, court costs) from the preparer may be prohibitive. For your own protection, you should always examine the completed return. Before you sign and file the return, thoroughly review it with your preparer and be sure you understand any entries that do not seem to be correct. Again, a knowledge of the tax law can help you catch errors or other misrepresentations made by a tax preparer before the return is filed.

**Example 5** Raul gives his tax return preparer a list of income and deduction items to be reported on his tax return. The income items total $50,000, and the deduction items total $14,000. When the preparer puts the information on the return, he omits $10,000 of the income and reports only $40,000 ($50,000 − $10,000) in income. In addition, the preparer includes a $2,000 deduction twice so that total deductions are reported as $16,000. As a result, Raul understates his taxable income by $12,000 ($36,000 correct taxable income − $24,000 reported taxable income).

**Discussion: If the IRS detects the errors on the return, Raul will have to pay the IRS the additional tax due on the $12,000 understatement plus penalties and interest. Depending on their agreement for preparing the return, Raul may or may not recover part of his costs from the preparer. If the preparer does not agree to reimburse Raul for his mistakes, Raul may take legal action to obtain the amount due from the preparer. However, this can be a costly process and may not be worth the additional tax, penalties, and interest due.**

Clearly, all taxpayers can benefit from a basic knowledge of the tax law. Although the federal income tax is only one of many taxes that government bodies use to raise revenue, it is by far the most important in terms of revenue produced and the number of taxpayers affected. Therefore, this book focuses on federal income tax law.

Federal income tax law is a complex array of statutory, administrative, and judicial authorities. Because of its ability to affect taxpayer's decisions, lawmakers frequently make changes in the tax law to achieve economic, social, and/or political objectives. This causes the tax law to be in constant evolution. Professional tax advisers spend a significant portion of their time maintaining their knowledge of this changing body of law. Fortunately, many aspects of the tax law have remained stable over time. The approach used in this book is to provide a conceptual framework for analyzing how particular transactions should be treated for federal income tax purposes. The book then presents the general operation of the tax law and explains it in terms of the basic concepts. Throughout the book, the focus of the discussion is on those aspects of the federal income tax that have remained stable over time. A knowledge of the basic operation of the tax law will enhance your ability to make the best decisions for your individual situation.

# Conceptual Foundations of the Tax Law

PART 1



Every society makes choices as to the tax systems that not only raise the necessary revenues to support government expenditures, but within that choice are also inherent reflections of societal values. Not only does a society choose a tax system but the tax system also becomes one of the basic institutions that in itself shapes and molds the society.

—Karen M. Yeager

iStock.com/carterdayne

# Federal Income Taxation—An Overview

1

Learning Objectives:

LO 1 Explain what constitutes a tax and the various types of tax rate structures that may be used to calculate a tax.

LO 2 Explain the major types of taxes in the United States.

LO 3 Identify the primary sources of federal income tax law.

LO 4 Define *taxable income* and other commonly used tax terms.

LO 5 Explain the IRS audit process and taxpayer rights within the process.

LO 6 Explain the calculation of taxable income for individual taxpayers and the unique personal deductions allowed to individuals.

LO 7 Develop a framework for tax planning and discuss the effect of marginal tax rates and the time value of money on tax planning.

LO 8 Make the distinction between tax avoidance and tax evasion.

LO 9 Explain ethical considerations related to tax practice.

## 1-1 INTRODUCTION

We have all heard the adage, "There's nothing certain but death and taxes." However, equating death and taxes is hardly a fair characterization of taxation. It is often stated that taxes are the price we pay for a civilized society. An early decision of the U.S. Supreme Court described a tax as "an extraction for the support of the government." Regardless of your personal view of taxation, society as we know it could not function without some system of taxation. People constantly demand that the government provide them with various services, such as defense, roads, schools, unemployment benefits, medical care, and environmental protection. The cost of providing the services that the residents of the United States demand is principally taxation. People are introduced to taxation at an early age. Remember the candy bar that had a price sticker of 90 cents yet actually cost 96 cents? The tax collector is all around us. Upon receiving their first paycheck, many are surprised that the $100 they earned resulted in a check of only $80 after taxes were deducted. The point is that taxes are a fact of life. Learning to deal with taxes, and perhaps using them to your advantage, is an essential element of success in today's world.

The federal income tax is a sophisticated and complex array of laws that imposes a tax on the income of individuals, corporations, estates, and trusts. Current tax law has developed over a period of more than 100 years through a dynamic process involving political, economic, and social forces. At this very minute, Congress is considering various changes in the tax law; the Internal Revenue Service (IRS) and the courts are issuing new interpretations of current tax law, and professional tax advisers are working to determine the meaning of all these changes.

The purpose of this book is to provide an introduction to the basic operation of the federal income tax system. However, before looking at some of the specifics, it is helpful to have a broad understanding of taxes and how the federal income tax fits into the overall scheme of revenue production. Toward this end, this chapter briefly discusses what constitutes a tax, how taxes are structured, and the major types of taxes in the United States before considering the federal income tax. Next, the primary sources of tax law authority are introduced. These sources provide the basis for calculating the tax and the unique terminology of federal income taxation. This chapter also introduces the tax calculation for individuals, the discussion of which serves as a reference for discussions in succeeding chapters. The next section of the chapter provides a framework for tax planning and a discussion of tax avoidance and tax evasion.

Because ethics is an important issue in the accounting profession, the chapter concludes with a brief discussion of the ethical considerations related to tax practice. The discussion provides the background that will help you detect ethical issues that you will face if you go on to practice in the tax area.

## 1-2 DEFINITION AND EVALUATION OF A TAX

LO 1
Explain what constitutes a tax and the various types of tax rate structures that may be used to calculate a tax.

Because this is a tax text, one starting point is to define what is meant by the term *tax*. Particular types of taxes and tax rules are often criticized as being loopholes, unfair, or creating an excessive burden on a particular group of taxpayers. The discussion that follows presents the four criteria commonly used to evaluate these criticisms. In addition, three types of tax rate structure are presented as an aid in evaluating whether a particular tax is "good" or "bad."

### 1-2a Definition of a Tax

What is a tax? The IRS defines a tax as "an enforced contribution, exacted pursuant to legislative authority in the exercise of the taxing power, and imposed and collected for the purpose of raising revenue to be used for public or governmental purposes. Taxes are not payments for some special privilege granted or service rendered and are, therefore, distinguishable from various other charges imposed for particular purposes under particular powers or functions of government."[1]

A tax could be viewed as an involuntary contribution required by law to finance the functions of government. The amount of the contribution extracted from the taxpayer is unrelated to any privilege, benefit, or service received from the government agency imposing the tax. According to the IRS definition, a tax has the following characteristics:

1. The payment to the governmental authority is required by law.
2. The payment is required pursuant to the legislative power to tax.
3. The purpose of requiring the payment is to provide revenue to be used for public or governmental purposes.
4. Special benefits, services, or privileges are not received as a result of making the payment. The payment is not a fine or penalty that is imposed under other powers of government.

Although the IRS definition states that the payment of a tax does not provide the taxpayer with directly measurable benefits, the taxpayer does benefit from, among other things, military security, a legal system, and a relatively stable political, economic, and social environment. Payments to a government agency that relate to the receipt of a specific benefit—in privileges or services—are not considered taxes. They are payments for value received or are the result of a regulatory measure imposed by the government agency.

**Example 1** Keith lives in Randal County, which enacted a law setting a 1% property tax to provide money for county schools. The 1% tax applies to all property owners in Randal County. All schoolchildren in the county will benefit from the tax, even if their parents do not own property or pay the tax. Is the 1% property tax a tax according to the definition?

**Discussion: The property tax is a tax. The tax is a required payment to a government unit. The payment is imposed by a property tax law. The purpose of the payment is to finance public schools. The tax is levied without regard to whether the taxpayer receives a benefit from paying the tax.**

**Example 2** Assume that in example 1, the tax is imposed on a limited group of property owners to finance the construction of sewer lines to their properties. Is the 1% tax a tax as defined by the IRS?

**Discussion: Each payer of the tax receives a direct benefit—a new sewer line. Therefore, the 1% tax payment is considered a payment to the government unit to**

**reimburse it for improvements to the taxpayer's property. The taxpayers would treat the payment as an investment in their property and not as a tax. The 1% tax in this case is a special assessment for local benefits. An assessment differs from a tax in that an assessment is levied only on a specific group of taxpayers who receive the benefit of the assessment.**

Certain payments that look like a tax are not considered a tax under the IRS definition. For example, an annual licensing fee paid to a state to engage in a specific occupation such as medicine, law, or accounting is not a tax because it is a regulatory measure that provides a direct benefit to the payer of the fee. A fee paid for driving on a toll road, the quarter deposited in a parking meter, and payments to a city for water and sewer services are payments for value received and are not taxes according to the IRS's definition. Fines for violating public laws and penalties on tax returns are not taxes. Fines and penalties are generally imposed to discourage behavior that is harmful to the public interest and not to raise revenue to finance government operations.

## 1-2b Standards for Evaluating a Tax

In *The Wealth of Nations*, Adam Smith identified four basic requirements for a good tax system. Although other criteria can be used to evaluate a tax, Smith's four points are generally accepted as valid and provide a basis for discussion of the primary issues regarding taxes. These requirements are equality, certainty, convenience, and economy. Although Smith clearly stated the maxims, taxpayers have different opinions as to whether the federal income tax strictly satisfies the four requirements.

1. **Equality**—A tax should be based on the taxpayer's ***ability to pay***. The payment of a tax in proportion to the taxpayer's level of income results in an equitable distribution of the cost of supporting the government.

The concept of equality requires consideration of both horizontal and vertical equity. **Horizontal equity** exists when two similarly situated taxpayers are taxed the same. **Vertical equity** exists when taxpayers with different situations are taxed differently but fairly in relation to each taxpayer's ability to pay the tax. This means that those taxpayers who have the greatest ability to pay the tax should pay the greatest proportion of the tax. These equity concepts are reflected to a great extent in the federal income tax. Certain low-income individuals pay no tax. As a person's taxable income level increases, the tax rate increases from 10 percent to 12 percent to 22 percent to 24 percent to 32 percent to 35 percent to 37 percent.

**Example 3** Tom and Jerry each earn $15,000 a year and pay $1,500 in tax.

**Discussion: The two taxpayers pay the same amount of tax on the same amount of income. Because they are treated the same, based on the facts given, horizontal equity exists.**

**A slight change of facts provides a different result. If Tom is married and supports his spouse and 3 children and Jerry is single with no one else to support, the tax appears unfair and not vertically equitable. The lack of vertical equity exists because the taxpayers' situations are no longer the same, yet they pay the same amount of tax on the same income.**

**Example 4** Assume that because of the size of his family, Tom (example 3) pays $500 in taxes. Jerry still pays $1,500.

**Discussion: In this situation, vertical equity is considered to be present. Because he presumably has a greater ability to pay tax, Jerry pays a larger amount of tax than Tom—Jerry's income, although equal to Tom's, supports fewer people.**

Some taxpayers consider inequitable the tax law provisions that treat similar income and deductions differently. For example, a person investing in bonds issued by a city does not have to pay tax on the interest income. In contrast, interest income earned on an investment in corporate bonds is taxed. People who operate proprietorships may deduct the cost of providing their employees with group term life insurance but may not deduct the cost of their own group insurance premium. If the proprietor incorporates, the cost of the insurance for both the shareholder-employee (owner) and employees can be deducted. Thus, the perception of equality often depends on the taxpayer's personal viewpoint. Because the concepts of equity are highly subjective, a tax rule considered equitable by one taxpayer is often considered unfair by a taxpayer who derives no benefit. Often, when evaluating the equality of a tax provision, taxpayers do not consider—or are not aware of—the economic, social, and administrative reasons for what may seem to be an inequity in the tax law.

**Example 5** Kate is a single mother who earns $10,000 a year. Maria and her husband, Ben, earn $75,000 a year. Kate and Maria each pay Neighborhood Day Care $2,000 per year for taking care of one child while they work. Because the payment is for qualified child care, Kate is entitled to a $700 reduction in her income tax because of her low income level. Because of their high income level, Maria and Ben receive only a $400 reduction in their income tax. Who is more likely to view this treatment as being inequitable?

**Discussion: Maria and Ben may view the tax rule as unfair because Kate receives a larger reduction in tax for the same amount of payment for day care. However, there is increasing emphasis on tax relief for families. Congress has decided that it is important that children be adequately cared for while parents are at work. Thus, Kate's family is given a larger tax break to help provide child care. Without the larger tax reduction, Kate might not be able to afford to pay child-care costs. The difference in treatment could also be based on the ability to pay child-care costs. In addition, the difference in treatment depicts a situation of vertical equity. Because Maria and Ben have higher incomes, vertical equity requires that they pay a higher tax (through receiving a smaller tax credit).**

> **2. Certainty**—A taxpayer should know when and how a tax is to be paid. In addition, the taxpayer should be able to determine the amount of tax to be paid.

Certainty in the tax law is necessary for tax planning. An individual's federal income tax return is due on the fifteenth day of the fourth month (usually April 15) after the close of the tax year. A corporation's return is due on the fifteenth day of the fourth month after the close of its tax year.[2] The balance of tax due with the return is usually paid by check to the IRS. However, determining the amount of tax due may not be so simple. When planning an investment that will extend over several tax years, the ability to predict with some degree of certainty how the results of the investment will be taxed is important to the investment decision. Frequent changes in the tax law create uncertainty for the tax planner. In addition to these legislative amendments to the tax law, the IRS and the courts issue a constant stream of decisions and interpretations on tax issues, which results in a tax law that is in a continual state of refinement. However, for the average individual taxpayer, who has wages subject to withholding, receives some interest income, owns a home, pays state and local taxes, and perhaps donates to a church or other charities, there is little complexity and a great deal of certainty in the tax law despite the numerous changes to the tax system.

> **3. Convenience**—A tax should be levied at the time it is most likely to be convenient for the taxpayer to make the payment. The most convenient time for taxpayers to make the payment is as they receive income and have the money available to pay the tax.

Most taxpayers would argue that it is not convenient to keep records, determine the amount of tax due, and fill out complex forms. However, certain aspects of the income tax law make it more convenient than it might be otherwise. Based on the **pay-as-you-go concept**, taxes are paid as close to the time the income is earned as is reasonable. The pay-as-you-go system results in the collection of the tax when the taxpayer has the money to pay the tax. This tax payment system applies to all taxpayers, including the self-employed and those who earn their income from investing activities. This system is discussed in more detail later in this chapter.

The federal income tax is based on self-assessment and voluntary compliance with the tax law. Taxpayers determine in privacy the amount of their income, deductions, and tax due. The tax calculated by the taxpayer is considered correct unless the IRS detects an error and corrects it or selects the return for an audit. The federal income tax system relies on the honesty and integrity of taxpayers in determining their tax payments. This system of self-assessment and voluntary compliance promotes convenience for taxpayers.

4. **Economy**—A tax should have minimum compliance and administrative costs. The costs of compliance and administration should be kept at a minimum so that the amount that goes to the U.S. Treasury is as large as possible.

The IRS operates on a budget of about one-half of 1 percent of the total taxes collected. However, the IRS's budget does not reflect the full cost of administering the tax law. A taxpayer's personal cost of compliance can be substantial. Taxpayers often need to maintain accounting records for tax reporting in addition to those that are necessary for business decisions. A corporation, for example, might use different depreciation methods and asset lives for financial reporting and for income tax. The taxpayer's personal cost also includes fees paid to attorneys, accountants, and other tax advisers for tax-planning, compliance, and litigation services.

## 1-2c Tax Rates and Structures

Tax rates are often referred to as a *marginal rate*, an *average rate*, or an *effective rate*. In addition, a tax rate structure is frequently described as being *proportional*, *regressive*, or *progressive*. Because a tax rate structure indicates how the average tax rate varies with changes in its tax base, examining a rate's structure helps in understanding and evaluating the effect of a tax.

To compute a tax, it is necessary to know the tax base and the applicable tax rate. The tax is then computed by multiplying the tax base by the tax rate:

$$\text{Tax} = \text{Tax base} \times \text{Tax rate}$$

A **tax base** is the value that is subject to tax. The tax base for the federal income tax is called **taxable income**. Other common tax bases include the dollar amount of a purchase subject to sales tax, the dollars of an employee's wages subject to payroll tax, and the assessed value of property subject to property tax.

### Tax Rate Definitions

When working with the federal income tax, different measures of the rate of tax paid from one year to the next are often compared to evaluate the effectiveness of tax planning and to help make decisions about future transactions. Three different rates are commonly used for these comparisons:

- The marginal tax rate
- The average tax rate
- The effective tax rate

The **marginal tax rate** is the rate of tax that will be paid on the next dollar of income or the rate of tax that will be saved by the next dollar of deduction. The marginal tax rate is used in tax planning to determine the effect of reporting additional income or deductions during a tax year. One objective of tax planning is to minimize the marginal rate and to keep the marginal rate relatively constant from one year to the next. The marginal tax rates for an individual taxpayer are 10 percent, 12 percent, 22 percent, 24 percent, 32 percent, 35 percent, and 37 percent.[3] If you know a person's taxable income (the tax base), you can find the marginal tax rate in the tax rate schedules in Appendix B.

**Example 6** Carlos has an asset he could sell this year at a $10,000 profit, which would increase his marginal tax rate from 12% to 22%. If he waits until next year to sell the asset, he is sure his other income will be less and the $10,000 gain will be taxed at 12%. Should Carlos sell the asset this year or wait until next year?

**Discussion: By waiting until next year to sell the asset, Carlos's tax savings on the sale are $1,000 [$10,000 × (22% – 12%)]. In addition, he will postpone the payment of the tax interest-free for a year (a time value of money savings). Assuming that he can sell the asset early in the next year and does not need the proceeds from the sale before next year, he should wait until next year to sell the asset to take advantage of the lower marginal tax rate and the time value of money savings on the tax to be paid on the gain.**

The **average tax rate** is the total federal income tax divided by taxable income (the tax base). This is the average rate of tax on each dollar of income that is taxable. The **effective tax rate** is the total federal income tax divided by the taxpayer's economic income (taxable income plus nontaxable income). Economic income is a broader base; it includes all the taxpayer's income, whether it is subject to tax or not. The effective tax rate is the average rate of tax on income from all taxable and nontaxable sources.

**Example 7** Assume that in example 6, Carlos sells the asset in 2021 and reports taxable income of $40,000. Also, Carlos collects $50,000 on a life insurance policy that is not taxable income. Carlos's tax on $40,000 is $4,601 (using the tax rate schedules in Appendix B). In addition, the only difference between Carlos's economic income and his taxable income is proceeds from the life insurance policy. What are Carlos's marginal, average, and effective tax rates?

**Discussion: Based on the facts given, Carlos's marginal tax rate is 12% (from the tax rate schedules). His average tax rate is 11.50% ($4,601 ÷ $40,000). The effective tax rate on his economic income of $90,000 ($40,000 in taxable income + $50,000 in nontaxable income) is 5.11% ($4,601 ÷ $90,000) and is much less than both the marginal and average tax rates.**

## Tax Rate Structures

Tax rate structures are described as being proportional, regressive, or progressive. The structures explain how the tax rates vary with a change in the amount subject to the tax (the tax base).

**Proportional Rate Structure** A **proportional rate structure** is defined as a tax for which the average tax rate remains the same as the tax base increases. This rate structure is also referred to as a *flat tax*. If you charted a proportional tax rate structure on a graph, it would look like Chart 1 in Figure 1-1.

If a tax rate is proportional, the marginal tax rate and the average tax rate are the same at all levels of the tax base. As the tax base increases, the total tax paid will increase at a constant rate. Examples of proportional taxes are sales taxes, real estate and personal property taxes, and certain excise taxes, such as the tax on gasoline. The sales tax is a fixed percentage of the amount purchased, property tax is a constant rate multiplied by the assessed value of the property, and the gas tax is a constant rate per gallon purchased.

**Example 8** Ji-woo bought a new suit for $350. The sales tax at 7% totaled $24.50. Steve bought a new lawn tractor for $3,500. At 7%, the sales tax he paid came to $245. Is the sales tax proportional?

**Discussion: Ji-woo's and Steve's marginal tax rate is 7%. In addition, Betsy's average tax rate is 7% ($24.50 ÷ $350), the same as Steve's (7% = $245 ÷ $3,500). The sales tax is proportional because the marginal and average tax rates are equal at all levels of the tax base (the selling price).**

**Regressive Rate Structure** A **regressive rate structure** is defined as a tax in which the average tax rate decreases as the tax base increases. On a graph, a regressive tax rate structure would look like Chart 2 in Figure 1-1.

*Figure 1-1*

## Tax Rate Structures

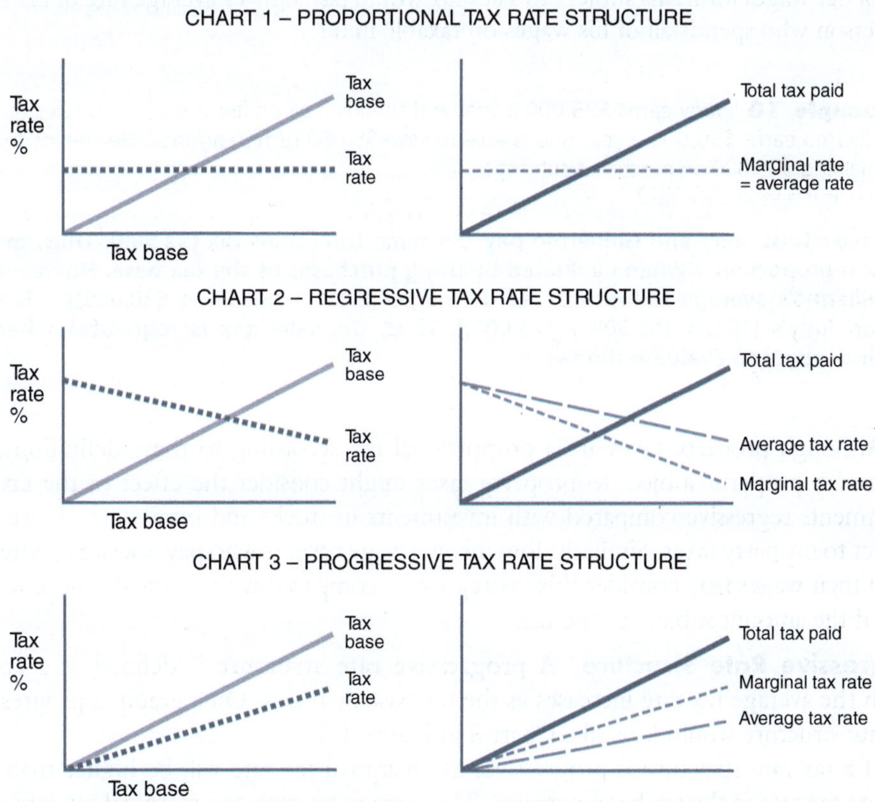


If a tax rate structure is regressive, the marginal tax rate will be less than the average tax rate as the tax base increases. Note that although the average tax rate and the marginal tax rate both decrease as the tax base increases, the total tax paid will increase. As a result, a person with a low tax base will pay a higher average and a higher marginal rate of tax than will a person with a high tax base. The person with the high tax base will still pay more dollars in total tax. Although a pure regressive tax rate structure (as defined earlier) does not exist in the United States, example 9 illustrates a regressive tax.

**Example 9** Each year, Alan purchases $4,000 worth of egg rolls and Tranh purchases $17,000 worth of egg rolls. A tax is levied according to the dollar value of egg rolls purchased per the following tax schedule:

| Tax Rate Schedule | | Alan | | Tranh | |
|---|---|---|---|---|---|
| **Base** | **Rate** | **Purchases** | **Tax** | **Purchases** | **Tax** |
| $-0- < $5,001 | 10% | $4,000 | $ 400 | $ 5,000 | $ 500 |
| $5,001 < $10,001 | 7% | | | 5,000 | 350 |
| More than $10,000 | 5% | | | 7,000 | 350 |
| Totals | | $4,000 | $ 400 | $17,000 | $1,200 |
| Marginal tax rate | | | 10% | | 5.0% |
| Average tax rate | | | 10% | | 7.1% |

**Discussion: This tax rate schedule is regressive. The average tax rate applicable to Alan (10%) is greater than the average tax rate for Tranh (7.1%), even though Tranh's tax base is higher. Note that Tranh pays more total tax ($1,200) than Alan ($400).**

If a different base is used to evaluate the tax rate structure, the same tax that may be viewed as proportional by one taxpayer may be considered regressive by another taxpayer. For example, using total wages as the tax base for evaluation, a person who spends part of her wages for items subject to sales tax would pay a lower average rate of tax than the person who spends all of his wages on taxable items.

**Example 10** Judy earns $25,000 a year and spends it all on items subject to sales tax. Guillermo earns $30,000 a year and is able to save $5,000 of his earnings. He spends the remaining $25,000 on purchases subject to sales tax. If the sales tax rate is 10% of purchase price, is it a regressive tax?

**Discussion: Judy and Guillermo pay the same total sales tax ($2,500). Thus, the tax is proportional when evaluated by using purchases as the tax base. However, Guillermo's average tax rate based on wages [8.3% = ($2,500 ÷ $30,000)] is less than Judy's [10% = ($2,500 ÷ $25,000)]. Thus, the sales tax is regressive when using wages to evaluate the tax.**

Although property taxes are a proportional tax according to these definitions, an investor in property subject to property taxes might consider the effect of the tax on investments regressive compared with investments in stocks and bonds, which are not subject to property taxes. Similarly, low-income wage earners who pay Social Security tax on all their wages may consider this tax regressive compared with a person whose wages exceed the amount subject to the tax.

**Progressive Rate Structure** A **progressive rate structure** is defined as a tax in which the average tax rate increases as the tax base increases. On a graph, a progressive tax rate structure would look like Chart 3 in Figure 1-1.

If a tax rate structure is progressive, the marginal tax rate will be higher than the average tax rate as the tax base increases. The average tax rate, the marginal tax rate, and the total tax all increase with increases in the tax base. A person with a low tax base will pay both lower average and marginal rates of tax than will a person with a high tax base.

The progressive tax rate structure reflects the embedding in the federal income tax rates of Adam Smith's equality criterion. Recall that according to this criterion, taxpayers should pay according to their ability to pay the tax. The use of progressive rate structures, wherein people with higher taxable income levels pay higher marginal tax rates, promotes equality.

**Example 11** Doug reports $22,000 a year in taxable income from wages he earns watering the greens at the Hot Water Golf Course. Shawana earns $47,000 in annual taxable income as a first grade teacher.

**Discussion: Doug and Shawana's 2021 income taxes using the single taxpayer rates are as follows:**

| | Doug's Tax (income: $22,000) | Shawana's Tax (income: $47,000) |
|---|---|---|
| Tax on income of $9,950 @ 10% | $ 995 | $ 995 |
| Tax on income from $9,950 to $40,525 @ 12% | 1,446 | 3,669 |
| Tax on income above $40,525 @ 22% | -0- | 1,425 |
| Total tax | $2,441 | $6,089 |
| Marginal tax rate | 12% | 22% |
| Average tax rate | 11.1% | 12.96% |

**Discussion: As a result of Shawana's larger tax base and the progressive tax rates, her marginal and average tax rates are higher than Doug's. Thus, the tax rate structure of the federal income tax promotes equality among taxpayers.**

# 1-3 MAJOR TYPES OF U.S. TAXES

LO 2 Explain the major types of taxes in the United States.

The federal, state, and local governments use a variety of taxes to fund their operations. Figure 1-2 shows the average number of days worked to pay various taxes in 2019. On average, over 30 percent of the year is devoted to paying various taxes. An analysis of the revenue sources shows that 70 of the 75 days spent working to pay federal taxes were devoted to payment of the income tax (individual and corporate) and social insurance taxes. It should also be noted that social insurance taxes (26 days) provide almost as much revenue to the federal government as individual income taxes (42 days). Although this text covers the basic operation of the federal income tax, it is helpful to have a basic understanding of the other taxes levied by governments. As will be seen throughout the text, many taxes affect and interact with the rules for the federal income tax. Each major type of tax is discussed briefly in turn. Do not be concerned with the mechanics of the taxes at this point. Focus only on their general nature.

## 1-3a Income Taxes

The federal government levies a tax on the income of individuals, corporations, estates, and trusts. Most states also tax the income on these taxpayers, and a few local governments also impose an income tax on those who work or live within their boundaries. The income tax is levied on a *net* number—taxable income. In its simplest form, taxable income is the difference between the total income of a taxpayer and the deductions allowed that taxpayer. Thus, the study of income taxation is really the study of what must be reported as income and what is allowed as a deduction from that income to arrive at taxable income.

Each of the three government units that impose an income tax has its own set of rules for determining what is included in income and what is deductible from income to arrive at taxable income. Because most state and local governments begin their taxable income

Figure 1-2

**Average Number of Days Worked to Pay Taxes by Type of Tax and Level of Government Calendar Year 2019**

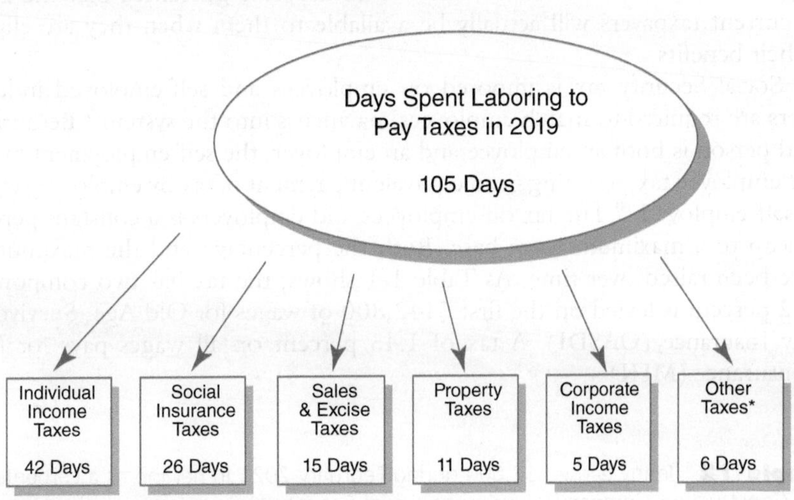


*Includes other business taxes.
Note: Due to rounding, components do not add up to total.
Sources: Tax Foundation calculations.

calculations in relation to the federal income tax computation, an understanding of the federal income tax rules is essential for calculating most income taxes. This book makes no attempt to cover the myriad state and local income tax rules.

Income taxes are determined on an annual basis. However, the United States uses a pay-as-you-go collection system under which taxpayers pay an estimate of their tax as they earn their income. Employers must withhold income taxes from wages and salaries of their employees and remit them on a timely basis to the appropriate government body.[4] When taxpayers file their tax returns, these prepaid amounts are credited against their actual bill, resulting in either a refund of taxes, if the prepaid amount is greater than the actual tax, or an additional tax due, if the prepaid amount is deficient.[5] Self-employed taxpayers and those with other sources of income that are not subject to withholding (e.g., dividend and interest income) must make quarterly estimated tax payments that are applied against their tax bills upon filing of the return.[6]

## 1-3b Employment Taxes

All employees and their employers pay taxes on the wages earned by employees. Employees pay **Social Security taxes** that are matched by their employers.[7] Self-employed individuals pay the equivalent of both halves of the Social Security tax by paying the **self-employment tax**.[8] In addition to the Social Security tax, employers pay unemployment compensation taxes to both the federal and state governments.

### Social Security Taxes

Under the Federal Insurance Contribution Act (FICA), a tax is levied on wages and salaries earned. The Social Security system was originally designed to provide retirement benefits to all individuals who contributed to the system. This function has been expanded to include many other social programs, such as medical insurance, disability benefits, and survivor's benefits. The result of this expansion of coverage has been a great increase in the amount of Social Security taxes paid by workers and employers. It should be stressed that the Social Security system is not a "funded" system. Current payments into the system are used to pay current benefits; technically, any excess is placed in a fund. However, the federal government often borrows against this "fund" to pay general government expenses. Thus, there is no absolute guarantee that the amounts paid by current taxpayers will actually be available to them when they are eligible to receive their benefits.

The Social Security tax is imposed on employees and self-employed individuals. Employers are required to match employees' payments into the system.[9] Because a self-employed person is both an employee and an employer, the self-employment tax rate is twice the employee tax, resulting in an equivalent payment of tax by employee/employer and the self-employed.[10] The tax on employees and employers is a constant percentage of wages up to a maximum wage base. Both the percentage and the maximum wage base have been raised over time. As Table 1-1 shows, the tax has two components. A tax of 6.2 percent is levied on the first $142,800 of wages for Old Age, Survivors, and Disability Insurance (OASDI). A tax of 1.45 percent on all wages pays for Medical Health Insurance (MHI).

**Example 12** Jenny earned $2,000 during February 2021 in her job as a carpenter for Acme Construction Company. How much Social Security tax must be paid by Jenny and Acme on her February earnings?

**Discussion: Jenny must pay 6.2% (OASDI) and 1.45% (MHI) on the first $142,800 of income earned in 2021. Thus, Jenny must pay $153 [($2,000 × 6.2%) + ($2,000 × 1.45%)] in Social Security taxes on her wages. Acme must match the $153 in Social Security taxes Jenny paid on the wages.**

Table 1-1

## Social Security Tax Rates for Employees and Employers

| Year | OASDI[1] | MHI[2] | Total | Maximum Wage Base | Maximum Tax Paid |
|---|---|---|---|---|---|
| 2017 | 6.20 | | 6.20 | $127,200 | $7,886 |
| | | 1.45 | 1.45 | Wages earned | No maximum |
| | | | 7.65 | | |
| 2018 | 6.20 | | 6.20 | $128,400 | $7,961 |
| | | 1.45 | 1.45 | Wages earned | No maximum |
| | | | 7.65 | | |
| 2019 | 6.20 | | 6.20 | $132,900 | $8,240 |
| | | 1.45 | 1.45 | Wages earned | No maximum |
| | | | 7.65 | | |
| 2020 | 6.20 | | 6.20 | $137,700 | $8,537 |
| | | 1.45 | 1.45 | Wages earned | No maximum |
| | | | 7.65 | | |
| 2021 | 6.20 | | 6.20 | $142,800 | $8,854 |
| | | 1.45 | 1.45 | Wages earned | No maximum |
| | | | 7.65 | | |

[1]Old Age, Survivors, and Disability Insurance
[2]Medical Health Insurance

**Example 13** Chandra earned $145,000 as the administrator of the Local Accounting Program in 2021. How much Social Security tax does Chandra pay in 2021?

**Discussion: Chandra pays the maximum OASDI of $8,854 (6.2% × $142,800) and $2,102 (1.45% × $145,000) of MHI for a total Social Security payment of $10,956. Her employer is required to pay the same amount on Chandra's behalf.**

As with income taxes, Social Security taxes are withheld from the employee's pay by the employer and remitted to the federal government with the employer's Social Security payment and other federal tax withholdings.

**Example 14** Assume that in example 12, Acme also withheld $312 in federal income tax and $87 in state income tax from Jenny's February earnings. What is Jenny's actual take-home pay for February?

**Discussion: Jenny's February take-home pay is $1,448 after withholding for income tax and Social Security. Out of her earnings of $2,000, $153 is withheld for payment of Social Security tax, $312 for federal income tax, and $87 for state income tax. Acme must pay these taxes to the appropriate government units on a timely basis. Acme will also remit its $153 in Social Security taxes on Jenny's wages when it makes Jenny's payments.**

Self-employed individuals pay a tax equal to the sum of the employee's and employer's payments. Thus in 2021, net self-employment income is subject to a tax of 12.4 percent (6.2% × 2) on the first $142,800 of income for OASDI and 2.9 percent (1.45% × 2) on all net self-employment income for MHI. Because employees are not taxed on the Social Security contribution made on their behalf by their employers, self-employed taxpayers are allowed to deduct one-half of their self-employment tax as a business expense to equalize the tax treatments of employees and the self-employed.

**Example 15** Assume that in example 13, Chandra's $145,000 in earnings constitutes net self-employment income rather than wages as an employee. How much self-employment tax must Chandra pay on her self-employment income?

**Discussion: Chandra pays $17,707 (12.4% × $142,800) of OASDI and $4,205 (2.9% × $145,000) of MHI, for a total self-employment tax of $21,912. Note that this is equal to the total tax paid by Chandra and her employer ($10,956 × 2) in example 13. Because Chandra is self-employed, she must pay the equivalent of the employee's and employer's tax.**

### Unemployment Taxes

Employers must also pay state and federal unemployment taxes on wages paid to employees to fund unemployment benefits. The Federal Unemployment Tax (FUTA) is 6.2 percent of the first $7,000 in wages paid to each employee. Unemployment taxes do not have to be paid for employees who earn less than $1,500 per calendar quarter and certain classes of agricultural workers. Because each state also levies an unemployment tax, employers are allowed a credit of up to 5.4 percent for the state unemployment taxes they pay. Thus, the minimum FUTA tax rate is 0.8 percent (6.2% − 5.4%).

## 1-3c Sales Tax

Many state and local governments raise significant amounts of revenue from a sales tax. A sales tax is based on a flat percentage of the selling price of a product or service. In contrast to income and employment taxes, which are based on the income of taxpayers, a sales tax is based on a taxpayer's consumption of goods and services. The business that sells the goods or services subject to the tax collects the tax for the government. However, the tax is still paid by the taxpayer purchasing the goods or services. Each government unit that imposes a sales tax determines which goods and/or services are subject to the tax. Thus, not all goods and services are subject to a sales tax. For example, medical services are typically exempted from the tax. Other items that are often exempted from the sales tax are food, farm equipment, and sales to tax-exempt organizations.

## 1-3d Property Taxes

A tax on the value of property owned by taxpayers is called a *property tax*. In general, **real property** is land and any structures that are permanently attached to it, such as buildings. All other types of property are referred to as **personal property**. Because real property is immobile and difficult to conceal from tax assessors, local governments such as cities, counties, and school districts prefer it as a revenue source.

Property taxes are referred to as **ad valorem taxes**, because they are based on the value of the property being taxed. However, most property taxes are not based on the true fair market value of the property. Rather, the assessed value of the property is used to determine the tax. The *assessed value* of property varies widely but is typically 50 to 75 percent of the estimated market value of the property. Market values are determined by the designated assessment authority (e.g., the county assessor) based on various factors such as recent comparable sales, replacement cost per square foot, and other local market conditions. The assessed value is then computed as the predetermined percentage of the assessor's valuation.

**Example 16** Maria Corporation owns a piece of land that it purchased for $6,000 in 2009. During the current year, the county tax assessor determines that the fair market value of the land is $8,000. In the county in which the land is located, assessed values are 50% of the fair market value. What is the assessed value of Maria Corporation's land?

**Discussion: Maria Corporation's assessed value is $4,000 ($8,000 × 50%). Note that the local authority can increase or decrease property taxes on the land by varying the percentage of fair market value that is subject to tax. Thus, if the county raised the percentage to 75%, the corporation would pay property tax based on an assessed value of $6,000 ($8,000 × 75%).**

Taxes on personal property are not as common as taxes on real property. The mobility and ease of concealment of personal property make the collection of a personal property tax administratively difficult. However, many local governments continue to selectively impose personal property taxes on types of property that are easier to track. Because of the relatively small number of establishments, property taxes on business property are still widely used. In addition, automobiles and boats are often assessed a personal property tax as part of their annual licensing fee.

**Example 17** State A imposes an annual tag fee on automobiles. The licensing fee is $20. A personal property tax is also levied, based on the initial selling price of the automobile and its age. During the current year, Darla paid a $94 tag fee on her automobile. How much of the fee is a personal property tax?

**Discussion:** **Darla's personal property tax on the automobile is $74 ($94 − $20). The $20 licensing fee is not a tax.**

## 1-3e Other Taxes

Income taxes, employment taxes, sales taxes, and property taxes are the primary revenue producers for the various forms of government. However, businesses and individuals pay a number of other taxes. The most important of these are excise taxes and wealth transfer taxes. In addition, state and local governments impose taxes on certain occupations (e.g., liquor dealers) and franchise taxes for the privilege of doing business within their jurisdictions.

### Excise Taxes

Excise taxes are imposed on various products and services. The federal government imposes excise taxes on a vast array of products and some services. Many states also levy excise taxes on the same products and services. An excise tax differs from a sales tax in that it is not based on the sales value of the product. Rather, an excise tax is typically imposed on a quantity, such as a gallon of gasoline or a pack of cigarettes. Some products subject to excise taxes include:

| | | | |
|---|---|---|---|
| alcohol | fishing equipment | bullets | tobacco |
| coal | gasoline | telephone services | |
| diesel fuels | guns | tires | |

### Wealth Transfer Taxes

Transfers of wealth between taxpayers are taxed by the federal gift tax and the federal estate tax. Most states also impose taxes on the value of an estate. These taxes are essentially a tax on the right to transfer property to another. **Gift taxes** are paid by the donor of property—the person making the gift. The person who receives the gift, the donee, is not subject to either the gift tax or income tax on the gift. The **estate tax** is paid by the administrator (called the *executor*) of a deceased taxpayer's estate from the assets of the estate. Both the gift tax and the estate tax are based on the fair market value of the property being transferred. In addition, there are numerous exclusions from both taxes, the effect of which is to tax only relatively large gifts and estates. Although gift and estate taxes are vaguely familiar to many people, they are relatively minor revenue producers. However, a basic understanding of the operation of the two taxes will aid in understanding some of the income tax issues related to gifts and estates that are discussed later in the text.

**Federal Gift Tax** A gift tax is imposed on the fair market value of gifts made between individuals.[11] Neither the donor nor the donee is subject to income tax on gifts. The donor of the gift property is responsible for reporting and paying the gift tax. The gift tax has several exclusions, the most basic of which is an annual exclusion of $15,000 per donee.[12] Under this provision, taxpayers can give as many individuals as they wish as much as $15,000 a year each and pay no gift tax. A married couple can use this exclusion to make tax-free gifts of up to $30,000 per person per year. The annual gift exclusion is indexed for inflation for gifts made after December 31, 2003. Taxpayers are also allowed to make unlimited gifts to their spouses and to charities without payment of the gift tax.

**Example 18** Ansel and Hanna gave their daughter a new car for graduation. The car cost $18,000. Is the gift subject to the gift tax?

**Discussion:** **Ansel and Hannah each are entitled to give $15,000 to any person each year. Therefore, they may make gifts of up to $30,000 to an individual without incurring any gift tax. Because the fair market value of the car is less than $30,000, it is not subject to gift tax.**

**Example 19** On their 25th wedding anniversary, Ansel gave Hannah a diamond ring that cost $50,000. Is the gift subject to the gift tax?

**Discussion:** **Gifts to a spouse are not subject to gift tax, regardless of the value transferred. Therefore, the ring is not subject to the gift tax.**

As these examples illustrate, the most common forms of gifts, such as those for birthdays, graduations, weddings, and anniversaries, are not subject to the gift tax. However, when a gift is made that is not totally excludable under one of these provisions, the taxpayer may use the unified donative-transfers credit to avoid payment of the gift tax.[13] The **unified donative-transfers credit** allows a lifetime credit against gift and estate taxes. The credit is equivalent to be able to exclude $11.7 million in property from the gift and/or the estate tax in 2021.

**Federal Estate Tax** The estate tax is levied on the fair market value of the assets a taxpayer owned at death.[14] The executor of the estate is responsible for valuing the assets of the estate, administering the assets before their distribution to the heirs, paying the estate taxes, and distributing the assets to the estate's beneficiaries. As with the gift tax, several exclusions and the unified donative-transfers credit limit taxation of estates to those estates that are fairly substantial.[15] The fair market value of the estate's assets is reduced by funeral and administrative costs, debts owned by the taxpayer, amounts bequeathed to charities, and the marital deduction for property passing to the surviving spouse. The marital deduction is unlimited—all amounts that pass to a surviving spouse are exempt from the estate tax. Judicious use of the marital deduction and the donative-transfers credit lets the value of most estates go untaxed at the death of the first spouse. Because the unified donative-transfers credit is a cumulative lifetime amount that applies to both gifts and property passing through the estate, careful planning is required to minimize the lifetime tax on gifts and property held at death. Suffice it to say that the gift and estate tax provisions can be quite complex. Taxpayers with substantial assets should seek competent professional advice in planning their estates to minimize the liability for these taxes.

Although the transfer of property from an estate to the heirs of the decedent has no income tax effect, the estate itself is subject to income tax while it holds the assets of the decedent. The executor of the estate must file an income tax return that reports the income and the deductions related to the assets of the decedent for the period between the date of death and the final distribution of the estate's assets.

## Health Care Related Taxes

The Affordable Care Act[16] implements a number of taxes to pay for the cost of subsidizing health care for those who cannot afford to purchase health insurance. Beginning in 2013, the following tax increases are imposed on individuals.

**Increased HI for higher income workers and self-employed taxpayers** For tax years beginning after December 31, 2012, an additional 0.9 percent hospital insurance (HI) tax applies wages received in excess of the threshold amount ($250,000 for a married couple filing jointly, $125,000 for a married individual filing a separate return, and $200,000 for all other taxpayers). For married individuals filing a joint return, the tax is imposed on the combined wages of the spouses. The additional 0.9 percent HI tax also applies to net self-employment in excess of the threshold amounts. The HI tax is in addition to the Social Security taxes imposed on wages and self-employment income.

**Example 20** Cinda earns $220,000 as an analyst at Lovekamp Securities in 2021. What is her total Social Security tax in 2021?

**Discussion: Cinda pays the $8,854 ($142,800 × 6.2%) maximum OASDI, $3,190 ($220,000 × 1.45%) of MHI, and $180 [($220,000 − $200,000) × 0.9%] of HI, for a total Social Security tax of $12,224. If the $220,000 was Cinda's net self-employment income, the OASDI and MHI taxes would double to $17,708 and $6,380, but the HI tax would remain $180.**

**Surtax on unearned income of higher-income individuals** For tax years beginning after December 31, 2012, a 3.8 percent Medicare contribution tax on unearned income is imposed on individuals, estates, and trusts. For individuals, the tax is imposed on the lesser of net investment income or modified adjusted gross income in excess of the threshold amount ($250,000 for a married couple filing jointly, $125,000 for a married individual filing a separate return, and $200,000 for all other taxpayers).

**Example 21** In example 20, assume that Cinda also has $10,000 in net investment income. If her modified adjusted gross income is $204,000, what is Cinda's Medicare contribution tax?

**Discussion: Cinda must pay a 3.8% tax on the lesser of ($10,000 net investment income) or $4,000 ($204,000 modified adjusted gross income – $200,000). Her Medicare contribution tax is $152 ($4,000 × 3.8%). NOTE: If Cinda's modified adjusted gross income was $216,000, her tax would be $380 [$10,000 < ($216,000 – $200,000) × 3.8%].**

**Limitation on contributions to health FSAs** For 2021, contributions to health flexible spending arrangements (health FSAs) are limited to $2,750. The original $2,500 limitation is adjusted annually for inflation for tax years beginning after December 31, 2013.

**Indoor tanning excise tax** Amounts paid for indoor tanning services performed after June 30, 2010, are subject to a 10 percent excise tax. Tanning salons are responsible for collecting the excise tax and paying over the tax on a quarterly basis. Tanning salons that fail to collect the tax from patrons are liable for the excise tax.

## 1-4 SOURCES OF FEDERAL INCOME TAX LAW

LO 3 Identify the primary sources of federal income tax law.

This text contains a general discussion of the federal income tax and by itself should not be considered a substitute for the original sources of the tax law. Before making a final decision about a tax issue, you should review the appropriate original source of the tax rule on which you are going to rely. Thus, it is important to be aware of the legislative, administrative, and judicial sources of tax law. These sources are frequently referred to as *primary sources* of tax law. The discussion that follows briefly outlines the primary sources. A more detailed discussion of the primary authorities is contained in Chapter 16, Tax Research. The remainder of this text generally will not make specific references to sources of tax law. Instead, this book makes generic reference to "tax law" to simplify the discussion.

The end of each chapter includes a list of applicable sources keyed to footnote numbers in the chapter and a brief summary of each source. For those who wish to read the primary sources, they are available in most university and public libraries. Briefly, our citations follow common tax practice, with deference to *The Bluebook: A Uniform System of Citation* (Harvard Law Review Association) and the *Chicago Manual of Style* (University of Chicago Press). For example, *Sec. 61* refers to Section 61 of the Internal Revenue Code of 1986 as amended. *Reg. Sec. 1.61-2* refers to the second Treasury regulation issued that interprets Section 61. *Helvering v. Gregory*, 69 F.2d 809 (2d Cir. 1934), is a citation to a 1934 court case that was decided by the U.S. Court of Appeals for the Second Circuit. The case is located in volume 69 of the *Federal Reporter* case series, beginning at page 809. A complete explanation of all citations and how to locate the primary sources can be found in Chapter 16.

The federal income tax law dates to 1913 and has been amended, revised, and reworked numerous times since. The current statutory source of federal income tax law is the **Internal Revenue Code of 1986**, as amended (referred to as the *Code*). The tax law is laid out in the Code by section number. Thus, the basic reference to a particular tax law provision is to the section of the Code in which the law is stated. Often, particular tax treatments are referred to by their Code section number. For example, Section 179 lets a taxpayer deduct a portion of the cost of qualifying depreciable property in the year of acquisition (rather than depreciating it over its tax life). Tax practitioners refer to this election as the *Section 179 election*. Therefore, when appropriate, references to Code sections will include the popular terminology associated with that section.

The Internal Revenue Service is the branch of the Treasury Department that is responsible for interpreting and administering the tax law. The Treasury provides overall interpretive guidance on the Code by issuing **Treasury regulations.**[17] Regulations undergo an intensive review and public comment process before they are issued. Because of this intensive review, interpretations of regulations generally carry considerable authority, sometimes approaching that of the Code.

In fulfilling its administrative function, the IRS issues revenue rulings, revenue procedures, and a variety of other pronouncements that provide guidelines on the interpretation of the Code. Because the IRS issues several hundred rulings each year, they do not undergo the extensive review process accorded regulations. As such, they are given less weight as an authority than a Treasury regulation.

In addition to providing interpretive guidance, the IRS has responsibility for ensuring taxpayers' compliance with the tax law. During 2020, the IRS processed 159.4 million income tax returns. In 2019, the IRS provided tax preparation assistance to 67.3 million taxpayers, and in 2014 it audited 1.4 million tax returns filed by individual taxpayers. When audited by the IRS, taxpayers are allowed to present their reasoning for the items in question on their return. As might be expected, disputes often arise between taxpayers and the IRS concerning its interpretations and enforcement of the tax law. Most disputes are resolved through the IRS appeals process. However, taxpayers who are dissatisfied with the result of the appeals process are entitled to take their disputes to court for settlement.

Court decisions establish precedent in the interpretation of the tax law. Taxpayers and the IRS are generally bound by the interpretation of a court on a particular issue. However, the loser of an initial court case may appeal the decision to a U.S. Circuit Court of Appeals. A loss at the appellate level may be further appealed to the U.S. Supreme Court. However, the Supreme Court limits its review of tax cases to those of major importance (e.g., a constitutional issue) or to resolving conflicting decisions in the appellate courts. A Supreme Court decision is not subject to review—it is the final interpretation of the law. Only Congress can override an interpretation of the Supreme Court by amending the Code section in question.

Tax information is also published in a variety of secondary sources. These resources include tax reference services, professional tax journals, tax newsletters, and textbooks. Secondary sources are useful when researching an issue, and they are often helpful for understanding the primary sources. However, you should exercise care when using secondary sources because their interpretations are not authoritative.

## 1-5 FEDERAL INCOME TAX TERMINOLOGY

LO 4

Define *taxable income* and other commonly used tax terms.

Individuals, corporations, and certain estates and trusts are subject to tax on their federal taxable income. Federal taxable income is defined by the tax law and differs from both financial accounting and economic measures of income. The general computational framework for determining the taxable income of all taxpayers is shown in Exhibit 1-1.

*Exhibit 1-1*

### Income Tax Computational Framework

Income "Broadly Defined" (includes income from all sources)

| | |
|---|---|
| Minus: | Excluded income |
| Equals: | Gross income |
| Minus: | Deductions |
| Equals: | Taxable income |
| × | Tax rate (schedule of rates) |
| Equals: | Income tax |
| Minus: | Tax credits |
| | Tax prepayments |
| Equals: | Tax (refund) due with return |

Both the terms used in the computations and the order of the computational framework are prescribed in the tax law.

## 1-5a Income

The term *income* is used in several ways. Therefore, always be sure you understand the context in which the term is used. As broadly defined, income includes both taxable and nontaxable types of income. This definition includes all income that belongs to the taxpayer. *Gross income* is a more restrictive term. As Exhibit 1-1 shows, **gross income** is income broadly defined minus income items that are excluded from taxation.[18] Items of gross income are included in the computation of taxable income. Generally, gross income is the starting point for reporting income items on a tax return. Chapter 3 discusses the most commonly encountered gross income items.

A fundamental rule in regard to income is that an item is included in gross income unless it is specifically excluded by the tax law. **Exclusions** represent increases in a taxpayer's wealth and recoveries of the taxpayer's capital investment that Congress has decided should not be subject to income tax. Thus, income exclusions are not counted as gross income. Common income exclusions include inheritances, gifts, and interest on certain municipal bonds. Exclusions are discussed in Chapter 4.

Although not an explicit part of the income tax computation, deferrals of income and deductions are also found in the tax law. A **deferral** is an item that does not affect the current period's taxable income but will affect taxable income in a future tax year. Thus, a deferral is like an exclusion in that it does not have a current tax effect. However, it differs in that an exclusion is *never* subject to tax, whereas a deferral *will be* subject to tax at some point in the future.

Taxable income is a net number and is the tax base. Taxable income is determined by subtracting deductions from gross income. Taxable income is the tax base that is multiplied by the applicable tax rate to compute the federal income tax. Taxable income is usually different from financial accounting income computed by using generally accepted accounting principles.

The differences between financial accounting income and taxable income generally arise because taxable income is computed according to the rules prescribed by the tax law. Tax accounting rules are not based on generally accepted accounting principles (GAAP). GAAP are concerned with determining the "true income" for an annual period. The income tax is geared to producing and collecting tax revenues and providing incentives for particular economic and social transactions. An important difference between the two objectives is that the income tax system attempts to collect the tax on income in the period during which the taxpayer has the resources to pay the tax. Under GAAP, having the resources to pay taxes is of no concern. As a result, specific income and deduction items may be accelerated, deferred, or permanently excluded from the current year's taxable income computation, as opposed to the GAAP treatment. For example, prepaid rental income may be amortized over the lease period for financial reporting but must be reported in full in the year it is collected for tax reporting. Another example is the treatment of depreciable property. For tax purposes, assets must be depreciated by using a statutorily determined recovery period, without regard for their actual useful life. For financial reporting, the same asset is depreciated over its useful life. These are but two examples of income and deduction items that are different for financial and taxable income and that will be discussed throughout the text.

Income is also referred to as *ordinary income*. **Ordinary income** is the recurring income earned by a taxpayer for a tax year.[19] It is the common type of income that people and businesses expect to earn. Ordinary income typically includes business profits, rent from property, interest on investments, dividend income, and wages. Ordinary income is subject to tax using regular tax rates and computations explained in later chapters. That is, ordinary income receives no special treatment under the laws.

Income also results from gains. A **gain** is the difference between the selling price of an asset and its tax cost and is the result of disposing of the asset.[20] Usually, a gain will be the result of a sale of a single asset. Most gains produce ordinary income. However, gains on the sale of certain types of assets receive special treatment in the determination of taxable income and the tax liability. These gains are called *capital gains* and result from the sale of capital assets.

## 1-5b Deductions

**Deductions** are amounts that the tax law specifically allows as subtractions from gross income. Deductions are a matter of legislative grace. The concept of legislative grace gives us a basic rule to follow to determine items that qualify for deduction. The rule is that an item may not be deducted unless the tax law specifically permits it. Deductions are characterized as *expenses* and *losses*.

An **expense** is a current period expenditure that is incurred to earn income. Deductions for expenses are limited to those incurred in a trade or business,[21] in an income-producing activity (investment activity),[22] and certain specifically allowed personal expenses of individuals. Trade or business expenses and income-producing expenses must be ordinary, necessary, and reasonable in amount to be deductible. Allowable personal expenses are deductible as itemized deductions and are subject to strict limitations.

The term **loss** refers to two distinctly different types of events. A loss occurs when an asset is disposed of for a selling price that is less than its tax cost. This type of loss is referred to as a **transaction loss** and represents a loss of capital invested in the asset. In later chapters, it will be necessary to apply limits to the amount of a loss that can be deducted in a tax year. To apply the limits, losses are characterized as personal, business, or capital. These limits deny deductions for most personal losses, place a cap on the amount of capital losses that may be deducted in the year of the loss, and allow business losses to be fully deducted as incurred.

The second type of loss is an annual loss. An **annual loss** results from an excess of allowable deductions for a tax year over the reported income for the year. The treatment of the annual loss depends on the activity in which the loss is incurred. Chapter 7 discusses the limitations on and treatment of all losses, transaction and annual.

## 1-5c Income Tax Rates

The 2021 tax rate schedules for two classes of individual taxpayers and corporations are reproduced in Table 1-2 (p. 1-22).[23] A full set of tax rates for individuals and corporations for 2021 is reproduced in Appendix B. The income tax is calculated by multiplying taxable income by the applicable tax rates. Each year, the IRS publishes new tax rate schedules that are adjusted for cost-of-living increases. The Tax Cuts and Jobs Act provides a new metric for calculating these cost of living increases. Before January 1, 2018, the IRS used CPI to adjust the tax rate schedules for changes in cost of living. On January 1, 2018, the IRS began to use the Chained Consumer Price Index for All Urban Consumers C-CPI-U. It is expected that C-CPI-U will show inflation growing at a slower rate than did CPI. Adjusting the tax rate schedules for changes in the cost of living helps minimize a hidden tax that results from inflation.

Assume the following information (as shown in Exhibit 1-2): A single taxpayer's taxable income in 2020 was $40,400. The rate of inflation in 2020 was 1.0 percent, and the taxpayer was able to keep up with inflation by increasing her income. Her taxable income goes up by $404 to $40,804 ($40,400 × 1.01%) in 2021. At this point, the taxpayer is no better or worse off in 2021 than in 2020. Her income increases merely kept up with the rate of inflation. The top panel of Exhibit 1-2 shows that failure to adjust the 2021 tax rates for the 1.0 percent inflation rate results in $89 in additional tax. The increased tax is attributable to two sources. First, the increased income results in additional tax even if the marginal rate stays the same from the first to the second year. Second, the problem worsens when the inflated income pushes the

Exhibit 1-2

## The Hidden Inflation Tax

| | Tax Year | |
|---|---|---|
| | 2020 | 2021 |
| Taxable income | $40,400 | $ 40,400 |
| Increase in taxable income due to inflation | | $ 404 |
| Inflation-adjusted taxable income | $40,400 | $ 40,804 |
| Tax using 2020 single taxpayer rates: | | |
| Tax on base amount | $ 4,618 | $ 4,618 |
| Excess taxed at marginal rate | | |
| 22% | $ 61 | $ 149 |
| Total tax | $ 4,678 | $ 4,767 |
| Additional tax resulting from inflation | | $ 89 |
| Tax on $40,804 at 2021 tax rates | | |
| Tax on $40,525 | | $ 4,664 |
| Tax on income in excess of $40,525 | | |
| ($40,800 − $40,525) × 22% | | $ 61 |
| Tax at 2021 rates | | $ 4,725 |
| 2020 After-tax income $40,400 − $4,678 | | $ 35,722 |
| 2020 Inflation rate adjustment | | × 1.010 |
| 2021 Real after-tax income | | $ 36,079 |
| Actual 2021 after-tax income $40,804 − $4,725 | | $ 36,079 |

taxpayer into a higher marginal tax bracket (tax bracket creep) causing additional tax Thus, the taxpayer is worse off, because she pays $89 more tax on the same deflated income when tax rates are not adjusted for inflation. The net result is an increase of after-tax income of only $315 ($404 − $89), which is less than the rate of inflation.

The bottom panel of Exhibit 1-2 calculates the tax using the actual 2020 rates, which are adjusted for the 1.0 percent inflation rate. The tax on a 2021 taxable income of $40,804 is $4,725. This is a reduction of $42 ($4,767 − $4,725) over the tax calculated using 2020 rates on the same income. The adjustment for inflation in the tax rate brackets leaves the taxpayer with the same inflation-adjusted after-tax income in 2021 [($40,400 − $4,678) × 1.010% = $35,722 ($40,804 − $4,725)] that the taxpayer had in 2020. Thus, the adjustment of the tax brackets for inflation each year ensures that taxpayers whose income merely keeps pace with inflation will not realize a decrease in real after-tax income.

## 1-5d Tax Prepayments

The pay-as-you-go system requires the payment of tax as the income is earned and when the taxpayer has the resources available to pay the tax. Tax prepayments are subtracted from the income tax liability to determine whether the taxpayer has underpaid and owes additional tax with the return (tax due) or is entitled to a refund of overpaid taxes (refund due). Employees prepay taxes on wages through payroll-tax withholding. Other types of income, such as pensions and some gambling winnings, are also subject to the withholding of tax by the payer. The employer or other person withholding the tax pays the tax withheld to the IRS, to be credited to the taxpayer's account with the government.

Table 1-2

## 2021 Tax Rate Schedules

**Single Taxpayers**

| If Taxable Income Is Over | But Not Over | The Tax Is | of the Amount Over |
|---|---|---|---|
| $ 0 | $ 9,950 | ....... 10% | $ 0 |
| $ 9,950 | $ 40,525 | $ 995.00 + 12% | $ 9,950 |
| $ 40,525 | $ 86,375 | $4,664 + 22% | $ 40,525 |
| $ 86,375 | $164,925 | $ 14,751.00 + 24% | $ 86,375 |
| $164,295 | $209,425 | $ 33,603.00 + 32% | $164,295 |
| 209,425 | 523,600 | $ 47,843.00 + 35% | 209,425 |
| 523,600 | ....... | $157,804.25 + 37% | 523,600 |

**Married Taxpayers Filing Jointly and Surviving Spouse**

| If Taxable Income Is Over | But Not Over | The Tax Is | of the Amount Over |
|---|---|---|---|
| $ 0 | 19,900 | ....... 10% | $ 0 |
| 19,900 | $ 81,050 | $ 1,990.00 + 12% | 19,900 |
| 81,050 | 172,750 | 9,328.00 + 22% | 81,050 |
| 172,750 | 329,850 | 29,502.00 + 24% | 172,750 |
| 329,850 | 418,850 | 67,260.00 + 32% | 329,850 |
| 418,850 | $628,300 | 95,686.00 + 35% | 418,850 |
| 628,300 | | $168,993.50 + 37% | 628,300 |

**Corporate Tax Rate Schedule**

| If Taxable Income Is Over | But Not Over | The Tax Is | of the Amount Over |
|---|---|---|---|
| $ -0- | $ unlimited | ....... 21% | $ -0- |

Self-employed people and taxpayers with income not subject to withholding (trade or business income, interest income, dividend income, gains from sales of assets, etc.) are required to make quarterly payments of their current-year estimated tax payments. An individual usually makes quarterly payments on April 15, June 15, and September 15 of the tax year and on January 15 of the next year. This corresponds to the fifteenth day of the fourth, sixth, and ninth months of the tax year and the fifteenth day of the first month of the following year. A corporation makes its estimated tax payments on the fifteenth day of the fourth, sixth, ninth, and twelfth months of its tax year. Estates and trusts follow the estimated tax schedule used by individuals. Estimated tax payments, like withheld amounts, are subtracted as credits for the prepayment of tax.

## 1-5e Tax Credits

A **tax credit** is a direct reduction in the income tax liability. In effect, tax credits are treated like tax prepayments. As Exhibit 1-1 shows, a credit is not deducted to arrive at taxable income but is instead subtracted directly from the income tax liability. Thus, a tax credit is more valuable than a deduction of an equal amount, because the credit yields a larger reduction in the total tax due. Tax credits are often used as incentives to encourage taxpayers to enter into specific types of transactions that Congress feels will further some public purpose.

If a taxpayer's marginal tax rate is 24 percent, a $5,000 tax deduction has the same value as a $1,200 tax credit ($5,000 × 24%). Likewise, a $1,000 tax credit has the same value as a $4,167 deduction if the marginal rate is 24 percent ($1,000 ÷ 24%).

**Example 22** Jada and Martha, whose marginal tax rate is 24%, paid $1,000 for child care.

**Discussion: If the expenditure is treated as a credit, the tax they owe for the year will be reduced by the full $1,000. If the expenditure is treated as a deduction, their tax would be reduced by $240 ($1,000 × 24% marginal rate). Treatment of the expenditure as a credit would save them $760 more than treatment as a deduction.**

The most common business tax credits are discussed in Chapter 15. Individuals are also allowed tax credits for certain circumstances and activities. For example, individuals with dependents are allowed a credit of $2,000 for each qualifying dependent. Restrictions and limitations associated with this tax credit and other common individual tax credits are discussed in Chapter 8.

## 1-5f Filing Returns

In general, all income tax entities must file an annual tax return. (See Chapter 8 for individual filing requirements.) Returns for individuals, corporations, estates, and trusts must be filed on or before the fifteenth day of the fourth month following the close of the entity's tax year (April 15 for calendar-year taxpayers). Partnership and S Corporation tax returns are due on or before the fifteenth day of the third month following the close of the tax year (March 15 for calendar-year corporate taxpayers). Taxpayers who cannot complete and file their returns by the regular due date can apply for extensions for filing the return. Individuals are granted an automatic six-month extension by applying for the extension by the due date of the return. Corporations are allowed an automatic six-month extension; partnerships and trusts can automatically extend their filing date by three months. Filing an extension does not extend the time for paying the tax. Applications for automatic extensions must show and include payment of the estimated amount due with the final return.

**Example 23** Thelma procrastinates about preparing her tax return and determines that she cannot complete the return by April 15. She has withholdings and estimated tax payments totaling $8,600 and estimates that her total tax liability for the year will be $8,950. What must Thelma do to extend the date for filing her return?

**Discussion: Thelma can extend the period for filing her return to October 15 (six months from April 15) by filing the application for automatic extension by April 15. This only grants Thelma permission to delay the filing of the return. She must pay the $350 ($8,950 − $8,600) estimated tax she owes when she applies for the extension.**

Taxpayers and the government can correct errors on returns within a limited time period called the **statute of limitations**. Generally, once the statute of limitations has expired, corrections cannot be made. The general statute of limitations is three years from the due date of the return, not including extensions. The three-year statute of limitations has several exceptions, the most important of which deal with fraudulently prepared returns. The statute of limitations runs for six years when a taxpayer omits gross income in excess of 25 percent of the gross income reported on the return. The government can bring charges of criminal fraud against a taxpayer at any time. That is, neither the three-year nor the six-year statute of limitations protects a taxpayer who willfully defrauds the government.

The government corrects errors on taxpayers' returns through its audit process. Taxpayers correct errors on prior year returns by filing amended returns. Amended returns are not used to adjust returns for previous years. (See discussion of the tax benefit rule in Chapter 2.) An amended return should be filed only if a taxpayer finds that an item of income that should have been included in gross income was omitted in the original filing or if the taxpayer improperly included an item of income in a prior year. Taxpayers also should file amended returns if they find that they failed to take an allowable deduction or if they find that they took an improper deduction on an earlier return.

**Example 24** Geraldo Corporation incurred a net operating loss in 2020, its first year of operation. Because the controller knew that Geraldo was going to suffer a loss, he took no deductions for depreciation for 2020. Geraldo's independent auditor found the error in 2021 and advised Geraldo that it must take all allowable deductions in the proper year. Should Geraldo file an amended return for 2020?

**Discussion: Because the depreciation was not treated properly on the 2020 tax return, Geraldo should file an amended return that takes the proper depreciation deduction for 2020.**

**Example 25** Walstad Corporation is an accrual basis taxpayer. In 2020, Walstad determined that one of its customers with an accounts receivable balance of $40,000 was in bankruptcy. After conferring with the customer's lawyers, Walstad determined that it would be able to collect only $15,000 of the account and deducted the $25,000 uncollectible amount as a bad debt expense. In 2021, the customer's bankruptcy was settled, and Walstad received $10,000 as a final settlement of the account it had written off. Should Walstad file an amended return for 2020 and correct the bad debt deduction?

**Discussion: The actual bad debt is $30,000 ($40,000 − $10,000). The $25,000 bad debt deduction that Walstad took in 2020 was an estimate of the amount of the bad debt. Therefore, the deduction was not incorrect at the time the return was filed. Walstad should deduct the additional $5,000 ($30,000 − $25,000) of actual bad debt in 2021 to adjust the estimate. Amended returns are not filed to adjust estimates on prior year returns. Adjustments to estimates are made on the return for the year in which the actual amount of the deduction becomes known.**

# 1-6 THE AUDIT AND APPEAL PROCESS WITHIN THE IRS

LO 5
Explain the IRS audit process and taxpayer rights within the process.

The federal income tax system is based on self-assessment, which requires taxpayers to report and pay their taxes correctly. IRS examinations, or audits, can vary from a letter that requests supporting information by mail to a full-scale, continuous examination of large corporations in which teams of IRS agents work at each taxpayer's office. Taxpayers who do not agree to changes suggested by the IRS during an audit can appeal the matter to a higher administrative level within the IRS. Generally, taxpayers cannot be charged with any additional taxes, interest, or penalties without first being formally notified. Whenever settlement cannot be reached with the IRS, the taxpayer can initiate litigation in one of the trial courts.

## 1-6a Tax Return Selection Processes

The IRS cannot possibly examine every return that is filed. It does examine as many returns as possible, given its staffing and facility levels. Currently, this amounts to only about 2 percent of all returns filed. The IRS uses five general methods to verify that taxpayers are properly self-assessing their taxes. One of the most important is a computerized return selection program called the **Discriminant Function System (DIF)**. Through mathematical analysis of historical data, this program selects those returns with the highest probability of containing errors. Selected returns are typically examined only for specific items such as charitable contributions or employee business expenses. A related program is the **Taxpayer Compliance Measurement Program (TCMP)**. Returns are randomly selected from different income levels, and every item on the return is comprehensively audited. The results are used to set the parameters for the DIF computer selection program. The IRS suspended the TCMP audits in 1997 because of reductions in its budget.

Virtually all returns are checked for mathematical, tax calculation, and clerical errors during the initial processing of the returns. If an error is discovered under this **document perfection program**, the IRS recalculates the amount of tax due and sends an explanation to the taxpayer. Another program of increasing importance is called the

**information-matching program**. Information from banks, employers, and others on forms such as the W-2 for wages and withholding and the 2000 for miscellaneous income are matched to the taxpayer's return. For any omitted or incorrect items, the IRS recomputes the tax and sends an explanation to the taxpayer. Finally, a number of **special audit programs** are designed by the IRS and combine computer and manual selection based on various standards that are changed periodically. Some of the standards used include the size of the refund, the amount of adjusted gross income reported, and the amount or type of deduction claimed.

## 1-6b Types of Examinations

There are three basic types of IRS examinations. **Correspondence examinations** are those that can be routinely handled by mail. Most originate at the IRS service centers and involve routine requests for supporting documents such as canceled checks or some other written instruments. A written reply to the questions raised, along with copies of supporting documents, usually completes the examination.

**Office examinations** are conducted at the local district office of the IRS and usually involve middle-income, nonbusiness returns, and small sole proprietorships. The taxpayer is notified by letter of the date and time of the exam, as well as the items for which proof is requested. Most taxpayers appear for themselves, although some are represented by their return preparers or other tax advisers. The audit is relatively informal, and the IRS agent has considerable discretion in resolving factual questions such as substantiation of travel expenses. For questions of law, however, the agent must follow IRS policy as expressed in Treasury regulations, revenue rulings and procedures, and the like, even if court decisions indicate otherwise.

**Field examinations** are conducted at the taxpayer's place of business and can involve any item on the income tax return as well as any items on the payroll and excise tax returns. These examinations are handled by more-experienced IRS agents, and almost all taxpayers are represented by their tax advisers. As with office examinations, IRS agents must follow IRS policy on matters of law and are accorded a great deal of latitude in settling matters of fact.

## 1-6c Settlement Procedures

After the examination, the agent prepares a report, known as the revenue agent's report (RAR), describing how each issue was settled and the amount of any additional tax or refund due the taxpayer. The agent also prepares a waiver of restrictions on assessment (Form 870), which states that the taxpayer waives any restrictions against assessment and collection of the tax by the IRS. Both items are mailed to the taxpayer in a letter commonly called a 30-day letter, along with an IRS publication describing the taxpayer's appeal rights.

A signed Form 870 means that the taxpayer agrees to the proposed changes, but it is not binding on either the taxpayer or the IRS. The taxpayer merely agrees to pay the additional tax due while reserving the right to file for a refund in a subsequent court action. Generally, the IRS rejects a settlement reached by its agents only if there is fraud or a misrepresentation of a material fact.

## 1-6d Administrative Appeals

A taxpayer who does not agree with the agent's report may request a meeting with agents from the **IRS Appeals Division** within 30 days of the date of the letter. If the additional tax due exceeds $2,500, the taxpayer must include a written response to the agent's findings; the taxpayer's response is called a **protest letter**. When the amount is less than $2,500 or is the result of a correspondence or office examination, no written protest is required.

The administrative appeal process allows taxpayers one additional opportunity to reach a settlement before resorting to the courts. The appeals division has the authority to consider the hazards of litigation. For example, when the facts or the law are uncertain, or both, the appeals division may settle issues it does not want to litigate, even if the IRS position has some merit. After what may be lengthy negotiation, taxpayers who finally reach an agreement with the IRS, or who simply don't want to pursue the matter, sign the Form 870 (or Form 870-AD, if the IRS has conceded some issues) and pay the full amount of the deficiency plus any penalties and interest.

Taxpayers unable to reach an agreement in the appeals division, or who have bypassed the appeals division by failing to respond to the 30-day letter, are sent a statutory notice of deficiency. This letter is the official notification by the IRS that it intends to assess or charge the taxpayer for some additional taxes, and is commonly referred to as a 90-day letter.

Taxpayers who are not interested in going to court can simply wait 90 days to have the deficiency formally assessed and then pay any additional amounts due. Taxpayers who want to litigate in district court or the claims court first must pay the amounts due and file for a refund in the court of their choice. Taxpayers who do not want to pay first must file a petition with the U.S. Tax Court within 90 days of the date of the letter. The decision to take an unresolved issue to court involves a number of additional factors and typically is made only with the advice of legal counsel specializing in tax litigation.

# 1-7 INDIVIDUAL INCOME TAX CALCULATION

The general tax calculation presented in Exhibit 1-1 applies to all taxpayers. However, the tax law modifies this calculation for individuals to take into account the unique characteristics of individual taxpayers.

The calculation of an individual's taxable income is outlined in Exhibit 1-3. Note that the general flow remains the same—deductions are subtracted from gross income to arrive at taxable income. Gross income is determined under the general tax formula. The distinguishing feature of the individual taxable income calculation is that deductions are broken into two classes—deductions for adjusted gross income and deductions from adjusted gross income. This dichotomy of deductions results in an intermediate income number called the **adjusted gross income (AGI)**.[24] In fact, it will become clear in the discussion that follows, this is a very important income number, because it is used to limit the deductions from adjusted gross income of an individual taxpayer. Deductions are discussed in more detail in later chapters. However, at this point, a general knowledge of the computational form and allowable deductions of individuals is necessary. Each type of deduction is discussed in turn.

*Exhibit 1-3*

## Individual Income Tax Formula

| | | |
|---|---|---|
| | All sources of income (broadly defined) | $ XXX |
| Minus: | Exclusions from income | (XXX) |
| Equals: | Gross income | $ XXX |
| Minus: | Deductions *for* adjusted gross income | |
| | Trade or business expenses | |
| | Rental and royalty expenses | |
| | Other specifically allowable deductions | (XXX) |
| Equals: | **ADJUSTED GROSS INCOME** | $ XXX |
| Minus: | Deductions *from* adjusted gross income | |
| | Personal deductions: the greater of | |
| | 1. itemized deductions (allowable personal expenses and certain other allowable deductions) | |
| | OR | |
| | 2. individual standard deduction | (XXX) |
| Equals: | Taxable income | $ XXX |

## 1-7a Deductions for Adjusted Gross Income

LO 6
Explain the calculation of taxable income for individual taxpayers and the unique personal deductions allowed to individuals.

Individuals are always allowed to deduct the qualified expenses they incur as **deductions for adjusted gross income**. In contrast to deductions from adjusted gross income, deductions in this class are not subject to reduction based on the income of the taxpayer. That is, once the allowable amount of an expenditure in this category has been determined, it is not subject to further reduction based on the income of the taxpayer. The allowable deductions for adjusted gross income are generally those that are incurred in a trade or business of the taxpayer or that are related to the earning of other forms of income. In addition, several other specifically allowed items are deductible for adjusted gross income. Deductions for adjusted gross income include:

Trade or business expenses
Rental and royalty expenses
Capital loss deductions
Contributions to individual retirement accounts (IRAs)
Reimbursed employee business expenses
1/2 of self-employment taxes paid
Self-employed medical insurance premiums
Up to $2,500 of interest on qualified student loans

Although these expenditures are not limited by the income of the taxpayer, other limitations in the tax law may reduce the current period's tax deduction. For example, the allowable deductions for rental properties may be limited by either the vacation home rules or the passive activity loss rules. Losses on the sale of capital assets are deductible but are first netted against capital gains. If the result is a net capital loss, the current year's deduction is limited to a maximum of $3,000.[25] These losses and other limits are covered in the chapters on deductions and losses. The important point to remember for now is that once the allowable amount of a deduction for adjusted gross income has been determined, it is not subject to further reduction. In addition, there is no preset minimum allowable amount of deductions for adjusted gross income.

## 1-7b Deductions from Adjusted Gross Income

Individuals are allowed to deduct certain personal expenditures and other specified nonpersonal expenditures as **deductions from adjusted gross income**. These deductions are commonly referred to as **itemized deductions**. Note in Exhibit 1-3 that individuals deduct the greater of their allowable itemized deductions or the standard deduction.[26] The **standard deduction** is an amount that Congress allows all taxpayers to deduct regardless of their actual qualifying itemized deduction expenditures. Thus, taxpayers itemize their deductions only if their total allowable itemized deductions exceed the standard deduction. For 2021, the standard deduction is $12,550 for a single individual and $25,100 for a married couple.

**Example 26** Festus is a single taxpayer with total allowable itemized deductions of $1,800 in 2021. What is Festus's allowable deduction from adjusted gross income?

**Discussion: Festus deducts the larger of his $1,800 in itemized deductions or the $12,550 standard deduction for a single individual. In this case, Festus deducts the $12,550 standard deduction.**

**Example 27** Assume that in example 26, Festus's total allowable itemized deductions are $12,700 in 2021. What is his allowable deduction from adjusted gross income?

**Discussion: Festus would deduct the $12,700 in actual itemized deductions because it exceeds his $12,550 standard deduction.**

As these examples illustrate, just because a particular expenditure is allowed as an itemized deduction does not necessarily mean that a taxpayer incurring the expense will actually deduct it. Itemized deductions reduce taxable income only when a taxpayer's total itemized deductions exceed the allowable standard deduction.

In addition to giving all taxpayers some minimum amount of deduction, the standard deduction eliminates the need for every taxpayer to list every qualifying personal expenditure. This makes it easier for taxpayers with small amounts of qualifying expenditures to comply with the tax law and relieves the government from having to verify millions of deductions that would have been claimed as a result of itemizing. Thus, the standard deduction is an important tool that the government uses to promote income tax law compliance by removing the burden of record-keeping and reporting for relatively small amounts of deductible items.

In the deduction classification scheme, specifically allowed personal expenditures are classified as itemized deductions.[27] Many allowable itemized deductions are subject to an income limitation. That is, the amount of the qualifying expenditure must be reduced by a percentage of the taxpayer's adjusted gross income to determine the actual deduction. The effect of using this type of income limitation is to disallow deductions for amounts that are small in relation to the taxpayer's income.

**Example 28** Qualifying medical expenses are deductible to the extent that they exceed 10% of a taxpayer's adjusted gross income. During the current year, Li has an adjusted gross income of $40,000 and incurred $5,200 in qualified medical expenses. What is Li's itemized deduction for medical expenses?

**Discussion: Li must reduce the $5,200 of qualified medical expenses by $4,000 ($40,000 × 10%), resulting in deductible medical expenses of $1,200.**

**Note that the effect of the limitation is to allow larger deductions for taxpayers with smaller incomes. Another taxpayer incurring the same $5,200 in expenses who had an adjusted gross income of only $25,000 would be allowed to deduct $2,700 [$5,200 − ($25,000 × 10% = $2,500)] of the medical expenses.**

The following list is intended to acquaint you with the categories of itemized deductions available to individuals. At this point, you should note the types of personal expenses that are allowed as a deduction. Do not be concerned about the detailed deduction requirements and limitations. These issues are explained in more detail in Chapter 8.

*Medical Expenses*—Unreimbursed medical expenses are deductible to the extent that they exceed 10 percent of adjusted gross income. Medical expenses include the cost of medical insurance, physicians, hospitals, glasses and contact lenses, and a multitude of other items. Because of the AGI limit, many taxpayers benefit from these deductions only when there is a major illness in the family.[28]

*Taxes*—State, local, and foreign income taxes, real estate taxes, and state and local personal property taxes not in excess of $10,000 may be deducted.[29]

*Interest*—An individual's itemized deduction for personal interest expense is limited to the following:[30]

- Home mortgage interest related to the acquisition of a home
- Investment interest expense

*Charitable Contributions*—Gifts to qualified charitable organizations may be deducted. Generally, the deductible contribution may not exceed 60 percent of the taxpayer's adjusted gross income.[31]

LO 7
Develop a framework for tax planning and discuss the effect of marginal tax rates and the time value of money on tax planning.

## 1-8 TAX PLANNING

The objective of tax planning is to maximize after-tax wealth. An effective tax plan results in a reduction of taxes for the planning period. Because a planning period may be two or more years, focusing on reducing tax for one year without considering any offsetting effects for other years can lead to excessive tax payments. The traditional planning technique of deferring income and accelerating deductions may not always be the best tax plan. The traditional technique considers only the time value of money savings that can be obtained from delaying tax payments on income or receiving tax savings from deductions sooner. Although the time value of money must always be considered, changes in marginal tax rates from one year to the next can have effects that offset the time value of money. Thus in many cases, changes in both the marginal tax rate and the time value of money must be considered when developing a tax plan. The mechanics of tax planning demonstrate basic techniques that can be used to help make tax-planning decisions. The planning discussion concludes by pointing out that tax avoidance is acceptable but tax evasion is not.

## 1-8a Mechanics of Tax Planning

The mechanics of tax planning focus on the issues of timing and income shifting. The timing question to be answered is when income and deductions should be claimed to save the most *real tax*. To make decisions involving timing, it is necessary to compare the tax effects of changes in marginal tax rates and the time value of money. To make the optimal choice among different alternatives, the calculations must be done to determine the *real* after-tax cost of each alternative. Income shifting involves moving income among related taxpayers to achieve the lowest marginal taxes (and lowest total tax) on the entire income of the related taxpayers. Shifting is commonly done by transferring income-producing property among family members and by using corporations that taxpayers control to shift income into the lowest marginal tax rates.

### Timing Income and Deductions

A taxpayer's marginal tax rate and the time value of money must be considered in tax planning. The traditional technique of deferring income and accelerating deductions relies solely on the time value of money savings from delaying the tax payment or receiving the tax deduction savings earlier. For example, a taxpayer who expects to be in a 24 percent marginal tax bracket for the next several years might be indifferent about reporting $1,000 in extra income in 2021 or 2022. Regardless of which year the income is reported, the taxpayer pays $240 in tax and keeps $760 ($1,000 − $240) in after-tax income. When the present value of the tax payment is considered (see Table 1-3 for present values factors), it becomes clear that choice of years does make a difference. If the taxpayer's applicable interest rate is 10 percent and the marginal rate is expected to remain the same, deferring payment of the tax until 2022 results in an interest-free loan. The present value of the tax savings is $22:

| | |
|---|---|
| Tax paid in 2022 | $ 240 |
| 10% present value factor | ×0.909 |
| Present value of tax paid in 2022 | $ 218 |
| Present value of tax paid in 2021 | 240 |
| Real tax savings by deferring income | $ 22 |

If the marginal rate is expected to decrease to 12 percent in 2022, the taxpayer has a greater incentive to defer the income. By deferring the income to 2022, the taxpayer receives the benefit of an interest-free loan for one year plus the benefit of the lower marginal tax rate. Deferring the income to 2022 would result in a real tax benefit of $144:

| | |
|---|---|
| Tax paid in 2022 ($1,000 × 12%) | $ 120 |
| 10% present value factor | ×0.909 |
| Present value of tax paid in 2022 | $ 109 |
| Present value of tax paid in 2021 | 240 |
| Real tax savings by deferring income | $ 131 |

Table 1-3

## Present Value Tables

Present Value of a Single Payment

| Year | 5% | 6% | 7% | 8% | 9% | 10% | 12% |
|---|---|---|---|---|---|---|---|
| 1 | 0.952 | 0.943 | 0.935 | 0.926 | 0.917 | 0.909 | 0.893 |
| 2 | 0.907 | 0.890 | 0.873 | 0.857 | 0.842 | 0.826 | 0.797 |
| 3 | 0.864 | 0.840 | 0.816 | 0.794 | 0.722 | 0.751 | 0.712 |
| 4 | 0.823 | 0.792 | 0.793 | 0.735 | 0.708 | 0.683 | 0.636 |
| 5 | 0.784 | 0.747 | 0.713 | 0.681 | 0.650 | 0.621 | 0.567 |
| 6 | 0.746 | 0.705 | 0.666 | 0.630 | 0.596 | 0.564 | 0.507 |
| 7 | 0.711 | 0.665 | 0.623 | 0.583 | 0.547 | 0.513 | 0.452 |
| 8 | 0.677 | 0.627 | 0.582 | 0.540 | 0.502 | 0.467 | 0.404 |
| 9 | 0.645 | 0.592 | 0.544 | 0.500 | 0.460 | 0.424 | 0.361 |
| 10 | 0.614 | 0.558 | 0.508 | 0.463 | 0.422 | 0.386 | 0.322 |

Table 1-3 shows how much $1 to be paid at a future date is worth today at the discount rate indicated.

If the taxpayer expects the marginal tax rate to increase to 35 percent next year, the income should be reported in 2021. Deferring the income to 2022 would have a real tax cost of $78:

| | |
|---|---|
| Tax paid in 2022 ($1,000 × 35%) | $ 350 |
| 10% present value factor | ×0.909 |
| Present value of tax paid in 2022 | $ 318 |
| Present value of tax paid in 2021 | 240 |
| Real tax savings by not deferring income | $ 78 |

The same approach can be used to determine the best timing for a deduction. However, keep in mind that deductions are the opposite of income—they reduce taxes paid. Therefore, the optimal choice for deductions is to maximize the real after-tax reduction in taxes paid. In many situations, it may be necessary to compare the offsetting effects of income and deduction items.

**Example 29** Lanny's marginal tax rate for 2021 is 24%. Lanny has $20,000 in income and $10,000 in deductions that could be reported in 2021 or deferred to 2022. Lanny expects his 2022 marginal tax rate to be 35% and the applicable interest rate to be 10%. When should the items be reported if both the income and deductions must be reported in the same year?

**Discussion: The result of reporting both the income and the deductions in 2021 as compared with 2022 is as follows:**

| | 2021 | 2022 |
|---|---|---|
| Increase in income | $ 20,000 | $ 20,000 |
| Less: Increase in deductions | (10,000) | (10,000) |
| Net increase in taxable income | $ 10,000 | $ 10,000 |
| Marginal tax rate | × 24% | × 35% |
| Tax on net increase in income | $ 2,400 | $ 3,500 |
| Present value factor | | × 0.909 |
| Present value of tax in 2021 | $ 2,400 | $ 3,182 |

**Discussion: Lanny should report the items in 2021 to save $782 in real tax cost.**

**Example 30** If Lanny could report the income or deductions separately, when should the income and the deductions be reported to maximize the tax savings?

**Discussion: The tax cost of reporting each item must be considered separately and the total result compared with reporting both items in 2021 (which was previously determined to be the optimal same-year reporting).**

**Income**

| | Report Income In | |
|---|---|---|
| | **2021** | **2022** |
| Increase in taxable income | $ 20,000 | $ 20,000 |
| Marginal tax rate | × 24% | × 35% |
| Increase in tax | $ 4,800 | $ 7,000 |
| Present value factor | | × 0.909 |
| Present value of tax in 2021 | $ 4,800 | $ 6,363 |
| Net tax savings from reporting in 2021 | $ 1,563 | |

**Deductions**

| | Report Deduction In | |
|---|---|---|
| | **2021** | **2022** |
| Decrease in taxable income | $ 10,000 | $ 10,000 |
| Marginal tax rate | × 24% | × 35% |
| Tax savings from deduction | $ 2,400 | $ 3,500 |
| Present value factor | | × 0.909 |
| Present value of tax savings | $ 2,400 | $ 3,182 |
| Net tax savings from reporting in 2022 | $ 782 | |

**Discussion: If Lanny reports the $20,000 of income in 2021, he has a real tax savings of $1,563. Deferring the reporting of the $10,000 in deductions until 2022 results in a real tax savings of $782. Thus, by reporting each item separately in the period that is optimal, he saves $2,345. This compares with a savings of $782 when both income and deductions are reported in the same tax year.**

In summary, there are four general rules of thumb when planning the timing of income and deductions. Two are based on time value of money propositions, and two are based on marginal tax rate considerations:

**Time Value of Money**

**1.** Defer recognition of income.

**2.** Accelerate recognition of deductions.

**Marginal Tax Rate**

**3.** Put income into the year with the lowest expected marginal tax rate.

**4.** Put deductions into the year with the highest expected marginal tax rate.

These general rules of thumb can be used in most situations. However, if there is a conflict between the time value rule and the marginal tax rate rule, the only way to determine the optimal strategy is to calculate the real tax cost of each. Table 1-4 summarizes the rules of thumb and indicates when calculation of the real tax cost is necessary.

## Income Shifting

Income shifting is a method commonly used to reduce taxes. The basic idea behind income shifting is to split a single stream of income among two or more taxpayers to lower the total tax paid. The total tax paid is lower because of the progressive tax rate structure.

*Table 1-4*

## Summary of Tax-Planning Rules

| Type of Item | Marginal Tax Rate: Increasing | Decreasing | Unchanged |
|---|---|---|---|
| Income | Calculate | Defer | Defer |
| Deduction | Calculate | Accelerate | Accelerate |

For example, if a taxpayer in the 22-percent marginal tax rate bracket can shift $1,000 in income to another taxpayer who is in the 10-percent marginal tax rate bracket, $120 [$1,000 × (22% − 10%)] of tax will be saved on the $1,000 in income. Obviously, taxpayers shifting income will want the income to go to taxpayers whom they want to benefit, such as children or grandchildren.

**Example 31** A married taxpayer has $100,000 in taxable income in 2021. The taxpayer has two children who have no taxable income. What are the tax savings if the taxpayer can legally shift $5,000 in income to each of her children?

**Discussion: The taxpayer saves $1,500 in tax by shifting $5,000 in taxable income to each child. Using the rates for married taxpayers, the tax on $100,000 in taxable income is $13,497:**

$9,328 + 22% ($100,000 − $81,050) = $13,497

**By splitting the income into three streams, the taxpayer pays tax on $90,000, and each child pays tax (at single-taxpayer rates) on $5,000. This results in a tax of $12,297.**

| | |
|---|---|
| Tax on $90,000 for a Married Couple | |
| $9,328 + 22% ($90,000 − $81,050) = | $11,297 |
| Tax on $5,000 for a Single Person | |
| $5,000 × 10% = $500 × 2 = | 1,000 |
| Total tax paid | $12,297 |

**The result of the income shift to the children is a reduction in the total tax paid on the $100,000 in taxable income of $1,200 ($13,497 − $12,297).**

It should be noted that numerous provisions in the tax law make it difficult to get the full advantage of income shifting. For example, merely directing that some of your income be paid to your children will not shift the income for tax purposes. To shift income to family members, you will generally need to transfer ownership of income-producing property to the children in order to shift the income from the property. Unless the parents are willing to give up ownership of income-producing property, income shifting to children is difficult to achieve. Even if a valid transfer of property ownership is made, if the child is younger than 18, provisions exist to take away much of the marginal rate advantage of such a shift.

Historically a popular income shifting technique used by owners of a business has been to incorporate the business and split the income between themselves and the corporation. The current law contains a 21 percent flat corporate tax rate. This means that income splitting with a corporation will only work when an individual has an effective tax rate greater than 21 percent. The following two examples illustrate this effect.

**Example 32** Assume that the $100,000 in taxable income in example 31 comes from a business owned by the taxpayer. If the taxpayer incorporates the business and pays herself a salary of $50,000, what is the tax savings?

**Discussion: Splitting the income between the taxpayer and a corporation results in a tax increase of $2,395. The taxpayer pays tax on $50,000, and the corporation pays tax on $50,000 ($100,000 income − $50,000 salary). This results in a tax of $16,105:**

| | |
|---|---|
| Tax on $50,000 for a Married Couple | |
| $1,990 + 12% ($50,000 − $19,900) = | $ 5,602 |
| Tax on $50,000 for a Corporation | |
| $50,000 × 21% = | 10,500 |
| Total tax paid | $16,102 |

**Before incorporation, the tax paid by the married couple was $13,497. The incorporation and split of the income actually costs the couple an additional $2,605 ($16,102 − $13,497) in tax.**

**Example 33** Assume the business in Example 32 earns $400,000 in income. If $100,000 of the income is reported on the taxpayer's individual return, and $300,000 is reported by the corporation, how much is the tax savings?

| | |
|---|---|
| Tax on $400,000 for a Married Couple | |
| $67,260 + 32% (400,000 − $329,850) = | $ 89,654 |
| Tax on $100,000 for a Married Couple | |
| $9,328 + 22% (100,000 − $81,050) = | $ 13,497 |
| Tax on $300,000 for a Corporation | |
| $300,000 × 21% = | $ 63,000 |
| Total | $ 76,497 |
| Tax Savings | $ 13,157 |

**Discussion: Taxpayers only benefit from income splitting with a corporation if their marginal tax rate exceeds 21%, the flat rate of tax imposed on corporations under the 2017 Tax Cuts and Jobs Act.**

Numerous other income-shifting techniques can be used by owners of a business. These include shifting income by employing children and using fringe-benefit packages to get tax-subsidized health care. It should be noted that careful planning is required to gain the optimal tax advantage from such shifting plans. The tax law contains many provisions designed to block blatant shifting schemes that lack economic substance. These provisions are discussed throughout the remainder of the text as they apply to the study of income and deductions.

## 1-8b Tax Evasion and Tax Avoidance

LO 8
Make the distinction between tax avoidance and tax evasion.

Taxpayers do not have to pay more income tax than is required by the tax law. In fact, taxpayers may plan transactions to make their tax bills as low as possible. In this regard, Judge Learned Hand stated: "[A] transaction, otherwise within an exception of the tax law, does not lose its immunity because it is actuated by a desire to avoid, or, if one choose, to evade, taxation. Any one may so arrange his affairs that his taxes shall be as low as possible; he is not bound to choose that pattern which will best pay the Treasury; there is not even a patriotic duty to increase one's taxes."[32]

**Tax evasion** occurs when a taxpayer uses fraudulent methods or deceptive behavior to hide the actual tax liability. Tax evasion usually involves three elements:

- Willfulness on the part of the taxpayer
- An underpayment of tax
- An affirmative act by the taxpayer to evade the tax

Tax evasion often involves rearranging the facts about a transaction to receive a tax benefit. An intentional misrepresentation of facts on a tax return to avoid paying tax is not acceptable taxpayer behavior. Tax evasion is illegal and is subject to substantial penalties. Note that unintentional mathematical or clerical errors on the return are not generally considered tax evasion.

Tax planning uses tax avoidance methods. **Tax avoidance** is the use of legal methods allowed by the tax law to minimize a tax liability. Tax avoidance generally involves planning an intended transaction to obtain a specific tax treatment. Further, tax avoidance is based on disclosure of relevant facts concerning the tax treatment of a transaction.

**Example 34** Ted, an accountant, uses the cash method of accounting. To avoid reporting additional income in 2021, he does not send his December bills to clients until January 2, 2022.

**Discussion: The income was properly reported when collected in 2022. Under the cash method of accounting, Ted properly reported income when his clients paid him. Ted's activity involves permissible tax avoidance.**

**Example 35** Ken, a painter, spent all the cash he received for his art work. He deposited payments he received by check to his business bank account. When he filed his tax return, he intentionally did not report the cash receipts as income.

**Discussion: Ken is engaged in tax evasion. Ken's method of reducing his tax is illegal, and he is subject to substantial penalties.**

At this point, you are probably wondering, "How will the IRS ever know?" Most people are aware that it is almost impossible for the government to track every cash receipt of income. In fact, the probability that the IRS will detect underreporting of cash income is quite low. This has led many taxpayers to play the "audit lottery," omitting cash income or overstating deductions because they know that they probably will not be caught. The IRS estimates that this behavior results in a loss of more than $300 billion per year in tax revenue. This loss must be made up through higher taxes on honest taxpayers. It is clear that if taxpayers were more honest in their reporting of income and deductions, everyone's taxes could be lowered. There is no clear-cut, cost-efficient solution to the evasion problem. However, as future professionals and taxpayers, you should recognize your obligations to your profession and the country when it comes to tax evasion situations. Only through education and ethical taxpayer behavior will the tax evasion problem be resolved. Keep in mind that avoiding detection by the IRS does not somehow magically transform a fraudulent act into allowable behavior. The idea that something is not illegal unless one is caught is an idea that should have died ages ago.

## 1-9 ETHICAL CONSIDERATIONS IN TAX PRACTICE

LO 9
Explain ethical considerations related to tax practice.

The field of tax practice is virtually unregulated—anyone who wishes to can prepare tax returns for a fee. However, anyone who prepares tax returns for monetary considerations, or who is licensed to practice in the tax-related professions, is subject to various rules and codes of professional conduct. For example, the Internal Revenue Code contains provisions (see Exhibit 1-4 for a list of preparer penalties) that impose civil and criminal penalties on tax return preparers for various improprieties.

All tax practitioners are subject to the provisions of *IRS Circular 230*, "Regulations Governing the Practice of Attorneys, Certified Public Accountants, Enrolled Agents, and Enrolled Actuaries Before the Internal Revenue Service." Tax attorneys are subject

*Exhibit 1-4*

## IRC Violations with Penalties for Tax Return Preparers

Understatement of taxpayer's liability because of unrealistic positions
Understatement of taxpayer's liability because of willful or reckless conduct
Failure to furnish a copy of a return to the taxpayer
Failure to sign a return
Failure to furnish identifying information
Failure to retain a copy or a list of returns prepared
Failure to file correct information returns
Negotiation of tax refund check
Improper disclosure or use of information on taxpayer's return
Organizing (or assisting in doing so) or promoting and making or furnishing statements with respect to abusive tax shelters
Aiding and abetting an understatement of tax liability
Aiding or assisting in the preparation of a false return

to the ethical code of conduct adopted by the state(s) in which they are licensed to practice. Certified Public Accountants (CPAs) who are members of the American Institute of Certified Public Accountants (AICPA) are governed by the institute's Code of Professional Conduct. The AICPA's Statements on Standards for Tax Services (SSTS) provide seven advisory guidelines for CPAs who prepare tax returns. Although tax practitioners who are not members of the AICPA are not bound by the Code of Professional Conduct and the Statements on Standards for Tax Services, the rules and guidelines contained in them provide useful guidance for all return preparers.

The AICPA Code of Professional Conduct is a set of rules that set enforceable ethical standards for members of the institute. The standards are broad and apply to all professional services that a CPA may render, including tax advice and tax return preparation. For example,

1. Rule 102 requires CPAs to perform professional services with objectivity and integrity, and to avoid any conflict of interest. CPAs should neither knowingly misrepresent facts nor subordinate their judgment to that of others in rendering professional advice.
2. Rule 202 requires compliance with all standards that have been promulgated by certain bodies designated by the AICPA's governing council.
3. Rule 301 states that CPAs will not disclose confidential client data without the specific consent of the client, except under certain specified conditions.

The seven SSTS provide guidance on what constitutes appropriate standards of tax practice. The statements are intended to supplement, not replace, the Code of Professional Conduct. Because they specifically address the problems inherent in tax practice, each statement is briefly described here. The full text of the SSTS can be found by going to www.cengage.com.

SSTS No. 1: *Tax Return Positions.* CPAs should not recommend that a position be taken on a return unless they believe that, if the position is challenged, it is likely to be sustained, which is known as the *realistic possibility standard.* CPAs should not prepare a return or sign as preparer of a return if they know the return takes a position that could not be recommended because it does not meet the realistic possibility standard. However, a CPA may recommend any return position that is not frivolous, so long as the position is adequately disclosed on the return. SSTS Interpretation No. 1-1 (reproduced in Appendix D) contains the AICPA interpretation of the realistic possibility standard.

SSTS No. 2: *Answers to Questions on Returns.* A CPA should make a reasonable effort to obtain from the client and provide appropriate answers to all questions on a tax return before signing as preparer. Where reasonable grounds exist for omission of an answer, no explanation for the omission is required, and the CPA may sign the return unless the omission would cause the return to be considered incomplete.

SSTS No. 3: *Procedural Aspects of Preparing Returns.* A CPA may in good faith rely upon, without verification, information furnished by the client or third parties. Reasonable inquiries should be made if the information furnished appears to be incorrect, incomplete, or inconsistent. The CPA should use previous years' returns whenever possible to avoid omissions. In addition, the CPA may appropriately use information from the tax return of another client if the information would not violate the confidentiality of the CPA-client relationship and is relevant to and necessary for proper preparation of the return.

SSTS No. 4: *Use of Estimates.* A CPA may prepare returns using estimates provided by the taxpayer if it is impracticable to obtain exact data and the estimates are reasonable, given the facts and circumstances.

SSTS No. 5: *Departure from a Position Previously Concluded in an Administrative Proceeding or Court Decision.* If a CPA follows the standards in SSTS No. 1, the result of an administrative proceeding or court decision with respect to a prior return of the taxpayer does not bind the CPA as to how the item should be treated in a subsequent year's return.

SSTS No. 6: *Knowledge of Error: Return Preparation and Administrative Proceedings.* A CPA who becomes aware of an error in a previous year's return—or of the client's failure to file a required return—should promptly inform the client and recommend measures to correct the error. The CPA may not inform the IRS of the error except when required to do so by law. If the client does not correct the error, the CPA should consider whether to continue the professional relationship and must take reasonable steps to ensure that the error is not repeated if the relationship is continued. When a CPA becomes aware of an error in a return that is the subject of an administrative proceeding, the CPA should promptly inform the client of the error and recommend measures to be taken. The CPA should request the client's consent to disclose the error to the IRS but should not disclose the error without consent unless required to do so by law. If the client refuses disclosure, the CPA should consider whether to withdraw from representing the client in the administrative proceeding and whether to continue a professional relationship with the client.

SSTS No. 7: *Form and Content of Advice to Clients.* A CPA should use judgment to ensure that advice given to a client reflects professional competence and appropriately serves the client's needs. For all tax advice given to a client, the CPA should adhere to the standards of SSTS No. 1, pertaining to tax return positions. A CPA may choose to notify a client when subsequent developments affect advice previously given on significant tax matters but is under no strict obligation to do so.

# CHAPTER SUMMARY

Taxes are a fact of everyday life. Taxes are levied on income, products, property holdings, and transfers of wealth. The federal income tax is the largest revenue producer of all the taxes in use in the United States. Therefore, a solid understanding of the basic rules of the income tax system is essential to maximize your after-tax income.

The term *tax* has been defined, and concepts have been examined that will help you reach your own conclusions about whether a tax is "good" or "bad." Keep these evaluations in mind as you continue through the text and as you read articles on proposed tax legislation.

The income tax law is a complex body of constantly changing information that is issued by legislative, administrative, and judicial sources. When evaluating a particular tax rule, it may be necessary to consult resources in all three areas.

Tax terms used in income tax computation have been defined in this chapter. Subsequent chapters explain the terms and build on the basic information. When you encounter a new term in later chapters, do not hesitate to refer to this chapter to see how the new term fits into the computational framework.

The study of federal income taxation will help you evaluate how business and personal financial decisions influence the amount of income tax you will have to pay. Awareness of basic income tax concepts will help you recognize opportunities to minimize compliance costs, save taxes, avoid IRS penalties, and make more informed business decisions.

The practical approach to tax planning discussed in this chapter does not require you to be a tax specialist to become an effective tax planner. In later chapters, you will be asked to solve tax-planning problems that require you to make decisions about when an item of income or deduction should be reported. When solving these problems, you will need to consider the effects of changes in the marginal tax rate and the time value of money.

Finally, always be aware of the difference between tax evasion and tax avoidance. Avoid tax evasion—it is illegal. Tax avoidance is legal and is expected of taxpayers.

## KEY TERMS

adjusted gross income (AGI) (p. 1-26)
ad valorem taxes (p. 1-14)
annual loss (p. 1-20)
average tax rate (p. 1-8)
certainty (p. 1-6)
convenience (p. 1-6)
correspondence examinations (p. 1-25)
deductions (p. 1-20)
deductions for adjusted gross income (p. 1-27)
deductions from adjusted gross income (p. 1-27)
deferral (p. 1-19)
Discriminant Function System (DIF) (p. 1-24)
document perfection program (p. 1-24)
economy (p. 1-7)
effective tax rate (p. 1-8)
equality (p. 1-5)
estate tax (p. 1-15)
exclusions (p. 1-19)
expense (p. 1-20)
field examinations (p. 1-25)
gain (p. 1-19)
gift taxes (p. 1-15)
gross income (p. 1-19)
horizontal equity (p. 1-5)
information-matching program (p. 1-25)
Internal Revenue Code of 1986 (p. 1-17)
IRS Appeals Division (p. 1-25)
itemized deductions (p. 1-27)
loss (p. 1-20)
marginal tax rate (p. 1-7)
office examinations (p. 1-25)
ordinary income (p. 1-19)
pay-as-you-go concept (p. 1-6)
personal property (p. 1-14)
progressive rate structure (p. 1-10)
proportional rate structure (p. 1-8)
protest letter (p. 1-25)
real property (p. 1-14)
regressive rate structure (p. 1-8)
self-employment tax (p. 1-12)
Social Security taxes (p. 1-12)
special audit programs (p. 1-25)
standard deduction (p. 1-27)
statute of limitations (p. 1-23)
taxable income (p. 1-7)
tax avoidance (p. 1-34)
tax base (p. 1-7)
tax credit (p. 1-22)
tax evasion (p. 1-33)
Taxpayer Compliance Measurement Program (TCMP) (p. 1-24)
transaction loss (p. 1-20)
Treasury regulations (p. 1-18)
unified donative-transfers credit (p. 1-16)
vertical equity (p. 1-5)

## PRIMARY TAX LAW SOURCES

[1]Rev. Rul. 77–29.

[2]Sec. 6072—Specifies the general rules for due dates of tax returns.

[3]Sec. 1—Imposes a tax on the taxable income of different classes of individual taxpayers; provides tax rates by class of taxpayer and requires adjustment of rate schedules each year for inflation; limits the tax rate on net long-term capital gains to 0 percent, 15 percent, and 20 percent.

[4]Sec. 3402—Requires employers to withhold estimates of taxes on wages and salaries paid to employees.

[5]Sec. 31—Provides that amounts withheld as tax from salaries and wages are allowed as credits against that year's tax liability.

[6]Sec. 6654—Provides that all individuals must pay estimated taxes when their tax liability is expected to be greater than $1,000; imposes a penalty for not paying the proper amount of estimated tax.

[7]Sec. 3101—Imposes the Social Security tax on employees; provides rates of tax to be paid.

[8]Sec. 1402—Defines *self-employment income* and provides for the tax to be paid on base amounts as specified in the Social Security Act for each tax year.

[9]Sec. 3111—Imposes the Social Security tax on employers for wages paid to employees.

[10]Sec. 1401—Provides the tax rates for self-employment taxes.

[11]Sec. 2501—Imposes a tax on transfers of property by gift.

[12]Sec. 2503—Allows exclusion from gift tax of gifts up to $15,000.

[13]Sec. 2505—Allows unified credit against taxable gifts.

[14]Sec. 2001—Imposes a tax on the assets of an estate. Provides tax rates on estate assets and for unlimited marital exclusion.

[15]Sec. 2010—Provides for unified tax credit against tax liability of an estate.

[16]Patient Protection and Affordable Care Act, P.L. 11–148 and Health Care and Education Reconciliation Act of 2010, P.L. 111–152—Imposes new taxes on individuals and businesses to pay for health care costs of those who cannot afford health insurance.

[17]Sec. 7801—Directs the secretary of the Treasury to issue the regulations necessary to implement and interpret the tax law.

[18]Sec. 61—Provides the general definition of *gross income* as all income from whatever source derived.

[19]Sec. 64—Defines *ordinary income* as income that does not result from the sale or exchange of property that is not a capital asset or an asset described in Sec. 1231.

[20]Sec. 1001—Prescribes the calculation of gains and losses for dispositions of property;

defines *amount realized* for purposes of determining gain or loss for dispositions.

[21]Sec. 162—Allows the deduction of all ordinary and necessary expenses incurred in a trade or business of the taxpayer.

[22]Sec. 212—Allows the deduction of all ordinary and necessary expenses incurred in a production-of-income activity of the taxpayer.

[23]Sec. 11—Imposes an income tax on corporations and provides the applicable tax rate schedules.

[24]Sec. 62—Defines *adjusted gross income* for individual taxpayers and specifies the deductions allowed as deductions for adjusted gross income.

[25]Sec. 1211—Sets forth the limit on deductions of capital losses of corporations and individuals.

[26]Sec. 63—Defines *taxable income.* Allows individual taxpayers to deduct the greater of their allowable itemized deductions or the standard deduction. Standard deduction amounts are specified and are required to be adjusted annually for inflation.

[27]Sec. 211—Generally allows specific personal expenditures as itemized deductions of individuals.

[28]Sec. 213—Allows the deduction of medical expenses as an itemized deduction for individual taxpayers; defines *medical expenses* and prescribes limitations on the amount of the deduction.

[29]Sec. 164—Specifies the allowable deductions for taxes.

[30]Sec. 163—Specifies the allowable deductions for interest.

[31]Sec. 170—Allows the deduction of contributions to qualified charitable organizations.

[32]Helvering v. Gregory, 69 F.2d 809 at 810 (2d Cir. 1934).

# DISCUSSION QUESTIONS

1. **LO1** Briefly state Adam Smith's four requirements for a good tax system.
2. **LO1** Based on the discussion in the chapter, evaluate how well each of these taxes meets Adam Smith's four requirements:
   a. Income tax
   b. Employment taxes
3. **LO1, 2** Based solely on the definitions in the chapter, is the Social Security tax a proportional, regressive, or progressive tax? Explain, and state how the tax might be viewed differently.
4. **LO1, 2** Based solely on the definitions in the chapter, is the sales tax a proportional, regressive, or progressive tax? Explain, and state how the tax might be viewed differently.
5. **LO2** As stated in the text, the federal income tax is the largest revenue-producing tax in use in the United States. Why do you think the income tax produces more revenue than any other tax?
6. **LO2** How are federal, state, and local income taxes collected by the government? Consider the cases of an employee and a self-employed taxpayer.
7. **LO2** How is a sales tax different from an excise tax?
8. **LO2** Who is responsible for collecting sales and excise taxes? Who actually pays the tax?
9. **LO2** Why is a tax on real property used more often than a tax on personal property?
10. **LO2** The gift tax is supposed to tax the transfer of wealth from one taxpayer to another. However, the payment of gift tax on a transfer of property is relatively rare. Why is gift tax not paid on most gifts?
11. **LO2** The estate tax is a tax on the value of property transferred at death. Why is payment of the estate tax not a common event?
12. **LO2** What is the basis for valuing assets transferred by gift and at death?
13. **LO2** Who is responsible for reporting and paying gift taxes? estate taxes?
14. **LO3** Identify three primary sources of tax law.
15. **LO3** Explain why the following statement is not necessarily true: "If the IRS disagrees, I'll take my case all the way to the Supreme Court."
16. **LO4** What is the federal income tax base?
17. **LO4** What is an exclusion?
18. **LO4** How is a deferral different from an exclusion?
19. **LO4** How is gross income different from income?
20. **LO4** What are the three basic tests that an expense must satisfy to be deductible?
21. **LO4** What is the difference between an expense and a loss?
22. **LO4** How is a transaction loss different from an annual loss?
23. **LO4** How does the legislative grace concept help identify amounts that qualify for deduction?
24. **LO4** Based on the example in Exhibit 1-2, explain how inflation can have two effects that result in a hidden tax.
25. **LO4** Explain the pay-as-you-go system.
26. **LO4** What is a tax credit?
27. **LO4** How is a tax credit different from a tax deduction?
28. **LO4** If you were in the 24 percent marginal tax bracket and you could choose either a $1,000 tax

credit or a $3,000 tax deduction, which would give you the most tax savings? Why?

29. **LO5** What is the statute of limitations, and what role does it play in the filing of tax returns?

30. **LO5** Briefly describe the types of programs used by the IRS to select a return for audit.

31. **LO5** What are the three types of IRS examinations?

32. **LO5** What is included in the 30-day letter, and what options does the taxpayer have after receiving one?

33. **LO5** What does the 90-day letter represent, and what are the choices the taxpayer has after receiving one?

34. **LO6** How is the calculation of taxable income for an individual different from the calculation of a corporation's taxable income?

35. **LO6** How do deductions for adjusted gross income and deductions from adjusted gross income of an individual differ?

36. **LO6** What is the purpose of the standard deduction for individuals?

37. **LO7** Haru is studying finance at State University. To complete the finance major, he has to take a basic income tax course. Because Haru does not intend to be a tax expert, he considers the course a waste of his time. Explain to Haru how he can benefit from the tax course.

38. **LO7** Evaluate the following statement: "The goal of good tax planning is to pay the minimum amount of tax."

39. **LO7** It has often been said that only the rich can benefit from professional tax planning. Based on the information presented in this chapter, why is this statement at least partially true?

## PROBLEMS

40. **LO1** State whether each of the following payments is a tax. Explain your answers.
    a. To incorporate his business, Alex pays the state of Texas a $2,000 incorporation fee.
    b. The city paves a road and assesses each property owner on the road $4,000 for their share of the cost.
    c. The city of Asheville charges each residence in the city $10 per month to pick up the trash.
    d. Rory pays $450 of income tax to the state of California.
    e. Lanny is fined $45 for exceeding the speed limit.

41. **LO1** Explain why each of the following payments does or does not meet the IRS's definition of a tax:
    a. Jack is a licensed beautician. He pays the state $45 each year to renew his license to practice as a beautician.
    b. Polly Corporation pays state income taxes of $40,000 on its $500,000 of taxable income.
    c. Winona pays $15 annually for a safety inspection of her automobile that is required by the state.
    d. The Judd Partnership owns land that is valued by the county assessor at $30,000. Based on this valuation, the partnership pays county property taxes of $800.
    e. Andrea fails to file her income tax return on time. She files the return late, and the IRS assesses her $25 for the late filing and $5 for interest on the tax due from the due date of the return until the filing date.

42. **LO1** Aliyah is single with a gross income of $120,000 and a taxable income of $98,000. In calculating gross income, she properly excluded $10,000 of tax-exempt interest income. Using the tax rate schedules in the chapter, calculate Aliyah's
    a. Total tax
    b. Marginal tax rate
    c. Average tax rate
    d. Effective tax rate

43. **LO1** A taxpayer has $95,000 of taxable income for the current year. Determine the total tax, the marginal tax rate, and the average tax rate if the taxpayer is a
    a. Single individual
    b. Married couple
    c. Corporation

44. **LO1** Rory earns $70,000 per year as a college professor. Latesia is a marketing executive with a salary of $180,000. With respect to FICA taxes, what are Rory's and Latesia's
    a. Total FICA taxes?
    b. Marginal FICA tax rates?
    c. Average FICA tax rates?
    d. Effective FICA tax rates?
45. **LO1** For each of the following, explain whether the rate structure is progressive, proportional, or regressive:
    a. Plymouth County imposes a 5 percent tax on all retail sales in the county. Taxpayers with incomes less than $12,000 receive a refund of the tax they pay.
    b. The country of Zambonia imposes a 10 percent tax on the taxable income of all individuals.
    c. Regan County imposes a property tax using the following schedule:

| Assessed Value | Tax |
|---|---|
| $ -0- to $10,000 | $ 40 |
| $10,001 to $40,000 | $ 40 + 1% of the value in excess of $10,000 |
| $40,001 to $80,000 | $ 340 + 2% of the value in excess of $40,000 |
| $80,001 and above | $1,140 + 3% of the value in excess of $80,000 |

    d. The city of Thomasville bases its dog licensing fee on the weight of the dog per the following schedule:

| Weight (in pounds) | Tax Rate |
|---|---|
| 0 to 40 | $ 2 + 50% of weight |
| 41 to 80 | $22 + 40% of weight in excess of 40 lbs. |
| 81 and above | $36 + 30% of weight in excess of 80 lbs. |

46. **LO1** The country of Boodang is the leading producer of sausage. Boodang imposes three taxes on its residents and companies to encourage production of sausage and discourage its consumption. Each tax applies as follows:
    - Income tax—Rates apply to each taxpayer's total income:

| | |
|---|---|
| $ -0- –$ 50,000 | 5% of total income |
| $ 50,001–$200,000 | $ 2,500 + 10% of income in excess of $ 50,000 |
| $200,001–$500,000 | $17,500 + 20% of income in excess of $200,000 |
| $500,001 or more | 40% of total income |

    In calculating total income, sausage workers are allowed to deduct 25 percent of their salaries. Companies that produce sausage are allowed to deduct 50 percent of their sales. No other deductions are allowed.
    - Sausage tax—All sausage purchases are subject to a 100 percent of purchase price tax. Residents who consume less than 10 pounds of sausage per year are given a 50 percent rebate of the sausage tax they paid.
    - Property tax—Taxes are based on the distance of a taxpayer's residence from state-owned sausage shops per the following schedule:

| | |
|---|---|
| 0–2 miles | $15,000 per mile |
| 2 miles–5 miles | $ 5,000 per mile |
| 5 miles or more | $ 2,000 per mile |

    Given the definitions in the chapter, are Boodang's taxes progressive, proportional, or regressive? Evaluate and discuss each tax and the aspect(s) of the tax that you considered in making your evaluation.
47. **LO2** Joe Bob is an employee of Rollo Corporation who receives a salary of $18,000 per month. How much Social Security tax will be withheld from Joe Bob's salary in
    a. March?
    b. November?

48. **LO2** Return to the facts of problem 47. Assume that each month, Joe Bob has $2,800 in federal income tax and $900 in state income tax withheld from his salary. What is Joe Bob's take-home pay in
   a. March?
   b. November?

49. **LO2** Gosney Corporation has two employees. During the current year, Clinton earns $80,000 and Trahn earns $150,000. How much Social Security tax does Gosney have to pay on the salaries earned by Clinton and Trahn?

50. **LO2** Eric is a self-employed financial consultant. During the current year, Eric's net self-employment income is $160,000. What is Eric's self-employment tax?

51. **LO2** Darrell is an employee of Whitney's. During the current year, Darrell's salary is $136,000. Whitney's net self-employment income is also $136,000. Calculate the Social Security and self-employment taxes paid by Darrell and Whitney. Write a letter to Whitney in which you state how much she will have to pay in Social Security and self-employment taxes and why she owes those amounts. Communication Skills

52. **LO4** Classify the following items as ordinary income, a gain, or an exclusion:
   a. The gross revenues of $160,000 and deductible expenses of $65,000 of an individual's consulting business
   b. Interest received on a checking account
   c. Sale for $8,000 of Kummel Corporation stock that cost $3,000
   d. Receipt of $1,000 as a graduation present from grandfather
   e. Royalty income from an interest in a gold mine

53. **LO4** Classify the following items as ordinary income, a gain, or an exclusion:
   a. The salary received by an employee
   b. Dividends of $400 received on 100 shares of corporate stock
   c. Sale for $10,000 of an antique chair that cost $3,500
   d. Rental income from an apartment building
   e. Receipt of an automobile worth $20,000 as an inheritance from Aunt Ruby's estate

54. **LO4** Explain why each of the following expenditures is or is not deductible:
   a. Lumbar, Inc., pays $12,000 as its share of its employees' Social Security tax. The $12,000 is deductible.
   b. Luis pays a cleaning service $250 per month to clean his real estate office. The $250 is deductible.
   c. Janice pays a cleaning service $75 per month to clean her personal residence. The $75 is not deductible.
   d. Leyh Corporation purchases land to use as a parking lot for $35,000. The $35,000 is not deductible.
   e. Martin spends $50 per month on gasoline for the car he uses to drive to his job as a disc jockey. The $50 is not deductible.

55. **LO4** Classify each of the following transactions as a deductible expense, a nondeductible expense, or a loss:
   a. Nira sells for $4,300 stock that cost $6,000.
   b. Chiro Medical, Inc., pays $2,200 for subscriptions to popular magazines that it places in its waiting room.
   c. Lawrence pays $200 for subscriptions to fly-fishing magazines.
   d. The Mendota Partnership pays $200,000 to install an elevator in one of its rental properties.
   e. Sterling Corporation pays $6,000 for lawn maintenance at its headquarters.

56. **LO6** Based on the following information, what are the taxable income and tax liability for a single individual?

| | |
|---|---|
| Total income | $118,000 |
| Excludable income | 2,000 |
| Deductions for adjusted gross income | 2,500 |
| Deductions from adjusted gross income | 8,000 |

57. **LO6** Based on the facts in problem 56, for a couple filing jointly, determine their adjusted gross income, taxable income and tax liability.

Communication Skills

58. **LO6** Jasmine's 2021 income tax calculation is as follows:

| | |
|---|---|
| Gross income | $120,000 |
| Deductions for adjusted gross income | (3,000) |
| Adjusted gross income | $117,000 |
| Deductions from adjusted gross income: | |
| Standard deduction | ($12,550) |
| (Total itemized deductions are $2,300) | |
| Taxable income | $104,450 |

Before filing her return, Jasmine finds an $8,000 deduction that she omitted from these calculations. Although the item is clearly deductible, she is unsure whether she should deduct it for or from adjusted gross income. Jasmine doesn't think it matters where she deducts the item because her taxable income will decrease by $8,000 regardless of how the item is deducted. Is Jasmine correct? Calculate her taxable income both ways. Write a letter to Jasmine explaining any difference in her taxable income arising from whether the $8,000 is deducted for or from adjusted gross income.

Communication Skills

59. **LO7** Since graduating from college, Mabel has used the firm of R&P to prepare her tax returns. Each January, Mabel receives a summary information sheet, which she fills out and sends to R&P along with the appropriate documentation. Because she has always received a refund, Mabel feels that R&P is giving her good tax advice. Write a letter to Mabel explaining why she may not be getting good tax advice from R&P.

60. **LO7** Michiko and Saul are planning to attend the same university next year. The university estimates tuition, books, fees, and living costs to be $12,000 per year. Michiko's father has agreed to give her the $12,000 she needs to attend the university. Saul has obtained a job at the university that will pay him $14,000 per year. After discussing their respective arrangements, Michiko figures that Saul will be better off than she will. What, if anything, is wrong with Michiko's thinking?

61. **LO7** Inga, an attorney, completed a job for a client in November 2021. If she bills the client immediately, she will receive her $10,000 fee before the end of the year. By delaying the billing for a month, she will not receive the $10,000 until 2022. What factors should Inga consider in deciding whether she should delay sending the bill to the client?

62. **LO7** Art is in the 24 percent marginal tax bracket for 2021. He owes a $10,000 bill for business expenses. Because he reports taxable income on a cash basis, he can deduct the $10,000 in either 2021 or 2022, depending on when he makes the payment. He can pay the bill at any time before January 31, 2022, without incurring the normal 8 percent interest charge. If he expects to be in a 32 percent marginal tax bracket for 2022, should he pay the bill and claim the deduction in 2021 or 2022?

63. **LO7** Elki would like to invest $50,000 in tax-exempt securities. He now has the money invested in a certificate of deposit that pays 5.75 percent annually. What rate of interest would the tax-exempt security have to pay to result in a greater return on Elki's investment than the certificate of deposit? Work the problem assuming that Elki's marginal tax rate is 12 percent, 22 percent, 24 percent, and 32 percent.

64. **LO7** Leroy and Amanda are married and have three dependent children. During the current year, they have the following income and expenses:

| | |
|---|---|
| Salaries | $120,000 |
| Interest income | 45,000 |
| Royalty income | 27,000 |
| Deductions for AGI | 3,000 |
| Deductions from AGI | 9,000 |

a. What is Leroy and Amanda's current year taxable income and income tax liability?

b. Leroy and Amanda would like to lower their income tax. How much income tax will they save if they validly transfer $5,000 of the interest income to each of their children? Assume that the children have no other income and that they are entitled to a $1,100 standard deduction.

65. **LO8** For each of the following situations, state whether the taxpayer's action is tax evasion or tax avoidance.

a. Tom knows that farm rent received in cash or farm produce is income subject to tax. To avoid showing a cash receipt on his records, he rented 50 acres for 5 steers to be raised by the tenant. He used 2 of the steers for food for his family and gave 3 to relatives. Because he did not sell the livestock, he did not report taxable income.

b. Betty applied for and received a Social Security number for Kate, her pet cat. Surprised by how easy it was to get a Social Security number, she decided to claim a dependent exemption on her tax return for Kate. Other than being a cat, Kate met all the tests for a dependent.

c. Glen has put money in savings accounts in 50 banks. He knows a bank is not required to report to the IRS interest it pays him that totals less than $10. Because the banks do not report the payments to the IRS, Glen does not show the interest he receives as taxable income. Although Glen's accountant has told him all interest he receives is taxable, Glen insists that the IRS will never know the difference.

d. Bob entered a contract to sell a parcel of land at a $25,000 gain in 2020. To avoid reporting the gain in 2020, he closed the sale and delivered title to the land to the buyers on January 2, 2021.

e. Asha's taxable income for 2021 puts her in the 32 percent marginal tax bracket. She has decided to purchase new equipment for her business during 2022. A special election allows Asha to treat the $25,000 of the cost of the equipment as a current period expense. Because she expects to be in a lower tax bracket next year, Asha buys and begins using $25,000 worth of the equipment during December 2021. She claims a $25,000 expense deduction under the special election for 2021.

66. **LO8** In each of the following situations, explain why the taxpayer's action is or is not tax evasion:

a. Jamal owns an electrical appliance repair service. When a client pays him in cash, he gives the cash to his daughter Tasha. Jamal does not report the cash he gives to Tasha in his business income. Tasha has no other income, and the amount of cash that she receives from Jamal is small enough that she is not required to file a tax return.

b. Roberta and Dudley are married. Roberta usually prepares their tax return. However, she was in the hospital and unable to prepare the return for 2020, so Dudley did it. In preparing their 2021 return, Roberta notices that Dudley included $1,000 of tax-exempt municipal bond interest in their 2020 gross income. To correct this mistake, Roberta takes a $1,000 deduction on the 2021 return.

c. In 2021, Hearthome Corporation receives notice that the IRS is auditing its 2019 return. In preparing for the audit, Hearthome's controller, Monique, finds a mistake in the total for the 2019 depreciation schedule that resulted in a $5,000 overstatement of depreciation expense.

d. While preparing his tax return, Will becomes unsure of the treatment of a deduction item. He researches the issue and can find no concrete tax law authority pertaining to the particular item. Will calls his buddy Dan, an accounting professor, for advice. Dan tells Will that if the law is unclear, he should treat the deduction in the most advantageous manner. Accordingly,

Will deducts the full amount of the item, rather than capitalizing and amortizing it over five years.

e. Sonja is a freelance book editor. Most companies for which she works pay her by check. In working out the terms of a job, a new client agrees to pay her by giving her a new computer valued at $3,600. In preparing her tax return, Sonja notes that the client failed to report to the IRS the value of the computer as income for Sonja. Aware that her chances of getting caught are small, Sonja does not include the $3,600 value of the computer in her gross income.

## ISSUE IDENTIFICATION PROBLEMS

In each of the following problems, identify the tax issue(s) posed by the facts presented. Determine the possible tax consequences of each issue that you identify.

67. Marla had $2,100 in state income taxes withheld from her 2021 salary. When she files her 2021 state income tax return, her actual state tax liability is $2,300.

68. While reading a State College alumni newsletter, Linh is surprised to learn that interest paid on student loans is deductible. Linh graduated from college two years ago and paid $1,200 in interest during the current year on loans that he took out to pay his college tuition.

69. Victoria's son needs $5,000 for tuition at the Motown School of Dance. Victoria, who is in the 32 percent marginal tax rate bracket, intends to pay the tuition by selling stock worth $5,000 that she paid $2,000 for several years ago.

70. Joey and Camilla are married and have three children, ages 8, 16, and 18. They own a commercial cleaning business that is organized as a sole proprietorship and makes $140,000 annually. They have $30,000 of other taxable income (net of allowable deductions).

## TECHNOLOGY APPLICATIONS

Communication Skills

71. Audrey opened Hardy Consulting Services during the current year. She has one employee, Deng, who is paid a salary of $30,000. Audrey is confused about the amount of federal unemployment tax she is required to pay on Deng's salary. The state unemployment tax rate is 4 percent. Audrey has asked you to determine how much federal unemployment tax she is required to pay on Deng's salary. Write Audrey a letter explaining the amount of federal unemployment tax she must pay.

Communication Skills

72. Shawna earns $95,000 as a biologist for Berto Corporation. She also consults with other businesses on compliance with environmental regulations. During the current year, she earns $70,000 in consulting fees. Determine the amount of self-employment tax Shawna owes on her consulting income.

Spreadsheet

73. Using the information below, prepare a spreadsheet that will calculate an individual's taxable income. The spreadsheet should be flexible enough to accommodate single and married taxpayers as well as changes in the information provided below.

| | |
|---|---|
| Number of dependent children | 2 |
| Salary | $75,000 |
| Interest | 8,000 |
| Deductions for adjusted gross income | 2,800 |
| Deductions from adjusted gross income | 14,000 |

# DISCUSSION CASES

74. A value-added tax has been the subject of much debate in recent years as a tax to use to help reduce the deficit. Various forms of value-added taxes are used throughout Europe, Canada, and in many other countries. To acquaint yourself with the basic operation of a value-added tax, read the following article:
Peter Chin and Joel G. Siegel, "What the Value-Added Tax Is All About," *TAXES—The Tax Magazine*, January 1990, pp. 3–13.

    After reading the article, consider the following circumstances:
Joe is married and has 2 children. A brain surgeon, he earns about $300,000 annually from his medical practice and averages about $250,000 in investment income. Jane, Joe's wife, spends most of her time doing volunteer work for charitable organizations. Tom is also married and has 5 children. He earns $40,000 per year working as a maintenance man for Joe.

    While Joe was working late one night, he and Tom had a serious disagreement about two new tax bills recently introduced to help reduce the deficit. The first bill would levy a 10 percent value-added tax on all goods and services. A second bill introduced at the same time would add an additional 10 percent tax to each of the seven current tax rate brackets (i.e., 10 percent would become 20 percent, 12 percent would become 22 percent, 22 percent would become 32 percent, 24 percent would become 34 percent, 32 percent would become 42 percent, 35 percent would become 45 percent, and 37 percent would become 47 percent).

    Joe is concerned that the imposition of a value-added tax would mean that fewer people could afford medical treatment. Both his patients and his practice would suffer from the tax. Tom strongly disagrees with Joe. He thinks that Joe does not want to pay his fair share of taxes. Tom charges that Joe can afford to hire tax accountants to help him avoid paying higher income taxes, even with the higher tax rates. By enacting a value-added tax, Tom believes, high-income taxpayers like Joe will have to pay up. He thinks it is the only fair way to raise taxes to bring down the deficit.

    After several hours of arguing, neither could convince the other that he was wrong. Joe finally ended the discussion by saying that he would get an independent person knowledgeable in tax law to decide who is right.

    You work for the firm that prepares Joe's tax return and advises him on managing his finances. The tax partner of your firm asks you to prepare a memorandum discussing the merits and deficiencies of the two proposals as they apply to Joe and Tom. In your memorandum, you are directed to specifically consider the following and provide a response:

    a. What is a value-added tax, and how does it work?
    b. Evaluate the rate structures of the two proposed taxes. Are they proportional, progressive, or regressive?
    c. What, if anything, is wrong with Tom's and/or Joe's point of view? Be sure to explain this part in depth.

75. Nora and Vanessa are married and have 2 dependent children. This is a summary of their 2021 tax return:

| | |
|---|---|
| Adjusted gross income | $107,837 |
| Deductions from adjusted gross income: | |
| Standard deduction | $ 25,100 |
| Taxable income | $ 82,737 |
| Tax liability | $ 9,699 |

a. Assuming that Nora and Vanessa's 2021 adjusted gross income will increase at an estimated 2.5 percent rate of inflation and that the standard deduction amounts does not change, calculate their 2022 taxable income. Calculate the tax liability on this income using the 2021 tax rate schedules (see Appendix B).
b. Calculate Nora and Vanessa's projected 2022 taxable income and tax liability, assuming that their adjusted gross income will increase by 2.5 percent and that all other inflation adjustments are made. Compare these calculations with those in part a, and explain how the inflation adjustments preserve Nora and Vanessa's after-tax income.

## TAX PLANNING CASES

Communication Skills

76. Bonnie is married and has one child. She owns Bonnie's Rib Joint, which produces a taxable income of approximately $120,000 per year.
   a. Assume that Bonnie's taxable income is $40,000 without considering the income from the rib joint. How much tax will she pay on the $120,000 of income from the rib joint?
   b. You work for the firm that prepares Bonnie's tax return. Bonnie has asked the partner for whom you work to advise her on how she might lower her taxes. The partner has assigned you this task. Draft a memorandum to the partner that contains at least two options Bonnie could use to lower her taxes. For each option, explain the calculations that support the tax savings from your recommendation.

## ETHICS DISCUSSION CASE

77. Return to the facts of problem 65. Assume that you are the CPA in charge of preparing the tax return for each of the taxpayers in the problem. Based on the Statements on Standards for Tax Services (which can be found at https://future.aicpa.org/resources), explain what you should do in each case. Your discussion should indicate which, if any, of the eight statements is applicable and your obligations with regard to each applicable statement. If the facts are not sufficient to determine whether a statement applies to a situation, discuss the circumstances in which the statement would apply.

# Income Tax Concepts

2

Learning Objectives:

LO 1 Explain the operation of the U.S. income tax as a system and how concepts, constructs, and doctrines provide overall guidance in the tax treatment of items that affect taxable income.

LO 2 Identify the general concepts that underlie the tax system and explain how the concepts affect taxation.

LO 3 Explain the effect of accounting concepts, how such concepts provide guidance in determining when an item of income should be included in gross income, and when an expense item is deductible.

LO 4 Explain income concepts and the how they aid in determining which items constitute gross income for tax purposes.

LO 5 Explain deduction concepts and how such concepts affect what may be deducted for income tax purposes.

## 2-1 INTRODUCTION

LO 1
Explain the operation of the U.S. income tax as a system and how concepts, constructs, and doctrines provide overall guidance in the tax treatment of items that affect taxable income.

The federal income tax is based on a system of rules and regulations that determine the treatment of various items of income and expense. The key point to be made is that federal income taxation is based on a *system*. In fact, it shares the characteristics of any type of system. We are all familiar with systems; our society is organized by systems of rules. Some systems are natural and afford us little leeway in abiding by them. For example, gravity is part of the environmental system in which we live and a force that cannot be overcome without great difficulty. Because of our knowledge of and experience with the concept of gravity, we have learned that we must be aware of its effects on our behavior. For example, because of the effect of gravity, you cannot walk off a cliff without suffering grave consequences.

Most of the legal and social systems we deal with every day are artificial. That is, people make rules and prescribe actions to enforce them. In these systems, detailed rules are developed for general concepts. For example, all states have testing requirements that must be met to get a driver's license. A person who moves from one state to another generally has no problem passing the test in the new state because the general concepts involved in driving an automobile do not change from location to location.

Artificial systems are distinguished from natural systems by exceptions to the general rules of the system. These exceptions are necessary to meet specific needs. Returning to our driving example, we know that most states permit you to make a right turn at a red light after making a complete stop (i.e., the general rule). However, traffic experts have determined that some intersections are so hazardous that the general rule cannot be followed. The result is an exception to the law—we cannot make a right turn on red after a complete stop at some intersections. How do we identify those instances in which we may not make a right turn on red? Simple—the rules provide that an appropriately labeled sign be posted to alert us to the exception.

As with all artificial systems, the federal income tax system has been developed around general concepts that guide us in its application to various types of transactions. There are, of course, exceptions that do not follow from the application of the general concepts. These exceptions generally stem from the desire to use the tax system to promote some social, economic, or political goal. For example, the income tax law provides an exclusion from income for employer-provided health insurance policies. This payment of the employee's expenses by the employer could be taxed. However, to encourage employers to provide health-care coverage for their employees (a social goal), Congress has excluded such payments from the employee's income. Another example of an exception involves losses on the sale of stocks. Net loss deductions on the sale of stocks by individuals are limited to $3,000 per year. However, to encourage investment in small companies (an economic goal), a special provision in the tax law allows the deduction of up to $50,000 in losses from an investment in the stock of a new company. The only effective way to learn the exceptions in the tax law is through experience and study. That is, there are no explicit "no right turn on red" signs in the tax law. The major exceptions to the general concepts of taxation are presented in this book, but the focus is on developing the ability to determine the treatment of transactions by applying the general concepts of taxation.

This chapter groups income tax concepts by their major function(s) within the income tax system. The four major groupings for discussion purposes are *general concepts, accounting concepts, income concepts,* and *deduction concepts.* Throughout the remaining chapters, the text constantly refers to these concepts to help explain the tax treatments being presented. You must understand these concepts, so we suggest that you return to this chapter and review the applicable concepts before you begin reading a new chapter. To help you, each chapter begins with a summary of the concepts applicable to the chapter's material.

Before beginning the discussion of the concepts, it is necessary to introduce a bit of terminology used throughout the remainder of the book. A **concept** is a broad principle that provides guidance on the income tax treatment of transactions. Because a specific concept covers many transactions, concepts are broad. A **construct** is a mechanism that has been developed to implement a concept. A **doctrine** is a construct that has been developed by the courts. Thus, constructs and doctrines are the interpretive devices necessary to apply a concept. When this book refers to a concept, the text includes all its related constructs and doctrines. An example of a concept is the annual accounting period concept; it requires all income tax entities to report their results on an annual basis. To properly identify the income of each annual period, each entity must select an accounting method. In this example, *annual accounting period* is the concept, and *accounting method* is the construct necessary to implement the concept. Thus, when we talk about the annual accounting period concept, the accounting method construct is implicitly a part of the concept.

This chapter introduces and discusses the fundamental concepts of income taxation. The discussion of each concept includes the fundamental constructs and doctrines necessary to begin the study of income taxation.

## 2-2 GENERAL CONCEPTS

LO 2
Identify the general concepts that underlie the tax system and explain how the concepts affect taxation.

General concepts provide guidance on the overall operation and implementation of the income tax system. As such, these concepts apply to almost every aspect of the system, be it an accounting issue, an income issue, or a deduction issue.

### 2-2a Ability-to-Pay Concept

A fundamental concept underlying the income tax structure is the **ability-to-pay concept**. This concept states that the tax levied on a taxpayer should be based on the amount that the taxpayer can afford to pay. The first result of this concept is that the income tax base is a *net* income number (i.e., income minus deductions and losses) rather than a *gross* figure such as total income received. Therefore, the tax base recognizes different deduction levels incurred by taxpayers as well as different levels of income.

**Example 1** Jerry and Marta each have a total income of $65,000. Jerry's allowable deductions are $20,000, and Marta's allowable deductions are $35,000.

**Discussion: Although Jerry and Marta have identical total incomes, Jerry's allowable deductions are $15,000 less than Marta's. Thus, Jerry has a greater ability to pay taxes than does Marta. Allowing deductions in the income tax base recognizes taxpayers' varying abilities to pay.**

The example of Jerry and Marta illustrates that the notions of *income* and *deduction* are fundamental constructs that are used to implement one aspect of the ability-to-pay concept. Losses and tax credits also reduce the amount of tax due and are related to a taxpayer's ability to pay tax. These constructs were defined and discussed in Chapter 1, and we will not elaborate further at this juncture. However, we would note that the study of income taxation is essentially the study of what makes up these constructs. It is important to remember that these constructs are really the basic elements of the system.

A second aspect of the ability-to-pay concept is the use of a progressive tax rate structure. Recall that a progressive tax is one in which higher levels of the tax base are subjected to increasingly higher tax rates. Individuals with large taxable incomes pay a higher marginal tax rate than do individuals with small taxable incomes. Thus, both the tax base—taxable income—and the tax rate applied to the base are determined by the taxpayer's ability to pay tax. It should be noted that the ability-to-pay concept is undermined by provisions that exclude certain types of income from the tax base. That is, to the extent that a taxpayer has income that is not subject to tax because of an allowable exclusion, the taxpayer is being taxed at less than her or his ability to pay.

**Example 2** Dewitt and Gloria are a retired couple with a taxable income of $32,000. The primary source of their taxable income is Gloria's pension and taxable dividends and interest. In addition, Dewitt and Gloria own municipal bonds that pay annual interest of $14,000 that is not included in their taxable income. What is the effect of the exclusion of the bond interest on the ability-to-pay concept?

**Discussion: Because the $14,000 in interest from the bonds is available to pay Dewitt and Gloria's taxes, the exclusion of the interest from the tax base allows them to pay less tax than they could afford to pay. This effect is somewhat mitigated by the lower interest rates found on tax-exempt bonds when compared with taxable bonds. That is, by investing in municipal bonds, Dewitt and Gloria have accepted a lower interest rate than they could have obtained by investing in taxable bonds. Thus, they have paid some implicit tax on the bonds (although none of it goes to the federal government) by accepting the lower tax-exempt bond rate.**

## 2-2b Administrative Convenience Concept

Throughout the discussion of the income tax, a particular item often is not treated consistently with the basic concept applicable to the situation. Many of these treatments result from the **administrative convenience concept**. This concept states that items may be omitted from the tax base whenever the cost of implementing a concept exceeds the benefit of using it. The cost is generally the time and effort for taxpayers to accumulate the information necessary to implement the concept as well as the cost to the government of ensuring compliance with the concept. The benefit received from implementation is generally the amount of tax that would be collected. Thus, many items that meet the definition of *income* are not taxed because the cost of collecting the information necessary to ensure compliance would be greater than the tax produced by the income.

**Example 3** Bravo Company provides a break room for its employees. Free coffee is provided to the employees there at a cost to Bravo of ten cents per cup. Leroy is an employee of Bravo Company who drinks three cups of coffee in the break room on an average day. Is Leroy taxed on the free coffee he receives from Bravo Company?

**Discussion: Under general concepts of income recognition (discussed later in this chapter and in depth in Chapter 3), Leroy receives income when he drinks the free coffee provided by his employer. This is, in effect, a form of compensation Bravo provides to its employees. However, the cost of each employee's tracking their consumption of coffee, as well as the cost of the government's ensuring that all employees include the cost of their free coffee in their income, exceeds the additional tax that would be collected. Thus, under the administrative convenience concept, Leroy is not taxed on the free coffee.**

Another aspect of this concept relates to deductions for individuals. The tax law lets individuals take deductions for certain personal expenditures (e.g., medical expenses, charitable contributions). However, many individuals incur only small amounts of these allowable personal deductions. In these situations, the tax law lets a taxpayer take a standard deduction in lieu of accumulating the information necessary to deduct the actual allowable deductions. This treatment saves taxpayers' time in accumulating and reporting deduction information and the government's time in ensuring the accuracy of the information reported (i.e., the standard deduction does not need to be audited).

**Example 4** Tara believes that she probably does not have a significant amount of allowable personal deductions in 2021. Even if she searches her records, she figures it's unlikely she can document more than $12,550, the 2021 standard deduction for a single taxpayer.

**Discussion: Tara may elect to deduct the $12,550 standard deduction. This relieves her of having to document her small amount of allowable personal deductions, and the government incurs no cost to ensure that her deductions are correct. When taxpayers' allowable personal deductions are close to the amount of their allowable standard deduction, it is more convenient for them to deduct the allowable standard deduction than spend a lot of time trying to document deductions that may provide very little tax savings.**

## 2-2c Arm's-Length Transaction Concept

In seeking to pay the minimum amount of tax, taxpayers often structure transactions that may not reflect economic reality. In many such cases, the transaction is not given any tax effect because the transaction is deemed not to conform with the **arm's-length transaction concept**. An arm's-length transaction is one in which all parties have bargained in good faith and for their individual benefits, not for the benefit of the transaction group. Transactions that are not made at arm's length are generally not given any tax effect or are not given the intended tax effect.

**Example 5** Bo, the sole shareholder of Shoe Company, owns a shoe-stretching machine for which he paid $15,000 and that is worth $18,000. He sells the machine to Shoe Company for $5,000. Can Bo deduct the loss on the sale of the machine to Shoe Company?

**Discussion: Because Bo was, in effect, negotiating with himself when he sold the machine to Shoe Company, the transaction was not made at arm's length, and Bo will not be allowed to deduct the loss on the sale. NOTE: Bo can deal at arm's length with Shoe Company. However, the tax law assumes that related parties (defined subsequently) do not transact at arm's length. One effect of this assumption is that losses on sales to related parties are always disallowed, even if the transaction is made at arm's length and the price reflects fair market value.**

As example 5 shows, transactions that are not made at arm's length generally involve an element of self-dealing. The tax law has formally incorporated the notion of self-dealing through a set of **related party provisions**.[1] Some of the more-common related party relationships (as depicted in Figure 2-1) are:

1. Individuals and their families. Family members include a spouse, brothers, sisters, lineal descendants (children, grandchildren), and ancestors (parents, grandparents).
2. Individuals and a corporation (or a partnership) if the individual owns more than 50 percent of the corporation (or the partnership).
3. A corporation and a partnership if the same person owns more than 50 percent of both the corporation and the partnership.

Note that all these relationships have the potential for self-dealing, either because of family relationships or a substantial ownership interest in an entity. The more-than-50-percent test for corporations and partnerships is based on the level of ownership necessary to control the actions of these entities. In example 5, Bo and Shoe Company are related parties because Bo owns more than 50 percent of Shoe Company and effectively controls Shoe Company's actions. Thus, when Bo deals with Shoe Company, he really deals with himself. In trying to circumvent the related party rules, individuals might

*Figure 2-1*

## Related Party Relationships

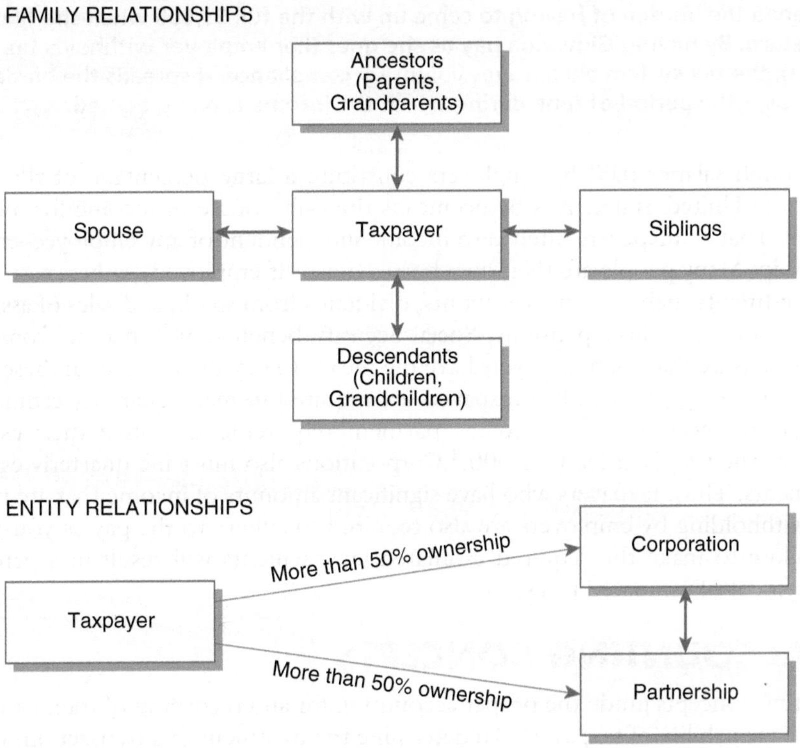


reduce their direct ownership in a corporation or a partnership by distributing ownership among family members, other corporations, or partnerships that they control. This effort is stymied by the **constructive ownership rules**, which state the relationships within which an individual is deemed to indirectly own an interest actually owned by another person or entity. These rules can be complex and are beyond the scope of this text.

## 2-2d Pay-as-You-Go Concept

The U.S. income tax system is one in which voluntary compliance is essential to the operation of the system. Most taxpayers comply with the requirement that they file a return each year and pay the tax due on their taxable income. However, the payment of the entire tax bill at the end of the year could be unduly burdensome for those taxpayers who do not have the foresight to save money for the payment of the tax or who do not have the ability to adequately estimate the amount of the tax they owe. To alleviate situations in which taxpayers are faced with a huge tax bill at the end of the year, the **pay-as-you-go concept** requires taxpayers to pay tax as they generate income. This concept is implemented through withholding and estimated tax payment requirements. The withholding provisions require employers to withhold amounts from each employee's paycheck to pay the tax on the income in that check. The withheld amounts are remitted to the government, and taxpayers receive credit on their tax returns for the tax paid through withholding. This minimizes the probability of a taxpayer facing a huge tax bill at the end of the year. Note that the taxpayer might pay too much tax through this process. In such cases, the government simply refunds the excess tax that has been paid.

**Example 6** Giovanna is a machinist who works for Adilia Company. During the current year, she earned $32,500 and had $2,850 of federal income tax withheld from her paycheck. In filing her return, Giovanna's actual tax was determined to be $3,000. How much tax must Giovanna pay when she files her return for the current year?

**Discussion: Although Giovanna's actual tax is $3,000, she has already paid in $2,850 through withholding. Therefore, she has to pay only $150 ($3,000 – $2,850) when she files her current year's return. NOTE: The withholding provisions ease for Giovanna the burden of having to come up with the full $3,000 when she files her tax return. By having Giovanna pay as she goes (her employer withholds tax payments), the tax system encourages voluntary compliance; it spreads the burden of taxes over the period of time during which the income is being earned.**

Although salaries paid by employers constitute a large percentage of the income taxed in the United States, it is by no means the only source of income for individual taxpayers. That is, taxpayers often earn income independent of any employee–employer relationship. Many people are their own bosses (i.e., self-employed), others earn income from investments such as savings accounts, dividends from stock, and sales of assets, and retired individuals collect pensions, Social Security benefits, and income from investments. To ensure that such taxpayers have the means to pay the tax due on these various sources of income, all individual taxpayers are required to make quarterly estimated tax payments—to meet the estimated tax payment requirements—when their estimated tax due for the year is at least $1,000.[2] Corporations also must file quarterly estimated tax payments. Thus, taxpayers who have significant amounts of income that are not subject to withholding by employers are also required to adhere to the pay-as-you-go concept. Failure to make the required estimated tax payments will result in a penalty for underpayment of estimated taxes.

## 2-3 ACCOUNTING CONCEPTS

LO 3

Explain the effect of accounting concepts, how such concepts provide guidance in determining when an item of income should be included in gross income, and when an expense item is deductible.

Accounting concepts guide the proper accounting for and recording of transactions that affect the tax liability of taxpayers. To determine the treatment of a transaction, we must first identify the appropriate taxpaying unit. Next, we must ascertain the rationale that controls its tax treatment in order to record it. Finally, the transaction must be reported in the correct tax period. These ideas appear to be rather simplistic and part of basic bookkeeping. That is partly true. However, without these basic accounting concepts, the tax system could not function in an orderly and efficient manner. Perhaps even more important, without these concepts, taxpayers could manipulate their affairs so as to avoid paying taxes for many years.

### 2-3a Entity Concept

The most basic accounting concept is the **entity concept**. According to the entity concept, each tax unit must keep separate records and report the results of its operations separate and apart from other tax units. The tax law requires that all tax units be classified as one of two basic entity types: taxable or conduit. The characteristics and unique features of each of the taxable and conduit entities are discussed in detail in Chapters 13 and 14.

**Taxable entities** are those that are liable for the payment of tax. That is, taxable entities must pay a tax based on their taxable income. The four entities responsible for the payment of income tax are individuals; regular, or C corporations; estates; and some trusts.

**Conduit entities** are nontaxable reporting entities. A conduit entity is one in which the tax attributes (income, deductions, losses, credits) of the entity flow through the entity to the owner(s) of the entity for tax purposes. The entities record transactions undertaken by the entity and report the results to the government. However, these entities pay no tax on the results of their operations. Rather, the tax characteristics (i.e., the income, deductions, losses, tax credits) of the operating results are passed through the conduit entity and are taxed to its owners. NOTE: All conduit entities are owned by one or more taxable entities. Two types of conduit entities authorized by the tax law are partnerships and subchapter S corporations.[3,4] Hereafter, any reference to a corporation means a taxable C corporation. Conduit corporations are referred to as *S corporations.*

Trusts are a mixture of taxable and conduit entities. A trust is an arrangement in which a trustee manages assets for the benefit of another, referred to as the *beneficiary*. The trust reports the results of its operations to the government (a conduit characteristic).

Any income distributed by the trust to the beneficiary is taxable to the beneficiary. However, the trust must pay income tax on any income that is earned but not distributed to the beneficiary (a taxable entity characteristic). Thus, trusts are both taxable and conduit entities in that they are taxed on income that is retained and are not taxed on income that is distributed.

To illustrate the relationship between the two basic types of entities, consider a 100-percent owner of a corporation. The corporation is recognized as an entity separate from its owner for purposes of recording transactions. That is, the owner cannot commingle personal transactions with those of the corporation for tax purposes. All income, deductions, losses, and credits attributable to the operation of the business are identified and recorded on the books of the corporation. The summarized results of these transactions are then reported on the corporation's tax return, and a tax is paid on the corporate taxable income. The owner of the corporation includes as income on an individual tax return only any salary or dividends she or he receives from the corporation. However, a different result is obtained if the corporation is organized as an S corporation. As a conduit entity, the S corporation still identifies and records on its books only those items that are attributable to the operation of the corporation. The summarized results of the transactions are reported to the government, but the S corporation pays no tax on its income. Rather, the income of the S corporation is reported on the tax return of the owner, along with the owner's other items of income and deductions, and a tax is paid based on the owner's taxable income. The 2017 Tax Cuts and Jobs Act added a new deduction for noncorporate taxpayers on qualified business income (QBI). The QBI deduction, also referred to as the "pass-through deduction," generally allows a taxpayer to deduct from taxable income 20 percent of the business income minus business expenses.[5] This deduction is discussed in greater detail in Chapters 6 and 13.

**Example 7** Martina and Fran each own 50% of the stock of Card Corporation. During the current year, Card Corporation had a taxable income of $80,000 and paid a total of $20,000 in dividends. What are the tax effects of Card Corporation's income and dividend distributions?

**Discussion: As a separate and distinct taxable entity, Card Corporation must pay the tax on its $80,000 in taxable income. Martina and Fran each must include the $10,000 in dividends she received from Card Corporation in her calculation of taxable income. Note that the dividends are being taxed twice—once when included as income by the corporation and again when distributed to the shareholders.**

**Example 8** Assume the same facts as in example 7, except that Card Corporation is an S corporation. What are the tax effects of Card Corporation's income and dividend distributions?

**Discussion: An S corporation is a conduit entity. The $80,000 is Qualified Business Income. The S corporation is entitled to deduct 20% of its Qualified Business Income, so $64,000 of income flows through to the owners and is included on their tax returns. Card Corporation pays no income tax. Martina and Fran each must include $32,000 in income on her individual tax return. Because the $64,000 is being taxed to the owners, the dividends paid are not taxed again to the owners. Rather, the dividends are considered a repayment of their investment that reduces the amount invested in the stock of the corporation.**

The distinction between entities becomes blurred when a business is owned as a sole proprietorship. Although not technically a conduit entity, the sole proprietorship does not pay tax on its income. The books of the sole proprietorship are kept separate and distinct from the personal transactions of the owner. However, the income tax attributes of the business are reported on the owner's return, in much the same manner as a conduit entity.

**Example 9** Karina is a machinist for Silver Marine Company. At nights and on weekends, she repairs washing machines and dryers. During the current year, Karina's income from her repair business was $10,000, and she incurred $3,500 in expenses to produce this income. She also earned a salary of $30,000 from Silver Marine and had $400 in interest income from a savings account. How should Karina treat these items on her tax return?

**Discussion: Karina's repair business is a sole proprietorship, which is similar to a conduit entity. In accounting for the repair business, she must keep the results of the repair business separate from her other taxable transactions. The business income of $10,000 and business expenses of $3,500 result in an income of $6,500 from the repair business. She would be allowed a QBI deduction of $1,300 ($6,500 × 20%). The $5,200 ($6,500 − $1,300) in business income is then added to her salary and interest income on her individual return, and Karina pays tax on the sum of all her income.**

The result for our sole proprietor appears to be much ado about nothing. However, two important aspects of this entity treatment prevent income manipulation. First, because the commingling of business and personal transactions is not allowed, owners cannot turn nondeductible personal items into deductible business expenses. The classic example of this separation is interest expense. As we shall see in Chapter 5, all interest paid on debt incurred in a trade or business (i.e., the sole proprietorship) is fully deductible, whereas interest paid on debt used for personal purposes (other than qualified home mortgage interest and education loan interest) is not deductible. The entity concept requires the owner to identify these two types of interest for each entity and deduct them according to the rules for that entity. Without such a split, business owners would effectively be allowed to deduct all their interest, and basic wage earners would get no deduction for interest on their personal debts. This treatment would result in an inequity most taxpayers would not tolerate.

**Example 10** In example 9, assume that Karina owns a van that she uses on repair calls. She also drives the van to work at Silver Marine and for various other personal purposes such as trips to the store, taking the kids to school, and so on. How should Karina account for the van and its operating costs?

**Discussion: For tax purposes, the van is viewed as two distinct assets. One asset is used in her repair business, whereas the other asset is used as a personal vehicle. Karina must keep records that adequately document the use of the van in her repair business. She can deduct the costs incurred in using the van in her repair business. The costs incurred for her personal use of the van are not deductible. This separation of business and personal use is required by the entity concept.**

The second major aspect of the reporting of a conduit entity's income on the return of the owner of the entity is that, with the exception of the 20 percent deduction for QBI from pass-through entities, conduit entities are not useful in income-shifting strategies. This results from the progressive nature of the federal income tax. Recall that in a progressive tax rate structure, the higher your taxable income is, the greater your marginal tax rate becomes. If each conduit entity paid tax on its separate income, taxpayers would be able to arrange their affairs into a multitude of conduit entities, all of which are taxed at the lowest marginal income tax rate. Under such circumstances, the income tax would effectively become a flat tax at the lowest tax rate instead of the progressive rate desired. By passing the income through to the owners of the conduit entity, income shifting by using such entities is not an effective tax-planning strategy. As an aside, it should be noted that the tax laws' requirement that taxable entities aggregate results from all their income-producing activities also contains a positive element. That is, if the conduit entity posts a loss from its operations, the taxable entity or entities that own the conduit are generally allowed to use this loss to offset income from other sources.

**Example 11** Assume the same facts as in example 9, except that Karina's repair income was $8,000 and her expenses for producing this income were $11,000. How should Karina treat this on her tax return?

**Discussion: The loss from the repair business flows through to Karina's individual return. The $3,000 loss is deductible on Karina's individual tax return, reducing the tax she would have paid on her other income.**

## Assignment-of-Income Doctrine

One corollary of the entity concept is the judicially developed **assignment-of-income doctrine.**[6] According to this doctrine, all income earned from services provided by an entity is to be taxed to that entity, and income from property is to be taxed to the entity that owns the property. Merely directing payment of income (i.e., assigning income) that has been earned by one entity to another, although legal, does not relieve the owner of the income from paying tax. Thus, it is not possible to avoid the payment of tax on wages earned by simply having them paid to someone else. Although you may legally assign the right to receive income to another, the income tax is imposed on the person who earns the income.

**Example 12** Allison owns a landscaping business. She has a 2-year-old son, Jeffrey. To provide funds for Jeffrey's college education, Allison has every tenth customer make her or his check payable to Jeffrey. Allison deposits the checks in a savings account in Jeffrey's name. Is Allison taxed on the amounts paid to Jeffrey?

**Discussion: Under the assignment-of-income doctrine, Allison cannot escape taxation on the income from her labor by directing the payments to Jeffrey. Allison is taxed on all income earned by the landscaping business, regardless of who receives payment for the services.**

Similarly, the owner of a building cannot escape taxation on the income from the building by having the rents paid to another entity. The only legal way for the building owner to pass the taxability of the income to the other entity is to legally transfer ownership of the building to that entity.

**Example 13** Isabella owns a house that she rents out to college students attending State University. Her grandson, Andy, is a student at State University. To help Andy with his college expenses, Isabella has her tenants pay the rent to Andy. Is Isabella taxed on the rental income?

**Discussion: Because Isabella owns the rental property, she is taxed on all rents, whether she or Andy receives the payments. Under the assignment-of-income doctrine, the owner of property is taxed on the income of the property, regardless of who actually receives the income.**

**Discussion: For Isabella to avoid payment of tax on the rental income, she would have to make a valid gift of the house to Andy. This would make Andy the owner of the property and thus taxable on the rental income. Andy would pay no income tax on the receipt of the gift property. Isabella may or may not have to pay a gift tax on such a transfer.**

## 2-3b Annual Accounting Period Concept

The second accounting concept is that of an annual accounting period. The **annual accounting period concept** states that all entities must report the results of their operations on an annual basis and that each taxable year is to stand on its own, apart from other tax years.[7] The most basic result of this concept is that all entities must choose an annual accounting period for reporting their results to the government. The two basic types of accounting periods are calendar years, which end December 31, and fiscal years, which end on the last day of any other month the taxpayer chooses. Although all entities are allowed to choose their accounting period, most individuals elect to be calendar-year taxpayers. This book assumes the taxpayer is using the calendar year unless otherwise noted. The election of a fiscal year carries some important restrictions, the most important of which are discussed in Chapter 13.

### Accounting Method

An important outgrowth of the annual accounting period requirement is that each taxpayer must select an **accounting method** to determine the year(s) in which taxable transactions are to be reported.[8] The two basic allowable methods are the **cash basis of accounting** and the **accrual basis of accounting**. Taxpayers using the cash basis are taxed on income as it is received and take deductions as they are paid. In contrast, accrual basis taxpayers report their income as it is earned and take deductions as they are incurred, without regard to the actual receipt or payment of cash. At this point, a simple example will illustrate the basic differences between the two methods of accounting.

**Example 14** Steen, Inc., is in the carpet-cleaning business. In December 2021, Steen cleans Gary's business office and bills him $200. Gary pays Steen in January 2022.

**Discussion:** **Assume that both Steen, Inc., and Gary are cash basis taxpayers. Although Steen earns the $200 during 2021, it is not taxed on the $200 until payment is received in 2022. Similarly, Gary takes the deduction for the carpet-cleaning expense in 2022 when he makes the payment.**

**Example 15** Assume that in example 14, both Steen, Inc., and Gary are accrual basis taxpayers.

**Discussion:** **Steen must include the $200 in the year in which it was earned, 2021, and Gary takes his deduction in the year the carpet-cleaning expense is incurred, 2021.**

**Discussion:** **Assume that Steen, Inc., is on the cash basis and Gary is on the accrual basis of accounting. Steen does not include the $200 in income until it is received in 2022. Gary deducts the carpet-cleaning expense in the year incurred, 2021.**

Note that the use of the cash method violates generally accepted accounting principals (GAAP), which require books to be kept using the accrual method. The accrual method used for tax purposes is generally the same as that used in financial accounting under GAAP. However, various limitations and exceptions apply to the application of each method. The most important of these are discussed as they apply to income recognition in Chapter 3 and to deductions in Chapter 5.

## Tax Benefit Rule

The requirement that each tax year stand on its own, apart from other tax years, leads to some problems when circumstances arise in which one transaction could affect more than one year. This has led to development of the **tax benefit rule**. Under this rule, any deduction taken in a prior year that is recovered in a subsequent year is reported as income in the year it is recovered, to the extent that a tax benefit is received from the deduction.[9] The tax benefit received means the amount by which taxable income was actually reduced by the deduction recovered. Consider the following examples:

**Example 16** Rayson Corporation is an accrual basis taxpayer selling widgets for cash and on account. Late in 2019, Rayson sells $500 worth of widgets on account to Tom. In 2020, before any payment is made to Rayson, Tom is sentenced to 20 years in prison for embezzlement. How should the corporation account for this series of events?

**Discussion:** **Because Rayson Corporation is on the accrual basis, it includes the $500 sale to Tom as income in the year of the sale, 2019. The tax law does not generally allow taxpayers to use the allowance method of accounting for bad debts, so Rayson must wait until it determines that Tom's debt is worthless to take a bad debt deduction. Going to jail for 20 years is enough evidence that Tom won't pay the debt, so Rayson should take a bad debt deduction of $500 in 2020. The recognition of the bad debt in 2020 stems from the annual accounting period concept requirement that the events of each tax year stand alone. Rayson Corporation does not go back to amend the income reported in 2019.**

**Example 17** While Tom is in prison, his aunt dies and leaves him a considerable inheritance. He had always felt badly about not paying Rayson Corporation for the widgets, so in 2021, he sends Rayson a check for the $500. How should Rayson account for the $500?

**Discussion:** **Because Rayson Corporation took a deduction for Tom's bad debt in 2020, the tax benefit rule requires it to include the $500 in its 2021 income. Note again that there is no attempt to adjust the prior year's income. The events of each tax year stand apart from each other under the annual accounting period concept.**

As these examples demonstrate, the tax benefit rule has its most common applications in situations in which an annual accounting period and an accounting method interact. It is necessary to put accrual basis and cash basis taxpayers in the same position after accounting for all years involved. In example 16, if Rayson Corporation had been a cash basis taxpayer, it would have recognized no income from the initial sale to Tom, because it never received payment. However, when Rayson received the $500 payment in 2021, it would have been included in income under the cash basis. Thus, over the three-year period, both a cash basis and an accrual basis taxpayer would have recognized income of $500 from the transactions in examples 16 and 17.

## Substance-over-Form Doctrine

The accounting concepts, constructs, and doctrines presented to this point require that all transactions be traced to and recorded by the entity responsible for that transaction in accordance with the method of accounting selected by that entity. Occasionally, the basis for recording the transaction is not clear. That is, taxpayers attempting to avoid taxation sometimes carefully sculpt transactions that are unrealistic in the ordinary sense.

**Example 18** Bill is the sole proprietor of Bill's Sub Shop. To lower his tax on the income from the sub shop, Bill "employs" his three-year-old daughter as a janitor at a salary of $200 per week. Is Bill's employment of his daughter unrealistic?

**Discussion: Because it is unlikely that a three-year-old could perform such services, Bill's characterization of his daughter as an employee is unrealistic.**

Although the courts have consistently held that taxpayers are under no legal obligation to pay more tax than the law prescribes (i.e., tax avoidance is a legal activity), the courts have also said that transactions must bear some semblance of reality. This judicially created concept is referred to as the **substance-over-form doctrine**. The doctrine states that the taxability of a transaction is determined by the reality of the transaction, rather than some (perhaps contrived) appearance.[10] This is generally interpreted to mean that a transaction is to be taken at its face value only when it has some business or economic purpose other than the avoidance of tax.

**Example 19** In example 18, should Bill be allowed to deduct the salary paid to his daughter?

**Discussion: Because the payment of the salary to his daughter is unrealistic under the circumstances, Bill would not be allowed a deduction for salary. This arrangement lacks economic substance and is solely for the purpose of tax avoidance. Thus, the form of the arrangement (daughter as an employee) is ignored, and the tax treatment is based on the substance of the transaction (a gift to his daughter, which is not deductible).**

When might substance over form apply? This is a difficult and subjective question that has no hard-and-fast answers that apply in every situation. However, a few factors should alert us to the possibility of this doctrine being invoked by the IRS. The major element to look for is whether the transaction has economic substance. Most legitimate business transactions are made at arm's length between two parties, neither of which stands to benefit by mutual manipulation of the transaction. Consider the following examples:

**Example 20** Selma is the president and chief executive officer of Megainternational Corporation. Megainternational is a large, publicly held corporation that operates in more than 50 countries around the world. During the current year, Selma receives a salary of $1,000,000. Can Megainternational deduct the $1,000,000 salary paid to Selma?

**Discussion: Megainternational can deduct the entire $1,000,000 in salary paid to Selma. The salary contract was negotiated at arm's length between Selma and Megainternational. Because Megainternational is a publicly held corporation, Selma is not able to exert undue influence over her contract, and the salary paid to her would be typical of such a position.**

**Example 21** Tyrone is the president and chief executive officer of Florence Dunes Company. Florence is a corporation that is wholly owned by Tyrone and his wife, Dahlia. Florence pays Tyrone a salary of $300,000 during the current year and a bonus of $200,000. The bonus is paid even though Florence has only $250,000 in income. Although Florence has been in business for more than 10 years, it has never paid a dividend. Can Florence deduct the $500,000 in salary and bonus it pays to Tyrone?

**Discussion: Because Florence is wholly owned by Tyrone and Dahlia, salary payments to the owners are subject to extra scrutiny. All deductions are subject to the requirement that they be reasonable under the facts and circumstances. In Tyrone's case, the first question is whether the $300,000 salary is reasonable when compared with the salaries paid by comparable companies to executives who do not control the corporation. Any portion of the salary that is unreasonable is considered a dividend paid to the owner. Dividends are not deductible expenses of a corporation.**

**Tyrone's bonus payment is suspicious under the circumstances. Because Florence has never paid a dividend, the payment of such a large bonus relative to the income of the corporation to a 100-percent owner appears to be more in the nature of a dividend distribution. Thus, although the form of the payment is a salary bonus, the substance of the payment is that of a dividend distribution under the facts presented. It is unlikely that the bonus can be deducted as a salary payment by Florence.**

## 2-4 INCOME CONCEPTS

LO 4
Explain income concepts and the how they aid in determining which items constitute gross income for tax purposes.

Income concepts determine what constitutes taxable income, explain why one type of income is taxed differently than other income, and establish the period in which income is to be reported.

### 2-4a All-Inclusive Income Concept

The broadest income concept is the **all-inclusive income concept**. Under this concept, all income received is considered taxable unless some specific provision can be found in the tax law that excludes the item in question from taxation. Income can be received in any form: cash, property, services, and so on. Thus, the tax law always starts with the proposition that anything of value received is taxable.[11] Many situations dealing with income recognition are covered in Chapter 3, so we are using only one example here to illustrate the pervasive nature of this concept.

**Example 22** Felicia is a tax accountant with Oil Rich Company. Alice is a plumber. Both are cash basis taxpayers. Felicia had a problem with her plumbing that Alice fixed. The normal charge for this service would have been $300. However, Alice agreed to waive her fee in exchange for some tax advice from Felicia relating to her business. Does either Felicia or Alice have taxable income from this agreement?

**Discussion: Both Felicia and Alice have income from rendering services, Alice from the plumbing repair and Felicia from the provision of tax advice. Although income was never reduced to cash by either party, both received something of value in exchange for their services. Alice should report the $300 as income when she receives the promised tax advice. Felicia should report $300 of income when Alice fixes her plumbing.**

We noted earlier that certain items of income are not subject to tax. How do we know which items are taxable and which are not? As with all exceptions to the general concepts, only study and experience in working with the tax laws provide answers. Chapter 4 discusses some major income items that are excluded from taxation.

### 2-4b Legislative Grace Concept

Exclusions are based on the **legislative grace concept**. This concept states that any tax relief provided to taxpayers is the result of specific acts of Congress that must be applied and interpreted strictly. Note that relief from taxes on income received can take several forms. Income can be either permanently excluded from tax, or it may be deferred for taxation in a future period (resulting in a time value of money savings). *Legislative grace* means that only Congress can grant an exclusion from income, and the exclusion must be taken in its narrowest sense. An example illustrates these two related notions.

**Example 23** Jorge receives 200 shares of MNO Corporation common stock as a gift from his grandfather. At the date of the gift, the shares have a fair market value of $20,000. During the current year, Jorge receives dividends totaling $2,000 on the stock. Recall that the tax law excludes the value of a gift from the gross income of the recipient. What are the tax effects for Jorge of the gift from his grandfather?

**Discussion: The receipt of the stock as a gift from the grandfather is specifically excluded from Jorge's income by the tax law. However, the exclusion applies only to the value of the gift received and does not exclude from tax any subsequent income Jorge receives on the gift property.[12] Therefore, Jorge is taxed on the $2,000 in dividends received on the stock.**

One other form of tax relief that Congress has provided is special treatment for certain types of income. Most income received and allowable losses incurred by taxpayers are simply added to (or deducted from, in the case of losses) the income tax return of the taxpayer and taxed according to the taxpayer's marginal tax rate. In tax jargon, this is referred to as *ordinary income (loss)*. Congress has created a special class of income treatment for gains and losses arising from the sale of capital assets. A **capital asset** is generally defined as any asset that is *not* a receivable, inventory, real or depreciable property used in a trade or business, or certain intangible assets, such as copyrights.[13] Thus, capital assets primarily consist of stocks, bonds, and other investment-related assets. In addition, all personal use assets (home, furniture, clothing, automobile, etc.) of individual taxpayers are capital assets.

The gains and losses from the sale of capital assets, known as **capital gains** and **capital losses**, must be separated from other gains and losses and aggregated through a prescribed netting procedure before they enter into the taxpayer's income calculation. Net long-term capital gains are currently given preferential treatment through a reduction in the tax rate that must be paid on this type of income. Currently, the tax rate paid on net long-term capital gains is 15 percent (zero percent if the taxpayer's AGI is below $80,800 married filing jointly, 20 percent if the taxpayer's AGI exceeds $501,600 married filing jointly), versus the top marginal tax rate of 37 percent for individual taxpayers. If the netting procedure results in a net capital loss for the year, only $3,000 of the net capital loss can be deducted from an individual's tax return per year.[14] Chapter 3 provides an overview of capital gains, whereas Chapter 11 covers capital gains and losses in more detail. For now, just remember that capital gains and losses are treated differently than all other types of income and losses.

## 2-4c Capital Recovery Concept

Once it has been determined that an item of taxable income has been received, the next logical step is to determine the amount of the income that belongs in the calculation of taxable income. In most cases, this is straightforward. However, sales of investment and/or business assets require more guidance. The **capital recovery concept** states that no income is taxed until all capital previously invested in the asset is recovered.[15] That is, on any asset purchased, all investment in the asset must be recorded to determine the amount of profit (or loss) made upon disposition of the asset. The amount invested in an asset is referred to as its **basis**.[16]

**Example 24** Earl purchases 100 shares of ABC Company's common stock at a total cost of $1,000. When he sells the stock, one lot of 50 shares is sold for $600 and the other 50 shares are sold for $300. What are the tax effects of these sales?

**Discussion: Because there are two separate sales of the stock at different prices, each sale must be considered separately. Each 50-share lot has a basis of $500 (half the $1,000 purchase price). The lot sold for $600 results in a $100 ($600 – $500) taxable gain. That is, Earl has recovered $100 more than he invested in the 50 shares.**

**The 50 shares sold for $300 result in a loss of $200 ($300 – $500). Note that a loss is nothing more than invested capital that has not been recovered. Because of the capital recovery concept, we recognize gains only when the recovery from the disposition of an asset is greater than the amount invested in the asset. A loss results when all the capital invested in an asset is not recovered upon its disposition.**

## 2-4d Realization Concept

A crucial question regarding income items is when to recognize the income (i.e., in which accounting period it should be taxed). In this regard, the taxpayer's accounting method resolves many of the problems. However, some general concepts provide additional guidance. The most basic recognition concept is the **realization concept**. This concept states that no income is recognized for tax purposes (i.e., is included in taxable income) until it has been realized by the taxpayer. In most cases, realization occurs when an arm's-length transaction takes place: Goods are sold, services are rendered, and so on. Mere changes in value without the advent of a realization event—in which the taxpayer receives the change in value—do not result in a taxable recognition.[17]

**Example 25** Assume that in example 24, Earl purchases the 100 shares of ABC common stock on July 2, 2020. On December 31, 2020, the 100 shares have a fair market value of $1,200. The first lot of 50 shares is sold for $600 on February 5, 2021. As of December 31, 2021, the remaining 50 shares have a fair market value of $400. What is Earl's recognized income from the stock in 2020? in 2021?

**Discussion: Although the shares gain $200 in value as of December 31, 2020, Earl still holds the shares and has not realized the increase in value. Therefore, the change in value does not result in a recognition of income in 2020. He realizes the $100 gain from the sale of the first 50 shares in 2021 and reports it in that year. The loss in value of $100 as of December 31, 2021, has not been realized, so Earl cannot deduct this loss in value until he realizes it through sale.**

### Claim-of-Right Doctrine

To aid in determining when a realization has occurred, the **claim-of-right doctrine** states that a realization occurs whenever an amount is received without restriction as to its disposition.[18] An item is received without restriction when the receiver has no definitive obligation to repay the amount received. Income received under a claim of right is reported in the year of receipt. If income is realized under a claim of right and a repayment of part or all of the receipt occurs in a later year, it is accounted for as a deduction in the year of repayment because of the annual accounting period concept. When a taxpayer receives amounts with their use restricted in some substantial manner, those amounts are not realized until the restriction is removed.

**Example 26** Sadie, a landlord and a cash basis taxpayer, enters into a 1-year lease agreement with Bob, a tenant, on December 1, 2021. The agreement calls for a monthly rent of $500, with payment of first and last months' rents upon signing. In addition, Bob is required to pay a $100 cleaning deposit that is to be returned at the end of the lease if the property is returned in good condition. What are the tax effects for Sadie of receiving the $1,100?

**Discussion: The first and last months' rents are taxable when received. Sadie is on a cash basis and has an unrestricted right to the use of the rent payments. However, she must return the cleaning deposit at the end of the lease if Bob abides by its terms. Because of this restriction, Sadie does not have a claim of right to the cleaning deposit when she receives it, and it is not taxed at that time. If Sadie keeps all or part of the deposit at the end of the lease, it is included in her income at that time.**

**Example 27** Assume that in example 26, Sadie sells the building in 2022 before the end of the lease term. Because of the sale, Sadie returns the last month's rent prepayment to Bob. How should Sadie account for the repayment of the last month's rent?

**Discussion: Because Sadie had previously included the last month's rent in her 2021 income, she is allowed to deduct the repayment in 2022. NOTE: The mere possibility that a repayment might be required does not negate Sadie's unrestricted use of the rent prepayment when she receives it.**

Note that the claim-of-right doctrine applies when something of value has been received by the taxpayer. The question to be answered in such cases is whether the receipt has resulted in a realization of income. If the taxpayer has a clear obligation to repay the amount received, *the taxpayer* does *not* have a claim of right to the amount and *is not taxable* on the receipt. However, if there is no clear and definitive obligation to repay, the taxpayer is deemed to have received income.

**Example 28** Herbert Corporation borrowed $10,000 from Local Bank to purchase a stamping machine. Herbert will repay the $10,000 by making monthly payments with interest at 7% over the next 6 years. Does Herbert Corporation have income from the receipt of the $10,000 it borrowed from Local Bank?

**Discussion: Because Herbert Corporation is obligated to repay the $10,000 loan, it does not have a claim of right and is not required to recognize the $10,000 as income.**

## Constructive Receipt Doctrine

An accrual basis taxpayer recognizes income when it has been earned, whereas a cash basis taxpayer recognizes income when it is received. Whether a receipt has occurred is not critical for accrual basis taxpayers. However, a major question for cash basis taxpayers is when is income received? That is, is income received only when it has been physically received in the form of cash? The all-inclusive income concept tells us that income can be received in any form—cash, property, or services. Thus, it is not necessary for a cash basis taxpayer to reduce the income to cash to be in receipt of income. A more fundamental problem is what constitutes a receipt. Based on the **constructive receipt doctrine**, cash basis taxpayers are deemed to be in receipt of income when it is credited to their accounts or otherwise made unconditionally available to them.[19] For example, interest income is taxed on the day it is credited to a savings account, regardless of when the taxpayer actually withdraws it. That is, the interest income is available for use by the taxpayer when it is credited to the account and is taxed at that time. Physical possession of the interest income is not required for it to be taxed. Note that this is not a problem for an accrual basis taxpayer—the interest income would be taxed in the period in which the income was earned, regardless of when the actual payment was received. Once income has been made unconditionally available, taxpayers cannot turn their backs on it and thus select the year for taxation.[20] To be considered unconditionally available, the taxpayer must be aware that the income is available for use.

**Example 29** At the December 12, 2021, meeting of the board of directors of Gould Company, the board awards bonuses to all officers in the amount of 5% of their annual compensation. The bonuses are to be paid in December. Samantha, the controller of Gould Company, requests that her bonus not be paid until January 2022. In what year is Samantha taxed on the bonus?

**Discussion: Because the board made the bonus unconditionally available to Samantha in December, she is in constructive receipt of the bonus in 2021 and is taxed as if she received the bonus in that year.**

However, income is *not* constructively received if the taxpayer's control of its receipt is subject to substantial limitations or restrictions.

**Example 30** Aardvark Corporation mails its annual dividend checks to shareholders on December 31, 2021. Alana receives her dividend check on January 4, 2022. In what year is the dividend taxable to Alana?

**Discussion: Because Alana does not have any control over the dividend check and does not have unrestricted use of the check until she receives it on January 4, 2022, she is taxed on the dividend in 2022. Although she knows that the check is coming, it is not available for use as of December 31, 2021.**

**Example 31** Assume that Aardvark Corporation policy is to mail its annual dividend checks to shareholders so that the checks arrive on or before December 31 of each year. Alana has been a shareholder of Aardvark for 5 years. Alana's dividend check arrives in her mailbox on December 31, 2021. However, Alana is out of town to visit relatives for the holiday and does not return until January 4, 2022, at which time she deposits the check in her checking account. In what year is the dividend taxable to Alana?

**Discussion: Because the dividend is made annually, Alana is aware that the check is coming. She is taxed on the dividend in 2021 because it is available to her on December 31 and she knew that the check was coming.**

**Example 32** Paul is selected as the outstanding player in the Super Bowl on December 31, 1967. He is awarded a car worth $10,000, which he picks up 3 days later at the dealer that supplied the car. When is Paul taxed on the award?

**Discussion: As long as Paul could not have picked up the car under any condition on December 31, it is not made unconditionally available to him until the first date on which he can pick it up. Therefore, he is taxed on the value of the car in 1968.**[21]

These are just a few applications of the constructive receipt doctrine. More detail on different types of restrictions and conditions is covered in the discussion of income sources in Chapter 3. At this point, the important point to remember is that cash basis taxpayers do not have to actually receive cash to trigger income recognition; the only requirement is that the income be unconditionally within their control.

### Comparing Claim of Right and Constructive Receipt

One of the most difficult problems encountered by beginning tax students is determining when the claim-of-right and constructive receipt doctrines apply. Figure 2-2 presents a time line that differentiates the two doctrines. In Figure 2-2, note that the constructive receipt doctrine applies when an item of income has not yet been physically received by the taxpayer. The question to be answered in determining whether the item is currently taxable is whether the taxpayer has the income within their control. This is in contrast to the claim-of-right doctrine where an amount has been received. The question in this case is whether the amount received is currently taxable.

## 2-4e Wherewithal-to-Pay Concept

The income tax system is philosophically based on the ability-to-pay concept. Features such as progressive tax rates and taxation based on the net income of a taxpayer are derived from the concept that the amount of tax paid should be in relationship to the ability of the taxpayer to pay the tax. Ability to pay the tax in the current tax year is also important for income-recognition purposes. To distinguish general ability-to-pay principles and income-recognition applications, we use the **wherewithal-to-pay concept**. This concept states that income should be recognized and a tax paid on the income when the taxpayer has the resources to pay the tax. Although this would generally require that the transaction in question provide cash to pay the tax, the receipt of other asset forms and relief from debts are considered forms of receipt with which tax can be paid.[22] NOTE: The concept applies equally to both cash and accrual basis taxpayers.

The wherewithal-to-pay concept provides the rationale for the deferral of recognition on several types of realized gains.

Figure 2-2

## Constructive Receipt and Claim of Right

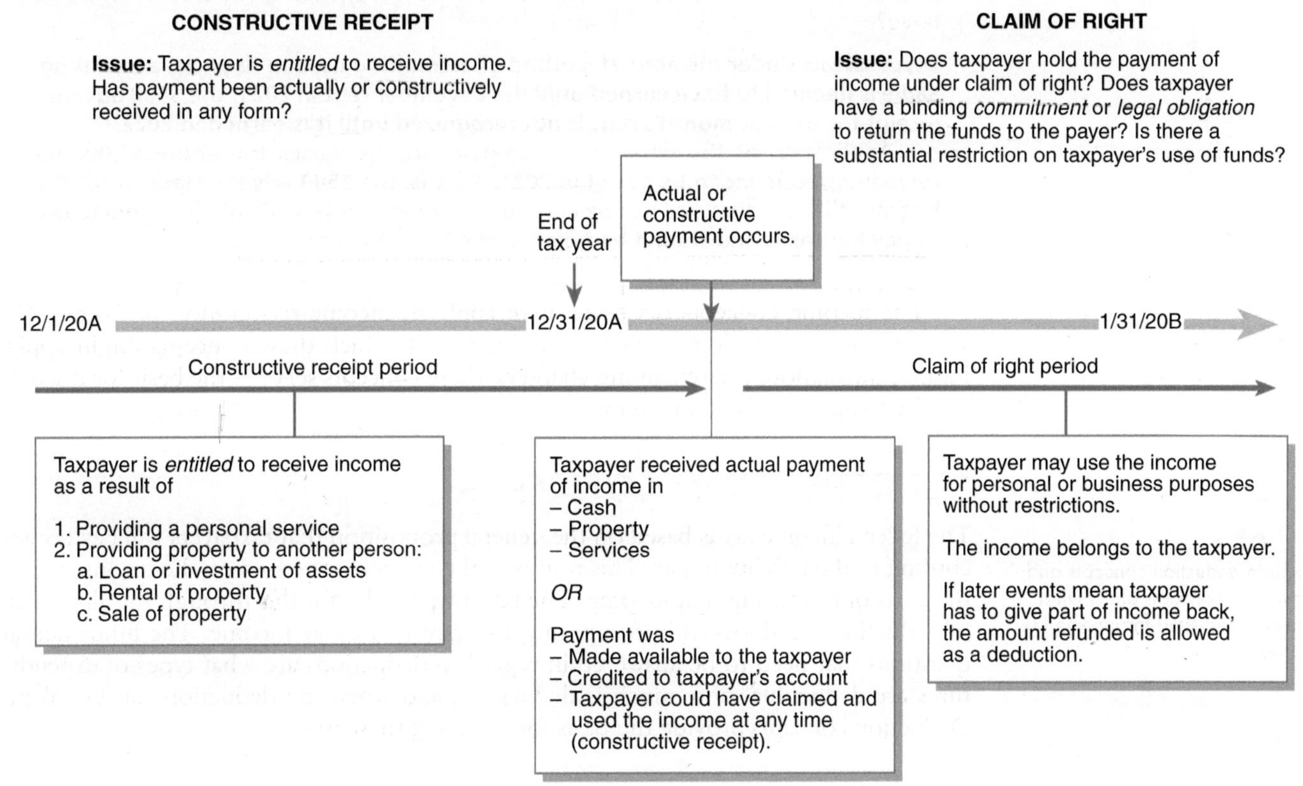


**Example 33** Liu exchanges his dental office building with a basis of $600,000 that he uses in his dental practice for a new dental office building. The new building cost $3,000,000, but Liu is given a trade-in value of $1,000,000 for his old building and has to pay only $2,000,000 out of pocket for the new building. Has Liu realized a gain from the exchange? If so, is the gain available to pay tax?

**Discussion: An exchange does constitute a realization. Liu has disposed of the building in an arm's-length transaction and converted its value toward the purchase of the new building. The substance of the transaction is a sale of the old building for $1,000,000 and the purchase of the new building for $3,000,000.**

**Although Liu has realized a gain of $400,000 ($1,000,000 – $600,000) on the exchange, all the gain has been reinvested in the purchase of the new building, and none of the $1,000,000 he received for his old building is available to pay the tax on the $400,000 gain.**

Liu's building transaction is an example of a like-kind exchange. Because Liu exchanged real property that is of like kind (in this case, one dental office building for another dental office building), the tax law allows him to defer recognition of the gain until he disposes of the new building in a transaction that gives him cash (or other assets) with which to pay the tax. Like-kind exchanges and other types of transactions in which gains are deferred under the wherewithal-to-pay concept are discussed in Chapter 12.

Another important application of this concept is the acceleration of income recognition by accrual basis taxpayers on advance receipts for goods and services. In general, accrual basis taxpayers recognize income in the tax year in which the income is earned, without regard to when cash payment is actually received. However, when an accrual basis taxpayer receives an advance payment for goods and services, the IRS takes the position that the taxpayer is in the best position to pay the tax in the period in which the cash is received rather than when it is earned.[23]

**Example 34** Return to the facts of example 26. Assume that Sadie, the landlord, is an accrual basis taxpayer. She receives the first and last months' rent on the 1-year lease in December 2021. In which year(s) should the $1,000 first and last months' rent receipts be taxed?

**Discussion: Under the accrual method of accounting used in financial accounting, Sadie is deemed to have earned only the December rent in 2021; the $500 advance receipt for the last month's rent is not recognized until it is earned in 2022.**

**Application of the wherewithal-to-pay concept causes the entire $1,000 received in December to be taxed in 2021. That is, the $500 advance receipt for the last month's rent that will not be earned until next year is available for Sadie to use to pay her taxes and should be taxed at the time she receives it.**

The income concepts discussed here apply to income-recognition problems. No attempt has been made to cover every situation in which these concepts might apply. Rather, throughout the remaining chapters, these concepts serve as the basis for discussing the treatment of income items.

## 2-5 DEDUCTION CONCEPTS

LO 5
Explain deduction concepts and how such concepts affect what may be deducted for income tax purposes.

The federal income tax is based on the general proposition that taxpayers will pay tax according to their ability to pay. This results in the tax being assessed on the income net of the costs of producing that income. The tax law provides for this through the allowance of deductions (and losses) in computing a taxpayer's taxable income. The fundamental questions that need to be answered in regard to deductions are what types of expenditures are deductible, how much is deductible, and when the deduction can be taken. Deduction concepts provide the basis for resolving these issues.

### 2-5a Legislative Grace Concept

The most fundamental deduction concept is that of legislative grace. Applied to deductions, this concept means that deductions are allowed only as a result of a specific act of Congress and that any relief granted in the form of a deduction must be strictly interpreted. In contrast to the all-inclusive income approach to the recognition of income—where we assume that everything is taxable unless we can find a provision exempting an item from tax—deductions must be approached with the philosophy that nothing is deductible unless a provision in the tax law allows the deduction.

### 2-5b Business Purpose Concept

The allowance of deductions is governed by the **business purpose concept**.[24] This concept means that a deduction is allowed only for an expenditure that is made for some business or economic purpose that exceeds any tax avoidance motive. This concept has been interpreted to mean that the expenditure was made in connection with a profit-seeking activity.[25] Note that a transaction may be entered into for a profit and for the additional profit from the tax savings associated with the deductibility of the expenditures related to the transaction. Two general types of expense deductions in the tax law embody this profit motive requirement: expenses incurred in a trade or business[26] and those related to the production of income.[27] These two general types of expenses are commonly referred to as **trade or business expenses** and **production of income expenses.**

A third category of expenses that is specifically disallowed (with a few specific exceptions) is those expenses that are personal in nature, known as **personal expenses**.[28] As stated in Chapter 1, the tax law does allow individuals to deduct certain personal expenditures from adjusted gross income. The list of deductible personal expenses includes medical expenses, home mortgage interest, income and property taxes, and charitable contributions. Recall that some of these expenses are subject to limitations and are deductible only if they exceed the taxpayer's allowable standard deduction amount.

To determine the tax treatment of any expenditure, the motive behind the transaction must be determined. Based on the motive—profit or personal purposes—it is categorized in one of these general classes:

1. Trade or business expenses
2. Expenses for the production of income
3. Personal expenses

Distinguishing a personal expenditure (category 3) from a profit-motivated activity (i.e., categories 1 and 2) is generally a fairly easy task.

**Example 35** Peter pays $1,000 for a new couch for his home. Is this a personal expenditure?

**Discussion: As long as the couch is not used in Peter's trade or business or is not held as an investment by Peter, its use is personal and no deduction would be allowed for the purchase of the couch.**

**Example 36** Peter purchases a couch for the reception area of his optometry practice. What is the proper treatment of the couch?

**Discussion: Because providing a place for clients to sit while they wait is something that businesses normally do, the couch is properly classified as related to his trade or business of optometry. Peter can therefore take the deductions allowed for the couch.**

A more difficult task is distinguishing a trade or business activity from a production of income activity. This is covered in depth in Chapter 5, but consider the following examples:

**Example 37** Roger owns Gould Trucking Company. The physical layout of the company's location includes an office building, a parking lot for his trucks, and a maintenance shop. During the current year, Roger purchases the house next door to his trucking company and rents it out to individuals unrelated to the trucking company. Is the house an investment activity or part of his trucking business?

**Discussion: Because Roger purchased the house to produce rents, which is an investment activity unrelated to his trucking business, it is considered an investment activity. He must account for the house and any related expenses under the rules for investments, not as part of his trade or business of trucking.**

**Example 38** Assume that instead of renting the house out, Roger lets his drivers stay in the house during rest periods between trucking runs. How should the house be treated?

**Discussion: In this case, the use of the house is related to his trucking business. Therefore, the house is considered a trade or business asset and is accounted for under the rules for trade or business assets.**

Once the general category to which an expenditure belongs has been determined, the tax law provides specific rules regarding deductibility for each category. For example, business expenses are generally limited only by the reasonableness (i.e., what a prudent businessperson would pay in the same circumstances) of their amount, whereas production of income of individuals are often subject to a limitation based on the income of that taxpayer. Losses incurred in a trade or business are fully deductible, but losses from the sale of personal use assets (automobile, furniture, clothing, personal residence, etc.) are generally not deductible. These are just a few general examples of the importance of distinguishing the activity in which an expenditure has been incurred. Chapters 5 through 7 discuss the specifics of differences in deductions and losses in the three classes of expenditures. For now, consider the following treatments of the sale of an automobile:

**Example 39** Juana owns an automobile that has a basis of $8,000. She sells the automobile for $5,000. How much of the $3,000 loss can Juana deduct on her tax return?

**Discussion: The deductibility of the loss depends on the use of the automobile. If Juana uses the automobile in a business, the loss would be fully deductible. However, if the use of the automobile were purely personal, no loss on the sale would be allowed.**

**Example 40** Assume that Juana sells the automobile for $9,000, resulting in a $1,000 gain. Is the gain taxable in all cases?

**Discussion: Yes, the gain would be taxed even if it were used for purely personal purposes. Remember that the all-inclusive income concept requires that all income be taxed unless specifically excluded by the tax law. There is no exclusion in the tax law for income from the sale of personal use assets.**

Certain personal expenditures, referred to as *itemized deductions,* for medical care, charitable contributions, and home mortgage interest are allowed as deductions.[29] Congress feels that these items are necessary living expenditures that are not available for the payment of tax. To create some equity for taxpayers of different means and for administrative convenience, a minimum deduction for these types of expenditures (itemized deductions) is allowed to all individual taxpayers through the provision of a standard deduction.

**Example 41** Mary and Tom are both single taxpayers. Mary makes a salary of $50,000 and Tom makes $20,000. Mary has total allowable itemized deductions of $13,000 for 2021. Tom's total allowable itemized deductions are $2,000. The standard deduction for a single taxpayer in 2021 is $12,550. Given these facts, what are Mary's and Tom's total allowable deductions for 2021?

**Discussion: Because Mary's itemized deductions exceed the standard deduction, she is allowed to deduct her actual $13,000 in expenditures. Tom's itemized deductions are less than the minimum allowable standard deduction, so he is allowed to deduct the $12,550 standard deduction in lieu of his $2,000 in actual expenditures.**

The allowance of a standard deduction is unique to individual taxpayers. The standard deduction amount does not apply to other tax entities, which may take only those deductions that are based on the business purpose concept in connection with a profit-motivated activity.

## 2-5c Capital Recovery Concept

After establishing the category of an expenditure, the next question to be answered is how much of the expenditure can be deducted. In general, the amount of a deduction can never exceed its cost. This is derived from the capital recovery concept discussed earlier. Under this concept, no income is realized until the amount invested has been recovered. The amount of investment in an asset is referred to as the asset's *basis.* Thus, the amount invested in an item, its cost, is the maximum amount that can be deducted in determining taxable income.

**Example 42** Wojo's Warblers, Inc., sells miniature porcelain birds. Wojo's purchased a shipment of the birds several months ago at a per-unit cost of $45. Wojo's recently sold the entire shipment for $65 per unit. It will cost $50 per unit to replace the birds sold. How much income does Wojo's, Inc., have from the sale of each bird?

**Discussion: Although it will cost Wojo's $50 to replace each porcelain bird, its income calculation is based on the amount actually invested in each bird. Therefore, the per-bird profit is $20 ($65 – $45).**

The year(s) in which expenditures may be deducted is generally determined by the taxpayer's accounting method. However, even cash basis taxpayers cannot deduct capital expenditures in total in the period in which they are paid.[30] The main characteristic of a **capital expenditure** is that its usefulness extends substantially beyond the end of the tax year in which the expenditure is made.[31] The classic example of a capital expenditure is the purchase of a long-lived asset such as a building.

**Example 43** In 2021, Amy Corporation, a cash basis taxpayer, purchases a computer to use in its consulting business. Amy pays $15,000 for the computer, which it expects to be able to use in its business for at least 5 years. When can Amy Corporation deduct the $15,000 investment in the computer?

**Discussion: Because the use of the computer extends beyond the end of 2021, Amy cannot deduct the entire $15,000 in 2021, even though it is on the cash basis. Amy Corporation must capitalize the $15,000 cost and deduct it over its tax life through depreciation deductions. Specific rules for depreciating property for tax purposes are covered in Chapter 10.**

In example 43, the computer would have an original basis equal to its cost, $15,000. As depreciation deductions are taken on the computer, the investment is being recovered against current period income. Therefore, the basis must be reduced whenever part of the investment is recovered through a tax deduction. To understand why the basis is reduced for recoveries, consider the following example:

**Example 44** Amy Corporation takes depreciation on its computer at $3,000 per year. At the end of 5 years, when total depreciation taken has amounted to $15,000, it sells the computer for $5,000. What is Amy Corporation's gain or loss on the sale of the computer?

**Discussion: Amy Corporation's gain is $5,000. When the computer is sold, it has no capital investment remaining in the computer because it has deducted the entire $15,000 cost against income during the 5 years it used the computer.**

**Note that if the basis were not reduced for the depreciation deductions taken, Amy Corporation would have a loss of $10,000 ($5,000 − $15,000) on the sale. Allowing the corporation to deduct a $10,000 loss and $15,000 of depreciation would result in a total deduction of $25,000. This would be a violation of the capital recovery concept, which limits deductions to the amount invested in an asset.**

Similarly, any additional capital expenditures pertaining to the computer would be added to the computer's basis for recovery over the remaining tax life. Because the amount of capital invested in a long-lived asset varies throughout its tax life because of these adjustments to its basis, the investment in an asset is more appropriately referred to as its *adjusted basis*.[32] An asset's **adjusted basis** is the amount of unrecovered investment in it after considering increases and decreases in the original amount invested in the asset.[33]

For any given expenditure, a deduction for the expenditure can take place at three points in time:

- In the period paid or incurred
- Over the useful life of the expenditure
- Upon disposition of the asset created by the expenditure

When the benefit of expenditures does not extend beyond the end of the current tax year, the expenditures are deducted in the year in which they are incurred (accrual basis) or paid (cash basis). These are the normal, recurring expenditures commonly made to produce the income being generated. Examples of currently deductible expenditures include salaries, rental payments, supplies, bank charges, and utilities.

Expenditures that benefit more than the current tax year must be capitalized. If the asset created by the expenditure is depreciable in nature, its cost is recovered by depreciation deductions over its useful tax life.[34] Long-lived assets that do not depreciate are recovered through amortization over the useful life of the asset. To be depreciable or amortizable, the asset must have a determinable life or period of usefulness to which the cost can be attributed.

**Example 45** Joe, a cash basis taxpayer, prepays the rent on his business building for 3 years on July 1, 2021. The monthly rent is $1,000, resulting in a $36,000 prepayment. How much rent can Joe deduct from 2021 through 2024?

**Discussion: Although Joe uses the cash method of accounting, the rent prepayment benefits tax years 2021, 2022, 2023, and 2024, and must be capitalized and amortized according to the number of rental months in each year. In 2021, the building is rented for 6 months, resulting in a $6,000 deduction. In 2022 and 2023, Joe can deduct 12 months of rent, $12,000, with the remaining $6,000 deductible in 2024.**

Assets such as land and common stock that do not have determinable lives are neither depreciable nor amortizable. Capital recovery on this type of asset does not take place until there is a disposition of the asset.

**Example 46** The Stephanie Partnership purchases some land in 2017 for $20,000. The land is held until 2021, when it is sold for $30,000. What deductions can the partnership take on the land and when can it take them?

**Discussion: Land is not a depreciable asset because it has no determinable life, so no capital recovery deductions are allowed until the land is sold. In 2021, Stephanie recognizes a gain of $10,000 from the sale of the land. That is, the $20,000 basis is deducted from the $30,000 selling price.**

It is possible for capital recovery to occur at more than one point in time for any given asset.

**Example 47** Raul purchases a heavy-duty truck for use in his construction business in 2019 at a cost of $1,040,000. He uses the truck until 2021, when it is sold for $8,000. How much can Raul deduct in 2019, 2020, and 2021 for use of the truck, and what is his gain or loss on the sale of the truck?

**Discussion: The heavy-duty truck is eligible for a special-election-to-expense (the Section 179 election to expense, discussed in Chapter 10) deduction of $1,020,000 in the year of purchase, 2019.[35] In addition, the remaining $20,000 of cost can be depreciated over 5 years for tax purposes. Under the rules for straight-line depreciation (discussed in Chapter 10), Raul is allowed a depreciation deduction of $2,000 in 2019, $4,000 in 2020, and $2,000 in 2021. This leaves him an adjusted basis of $12,000 at the date of the sale and a loss on the sale of $4,000:**

**Calculation of Adjusted Basis**

| | |
|---|---|
| Original basis | $ 1,040,000 |
| Less: amounts recovered (deducted) against income | |
| First year election to expense | (1,020,000) |
| Depreciation | |
| 2019 | (2,000) |
| 2020 | (4,000) |
| 2021 | (2,000) |
| Total recovered through deductions against income | $ (1,028,000) |
| Adjusted basis at date of sale | $ 12,000 |

**Calculation of Loss on Sale**

| | |
|---|---|
| Selling price | $ 8,000 |
| Less: adjusted basis | (12,000) |
| Loss on sale | $ (4,000) |

**Discussion: In this example, Raul recovers his $1,040,000 investment in the truck as follows: (1) $1,020,000 in the year of purchase through the election to expense, (2) $8,000 in depreciation during the period he uses the truck, and (3) $12,000 recovered against the $8,000 selling price when the truck is sold.**

These deduction concepts are applicable to all deduction situations. As with the other concepts presented, this chapter does not attempt to cover all applications of the deduction concepts. Throughout the remaining chapters, the discussion of deductions is presented with reference to the applicable deduction concepts.

# CHAPTER SUMMARY

The federal income tax is based on a system of rules and regulations. These rules and regulations are based on general concepts that can be used to determine the income tax treatment of most transactions. As with all systems devised by human beings, the federal income tax system contains exceptions to the treatments prescribed by the system's concepts. Throughout the remaining chapters, the treatment of various transactions is developed by reference to the applicable concepts. To deal with the federal income tax system effectively, knowledge of the concepts on which it is based is essential. This chapter has presented the basic tax concepts and categorized them according to their use within the tax system: general, accounting, income, and deduction concepts. For reference purposes, each category is summarized in Table 2-1.

*Table 2-1*

## Income Tax Concepts with Related Constructs and Doctrines

| General Concepts | Accounting Concepts | Income Concepts | Deduction Concepts |
|---|---|---|---|
| **Ability to Pay** | **Entity** | **All-Inclusive Income** | **Legislative Grace** |
| Income, exclusions, deductions, losses, tax credits | Taxable/Conduit | | |
| Progressive rate structure | Assignment of income | **Legislative Grace** | **Business Purpose** |
| | | Capital asset | |
| **Administrative Convenience** | **Annual Accounting Period** | Capital gains and losses | **Capital Recovery** |
| Standard deduction | Accounting method | | Basis |
| | Tax benefit rule | **Capital Recovery** | Capital expenditure |
| | Substance over form | Basis | |
| **Arm's-Length Transaction** | | | |
| Related party | | **Realization** | |
| Constructive ownership | | Claim of right | |
| | | Constructive receipt | |
| **Pay as You Go** | | | |
| Withholding | | **Wherewithal to Pay** | |
| Estimated tax payments | | | |

# KEY TERMS

ability-to-pay concept (p. 2-2)
accounting method (p. 2-9)
accrual basis of accounting (p. 2-9)
adjusted basis (p. 2-21)
administrative convenience concept (p. 2-3)
all-inclusive income concept (p. 2-12)
annual accounting period concept (p. 2-9)
arm's-length transaction concept (p. 2-4)
assignment-of-income doctrine (p. 2-8)
basis (p. 2-13)
business purpose concept (p. 2-18)
capital asset (p. 2-13)
capital expenditure (p. 2-20)
capital gains (p. 2-13)
capital losses (p. 2-13)
capital recovery concept (p. 2-13)
cash basis of accounting (p. 2-9)
claim-of-right doctrine (p. 2-14)
concept (p. 2-2)
conduit entity (p. 2-6)
construct (p. 2-2)
constructive ownership rules (p. 2-5)
constructive receipt doctrine (p. 2-15)
doctrine (p. 2-2)
entity concept (p. 2-6)
legislative grace concept (p. 2-12)
pay-as-you-go concept (p. 2-5)
personal expense (p. 2-18)
production of income expenses (p. 2-18)
realization concept (p. 2-14)
related party provisions (p. 2-4)
substance-over-form doctrine (p. 2-11)
taxable entity (p. 2-6)
tax benefit rule (p. 2-10)
trade or business expense (p. 2-18)
wherewithal-to-pay concept (p. 2-16)

# PRIMARY TAX LAW SOURCES

[1]Sec. 267—Defines related parties and limits deductibility of certain transactions between related parties.

[2]Sec. 6654—Provides that all individuals must pay estimated taxes when their tax liability is expected to be greater than $1,000; imposes a penalty for not paying the proper amount of estimated tax.

[3]Sec. 701—Provides that partners, not the partnership, are responsible for payment of tax on the income of the partnership.

[4]Sec. 1336—Prescribes the taxation of income of S corporations.

[5]Sec. 199A—Generally provides a deduction from taxable income of 20 percent of Qualified Business Income (QBI).

[6]Lucas v. Earl, 281 U.S. 111 (1930)—Established the assignment-of-income doctrine in holding that salaries and fees earned by the taxpayer but paid to his wife under a valid agreement were still income to the taxpayer who earned the income.

[7]Burnet v. Sanford & Brooks Co., 282 U.S. 359 (1931)—Held that the transactions of each tax year should stand separate and apart from transactions of other tax years.

[8]Sec. 446—Sets general rules for methods of accounting, including the allowance of the cash and accrual methods; requires that the method selected by a taxpayer clearly reflect income.

[9]Sec. 111—Establishes the tax benefit rule.

[10]U.S. v. Phellis, 257 U.S. 156 (1921)—Made the first application of the substance-over-form doctrine; held that the substance of a transaction should be considered and the form of a transaction can be disregarded in applying the provisions of the tax law.

[11]Sec. 61—Provides the general definition of *gross income* as all income from whatever source derived.

[12]Willcuts v. Bunn, 282 U.S. 216 (1931)—Determined that gain on the sale of tax-exempt securities is taxable income.

[13]Sec. 1221—Defines *capital assets.*

[14]Sec. 1211—Sets forth the limit on deductions of capital losses of corporations and individuals.

[15]Sec. 1001—Prescribes the calculation of gains and losses on dispositions of property; defines *amount realized* for purposes of determining gain or loss on dispositions.

[16]Sec. 1012—Defines *basis* of property: The general rule for the initial basis of a property is its cost.

[17]Eisner v. Macomber, 252 U.S. 189 (1920)—In holding that a stock dividend did not constitute gross income, determined that increases in value that have not been realized are not subject to tax.

[18]North American Oil Consol. v. Burnet, 286 U.S. 417 (1932)—Established the claim-of-right doctrine in holding that an amount received under the clear control of the taxpayer was income even if some portion of the amount received might have to be repaid in the future.

[19]Reg. Sec. 1.446-1—Requires all items that constitute gross income to be included in gross income in the tax year in which the item is actually or constructively received.

[20]Hamilton National Bank of Chattanooga v. CIR, 29 B.T.A. 63 (1933)—Held that "a taxpayer may not deliberately turn his back upon income and thus select the year for which he will report it."

[21]Hornung v. CIR, 47 T.C. 428 (1967)—Held that the value of an automobile received by a football player as most valuable player in a championship game was not included in income until the player had actual possession made available to him.

[22]Reg. Sec. 1.61-1—States that income can be realized in any form, including cash, services, and property received.

[23]Reg. Sec. 1.61-8—States that advance receipts of rents are included in gross income in the year of receipt, regardless of the taxpayer's accounting method.

[24]Helvering v. Gregory, 293 U.S. 465 (1935)—Originated the business purpose concept; held that the transaction in question had no business purpose, therefore the applicable tax law did not apply.

[25]CIR v. Transport Trading & Terminal Corp., 176 F.2d 510 (2d Cir. 1949)—Expanded the application of the business purpose concept enunciated in *Helvering v. Gregory* to include any tax law provisions pertaining to commercial transactions.

[26]Sec. 162—Allows the deduction of all ordinary and necessary expenses incurred in a trade or business of the taxpayer.

[27]Sec. 212—Allows the deduction of all ordinary and necessary expenses incurred in a production-of-income activity of the taxpayer.

[28]Sec. 262—Provides the general rule for the disallowance of deductions for personal expenditures by individuals.

[29]Sec. 211—Generally allows specific personal expenditures as itemized deductions of individuals.

[30]Sec. 263—Provides the general rule that disallows current period deductions for capital expenditures.

[31]Reg. Sec. 1.461-1—Specifies that expenditures that create an asset with a life expectancy that extends substantially beyond the end of the tax year must be capitalized.

[32]Sec. 1011—Provides general rules for determining the adjusted basis of property.

[33]Sec. 1016—Provides the general rules for adjustments to basis of property for capital expenditures and recoveries of capital subsequent to purchase.

[34]Sec. 167—Allows a depreciation deduction for property subject to exhaustion and wear and tear on property used in a trade or business or held for the production of income.

[35]Sec. 179—Provides an election to expense up to $1,000,000 of the cost of depreciable tangible personal property in the year of purchase and is indexed for inflation in tax years after 2018.

# DISCUSSION QUESTIONS

1. **LO1** This chapter compared the operation of the income tax system with the operation of other systems we have devised to govern our everyday lives. Choose an example of a system you deal with in your everyday life, and explain part of its operation in terms of concepts, constructs, and exceptions to the general concepts and constructs.
2. **LO2** The chapter stated that the ability-to-pay concept is fundamental to the operation of the income tax system. What is the ability-to-pay concept, and what two basic aspects of the income tax system are derived from the concept? What might the tax system be like without this concept?
3. **LO2** What is an arm's-length transaction? What is its significance to income taxation?
4. **LO2** Explain how the related party construct and the arm's-length transaction concept interact.
5. **LO2** Why is the pay-as-you-go concept important to the successful operation of the income tax system? What other types of taxes are based on this concept?
6. **LO3** What is the difference between a taxable entity and a conduit entity?
7. **LO3** Why is the tax benefit rule necessary? That is, which concept drives the need for this construct? Explain.
8. **LO3** What are the two basic methods of accounting that may be used by taxpayers? How do the two basic methods differ?

9. **LO4** What is the effect of the capital recovery concept on income recognition?
10. **LO4** Chapter 1 discussed how gross income is equal to all income received, less exclusions. Which concepts form the basis for this calculation of gross income? Explain.
11. **LO4** What is capital gain income? How is it different from ordinary income?
12. **LO4** Why does the doctrine of constructive receipt apply only to cash basis taxpayers?
13. **LO4** How is the wherewithal-to-pay concept different from the ability-to-pay concept?
14. **LO5** Explain how the business purpose concept provides the basis for determining which expenses are deductible.
15. **LO5** What is a capital expenditure?
16. **LO4, 5** The legislative grace concept is both an income concept and a deduction concept. Explain how the application of the concept differs for income items and deduction items.
17. **LO4, 5** The capital recovery concept is both an income concept and a deduction concept. Explain how the application of the concept differs for income items and deduction items.

## PROBLEMS

18. **LO2** Which of the following are based on an ability to pay? Explain.
    a. State Y collects a sales tax of 5 percent on all purchases of goods and services.
    b. State X collects a sales tax of 5 percent on all purchases of goods and services but gives low-income families a tax credit for sales taxes.
    c. Students at State University are given free parking in designated lots. Faculty and staff members must pay $125 per year for parking at State University.
    d. Barton City charges all customers a flat monthly rate of $10 for garbage pickup.
19. **LO2** Which of the following are based on an ability to pay? Explain.
    a. Local County assesses property taxes at the rate of 1 percent of assessed value.
    b. The university library lets all students, faculty, and staff members check out books free. Students who do not return books by the due date are fined $1 for each day the book is late. Staff members are fined 50 cents for each day a book is late. Faculty members are not fined when they return books late.
    c. The country of Lacyland assesses an income tax based on the following schedule:

| Taxable Income | Income Tax |
|---|---|
| $ –0– to $20,000 | 20% of taxable income |
| $20,001 to $60,000 | $ 4,000 + 15% of taxable income in excess of $20,000 |
| $60,001 and above | $10,000 + 10% of taxable income in excess of $60,000 |

    d. State Z imposes a 10-cent-per-gallon tax on gasoline but gives low-income taxpayers a tax credit for gasoline taxes paid.
20. **LO2** Sheila, a single taxpayer, is a retired computer executive with a taxable income of $100,000 in the current year. She receives $30,000 per year in tax-exempt municipal bond interest. Adam and Tanya are married and have no children. Adam and Tanya's $100,000 taxable income is comprised solely of wages they earn from their jobs. Calculate and compare the amount of tax Sheila pays with Adam and Tanya's tax. How well does the ability-to-pay concept work in this situation?
21. **LO2** Andrew and Yuna each receive a salary of $80,000. Neither Andrew nor Yuna has any other source of income. During the current year, Yuna paid $800 more in tax than Andrew. What might explain why Yuna paid more tax than Andrew when they both have the same income?

22. **LO2** Which of the following are related parties?
    a. Harvey and his sister Janice.
    b. Harvey and the Madison Partnership. Harvey owns a 60 percent interest in the partnership. Three of Harvey's friends own the remaining partnership interest.
    c. Harvey and his grandfather Maurice.
    d. Harvey and Noti Corporation. Harvey owns 40 percent of Noti Corporation. Three unrelated parties own 20 percent each.
    e. Harvey and his uncle, Elmer.
23. **LO2** In each of the following cases, determine whether Inez is a related party:
    a. Inez owns 500 shares of XYZ Corporation's common stock. XYZ has 50,000 shares of common stock outstanding.
    b. Inez owns a 40 percent interest in the Tetra Partnership. The other 60 percent interest is owned by 3 of Inez's friends.
    c. Inez owns 40 percent of the stock in Alabaster Company. Her husband, Bruce, owns 30 percent and her brother-in-law, Michael, owns the remaining 30 percent.
    d. Inez is a 100 percent owner of Nancy Corporation.

Communication Skills

24. **LO2** Doiko Corporation owns 90 percent of the stock in Nall, Inc. Trebor owns 40 percent of the stock of Doiko. Trebor's sister owns the remaining 60 percent of Doiko. During the current year, Trebor purchased land from Nall for $43,000. Nall had purchased the land for $62,000. Write a memorandum to the controller of Nall, Inc., explaining the potential tax problem with the sale of the land to Trebor.
25. **LO3** Ed runs an auto repair business out of the garage attached to his personal residence. How should he account for each of the following items?
    a. Cash received from repair services, $28,000.
    b. Interest paid on his home mortgage, $7,300.
    c. Power jack hoist purchased at a cost of $12,000.
    d. Electricity bills, $3,600. (Ed does not have separate electricity service to the garage.)
    e. Checks received from customers that were returned by his bank, $1,600. The bank charged Ed's account $35 for processing the bad checks.
    f. Telephone bill for phone in the garage, $420. (Ed has a separately listed phone in his house.)
    g. Advertising in the local newspaper, $800.
    h. Interest paid on home furniture loan, $600.
26. **LO3** Jie owns a lawn mower repair business. Her repair shop is in a building she constructed on the lot on which her personal residence is located. How should Jie account for each of the following?
    a. Interest paid on her home mortgage, $9,200. Interest of $4,000 is paid on a separate loan that she used to construct the repair shop.
    b. Property taxes, $1,800.
    c. Electricity bills, $3,800. (Jie is not billed separately for electricity service to her repair shop.)
    d. Cost of remodeling the kitchen, $3,200.
    e. Telephone bills, $970. Jie uses one telephone number for her residence and her business. The cost of having an extra line to the shop is $30 per month. The $970 includes a charge of $250 for an ad in the business section of the telephone directory.
    f. Cost of operating her van for one year, $7,800. Jie uses the van in her repair business and for personal use.
27. **LO3** Aiko, Lani, and Charlie own the 3-Star Partnership, sharing profits and losses 20:50:30. During the current year, 3-Star has total gross income of $500,000 and total allowable deductions of $300,000. How should each of the following taxpayers account for 3-Star's results? Explain.
    a. 3-Star Partnership
    b. Aiko
    c. Lani
    d. Charlie

28. **LO3** Wendy owns 20 percent of the common stock of Britton Company. During the current year, Britton reported a taxable income of $90,000 and paid $40,000 in cash dividends. What are the income tax effects for Wendy of her investment in Britton Company if Britton is organized as
    a. A corporation?
    b. An S corporation?

29. **LO3** Binh owns several businesses. The total income generated by all his businesses puts him in the highest marginal tax bracket. Seeking to lower the overall tax on his business income, Binh is thinking of creating two S corporations and putting half his business interests in each. Will this arrangement lower his overall tax? Write a letter to Binh in which you explain the tax effects of organizing his businesses as two S corporations. In your letter, suggest an alternative plan that might lower his tax. Communication Skills

30. **LO3** Christie purchases a one-third interest in the Corporate Capital Partnership (CCP) in 2020 for $40,000. During 2020, CCP earns an income of $90,000, and Christie withdraws $30,000 in cash from the partnership. In 2021, CCP suffers a loss of $30,000, and Christie withdraws $10,000. What are the tax consequences for Christie of this investment in 2020 and 2021?

31. **LO3** Arnie is a self-employed handyman. During the current year, customers pay him $10,000 in cash for his services. Arnie gives the $10,000 to his daughter, Ariel, who uses it to pay college expenses. Is Arnie or Ariel taxed on the $10,000? Explain.

32. **LO3** Esmeralda is an attorney. Before 2021, she is employed by the law firm of Ellis and Morgan (E&M). Esmeralda is not a partner in E&M; her compensation consists of a fixed salary and a percentage of any fees generated by clients she brings or refers to the firm. In January 2021, she becomes a partner in the law firm of Thomas, Gooch, and Frankel (TGF). As a partner, Esmeralda agrees to turn over to TGF any income from the practice of law from the date of her admittance to the practice. In leaving E&M, it is agreed that she will continue to receive her percentage of fees from clients she referred to E&M during her employment there. In return, Esmeralda agrees that, upon request, she will consult with E&M attorneys regarding those clients. During 2021, she consults with two of her former E&M clients and receives $12,000 from E&M per their agreement. The $12,000 consists of $10,000 as a percentage of fees for client referrals after she left E&M and $2,000 as a percentage for work done before she left E&M. Esmeralda turns the $12,000 over to TGF per her partnership agreement. Write a letter to Esmeralda explaining whether she is taxed on the $12,000 she receives from E&M. Communication Skills

33. **LO3** For each of the following situations, determine the proper year for recognition of the income or deduction if the taxpayer is (1) a cash basis taxpayer and (2) an accrual basis taxpayer:
    a. Tindle Corporation purchases office supplies costing $600 on December 21, 2021. Tindle pays for the office supplies on January 18, 2022.
    b. Raashan pays his employee, Sara, $22,450 in salary up to December 23, 2021. As of December 31, 2021, Raashan owes Sara $560 for the period of December 23 through December 31. The $560 is to be paid on the next pay date, which is January 5, 2022.
    c. Jerri paints Roland's house in December 2021. Roland pays Jerri's bill in January 2022.
    d. Devi sells Aaron a car on August 1, 2021, for $36,000. The terms of the sale call for Aaron to pay Devi $18,000 on August 1, 2021, and $9,000 on August 1, 2022 and 2023.
    e. Barnie's Paint Barn purchases new spray painters on January 15, 2021, at a cost of $3,000. The spray painters have an estimated useful life of 10 years, but the tax life is five years.

34. **LO3** For each of the following situations, determine the proper year for recognition of the income or deduction if the taxpayer is (1) a cash basis taxpayer and (2) an accrual basis taxpayer:
   a. Helen fixes Mark's plumbing in November 2021. Mark receives the bill in December 2021 but does not pay Helen until January 2022.
   b. The Outback Brewing Company purchases a new delivery van on October 30, 2021. The purchase is financed with a note that will be paid off over three years. Outback expects to use the van for three years, but the tax life of the van is five years.
   c. Morbid Marble Mortuaries, Inc., sells a headstone to Lorissa for $6,000. The terms of the sale call for Lorissa to pay $3,000 in the year of the sale and $1,000 in each of the succeeding three years.
   d. Maury's Computer Consultants, Inc., performs work for Janis in 2021. Maury's bills Janis in 2021, but no payment is received. In 2022, Janis files for bankruptcy, and Maury's determines that it will be able to collect nothing on her account.
35. **LO3** Tim has state income taxes of $4,500 withheld from his salary during 2020. On his 2020 federal income tax return, Tim properly deducts the $4,500 as state taxes paid. Upon filing his 2020 state income tax return, he determines that his actual state income tax for 2020 is only $3,900, and the state sends him a $600 refund. What are the tax consequences of the refund? Explain in terms of the concepts presented in the chapter. How would your answer change if Tim's actual state income tax is $4,900 and he has to pay $400 with his state return?
36. **LO3** Jamal Corporation is an accrual basis taxpayer. In 2020, Jamal writes off a $1,000 account receivable from a customer who has died. In 2021, the former customer's estate sends Jamal a check for $600. What are the tax effects of the receipt of the $600 in 2021? Explain. How would your answer be different if Jamal Corporation were a cash basis taxpayer?
37. **LO3** Angela enrolls as a student at Local College during the current year. Before she starts school, her parents lend Angela $80,000 with the stipulation that she will lend the entire $80,000 back to them. The loan is evidenced by a noninterest-bearing note payable in 10 years. Several days later, Angela returns the $80,000 to her parents in exchange for their $80,000 note secured by a mortgage on their personal residence. The note has an 8 percent interest rate and requires monthly interest payments, with the principal due in 10 years. Angela's parents pay her $6,400 in interest on the loan during the current year. Mortgage interest on a principal residence is deductible as an itemized deduction. Discuss whether Angela's parents should be allowed a deduction for the $6,400 in interest paid to Angela.
38. **LO2, 3** For each of the following tax treatments, determine the concept, construct, or doctrine that provides the rationale for the treatment:
   a. Lester purchases some stock for a total cost of $2,500. On December 31, 2020, the stock is worth $2,800. In August 2021, he sells the stock to his brother Rufus for $2,000. Lester has no income from the stock in 2020, and he is not allowed to deduct the $500 loss on the sale of the stock to Rufus in 2021.
   b. Kerry is an employee of Ross Company. During the year, Ross withholds federal income taxes of $3,500 from her salary. Her tax liability for the year is only $3,200, so she receives a refund of $300.
   c. Catherine is a city government employee. She often uses the city's photocopier to make personal photocopies and has her secretary type an occasional personal letter. The value of these services for the current year is approximately $55 but is not included in Catherine's gross income.
   d. Dante's allowable personal deductions are only $2,800 this year, so he deducts the standard deduction in computing his taxable income.

39. **LO2, 3** For each of the following tax treatments, determine the concept, construct, or doctrine that provides the rationale for the treatment:
   a. During the current year, Trafalger Corporation pays $475,000 in estimated tax payments. Trafalger determines that its actual tax liability is $490,000, so it pays only $15,000 with its tax return.
   b. The Parsnip Partnership is an accrual basis taxpayer. During 2020, Parsnip deducted as a bad debt expense a $5,000 account receivable that it determined it could not collect. In 2021, Parsnip receives a $1,000 payment on the account. Parsnip must include the $1,000 in its 2021 gross income.
   c. Kuri sells land for $30,000; its cost was $20,000. Under the sales agreement, the buyer is to pay Kuri's son $10,000 of the sales price. Kuri must recognize a gain of $10,000 on the sale.
   d. Jevon owns 20 percent of the stock of Cowdery, Inc., an S corporation. During the current year, Cowdery reports income of $45,000 and pays no dividends. Jevon must include $9,000 in gross income.

40. **LO4** Postum Partnership purchases a building in 2018 for $250,000. It deducts $5,600 in depreciation on the building in 2018, $6,400 in 2019, $6,400 in 2020, and $3,200 in 2021. It sells the building in 2021 for $260,000. What is the partnership's gain or loss on the sale of the building?

41. **LO4** Chelsea, who is single, purchases land for investment purposes in 2016 at a cost of $22,000. In 2021, she sells the land for $38,000. Chelsea's taxable income without considering the land sale is $100,000. What is the effect of the sale of the land on her taxable income, and what is her tax liability?

42. **LO4** George purchases stock in Dodo Corporation in 2017 at a cost of $50,000. In 2021, he sells the stock for $32,000. What is the effect of the sale of stock on George's taxable income? Assume that George sells no other assets in 2021.

43. **LO4** Determine whether the taxpayer in each of the following situations has realized income. Explain why there has or has not been a realization, and determine the amount of income to be reported.
   a. Alfredo owns a one-third interest in Bayou Partnership. During the current year, Bayou's taxable income is $45,000.
   b. Janet owns a pest-control service. She charges customers $50 per month for basic pest control. Alternatively, customers can pay a lump sum of $500 for one year of basic monthly pest control. During the current year, Janet receives $13,000 in monthly payments and $26,000 in one-year prepayments.
   c. Monte owns 1,000 shares of Ali, Inc., common stock. During the current year, Ali declares and distributes a 20 percent stock dividend. As a result, Monte receives an additional 200 shares of stock.
   d. Rogers Trucking Company owes Big Truck Sales, Inc., $200,000 for the purchase of 3 trucks. Rogers is having a bad year and is unable to make full payment on the debt to Big Truck. Rather than foreclose on Rogers, Big Truck reduces the debt to $170,000 so that Rogers can stay in business.

44. **LO4** Determine whether the taxpayer in each of the following situations has realized income. Explain why there has or has not been a realization, and determine the amount of income to be reported:
   a. Ramrod Development Company purchases land costing $230,000. Ramrod subdivides the land into 100 lots, incurring legal fees of $20,000. It also spends $50,000 to install utility and sewer connections to each lot. The lots are priced to sell at $50,000 each, but none sold during the year.
   b. Eugene is a computer consultant. Rashid is an accounting professor. Rashid needs help installing new software on his home computer. Eugene offers to install the software if Rashid will help him set up the books for a new company he is forming. Eugene installs the software in December. Rashid sets up the books in February.

c. Sasha is an employee of Chasteen Hair Products. Chasteen provides all employees with free medical coverage. During the current year, the cost of Sasha's coverage is $1,900.

d. In November, Ira wins an all-expense-paid trip for two to the Super Bowl in January. He plans to take his best friend to the game. The estimated value of the trip is $4,300.

45. **LO4** Shannon signs a $100,000 contract to develop a plan for integrating the computer operations of State University in December. Under the contract, she receives a $30,000 advance against future payments on the contract upon signing the contract. The contract stipulates that if Shannon does not produce an acceptable plan, she must repay any portion of the advance not earned to date. Does Shannon have any income from the receipt of the advance? Explain in terms of the income tax concepts presented in the chapter.

46. **LO4** Determine whether the taxpayer in each of the following situations has a claim of right to the income received:

a. Trigger, Inc., receives a $5,000 stud fee for services rendered by one of its prized horses. Under its standard contract, Trigger will return the fee if a live foal is not born.

b. Orville works as a salesman for Brewster Company. He receives a travel allowance of $1,000 at the beginning of each quarter. At the end of each quarter, he must make a full accounting of his travel expenses and reimburse Brewster for any of the $1,000 not spent on approved travel.

c. Assume that in part b, Orville is not required to account for his actual travel expenses for Brewster and is not required to return unused portions of the travel advance.

d. Arco Architecture, Inc., receives $10,000 from a client for work done by a subcontractor on the client's project. Arco, in turn, pays $10,000 to the subcontractor.

47. **LO4** Determine whether the taxpayer in each of the following situations has a claim of right to the income received:

a. Sulley's Spa Spot sells hot tubs that have a two-year warranty. The warranty provides for the replacement of all parts and the cost of labor to replace the parts. In addition, Sulley's may replace the hot tub in lieu of repairing it. During the current year, Sulley's hot tub sales total $250,000. Sulley's estimates that 10 percent of all hot tubs sold will require warranty work.

b. In 2019, Retro Fit Construction Company purchased equipment by borrowing $100,000 from Fifth State Bank. After paying off $30,000 of the loan, Retro has financial problems in the current year and cannot afford to make its regular payment. Rather than have Retro default on the loan, Fifth State Bank agrees to reduce the debt to $50,000.

c. Larry's Lawncare Service provides lawn mowing and fertilization services to residential customers. Customers can pay by the month, or they can purchase a one-season contract for $1,000. The contracts obligate Larry's to provide the necessary mowing and fertilization from April through October. In September, Larry's has a "pre-season" sale that lets current customers purchase next season's contract for $800. Fourteen customers buy the discounted contract in September.

d. Alexander Associates does computer consulting for Bertman, Inc., in September. Bertman pays Alexander's $3,000 bill for the work in October 2021. In late November, Bertman's computer system crashes and Bertman sues Alexander, seeking reimbursement of $3,000. The lawsuit is scheduled for court in March 2022.

48. **LO4** Consider the following two situations. Although they are similar, their treatments are exactly opposite. Identify the concept underlying both treatments, and explain why the concept treats the two situations differently.

a. Sam is an employee of Dunbar Company. The company regularly mails salary checks to employees to arrive on or before the last day of each month. Sam's regular paycheck arrives at his house on December 31, 2021, but Sam is away on a ski trip and does not return until January 2, 2022. Sam deposits the check in his bank account the following day. The check is included in Sam's 2021 income.
b. Percy is an employee of Daly Company. In November 2021, Percy's position is eliminated in a "streamlining" of company costs. As part of the cost reduction program, Percy is entitled to severance pay; however, his boss tells him that it will be three or four months before the severance payments are made. The check arrives by mail on December 31, 2021, while Percy is away on a ski trip. He returns on January 2, 2022, and deposits the check in his bank account the following day. The severance pay check is not taxable until 2022.

49. **LO4** Determine whether the taxpayer in each of the following situations is in constructive receipt of income. If not, explain when the income will be constructively received.
   a. Kenji is president of Wright Company. On December 14, 2021, the board of directors votes to give him a $25,000 bonus. Kenji receives the bonus on January 4, 2022.
   b. Regan is an employee of BIF Manufacturing, earning $3,000 per month. She purchases merchandise from BIF costing $2,000 in January of the current year. To pay for the merchandise, BIF agrees to deduct $75 per month from her pay, reducing it to $2,925 per month before other withholdings.
   c. Marnie owns $50,000 par value of 6 percent coupon bonds. The interest coupons may be clipped and redeemed on May 30 and November 30 each year. Marnie does not redeem the November 30, 2021, coupon interest until January 8, 2022.

50. **LO4** Using the income concepts presented in this chapter, discuss whether the taxpayer has realized income in each of the following situations:
   a. Adco Corporation pays the health insurance premiums for all its employees. Adrian is an employee of Adco. Health insurance premiums Adco pays for Adrian cost $1,150 for the current year.
   b. The Sung Partnership buys a parcel of unimproved land for $32,000. Sung spends an additional $22,000 to put in roads and sewerage and to grade the property for subdividing. The property is subdivided into 15 lots and offered for sale at $10,000 per lot.
   c. Doctors and nurses at Valley View Hospital are allowed to eat free of charge in the hospital cafeteria during their shifts. Sue, a doctor, eats meals valued at $1,900 during the current year.
   d. Wayman wins the golf championship at his country club. In addition to a handsome trophy, he receives merchandise worth $500 for winning the tournament.
   e. Rock signs a contract to play football for the Rangers. In addition to a salary of $1,000,000 per year for five years, he is to receive a signing bonus of $5,000,000 to be paid 10 years from the date the contract was signed.

51. **LO4** Nina leases a building to Downtown Computer Systems for $5,000 per month under a five-year lease. The terms of the lease provide that any improvements to the building made by Downtown revert to Nina upon termination of the lease. Downtown remodels the building at a cost of $40,000. At the end of the lease, the fair market value of the remodeling improvements is $50,000. Nina sells the building one year later for $250,000.
   a. List three points at which Nina might recognize income from the improvements made by Downtown Computer Systems.
   b. According to the income concepts presented in the chapter, when should Nina recognize income from the lease? Explain.
   c. Would your answer to part b be different if the lease provides that any improvements made by Downtown Computer Systems can be deducted from the rental payment made to Nina?

52. **LO4** For each tax treatment described, determine the applicable income tax concept(s), and explain how it forms the basis for the treatment:
   a. Jackson owned coupon bonds with detachable interest coupons. He detached coupons worth $5,000 and gave them to his son to buy a car. Jackson is taxed on the $5,000 of interest, even though he never actually received the interest.
   b. Joan's barn on her ranch was destroyed by a tornado. The barn had an adjusted basis of $24,000. Joan received insurance proceeds of $35,000 and built a new barn costing $40,000. Joan does not have to recognize the gain realized on the barn in the current period.
   c. Elvis borrowed $30,000 from University Credit Union to purchase a new X car. He is not taxed on the receipt of the $30,000.
   d. Kelley lost the diamond ring she received from her husband, Ian. The ring had a basis of $2,000, and she received $3,000 from her insurance company. Kelley used the money to pay off medical bills. Kelley must recognize a $1,000 gain on the loss of her ring.

53. **LO5** During the current year, Errol starts a management consulting service which he operates from an office in his home. He uses one room of the house as his office. He purchases office furniture for $6,000 and a computer for $3,000. He uses the computer primarily in his consulting business but also uses it to track his personal investments and for other personal purposes. What tax problems might Errol face regarding his office, the furniture, and the computer? Explain.

54. **LO5** For each of the following situations, determine the deduction concepts involved, and explain how they form the basis for the tax treatment described:
   a. Individuals are allowed to deduct medical expenses.
   b. Happy Burgers, Inc., owns a chain of drive-in restaurants in California. Seeking to expand its operations, Happy spends $90,000 investigating locations in Oregon. Happy decides that expanding into Oregon is not a wise move, but it is allowed to deduct the $90,000.
   c. Lage's Licorice Company suffers a fire in one of its warehouses. Equipment that cost $40,000 and that had been depreciated $15,000 is destroyed. The equipment, which cost $50,000 to replace, is uninsured. Lage is allowed to deduct a loss of $25,000 on the equipment.
   d. While Ray is out to dinner one night, someone breaks into his personal car. The thief steals his stereo and his golf clubs. The fair market value of the items stolen is $300. Because he has a $500 deductible on his insurance policy, he receives no reimbursement from his auto insurance. To make matters worse, no tax deduction for his loss is allowed.

55. **LO5** For each of the following situations, determine the deduction concepts involved, and explain how they form the basis for the tax treatment described:
   a. Jamie sells her personal residence at a loss of $9,000. She is not allowed a deduction for the loss.
   b. Jamie sells a building used in her business at a loss of $9,000. She is allowed to deduct a $9,000 loss on the sale of the building.
   c. Last year, Gardner Corporation purchased equipment costing $10,000. The equipment was eligible for a special expense election, and Gardner deducted the $10,000 cost in the year of purchase. Gardner is not allowed a depreciation deduction on the equipment in the current year.
   d. The Orlando Jams Partnership borrows $500,000 to use as working capital. During the current year, the partnership pays $45,000 in interest on the loan and repays $100,000 of the loan principal. Orlando can deduct the $45,000 interest payment but cannot deduct the repayment of the loan principal.

Communication Skills

56. **LO5** Sidney lives in Hayes, Kansas. He owns land in Cotulla, Texas, that he inherited from his father several years ago. The land is unimproved and has never produced income. On January 26, 2021, Sidney receives a statement of delinquent taxes on the property for 2018, 2019, and 2020 for $120. On February 10, 2021,

Sidney and his wife, Ellen, start to drive to Cotulla; they arrive on February 20 and pay the taxes on the same day. The cost of the trip for Sidney and Ellen is $450. Sidney and Ellen would like to deduct the cost of the trip. Write a letter to Sidney and Ellen in which you explain what they can deduct.

57. **LO5** Explain why the legal fees paid in the following three situations are treated differently for income tax purposes:
    a. Jim pays $10,000 in legal fees in obtaining a divorce. None of the $10,000 is deductible.
    b. Camella invents and patents a device that shells nuts. When she learns that another company is selling copies of her device, she pays an attorney $10,000 to enforce her patent. The $10,000 is fully deductible.
    c. Melody pays $10,000 in legal fees for advice relating to investments she owns. Only $6,000 of the fees is deductible.

58. **LO5** Explain why the loss resulting from the sale of a computer in the following three situations is treated differently for income tax purposes:
    a. Monica sells her personal computer at a loss of $1,300. None of the loss is deductible.
    b. Omar sells a computer used in his carpeting business at a loss of $4,300. The loss is fully deductible.
    c. Jerry sells his computer at a loss of $3,800. Jerry used the computer to keep track of his investment portfolio. Only $3,000 of the loss is deductible.

59. **LO5** A truck owned by Duster Demolition Services is involved in an accident. The truck originally cost $40,000, and $25,000 of depreciation had been taken on the truck as of the date of the accident. The cost of repairing the truck is $10,000, for which the insurance company reimburses Duster $8,000.
    a. How much of a loss, if any, is Duster entitled to deduct as a result of the accident?
    b. What is the adjusted basis of the truck after the accident?

60. **LO5** Determine the proper treatment of each of the following expenditures:
    a. Zoe purchases land costing $8,000. During the current year, she pays $2,000 to have utilities and sewer lines installed on the property. Zoe also pays $600 in interest on the loan used to obtain the land and $300 in property taxes on the land.
    b. On August 2, Carruth Corporation pays $11,000 for a two-year fire insurance policy on its manufacturing facility.
    c. The Freeborn Partnership purchases a rental property costing $125,000. Before it rents out the building, Freeborn repaints it at a cost of $2,000 and spends $1,200 on minor repairs. After the property is rented, a pipe bursts, requiring $2,000 in repairs.
    d. Aqua Robotics, Inc., purchases and pays for supplies costing $1,400 on December 26. As of December 31, the company has not used $1,200 worth of the supplies.

61. **LO5** Determine the taxpayer's adjusted basis in each of the following situations. If any changes are made in the original basis of the asset, explain why they are necessary.
    a. Simone purchases 300 shares of Wilguess, Inc., stock in 2019 for $6,300. In 2019 and 2020, Wilguess pays cash dividends of $2 per share. In 2021, Wilguess pays a 40 percent stock dividend (nontaxable), and Simone receives an additional 120 shares of stock.
    b. Symbol Corporation purchases a building in 2018 at a cost of $240,000. Annual maintenance costs on the building are $80,000. In 2020, Symbol adds a wing to the building at a cost of $60,000. In 2021, the building is painted at a cost of $25,000. Symbol deducts $4,800 in depreciation in 2018, $7,300 in 2019, and $8,100 in 2020 and 2021.
    c. Lorissa purchases land as an investment in 2019 for $33,000. Property taxes on the property are $400 per year. In 2020, Lorissa is assessed $2,000 by the

county assessor for her share of a sidewalk that the county builds adjacent to the land. Lorissa pays the assessment in 2021.

d. The Barton Brothers Partnership purchases a computer in 2019 for $8,000. The partnership elects to deduct the entire cost of the computer in 2019. In 2021, Barton Brothers spends $300 to repair the computer.

62. **LO5** Davidson Industries manufactures golf course maintenance equipment. The equipment comes with a four-year warranty. Davidson's engineers estimate that approximately 10 percent of the equipment will be defective and require payment under the warranty. Discuss the propriety of allowing Davidson a deduction for warranty costs in the current year if:
   a. Davidson is a cash basis taxpayer.
   b. Davidson is an accrual basis taxpayer.

## ISSUE IDENTIFICATION PROBLEMS

In each of the following problems, identify the tax issue(s) posed by the facts presented. Determine the possible tax consequences of each issue that you identify.

63. Ahmed bought some stock several years ago for $8,000. He is thinking of selling it and has 2 offers. His broker told him he could sell the stock for $8,300 and would have to pay a $600 commission, for a net realization of $7,700. His sister Layla offered to pay Ahmed $7,700 with no commissions paid on the transaction.

64. Henrietta is the president and sole shareholder of Clutter Corporation. In 2018, Henrietta transferred ownership of her personal residence to the corporation. As part of the transfer, Clutter Corporation assumed Henrietta's mortgage on the house. At the same time, she and the corporation entered into an agreement that lets Henrietta lease the property for as long as she wants at an amount approximating the monthly mortgage payments on the house. During the current year, Clutter paints the house at a cost of $5,000, makes other repairs totaling $3,000, and adds an entertainment room at a cost of $30,000. Current-year property taxes and interest paid by Clutter on the house are $1,400 and $18,000, respectively. Henrietta paid $18,000 in rent to Clutter.

65. Milton is an inventor who has also written several successful mystery novels. Because he didn't really need the income from the novels, Milton wrote them under an assumed name and had the royalties paid to Hammer Corporation. When Milton incorporated Hammer, he gave all the stock to his three sons. The sons are employed by the corporation, with salaries approximately equal to the royalties earned each year from the novels.

66. Jerry and his husband, Antonio, own a successful concrete company that is organized as a corporation. Jerry spends all his time running the company, whereas Antonio has a full-time job as a legal secretary. The corporation pays Antonio a salary of $45,000 a year as vice president.

67. The Perry Development Partnership purchases 40 acres of land for $30,000. It spends $8,000 subdividing the land into 2-acre parcels and $17,000 to install a sewer line and utilities to each parcel. Perry intends to sell the 2-acre parcels for $12,000, but none of them are sold by the end of the current year.

68. Ayah signs a contract to write a book for East Publishing Company in the current year. Under its terms, she receives a $5,000 advance against future royalty payments upon signing the contract. The contract provides that if Ayah does not write a suitable book or if the book's royalties are insufficient to cover the advance, she must repay any portion not earned.

69. Aretha is an executive vice president of Franklin, Inc. On December 18, 2021, the Franklin, Inc., board of directors awards her a $20,000 bonus. Aretha asks Franklin's controller to delay processing the bonus check until January. The controller

agrees to her request, and she receives the $20,000 bonus check on January 10, 2022.

70. Arnold is a college professor specializing in robotics. During the current year, he attends a meeting on robotics in San Diego. Because of the desirable location of the meeting, he takes along his wife, Hortense, and their 2 children. The meeting lasts for 3 days, but Arnold and his family stay for 2 weeks.

71. Doris purchases a ski cabin in Montana during the current year. She hires a real estate management company to rent out the cabin on a daily basis. The real estate management company tells Doris to expect an average of 70 rental days per year. Doris intends to use the cabin for her vacation 3 weeks during the year.

# TECHNOLOGY APPLICATIONS

72. **RIA RESEARCH EXERCISE** Use the RIA Checkpoint research database to answer the following questions. Cut and paste the relevant Internal Revenue Code and Treasury Regulation section(s) into your solution and explain how the authority answers the tax issue in question. Give the most specific citation applicable [e.g., Sec. 168(a)(1)] that answers the question. NOTE: If the answer can be found in both the code and regulations, you must provide both authorities.

the answer company™ THOMSON REUTERS®

Research Skills

   a. Carol went and lobbied before the federal government concerning proposed changes to the new pension regulations. She incurred $2,300 in expenses. What code section and/or regulation disallows a deduction for these expenses?
   b. Marsha is self-employed and paid $4,000 in self-employment taxes during the year. What code section and/or regulation lets her deduct 50 percent of these taxes as a deduction for adjusted gross income?
   c. Hamid dies in an automobile accident. He is covered by a $500,000 life insurance policy that is payable to his wife, Janet. What code section and/or regulation excludes the $500,000 from Janet's gross income?
   d. Roy and Deanna are married and have two children, ages 13 and 19. They are aware that they are eligible for a child tax credit, but do not know if their children qualify them for the credit. What code section and/or regulation defines a child for purposes of the child tax credit?

73. **RIA RESEARCH EXERCISE** Use the RIA Checkpoint research database to answer the following questions. Cut and paste the relevant Internal Revenue Code and Treasury Regulation section(s) into your solution and explain how the authority answers the tax issue in question. Give the most specific citation applicable [e.g., Sec. 168(a)(1)] that answers the question. Note: If the answer can be found in both the code and regulations, you must provide both authorities.

the answer company™ THOMSON REUTERS®

Research Skills

   **1.** Melinda takes classes costing $3,500 that are paid for by her employer's educational assistance plan.
      a. What code section and/or regulation allows the exclusion of payments from an employer's educational assistance plan?
      b. What code section and/or regulation limits the amount that can be excluded?
      c. What code section and/or regulation defines the elements of an employer's educational assistance plan that must be met for employees to be allowed an exclusion for payments received from the plan?
      d. What code section and/or regulation defines what types of expense payments from an employer's educational assistance plan can be excluded from the employee's gross income?

   **2.** Billy's Barbeque has assets of $60,000 and liabilities of $100,000. To assist Billy's, its bank agrees to reduce the amount due on a loan from $65,000 to $50,000.
      a. What code section and/or regulation specifically includes discharges of debt in gross income?

b. What code section and/or regulation allows certain discharges of debt to be excluded from gross income?
c. What code section and/or regulation defines the condition that must be met to exclude a discharge of debt from gross income?
d. What code section and/or regulation limits the amount of debt discharge that can be excluded?

Research Skills

74. The assignment of income doctrine states that income is taxed to the entity owning the income, regardless of who actually receives the income. That is, income taxation cannot be escaped by assigning the payment of income to another entity. Find the court case that led to this doctrine and explain the facts surrounding the court's decision.

Research Skills

75. Under a reimbursement plan that has been in effect for five years, Simmons Corporation advances travel expenses to its sales employees. The advances are deducted from the employees' commissions as they are earned. The employees have an unconditional obligation to repay any advances not repaid through the commission offset. Up to the current year, the sales employees' commissions have never been sufficient to fully offset the advances made under the plan. To boost morale, Simmons charges off the balance of the advances. What are the tax effects of the reimbursement plan and the subsequent write-off of the advance balances?

Tax Form

76. Kimberly Cerny is a graduate student. She is 22 years old and works part-time as a graduate assistant in the biology department. In the summer, Kimberly was an intern at Neutrobio, Inc. Details regarding her salary and withholdings from her employment follow.

| | Biology Department | Neutrobio, Inc. |
|---|---|---|
| Salary | $ 2,600 | $ 3,600 |
| Federal withholding | 260 | 302 |
| State withholding | 97 | 114 |
| Social Security | 168 | 275 |

Kimberly also received $1,200 in interest from a savings account that was set up by her grandparents to help pay her college expenses. Kimberly lives at 499 Hillside Drive, Portland, Oregon, 97208. She is a dependent of her parents, her Social Security number is 324-99-8020, and she does not wish to contribute to the Presidential Campaign Election Fund. She has asked you to help her with her federal income tax return. Prepare Form 1040 for Kimberly. Forms and instructions can be downloaded from the IRS website (www.irs.gov).

## DISCUSSION CASES

77. The controller of Newform Oil Company has come to you for advice. Newform recently cleared a forested area and began drilling an oil well on the site. The well is a gusher, and Newform's geologists estimate that it will produce for at least 10 years. Environmental restoration laws will require Newform to completely reforest and restore the oil well site when the well is taken out of production. An engineering firm hired by Newform estimates that the cost of complying with the environmental requirements will be $8,000,000. For financial accounting purposes, Newform intends to amortize the estimated cost over the 10-year expected life. In addition, it plans to put $500,000 per year into an account that should provide the $8,000,000 necessary to perform the restoration.

The controller would like your advice on the deductibility of the costs of restoration. That is, when can Newform deduct the costs and how much can it deduct?

Based on the concepts discussed in this chapter, explain what you think is the proper treatment of the restoration costs for tax purposes.

78. The Prevetti Partnership is engaged in the purchase and management of apartment complexes. The partnership entered into an agreement with Parsnip Development Company on July 1 of the current year to purchase the Perry Apartments. The sales agreement stated the purchase price of $5,000,000. It also provided for "other payments to seller," composed of a $500,000 payment for a covenant not to compete, $50,000 for the seller's management advice during the ownership transition, and a financing fee of $100,000. In addition, the seller is to receive the first $400,000 of the rent collected by Prevetti. The purchase was completed on August 5. Monthly rentals on the property are $90,000. Prevetti paid Parsnip the first $400,000 of rent it collected per the purchase agreement. How much rental income does the Prevetti Partnership have for the current year? Explain.

## TAX PLANNING CASES

79. Biko owns a snowmobile manufacturing business, and Miles owns a mountain bike manufacturing business. Because each business is seasonal, their manufacturing plants are idle during their respective off-seasons. Biko and Miles have decided to consolidate their businesses as one operation. In so doing, they expect to increase their sales by 15 percent and cut their costs by 30 percent. Biko and Miles own their businesses as sole proprietors and provide the following summary of their 2020 taxable incomes:

| | Biko | Miles |
|---|---|---|
| Business income | | |
| Sales | $ 600,000 | $ 450,000 |
| Cost of goods sold | (400,000) | (300,000) |
| Other expenses | (100,000) | (75,000) |
| Business taxable income | $ 100,000 | $ 75,000 |
| Other taxable income | | |
| (net of allowable deductions) | 20,000 | 35,000 |
| 2020 taxable income | $ 120,000 | $ 110,000 |

Biko and Miles don't know what type of entity they should use for their combined business. They would like to know the tax implications of forming a partnership versus a corporation. Under either form, Biko will own 55 percent of the business and Miles will own 45 percent. They each require $60,000 from the business and would like to increase that by $5,000 per year.

Based on the information provided, do a three-year projection of the income of the business and the total taxes for a partnership and for a corporation. In doing the projections, assume that after the initial 30 percent decrease in total costs, their annual costs will increase in proportion to sales which continue to grow at 15 percent. Also, assume that their nonbusiness taxable income remains unchanged. Use the 2021 tax rate schedules to compute the tax for each year of the analysis. Ignore the impact of the Qualified Business Income (QBI) deduction available under the partnership option.

## ETHICS DISCUSSION CASE

80. You are a CPA who has been preparing tax returns for Sign, Seal, and Deliver, a midsize CPA firm, for the last five years. During the current year, you are assigned the individual return of a new client, Guadalupe Piaz. Guadalupe has completed and returned the tax return questionnaire that the firm sent to her. Communication Skills

In reviewing the questionnaire, you notice that Guadalupe has included an entry for $10,000 in cash dividends received from Quinn Corporation. However, there is no supporting documentation for the dividend payment in the information Guadalupe provided.

What concerns you is that until this year, you had prepared the tax return for Quinn Corporation. (It was reassigned to another firm member when you were promoted late last year.) You know that Quinn Corporation was organized as an S corporation during the years that you prepared the return. During that period, Quinn was equally owned by three shareholders, and Guadalupe was not among them. In addition, the corporation was highly profitable, averaging approximately $6,000,000 per year in taxable income. Given this information, what are your obligations under the Statements on Standards for Tax Services (which can be found at www.aicpa.org.) Write a memorandum to your supervisor explaining your concerns and what actions, if any, you will need to take before you can prepare Guadalupe's return.

# Gross Income



PART 2

A tax can be a means for raising revenue, or a device for regulating conduct, or both.

—Felix Frankfurter

iStock.com/malerapaso

# Income Sources

3

Learning Objectives:

LO 1 Explain the historical development of what constitutes gross income and how it affects the current view of gross income.

LO 2 Distinguish earned income from unearned income, and explain the tax problems associated with each type of income.

LO 3 Identify sources of income that result from transfers from others and explain the tax rules for each type of income.

LO 4 Explain imputed income and identify the common sources of such income and their tax treatments.

LO 5 Provide an overview of the tax treatment of capital gain income.

LO 6 Explain the primary accounting methods used for tax purposes and how income is recognized under each method: the cash method, the accrual method, and the hybrid method.

LO 7 Explain the exceptions to the general rules of income recognition for each of the accounting methods.

## concept review

### GENERAL CONCEPTS

**Ability to pay** A tax should be based on the amount that the taxpayer can afford to pay, relative to other taxpayers pg. 2-2

**Administrative convenience** Those items for which the cost of compliance would exceed the revenue generated are not taxed pg. 2-3

**Arm's-length transaction** A transaction in which all parties have bargained in good faith and for their individual benefit, not for the benefit of the transaction group. pg. 2-4

**Related party** Family members, corporations that are owned by family members, and certain other relationships between entities in which the power to control the substance of a transaction is evidenced through majority ownership. pg. 2-4

### ACCOUNTING CONCEPTS

**Annual accounting period** All entities must report the results of their operations on an annual basis (the tax year). Each tax year stands on its own, apart from other tax years. pg. 2-9

**Assignment of income** The tax entity that owns the income produced is responsible for the tax on the income, regardless of which entity actually receives the income. pg. 2-8

**Conduit entity** An entity for which the tax attributes flow through to its owners for tax purposes. pg. 2-6

**Substance over form** Transactions are to be taxed according to their true intention rather than some form that may have been contrived. pg. 2-11

**Tax benefit rule** Any deduction taken in a prior year that is recovered in a subsequent year is income in the year of recovery, to the extent that a tax benefit was received from the deduction. pg. 2-10

### INCOME CONCEPTS

**All-inclusive income** All income received is taxable unless a specific provision in the tax law either excludes the income from taxation or defers its recognition to a future tax year. pg. 2-12

**Capital recovery** No income is realized until the taxpayer receives more than the amount invested to produce the income. The amount invested in an asset represents the maximum amount recoverable. pg. 2-13

**Claim of right** A realization occurs whenever an amount is received without any restriction as to its disposition. pg. 2-14

**Constructive receipt** Income is deemed to be received when it is made unconditionally available to the taxpayer. pg. 2-15

**Legislative grace** Any tax relief provided is the result of a specific act of Congress that must be strictly applied and interpreted. All income received is taxable unless a specific provision in the tax law excludes the income from taxation. Deductions must be approached with the philosophy that nothing is deductible unless a provision in the tax law allows the deduction. pg. 2-12

**Realization** No income or loss is recognized until it has been realized. A realization involves a change in the form and/or substance of a taxpayer's property rights that results from an arm's-length transaction. pg. 2-14

**Wherewithal to pay** Income is recognized in the period in which the taxpayer has the means to pay the tax on the income. pg. 2-16

## 3-1 INTRODUCTION

The first step in calculating the taxable income for any tax entity is determining its gross income. Gross income equals all income received, less exclusions from income. Therefore, all items of income realized during the period under consideration must first be identified. Next, the income items are analyzed and segregated into those that are taxable and those that are excluded from taxation. Finally, the proper tax year for recognition of the income items must be determined. The purpose of this chapter is to introduce the basis for identifying income sources and to discuss those sources that present particular problems. In addition, a brief overview of the tax treatment of capital gains and losses is presented. The chapter also considers the effect of an entity's accounting method on the recognition of income and exceptions to the general methods of accounting. Exclusions from income tax are discussed in Chapter 4.

## 3-2 WHAT CONSTITUTES INCOME

LO 1
Explain the historical development of what constitutes gross income and how it affects the current view of gross income.

The all-inclusive income concept provides the basis for calculating gross income. Under this concept, any income received is assumed to be taxable unless some provision in the tax law allows its exclusion. This concept is the basis of the Internal Revenue Code's definition of *gross income*:

SECTION 61 GROSS INCOME DEFINED

(a) General Definition—Except as otherwise provided in this subtitle, gross income means all income from whatever source derived, including (but not limited to) the following items:
(1) Compensation for services, including fees, commissions, and similar items;
(2) Gross income derived from business;
(3) Gains derived from dealings in property;
(4) Interest;
(5) Rents;
(6) Royalties;
(7) Dividends;
(8) Annuities;
(9) Income from life insurance and endowment contracts;
(10) Pensions;
(11) Income from discharge of indebtedness;
(12) Distributive share of partnership gross income;
(13) Income in respect of a decedent; and
(14) Income from an interest in an estate or trust.

The phrase "all income from whatever source derived" is the statutory equivalent of the all-inclusive income concept's requirement that any income received is initially considered taxable. This phrase has been part of the income tax law since the Sixteenth Amendment to the Constitution empowered Congress in 1913 to "lay and collect taxes on *incomes, from whatever source derived*" [emphasis added]. In Section 61 of the Code, the phrase "except as otherwise provided" allows items to be excluded from gross income if the specific exclusion is found in the Internal Revenue Code.

The realization concept requires that income be realized before it is included in gross income. However, nothing in the definition of gross income in the Internal Revenue Code requires that income be *realized* before it is *recognized*. Although absent from the Internal Revenue Code, the realization concept was developed primarily by the courts in response to cases requiring an interpretation of the statutory definition of *income*. As a result, the concept has been adopted by the Internal Revenue Service in the regulation that interprets the definition of gross income:

> (a) General Definition. Gross income means all income from whatever source derived unless excluded by law. Gross income includes income *realized* in any form, whether in money, property, or services. Income may be *realized*,

> therefore, in the form of services, meals, accommodations, stock, or other property, as well as in cash.[1]

Thus, a better working definition would be that gross income includes all income realized from whatever source derived, unless specifically excluded.

At first glance, the statutory and administrative definitions of income appear to be quite simple and straightforward. However, a linguist would no doubt be bothered by the circular nature of the definition: Gross income means all income. In fact, no definition of the term *income* exists in the Internal Revenue Code. Thus, the threshold question of whether a particular item is or is not income is not answered by these definitions of gross income. Perhaps wisely, Congress has never seen fit to attempt to define the term *income*. Do you think that drafters of tax legislation in 1913 could have foreseen the complexities of business in the 21st century and been able to draft a precise definition of income to cover such items as incentive stock options and gains from currency translations? By not providing a precise definition, what constitutes income evolves with changes in society. In this regard, the courts have played a major role in guiding taxpayers on the treatment of various transactions in which it is not clear whether the statutory definition of income has been met.

## 3-2a Income Is Derived from Labor and Capital

In 1920, the U.S. Supreme Court considered the first case addressing the concept of income. In determining that specific provisions in the tax law that included stock dividends as taxable income were unconstitutional, the Supreme Court said, "Income may be defined as the gain derived from capital, from labor, or from both combined, provided it be understood to include profit gained through sale or conversion of capital assets."[2]

This initial attempt at defining income implies that income could be generated from only two sources: capital and labor. The Court also emphasized the necessity of a realization as a precondition to the existence of income:

> Here we have the essential matter: *not* a gain *accruing* to capital, not a *growth or* increment of value *in* the investment; but a gain, a profit, something of exchangeable value *proceeding from* the property, *severed from* the capital however invested or employed, and *coming in*, being "*derived*"—that is, *received* or *drawn* by the recipient (the taxpayer) for his *separate* use, benefit and disposal; *that* is income derived from property. Nothing else answers the description. [Court's emphasis][3]

In fact, a vast majority of items we commonly think of as income fit nicely into this definition: wages, income from a sole proprietorship (income from labor), interest, dividends, rental income, and royalty income (income from capital). However, this definition did not contemplate sources of income that were not returns from labor or capital, such as windfalls. Consider the following examples:

**Example 1** Lee is playing golf one day and hits an enormous hook into the woods. While searching for his ball, he finds a tattered sack full of $100 bills. The police are never able to locate the owner, and Lee is allowed to keep the money, which totals $50,000. Does Lee have income from finding this money?

**Discussion: Given the Supreme Court's definition, it would seem that such a windfall would not be considered as "derived from capital, from labor, or from both combined." However, it would appear that such a "treasure trove," as it is referred to in income tax jargon, would fit the statutory definition of "income from whatever source derived." In fact, the courts have said that such treasure troves do constitute income.[4]**

**Example 2** Johnson, Inc., leases a lot and a building to Wenona Corporation under a 99-year lease that lets Wenona remodel the building at its own cost. The lease provides that all improvements are Johnson's property upon termination of the lease. Twenty years after remodeling the building, Wenona defaults on the lease payment, and Johnson repossesses the property. The net increase in the value of the property from the remodeling of the building is $50,000. Does Johnson, Inc., have taxable income when it retakes possession of the building?

**Discussion: On similar facts, in 1940 the Supreme Court held that Johnson, Inc., was taxable on the increase in the value of the property attributable to the remodeling of the building at the time it repossessed the property.[5]**

Although the Court's decision on the facts in example 2 would appear to fit the notion of income "derived from capital," it does not square with the requirement that income be realized by "severing" it from the capital investment and that it be "*received* or *drawn* by the recipient (the taxpayer) for his *separate* use, benefit and disposal." In addressing this issue, the Court said:

> While it is true that economic gain is not always taxable as income, it is settled that the realization of gain need not be in cash derived from the sale of an asset. Gain may occur as a result of exchange of property, payment of the taxpayer's indebtedness, relief from a liability, or other profit realized from the completion of a transaction. The fact that the gain is a portion of the value of property received by the taxpayer in the transaction does not negative its realization.[6]

This decision severely weakened the earlier realization requirement by suggesting that any definitive event could be properly considered a realization of income. At this point, there was no requirement that the income be severed from the capital and available for use by the taxpayer. However, in reaction to this decision, Congress adopted a provision in 1942 that excluded from gross income such increases in the value of property upon termination of a lease, to the extent that the lessee's improvements did not constitute a payment in lieu of rent.[7] This exclusion is discussed in Chapter 4.

## 3-2b Income as an Increase in Wealth

As can be seen from the discussion of court cases that define income, the courts increasingly diluted the original judicial requirement that income be derived from capital or labor and that recognition of the income required a realization. In 1955, the Supreme Court closed the circle on its original definition in a case involving the taxability of punitive damages awarded in an antitrust action. In finding that such windfall profits were taxable income, the Court did not even attempt to reconcile its decision with the earlier "gain derived from capital or labor" requirement. Rather, the Court relegated this concept to minor status in determining that *any* increase in the wealth of the taxpayer that has been realized is subject to income tax:

> But it [income derived from capital or labor] was not meant to provide a touchstone to all future gross income questions.... Here we have instances of *undeniable accessions to wealth, clearly realized* and over which the taxpayers have *complete dominion.* The mere fact that the payments were extracted from the wrongdoers as punishment for unlawful conduct cannot detract from their character as taxable income to the recipients.... We find no ... evidence of intent to exempt these payments. [emphasis added][8]

Thus, the Court adopted a much broader concept of income, "undeniable accessions to wealth," as its interpretation of "income from whatever source derived." The notion of income as an increase in wealth is not new or, for that matter, surprising. Economists have long argued that the true measure of income is the change in wealth for the period under consideration. Using the economist's definition of income, all gains received during the period, whether realized or not, are considered income. Where the tax law deviates from the economists' notion of income is in the requirement that the increase in wealth be "clearly realized." Note also that the tax law definition of income not only requires a realization but also that the taxpayer have "complete dominion" over the realized income. The requirement of complete dominion means that the taxpayer must have a claim of right to the income. Recall that the claim of right doctrine says that any amount received without restriction as to its disposition is income in the period received.

### 3-2c What Constitutes Income: Current View

Given this brief historical account of how the concept of income developed, what is considered income today? Although the courts continue to consider the issue, no significant developments have occurred since the Supreme Court determined that any increase in wealth that has been realized constitutes income. Thus, it is safe to say that the first requirement is that the taxpayer experiences an increase in wealth. An increase in wealth can be through an increase in net worth or through consumption.

**Example 3** Tran purchases 100 shares of XYZ Company stock during the current year at a cost of $2,000. As of December 31, the shares of stock are worth $2,500. Does Tran experience an increase in wealth during the year as a result of this stock purchase?

**Discussion: Tran's wealth increases as a result of the stock purchase. Her net worth increases by $500 over what it was before she purchased the stock.**

**Example 4** Cara's car needs new spark plugs. She calls Local Service Station and learns that it will cost $50 to get the job done. Rather than pay the $50, Cara purchases the spark plugs for $15 and installs them herself. Has Cara's wealth increased as a result of installing the spark plugs herself?

**Discussion: Cara's wealth has increased by the $35 she saved by doing the job herself. Through consumption of the labor and overhead involved in the $50 charged by Local, her net worth has increased by the $35 she saved.**

Although an increase in wealth is a necessary condition for the recognition of income, it alone is not sufficient to trigger taxation. Before an increase in wealth becomes taxable (i.e., is recognized income), it must also be realized. As stated previously, realization is not an explicit statutory requirement for the recognition of income; however, over the years, the concept has become so basic to the structure of the tax system that the general premise of the requirement is simply not challenged. What typically is challenged by taxpayers is what constitutes a realization. A reasonable working definition contains the following two elements:

- A change in form and/or substance of the taxpayer's property (or property rights)
- The involvement of a second party in the income process

The most common forms of income realization involve the receipt of something of value (cash, stock, services) for a service rendered or the sale, exchange, or lease of a property.

**Example 5** Return to the facts of example 3. Does Tran realize any income from her dealings in XYZ Company's stock?

**Discussion: Although Tran's wealth increases through the increase in the value of the stock, she has not realized that wealth through sale, exchange, or other disposition of the stock. That is, the form of her property (stock) has not been changed through a transaction with another party.**

**Example 6** Return to the facts of example 4. Has Cara realized the increase in wealth she obtained by repairing the car herself?

**Discussion: Cara has had a change in the form of her property through the repairs, but because no second party was involved, she would not be considered to have a realization of income.**

In general, any increase in wealth that has been realized by a taxpayer must be recognized (i.e., included in gross income) for tax purposes in the period in which the realization occurs. However, this general rule has several exceptions. As previously stated, some income realizations are excluded by law and therefore are never recognized for tax purposes. The tax laws also provide for deferral of gains on certain types of property transactions in which the wherewithal to pay tax from the transaction is lacking. The recognition of gains from this class of transactions is deferred to a future period when a transaction occurs that provides the cash to pay the tax.

**Example 7** Duc's business automobile, which had an adjusted basis of $2,000, was destroyed in a tornado. Duc received a check for $6,000 from his insurance company. He used the $6,000 as a down payment on a new business automobile costing $30,000. Has Duc realized a gain from the destruction of his old automobile? If so, must he recognize the gain in the period of the destruction of the automobile?

**Discussion: Duc has realized a gain of $4,000 ($6,000 in insurance proceeds—the adjusted basis of $2,000) on the destruction of his automobile. He realized a gain because he received something of value, $6,000 in cash, for his old automobile in a transaction with another party.**

**Duc will not have to recognize the gain (include the gain in gross income) on the destruction of his automobile in the current period. When the entire proceeds from the casualty are reinvested in a qualifying replacement asset, the tax law allows the deferral of gains from casualties on business property that has been replaced. In this case, Duc reinvested the entire $6,000 he received for his old automobile and has no cash remaining to pay the tax on the gain.**

**Although Duc does not have to pay tax on the gain in the current period, he will pay tax on the gain when he disposes of the new business automobile in a taxable transaction. Chapter 12 discusses the rules for deferrals of gains and the mechanics of the calculations to ensure that the tax is eventually paid on the gain.**

## 3-3 COMMON INCOME SOURCES

This chapter discusses four categories of income sources to provide a framework for working with income sources. The first two categories are based on the Supreme Court's early definition of income as being derived from labor, which is referred to as *earned income*, and income derived from capital, referred to as *unearned income*. The third category consists of transfers from others. The fourth category considers taxable sources of imputed income.

### 3-3a Earned Income

LO 2 Distinguish earned income from unearned income, and explain the tax problems associated with each type of income.

The most common form of income for individuals is compensation paid for their services. That is, individuals provide their labor for the production of goods and services. In return for their labor, they are compensated by the entity for which they are performing the work. Providing labor for compensation produces **earned income**. All amounts paid by an employer to or on behalf of an employee are taxable unless specifically excluded by law. In addition, income generated from the operation of a business is considered earned by the owner. Income from illegal activities (gambling, drugs, extortion, etc.) is also considered earned and subject to tax.[9] The most common forms of earned income are:

1. Wages, salaries, tips, bonuses, and commissions
2. Income from the active conduct of a trade or business
3. Income from the rendering of services
4. Income from the performance of illegal activities

The taxability of earned income sources is undisputed. However, two problems often arise with this type of income. The first problem stems from a desire to take advantage of the progressive nature of the tax rate schedules by transferring income earned by a high marginal tax rate payer to a family member who is in a lower tax bracket. These attempts are foiled by the assignment-of-income doctrine, which requires the entity earning the income to pay the tax on the income, regardless of who actually receives the income.

**Example 8** Thelma has a successful carpet-cleaning business. To lower her taxes, she instructs every fifth client to make the check out to Thelma's son. Her son is a college student who does not work and uses the checks received from Thelma's business to pay for his college expenses. Who is taxed on this income?

**Discussion: Because the payments made to the son were earned by Thelma, she must include the payments in her taxable income. Therefore, this scheme results in no tax savings to Thelma. NOTE: There are legal ways for Thelma to transfer taxability of**

**the income earned from her carpet-cleaning business to her son. The simplest method would be to employ her son in the business and pay him a reasonable salary for his labor. This would lower Thelma's taxable income through a deduction for compensation and transfer the income to her son for taxation at a lower marginal tax rate.**

Taxpayers may also attempt to transfer income to establish a basis for taking business deductions.

**Example 9** Michael has a computer in a separate room of his house that he uses to perform work related to his employment as an engineer for Ajax Corporation as well as for personal purposes. Because he is not considered to be in a trade or business, the tax law does not allow a deduction for either the office or the computer. Michael's wife, Daniela, does the bookkeeping and payroll work for several small businesses. To establish a trade or business for himself, Michael has the payments for Daniela's bookkeeping services made out to him. Who is taxed on this income?

**Discussion: No marginal tax rate savings result from the transfer of income from Daniela to Michael, because Michael and Daniela commingle their respective incomes on their joint tax return. The tax benefit to be derived from such a scheme would be the additional deductions Michael could take for the office and the computer, if he can establish their use in the business of bookkeeping. However, under the assignment-of-income doctrine, Daniela would still be deemed to have earned the payments for her services, and Michael could not claim the checks he receives as income he earned in a trade or business. Thus, he could not take any deductions for the office or the computer.**

The second concern with earned income is what constitutes a receipt of income. Typically, earned types of income are received in cash. However, if receipts of cash were the sole source of earned income, clever taxpayers could arrange their affairs to receive significant amounts of their income in other forms, thus avoiding tax. To counter such tax avoidance schemes, a **cash-equivalent approach** is used to measure receipts of income. Under this approach, the receipt of anything with a fair market value will trigger recognition of income. Thus, income can be realized in the form of property, services, meals, lodging, stock, and so on.

**Example 10** Betty agrees to clean Shiro's house once a week, in return for which Shiro agrees to mow Betty's lawn once a week. Betty usually charges $30 to clean a house, which is what Shiro charges to mow a lawn. Do Betty and/or Shiro have taxable income from this arrangement?

**Discussion: Yes, both have income of $30 per week from this arrangement. Each receives something of value in return for her or his services. Therefore, they are taxed as if they had paid each other cash.**

Under the constructive receipt doctrine, a cash basis taxpayer does not have income until there is an actual or constructive receipt of the income earned. Therefore, a cash basis taxpayer who sells merchandise or performs services on general account does not recognize income until the account is paid with something of value. However, if the customer of such a taxpayer gives the taxpayer a promissory note for the amount due, the fair market value of the note is considered a receipt of property and is taxable when received.

**Example 11** Farnsworth, a cash basis taxpayer, puts a new roof on EM Corporation's warehouse in late November and bills it $3,000. EM pays the bill in January. When is Farnsworth taxable on the $3,000 roofing job?

**Discussion: Because Farnsworth does not receive something of value until January, the $3,000 is not included in his taxable income until then.**

**Example 12** Assume that in example 11, EM Corporation gives Farnsworth a valid note payable for $3,000 when he completes the roofing job in November. Farnsworth does not discount the note, although local banks typically discount such personal notes by 30%. EM pays the note in full in January. How does this affect Farnsworth's recognition of income?

**Discussion: Because Farnsworth could have converted the note to cash upon receipt, the amount of cash he could have received from discounting the note, its fair market value, is taxable upon receipt. Therefore, $2,100 [$3,000 – (30% × $3,000)] is taxable in the year Farnsworth receives the note. The remaining $900 is taxable when he receives full payment on the note the following January.**

## 3-3b Unearned Income

LO 2 Distinguish earned income from unearned income, and explain the tax problems associated with each type of income.

The **unearned income** category of income includes the earnings from investments and gains from the sale, exchange, or other disposition of investment assets. The distinguishing features of this type of income are that it constitutes a return on an investment and producing the income does not require any labor by the owner of the investment. The most common forms of unearned income are:

1. Interest income
2. Dividend income
3. Income from rental and royalty-producing activities
4. Income from annuities
5. Income from conduit entities
6. Gains from the sale of investments producing any of the five forms of unearned income

As with earned sources of income, the inclusion of unearned types of income in the tax base is not controversial. However, a few practical difficulties do arise.

### Rental and Royalty Income

The first problem deals with the definition of *rental and royalty income*. Technically, the tax law defines these two types of income as gross income from the property, less the related expenses to produce the income.

**Example 13** Ali Corporation owns an apartment building and rents out the units. During the current year, Ali receives total rents of $15,000 and incurs costs of $13,000 related to the apartments. What is Ali Corporation's rental income for the current year?

**Discussion: Ali Corporation has rental income of $2,000 ($15,000 – $13,000).**

**Example 14** Assume that utility and maintenance costs are higher than expected, Ali's total expenses related to the apartments are $18,000. What is Ali's rental income?

**Discussion: Ali Corporation does not have any rental income. Rather, it has a rental loss of $3,000, the deduction of which is subject to the rules for deducting losses, discussed in Chapter 7.**

### Annuities

The second item to consider is the taxation of annuities. An **annuity** is a string of equal payments received over equal time periods for a determinable period. The purchase of annuity contracts has become increasingly popular in recent years as a way to guarantee income during retirement. A typical annuity is illustrated in the top panel of Exhibit 3-1. In the typical annuity situation, an individual pays a certain sum now, in return for which the seller of the annuity promises to make set payments for a period of time in the future. The payments are calculated to provide the purchaser with a predetermined rate of return *on* the investment. The problem with these arrangements is determining how much of each payment is a return *of* the original capital investment and how much is a return on the investment. Recall that the capital recovery concept exempts returns of capital from taxation; only returns on capital are taxable sources of income.

**Example 15** Susan purchased an annuity contract for $30,000. Under the contract, when Susan reaches 62, she is to receive $500 per month for 15 years. How much income will Susan earn in total from this investment?

**Discussion: Susan will receive payments totaling $90,000 ($500 × 12 × 15) from the contract, resulting in a total profit of $60,000 ($90,000 – $30,000).**

*Exhibit 3-1*

## Annuities

General Operation of an Annuity

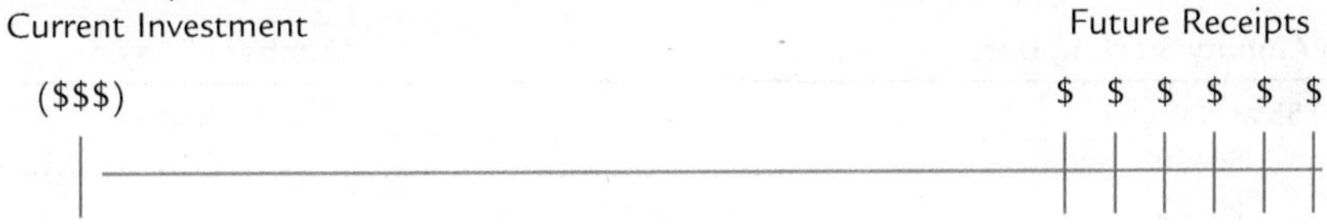


**Annuity Exclusion Ratio**

$$\frac{\text{Cost of the contract}}{\text{Number of the payments}} = \text{Exclusion per payment}$$

Amount of each payment taxable = Contract payment − Amount excluded

In example 15, the major tax problem is determining when to recognize the $60,000 earnings from her investment. Although it is clear that she will not realize any income until she begins receiving payments on the contract, taxation once the payments begin is more controversial. A strict application of the capital recovery concept would exempt the first $30,000 as a repayment of capital investment. However, the tax law views the amounts paid out under the contract as being partly a return *of* her original capital investment (excluded) and partly a return *on* her capital investment (taxable income).[10]

The annuity exclusion ratio is used to determine the amount of each payment that is excluded from income. The **annuity exclusion ratio** is the cost of the contract divided by the number of payments expected from the contract. (See the bottom panel of Exhibit 3-1.) When the number of payments on an annuity contract is fixed, the computation is straightforward. The cost of the contract divided by the number of payments to be received gives the excludable portion of each payment.

**Example 16** Susan begins receiving payments on the contract on January 2, 2021. How much of each $500 payment that she receives from the contract is taxable?

**Discussion: Because the contract is based on a fixed number of payments, Susan uses the annuity exclusion ratio based on the actual payments to determine the taxable portion of each payment. The exclusion ratio on the contract is $30,000 ÷ 180 (12 × 15) = $167. Therefore, $167 of each $500 payment is not taxable, because it is considered a return of her $30,000 investment. The remaining $333 is taxed as a return on capital.**

For annuities making payments until the death of the taxpayer, the calculation becomes more complicated because an estimate of the number of payments that will be made under the annuity contract must be used. The method of estimation to use depends on the date the annuity begins to make payments. If the annuity payments began on or before November 18, 1996, the number of payments under the contract is determined by the taxpayer's life expectancy at the date the payments began.

If the annuity payments begin after November 18, 1996, the taxpayer must use the "simplified method" to determine the return of capital for each monthly payment. Under this method, the number of anticipated monthly payments is determined based on the age(s) of the taxpayer(s) at the annuity starting date. The simplified method requires the use of a standard set of expected payments for a single taxpayer and a separate table of expected payments when the annuity will continue to be paid to a survivor after the death of the taxpayer. Table 3-1 provides the number of monthly payments to be used by a single taxpayer, and Table 3-2 provides the number of monthly payments when more than one taxpayer will receive payments under the contract.

Table 3-1

## Number of Monthly Annuity Payments Using the Simplified Method, Single Taxpayer

| Age on Annuity Starting Date | Number of Payments |
|---|---|
| 55 and under | 360 |
| 56–60 | 310 |
| 61–65 | 260 |
| 66–70 | 210 |
| 71 and over | 160 |

Table 3-2

## Number of Monthly Annuity Payments Using the Simplified Method, More Than One Taxpayer

| Combined Age of Taxpayers on Annuity Starting Date | Number of Payments |
|---|---|
| 110 and under | 410 |
| 111–120 | 360 |
| 121–130 | 310 |
| 131–140 | 260 |
| 141 and over | 210 |

**Example 17** Assume the same facts as in example 16, except that the payments are to continue until Susan dies. How much of each $500 payment is taxable?

**Discussion: Susan must use the simplified method to determine the portion of each $500 payment that is excluded. Because Susan is age 62 when she receives her first payment, the number of monthly payments is 260. This gives a monthly exclusion on the contract of $115 ($30,000 ÷ 260). The remaining $385 ($500 − $115) is taxable as a return on investment.**

The anticipated monthly payments in the simplified method approximate life expectancies. However, life expectancies are merely averages. As such, few people die at their average life expectancy. Some people die before the average, whereas others outlive their life expectancies. Therefore, in most cases, adjustments are required to ensure that proper capital recovery of the annuity investment is made.

**Example 18** Using the same facts as in example 17, assume that Susan lives for 25 years and receives payments totaling $150,000 under the contract. How is Susan taxed on these payments?

**Discussion: Because we do not know how long Susan will live when the payments start, we figure the monthly exclusion and income as in example 17. That is, she will exclude $115 per month.**

**After she receives the 260th payment, Susan will have excluded her entire $30,000 investment. At that time, her capital investment will have been fully recovered. Susan receives 300 (25 years × 12) payments on the contract. Therefore, payments 261 through 300 will be fully taxable.**

**Note that during the 25 years of payments, Susan will recognize $120,000 ($150,000 received – the $30,000 investment) income.**

| | | | |
|---|---|---|---|
| Payments | 1–260: | $ 100,000 | ($385 × 260) |
| Payments | 261–300: | $ 20,000 | ($500 × 40) |

What happens when an annuity owner dies before her life expectancy? In this case, her capital recovery is incomplete; she has not fully recovered her capital investment through an exclusion. To allow full recovery of capital in this situation, the tax law permits a deduction in the year of death for the unrecovered portion of the annuity investment.

**Example 19** Assume the same facts as in example 17, except that Susan dies on June 15, 2030.

**Discussion: Susan receives $3,000 (6 payments × $500) in 2030. She excludes $690 ($115 × 6), and $2,310 ($3,000 – $690) is included in her 2030 gross income.**

**Up to her death, Susan has received 114 payments (9 years + 6 months in 2030) and excluded $13,110 ($115 × 114) of her $30,000 investment. The remaining $16,890 ($30,000 – $13,110) of her original investment, which was not recovered, is deductible on her 2030 tax return. Therefore, over the period she receives payments on the annuity, she will have recovered her $30,000 investment through $13,110 of excluded income and a deduction of $16,890 in the year of her death.**

Note the effect of the annual accounting period concept on the reporting of annuities. This concept requires not only an annual reporting of income but also embodies the notion that the events of each tax year are to stand apart from the events of other years. Thus, we do not go back and adjust the annuity calculations on prior years' returns when we know the true number of payments. Rather, we apply the capital recovery concept as it applies to the individual year in question.

As a final note on annuities, the exclusion ratio is used when the taxpayer receives amounts that represent both a return of investment in the contract and a return on the investment in the contract. Many pension plans are structured so that amounts paid into the plan by the employee and the employer are excluded from current taxation. Such plans are called *qualified plans* and allow the deferral of tax on payments into the plan and earnings on the plan's assets until they are withdrawn. As such, the taxpayer has no previously taxed capital investment in the plan. Therefore, all amounts paid from the plan are subject to tax.

**Example 20** Agatha worked for Crystal Company for more than 30 years. As part of her employment contract, Crystal matched contributions Agatha made to a qualified plan. None of the payments to the plan or the earnings on the plan investment was subject to tax. Over the years, Agatha accumulated $420,000 in her pension plan. At retirement, she will receive $850 per month from the plan. How much of the monthly payment is subject to tax?

**Discussion: Because the $420,000 in the pension plan is income that has not been taxed, the full amount of each payment is subject to tax. Agatha must include all payments she receives from the plan in her gross income in the year she receives the payments.**

## Calculation of Gain/Loss on Sale of Investments

Another aspect related to unearned income is the calculation of gains or losses from sales, exchanges, or other dispositions of investment property. Again, this is not a particularly perplexing problem. However, you should keep in mind what constitutes a gain. A gain is the result of a realization in excess of capital investment.[11] The amount of unrecovered capital investment in a property is its adjusted basis.[12] More formally,

| | |
|---|---|
| | Proceeds from sale of property |
| Less: | Selling expenses |
| Equals: | Amount realized from sale of property |
| Less: | Adjusted basis of property sold |
| Equals: | Gain (loss) on sale |

**Example 21** The Alima Partnership buys a rental property in 2019 for $70,000. In 2021, after deducting depreciation of $5,000, Alima sells the rental property for $90,000 and pays a $6,000 commission on the sale. What is Alima's gain or loss on the sale of the rental property?

**Discussion: The Alima Partnership realizes $84,000 ($90,000 – the $6,000 commission) from the sale. Because Alima has already recovered $5,000 of its investment through depreciation deductions, the adjusted basis for the rental property is $65,000 ($70,000 – $5,000). This results in a gain of $19,000 ($84,000 – $65,000).**

Note that property dispositions can also result in losses. A loss results when a property is disposed of at less than its adjusted basis. That is, a loss represents incomplete capital recovery.

**Example 22** Assume that in example 21, the Alima Partnership is able to sell its rental property for only $60,000 and pays a $3,000 commission on the sale. What is Alima's gain or loss on the sale of the rental property?

**Discussion: In this case, the Alima Partnership realizes only $57,000 ($60,000 – $3,000) on the sale, resulting in a loss on the sale of $8,000 ($57,000 – $65,000). Note that the $8,000 loss represents Alima's unrecovered investment in the rental property. Letting Alima deduct the $8,000 loss fully recovers its original $70,000 investment:**

| | |
|---|---|
| Capital deducted as depreciation | $ 5,000 |
| Capital deducted against sales price | 57,000 |
| Capital deducted as a loss | 8,000 |
| Total amount invested | $ 70,000 |

### Income from Conduit Entities

The last consideration related to unearned forms of income is the recognition of income from conduit entities (primarily S corporations and partnerships). Recall that a conduit entity is not taxed on its income; rather, the income from the conduit flows to the owner(s) of the entity for taxation. Thus, taxpayers who own investments in such entities must recognize their share of the conduit's income on their tax return.[13] Conversely, distributions from a conduit entity are not taxed; they are merely a return of capital investment in the entity.

**Example 23** Ansel owns a 20% interest in Forrest, Inc. Forrest is organized as an S corporation and has operating income of $80,000 in the current year. Forrest also distributes $20,000 in dividends. What amount of income must Ansel recognize from his ownership in Forrest, Inc.?

**Discussion: Ansel must recognize his proportionate share of Forrest's income, $16,000 (20% × $80,000). Because he is taxed on his share of Forrest's income, the $4,000 in dividends (20% × $20,000) received is not taxed; it is considered a return of his investment, which reduces the basis of his investment in Forrest.**

**Example 24** Assume that in example 23, Forrest, Inc., is a corporation. What amount of income must Ansel recognize from his ownership in Forrest, Inc.?

**Discussion: As a corporation, Forrest is taxed on the $80,000 in income it earned; the income does not flow to the owners. Ansel is taxed on the $4,000 in dividends he receives from Forrest.**

## concept check

The *all-inclusive income concept* taxes all income received unless a specific provision in the tax law either excludes the income from taxation or defers its recognition to a later period. The realization concept taxes income when an increase in wealth occurs in an *arm's-length transaction.* All earned and unearned income realized by a cash basis taxpayer is taxable in the period in which the income is actually or constructively received. The *assignment of income doctrine* prevents taxpayers from directing income they have produced to other entities for taxation. The *capital recovery concept* lets taxpayers recover invested capital tax-free; only returns on invested capital are taxed.

## 3-3c Transfers from Others

LO 3
Identify sources of income that result from transfers from others and explain the tax rules for each type of income.

As the discussion of what constitutes income indicated, not all income is the result of labor or capital. Tax entities, particularly individuals, sometimes receive amounts that are neither earned nor unearned, yet they constitute realizations of increases in wealth and as such are taxable to the recipient. In this area are five common sources of taxable transfer income:

- Prizes and awards
- Unemployment compensation
- Social Security benefits

- Alimony received
- Death benefit payments

## Prizes and Awards

With two exceptions, any prizes or awards received are taxable to the recipient.[14] One way to avoid tax on the receipt of a prize or award is to immediately transfer the prize or award to a government body or other qualified charitable organization such as a church, school, or charity. This exclusion is available only for certain awards, such as those for literary, scientific, or charitable achievements for which the taxpayer did not take action to obtain the award and for which no future services must be performed as a condition of receiving the award. Thus, winnings on game shows cannot be excluded, even if they are immediately transferred to a local charity because the contestant voluntarily entered the contest.

**Example 25** Letisha receives the outstanding teacher award at State University. The award includes a cash prize of $5,000. Is the $5,000 taxable to Letisha?

**Discussion: If Letisha keeps the $5,000, she will have to include it in her gross income. However, if she was chosen from among all teachers at State University and the award does not require her to perform a specific future service, she can avoid taxation by transferring the check to a government body or charitable organization.**

The second class of awards that may be excluded is employee achievement awards that are paid in the form of property and are based on length of service or on safety achievements. The maximum dollar exclusion for such awards is $400 per employee per year. However, if the award comes from a qualified plan, the individual limit is raised to $1,600. A qualified plan is a formal written plan or program to award all employees who qualify under the plan's requirements. The plan must not discriminate in favor of highly compensated employees.

**Example 26** At her retirement party, Tova receives a Rolex watch worth $1,200 in recognition of her 30 years of service to her employer. Is the receipt of the watch taxable to Tova? If so, how much income must she recognize?

**Discussion: Because the watch is an award of property that was given in recognition of length of service, at least $400 of the $1,200 fair market value of the watch may be excluded. If Tova's watch is given as part of a qualified plan, she may exclude the entire $1,200 from her taxable income, because it is worth less than the $1,600 limit for such plans.**

While the 2017 Tax Cuts and Jobs Act (TCJA) does not change the tax treatment of employee achievement awards, it does provide a definition of tangible personal property. Tangible personal property does not include cash, cash equivalents, gifts cards, gift coupons, gift certificates, vacations, meals, lodging, tickets for theater or sporting events, stock, bonds or similar items, and other nontangible personal property.

## Unemployment Compensation

Amounts received from state unemployment compensation plans are considered substitutes for earned income and are always taxable to the recipient.[15] Unemployment compensation is designed to aid individuals who become unemployed until they can find new employment. A similar type of benefit paid by states to individuals is workers' compensation. Workers' compensation is paid to employees who are injured on the job and cannot continue to work as a result of their injuries. A specific exclusion from income is provided for workers' compensation payments and is discussed in Chapter 4.

## Social Security Benefits

Before 1984, Social Security benefits were excluded from taxation. The exclusion was evidently based on administrative convenience because the tax law contained no specific exclusion for such payments. This made some sense, because the payments made by an employee into the fund are not exempt from tax. However, the matching portion paid by the employer is not taxable to the employee. Thus, under the capital recovery concept, it could be said that half of each payment received from Social Security represented a return of the taxpayer's investment and was therefore excluded, much like the annuities discussed earlier. However, when Congress decided to begin taxing Social Security benefits

Exhibit 3-2

## Calculation of Taxable Portion of Social Security Benefits Received (50-percent formula)

The taxable portion of Social Security is equal to the lesser of

1. one-half of the Social Security benefits received during the year

OR

2. one-half of the amount by which modified adjusted gross income exceeds the base amount

Where

**Modified adjusted gross income** = Adjusted gross income + one-half of the Social Security benefits received during the year + any foreign earned income exclusion + any tax-exempt interest

And

**Base amount** = $25,000 for an unmarried individual
$32,000 for a married couple, filing jointly
$ -0- for all others

in 1984, politicians were concerned about taxing those whose main source of income came from Social Security. That is, Congress questioned the ability of lower income taxpayers to pay the tax. To negate this possibility, Congress used a lesser-of formula to determine the amount of Social Security to include in gross income; the formula allows lower-income taxpayers to escape taxation on Social Security benefits.[16] Calculation of the taxable portion of Social Security benefits before 1994 is presented in Exhibit 3-2.

Although the second formula seems unduly complex, modified adjusted gross income serves as a "floor" value under which no Social Security benefits are taxed. Note that as long as the taxpayer's modified adjusted gross income is less than the base amount, none of the Social Security benefits is subject to tax. Thus, people with relatively modest incomes are not taxed on Social Security benefits.

Recall from Chapter 1 that adjusted gross income (AGI) is defined as gross income less deductions for adjusted gross income. Deductions allowable for AGI include trade or business expenses, rental and royalty expenses, reimbursed employee business expenses, payments into pension accounts (e.g., IRAs), and certain other business- and investment-related expenses. As such, adjusted gross income provides a measure of the individual's ability to pay tax. In the second formula, the two major additions to AGI, for the foreign earned income exclusion and tax-exempt interest (both discussed in Chapter 4), are there to ensure that individuals with large, untaxed economic incomes pay some tax on Social Security benefits.

**Example 27** Judith is a single individual who receives $4,000 in Social Security benefits during 1993. Her adjusted gross income before considering the taxability of the Social Security benefits is $10,000. How much of the $4,000 is taxable?

**Discussion: None of the $4,000 is included in Judith's gross income because her modified adjusted gross income falls below the $25,000 floor value for taxation of unmarried taxpayers. Per the formulas in Exhibit 3-2, Judith includes in income the *lesser* of**

no tax

$$\tfrac{1}{2}(\$4{,}000) = \$2{,}000$$

OR

$$\tfrac{1}{2}(\$10{,}000 + \$2{,}000 - \$25{,}000) < 0$$

**Example 28** Jack and Bettina receive the following income during 1993:

| | |
|---|---|
| Retirement pay | $23,000 |
| Tax-exempt bond interest | $10,000 |
| Social Security benefits | $ 6,000 |

How much of the $6,000 must be included in their gross income?

**Discussion:** **Social Security benefits of $2,000 are taxable per the following formulas:**
**The lesser of**

½($6,000) = $3,000
OR
½($23,000 + $3,000 + $10,000 − $32,000) = ½($36,000 − $32,000) = $2,000

Note that if Jack and Bettina were not required to include their tax-exempt interest in the Social Security benefits calculation, their income ($26,000) would have fallen below the base amount for a married couple ($32,000) and no part of their benefits would have been taxed. Thus, the adjustment for tax-exempt interest has made a portion of their benefits taxable in accord with Congress's intent: to apply the tax to individuals with large economic incomes.

**Example 29** Ruth is a retired executive whose adjusted gross income for 1993 is $80,000. In addition, she receives $5,000 in Social Security benefits. How much of the $5,000 must be included in Ruth's gross income?

**Discussion:** **Ruth must include $2,500 in her gross income per the following formula:**
**The lesser of**

½($5,000) = $2,500
OR
½($80,000 + $2,500 − $25,000) = $28,750

Example 29 illustrates how once a taxpayer's modified adjusted gross income reaches the level at which formula 2 exceeds one-half of the Social Security benefits, the maximum amount of Social Security subject to tax is one-half of the benefits received, no matter how much the taxpayer's income increases. Thus, formula 1 establishes a "ceiling" value for the taxation of Social Security benefits received before 1994.

For tax years after 1993, a second-tier inclusion rule applies to higher-income taxpayers. The second tier applies to unmarried individuals with modified adjusted gross incomes greater than $34,000 and married couples filing joint returns with modified adjusted gross incomes exceeding $44,000. The rules discussed earlier (the 50-percent formula) remain in effect for taxpayers with modified adjusted gross incomes that are less than these amounts.

For tax years after 1993, taxpayers with modified adjusted gross incomes above the threshold levels of $34,000 and $44,000 have to make an additional computation to determine the amount of Social Security benefits that they must include in gross income. As outlined in Exhibit 3-3, the new second-tier rule increases the taxable portions in the original Social Security formulas from 50 percent to 85 percent. In addition, formula 2 is increased by the amount of Social Security included under the 50-percent formula or a fixed amount ($4,500 for unmarried individuals, $6,000 for married taxpayers filing joint returns), whichever is less. This change in formula 2 requires taxpayers subject to the second-tier rules to calculate the amount of Social Security they would have included in their gross income under the 50-percent formula.

**Example 30** Assume the same facts as in example 27, except that the tax year is 2021. How much of the $4,000 in Social Security benefits is included in Judith's gross income?

**Discussion:** **None of the $4,000 is included in Judith's gross income because her modified adjusted gross income is below the $25,000 floor value for unmarried individuals. Note that the new second-tier rule does not apply to Judith, and her Social Security benefits will not be subject to tax.**

**Example 31** Dieter and Luann are a married couple whose adjusted gross income is $42,000. In addition, they receive $10,000 in Social Security benefits. How much of the $10,000 must be included in Dieter and Luann's gross income?

**Discussion:** **Dieter and Luann's modified adjusted gross income is $47,000 [$42,000 + $5,000 (½ × $10,000)]. Because their modified adjusted gross income exceeds the**

**Exhibit 3-3**

## Calculation of Second Tier for Inclusion of Social Security Benefits Received

The taxable portion of Social Security is equal to the lesser of

1. 85% of the Social Security benefits received during the year

OR

2. The sum of
   a. 85% of the amount by which modified adjusted gross income exceeds the base amount
   PLUS
   b. The smaller of the amount of Social Security benefits included in gross income under the 50% formula

   OR

   $4,500 for an unmarried individual
   $6,000 for a married couple filing jointly

   Where

   **Modified adjusted gross income** = Adjusted gross income + one-half of the Social Security benefits received during the year + any foreign earned income exclusion + any tax-exempt interest

   And

   Base amount = $34,000 for an unmarried individual
   $44,000 for a married couple filing jointly
   $ -0- for all others

**$44,000 base amount, they are subject to the second-tier rule. Under the 50% formula, their taxable Social Security is $5,000:**

**The lesser of**

½($10,000) = $5,000
OR
½($47,000 − $32,000) = $7,500

**Under the second-tier rule, Dieter and Luann must include $7,550 of the Social Security benefits in gross income:**

*The lesser of*

| | |
|---|---|
| 1. 85% × $10,000 = | $8,500 |
| OR | |
| 2. The sum of | |
| a. 85% × ($47,000 − $44,000) = | $2,550 |
| b. the smaller of | |
| $5,000 (amount included under the 50% formula) | |
| OR | |
| $6,000 | $5,000 |
| Equals | $7,550 |

## Alimony Received

In divorce situations, one spouse often makes payments to a former spouse. These payments may be to provide for the support of children (called **child support payments**), they may be simply a sharing of income between the two parties (called **alimony**), or they may constitute a division of marital property (**property settlement**). Child support payments are not taxable to the recipient regardless of how the recipient actually spends the money.[17] However, payments made pursuant to a divorce agreement before December 31, 2018, are a sharing of current income (alimony) and are taxable to the recipient and deductible for adjusted gross income by the payer. That is, alimony is an allowable transfer of income from one former spouse to another. To be considered alimony, all the following conditions must be met:[18]

1. The payment must be in cash.
2. The payment must be in a written agreement (either a separation or divorce agreement).

3. The written agreement must not specify that the payments are for some other purpose (i.e., child support).
4. The payer and the payee cannot be members of the same household at the time of the payment.
5. There is no liability to make payments for any period after the death of the payee.

These requirements are intended to ensure that both parties to the agreement concur on the amount of alimony being paid.

One controversial tax aspect of these agreements involves property settlements. Payments and transfers pursuant to property settlements between spouses do not have any income tax consequences.

**Example 32** Walt and Janice are divorced during the current year. As part of the divorce settlement, Walt pays Janice $100,000 for her interest in their home (the home has a fair market value of $200,000) and agrees to pay Janice $12,000 per year in alimony. The home has an adjusted basis to Walt and Janice of $120,000. What are the tax effects of the payments Walt makes to Janice?

**Discussion: The $100,000 payment to Janice is not a taxable disposition by Janice, and no deduction is allowed to Walt, because it is a property settlement payment. The $12,000 per year of alimony is included in Janice's gross income and is deductible for adjusted gross income by Walt.**

A final problem in the alimony area is the attempt to disguise child support payments as alimony. To counter this problem, the tax law requires that any reductions in alimony payments that are the result of a contingency related to a child are classified as child support payments.[19]

**Example 33** Ben and Diane are divorced in the current year. As part of their divorce agreement, Ben is to pay Diane alimony of $500 per month until their son reaches age 18, at which time the payments will be reduced to $200 per month. What are the tax effects of the payments Ben makes to Diane?

**Discussion: Because the payments are to be reduced to $200 when their child reaches age 18 (a contingency related to a child), only $200 per month of all payments made are considered alimony. The remaining $300 is a nondeductible child support payment.**

For divorce or separation agreements executed or modified after December 31, 2018, the 2017 Tax Cuts and Jobs Act changes the tax treatment of alimony. The payment is no longer included as income to the recipient, and the payor is no longer allowed a deduction for the payment.

### Death Benefit Payments

When an employee dies, the employer often makes payments to surviving dependents to help them out financially while they adjust to life without the income of the deceased. Until August 19, 1996, the tax law allowed one $5,000 exclusion for death benefits paid to deceased employees' beneficiaries. **Death benefit payments** received after August 19, 1996, are no longer allowed the exclusion and are included in the gross income of the beneficiaries.

## 3-3d Imputed Income

LO 4 Explain imputed income and identify the common sources of such income and their tax treatments.

Two major sources of income that are untaxed under current law are the goods and services produced by individuals for personal consumption and individuals' use of their personal residence and other durable goods. To understand why these items constitute income under the principles described earlier in the chapter, consider the following example:

**Example 34** Jana has a garden in which she grows tomatoes for her personal consumption. The full cost of producing the tomatoes amounts to $40. At current prices, it would have cost $100 to purchase the tomatoes. Does Jana have income from growing and consuming her tomatoes?

**Discussion: Although Jana's wealth has increased by $60 from growing and consuming her own tomatoes rather than purchasing them, she does not have to recognize the $60 as income. The key factor in the nonrecognition of the income is that the $60 increase in wealth was not realized in an arm's-length transaction with another party. Note that if Jana had sold the tomatoes for $100 and used the money for other purposes, she clearly would have realized the income, and the $60 increase in wealth would be subject to tax.**

This example of income from in-kind consumption is but one of many types of **imputed income** from which taxpayers profit on a daily basis but are not subject to taxation. The primary reason that these kinds of income are not taxed is that there is no realization of the income. In addition, even if in-kind consumption were considered a realization, such income would not be taxed because it would be administratively inconvenient: Imagine the nightmare of having to keep track of all the tasks you perform for yourself rather than hiring someone else to do the work! How could the government audit this type of income?

Although the vast majority of imputed income is not taxed, the tax law does identify several specific items of imputed income that must be taxed. The three most common forms of imputed income subject to tax are:

- Below market-rate loans
- Payment of expenses by others
- Bargain purchases

## Below Market-Rate Loans

Before 1984, a common tax-planning technique that taxpayers used to shift income from high marginal tax rate taxpayers to low marginal tax rate taxpayers was the use of an interest-free loan, called a **below market-rate loan**. The savings that could have been realized from such a plan are illustrated in the following example:

**Example 35** Binh, who is in the 35% marginal tax rate bracket, lends his son Chee $50,000 interest-free. Chee, who is a 15% marginal tax rate payer, puts the money in a savings account earning 10%. How much tax does the family save through this arrangement?

**Discussion: If Binh invested the $50,000 at the same earnings rate, the tax savings would be $1,000. That is the difference between the tax Binh would have paid on the $5,000 in interest, $1,750 ($5,000 × 35%), and the tax paid by Chee on the $5,000 in interest, $750 ($5,000 × 15%).**

In 1984, Congress curtailed some advantages of interest-free loans by enacting provisions that consider such loans as consisting of two transactions: a normal interest-bearing loan (at the current federal rate of interest) and an exchange of cash between the lender and the borrower to pay the interest on the loan. The imputed exchange of cash is the amount of cash necessary for the borrower to pay the lender the interest on the loan. A conventional interest-bearing loan and an interest-free loan are compared in Figure 3-1.

Under the imputed interest rules,[20] the lender is deemed to have interest income at the federal rate of interest, whereas the borrower is deemed to have made a payment (first imputed cash payment) of the interest (step 2 at the bottom of Figure 3-1). The imputed payment of cash (second imputed cash payment) from the lender to the borrower (step 3 at the bottom of Figure 3-1) may also produce taxable income to the borrower, depending on the type of loan.

The three basic types of loans are:

- Gift loans
- Employment-related loans
- Corporation/shareholder loans

A gift loan is one made between family members. The imputed cash exchange on these loans is considered a gift from the lender to the borrower and is not subject to tax. (The exclusion for gifts is covered in Chapter 4.)

Figure 3-1

## Imputed Interest Rules

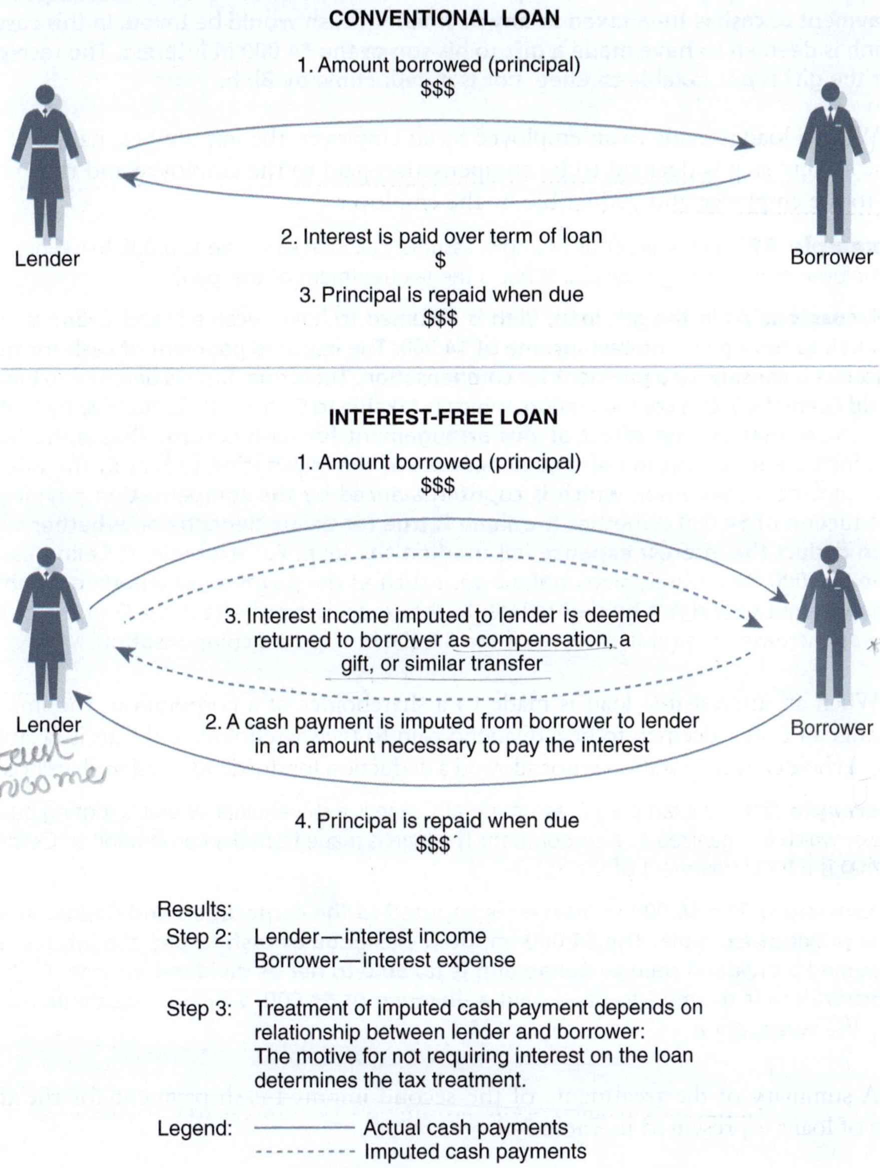


**Example 36** What is the tax treatment of the loan Binh made to Chee in example 35 if the federal rate of interest is 8%?

**Discussion: The first step in accounting for an interest-free loan is to determine the amount of imputed interest on the loan using the applicable federal rate of interest. In this case, the amount of imputed interest is $4,000 ($50,000 × 8%). This is the amount of interest income the lender is deemed to have earned (and the borrower is deemed to have paid) from the making of the loan. In this case, interest income of $4,000 is imputed to Binh, and interest expense of $4,000 is imputed to Chee. Binh, therefore, includes $4,000 of interest in his gross income. Chee has interest expense of $4,000, the deductibility of which depends on how he uses the money. (Interest deductions are discussed in Chapter 5.) NOTE: Because this is a gift loan of less than $100,000, the amount of interest imputed may be less than the $4,000 federal rate. See examples 39–41.**

**The second step is to give effect to the motive for the nonpayment of interest on the loan. This is done by assuming that the lender gave the borrower the cash with which to pay the interest imputed on the loan in the first step. This imputed payment of cash is then taxed as any payment of cash would be taxed. In this case, Binh is deemed to have made a gift to his son of the $4,000 in interest. The receipt of the gift is not taxable to Chee, nor is it deductible by Binh.**

When a loan is made to an employee by an employer, the imputed exchange of cash in the second step is deemed to be compensation paid to the employee and thus is taxable to the employee and deductible by the employer.

**Example 37** In the previous example, assume that Binh lends the $50,000 to Celine, an employee of his roofing business. What is the tax treatment of the loan?

**Discussion: As in the gift loan, Binh is assumed to have received (and Celine is assumed to have paid) interest income of $4,000. The imputed payment of cash for the interest is considered a payment for compensation. Therefore, Binh is deemed to have paid Celine $4,000 in compensation, which is taxable to Celine and deductible by Binh.**

**Note that the net effect of this arrangement for Binh is zero. That is, he has an increase in his income of $4,000 because of the imputation to him of the interest income on the loan, which is counterbalanced by the compensation payment deduction of $4,000. Whether the same is true for Celine depends on whether she can deduct the interest expense imputed on the loan. For example, if Celine uses the $50,000 for a purely personal purpose such as the payment of a personal debt, the interest would not be deductible. In that case, the net effect for Celine would be an increase in taxable income of the $4,000 in imputed compensation.**

When an interest-free loan is made to a shareholder of a corporation, the imputed exchange of cash is deemed to be a dividend paid to the shareholder and thus is taxable to the shareholder. A corporation is not allowed a deduction for dividends paid to shareholders.

**Example 38** In example 37, assume that Celine is a shareholder of Binh's roofing business, which is organized as a corporation. The loan is made from the corporation to Celine. What is the tax treatment of the loan?

**Discussion: The $4,000 in interest is imputed to the corporation and Celine, as in the previous example. The $4,000 imputed exchange of cash to pay the interest is deemed a dividend paid to Celine and is taxable to her as dividend income. Binh's corporation is deemed to have paid a dividend of $4,000, which is not deductible by the corporation.**

A summary of the treatments of the second imputed cash payment for the three types of loans is presented in Table 3-3.

*Table 3-3*

## Treatment of Second Imputed Cash Payment

| Type of Loan | Lender | Borrower |
|---|---|---|
| **Gift loans** | Imputed payment is a gift made to the borrower—*no income tax effect.* | Imputed payment is a gift received from the lender—*no income tax effect.* |
| **Employment-related loans** | Imputed payment is compensation paid to the borrower—*lender gets a deduction for compensation paid.* | Imputed payment is compensation received by the borrower—*borrower has compensation income.* |
| **Shareholder loans** | | |
| **1. Loan to a shareholder** | 1. Imputed payment is a dividend paid to the borrower—*lender gets no deduction for dividends paid.* | 1. Imputed payment is a dividend received from the lender—*borrower has dividend income.* |
| **2. Loan to the corporation** | 2. Imputed payment is a contribution to corporate capital—*no deduction allowed to lender (added to basis in stock).* | 2. Imputed payment is receipt of contributed capital—*no income imputed to the borrower.* |

**Exceptions to Imputed Interest Rules** There are two exceptions to the rules for interest-free loans. First, any loan of $10,000 or less is exempted from the imputed interest rules. This exception is for administrative convenience; it would be very costly to keep track of all small loans that people make to friends and relatives. Therefore, a small amount of income can still be shifted through the use of $10,000 interest-free loans.

The second exception is for gift loans of $100,000 or less. On such loans, the imputed interest on the loan cannot exceed the borrower's net investment income (investment income less the costs of producing the income) for the year. Further, if the borrower's net investment income for the year does not exceed $1,000, the imputed interest is deemed to be zero; the loan has no tax effect. Therefore, gift loans that do not produce much income for the borrower or that are used for in-kind consumption by the borrower escape the imputed interest rules.

**Example 39** Allegra lends her daughter Elena $50,000, which she uses to purchase a new house. The loan is interest-free, the federal rate of interest is 8%, and Elena has $600 in investment income for the year. What are the tax consequences of the loan?

**Discussion: Because this is a gift loan of less than $100,000, the imputed interest is limited to Elena's net investment income for the year. However, because Elena's investment income is less than $1,000, no interest is imputed on the loan. Therefore, the loan has no income tax effects for either Allegra or Elena.**

**Example 40** Assume the same facts as in example 39, except that Elena's investment income is $2,500.

**Discussion: In this case, interest on the gift loan would be imputed at $2,500, Elena's investment income. Allegra would have interest income of $2,500, and Elena would have interest expense of $2,500.**

**Example 41** Assume the same facts as in example 39, except that Elena's investment income is $6,000.

**Discussion: In this case, interest at the federal rate of $4,000 ($50,000 × 8%) is less than Elena's investment income of $6,000. Therefore, interest of $4,000 is imputed on the loan. That is, none of the special exceptions for gift loans is applicable. NOTE: Interest is never imputed at a rate greater than the applicable federal interest rate.**

## Payment of Expenses by Others

Whenever one taxpayer pays another taxpayer's expenses, the taxpayer who received the benefit of the payment has realized an increase in wealth and is taxed on the payment, unless the payment constitutes a valid gift. (Gifts are excluded from income.)[21] The more common situations involve payments of expenses of an employee by an employer, taxes of the lessor paid by the lessee of property, and the payment of the personal expenses of the principal shareholder of a closely held corporation. (A closely held corporation is one in which five or fewer shareholders own more than 50 percent of the stock of the corporation.)

**Example 42** Ramona is the president of DEF, Inc. Her employment contract states that DEF is to pay Ramona a salary of $100,000 and the federal income tax due on the salary. In the current year, the tax on Ramona's DEF salary totals $27,000, which is paid by DEF. What is Ramona's gross income from DEF?

**Discussion: The payment of the $27,000 of tax on Ramona's salary is considered compensation income paid to Ramona. Therefore, her gross income from DEF is $127,000.**

**Example 43** Joe lost his job this year. Because he was having trouble paying all his bills, his grandfather agrees to pay Joe's home mortgage until he can find a new job. His grandfather makes payments on Joe's mortgage totaling $10,000 during the current year. What are the tax effects of the payment of Joe's mortgage by his grandfather?

**Discussion: The payment of the mortgage is not meant to be compensation from grandfather to Joe; rather, it is in the nature of a gift from grandfather to Joe to help him through his tough economic times. Therefore, the payments are not taxable to Joe. (Gifts are excluded from income.)**

These two examples illustrate the key consideration in determining whether the payment of an expense by another is taxable: intent to compensate. That is, when payments are made on behalf of another in an employment or other business-related context, they are generally taxable. Payments made on behalf of family members that are unrelated to employment or other business matters are generally considered nontaxable gifts.

### Bargain Purchases

Ordinarily, when taxpayers astutely purchase property for less than it is worth, they are not taxed immediately on the increased wealth resulting from the purchase. Any such gain will be reflected when the property is sold. However, a true **bargain purchase** is taxable to the buyer. Such a purchase occurs when the difference between the purchase price and the fair market value represents an effort by the seller to confer an economic advantage to the buyer.[22] That is, the purchase price does not result from an arm's-length transaction. As such, bargain purchases are typically found in employer/employee purchases and other instances in which the seller perceives some ultimate advantage in selling the property to a particular taxpayer at less than fair market value.

**Example 44** Sterling is an employee of Shelf Road Development Company. The company recently subdivided some property and offered lots for sale at a price of $50,000. Shelf sells Sterling a lot for $20,000. How much gross income does Sterling have from the purchase of property?

**Discussion: The difference between the $50,000 fair market value and the $20,000 purchase price—$30,000—is taxable to Sterling as compensation. The purchase price, an attempt to compensate Sterling, is not the result of an arm's-length bargain.**

**Example 45** Karolina wants to purchase a new Bugatti roadster. She knows that such cars usually sell for about $50,000. However, she finds a dealer who is having financial difficulties and she is able to purchase a Bugatti for only $40,000. Does Karolina have gross income from the purchase of the Bugatti?

**Discussion: Because the dealer gains no long-term benefit from selling the car to Karolina for $40,000, her astute purchase is not considered a bargain purchase for tax purposes. Further, the purchase price is the result of an arm's-length transaction. Therefore, she is not taxed on the $10,000 below market-value purchase.**

### concept check

Under the *legislative grace concept*, only items of income that Congress has specifically excluded from taxation are not included in gross income. Therefore, realized increases in wealth are subject to tax unless a specific exclusion from income exists. In addition, Congress can specify both the amount and the form of relief based on a taxpayer's *ability to pay* the tax. The *substance over form doctrine* requires that transactions be taxed according to their true intention. Below market-rate loans are recast as loans bearing interest at the federal rate, and the motive for not requiring an interest payment determines the tax treatment. Similarly, attempts to compensate employees through payment of another's expenses or bargain purchases, and similar business relationships, are characterized according to their compensatory intentions.

## 3-4 CAPITAL GAINS AND LOSSES—AN INTRODUCTION

LO 5 Provide an overview of the tax treatment of capital gain income.

Whenever a property is sold, exchanged, or otherwise disposed of, a realization occurs, and the entity owning the property must calculate the gain or loss resulting from the disposition of the property. The income tax provisions governing property transactions are an important part of the income tax system. Chapters 9 through 12 discuss in detail various aspects of income tax accounting for the acquisition, use, and disposition of property. However, because of their importance in the income tax system, we briefly discuss capital gains and losses at this point.

A capital gain or a capital loss results from the sale or other disposition of a capital asset. As discussed in Chapter 2, a **capital asset** is any asset that is not a receivable, an item of inventory, depreciable property used in a trade or business, or real property used in a trade or business.[23] Thus, the most common capital assets are investment assets (stocks, bonds, rental property held for investment, etc.) and assets used for personal use purposes (home, furniture, clothing, personal automobile, etc.) by individuals.

The 2017 Tax Cuts and Jobs Act (TCJA) amended the types of assets that are excluded from being capital assets to include patents, inventions, models or designs (whether or not patented), and secret formulas or processes, which are held either by the taxpayer who created the property or by a taxpayer with a substituted or transferred basis from the taxpayer who created the property (or for whom the property was created).

Since 1921, the tax law has provided some form of preferential tax treatment for capital gains. For example, until 1987, individuals were allowed to deduct 60 percent of any net long-term capital gains. This meant that only 40 percent of net long-term capital gains was subject to tax. During most of this time, the top marginal tax rate was 50 percent, resulting in a maximum tax rate on long-term capital gains of 20 percent (50% × 40%). Although the 60-percent capital gains deduction was repealed in 1987, all the mechanisms for accounting for capital gains and other limitations were left in place. Because of the tax benefits afforded to sales of capital assets, accounting for capital gains and losses is an important aspect of our tax system. The basic aspects of accounting for capital gains and losses are discussed in the sections that follow. More detailed analysis is provided in Chapter 11.

## 3-4a Capital Gain-and-Loss Netting Procedure

The income tax law determines the treatment of capital gains and losses on an annual basis. That is, all capital gains and losses occurring during a tax year are aggregated through a prescribed netting procedure to determine the net effect of all capital asset transactions for the year.[24] The special tax treatments (if any are applicable) are applied only to the net results for the year, not to individual transactions.

Exhibit 3-4 outlines the procedure for determining the net long-term capital gains or losses for the year. The first step requires identification of the year's gains and losses by the type of gain. Gains and losses must be identified as long-term or short-term. In addition, collectibles gains and losses, gains on qualified small business stock, and unrecaptured Section 1250 gains must be separately identified at this step. Whether a gain or loss is short term or long term depends on its holding period. As the phrase indicates, the **holding period** is how long the taxpayer owned the asset that was sold. Assets held for more than 12 months produce **long-term capital gains** and **long-term capital losses**. Assets held for one year or less produce **short-term capital gains** and **short-term capital losses**.[25] Sales of collectibles that are held for more than 12 months produce **collectibles gains** and **collectibles losses**.[26] Collectibles include works of art, rugs, antiques, metals, gems, stamps, coins, and alcoholic beverages. Gains on qualified small business stock and unrecaptured Section 1250 gains are defined and discussed in Chapter 11. Distinguishing among the various types of gains and losses is important

*Exhibit 3-4*

## Capital Gain-and-Loss Netting Procedure

**Step 1** Identify all capital gains and losses occurring during the year as being short-term gains and losses, long-term gains and losses, collectibles gains and losses, gains on qualified small business stock, and unrecaptured Section 1250 gains.

**Step 2** Combine all long-term gains and losses to determine a net long-term position for the year. Collectibles gains and losses, gains on qualified small business stock, and unrecaptured Section 1250 gains are treated as being held long-term. Combine all short-term gains and losses to determine a net short-term position for the year.

| | | |
|---|---|---|
| Long-term gains | $ XXX | |
| Long-term losses | (XXX) | |
| Net long-term gain (loss) | | $XXX or $(XXX) |
| Short-term gains | $ XXX | |
| Short-term losses | (XXX) | |
| Net short-term gain (loss) | | $XXX or $(XXX) |

**Step 3** If the positions determined in step 2 are opposite (i.e., one is a gain and one is a loss), net the two positions together to obtain either a gain or a loss position for the year.

If the positions determined in step 2 are the same (i.e., either both are gains or both are losses), no further netting is necessary.

because each category is accorded different treatment in determining the income tax liability of a taxpayer.

The second step in the netting procedure is to reduce the gains and losses for the year into one net long-term position (either a gain or a loss) and one net short-term position (either a gain or a loss). For purposes of this netting, collectibles gains and losses, gains on qualified small business stock, and unrecaptured Section 1250 gains are considered to be held long-term. At this stage, all capital gains and losses for the year have been reduced to two numbers—one for the effect of long-term gains and losses and another for short-term gains and losses.

**Example 46** Astrid has the following capital gains and losses for the current year:

| | |
|---|---|
| Long-term capital gains | $ 13,000 |
| Long-term capital losses | (4,000) |
| Short-term capital gains | 8,000 |
| Short-term capital losses | (10,000) |
| Collectibles gains | 7,000 |
| Collectibles losses | (3,000) |

What are Astrid's net long-term and net short-term capital gain or loss positions for the year?

**Discussion: Collectibles gains and losses are treated as long-term gains and losses in the netting procedure. Astrid has a net long-term capital gain of $13,000 and a net short-term capital loss of $2,000 for the current year:**

| Long-Term Gain/Loss Netting | |
|---|---|
| Long-term capital gain | $13,000 |
| Long-term capital loss | (4,000) |
| Collectibles gains | 7,000 |
| Collectibles losses | (3,000) |
| Net long-term capital gain | $13,000 |

| Short-Term Gain/Loss Netting | |
|---|---|
| Short-term capital gain | $ 8,000 |
| Short-term capital loss | (10,000) |
| Net short-term capital loss | $ (2,000) |

After the capital gain-and-loss transactions for the year have been reduced to a long-term and a short-term position for the year, the next step is to reduce the capital gain position for the year to either a gain or a loss on capital asset transactions for the year. Thus, if the short- and long-term positions are opposite (one is a gain and one is a loss), the two positions must be netted together to determine whether a gain or a loss has resulted from the taxpayer's capital asset transactions for the year.

**Example 47** Return to the facts of example 46. What is Astrid's net capital gain or loss for the year?

**Discussion: Astrid has a net long-term capital gain of $11,000 for the year. Because the first netting resulted in a long-term capital gain and a short-term capital loss, one more netting is necessary to determine Astrid's net capital gain position for the year:**

| | |
|---|---|
| Net long-term capital gain | $ 13,000 |
| Net short-term capital loss | (2,000) |
| Net long-term capital gain | $ 11,000 |

**Note that the effect of the netting procedure is to summarize all of Astrid's capital gains and losses for the year in a net gain position. This is the purpose of the procedure—to reduce all capital gains and losses occurring during the year into either a net gain or a net loss position.**

If the first netting produces short- and long-term positions that are the same (both are gains or both are losses), the taxpayer's gain or loss position for the year is known and no further netting is necessary.

**Example 48** Milton has the following capital gains and losses for the current year:

| | |
|---|---|
| Long-term capital gain | $ 3,000 |
| Long-term capital loss | (1,000) |
| Short-term capital gain | 6,000 |
| Short-term capital loss | (2,000) |

What is Milton's net capital gain or loss position for the current year?

**Discussion: The first netting results in a net long-term capital gain of $2,000 and a net short-term capital gain of $4,000:**

**Long-Term Gain/Loss Netting**

| | |
|---|---|
| Long-term capital gain | $ 3,000 |
| Long-term capital loss | (1,000) |
| Net long-term capital gain | $ 2,000 |

**Short-Term Gain/Loss Netting**

| | |
|---|---|
| Short-term capital gain | $ 6,000 |
| Short-term capital loss | (2,000) |
| Net short-term capital gain | $ 4,000 |

**Because both the long- and short-term positions are gains, it is clear that Milton has a gain in his capital asset transactions for the year. Therefore, no further netting is necessary. He will report a long-term capital gain of $2,000 and a short-term capital gain of $4,000 on his current year's tax return.**

After the net capital gain or loss position for the year has been determined, each of the various types of gains and losses is subject to special rules in the calculation of the taxpayer's taxable income and income tax liability. The 2017 TCJA retains the maximum rates on net capital gains and qualified dividends; however, it sets the point at which the rates (15 percent and 20 percent) change based on the 2018 tax rate schedule and indexes them for inflation using C-CPI-U for tax years after December 31, 2018.

For 2021, the 15 percent breakpoint is: $80,800 for joint returns and surviving spouses, $54,100 for heads of household, $2,700 for trusts and estates, and $40,400 for single individuals and for married filing separately. The 20-percent breakpoint is $501,600 for joint returns and surviving spouses, $250,800 for married filing separately, $473,750 for heads of household, $13,250 for estates and trusts, and $445,850 for single individuals. These rules are outlined in Table 3-4 and discussed in the next section. One thing you should note is that the tax treatments are applied to the net gain or loss for the entire tax year, not for individual gains and losses occurring during the year.

*Table 3-4*

## Treatment of Capital Gains and Losses (Individuals)

| Capital Gain/Loss Position | Holding Period | Tax Treatment |
|---|---|---|
| Short-term capital gain | 12 months or less | Ordinary income |
| Adjusted net capital gain | More than 12 months | Based on the breakpoints for 15% and 20%. |
| Unrecaptured Section 1250 gain | More than 12 months | Taxed at a maximum rate of 25% |
| Net collectibles gain | More than 12 months | Taxed at a maximum rate of 28% |
| Gain on qualified small business stock | More than 5 years | 50% of gain is excluded. Remaining gain is taxed at a maximum rate of 28% |
| Short-term capital loss | 12 months or less | Deductible loss for AGI; limited to $3,000 per year with indefinite carryforward of excess loss to future year's netting |
| Long-term capital loss | More than 12 months | Deductible loss for AGI; limited to $3,000 per year with indefinite carryforward of excess loss to future year's netting Any short-term losses are applied against the $3,000 limit before long-term losses are deducted |

## 3-4b Tax Treatment of Capital Gains

In calculating taxable income, net capital gains are added to gross income. The preferential treatments accorded to the various types of capital gains are applied in the calculation of the income tax liability. **Net short-term capital gains** receive no preferential tax treatment and are taxed at the taxpayer's marginal tax rate. *Adjusted net capital gains* are taxed at 15 percent and 20 percent based on the previously discussed breakpoints. Eligible *dividend income* is taxed at the zero, 15 percent, or 20 percent long-term capital gain rates. Unrecaptured Section 1250 gains are taxed at a maximum rate of 25 percent. **Net collectibles gains** are taxed at a maximum rate of 28 percent. One-half of the gain on qualified small business stock is excluded from income. The remaining gain is taxed at a maximum rate of 28 percent.

To calculate the capital gains tax, a series of nettings is done to determine the composition of the net long-term capital gain. **Adjusted net capital gain** is defined as the net long-term gain from the netting procedure minus the 28 percent rate gain and the unrecaptured Section 1250 gain plus eligible dividend income.

| | |
|---|---|
| | Long-term capital gain from netting procedure |
| Minus: | 28 percent rate gain |
| Minus: | Unrecaptured Section 1250 gain |
| Plus: | Eligible dividend income |
| Equals: | Adjusted net capital gain |

The 28 percent rate gain is equal to the sum of the net collectibles gain and gain on qualified small business stock reduced by net short-term capital losses and any long-term capital loss carryovers from previous years. If the 28 percent rate gain is negative, the remaining loss is netted against unrecaptured Section 1250 gains.[27]

| | |
|---|---|
| | Net collectibles gain |
| Plus: | Gain on qualified small business stock |
| Minus: | Short-term capital loss |
| Minus: | Long-term capital loss carryover |
| Equals: | 28 percent rate gain |

The practical effect of this offsetting of losses is that the long-term capital gain from the netting procedure is accorded the most favorable rates first. That is, the net long-term capital gain from the netting procedure is first allocated to the gain taxed at 15 percent (adjusted net capital gain), then to the gain taxed at 25 percent (unrecaptured Section 1250 gain), and last to the gain taxed at 28 percent (net collectibles gain and gain on qualified small business stock).

**Example 49** In example 47, Astrid had a net long-term capital gain of $11,000:

| | | |
|---|---|---|
| Short-term capital gain | $ 8,000 | |
| Short-term capital loss | (10,000) | $ (2,000) |
| Long-term capital gain | $ 13,000 | |
| Long-term capital loss | (4,000) | |
| Collectibles gains | 7,000 | |
| Collectibles losses | (3,000) | 13,000 |
| Net long-term capital gain | | $11,000 |

Astrid is single and has other taxable income of $180,000. What is her taxable income and income tax liability?

**Discussion: Astrid adds the $11,000 net long-term capital gain to her gross income, increasing taxable income to $191,000. Astrid's $11,000 net long-term capital gain consists of three parts:**

| | | |
|---|---|---|
| Short-term capital gain | $ 8,000 | |
| Short-term capital loss | (10,000) | |
| Net short-term capital loss | | $ (2,000) |
| Long-term capital gain | $ 13,000 | |
| Long-term capital loss | (4,000) | |
| Net long-term capital gain | | $ 9,000 |

| | | |
|---|---|---|
| Collectibles gains | 7,000 | |
| Collectibles losses | (3,000) | |
| Net collectibles gain | $ 4,000 | |

**In computing her tax liability, the 28% rate gain is $2,000 ($4,000 collectibles gain – $2,000 short-term capital loss). Her adjusted net capital gain is $9,000 ($11,000 – $2,000). This is equivalent to allocating the $11,000 net long-term capital gain first to the $9,000 adjusted net capital gain, leaving a net collectibles capital gain of $2,000 ($11,000 – $9,000). The adjusted net capital gain is taxed at 15%. In 2021 single individuals begin paying a 32% marginal tax rate at a taxable income of $164,925. Because Astrid's taxable income is greater than this amount, her marginal rate is 32% and the $2,000 net collectibles gain is taxed at the 28% maximum rate. Her income tax liability is $40,337:**

| | |
|---|---|
| Tax on $180,000 ordinary income—<br>$33,603.00 + [32% × ($180,000 – $164,925)] | $ 38,427 |
| Tax on $2,000 net collectibles capital gain—$2,000 × 28% | 560 |
| Tax on $9,000 net long-term capital gain—$9,000 × 15% | 1,350 |
| Income tax liability | $40,337 |

**Without the favorable treatment accorded capital gains, Astrid's income tax liability would have been $41,947. Astrid saves $1,610 ($41,947 – $40,337) from the capital gain rate provisions.**

**Example 50** Lane has the following capital gains and losses during the current year:

| | |
|---|---|
| Short-term capital loss | $ (8,000) |
| Collectibles gain | 6,000 |
| Long-term capital gain | 12,000 |

Lane is single and has taxable income from other sources of $45,000. What is her taxable income and her income tax liability?

**Discussion: Lane has a $10,000 net long-term capital gain:**

| | | |
|---|---|---|
| Short-term capital loss | | $ (8,000) |
| Collectibles gain | $ 6,000 | |
| Long-term capital gain | 12,000 | 18,000 |
| Net long-term capital gain | | $10,000 |

**The 28 percent rate gain is negative and all of the $10,000 net long-term capital gain is adjusted net capital gain:**

| | |
|---|---|
| Collectibles gain | $ 6,000 |
| Short-term capital loss | (8,000) |
| 28 percent rate gain | $ (2,000) |
| Long-term capital gain | $12,000 |
| 28 percent rate gain | (2,000) |
| Adjusted net capital gain | $10,000 |

**Her taxable income is $55,000 and her income tax liability is $7,149:**

| | |
|---|---|
| Tax on $45,000 ordinary income—<br>$4,664.00 + [22% × ($45,000 – $40,525)] | $5,649 |
| Tax on $10,000 adjusted net capital gain—$10,000 × 15% | 1,500 |
| Total income tax liability | $7,149 |

The Affordable Care Act adds a surtax on unearned income of higher income individuals. For tax years beginning after December 31, 2013, a 3.8 percent Medicare contribution tax on unearned income is imposed on individuals, estates, and trusts. For individuals, the tax is imposed on the lesser of net investment income or modified adjusted gross income in excess of the threshold amount ($250,000 for a married couple filing jointly, $125,000 for a married individual filing a separate return, and $200,000 for all other taxpayers). Because capital gains are unearned income, taxpayers with adjusted gross income above the threshold amount will incur an additional 3.8 percent tax on their net capital gains.[28]

**Example 51** In example 49, if Astrid's modified adjusted gross income is $225,000, what is the tax on her $11,000 long-term capital gain?

**Discussion: Because Astrid's modified adjusted gross income is greater than $200,000, she must pay the Medicare surtax on her long-term capital gain. The 3.8% tax is imposed on the lesser of $11,000 (net investment income) or $25,000 ($225,000 modified adjusted gross income >$200,000 single taxpayer threshold amount). The tax on her $11,000 long-term capital is $2,328:**

| | |
|---|---|
| Tax on $2,000 net collectibles capital gain—$2,000 × 28% | $ 560 |
| Tax on $9,000 net long-term capital gain—$9,000 × 15% | 1,350 |
| Medicare surtax on net long-term capital gain—$11,000 × 3.8% | 418 |
| Tax on long-term capital gain | $2,328 |

**Example 52** In example 51, if Astrid's modified adjusted gross income is $490,000, what is the tax on her $11,000 long-term capital gain?

**Discussion: As in example 51, Astrid must pay the 3.8% Medicare surtax on her $11,000 long-term capital gain. Because her taxable income exceeds $445,850, the tax on her net long-term capital gain is 20%. The tax on her $11,000 long-term capital gain is $2,778:**

| | |
|---|---|
| Tax on $2,000 net collectibles capital gain—$2,000 × 28% | $ 560 |
| Tax on $9,000 net long-term capital gain—$9,000 × 20% | 1,800 |
| Medicare surtax on net long-term capital gain—$11,000 × 3.8% | 418 |
| Tax on long-term capital gain | $2,778 |

## 3-4c Tax Treatment of Dividends

Corporate dividends are subject to double taxation—once as earned by the corporation and again as the earnings are distributed as dividends. To alleviate the double taxation of dividends, **eligible dividends** received are taxed at the long-term capital gain rates (0 percent, 15 percent, or 20 percent).[29] Eligible dividends include dividends from a domestic corporation or a qualified foreign corporation. A qualified foreign corporation is any foreign corporation whose stock is traded on an established U.S. securities market or any corporation incorporated in a U.S. possession. Dividends passed through to investors by a mutual fund or other regulated investment company, partnership, or real estate investment trust, or held by a common trust fund are eligible for the reduced rate so long as the distribution would otherwise be classified as an eligible dividend.

Eligible dividends do not include dividends paid by credit unions, mutual insurance companies, farmers' cooperatives, tax-exempt cemetery companies, nonprofit voluntary employee benefit associations, employer securities owned by an employee stock ownership plan, corporations exempt from tax under Section 501 or 521, mutual savings bank, savings and loan, domestic building and loan, cooperative bank, any other type of bank eligible for a dividends paid deduction, stock owned less than 60 days in the 120-day period surrounding the ex-dividend date, stock purchased with borrowed funds if the dividend was included in investment income in determining the investment interest deduction, stock with respect to which related payments must be made with respect to substantially similar or related property, and substitute payments in lieu of a dividend made with respect to stock on loan in a short sale.

Although dividends are taxed at the reduced capital gains rates, they are not included in the capital gain and loss netting procedure. Rather, eligible dividends are added to adjusted net capital (which can be zero). This ensures that taxpayers get rate relief on dividends even when they suffer net capital losses.

**Example 53** Claire has the following capital gains and losses in 2021:

| | |
|---|---|
| Short-term capital loss | $ 6,000 |
| Long-term capital gain | 1,500 |
| Collectibles gain | 2,500 |

In addition, Claire receives $800 in qualifying dividends in 2021. If Claire is in the 32 percent marginal rate bracket, what is the effect of her capital asset transactions and dividend income on her 2021 taxable income and income tax liability?

**Discussion: Claire has a $2,000 net short-term capital loss. Her adjusted net capital gain is $800 and she has a $2,000 net capital loss deduction.**

| | | |
|---|---|---|
| Short-term capital loss | | $(6,000) |
| Long-term capital gain | $1,500 | |
| Collectibles gain | 2,500 | 4,000 |
| Net short-term capital loss | | $(2,000) |

**The $800 in dividend income is included in gross income and added to the adjusted net capital gain (which is zero) and taxed at 15%. Claire can deduct the $2,000 net short-term capital loss, resulting in a $1,200 ($800 − $2,000) decrease in taxable income. Her income tax liability is reduced by $440:**

| | |
|---|---|
| Tax savings from capital loss deduction—$2,000 × 32% | $ 640 |
| Tax on dividend income—$800 × 15% | (120) |
| Reduction in income tax liability | $ 520 |

**Note that if the dividends were included in the capital gain and loss netting, Claire's net capital loss would be reduced to $1,200 and her tax savings would be $384 ($1,200 × 32%). By not including the dividends in the capital gain and loss netting procedure, Claire saves $136 ($520 − $384) in tax.**

## 3-4d Tax Treatment of Capital Losses

**Net capital losses** of individuals are deductible up to an annual limit of $3,000.[30] Capital losses are deductible as a deduction *for* adjusted gross income. Any capital loss in excess of the $3,000 limit is carried forward to the next year and is used in the next year's capital gain-and-loss netting.[31]

**Example 54** Chalmer has a net long-term capital gain of $6,000 and a net short-term capital loss of $17,000 in the current year. What is the effect of Chalmer's capital asset transactions on his taxable income?

**Discussion: Because the long- and short-term positions are opposite, they are netted together, resulting in a net short-term capital loss of $11,000 ($6,000 − $17,000). Chalmer can deduct $3,000 of the loss as a deduction for adjusted gross income in the current year. The remaining $8,000 loss is carried forward to next year as a short-term capital loss and used in next year's capital gain-and-loss netting.**

When an individual has both a net short-term capital loss and a net long-term capital loss in the same year, the short-term loss must be used toward the $3,000 annual limit before any long-term loss is deducted.[32]

**Example 55** During the current year, Zerenda has a $2,000 net short-term capital loss and a $5,000 net long-term capital loss. What is the effect of Zerenda's capital asset transactions on her taxable income?

**Discussion: Because the long-term and short-term positions are both losses, no netting is necessary. Zerenda deducts $3,000 of the total loss as a deduction for adjusted gross income. The $3,000 loss deduction is composed of the $2,000 short-term loss and $1,000 of the long-term loss. The remaining $4,000 ($5,000 − $1,000) of the long-term loss is carried forward to the next year as a long-term capital loss and used in next year's capital gain-and-loss netting.**

One thing to remember when dealing with personal use assets (which are capital assets) is that gains on the sale of personal use assets are taxable under the all-inclusive income concept. However, losses on personal use assets are disallowed. Therefore, if a personal use asset is sold at a gain, the gain is a capital gain and subject to the rules for capital gains. A loss on the sale of a personal use asset is not deductible and does not enter into the capital gain netting procedure.

**Example 56** Morgan sells for $3,400 a diamond necklace she purchased in 1998 at a cost of $2,000. Larry sells his personal truck, for which he paid $12,000, for $5,000. What are the effects of the sales on Morgan's and Larry's incomes?

**Discussion: Morgan has a long-term capital gain of $1,400 ($3,400 – $2,000) from the sale of her necklace. The $1,400 gain must be combined with her other capital gains and losses in the capital gain-and-loss netting procedure. Larry's loss of $7,000 ($5,000 – $12,000) on the sale of his truck is a nondeductible personal use loss. Therefore, the loss has no effect on his taxable income.**

## 3-4e Capital Gains and Losses of Conduit Entities

All items of income—gains, losses, deductions, and credits—of a conduit entity flow through the entity and are reported directly by the owners of the conduit. However, many items realized at the conduit level receive special treatment on the owners' tax returns. To provide owners with the information necessary to prepare their returns properly, a conduit entity is required to report each owner's share of the "ordinary" taxable income or loss separately from those items that receive special treatment.[33] The ordinary taxable income or loss is the income that results from income, gains, losses, and deductions that receive no special treatment. Because capital gains and losses are aggregated in the netting process on an owner's return, they must be allocated to each owner.

**Example 57** Parnell and Isis are equal partners in the Steiner Partnership. Steiner has total income of $70,000, consisting of the following items in the current year:

| | |
|---|---|
| Gross income from sales | $120,000 |
| Trade or business expenses | (90,000) |
| Operating income | $ 30,000 |
| Long-term gain on investment property | 50,000 |
| Short-term loss on Webto stock | (10,000) |
| Total income | $ 70,000 |

How do Steiner's results affect Parnell and Isis?

**Discussion: As equal partners, Parnell and Isis share the partnership items equally. Each reports $15,000 (50% × $30,000) in ordinary income from the partnership. In addition, each will have a long-term capital gain of $25,000 and a short-term capital loss of $5,000 that each must include in his or her capital gain-and-loss netting.**

**Example 58** Assume that in addition to the items reported to her in example 57, Isis has the following income items:

| | |
|---|---|
| Salary from Webto Corporation | $64,000 |
| Dividend income | 4,000 |
| Long-term capital loss | (14,000) |

What is Isis's adjusted gross income?

**Discussion: Isis's adjusted gross income is $89,000:**

| | |
|---|---|
| Salary from Webto Corporation | $64,000 |
| Dividend income | 4,000 |
| Ordinary income from Steiner Partnership | 15,000 |
| Net long-term capital gain ($25,000 – $14,000 – $5,000) | 6,000 |
| Adjusted gross income | $89,000 |

**Note that if the Steiner Partnership were not required to report its capital gains and losses separately, Isis's adjusted gross income would be $100,000 [(1/2 × $70,000) + $64,000 + $4,000 – $3,000] because of the limitation on capital loss deductions. Because capital gains and losses are reported separately from the partnership's ordinary income, Isis's $14,000 long-term capital loss is deducted against the $25,000 long-term capital gain from the partnership and is not subject to the capital loss limitations. In addition, the $4,000 in dividend income is added to the $6,000 net long-term capital gain and taxed at 15%.**

## 3-5 EFFECT OF ACCOUNTING METHOD

Once an income item has been identified as taxable, the tax year for recognition must be determined. In general, the taxpayer's accounting method dictates the proper period for inclusion. The two basic accounting methods allowed for tax purposes are the cash method and the accrual method.[34] We will discuss each method and its general income-recognition criteria in turn. Within each of the two basic accounting methods are exceptions to the treatments prescribed by the methods. These exceptions are generally designed to either discourage tax avoidance schemes or are based on the wherewithal-to-pay concept, which states that income should be taxed when the taxpayer has the means to pay the tax.

### 3-5a Cash Method

LO 6

Explain the primary accounting methods used for tax purposes and how income is recognized under each method: the cash method, the accrual method, and the hybrid method.

Taxpayers using this method of accounting recognize income when it is actually or *constructively* received. Recall that reduction to cash is not necessary to trigger income recognition because of the cash-equivalent approach to income recognition under the cash method of accounting. All that is required is that something with a fair market value (property, services, etc.) be received. Under the constructive receipt doctrine, income is received when it is made unconditionally available to the taxpayer and is subject to the taxpayer's complete control.

Because of its simplicity (a checkbook is all the record keeping that is required), most individuals use the cash method. In addition, this method gives taxpayers a somewhat limited ability to determine the year of taxation by accelerating or deferring cash receipts.

**Example 59** Harold is a cash basis taxpayer who repairs and maintains air conditioners and heating units in his spare time. The current year has been a good one for Harold, and he expects to be in the top marginal tax bracket. Next year, he plans to expand his business with a resulting increase in expenses and a drop in his marginal tax rate. What can Harold do to lower his tax bill?

**Discussion: To lower his taxes, Harold should defer receipt of some of his repair and maintenance income until next year, when his marginal tax rate will be lower. This can be accomplished by delaying billings to customers until next year or by easing any credit terms he extends to customers.**

Because of this ability to determine the year of taxation using the cash method, several restrictions are placed on the use of the method by certain types of taxpayers. These restrictions are discussed in more detail in Chapter 13. The most basic restriction on the use of the cash method is that taxpayers who sell inventories must account for sales, purchases, and inventories using the accrual basis.[35] However, for tax years beginning after December 31, 2017, the 2017 TCJA does not require a taxpayer to use the accrual method if the taxpayer meets the $26 million gross receipts test. The taxpayer can treat the inventories as nonincidental materials and supplies, or to follow the same rules as it does for financial accounting.

#### Exceptions Applicable to the Cash Method

LO 7

Explain the exceptions to the general rules of income recognition for each of the accounting methods.

The major income-recognition exception for cash basis taxpayers is for investments in **original issue discount (OID) securities**. An OID security is a debt instrument that has interest payable at maturity rather than throughout the life of the debt. Before the OID rules were codified, cash basis taxpayers could defer interest income by purchasing OID instruments.

**Example 60** First Financial, Inc., loans Heywood $10,000 on an interest-only basis, with interest payable annually at 10% for 3 years. Under the agreement, Heywood pays $1,000 in interest at the end of each year for 3 years. The $10,000 loan balance is repaid at the end of the third year. How much income does First Financial recognize each year?

**Discussion: This is a conventional debt situation wherein interest is received throughout the term of the loan and is recognized accordingly. The $1,000 in interest received each year would be included in First Financial's gross income.**

**Example 61** As an alternative, First Financial could lend the money on a discount basis. As an OID debt, the face amount of the debt would be $13,310, payable at the end of 3 years, and Heywood would still receive the $10,000 at the inception of the loan. If First Financial is a cash basis taxpayer, how would it recognize the interest under the general rules for the cash method?

**Discussion: Under the cash method, First Financial would recognize no income until it receives payment at the end of the third year. At that time, First Financial would recognize the difference between the amount received at maturity and the amount Heywood actually received as income, $3,310 ($13,310 − $10,000). Note that First Financial receives slightly more interest under this arrangement, because interest is being earned on the annual interest payment that is not being made throughout the 3 years.**

Current tax law requires that all OID securities with a maturity of more than one year be accounted for on the accrual basis, using the effective interest method.[36] The intent of this provision is to discourage cash basis investors from deferring income using OID instruments.

**Example 62** What is the proper income recognition for First Financial in example 61?

**Discussion: Because the loan is made on an OID basis and has a term of more than one year, First Financial must recognize the interest annually, using the effective interest method. Under this method, the book value of the debt is increased each year for the prior year's interest, which was accrued but not paid. Interest is calculated as the product of the book value outstanding throughout the year and the rate of interest charged on the loan.**

| | |
|---|---|
| Year 1 $10,000 × 10% = | $ 1,000 |
| Year 2 ($10,000 + $1,000) × 10% = | 1,100 |
| Year 3 ($10,000 + $1,000 + 1,100) × 10% = | 1,210 |
| Total income recognized = | $ 3,310 |

Series E and EE **savings bonds** issued by the U.S. government are OID securities that are exempt from the OID rules.[37] Taxpayers purchasing these bonds are not required to amortize interest income during the life of the bonds, although they may elect to amortize all such bonds they hold currently. If such an election is made, they must amortize interest on any bonds they purchase in the future.

**Example 63** Henry purchases for $650 a Series EE savings bond with a face value of $1,000 in the current year. The savings bond matures in 10 years and is priced to yield a 6% annual return. How should Henry account for the interest income related to the savings bond?

**Discussion: Because Series EE savings bonds are exempted from the OID rules, Henry will not have to recognize interest on the bond until he cashes it in. If Henry cashes in the bond at maturity, he will receive the $1,000 face value of the bond. At that time, he would recognize $350 ($1,000 − $650) in interest income. NOTE: Henry may elect to amortize the interest earned on the bond each year, using the effective interest method. However, if he makes this election, any other Series EE bonds he owns, as well as any others he may purchase in the future, must also be amortized. That is, you must use the same accounting method for all such bonds.**

## 3-5b Accrual Method

Taxpayers using this method recognize income when it is *earned*, regardless of the actual period of receipt. Income is considered earned when (1) all events have occurred that fix the right to receive the income, and (2) the amount of income earned can be determined with reasonable accuracy.[38] In most cases, these recognition criteria parallel the recognition rules for financial accounting. Some significant differences between the two are discussed later.

Two important aspects of the accrual method should be noted at this point. First, the checkbook approach commonly used by cash basis taxpayers is not sufficient to account for the many accruals and deferrals of income required by the accrual method. Thus, this is a more costly method. Second, accrual basis taxpayers have little control over the timing of their income, because the earning of the income, not the receipt of payment, is the critical recognition event.

**Example 64** Assume the same facts as in example 59, except that Harold has elected to be an accrual basis taxpayer.

**Discussion: Harold must recognize the income from the performance of his repair and maintenance services in the year in which they are performed, not when he receives payment for them. Therefore, he has little ability to control the timing of his income recognition to take advantage of marginal rate differences between tax years.**

## Exceptions Applicable to the Accrual Method

LO 7 Explain the exceptions to the general rules of income recognition for each of the accounting methods.

The receipt of prepaid income by accrual basis taxpayers is generally taxable in the tax year in which payment is received (under the wherewithal-to-pay concept). Thus, advance receipts of rent, interest, and royalties are taxable when the cash payment is received, even for accrual basis taxpayers.[39]

Accrual basis taxpayers are allowed to defer prepaid income in certain limited situations.[40] Prepaid income to which the exception applies includes advance payments received for services, the sale of goods, the use of intellectual property, the occupancy of space or the use of property if the occupancy or use is ancillary to the provision of services (e.g., advance receipts for hotel rooms), guaranty or warranty contracts ancillary to the preceding items, subscriptions, and membership in an organization. Prepaid income that is not allowed the deferral exception includes rents (other than those described above), insurance premiums, and payments with respect to financial instruments, including prepaid interest.

Under the **deferral method**, the taxpayer must include the advance payment in gross income in the year of receipt to the extent the advance payment is included in gross receipts for financial accounting purposes. The remaining income from the advance payment must be included in gross income in the next tax year (regardless of when it is included for financial accounting purposes).

**Example 65** On July 1, 2021, Toy's Termite Service, Inc., receives $1,200 on a one-year service contract. Under the contract, Toy's is to perform pest control once per month. Assuming that Toy's uses the accrual method of accounting, when should the $1,200 be recognized for tax purposes?

**Discussion: An advance receipt for services income is eligible for the deferral method. Toy's may recognize the amount of income it recognizes for financial accounting purposes in 2021. Six months of the services are to be performed in 2021 and 2022, resulting in the recognition of $600 in 2021 with the remaining $600 of income recognized in 2022. NOTE: If Toy's uses the cash method of accounting, the entire $1,200 is taxable in the year of receipt. The deferral method is an exception for accrual basis taxpayers.**

It should be noted that the deferral method is applicable only in very limited situations. For example, advance receipts for rents and interest are never deferred; they are always taxable in the year of receipt.

**Example 66** Assume the same facts as in example 65, except that the $1,200 advance receipt is for a 2-year service contract. When should Toy's recognize the income from the contract?

**Discussion: Under the deferral method, Toy's will include the amount of the prepayment in gross income that it recognizes for financial accounting purposes in 2021. Six of the 24 months of services will be performed in 2021 and Toy's will recognize $300 [($1,200 ÷ 24 = $50 per month) × 6 months = $300] in its 2021 gross income. The remaining $900 ($1,200 − $300) from the contract must be recognized in 2022. Note that Toy's will recognize $600 in 2022 and $300 in 2023 for financial accounting purposes. The deferral method allows only a one-year deferral of income on advance receipts qualifying for the exception.**

The second exception to the general rule for prepayments is for prepaid receipts received for goods. To use the accrual method to account for advance receipts for goods, the prepayment must be less than the cost of the goods and must be deferred for financial accounting purposes.[41]

**Example 67** Anne wants to buy a new car, but none of the dealers in her area has the car she wants. Local Car Sales, Inc., agrees to order the car she wants from the factory. The agreed-upon price for the car is $17,500, and Anne agrees to give Local a $500 deposit on the order, the balance to be paid upon delivery. Local receives the deposit on December 27, 2021. The car arrives the following February, and Anne pays Local the $17,000 balance due on the car. How should Local Car Sales, Inc., account for the $500 deposit received in 2021?

**Discussion: Assuming that the $500 deposit is less than the cost of the car to Local, Local may defer recognition of the deposit until 2022 provided that it also defers recognition for financial accounting purposes.**

## 3-5c Hybrid Method

The **hybrid method of accounting** allows the taxpayer to account for sales of merchandise and the related cost of goods sold on the accrual basis and all other items of income and expense on the cash basis. Thus, the hybrid method is a mixture of the accrual and cash methods. This method is most commonly used by taxpayers who have inventories and therefore must use the accrual method to account for sales and the cost of goods sold from inventories. Such taxpayers must still use the cash method to account for other revenues and must use the cash method for all other expenses.

**Example 68** Sunshine is a cash basis taxpayer who repairs and maintains hot tubs in her spare time. She also sells hot tubs. How must Sunshine account for sales of the hot tubs?

**Discussion: Sunshine must use the accrual method to account for sales and calculate cost of goods sold for the hot tubs. However, she may elect to use the hybrid method of accounting, which would let her use the cash method for her service income and for all other expenses.**

## 3-5d Exceptions Applicable to All Methods

LO 7

Explain the exceptions to the general rules of income recognition for each of the accounting methods.

Certain taxpayers must use two major income-recognition methods, regardless of their accounting methods. These methods relate to installment sales of property and accounting for long-term construction contracts.

### Installment Sales

An **installment sale** occurs whenever property is sold and at least one payment is received in a tax year subsequent to the year of sale. Taxpayers who are not dealers in the particular type of property but who make casual sales of property must recognize income from the sale by using the installment method, unless they elect to recognize the entire gain in the year of the sale.[42] The installment method is based on the wherewithal-to-pay concept and recognizes income proportionally as the selling price is received.[43]

**Example 69** Lene purchases a tract of land in 2017 at a cost of $20,000 as a speculative investment. In 2021, she sells the land for $50,000. The terms of the sale require the buyer to pay Lene $10,000 in 2021, $20,000 in 2022, and $20,000 in 2023 with interest at 8% on the outstanding balance. How much income must Lene recognize in 2021 through 2023?

**Discussion: Because Lene is not a dealer in property, she must use the installment method, unless she elects to recognize the entire $30,000 ($10,000 + $20,000 + $20,000 − $20,000) gain in 2022. Under the installment method, the gain is recognized proportionately as the $50,000 selling price is received.**

| | |
|---|---|
| 2021 | $10,000 × ($30,000 ÷ $50,000) = $6,000 |
| 2022 & 2023 | $20,000 × ($30,000 ÷ $50,000) = $12,000 |

**In addition, Lene has interest income of $3,200 ($40,000 × 8%) on the outstanding balance in 2022 and $1,600 ($20,000 × 8%) in 2023.**

The use of the installment method by other taxpayers has been severely restricted in recent years (i.e., dealers in property generally cannot use the installment sales method).

### Long-Term Construction Contracts

Taxpayers in the construction industry typically undertake projects that span a number of years and must be accounted for by using the **percentage-of-completed-contract method**. As the name of the method implies, income is recognized according to the amount of work completed on the contract each year. The work completed must be based on costs incurred during the year in relation to the estimated total costs of the project.

**Example 70** Acme Construction Corporation enters into a 3-year contract in 2021 to construct a bridge for Garden City. The contract price for the bridge is $10,000,000, and Acme estimates its total cost of building the bridge to be $8,000,000. In 2021, Acme's actual costs were $2,000,000. How much gross income from the contract must Acme report in 2021?

**Discussion: Using the percentage-of-completion method, Acme reports gross income from the contract of $2,500,000 in 2021.**

$$\text{Work completed} = (\$2{,}000{,}000 \div \$8{,}000{,}000) = 25\%$$
$$\text{Grossincome} = 25\% \times \$10{,}000{,}000 = \$2{,}500{,}000$$

With the passage of the 2017 TCJA, a taxpayer who meets the $25 million gross receipts test (increased to $26 million in 2021) and enters into a contract after December 31, 2017, for the construction or improvement of real property is not required to use the percentage of completion me-thod if the work will be completed within two years after the date construction begins.

To ensure that contractors do not manipulate their income by inaccurately estimating contract costs, a look-back rule is applied at the completion of the contract, and interest is charged on any deficient income reporting.

# CHAPTER SUMMARY

This chapter focused on the determination of taxable income sources. In general, a taxpayer is in receipt of income when an increase in wealth is realized. Realization requires a change in the form or substance of a taxpayer's property or property rights and the involvement of a second party in an arm's-length transaction.

The four primary sources of income are earned income (income from labor), unearned income (income from investments), transfers from others (increases in wealth that are not the result of either labor or investment), and imputed income (increases in wealth realized because another party confers an economic advantage). Within each of these categories are various problems of realization and recognition. In most instances, application of the income tax concepts provides a solution to the problem. In other cases, the treatment is prescribed by law and must be learned through study and experience. To aid you in reviewing these sources of income, Table 3-5 classifies the income items discussed in this chapter and summarizes the major problems within each category of income.

Capital gains and losses are subject to special reporting rules. All capital gains and losses for a tax year are segregated from other forms of income and subjected to the capital gain-and-loss netting procedure. The purpose of the capital gain-and-loss netting procedure is to reduce a taxpayer's capital gain and loss transactions for the tax year to a net figure that represents the gain or loss for the year. Net long-term capital gains of individuals and eligible dividend income are taxed at a rate of 15 percent and 20 percent based on breakpoints that are adjusted annually for inflation. Up to $3,000 of net capital losses of individuals are deductible for adjusted gross income. Any excess losses are carried forward to the next year's netting.

The period in which an item of income is recognized is determined by the taxpayer's method of accounting. The two basic accounting methods are the cash method and the accrual method, although some taxpayers may use a combination of the two methods called the *hybrid method*. Exceptions to the general recognition rules exist for certain installment sales and long-term construction contracts. Other specific recognition exceptions exist for both the cash and the accrual methods.

Table 3-5

## Income Sources by Class of Income

| | Income Sources | Major Problems |
|---|---|---|
| **Earned Income** | Wages and salaries<br>Tips, commissions, bonuses<br>Income from sole proprietorship—either the active conduct of a trade or business or the rendering of services<br>Income from illegal activities—gambling, drug dealing, racketeering, etc. | Assignment of income<br>What is a receipt? |
| **Unearned Income** | Income from investments—interest, dividends, rental income, royalty income, income from annuities, gains (losses) from the sale of investments<br>Income from investment in conduit entities | Definition of income from rents and royalties<br>Capital recovery on annuities<br>Calculation of gain (loss)<br>Income from conduit entity |
| **Transfers from Others** | Prizes and awards<br>Unemployment compensation<br>Social Security benefits<br>Alimony received—agreements executed before 1/1/19.<br>Death benefit payments | Exception for prizes and awards given to charity<br>Exception for employee awards for length of service or safety<br>Calculation of taxable portion of Social Security benefits<br>Front loading of alimony payments to disguise a property settlement<br>Child support payments disguised as alimony |
| **Imputed Income** | Below market-rate loans<br>Payment of expense by others<br>Bargain purchases | Exceptions for below market-rate loans<br>Gift vs. compensation for payment of expenses by others<br>Compensatory nature of bargain purchase |

# KEY TERMS

adjusted net capital gain (p. 3-28)
alimony (p. 3-18)
annuity (p. 3-10)
annuity exclusion ratio (p. 3-11)
bargain purchase (p. 3-24)
below market-rate loan (p. 3-20)
capital asset (p. 3-24)
cash-equivalent approach (p. 3-9)
child support payments (p. 3-18)
collectibles gains (p. 3-25)
collectibles losses (p. 3-25)
death benefit payments (p. 3-19)
deferral method (p. 3-35)
earned income (p. 3-8)
eligible dividends (p. 3-30)
holding period (p. 3-25)
hybrid method of accounting (p. 3-36)
imputed income (p. 3-20)
installment sale (p. 3-36)
long-term capital gain (p. 3-25)
long-term capital loss (p. 3-25)
net capital loss (p. 3-31)
net collectibles gain (p. 3-28)
net short-term capital gain (p. 3-28)
original issue discount (OID) security (p. 3-33)
percentage-of-completed-contract method (p. 3-37)
property settlement (p. 3-18)
savings bond (U.S. government-issued) (p. 3-34)
short-term capital gain (p. 3-25)
short-term capital loss (p. 3-25)
unearned income (p. 3-10)

# PRIMARY TAX LAW SOURCES

[1]Reg. Sec. 1.61-1—States that income can be realized in any form, including cash, services, and property received.

[2]Eisner v. Macomber, 252 U.S. 189 at 207 (1920)—In holding that a stock dividend did not constitute gross income, determined that income is derived from labor and capital.

[3]Eisner v. Macomber at 207.

[4]Cesarini v. Comm., 428 F.2d 812 (6th Cir. 1970)—In determining that cash found in a purchased piano was included in gross income, established that "treasure troves" constitute gross income.

[5]Helvering v. Bruun, 309 U.S. 461 (1940)—Held that a landlord realized gain on the forfeiture of a leasehold for the nonpayment of rent and that the increase in the value of the property was taxable even though the gain was not severed from the property. (Subsequently overturned by enactment of Sec. 109.)

[6]Helvering v. Bruun at 469.

[7]Sec. 109—States that gross income does not result from increases in the value of a property at the termination of a lease.

[8]Glenshaw Glass v. Comm., 348 U.S. 426 at 430–431 (1955)—Determined that income consists of undeniable accessions to wealth that are completely controlled by the taxpayer.

[9]Reg. Sec. 1.61-15—States that income from illegal activities is included in gross income.

[10]Sec. 72—Describes the general rules for the taxation of annuities and presents the formula for determining the amount of each payment that is taxable.

[11]Sec. 1001—Prescribes the calculation of gains and losses on dispositions of property; defines *amount realized* for purposes of determining gain or loss on dispositions.

[12]Sec. 1016—Provides the general rules for adjustments to basis of property for capital expenditures and recoveries of capital subsequent to purchase.

[13]Reg. Sec. 1.61-13—States that a partner's share of the partnership's income is included in the gross income of the partner.

[14]Sec. 74—States that prizes and awards are taxable; details situations under which a qualified prize or award may be excluded from income.

[15]Sec. 85—States that unemployment compensation payments received are taxable.

[16]Sec. 86—States that Social Security payments received are taxable for high-income taxpayers; provides the formula for determining the taxable portion of Social Security payments.

[17]Reg. Sec. 1.71-1—States that child support payments are not taxable.

[18]Sec. 71—States that *alimony* received is taxable; defines alimony and presents the required recapture for front loading of alimony payments.

[19]Reg. Sec. 1.71-IT—Discusses what constitutes a contingency related to a child.

[20]Sec. 7872—Prescribes the treatment of below market-rate (interest-free) loans and the exceptions to the below market-rate rules.

[21]Old Colony Trust Co. v. CIR, 279 U.S. 716 (1929)—Determined that the payment of a corporate officer's state and federal taxes by the corporation constituted gross income to the officer; established that payment of another's expense in an employment-related setting is compensation that is included in gross income.

[22]CIR v. Smith, 324 U.S. 695 (1945)—Held that selling stock to an employee at less than its fair market value constituted compensation received by the employee; established that a "bargain purchase" in an employment-related setting is included in gross income.

[23]Sec. 1221—Defines *capital assets.*

[24]Sec. 1222—Defines *short-term and long-term capital gains and losses*; prescribes the netting procedure used for capital gains and losses.

[25]Sec. 1223—Defines *holding period* for purposes of determining short-term and long-term classification of capital gains and losses.

[26]Sec. 1(h)—Defines *collectibles gains and losses* and *unrecaptured Section 1250 gains.* Prescribes the tax rates to be paid on capital gains.

[27]IRS Restructuring and Reform Act of 1998, Sec. 5000—Provides the netting rules for capital gains and losses in calculating the tax on capital gains.

[28]The Affordable Care Act of 2013 levied a surtax on unearned income of higher income individuals.

[29]Jobs and Growth Tax Relief Reconciliation Act of 2003—Reduces the tax rate on eligible dividend income to 15 percent (0 percent for taxpayers in the 10 percent or 15 percent brackets).

[30]Sec. 1211—Sets forth the limit on deductions of capital losses of corporations and individuals.

[31]Sec. 1212—Allows the carryforward of disallowed capital losses by individuals.

[32]Reg. Sec. 1.1211-1—Requires the deduction of short-term capital losses before long-term capital losses in determining the current year's capital loss deduction.

[33]Sec. 703—Requires a partnership to state separately the items of income, gain, losses, deductions, and credits provided in Sec. 702 in computing its taxable income. Sec. 702 requires partners to separately account for their share of capital gains and losses, gains and losses on the sale of certain types of business property, charitable contributions, foreign taxes, and other items as prescribed by the secretary of the Treasury. Sec. 1366 contains similar provisions for S corporations.

[34]Sec. 446—States general rules for methods of accounting, including the allowance of the cash and accrual methods.

[35]Reg. Sec. 1.446-1—Requires the use of the accrual method for sales and cost of goods sold for sales of inventories; allows accounting of other income and expenses with the cash basis. (The hybrid method is an acceptable accounting method.)

[36]Sec. 1273—Prescribes the methods for determining the amount of original issue discount to include in gross income.

[37]Sec. 1272—Provides for the inclusion of original issue discount on debt instruments in gross income. Allows the exclusion of U.S. savings bonds from the OID rules.

[38]Sec. 451—Sets forth general rules for taxable year of inclusion of gross income items.

[39]Reg. Sec. 1.61-8—States that gross income includes rental and royalty income and that advance receipts of rent are included in gross income in the year of receipt, regardless of the taxpayer's accounting method.

[40]The 2017 Tax Cut and Jobs Act - codifies in Sec. 452 Rev. Proc. 2004-34.

[41]Reg. Sec. 1.451-5—Specifies the conditions under which an accrual basis taxpayer can defer recognition of income from an advance receipt for goods.

[42]Sec. 453—Prescribes the required treatment of installment sales of property.

[43]Temp. Reg. Sec. 15a.453-1—Provides the calculations for determining the amount of income to be recognized under the installment method of accounting.

# DISCUSSION QUESTIONS

1. **LO1** How is the definition of *income* for income tax purposes different from the definition used by economists to measure income?

2. **LO1** One of Adam Smith's four criteria for evaluating a tax is certainty. Does the income tax definition of *gross income* promote certainty in the U.S. tax system? Explain.

3. **LO1** What is the difference between realized income and recognized income?

4. **LO1** Buford purchased a new automobile in March for $23,000. In April, he receives a $500 rebate check from the manufacturer. The rebate was paid to all customers who purchased one of the manufacturer's automobiles in March. Should Buford include the $500 rebate in his gross income? Explain.

5. **LO1** What is a cash equivalent? How does a cash equivalent affect the reporting of income?
6. **LO2** What type of income does a sole proprietor of a business receive?
7. **LO2** What is the difference between earned income and unearned income?
8. **LO2** How is the gross income from a rental property or a royalty property determined?
9. **LO2** Explain how the capital recovery concept applies to the taxation of annuities. Consider both purchased annuities and pension payments in your answer.
10. **LO2** Explain the difference in determining the amount of income recognized from a conduit entity versus a taxable entity.
11. **LO2** What effect does an asset's adjusted basis have in determining the gain or loss realized upon its sale?
12. **LO2** This chapter noted that returns on investment are taxable, whereas returns of investment are not taxable. What is the conceptual basis for this treatment? Cite examples of each type of return, and explain why they are or are not taxable.
13. **LO3** Prizes and awards are generally taxable. Under what conditions is the receipt of a prize or award not taxable?
14. **LO3** Are Social Security benefits taxable? Explain.
15. **LO3** How is the taxation of an alimony payment different from the taxation of a child support payment?
16. **LO3** What incentive does a taxpayer have to disguise a property settlement as an alimony payment?
17. **LO4** Does the tax treatment of below market-rate loans violate any income tax concepts? If so, how? Explain.
18. **LO4** Evaluate the following statement: Whenever another person pays an expense for you, you are in receipt of taxable income.
19. **LO4** What is a bargain purchase?
20. **LO5** How is capital gain income treated differently from other forms of income?
21. **LO5** What is the purpose of the capital gain-and-loss netting procedure?
22. **LO5** Are all losses realized on the sale of capital assets deductible?
23. **LO5** Why is it important that a conduit entity separate the reporting of its capital gains and losses from its report of other forms of income?
24. **LO6** Detail any significant differences in the recognition of income using the cash method and using the accrual method of accounting.
25. **LO6** Explain the hybrid method of accounting.
26. **LO7** How does the wherewithal-to-pay concept affect the tax treatment of prepaid income?
27. **LO7** Under what circumstances can the following taxpayers defer recognition of prepaid income beyond the year of receipt?
    a. A cash basis taxpayer
    b. An accrual basis taxpayer
28. **LO7** What is an installment sale?
29. **LO7** How is the degree of completion of a long-term construction contract determined?

## PROBLEMS

30. **LO1** Mitch travels extensively in his job as an executive vice president of Arthur Consulting Company. During the current year, he used frequent flier miles that he had obtained during his business travel to take his family on a vacation to Europe. The normal airfare for the trip would have been $6,000.
    a. Discuss whether Mitch has realized income from the use of the frequent flier miles for personal purposes.
    b. Will Mitch have to recognize any income from the use of the frequent flier miles? Explain.
31. **LO1** Two Sisters is a partnership that owns and operates a farm. During the current year, the partnership raised and harvested hay at a cost of $20,000. It then traded half the hay for quarter horse breeding stock—young horses worth $30,000. Two Sisters fed the remainder of the hay to the horses, which were worth $50,000 at the end of the year. How much income does the partnership have from these transactions during the current year?
32. **LO1** Darcy borrowed $4,000 in 2018 from her employer to purchase a new computer. She repays $1,000 of the loan plus 6 percent interest on the unpaid balance in 2018, 2019, and 2020. After closing a big deal in 2021, she receives the original loan agreement stamped "paid in full" across the face. Does Darcy have to recognize any income from the cancellation of the loan in 2021? Explain.

33. **LO1** In December, Hilga sells her German language translation business to Chia-Ching. The sales agreement includes a provision that for an extra $6,000, Hilga will not open another German language translation business in the area for two years. Chia-Ching pays Hilga the $6,000 in January. In June, Hilga opens a European language translation business in a neighboring state and advertises it in Chia-Ching's locality. Has Hilga realized income? If so, when does she realize the income?

34. **LO1** How much taxable income should each of the following taxpayers report?
    a. Kimo builds custom surfboards. During the current year, his total revenues are $90,000, and he incurs $30,000 in expenses. Included in the $30,000 is a $10,000 payment to Kimo's five-year-old son for services as an assistant.
    b. Manu gives hula lessons at a local bar. During the current year, she receives $9,000 in salary and $8,000 in tips. In addition, she engages in illegal behavior, for which she receives $10,000.

35. **LO2** In each of the following cases, determine who is taxed on the income:
    a. For $200, Lee purchases an old car that is badly in need of repair. He works on the car for three months and spends $300 on parts to restore it. Lee's son Jason needs $2,000 to pay his college tuition. Lee gives the car to Jason, who sells it for $2,000 and uses the money to pay his tuition.
    b. Erica loans a friend $20,000. The terms of the loan require the payment of $2,000 in interest each year to Erica's daughter. At the end of four years, the $20,000 loan principal is to be repaid to Erica. Erica's daughter will use the $2,000 to pay her college tuition.

36. **LO2** Determine whether Frank or Dorothy, Frank's friend, is taxed on the income in each of the following situations:
    a. Frank owns 8 percent bonds with a $10,000 face value. The bonds pay interest annually on June 30. On September 30, Frank makes a bona fide gift of the bonds to Dorothy.
    b. A few years ago, Frank wrote a best-selling book about computers. On August 1, he instructs the publisher to pay all future royalties to Dorothy.
    c. Frank owns 1,000 shares of Pujan stock. On May 1, Pujan declares a $12-per-share dividend to shareholders of record as of June 1. On May 15, Frank gives the Pujan stock to Dorothy. She receives the $12,000 dividend on June 30.

37. **LO2** In each of the following cases, determine who is taxed on the income:
    a. Camille owns several rental properties that produce $3,000 in income each month. Because of the age of the properties, Camille is concerned about her potential liability from accidents on the property. On June 1, she forms the CAM Rental Corporation and transfers ownership of the rental properties to the corporation. The tenants continue to pay Camille the monthly rent, which she deposits in her personal checking account.
    b. Jimbob owns royalty interests in several oil wells. On March 1, Jimbob instructs the payers of the royalties to pay half of each royalty payment to his son Joebob.
    c. Assume the same facts as in part b, except that on March 1, Jimbob gifts a half interest in each royalty contract to Joebob.

38. **LO1** Determine whether any income must be recognized in each of the following situations, as well as who must report income, how much that taxpayer should report, and when that taxpayer will report the income:
    a. Patz Corporation owns a gourmet restaurant. The restaurant needs to remodel its kitchen but is short of cash. Dennis owns Tucky's Accessories, a restaurant supply store. The manager of Patz makes a deal with Dennis to have Tucky's do the kitchen remodeling, in exchange for which Patz will cater Tucky's company picnic. Tucky's does the remodeling and Patz caters the picnic. It costs Patz $800 to cater the picnic, a job for which it would have charged $1,500.
    b. Geraldo is a sales manager who enjoys collecting antique guns. Geraldo attends various shows around the country at which collectors and dealers sell

and trade guns. During the current year, Geraldo sells 3 guns for a total of $6,200 (the cost of the guns to Geraldo was $4,000) and purchases 2 guns at a total cost of $2,400. In addition, he exchanges a gun for which he had paid $700 for another gun worth $800.

39. **LO2** Partha owns a qualified annuity that cost $52,000. Under the contract, when he reaches age 65, he will receive $500 per month until he dies. Partha turns 65 on June 1, 2021, and receives his first payment on June 3, 2021. How much gross income will Partha report from the annuity payments in 2021?

40. **LO2** Minnie owns a qualified annuity that cost $78,000. The annuity is to pay Minnie $650 per month for life after she reaches age 65. Minnie turns 65 on September 28, 2021, and receives her first payment on November 1, 2021.
    a. How much gross income does Minnie have from the annuity payments she receives in 2021?
    b. Shortly after receiving her payment on October 1, 2036, Minnie is killed in an automobile accident. How does the executor of Minnie's estate account for the annuity on her return for the year 2036?
    c. Assume that the accident does not occur until November 1, 2045. How does the executor of Minnie's estate account for the annuity on her 2045 return?

41. **LO2** Duc has been employed by Longbow Corporation for 25 years. During that time, he bought an annuity at a cost of $50 per month ($15,000 total cost). The annuity will pay him $200 per month after he reaches age 65. When Duc dies, his wife, Annika, will continue to receive the annuity until her death. Duc turns 65 in April 2021 and receives 8 payments on the contract. Annika is age 60 when the annuity payments begin.
    a. How much gross income does Duc have from the contract in the current year?
    b. Assume that Duc dies on April 2, 2031. How does Annika account for the contract in 2031?
    c. Assume the same facts as in part b and that Annika dies on August 4, 2038. How does the executor of Annika's estate account for the contract in the year of her death?

42. **LO2** Hank retires this year after working 30 years for Local Company. Per the terms of his employment contract, Hank is to receive a pension of $600 per month for the rest of his life. During the current year, he receives 7 pension payments from Local. At the time of his retirement, Hank is single and 67 years old.
    a. How much taxable income does Hank have if his employer's plan was noncontributory (i.e., Local Company paid the entire cost of the plan; Hank made no contributions to it)?
    b. How would your answer change if Hank had contributed $42,000 to the pension plan? Assume that the $42,000 had been included in Hank's income (i.e., he has already paid tax on the $42,000).
    c. What if Hank had contributed $42,000 to the plan and none of the $42,000 were taxed (i.e., the tax law allows certain pension contributions to go untaxed during the contribution period)?

43. **LO2** Ratliff Development Corporation purchases a tract of land in 2020 at a cost of $120,000 and subdivides the land into 30 building lots. The cost of subdividing is $6,000. In 2020, Ratliff installs roads and utilities at a cost of $36,000 and pays property taxes totaling $2,000 in 2020 and 2021. Interest paid on the loan used to purchase the land is $10,000 in 2020 and $6,000 in 2021. In 2021, Ratliff sells 10 lots for a total of $350,000. What is the corporation's gain or loss on the sale of the lots?

44. **LO2** The Rosco Partnership purchases a rental property in 2016 at a cost of $150,000. From 2016 through 2021, Rosco deducts $14,000 in depreciation on the rental. The partnership sells the rental property in 2021 for $160,000 and pays $9,000 in expenses related to the sale. What is Rosco's gain or loss on the sale of the rental property?

45. **LO2** Reddy owns common stock with a market value of $30,000. The stock pays a cash dividend of $1,200 per year (a 4 percent annual yield). Reddy is considering selling the stock, which she purchased 13 years ago for $10,000, and using the proceeds to purchase stock in another company with a 10 percent annual dividend yield. If Reddy's goal is to maximize future dividends on her common stock investments, should she make the sale and purchase the new shares? Assume that Reddy is in the 24 percent marginal tax rate bracket.

46. **LO2** How much income should the taxpayer recognize in each of the following situations? Explain.
   a. Julius owns a 25 percent interest in the Flyer Company, which is organized as a partnership. During the current year, he is paid $14,000 by Flyer as a distribution of earnings. Flyer's taxable income for the year (calculated without any payments made to partners) is $60,000.
   b. Felix owns 1,000 shares of Furr Company, which is a publicly traded corporation. Furr has 1,000,000 shares of stock outstanding during the current year. The company has a net income of $2,500,000 and pays out a $3 per share dividend during the current year.
   c. Andrea is the sole proprietor of Andrea's Art Shop. During the current year, Andrea's has total revenue of $157,000 and total expenses of $110,000. Andrea draws a monthly salary of $2,600 from the shop that is not included in the $110,000 in expenses.
   d. Maryanne owns 50 percent of the stock of Sterling Safe Company, an S corporation. During the current year, Sterling has a taxable income of $300,000 and pays out dividends of $120,000 to its shareholders.
   e. Assume the same facts as in part d, except that Sterling incurs a loss of $60,000 during the current year.

47. **LO2** Devi is the chief executive officer of Nishida Limited. Devi owns 20 percent of the common stock of Nishida. During the current year, Devi's salary is $60,000 and he receives a $30,000 bonus. Nishida has taxable income of $200,000 and pays $80,000 in cash dividends. How much gross income does Devi have if
   a. Nishida is a corporation?
   b. Nishida is an S corporation?

48. **LO3** Pablo wins a new automobile on a television game show. The car has a listed sticker price of $31,500. A dealer advertises the same car for $30,000. How much income does Pablo have from the receipt of the car? Explain.

49. **LO3** Determine the amount of income that must be recognized in each of the following cases:
   a. Ramona is a production supervisor for White Company. During the current year, her division had no accidents, and White rewarded the achievement with a $200 cash award to each employee in the division.
   b. Lenny retires from the Brice Company this year. At his retirement reception, the company gives him a set of golf clubs valued at $600 in appreciation of his years of loyal service.
   c. Fatima is named Humanitarian of the Year by Local City for her volunteer service. She receives a plaque and an all-expense-paid trip to Washington, D. C., where she will meet the president. The value of the trip is $1,400.
   d. Sook is a college professor specializing in computer chip development. During the current year, he publishes a paper that explains the design of a revolutionary new chip. Softmicro, Inc., awards him $10,000 for the best breakthrough idea of the year. Sook uses the money to purchase a computer workstation to use in his research.

50. **LO2, 3** Has the taxpayer in each of the following situations received taxable income? If so, when should the income be recognized? Explain.
   a. Charlotte is a lawyer who specializes in drafting wills. She wants to give her husband a new gazebo for Christmas. In November, she makes a deal with Joe,

a local handyman, to build a gazebo. In return, Charlotte is to draft a will for Joe's father. The gazebo normally would cost $3,000, which is approximately what Charlotte would charge for drafting the will. Joe builds the gazebo in time for Christmas. Charlotte drafts the will and delivers it to Joe the following January.

b. Ed buys 500 shares of Northstar stock in January 2020 for $4,000. On December 31, 2020, the shares are worth $4,600. In March 2021, Ed sells the shares for $4,500.

c. Dayo is the director of marketing for Obo, Inc. In December, the board of directors of Obo votes to give Dayo a $10,000 bonus for her excellent work throughout the year. The check is ordered and written on December 15 but is misplaced in the mail room and is not delivered to Dayo until January 5.

d. John is unemployed. During the current year, he receives $4,000 in unemployment benefits. Because the unemployment is not enough to live on, John sells drugs to support himself. His total revenue for the year is $120,000. The cost of the drugs is $60,000.

51. **LO3** Elwood is retired. During the current year, he receives $10,000 in Social Security benefits. In addition, he receives $6,000 in cash dividends on stocks that he owns and $8,000 in interest on tax-exempt bonds. Assuming that Elwood is single, what is his gross income if

a. He receives no other income?

b. He also receives $11,000 in unemployment compensation?

c. He sells some land for $80,000? He paid $45,000 for the land.

52. **LO3** Hermano and Rosetta are a retired couple who receive $10,000 in Social Security benefits during the current year. They also receive $3,000 in interest on their savings account and taxable pension payments of $28,000. What is their gross income if

a. They receive no other income?

b. They receive $13,000 in interest from tax-exempt bonds they own?

53. **LO3** Upon returning from lunch, you find the following message on your voice mail:

This is Jarrett Ogilvie. I'm not one of your clients, but I need some advice. I received a statement in the mail from the Social Security Administration reporting the $8,500 I received from them last year. It says that a portion of my Social Security may be taxable. Last year was the first year I ever received Social Security and I'm confused. I thought Social Security wasn't taxable. Could you call me and explain this?

What facts will you need from Jarrett to determine what portion, if any, of the $8,500 of Social Security benefits is taxable? In your answer, explain how different facts may lead to different taxable amounts.

54. **LO3** Will and Janine are divorced and their agreement is finalized in 2017. Will is to have custody of their two children and will receive their house as part of the divorce settlement.

The house, which Will and Janine bought for $60,000, is worth $100,000. Janine is to receive one of their automobiles, for which they paid $21,000 and which is now worth $9,000. Will will get the other automobile, which cost $6,000 and is worth $2,000. Janine is to pay Will alimony of $900 per month. However, the alimony payment is to be reduced by $200 per month as each child reaches age 18 or if a child should die or marry before reaching age 18.

a. What are the tax effects of the divorce settlement for Will and Janine?

b. Assume Will and Janine are divorced in 2021 what are the tax effects of their divorce?

55. **LO4** Which of the following interest-free loans are subject to the imputed interest rules?

a. Alamor Corporation loans Sandy, an employee, $8,000. The loan is to be repaid over four years. Sandy uses the proceeds to buy a used automobile. She has $1,100 in investment income during the current year.

b. Trinh loans her son Jimmy $80,000. The loan is to be repaid over 20 years. Jimmy uses the loan to purchase a cabin in the mountains. He has $300 in investment income during the current year.
c. Abdula Corporation loans Augie, an employee, $80,000. The loan is to be repaid over 20 years. Augie uses the loan to purchase a new house. He has $300 in investment income during the current year.
d. Isabel owns 10 percent of Marcos Corporation. Isabel loans Marcos $20,000 to use for working capital. The loan is to be repaid over five years. Marcos has no investment income during the current year.
e. Stuart loans his sister Sima $120,000. The loan is to be repaid over 20 years. Sima uses the loan to purchase a new home. She has no investment income during the current year.

56. **LO4** Laura makes the following interest-free loans during the current year. Discuss the income tax implications of each loan for both Laura and the borrower. In all cases, the applicable federal interest rate is 8 percent.
a. On April 15, Laura loans $30,000 to her brother Hyun to pay his income taxes. Hyun is financially insolvent and has no sources of investment income.
b. On March 1, Laura loans $12,000 to her secretary, George. He uses the money as a down payment on a new house.
c. On July 1, Laura loans her father $150,000. He uses the money to buy a franchise to open a yogurt store. He makes $5,000 on the yogurt store during the current year.
d. On January 1, Laura loans $70,000 to Lotta, Inc. She is the sole shareholder of Lotta, Inc., which is organized as a corporation.

57. **LO4** On January 1, Wilton loans Andy $90,000. The loan is to be repaid in five years with no interest charged. The applicable federal rate is 5 percent. Discuss the treatment of the loan for both Wilton and Andy in each of the following independent situations:
a. Andy is Wilton's son, and he uses the loan to purchase a new home. Andy has investment income of $600 during the year.
b. Andy is Wilton's son, and he uses the loan to purchase investment property. Andy's net income from all investments for the year is $1,800.
c. Assume the same facts as in part b, except that Andy is an employee of Wilton's.
d. Assume the same facts as in part b, except that Andy is a shareholder in Wilton's corporation, which makes the loan to Andy.

58. **LO4** Determine whether the following taxpayers have gross income from the payment of their expenses:
a. Julia's mother, Henrietta, is short of cash when it comes time to pay her property taxes. Julia pays Henrietta's property taxes of $350.
b. Kurt fell asleep at the wheel one night and crashed his car into a telephone pole. Repairs to the car cost $600. Kurt isn't covered by insurance and doesn't have the cash to pay the repair shop. Because he needs his car in his job as a salesman, his employer pays the repair bill.
c. Leonard leases a building from the PLC Partnership for $800 per month. The lease agreement requires Leonard to pay the property taxes of $1,100 on the building.
d. On July 1, Gino bought some land from Harco Corporation for $14,000. As part of the sales agreement, Gino agrees to pay the property taxes of $700 for the year. Harco had paid $10,000 for the land.

59. **LO4** Reggie works during the summer for Dan the Screenman. Dan pays Reggie $4,300 in salary, saves Reggie $200 on free screens for Reggie's father's house, and agrees to pay Reggie's fall college tuition of $2,100. How much gross income does Reggie have from this arrangement?

60. **LO4** Aziza is the sole owner of Azi's Fast Pizza. During the current year, Azi's replaces its fleet of delivery vehicles. Aziza's son purchases one of the old vehicles for

$500, its tax basis to Azi's. Similar vehicles are sold for $4,000. What tax problem is posed by this situation? Explain who, if anyone, should report income from the transaction.

61. **LO4** Determine whether the taxpayer has income that is subject to taxation in each of the following situations:
   a. Capital Motor Company is going out of business. As a result, June is able to purchase a car for $12,000; its original sticker price was $25,000.
   b. Chuck is the sole owner of Ransom, Inc., a corporation. He purchases a machine from Ransom for $10,000. Ransom had paid $50,000 for the machine, which was worth $30,000 at the time of the sale to Chuck.
   c. Gerry is an elementary school teacher. She receives the Teacher of the Month Award for February. As part of the award, she gets to drive a new car supplied by a local dealer for a month. The rental value of the car is $400 per month.
   d. Payne has worked for Stewart Company for the last 25 years. On the 25th anniversary of his employment with Stewart, he receives a set of golf clubs worth $1,200 as a reward for his years of loyal service to the company.
   e. Anna enters a sweepstakes contest that was advertised on the back of a cereal box, and wins $30,000. The prize will be paid out in 30 annual installments of $1,000. She receives her first check this year.
   f. Terry buys an antique vase at an estate auction for $780. Upon returning home, she accidentally drops the vase and finds that a $100 bill had been taped inside it.

62. **LO5** Pedro purchases 50 shares of Piper Company stock on February 19, 2018, at a cost of $4,300. He sells the 50 shares on July 2, 2021, for $9,000. On March 14, 2021, Pedro purchases 100 shares of Troxel stock for $9,700. He sells the Troxel shares on December 18, 2021, for $6,600. What is the effect of the stock sales on Pedro's 2021 income?

63. **LO5** Rikki has the following capital gains and losses for the current year:

| | |
|---|---|
| Short-term capital gain | $ 1,000 |
| Long-term capital gain | 11,000 |
| Long-term capital loss | 3,000 |
| Collectibles gain | 8,000 |
| Collectibles loss | 2,000 |

What is the effect of the capital gains and losses on Rikki's taxable income and her income tax liability? Assume that Rikki is in the 32 percent marginal tax rate bracket.

64. **LO5** Polly has the following capital gains and losses for the current year:

| | |
|---|---|
| Short-term capital gain | $ 1,000 |
| Short-term capital loss | 8,000 |
| Long-term capital gain | 5,000 |
| Collectibles gain | 16,000 |
| Collectibles loss | 3,000 |

What is the effect of the capital gains and losses on Polly's taxable income and her income tax liability? Assume that Polly is in the 35 percent marginal tax rate bracket and her adjusted gross income is $225,000.

65. **LO5** Erin, a single taxpayer, has a taxable income of $168,000 in the current year before considering the following capital gains and losses:

| | |
|---|---|
| Short-term capital gain | $ 3,000 |
| Long-term capital gain | 22,000 |
| Unrecaptured Section 1250 gain | 14,000 |

In addition, Erin has an $8,000 long-term capital loss carryover from last year. What are the effects of these transactions on Erin's taxable income and her income tax liability?

66. **LO5** Jason and Jill are married and have a six-year-old daughter. During the year, they sell one acre of land for $80,000. Three years ago, they paid $70,000 for two acres of land. Their other income and deductions are as follows:

| | |
|---|---|
| Jill's commissions | $ 82,000 |
| Jason's salary | 46,000 |
| Dividend income | 5,000 |
| Interest income | 8,000 |
| Short-term loss on sale of stock in Nippon Inc. | 15,000 |
| Deductions for adjusted gross income | 28,000 |

Calculate Jason and Jill's taxable income and income tax liability for the current year.

67. **LO5** Jennifer is single and has the following income and expenses:

| | |
|---|---|
| Salary | $ 76,000 |
| Interest income | 5,000 |
| Dividend income | 9,000 |
| Long-term capital gain | 10,000 |
| Short-term capital loss | 14,000 |
| Deductions for AGI | 3,000 |
| Deductions from AGI | 14,000 |

Calculate Jennifer's taxable income and income tax liability.

68. **LO5** Herbert and Geraldine have a taxable income of $28,000 before considering the gain they realize on the sale of 500 shares of Olebolla Corporation common stock for $26 per share. Herbert had acquired the shares for $3 per share while he worked for Olebolla through the company's employee incentive program. He retired from the company five years ago. What is the effect of the sale on Herbert and Geraldine's taxable income and their income tax liability?

69. **LO5** Jawan has the following capital gains and losses in the current year:

| | |
|---|---|
| Short-term capital gain | $ 500 |
| Short-term capital loss | 3,000 |
| Long-term capital gain | 6,000 |
| Long-term capital loss | 12,000 |
| Collectibles gain | 2,000 |

What is the effect of the capital gains and losses on Jawan's taxable income?

70. **LO5** Refer to problem 71. In the following year, Jawan has the following capital gains and losses:

| | |
|---|---|
| Short-term capital loss | $ 1,300 |
| Long-term capital gain | 8,600 |
| Long-term capital loss | 4,100 |

What is the effect of the capital gains and losses on his taxable income?

71. **LO5** During the current year, Inge sells stock purchased three years ago at a loss of $9,000. She also owns a 10 percent interest in Chatham, Inc., which is organized as an S corporation. Chatham reports ordinary income of $80,000 and a short-term capital gain of $30,000 during the current year. What are the effects of these two investments on Inge's taxable income?

72. **LO5** Ozzello Property Management is organized as a partnership. The owners, Lorenzo, Erwin, and Michelle, share profits and losses 30:30:40. Ozzello has the following results for the current year:

| | |
|---|---|
| Management fees | $230,000 |
| Long-term gain on sale of investments | 22,000 |
| Short-term loss on sale of investments | 4,000 |
| Salaries paid to employees | 67,000 |
| Office rent | 43,000 |
| Office expenses | 19,000 |

Determine each partner's share of Ozzello's taxable income for the current year.

73. **LO5** Ramona owns 20 percent of the stock of Miller, Inc. Miller reports the following items for the current year:

| | |
|---|---|
| Sales | $3,400,000 |
| Gain on sale of stock held for two years | 250,000 |
| Cost of goods sold | 1,800,000 |
| Operating expenses | 900,000 |
| Dividends paid to stockholders | 180,000 |

What are the effects on Ramona's taxable income if Miller, Inc., is organized as

a. A corporation?

b. An S corporation?

Communication Skills

74. **LO5** Chloe and Emma start a new business, Cement Sidewalks and Accessories (CSA), during the current year. CSA is organized as a partnership. Chloe owns 40 percent of CSA; Emma owns the remaining 60 percent. Chloe and Emma come to your firm for advice on the tax consequences of their business. Your supervisor gives you the following information, as prepared by Chloe and Emma for their first year of operation:

| | |
|---|---|
| Sales | $ 210,000 |
| Cost of materials | (95,000) |
| Labor costs | (90,000) |
| Other expenses | (55,000) |
| Loss on sale of stock | (18,000) |
| Cash withdrawals by partners | (70,000) |
| Loss | $ (118,000) |

Prepare a memo for your supervisor explaining the ramifications of CSA's first-year results for Chloe's and Emma's tax liabilities.

75. **LO6** During the last five months of the year, Dwana opens a new Internet telecommunications business called Dwan-Com. Dwan-Com bills $50,000 of revenues, but receives only $40,000 cash. Dwan-Com incurs $3,000 of supply expenses, and $41,000 of labor costs. Dwan-Com pays for $2,200 of the supplies and $38,000 of the labor costs in the current year. Dwan-Com is a c-corporation.

a. What is Dwan-Com's taxable income if it elects the cash method of accounting?

b. What is Dwan-Com's taxable income if it elects the accrual method of accounting?

c. What method of accounting do you recommend that Dwan-Com elect?

76. **LO6** Bonnie opens a computer sales and repair service during the current year. Her records for the year show:

| | Sales Made | Cash Received | Liability Incurred | Cash Paid |
|---|---|---|---|---|
| Repair revenue | $ 30,000 | $ 22,000 | | |
| Computer sales | 26,000 | 18,000 | | |
| Computer purchases | | | $ 55,000 | $ 27,500 |
| Employee wages | | | 12,000 | 10,000 |
| Supplies, utilities, etc. | | | 9,000 | 6,000 |

Bonnie has computers on hand on December 31 that cost $40,000 and have a retail selling price of $65,000.

Bonnie needs help figuring her taxable income. Is more than one income figure possible? If so, explain why, and compute taxable income under the various methods.

77. **LO6** Arlene is a lawyer. She begins the current year with $12,000 in accounts receivable from customers. During the year, she bills customers $210,000 in fees and receives $180,000 in payments on account. She writes off $8,000 of the

receivables as uncollectable, leaving her a year-end receivable balance of $34,000. What is Arlene's gross income if

a. She uses the cash basis of accounting?
b. She uses the accrual basis of accounting?

78. **LO6, 7** Determine how much interest income Later Federal Loan Company, a cash basis taxpayer, must recognize on each of the following loans in 2021:
   a. A $10,000, 8.5 percent, 6-month loan made on October 1, 2021. The principal and interest are due on April 1, 2022.
   b. A $10,000, six-month loan, discounted at 8 percent on October 1, 2021. Later gives the borrower $9,615, and the borrower must repay the $10,000 face amount on April 1, 2022.
   c. A $10,000, two-year loan, discounted at 6 percent on October 1, 2021. Later gives the borrower $8,900; the $10,000 face amount is to be repaid on October 1, 2023.

79. **LO6, 7** In January 2021, Conan, a cash basis taxpayer, purchases for $4,000 a Series EE savings bond with a maturity value of $4,800 (a 6 percent annual yield). At the same time, he also purchases for $5,000 a three-year bank certificate of deposit with a maturity value of $6,650 (a 10 percent annual yield). Both securities mature in 2023. Must Conan recognize any income in 2021? How much income must Conan recognize in 2023?

80. **LO6, 7** Lorene, Inc., owns an apartment complex. The terms of Lorene's lease agreement require new tenants to pay the first and last month's rent and a cleaning deposit at the inception of the lease. The cleaning deposit is returned when tenants move out and leave their apartment in good condition. If the apartment is not in good condition, Lorene hires a cleaning company and uses the tenant's deposit to pay the cleaning bill, with any excess deposit returned.

    During the current year, Lorene receives monthly rents totaling $28,000, last month's rent deposits from new tenants of $8,000, and cleaning deposits of $7,000. Lorene keeps $5,000 in cleaning deposits to pay the cleaning company bill on apartments that are not left in good shape (the $5,000 is the actual cost that is paid in cash to the cleaning company) and returns $4,000 in deposits. Lorene's expenses related to the rental property (other than the cleaning costs) are $14,000. What is Lorene, Inc.'s gross income from the rental property if Lorene is a cash basis taxpayer? an accrual basis taxpayer?

81. **LO7** Determine the proper year(s) for reporting the income in each of the following cases:
   a. Lagoon Inc., an accrual basis taxpayer, owns an amusement park. The park is open April through September. In October, Lagoon begins selling discounted season passes for the upcoming season. By the end of the year, Lagoon has received $40,000 from the advance sale of the discounted passes.
   b. Arnie sells and repairs televisions. In December of the current year, a customer special-orders a television that retails for $2,600 (Arnie's cost is $1,300). Arnie requires the customer to prepay $1,500 as a condition of placing the order.
   c. Quick Systems, Inc., an accrual basis taxpayer, leases out computer equipment. During December, Quick receives $22,000 from customers as advance rent for January.
   d. Trinh is a service representative for Harrington Corporation. Trinh and Harrington are cash basis taxpayers. In addition to her salary, Trinh receives a bonus equal to 5 percent of all receipts collected from her customers during the year. On December 30, a customer gives her a $5,000 check payable to Harrington for Trinh's work during the current year. Trinh returns to her office on January 3 and promptly gives the check to the company's controller.

82. **LO7** How much income would an accrual basis taxpayer report in 2021 in each of the following situations?
   a. Toby's Termite Services, Inc., provides monthly pest control on a contract basis. Toby sells a one-year contract for $600 and a two-year contract for $1,080. In October, Toby sells 10 one-year contracts and five two-year contracts.

b. John's Tractor Sales receives a $150 deposit from a customer for a new tractor that the customer orders in December. The tractor arrives the following February, at which time the customer pays the remaining $9,800 of the agreed-upon sales price.
c. A customer of First Financial Lending sends First Financial two $600 checks in December in payment of December and January interest on a loan.
d. First Financial Lending receives interest payments totaling $8,400 in January 2022 in payment of December 2021 interest on loans.

83. **LO7** Daryl purchases land in 2017 at a cost of $65,000. In 2021, he sells the land for $100,000.
a. How much gain or loss does Daryl realize on the sale of the land?
b. Assume that the sales contract on the land calls for the buyer to pay Daryl $40,000 at the time of sale and $15,000 per year for the next four years with interest on the unpaid balance at 8 percent. How much income must Daryl recognize in 2021? In 2022?

84. **LO7** In 2018, Patricia purchases a rental property as an investment at a cost of $60,000. From 2018 through 2021, she takes $7,000 in depreciation on the property. In 2021, Patricia sells the rental property for $80,000, payable at $20,000 per year for four years with interest on the unpaid balance at 10 percent.
a. How much income or loss must Patricia recognize in 2021?
b. Assume that in addition to the sale of the rental property, Patricia sells other capital assets that result in a loss of $28,000. What would you recommend that Patricia do regarding the gain on the sale of the rental property?

85. **LO7** WCM Builders enters into a contract to build a shopping mall in 2020 for $6,000,000. Completion of the mall is expected to take 27 months and cost WCM $3,600,000. Upon signing the contract, WCM receives $600,000. During 2021, WCM incurs costs of $1,200,000 and receives a $1,000,000 progress payment. WCM's forewoman estimates that the job is 50 percent complete at the end of 2021. How much income must WCM recognize in 2021 from the work done on the mall?

86. **LO7** Quapaw Construction Company enters into an agreement with Paine County to resurface 30 miles of highway. The contract is for $600,000. Quapaw estimates its total cost of the project to be $500,000. During the current year, Quapaw completes 18 miles of resurfacing, incurs $250,000 in actual costs, and receives $300,000 in advance payments on the project. How much income will Quapaw have to recognize during the current year?

## ISSUE IDENTIFICATION PROBLEMS

In each of the following problems, identify the tax issue(s) posed by the facts presented. Determine the possible tax consequences of each issue that you identify.

87. During her vacation, Janita found a gold bar from a sunken ship while she was scuba diving off Texas.

88. Herman sells his carpet-cleaning business to Elki. As part of the sales agreement, Elki pays Herman $3,000 for his agreement not to open another carpet-cleaning business in the area for three years.

89. In 2015, Awnings, Inc., issues $200,000 of 15 percent, 20-year bonds payable at par. During 2021, when Awnings' bonds are trading at 93, the company purchases and retires $100,000 par value of the bonds.

90. Merlene owns a bookstore. The store needs repainting, but she is short of cash to hire a painter. Fred is a painter who enjoys fine mystery novels. Merlene makes a deal with Fred to have him paint the bookstore for any 30 mystery novels Merlene has in stock. Fred paints the store and selects novels that cost Merlene $250 and had a retail selling price of $480.

91. Simon and Sherry divorce during the current year. As part of their property settlement, Simon gives Sherry 25 percent of the stock in his 100 percent-owned corporation, Hobday, Inc. The stock has a fair market value of $80,000. Rather than pay Sherry any alimony, Simon agrees to make her a vice president of Hobday with an annual salary of $70,000. In her position, Sherry has no responsibilities or involvement with the company.
92. Gilbert got married this year. Because he couldn't afford a wedding reception, his employer gave him the $5,000 he needed to pay for it.
93. Meek, Inc., remodeled its offices this year. Renee, the executive vice president, bought the desk, couch, and lamp set that had been in her office for $200.
94. RealTime Rentals leases space on its Internet server. Its standard one-year lease agreement requires new customers to pay the first and last months' rent upon signing the lease and a $500 deposit that is returned after the customer has been with RealTime for one year.
95. Tonya purchased land for investment purposes in 2018 for $21,000. In 2021, she sells the land for $36,000. The terms of the sale require the purchaser to pay Tonya $12,000 per year for three years with interest of 6 percent on the unpaid balance. Tonya also sells stock that she paid $28,000 for in 2019 for $16,000.

## TECHNOLOGY APPLICATIONS

96. Gloria sells land that she held as an investment for $2,000 to the Lacy for Senate Campaign Committee. Gloria purchased the land 20 years ago for $2,000. The chairman of the Lacy for Senate Campaign Committee intends to sell the land at an auction of Lacy supporters and use the proceeds to purchase television commercial time. He believes that he can sell the land for at least $15,000 to a Lacy supporter at the auction. Tax Simulation

    REQUIRED: Determine the income tax treatment of Gloria's sale to the Lacy for Senate Campaign Committee. Use a tax research database and find the relevant authority(ies) that form the basis for your answer. Your answer should include the exact text of the authority(ies) and an explanation of the application of the authority to Gloria's sale. If there is any uncertainty regarding the tax treatment of the sale, explain what is uncertain and what you need to know to resolve the uncertainty.

97. A stock appreciation right (SAR) entitles the holder of the right to a cash payment equal to the difference between the fair market value of the stock on the date the SAR is exercised and the fair market value of a share on the date the SAR is granted. In 2019, L&M Corporation grants 1,000 SARs to Jasmine, an employee of L&M. On the date of the grant, the L&M stock sells for $30 per share. On December 31, 2019, the stock sells for $40; it sells for $50 on December 31, 2020, and for $55 on December 31, 2021. Jasmine exercises the SARs on December 31, 2021. When does she recognize income from the SARs, and what is the character of the income recognized? Research Skills
98. Julio and Rosetta are retired and receive $12,000 in Social Security benefits during the current year. They also receive $10,000 in interest and taxable pension payments of $30,000. Prepare a spreadsheet calculating the amount of Social Security income that is included in their gross income and their adjusted gross income. The spreadsheet should be able to handle changes in their marital status (e.g., if Julio dies) or their income. Spreadsheet Skills

Tax Form

99. Marvin and Tracy Peery's 2020 taxable income is $87,830 before considering the effect of their investment activities. The details of their 2020 sales of investment assets follow:

| Security | Sale Date | Purchase Date | Sales Price | Commissions Paid | Basis |
|---|---|---|---|---|---|
| Jobe Tool Inc. | 02/19/20 | 11/15/19 | $14,500 | $400 | $11,000 |
| Gilly Corporation | 04/30/20 | 03/02/18 | $ 8,800 | $300 | $ 2,900 |
| Skyelab Inc. | 12/14/20 | 04/30/18 | $ 8,000 | $275 | $ 8,525 |

The Form 1099 Marvin and Tracy received from their broker indicated total sales of $30,325 (i.e., sales were reported net of commissions). In addition, on July 19, Marvin sells a Barry Sanders football card for $600. He paid $20 for the card in June 2006.

Marvin and Tracy ask you to prepare their 2020 Schedule D. Their 2019 schedule D indicates that they had a $4,500 net long-term capital loss in 2019. Marvin's Social Security number is 567-22-3495 and Tracy's is 654-33-8790. Forms and instructions can be downloaded from the IRS Web site (www.irs.gov).

## DISCUSSION CASES

100. Yung is the sole owner of Southern Hills Insurance Agency. His primary business is the sale of fire and casualty policies. He has recently expanded his business by selling life insurance policies. Under his agreement with Heart Life Insurance Company, he receives a basic commission on each policy he sells. The basic commission is equal to the cost of the insurance minus the first year's premium. Under the agreement, Yung collects the cost of the insurance policy and remits the first-year premium to the company. He is also entitled to an override commission, which is paid on subsequent years' premiums. To build up his life insurance business, Yung enters into separate contracts with clients in which he agrees to act as an insurance consultant for a fee that is equal to the first-year premium. The client pays Yung the fee, which he remits to Heart Life. This contract effectively waives Yung's basic commission and offers the insurance at a discounted price, a practice that is illegal under state law. During the current year, Yung sold policies that had a cost of $50,000 and first-year premiums of $18,000 (which were remitted to Heart Life). He also received $11,000 in override commissions from policies sold in previous years. How much income must Yung report from the life insurance policies in the current year? Explain.

101. Kerry is employed as a ticket vendor at an off-track betting parlor in New York. No credit is extended to customers, and employees are not allowed to bet on races. Kerry is a compulsive gambler and occasionally places bets without paying for them. In the past, she has always managed to cover her bets without being detected by her employer. Earlier this year, Kerry ran up $80,000 in bets that she did not pay for and won only $33,000. She was unable to cover this large loss and turned herself in to her employer. Kerry was convicted of grand larceny and sentenced to five years of probation, required to perform 200 hours of community service, and pay a $500 fine. Her employer was liable to the racetrack for the bets she had made and obtained a judgment against her for the $47,000 shortfall it had to pay because of her indiscretions. How much, if any, gross income must Kerry recognize from her illegal betting?

## TAX PLANNING CASES

102. Nick and Jolene are married. Nick is 61 and retired in 2020 from his job with Amalgamated Company. Jolene is 56 and works part-time as a special education

teacher. Nick and Jolene have a substantial amount of investment savings and would like to reorganize it to achieve the best after-tax return on their investments. They give you the following list of projected cash receipts for 2021:

| | |
|---|---|
| Jolene's salary | $ 29,000 |
| Nick's pension—fully taxable | 12,500 |
| Interest income | 4,000 |
| Dividend income | 2,500 |
| Social Security benefits | 7,000 |
| Farmer's Fund annuity | 6,000 |

In addition, Nick tells you that he owns a duplex that he rents out. The duplex rents for 2021 are $18,000, and Nick estimates expenses of $22,000 related to the duplex. The annuity was purchased 18 years ago for $20,000, and pays $500 per month for 10 years.

Nick and Jolene's investments consist of the following:

| | |
|---|---|
| 6-month certificates of deposit (CDs) | $ 100,000 |
| 1,000 shares of Lardee's common stock (current market value = $7 per share, projected 2020 dividend = $1 per share)—cost | 10,000 |
| 2,000 shares of Corb Company common stock (current market value = $20 per share, projected 2020 dividend = $.75 per share)—cost | 20,000 |

a. Assuming that Nick and Jolene have total allowable itemized deductions of $18,000 in 2021. Determine their 2021 taxable income and tax liability based on the projections they gave you.

b. The six-month CDs consist of two $50,000 certificates, both of which yield 4 percent interest. One CD matures on January 3, 2021. Nick's banker tells him that he can renew the CD for one year at 4 percent. Nick's stockbroker tells him that he can purchase tax-exempt bonds with a yield of 3 percent. Nick would like you to determine whether the tax-exempt bonds provide him a better after-tax return than the CD.

c. Jolene is concerned that they are not getting the best return on their Corb Company stock. When they purchased the stock in 2010, the $.75 per share dividend was yielding 10 percent before taxes. However, the rise in market value has far outpaced the dividend growth, and it is yielding only 3.75 percent, based on the current market value. Jolene thinks they should sell the stock and purchase either the 3 percent tax-exempt securities or the 4 percent CD if it would be a better deal from an income tax viewpoint. Calculate the tax effect on their 2021 income of selling the shares, and determine whether they should sell the shares and invest the after-tax proceeds in tax-exempt securities or the 4 percent CD. Do this calculation after you have determined the best option regarding the CD that matures in January.

103. Peter is a professor of mathematics at State University. His lifetime avocation has been sailing, and he owns an oceangoing sailing vessel. He plans to retire in five years and spend the remainder of his life "plying" the South Pacific, visiting exotic ports of call. Accordingly, in five years, he plans to convert all his assets into a single-life annuity that is payable monthly into a bank account which he can access from anywhere in the world.

He currently owns four residential lots in Miller Beach that he purchased as an investment in 1988 for $6,000. Peter has received an offer of $140,000 for the lots. He estimates that the lots will appreciate during the next five years at an 11 percent annual rate.

If he sells the lots, Peter will invest the proceeds in his portfolio of stocks. He invests in growth securities paying negligible dividends that provide their return through appreciation. Peter expects his security portfolio to increase an average of 12 percent per annum. The risk of real estate in Miller Beach is approximately equal to that of growth stocks.

Peter asks you to evaluate each of the following alternatives and make a recommendation on which course of action he should pursue.

Alternative 1. Sell the beach property now, reinvest the net proceeds in stock, sell the stock in five years, and retire.

Alternative 2. Continue to hold the beach property for another five years, sell the lots, and retire.

## ETHICS DISCUSSION CASE

Communication Skills

104. The Gallery is an indoor recreational facility. It employs 95 minimum-wage employees and 7 management-level staffers. During the past month, all employees participated in a promotion to enhance sales by distributing discount coupons to potential customers. The employee who had the most coupons redeemed was to receive a $150 credit toward the purchase of a mountain bike. The general manager won the coupon promotion. After accepting the $150 credit, he instructed the controller, Aretha, not to include the $150 on his pay stub or on his Form W-2. Aretha is a CPA and a member of the AICPA. You prepare the tax return for the gallery. Aretha has advised you of the situation regarding the general manager; she is concerned about the effect on her career of following the general manager's instructions. Prepare a letter to Aretha explaining the potential ramifications of following the general manager's instructions and what actions, if any, she should take to avoid adverse career effects

# Income Exclusions

4

## Learning Objectives:

LO 1 Explain the requirements for the exclusion of an item of income and the rationale for excluding items from gross income.

LO 2 Identify the allowable exclusions for donative items of income: gifts, inheritances, life insurance proceeds, and scholarships.

LO 3 Describe the effect of employment-related exclusions on the after-tax compensation of employees.

LO 4 Explain the nontaxable fringe benefits that a business may provide to its employees.

LO 5 Identify payments that represent returns of human capital and are excluded from income as capital recoveries: workers' compensation, damage payments for personal physical injuries, and medical expense reimbursement payments.

LO 6 Explain the exclusions from income allowed for investment-related items: municipal bond interest, stock dividends, discharge of indebtedness, and improvements by a lessee.

## concept review

### GENERAL CONCEPTS

**Administrative convenience** Those items for which the cost of compliance would exceed the revenue generated are not taxed. pg. 2-3

### ACCOUNTING CONCEPTS

**Substance over form** Transactions are to be taxed according to their true intention rather than some form that may have been contrived. pg. 2-11

**Tax benefit rule** Any deduction taken in a prior year that is recovered in a subsequent year is income in the year of recovery, to the extent that a tax benefit was received from the deduction. pg. 2-10

### INCOME CONCEPTS

**All-inclusive income** All income received is taxable unless a specific provision can be found in the tax law that either excludes the income from taxation or defers its recognition to a future tax year. pg. 2-12

**Claim of right** A realization occurs whenever an amount is received without any restriction as to its disposition. pg. 2-14

**Legislative grace** Any tax relief provided is the result of a specific act of Congress that must be strictly applied and interpreted. All income received is taxable unless a specific provision in the tax law excludes the income from taxation. Deductions must be approached with the philosophy that nothing is deductible unless a provision in the tax law allows the deduction. pg. 2-12

**Realization** No income (or loss) is recognized until it has been realized. A realization involves a change in the form and/or the substance of a taxpayer's property rights that results from an arm's-length transaction. pg. 2-14

**Wherewithal to pay** Income is recognized in the period in which the taxpayer has the means to pay the tax on the income. pg. 2-16

### DEDUCTION CONCEPTS

**Basis** This is the amount of unrecovered investment in an asset. As amounts are expended and/or recovered relative to an asset over time, the basis is adjusted in consideration of such changes. The **adjusted basis** of an asset is the original basis, plus or minus the changes in the amount of unrecovered investment. pgs. 2-13, 2-21

**Capital recovery** No income is realized until the taxpayer receives more than the amount invested to produce the income. The amount invested in an asset represents the maximum amount recoverable. pg. 2-13

# 4-1 INTRODUCTION

LO 1
Explain the requirements for the exclusion of an item of income and explain the rationale for excluding items from gross income.

After identifying all the sources of income received during an accounting period, the next step in calculating taxable income is determining which, if any, of the income sources do not have to be included in the current period's gross income. This step requires identification of income items that are subject to exclusion or deferral. The all-inclusive income concept considers taxable any income received unless a specific provision can be found that exempts the item from taxation. Under the legislative grace concept, only Congress can provide such tax relief. In addition, tax relief provisions are strictly applied and interpreted, thereby explicitly limiting the scope of any tax relief provision to that which Congress intended.

Congress has chosen to exempt certain items that meet the definition of *gross income* for several reasons. Some of the relief provisions are designed as equity measures that relieve the item from double taxation. Other provisions are meant as incentives for taxpayers to engage in specific activities. Most incentive provisions have as their goal some social objective, such as encouraging firms to provide medical coverage for their employees. As the provisions are introduced, the chapter states the rationale for providing the relief.

This chapter discusses the most common exclusions found in the tax law. Because they represent exceptions to the general concepts of income recognition, exclusions are an area of the tax law that can be mastered only through exposure and study. The more you encounter and work with these items, the more familiar they will become. In addition, this chapter introduces several common deferral provisions. Recall from Chapter 1 that the difference between an exclusion and a deferral of income is that an exclusion is permanent—it is never subject to taxation. On the other hand, a deferral is not taxed in the current period but will be taxed in some future period(s). Most deferrals are a result of the wherewithal-to-pay concept and are not taxed currently because the transaction has not produced the cash with which to pay the tax.

Exhibit 4-1 lists the titles of the Internal Revenue Code sections that allow the various exclusions. As you can see from the list, the number of exclusions and the topics they cover is formidable. The discussion in this chapter focuses on those exclusions that have the widest application. To provide a frame of reference for your study of exclusions, they are grouped into four categories: donative items, employment-related exclusions, returns of human capital, and investment-related exclusions.

# 4-2 DONATIVE ITEMS

LO 2
Identify the allowable exclusions for donative items of income: gifts, inheritances, life insurance proceeds, and scholarships.

Items in this category are receipts of wealth that the receiver has not earned and for which no future services are to be rendered as a result of the transfer, nor are they the result of an investment. Because they represent realized increases in wealth, items in this class fit the definition of *income*. However, Congress has determined that such items should not be taxed either for equity or incentive reasons. Donative items include gifts and inheritances, life insurance proceeds, and scholarships.

## 4-2a Gifts

The value of property acquired by **gift** has been excluded from income taxation since 1913. Gifts received are not subject to income taxation.[1] However, the donor (person making the gift) is subject to the gift tax rules on the making of a gift. Thus, the exclusion of gifts from income tax is an equity measure that prevents a double tax on a gift. However, neither Congress nor the Treasury has ever attempted to provide a strict definition of what constitutes a gift. The most authoritative definition was developed by the U.S. Supreme Court in 1960:

> A gift in the statutory sense, ... proceeds from a detached and disinterested generosity, ... out of affection, respect, admiration, charity, or like impulses, ... And in this regard, the most critical consideration, as the Court was agreed in the leading case here, is the transferor's "intention."... What controls is the intention with which payment, however voluntary, has been made.[2]

Exhibit 4-1

## Income Exclusions by Internal Revenue Code Section

| | |
|---|---|
| Sec. 101 | Certain death benefits |
| Sec. 102 | Gifts and inheritances |
| Sec. 103 | Interest on state and local bonds |
| Sec. 104 | Compensation for injuries or sickness |
| Sec. 105 | Amounts received under accident and health plans |
| Sec. 106 | Contributions by employers to accident and health plans |
| Sec. 107 | Rental value of parsonages |
| Sec. 108 | Income from discharge of indebtedness |
| Sec. 109 | Improvements by lessee on lessor's property |
| Sec. 110 | Lessee construction allowances for short-term lenses |
| Sec. 111 | Recovery of tax benefit items |
| Sec. 112 | Certain combat pay of members of the armed forces |
| Sec. 115 | Income of states, municipalities, etc. |
| Sec. 117 | Qualified scholarships |
| Sec. 118 | Contributions to the capital of a corporation |
| Sec. 119 | Meals or lodging furnished for the convenience of the employer |
| Sec. 120 | Amounts received under group legal services plans |
| Sec. 121 | Exclusion of gain from sale of principal residence |
| Sec. 122 | Certain reduced uniformed services retirement pay |
| Sec. 123 | Amounts received under insurance contracts for certain living expenses |
| Sec. 125 | Cafeteria plans |
| Sec. 126 | Certain cost-sharing payments |
| Sec. 127 | Educational assistance programs |
| Sec. 129 | Dependent care assistance programs |
| Sec. 130 | Certain personal injury liability assignments |
| Sec. 131 | Certain foster care payments |
| Sec. 132 | Certain fringe benefits |
| Sec. 134 | Certain military benefits |
| Sec. 135 | Income from U.S. savings bonds used to pay higher education tuition and fees |
| Sec. 136 | Energy conservation subsidies provided by public utilities |
| Sec. 137 | Adoption assistance programs |
| Sec. 138 | Medicare + Choice MSA |
| Sec. 139 | Disaster relief payments |
| Sec. 139a | Federal subsidies for prescription drug plans |

In most situations, the intention to make a gift is clear. People make gifts to friends and relatives all the time "out of affection, respect, admiration, charity, or like impulses" with no expectation of any consideration in return.

**Example 1** Odom gives his daughter Althea a new car worth $18,000 when she graduates from college. Does Althea have taxable income from the receipt of the car?

**Discussion: It is unlikely that Odom is attempting to compensate his daughter; he gave her the car out of affection and respect for her accomplishments, and it therefore constitutes an excludable gift.**

Recall that the legislative grace concept requires a strict application and interpretation of the exclusion for gifts. Thus, only the receipt of a gift is a nontaxable event; any subsequent earnings from property received as a gift are subject to taxation. Subsequent earnings may be in the form of income flows from the property (interest, dividends, rents, royalties, etc.) or gains from the sale of the property.

**Example 2** For Christmas, Zane's uncle Bob gives him 100 shares of ABC Company stock that has a fair market value of $200. Sometime later, Zane receives a cash dividend of $50 on the stock. Does Zane have any taxable income from the stock?

**Discussion: The receipt of the stock is a gift, the value of which is excluded from Zane's income. However, the exclusion applies only to the receipt of the gift; any subsequent earnings on the gift property are subject to tax. Thus, Zane must**

**include the $50 dividend in his taxable income. NOTE: If the dividend had already been declared when Bob made the gift, Bob would have been taxed on the dividend under the assignment-of-income doctrine. Under such circumstances, the cash dividend would have been an additional gift.**

The major problem with gifts involves those made in a business setting. Per the standard outlined, the donor's intent in making the gift is controlling. That is, if the gift was meant to be compensation for past, present, or future services, it is not really a gift but is taxable as compensation.

**Example 3** Over the years, Albert has provided Phillip with the names of many potential customers. Albert never expected anything but his friendship in return. In the current year, Phillip has a particularly good year and decides to give Albert a new automobile worth $20,000 for being such a good friend through the years. Does Albert have income from the receipt of the automobile?

**Discussion: On similar facts, in 1960 the Supreme Court held that the automobile did not constitute a gift, although both parties testified that nothing was owed between the two and that the automobile was meant to be a present. The Court felt that the nature of their past relationship indicated that the automobile was either compensation for past customer leads or an inducement to Albert to continue providing such information in the future.**

As example 3 illustrates, gifts between individuals who also engage in business with one another are always suspect. In most cases, such "gifts" have some compensatory element to them and as such do not meet the income tax definition of a gift. Note that the treatment of business gifts is an application of the substance-over-form doctrine, which taxes transactions according to their true intention rather than their technical form.

## 4-2b Inheritances

As with gifts, the value of property received by **inheritance** has been excluded from taxation since 1913. The rationale for exclusion follows that for a gift—property held in an estate is subject to an estate tax; thus, the income tax exclusion for inheritances avoids a double taxation of the property of a deceased taxpayer. There are no particular problems in this area. Remember, the legislative grace concept requires that exclusions be strictly applied. In the case of inherited property, the exclusion is limited to the value of property received. Any subsequent earnings from the inherited property are not excludable.[3]

**Example 4** Elinor receives 100 shares of Pleasing Pools common stock worth $6,000 from the estate of her uncle Frank. She subsequently receives dividends totaling $200 on the stock. What are the tax effects for Elinor of receiving the stock?

**Discussion: Elinor is not taxed on the $6,000 value of the stock received from the inheritance. However, she is taxed on the income received from the stock subsequent to its receipt and must include the $200 dividend in her gross income.**

**Example 5** Elinor holds the stock she received from her uncle's estate for two years, after which she sells it for $8,500. Does Elinor have a taxable gain from the sale of the stock?

**Discussion: Elinor is taxed on the gain from the sale of the stock. Her taxable gain is $2,500 ($8,500 − $6,000). Note that the $6,000 fair market value of the stock received from the estate becomes Elinor's basis. Because the value of the inheritance (in this case $6,000) must never be taxed, it is permanently excluded from income. Therefore, under the capital recovery concept, Elinor does not have income unless she receives more than $6,000 for the stock upon disposition.**

## 4-2c Life Insurance Proceeds

Payments from life insurance upon the death of the insured are generally excluded from income tax,[4] although **life insurance proceeds** may be included in the decedent's gross estate and subject to the estate tax. Life insurance proceeds resemble inheritances, which are excluded from income taxation. Thus, the exclusion of life insurance proceeds provides equity with other forms of inherited property.

**Example 6** Alice's husband, Ralph, dies this year. Ralph has a $200,000 life insurance policy that names Alice as the beneficiary. Alice invests the $200,000 in a certificate of deposit that earns 6% annually. What are the tax effects of the receipt of the $200,000 for Alice?

**Discussion: The receipt of the $200,000 face value of the policy is excludable under the provision for receipt of life insurance proceeds. However, the subsequent earnings on the proceeds, $12,000 per year, are subject to tax.**

The life insurance proceeds exclusion applies to such payments even if the payments are received in installments, although any earnings included in the installment payments are taxable.

**Example 7** Assume the same facts as in example 6 except that Alice elects to take the proceeds in installments of $32,000 per year for 10 years. What are the tax consequences of the receipt of the annual installments?

**Discussion: The $200,000 face value of the policy is excludable. However, Alice will receive a total of $320,000 under the installment plan. Thus, she must recognize the $120,000 ($320,000 − $200,000) in earnings as they are received. The payments are in the form of an annuity, so the annuity formula described in Chapter 3 is used to determine the taxable portion of each payment:**

**Annuity Exclusion Formula**

$$\text{Amount excluded} = \frac{\text{Cost of contract}}{\text{Number of payments}}$$

$$\text{Amount excluded} = \frac{\$200{,}000}{10} = \$20{,}000$$

$$\text{Taxable amount} = \$32{,}000 - \$20{,}000 = \$12{,}000$$

**Note that this treatment is consistent with the treatment in example 6. In both cases, Alice invests the $200,000 proceeds at a 6% annual return. In example 7, the fact that she makes the investment with an insurance company does not provide her with any tax relief. It is taxed as any investment of the proceeds would be taxed.**

An exception to the exclusion for life insurance proceeds is made for amounts paid to the owner of a policy that was obtained for a consideration (i.e., purchased). That is, if a taxpayer purchases or otherwise obtains for some valuable consideration a policy on the life of another, the receipt of the insurance proceeds is considered the realization of an investment.

**Example 8** Athena owns a life insurance policy on herself that has a face value of $50,000. During a financial crisis, she assigns the proceeds of the policy to Helena for $10,000. Helena subsequently pays premiums on the policy totaling $20,000 before Athena dies. What is the tax effect of Helena's receipt of the $50,000 life insurance proceeds?

**Discussion: Because Helena purchased the policy for a consideration, the receipt of the $50,000 is taxable. Under the capital recovery concept, she is allowed to recover her $30,000 investment in the policy before she recognizes any income. Therefore, she has a realized and recognized gain of $20,000 on the receipt of the life insurance proceeds.**

This exception to the life insurance exclusion provisions does not apply to policies owned by partners or partnerships in which the insured is a partner or a corporation in which the insured is an officer or a shareholder. Payments on such contracts are excluded, because they are deemed to be for legitimate business purposes rather than for speculative gain. This type of life insurance on the death of a partner or a key employee is usually used to fund buy-out agreements and is necessary to ensure continuation of the business in most cases.

**Example 9** Nina and Chen are partners in a consulting business. The business has been highly profitable, and each has a considerable equity interest in the partnership. When they realize that paying off each other's estate in the event of death would drain the business of all its resources, the partnership purchases life insurance payable to the partnership for $500,000 on both Nina and Chen. After several years, Chen dies in an automobile accident, and the partnership receives the $500,000. At that time, Chen's equity in the partnership is $400,000, which is paid to his estate. Is the partnership in receipt of taxable income?

**Discussion: Because the partnership is the owner of the policy that was taken out for legitimate business reasons (to ensure continuity of the business), the $500,000 received by the partnership is excluded from taxation. Note that this is the case even though only $400,000 was required to settle Chen's account. The $100,000 windfall for the partnership remains tax-free.**

The payment-of-consideration exception to the exclusion for life insurance proceeds also does not apply to accelerated death benefits received under a life insurance policy by a terminally or chronically ill individual. Generally, accelerated death benefits for terminally or chronically ill people are excludable, although certain limits may apply.

### 4-2d Scholarships

A college student who is a candidate for a degree may exclude the value of a **scholarship** if the award does not require the student to perform any future services such as teaching, grading papers, or tutoring.[5] That is, the scholarship must be gratuitous in nature and not merely a form of compensation for past, present, or future services.

**Example 10** Diane receives a $1,000 scholarship to the College of Agriculture. The college gives such scholarships annually to students in the top 10% of their class. There are no other criteria or obligations for the receipt of the scholarship. Is the scholarship eligible for exclusion?

**Discussion: Because the scholarship is based solely on merit and does not require Diane to provide any services to the college, it is eligible for the exclusion for scholarships.**

**Example 11** Luciana receives a graduate assistant scholarship from the School of Accounting to aid her in her graduate studies. As part of the scholarship, which pays $300 per month, she is to work for an accounting professor for 10 hours per week, grading papers and assisting the professor in her duties. Is the scholarship eligible for exclusion?

**Discussion: Because Luciana is required to perform services in return for her scholarship, the $300 per month that she receives is not eligible for exclusion as a scholarship.**

The amount of the exclusion is limited to the direct costs of the student's college education. Direct costs consist of the student's tuition, fees, books, supplies, and other equipment required for the student's course of instruction.[6] Amounts received in excess of the direct costs of the education are taxable. This puts students receiving scholarships on an equal footing with nonstudents regarding personal living expenses. That is, individuals are not allowed to deduct personal living expenses. Therefore, students who receive amounts for personal living expenses must include such amounts in income to provide equity with nonstudents, who are effectively taxed on income they spend for personal living expenses. Thus, scholarships that are specified as being for the payment of a student's room and board are fully taxable.

**Example 12** Jada receives a scholarship for $10,000 to attend Local University. The cost of her tuition, books, fees, and supplies totals $9,000 for the year. How much of the $10,000 scholarship is taxable?

**Discussion: Jada may exclude only the $9,000 she spends on the direct costs of her college education. The remaining $1,000 is included in her gross income.**

## 4-3 EMPLOYMENT-RELATED EXCLUSIONS

LO 3
Describe the effect of employment-related exclusions on the after-tax compensation of employees.

The largest class of exclusions is certain payments made to or on behalf of an employee by an employer. This category of exclusions is costly in terms of the tax revenue lost to the government because these payments are deductible by the employer and yield no tax revenue because of the exclusion from income granted the employee. These relief provisions are intended to provide equity in cases of double taxation and act as incentives to employers and employees to engage in the specified activity.

## 4-3a Foreign-Earned Income

U.S. citizens are subject to tax on all income they receive, regardless of the source. Thus, taxes are levied on worldwide income. To provide relief from double taxation for U.S. citizens working in foreign countries, the tax law allows individuals two options. First, taxpayers may include the **foreign-earned income** in their taxable income, calculate the U.S. tax on the income, and take a tax credit for any foreign taxes paid.[7] The amount of the allowable tax credit is the lesser of (1) the actual foreign taxes paid, or (2) the U.S. tax that would have been paid on the foreign-earned income. Under the second option, individuals may exclude up to $108,700 (2021) in foreign-earned income for each full year they work in a foreign country.[8] To take advantage of the exclusion option, an individual either must be a bona fide resident of the foreign country or must be present in the foreign country for 330 days in any 12 consecutive months. The tax under the exclusion option is equal to the difference between the tax on taxable income without the exclusion and the tax on the amount excluded:

| | |
|---|---|
| Tax on taxable income without exclusion | $ XXX |
| Less: Tax on exclusion amount | (XXX) |
| Equals: Tax on taxable income | $ XXX |

Selection of the most tax-advantageous option will depend on the amount of income earned abroad as well as the relative marginal tax rates between the foreign country and the United States. Thus, to select the optimal choice in a given situation, both options must be calculated to determine which one results in the lower net tax payable.

**Example 13** Rollie works on a drilling rig in South America during all of the current year. He earns $90,000 from this job and pays $19,000 in tax to the appropriate South American government. Rollie is single, and his taxable income without considering his $90,000 salary is $30,000. Should he elect the tax credit or the exclusion option?

**Discussion: Rollie should elect the option that minimizes the amount of U.S. tax paid on the foreign income. Under the exclusion option, Rollie's taxable income is $30,000 ($90,000 + $30,000 – $90,000) and his tax liability is $7,200. If he elects to take the foreign tax credit, his taxable income is $120,000 ($90,000 + $30,000) and his tax liability is $5,705. The tax credit option results in a tax savings of $1,495 ($7,200 – $5,705).**

| | |
|---|---|
| Exclude $90,000 from taxable income: | |
| Tax on $120,000 – $14,751.00 + [24% × ($120,000 – $86,375)] | $ 22,821 |
| Less: Tax on $90,000 – $14,751.00 + [24% × ($90,000 – $86,375)] | $ 15,621 |
| Equals: Tax on $30,000 | $ 7,200 |
| Foreign Tax Credit: | |
| Tax on $120,000 – $14,751.00 + [24% × ($120,000 – $86,375)] | $ 22,821 |
| Tax credit for South American taxes paid* | $ 17,116 |
| Net tax due | $ 5,705 |
| Tax savings using credit option | $ 1,495 |

**The foreign tax credit cannot exceed the amount of U.S. tax that would have been paid on the South American income. In this case, the U.S. tax on the South American income is $17,116 [$22,821 × ($90,000 ÷ $120,000)] and Rollie is allowed a foreign tax credit for the limited amount of $17,116.*

## 4-3b Payments Made on Behalf of an Employee

LO 4 Explain the nontaxable fringe benefits that a business may provide to its employees.

Recall from the discussion of income sources in Chapter 3 that when one person pays the expenses of another in an employment setting, the person whose expenses are paid generally has taxable income. However, the tax law does exempt from taxation the payment of the following employee expenses by an employer:

- Payments to qualified pension plans
- Group term life insurance
- Health and accident insurance premiums
- Meals and lodging provided by the employer

The favorable tax treatment accorded these items has encouraged employers to provide more and more of an employee's compensation in the form of excludable fringe benefits. This is quite advantageous to the employee, as the following example illustrates:

**Example 14** Lacy Corporation offers its employees various fringe-benefit package options. Under one of Lacy's options, an employee may participate in the company's accident and health insurance plan or may take the cost of the plan, $1,200 per year, in cash.

**Discussion: As discussed later, health and accident insurance premiums paid by an employer on behalf of an employee are excludable from income. Assuming that an employee would ordinarily purchase such insurance, selection of this option effectively increases that person's after-tax compensation from Lacy Corporation by $1,200. An employee who elects to take the $1,200 in cash will be taxed on the receipt of cash. Assuming a 24% marginal tax rate, an employee taking the cash option would have only $912 [$1,200 – (24% × $1,200)] to purchase insurance after paying the tax. In most cases, the employee could not purchase a comparable insurance plan for this amount and would be worse off by electing the cash option.**

This example illustrates the tremendous advantage of employer-provided benefits. Employees get benefits at no tax cost that they would otherwise purchase. This use of before-tax compensation can greatly increase the employee's effective pay rate. If the benefit is clear for the employee, what is the incentive for the employer to provide these tax-free benefits? The employer realizes a tax saving from a deduction for the payment of the tax-free benefit as an ordinary and necessary business expense, but it would get the same deduction for any form of compensation paid to the employee. The key for the employer is that the market for employees demands that each employee be paid a certain wage. Thus, the employer will pay the same price for labor whether the payment is totally in cash or a combination of cash and tax-free benefits. It makes sense for firms to increase their effective compensation to employees by providing the tax-free benefits: $1,000 in cash compensation is not worth as much after taxes as the same $1,000 in compensation paid in the form of tax-free benefits. In this way, employers are able to increase their employees' real after-tax compensation without an increase in cash outflow. In addition, the tax-free fringe benefits are generally not subject to payroll taxes (e.g., Social Security, unemployment tax), reducing the cost of compensation for the employer.

Although some qualifications for exclusion are quite complex, the discussion that follows is designed to provide an overview of the tax-free benefits that an employer can provide to an employee. Therefore, most of the complexities involved in the exclusions are omitted.

## Payments to Qualified Pension Plans

The income tax law provides many ways for individuals to provide for their retirement on a tax-deferred basis. Those who are not covered by an employer-provided pension plan can set up an individual retirement account (IRA) and deduct contributions made to the account for adjusted gross income.[9] Self-employed individuals are allowed to establish either an IRA or what is referred to as a *Keogh plan* and deduct amounts paid into the plan for adjusted gross income.[10] In addition to the tax deductions allowed for payments into such plans, any earnings on the assets in the plans are not subject to tax as the income is earned. Rather, the retirement plan is taxed when amounts are drawn from the plan. Thus, retirement plans defer current income until the taxpayer retires. The operation of IRAs and the deduction limits are discussed in Chapter 6.

Many companies provide pension plans for their employees. Several allowable variations of such plans permit employers and employees to make payments into the plans and receive the same tax treatment as IRA and Keogh plans. Such plans are referred to as **qualified pension plans**.[11] Payments made by an employer to an employee's account in a qualified pension plan are not taxable in the period in which the payments are made. The tax on such payments is deferred until the employee actually withdraws the payments from the plan.[12] As such, this is not a true exclusion on which a tax is never paid but a deferral of income-recognition to a future period. An added benefit of a qualified pension plan is that the *earnings* on amounts paid into such plans are not taxed until they are withdrawn by the employee. The deferral of income through pension plan payments is mentioned in this chapter because of the growing popularity of employer-sponsored pension plans as an employee fringe benefit.

**Example 15** Linda is an employee of Ross Company. Ross has a qualified pension plan for its employees under which it contributes 5% of each employee's salary to the plan each year. Linda's salary for the current year is $30,000, resulting in a pension plan payment of $1,500. How is Linda taxed on the $1,500?

**Discussion: Because Ross Company's plan is qualified, the $1,500 payment is not taxed to Linda in the current period. When Linda withdraws the $1,500 from the plan (either at retirement or when she leaves the company), she will be taxed on amounts paid into the plan by Ross as well as any earnings on the amounts in her pension plan.**

In addition to the deferral of amounts paid into qualified pension plans by employers, employees may defer taxation of any amounts that they pay into such plans until they withdraw amounts from the plan.

**Example 16** Assume that in example 15, Ross Company's pension plan allows employees to contribute up to 5% of their annual earnings to the plan. What is the tax effect to Linda if she contributes the maximum allowed under the plan?

**Discussion: Linda can contribute a maximum of $1,500 of her $30,000 salary. Because Linda is not taxed on the contribution now, her gross salary from Ross Company is reduced to $28,500 ($30,000 − $1,500) by the contribution to the plan. As with the employer's contribution, Linda will be taxed on her contribution when she withdraws it from the plan.**

What is the benefit derived from payments to pension plans? First, by deferring tax on payments to the plan until a future period, a time value of money savings is effected on the tax being deferred. The second benefit is that the earnings in the plan accumulate tax-free, allowing a larger buildup of funds at retirement than if the earnings were taxed as they were earned. Last, employees often have less income when they retire, resulting in a tax on the deferred income at a lower marginal tax rate.

## Group Term Life Insurance

One of the most popular employee benefits is the exclusion of the premiums paid by an employer on the first $50,000 face amount of **group term life insurance**. This exclusion is available only for term insurance that is provided to a group of employees on a nondiscriminatory basis.[13] Payments made on whole life policies, term insurance purchased for individuals (not a group policy), or plans that discriminate in favor of highly compensated individuals are not eligible for exclusion. This provision is intended to encourage employers to provide life insurance to all their employees so that their families have a cushion if the employee dies while still working (a social goal). If an employee's qualified group term policy has a face value greater than $50,000, the premiums paid on the coverage in excess of $50,000 are taxable to the employee. That is, only the premiums paid on $50,000 of group term life insurance are excludable from the employee's income. The IRS provides a table that calculates the income from premiums paid in excess of the $50,000 exclusion.[14] This table is reproduced in Table 4-1. Note that the premium cost is related to the employee's age and is stated per $1,000 of coverage.

**Example 17** Jim is an employee of Panko Builders with an annual salary of $40,000. Panko provides group term life insurance to all its employees at twice their annual salaries. Jim's $80,000 of group term life insurance costs Panko $400 during the current year. How much taxable income does Jim receive from the provision of the life insurance if he is 33?

**Discussion: Jim is allowed to exclude the premiums paid on the first $50,000 of the group term life insurance. The premiums paid on the $30,000 of excess coverage must be included in his gross income as compensation from Panko. Using Table 4-1, the amount of the premiums taxed to Jim is $29 (rounded):**

| | |
|---|---|
| Cost per $1,000 of coverage for 33-year-old | $ .96 |
| Coverage in excess of $50,000 | × 30 |
| Gross income from excess coverage | $ 29 |

Table 4-1

## Gross Income from Group Term Life Insurance in Excess of $50,000

| | Includable Income per $1,000 | |
|---|---|---|
| Employee's Age | Monthly | Annually |
| Under 25 | $ .05 | $ .60 |
| 25 to 29 | .06 | .72 |
| 30 to 34 | .08 | .96 |
| 35 to 39 | .09 | 1.08 |
| 40 to 44 | .10 | 1.20 |
| 45 to 49 | .15 | 1.80 |
| 50 to 54 | .23 | 2.76 |
| 55 to 59 | .43 | 5.16 |
| 60 to 64 | .66 | 7.92 |
| 65 to 69 | 1.27 | 15.24 |
| 70 and older | 2.06 | 24.72 |

**Example 18** Assume that Panko also provides $100,000 of whole life insurance to all management-level employees. Jim is in a management-level position. The cost of his $100,000 policy to Panko is $1,800. How much taxable income does Jim receive from the provision of the whole life insurance?

**Discussion: There is no exclusion for the provision of whole life insurance to employees. Therefore, Jim must include the $1,800 cost of the policy in his gross income as compensation from Panko.**

### Health and Accident Insurance Premiums

Premiums paid by an employer to purchase **health and accident insurance** coverage for employees (and their dependents) are excluded from the employee's income.[15] The exclusion also applies to companies that choose to "self-insure" by making payments to a fund that is used to pay employees' medical expenses. However, if a **self-insured medical plan** discriminates in favor of highly compensated employees, the amounts paid for medical expenses of highly compensated employees covered by the plan are included in the individual's taxable income.

**Example 19** Rory is an employee of Royce Company. Royce provides health and accident insurance for all its employees. During the current year, Royce pays $1,300 for each employee for coverage under the plan. Does Rory have taxable income from the payment of the premiums?

**Discussion: The $1,300 is not taxable to Rory because it is a payment for a health and accident insurance plan premium that is not discriminatory.**

**Example 20** Cory is a senior vice president of Discriminator Corporation. The corporation has a self-insured health and accident plan that covers only its executive officers. Discriminator makes monthly payments to a fund that is used to reimburse the executives for any medical expenses they incur. During the current year, Cory incurs $3,700 in medical expenses, all of which are reimbursed by the plan. Does Cory have taxable income from the payment of her medical expenses by the plan?

**Discussion: Because the plan discriminates in favor of highly compensated employees (only executive officers are covered), all payments from the plan are taxable to Cory. Thus, Cory must include the $3,700 reimbursement in her gross income.**

Note that the exclusion is allowed only for the premiums paid by an employer to buy health and accident insurance on a nondiscriminatory basis. The taxation of payments made to the employee from such plans is discussed in the section on returns of human capital.

### Meals and Lodging Provided by the Employer

The value of meals provided to an employee free of charge may be excluded from the employees' income if the meals are provided on the employer's business premises and the provision of the meals is "for the convenience of the employer."[16] Note that the exclusion is for the **meals provided by the employer**; cash meal allowances are generally taxable because they are not meals provided by the employer.[17] To satisfy the convenience-of-the-employer requirement, the provision of the meals must have a substantial noncompensatory business purpose. Employers have historically been allowed a deduction for the full cost of meals provided for the convenience of the employer and on the employer's premises. For the period beginning on January 1, 2018, and ending on December 31, 2025, the 2017 Tax Cuts and Jobs Act (TCJA) applies a 50 percent limit on the deductibility of these meals. The Concolidated Appropriations Act of 2021 contains a temporary provision which allows a 100 percent deduction for calendar years 2021 and 2022 for meals purchased in restaurants. A more comprehensive discussion is found in Chapter 6. For tax years beginning after December 31, 2025, the meal expenses become nondeductible. While the 2017 TCJA limits the deduction, the tax law continues to allow the employee to exclude these benefits from income.

**Example 21** Hilda is a server at Jiffy Fast Foods. To encourage employees to stay on the premises during their food breaks, Jiffy allows employees to eat one free meal per shift. Is the value of the meals she receives from Jiffy taxable for Hilda?

**Discussion: Because the provision of the meals serves a business purpose (keeping employees close at hand during their meal breaks), the value of the meals is excluded from Hilda's income. Note that this is the case even if Hilda eats her free meal before or after her shift starts.**

**Example 22** Blue Trucking Company gives all its drivers meal vouchers that are honored at various truck stops on the company's routes. The drivers pay for their meals with the vouchers, which are then billed to Blue Trucking Company. Brian, a driver for Blue, consumed meals costing a total of $3,900 during the current year. Can he exclude the value of the meals provided by Blue?

**Discussion: Because the meals were not provided on Blue's business premises, they are taxable as compensation to Brian. He must include the $3,900 worth of meals in his gross income.**

To exclude the value of **employer-provided lodging**, the lodging must meet an additional requirement: The acceptance of the lodging must be a condition of employment. That is, the employee has no choice but to live in the employer-provided housing.

**Example 23** Nadia is an employee of Arctic Pipeline Company. Because the construction site of a new pipeline is in a remote area, all employees are required to live in temporary quarters erected at the construction site by Arctic. The cost of the lodging to Arctic is estimated at $7,200 per employee per year. Does Nadia have taxable income from the provision of the lodging?

**Discussion: Because the lodging on the employer's business premises (the job site) is for the convenience of the employer (employees can work more hours if they don't have to make a long commute) and is required as a condition of employment, it is not taxable to the employee. Therefore, Nadia may exclude the $7,200 of employer-provided housing from her gross income.**

## General Fringe Benefits

The tax law also allows the exclusion of four general types of employment-related fringe benefits:

- No-additional-cost services
- Employee discounts
- Qualified retirement planning services
- Working-condition fringes
- De minimis fringe benefits[18]

**No-additional-cost services** and **employee discounts** must be made available to employees on a nondiscriminatory basis and must also be in the same line of business in which the employee works. For example, a hotel chain may let hotel employees stay free at any of its hotels on a space-available basis with no tax consequences to the employee. However, if the hotel chain also gives free hotel rooms to employees of its rental car business, the fair market value of the hotel room is taxable to the employee. Reciprocal agreements between companies in the same line of business are allowed.

**Example 24** Marshall is an employee of Deloitte Airlines. Deloitte and Ernst Air have a reciprocal agreement under which their employees may fly free of charge on each other's planes on a space-available basis. Marshall used the agreement to take two free flights on Ernst Air that would have cost him $880 if he had paid the regular fare. Is Marshall taxed on the value of the free flights?

**Discussion: Because Marshall is an airline employee and the free flights are available to all employees, he is allowed to exclude the value of any flights on either Deloitte or Ernst as a no-additional-cost service. Therefore, the free flights are not taxable to Marshall.**

**Example 25** Assume that Deloitte also owns a finance company. Employees of the finance company are allowed to take free flights only on Deloitte Airlines on a space-available basis. Janelle is a financial analyst with Deloitte's finance company. She took two free flights on Deloitte that would have cost $1,060 if she had paid the regular fare. Is Janelle taxed on the value of the free flights?

**Discussion: Because Janelle does not work in the same line of business as the free service, she is not allowed to exclude the value of the free flights. She must include the $1,060 value of the flights in her gross income.**

To exclude employee discounts, the discount must be made available to all employees on a nondiscriminatory basis and the goods and/or services provided must be in the same line of business. Note that the exclusion for discounts would ordinarily constitute a bargain purchase. The distinguishing feature between a valid employee discount and a taxable bargain purchase is that employee discounts must be made available to all employees in order to be excluded. Bargain purchases are essentially employee discounts that are made available only to select employees. The excludable discount on goods is limited to the gross profit percentage on the goods purchased (i.e., employees can't buy goods below the employer's cost tax-free). Excludable service discounts are limited to 20 percent. Any employee discount on services in excess of 20 percent is taxable to the employee. (The first 20 percent of the discount is excludable.)

**Example 26** All-City Hardware lets all its employees buy its products at a 25% discount. All-City marks up all its products by a minimum of 100% of its cost. Arnold is a store employee who bought various tools that normally retail for $200 (cost to All-City of $100) for $150 during the current year. Is Arnold taxed on the $50 discount?

**Discussion: Because the discount is available to all employees and does not exceed All-City's gross profit percentage (100% markup on cost equals a gross profit percentage of 50%), the discount is excludable from Arnold's gross income.**

**Example 27** In addition to the tools, Arnold buys a used delivery truck from All-City. The truck is worth $8,000, but All-City sells it to Arnold for $5,000 because he has been such a good employee through the years. Is Arnold taxed on the $3,000 discount?

**Discussion: Because the discount on the truck is not available to all employees, Arnold is taxed on the $3,000 as a bargain purchase.**

**Qualified retirement planning services** include any retirement planning advice or information provided to an employee and the employee's spouse by an employer that maintains a qualified retirement plan for its employees.[19] To qualify for exclusion, the retirement planning services must be available on substantially the same terms to all employees who normally receive information and education about the plan.

A **working-condition fringe benefit** is any item provided to the employee that would have been deductible by the employee as an employee business expense if the employee had paid for the item. This class of fringe benefits includes dues to professional organizations, professional journals, uniforms, and so on.[20] Although not normally deductible as an employee business expense, the payment of parking by an employer is designated as a working-condition fringe benefit. Similar to the limit on the deductibility of meals for the convenience of the employer, the 2017 TCJA does not allow an employer to deduct these expenses. However, the tax law continues to allow the employee to exclude a portion of these benefits from income. Since 1993, Congress has limited the amount of employer-provided parking that is excludable from income. The limit is $270 per month for 2021 ($270 in 2020). In contrast to discounts on goods and services, working-condition fringes can be given on a discriminatory basis. For example, a company can provide free parking only to its officers and the fringe benefit will remain tax free—up to the $270 per month maximum exclusion.

**De minimis fringe benefits** are those items that are too small to permit a reasonable accounting.[21] This would include such items as personal use of the office photocopier and free coffee in the employees' break room. Also included in this category would be employee parties and small holiday gifts, such as a Christmas ham. This exclusion is based on administrative convenience—the cost of accumulating the information necessary to tax such items would exceed the revenue derived from taxing the items.

### Other Benefits Paid by an Employer

Several other employer-paid fringe benefits are also excludable from income. An employee may exclude up to $5,000 per year of employer-provided child and dependent care services.[22] The value of the use of an **employer's athletic facility** may also be excluded if the facility is on the employer's premises and substantially all its use is by employees and their families. In addition, up to $5,250 in payments made for such costs as tuition and books is excludable if the payments are made from a nondiscriminatory **educational assistance program**.[23]

## 4-3c Employer Benefit Plans

As the number of tax-free benefit options proliferated in the late 1970s and early 1980s employers began to realize that they could not afford to offer all benefits to all employees. Further, every employee did not derive the maximum benefit from every type of benefit. For example, single individuals with no dependents receive no benefit from employer-provided child and dependent care. In response to this situation, firms developed cafeteria plans. In a **cafeteria plan**, a menu of tax-free benefits is offered at the employer's cost. The rules for cafeteria plans let employers offer any benefit that is specifically excluded by the tax law in their plans.[24] Each employee is allowed to choose a certain dollar amount of benefits from the menu or may choose to take the cash cost of the benefits. That is, employees who do not want to take all their allowable dollar amount in tax-free benefits can take the cash equivalent of the benefits. Employees who choose the tax-free benefits are not taxed on the value of the benefits. However, those who elect to receive cash are taxed on the amount of cash received. To receive this favorable treatment, the employer must make the benefits of the plan available to all employees on a nondiscriminatory basis. All benefits received from a plan that discriminates in favor of highly compensated employees are included in gross income.

**Example 28** Theodore is the chief financial officer of CEO Corporation. CEO has a cafeteria plan that lets all employees select from a menu of tax-free benefits a total of 5% of their annual compensation. Theodore's annual salary is $100,000, allowing him to select $5,000 in benefits from the plan. Under the plan, he selected $50,000 worth of group term life insurance and health and accident insurance at a cost to the company of $4,000. He took the remaining $1,000 of allowable benefits in cash. What are the tax consequences to Theodore of the cafeteria plan?

**Discussion: The plan is nondiscriminatory because it covers all employees and allows benefits in proportion to their salaries. Therefore, Theodore can exclude the value of the tax-free benefits (group term life insurance and health insurance) he selected. He must include in his gross income the $1,000 of benefits he took in cash.**

Another type of plan that has gained popularity is the **flexible benefits plan** or **salary reduction plan**.[25] With this type of plan, the employee has an annual amount withheld from their salary that is used to pay medical care expenses or child-care costs. As the costs are incurred, the employer reimburses the employee from the account. Amounts paid into the account by the employee are not included in the employee's gross income, thus the term *salary reduction plan*. The Patient Protection and Affordable Care Act limits contributions to these plans to $2,750 (2021). These plans let employees pay for medical costs and child care with before-tax dollars rather than after-tax dollars.

**Example 29** Bale Corporation has a flexible benefits plan that lets employees have amounts withheld from their salaries to pay for unreimbursed medical costs and child-care costs. Melchior is an employee of Bale whose annual salary is $45,000. Melchior has Bale withhold $2,750 under the plan to pay for health and accident insurance, dental costs, eyeglasses, and so on for his dependents. During the year, Melchior incurs $9,500 in such costs, and Bale reimburses him the $2,750 that had been withheld. What is the tax effect on Melchior of the flexible benefits plan?

**Discussion: Melchior's salary is reduced by the $2,750 he paid into the plan, leaving him with a gross income of $42,250. He is not taxed on the amounts he is paid for reimbursements from the plan ($2,750 in this case).**

**Note that Melchior has been able to pay for $2,750 of his costs with before-tax dollars. Without such a plan, Melchior still would have spent the $2,750, but the income would have been subject to tax. Therefore, he would have had to make more than $2,750 before taxes to have $2,750 after taxes to pay for these expenses.**

One final note on this type of plan: The regulations governing these plans do not let the company return unused payments to the employee. The employee makes an annual election of the amount she or he wants put into the plan. Any amounts put into a flexible benefits or salary reduction plan that are not spent during the year are retained by the plan and are not available to the employee in subsequent years. That is, the employee loses any payments that are not reimbursed during the plan year.

**Example 30** Assume that in example 29, Melchior spends only $2,000 of the $2,750 he paid in during the year. What is the effect on Melchior?

**Discussion: Melchior is still allowed to exclude the $2,750 he paid into the plan, reducing his gross income to $42,250. However, the plan would keep the $750 he paid in but did not spend. It would not be available for Melchior to use to pay his expenses in the next plan year.**

## Health Savings Accounts

The favorable tax treatment accorded medical insurance premiums and reimbursements of medical expenses is intended to encourage employers and employees to purchase adequate medical coverage. In recent years, concern about the rising cost of health care has prompted legislators to consider other policies to encourage adequate health care while controlling the rate of increase in health-care costs. In 2003, Congress created **Health Savings Accounts (HSAs)** to encourage taxpayers to more closely monitor their spending for medical services. This is accomplished by giving a significant tax benefit to taxpayers who agree to shoulder a larger share of their own health costs, with the expectation that they will pay more attention to how they are spending their medical dollars. To be eligible to make contributions to an HSA, an individual must be covered by a high-deductible health plan and no other health plan. A high-deductible health plan has a deductible that is at least $2,800 for family coverage ($1,400 single coverage) in 2021.

Both the employer and employee can contribute to an HSA—contributions made by an employer to an employee's HSA are excluded from gross income and employee contributions are deductible for adjusted gross income. Distributions from an HSA for qualified medical expenses are excludible from gross income.[26] Unlike a flexible benefits plan, unused amounts from one year's contributions are carried forward to pay future medical expenses. The earnings on amounts in an HSA are excluded from gross income, allowing taxpayers to save tax-free for the payment of their future medical expenses. The maximum aggregate annual contribution to an HSA is $7,200 for family coverage ($3,600 single coverage) in 2021.

**Example 31** Aria works for Bond Corporation. Bond offers employees a high-deductible medical insurance plan ($1,400) with a $600 contribution to the employees' HSA. Aria elects to contribute the maximum to the plan. During the year, she spends $250 from the HSA on qualified medical expenses and the account earns $18. If Aria's salary is $62,000, what is the effect of her participation on her adjusted gross income?

**Discussion: Aria's adjusted gross income from Bond is $59,000 ($62,000 − $3,000). Aria is not taxed on Bond's $600 contribution to her HSA but can deduct her $3,000**

**($3,600 maximum aggregate contribution – $600 employer contribution) contribution for adjusted gross income. Aria is not taxed on either the $250 spent on qualified medical expenses or the $18 of earnings on the HSA.**

## concept check

All exclusions from income result from the *legislative grace concept.* Only income items that are specifically excluded by the tax law are not subject to tax. This concept also requires income exclusions to be strictly applied and interpreted. Therefore, any subsequent earnings received on gifts, inheritances, and life insurance proceeds are subject to tax. Exclusions for donative items provide relief from double taxation and/or encourage social goals. Most employment-related exclusions encourage employers to provide employees with benefits that the government would have to provide if the employee did not purchase them.

# 4-4 RETURNS OF HUMAN CAPITAL

LO 5
Identify payments that represent returns of human capital and are excluded from income as capital recoveries: workers' compensation, damage payments for personal physical injuries, and medical expense reimbursement payments.

Individuals often receive payments that are intended either to reimburse them for the costs of injuries or to compensate them for injuries in such a way as to "make them whole." Such payments are not deemed to increase wealth; rather, they are viewed as a return of human capital lost because of injury or sickness. As such, they are treated as a capital recovery that is not subject to tax. However, payments that are meant to replace lost income do not constitute returns of human capital and are generally taxable. Various types of payments received as compensation for injury or sickness are excluded from gross income. The list of excluded payments includes:

- Workers' compensation payments received as compensation for personal injury or sickness
- Damage payments received on account of personal physical injury or physical sickness
- Payments received for personal injuries or sickness that are paid from health and accident policies purchased by the taxpayer
- Payments received from employer-provided health and accident insurance if the payments:
  1. Are made for the permanent loss or loss of use of a member or function of the body, or for permanent disfigurement of the body; or
  2. Are based on the nature of the injury and are computed without reference to the period of time the employee is absent from the workplace; or
  3. Are payments received to reimburse the taxpayer for expenses incurred for medical care.

## 4-4a Workers' Compensation

Payments from a state **workers' compensation** fund are excluded from taxation. These payments are made to workers who become unable to work as a result of a work-related injury. Although the payments are somewhat of a substitute for earned income, Congress has provided relief from taxation for such payments because they are related to an injury suffered on the job and help taxpayers through the period they are recovering from their injuries. As such, they help restore the human capital of the individual. Note that this is not true for unemployment compensation benefits. Unemployment compensation is meant to be a substitute for income and is therefore subject to tax.

## 4-4b Damage Payments for Personal Physical Injury or Physical Sickness

Prior to 1996, damage payments received for any personal injury or sickness were excluded from taxation. The courts interpreted personal injury as any personal wrong committed against the taxpayer, such as libel, slander, breach of promise to marry, invasion of privacy, assault, and battery. In 1996, Congress limited the exclusion to **compensatory damage payments** received for a **personal physical injury** or personal physical sickness and medical payments for emotional distress.[27] Under this provision, if the action creating the payment has as its origin a physical injury or physical sickness, all payments received (other than punitive damage payments) are excluded, whether or not the recipient is the injured party. Thus, damage payments (other than punitive damages) to a spouse for loss of consortium due to a physical injury are excluded as damages related to a physical injury.

**Example 32** Rose is hit by an automobile while riding her bicycle to work. Although she is not hospitalized, she is traumatized and unable to work for 2 weeks. The insurance company of the driver of the automobile pays her $2,000 for her pain and suffering, $1,000 for her emotional distress, and $650 for the wages she lost while she was unable to work. How much of the $3,650 Rose received is included in her gross income?

**Discussion: None of the $3,650 is taxable. Because the damage payments originate from a claim based on a personal physical injury, they are excluded from income.**

**Example 33** Elliot works as a corner grocer. A feature on the local news portrays him as having links to organized crime. Elliot is outraged, the allegation is false, and he sues the television station for libel. The court awards Elliot $5,000 for the emotional distress he suffered and $60,000 for the loss of his business reputation. How much of the $65,000 is included in Elliot's gross income?

**Discussion: The $65,000 is taxable. Because the origin of the damage payments is a nonphysical personal injury, none of the payments is excluded. Compare this result with that of Rose in example 32. Rose also received loss of income and emotional distress payments, but they are excluded because they result from a claim based on a personal physical injury.**

In addition to compensatory damages, the courts often award **punitive damages** and/or **loss-of-income damages**. Historically, the treatment of such payments was controversial and resulted in much litigation. In 1996, Congress eliminated the controversy by restricting the exclusion for loss-of-income damage payments to payments received that are related to personal physical injury or personal physical sickness and by making all punitive damages taxable regardless of the action creating the payment.[28]

**Example 34** Assume that in example 32, Rose had sued the driver of the automobile. In addition to the other payments, the court awarded her $10,000 in punitive damages for the driver's gross negligence. Are the punitive damages included in Rose's gross income?

**Discussion: Even though the punitive damages relate to a physical injury, they are included in Rose's gross income. All punitive damages received are included in gross income and cannot be excluded as personal physical injury or personal physical sickness payment.**

## 4-4c Payments from Health and Accident Policies

Health and accident insurance policies may be provided by an employer to an employee, or they may be purchased separately by the taxpayer. In either case, payments for medical expenses from such policies are excluded because they make the taxpayer whole.[29]

An important distinction between employer- and taxpayer-purchased policies is that all health and accident insurance payments from policies purchased by an individual taxpayer are excluded from taxation. The exclusion for payments from employer-provided policies is limited to those for medical care, loss of body parts, or payments made for specific types of injuries. Thus, amounts received as **disability payments** (sick pay or wage-continuation plans) from an employer-provided health and accident plan would be included in gross income. However, the same payments made from a plan purchased by the individual taxpayer would be excluded from gross income. The disparity in treatment is apparently an additional incentive Congress has provided to individuals to purchase adequate health insurance. Figure 4-1 summarizes the tax treatment of payments received from health and accident policies.

**Example 35** Sean is severely injured in an automobile accident. The costs of his medical care total $8,000. His employer-sponsored plan pays $6,400 of the medical costs and $2,200 in sick pay. In addition, a policy that he had purchased separately pays the remaining

Figure 4-1

## Taxability of Payments Received from Health and Accident Policies

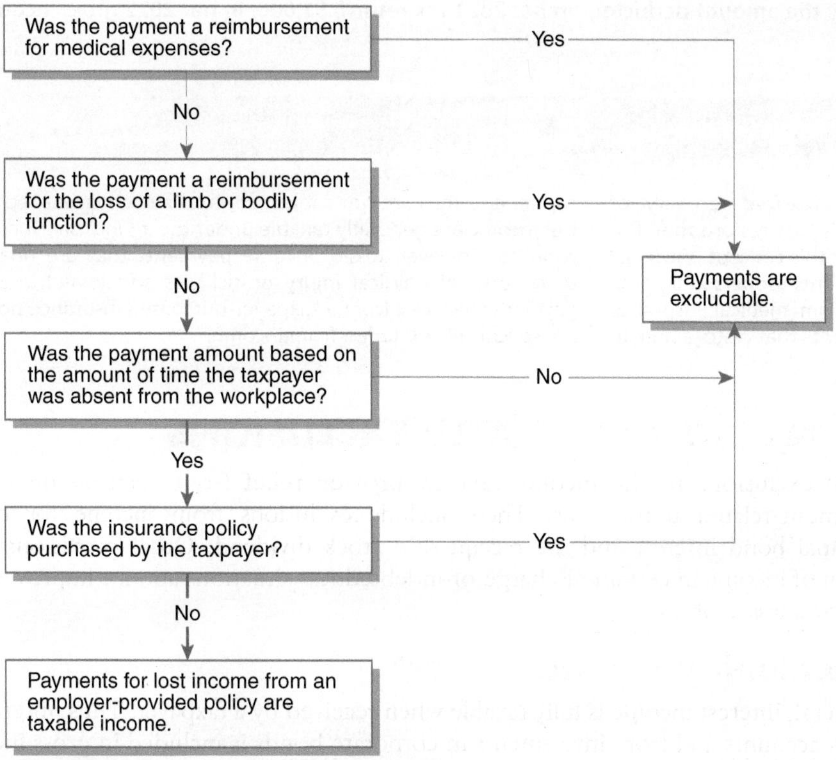


$1,600 of his medical costs and an additional $1,000 for income lost while he was unable to work. What are the tax consequences of the receipt of the payments from the two plans?

**Discussion: The $8,000 in reimbursed medical care expenses is excludable. The $6,400 payment from his employer-provided plan was for medical expenses and is excludable. The remaining $1,600 of medical expense payments came from a plan that Sean purchased and is also excludable. The $1,000 lost-income payment from his personal plan is also excludable because Sean purchased the policy. However, the $2,200 in sick pay from his employer's plan is not excludable and must be included in his gross income. Payments for loss of income are excluded only if the payment comes from a policy that the taxpayer purchased. All other payments for loss of income are included in gross income.**

A problem sometimes arises with reimbursements for medical care when an individual takes an allowable medical deduction for unreimbursed medical expenses in one tax year and then is reimbursed for those expenses in a subsequent year. Individuals are allowed to deduct unreimbursed medical expenses only to the extent that they exceed 10 percent of the individual's adjusted gross income. (The specifics of this deduction are covered in Chapter 8.) Under the tax benefit rule, any reimbursed amount that was deducted in a prior year must be included in taxable income in the year of the reimbursement, to the extent that a tax benefit was received from the deduction.

**Example 36** Jo is seriously injured in a skiing accident late in 2021. The cost of her medical care, which she pays in cash, is $5,000. Because she believes that her insurance company will not reimburse her for these costs, she correctly includes the $5,000 in medical costs as a deduction on her 2021 tax return, which she files in February 2022. Because of the limitations on medical deductions, her actual medical deduction is for only $1,000 of the $5,000. In May 2022, her insurance company reimburses her for $4,500 of the medical costs. What is the proper treatment of the $4,500 reimbursement?

**Discussion: Because the medical costs she deducts on her 2021 return are reimbursed in 2022, Jo must include the reimbursement in her 2022 gross income to the extent she receives a tax benefit from the deduction. In this case, her actual deduction is only $1,000 because of the medical deduction limitations. Therefore, she includes only the amount deducted on her 2021 tax return, $1,000, in her 2022 gross income.**

## concept check

The *capital recovery concept* allows tax-free recovery of invested capital. Payments to individuals that restore their human capital are exempt from tax under this concept. Workers' compensation payments, damage payments for personal physical injuries, and payments received from medical insurance policies for medical expenses are payments that restore human capital and thus are not subject to tax. Payments that replace lost income are generally taxable under the *all-inclusive income concept*. However, loss-of-income payments that are related to a personal physical injury or sickness and loss-of-income payments received from a taxpayer-purchased insurance policy are specifically excluded from income.

# 4-5 INVESTMENT-RELATED EXCLUSIONS

LO 6

Explain the exclusions from income allowed for investment-related items: municipal bond interest, stock dividends, discharge of indebtedness, and improvements by a lessee.

Several exclusions in the income tax law provide relief from taxation on certain investment-related transactions. These include exclusions from income for certain municipal bond interest and the receipt of a stock dividend. Other provisions allow deferral of income in certain discharge-of-indebtedness situations and for improvements made by a lessee of property.

## 4-5a Municipal Bond Interest

In general, interest income is fully taxable when received by a taxpayer. Thus, interest on savings accounts and from investments in corporate bonds is included in gross income. However, the tax law provides an exclusion for interest earned on bonds issued by state and local governments (e.g., cities, counties, state agencies such as turnpike authorities) of the United States as well as those of U.S. possessions (e.g., Guam, Puerto Rico),[30] called **municipal bond interest**. Note that the exclusion from tax does not include interest on U.S. government obligations such as Treasury bills, nor does it apply to interest received on foreign government obligations.

**Example 37** During the current year, Jorge receives the following interest payments:

| | |
|---|---|
| General Motors bonds | $ 350 |
| Province of Ontario bonds | 220 |
| State of Oklahoma bonds | 330 |
| Puerto Rico Port Authority bonds | 100 |
| Total interest received | $1,000 |

How much of the $1,000 in interest is taxable to Jorge?

**Discussion: Only interest on the debt obligations of state and local governments of the United States and its possessions is excluded from gross income. This would include the interest Jorge received on the state of Oklahoma bonds and the Puerto Rico bonds, a total of $430. The interest on the General Motors bonds and the Ontario bonds is fully taxable. Thus, Jorge has taxable interest income of $570.**

Municipal bond interest is excluded because it lets municipalities raise money for projects at lower interest rates than comparable taxable bonds.

**Example 38** ALF Corporation is considering investing in some bonds. ALF's broker has told the company that it can buy city of Nashville tax-exempt bonds at a yield of 6%. Assuming that ALF is taxed at 21%, what would a fully taxable bond of the same risk have to yield to provide an equivalent return?

**Discussion:** Because tax will have to be paid on the taxable bond, it will have to have a higher before-tax yield to provide the same 6% after-tax return on the city of Nashville bonds. To find the after-tax equivalent return, equate the 6% return to the after-tax return, X, *and solve*:

$$\begin{aligned} 0.06 &= X - 0.21X \\ 0.06 &= X(1 - 0.21) \\ 0.06 &= X(0.79) \\ 0.06 \div 0.79 &= X \\ 0.0759 &= X \end{aligned}$$

Therefore, any taxable bond with a pretax yield greater than 7.59% will provide ALF with a higher after-tax return than the Nashville bonds.

## 4-5b Stock Dividends

The Supreme Court ruled in 1920 that the receipt of a **stock dividend** does not constitute a realization of income.[31] That is, a dividend paid in stock of the same company (either a stock dividend or a stock split) is merely "slicing the pie" into small ownership units, with no resulting increase in shareholder wealth. The value of a shareholder's interest does not change; it is merely spread over more ownership units.

**Example 39** Imelda owns 100,000 shares of Smith common stock, for which she paid $1,200,000 several years ago. During the current year, when Smith had a total of 1,000,000 shares outstanding, the company declared and distributed a 20% stock dividend. Imelda received 20,000 new shares (of the 200,000 issued) from the dividend. What are the tax consequences for Imelda from the receipt of the dividend?

**Discussion:** Imelda's wealth has not increased from the receipt of the shares. Before the dividend, she owned 10% (100,000 ÷ 1,000,000) of Smith. After the dividend, she still owns 10% (120,000 ÷ 1,200,000). Therefore, she has not realized an increase of wealth from the dividend and is not taxed on the value of the 20,000 shares received. NOTE: Imelda's original 100,000 shares had a basis of $12 per share ($1,200,000 ÷ 100,000). She now owns 120,000 shares with a total basis of $1,200,000. Thus, her basis per share is now $10 ($1,200,000 ÷ 120,000).

**Example 40** After making the stock dividend, Smith paid a cash dividend of $2 per share on the 1,200,000 shares outstanding. Imelda received $240,000 from the dividend. What are the tax effects of the dividend for Imelda?

**Discussion:** The exclusion from tax is only for the shares of stock received from a stock dividend. Any subsequent cash dividends received on the stock are fully taxable. Imelda must include the $240,000 cash dividend in her gross income.

However, if the receiver of the stock dividend has the option to receive cash in lieu of stock, the dividend is taxed as if the cash option had been selected.[32] In this case, the shares of stock are deemed to have a cash equivalent and thus are taxable.

**Example 41** Opubco, Inc., a public utility, declares a 10% stock dividend when its stock is selling for $50 per share. Stockholders have the option of receiving $5 cash per share in lieu of the stock. Ginny owns 1,000 shares of Opubco stock. She elects to take the 100 additional shares of Opubco stock. What is the tax effect of the receipt of the stock dividend for Ginny?

**Discussion:** Because Ginny could have received cash instead of the shares of stock, she is taxed on the fair market value of the shares received, resulting in taxable income of $5,000 (100 × $50). Her basis in the 100 shares she actually received is the taxable income reported, $5,000.

## 4-5c Discharge of Indebtedness

Under the general principles of income recognition, the borrowing of money is not a taxable event, because the borrower is under an obligation to repay the loan. Similarly, the repayment of the loan principal does not generate taxable income. However, if a lender forgives all or a portion of the debt of the borrower, the borrower realizes an increase in wealth from the reduction of liability. That is, the borrower who is relieved of a debt has obtained a claim of right to the amount of debt forgiven. This increase in wealth, known as a **discharge of indebtedness**, is generally taxable to the borrower.

**Example 42** Leonard borrowed $17,000 from his employer to buy a new car. Several years later, when Leonard had paid the debt down to $3,000, his employer told Leonard he no longer owed the debt as a bonus for Leonard's hard work and devotion to the company. Is Leonard taxed on the forgiveness of the $3,000 owed on the loan?

**Discussion: Leonard is taxed on the $3,000. His wealth has increased as a result of the extinguishment of the liability, and he now has obtained a claim of right to the $3,000, because he is no longer under any obligation to repay.**

The tax law provides an exception to the general rule of taxability of a discharge of indebtedness when the borrower is insolvent (liabilities exceed assets), both before and after the forgiveness of the debt.[33] This exception includes any debt reductions as a result of a bankruptcy proceeding.

**Example 43** Because of a slump in the real estate market, Koka Properties, Inc., is having trouble paying its debts. The value of Koka's assets is $400,000, and its liabilities are $600,000. To help Koka restore stability, its bank forgives a $100,000 line of credit loan it had made to Koka several years earlier. What are the tax effects of the $100,000 forgiveness of debt?

**Discussion: Because Koka is still insolvent ($400,000 – $500,000) after the debt reduction, it does not have to recognize the $100,000 forgiveness as income.**

However, if the discharge makes the debtor solvent, the debtor must recognize income to the extent that the debtor is solvent after the debt reduction. That is, a taxpayer who has a positive net worth after the forgiveness of debt is deemed to have the wherewithal to pay, up to the amount of the solvency.

**Example 44** In example 43, what would the tax effects be if Koka's bank line of credit, which was forgiven, had been $250,000?

**Discussion: The tax law provides that income from the discharge of indebtedness is excluded only if the borrower is insolvent after the discharge. Therefore, income must be recognized to the extent that the borrower is solvent after the debt reduction. Applying this to Koka, its net worth after the discharge is $50,000 ($400,000 – $350,000), which must be included in its gross income.**

When a taxpayer is allowed to exclude discharge of indebtedness income because of insolvency, any tax attributes the taxpayer has in relation to the debt must be reduced by the amount of the exclusion. Tax attributes that must be reduced include net operating loss carryforwards, capital loss carryforwards, and the basis of property purchased with the debt.

The exclusion applies to restructures of acquisition debt, loss of a principal residence in a foreclosure, or short sales of a principal residence. A short sale of a principal residence is a sale in which the sales proceeds are insufficient to pay off the mortgage debt and the lender forgives the balance of the mortgage. The taxpayer's basis in the residence must be reduced by any excluded debt.

**Example 45** Grace owns a principal residence subject to a $300,000 mortgage, all of which is qualified principal residence indebtedness. Because she has been unable to make the payments on the mortgage, the bank forecloses on the home and sells it for $240,000 in satisfaction of Grace's debt. How much income does Grace have to recognize from the foreclosure and forgiveness of the debt on the residence?

**Discussion: Grace has $60,000 ($300,000 − $240,000) of debt discharge income. However, because the amount of the discharge is less than the qualified principal residence indebtedness, she can exclude the $60,000 from gross income.**

**Discussion: The result would be the same if the bank had restructured the loan and reduced the mortgage to $240,000. Grace would have to reduce her basis in the residence by the $60,000 of excluded debt discharge income.**

**Discussion: The result would be the same if Grace had sold the property for $240,000 and the bank canceled the remaining $60,000 of debt (short sale of residence).**

## 4-5d Improvements by a Lessee

The tax law provides that a property owner does not have income when a lessee makes improvements to the owner's property or when such improvements revert to the property owner at the termination of the lease.[34] This allows the property owner to defer the gain in the value of the property from the improvements until the property is sold, at which time the owner will have the wherewithal to pay the tax on the increased value from the **improvements by a lessee**.

**Example 46** Natasha leased a building from Rudy Corporation under a 10-year lease that provided that any improvements made by Natasha would revert to Rudy at the expiration of the lease. Natasha added a wing to the building at a cost of $40,000. When the lease ended, the new wing increased the value of the property by $75,000. Does Rudy Corporation have any income from the addition of the new wing by Natasha?

**Discussion: Rudy will not be taxed on the increased value of the property until it sells or otherwise disposes of the property in a taxable transaction. At that time, the $75,000 increase in value will be reflected in any gain from the property's disposition.**

The exclusion from income for improvements by a lessee does not apply when the improvements are made in lieu of rent. When that is the case, the lessee is paying the rent in the form of the improvement rather than in cash. Under the cash-equivalent approach to income recognition, the value of such improvements is included in income.[35]

**Example 47** Andrea leased a building from Petros for $2,000 per month. The bathroom was in need of repair, so Petros agreed to reduce Andrea's rent by the cost of repairing the bathroom. Andrea paid $1,800 to have the bathroom repaired and paid Petros only $200 for the next month's rent. What are the tax effects to Petros of the payment of the repair costs by Andrea?

**Discussion: Because the repair improvement was made in lieu of a rental payment, the $1,800 is considered a rental payment received by Petros. It is not excludable as an improvement by a lessee.**

**Although Petros recognizes income from the repairs, he is allowed a deduction for the repair cost as an ordinary and necessary expense. The net effect of this situation for Petros is no increase in his income. This effect follows from the substance of the transaction: If Andrea had paid Petros the $2,000 monthly rent and Petros then reimbursed Andrea for the repairs, Petros would include the repairs in income through the rent payment and deduct the repair expense payment.**

# CHAPTER SUMMARY

All income received by a taxpayer is taxable unless specifically excluded by the tax law. Excludable forms of income must be identified to determine a taxpayer's gross income. Exclusions from income are a result of the *legislative grace concept*. Under this concept, only Congress can provide relief from tax. Any relief provided must be strictly applied and interpreted. As applied to exclusions, this means that a specific provision must be found in the tax law before an income item can be excluded from taxation. Exclusions from income are usually meant to avoid double taxation or to provide incentive for taxpayers to enter into a tax-favored transaction. Often, amounts are excluded from taxation based on the *wherewithal-to-pay concept*, under which amounts are taxed when the means are available to pay the tax.

This chapter identified and discussed four general classes of exclusions: donative items, employment-related exclusions, returns of human capital, and investment-related exclusions. Because all these exclusion items represent departures from the general concepts of income recognition, there is no hard-and-fast method for learning the various types of exclusions. To aid in your study of exclusions, Table 4-2 summarizes by category the exclusions discussed in this chapter and points out the major problems involved within each category. At the completion of the chapter, you should be able to compute the gross income for most common situations faced by taxpayers.

*Table 4-2*

**Income Exclusions by Category**

| | Exclusions | Major Problems |
|---|---|---|
| **Donative Items** | Gifts<br>Inheritances<br>Life insurance proceeds<br>Scholarships | What is a gift?<br>No exclusion for future earnings on amounts excluded for gifts, inheritances, life insurance proceeds<br>Only direct costs of education excludable for scholarships |
| **Employment-related Exclusions** | Foreign-earned income<br>Employer-provided benefits<br>Pension plan payments<br>Group term life insurance<br>Health/accident insurance<br>Meals and lodging<br>No additional cost services<br>Employee discounts<br>Qualified retirement planning services<br>Working-condition fringes<br>De minimis fringes<br>Child care<br>Athletic facilities<br>Educational assistance<br>Employee benefit plans<br>Cafeteria plans<br>Flexible benefits/salary reduction plans<br>Health Savings Accounts | Nondiscrimination requirement for most benefits<br>Each benefit has specific requirements and/or limitations |
| **Returns of Human Capital** | Workers' compensation<br>Damages for personal physical injury<br>Payments from employee-purchased health/accident plan<br>Payments from employer-provided health/accident insurance for medical expenses | Payments for lost income-wage continuation/disability payments<br>Tax benefit rule for medical expenses reimbursed in a year subsequent to deduction |
| **Investment-related Exclusions** | Municipal bond interest<br>Stock dividends<br>Discharge of indebtedness—insolvent debtor<br>Improvements by a lessee | Taxability of gain on disposition of tax-exempt securities/nontaxable dividend shares<br>Cash option on stock dividend<br>Insolvent debtors who become solvent after discharge of debt<br>Improvements made in lieu of rent |

Reinforce this chapter's concepts by going to **www.cengage.com**

# KEY TERMS

cafeteria plan (p. 4-13)
compensatory damage payments (p. 4-15)
de minimis fringe benefits (p. 4-13)
disability payments (p. 4-16)
discharge of indebtedness (p. 4-20)
educational assistance program (p. 4-13)
employee discount (p. 4-11)
employer-provided lodging (p. 4-11)
employer's athletic facility (p. 4-13)
flexible benefits plan (p. 4-13)
foreign-earned income (p. 4-7)
gift (p. 4-2)
group term life insurance (p. 4-9)
health and accident insurance (p. 4-10)
Health Savings Account (HSA) (p. 4-14)
improvements by a lessee (p. 4-21)
inheritance (p. 4-4)
life insurance proceeds (p. 4-4)
loss-of-income damages (p. 4-16)
meals provided by the employer (p. 4-11)
municipal bond interest (p. 4-18)
no-additional-cost services (p. 4-11)
personal physical injury (p. 4-15)
punitive damages (p. 4-16)
qualified pension plan (p. 4-8)
qualified retirement planning services (p. 4-12)
salary reduction plan (p. 4-13)
scholarship (p. 4-6)
self-insured medical plan (p. 4-10)
stock dividend (p. 4-19)
workers' compensation (p. 4-15)
working-condition fringe benefit (p. 4-12)

# PRIMARY TAX LAW SOURCES

[1]Sec. 102—States that the value of property received by gift or inheritance is excluded from gross income.

[2]Comm. v. Duberstein, 363 U.S. 278 at 283 (1960)—Held that a Cadillac received by a taxpayer from a businessman to whom he occasionally gave names of potential customers was not a tax-free gift.

[3]Reg. Sec. 1.102-1—States that property received by gift or inheritance is not subject to income tax, but income earned on such property subsequent to receipt is not excluded.

[4]Sec. 101—States that life insurance payments are excluded from gross income.

[5]Sec. 117—States that qualified scholarships are excluded from gross income and the amount of the exclusion is limited to qualified tuition and related expenses.

[6]Prop. Reg. Sec. 1.117-6—Defines *scholarships* and discusses the types of expenditures that are excludable as direct education costs.

[7]Sec. 901—Allows a tax credit for foreign taxes paid on earned income.

[8]Sec. 911—Allows the exclusion of up to $80,000 of foreign-earned income from gross income in lieu of the tax credit provided by Section 901. After 2006, the $80,000 exclusion is indexed for inflation and is $108,700 in 2021 ($107,600 in 2020).

[9]Sec. 219—Allows a deduction for adjusted gross income for contributions to qualified retirement accounts.

[10]Sec. 401—Allows self-employed individuals to establish retirement accounts that allow deductions for contributions comparable to those provided by employer-sponsored pension plans.

[11]Sec. 401—Prescribes the requirements for a qualified employer-provided retirement plan.

[12]Sec. 402—Prescribes the tax treatment of qualified employer-provided pension plans.

[13]Reg. Sec. 1.79-4T—Discusses the nondiscrimination rules as they apply to the provision of group term life insurance to employees.

[14]Reg. Sec. 1.79-3—Specifies the taxability of premiums paid on group term life insurance in excess of $50,000.

[15]Sec. 106—States that gross income does not include payments for health and accident insurance coverage by an employer for an employee.

[16]Sec. 119—Provides an exclusion from gross income for meals and lodging provided by an employer to an employee.

[17]Reg. Sec. 1.119-1—Defines terms for purposes of the exclusion for meals and lodging provided by an employer.

[18]Sec. 132—Excludes no-additional-cost services, qualified employee discounts, working-condition fringes and de minimis fringe benefits from gross income; also provides that employer-provided parking and on-premises athletic facilities are excludable fringe benefits.

[19]Sec. 132(a)(7)—Allows exclusion of qualified retirement planning services.

[20]Reg. Sec. 1.132-5—Discusses working-condition fringes and gives examples of qualifying working-condition fringe benefits.

[21]Reg. Sec. 1.132-6—Discusses de minimis fringe benefits and provides examples of such benefits.

[22]Sec. 129—Excludes up to $5,000 per year for employer-provided dependent care.

[23]Sec. 127—Excludes up to $5,250 in reimbursements to an employee from an employer's qualified educational assistance plan.

[24]Sec. 125—Provides an exclusion for benefits selected under a cafeteria plan; defines a *cafeteria plan* and describes the types of benefits it may offer.

[25]Prop. Reg. Sec. 1.125-1—Provides information about cafeteria plans in a question-and-answer format; question 7 answers questions relating to what constitutes a flexible benefits (salary reduction) plan.

[26]Sec. 223—Defines a Health Savings Account (HSA) and allows a deduction for contributions to an HSA. Sets a limit on the amount of the contribution to and provides the tax treatment of reimbursements from an HSA.

[27]Sec. 104—Limits the exclusion for damage payments to any damages (other than punitive damages) received for personal physical injury or sickness.

[28]Conference Committee Report, H.R. Rep. No. 3448, 104th Cong., 2nd Sess. (1996)—Provides that all punitive damage payments received after August 19, 1996, are taxable regardless of the origin of the claim for the damages.

[29]Sec. 105—States that payments for medical expenses from an employer-provided plan are excluded from gross income.

[30]Sec. 103—States that interest received on state or local government bonds is excluded from gross income.

[31]Eisner v. Macomber, 252 U.S. 189 (1920)—Held that a stock dividend did not constitute gross income.

[32]Sec. 305—States that stock dividends with a cash option are taxable.

[33]Sec. 108—Provides an exclusion from gross income for the discharge of indebtedness of an insolvent taxpayer.

[34] Sec. 109—States that the value of improvements made to a lessor's property by a lessee are not income to the lessor at the termination of the lease.

[35] Reg. Sec. 1.109-1—States that improvements made by a lessee to a lessor's property that are in lieu of rental payments are included in gross income as income from rents.

# DISCUSSION QUESTIONS

1. **LO1** What are the two reasons most commonly advanced for excluding items from income? Give examples of each, and explain how they accomplish the purpose of the exclusion.
2. **LO1** What is the difference between an exclusion of income and a deferral of income?
3. **LO2** How can gifts be used to lower the overall tax paid by a family?
4. **LO2** Why are life insurance proceeds excluded from the gross income of the beneficiary of the policy?
5. **LO2** Explain the circumstances under which a scholarship would not be excluded from gross income.
6. **LO3** What tax relief is provided to U.S. citizens who earn income in a foreign country and pay taxes in that country?
7. **LO4** How do employees benefit from payments made into a qualified pension plan on their behalf?
8. **LO4** Distinguish group term life insurance from whole life insurance.
9. **LO4** What is the difference in the tax treatment of a medical insurance plan that is purchased from a third-party insurer and a self-insured medical reimbursement plan?
10. **LO4** What is a Health Savings Account?
11. **LO4** What is the difference between a qualified employee discount and a bargain purchase by an employee?
12. **LO4** What is the difference between a cafeteria plan and a flexible benefits (salary reduction) plan?
13. **LO5** Why are workers' compensation payments treated differently from unemployment compensation payments for tax purposes?
14. **LO5** What is a personal physical injury for purposes of excluding damage payments received?
15. **LO5** Are punitive damages taxable? Explain.
16. **LO5** Are payments for loss of income taxable? Explain.
17. **LO5** Discuss the difference in the tax treatment of payments received from an employer-provided health and accident insurance policy and a health and accident insurance policy purchased by the taxpayer.
18. **LO6** What is the purpose of excluding municipal bond interest from gross income?
19. **LO6** Are all stock dividends received excluded from gross income?

# PROBLEMS

20. **LO1** Throughout the textbook, it has been stated that tax relief can come in several forms. Assuming that the taxpayer in question is in a 24 percent marginal tax rate bracket and the time value of money is 6 percent, determine the tax value of the following forms of relief:
    a. A $2,000 item of income that is excluded from income
    b. A $2,000 expenditure that is deductible in computing taxable income
    c. A $2,000 expenditure that is eligible for a 10 percent tax credit
    d. A $2,000 item of income that is deferred for five years (assume no change in the marginal tax rate.)
21. **LO2** A fire extensively damaged a small Alaska town where Intech Company had its primary plant. Intech decided to give $200 to each household that lost its residence. About 12 percent of the payments were made to Intech employees. Is the receipt of $200 by some Intech employees taxable as compensation or excludable as a gift?
22. **LO2** On May 1, Raisa received a $10,000, 9 percent bond of Altomba Corporation as a graduation present from her aunt Lenia. The bond pays interest on June 30 and December 31. What are the tax effects of this transfer for Raisa and Lenia for the current year?
23. **LO2** During the current year, Alexis gives her daughter Tabatha stocks worth $80,000 on the condition that she pay her son Rory the first $7,000 in dividends

on the stock each year. Discuss the taxability of this arrangement in each of the following cases:

a. The stocks pay total dividends of $8,000. Tabatha pays Rory $7,000 under the agreement.

b. The stocks pay total dividends of $5,500. Tabatha pays Rory $5,500 under the agreement.

24. **LO2** Herman inherits stock with a fair market value of $100,000 from his grandfather on March 1. On May 1, Herman sells half the stock at a gain of $10,000 and invests the $60,000 proceeds in Jordan County school bonds. The bonds' annual interest rate is 6 percent which is paid on July 31 and January 31. On October 15, Herman receives a $2,200 dividend on the remaining shares of stock. How much gross income does Herman have from these transactions?

25. **LO2** Fatima inherits a rental property with a fair market value of $90,000 from her aunt on April 30. On May 15, the executor of the estate sends her a check for $7,000. A letter accompanying the check states that the $7,000 comes from the rent received on the property since her aunt's death. Fatima receives $6,600 in rent on the property during the remainder of the year and pays allowable expenses of $4,200 on the property. How much gross income does Fatima have from these transactions?

26. **LO2** Allison dies during the current year. She is covered by a $1,000,000 life insurance policy payable to her husband, Bob. Bob elects to receive the policy proceeds in 10 annual installments of $120,000. Write a letter to Bob explaining the tax consequences of the receipt of each installment. Communication Skills

27. **LO2** Earl is a student at Aggie Tech. He receives a $5,000 general scholarship for his outstanding grades in previous years. Earl is also a residence hall assistant, for which he receives a $1,000 tuition reduction and free room and board worth $6,000 per year. Earl's annual costs for tuition, books, and supplies are $8,000. Does Earl have any taxable income from the scholarship or the free room and board?

28. **LO2** Assume the same facts as in problem 27, except that Earl is not a residence hall assistant and his general scholarship is for 10,000.

29. **LO2** Fawn receives a $2,500 scholarship to State University. Discuss the taxability of the scholarship under each of the following assumptions:

a. The scholarship is paid from a general scholarship fund and is awarded to students with high academic potential. Recipients are not required to perform any services to receive the scholarship.

b. The scholarship is paid by the finance department. Recipients are required to work 10 hours per week for a professor designated by the department.

30. **LO2** Determine whether the taxpayers in each of the following situations have realized taxable income:

a. Alexander inherited a tract of land from his uncle who died during the current year. A friend of Alexander's who is a petroleum engineer told him he thought there might be oil on the land. Alexander had the land surveyed, and an oil deposit worth an estimated $5,000,000 was discovered on the property.

b. Mickey was given two tickets to the World Series by a friend. Mickey sold the tickets for $500 apiece.

c. Hannah is the purchasing agent for Slim Diet Centers. Harold, a salesman who does considerable business with Hannah, gave her a set of golf clubs worth $750. Harold told Hannah that he was giving her the clubs to show his appreciation for being such a good friend throughout their business dealings.

d. Melanie's father died during the current year. She was the beneficiary of a $200,000 insurance policy on her father's life. She received the proceeds on August 1 and immediately invested in a bank certificate of deposit with a 9 percent annual earnings rate.

31. **LO2** Armando, a manager for Petros Pizza Pies (PPP), dies in an accident on July 12. PPP pays his wife, Penelope, $600 in salary that had accrued before Armando died. Armando was covered by a $90,000 group term life insurance policy, which is also paid to Penelope. In addition, the board of directors of PPP authorizes payment of $6,000 to Penelope and $4,000 to their child in recognition of Armando's years of loyal service and contributions to the success of the company. What are the tax consequences of the payments to Penelope and her child?

Communication Skills

32. **LO2** Lucinda, a welder for Big Auto, Inc., dies in an automobile accident on March 14 of this year. Big Auto has a company policy of paying $5,000 to the spouse of any employee who dies. In addition to the $5,000 payment, Big Auto pays Harvey, Lucinda's husband, $1,600 in salary and $1,100 in vacation pay Lucinda had earned before her death. Harvey also collects $120,000 from a group term life insurance policy Big Auto provided as part of Lucinda's compensation package. Lucinda had contributed to a qualified employer-sponsored pension plan. Big Auto had matched Lucinda's contributions to the plan. The plan lets the beneficiary of an employee who dies before payments begin take the plan balance as an annuity or in a lump sum. Harvey elects to take the $250,000 plan balance in a lump sum. Write a letter to Harvey explaining the tax consequences of each payment he receives.

33. **LO3** Joan is a single individual who works for Big Petroleum, Inc. During all of 2021, she is stationed in West Africa. She pays West African taxes of $20,000 on her Big Petroleum salary of $92,000. Her taxable income without considering her salary from Big Petroleum is $36,000. How should Joan treat the salary she receives from Big Petroleum on her 2021 U.S. tax return?

Communication Skills

34. **LO3** Boris is an unmarried systems specialist with a public accounting firm. During all of 2021, he is on temporary assignment in London. He pays $21,000 in British income tax on his $100,000 salary. Boris knows little about taxes and seeks your advice on the taxability of the salary he earns while in London. Write Boris a memorandum explaining the tax treatment of his London salary. Assume that Boris has no other income sources and that he does not itemize deductions.

35. **LO4** Zoie has worked for Humple Manufacturing for 16 years. Humple has a pension plan that matches employee contributions by up to 4 percent of an employee's salary. Zoie, age 60, is ready to retire. She has contributed $20,000 to the plan. Under Humple's pension plan, Zoie will receive $1,000 per month until she dies. Assume that Zoie is expected to live 25 more years. She wants to know the tax consequences of each pension payment that she will receive.
    a. Assume Humple's plan is a qualified pension plan.
    b. Assume Humple's plan is not a qualified plan. Zoie has paid tax on all contributions into and earned by the plan.

36. **LO4** Hashem works for Close Corporation for 24 years. Close has a qualified, noncontributory pension plan that pays employees with more than five years of service $100 per month per year of service when they reach age 65. Hashem turns 65 in February of this year and retires in June. Payments from Close's plan begin in July. In preparing for his retirement, Hashem purchased an annuity 15 years ago for $26,000. The annuity pays $775 per month for life beginning at age 65. Hashem begins receiving the annuity payments in March. How much gross income does Hashem have from the receipt of the payments from Close and the annuity in the current year?

Communication Skills

37. **LO4** Bear Company provides all its employees with a $10,000 group term life insurance policy. Elk Company does not provide any life insurance but pays $10,000 to survivors of employees who die. Jackie, an employee of Bear Company, and her sister-in-law, Rosetta, an employee of Elk Company, both die during the current year. Their husbands, Bo and Carl, do not understand the tax effects of the $10,000 payments they receive. Write a letter to Bo and Carl explaining the tax effects of the $10,000 payments each receives.

38. **LO4** Horace is an employee of Ace Electric Company. Ace provides all employees with group term life insurance equal to twice their annual salary. How much gross income does Horace have under each of the following assumptions?
    a. Horace is 26 and earns $16,000 per year.
    b. Horace is 26 and earns $42,000 per year.
    c. Horace is 63 and earns $42,000 per year.
    d. Horace is 46 and earns $90,000 per year.

39. **LO4** Abe is an employee of Haddock, Inc. Haddock provides basic health and accident insurance to all its employees through a contract with Minor Accident Insurance Company. Because the Minor policy does not cover 100 percent of medical costs, Haddock provides all executive officers with a self-insured plan to pay any medical costs not covered by Minor's policy. Abe is eligible for both plans. During the current year, premiums on the Minor policy for Abe were $1,450. Abe is reimbursed for $1,900 of his medical costs from the self-insured plan.
    a. What are the tax consequences to Abe of the payments made by Haddock?
    b. What difference would it make if all employees were covered under both plans?

40. **LO4** Faldo, Inc., provides medical coverage to employees through a self-insured plan. Nick, the president of Faldo, receives $3,400 in medical expense reimbursements from the plan during the current year. Discuss the tax consequences to Nick under the following circumstances:
    a. All employees are fully covered by the plan.
    b. All employees are covered by the plan. However, only Faldo's executive officers are fully reimbursed for all expenses. All other employees are limited to a maximum reimbursement of $1,000 per year.

41. **LO4** Hamid's employer provides a high-deductible health plan ($1,400 deductible) and contributes $500 to each employee's Health Savings Account (HSA). Hamid makes the maximum allowable contribution to his HSA. During the year, he spends $300 on qualified medical expenses and the HSA earns $18. What is the effect of Hamid's participation in the HSA on his adjusted gross income?

42. **LO4** Tia is married and is employed by Carrera Auto Parts. In 2021, Carrera established high-deductible health insurance for all its employees. The plan has a $2,800 deductible for married taxpayers. Carrera also contributes 5 percent of each employee's salary to a Health Savings Account. Tia's salary is $30,000 in 2021 and $32,000 in 2022. Tia makes the maximum allowable contribution to her HSA in 2021 and 2022. She received $600 from the HSA for her 2021 medical expenses. In 2022, she spends $1,400 on medical expenses from her HSA. The MSA earns $28 in 2021 and $46 in 2022.
    a. What is the effect of the HSA transactions on Tia's adjusted gross income?
    b. How much does Tia have in her HSA account at the end of 2022?

43. **LO4** Adam works during the summer as a fire watcher for the Oregon forest service. As such he spends three weeks in the woods in a forest service watchtower and then gets a week off. Because of the remoteness of the location, groceries are flown in by helicopter to Adam each week. Does Adam have any taxable income from this arrangement? Explain.

44. **LO4** Don is the production manager for Corporate Manufacturing Facilities (CMF). CMF works three production shifts per day. Because Don is so integral to CMF's operations, the company requires him to live in housing that CMF owns so he can be available for any emergencies that arise throughout the day. The housing is located four blocks from the CMF plant. Is Don taxed on the value of the housing? Explain.

45. **LO4** Determine whether the taxpayer has received taxable income in each of the following situations. Explain why any amount(s) may be excluded:
   a. Jim is an employee of Fast Tax Prep, Inc. All employees of Fast Tax Prep are eligible for a 50 percent discount on the preparation of their income tax returns. Jim's tax return preparation would normally have cost $300, but he paid only $150 because of the discount.
   b. Mabel is a lawyer for a large law firm, Winken, Blinken, and Nod. Winken pays Mabel's annual license renewal fee of $400 and her $300 annual dues to the American Lawyers' Association. Mabel also takes advantage of Winken's educational assistance plan and receives payment for the $6,000 cost of taking two night school courses in consumer law.
   c. Gomez Company runs a nursery near its offices. Employees are allowed to leave their children at the nursery free of charge during working hours. Nonemployees may also use the facility at a cost of $300 per month per child. Dolph is an employee of Gomez with two children who stay at Gomez's facility while Dolph is at work.
   d. At the sporting goods store where Melissa works, her employer lets all employees buy goods at a 40 percent discount. Melissa purchases for $300 camping and fishing supplies that retail for $500. The goods had cost her employer $250.

46. **LO4** Courtney is an employee of Fremont Company. An average of three times a week, she works out during her lunch hour at a health club provided by Fremont. Discuss the taxability of Fremont's provision of the health club in the following situations:
   a. The health club is owned by Fremont and is located on its business premises. All employees and their dependents are allowed to use the facility. The cost of joining a comparable facility is $60 per month.
   b. The health club is located in Fremont's office building but is owned by Manzer Fitness World. Fremont pays the $60 per month health club dues.
   c. Fremont is in the health club business. The health club is used primarily by customers, although several employees, including Courtney, use it, too.

47. **LO4** Dow, 42, is a manager for Winter Company. In addition to his $90,000 salary, he receives the following benefits from Winter during the current year:
   - Winter pays all its employees' health and accident insurance. Premiums paid by Winter for Dow's health insurance are $1,800.
   - Winter provides all employees with group term life insurance coverage equal to their annual salary. Premiums on Dow's $90,000 in coverage are $900.
   - Winter has a flexible benefits plan in which employees may participate to pay any costs not reimbursed by their health insurance. Dow has $2,700 withheld from his salary under the plan. His actual unreimbursed medical costs are $3,430. Winter pays Dow the $2,700 paid into the plan during the year.
   - All management-level Winter employees are entitled to employer-provided parking. The cost of Dow's parking in a downtown garage is $4,800 for the year.
   - Winter pays Dow's $150 monthly membership fee in a health club located in the building in which Dow works. Dow uses the club during his lunch time and on weekends.

   Compute Dow's gross income for the current year.

48. **LO4** Becky, 45, is a senior vice president for South Publishing Company. During the current year, her salary is $125,000 and she receives a $25,000 bonus. South matches employee contributions to its qualified pension plan up to 10 percent of an employee's annual salary before bonuses. Becky contributes the maximum to the plan. She also receives the following benefits from South during the year:
   - South has a cafeteria plan that lets all employees select tax-free benefits or the cash equivalent on 5 percent of their annual salary before any bonus or pension plan payments. Becky uses the plan to buy health and accident insurance for her

daughter at a cost of $1,600, group life insurance coverage of $200,000 at a cost of $1,300, and child care at a cost of $2,800. She takes the remaining $550 in cash.

- All executive officers' medical expenses are covered by a self-insured medical reimbursement plan. Becky is fully reimbursed for her $600 in medical expenses.
- South pays the employee's share of Social Security taxes on all executive employees' regular salaries.
- Executive officers are provided with covered parking at company headquarters. All other employees must pay for their own parking. Becky's free parking is worth $4,500 this year.
- Becky belongs to several professional organizations. South pays her dues of $850. In addition, South pays the dues for all executive officers at one social club. South pays Becky's $3,600 country club membership.
- The executive officers eat lunch in a private dining room at company headquarters. The purpose of the dining room is to encourage the officers to interact in an informal setting. They often discuss business but are not required to follow an agenda. The value of the meals Becky ate in the dining room this year is estimated at $1,900.

Compute Becky's gross income from South Publishing Company for the current year.

49. **LO4** Camila, 43, is an employee of Primus University. Her annual salary is $44,000. Primus provides all employees with health and accident insurance (Camila's policy cost $1,800) and group term life insurance at twice their annual salary rounded up to the nearest $10,000 ($90,000 of coverage for Camila). In addition, Primus pays the first $1,000 of each employee's Social Security contribution. The university has a qualified pension and a flexible benefits plan. Camila has $4,000 of her salary withheld and paid (and Primus matches the payment) into the pension plan. She also elects to have $1,300 of her salary paid into the flexible benefits plan. Because her medical costs are lower than expected, Camila gets back only $1,250 of the $1,300 she paid into the plan. What is Camila's gross income for the current year?

50. **LO4** Theresa is an employee of Hubbard Corporation with an annual salary of $60,000. Hubbard has a cafeteria plan that lets all employees select a total of 10 percent of their annual salary from a menu of nontaxable fringe benefits. Theresa selects medical insurance that costs the company $4,200, and $50,000 worth of group term life insurance that costs the company $1,000, and takes the remainder in cash. What is the effect of Hubbard's cafeteria plan on Theresa's gross income?

51. **LO5** Determine the taxability of the damages received in each of the following situations:
    a. Helio Corporation sues Wrongo Corporation, charging that Wrongo made false statements about one of Helio's products. Helio claims that the statements injured its business reputation with its customers. The court awards Helio $2,000,000 in damages.
    b. Lien is injured when a chair on a ski lift she is riding on comes loose and crashes to the ground. Lien sues the ski resort and receives $12,000 in full payment of her medical expenses, $4,000 for pain and suffering, and $6,500 for income lost while she recovers from the accident. The company that manufactured the ski lift also pays Lien $50,000 in punitive damages.
    c. A major broadcasting company reports that Dr. Henry Mueller was engaged in Medicare fraud. The doctor is incensed and sues the company for libel. The court rules that the report was made with reckless disregard for the truth and awards Mueller $20,000 for the humiliation he suffered because of the allegation, $200,000 for loss of his business reputation, and $150,000 in punitive damages.

52. **LO5** May was injured when a forklift tipped over on her while she was moving stock in the company warehouse. Because of her injuries, she could not work for

three weeks. Her employer paid her $400, which was half her normal wages for the three-week period. She also received $600 in workers' compensation for the injury. May is required to include the $400 she received from her employer in her gross income but excludes the $600 workers' compensation payment. Discuss why the payments are taxed differently.

53. **LO5** Bill was severely injured when he was hit by a car while jogging. He spent one month in the hospital and missed three months of work because of the injuries. Total medical costs were $60,000. Bill received the following payments as a result of the accident:
    - His employer-provided accident insurance reimbursed him for $48,000 of the medical costs and provided him with $3,800 in sick pay while he was out of work.
    - A private medical insurance policy purchased by Bill paid him $12,000 for medical costs.
    - His employer gave Bill $6,000 to help him get through his rehabilitation period.
    - A separate disability policy that Bill had purchased paid him $4,000.

    How much gross income does Bill have as a result of the payments received for the accident?

54. **LO5** Determine the tax treatment of the payments received in each of the following cases:
    a. Anastasia is covered by her employer's medical insurance policy. During the current year, the policy reimburses her for $960 of the $1,200 in medical costs she incurred.
    b. Alfredo, who is self-employed, is injured in a snowmobile accident. The insurance he purchased covers $3,200 of the $3,900 in medical costs related to the accident. It also pays him $2,000 to cover the income he loses during his recuperation.
    c. Libby is injured when a company truck backs over her at a warehouse. The company pays her $2,200 in medical expenses from its self-insured medical reimbursement plan. (All employees are covered by the plan.) During her recuperation, the company pays her normal $1,300 salary. In addition, she receives $600 from an insurance policy the company purchased to cover its liability to injured employees.
    d. Shortly after beginning work for El Dorado Corporation, Manny is injured when a lathe he is operating breaks his leg. Because he has not worked for the company long enough to qualify for employee medical insurance coverage, the company pays his $800 medical bill.

55. **LO6** Determine Rona's gross income from the following items she receives during the current year:

| | |
|---|---|
| Interest on savings account | $ 300 |
| Dividends on Microsoft stock | 200 |
| Interest on Guam development bonds | 2,000 |
| Dividend on life insurance policy | 200 |
| (The company is a mutual life insurance company, and the dividend is a return of part of the premium she paid on the policy.) | |

In addition, Rona owns 1,000 shares of Cochran Corporation common stock. Cochran has a dividend reinvestment plan through which stockholders can receive a stock dividend equal to 4 percent of their holdings in lieu of a cash dividend of equal value. Rona takes the 40 shares of stock, which are worth $3 per share.

56. **LO6** Horatio owns Utah general purpose bonds with a face value of $50,000 that he purchased last year for $52,000. During the current year, Horatio receives $2,400 in interest on the bonds. In December, Horatio sells the bonds for $48,000. What is the effect of the bond transactions on Horatio's gross income for the current year?

57. **LO6** Determine the amount of gross income Elbert must recognize in each of the following situations:
   a. In October, Elbert sells city of Norfolk bonds with a face value of $6,000 for $5,800. Elbert had purchased the bonds two years ago for $5,200, and had received $450 in interest on the bonds before he sold them.
   b. Elbert owns 1,000 shares of Tortoise, Inc., common stock for which he had paid $8,000 several years ago. Tortoise declares and distributes a 20 percent stock dividend during the current year. On December 31, Tortoise common stock is selling for $10 per share.
   c. In December, Elbert sells city of Quebec bonds with a face value of $7,600 for $7,200. Elbert had purchased the bonds in January for $7,700 and received $950 in interest on the bonds before he sold them.

58. **LO6** Maysa is considering making an investment in municipal bonds yielding 4 percent. What would the yield on a taxable bond have to be to provide a higher after-tax return than the municipal bond if Maysa is in a 33 percent marginal tax rate bracket?

59. **LO6** Return to the facts of problem 58. Assume that Maysa bought $5,000 par value of Rondo Corporation bonds for $4,500. The bonds pay 8 percent interest annually. Three years later, the price of the bonds has increased to $6,200. Maysa can purchase municipal bonds yielding 5.5 percent. Should she sell the Rondo Corporation bonds and buy the municipal bonds?

60. **LO6** Vito is having financial difficulties. Among other debts, he owes More Bank $300,000. Rather than lend Vito more money to help him out, More Bank agrees to reduce his debt to $200,000.
   a. How much gross income must Vito recognize if his assets total $600,000 and his liabilities are $400,000 before the forgiveness of debt?
   b. Assume the same facts as in part a, except that Vito's liabilities are $800,000 before the forgiveness of debt.

61. **LO6** Determine the amount of income that must be recognized in each discharge of indebtedness situation that follows:
   a. Marvin owes Central State Bank $80,000. The bank agrees to reduce the debt to $60,000. Prior to the debt reduction, Marvin's assets total $350,000 and his liabilities are $330,000.
   b. Assume the same facts as in part a, except that Marvin's liabilities are $400,000 before the forgiveness of debt.

62. **LO6** Helena has assets of $130,000 and liabilities of $160,000. One of her debts is for $120,000. Discuss the tax consequences of the reduction of this debt in each of the following circumstances:
   a. The debt was incurred by Helena for medical school expenses. She borrowed $120,000 from her grandfather, who agreed to reduce the debt to $80,000 because Helena had done so well in school.
   b. The debt was incurred to buy property used in Helena's business. To help Helena get back on her feet, the bank that loaned her the money agreed to reduce the debt to $80,000.
   c. The debt was incurred to buy equipment used in Helena's business. Because the equipment did not perform as advertised by the manufacturer who had financed the purchase, the manufacturer agreed to reduce the debt to $80,000.

63. **LO6** Paulsons Partnership owns a building that it has rented out to Corner Grocery Store for the last 10 years. Corner goes out of business and returns the property to Paulsons. Corner had made improvements to the store costing $30,000 during the 10-year lease period. The partnership had paid $60,000 for the building, which is now worth $200,000. Does Paulsons have any gross income from the ending of the lease? Discuss when Paulsons will recognize any income from the building.

Communication Skills

64. **LO6** Jonas owns a building that he leases to Dipper, Inc., for $5,000 per month. The owner of Dipper has been complaining about the condition of the restrooms and has proposed making improvements that will cost $24,000. Dipper's owner is willing to pay to have the improvements made if Jonas will reduce the monthly rent on the building to $4,000 for one year. Write a letter to Jonas explaining the tax effects for Jonas of the proposal by Dipper's owner.

## ISSUE IDENTIFICATION PROBLEMS

In each of the following problems, identify the tax issue(s) posed by the facts presented. Determine the possible tax consequences of each issue that you identify.

65. A tornado extensively damaged the community in which Bodine Company had its primary manufacturing facilities. Bodine gives $1,000 to each household that suffered damage from the tornado to help residents while repairs are being made. Some (but not all) of the payments are made to Bodine employees.
66. Kermit receives a $1,000, 6 percent bond of General Foods, Inc., from his uncle Ed as a graduation present. The bond pays interest on June 30 and December 31. Kermit receives the bond on May 1.
67. Hersh inherits $50,000 from his grandfather. He receives the money on January 1 and immediately invests $25,000 in General Motors bonds that pay 8 percent annual interest and $25,000 in Lane County highway improvement bonds with a 6 percent annual interest rate.
68. Than's grandmother dies and leaves him jewelry worth $40,000. In addition, he is the beneficiary of a $100,000 life insurance policy that his grandmother had bought before she retired.
69. Binh met Anika 10 years ago at a cocktail party. Anika was a wealthy investor with extensive holdings in the oil and gas industry. Binh was a real estate agent earning about $35,000 a year. Several months later, they decided to live together, and Anika promised to leave Binh her entire estate. In the ensuing years, they had an intimate, marriage-like relationship, attending social, business, and family functions together. Anika died in 2019. No will was found immediately. A few months after Anika's death, her sister found a one-page paper signed by Anika. The paper left Anika's entire estate to her brothers and sisters and named her sister as executor of the estate. Binh sued Anika's estate and won a judgment of $2 million for services rendered to Anika during their relationship. The estate appealed the decision, which was affirmed as to liability but reversed and remanded for a new trial on the amount of the judgment. Binh and the estate subsequently worked out an agreement in which the estate paid Binh $1.2 million to settle his claim.
70. Ariel has worked for Sander Corporation for 30 years. Sander has a pension plan in which it matches employee contributions by up to 5 percent of the employee's salary. Ariel, who is single, retires during the current year when she is 66 years old. Her pension plan contains payments and earnings of $300,000, half of which are attributable to payments made by Ariel and half attributable to payments made by Sander. Under the plan, Ariel is to receive $2,000 per month until she dies.
71. Ikleberry is a self-employed fisherman. He buys a health insurance policy by donating 1,000 salmon filets to the Nordisk Insurance Company's annual Christmas party. During the year, Ikleberry receives $321 in reimbursements from the plan.
72. Salina is an apartment manager and is paid $6,000 per year. The owner of the apartments offered her the option of a $300-per-month living allowance or the use of an apartment rent-free. Salina chose to live in the apartment, which normally rents for $400 per month.

73. Taki was injured in an airplane crash. He sues the airline and receives $4,400 for his pain and suffering, $3,300 for lost wages while he recuperated from his injuries, and $7,000 in punitive damages. He also uses $1,000 from his Medical Savings Account to pay for medical expenses related to the crash. Taki had deposited $1,400 in the account during the year.
74. Sonya purchases a house for $65,000. The seller had listed the house for sale at $80,000 but got into financial trouble and had to accept Sonya's $65,000 offer to avoid bankruptcy.
75. Bud borrows $20,000 from a friend. Before he can repay any of the loan, the friend dies. His friend's will provides that any amounts owed to him are to be forgiven upon his death.
76. Perry Corporation leases a building to Jimison Corporation for $10,000 per month. The terms of the lease provide that any improvements to the building will revert to Perry upon termination of the lease. During the current year, Jimison adds a wing to the building at a cost of $50,000.

## TECHNOLOGY APPLICATIONS

77. In April, a tornado damages the house owned by Malik and John. The damaged residence required extensive repairs, making it necessary for Malik and John to move into a motel and eat their meals in restaurants. During the repair period they incur $1,200 for lodging at a motel, $800 for meals (their normal grocery costs would have been $220), and $150 for laundry services (Malik usually does the laundry, but the $150 includes $40 in dry cleaning costs they would have incurred if they hadn't moved out of their residence). Included in the cost of the meals is $250 for lunches they normally would have incurred. They continue to make the $785 mortgage payment on their residence but their home utility expenses are only $80 (they normally would have paid $240 for utilities if they had occupied the residence). Their insurance company reimburses them $2,150 for the living expenses they incur while their residence is being repaired. **Tax Simulation**

    REQUIRED: Determine the income tax treatment of the receipt of the $2,150 from the insurance company. Search a tax research database and find the relevant authority(ies) that forms the basis for your answer. Your answer should include the exact text of the authority(ies) and an explanation of the application of the authority to Malik and John's facts. If there is any uncertainty about the validity of your answer, indicate the cause for the uncertainty.

78. Oliver and James are equal owners of OJ Company. During the current year, when OJ Company is insolvent by $100,000, a creditor reduces one of OJ's debts by $50,000. For the year, OJ incurs a $20,000 operating loss. Oliver and James are both solvent. Oliver's basis in OJ is $30,000; James's basis is $40,000. Determine the effect of OJ's debt discharge and net operating loss on Oliver and James assuming that **Research Skills**
    a. OJ is organized as a partnership.
    b. OJ is organized as an S corporation.
79. Imani receives a two-year scholarship to Big University. The scholarship stipulates that, to improve her teaching skills, she must spend her first year teaching at an affiliated school. She will be paid her scholarship by the affiliated school based on the level of pay for the teaching duties she is assigned. Upon completion of the first year, Imani will return to Big University and work on the research required to obtain her degree. During the second year, she will receive her scholarship from Big University. Is Imani's scholarship taxable? **Research Skills**

Tax Form

80. Christina Ruiz provides you with the following information regarding her investment income.

| | |
|---|---|
| Interest received: | |
| Cavendar State Bank checking account | $ 43 |
| Federal Employee's Credit Union | 881 |
| City of Singapore bonds | 990 |
| New Jersey Urban Development bonds | 382 |
| Dividends received: | |
| Ford Motor Company | $120 |
| New Core preferred stock | 220 |
| Northwestern Publishing Inc. | 400 |

In addition, Northwestern Publishing Inc. issued a 5 percent stock dividend on August 15. Christina received 25 dividend shares, which were trading at $23 per share on August 15. Prepare Christina's Schedule B. Her Social Security number is 568-33-2541. Forms and instructions can be downloaded from the IRS website (www.irs.gov).

## INTEGRATIVE PROBLEMS

81. Edna, 63, is a widow and works for Rhododendron Corporation. Her annual salary is $40,000. Rhododendron provides the following benefits to all employees:
    - Medical insurance—The cost of Edna's policy is $1,800. She incurs $950 in valid medical expenses and is reimbursed for $760 of the expenses by the company policy.
    - Group term life insurance—Each employee is provided with $90,000 worth of coverage under the policy.
    - Qualified pension plan—Rhododendron matches employee contributions up to $2,000. Edna contributes 8 percent of her salary to the plan.

    Edna has the following other items that may affect her current-year taxes:

    a. She receives $125 per month from a qualified annuity. The annuity cost $9,100. Edna is to receive the annuity for life. She began receiving the payments in January, when her life expectancy was 15 years.

    b. She receives a $200 refund of last year's state income taxes during the current year. Last year, her itemized deductions totaled $6,900. In the current year, Edna's itemized deductions are $4,300.

    c. She has a separate medical policy she purchased to cover costs that her employer-provided policy does not cover. She pays $1,400 for the policy, which reimburses her for $350 of her medical expenses.

    d. She owns 6 percent Puerto Rico bonds with a face value of $40,000. The bonds pay interest annually on December 20.

    e. She sells stock she owned for $26,000 on July 1. She had paid $32,000 for the stock three years earlier. Edna invests the proceeds from the sale of the stock in a money-market savings account that pays 4 percent interest.

    f. Her brother dies and leaves her the farm he had inherited from their father. The farm is valued at $160,000. Edna leases the farm to a local farmer and receives $8,000 in rent during the current year.

    g. On April 1, she gives $5,000 of Kao Corporation bonds she owns to her granddaughter. The bonds pay annual interest of 8 percent on December 31.

    h. She receives a watch worth $300 from Rhododendron for her 20 years of loyal service. Rhododendron does not routinely give out length-of-service awards.

    i. She sells land that she had held as an investment for $19,000 on October 1. She had paid $17,000 for the land two years earlier. Edna invests the proceeds in state of Oregon bonds that pay 4 percent interest annually on December 31.

    Compute Edna's gross income, adjusted gross income, taxable income, and her income tax liability. Edna has no dependents.

82. Carmin Kovach is single and has two children from her previous marriage. Anika, 9, lives with Carmin. Julius, 11, lives with his father, Ray. Carmin pays alimony of $400 per month to Ray. The payments are to continue until Julius reaches age 18, when they will be reduced to $100. Communication Skills

Carmin is 34 and employed as a nuclear engineer with Atom Systems Consultants, Inc. (ASCI). Her annual salary is $80,000, and ASCI has an extensive fringe benefits program for its employees.

ASCI has a qualified pension plan that covers all employees. Under the plan, ASCI matches any contribution to the plan up to 8 percent of the employee's annual salary. Carmin makes the maximum allowable contribution of $6,400, and it is matched by ASCI.

ASCI provides medical coverage to all employees but not to their dependents. Carmin's medical coverage costs ASCI $3,000 during the current year. She receives $980 in reimbursements for her medical costs. ASCI also provides employees with a flexible benefits plan. Carmin pays $2,500 into the plan. She uses $2,400 to purchase medical coverage for Anika. Her medical, dental, and optometry costs not covered by insurance total $1,900; the flexible benefits plan reimburses her $100 for these costs.

ASCI also provides employees with group term life insurance of twice their annual salary, up to a maximum coverage of $150,000. Carmin's group term life insurance premiums cost $400. Because of the sensitive and sometimes dangerous nature of her work, ASCI also provides Carmin with a $300,000 whole life insurance policy. The whole life insurance policy costs $490.

Taking advantage of ASCI's educational assistance program, during the fall Carmin enrolls in two law school classes at a local university. ASCI pays her tuition, fees, books, and other course-related costs totaling $2,300.

Carmin also receives certain other fringe benefits not available to all employees. She receives free parking in the company's security garage that would normally cost $290 per month. In addition, ASCI pays the $1,000 cost of her nuclear engineer's license and $600 per year in professional association dues and professional magazine subscriptions. ASCI also pays Carmin's $900 dues to a health club that is located in the same building as her office.

Carmin routinely enters sweepstakes contests. This year, she is notified that she has won $5,000 in a breakfast cereal promotion. The prize is to be paid equally over 10 years. She receives the first payment December 28, although she doesn't deposit the check in her checking account until January 3.

In February, Carmin's father dies. Social Security pays her $600 as a survivor's benefit. She also receives stock valued at $30,000 and her father's house, which has a value of $90,000, as her share of her father's estate.

Carmin rents out her father's house on August 1. The monthly rent is $400, and the lease agreement is for one year. The lease requires the tenant to pay the first and last months' rent and a $400 security deposit. The security deposit is to be returned at the end of the lease if the property is in good condition. On August 1, Carmin receives $1,200 from the tenant per the terms of the lease agreement. In November, the plumbing freezes and several lines burst. The tenant has the repairs made and pays the $300 bill. In December, he reduces his rental payment to $100 to compensate for the plumbing repairs. Carmin pays other deductible costs for the rental that total $2,680. The allowable depreciation on the rental house is $1,080.

Carmin owns several other investments. She receives the following amounts (all in cash) from the stocks and bonds she owns:

| | |
|---|---:|
| General Dynamics common stock | $ 300 |
| City of Toronto bonds | 1,600 |
| State of Nebraska bonds | 400 |
| New Jersey economic development bonds | 300 |
| Grubstake Mining Development stock | 1,000 |

Carmin owns 1,000 shares of Grubstake Mining Development common stock. Grubstake is organized as an S corporation and has 100,000 shares outstanding. Grubstake reports taxable income of $200,000 during the current year.

Carmin sells the following securities during 2021:

| Security | Sale Date | Purchase Date | Sale Price | Commission Paid | Basis |
|---|---|---|---|---|---|
| Nebraska Bonds | 3/14/21 | 10/22/17 | $1,900 | $ 80 | $1,710 |
| Cassill Corporation Stock | 10/18/21 | 2/19/20 | $8,900 | $450 | $9,630 |

Carmin purchased 500 shares of General Dynamics stock on July 22, 2018, at a cost of $2,200. On June 15, 2021, she receives 50 shares of General Dynamics stock as a dividend. The fair market value of General Dynamics stock on June 15, 2021, was $3.50 per share.

Carmin slips on a wet spot in front of a computer store during the current year. She breaks her ankle and is unable to work for two weeks. She incurs $1,300 in medical costs, all of which are paid by the owner of the store. The store also gives her $1,000 for pain and suffering resulting from the injury. ASCI continues to pay her salary during the two weeks she misses because of the accident. ASCI's plan also pays her $1,200 in disability pay for the time she is unable to work.

Calculate Carmin's adjusted gross income on her 2021 tax return. Then do one or both of the following, according to your professor's instructions:

a. Include a brief explanation of how you determined each item that affected adjusted gross income and any items you excluded from gross income. Your solution to the problem should contain a list of each item included in adjusted gross income and its amount, with the explanations attached.

b. Write a letter to Carmin explaining how you determined each item that affected adjusted gross income and any items you excluded from gross income. You should include a list of each item included in adjusted gross income and its amount.

# DISCUSSION CASES

83. Germaine, 22, is a single individual with no dependents who recently graduated from college. She has job offers from two firms. Germaine likes both companies equally well and has decided to base her decision on which company offers more. Details of each job offer are as follows:

Company A—Annual salary of $44,000, employer-provided health and accident insurance (employer cost: $2,400), group term life insurance coverage at twice the annual salary (premiums for $88,000 worth of coverage are $460), employer-provided day-care facility (employer's cost per dependent is $150 per month), and company-provided parking ($900 per year).

Company B—Annual salary of $46,000, a cafeteria plan under which employees can choose benefits of up to 10 percent of annual salary or take the cash equivalent. In addition, the company has a flexible benefits plan in which employees may participate by setting aside up to 10 percent of annual salary per year for payment of unreimbursed medical expenses.

Explain the tax effects of the two job offers and the income Germaine can expect from each offer. Assume that she has no other income sources and that she uses the standard deduction.

84. Marlo and Merlin's son, Alex, needs $20,000 to start a business. They have $30,000 in securities that they can use to give him the capital he needs. Pertinent information regarding the securities is given below:

| | Fair Market Value | Basis | Purchase Date |
|---|---|---|---|
| Security A | $10,000 | $ 7,000 | 2/10/17 |
| Security B | $10,000 | $ 5,000 | 2/14/14 |
| Security C | $10,000 | $14,000 | 3/19/13 |

Marlo and Merlin are in the 24 percent marginal tax rate bracket; Alex is in the 12 percent marginal tax rate bracket. Neither Marlo, Merlin, nor Alex has any other capital asset transactions during the year. Alex's basis in any of the securities gifted to him will be the lesser of his parents' basis or the fair market value of the security. Discuss the tax effects of alternate methods of transferring $20,000 to Alex, and devise an optimal plan for making the transfer.

## TAX PLANNING CASES

85. Reggie wants to invest $10,000. His options are
    a. Gibraltar Corporation bonds with an annual interest rate of 8 percent.
    b. State of Hawaii bonds with an annual interest rate of 5 percent.
    c. Series EE savings bonds; a $10,000 investment will pay $14,300 in five years.

    Assume that Zane is a 24 percent marginal tax rate payer, the time value of money is 6 percent, and Zane intends to hold any amounts invested for five years. Which option will provide the greatest after-tax return, ignoring state income tax implications? Would your answer change if Zane's marginal tax rate is 32 percent?

86. Leyh's Outdoor Adventures, Inc., would like to begin providing life insurance coverage for its employees. Three employees are officers; each earns $100,000 per year. The other three employees each earn $40,000 per year. Ricardo, president of Leyh's, comes to you for advice on how to provide the coverage. He provides three alternatives, each of which will cost Leyh's $15,000 per year (an average of $2,500 per employee): Communication Skills

    Option 1—Give each employee $2,500 to purchase coverage.

    Option 2—Buy a group term life insurance policy under which each employee would be covered for an amount equal to twice her or his annual salary.

    Option 3—Buy a whole life insurance policy under which each employee would receive $100,000 worth of coverage.

    Ricardo asks you to evaluate these options and advise him on the tax consequences of each. Write a letter to Ricardo explaining the tax effects of each option. Include your recommendation of the option that provides the greatest overall tax benefits.

## ETHICS DISCUSSION CASE

87. You are a CPA working for a local firm and have been assigned the 2021 tax return of Bobby Crosser. In going over the data that Bobby gave the firm, you are surprised to see that he has reported no dividend income or gains from the sale of stock. You recently prepared the 2021 gift tax return of Bobby's aunt Esther. In that return, Esther reported a gift of stock to Bobby on January 6, 2021. The stock had a fair market value of $50,000, and Esther's basis in the stock (which became Bobby's basis) was $5,000. What are your obligations under the Statements on Standards for Tax Services (which can be found at www.aicpa.org)? In your discussion, state which standard(s) may apply to this situation and what might result from applying the standard(s).

# Deductions

PART 3



As you journey through life … always try to give something back.… But be sure whatever you give back qualifies as a tax deduction.

—Chris Browne ("Hagar the Horrible")

Shamleen/Shutterstock.com

# Introduction to Business Expenses

5

Learning Objectives:

LO 1 Determine the tax concepts that allow for deductions.

LO 2 Explain the reporting of allowable deductions by individuals, corporations, and conduit entities.

LO 3 Identify the criteria used to classify expenditures as trade or business, production of income, or personal.

LO 4 Explain the difference between mixed-use assets and mixed-use expenditures and the tax treatment of such assets and expenditures.

LO 5 Explain the ordinary, necessary, and reasonable requirements for the deduction of trade or business and production-of-income expenses.

LO 6 Identify the general classes of expenditures for which a deduction is not allowed.

LO 7 Determine the tax treatment associated with mixed-use expenses in the areas of hobby expenses, vacation home expenses, and home office expenses.

LO 8 Explain the general rules for deducting expenses under the cash and accrual method.

LO 9 Explain the requirements for the deduction of related party expenses.

LO 10 Identify deductions allowed in calculating financial income versus taxable income and the timing, if any, of these deductions.

## concept review

### GENERAL CONCEPTS

**Ability to pay** A tax should be based on the amount that the taxpayer can afford to pay, relative to other taxpayers. pg. 2-2

**Administrative convenience** Those items for which the cost of compliance would exceed the revenue generated are not taxed. pg. 2-3

**Arm's-length transaction** A transaction in which all parties to the transaction have bargained in good faith and for their individual benefit, not for the benefit of the transaction group. pg. 2-4

**Related party** Family members and corporations that are owned by family members are considered related parties, as are certain other relationships between entities in which the power to control the substance of a transaction is evidenced through majority ownership. pg. 2-4

### ACCOUNTING CONCEPTS

**Accounting method** A taxpayer must adopt an accounting method that clearly reflects income. pg. 2-9

**Annual accounting period** All entities report the results of their transactions on an annual basis (the tax year). Each tax year stands on its own, apart from other tax years. pg. 2-9

**Conduit entity** An entity for which the tax attributes flow through to its owners for tax purposes. pg. 2-6

**Entity** All items of income, deduction, and so on are traced to the tax unit responsible for the item. pg. 2-6

**Tax benefit rule** Any deduction taken in a prior year that is recovered in a subsequent year is income in the year of recovery, to the extent that a tax benefit was received from the deduction. pg. 2-10

### INCOME CONCEPTS

**Basis** This is the amount of unrecovered investment in an asset. As amounts are expended and/or recovered relative to an asset over time, the basis is adjusted in consideration of such changes. The **adjusted basis** of an asset is the original basis, plus or minus the changes in the amount of unrecovered investment. pgs. 2-13, 2-21

**Wherewithal to pay** Income is recognized in the period in which the taxpayer has the means to pay the tax on the income. pg. 2-16

### DEDUCTION CONCEPTS

**Business purpose** To be deductible, an expenditure or a loss must have a business or other economic purpose that exceeds any tax avoidance motive. The primary motive for the transaction must be to make a profit. pg. 2-18

**Capital recovery** No income is realized until the taxpayer receives more than the amount invested to produce the income. The amount invested in an asset represents the maximum amount recoverable. pg. 2-13

**Legislative grace** Any tax relief provided is the result of a specific act of Congress that must be strictly applied and interpreted. All income received is taxable unless a specific provision in the tax law excludes the income from taxation. Deductions must be approached with the philosophy that nothing is deductible unless a provision in the tax law allows the deduction. pg. 2-12

## 5-1 INTRODUCTION

LO 1

Determine the tax concepts that allow for deductions.

Chapter 1 pointed out that deductible expenditures are grouped into three broad categories: business expenses, losses, and other itemized deductions. This chapter focuses on the general requirements for deducting business expenses. Specific business-expense deductions are the topic of Chapter 6, deductions for losses are discussed in Chapter 7, and itemized deductions that are specific to individual taxpayers are fully discussed in Chapter 8. The 2017 Tax Cuts and Jobs Act limits the amount of business interest that is deductible and also created the qualified business income (QBI) deduction which reduces the taxable income that flows through from a partnership, S corporation, sole proprietorship to a noncorporate taxpayer. Because Chapter 5 is conceptual in nature, the examples used in this section do not reflect the limit on business interest and/or consider the QBI deduction. Both of these deductions will be discussed in Chapter 6.

Tax **deductions** are a matter of legislative grace. As a result, two restrictions immediately apply to deductions. First, only deductions allowed by the tax law may be subtracted to compute taxable income. The deduction provisions are part of Congress's approach to implementing the ability-to-pay concept. By allowing deductions, Congress is, in effect, recognizing the inequity that could result from imposing a tax on gross income rather than taxable income. Therefore, Congress allows deductions for the costs of earning income and certain other expenditures. Second, a deduction is allowed for an item only if all the requirements for the deduction are satisfied. Because deductions are intended to provide relief from tax, the deduction rules are strictly interpreted and applied. Thus, a deduction is not allowed merely because a taxpayer thinks it is fair or equitable to use the expenditure to reduce income.

**Example 1** Maddie earns $25,000 in wages as a county property tax assessor. John owns and operates his own business selling Slippery Oil. John's Slippery Oil sales are $60,000, the cost of the oil sold is $25,000, and he has other business expenses of $10,000.

**Discussion: Maddie should report $25,000 in wages as gross income. Because the tax law allows a deduction for the cost of sales and business expenses, John has a gross income of $35,000 ($60,000 − $25,000) and reports $25,000 in taxable income from his business ($35,000 − $10,000). After recovering his expenses, John pays tax on his increase in wealth according to the ability-to-pay concept. Compared with Maddie's tax treatment, it is inequitable to tax John on his gross income and deny him a deduction to recover the amounts he invests to earn a profit.**

**Example 2** Rahul and Margot are both self-employed practicing CPAs, specializing in tax. Rahul enrolls in law school so he can take tax courses. He intends to get a law degree. Margot enrolls in a master's program in tax to improve her skills as a tax accountant. Eventually, Margot hopes to earn a master's degree.

**Discussion: Both Rahul and Margot have incurred expenses to improve or maintain their skills as practicing tax accountants. However, Rahul cannot deduct his expenses. Educational expenses that qualify a person for a new profession (the practice of law) are not deductible. Margot's expenses are deductible because they relate to her job and do not qualify her for a new profession.[1] Although treating Rahul differently from Margot seems unfair, Rahul did not satisfy all the requirements of the tax law to claim an educational expense deduction.**

To deduct a **business expense**, the expenditure must have a *business purpose* that is unrelated to its tax effect. Under the business purpose concept, there must be a business purpose for the expenditure that exceeds any tax-avoidance motive. Failure to establish a business purpose for the expense can result in the loss of the deduction. In most instances, a business purpose can be established by showing that the expense was related to a profit-motivated transaction. When the taxpayer has both business and personal reasons for an expenditure, the taxpayer risks losing the deduction. For these expenditures, the taxpayer will need to show that the business purpose was the primary or dominant motive for the transaction.

**Example 3** Zoltan is a physician who has not seen his sister for more than 10 years because she lives in Kenya. He would like to visit her and write a book about his experiences. He has never written a book. Because his trip has a business purpose—to write a book—Zoltan intends to deduct the full cost of his trip as a business expense. Has Zoltan met the dominant motive requirement for deducting the cost of the trip?

**Discussion: Because Zoltan has several motives for making the trip, he will have to prove that the dominant motive is a business purpose. Based on the facts, it would appear that Zoltan is not entitled to a deduction because the primary purpose of his trip is personal (to visit his sister). Because Zoltan has no experience in writing travel books, he would have a hard time proving that writing the book is his dominant motive.**

*Gross income* has been defined to include only the excess of an individual's capital investment. As a result, the expenditure or consumption of capital to earn income results in a tax deduction. The capital recovery concept limits the amount of a deduction to the amount of the expenditure or the taxpayer's investment in an asset. As a result of this concept, the deduction for an item may not exceed the taxpayer's cost. For example, the payment of a $500 business expense is limited to a $500 deduction. In this chapter, basis is used to identify the amount that can be deducted under the capital recovery concept. *Basis* is a technical term that was introduced as a construct in Chapter 2 and is discussed in detail in Chapter 9. For discussion purposes, think of basis as the cost of an asset or the dollar amount of a specific expenditure. Thus, basis represents the maximum amount of an expenditure that can be deducted as a recovery of capital.

The accounting concepts discussed in Chapter 2 influence the tax treatment of deductions. Although a deduction of basis is allowed under the capital recovery concept, the entity concept requires the taxpayer claiming the deduction to own the capital being deducted as a recovery. Thus, the entity concept prevents one taxpayer from deducting another taxpayer's expenditures.

**Example 4** Miranda is a public accountant and is required by state law to have a license to practice public accounting. When the state license renewal fee comes due, Miranda is short of money and cannot renew her license. Miranda's mother pays the license renewal fee for her so she can continue working as a public accountant. Can Miranda deduct the fee as a business expense?

**Discussion: The license renewal fee is Miranda's business expense, and only she can deduct the payment of the fee. Because Miranda does not pay the license renewal fee, she is not allowed a deduction for the business expense. Because the license renewal fee is not Miranda's mother's expense, her mother cannot deduct the payment of the expense. Based on these facts, neither Miranda nor her mother can deduct the payment of the license renewal fee.**

**Note that the bad tax result here can be avoided if Miranda's mother either gifts or makes a valid loan to Miranda of the money necessary to pay the licensing fee and Miranda makes the payment from her own funds.**

The annual accounting period concept requires the taxpayer to use an acceptable accounting method to determine the year in which a deduction should be reported. Once an accounting method is adopted, it should be used as the basis for the systematic and consistent allocation of expenses to the proper tax years. Failure to claim an expense in the correct year can result in loss of the deduction. If an expenditure, such as utilities or office supplies, benefits only one tax year, it is allowed as a deduction in the year benefited. When an expenditure benefits more than one accounting period, the expenditure is usually allocated, based on the annual accounting period concept, to the proper tax years by using an acceptable accounting method. Examples of expenses that may need to be allocated are prepaid rent, prepaid interest, and prepaid insurance as well as depreciation on buildings and equipment. If the expenditure has an indefinite life, it is normally not deducted until the accounting period in which the asset is disposed of, abandoned, or proved to have lost its value. Thus, assets such as securities and land that do not have definite useful lives are not subject to amortization or depreciation for tax purposes.

As deductions are more closely examined in the rest of this chapter, the concepts discussed in Chapter 2 will be related to the specific rules and requirements for a deduction. The discussion and examples throughout this chapter consider deduction issues from the points of view of individuals, corporations, and conduit entities (partnerships and S corporations). Situations in which a tax rule applies only to individual taxpayers will be pointed out.

## 5-2 REPORTING DEDUCTIONS

LO 2
Explain the reporting of allowable deductions by individuals, corporations, and conduit entities.

The phrases **deductions for adjusted gross income** and **deductions from adjusted gross income** identify where in the tax computation an individual taxpayer deducts an allowable expense. Because all of a corporation's expenses are related to a business purpose, it is not necessary to use these two phrases when discussing its deductions; a corporation does not have personal expenses similar to those of an individual, which are deducted from adjusted gross income. Thus, the term **adjusted gross income** is unique to the individual tax computation.

Chapter 1 introduced an income tax computational framework as an overview of the federal income tax computation. At this point, we expand the framework for computing an individual's income tax (see Exhibit 5-1) to illustrate how individuals deduct various expenses. This chapter discusses the distinctions among *trade or business, production of income*, and *personal expenses.* Note in Exhibit 5-1 that trade or business expenses are deducted for adjusted gross income and prior to the adoption of the 2017 Tax Cut and Jobs Act some production of income expenses were treated as deductions from adjusted gross income. Now the only allowed production of income expenses that are deductible are expenses related to the production of rent and royalty income, which are deductible for adjusted gross income.

Trade or business expenses, expenses related to the production of rent and royalty income, losses on sales of property used in a trade or business, and capital losses (limited to $3,000) are deducted from gross income to compute adjusted gross income. As a result of legislative grace, these deductions receive more favorable treatment than deductions from adjusted gross income. Unless the passive activity rules discussed in Chapter 7 apply, trade or business expenses and losses and rent expenses are fully allowed as deductions for adjusted gross income in computing taxable income.

*Exhibit 5-1*

### Individual Income Tax Computation Framework

| | |
|---|---|
| **Income "broadly defined"** (includes income from all sources) | |
| **Minus:** | **Excluded sources of income** |
| **Equals:** | **Gross income** |
| **Minus:** | **Deductions for adjusted gross income** |
| | Trade or business expenses |
| | Rent or royalty expenses |
| | Trade or business losses |
| | Capital loss deduction ($3,000 maximum) |
| | Other specifically allowable deductions |
| **Equals:** | **Adjusted gross income** |
| **Minus:** | **Deductions from adjusted gross income** |
| | The greater of: |
| | 1. Standard deduction |
| | or |
| | 2. Allowable itemized deductions: |
| | Deductible personal expenditures |
| | Medical expenses |
| | Home mortgage interest |
| | Property taxes/state income taxes – Limited to $10,000 |
| | Charitable contributions |
| | Personal casualty losses from a federal disaster |
| **Equals:** | **Taxable income** |
| **Minus:** | **Qualified Business Income (QBI) Deduction** |

The allowable deduction from adjusted gross income is the greater of the taxpayer's standard deduction amount or allowable itemized deductions.[2] **Itemized deductions** consist of allowable personal expenditures.[3] Some itemized deductions are subject to income limitations. For example, the total of state and local income taxes and property taxes are limited to $10,000.[4] As a result, deductions from adjusted gross income receive less favorable treatment than deductions for adjusted gross income. The computation of allowable personal itemized deductions and the applicable limitations are discussed in Chapter 8.

## 5-2a Conduit Entity Reporting

**Conduit entities** (partnerships and S corporations) are not subject to tax. The entity concept requires all deduction items to be traced to the tax unit responsible for taxation of the item. Rather, the taxable income from the conduit flows through to each owner, and each is taxed on their individual tax return. As discussed in Chapter 3, a conduit entity reports some income items (i.e., capital gains) separately to the partner or shareholder because these items are subject to special tax rules. Therefore, these items are not included in the calculation of a conduit entity's ordinary taxable income or loss.[5] Certain deductions are also subject to special tax rules—typically limitations on the amount that can be deducted by the owners—and must be reported separately. For example, charitable contributions of individuals are itemized deductions that would be deductible only if the taxpayer itemized their deductions. Therefore, as with some income items, not all deductions of a conduit entity are used in calculating ordinary taxable income or loss.

**Example 5** The Hackett Group (HG), a partnership, operates a management consulting firm; it consists of three equal partners Iman, Nancy, and Neil. HG's taxable income for the year is $255,000, consisting of the following:

| | |
|---|---|
| Sales revenues | $ 1,500,000 |
| Short-term capital gains | 27,000 |
| Trade and business expenses | (1,260,000) |
| Charitable contributions | (12,000) |
| Taxable income | $ 255,000 |

How must the Hackett Group report its results to Iman, Nancy, and Neil for tax purposes?

**Discussion: Because the Hackett Group must report each partner's share of short-term capital gain and charitable contributions, the Hackett Group cannot divide the partnership's taxable income of $255,000 equally and report ordinary taxable income of $85,000 ($255,000 ÷ 3) to each partner. Rather the Hackett Group uses only the partnership's sales revenue and business expenses to calculate the ordinary taxable income for each partner. As a result, each partner's taxable income is $80,000 [($1,500,000 − $1,260,000 = $240,000) ÷ 3]. The Hackett Group must report to each partner $9,000 of short-term capital gains and $4,000 of charitable contributions. As discussed briefly, charitable contributions are considered itemized deductions subject to special rules, so these items cannot be used to calculate the partnership's ordinary taxable income.**

**Example 6** Assume the same facts as in example 5. Neil is single, and without considering the above information, his adjusted gross income is $25,000 and he has other itemized deductions of $6,000. What is the effect on Neil's taxable income of stating the charitable contributions separately?

**Discussion: If the Hackett Group did not report both the short-term capital gain and charitable contributions separately, Neil's ordinary taxable income from the Hackett Group would be $85,000 ($255,000 ÷ 3). He would have an adjusted gross income of $110,000 ($25,000 + $85,000), itemized deduction of $4,000, which would not be deductible since his standard deduction is $12,550 and his taxable income would be $97,450.**

**Because the short-term capital gain and charitable contributions receive special tax treatment, HG must report these items separately. Neil's share of the ordinary income is $80,000 and his adjusted gross income is $114,000 ($80,000 + $25,000 + $9,000) and Neil's taxable income is $101,450 ($114,000 − $12,550). Because HG reports these items separately, Neil's taxable income increases by $4,000. Neil receives no benefit for the $4,000 of HG's charitable contributions allocated to him. Note: As discussed earlier in this chapter, Neil will be allowed a QBI deduction that will reduce his taxable income. This will be discussed in Chapter 6.**

In essence, the owner and not the conduit entity is subject to tax. The conduit is viewed as only a form of organization, with the income and deductions flowing through to each owner. This ensures that income and deductions of a conduit are treated similarly to income and deductions incurred by an individual taxpayer. As example 6 illustrates, it is important that a conduit entity report separately any deduction that receives special tax treatment. The following is a list of commonly incurred deductions that a conduit entity must report separately:

- Charitable contributions
- Section 179 expense
- Nondeductible expenses

## 5-3 CLASSIFICATION OF DEDUCTIONS

LO 3
Identify the criteria used to classify expenditures as trade or business, production of income, or personal.

Proper application of the ability-to-pay and legislative grace concepts requires the separation of expenditures that qualify for deduction from those that are not allowed by the tax law. The basic test to be applied to obtain the initial classification of expenditures is whether the expenditure is related to a profit-motivated transaction or is motivated by personal needs and wants. Thus, expenditures are initially classified as profit-motivated or personal expenditures. Figure 5-1 illustrates this classification scheme.

### 5-3a Profit-Motivated Expenditures

As discussed in Chapter 1, a taxpayer may legitimately plan transactions to avoid the payment of tax. Because business profits reflect tax costs and savings, the tax effect of a transaction is an important planning consideration. A legitimate business reason for entering a transaction is to save taxes. However, the tax law prohibits deductions that are motivated solely by the expected tax benefits (savings). To be deductible, the business purpose concept requires an expenditure to have a bona fide business reason other than

*Figure 5-1*

**Classification of Deductions of an Individual**

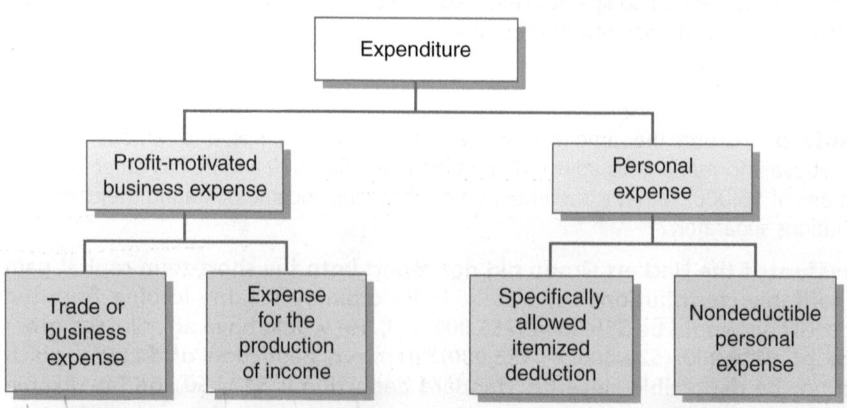

tax avoidance. If the sole purpose of a transaction is tax savings, it will not be allowed as a deduction.

The courts maintain that the presence of a business purpose does not always require that a transaction be recognized. Where objective evidence indicates no potential for economic profit apart from tax savings, a transaction can be disregarded.[6] Thus, to be deductible, the dominant motive for incurring a business expense must be to earn a profit that is independent of any tax savings. Therefore, only expenses that satisfy the requirement that profit be the **dominant motive** are classified as business expenses.

**Example 7** Harry's son Junior wants to open a motorcycle dealership. Because Junior is short of funds, Harry purchases a building for the dealership and leases it to Junior. No lease is signed, but Harry tells Junior not to worry about paying rent until the dealership begins to show a profit. In addition, Harry agrees not to sell the building without Junior's approval. Is Harry's dominant motive in acquiring the building to obtain a profit?

**Discussion: On the facts presented, Harry's dominant motive in acquiring the building is to help his son get his business established. Because there is no formal rental agreement and Harry will not sell the building without Junior's approval, the purchase of the building and the payment of costs related to the building are in the nature of a gift. Harry is not attempting to profit from either rental payments or potential appreciation in the value of the business. Therefore, any expenditures Harry makes regarding the building are not classified as business expenses. As personal expenses, only those personal expenses specifically allowed by the tax law (property taxes) are deductible.**

Recall from Chapter 2 that the business purpose concept means that the taxpayer's dominant motive for an expenditure is to earn an economic benefit (profit) before considering the effects of tax savings. Thus, profit-motivated expenses, or expenses related to a business purpose, are deductible as business expenses. Throughout the remainder of this text, reference to a *business expense* means that the expenditure satisfies the dominant profit-motive requirement.

Based on the legislative grace concept, business expenses are grouped into two main categories:

- Trade or business expenses
- Expenses for the production of income

Both classifications apply to individuals and certain conduit entities (partnerships, S corporations, etc.). However, production-of-income expenses do not apply to corporations. A corporation's expenses are always classified as trade or business expenses, regardless of the underlying business purpose. The deductions allowed under these two provisions of the tax law are the types of expenses that you would expect to find on a typical income statement. For example, on an income statement, you expect to find employee wages, depreciation expense, advertising, and similar items subtracted from income to determine net income. Thus, you are already familiar with several types of expenses that are allowed as business deductions.

## 5-3b Trade or Business or Production-of-Income Expenses?

Because business expenses are classified either as related to a trade or business or for the production of income, it is necessary to look at these two classifications more closely. Although many of the same kinds of expenses can be deducted in these two categories, the tax result can be significantly different. As explained later, classification of an activity as either a trade or business or for the production of income depends on the facts related to the particular activity. No single definition applies to all situations. Because both types of activities must be profit-motivated, a trade or business will most likely be identified by the extent of the taxpayer's involvement and whether the intent is to earn a living from the activity.

## Trade or Business Expenses

If a taxpayer's activities qualify as a trade or business, the related expenses are fully deductible. As you can see from the following excerpt from the tax law, **trade or business expenses** is broadly defined:

SEC. 162. TRADE OR BUSINESS EXPENSES

(A) IN GENERAL—There shall be allowed as a deduction all the ordinary and necessary expenses paid or incurred during the taxable year in carrying on any trade or business, including—

(1) a reasonable allowance for salaries or other compensation for personal services actually rendered;

(2) traveling expenses (including amounts expended for meals and lodging other than amounts that are lavish or extravagant under the circumstances) while away from home in the pursuit of a trade or business; and

(3) rentals or other payments required to be made as a condition to the continued use or possession, for purposes of the trade or business, of property to which the taxpayer has not taken or is not taking title or in which he has no equity.

A taxpayer may deduct "all the ordinary and necessary expenses" of operating a "trade or business." But what is a trade or business? The Internal Revenue Code contains at least 50 references to a trade or business without defining the phrase. The Treasury regulations are also silent on the definition of a trade or business. Therefore, the task has been left to the courts. One interpretation observed for many years was that taxpayers who held themselves out as engaged in the selling of goods or services were engaged in a trade or business. Although noting that a person selling goods or services would usually be engaged in a trade or business, the Supreme Court rejected these activities as the single appropriate test for a trade or business in 1987. Instead, the Court took a broader view of what constituted a trade or business.

The Court has stated that to be engaged in a trade or business, a taxpayer must meet the following requirements:

- Profit motivation—The primary purpose for engaging in the activity must be to earn income or a profit.
- Continuous and regular activity—There must be continuity and regularity in the taxpayer's involvement in the activity.
- Livelihood, not a hobby—The activity must not be sporadic, a hobby, or an amusement diversion.[7]

The Court went on to say that whether an activity meets these tests must be determined by examining the facts in each case. In this regard, the Court noted that taxpayers meeting the prior "holding out as a seller of goods and services" test would normally meet the requirements for being engaged in a trade or business.

As a general rule, an employee is usually engaged in the trade or business of rendering services to the employer. The most common problem encountered in delineating a trade or business activity from a production-of-income activity involves dealings in securities. A person who transacts business in securities may be an active investor, an active trader, or a dealer in securities. Unlike active traders and dealers, active investors are not considered to be in a trade or business.

An **active investor** is a person who continually, regularly, and extensively manages her or his own portfolio with a view toward long-term appreciation in the portfolio's value and not short-term profit. An active investor's income is earned from interest, dividends, and gains from long-term holdings of securities, and the investment expenses are deductible only as miscellaneous itemized deductions. An active investor is never deemed to be engaged in a trade or business.

An **active trader** earns a livelihood buying and selling securities for personal profit. The main source of an active trader's income is from selling securities for more than they cost to make a profit. The securities are typically held for a short time before they are sold, with the active investor trying to capture the short-term swings in the market. Thus, an active trader may be distinguished from the active investor by the nature of the investing activities and the source of income. If the trader's activities are frequent and substantial, the trader will be deemed to be engaged in a trade or business, and the expenses will be deductible for adjusted gross income.

Distinguishing a trader from an active investor is often quite difficult. The determination of whether a taxpayer should be classified as a trader or an active investor is best left to a tax expert.

A **securities dealer** purchases a security expecting to realize a profit from selling it to a customer for a fee or commission. The dealer acts as an agent who performs the services of a wholesaler or retailer in bringing together a buyer and a seller. Dealers have customers with whom they deal to earn a profit. Dealers are deemed to be engaged in a trade or business.

## Expenses for the Production of Income

If the taxpayer's business activity fails to qualify as a trade or business, expenses related to the production of income may still be deductible under Section 212 of the Internal Revenue Code. Although the formal tax term for these deductions is *nonbusiness expenses*, we will refer to these items as **investment expenses**, consistent with the terminology used by most taxpayers. The tax law provides a broad definition of **production-of-income expenses** that an individual taxpayer can deduct:

SEC. 212. EXPENSES FOR THE PRODUCTION OF INCOME.

In the case of an individual there shall be allowed as a deduction all the ordinary and necessary expenses paid or incurred during the taxable year—

(1) for the production or collection of income;
(2) for the management, conservation, or maintenance of property held for the production of income, or
(3) in connection with the determination, collection, or refund of any tax.

The objectives of Section 212 are to tax the net profits of income-motivated transactions and to allow individuals a deduction for costs of complying with the tax law. However, expenses deducted under this provision receive less-favorable treatment than trade or business expenses. Generally, expenses related to earning rent and royalty income are treated the same (as deductions for adjusted gross income), whether they are considered to be for the production of income or trade or business expenses.

**Example 8** Grady owns a large portfolio of stocks, bonds, and other securities. What is the treatment of Grady's securities activities in each of the following cases?

**Case A**

Grady spends all his time managing his portfolio. He continually trades securities to obtain a profit from short-term price increases. Grady rarely holds a security for the dividend or interest income it may produce or for long-term appreciation in value. He has no other job and receives the bulk of his income from his securities dealings.

**Case B**

Grady is employed as a chemist for Dough Company. He spends an average of 5 hours per week studying investment materials and making investment decisions. Grady primarily invests in securities for their dividend and interest income and long-term appreciation potential. Because his portfolio is quite extensive, more than half his income comes from his security investments.

**Discussion: In case A, Grady's activities constitute a trade or business. His primary motive is profit, he engages in the activity on a continual and regular basis, and his securities activities are his livelihood. Grady's business expenses are deductible for adjusted gross income. In addition, gains and losses from his securities dealings are considered gains and losses from a trade or business.**

**In case B, Grady's security dealings are a production-of-income activity. He receives a substantial portion of his income from his securities, but they are not his livelihood, nor does he engage in the activity with the continuity and regularity of a trade or business. Therefore, the gains and losses Grady has from selling the securities are capital gains and losses. *Note:* Prior to the adoption of the 2017 Tax Cut and Jobs Act his investment expenses would have been deductible as a miscellaneous itemized deduction.**

## 5-3c Rental Activity

Depending on the extent of the taxpayer's activities related to renting out real estate, the activity could be deemed either a trade or business or an investment activity. For many years, the mere rental of a single piece of improved real estate was considered a trade or business, whereas the rental of unimproved real estate was subject to an "all the facts and circumstances" test to determine the classification of the rental activity.[8] Improved real estate is land that has a building or other capital improvement on it. Unimproved real estate is raw land without a building or other structure on it. In recent years, several courts have begun to apply a facts-and-circumstances test to both improved and unimproved real estate to determine whether rental property is a trade or business or an investment asset. The courts have looked to the scope of the rental activities and the extent of the taxpayer's involvement with the rental operations to classify the property.

For example, the U.S. Tax Court considered whether a rental activity was a trade or business for purposes of the home office deduction.[9] The court indicated that, as a matter of law, a rental activity is not automatically a trade or business. Classification as a trade or business depends on the facts related to the taxpayer's activities. In examining the facts, the Tax Court looked at the scope of ownership and management activities in classifying a rental activity as a trade or business instead of an investment activity. The IRS has stated that rental property must produce income from an active trade or business, as opposed to income that would be earned on portfolio investments (e.g., stocks, bonds), to qualify as property used in a trade or business.

**Example 9** Frank agrees to lease land in downtown Chicago to Sleepytime Motels for 99 years. Under the lease, Sleepytime has the right to construct a motel on the land. Sleepytime is responsible for all expenses, claims, and liabilities related to the property. In the event of default on the lease, Frank has the right to assume ownership of the building and possession of the property. Is Frank's rental activity a trade or business or a production-of-income activity?

**Discussion: Because Frank is not actively involved in the management of the property, the income earned is similar to the income that is earned by an investor in stocks or bonds. Thus, the lease described does not constitute a trade or business. Frank's rental activity is considered a production-of-income activity.**

**Example 10** Yolanda owns two rental properties. She obtains tenants for the properties, makes repairs, provides maintenance, pays expenses related to the properties, and is subject to claims and liabilities arising from the rental properties. Is Yolanda's rental activity a trade or business or a production-of-income activity?

**Discussion: Because Yolanda actively manages the two properties, pays expenses related to them, and is liable for claims on the properties, she is deemed to be engaged in a trade or business.**

Note in Exhibit 5-1 that rental expenses are deductible for adjusted gross income. This is true whether the rental activity is classified as a trade or business or for the production of income. Therefore, the proper classification of rental deductions is not an issue in preparing a taxpayer's return. However, when the taxpayer decides to sell the property, the classification becomes important. Disposal of rental property at a gain results in similar tax treatment whether the property is classified as a trade or business or an investment asset. However, if the rental property is disposed of at a loss, the full amount of the loss can be deducted in the year of the sale only if the property is used in a trade or business (Exhibit 5-1). Investment property sold at a loss is classified as a capital loss. Although net capital losses are also deducted for adjusted gross income, a capital loss may be limited to a $3,000 deduction each year until it is fully used. Because of the limitation on capital losses, classification of rental real estate as an investment asset is usually less desirable than classification as a trade or business asset when the property is sold at a loss.

**Example 11** Frank sells the property in example 9 at a $10,000 loss during the current year. How much of the loss can Frank deduct?

**Discussion: Because Frank's rental activity is a production-of-income activity, the $10,000 is a capital loss. The $10,000 loss would be included in the capital gain-and-loss netting. If Frank had no other capital gains and losses during the year, he could deduct only $3,000 of the loss, with the remaining $7,000 of loss carried forward to next year.**

**Example 12** Assume that Yolanda sells one of her rental properties in example 10 at a $10,000 loss during the current year. How much of the loss can Yolanda deduct?

**Discussion: Because Yolanda's rental activities constitute a trade or business, the $10,000 loss on the sale of the rental property is deducted in full as a trade or business loss.**

The trade or business versus investment characterization of rental real estate is also important if the taxpayer wants to claim deductions or credits, such as home office expenses, that are available only to a trade or business activity.

## 5-3d Personal Expenditures

An individual's personal expenditures are also grouped into two categories: allowable personal itemized deductions and nondeductible personal expenses. In contrast to expenditures for a business purpose in which all ordinary and necessary expenses are deductible, the tax law severely limits deductions for personal expenditures. As shown in Exhibit 5-1, allowable personal expenses are deductible from adjusted gross income. In addition, most personal itemized deductions are subject to a limit based on the taxpayer's adjusted gross income. A major problem in determining an individual's personal itemized deductions is that many assets and expenses are used for both business and personal purposes. Proper accounting for such assets and expenses requires segregation of the business portion from the personal portion.

## 5-3e Mixed Business and Personal Expenditures

LO 4
Explain the difference between mixed-use assets and mixed-use expenditures and the tax treatment of such assets and expenditures.

These categories of expenditures, *mixed-use assets* and *mixed-use expenditures*, present special problems for individual taxpayers. A person's expenses related to mixed-use assets and mixed-use expenditures must be analyzed and allocated between profit-motivated and personal expenditures. To the extent an expense is related to a profit-motivated transaction, it is treated as a business expense. Unless the personal expenditure qualifies as an itemized deduction, it is not deductible.

## Mixed-Use Assets

A **mixed-use asset** is an asset that is used both to earn income and for personal purposes. For tax purposes, the single asset is effectively treated as two separate assets. One is a business asset, and the other is a personal use asset. For example, a taxpayer may own one car that he uses to travel for his business and to provide local transportation for his family. To deny a deduction for the business use of the car would violate both the ability-to-pay and capital recovery concepts. Because the income earned using the car is taxable, a deduction is allowed for the expense related to the business use of the car. The cost of using the car to provide local transportation for the family is a personal expense that is not deductible. Thus, an expense that is related to using a mixed-use asset must be reasonably allocated between business and personal use. The portion of the expense reasonably allocated to business use is treated the same as other expenses that are related to the profit-motivated activity. An expense allocated to personal use cannot be deducted unless it qualifies as a specifically allowed itemized deduction.

**Example 13** Aaron purchases a computer in 2020 at a cost of $8,000. He uses the computer in his dry-cleaning business and for personal purposes after work and on weekends. During 2020, Aaron's records indicate that 75% of the computer's use is for business purposes and 25% for personal purposes. How should Aaron treat the computer for tax purposes?

**Discussion: Aaron must treat the computer as two separate assets for tax purposes. For purposes of computing depreciation on the computer, only $6,000 ($8,000 × 75%) of the cost can be depreciated for tax purposes. The remaining $2,000 of cost is considered a personal use asset. Depreciation is not allowed on personal use assets.**

**Example 14** Aaron sells the computer in 2022 for $4,000. His business use remains at 75% for 2021 and 2022. Aaron properly deducts $2,400 in depreciation on the computer for 2020 through 2022. What is Aaron's taxable gain or loss on the sale of the computer?

**Discussion: Aaron must treat the sale of the computer as the sale of two assets—one a business asset and one a personal asset. The $4,000 sales price and the $8,000 purchase price must be allocated between business and personal use:**

| | | | Business | Personal |
|---|---|---|---|---|
| Selling price— | $4,000 × 75% | | $ 3,000 | |
| | $4,000 × 25% | | | $ 1,000 |
| Less: Adjusted basis | | | | |
| Original cost— | $8,000 × 75% | $ 6,000 | | |
| | $8,000 × 25% | | | (2,000) |
| Less: Depreciation | | (2,400) | (3,600) | |
| Loss on sale | | | $ (600) | $(1,000) |

**The $600 loss on the business portion of the computer is deductible as a business loss. However, the $1,000 loss on the personal use portion is a nondeductible personal use loss.**

## Mixed-Use Expenditures

Mixed-use expenditures are also subject to special treatment. **Mixed-use expenditures** are expenses that are incurred for both profit and personal reasons. As with mixed-use assets, these expenditures must be allocated between business and personal use and deducted according to the rules for each use. In addition, certain types of mixed-use expenditures (e.g., hobby and vacation home expenses, which are discussed later in this chapter) are subject to special rules designed to prevent taxpayer abuse by disallowing all or part of an otherwise-deductible expenditure.

**Example 15** Pam travels to San Diego for 4 days primarily for business reasons. Her airfare costs $800, and she incurs expenses of $200 a day for lodging and incidentals. Because Pam has never been to San Diego, she stays 2 extra days to visit the zoo and to tour the city. How much of her costs can be deducted as a business expense?

**Discussion: Pam has incurred mixed-use expenditures. The expense relates to a business trip and a personal vacation. Because the primary motive for making the trip (as evidenced by spending more days on business than for personal purposes) was to conduct business, Pam can deduct the full $800 airfare. She can also deduct $200 for each day she was in San Diego to conduct business. Pam cannot deduct any part of the $200 per day for lodging and incidentals for the 2 extra days she stayed for personal reasons.**

## concept check

For an expense to be deductible under the business purpose concept, it must have a business or other economic purpose that exceeds any tax avoidance motive. The primary motive for the transaction must be to make a profit. In addition, the legislative grace concept requires that any tax relief provided is the result of a specific act of Congress that must be strictly applied and interpreted. Deductions must be approached with the philosophy that nothing is deductible unless a provision in the tax law allows the deduction. Under the entity concept, all items of income and deduction are traced to the tax unit responsible for the item. Therefore, a taxpayer who uses an asset for both business and personal use (i.e., a mixed-use asset) or has expenses that are incurred for both business and personal reasons (i.e., mixed-use expenses) must separate the business portion from the personal portion. The capital recovery concept limits the deduction to the amount invested in the asset. The annual accounting period concept requires all entities to report the results of their operations on an annual basis. As a result, if an asset has a tax life that extends substantially beyond the end of the tax year, this concept requires the taxpayer to recover the cost of the asset over its tax life.

# 5-4 TESTS FOR DEDUCTIBILITY

In classifying expenditures, only expenses that have a business purpose are treated as deductible trade or business and investment expenses. In addition to having a business purpose, these expenses must also be:

- Ordinary
- Necessary
- Reasonable in amount

Note that all three requirements must be met to deduct a trade or business or an investment expense. Deductible trade or business and investment expenses may *not* be any of the following:

- A personal expense
- A capital expenditure
- A payment that frustrates public policy
- An expense related to tax-exempt income
- Another person's expense

The discussion that follows examines each requirement for determining deductible business and investment expenses.

LO 5

Explain the ordinary, necessary, and reasonable requirements for the deduction of trade or business and production-of-income expenses.

## 5-4a Ordinary, Necessary, and Reasonable in Amount

Trade or business and investment-related activities are allowed a deduction for the ordinary and necessary expenses of earning income. In addition, the tax law provides that a trade or business can deduct reasonable salaries. According to the IRS and the courts, an expense must be reasonable in amount to be ordinary and necessary.[10] Thus, the portion of an expense that is not reasonable in amount will not be deductible because it is not ordinary or necessary. Because of their importance in identifying deductible business expenses, these terms need further consideration.

## Ordinary Expense

An expenditure must qualify as an ordinary expense to be deductible. The term *ordinary* is generally interpreted to have two meanings. First, the expense must be of a kind commonly incurred in the particular income-earning activity.[11] Thus, the expense is said to be customary or usual in the activity. An **ordinary expense** is one that is normal, common, and accepted under the circumstances of the business community. In addition, although the expense must be common to the income-earning activity, it does not have to be a regularly recurring item for the taxpayer.

**Example 16** Kara owns and operates a pet shop. One day, a customer is bitten by a snake. Although the accident is the customer's fault, he sues Kara for $25,000. After Kara pays her lawyer $2,500 to defend her, the customer drops the suit. Are the legal fees an ordinary expense for Kara?

**Discussion: Lawsuits by customers are a common occurrence in today's business environment. The cost of defending the business against the disgruntled customer is a normal cost of doing business, although it is not a recurring expense. The legal fees satisfy the ordinary test.**

**Example 17** The Russo Company, which raises hogs, enters into a contract with the local feed mill to buy hog feed. Under the terms of the agreement, Russo agrees to purchase a quantity of grain and pay for it in advance. The mill agrees to deliver the feed as needed and to charge the deliveries against Russo's advance payment at the lower of the market price on delivery or the maximum price in the contract. Is the advance payment for the hog feed an ordinary expense?

**Discussion: The payment for the grain qualifies as an ordinary expense. The advance purchase of the grain for feeding livestock is the normal way farmers conduct their business. By ensuring that the grain is available, Russo can better plan the scope of its farm operations for the coming months.**

As these examples illustrate, an ordinary expense may or may not occur frequently. Also, the determination of what is usual or customary depends on the nature of the taxpayer's business. A typical expense for a pet shop (bird seed) is not a typical expense for an auto mechanic (repair parts).

The second meaning of *ordinary* is that the expenditure is an expense that is assignable to the current accounting period. A capital expenditure that provides future benefits cannot be deducted now.[12] Capital expenditures that benefit more than one tax year are allocated by means of a depreciation, depletion, or amortization deduction to the accounting periods receiving benefit from the use of the asset.

**Example 18** Gustav Brothers, a partnership, buys a $300,000 machine in the current year to use in its business. The machine has a 7-year tax life. When can the partnership deduct the cost of the machine?

**Discussion: The machine is to be used to earn income during several tax years. As a result, its cost must be capitalized and allocated to the years benefited by the use of the machine. The deductions allowed for depreciation are discussed in Chapter 10.**

## Necessary Expense

An expense must also be necessary to be deductible. The courts have defined a **necessary expense** as one that is "appropriate and helpful" to the taxpayer's income activity.[13] An expense will be considered necessary if a reasonable and prudent businessperson would incur the expense in a similar situation. It is important to note that the term *necessary* does not mean that the expense must be essential to the continued existence of the income activity to be deductible. In most cases, the courts have tended to accept the taxpayer's judgment of the business necessity of the expenditure rather than attempt to determine the commercial value of the expenditure.

**Example 19** A tax lawyer purchases a large red, white, and blue flag with the numerals 1040 for his yacht. While using his yacht, many people inquire about the flag, and the tax attorney obtained a few customers as a result of such contact. Can the lawyer deduct the cost of operating his yacht as a promotional expense?

**Discussion: On similar facts, the Tax Court determined that operating the yacht is not the ordinary method of promoting the taxpayer's business. Further, the court determined that the expenses of the yacht were so personal in nature that they could not be necessary in the common sense of the word.**

**Example 20** Buster, Inc., is a women's clothing store in Fashion City. One day a year, the company pays $500 to publish a full-page advertisement in the town newspaper to announce its annual clothing sale. Is the cost of the advertisement deductible?

**Discussion: The $500 paid for the sale advertisement is deductible. The expense satisfies both the ordinary and necessary tests. It is customary for clothing retailers to advertise their merchandise. In addition, the advertisement helps the business because it both promotes the store to the public and attracts the attention of customers, and gives them an incentive to shop at the store—to take advantage of the sale prices.**

### Reasonable in Amount

An expense must also be reasonable in amount to be deductible. An expense does not satisfy the ordinary and necessary tests unless it is reasonable in amount. The reasonableness test most often becomes an issue in transactions involving related parties. When unrelated parties are dealing at arm's length in their own best interests, the result of the negotiations will normally be a fair market value. However, related parties have incentives to shift income by charging prices higher or lower than what would be paid in an arm's-length transaction, so these costs would not constitute **reasonable expenses**.

**Example 21** Tara operates a shoe store in a building she rents from her father for $1,000 per month. Comparable store space is readily available for rent at $400 per month. Is the rental payment reasonable?

**Discussion: Tara is allowed a $400 rent expense deduction unless she can establish that the location or other unique features of her father's building justify a higher rent than other, comparable store space. Unless Tara can prove otherwise, the $600 excess payment is considered a nondeductible payment to her father (a gift).**

**Example 22** Roy pays Sally $100 per week to clean his medical office. When Sally became ill, he hired his daughter, Janice, to fill in and keep the office tidy. Roy pays Janice $300 a week. How much of the $300 payment is reasonable?

**Discussion: Of the $300 per week paid Janice, he is allowed to deduct only $100, because that is the amount he pays Sally. Unless Roy can prove otherwise, Janice's $300 weekly salary is considered excessive because he normally pays $100 a week for the same services.**

**Note: In each of these examples, the apparently unreasonable compensation is paid to a related party. It is unlikely that the taxpayers in these examples would pay the same amounts had the transaction been with an unrelated party.**

## 5-4b Not a Personal Expense

LO 6 Identify the general classes of expenditures for which a deduction is not allowed.

The tax law specifically disallows a deduction for personal, living, and family expenses.[14] Because deductions are a matter of legislative grace, this rule eliminates deductions for expenditures that do not have a business purpose, such as:

- Premiums the insured taxpayer pays for life insurance
- Insurance premiums paid on the taxpayer's home and personal property
- Expenses of maintaining a home such as rent, utilities, and maintenance
- Losses from disposing of property held for personal, living, or family purposes

- The cost of transportation, meals, or lodging unless they are related to a trade or business, the production of income, charitable contributions, or medical expenses; the personal cost of commuting to work and back is not deductible
- Legal fees and costs of obtaining a divorce; the portion of the attorney's fee paid to obtain alimony or other taxable income is allowed as a deduction for the production of income

Frequently, an expense is incurred for both business and personal reasons. Does the business purpose automatically qualify the expense for deduction? According to the IRS and the courts, the answer is no. To be deductible, the expense must bear a proximate relationship to the income-producing activity.[15] In addition, the primary or dominant motivation for incurring the expense must be the business purpose. A significant business motivation is not enough.

**Example 23** Atman and Sarita are good friends. Atman also supplies Sarita with artwork that she sells to customers in her interior decorating business. Atman takes Sarita to dinner at the Greyhouse. During the meal, they discuss business, and Sarita agrees to buy several pieces of art. Atman pays for the meal. Is the cost of the meal a business expense or a personal expense?

**Discussion: If Atman takes Sarita to dinner just to spend time with a friend, the fact that the conversation drifts to business does not result in a business deduction for the meal. Because the dominant motive for the expense is personal, the expense is not deductible.**

**If Atman takes Sarita to dinner so he can discuss his artwork and to solicit an order for paintings and the event centered on a business discussion, Atman can deduct the cost of the meal as a business expense because the dominant motive is business.**

## 5-4c Not a Capital Expenditure

A **capital expenditure** that results in an asset that benefits future accounting periods is not allowed as a current deduction because the useful life extends substantially beyond the end of the tax year.[16] Capital expenditures include the cost of acquiring land, buildings, machinery, equipment, furniture, and fixtures; the cost of perfecting or defending title to property; and purchased goodwill. Amounts paid for freight and installation charges related to getting an asset to the taxpayer's location and set up are included in the asset's basis. If the taxpayer constructs an asset for their own business, the property's basis includes both the direct and indirect costs of production. If an asset has a useful life that extends substantially beyond the end of the tax year of the expenditure, its immediate deduction is generally not allowed.

**Example 24** Paula buys Colleen's advertising agency. As part of the purchase price, she pays Colleen $12,000 not to open another advertising agency in the area for 3 years. Can Paula deduct the $12,000 as a current business expense?

**Discussion: The $12,000 payment (known as a *covenant not to compete*) will benefit Paula's business for 3 years by not having Colleen as a competitor during that period. Thus, the benefit of the payment extends substantially beyond the end of the tax year and must be capitalized and amortized as an intangible asset.**

The capital recovery and the annual accounting period concepts require deduction of an asset's basis through depreciation, amortization, depletion, or as a reduction in the amount realized on the asset's disposition. For example, assets with a limited life, such as buildings and equipment, are subject to a depreciation expense deduction. The cost of assets with an indefinite useful life, such as land, are permanently capitalized until the asset's disposition. Based on the administrative convenience concept, tools that wear out and are thrown away within one year can be deducted in the year of purchase. Contrary to the general rule, by legislative grace, Congress lets taxpayers take a current deduction for certain long-lived assets. For example, a taxpayer can elect to expense certain depreciable business assets (Section 179 election).

The commission paid on the acquisition of a security is not a current deduction. When a commission is paid on the purchase of a security, it is considered part of the cost of buying the asset and is added to the security's basis. When the security is sold, the basis is deducted from the sale price as a capital recovery. The commission paid on the sale of a security is a reduction in the amount realized on the sale.

**Example 25** Bao purchases 100 shares of Calvinator Corporation stock for $100 per share. She also pays a commission on the purchase of $400. What is the basis of the 100 shares of stock?

**Discussion: The basis of the stock is the cost of obtaining it. Because the commission is part of the cost of acquiring the stock, it is added to basis; commissions are not current period expenses. Therefore, the cost of the 100 shares of stock is $10,400 [(100 × $100) + $400].**

**Example 26** Bao sells the 100 shares of stock purchased in example 25 for $130 per share. She pays a commission of $600 on the sale. What is Bao's gain or loss on the sale of the stock?

**Discussion: Bao has a gain of $2,000 on the sale. The $600 commission is a reduction of the amount realized on the sale; it is not a current period expense:**

| | |
|---|---|
| Selling price (100 × $130) | $ 13,000 |
| Less: Commissions | (600) |
| Amount realized from sale | $ 12,400 |
| Less: Basis of shares sold | (10,400) |
| Gain on sale | $ 2,000 |

## Repair-and-Maintenance Expense

The difference between a capital expenditure that results in an asset and a **repair-and-maintenance expense** is important. Repair-and-maintenance expenses are allowed as a deduction in the current accounting period.[17] Repairs include repainting an office, fixing a leaking water or gas line, patching a roof, and replacing a broken glass in a window. These expenses generally include the costs of keeping business assets in normal operating condition. Unlike improvements and replacements, repairs do not appreciably extend an asset's useful life or materially add to its value. Improvements, such as rewiring or putting a new roof on a building, should be capitalized, because they either extend useful life or add to the value of the property. A **replacement**, such as a major overhaul of a machine, that extends the life of an asset should also be capitalized. In addition, expenditures made as part of a plan to recondition, improve, or alter an asset (called *betterments*) should be capitalized as assets, although if considered separately, the individual expenditures might qualify as repairs.[18] The costs of improvements, replacements, and betterments should be deducted in the accounting periods benefited by their use, based on an acceptable depreciation or amortization method.

## Start-up Costs

Capital expenditures can also include start-up costs. **Start-up costs** are related to investigating and creating a new active trade or business. The start-up costs to be capitalized are the expenses incurred before the new business begins its activities. Start-up costs could include:

- Surveys and analyses of markets, facilities, and labor force
- Travel to develop the business and locate potential customers and suppliers
- Advertising the new business
- Salaries to train employees
- Salaries for executives and consultants
- Other expenses such as legal and accounting fees

The items included as capitalized start-up costs must be similar to expenses that would be deductible in expanding an existing business.

Up to $5,000 of start-up costs can be deducted in the year in which the new business begins operation. Start-up costs in excess of $5,000 are amortized over 180 months, beginning in the month the business begins operations. The $5,000 deductible amount is phased out on a dollar-by-dollar basis when start-up costs exceed $50,000 (i.e., can only amortize if start-up costs exceed $55,000).[19] Therefore, the deduction for start-up costs can be viewed as consisting of two parts. The first is a $5,000 current deduction and a second part that allows any remaining start-up costs to be amortized over 180 months. For example, a taxpayer with $25,000 of start-up costs would receive a one-time current deduction of $5,000 with the remaining $20,000 ($25,000 − $5,000) of start-up costs amortized over 180 months. If the taxpayer does not elect to amortize the start-up costs, they become locked in and can be deducted only upon disposition of the business. If the taxpayer does not enter the new business, expenses related to investigating it are not deductible.[20] The transaction is given this treatment because the taxpayer's motivation is deemed to be primarily personal before a new business is begun. A taxpayer's efforts to investigate a business do not establish a business purpose for the expenditures.

It is important to note that a taxpayer operating an existing trade or business can claim a current deduction for the cost of investigating, expanding, or establishing new locations for the same line of business. The investigation costs are considered an ordinary and necessary expense of the existing trade or business and therefore fully deductible when incurred. However, an existing business entering an unrelated trade or business is subject to the same capitalization rules as a new business.[21] If the unrelated business is not acquired, the investigation expenses are nondeductible.

**Example 27** Jason has operated Main Street Cafe for 15 years. He would like to branch out by opening another cafe in a nearby city. Jason incurs $40,000 of costs investigating the feasibility of opening the second cafe. Can he deduct these costs?

**Discussion: Whether Jason decides to expand his business and open a second cafe or not, he can deduct the costs of investigating a location for a second cafe as a current deduction. Because the expenses are related to opening a business that is related to Jason's existing business, they are allowed as a current deduction, no matter what he decides.**

**Example 28** What would happen if Jason, in example 27, investigates opening a retail store selling speedboats?

**Discussion: The retail speedboat store would be a new business because it is unrelated to his cafe business. If Jason decides not to enter the retail boat business, he cannot deduct any investigation expenses. They are considered nondeductible personal expenses. If Jason acquires the retail store, he can deduct $5,000 of the start-up costs. The remaining $35,000 ($40,000 − $5,000) in start-up costs is amortized over 180 months, beginning in the month the retail speedboat store begins operations.**

**Example 29** Assume that in example 28, Jason opens the retail speedboat store in October of the current year and incurs $53,000 of start-up costs. What amount can Jason deduct for start-up costs in the current year?

**Discussion: Jason can deduct $2,850 ($2,000 + $850) of the start-up costs. Because his start-up costs exceed $50,000, Jason can only receive a one-time deduction of $2,000 [$5,000 − $3,000 ($53,000 − $50,000)]. The remaining $51,000 ($53,000 − $2,000 one-time deduction) of start-up costs is amortized over 180 months, beginning in October. The amortized amount of Jason's start-up costs is $850 [($51,000 ÷ 180) × 3 months]. Note: In subsequent years, Jason will deduct $3,400 [$51,000 ÷ 180) × 12 months] of the start-up costs each year.**

The costs of organizing a corporation or partnership must also be capitalized. Organization costs are those costs incurred to organize a corporation or a partnership. Such costs include legal, accounting, filing, and other fees and costs incidental to the start-up of a corporation or a partnership. They are similar to start-up costs in that they are incurred before the entity is legally organized. As such, they are subject to the same rules outlined above for start-up costs.[22]

## 5-4d Not Frustrate Public Policy

In a long series of cases before 1970, the courts disallowed deductions (usually for fines and penalties) for expenditures that the courts thought were frustrating public policy by encouraging unlawful conduct.[23] The courts' rationale was that it was neither ordinary nor necessary to violate the law. In 1969, Congress preempted the court battles by amending Section 162 to disallow certain categories of payments. The following payments are explicitly stated in the tax law as nondeductible expenditures:

- Direct or indirect illegal bribes or kickbacks to government officials and employees, including payments to federal, state, local, and foreign government officials and employees as well as officials and employees of a government agency.
- Direct or indirect payments to any person of an amount that constitutes an illegal bribe, kickback, or other illegal payment under federal or state law (if the state law is generally enforced).
- Bribes, kickbacks, or rebates by a provider of services, supplier, physician, or other persons who furnish items or services under Medicare or Medicaid.
- Fines, penalties, or similar payments to a governmental unit for the violation of any law.
- Certain damage payments for violation of the antitrust laws.
- Effective December 20, 2017, expenses incurred for the settlement, payout, or attorney fees related to sexual harassment or sexual abuse if such payments are subject to a nondisclosure agreement.

**Example 30** Rapid Trucking Company incurred several weight overload fines. Although Rapid took reasonable precautions to avoid violating the overall weight limit, loads that shifted during transit resulted in violations of the axle-weight limit. Can Rapid deduct the overload fines?

**Discussion: Even if Rapid Trucking Company had exercised all due care and incurred the overweight fines without willful intent, the fines would not be allowed as a deduction. A deduction for fines is specifically disallowed as being in violation of public policy.**

**Example 31** Chitsa is a tax return preparer. She forgot to sign tax returns she prepared for her clients. As a result, she was fined $50 for each unsigned return. Can Chitsa deduct the fines as a cost of doing business?

**Discussion: The tax law requires a return preparer to sign each return prepared for a fee. A $50 penalty is assessed for each return not properly signed. The penalties paid by Chitsa are not deductible as an expense related to her tax return preparation business.**

### Expenses of an Illegal Business

Although the tax law specifically denies a deduction for the listed expenditures on the basis that they are illegal payments, a taxpayer can deduct the legal ordinary and necessary expenses related to carrying on an illegal trade or business.[24]

**Example 32** Bert is engaged in the business of illegally trafficking in liquor, gambling, and betting on horse races. The business is operated out of the Overflow Club. Under state law, the activities are illegal. What expenses may Bert deduct against his illegal income?

**Discussion: Bert's income from the illegal activities is taxable under the all-inclusive income concept. The payment of fines for breaking the law and bribes paid to protect the business from raids and arrests by state and county law officers are not deductible. However, legitimate expenses incurred in the illegitimate business are deductible. Among the allowable expenses are rent, utilities, and employee wages.**

A special provision in the tax law denies all deductions other than cost of goods sold for individuals engaged in the illegal trafficking of controlled substances (drugs).[25]

### Lobbying Expenses and Other Political Activities

Relying on the ordinary and necessary requirement for deducting business expenses, in 1918 the Treasury Department promulgated regulations that denied deductions for expenditures for the promotion or defeat of legislation, and political contributions. With minor changes in language, these restrictions have been retained. The denial of such deductions has been upheld by the courts on the grounds that money was an "insidious influence" on politics.

Contributions to political campaigns and expenditures to influence public opinion about legislation, a referendum, or how to vote in an election are not deductible. This denial of deductions extends to advertising in a political party's convention program, admission to political fund-raising dinners, and events such as an inaugural ball, parades, and concerts.

**Example 33** The accounting firm of Williams, Daniels, and Thomas contributes $100 to a political campaign fund. The objective of the group managing the fund is to defeat a senator who has proposed legislation unfavorable to CPAs and to support candidates who favor CPAs' positions. Can the firm deduct the $100 payment?

**Discussion: The firm's political contribution is not allowed as a deduction because the fund supports the election of a candidate and attempts to influence public opinion concerning the suitability of the senator to hold office.**

Before 1994, costs incurred for lobbying in favor of or against legislation of direct interest to the taxpayer's trade or business were deductible. Under this exception to the general rule disallowing political expenditures, the taxpayer was allowed to deduct **lobbying expenses** such as traveling, preparing testimony, and communicating the taxpayer's view directly to legislators or the legislative body. The taxpayer was also permitted to deduct membership dues paid to lobbying organizations. Congress changed these rules to generally disallow deductions for expenses incurred in connection with influencing federal or state legislation or for expenses (including dues to lobbying organizations) associated with attempting to influence officials in the federal executive branch.[26] The 2017 Tax Cut and Jobs Act now disallows the deduction for lobbying expenses with respect to legislation before local government bodies. Therefore, the only expenses that are deductible are those incurred to monitor legislation. An example would be the deduction for travel expenses to the state capital to monitor and observe the discussion on new tax legislation.

## 5-4e Not Related to Tax-Exempt Income

Expenses incurred to earn tax-exempt income are not allowed as a deduction.[27] Allowing the deduction of these expenses would violate the ability-to-pay concept by giving the taxpayer the double benefit of excluding income while deducting the related expenses. Frequently, taxpayers have to allocate investment expenses to both taxable and tax-exempt income. When making the allocation, expenses directly related to a class of income are allocated to that income. Expenses indirectly related to more than one class of income are allocated among the various classes of income by using a reasonable accounting method. One reasonable method of allocating indirect expenses is by total investment income.

**Example 34** Clemons incurs $5,000 in investment expenses related to earning $3,000 in interest on taxable bonds and $3,600 in interest on tax-exempt bonds. The expenses are not directly allocable to either class of income. How much of the $5,000 in investment expenses can Clemons deduct as a production-of-income expense?

**Discussion: Clemons can deduct only the portion of the expenses that is incurred to produce taxable income. The portion attributable to the production of tax-exempt income is not deductible. The investment expenses are allocated to the classes of interest income as follows:**

| Bonds | Total Investment Income | % of Total Income | Investment Expenses |
|---|---|---|---|
| Taxable interest income | $3,000 | 45.5% | $2,273 |
| Tax-exempt interest income | 3,600 | 54.5 | 2,727 |
| Totals | $6,600 | 100.0% | $5,000 |

**Clemons is allowed a deduction for the expenses related to the taxable bonds ($2,273). The investment expenses related to tax-exempt bonds ($2,727) are not deductible.**

### 5-4f Expenditure Must Be for Taxpayer's Benefit

To be deductible, an expenditure must be for the taxpayer's benefit or be a payment of the taxpayer's obligation. A payment of another person's obligation does not result in a tax deduction for either person. The person making the payment cannot deduct an expense that is not related to her or his business because the payment lacks a business purpose.[28] The person for whom the debt is paid is not entitled to another entity's deduction for a capital recovery.

**Example 35** Marty's mother, Mary, owes $5,000 in back property taxes. To help her out of financial difficulty, Marty pays the property taxes. Can either Marty or Mary take a deduction for the property taxes paid by Marty?

**Discussion: Although property taxes are allowed as a personal itemized deduction, subject to limitations, Marty may not claim a deduction for payment of his mother's obligation. The property taxes were not Marty's obligation, and he did not benefit from the use of the property subject to the taxes. Mary may not deduct the payment of taxes because she did not pay the expense.**

**To make sure that a deduction is allowed for the taxes, Marty could have made a gift of the $5,000 to Mary and had her pay the taxes directly.**

An exception to the disallowance of the payment of another's expenses is made in the case of medical expenses of a dependent. All medical expenses paid on behalf of a taxpayer's dependent are deductible by the taxpayer, subject to the limitations on medical expense deductions.

## 5-5 LIMITED MIXED-USE EXPENSES

LO 7 Determine the tax treatment associated with mixed-use expenses in the areas of hobby expenses, vacation home expenses, and home office expenses.

As indicated earlier in the chapter, mixed-use expenses and expenses related to using mixed-use assets must be analyzed and allocated between business and personal expenses. The discussion that follows examines the three areas that Congress has determined have the greatest potential for abuse: hobby, vacation home, and home office expenses. The common thread among all three activities is that they are entered into by individuals who have an incentive to attempt to convert personal expenditures within the activity to deductible business expenses. Thus, detailed rules have been written to prevent this from happening. The legislative grace, ability-to-pay, business purpose, and capital recovery concepts all apply to these deductions and indicate that these expenses should be allowed to the extent they are incurred to earn income. As these topics are discussed, note the similarities in the calculation of the deductions and how the income from the mixed activity limits the amount deductible. The common denominator among all three mixed-use activities is that business expenses in excess of income earned in a hobby, vacation home, or home office activity are not deductible because they lack a business purpose.

### 5-5a Hobby Expenses

A taxpayer may engage in an income-earning activity primarily for personal reasons that prevents its qualifications as a trade or business or an investment activity. The activity may be carried on mainly for recreation and personal enjoyment, with profitability a secondary concern. In tax law jargon, this type of activity is referred to as a **hobby**, because it lacks a business purpose. However, the legislative grace, ability-to-pay, and capital recovery concepts all indicate that hobby income should be taxed only to the extent it exceeds the related expenses.

The hobby rules apply when a taxpayer has income and expenses in an activity without a predominant profit motive. The tax law considers nine factors in determining whether an activity that earns income is profit-motivated and should be treated as a business or is subject to the hobby rules. These factors are:

- Whether the taxpayer carries on the activity in a businesslike manner
- Expertise of the taxpayer or the taxpayer's reliance on advice of experts
- Time and effort the taxpayer spends to carry on the activity
- Expectation that the assets used in the activity will appreciate in value

- Taxpayer's success in similar activities
- Taxpayer's history of income or losses in the activity
- Amount of occasional profits, if any
- Taxpayer's financial status
- Elements of personal pleasure or recreation in the activity[29]

The courts consider and weigh all these factors in determining whether a taxpayer's activity constitutes a hobby. An activity's classification as a hobby is based on all the facts and circumstances presented by the taxpayer. Thus, the classification is subjective and is not determined by a single factor or by the presence of more factors indicating a hobby than a profit objective. The courts also will consider other factors relevant to the taxpayer's situation that may indicate a profit motive. In many situations, the determination of whether an activity is a hobby is best left to a tax expert.

A taxpayer's deductible hobby expenses cannot exceed the gross income from the hobby.[30] The expenses in excess of income are referred to as **hobby losses.** Hobby losses are not deductible. Hobby deductions must be computed in a specific order. First the deductions are grouped into three categories:

1. Expenses that could be deducted as either business expenses or itemized deductions (e.g., home mortgage interest and property taxes)
2. Expenses related to the hobby that would be deductible if the hobby had qualified as a business (e.g., supplies, utilities, repairs, auto expenses)
3. Depreciation on assets used to carry on the hobby activity

Category 1 expenses are deducted from hobby income first. If any income remains, category 2 expenses are deducted. Category 3 expenses can then be deducted to the extent that any income remains after deducting categories 1 and 2. However, with the passage of the 2017 Tax Cut and Jobs Act, a taxpayer's deduction for taxes paid is limited to $10,000. This limitation could restrict the amount of Category 1 expenses allowed to offset gross income. hobby expenses in categories 2 and 3 are no longer deductible as miscellaneous itemized deductions reduced by 2 percent of adjusted gross income. The TCJA suspends the deduction for miscellaneous itemized deductions for expenses prior to January 1, 2026. Thus, the benefit of hobby deductions is limited in two ways: The expenses are allowed only to the extent of hobby income, and only category 1 expenses are deductible as an itemized deduction. If a taxpayer uses the standard deduction instead of listing the actual itemized deductions, all benefit from the hobby deduction is lost.

**Example 36** Valeria is a physician. As a hobby, Valeria operates a farm where she raises animals. During the year, Valeria has gross income of $18,000 from the farm and pays the following expenses:

| | |
|---|---|
| Property taxes on the farm | $ 6,000 |
| Labor, feed, and veterinary costs | 10,000 |
| Depreciation on farm building and equipment | 4,000 |

How much of the $20,000 that Valeria incurs as expenses can she deduct?

| | |
|---|---|
| Gross income | $ 18,000 |
| Less: Category 1 expenses (property tax) | (6,000) |
| Balance of income | $ 12,000 |
| Less: Category 2 expenses (labor, feed, veterinary) | (10,000) |
| Balance of income | $ 2,000 |
| Less: Category 3 expenses (depreciation limited to $2,000) | (2,000) |
| Balance of income | $ -0- |

**Discussion: Valeria will report $18,000 of income in gross income. She can deduct $6,000 in taxes as an itemized deduction. The remaining $12,000 are not deductible since the deductibility of miscellaneous deductions has been suspended. In addition, she cannot deduct the $2,000 in excess of income from depreciation since it is considered a nondeductible hobby loss. Note: Property taxes are itemized deductions that are subject to limitations and will be discussed in Chapter 8.**

## 5-5b Vacation Home Expenses

A **vacation home** can be a house, apartment, condominium, mobile home, boat, or similar property. A taxpayer who owns a vacation home that is used for family vacations and then rented to unrelated people during the remainder of the year is subject to special rules. The deductibility of vacation home rental expenses depends on the rental income and the extent of the taxpayer's personal use of the home.

Table 5-1 summarizes the treatment of vacation home expenses.[31] As the table shows, if the taxpayer rents out the vacation home for a minimal period during the year (14 days or fewer), the dwelling is not considered to have been used for business purpose and is treated as a personal residence. For administrative convenience, the rental income is not reported and rent expenses are not deducted. As discussed in Chapter 8, home mortgage interest and property taxes on the property can be deducted as a personal itemized deduction.

**Example 37** Amber owns a summer cabin that she and her family use for personal purposes from May through August of each year. In August, Expando Corporation pays Amber $1,000 to rent her cabin for 5 days. Amber's expenses related to the cabin include $5,000 in taxes and interest and $2,000 in utilities and maintenance for the year. What is the proper treatment of the summer cabin income and expense?

**Discussion: Because the cabin is rented for 14 days or fewer, Amber does not have to report the $1,000 received from Expando Corporation as rental income. The cabin is considered a personal residence, and Amber may not deduct any expense related to the rental use of the vacation home by Expando. She can deduct the property taxes and interest as personal itemized deductions.**

If the home is rented for more than 14 days and used for personal use for a minimal length of time (the greater of 14 days or 10 percent of the days rented), the property is treated the same as investment rental property. Expenses allocable to the personal use of the dwelling are not deductible. Expenses related to rental use that have a business purpose are deducted just as they would be for any other profit-motivated transaction.

As the third row of Table 5-1 shows, using the vacation home for more than 14 days as rental property and using it for more than 14 days as a personal vacation home limits the deduction for expenses to the amount of the rental income. Expenses that have a business purpose are deducted in the same order as for hobby expenses. But unlike a hobby loss, vacation home expenses in excess of current income can be carried forward indefinitely for use in a later year in which there is enough rental income to offset them. The IRS requires that the taxpayer allocate vacation home expenses between personal and rental by using the ratio of personal days to total days of use (sum of personal days and rental days).[32]

*Table 5-1*

### Summary of Vacation Home Use Tests

| Rent Period | Personal Use Period | Tax Result |
|---|---|---|
| 14 days or fewer | Remainder of year. | A personal residence. Do not report income and do not deduct rent expenses. |
| More than 14 days | 14 days or fewer, or 10% or less of the number of days rented at a fair rental price, whichever is longer. | A rental property. Report like any other rental property. Expenses must be allocated between rental and personal use. |
| More than 14 days | More than 14 days, or more than 10% of the number of days rented at a fair rental price, whichever is longer. | A vacation home. Report rental income and allocate rental expenses using specified priority. Expenses are limited to gross rental income. A loss cannot be deducted. |

**Example 38** Latoya owns a cabin that she uses 20 days for her family's vacation during the current year. The cabin is rented to others for 40 days, for which she receives gross rental income of $5,500. Her total expenses of maintaining the cabin are

| | |
|---|---|
| Interest and property taxes | $6,000 |
| Utilities, insurance, and repairs | 1,500 |
| Depreciation expense | 4,500 |

What are Latoya's allowable deductions on the cabin?

**Discussion: Because Latoya uses the property for personal use for more than 14 days, the total deductions allocable to the rental are limited to rental income. The first step is to allocate the expenses to rental use and personal use.**

| | | | Amount Allocated to | |
|---|---|---|---|---|
| | Total Cost | Rent Use Ratio | Rental Use | Personal Use |
| Interest and property taxes | $6,000 | 40/60 | $4,000 | $2,000 |
| Utilities, insurance, repairs | 1,500 | 40/60 | 1,000 | 500 |
| Depreciation expense | 4,500 | 40/60 | 3,000 | 1,500 |

**Latoya's deductions for the rental are limited to the $5,500 in gross rental income. Further, the $5,500 in deductions must be taken from the expenses in the same order as deductions for hobby expenses:**

| | |
|---|---|
| Gross rental income | $ 5,500 |
| Less: Deductions allowable as either itemized deductions or as rental expenses (interest and property taxes). | (4,000) |
| Balance of income | $ 1,500 |
| Less: Deductions allowable only as a rental expense (utilities, insurance, repairs). | (1,000) |
| Balance of income | $ 500 |
| Less: Depreciation. Limited to the balance of income after other expenses. | (500) |
| Balance of income | $ -0- |

**The $2,500 ($3,000 − $500) in depreciation that is disallowed because of the income limitation is carried into future years for deduction if there is enough rental income to absorb the expense. In addition, Latoya can deduct the $2,000 of personal interest and property taxes as a personal itemized deduction. Assuming that Latoya itemizes deductions, the net effect of the cabin on her income is a reduction of $2,000 because of the deductions for personal itemized interest and property taxes.**

## 5-5c Home Office Expenses

A taxpayer who operates a trade or business from home can claim a deduction for expenses related to its business use. Expenses such as mortgage interest, real property taxes, insurance, utilities, repairs, and depreciation can be allocated on a reasonable basis to the area of the home used for a business purpose. This deduction is commonly referred to as the **home office deduction**. To claim a deduction, strict tests must be satisfied.

A specific part of the home must be used exclusively for carrying on a trade or business. A taxpayer who does not have another business location can deduct the cost of using an area in the home for storing inventory on a regular basis. If a room is used for a trade or business and is also used for investing or personal activities, the exclusive use test is not met and no deduction for home office expenses is allowed.

The home office area must also be regularly used as the principal place to conduct a trade or business belonging to the taxpayer or as a place to meet or deal with patients, clients, or customers in the normal course of the trade or business.[33] If the portion of the home used for business is a separate structure, the taxpayer needs only to show that it was used in connection with a trade or business. If these tests are met, the taxpayer can deduct expenses related to using part of the home for business.

In addition, a taxpayer who uses a home office to conduct substantial administrative or management activities and has no other fixed location to conduct these activities is allowed to deduct the cost of a home office. The taxpayer must still use the home office exclusively and on a regular basis in carrying on a trade or business.[34]

Employees who use an office in their home to conduct business for their employer must meet an additional test. Employee use must be "for the convenience of the employer" and "required as a condition of employment" before any deductions for a home office may be taken.[35] Because most employee use of a home office is for the convenience of the employee (i.e., people work at home because they want to, not because they are required to), most employee situations will not result in a deduction for home office expenses.

**Example 39** Reginald is an engineer for Arclight Petroleum Company. Rather than work late at the office, he often takes home Arclight work, which he works on in an office in his home. Reginald prefers to bring work home so that he can have dinner with his family and not have to return to his office late at night or on weekends. Can Reginald deduct any of the costs of maintaining the home office?

**Discussion: Because Reginald's use of the office is related to his employment with Arclight, he must prove that the use of the home office is for Arclight's convenience and that it is required as a condition of his employment. Given these facts, Reginald's use is for his convenience, not Arclight's. Thus, the deduction would not be allowed. In addition, it is doubtful that Arclight requires Reginald to maintain an office in his home to maintain employment, which is also required for deductibility.**

Expenses of maintaining the home are allocated between the home office and the areas used as a residence. The expenses may be allocated on the basis of the number of rooms or on the basis of square footage of floor space in the home. The method chosen should reasonably reflect the area used as an office. The home office deduction follows the same computational pattern as the hobby and vacation home deductions discussed earlier. However, the income limitation is based on income earned from the home office activity after deducting all other business expenses that are unrelated to the use of the home office. If the home office deductions exceed the income limitation, the excess may be carried forward and used to reduce income in a later year.

**Example 40** Kendall uses 1 room in her home as the primary location for her business. Her home has 6 rooms and is 2,500 square feet. The office area is 300 square feet or 12% of the total area. For the current year, she has $15,000 in mortgage interest and real estate taxes and $8,000 in insurance, repairs, and maintenance related to her home. Kendall determines that depreciation on the house for the current year is $4,000. She has $21,000 in income and $17,800 in other business expenses. What is Kendall's allowable home office deduction for the current year?

**Discussion: Kendall's home office deduction cannot exceed her income from the home office activity after deducting all other business expenses that are unrelated to the home office. Thus, her maximum home office deduction is $3,200 ($21,000 − $17,800). The amounts that Kendall can deduct for her home office are**

| | |
|---|---|
| Income limitation on home office expenses ($21,000 − $17,800) | $3,200 |
| 1. Deduct expenses otherwise allowed as a deduction under other tax rules: | |
| Interest and taxes ($15,000 × 12%) | (1,800) |
| Balance of income | $1,400 |

| | | |
|---|---|---|
| 2. Deduct office expenses not otherwise allowed as a deduction: | | |
| Insurance, repairs, and other expenses ($8,000 × 12%) | | (960) |
| Balance of income | | $ 440 |
| 3. Deduct depreciation on office portion of residence: | | |
| Current-year depreciation | $ 4,000 | |
| Business percentage | × .12 | |
| Depreciation on office | $ 480 | |
| Deduction limited to balance of income | | (440) |
| Balance of income | | $ -0- |

**The $40 ($480 − $440) in depreciation that was not allowed as a deduction in the current year because of the income limitation can be carried forward to next year.**

You should be aware of two important points concerning the operation of a business from home. First, the expenses of operating the business that are not related to the home office are allowed as a deduction, even if the home office expense is disallowed because of the income limitation. Second, to deduct telephone expenses relating to a home office, the taxpayer must have a separate phone line (i.e., phone number) for the business. If the taxpayer has only one phone, the basic phone charge cannot be deducted; only long distance business-related phone calls are allowed as a deduction.

**Example 41** Alvin operates his business from home. His sales for the year total $50,000. He incurs $55,000 in travel expenses, employee wages, depreciation on equipment, and other expenses unrelated to his home office. The residence expenses allocated to the home office using the approach illustrated total $2,000. What are Alvin's allowable deductions?

**Discussion: Alvin's deductible loss from his business before considering a home office deduction is $5,000 ($50,000 − $55,000). He cannot deduct any of his home office expense in the current year because of the income limitations. However, the $2,000 in home office expenses can be carried forward to next year and deducted if he has enough income.**

## concept check

For an expense to be deductible under the business purpose concept it must have a business or other economic purpose that exceeds any tax avoidance motive. The primary motive for the transaction must be to make a profit. Under the entity concept, all items of income and deduction are traced to the tax unit responsible for the item. Therefore, taxpayers that use an asset for both business and personal use (e.g., vacation home, home office) must allocate the expenses associated with the asset between business use and personal use. Under the ability to pay concept, a taxpayer's tax liability must be based on the amount the taxpayer can afford to pay, relative to other taxpayers. The legislative grace concept requires that any tax relief provided is the result of a specific act of Congress that must be strictly applied and interpreted. Therefore, losses must be approached with the philosophy that a loss is not deductible unless a provision in the tax law allows it. Through these two concepts Congress allows deductions for expenses of hobbies, vacation homes, and home offices, but specifically limits the deductions to the income generated from the activity.

# 5-6 TIMING OF DEDUCTIONS—EFFECT OF ACCOUNTING METHOD

LO 8

Explain the general rules for deducting expenses under the cash and accrual method.

The annual accounting period concept requires taxpayers to determine the expenses that can be deducted for each tax year. To assign expenses to the correct year, the tax law requires the taxpayer to adopt an accounting method that clearly reflects income. A taxpayer's **accounting method** refers to the overall method used to compute income and deductions belonging to the tax year. It also refers to the method used to compute the amount of particular income or deduction items. For example, the taxpayer may determine net income for a business using either the cash or the accrual method. In addition, to calculate the deduction for automobile expenses, the taxpayer must elect to use either the actual cost method or the standard rate method (as discussed in Chapter 6).

If the taxpayer adopts a method of accounting that does not fairly reflect income (such as accrual method for expense and the cash method for income), the IRS can designate the method to be used by the taxpayer.[36] The accounting method adopted by the taxpayer is important because it controls the timing of a deduction. Deduction of an expense in the wrong accounting period is not allowed.

**Example 42** Craig pays $100 for supplies on December 28, 2021. His taxable income for 2021 is the lowest it has ever been, and he does not need more deductions for the year. Although he uses the cash method of accounting and normally expenses supplies when he buys them, he decides to save the $100 deduction until 2022. He reasons that his actions are proper because he has not used the supplies. When should Craig deduct the cost of the supplies?

**Discussion: Given his accounting method, Craig must deduct the expenses in 2021. He must use a method of accounting that fairly reflects income and apply that method on a consistent basis. As a cash basis taxpayer, Craig must deduct the $100 supplies expense in 2021. Under the cash method, he cannot take the deduction in 2022.**

## 5-6a Cash Method

A cash basis taxpayer may claim a deduction in the year an expense is paid. The basic question to be answered then is when does payment occur? If a check is honored when it is taken to the bank for deposit, an expense is generally considered paid on the date the taxpayer gives or mails the check to the creditor. If the check is not honored when presented for payment, the timing of the deduction is not clear. Depending on the facts that caused the check to be dishonored, the deduction could be delayed until the check is made good. If the check is intended as payment of the debt but is not honored because of clerical errors, the deduction is allowed when the check is mailed (if it is promptly paid). If the taxpayer does not have the funds to pay the check and intends for the check to be a promise to pay in the future (i.e., a note), the deduction is allowed in the year the check (note) is paid.

**Example 43** On December 31, 2021, Leilani, a cash basis taxpayer, mails a $500 check to her attorney to pay for legal fees related to her business. The attorney receives the check on January 2 and deposits it in her account. When can Leilani deduct the legal fees?

**Discussion: If the check is honored by the bank when it is presented for payment, Leilani can claim the deduction when she mailed it—in 2021—although the check was not cashed until 2022.**

**If the check bounces because Leilani does not have sufficient funds for the check to clear, the deduction is not allowed until sufficient funds are deposited and the check clears or Leilani makes some other form of payment to the lawyer.**

When a property or service is used to pay an expense, payment occurs when the taxpayer gives the property or renders the service to the creditor. If property or services are used to pay an expense, the amount deductible is generally the fair market value of the property or services given the creditor. However, a cash basis taxpayer will have to recognize the fair market value of services used to pay an expense as income and then deduct the expense incurred in providing the service. When the fair market value of an asset is more or less than its basis, the transfer of property will result in a realized gain or loss.

**Example 44** Sandra has worked out an agreement with a local radio station for advertising. The radio station will run 30-second commercials in exchange for interior decorating services offered by her business. During the current year, she provides enough interior decorating services to compensate the radio station for $2,500 worth of advertising. Her expenses related to performing the services total $1,200. How should Sandra treat this arrangement?

**Discussion: Sandra should deduct $2,500 in advertising expense and report $2,500 in service sales related to the advertising contract. Her $1,200 in expenses related to doing the work for the radio station are deductible as normal business expenses.**

Payment of an expense by charging it to a credit card is treated as payment on the date the transaction is charged to the card.[37] It does not matter when the taxpayer pays the credit card company. If a taxpayer gives their own note payable to a creditor, or the creditor charges an item on an open account, the expense is not considered paid until the note or open account is paid off. On the other hand, a taxpayer may go to the bank and borrow money, give the bank a note for the loan, and then use the money to pay expenses. Expenses paid with borrowed money are allowed as a deduction regardless of when the loan is repaid.

**Example 45** Laval owes $3,000 in expenses that are tax deductible. However, he does not have the cash to write a check. How can Laval obtain a current deduction for the expenses?

**Discussion: If Laval charges the expenses to a credit card, he is deemed to have paid the expense on the date of the charge and can take a deduction on the charge date. He can pay the credit card balance when he has the money.**

**If the expenses are not payable by credit card, Laval could borrow the money from a friend or a bank and give his note in return. He could use the cash to pay the expense and claim a deduction on the payment date. He could repay the note when he has the funds.**

**If Laval pays the expense by giving a note directly to the creditor, the expense is not deductible until the note is paid.**

A cash basis taxpayer may deduct prepaid expenses in the year paid if the prepayment does not create an asset that extends substantially beyond the year of payment. Thus, the late 2020 purchase of office supplies to be used in January 2021 is deducted when the supplier is paid in 2021. However, the IRS has said that if $1,000 in business insurance is prepaid for one year on July 1, 2021, the expense must be allocated by charging $500 to 2021 and $500 to 2022. The courts differ with the IRS on this issue. The courts have held that a prepayment of an expense that will be used up before the end of the tax year following the year of prepayment can be deducted when paid.[38] That is, such prepayments are deemed not to extend substantially beyond the tax year. This is referred to as the **one-year rule for prepaid expenses**. To qualify a prepaid expense under the one-year rule, the taxpayer must show that the payment is required by the creditor and that the payment does not distort income.

**Example 46** Woody rents his office building. According to his 15-year lease, he is required to pay the $12,000 rent in advance on August 1 for the period September 1 through August 31. Woody has complied with the lease terms for the last 3 years. Can he deduct the $12,000 in the year it is paid?

**Discussion: Woody can deduct the $12,000 annual rent when paid. Because the terms of the lease require the prepayment, the deduction will not distort income, and because it is used up before the end of the tax year following the year of prepayment, he will not need to amortize the expense. Note that a prepayment that extends beyond 1 year (e.g., a 2-year rent prepayment) is allocated to the periods benefited by the expense.**

Prepaid taxes are deductible in the year paid, even if the prepayment results in a refund in a later year. Under the tax benefit rule, the tax refund is reported as income.

**Example 47** Plain County assesses property taxes annually on December 1. The taxes are not due until March 1. Hortense always pays her property taxes before December 31. When can Hortense deduct the tax payments?

**Discussion: Although Hortense is not under a legal obligation to pay the taxes until March 1, the taxes are deductible when paid in December under the one-year rule.**

**Example 48** Charles has $2,200 in state income taxes withheld from his paycheck during 2021. How much of the $2,200 can Charles deduct in 2021?

**Discussion: State income taxes are deductible as a personal itemized deduction. Assuming that Charles itemizes his deductions on his 2021 tax return, he can deduct the $2,200 in state income taxes paid during 2021.**

**Example 49** Assume that after deducting the $2,200 in state income taxes, Charles files his state tax return and receives a refund of $300. How should Charles treat the $300 refund?

**Discussion:** Under the tax benefit rule, the $300 refund is a recovery of an expense deducted in a prior year. Therefore, Charles must include the $300 in his gross income in the year of receipt, 2022. Note: The $300 is not a reduction of 2022 state taxes paid. Also, if Charles does not itemize his deductions in 2021, the refund in 2022 is not included in his gross income because he receives no tax benefit from the state income tax deduction.

Prepaid interest is not generally deductible under the one-year rule. The tax law effectively requires all interest to be accounted for with the accrual method.[39] In essence, prepaid interest is payment for the use of money over time. As a result, it is allocated to the periods in which the money is used. The only exception to this rule is the payment of "points" on a loan used to purchase or construct a principal residence. The treatment of points is discussed further in Chapter 8.

**Example 50** On April 1, 2021, Tasi borrows $10,000 from his bank. The $10,000, 10% interest, 1-year note is due on March 31, 2022. To increase his expenses for 2021, Tasi prepays the $1,000 in interest on the note on December 31, 2021. How much of the $1,000 of prepaid interest is deductible in 2021?

**Discussion:** Because interest expense is a charge for the use of money over a period of time, Tasi must allocate the prepaid interest to the time period in which the money is used. Tasi may deduct only the interest related to the period of April 1 through December 31, 2021, $750 [$1,000 × (9 ÷ 12)] in 2021. The remaining $250 in prepaid interest is not allowed as a deduction until it accrues in 2022.

## 5-6b Accrual Method

An accrual basis taxpayer may deduct expenses in the year in which two tests are met. The first test is called the *all-events test*. The **all-events test** is met when all the events have occurred that determine that a liability exists and the amount of the liability can be determined with reasonable accuracy.

**Example 51** Hunter manufactures and sells electronic components for radar. The electronic components are fully warranted against defects for 3 years from the date of sale. Based on experience, Hunter knows that 5% of the components will be returned under the terms of the warranty. He estimates warranty costs related to 2021 sales at $15,000. Does Hunter satisfy the all-events test with regard to the $15,000 of estimated warranty expense?

**Discussion:** Although Hunter can reasonably anticipate $15,000 in warranty costs for 2021, the liability does not satisfy the all-events test. Because the actual payee and the nature of the claim are unknown, the amount of the warranty expense must be estimated. Thus, the warranty liability is not fixed, and it is not determinable with reasonable accuracy. None of the estimated warranty expenses is allowed as a tax deduction until the parts are actually returned and the warranty obligation becomes certain. Note: This treatment differs from financial accounting. In financial accounting, reasonable estimates of expenses are sufficient to fix the liability for the expense. Tax accounting differs in the requirement that the payee be known before an amount is considered fixed.[40]

The second test requires economic performance to have occurred with regard to the liability. Economic performance occurs when services or property are provided to the taxpayer or when the taxpayer uses property. Table 5-2 summarizes when economic performance is considered to have occurred for several commonly accrued expenses. For example, interest accrues with the passage of time, and compensation of employees accrues as workers perform services. Only when the all-events test and the **economic performance test** have been met can an expense be accrued and deducted for tax purposes.

**Example 52** Assume in example 51 that in 2022, customers return defective components sold in 2020 and 2021. It costs Hunter $4,000 to replace the defective parts. When can Hunter deduct the $4,000?

**Discussion:** When the defective components are returned and they are replaced or the sale price is refunded, Hunter has satisfied the all-events test and economic performance has occurred. He may deduct the $4,000 in warranty expenses in 2022.

Table 5-2

## Summary of Economic Performance Tests

| Source of Expense | When Economic Performance Occurs |
|---|---|
| Taxpayer is to receive property or services from others | As taxpayer receives property or services |
| Taxpayer is to use property owned by others | As property is used by taxpayer |
| Taxpayer is to provide property or services to others | As taxpayer provides property or services to others |
| Taxpayer owes interest expense | With passage of time, as taxpayer uses money borrowed |
| Taxpayer owes compensation to employees | As employees render services |
| Taxpayer owes vacation pay to employees | When paid by taxpayer, or when accrued if paid within 2½ months after close of year |
| Payments required<br>• Under workers' compensation laws<br>• As payment of liability for tort | As payments are made by taxpayer |
| Payments for accrued recurring items<br>• Sales commissions<br>• Shipping costs | When paid by taxpayer if immaterial *or* for a material item if it is treated the same for financial purposes |
| Prepaid items<br>• Insurance<br>• Warranty contracts<br>• Service contracts | When paid only if immaterial *and* service is provided in a reasonable time after close of year |

The purpose of the economic performance test is to disallow a current deduction for costs that will not be paid in the near future. This contrasts with financial accounting for such costs, where an accrual is necessary to properly match expenses to the revenues being generated. In working with the income tax accrual method, you should keep in mind that matching expenses to revenues is not a general criterion that must always be satisfied. Rather, income tax accounting is designed to implement the ability-to-pay and wherewithal-to-pay concepts that assess the tax according to the amount available in the current period to pay taxes.

**Example 53** Big Oil Company enters into an offshore oil- and gas-drilling lease in 2021. In 2022, Big installs a platform and commences drilling. The terms of the lease obligate Big to remove its offshore platform and well fixtures upon abandonment of the well or termination of the lease. Based on past experience, Big estimates that the well will be productive for 10 years, after which it will cost $2,000,000 to remove the platform and fixtures. When can Big deduct the cost of removing the platform and fixtures for financial accounting purposes? for income tax purposes?

**Discussion: Proper matching of expenses to revenues for financial accounting purposes requires Big to accrue a portion of the estimated cost of removing the platform and fixtures over the life of the well. Therefore, Big will expense $200,000 ($2,000,000 ÷ 10 years) per year beginning in 2021. For income tax purposes, the cost of removing the platform and fixtures is not deductible until economic performance of the liability occurs. Thus, Big will not be able to deduct any of the costs until it begins removal and incurs costs related to the removal.**

**Example 54** Janson Corporation runs charter aircraft services. In 2021, Janson enters into a lease agreement with Dana Airlines to lease one of its aircraft for the next 4 years. The lease obligates Janson to pay Dana a base rental of $500,000 per year. In addition, Janson must pay $25 to a repair escrow account for each hour flown. The amounts in the escrow account are to be used by Dana to make necessary repairs to the aircraft. At the end of the lease, any amount remaining in the escrow account is to be returned to Janson. In 2021, the aircraft flies 1,000 hours, and Janson pays $25,000 into the escrow account. Repairs to the plane in 2022 cost $20,000. In 2022, $20,000 is released from the escrow account to pay Dana for the repairs. When can Janson deduct the costs associated with the lease?

**Discussion: Janson can deduct the $500,000 rental payment each year because both the all-events and economic performance tests are met as Janson uses the plane. However, the $25,000 paid into the escrow account for repairs is not deductible until economic performance occurs. Economic performance occurs when the repair service**

**is rendered. Janson must wait until the repairs are made in 2022 to deduct the $20,000. Note that under financial accounting rules the amounts paid into the escrow fund would be deducted as they are paid as a cost of using the plane that year.**

An exception to the economic performance test permits a taxpayer to take a current deduction for an item even if economic performance has not yet occurred. This is known as the *recurring item exception*. Use of this exception requires all of the following:

- That the all-events test is met without regard to economic performance
- That economic performance occurs within the shorter of
  a. 8½ months after the close of the year
  b. A reasonable time after the close of the year
- That the taxpayer consistently treats the item as incurred in the year the all-events test is met
- That the expense either is not material or the accrual of the expense results in a better matching of income and expense than accruing the expense in the year in which economic performance occurs[41]

Congress intended this exception to apply primarily to accrued expenses—those that have not yet been paid but that meet the all-events test and will be paid within a reasonable time after the close of the year.

**Example 55** Arturo has a commission agreement with his sales force. Under the agreement, he is to pay his salespeople a percentage of their net sales for 2021. Because of accounting requirements, he pays the salespeople their commissions in February 2022. When can Arturo deduct the commissions?

**Discussion: Under the matching exception, Arturo can deduct the accrued commissions in 2021. Although economic performance (payment of commissions) does not occur until 2022 deducting the payment in 2021 results in a better match of sales income and commission expense.**

Prepaid expenses qualify under the recurring item exception only if the expense is not material. A material prepaid expense (e.g., insurance) cannot qualify for the recurring item exception because deducting the total amount of the expense in the current period does not result in a better match of the expense with income. If an item is considered material for financial accounting purposes, it is treated as material for tax purposes. However, if an item is immaterial for financial purposes, it is not necessarily immaterial for tax purposes. For an item to qualify as immaterial for tax purposes, the actual amount of the item *and* its relationship to other items of income and expense for the entity must be immaterial.

**Example 56** Robin enters into a 1-year maintenance contract on July 1, 2021, by paying $12,000. The cost of the maintenance contract is a large expense relative to the total expenses of her business. For financial reporting, the expense is prorated, $6,000 to 2021 and $6,000 to 2022. When can Robin deduct the $12,000 cost of the maintenance contract?

**Discussion: Robin should deduct $6,000 in 2021 and $6,000 in 2022. Robin does not qualify for the recurring item exception because the item is material. She does not qualify under the matching criteria because taking a current deduction for the expense does not result in a better match of the expense with income.**

**Example 57** Robin enters into a 1-year maintenance contract on July 1, 2021, by paying $12,000. The cost of the contract is a minor expense relative to the total expenses of her business for both financial and tax purposes. For financial reporting, the expense is prorated, $6,000 to 2021 and $6,000 to 2022. When can Robin deduct the $12,000 cost of the maintenance contract?

**Discussion: Robin can deduct $12,000 in 2021. She qualifies for the recurring item exception because the item is immaterial. Note: Robin's prorating the expense for financial purposes does not affect her tax treatment.**

**Example 58** Claudio begins carrying a new line of clothing in his men's shop in 2021. He pays $5,000 for advertising the introduction of the new line in 2021. Claudio does not expect to have to run the advertising campaign in the future. When can he deduct the cost of the advertising?

**Discussion: Under the matching exception, Claudio should deduct $5,000 for advertising in 2021. According to the IRS, expenses such as advertising, which cannot be practically associated with income of a particular period, should be assigned to the period in which the costs are incurred. The matching requirement is satisfied if the taxpayer reports the advertising expense in the same accounting period for both financial and tax reporting.**

## 5-6c Related Party Accrued Expenses

LO 9
Explain the requirements for the deduction of related party expenses.

The tax law limits the timing of the deduction of accrued expenses payable to a related cash basis taxpayer. **Related parties** are members of an individual's family and business entities in which the person directly or constructively owns more than a 50-percent interest. The arm's-length transaction and business purpose concepts require that related party transactions be scrutinized closely to discourage unwarranted tax avoidance. The ownership of a controlling interest in a business entity permits the taxpayer to exert significant control over the timing of transactions between the business and the taxpayer. The objective of the related party limitations is to defer accrued expenses from transactions that lack economic substance. For example, an accrual basis corporation and a cash basis related party could time a transaction to permit a deduction for the corporation in one year with the income reported by the related party in a later year. Thus, the taxpayers would receive benefit from the interest-free use of the deferred tax payment. The benefit is the interest related to the present value of the deferred tax.

**Example 59** Kool Corporation, an accrual basis taxpayer, accrues a $10,000 bonus payable to Ivan for its year ending December 31, 2021. Kool pays the bonus to Ivan on February 28, 2022. Ivan owns 90% of Kool Corporation and reports his income on the cash basis. What tax savings might Ivan realize from the accrual?

**Discussion: Assuming a 32% marginal tax rate and an 8% interest rate (the present value factor for one year is 0.926), Ivan could save $237 by structuring the transaction to accelerate the deduction while deferring the income. The tax savings are solely the result of the timing of the transaction [($10,000 × 32%) − ($10,000 × 32% × 0.926)]. However, the related party rules discussed next prevent this result.**

The related party rules prevent the abuse in example 59 by requiring an accrual basis taxpayer to use a cash method of accounting for expenses that are paid to a cash basis related party. If an accrual basis taxpayer accrues an expense payable to a cash basis related party, the expense is not deductible until it is paid in cash and included in the related cash basis taxpayer's gross income.[42] Thus, the tax law requires a matching of the deduction with the related reporting of income to avoid potential tax avoidance. If both parties are accrual basis taxpayers, the problem does not arise. The accrual accounting method results in the transaction being recognized by the related parties at the same date.

**Example 60** What is the proper treatment of the bonus in example 59?

**Discussion: Kool Corporation may not deduct the accrued bonus for tax purposes until the cash is paid to Ivan and included in his taxable income. Thus, Ivan reports the $10,000 bonus as income in 2022 when it is received, and Kool Corporation deducts the expense in 2022. The related party rules require both parties to recognize the transaction on the same date.**

**If Ivan and Kool Corporation are both accrual basis taxpayers, they would both accrue the transaction for the year ended December 31, 2021, regardless of when the cash was paid. Ivan would report income, and Kool would claim a deduction for the expense in 2021.**

LO 10
Identify deductions allowed in calculating financial income versus taxable income and the timing, if any, of these deductions.

## 5-6d Financial and Taxable Income Differences

Financial accounting rules place a strong emphasis on the matching of expenses to the income generated during the period. In addition, conservatism dictates that expenses and losses be recognized for financial accounting purposes before they are actually incurred. As a result, financial accounting promotes the use of reasonable estimates of the expenses incurred to earn income. However, tax accounting rules emphasize objectivity in measuring taxable income to be sure the proper tax is collected each year. The tax law's objectivity is essential to protecting revenue collection. Because of the time value of money, deducting an expense too early reduces the time value of tax collections. Deducting an expense in the wrong year to receive the benefit of a higher marginal tax rate will also reduce the tax collections. Thus, the timing of deductions is a critical issue.

The all-events and economic performance tests create temporary differences between financial (book) and taxable income. For example, the tax law generally requires the use of the specific charge-off method (as discussed in Chapter 6) for computing a bad debt deduction. Financial accounting requires the use of the allowance method, which uses a reasonable estimate of the current year's bad debt deduction to be charged against income.

**Example 61** For financial reporting, Press Corporation estimates its bad debt expense to be 2% of credit sales. For 2021, Press records $500,000 in credit sales and $10,000 (2% × $500,000) in bad debt expense. However, a review of individual accounts receivable indicates that on the specific charge-off method, actual bad debts for 2021 total $6,000. How much can Press deduct for bad debts for tax purposes?

**Discussion: Although the allowance method is used to estimate bad debt expense for financial reporting, the specific charge-off method must be used for tax reporting. As a result, Press should deduct $10,000 in bad debt expense for financial income reporting and $6,000 in bad debt expense for tax income. The difference in the book and tax deductions results in a $4,000 temporary difference.**

For financial accounting, vacation pay accrues as it is earned by the employees. The economic performance requirement allows vacation pay as a deduction when paid or when accrued if payment occurs within 2½ months after the close of the year. Similar rules apply to allowances for warranties. Warranty repair allowances are estimated and deducted as sales are made for financial accounting, but tax accounting allows a deduction only when the taxpayer performs warranty services.

Other tax laws, which are discussed in this and later chapters in the text, also create differences between book and taxable income. These differences are temporary differences in some instances and permanent differences in others. For example, capital expenditures benefiting future tax years are not currently deductible. However, the tax law makes several exceptions to this requirement to promote economic and social objectives. Chapter 10 discusses a special provision that lets a business expense $1,050,000 of the cost of new equipment in the year it is purchased. For a small business, these expenditures could be a significant drain on working capital. Allowing an immediate tax deduction for the expenditure takes into account two concepts: The immediate tax reduction recognizes that an investment in capital expenditures may reduce the taxpayer's wherewithal to pay, and the election to expense assets adds administrative convenience by eliminating the need to make annual depreciation calculations and keep detailed records for small investments in business assets.

Other temporary differences are caused by the tax law calculation of depreciation. For example, current tax depreciation rules ignore an asset's salvage value and compute depreciation over a predefined statutory life instead of the asset's useful life. These tax rules have the effect of allowing deductions for tax purposes before they are allowed for book income. Because the capital recovery concept limits the total depreciation deduction to the investment in the asset for both book and tax purposes, the difference is in the timing of deductions.

The tax laws also create permanent differences between book and taxable income. Provisions in the tax law that limit the deduction of business gifts to $25 per donee, deny a deduction for excessive compensation paid to employees, and the federal income tax expense are examples of expenses that do not reduce taxable income but are deducted for financial reporting. As a result, these expenses create permanent differences between book and taxable income. On the other hand, the tax law allows deductions that are not recognized as expenses for financial reporting.

As discussed in Chapter 1, the standard deduction is a tax accounting construct. This construct makes the tax rate structure more progressive and enhances administrative convenience, which makes the tax law easier to enforce. The use of the standard deduction is foreign to financial reporting. Further, the tax law allows a percentage depletion deduction for certain natural resources. Percentage depletion is a tax deduction based on a percentage of income from the mineral source. The deduction is allowed even if the taxpayer has fully recovered the capital invested in the asset. This deduction violates both the capital recovery concept and financial reporting's cost depletion rules. However, Congress, in its exercise of legislative grace, has decided that it is desirable to violate the concept to provide tax incentives to promote the economic objective of developing natural resources. In doing so, the tax law has again introduced permanent differences between book and taxable income.

### concept check

The annual accounting period concept requires taxpayers to adopt an accounting method that clearly reflects income. Once an accounting method is adopted, it must be used as the basis for the systematic and consistent allocation of expenses to the proper tax years. Therefore, the taxpayer cannot choose to use the cash basis to report income and the accrual basis to report deductions. Alternatively, the taxpayer cannot report expenses on the cash basis in the current year and then switch to the accrual basis in the following year.

## CHAPTER SUMMARY

Tax deductions are a matter of *legislative grace*. Therefore, expenses incurred in a trade or business or for the production of income that have a *business purpose* are allowed as deductions. Personal expenditures are not deductible unless they are specifically allowed itemized deductions. A conduit entity is not subject to tax. Rather, deductions flow through to each owner and are treated similarly to deductions incurred by an individual taxpayer. Mixed-use expenditures and expenses related to using mixed-use assets must be analyzed to determine the business deductions allowed for such expenditures.

An activity will generally be considered a trade or business if it is profit-motivated and the taxpayer is regularly and continually involved in the activity to earn a livelihood. A profit-motivated activity that does not satisfy the continual and regular involvement or the livelihood requirements will usually be considered an income-producing activity. Trade or business expenses receive preferential treatment compared with expenses for the production of income in the individual income tax calculation. Trade or business expenses and losses, rent and royalty expenses, and capital losses of individuals (subject to the $3,000 annual limitation) are deducted for adjusted gross income. As a result, they are fully deductible unless the passive activity loss limitations apply.

To be deductible, a business expense must be ordinary, necessary, and reasonable in amount. A deductible expense may not be

- A personal living expense
- A capital expenditure
- An expenditure that frustrates a public policy
- Related to earning tax-exempt income
- An expenditure for another person's benefit

The deduction for hobby, vacation home, and home office expenses is limited to the amount of income earned from the activity. If these mixed-use expenses exceed the related income, the excess expenses are not allowed as a deduction from other sources of income such as wages, dividends, and interest. Taxpayers claiming deductions for a hobby, vacation home, or home office must observe strict requirements to be able to deduct the expenses.

The year in which a deduction is taken is determined by the taxpayer's *accounting method*. A cash basis taxpayer may deduct expenses when paid. An accrual basis taxpayer may deduct expenses when the all-events test is met and economic performance has occurred. Both cash and accrual basis taxpayers generally must allocate prepaid expenses and capital expenditures to the accounting period benefiting from the use of the asset. Accrued expenses owed to a related cash basis taxpayer are not allowed as a deduction until the item is paid and included in the cash basis taxpayer's income. Temporary and permanent differences between financial reporting income and taxable income arise from the tax law's emphasis on the *annual accounting period concept* and objectivity in measuring and reporting allowable deductions.

# KEY TERMS

accounting method (p. 5-28)
active investor (p. 5-10)
active trader (p. 5-10)
adjusted gross income (p. 5-6)
all-events test (p. 5-31)
business expense (p. 5-4)
capital expenditure (p. 5-18)
conduit entity (p. 5-7)
deductions (p. 5-4)
deductions for adjusted gross income (p. 5-6)
deduction from adjusted gross income (p. 5-6)
dominant motive (p. 5-9)
economic performance test (p. 5-31)
hobby (p. 5-23)
hobby loss (p. 5-24)
home office deduction (p. 5-26)
investment expense (p. 5-11)
itemized deduction (p. 5-7)
lobbying expense (p. 5-22)
mixed-use asset (p. 5-14)
mixed-use expenditure (p. 5-15)
necessary expense (p. 5-16)
one-year rule for prepaid expenses (p. 5-30)
ordinary expense (p. 5-16)
production-of-income expense (p. 5-11)
reasonable expense (p. 5-17)
related party (p. 5-34)
repair-and-maintenance expense (p. 5-19)
replacement (p. 5-19)
securities dealer (p. 5-11)
start-up costs (p. 5-19)
trade or business expenses (p. 5-10)
vacation home (p. 5-25)

# PRIMARY TAX LAW SOURCES

[1]Reg. Sec. 1.162-5—Allows the deduction of education expenses that maintain or improve skills required in the taxpayer's employment or that meet the express requirements of the taxpayer's employer or applicable laws in order to retain employment.

[2]Sec. 63—Defines *taxable income*; allows individual taxpayers to deduct the greater of their allowable itemized deductions or the standard deduction. Standard deduction amounts are specified and are required to be adjusted annually for inflation.

[3]Sec. 211—Generally allows specific personal expenditures as itemized deductions of individuals.

[4]Sec. 164 (b)(6)—Effective for tax years beginning after December 31, 2017, the deduction for state and local income taxes and property taxes is limited to $10,000.

[5]Sec. 703(a)—Requires that the taxable income of a partnership be computed in a manner similar to an individual's. However, certain deductions are not allowed, and the items listed in Sec. 702(a)(1) through 702(a)(7) must be reported separately. Likewise, Sec. 1363(b) requires that the taxable income of an S corporation be computed in a manner similar to an individual's. Also, certain deductions are not allowed [Sec. 703(a)], and the items listed in Sec. 1366(a) must be reported separately.

[6]Knetsch v. U.S., 348 F.2d 932 (Cl. Ct. 1965)—Disallowed deductions from an investment in which the sole anticipated gain was the tax savings from the investment.

[7]Comm. v. Groetzinger, 480 U.S. 23 (1987)—Provides the current criteria for determining what constitutes a trade or business.

[8]Hazard v. Comm., 7 T.C. 372 (1946)—Held that the rental of a single parcel of improved property constituted a trade or business.

[9]Curphrey v. Comm., 73 T.C. 766 (1980)—Held that the ownership and rental of real property does not automatically constitute a trade or business, that the ultimate determination is based on the facts and circumstances of each taxpayer, and that the scope of ownership and management activities is an important consideration.

[10]Comm. v. Lincoln Electric Co., 176 F.2d 815 (6th Cir. 1949)—Held that the reasonableness of a payment is an element to consider in determining whether the payment is ordinary and necessary.

[11]Deputy v. DuPont, 308 U.S. 488 (1940)—Held that an ordinary expense is one that is normal, usual, or customary in the particular business of the taxpayer.

[12]Comm. v. Tellier, 383 U.S. 687 (1966)—Held that the term *ordinary* distinguishes those expenditures that are currently deductible from those that are capital in nature.

[13]Welch v. Helvering, 290 U.S. 111 (1933)—Defines what constitutes an ordinary and necessary expense.

[14]Sec. 262—Provides the general rule for the disallowance of deductions for personal expenditures by individuals.

[15]U.S. v. Gilmore, 372 U.S. 39 (1963)—Held that the origin of an expense determines its deductibility.

[16]Sec. 263—Provides the general rule that disallows current period deductions for capital expenditures.

[17]Reg. Sec. 1.162-4—Allows the deduction as an ordinary and necessary business expense of incidental repairs that do not add to the value of the property or that do not appreciably prolong the life of the property.

[18]Reg. Sec. 1.263(a)-1—Defines the characteristics of a capital expenditure.

[19]Sec. 195—Provides the rules for amortization of start-up costs of a new business.

[20]Rev. Rul. 72-254—States that the expenses related to a general search for a new business are not deductible.

[21]The Colorado Springs National Bank v. U.S., 505 F.2d 1185 (10th Cir. 1974)—Held that the deductibility of the costs of investigating a new business depends on whether the business being investigated is in the same or a similar line of business in which the taxpayer is already engaged.

[22]Sec. 248—Allows a corporation to amortize the costs of organizing the corporation. For partnerships, similar rules are found in Sec. 709.

[23]Hoover Motor Express Co. Inc. v. U.S., 356 U.S. 38 (1958)—Held that payments contrary to public policy are not ordinary and necessary.

[24]Max Cohen v. Comm., 176 F.2d 394 (10th Cir. 1949)—Held that expenses related to an illegal business are deductible as ordinary and necessary business expenses.

[25]Sec. 280E—Specifically disallows the deduction of business expenses of drug dealers. (Cost of goods sold is not a business expense.)

[26]Sec. 162(e)—Disallows the deduction for certain lobbying and political expenditures.

[27]Sec. 265—Disallows the deduction of expenditures related to the production of tax-exempt income.

[28]Reg. Sec. 1.162-1—Disallows deductions for expenses that are not related to a taxpayer's own trade or business or production-of-income activities.

[29]Reg. Sec. 1.183-2—Sets forth the criteria for determining when an activity constitutes a hobby.

[30]Sec. 183—Limits the deductions allowed for hobbies.

[31]Sec. 280A—Limits the allowable deductions on home offices and vacation homes; defines requirements for home office expense

deduction and what constitutes a vacation home.

[32]Prop. Reg. Sec. 1.280A-3—Requires that all expenses related to a vacation home be allocated between rental use and personal use on the basis of the number of days of total use of the vacation home.

[33]Comm. v. Soliman, 113 S. Ct. 701 (1993)—Held that for purposes of determining what constitutes a principal place of business for purposes of the home office deduction, the home office must be the focal point of the taxpayer's business.

[34]Sec. 280A(c)(1)—A taxpayer is allowed a home office deduction if the taxpayer conducts substantial administrative or management duties in the office and has no other location available to perform these duties.

[35]Sec. 280A—See note 32.

[36]Sec. 446—Provides the general rules for methods of accounting, including what constitutes a permissible method.

[37]Rev. Rul. 73-39—States that an expense of a cash basis taxpayer is deductible in the year in which it is charged to a credit card, not the year in which the credit card payment is made.

[38]Martin J. Zaninovich v. Comm., 616 F.2d 429 (9th Cir. 1980)—Allowed the deduction of prepaid expenses by a cash basis taxpayer when the expense would expire before the end of the tax year following the year of the payment and the payment was required. This is the one-year rule for prepaid expenses by cash basis taxpayers.

[39]Sec. 461—Provides the general rules for determining the year in which a deduction may be taken, provides the criteria for the all-events and economic performance tests, and disallows the current deduction of prepaid interest.

[40]Hughes Properties Inc. v. U.S., 106 S. Ct. 2092 (1986)—Held that a liability must be fixed and determinable in that the payee is known before an expense can be accrued.

[41]Reg. Sec. 1.461-4—Explains the economic performance test and the application of the exception for recurring items.

[42]Sec. 267—Defines related parties and disallows accrual of deductions to a cash basis related party.

# DISCUSSION QUESTIONS

1. **LO2** All allowable deductions of individual taxpayers are classified as either for adjusted gross income or from adjusted gross income. Why are deductions for adjusted gross income usually more advantageous than deductions from adjusted gross income?
2. **LO3** Why does the computation of adjusted gross income apply only to individual taxpayers and not to other tax entities such as corporations?
3. **LO1** What is the fundamental requirement that must be satisfied to deduct a business expense?
4. **LO3** What are the two primary categories of business expense? Why is it necessary to classify business expenses in these two categories?
5. **LO3** Why must a conduit entity report certain deductions separately?
6. **LO2** What is the effect on a partner's individual tax return if a partnership does not report separately the partner's pro rata share of investment expenses and instead includes these expenses in determining the partnership's ordinary taxable income?
7. **LO1, 3** The rules for deducting business expenses assure that virtually all expenses related to a trade or business or a production-of-income activity are deductible at some time during the life of the activity. However, few personal expenditures are deductible. Why is there a difference in treatment of the expenses?
8. **LO2** Discuss how well the rules for deducting expenses implement the ability-to-pay concept.
9. **LO4** How are mixed-use expenditures and expenses related to mixed-use assets treated for tax reporting?
10. **LO3** What is the difference between a trade or business and a production of income activity and why is it important to distinguish between these two types of activities?
11. **LO5** What requirements must be met to deduct a trade or business expense? an expense related to the production of income?
12. **LO6** When are capital expenditures deductible?
13. **LO6** How do you distinguish a currently deductible expenditure from a capital expenditure? Give examples of each type of expenditure.
14. **LO6** Why are start-up costs related to the investigation of a business opportunity treated differently depending on the current trade or business of the taxpayer?
15. **LO6** Explain the rationale for not allowing a deduction for political and lobbying expenditures.
16. **LO6** Explain why the income tax concepts support a deduction for some expenses of an illegal business.
17. **LO6** Why are expenses related to the production of tax-exempt income not deductible?
18. **LO7** Explain the rationale for the treatment of deductions related to hobbies, vacation homes, and home offices.
19. **LO7** What is/are the requirement(s) for determining whether a residence used for personal purposes is a vacation home or a true rental property?
20. **LO7** Under what circumstances can a taxpayer deduct the costs of a home office?
21. **LO8** What is/are the criterion (criteria) for the deduction of an expense by a cash basis taxpayer?

22. **LO8** What constitutes the payment of an expense by a cash basis taxpayer?

23. **LO8** What are the criteria for the current deduction of a prepaid expense by a cash basis taxpayer?

24. **LO8** What tests must be met for an accrual basis taxpayer to deduct an expense?

25. **LO8** What is the general purpose of the economic performance test?

# PROBLEMS

26. **LO1** Alexandra is a veterinarian employed by Fast Vet Services. Susan is a self-employed veterinarian. During the current year, Alexandra and Susan have the same amounts of income and deductions. How does a deductible expense paid by Susan affect her taxable income differently than the payment of the same expense by Alexandra?

27. **LO1** Discuss how an individual would deduct each of the following expenditures. If more than one treatment is possible, discuss the circumstances under which each type of deduction would be obtained:
    a. Amos purchased 500 shares of Lietzke stock for $50 per share. He also paid $1,200 in commissions on the purchase.
    b. Dandy owns an optical store. She paid $2,000 in medical insurance premiums on her employees and $1,400 on a medical policy covering herself and her family.
    c. Oscar is a finance professor at State University. He purchased professional journals costing $400 that he uses to keep current on the latest developments in finance.
    d. Gerry is a nurse. He paid $350 for nursing uniforms.
    e. Edgar owns a rental property. His rental income for the year was $13,000, and his allowable expenses were $9,000.

28. **LO1** Determine how each of the following expenses would be deducted for tax purposes. If the expense is not deductible, explain why not.
    a. Chander paid $500 in interest on a loan he used to purchase equipment for his retail business.
    b. Peter paid $500 in interest on a loan he used to purchase 1,000 shares of Pickled Pepper stock.
    c. Portia paid $500 in interest on a loan she used to purchase her personal automobile.
    d. Jordan's primary source of income is his wholesale warehousing business. During the current year, he paid $8,000 in state income taxes.
    e. Alphonse is a professional golfer who likes to race cars in his spare time. He spent $60,000 on expenses related to racing cars during the current year.
    f. Barry is an insurance agent. He bought a golf cart and had his insurance company logo put on the golf cart to attract customers while he played golf.

29. **LO2** Andy, Azim, and Ashwin operate the Triple-A Steak House, a popular restaurant and bar. The three, who have been friends since childhood, are equal partners in the establishment. For the year, Triple-A reports the following:

| | |
|---|---:|
| Sales revenues | $ 800,000 |
| Short-term capital gains | 24,000 |
| Short-term capital losses | (12,000) |
| Business expenses | (560,000) |
| Charitable contributions | (6,000) |
| Taxable income | $ 246,000 |

How must the Triple-A Steak House report its results to each partner for tax purposes?

30. **LO2** Manuel and Fernando own and operate an electronics store, Electronica, as an S corporation. Manuel owns 70 percent, and Fernando owns 30 percent. For the current year, the store reports the following:

| | |
|---|---|
| Sales revenue | $1,000,000 |
| Long-term capital gains | 8,000 |
| Business expenses | (840,000) |
| Charitable contributions | (9,000) |
| Nondeductible expenses | (4,000) |
| Short-term capital losses | (15,000) |
| Operating income | $ 140,000 |

a. How must Electronica report its results to Manuel and Fernando for tax purposes?
b. In addition to the income and deductions from Electronica, Manuel is married and has interest and dividend income of $3,500, long-term capital gains of $1,500, and other itemized deductions of $14,500. What is his taxable income and his income tax liability?

Communication Skills

31. **LO3** DeShawn is a retired auto mechanic. Since retiring four years ago, he has made stained glass windows. Because he has only occasional sales, DeShawn treats this activity as a hobby. A friend of DeShawn's recommends him to a local merchant who is renovating her office and needs someone to make and install 15 new windows. The job takes DeShawn a month to complete, and he is paid $3,000. In preparing his tax return, DeShawn is unsure whether the $3,000 is subject to self-employment tax. The instructions accompanying his federal income tax return indicate that a payment is subject to self-employment tax only if an individual is engaged in a trade or business. Write a letter to DeShawn explaining whether he is engaged in a trade or a business.

32. **LO3** Max owns an office building that he rents for $750 a month. Under the terms of the lease, the tenant is responsible for paying all property taxes and costs related to the building's operation and maintenance. The only cost to Max in relation to the lease is an annual legal fee for renewing the lease. Is Max engaged in the trade or business of renting real estate? How would you classify his deduction for the attorney's fee?

33. **LO1** Don was a senior vice president of a bank until its officials found he had embezzled more than $1,000,000. Don had set up fictitious checking accounts and deposited the funds into the accounts. He then created fictitious loans to himself. The embezzled money was used for personal purposes and to keep the fictitious loan payments current. Thus, he created fictitious loans to make payments on prior fictitious loans. Don worked hard to keep the loans current so he would not be detected. Because of a tax audit, he is seeking your advice. If his embezzlement activity is a trade or business, he claims he should be able to deduct as an ordinary and necessary expense the payments on the loans to keep his actions secret. What advice would you give Don concerning his business and deductions? Explain.

34. **LO4** Hamid owns and lives in a duplex. He rents the other unit to an unrelated married couple for $850 per month. During the current year, he incurs the following expenses related to the duplex:

| | | |
|---|---|---|
| Mortgage interest | | $7,500 |
| Property taxes | | 1,100 |
| Utilities | | 1,450 |
| Repairs | | |
| Paint exterior of duplex | $2,200 | |
| Fix plumbing in rental unit | 320 | |
| Shampoo carpet in both units | 290 | |
| Fix dishwasher in Hamid's unit | 120 | 2,930 |
| Homeowner's association fee | | 480 |
| Insurance | | 800 |
| Special property tax assessment to pave sidewalks | | 3,100 |
| Depreciation (both units) | | 4,200 |

How should Hamid treat the expenditures related to the duplex? Explain.

35. **LO7** In 2021, Lucy acquires a car for $14,000. She uses the car in her advertising business and for personal purposes. Her records indicate the car is used 70 percent for business and that her total annual operating expenses, including depreciation, are $3,800.
   a. How should Lucy treat the operating costs of the car for tax purposes?
   b. In 2024, Lucy sells the car for $6,500. Her business use for 2022 through 2024 remains at 70 percent, and she properly deducted $5,880 in depreciation. What is her taxable gain or loss from the sale of the car?

36. **LO5** Big Star Auto regularly advertises on local television. Carla, the owner of Big Star, pays her six-year-old grandson $250 for each commercial in which he appears for Big Star. During the current year, the grandson appeared in 100 commercials. Big Star wants to deduct the full $25,000 as a business expense. The grandson will report the $25,000 as income. Write a letter to Carla explaining whether Big Star can deduct the advertising fee paid to her grandson. Communication Skills

37. **LO5** Discuss whether the following expenditures meet the ordinary, necessary, and reasonable requirements:
   a. Sadie owns 5 shares of Megaconglomerate stock. She spent $4,000 to attend the annual shareholders' meeting.
   b. Sam runs a successful medical practice. Because he has a substantial investment portfolio, he spent $3,000 to attend a seminar on investing strategies.
   c. Alana is a self-employed tax attorney. She spent $3,000 to attend the American Institute of Certified Public Accountants' annual conference on income tax developments.
   d. Kevin owns a large ranching operation. He is deeply religious and feels it is important that his employees have access to religious counseling. He hired an ordained minister to live on the ranch and be available to counsel his employees on any religious problems they might have.

38. **LO5** Discuss whether the following expenditures meet the ordinary, necessary, and reasonable requirements:
   a. The Brisbane Corporation is being sued in connection with allegations that it produced a faulty product. Brisbane has hired an expert witness to testify that the product was not faulty. The expert's standard fee is $200 per day plus expenses. Brisbane has agreed to pay her standard fee plus expenses and a bonus of $5,000 if the company wins the lawsuit.
   b. Shannon is a professor who teaches film study at Burwood College. Her annual salary is $45,000. She maintains an extensive library of films and books at her home. During the year, she spends $15,000 on new material for her library. Most of the material is available at the university library.
   c. Francis operates an ice cream store and rents the building from his aunt Shirley, who acquired it last year. He paid the previous owner $600 a month in rent. When Francis's lease expires, his aunt increases the rent to $750. Rent for a comparable building in the area is $850.
   d. Max owns a dairy farm in Wisconsin. During the year, he makes 10 phone calls to his sister Ruby, who is an accountant. The calls, which total $150, are for financial and business advice. Ruby prepares Max's business and personal tax returns.

39. **LO6** For each of the following situations, discuss whether the expense is currently deductible or must be capitalized:
   a. The Mickleham Hotel installs a $125,000 sprinkler system to comply with recently enacted fire regulations.
   b. The Healesville Corporation pays a real estate commission of $35,000 in acquiring its new office building.
   c. The Doverson Company pays $25,000 to repave its parking lot.
   d. The Watsonia Company pays $56,000 to add an air-conditioning system to its warehouse. The company had agreed to air condition the warehouse as part of a three-year labor agreement with its employees.
   e. Hua pays $600 to repair the walls and ceiling of his rental property after his tenant moves out.

Communication Skills

40. **LO6** Rebecca is the head chef at a local restaurant and is exploring the possibility of leaving her current job and opening her own restaurant in a nearby town. She has spent $15,000 investigating potential locations for the restaurant and $14,000 on an analysis of the demand for a restaurant specializing in Asian cuisine. Write a letter to Rebecca explaining the proper tax treatment of the investigation expenses.

41. **LO6** Neal and Ned spend $25,000 on travel, surveys, and financial forecasts to investigate the possibility of opening a bagel shop in the city. Because their suburban bagel shop has been so successful, they would like to expand their operations. What is the proper treatment of their expenditures if
   a. They open a bagel shop in the city?
   b. They decide not to open a bagel shop in the city?
   c. Answer a and b assuming they are investigating opening a computer store in the city and they operate a bagel shop in the suburbs.

42. **LO5, 6** What is the proper tax treatment for each of the following expenses?
   a. All apartment house construction in Sandy Beach must comply with local and state building codes. To ensure that these codes are observed, Rex, a city building inspector, regularly visits construction sites. Shoddy Construction deposits $20,000 in a fund to provide a scholarship for Rex's son to attend college. The payment is in appreciation for Rex's help in getting around a building code violation.
   b. Rachel operates a pharmacy. She pays a 10 percent commission on all Medicare and Medicaid business and a 5 percent commission on all other business sent her way by the Last Stop Nursing Home.
   c. Kelly is a registered nurse. She receives a $1,750-per-month salary working for a local clinic. Because Kelly is five minutes late to work two days in a row, the clinic fines her $25. Thus, her salary for the current month is $1,725.

43. **LO6** What is the proper tax treatment for each of the following expenses?
   a. Bernilyn, a commercial real estate broker, is late for a meeting with her boss when she is stopped and ticketed $150 for speeding. She is using a company car when she receives the ticket.
   b. Russell is an employee of the Dinsmore Corporation, a small plumbing repair business. He learns that his boss Simon, the sole owner of the business, was arrested 20 years ago for burglary. Because Simon needs access to homes and businesses to do his work, he pays Russell $100 per month for his silence.
   c. Anastasia owns a travel agency. The daughter of the president of her largest corporate client is getting married, and Anastasia insists on paying for her bridal shower at a local restaurant.
   d. The San Martin Construction Company pays local union officers $20,000 to ensure that San Martin continues to receive construction contracts. The payments are standard practice in the area.

44. **LO6** Are the following payments deductible?
   a. A contribution to a fund to finance Honest Abe's campaign for mayor.
   b. A contribution to the Hardcore Gamblers' Association to fund efforts to persuade the public to vote for pari-mutuel betting on licensed turtle races.
   c. George, who is in the import-export business, sends an employee to Washington, D.C., to monitor current legislation. The expenses for the one-week trip are $1,500.
   d. Ruth, a small business owner, incurs $3,000 in travel, lodging, and meal expenses to testify in Washington, D.C., on the effect on small business of new environmental regulations.

45. **LO6** During the current year, the Fremantle Corporation, a real estate development firm, incurs $2,200 of expenses lobbying and testifying before the city council to change the zoning rules. The firm also spends $3,500 testifying before the state legislature and lobbying to modify the existing law that restricts commercial building in areas that are classified as wetlands. Can Fremantle deduct the cost of these lobbying efforts?

46. **LO6** During the current year, Maureen pays Universal Brokerage House $1,600 for investment interest expense. The fee is not directly related to any particular investment owned by Maureen. The company provides her with the following summary of her investments: Communication Skills

| Type of Security | Fair Market Value of Securities | Income Earned |
|---|---|---|
| Taxable | $72,000 | $7,300 |
| Tax-exempt | $48,000 | $2,700 |

Write a letter to Maureen explaining the proper tax treatment of the $1,600 she paid for investment interest expense.

47. **LO6** Ying pays $300 of investment interest expense and provides investment advice. The interest is not directly related to any particular investment owned by Ying. She owns $40,000 worth of municipal bonds that pay her $2,400 in interest and $20,000 worth of bonds that pay her taxable interest of $2,000. What is the proper tax treatment of the interest paid of $300 fee?

48. **LO3, 6** Tracy and Brenda are equal partners in Crescent Home Furniture, which is organized as an S corporation. For the year, the company reports sales revenue of $330,000 and business expenses of $195,000. Crescent also earns $15,000 in taxable interest and dividend income and $3,700 in tax-exempt interest on its investments. The investment portfolio consists of $35,000 in tax-exempt securities and $100,000 in taxable securities. Not included in the business expenses is $3,400 Crescent paid as investment interest. As the staff accountant in charge of taxes for Crescent Home Furniture, write a memo to Judy, the accounting manager, explaining how the company must report its results to Tracy and Brenda. Communication Skills

49. **LO6** Determine the current tax deduction allowed in each of the following situations:
    a. Doug, John's son, buys a new car that is titled in Doug's name. John pays for Doug's auto license tag. The tag costs $220: $40 for registration plus $180 in property taxes based on the value of the auto. Doug qualifies as John's dependent for tax purposes. Doug uses the auto for personal transportation.
    b. Elvis owns Ace Auto Repair. His head mechanic is arrested for drunken driving. Because Elvis needs the mechanic back at work as soon as possible, he pays the $500 bail to get the mechanic out of jail. To keep him out of jail, he pays $450 in attorney's fees and the $500 fine the court imposes on the mechanic.

50. **LO6** Determine the current tax deduction allowed in each of the following situations:
    a. Sam owns and operates SoftPro, a software programming business. In June, the firm files for bankruptcy. Eighteen months earlier, Sam's attorney, Karl, had recommended SoftPro as a good investment to his clients. Three of Karl's clients each loaned SoftPro $40,000 at 12 percent interest. To avoid losing his three clients, Karl repays the $40,000 each client had loaned to SoftPro.
    b. During the year, Raven's mother is hospitalized for three weeks and incurs $36,000 of medical costs. Her mother's insurance company pays only $22,000 of the medical expenses. Because her mother could pay only $4,000 of the remaining medical costs, Raven pays the remaining $10,000. Raven's mother does not qualify as her dependent.

51. **LO7** As a hobby, Salome creates and sells oil paintings. During the current year, her sales total $8,000. How is the tax treatment of her hobby different from the treatment of a trade or business, if
    a. Her business expenses total $5,600?
    b. Her business expenses total $10,000?

52. **LO7** Sharon is single and a data-processing manager for the phone company. She also owns and operates a sports memorabilia store. Sharon goes to shows, subscribes to numerous magazines on sports memorabilia, and maintains a Web page on the Internet. She has been engaged in the activity for the last five years. During that time, she reported a net loss in two of the years and net income in the other three. Overall, her sports memorabilia activity has shown a slight loss, but the value of her collection over the five years has increased by 20 percent. Sharon rents a 600-square-foot storefront for $500 a month. Although the store is open only on Saturdays, she is usually in her office at the store two or three nights a week buying and selling sports memorabilia on the Internet. For the current year, if she has an adjusted gross income of $42,000 before considering the following income and expenses related to her sports memorabilia activity:

| | |
|---|---|
| Sale of memorabilia | $11,500 |
| Cost of items sold | 3,725 |
| Cost of new memorabilia acquired | 1,500 |
| Registration and booth fees | 750 |
| Transportation to memorabilia shows | 600 |
| Meals attending shows | 250 |
| Cost of magazines | 280 |
| Cost of Internet connection | 240 |
| Office utilities | 800 |
| Phone | 400 |
| Depreciation on computer | 200 |

a. What is her taxable income if Sharon is engaged in a trade or business?
b. What is her taxable income if she is engaged in a hobby?
c. What factors (e.g., facts, aspects) of Sharon's sports memorabilia activity indicate that it is a hobby? a trade or business?

53. **LO7** Lee and Ben own a winter retreat in Harlingen, Texas, that qualifies as their second home. This year they spent 40 days in their cabin. Because of its ideal location, it is easy to rent at $120 a day and was rented for 80 days this year. The total upkeep costs of the cabin for the year were as follows:

| | |
|---|---|
| Mortgage interest | $9,000 |
| Real and personal property taxes | 1,200 |
| Insurance | 750 |
| Utilities | 600 |
| Repairs and maintenance | 1,000 |
| Depreciation (unallocated) | 2,500 |

What is the proper treatment of this information on Lee and Sally's tax return?

54. **LO7** Mel and Helen own a beachfront home in Myrtle Beach, S.C. During the year, they rented the house for five weeks (35 days) at $800 per week and used the house for personal purposes 65 days. The costs of maintaining the house for the year were:

| | |
|---|---|
| Mortgage interest | $5,500 |
| Real property taxes | 4,500 |
| Insurance | 650 |
| Utilities | 1,000 |
| Repairs and maintenance | 480 |
| Depreciation (unallocated) | 3,500 |

a. What is the proper tax treatment of this information on their tax return?
b. What is the proper tax treatment if Helen and Mel rented the house for only two weeks (14 days)?

55. **LO7** Matilda owns a condominium on the beach in Rehoboth, Delaware. During the current year, she incurs the following expenses related to the property:

| | |
|---|---|
| Mortgage interest | $8,000 |
| Property taxes | 1,750 |
| Utilities | 1,050 |
| Maintenance fees | 600 |
| Repairs | 350 |
| Depreciation (unallocated) | 3,200 |

Determine the amount of Matilda's deductions in each of the following cases:

| Case | Rental Income | Rental Days | Personal Use Days |
|---|---|---|---|
| A | $12,000 | 365 | 0 |
| B | $ 3,800 | 80 | 20 |
| C | $ 600 | 14 | 86 |
| D | $ 9,050 | 275 | 25 |

56. **LO7** Hassad owns a rental house on Lake Tahoe. He uses a real estate firm to screen prospective renters, but he makes the final decision on all rentals. He also is responsible for setting the weekly rental price of the house. During the current year, the house rents for $1,500 per week. Hassad pays a commission of $150 and a cleaning fee of $75 for each week the property is rented. During the current year, he incurs the following additional expenses related to the property:

| | |
|---|---|
| Mortgage interest | $12,000 |
| Property taxes | 2,700 |
| Utilities | 1,400 |
| Landscaping fees | 900 |
| Repairs | 450 |
| Depreciation (unallocated) | 7,500 |

a. What is the proper tax treatment if Hassad rents the house for only one week (seven days) and uses it 50 days for personal purposes?
b. What is the proper tax treatment if Hassad rents the house for eight weeks (56 days) and uses it 44 days for personal purposes?
c. What is the proper tax treatment if Hassad rents the house for 25 weeks (175 days) and uses it 15 days for personal purposes?

57. **LO7** Ray, 83, is a used car dealer. He lives in a rural community and operates the business out of his home. One room in his six-room house is used exclusively for his business office. He parks the cars in his front yard, and when customers come along, they sit on the front porch and negotiate a sale price. The income statement for Ray's auto business is as follows: Communication Skills

| | | |
|---|---|---|
| Sales | | $110,000 |
| Cost of cars sold | | (78,000) |
| Gross profit | | $ 32,000 |
| Interest expense on cars | $4,200 | |
| Property tax on cars | 700 | |
| Gas, oil, repairs | 1,200 | |
| Loan fees | 3,200 | |
| Depreciation on equipment | 1,800 | (11,100) |
| Net profit | | $ 20,900 |

If Ray's home were rental property, the annual depreciation would be $2,900. The utilities and upkeep on the home cost Ray $6,400 for the year. Ray's mortgage interest for the year is $2,400. When asked about the loan fees, Ray bitterly responds that Jim, the bank loan officer, charges him 10 percent of his gross profit on cars financed through the bank. Ray says, "The money is under the table, and if I don't shell out the cash, Jim won't loan the money to my customers to buy my cars. Everybody goes to Jim—he's got the cash."

Write a letter to Ray explaining the proper treatment of this information on his tax return.

58. **LO7** Hromas uses a separate room in his home as an office. The room is 500 square feet of the total 2,000 square feet in the house. During the current year, Hromas incurs the following household expenses:

| | | |
|---|---|---|
| Mortgage interest | | $ 12,000 |
| Property taxes | | 1,400 |
| Insurance | | 450 |
| Utilities | | |
| Gas and electric | $2,100 | |
| Cable TV | 280 | |
| Phone ($15 per month for a separate phone number for the office) | 450 | 2,830 |
| House cleaning | | 1,820 |
| Long-distance phone calls (business-related) | | 670 |
| Depreciation (unallocated) | | 5,600 |

How much of a deduction is Hromas allowed for the cost of the home office in each of the following situations?

a. Hromas is an independent salesperson who uses the room exclusively to call customers who buy goods from him. During the current year, his sales total $83,000, cost of goods sold is $33,000, and he incurs other valid business expenses unrelated to the office of $25,000.

b. Hromas is an employee of Ace Computer Company. He uses the office primarily when he brings work home at nights and on weekends. He occasionally uses the office to pay personal bills and to study the stock market so he can make personal investments. His salary at Ace is $80,000 per year. He is not paid extra for the time he spends working at home.

59. **LO7** Charlotte owns a custom publishing business. She uses 500 square feet of her home (2,000 square feet) as an office and for storage. All her business has come from telemarketing (telephone sales), direct mailings, or referrals. In her first year of operation, she has revenues of $37,000, cost of goods sold of $25,900, and other business expenses of $8,100. The total expenses related to her home are:

| | |
|---|---|
| Home mortgage interest | $6,400 |
| Real property taxes | 2,100 |
| Insurance | 560 |
| Utilities | 800 |
| Repairs and maintenance | 600 |
| House cleaning | 960 |
| Depreciation (unallocated) | 5,000 |

What amount can Charlotte deduct for her home office?

60. **LO8** The Adelaide Advertising Agency, a cash basis taxpayer, bills its clients for services it renders and any out-of-pocket expenses it pays to third parties on behalf of its clients. For example, in creating a television commercial for a client, Adelaide charges the client for its staff time in creating the commercial and the third-party costs of filming and editing the commercial. During the year, Adelaide bills its clients $2,800,000. Of this amount, $600,000 is for expenses it pays to third parties. On December 31, the accounts receivable ledger shows a balance due to Adelaide of $400,000, $35,000 of which is for third-party expenses. How much of the third-party expenses can Adelaide deduct during the current year?

61. **LO8** On July 1, 2021, Andaria borrows $30,000 from the First Financial Bank. The loan is for one year at an annual interest rate of 10 percent. How much interest can Andaria deduct under each of the following situations?
   a. The bank deducts the interest from the loan proceeds.
   b. The $30,000 loan proceeds are due at the end of the loan, but Andaria pays interest on the loan each month.
   c. The interest and loan proceeds are due June 30, 2022.

62. **LO8** The Kane Corporation is an accrual basis taxpayer. State law requires that Kane acquire workers' compensation insurance from a third-party carrier or maintain a self-funded workers' compensation insurance plan. Kane has decided to create a self-funded workers' compensation plan and pay $6 per month (the state minimum) into the fund for each of its 800 employees. During the year, the corporation pays $52,500 in workers' compensation benefits to its employees. How much can Kane deduct as workers' compensation expense for the year? Discuss.

63. **LO8** Appliance Sales Corporation sells all types of appliances. In addition, it offers purchasers of its appliances the option of purchasing repair contracts. During the current year, Appliance estimates that repairs totaling $13,100 will be made under the contracts sold during the current year. Actual repair costs are $7,500 related to last year's contracts and $2,450 on contracts sold during the contract year. How much repair cost can Appliance deduct during the current year?

64. **LO8** Gonzo Company is an accrual basis taxpayer. It provides medical insurance for its employees through a self-insured reimbursement plan. Gonzo pays $150 per month per employee into the plan fund. The fund is then used to reimburse employees' medical expenses. During the current year, Gonzo pays $90,000 into the fund and pays medical reimbursement claims totaling $78,300. How much can Gonzo deduct for the provision of employee medical coverage? Discuss.

65. **LO8** Damon's Lawn and Garden Supply, an accrual basis taxpayer, is the exclusive dealer for Tru-Cut lawn mowers. In 2021, Damon's agrees to pay the Dash Corporation, the manufacturer of Tru-Cut, an additional $15 per lawn mower. In exchange, the Dash Corporation will provide advertising and promotion to Damon's for a two-year period. Damon's purchases and pays for 200 lawn mowers in 2021 and 350 lawn mowers in 2022. The Dash Corporation pays $2,750 for advertising and promotion in 2021 and $5,500 in 2022. How much of the amount paid to the Dash Corporation for advertising and promotion can Damon's deduct in 2021? in 2022?

66. **LO8** Joy incurs the following expenses in her business. When can she deduct the expenses if she uses the accrual method of accounting? the cash method?
   a. Joy rents an office building for $750 a month. Because of a cash flow problem, she is unable to pay the rent for November and December 2021. On January 5, 2022, Joy pays the $2,250 rent due for November, December, and January.
   b. Joy borrows $60,000 on a one-year note on October 1, 2021. To get the loan, she has to prepay $6,200 in interest.
   c. Joy owes employees accrued wages totaling $20,000 as of December 31, 2021. The accrued wages are paid in the regular payroll on January 5, 2022.
   d. Joy purchases $2,400 worth of supplies from a local vendor. The supplies are delivered on January 29, 2021. They are fully used up on December 30, 2021. Because of unusual circumstances, a bill for the supplies arrives from the vendor on January 10, 2022, and is promptly paid.
   e. While at a trade convention, Joy purchases some pens and paperweights to send out as holiday gifts to her clients. She charges the $700 cost to her credit card in December 2021. She pays the credit card bill in January 2022.

67. **LO8** The Parr Corporation incurs the following expenses. When can it deduct the expenses if it uses the accrual method of accounting? the cash method?
   a. Parr Corporation mails a check for $5,000 to the United Way on December 26, 2021. The company's canceled check shows that the United Way did not deposit the check until January 16, 2022.
   b. For 2021, Parr Corporation estimates its warranty expense to be 1.5 percent of sales. The company's sales for 2021 were $2,100,000. The actual warranty costs paid in 2021 were $40,000.
   c. On August 1, 2021, Parr Corporation borrows $225,000 on a one-year note. Because the company is experiencing a cash flow problem, the bank agrees to let Parr pay the interest when the note matures. In exchange, the interest rate on the note is 10 percent which is 3 percent above the current market rate.
   d. Parr Corporation advertises on radio and in the newspaper. During the year, the company is billed $16,500 for advertising. The beginning balance in the advertising payable account on January 1, 2021, is $2,500, and the ending balance on December 31, 2021, is $3,300.
   e. On August 1, 2021, Parr Corporation pays $3,200 for a one-year fire insurance policy for the period August 1, 2021 through July 31, 2022. Parr's insurance company requires the one-year prepayment, which the company makes every year.
68. **LO9** Kai, a cash basis taxpayer, is a 75 percent owner and president of Finnigan Fish Market. Finnigan, an S corporation, uses the accrual method of accounting. On December 28, 2021, Finnigan accrues a bonus of $40,000 to Kai. The bonus is payable on February 1, 2022. When is the bonus deductible? How would your answer change if Finnigan is a cash basis taxpayer?
69. **LO9** Lonnie owns 100 percent of Quality Company's common stock. Lonnie, the president of Quality, is a cash basis taxpayer. Quality is short of cash as of December 31, 2021, the close of its tax year. As a result, it is necessary to accrue a $50,000 bonus payable to Lonnie. As soon as the cash becomes available on January 15, 2022, Quality pays Lonnie the bonus in cash. When is the bonus deductible for the accrual basis corporation? How would your answer change if Lonnie is an accrual basis taxpayer?
70. **LO10** During the current year, Covino Construction makes $5,000 in political contributions to ten political candidates. What amount can Covino deduct for financial accounting purposes? for tax purposes?
71. **LO10** The Martin Corporation is an accrual basis taxpayer that manufactures cellular phones. The company provides a five-year limited warranty on its phones and estimates that warranty expenses will be 1.5 percent of sales. During the current year, Martin has sales of $12,000,000 and incurs $149,000 of warranty expenses. What amount can Martin deduct for financial accounting purposes? for tax purposes?

## ISSUE IDENTIFICATION PROBLEMS

In each of the following problems, identify the tax issue(s) posed by the facts presented. Determine the possible tax consequences of each issue that you identify.

72. Shuana works as a lawyer for a large law firm where professional dress is expected. Her friend, Carissa, is self-employed as a nurse and works as an independent contractor for hospitals throughout the city. Shuana spends $1,500 a year on clothing, shoes, and accessories that she wears to work. Carissa spends $500 on uniforms and shoes for her job.
73. Angela owns a duplex. She rents out one unit and lives in the other. During the current year, she pays $4,500 in interest on the loan she used to buy the duplex, $900 in property taxes on the duplex, and $1,200 in dues to the duplex association which maintains the grounds and the swimming pool.
74. Harry and Sydney each inherited 50 percent of the stock in their father's corporation when he died. Harry had been working for his father and wanted to retain

control of the business. Sydney was not really interested in the family business and wanted to sell her stock to outsiders. To retain control of the corporation, Harry made Sydney a vice president of the corporation with an annual salary of $200,000. The only requirements of the position were that Sydney not sell her stock and that she let Harry run the business.

75. Leonard owns an apartment complex. During the current year, he pays $14,000 to have all the apartments painted and recarpeted. Gena purchases an apartment complex during the current year. Before she can rent out the apartments, she pays $14,000 to have them painted and recarpeted.

76. In auditing the Philbin Corporation's repair expense account, Sara finds a $28,000 entry. Since the amount is so large, she obtains supporting documentation. The invoice lists the Fradin Roofing Company as providing the service, but no description of the work the company performed is attached to the invoice. However, a notation on the check says "office roof."

77. Gary and Wes operate a wholesale meat company. The company sells to restaurants, golf clubs, and other dining establishments. Recently they spent $20,000 for market and demographic surveys, financial projections, and real estate appraisals to help them decide whether to open a retail store.

78. Marcus is the vice president of human resources for Griffin Industries. He spent one week testifying before Congress on the impact health care legislation will have on small business. His trip cost $2,750.

79. Russell is employed as a prosecutor for the town of Swansee. He also works 15 to 20 hours a week raising purebred Labradors. Over the last seven years, he has reported an average net income from this activity of $7,000 per year. However, in two of those years, he had losses of $3,000 and $4,000. He believes he could make more money from the activity if he kept better records, was less stubborn, and listened more to the advice of his cousin who has won national awards in dog breeding.

80. Chin, a cash basis taxpayer, borrows $25,000 on a two-year loan from State Bank to purchase business equipment. Under the terms of the loan, State Bank deducts $4,500 in interest on the loan and gives Chin the $20,500 net proceeds. Chin will repay State Bank $25,000 in two years.

81. The Showgate Hotel Casino is an accrual basis taxpayer and maintains its records on a calendar year. It has 3,000 slot machines, one of them a progressive machine whose jackpot increases based on the amount wagered. The casino guarantees that a person who hits the jackpot will receive the lesser of 5 percent of the amount wagered to date or $250,000. On December 1, 2021, the progressive slot machine reaches the $250,000 maximum payoff. The following January, a hotel guest wins the $250,000 jackpot.

# TECHNOLOGY APPLICATIONS

82. **RIA RESEARCH EXERCISE** Use the RIA Checkpoint database to answer the following questions. Cut and paste the relevant Internal Revenue Code and Regulation section(s) into your solution and explain how the authority answers the tax issue in question. Give the most specific citation applicable [e.g., Section 168 (a) (1)] to the question. Note: If the answer can be found in both the code and regulations you must provide both authorities.

    the answer company™ THOMSON REUTERS®

    Research Skills

    1. Saoirse is a teacher. In her spare time, she enjoys painting watercolors. Occasionally she sells one of her paintings. Last year, Saoirse spent $800 on paint supplies and received $1,000 from the sale of her paintings. What code section and/or regulation allows Saoirse to deduct some of the expenses from her hobby?

2. Jerry, a salesman, sends his five best clients gift baskets on their birthdays. The gift baskets cost Jerry $50 each. What code section and/or regulation allows Jerry to deduct $25 of the price of each gift?
3. Peter undergoes a medical procedure to prevent him from snoring. His insurance company will not reimburse him for the $2,000 procedure since he does not suffer from sleep apnea and the company contends that the procedure is cosmetic surgery. What code section and/or regulation does not allow him to deduct the cost of the procedure if the medical procedure is considered cosmetic surgery?

the answer company™ THOMSON REUTERS®

Research Skills

83. **RIA RESEARCH EXERCISE** Use the RIA Checkpoint database to answer the following questions. Cut and paste the relevant Internal Revenue Code and Regulation section(s) into your solution and explain how the authority answers the tax issue in question. Give the most specific citation applicable [e.g., Section 168 (a) (1)] to the question. Note: If the answer can be found in both the code and regulations you must provide both authorities.

Carmela is single, 52 years old, and has an adjusted gross income of $66,000. Carmela is covered by a qualified employee pension plan and she contributes the maximum amount to her Individual Retirement Account (IRA).

a. What code section and/or regulation allows a deduction for contributions to an IRA?
b. What code section and/or regulation limits the amount that can be contributed to an IRA?
c. What code section and/or regulation allows an increased IRA contribution due to age?
d. What code section and/or regulation limits the amount of the IRA deduction for members of a qualified employee pension plan?

Tax Simulation

84. In April of the current year, the Mojena Corporation, a computer power supply manufacturer, was found guilty of price fixing under the Sherman Anti-Trust Act and fined $50,000. In addition, The United States sued Mojena under Section 4A of the Clayton Act for $140,000, of which $100,000 represents the actual damages (compensatory damages) resulting from the price fixing and $40,000 represents court costs. In July, Mojena Corp. pays the United States $190,000 ($50,000 + $100,000 + $40,000) in full settlement of the charges.

REQUIRED: Determine the amount Mojena can deduct on its tax return. Search a tax research database and find the relevant authority(ies) that form the basis for your answer. Your answer should include the exact text of the authority(ies) and an explanation of the application of the authority to Mojena's facts. If there is any uncertainty about the validity of your answer, indicate the cause for the uncertainty.

Research Skills

85. Spencer and Richard own S&R Sports, a regional chain of 15 sporting goods stores. They decide to expand their business by opening three new stores. The stores will employ 90 people, most of whom will work part-time. Over the years, S&R Sports has been able to keep its employee turnover lower than the competition by having its new employees attend a three-day training seminar. The cost of training the new employees will be $45,000. Explain whether S&R Sports can deduct the cost of training the new employees in the current year.

Research Skills

86. Calvin and Lorna live in Nebraska and own rental property in the Ozark Mountains. They have always prepared their own tax return and have allocated their rental expenses including their mortgage interest and property taxes using the ratio of personal days to total days of use. During the year, they rent the property for 75 days and use it for 25 days. They receive $8,500 in rental income and incur the following expenses:

| | |
|---|---|
| Mortgage interest | $7,500 |
| Property taxes | 1,800 |
| Insurance | 500 |
| Maintenance | 400 |
| Utilities | 650 |
| Depreciation (unallocated) | 4,200 |

One of Calvin's neighbors tells him that there is a better way to deduct the mortgage interest and property taxes on the rental that results in a greater tax deduction. Find authority for a different method for deducting mortgage interest and property taxes on Calvin and Lorna's rental property, and calculate the effect of that method on their taxable income.

87. Teresa owns a condominium in Florida. During the current year, she incurs the following expenses related to the property:

Spreadsheet Skills

| | |
|---|---|
| Mortgage interest | $10,200 |
| Property taxes | 1,500 |
| Utilities | 800 |
| Maintenance fees | 1,000 |
| Repairs | 600 |
| Depreciation (unallocated) | 5,000 |

Prepare a spreadsheet calculating Teresa's rental income or loss for each of the following cases. The spreadsheet should be prepared so that it will calculate the rental income or loss by changing the number of rental and personal days. A template to assist the student in solving this problem can be found at www.cengage.com.

| Case | Rental Income | Rental Days | Personal Use Days |
|---|---|---|---|
| A | $9,000 | 40 | 10 |
| B | $9,000 | 40 | 20 |
| C | $1,000 | 12 | 48 |

88. Mark Pari is a self-employed electrician who exclusively uses a room in his home to perform the administrative functions related to his business. The room is 250 square feet of the 2,500 total square feet of his home. Mark's income from his business before considering the cost of his home office is $62,890. He incurs the following expenses related to his home:

Tax Form

| | |
|---|---|
| Mortgage interest | $10,000 |
| Property taxes | 1,500 |
| Insurance | 600 |
| Gas and electric | 1,800 |
| Repairs and maintenance | 500 |
| Cable television | 350 |
| Phone ($15 per month for a separate phone number for the office) | 420 |
| House cleaning | 1,400 |
| Long-distance phone calls (business-related) | 670 |
| Kitchen renovations | 4,700 |

Assume that the home is worth $200,000. Mark's basis is 140,000, the value of the land is 20 percent of basis, and the applicable depreciation percentage is 2.564 percent. Complete form 8829 using the above information. Mark's Social Security number is 136-42-5677. Forms and instructions can be downloaded from the IRS website (www.irs.gov).

# COMPREHENSIVE PROBLEM

89. Carol is a single mother who owns a wholesale auto parts distributorship. The business is organized as a sole proprietorship. Her business has advanced, and she can no longer devote the time necessary to do her own tax return. Because she always has prepared her own return, Carol is familiar with most tax rules applicable to her business and personal affairs. However, she has come to you for advice with respect to a number of items she paid during the current year. You are to determine whether she can take a deduction for the expenditures in the current year.
    a. Carol purchased a small building on March 2 to use as a warehouse for her auto parts inventory. To purchase the building, she borrowed $180,000 on a 30-year loan and paid $20,000 in additional cash. Carol also incurred $3,200 in legal and other fees to purchase the building. The bank charged her $3,600 in points (prepaid interest) to obtain the loan. After acquiring the building, Carol spent an additional $25,000 to renovate it for use as a warehouse. The $25,000 included $8,000 for painting.
    b. Carol had her office building painted at a cost of $14,000 and paid $6,000 to have it landscaped. She paid for the building renovation in part a and the office building work by borrowing $60,000 on April 1 at 7 percent interest. (See part f for details of the interest payments.)
    c. On April 1, Carol prepaid a one-year fire insurance policy on her two buildings. The policy cost $1,500, and the insurer required the prepayment. On September 1, Carol prepaid a $5,000, two-year maintenance contract on the buildings.
    d. Carol started a self-insured medical reimbursement plan for her employees this year. Based on actuarial assumptions, she deposited $13,500 in a fund to pay employees' medical expenses. Actual payments from the fund totaled $11,200.
    e. Carol purchased a new automobile costing $32,000. She can document that her business use of the automobile came to 90 percent and that her out-of-pocket operating costs totaled $3,600.
    f. Carol paid the following interest on business-related loans:

| | |
|---|---|
| Warehouse | $15,300 |
| Office building | 4,000 |
| Renovation loan | 5,400 |

    The renovation loan was for $60,000. Because she spent only $45,000 renovating the new building and painting and landscaping the old one, she used the additional $15,000 to purchase city of Seattle bonds with a yield of 6 percent.
    g. Carol became active in politics and contributed $1,000 to the presidential campaign of an independent candidate. She made the contribution because she believed that, if elected, the candidate would institute policies beneficial to her business. The candidate lost the election and immediately started a grassroots lobbying organization. The purpose of the organization is to keep track of elected officials' campaign promises and report to the public when they vote contrary to their stated campaign promises. Carol paid $1,600 in dues to join the lobbying organization.
    h. Carol's oldest son began college during the current year. She paid his tuition and living expenses, a total of $13,300, out of the company's checking account. During the summer, her son worked for the business, and Carol paid him $4,300, the same amount she paid other college students working during the summer. Because she consults her son from time to time on the operation of the business, she thinks that at least some of the $13,300 should be deductible.

i. Carol has always itemized her deductions. This year, her mother and father retired and could no longer afford the mortgage interest and property taxes on their home. Rather than have them sell the house, Carol made the payments for them. They received a statement from their bank indicating that a total of $8,125 in mortgage interest and taxes were paid in the current year. Carol knows that mortgage interest and property taxes are deductible as itemized deductions and would like to add them to her personal interest and property tax payments.

j. Because of the success of her business, Carol has received many offers to invest in various business ventures. One offer was to establish a chain of nursing homes in Florida. Carol spent two weeks in Florida evaluating the prospects of the proposed venture and incurred costs of $2,100. After careful consideration, she decided the venture was too risky and decided not to expand into the health-care business.

# DISCUSSION CASES

90. Malloy Industries manufactures air conditioners. The machines used to manufacture the air conditioners usually are insulated with asbestos. Because of health risks associated with asbestos, the Occupational Safety and Health Administration (OSHA) lowered the permissible level of asbestos fibers in the air. In addition, employers who have asbestos-insulated buildings or machines are required to monitor the amount of asbestos fibers in the air to ensure that they do not exceed the permissible level. Malloy Industries, a leader in providing its employees with a safe and healthy work environment, decided to remove the asbestos insulation from its 45 machines and replace it with another insulation material. The company determined that it would be less expensive to remove the asbestos insulation from its machines than to monitor asbestos levels on a daily basis. The company has found that the replacement material is 10 percent less efficient than the asbestos insulation. Should Malloy Industries capitalize or deduct the expense of replacing the asbestos insulation? Explain.

91. Conrad purchases a condominium in Aspen, Colorado. Because of his hectic work schedule, Conrad is unsure how much he will be able to use the condo over the next few years. A friend of his who has a condo in Aspen tells him that the condominium is both a great investment and an excellent tax shelter. Conrad's friend has been able to rent his condominium for $1,000 per week. Conrad expects to incur the following expenses related to the condominium:

| | |
|---|---:|
| Home mortgage interest | $16,000 |
| Real property taxes | 5,500 |
| Insurance | 825 |
| Utilities | 2,150 |
| Condominium fee | 2,400 |
| Maintenance | 300 |
| Depreciation (unallocated) | 6,500 |

Conrad is somewhat hesitant to rent his new condo out for the entire year, just in case he can sneak away from work for a few days. Therefore, he wants to explore all his options. Explain the different tax treatments of his condominium expenses depending on the number of days he uses it.

92. During the current year, Benjamin and Valerie were notified that their 2019 tax return was being audited. The IRS commissioner has disallowed all the losses attributable to Valerie's cattle breeding and showing.

Valerie was raised on a small ranch where her family raised commercial cattle. When she was 18, she left to attend college, where she obtained an accounting degree. Valerie is now employed as a full-time accountant by Veltkamp, Stannebein & Bateson, a local accounting firm, and receives an annual salary of $45,000. Ben, a full-time househusband, takes care of their children, Kody and Jaycee.

In 2015, Valerie purchased 10 impregnated purebred Maine Anjou heifers, an exotic breed of cattle from France, for a total price of $16,375. She entered into a contract with a local farmer to obtain pastureland for her herd. The contract requires a payment of $20 a month from April through October for each cow and calf. From November through March, the cost of feeding each cow and calf is $1.50 per day. In February 2017, Valerie purchased a bull with an exceptional pedigree for $7,500 to improve the quality of her calves.

She sells any inferior animals to the meat market, keeps her best heifers for breeding, and shows her best bull calves in livestock shows. The livestock shows provide her with the opportunity to show and sell her exotic cattle. Until 2019, Valerie had been responsible for getting the animals ready to show, which requires approximately four hours per day from November through January. Unfortunately, Valerie was injured while working with one of her bulls and was forced to pay someone to finish breaking and showing the bulls. During the summer months, Valerie pays someone to watch the cattle so she can spend time with her family.

In 2015 and 2016, Valerie realized losses of $4,125 and $1,894, respectively. In 2017 and 2018, she realized gains of $3,000 and $750, respectively. For 2019, Valerie realized an operating loss of $1,200 and a casualty loss of $7,500 because her new bull was struck by lightning and killed. Valerie has maintained adequate records for all tax years since she began the cattle venture.

Explain whether Valerie's ranching activity is a trade or business.

## TAX PLANNING CASES

93. Rosita's grandmother dies in November 2020 and leaves her an investment portfolio worth $180,000. In January 2021, when Rosita receives ownership of the investments, the portfolio consists of $112,000 in tax-exempt securities and $68,000 in taxable securities. Her grandmother's accountant estimated that the tax-exempt securities would earn $8,175 in interest and the taxable securities would pay $7,140 in dividends in 2021. The investment interest expense related to the portfolio is estimated at $2,100. Rosita is single, has no other investments, and earns $60,000 as an engineer. She expects that her itemized deductions, not including the investment interest expense, will include state income taxes of $2,800, real estate taxes of $1,600, and home mortgage interest of $4,000.

   a. What is Rosita's projected taxable income for 2021?
   b. Assume that Rosita switches $40,000 from tax-exempt securities to taxable securities and the rate of return on both portfolios remains the same. In switching the securities, Rosita has a $10,000 gain on the sale of the tax-exempt securities and pays $1,500 in tax. Instead of reducing the value of her portfolio, she pays the tax from her other income. All the other information would remain unchanged, except that state income taxes would increase by $500. What is the effect on her taxable income of changing her investment strategy?
   c. Should Rosita switch $40,000 in her portfolio from tax-exempt securities to taxable securities? Explain.

94. Allison and Paul are married and have no children. Paul is a lawyer who earns a salary of $80,000. In November 2020, Allison quit her job as a copy editor and began exploring the possibility of breeding and showing horses. She would run the business on their property. Allison expects to travel to nine or ten horse shows during the year. While researching the activity, she came across an article entitled: "IRS Cracking Down on Horse Breeding—Is It Really a Business or Is It a Hobby?" She is unsure of the tax ramifications discussed in the article and has come to you for advice on whether her activity will be considered a business or a hobby. Allison provides you with the following projections of the 2021 income and expense items for the horse breeding and showing activity: Communication Skills

| | |
|---|---|
| Revenue: | |
| Sale of horses | $13,500 |
| Prizes | 4,200 |
| Expenses: | |
| Hay | $ 7,200 |
| Veterinarian fees | 3,100 |
| Utilities | 880 |
| Property taxes | 470 |
| Registration and papers for horses | 2,100 |
| Interest expense on the barn | 1,230 |
| Depreciation | 6,000 |

Paul and Allison expect to receive $6,000 in interest and dividend income, they will have an $8,000 net long-term capital gain, and their other itemized deductions will total $16,300 in 2021. Write a letter to Allison explaining the factors the IRS will use to determine whether she is engaged in a trade or business or a hobby. You should also provide her with a calculation of their taxable income and tax liability and explain the difference(s) caused by the classification of the horse breeding and showing activity as a business or as a hobby.

## ETHICS DISCUSSION CASE

95. Dan owns a successful sports bar in downtown Providence. The state is considering legislation that would restrict the sale of alcohol in restaurants and bars on Saturdays and Sundays until after 7 P.M. The association of Providence restaurant owners is thinking about hiring a lobbyist to fight the legislation. The lobbyist has told the association that the lobbying effort would cost each owner $6,000. Dan's accountant has informed him that his $6,000 contribution would not be deductible for tax purposes. Dan has told his 30 employees, most of whom are students at a local college, that if the legislation passes, he will have to lay off employees. In addition, he told them that most local restaurant owners cannot afford to pay a lobbyist $6,000 to fight the legislation because it is not tax deductible. Ann, one of Dan's employees and an accounting major, suggests that Dan pay each employee an extra $200 in salary (30 × $200 = $6,000) and that they forward the payments to the lobbyist. That way, Ann reasons, the cost will be deductible as salary expense. Dan tells his accountant about Ann's idea, and his accountant thinks it is great. In fact, he is so impressed with the idea that he has offered Ann a job when she graduates next spring. Do you think Ann's idea is a legal way to deduct the lobbying expenses? What ethical standards has Dan's accountant violated? (Refer to the Statements on Standards for Tax Services, which can be found at www.aicpa.org.)

# Business Expenses

6

## Learning Objectives:

LO 1 Explain the requirements for deducting meal expenses.

LO 2 Describe the two methods a taxpayer can use to deduct auto expenses and explain how each method is used in calculating the deduction.

LO 3 Describe the requirements for deducting travel expenses.

LO 4 Explain the tax treatment of business expenses that have specific deduction requirements: gifts, education expenses, employee compensation, and qualified business income.

LO 5 Describe the different tax treatment for business and nonbusiness bad debts.

LO 6 Explain the criteria for deducting business expenses that may have to be capitalized rather than deducted in the current period: insurance, taxes, and legal fees.

LO 7 Explain the tax treatment of reimbursed employee business expenses.

LO 8 Explain the tax treatment for deducting expenses specifically attributable to self-employed individuals.

LO 9 Explain the requirements for the deduction of contributions to an Individual Retirement Account.

LO 10 Explain the requirements for contributing to a Roth Individual Retirement Account and a Coverdell Education Savings Account.

LO 11 Identify the requirements for expenses Congress has allowed individuals to deduct for AGI: higher education and interest on student loans.

## concept review

### GENERAL CONCEPTS

**Ability to pay** A tax should be based on the amount that the taxpayer can afford to pay, relative to other taxpayers. pg. 2-2

**Administrative convenience** Those items for which the cost of compliance would exceed the revenue generated are not taxed. pg. 2-3

**Arm's-length transaction** A transaction in which all parties to the transaction have bargained in good faith and for their individual benefit, not for the benefit of the transaction group. pg. 2-4

**Related party** Family members and corporations that are owned by family members are considered related parties, as are certain other relationships between entities in which the power to control the substance of a transaction is evidenced through majority ownership. pg. 2-4

### ACCOUNTING CONCEPTS

**Accounting method** A taxpayer must adopt an accounting method that clearly reflects income. pg. 2-9

**Annual accounting period** All entities report the results of their transactions on an annual basis (the tax year). Each tax year stands on its own, apart from other tax years. pg. 2-9

**Assignment of income** The tax entity that owns the income produced is responsible for the tax on the income, regardless of which entity actually receives the income. pg. 2-8

**Entity** All items of income, deduction, and so on are traced to the tax unit responsible for the item. pg. 2-6

**Substance-over-form doctrine** Transactions are to be taxed according to their true intention rather than some form that may have been contrived. pg. 2-11

**Tax benefit rule** Any deduction taken in a prior year that is recovered in a subsequent year is income in the year of recovery, to the extent that a tax benefit was received from the deduction. pg. 2-10

### INCOME CONCEPTS

**Basis** This is the amount of unrecovered investment in an asset. As amounts are expended and/or recovered relative to an asset over time, the basis is adjusted in consideration of such changes. The **adjusted basis** of an asset is the original basis, plus or minus the changes in the amount of unrecovered investment. pgs. 2-13, 2-21

### DEDUCTION CONCEPTS

**Business purpose** To be deductible, an expenditure or a loss must have a business or other economic purpose that exceeds any tax avoidance motive. The primary motive for the transaction must be to make a profit. pg. 2-18

**Capital recovery** No income is realized until the taxpayer receives more than the amount invested to produce the income. The amount invested in an asset represents the maximum amount recoverable. pg. 2-13

**Legislative grace** Any tax relief provided is the result of a specific act of Congress that must be strictly applied and interpreted. All income received is taxable unless a specific provision in the tax law excludes the income from taxation. Deductions must be approached with the philosophy that nothing is deductible unless a provision in the tax law allows the deduction. pg. 2-12

# 6-1 INTRODUCTION

To deduct a business expense, the expenditure must have a bona fide business purpose. This means that you initially must classify an individual's expenses as either profit motivated or personally motivated. Itemized deductions are limited according to an individual's adjusted gross income and are discussed in Chapter 8. Because corporations are always considered to be in a trade or business and have no personal transactions, they do not compute adjusted gross income.

This chapter introduces and explains specific business expenses. Many other expenses may be deducted on a tax return. Because of space limitations, it is necessary to confine the discussion to expenses that are common to many different types of business. However, the concepts discussed in Chapter 2 provide a foundation for identifying most other deductible expenses.

In addition to determining that an expense has a business purpose and is ordinary, necessary, and reasonable in amount, you may want to review the other tests discussed in Chapter 5 as you continue to read this chapter.

The chapter also discusses those expenditures that Congress, through legislative grace, has specifically allowed in the calculation of adjusted gross income. With the exception of alimony, the discussion focuses on expenditures that either have a business purpose or that Congress has allowed to equalize the tax treatment of the expenditure among different taxpayers. For example, by allowing taxpayers who are not members of a qualified pension plan to deduct their contribution to an individual retirement account, Congress is attempting to provide these taxpayers with the same tax treatment that is provided to taxpayers who are members of a qualified pension plan.

# 6-2 BUSINESS EXPENSES

The discussion that follows focuses on deductible business expenses. Most common expenditures made in a trade or business, such as utility payments, wage payments, supplies, and rental payments, are not subject to any specific rules. However, certain types of expenses have both a business and a potential personal aspect. This can lead to abuse by taxpayers who attempt to convert nondeductible personal expenditures into deductible business expenses. The tax law contains specific rules to follow in those areas that have the most potential for abuse. The first category of deductions to be considered is meal, auto, travel, gift, and education expenses. As you read about these expenses, note the special requirements for the deduction, the types of expenses that qualify, the 50-percent limitation, and the records that are required. In the discussion of employee compensation, notice the adverse effects of excessive salary payments.

In addition, various types of deductions have special rules. The tax law makes a distinction between business and nonbusiness bad debts. As a result, the treatments of business and nonbusiness bad debts are significantly different for tax purposes. The discussion of other business expenses points out several instances in which an expenditure either is not deductible or must be treated as a capital expenditure.

## 6-2a Meal, Auto, Travel, Gift, and Education Expenses

Meal, auto, travel, gift, and education expenses are particularly troublesome for many taxpayers. Although the expenses are incurred for a business purpose, they often involve an element of personal benefit or enjoyment. As a result, these deductions are subject to significant restrictions and limitations. To be deductible, the expense must satisfy specific requirements and be properly documented. Even if the expense qualifies and the taxpayer keeps good records, only the business portion of the expense is allowed as a deduction. Because these deductions are a matter of legislative grace and the taxpayer receives personal benefit from the expense, the IRS closely monitors compliance with the requirements. The tax law in this area is sometimes very detailed and quite complex. The intent of the following discussion is to familiarize you with the basic requirements for deducting these expenses.

## Meals

LO 1
Explain the requirements for deducting meal expenses.

A taxpayer may deduct 50 percent of the costs of meals incurred for a business purpose.[1] The meal expense must be an ordinary and necessary expense of the business and not be lavish or extravagant under the circumstances and has a business purpose. The cost of a meal includes the amount spent for food, beverage, tax, and tip. The Consolidated Appropriations Act of 2021 contains a temporary provision which allows a 100% deduction for calendar years 2021 and 2022 for meals purchased in restaurants.

Notice 2018-76, states that 50 percent of the cost of business meals continues to be deductible so long as it meets the following five part test:

1) The expense is an ordinary and necessary business expense under Sec. 162(a) paid or incurred during the tax year when carrying on any trade or business;
2) The expense is not lavish or extravagant under the circumstances;
3) The taxpayer, or an employee of the taxpayer, is present when the food or beverages are furnished;
4) The food and beverages are provided to a current or potential business customer, client, consultant, or similar business contact; and
5) For food and beverages provided during or at an entertainment activity, they are purchased separately from the entertainment, or the cost of the food and beverages is stated separately from the cost of the entertainment on one or more bills, invoices, or receipts.[2]

A meal expense is related to the active conduct of the taxpayer's business if it meets all four of the following conditions:

- There is more than a general expectation of deriving income or a business benefit from the meal.
- A bona fide business activity takes place during the meal.
- The principal reason for providing the meal is to conduct business.
- The expenses are related to the taxpayer and people involved in the business activity.[3]

**Example 1** In 2021, Claudia is thinking of opening a second location of her hair salon and takes her real estate agent out to lunch at a local restaurant to discuss possible locations for the new store. Can Claudia deduct the cost of the lunch as a business expense?

**Discussion: There is a clear business purpose for the meal expense. Claudia will be able to deduct the full cost of the meal.**

**Example 2** Jane owns and operates a business that makes bridal gowns and accessories. She invites 20 of her best customers to her plant for a business meeting. The business meeting and a tour of her plant take most of the day. She has lunch for her customers catered at the plant so she can show them her new products. Are the meals deductible?

**Discussion: The cost of the lunches for her customers qualifies as a deductible expense since it serves a business purpose. Jane can deduct 50% of the meal expense. The 100% deduction allowed by the Consolidated Appropriations Act of 2021 applies only to meals purchased in restaurants.**

The cost of membership dues for business, social, athletic, and luncheon clubs is not deductible.[4] Although the dues at these facilities are not deductible, the cost of meals, assuming there is a valid business purpose, remains deductible, subject to the 50-percent limitation.

As a general rule, the meal expenses of people whose presence is necessary to conduct the business activity are deductible. The expenses of other people can be deducted if their presence serves a clear business purpose. If expenses are incurred for business and personal reasons, only the expenses that have a business purpose are deductible. Thus, expenses of social guests are nondeductible personal expenses. In addition, the tax law requires the taxpayer or an employee of the taxpayer to be present when meals and beverages are served for the cost to be deductible.

**Example 3** Tom gives a party at his place of business for his clients. Tom, six clients, and three social guests are present. The party costs Tom $1,000 for food and beverages. How much of the $1,000 can Tom deduct as a business expense?

**Under Notice 2018-76, the business portion of the cost is clearly a deductible business expense. The expense for Tom and his 6 clients is deductible because the expenditure has a business purpose. The expense related to the social guests is personal and not deductible. Tom's allowable meal costs of $700 [(7 ÷ 10) × $1,000] result in a deduction of $350 ($700 × 50%).**

As a further limitation, reciprocal meal expenses incurred by business associates is not permitted. Reciprocal meal expenses occur when people in a group take turns paying for meals for each other to attempt to make the expense tax deductible. That meal expense is treated according to its social substance rather than its business form (substance-over-form doctrine).

**Example 4** Vanessa is an audit partner in a public accounting firm. Once a month, she has dinner with two of her college roommates who are audit partners in other firms. The three alternate picking up the check. Although the conversation often begins with personal issues, inevitably most of the discussion is business. Vanessa has saved the receipts, totaling $275, from the dinners. Do the dinners qualify as valid meal expenses?

**Discussion: The dinners fail both the directly related test (no expectation of future profits) and the associated with test (no valid business purpose). The predominant motive for the dinner is personal. Vanessa cannot deduct the $275 as a meal expense. In essence, the three are engaging in reciprocal meals.**

Several exceptions to the 50-percent limitation let a business deduct the full cost of the meals. These exceptions also are exempt from the directly related test for the deductibility of meals. The more common situations in which a business expense for meals is fully deductible are:

- Expenses treated as compensation to an employee and subject to income tax withholding. This arises when the employer has a nonaccountable plan for reimbursing employees' expenses. This type of plan is discussed later in the chapter.
- Expenses incurred while performing services for another person who reimburses the expenses when the taxpayer specifically accounts for them. Note that the person who reimburses the expense is subject to the 50-percent limit.
- Recreational, social, or similar expenses primarily for the benefit of employees. The value of the entertainment is not income to employees under the de minimis fringe-benefit rule discussed in Chapter 4.
- Expenses for goods, services, and facilities that are taxable income to a recipient who is not an employee because the meal or entertainment expense represents a payment of compensation for services or a prize or an award.
- Expenses for goods, services, and facilities made available to the general public.

**Example 5** Rubin Corporation provides the food, beverages, and entertainment for a Fourth of July picnic for its employees and their families. This is an annual event that Rubin believes benefits its employees and the company. This year, the picnic costs $5,000. How much of the $5,000 in meals and entertainment cost can Rubin deduct?

**Discussion: Rubin Corporation can deduct the full $5,000, because the expense is for the recreational and social benefit of its employees. The expense is not subject to the 50% limitation. The value of the party is excluded from the employees' income under the de minimis fringe-benefit rule discussed in Chapter 4.**

Employers have historically been allowed a deduction for the full cost of meals provided for the convenience of the employer and on the employer's premises. For the period beginning on January 1, 2018, and ending on December 31, 2025, the Tax Cuts and Jobs Act applies the 50-percent cutback described above to these meal expenses. For tax years beginning after December 31, 2025, the meal expenses become nondeductible.

The deductible percentage for meals consumed away from home by individuals subject to the Department of Transportation hours-of-service limitations is 80 percent. Individuals who are allowed this increased deduction include certain air transportation employees (pilots, crew members, dispatchers, mechanics, and control tower personnel), interstate bus and truck drivers, certain railroad employees (engineers, conductors, train crews, dispatchers, and control operations personnel), and certain merchant mariners.

## Entertainment Expenses

The Tax Cuts and Jobs Act of 2017 repeals the deduction for entertainment expenses even if those expenses are directly related to the taxpayer's trade or business. The law states that after January 1, 2018, no deduction is allowed for:

1) An activity considered entertainment, amusement, or recreation,
2) Membership dues for any club organized for business, pleasure, recreation, or other social purposes, or
3) A facility, or portion of a facility, used in connection with entertainment, amusement, or recreation.

## Auto Expenses

LO 2
Describe the two methods a taxpayer can use to deduct auto expenses and explain how each method is used in calculating the deduction.

A taxpayer can choose one of two methods for computing a deduction for using an auto for business purposes. These methods are the standard mileage rate method and the actual cost method. Although the standard mileage rate method is the easier way to calculate the **auto expense**, it often results in a smaller deduction. On the other hand, the actual cost method may yield a larger deduction, but it requires more record keeping. The cost of commuting from home to work and back is considered a personal expense. Neither the use of a cell phone to contact customers while driving to and from work nor putting advertising on the car makes commuting deductible. As Figure 6-1 illustrates, a taxpayer's mileage or cost of travel is considered business-related if the travel is:

- Out of town
- From the taxpayer's home to their temporary workplace
- From the taxpayer's regular workplace to a temporary workplace
- From the taxpayer's regular workplace (or temporary workplace) to a second job[5]

However, the mileage between the taxpayer's second job and home is considered personal. On days when a taxpayer does not work at their regular job, the travel to and from the second job is considered commuting.

**Example 6** On a typical day, Carla drives 10 miles round-trip between home and her office. In addition, she drives 75 miles to meet customers and take care of other business needs. How many of the 85 miles she drives each day count as business-related miles?

**Discussion: Carla can deduct the cost of driving the 75 business miles. The cost of transportation to work and back home is personal and not deductible.**

**Example 7** Brendan works weekdays as a nurse at a local hospital that is 14 miles from his home. He also works as a waiter at a restaurant 2 nights during the week and on weekends. The weeknights he works at the restaurant, he leaves directly from the hospital. The restaurant is 6 miles from the hospital and 8 miles from his home. What portion of Brendan's travel is considered business-related?

**Discussion: The 14 miles (28 miles round-trip) from Brendan's home to the hospital are commuting and considered personal. The 6 miles from the hospital to the restaurant are business, and the 8 miles from the restaurant to his home are personal. The mileage to and from the restaurant on the weekend is considered personal because Brendan did not work at his regular job. NOTE: If during the week, Brendan went home before going to the restaurant, his business miles would be limited to his normal travel distance (6 miles).**

*Figure 6-1*

## Business-Related Travel

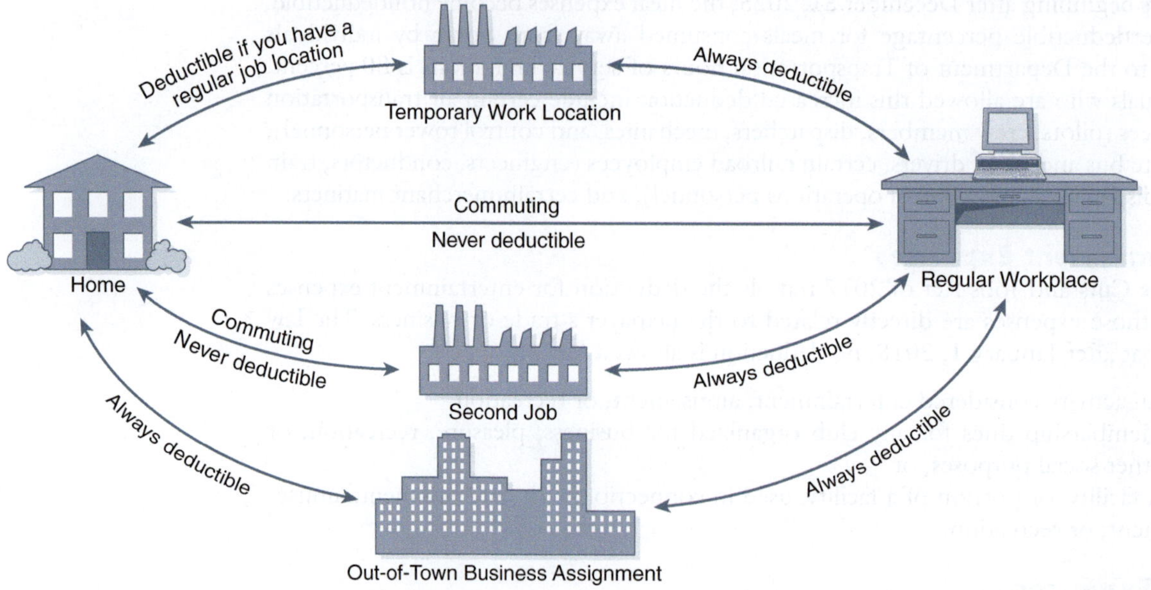


Regardless of which method the taxpayer chooses, the deduction can be disallowed for failure to keep records that support the date and amount of an expense that is deducted, the mileage allocations, and the business purpose for the expense.

**Standard Mileage Rate Method** To use the **standard mileage rate method**, which is based on administrative convenience, a taxpayer simply deducts 56 cents (57.5 cents in 2020) for each business mile the car was driven.[6] The standard mileage rate is an estimate of the cost of operating a car (gas, oil, repairs, insurance, depreciation, etc.). Because these costs change over time, the standard rate is adjusted each year. In addition to the standard mileage rate, the taxpayer can deduct direct out-of-pocket expenses that are unrelated to the operating costs of the car. These include the business portion of parking, tolls, interest, and property taxes. The property taxes must be based on the car's value. Interest is deductible only if the individual is self-employed. The standard mileage rate method is subject to several limitations and requirements that should be considered before it is used. For example, the standard mileage rate method may not be used by a business that operates more than five vehicles in the business at the same time.

**Example 8** José purchases a new car this year and drives it 10,000 miles for business purposes and 3,000 miles for personal use. What is José's deduction for the business use of the car if he elects to use the standard mileage rate method?

**Discussion: José can deduct $5,600 (10,000 × 56 cents) in auto expense based on his business mileage under the standard mileage rate method. No deduction is allowed for the personal use of the car. If he paid any parking fees or tolls out-of-pocket while on business, these expenses are also deductible.**

**Actual Cost Method** The actual cost method is a more flexible way to compute the auto expense deduction and often results in a larger tax savings. Using the **actual cost method**, a taxpayer can deduct depreciation, gas and oil, repairs, insurance, license, and other expenses of driving the car. As with the standard mileage rate, the taxpayer can deduct the business portion of the nonoperating costs of the car. If the car is used for both business and personal purposes, the expenses must be allocated according to the miles driven for each purpose. Only mileage driven for a business purpose results in a tax deduction. If the actual cost method is used, it is important to keep mileage records to support the allocation of expenses between business and personal use. The depreciation deduction under the actual cost method is subject to significant limitations, which are discussed in Chapter 10. The actual depreciation deduction is limited to statutory caps based on when the car was acquired. The 2021 statutory caps had not been issued by the time this book went to press, so the 2020 caps are used in example 9 and Chapter 10. For example, if a car was bought in 2020 and used 100 percent for business, the maximum depreciation deduction for 2020 is $18,100.[7] This limit changes each year of the car's depreciation life.

**Example 9** Nancy uses her car in her business of selling real estate. In 2020, she buys a new car and drives it 18,700 miles for business and 3,800 miles for commuting to and from the office and for other personal use. Depreciation, insurance, license, gas, repairs, and other operating expenses total $14,000. She can document that she paid $125 in tolls and parking while on business, and the interest expense on her car loan is $250. What is her deduction using the standard mileage rate method and the actual cost method?

**Discussion: If Nancy chooses to use the standard rate method, her car expense deduction is equal to 56 cents for each business-related mile driven plus any tolls and parking:**

| | |
|---|---|
| Standard rate deduction (18,700 miles × 56 cents) = | $10,472 |
| Tolls and parking (100% business) | 125 |
| Interest on car loan [(18,700 ÷ 22,500 = 83%) × $250] | 208 |
| Total deduction for business use of car | $10,805 |

**Because the tolls and parking were incurred while on business, they do not have to be allocated. The interest expense is based on the ratio of business-related miles to total miles.**

**Discussion: If Nancy chooses to use the actual cost method, her car expense deduction is determined by allocating the costs of operating the car between business and personal use:**

| | |
|---|---|
| Actual operating expenses | $14,000 |
| Business use percentage (18,700 ÷ 22,500) | × 83% |
| Business portion of operating expenses | $11,620 |
| Tolls and parking (100% business) | 125 |
| Interest on car loan (83% × $250) | 208 |
| Total deduction for business use of car | $11,953 |

**Tolls and parking incurred while on business do not have to be allocated. The interest expense is allocated according to the business use percentage. If Nancy is willing to keep the records necessary to support the actual cost method, she can obtain a larger car expense deduction than under the standard mileage rate method.**

## Travel Expenses

LO 3
Describe the requirements for deducting travel expenses.

A taxpayer can deduct travel expenses incurred while pursuing a business purpose. **Travel expenses** include transportation, lodging, 50 percent of the cost of meals (100% for 2021 and 2022 if purchased in a restaurant) and incidental expenses. Incidental expenses are items such as local transportation, telephone calls, laundry, and similar expenses that are necessary while traveling. For an expense to qualify as travel, the taxpayer must be away from her or his tax home overnight. A **tax home** is the general area in which the taxpayer conducts her or his principal business activity. To be *away overnight* means a period that is long enough to require the taxpayer to rest. Overnight is substantially longer than a normal workday and can be less than twenty-four hours. A one-day business trip usually will not satisfy the overnight test.

**Example 10** Theresa, a CPA, travels to Houston for 10 days in 2021. The business purpose for making the trip is to audit a client's accounting records. The airplane ticket cost $195, the hotel cost $85 a night, and she spends $40 a day on meals at restaurants and $15 a day for incidentals. She did not spend any time sightseeing or visiting friends. What is Theresa's deductible travel expense?

**Discussion: All of Theresa's travel expenses are allowed as a deduction because they are related to business. She can deduct:**

| | |
|---|---|
| Transportation | $ 195 |
| Lodging (10 days × $85) | 850 |
| Meals (10 days × $40) | 400 |
| Incidentals (10 days × $15) | 150 |
| Total deductible travel expense | $1,595 |

If the primary purpose of the travel is personal, incidental business activity will not change the nature of the trip. The taxpayer cannot deduct any transportation costs if the purpose of the trip is primarily personal. However, lodging, 50 percent of meals (100% for 2021 and 2022 if purchased in a restaurant) and incidental expenses directly related to conducting business while on a personal trip may be deducted. The primary purpose of a trip is determined by the facts and circumstances in each case. The time devoted to business activity compared with the time spent on personal activities is an important factor. If more than 50 percent of the total time is related to personal activities, the primary purpose generally is deemed personal.[8]

**Example 11** Using the facts in example 10, assume that Theresa spends 6 days visiting family in Houston and 4 days auditing her client's records. What is Theresa's deductible travel expense?

**Discussion: Because 60% (6 of 10 total days) of Theresa's time on the trip is related to personal activities, none of the transportation expense is deductible. She can deduct the other expenses to the extent related to business activities:**

| | |
|---|---|
| Transportation | $ -0- |
| Lodging (4 days × $85) | 340 |
| Meals (4 days × $40) | 160 |
| Incidentals (4 days × $15) | 60 |
| Total deductible travel expense | $560 |

If the primary reason for the trip is business (more than 50 percent of the trip is spent on business activities) and the taxpayer spends some time for personal activities, the tax result will be different. The cost of transportation is fully deductible, but a deduction for lodging, meals, and incidental expenses related to personal activities is not allowed.

**Example 12** Using the facts in example 10, assume that Theresa spends 3 days visiting family in Houston and 7 days auditing her client's records. What is Theresa's deductible travel expense?

**Discussion: Because more than 50% of Theresa's time on the trip is related to business activities, she can deduct all the transportation expense. She can also deduct the other expenses to the extent they relate to business activities:**

| | |
|---|---|
| Transportation | $ 195 |
| Lodging (7 days × $85) | 595 |
| Meals (7 days × $40) | 280 |
| Incidentals (7 days × $15) | 105 |
| Total deductible travel expense | $1,175 |

Expenses incurred by a spouse or a family member who accompanies the taxpayer on the trip are not allowed as a deduction, unless there is a bona fide business purpose for the person's presence and the spouse or family member is an employee of the taxpayer. An additional limitation is imposed on travel to attend a convention, seminar, or other meeting that qualifies as related to the production of income. Expenses for attending investment-related meetings are not deductible unless it can be shown the meeting is related to the taxpayer's trade or business.

**Example 13** Raul is a physician who invests in real estate partnerships. He travels from Dallas to Tulsa to attend a seminar on tax laws affecting real estate investments. Can Raul deduct the cost of attending the seminar?

**Discussion: Raul is an investor in real estate partnerships, and the travel is related to the production of income. Because the travel is not related to his medical practice (trade or business), the travel expenses are not deductible.**

**Example 14** Assume that in example 13, Raul is a tax attorney who represents clients who invest in real estate partnerships. Can he deduct the cost of attending the seminar?

**Discussion: Because the seminar is related to his trade or business as a tax attorney, Raul may deduct the allowable costs of attending the seminar as an expense incurred in his trade or business.**

**Example 15** Yusef is a self-employed insurance agent. He and his wife, Ruby, travel to Washington to attend an insurance conference. Ruby is an executive secretary for Rhody Corporation. She spends her time in Washington attending the sessions, taking notes, and setting up meetings for Yusef. Can Yusef deduct the cost of attending the seminar for both of them?

**Discussion: Ruby's presence at the conference serves a useful business purpose, but because she is not Yusef's employee, the expenses related to Ruby's travel are not deductible. If the hotel rate is the same for single or double occupancy, no part of the lodging is disallowed. But if different rates apply, Yusef can deduct only the cost of single occupancy (his own). All allowable costs Yusef incurs for his attendance at the conference are deductible because the seminar relates to his trade or business.**

## Business Gifts

A taxpayer can deduct up to $25 per year per donee for gifts to business customers. To apply the $25 limitation, direct and indirect gifts to a person must be counted. An indirect gift is one made to a related party, such as a taxpayer's spouse or child.

LO 4

Explain the tax treatment of business expenses that have specific deduction requirements: gifts, education expenses, employee compensation, and qualified business income.

**Example 16** Sam operates a retail store. To show his appreciation for the business of his 5 best customers, he sends candy to their spouses at their homes. The candy costs Sam $45 for each box. How much of the cost can he deduct as a business gift?

**Discussion: The gift of the candy to the spouse is an indirect gift to the customer. The $20 cost per box in excess of the annual donee limit is not deductible. Sam's deduction is limited to $125 (five gifts at $25 each).**

**Example 17** Assume that Sam also sends each of his 5 best customers custom-made desk clocks that cost $85 each. How much of the cost of the clocks is deductible as a business gift?

**Discussion: Because the annual limit of $25 per donee applies to both direct and indirect gifts, none of the cost of the clocks may be deducted as a business gift. The $25 limitation was exceeded on the gift to the spouse. Therefore, Sam is over the limit on his 5 best customers.**

The amount subject to the annual limit does not include incidental expenses that do not add value to the gift, such as gift wrapping, engraving, or delivering the item to the customer. An item that could be considered either a gift or an entertainment expense is generally considered entertainment and is not deductible.

## Substantiation Requirements

Meals, auto, travel, and gift expenses are subject to strict documentation requirements. The tax law requires the taxpayer to keep records that will show:

- The amount of the expense
- The time and place of travel or meal, or date and description of a gift
- The business purpose of the travel, meal, or gift
- The business relationship to the person receiving the meal or gift[9]

These are **substantiation requirements**, and failure to keep the records necessary to meet them can result in loss of the deduction.

## Education Expenses

Because education is viewed as a personal capital expenditure, individuals are not generally allowed to deduct education expenses. However, the tax law does let a taxpayer deduct education expenses if the **education expense** meets either of the following requirements:

- The education is a requirement—either by law or the taxpayer's employer—for the taxpayer's continued employment.
- The education maintains or improves the skills required in the taxpayer's trade or business.[10]

A taxpayer who is self-employed can deduct the cost of education expenses as an ordinary and necessary business expense. The effect is that the deduction for education expenses is *for* adjusted gross income.

**Example 18** Juan is a self-employed lawyer. State law requires that he attend 40 hours of continuing education each year, at least 8 hours of which must be on ethics. Juan attends four seminars (8 hours each) on estate taxes and an 8-hour seminar on ethics. The tuition for the four seminars came to $1,200; the ethics seminar cost $250. Can Juan deduct the cost of the continuing education seminars?

**Discussion: The cost of all the continuing education seminars is deductible as a business deduction. The 32 hours on estate taxes qualify because the courses either maintain or improve his skills. The cost of the ethics seminar is deductible because it is required by state law.**

Meeting one of the requirements for deducting an education expense does not guarantee that the expense is deductible. If the education is necessary to meet the minimum educational requirements of the taxpayer's job, the cost is not deductible. Also, if the education qualifies the taxpayer for a new trade or business, the expense is not deductible.[11]

**Example 19** Horace is a full-time student in computer science at State University. He works part-time as a programmer for a software developer. His employer has promised him a full-time job after he graduates. Can Horace deduct the cost of his college courses as an education expense?

**Discussion: The cost of Horace's college courses is not deductible. Although his courses are related to his job, he is not considered to be engaged in a trade or business because he is working only part-time. In essence, the college degree provides Horace with the qualifications needed to enter a new trade or business.**

A final limitation to note here is that travel that is in itself educational is not allowed as a deduction. For example, an art teacher who travels to New York City and Washington, D.C., to tour art galleries cannot deduct the cost of the travel even though it directly relates to teaching art. In contrast, if the teacher is an expert in a particular type of art and has to travel to Paris to verify the authenticity of an art object, the cost of the trip can be deducted.

In many cases, employers reimburse employees' education expenses. As discussed in Chapter 4, an employee can exclude from income up to $5,250 of education expenses reimbursed from a qualified educational assistance plan. In addition, the CARES Act and the CAA allow employers to make tax free payments of employees student loans up to $5,250 per year through 2025.

### concept check

For an expense to be deductible under the *business purpose concept*, it must have a business or other economic purpose that exceeds any tax avoidance motive. The primary motive for the transaction must be to make a profit. In addition, the *legislative grace concept* requires any tax relief provided to be the result of a specific act of Congress that must be strictly applied and interpreted. Therefore, deductions must be approached with the philosophy that nothing is deductible unless a provision in the tax law allows the deduction. Through this concept, Congress specifically limits the deduction for business meals to 50 percent of their actual cost. Under the *entity concept*, all items of income and deduction are traced to the tax unit responsible for the item. Therefore, when assets are used for both business and personal use (i.e., mixed-use assets) or when expenses are incurred for both business and personal reasons (i.e., mixed-use expenses), the business portion of the expense must be separated from the personal portion.

## 6-2b Compensation of Employees

The tax law provides for the deduction of reasonable salaries, wages, bonuses, and other compensation paid to employees. Thus, employee compensation is subject to two basic tests for deductibility. First, the payments must be for services actually performed by the employee. Second, the total payment for services of the employee must be reasonable in amount.[12] The determination of whether total compensation is excessive is made for each employee. When the compensation paid to an employee is found to be excessive, only a reasonable salary deduction is allowed. Whether compensation paid an employee is reasonable is decided by considering several factors, including:

- Employee's duties, responsibilities, and pay history
- Volume and complexity of the business
- Time required to do the work
- Ability and accomplishments of the employee
- General cost of living and the company pay policy
- Relationship of the compensation, the gross and net income of the business, and dividends paid to shareholders[13]

Whether the remuneration is **reasonable compensation** is usually a problem when the payment is made to a **related party**. Thus, reasonable compensation issues generally arise in connection with a closely held business. In addition, the business purpose of the payment may be questioned. Lack of a business purpose will result in disallowance of the total compensation paid the person.

**Example 20** Tina is the sole shareholder of Staple Manufacturing Corporation. She is the president of the corporation and pays herself $200,000 a year. Her son, who is the operations officer, is paid $60,000 a year. Her son seldom visits the plant because he is a full-time student at State University. The next-highest-paid employee, the general manager, is unrelated to Tina and is paid $50,000 a year. During an audit, the IRS determines that, based on comparable salaries in the area, a reasonable salary for Tina should be $90,000. Based on an examination of employee records, the IRS decides that Tina's son is not an employee. The salary paid Tina's son is a sham (an assignment of income from Tina). How much of the payments to Tina and her son is deductible by Staple?

**Discussion: The $110,000 ($200,000 − $90,000) excess salary paid to Tina is not a deductible expense of the corporation. The excess salary paid Tina is taxed as a dividend payment. The salary paid to her son is disallowed as a deduction for the corporation because it lacks a business purpose. Under the assignment-of-income doctrine, the payment of the son's salary is taxed as dividend income to Tina. Then, Tina is deemed to have made a gift to her son in the amount of the salary payments. The gift to the son is excluded from his income and is not deductible by Tina.**

The amount a publicly traded corporation can deduct as compensation expense is limited to $1,000,000. However, this limitation applies only to compensation paid to the chief executive officer, the chief financial officer, and the next three highest paid officers of the corporation. In addition, some items of compensation (e.g., contributions to a qualified pension plan) are not included for purposes of the $1,000,000 limitation. Although a detailed discussion of this topic is beyond the scope of this text, as a general rule, the salary paid to these individuals in excess of $1,000,000 is not deductible.[14]

**Example 21** Pamela is the chief executive officer of the Vanger Corporation. Her salary for the year is $1,250,000. What amount can the corporation deduct as salary expense?

**Discussion: Because Pamela is the chief executive officer of Vanger, the corporation can deduct as salary expense only $1,000,000 of the $1,250,000 paid to her.**

## 6-2c Bad Debts

LO 5 Describe the different tax treatment for business and nonbusiness bad debts.

The tax law permits a capital recovery deduction for the taxpayer's basis in business and investment bad debts.[15] To be deductible, the bad debt must be related to a transaction that had a business purpose. To determine how to report the deduction, the bad debt must first be identified as a business or a nonbusiness (investment) bad debt. If the debt arose from a transaction in the taxpayer's trade or business, the bad debt is deductible as a **business bad debt**. Other bad debts that are not related to the taxpayer's trade or business are considered **nonbusiness bad debts**. The use of the loan proceeds by the borrower does not affect the classification as business or nonbusiness. The distinction between the two classifications is important. A business bad debt is deductible just like any other business expense. A nonbusiness bad debt cannot be deducted if the debt is voluntarily forgiven or the forgiveness of the debt is intended as a gift. In addition, nonbusiness bad debts are deducted as a short-term capital loss. The important implication of the **capital loss** treatment is that the deduction may be limited to $3,000 each year until the loss is fully used.

**Example 22** Do-Rite, Inc., owes Kelly $10,000 for goods it purchased from Kelly on account. Because of financial difficulty, Do-Rite cannot repay the debt when it comes due in 2021. Kelly wants to deduct the $10,000 as a loss. How should she report the bad debt on her tax return?

**Discussion: An account receivable from the sale of merchandise to Do-Rite is related to Kelly's trade or business. Therefore, Kelly can deduct the $10,000 bad debt as a business expense in 2021.**

**Example 23** Assume in example 22 that Do-Rite owes Kelly the $10,000 because the owner of Do-Rite is a friend of Kelly's and Kelly made the company a temporary loan to help it through a cash-flow shortage. Kelly does not do any business with Do-Rite. How should Kelly report the bad debt on her tax return?

**Discussion: Because the loan is not related to Kelly's trade or business, the debt is a nonbusiness debt. Assuming Kelly does not have other capital gains or losses to report, she is permitted a $3,000 capital loss deduction in 2021, 2022, and 2023. The remaining $1,000 is deductible in 2024.**

**If Kelly forgives the $10,000 due from Do-Rite because the company is owned by her uncle and she wants to do him a favor, the forgiveness is considered to be a gift to her uncle and not allowed as a bad debt deduction.**

The amount deductible as a bad debt is limited to the taxpayer's basis in the receivable. As a result, the taxpayer's accounting method is an important factor in determining the amount deductible. If the receivable represents income owed to the taxpayer, the income must have been reported as taxable income before the taxpayer has a basis for claiming a deduction. Because of the basis limitation, a cash basis taxpayer normally cannot claim a bad debt expense deduction for accounts receivable. Because a cash basis taxpayer does not report income until cash is collected, there is no tax basis in the receivable to deduct. However, an accrual basis taxpayer reports taxable income as it is earned, regardless of when the cash is received, and has a tax basis for an uncollectible account.

**Example 24** Sylvia operates a successful consulting practice. During January 2021, she performs $5,000 in services for clients who still owe her as of December 31, 2022. She reviews her client files and determines that $3,000 in receivables is uncollectible. How much of a deduction is Sylvia allowed if she uses the accrual basis of accounting?

**Discussion: Using the accrual method of accounting, Sylvia would report $5,000 in income from the receivables in 2021. Because the income is reported on the accrual basis as it is earned, she has a $5,000 basis for the accounts receivable. In 2022, she can take a $3,000 bad debt deduction for the uncollectible accounts. The net result is that Sylvia's taxable income from these accounts is $2,000 for the 2-year period.**

**Example 25** Assume the same facts as in example 24 except that Sylvia uses the cash basis of accounting.

**Discussion: Using the cash method of accounting, Sylvia has not reported income from the receivables because they have not been collected. Therefore, she has no basis in the receivables and is not allowed a deduction. She reports $2,000 in taxable income when she receives cash from the collectible accounts. Note that this treatment gives Sylvia the same $2,000 in income that is reported on the accrual basis.**

The tax law permits a bad debt deduction using the **specific charge-off method**. Based on this accounting method, a business bad debt can be written off in the accounting period in which the facts known to the taxpayer indicate the account is fully or partially uncollectible.[16] If an account is partially written off in one year and later becomes fully uncollectible, the remaining balance of the account can be written off as a bad debt. A receivable may be uncollectible for several reasons. For example, the debtor may go out of business or become bankrupt, or the collateral securing the loan may be destroyed or become worthless, indicating collection of the account is unlikely. If an account is fully or partially written off and the amount of the write-off is later recovered, under the tax benefit rule, the recovered amount is reported as income in the year of collection.

**Example 26** Raquel Corporation owns and operates a furniture store. Because it has inventory, Raquel uses the accrual method of accounting. At the end of 2021, its accounts receivable total $75,000. Based on a review of the individual accounts, Raquel identifies $2,500 worth of accounts as uncollectible. For financial accounting purposes, Raquel's accountant estimates that $4,500 of its 2021 sales ultimately are uncollectible. How much can Raquel Corporation deduct on its 2021 tax return for bad debts?

**Discussion: Using the specific charge-off method, Raquel Corporation may deduct only the $2,500 in bad debts identified as uncollectible. The allowance method of accounting for bad debts, which is used for financial reporting, is not generally allowed for tax purposes.**

**Example 27** Assume that in 2022, Raquel in example 26 collects $1,000 of the accounts receivable it wrote off as a bad debt expense for 2021. What is the effect on Raquel's 2022 income from the collection of the bad debt?

**Discussion: Based on the tax benefit rule, the recovery of the $1,000 in bad debts deducted in 2021 must be reported as income when the accounts receivable are collected in 2022.**

Nonbusiness bad debts often result from loans to family and friends. To claim a bad debt deduction for these loans, the taxpayer may have to prove that the failure to collect the loan was not motivated by the intent to make a gift. Thus, the benefit of the bad debt deduction may depend on whether the taxpayer can prove that the loan was the result of a bona fide arm's-length transaction.

**Example 28** Wenona lends her uncle $15,000 to pay hospital and medical bills. She does not intend to charge any interest nor require him to sign a note. Her uncle promises to pay her back as soon as possible. Wenona's uncle dies without repaying her. Can she deduct the loan to her uncle as a nonbusiness bad debt?

**Discussion: Although her uncle defaulted on his debt, Wenona is likely to be denied a nonbusiness bad debt deduction. There is no evidence that a bona fide arm's-length loan was made to the uncle. None of the elements found in a bona fide loan is present in this situation: no note as evidence of the debt, no collateral for the loan, no provision for interest on the loan, no payment or due date, and no collection efforts on Wenona's part. She would have to prove that her intent was not to make a gift to her uncle to get a nonbusiness bad debt deduction.**

Like business bad debts, nonbusiness bad debts are accounted for using the specific charge-off method. Unlike a business bad debt, a deduction is not allowed for partial worthlessness of a nonbusiness bad debt. The nonbusiness bad debt can be deducted only when the taxpayer finally settles the loan for less than its basis.[17]

**Example 29** Katie owes Maria $5,000. The loan is related to Maria's business. In 2021, Katie files for bankruptcy. Maria talks to Katie's lawyers and determines that only 40% of the debt is collectible. In 2022, Maria receives $1,500 from the bankruptcy proceeding in full payment of the debt. How much of the bad debt can Maria deduct for 2021 and 2022?

**Discussion: Because the debt is a business bad debt, a deduction is allowed for partial worthlessness. Maria can deduct $3,000 ($5,000 × 60%), the amount estimated as uncollectible, for 2021. When the debt is finally settled in 2022, Maria can deduct the remaining $500 ($2,000 − $1,500) of the debt that she will not collect.**

**Note that if Maria had received $2,800 from the bankruptcy proceeding, she would have had gross income of $800 ($2,800 − $2,000) under the tax benefit rule.**

**Example 30** Assume that the loan in example 29 was a bona fide nonbusiness bad debt. How much of the bad debt can Maria deduct for 2021 and 2022?

**Discussion: A deduction is not allowed for the partial worthlessness of a nonbusiness bad debt. Maria must wait until 2022 when she knows the amount of the bad debt to take a deduction. At that time, Maria has a short-term capital loss of $3,500 ($5,000 − $1,500). If Maria has no other capital gains or losses in 2022, she may deduct only $3,000 of the short-term capital loss for 2022, with the remainder carried forward to 2023.**

Table 6-1 summarizes the rules for deductibility of bad debts.

*Table 6-1*

## Bad Debt Deductions

| | Business Bad Debts | Nonbusiness Bad Debts |
|---|---|---|
| **What is deductible?** | Any debt related to the taxpayer's trade or business | Any bona fide debt that is not related to the taypayer's trade or business |
| **Amount of deduction?** | Limited to the taxpayer's basis in the debt | Limited to the taxpayer's basis in the debt |
| **When is it deductible?** | Deductible in the year of partial or total worthlessness | Deductible when the exact amount of the worthlessness becomes known |
| **How is it deductible?** | Ordinary business expense | Short-term capital loss |

## 6-2d Other Business Expenses

Rent paid for the use of business property, business insurance, payroll taxes on employee compensation paid by the employer, property taxes on business property, interest on business indebtedness, utilities, dues to professional and business organizations, subscriptions to trade publications, supplies, and similar expenses incurred for a business purpose are allowed as a deduction. As you read the discussion of the deductions for insurance, taxes, and legal fees, pay close attention to the situations in which the expenditure is either disallowed as a deduction or required to be capitalized as an asset.

## 6-2e Qualified Business Income (QBI) Deduction

The Tax Cut and Jobs Act (TCJA) allows a deduction to taxpayers who own a pass-through business (i.e., a sole proprietorship, partnership, or S corporation). The deduction is based on the taxpayer's **Qualified Business Income (QBI)**, which is defined as the net income from the pass-through business after all business deductions and before any salaries to S corporation owners and guaranteed payments allocated to partners in a partnership.[18] The calculation of the QBI deduction is extremely complex, and because this book is conceptual in nature we have only provided simple examples to illustrate the concept of the QBI deduction.

Regardless of the type of pass-through business in which a taxpayer is engaged, when the taxpayer's taxable income is less than $164,900 (if single) or $329,800 (if married) the calculation of the QBI deduction is straightforward. The taxpayer's QBI deduction is the lesser of:

(1) 20 percent of their QBI
or
(2) 20 percent of their taxable income not including capital gains but before the QBI deduction.

The purpose of this QBI deduction is to have the average tax rate paid by those who report income from pass-through businesses to be more in line with the flat corporate tax rate of 21 percent. To help achieve this goal, the QBI deduction is permitted regardless of whether the taxpayer itemizes their deductions or takes the standard deduction.

**Example 31** Hanna is single and operates an antique store as a sole proprietorship. In 2021, the store has $115,000 of net income. Hanna does not itemize and has other income from interest and dividends of $5,000. What is Hanna's QBI deduction for 2021?

**Discussion: Hanna's QBI deduction is the lesser of 20% of her QBI or 20% of her taxable income. Her deduction based on her QBI is $23,000 ($115,000 × 20%). Her taxable income for purposes of calculating her QBI deduction would be $107,450 ($115,000 + $5,000 − $12,550) and includes the $115,000 of income from her antique store, $5,000 of interest and dividends, minus her standard deduction of $12,550. Her QBI based on taxable income is $21,490 ($107,450 × 20%). Therefore, her QBI deduction is $21,490 since it is less than $23,000.**

Owners of specific types of service businesses are only able to claim a QBI deduction if their taxable income is below certain levels. A specified service business is any business involving the performance of services in the fields of health, law, actuarial sciences, accounting, performing arts, consulting, athletics, financial services, brokerage services, or any trade or business where the principal asset of such business is the reputation or skill of one or more of its employees or owners.

A taxpayer who has income from a specified service business can use the full 20 percent deduction if their taxable income is less than $164,900 (if single) or $329,800 (if married). As taxable income increases, the deduction is gradually phased out over $100,000 for those filing married jointly or $50,000 if filing single. Therefore, there is no deduction for single taxpayers whose taxable income exceeds $214,900 or for married taxpayers whose taxable income exceeds $429,800. Exhibit 6-1 summarizes the tax treatment of QBI.

Exhibit 6-1

## 2021 QBI Deduction (QBID)

| | |
|---|---|
| | **Taxable income before QBID < $329,800 (Married), $164,900 (Single)** |
| All Businesses (General Rule) | Lesser of:<br>(1) 20% of QBI or<br>(2) 20% of taxable income (less any capital gains) before the QBID |
| | **Taxable income before QBID > $329,800 but < $429,800 (Married), [$164,900 and $214,900 (Single)]** |
| Specified Service Business | QBI deduction calculated under General Rule (see above) is phased out ratably as taxable income before QBID exceeds $329,800 (Married) [$164,900 (single)] |
| Other Businesses | W-2 limitation (see below) is phased in (Not covered in this course) |
| | **Taxable income before QBID > $429,800 (Married), [$214,900 (Single)]** |
| Specified Service Business | No QBI Deduction (Completely phased-out) |
| Other Businesses | Lesser of:<br>(1) 20% of QBI or<br>(2) 20% of taxable income (less any capital gains) before QBID<br>(3) Greater of<br>(a) 50% of W-2 wages or<br>(b) sum of 25% of W-2 wages plus 2.5% of original cost of depreciable property |

**Example 32** Assume the same facts as example 31, except that Hanna operates a consulting firm as a sole proprietorship and her net income is $192,450. What is Hanna's QBI deduction for 2021?

**Discussion: Since Hanna operates a business that is considered a specified service business, her QBI will be limited if her taxable income before considering the QBI deduction exceeds $164,900. Hanna's deduction based on her QBI is $38,490 ($192,450 × 20%). Hanna's taxable income is $184,900 ($192,450 + $5,000 − $12,550), and her QBI deduction based on taxable income before considering the phase-out is $36,980 ($184,900 × 20%). Therefore, because the $36,980 is lower, this is her QBI deduction before the phase out. Hanna's taxable income exceeds the beginning phase-out by $20,000 ($184,900 − $164,900), so she must reduce her QBI deduction by 40% ($20,000 ÷ $50,000). Hanna's QBI deduction is $22,188 [$36,980 × (1 − 0.40)].**

**Example 33** Assume the same facts as example 32, except that Hanna's income from the consulting firm is $247,000. What is Hanna's QBI deduction for 2021?

**Discussion: Hanna's taxable income before considering her QBI deductions is $239,450 ($247,000 + $5,000 − $12,550). Because Hanna is in a specified service business, and her taxable income exceeds $214,900, her QBI deduction is zero.**

For nonspecified service pass-through businesses (i.e., a manufacturing business), when the income from the pass-through entity exceeds the threshold limits of $214,900 (if single) or $429,800 (if married), additional rules that incorporate the amount of wages paid and capital investment of the flow-through entity apply. In these cases, the taxpayer's QBI deduction is the lesser of:

(1) 20 percent of their QBI
or
(2) 20 percent of their taxable income not including capital gains but before the QBI deduction
or

(3) the greater of
    (a) 50 percent of the W-2 wages paid by the business (including to the owners) or
    (b) the sum of 25 percent of W-2 wages paid by the business plus 2.5 percent of unadjusted depreciable property.

The law refers to unadjusted depreciable property as the original cost of the property before any depreciation expense.

**Example 34** Assume the same facts as example 33, except that Hanna has itemized deductions of $25,000. The QBI from the business is $400,000, W-2 wages are $140,000, and unadjusted depreciable property is $200,000. What is Hanna's QBI deduction for 2021?

**Discussion: The first step is to calculate Hanna's QBI deduction assuming there were no limitations and results in a QBI deduction of $80,000 ($400,000 x 20%). The second step is to calculate 20% of her taxable income before considering her QBI deduction, which is $75,000 ($400,000 – $25,000) x 20%. The third step is to determine which is greater (a) 50% of salaries paid by the business or (b) 25% of salaries paid by the business plus 2.5% of unadjusted depreciable property.**

| | | | |
|---|---|---|---|
| **(a)** | **50% × $140,000** | | **$70,000** |
| **(b)** | **25% × $140,000** | **$35,000** | |
| | **and** | | |
| | **2.5% × $200,000** | **5,000** | **$40,000** |

**Since $70,000 is greater than $40,000, it is used as the QBI for step 3. To determine Hanna's QBI deduction for her tax return we would use $70,000 since it is the lowest of three calculations.**

As discussed earlier, the calculation of the QBI deduction is very complex, and we have tried to only provide a brief introduction to this deduction. We have intentionally omitted calculation of self-employment tax and the deduction for 50 percent of self employment tax from the preceding examples to simplify these complex calculations. In addition, whereas the QBI deduction is not a deduction for adjusted gross income as many of the other deductions in this chapter, we felt the discussion was more appropriate in this chapter than in Chapter 8, which focuses on allowable personal deductions and credits.

## Interest Expense

The 2017 Tax Cuts and Jobs Act limits the deduction for business interest expense to 30 percent of the business's adjusted taxable income. The CARES Act increased this limit to 50% for 2019 and 2020. Adjusted taxable income is computed as earnings before interest, taxes, depreciation or depletion, and amortization. This is typically referred to as EBITDA. Any interest not deductible in the current year can be carried forward indefinitely. Taxpayers, other than tax shelters, are exempt from this limitation if their average annual gross receipts for the three-year period ending with the prior tax year do not exceed $25 million.[19]

**Example 35** For the last 3 years, Diggs corporation has averaged annual gross receipts of $30 million. This year, Diggs has EBITDA of $4,000,000, and it has incurred $1,500,000 in business interest expense. What can Diggs deduct as business interest in the current year?

**Discussion: Because Diggs' average annual gross receipts for the last 3 years exceeds $25 million, it is subject to the business interest expense limitation. Diggs can only deduct $1,200,000 ($4,000,000 × 30%) of business interest. The remaining $300,000 ($1,500,000 – $1,200,000) of interest can be carried forward indefinitely.**

## Insurance Expense

LO 6
Explain the criteria for deducting business expenses that may have to be capitalized rather than deducted in the current period: insurance, taxes, and legal fees.

Premiums paid for insurance to protect a taxpayer's business from loss are deductible. The types of insurance premiums that qualify for deduction include the following:

- Fire, theft, and other casualty insurance, and liability insurance
- Employees' group medical and group term life insurance, and workers' compensation insurance

- Employee performance and fidelity bonds to protect against losses caused by employees
- Business interruption and overhead insurance to reimburse the business for lost profits and overhead from casualty or other unexpected event. (However, premiums on an individual's disability income policy cannot be deducted.)

**Example 36** On July 1, 2021, Sook pays a $6,000 premium for a 3-year fire and casualty insurance policy on his business buildings and equipment. How much of the premium can Sook deduct for 2021?

**Discussion: Payment of the premium in advance results in a prepaid expense that benefits tax years 2021, 2022, 2023, and 2024. Regardless of Sook's accounting method, the $6,000 basis in the policy must be allocated to the periods benefited by the prepaid expense. The allocation results in a $1,000 [$6,000 × (6 ÷ 36 months)] insurance expense deduction for 2021.**

Except for qualified group term life insurance, life insurance premiums generally are not deductible. To qualify as a deduction, life insurance premiums must be viewed as additional compensation to the insured person. If the payer of the insurance premiums benefits directly or indirectly when the policy pays off on the insured's death, the premium cannot be deducted. Thus, insurance premiums on the life of the owner of a business, an officer of a corporation, an employee, or other person who has a financial interest in the taxpayer's business are not deductible unless they are treated as payment of compensation to the insured person. In addition, an entity other than the payer of the life insurance premiums must be the beneficiary of the policy for the premium to be deductible.

**Example 37** Radon Corporation pays a $5,000 premium on a whole life insurance policy on the life of Luke, a key employee in the company. If the corporation is the beneficiary of the policy, how much of the premium can Radon deduct?

**Discussion: Because Radon benefits directly or indirectly from the policy proceeds when Luke dies, the premium is not deductible. But recall from Chapter 4 that life insurance proceeds received upon the death of the insured are excluded from gross income.**

**Example 38** Assume that Luke, in example 37, is unrelated to Radon Corporation and its owners. Also, Luke's wife is the beneficiary of the life insurance policy. How much of the insurance premium can Radon deduct?

**Discussion: Because Radon is not a direct or indirect beneficiary of the policy, the $5,000 premium is allowed as a deduction for additional compensation paid to Luke. Luke will have to report the $5,000 premium paid by the corporation as income. His wife can exclude the proceeds of the policy from her income when Luke dies.**

## Taxes

A taxpayer is allowed a deduction for the payment of certain taxes incurred in a trade or business.[20] Some taxes are not allowed as a deduction, and others must be added to the basis of property owned by the taxpayer. Common types of deductible taxes include the following:

- State, local, and foreign real estate taxes
- State and local ad valorem personal property taxes (An ad valorem tax is based on the property's value.)
- State, local, and foreign income taxes
- Payroll taxes imposed on an employer (including the employer's share of the Social Security tax and unemployment taxes)
- Sales taxes, excise taxes, fuel taxes, franchise taxes, and other miscellaneous taxes[21]

Federal income tax and gift and estate taxes are not allowed as deductions in computing federal taxable income.[22] In addition, the taxes listed are deductible *only* when they are incurred in a trade or business. The itemized deduction allowed for taxes (discussed in Chapter 8) is far more restrictive than the deductions allowed for businesses.

**Example 39** Leslie Corporation pays the following taxes during the current year:

| | |
|---|---|
| Federal income tax | $50,000 |
| State and local income taxes | 15,000 |
| State and local real estate and personal property taxes | 2,000 |
| State and local sales taxes | 7,000 |

What is Leslie's deduction for taxes paid?

**Discussion: Except for the federal income tax, Leslie may deduct all the taxes listed. Leslie's deduction for taxes paid is $24,000. The $50,000 federal income tax is never allowed as a deduction.**

Sales taxes are deductible if they are paid for supplies and other items that are not capital expenditures. If the sales tax is related to the purchase of a long-lived asset, the tax must be added to the asset's basis. The sales tax is then deducted as a capital recovery through depreciation of the asset's basis.

**Example 40** Leslie Corporation purchases a new computer for use in its office. The computer costs $8,000 and is subject to a 10% sales tax. What is Leslie's deduction for the $800 in sales tax paid on the computer?

**Discussion: Because the sales tax is for the purchase of a depreciable asset, the $800 in tax is not currently deductible. The sales tax is added to the computer's basis as part of the cost of acquiring the asset. A deduction is allowed for depreciation of the computer's $8,800 tax basis.**

If real estate is purchased or sold during the year, real estate taxes must be allocated between the buyer and the seller. The tax is allocated according to the number of days each owned the property during the period of time to which the tax relates (the property tax year).[23]

**Example 41** Leslie Corporation sells land and a building on October 1, 2021. The property tax for the 2021 property tax year (a calendar year) is $13,600. Leslie pays its share of the property tax on the date the sale closes. What is Leslie's 2021 deduction for real estate taxes on the land and building?

**Discussion: Leslie may deduct the property taxes for the period it owned the land and building. Leslie's deduction would be $10,200—the taxes related to the period January 1 through September 30, 2021 [$13,600 × (9 ÷ 12)]. The buyer should deduct the property tax for the remainder of the property tax calendar year because that entity was the owner of the property.**

**Example 42** Assume that in example 41, the sales price of the building is $315,000. As part of the sales agreement, the buyer agrees to pay Leslie's share of the property taxes for 2021. Is Leslie allowed a deduction for property taxes on the building for 2021?

**Discussion: The payment of another's expense in a business setting is considered income for the entity for which the expense is being paid. Therefore, the payment of Leslie's $10,200 share of the property taxes must be included as part of the sales price of the building. Leslie is deemed to have received $325,200 for the building and to have paid $10,200 in property taxes. Each party to a real estate transaction must always recognize its share of the property taxes, regardless of which party actually pays the tax.**

When real estate taxes are related to **assessments for local benefits**, such as sidewalks, streets, sewers, and other improvements, the tax payment is not deductible. The tax imposed for local benefits is deemed to increase the value of the taxpayer's property and is considered a capital expenditure. As a result, the tax is added to the improved asset's basis. However, under the capital recovery concept, the taxpayer will recover the tax through depreciation, amortization, or upon its disposition.

**Example 43** The town of Guthrie imposes a special real estate tax assessment to put in new streets. Leslie Corporation has to pay $75,000 as its share of the new streets in front of its warehouse. What is Leslie's deduction for the $75,000 special property tax assessment it pays in 2021?

**Discussion: The special assessment for installing streets is deemed to increase the value of Leslie's property. As a result, the special assessment is added to Leslie's basis in the land. Thus, the $75,000 tax payment is not currently deductible. When Leslie disposes of the property, the capital recovery concept permits the capitalized tax to be deducted against the amount received on the sale of the property.**

### Legal Fees

Legal expenses are allowed as a deduction if they have a business purpose. To determine whether **legal fees** are deductible, one has to look to the origin of the expense. If the legal fee originates in a profit-motivated activity or qualifies as a specifically allowed itemized deduction, it is deductible. If the expense originates from a personal transaction, such as a divorce or the preparation of a will, the expense is not deductible.

**Example 44** Salvadore is being sued by a client who fell in his store and hurt himself. Salvadore spends $5,000 in legal fees to defend his business against his customer's claims. Can Salvadore deduct the legal fees?

**Discussion: The legal fees originated in Salvadore's business. Because the fees are an ordinary and necessary expense of doing business, Salvadore may deduct the $5,000 in legal expenses.**

**Example 45** Elissa, Salvadore's wife, has filed for divorce and has asked for a large property settlement. The only way Salvadore can pay Elissa the amount she is seeking is to sell his business. Salvadore pays $6,000 in legal fees related to the divorce. Can he deduct his legal fees?

**Discussion: Salvadore may not deduct the personal legal fees. The legal expenses did not arise from the conduct of his business. The fact that he may have to sell his business merely reflects the results of the legal claim that arose from a personal relationship.**[24]

**Example 46** Salvadore has been having a bad year. In August, he receives a letter from the IRS stating that he owes an additional $34,000 in income taxes. Salvadore pays his attorney $12,000 to settle the case with the IRS. Can he deduct the attorney's fees?

**Discussion: Salvadore will be able to deduct the attorney's fees to the extent the amount in dispute relates to his business, as an ordinary and necessary business expense.**

In addition to the disallowance of personal legal fees, certain legal fees may have to be capitalized as part of an asset's basis. For example, legal fees related to establishing ownership of property, defending title to property, or otherwise related to the acquisition or improvement of an asset are not deductible. These costs must be added to the affected asset's basis. However, the taxpayer can deduct legal fees paid to protect an existing business, its reputation, and goodwill.

## 6-3 INDIVIDUAL DEDUCTIONS FOR ADJUSTED GROSS INCOME

This category of deductions generally consists of those expenditures that have a business purpose as well as certain expenditures that Congress, through legislative grace, has specifically allowed in the calculation of adjusted gross income. The allowable **deductions for adjusted gross income** are listed in Exhibit 6-2.[25]

Exhibit 6-2

## List of Deductions Allowed for Adjusted Gross Income

Trade or business expenses (losses)
Reimbursed employee business expenses
Capital loss deduction
Rental and royalty expenses
Deduction for contributions to a retirement plan (other than an employer-provided plan)
Interest on qualified student loans
Net operating loss deduction
Fifty percent of the self-employment tax paid on business income
A self-employed person's medical insurance premiums
Interest reported as income that has been repaid as a result of cashing in a certificate of deposit before its due date (early withdrawal penalty)
Certain deductions of life tenants and income beneficiaries of property
Certain required repayments of supplemental unemployment insurance benefits
Reforestation expenses
Certain portion of lump-sum distributions from pension plans subject to the special averaging convention

It should be noted that expenditures in this category of deductions are *always* allowed as deductions. That is, after determining the allowable amount of each deduction, that amount is not subject to any income-level limitations and is always deductible. This is not always the case for deductions from adjusted gross income.

For reporting purposes, trade or business expenses, rent and royalty expenses, and reimbursed employee business expenses are subtracted directly from the related items of gross income. That is, the expenses are netted against their related gross income and reported as a net figure in the income tax calculation.

**Example 47** Koharu is the sole proprietor of a carpet-cleaning business. During the current year, she has gross income from the business of $93,000 and allowable expenses of $36,000. How should this information be reported on her return?

**Discussion: The allowable trade or business expenses are netted separately against the gross income, resulting in trade or business income of $57,000. In calculating taxable income, the $57,000 in trade or business income is reported as gross income.**

**Example 48** Assume the same facts as in example 47, except that Koharu's allowable trade or business expenses total $101,000.

**Discussion: In this case, the netting of expenses against income results in a loss of $8,000 ($93,000 − $101,000). Because it is a loss from a trade or business, it is deductible for adjusted gross income. Thus, the net figure of $8,000 is shown as a deduction for adjusted gross income.**

The remaining items discussed in this section of the chapter appear as separate deductions for adjusted gross income on the tax return. The discussion focuses on those expenditures that either have a business purpose or are expenses that Congress has allowed to equalize the tax treatment of the expenditure among different taxpayers

### 6-3a Reimbursed Employee Business Expenses

LO 7 Explain the tax treatment of reimbursed employee business expenses.

It has long been held that an employee is engaged in a trade or business. However, not all employee business expenses are deductible for AGI as trade or business expenses. That is, the tax law allows a deduction for adjusted gross income only for those employee business expenses that are reimbursed by the employer, known as *reimbursed employee business expenses.*[26] It is important to properly account for employee business expenses on the tax return. Unfortunately, Congress further complicated this distinction by restricting the deduction for adjusted gross income to those situations in which employees were reimbursed for their expenses under an accountable plan.

### Accountable Reimbursement Plans

An **employer reimbursement plan** is an **accountable plan** if employees are required to make an adequate accounting of their expenses with their employer and to return excess reimbursements to the employer. An adequate accounting requires that the employee give the employer adequate documentation to support the expenditure being reimbursed as a valid business expense. This would include details as to time, place, and amount of the expense as well as the business purpose for the expense. Plans that reimburse employees by preset amounts for meals, lodging, and/or mileage (called *per-diem payments*) are considered accountable plans if the employee is required to establish the business purpose for the payment and the per-diem amount does not exceed that paid by the federal government.

The treatment of reimbursements and expenses by the employee under an accountable plan depends upon the amount of reimbursement in relation to the actual expense. There are three scenarios:

- Reimbursement equals actual expenses. (Any excess reimbursement is returned to the employer.) In this case, the effect on the employee's income is a net change of zero. That is, the employee is neither in receipt of income from a reimbursement in excess of actual costs nor is the employee in a net deduction situation. No income is included in the employee's gross income, and no deductions are allowed.
- Reimbursement is less than actual expenses. The employee may be in a net deduction situation. The reimbursement must be included in the employee's gross income. The portion of the expenses reimbursed is deductible for adjusted gross income, thus canceling out the inclusion of the reimbursement in gross income. After December 31, 2017, unreimbursed employee business expenses are no longer deductible.
- Reimbursement is greater than actual expenses (i.e., excess reimbursement is not returned to the employer). In this case, the employee has net income because the reimbursement is greater than actual expenses. The excess reimbursement is included in the employee's gross income.

### Nonaccountable Reimbursement Plans

If an employer reimbursement plan is a **nonaccountable plan**, the employee must include the reimbursement (if any) in gross income. No deductions for adjusted gross income are allowed. As a matter of administrative convenience, employees (but not self-employed individuals) may choose to take deductions for meals and automobile mileage using the allowable federal per-diem rates rather than using actual costs.

For your reference, a summary of the reporting of reimbursements under the two types of plans is presented in Exhibit 6-3.

**Example 49** Santamaria Company requires its employees to adequately account for all reimbursed business expenses. Sarah, an account executive, submits for reimbursement the following valid business expenses:

| | |
|---|---|
| Transportation costs | $ 600 |
| Meals in restaurants | 600 |
| Lodging costs | 800 |
| Total costs | $ 2,000 |

What are the tax consequences if Santamaria reimburses Sarah the $2,000?

Exhibit 6-3

## Treatment of Employee Business Expenses

| Types of Plans | Gross Income Effect | Deduction for AGI | Deduction from AGI |
|---|---|---|---|
| *Accountable Plans* | | | |
| Reimbursement = Actual expenses | None | None | None |
| Reimbursement < Actual expenses | Full amount of reimbursement is included in the gross income. | Reimbursed expenses; no 50% rule for meals. | None |
| Reimbursement > Actual expenses | Excess reimbursement is included in gross income. | None | None |
| *Nonaccountable Plans* | | | |
| Reimbursement received | Full amount of reimbursement is included in gross income. | None | None |
| No reimbursement | None | None | None |

**Discussion: Because there has been an adequate accounting, Sarah has no tax effects. None of the reimbursement is included in her gross income, and she is allowed no deductions for the expenses. NOTE: In this case, the employer is the taxpayer who effectively gets the deduction for the business expenses.**

**Example 50** What are the tax consequences if Santamaria reimburses Sarah for $1,500 instead of $2,000?

**Discussion: In this case, Sarah is in a net deduction situation. The amount of the reimbursement, $1,500, is included in her gross income, and $1,500 of the expenses is deducted for AGI. Since Sarah is not reimbursed for $500 of the expenses, she is not allowed a deduction for this amount.**

**Example 51** Assume that Santamaria reimburses Sarah in the amount of $2,200 for the $2,000 in actual expenses. Although Santamaria's plan requires employees to return excess reimbursements, Sarah does not return the excess.

**Discussion: In this case, because the plan is an accountable plan, Sarah is deemed to have made an adequate accounting of the $2,000 in actual expenses. The excess reimbursement, $200, must be included in her gross income.**

**Note that Santamaria will deduct the same amount that was allowed in example 50. The employer may deduct the $200 excess reimbursement as wages paid to Sarah.**

**Example 52** Assume the same facts as in example 51, except that Sarah either does not have to make an adequate accounting or does not have to return any excess reimbursement. That is, Santamaria's plan is a nonaccountable plan.

**Discussion: In examples 50 and 51, the reporting is the same if the plan is nonaccountable. The reimbursement must be included in Sarah's gross income, and since miscellaneous itemized deductions are no longer deductible under the TCJA of 2017, Sarah is not allowed to deduct the actual costs.**

## 6-3b Deductions for Self-Employed Taxpayers

LO 8
Explain the tax treatment for deducting expenses specifically attributable to self-employed individuals.

The deductions for adjusted gross income that self-employed taxpayers are allowed to take for health insurance premiums and self-employment taxes are designed to provide some measure of equity in the treatment of employees and self-employed individuals. Recall that health insurance premiums paid by an employer for an employee are excluded from the employee's gross income. Because self-employed individuals are not employees, they cannot take advantage of this fringe benefit. To partially equalize the treatment of employees and self-employed individuals, the tax law lets self-employed individuals deduct the cost of their health insurance premiums as a deduction for adjusted gross income.[27] If the self-employed taxpayer or spouse is eligible to be covered by employer-provided medical insurance, the deduction for adjusted gross income is not allowed.

**Example 53** Rory is the sole proprietor of Rory's Western Wear. During 2021, he pays $1,800 for his own health insurance. How should Rory deduct the $1,800 health insurance cost?

**Discussion: Because Rory is self-employed, he can deduct the $1,800 of health insurance premiums as a deduction for adjusted gross income. If Rory's wife, Eleanor, is covered by medical insurance provided by her employer, the entire $1,800 can be deducted only as an itemized medical expense (discussed in Chapter 8).**

The second deduction for adjusted gross income that self-employed taxpayers may take is for one-half of the **self-employment tax** paid. The self-employment tax is the method through which self-employed individuals contribute to the Social Security system. The self-employment tax rate is 15.3 percent of net self-employment income. This is equal to the rate paid by employees (7.65 percent), which is matched by employers. The employer's payment into the employee's Social Security account is not taxed to the employee. The deduction of one-half of the self-employment tax equalizes the treatment for employees and self-employed individuals. In determining self-employment income, the net earnings from self-employment are reduced by one-half of the self-employment tax paid.[28] The effect of this provision is that only 92.35 percent [100 percent − (50 percent × 15.3 percent)] of the net earnings from self-employment is subject to the self-employment tax.

**Example 54** Ramona is the sole proprietor of Rangoon Foods. During 2021, Rangoon has a taxable income of $165,000. Assuming that Ramona has no other sources of self-employment income, what is Ramona's 2021 self-employment income subject to the self-employment tax?

**Discussion: Only 92.35% of the earnings from self-employment is subject to the self-employment tax. Thus, Ramona's net self-employment income is $152,378 ($165,000 × 92.35%).**

The amount of income subject to the self-employment tax is the lesser of the ceiling amount or 92.35 percent of self-employment earnings. The 15.3 percent self-employment tax rate consists of two components, Old Age, Survivors, and Disability Insurance (OASDI) and Medicare Health Insurance (MHI). The OASDI component is levied at 12.4 percent on the first $142,800 of self-employment income, and the MHI component is levied at 2.9 percent of total self-employment income.

An additional 0.9 percent Hospital Insurance tax (HI) is imposed on taxpayers (other than corporations, estates, or trusts) on self-employment income for the tax year in excess of $250,000 for a married couple filing a joint return, $125,000 for married taxpayers filing a separate return, and $200,000 for all other taxpayers. However, the additional HI tax is not eligible for the self-employment tax deduction.

**Example 55** In example 54, what are Ramona's 2021 self-employment tax and her deduction for self-employment taxes paid?

**Discussion: Ramona's self-employment tax is $22,126. Ramona is allowed to deduct $11,063, half of the self-employment tax, as a deduction for adjusted gross income.**

| | |
|---|---|
| OASDI on $142,800 of income: $142,800 × 12.4% | $17,707 |
| MHI on $152,378 of income: $152,378 × 2.9% | $4,419 |
| Self-Employment Tax | $22,126 |

**Discussion: If Ramona's net self-employment income was $220,000, then her self-employment tax is $24,267.**

| | |
|---|---|
| OASDI on $142,800 of income: $142,800 × 12.4% | $17,707 |
| MHI on $220,000 of income: $220,000 × 2.9% | 6,380 |
| HI tax on income in excess of $200,000: ($220,000 – $200,000) × .9% | 180 |
| Self-Employment tax | $24,267 |

**Ramona is allowed to deduct $12,044, one-half of the self-employment tax ($17,707 + $6,380) as a deduction for adjusted gross income. The additional $180 HI tax is not eligible for the deduction.**

## 6-3c Retirement Plan Contribution Deductions

Employees who participate in qualified employer pension plans are allowed to defer recognition of income paid into and earnings on assets in such plans until they are withdrawn from the plan. Recall from Chapter 4 that employees' payments into a qualified employer-sponsored pension plan are excluded from the employee's gross income. Taxpayers who do not have access to an employer-sponsored pension plan have several options under which they can accumulate assets for retirement in a tax-deferred manner. (See Chapter 15 for a detailed explanation of these plans.) These retirement plans are different from employer-provided plans in that the taxpayer makes contributions to the plan and takes deductions for adjusted gross income for the amounts contributed. As with employer-sponsored plans, earnings on amounts paid into these plans are deferred until they are withdrawn. The effect of this arrangement is to reduce adjusted gross income (and ultimately taxable income) by the amount contributed to the plan, providing the same tax relief as an employer-sponsored plan. Self-employed taxpayers are allowed to establish their own separate retirement savings plan (referred to as a *Keogh*, or *H.R. 10, Plan*). One type of plan in which all individuals may participate is an individual retirement account.

### Individual Retirement Accounts

LO 9 Explain the requirements for the deduction of contributions to an Individual Retirement Account.

An **individual retirement account (IRA)** is an individual trust account maintained for the exclusive benefit of an individual or their beneficiary. There are three types of individual retirement accounts: conventional IRAs, Roth IRAs, and Education IRAs. A conventional IRA can consist of either deductible contributions or non-deductible contributions. For administrative purposes, a taxpayer who makes both deductible and nondeductible contributions must maintain a separate IRA account for each type of contribution. Contributions to Roth IRAs and Education IRAs are nondeductible. Because the focus of this chapter is on business deductions and deductions for adjusted gross income, our discussion is limited to the contribution and deduction limits of each IRA. A more thorough discussion of each IRA is presented in Chapter 15.

## Conventional Individual Retirement Account

All taxpayers are allowed to contribute up to $6,000 (this amount is indexed for inflation) per year of their earned income to an individual retirement account. In addition, taxpayers who are at least 50 years old are allowed to make a "catch-up" contribution of $1,000 to their IRA account.[29] A husband and wife may contribute $12,000 ($6,000 × 2) to two separate IRA accounts as long as their total earned income exceeds $12,000.[30] The allowance of a deduction for an IRA contribution that benefits a nonworking spouse is referred to as the Kay Bailey Hutchison spousal IRA. However, the total amount contributed to each account cannot exceed $6,000.

**Example 56** Chong and Ling are married, and each has earned income. Chong makes $20,000 per year, and Ling earns $27,000 per year. What is the maximum amount they can contribute to their individual retirement accounts?

**Discussion: Because both Chong and Ling have earned income, each may contribute the $6,000 maximum to their own account, a total of $12,000.**

**Example 57** Assume that in example 56, only Ling works and Chong stays home with the children. What is the maximum amount they can contribute to their individual retirement accounts?

**Discussion: Even though Chong is a nonworking spouse, because their total earned income exceeds $12,000, they can contribute a total amount of $12,000, with no more than $6,000 contributed to each account.**

**Example 58** Assume the same facts as in example 57, except that Chong is 52 years old. What is the maximum amount Chong and Ling can contribute to their individual retirement accounts?

**Discussion: Because Chong is at least 50 years old, his maximum contribution is $7,000. Ling's maximum contribution does not change, and their total contribution limit is $13,000.**

An unmarried taxpayer who is not an active participant in a pension plan is allowed to deduct their entire contribution to an IRA account regardless of the amount of their adjusted gross income. This is also the case for a married taxpayer if both spouses are not active participants in a pension plan. The effect of the deduction is to reduce a taxpayer's earned income by the amount paid into the IRA and provides the taxpayer with the same tax treatment as an employee who participates in an employer-sponsored contributory pension plan. Earnings on IRA accounts are deferred until they are withdrawn.

**Example 59** Assume the same facts as in example 58, except that neither Chong nor Ling is covered by an employer-sponsored pension plan. If they each contribute the maximum allowable amount to their IRAs, what is their deduction for adjusted gross income?

**Discussion: Because neither Chong nor Ling is covered by an employer-sponsored pension plan, they may each contribute $6,000 to their plans and deduct $6,000 for adjusted gross income. This gives them a total deduction of $12,000 for adjusted gross income. The effect of the deduction is to reduce their individual earned incomes by the $6,000 contribution. Chong is taxed on only $14,000 ($20,000 − $6,000) of his earned income, and Ling is taxed on only $21,000 ($27,000 − $6,000) of her earned income.**

Unmarried taxpayers who participate in an employer-sponsored pension plan must reduce the amount of their IRA deduction proportionately when their adjusted gross income reaches $66,000 ($65,000 in 2020). The entire deduction must be reduced to zero when adjusted gross income reaches $76,000 ($75,000 in 2020). For married taxpayers, if both taxpayers are covered by an employer-sponsored plan, the amount of the IRA deduction must be reduced when adjusted gross income exceeds $105,000 ($104,000 in 2020) and is reduced to zero when adjusted gross income reaches $125,000 ($124,000 in 2020).[31] When adjusted gross income exceeds the top end of the range, no deduction is allowed. A general formula for calculating the IRA percentage reduction and computing the maximum deduction for a married couple follows:

$$\text{IRA Percentage} = \frac{\text{Adjusted gross income} - \$105{,}000}{\$20{,}000}$$

$$\text{Maximum IRA deduction} = \text{Maximum contribution} \times (1 - \text{IRA percentage})$$

**Example 60** Assume the same facts as in example 58, except that both Chong and Ling participate in an employer-sponsored pension plan. Chong and Ling continue to make the maximum contribution to their IRAs, and they have an adjusted gross income of $117,000. What is their allowable deduction for the $12,000 they contribute to their IRAs?

**Discussion: Because they both participate in an employer-sponsored pension plan, Chong and Ling must reduce their $12,000 IRA deduction proportionately for each dollar of adjusted gross income that exceeds $105,000. The entire deduction is reduced to zero when adjusted gross income reaches $125,000. Based on the reduction formula below, Chong and Ling must reduce the amount of their IRA deduction to $4,800 (i.e., $2,400 each):**

$$60\% = \frac{\$117{,}000 - \$105{,}000}{\$20{,}000}$$

$$\$4{,}800 = \$12{,}000 \times (1 - 60\%)$$

**Chong and Ling may still contribute the $12,000 maximum to their IRA accounts. It is only the amount of the allowable deduction that must be reduced when both taxpayers are covered by a separate pension plan, not the allowable contribution amount. The tax benefit of making nondeductible contributions is that the earnings on the contributions are allowed to accumulate tax-free until they are withdrawn. Chong and Ling do not have to make the maximum contribution to get the $4,800 deduction. They may choose to contribute only the deductible amount, or they may contribute another amount less than the $12,000 maximum.**

**Example 61** Assume the same facts as in example 60, except that Chong and Ling's adjusted gross income is $93,000. What is the amount of their IRA deduction?

**Discussion: Although they both participate in an employer-sponsored plan, their adjusted gross income is below the level at which the IRA deduction is reduced. Therefore, they are allowed to deduct their entire $12,000 contribution.**

If only one spouse participates in a qualified pension plan, the other spouse can still receive a deduction for their contribution to an individual retirement account (IRA). However, the deduction is reduced proportionately when the couple's adjusted gross income exceeds $198,000 ($196,000 in 2020) and is reduced to zero when adjusted gross income reaches $208,000 ($206,000 in 2020).

**Example 62** Ling and Chong are married, and each has earned income. Ling participates in an employer-sponsored pension plan while Chong's company does not have a pension plan. Ling and Chong make the maximum contribution to their IRAs and have adjusted gross income for the year of $130,000. What is their allowable deduction for the $12,000 they contribute to their IRAs?

**Discussion: Because Ling is an active participant in a pension plan and their adjusted gross income exceeds $124,000, Ling is not allowed a deduction for the $6,000 contribution to her IRA. However, Chong is allowed a deduction for his contribution because he is not an active participant in a pension plan and their adjusted gross income is less than $198,000.**

LO 10

Explain the requirements for contributing to a Roth Individual Retirement Account and a Coverdell Education Savings Account.

## Roth Individual Retirement Account

The major difference between the nondeductible **Roth IRA** and the conventional nondeductible IRA is that qualified distributions from a Roth IRA, including the income earned on the IRA assets, are not included in the taxpayer's gross income. Participation in a qualified pension plan does not restrict contributions to a Roth IRA. However, the amount contributed to a Roth IRA must be reduced by any contributions made to a deductible IRA. That is, total contributions made to all IRA accounts cannot exceed $6,000 per taxpayer. However, as with a conventional IRA, a taxpayer who is at least 50 years old is allowed an additional "catch-up" contribution to their IRA account. The maximum additional contribution is $1,000.

**Example 63** Kathryn and Michael are married and both participate in their employers' qualified pension plans. Their adjusted gross income is $80,000, and each contributes $4,000 to a deductible IRA. What is the maximum amount they each may contribute to a Roth IRA?

**Discussion: The maximum amount they each can contribute to a Roth IRA is $2,000. Each must reduce her or his maximum Roth IRA contribution amount of $6,000 by the $4,000 contribution made to the deductible IRA account.**

An unmarried taxpayer with adjusted gross income of $125,000 ($124,000 in 2020) or less is allowed to make a $6,000 nondeductible contribution to a Roth IRA. When the taxpayer's adjusted gross income exceeds $125,000 the amount that can be contributed is phased out ratably until no contribution is allowed when adjusted gross income equals $140,000 ($139,000 in 2020). Married taxpayers with adjusted gross income of $198,000 ($196,000 in 2020) or less may each contribute $6,000 to a Roth IRA. When a married couple's adjusted gross income exceeds $198,000, the amount that can be contributed is phased out ratably until no contribution is allowed when adjusted gross income equals $208,000 ($206,000 in 2020).[32] A general formula for calculating the amount of the allowable Roth IRA contribution for married taxpayers follows:

$$\text{Roth IRA Percentage} = \frac{\text{Adjusted gross income} - \$198{,}000}{\$10{,}000}$$

$$\begin{array}{c}\text{Maximum Roth}\\ \text{IRA contribution}\end{array} = \text{Maximum contribution} \times (1 - \text{Roth IRA percentage})$$

**Example 64** Assume the same facts as in example 63, except that Kathryn and Michael's adjusted gross income is $204,000. What is the maximum amount they may contribute to their Roth IRAs?

**Discussion: Because their adjusted gross income is greater than $125,000, they cannot make a deductible IRA contribution. They must reduce their $12,000 Roth IRA contribution proportionately for each dollar of adjusted gross income that exceeds $198,000. The entire contribution amount is reduced to zero when adjusted gross income exceeds $208,000. Kathryn and Michael must reduce the amount of their Roth IRA contribution to $4,800 (i.e., $2,400 each):**

$$60\% = \frac{\$204{,}000 - \$198{,}000}{\$10{,}000}$$

$$\$4{,}800 = \$12{,}000 \times (1 - 60\%)$$

## Coverdell Education Savings Account

Any taxpayer can make a nondeductible contribution of up to $2,000 to a **Coverdell Education Savings Account (CESA)** for the benefit of an individual who is not 18 years of age. However, the total amount contributed to an individual's CESA is limited to $2,000. The advantage of establishing a CESA is that the income earned on the IRA assets will accumulate tax-free and never be taxed to the beneficiary if the income is used to pay for qualified education expenses. In addition to expenses incurred for higher education, qualified education expenses include tuition paid for elementary (including kindergarten) and secondary education at a public, private, or religious school. Qualified educational expenses also include amounts paid for tutoring, computer technology, uniforms, transportation, and extended-day programs for a child attending an elementary or secondary school.

The amount an individual can contribute to a CESA is phased out ratably for married taxpayers filing a joint return with adjusted gross income between $190,000 and $220,000 and for all other taxpayers with adjusted gross income between $95,000 and $110,000.[33]

A general formula for calculating the allowable CESA contribution for an unmarried taxpayer follows:

$$\text{CESA Percentage} = \frac{\text{Adjusted gross income} - \$95,000}{\$15,000}$$

$$\begin{array}{l}\text{Maximum Coverdell} \\ \text{Education Savings} \\ \text{Account Contribution}\end{array} = \text{Maximum contribution} \times (1 - \text{CESA Percentage})$$

**Example 65** Howard is single, and his adjusted gross income for the year is $98,000. He has two sons, Jason and Brian, ages 16 and 13, respectively. What amount can Howard contribute to Coverdell Education Savings Accounts for Jason and Brian?

**Discussion: Because Howard's adjusted gross income exceeds $95,000, the amount he can contribute to each son's CESA must be reduced to $1,600:**

$$20\% = \frac{\$98,000 - \$95,000}{\$15,000}$$

$$\$1,600 = \$2,000 \times (1 - 20\%)$$

## 6-3d Interest on Education Loans

Interest paid on a **qualified education loan** is deductible for adjusted gross income. The loan must be for the benefit of the taxpayer, the taxpayer's spouse, or an individual who is a dependent of the taxpayer at the origination of the loan. The proceeds of the loan must have been used to pay for tuition, fees, room and board, or other necessary expenses. The maximum amount of interest that can be deducted is $2,500.[34] Any amount in excess of the maximum is considered personal interest and is not deductible.

LO 11 Identify the requirements for expenses Congress has allowed individuals to deduct for AGI: higher education and interest on student loans.

**Example 66** Upon graduating from Deekman University, Conchita begins working as a financial analyst for Cobblestone Securities. To finance her college education, she had borrowed $34,000 from a local bank. During the current year, she paid $2,600 in interest on her student loans. What amount can Conchita deduct as student loan interest if her adjusted gross income is $38,000?

**Discussion: Conchita is allowed a deduction for adjusted gross income of $2,500. The remaining $100 is considered personal interest and is not deductible.**

The interest deduction is phased out ratably for unmarried taxpayers with adjusted gross income between $70,000 and $85,000 and for married taxpayers with adjusted gross income between $140,000 and $170,000. The education interest deduction is phased out proportionately over a $15,000 ($30,000 married, filing jointly) range. In calculating the allowable deduction, the amount of the student interest that is subject to the phase-out is the lesser of the amount of interest paid or $2,500. The phase-outs are indexed for inflation. A general formula for calculating the allowable student interest deduction for an unmarried individual follows:

$$\text{Education Interest Percentage} = \frac{\text{Adjusted gross income} - \$70,000}{\$15,000}$$

$$\begin{array}{c}\text{Allowable Education} \\ \text{Interest Deduction}\end{array} = \begin{array}{c}\text{Lesser of student loan} \\ \text{interest paid or } \$2,500\end{array} \times \begin{array}{c}\text{(1 − Education Interest} \\ \text{Percentage)}\end{array}$$

**Example 67** Assume the same facts as in example 66, except that Conchita's adjusted gross income is $73,000 and the interest paid is $2,200. What amount can she deduct as student loan interest?

**Discussion: Because Conchita's adjusted gross income exceeds $65,000, the $2,200 maximum deduction must be reduced proportionately for each dollar of adjusted gross income that exceeds $70,000. Based on the reduction formula, Conchita must reduce her student loan interest deduction to $1,760:**

$$20\% = \frac{\$73,000 - \$70,000}{\$15,000}$$

$$\$1,760 = \$2,200 \times (1 - 20\%)$$

## 6-3e $300 Charitable Contribution Deduction for 2020 and 2021

The CARES Act provides a deduction for AGI for up to $300 in charitable contributions made in 2020. This deduction is for cash contributions only, not donated property. This provision allows nonitemizing taxpayers to benefit from a limited amount of their charitable contributions. The CAA of 2021 extended this deduction to 2021 and allows a married couple to claim $600 in 2021. The details of the charitable contribution deduction are discussed further in Chapter 8.[35]

### concept check

The *legislative grace concept* requires that any tax relief provided be the result of a specific act of Congress that must be strictly applied and interpreted. Deductions must be approached with the philosophy that nothing is deductible unless a provision in the tax law allows the deduction. Through this concept, Congress specifically allows the deduction for health insurance premiums of self-employed individuals.

# CHAPTER SUMMARY

Meal expenses are allowed as business deductions if the expenses are ordinary, necessary, reasonable in amount, and directly related to the active conduct of the taxpayer's business activity. However, only 50 percent of the meals expenses is deductible unless the meals are purchased in a restaurant. Auto expense deductions can be based on the actual cost of using a car for business or on a standard mileage rate method. Regardless of which method is used, the taxpayer must keep detailed records documenting the business use of the car. If the primary reason for making an out-of-town trip is a business purpose, the travel expenses for transportation, meals, lodging, and incidental expenses can be deducted. When time on the trip is devoted to vacation or personal activities, the amount of the deduction may be limited. A deduction is allowed for up to $25 per donee each year for business gifts. Proper documentation is necessary to be sure that meals, auto, travel, or gift expense will be allowed as a deduction.

The tax law allows a deduction for reasonable compensation to employees. Unless certain exceptions are met, the deduction for compensation paid to certain employees of a publicly traded corporation is limited to $1,000,000.

Business and nonbusiness bad debts are deductible only if there is a valid business purpose. Nonbusiness bad debts that are in fact gifts are not deductible. The bad debt deduction is determined using the specific charge-off method. Taxpayers who own a pass-through business (i.e., a sole proprietorship, partnership, or S corporation) are entitled to a deduction based on the taxpayer's Qualified Business Income (QBI). Deductions for interest, insurance, taxes, and legal fees are subject to special rules that limit the deduction or, in some instances, require capitalization of the expenditure as an asset.

Through legislative grace, Congress specifically allows certain expenditures of individuals to be deducted for adjusted gross income. Most of these deductions either have a business purpose or are allowed in an effort to equalize the tax treatment of the expenditure among different taxpayers.

All taxpayers are allowed to *contribute* $6,000 to an individual retirement account. A taxpayer who is at least 50 years old is allowed to make an additional contribution of $1,000. However, a deduction for the contribution is allowed only to those taxpayers who are not covered by an employer-provided retirement plan. If an unmarried taxpayer is covered by an employer-provided retirement plan, the allowable deduction is phased out ratably over a $10,000 range beginning at an adjusted gross income of $66,000. For married taxpayers, if both the husband and wife are covered by an employer-provided plan, the deduction is phased out ratably over a $20,000 range beginning at an adjusted gross income of $105,000. If only one spouse is covered by an employer-provided retirement plan, the allowable deduction for the spouse not covered by a plan is phased out ratably over a $10,000 range beginning at an adjusted gross income of $198,000.

The contribution to a Roth IRA is not deductible. The major benefit of a Roth IRA is that qualified distributions from a Roth IRA, including the income earned on the IRA assets, are not included in the taxpayer's gross income. Unmarried taxpayers with an adjusted gross income of less than $125,000 may contribute $6,000 to a Roth IRA. As with an IRA, a taxpayer who is at least 50 years old is allowed to make an additional contribution of $1,000. However, the amount contributed to a Roth IRA must be reduced by any contributions made to other IRA accounts. When an unmarried taxpayer's adjusted gross income exceeds $125,000, the amount that can be contributed is reduced ratably over a $15,000 range until no contribution is allowed when adjusted gross income exceeds $140,000. For married taxpayers with an adjusted gross income of less than $198,000, each spouse can contribute $6,000 to a Roth IRA. The amount that can be contributed is reduced ratably over a $10,000 range when adjusted gross income exceeds $198,000 and is fully phased out when adjusted gross income exceeds $208,000.

All taxpayers can make a nondeductible contribution of up to $2,000 to a Coverdell Education Savings Account for the benefit of an individual who is not 18 years of age. However, the total amount contributed to an individual's Coverdell Education Savings Account is limited to $2,000. For unmarried taxpayers, the amount of the contribution is phased out ratably over a $15,000 range beginning when adjusted gross income exceeds $95,000 and is fully phased out when adjusted gross income exceeds $110,000. For married taxpayers, the contribution is phased out ratably over a $30,000 range beginning when adjusted gross income exceeds $190,000 and is fully phased out when adjusted gross income exceeds $220,000.

A qualified education loan is one that is used to pay for tuition, fees, room and board, and other necessary education expenses. The maximum amount of interest that can be deducted is $2,500. Any amount in excess of the maximum is considered personal interest and is not deductible. The interest deduction is phased out ratably for single taxpayers over a $15,000 range beginning when adjusted gross income exceeds $70,000 and is fully phased out at $85,000. For married taxpayers, the phase out begins when adjusted gross income exceeds $140,000 and is fully phased out when adjusted gross income exceeds $170,000.

# KEY TERMS

accountable plan (p. 6-22)
actual cost method (p. 6-6)
assessment for local benefits (p. 6-19)
auto expense (p. 6-5)
business bad debt (p. 6-12)
business gift (p. 6-9)
capital loss (p. 6-12)
Coverdell Education Savings Account (CESA) (p. 6-28)
deductions for adjusted gross income (p. 6-20)
education expense (p. 6-10)
employer reimbursement plan (p. 6-22)
individual retirement account (IRA) (p. 6-25)
legal fees (p. 6-20)
nonaccountable plan (p. 6-22)
Qualified Business Income (QBI) (p. 6-15)
nonbusiness bad debt (p. 6-12)
qualified education loan (p. 6-29)
reasonable compensation (p. 6-11)
related party (p. 6-11)
Roth IRA (p. 6-27)
self-employment tax (p. 6-24)
specific charge-off method (p. 6-13)
standard mileage rate method (p. 6-6)
substantiation requirement (p. 6-10)
tax home (p. 6-7)
travel expenses (p. 6-7)

# PRIMARY TAX LAW SOURCES

[1]Sec. 274—Provides the limitations on deductions for meals and entertainment, and business gifts; requires that deductions for such items be substantiated by adequate records.

[2]Notice 2018-76 Provides guidance on when business meals continue to the 50% deductible under the TCJA.

[3]Reg. Sec. 1.274-2—Explains the general rules for meal and entertainment deductions; defines expenditures *directly related* and *associated with* business for purposes of determining the deductibility of entertainment costs.

[4]Sec. 274(a)(3)—Disallows deductions for dues of clubs organized for business, pleasure, recreation, or social purposes.

[5]Rev. Rul. 94-47—Further explains Rev. Rul. 90-23, which provides examples of allowable deductions for a taxpayer's daily transportation expenses.

[6]Notice 2021-5—Sets the 2021 standard mileage rate for determining automobile expenses at 57.5 cents per mile.

[7]Rev. Proc. 2019-26—Provides the maximum yearly depreciation deductions on automobiles purchased in 2019.

[8]Reg. Sec. 1.162-2—Allows deduction for travel expenses; provides treatment of business travel mixed with personal activities.

[9]Reg. Sec. 1.274-5T—Provides the substantiation rules that must be followed in deducting meals, entertainment, and travel expenses.

[10]Reg. Sec. 1.162-5(a)—Sets forth the types of educational expenses that are deductible.

[11]Reg. Sec. 1.162-5(b)—Sets forth the types of educational expenses that are not deductible.

[12]Reg. Sec. 1.162-7—Sets forth guidelines for deductions of compensation paid for personal services.

[13]Internal Revenue Service Manual 4233, Sec. 232—Provides the factors that the IRS considers in determining whether compensation is reasonable.

[14]Sec. 162(m)—Sets forth the rules for deducting compensation in excess of $1,000,000.

[15]Sec. 166—Specifies the allowable deductions for bad debts.

[16]Reg. Sec. 1.166-3—Allows a deduction for partial worthlessness of a business bad debt.

[17]Reg. Sec. 1.166-5—Defines *nonbusiness bad debt* and specifies the treatment as a short-term capital loss in the year the debt becomes worthless.

[18]Sec. 199 A—Sets forth the rules for taxpayers with income from pass through entities to be entltled to a Qualified Business Income (QBI) deduction.

[19]Sec. 163 (j)—Limits deduction for business interest to 30% of earnings before interest, taxes, depreciation, and amortization. Companies with average annual gross receipts of less than $25 million during the 3 prior years are not subject to this limitation.

[20]Sec. 164—Specifies the allowable deduction for taxes.

[21]Reg. Sec. 1.164-1—Specifies the types of taxes that are deductible as trade or business expenses.

[22]Reg. Sec. 1.164-2—Denies deductions for certain types of taxes.

[23]Reg. Sec. 1.164-6—Requires the apportionment of the deduction for real property taxes between the buyer and the seller of real property based on the number of days each party owned the property during the year.

[24]U.S. v. Gilmore 83 S. Ct. 623 (1963)—Held that the deductibility of legal expenses depends on whether the claim arises in connection with the taxpayer's business activities. The consequences of the transaction, in this case the sale of the business, are not a factor.

[25]Sec. 62—Defines *adjusted gross income* for individual taxpayers and specifies the deductions allowed as deductions for adjusted gross income.

[26]Reg. Sec. 1.62-2—Provides the rules for reimbursements of employee business expenses.

[27]Sec. 162(1)—Allows a self-employed individual to deduct for adjusted gross income medical insurance premiums paid during the year.

[28]Sec. 1402—Defines *self-employment income* and provides for the tax to be paid on base amounts as specified in the Social Security Act for each tax year; allows the reduction of self-employment income by one-half of the Social Security tax paid.

[29]Sec. 219 (b)(5)(B)—Allows a taxpayer who is at least 50 years old to make an additional "catch-up" contribution of $1,000 to a conventional individual retirement account or a Roth Individual Retirement Account.

[30]Sec. 219(c)—Allows a nonworking spouse to contribute into an individual retirement account as long as the total earned income of both spouses exceeds the annual IRA deduction amount.

[31]Sec. 219—Allows a deduction for contributions to an individual retirement account; prescribes the maximum amounts deductible and limitations on deductions for active participants in other pension plans.

[32]Sec. 408A—Allows a taxpayer to contribute to a Roth Individual Retirement Account; prescribes the limitations on contributions for taxpayers whose adjusted gross income exceeds certain thresholds.

[33]Sec. 530—Allows a taxpayer to contribute to a Coverdell Education Savings Account; prescribes the limitations on the amount each account can receive during the year and limits contributions for taxpayers whose adjusted gross income exceeds certain thresholds.

[34]Sec. 221—Allows a taxpayer to deduct interest on qualified education loans and prescribes the maximum amount of interest that can be deducted and the limitation on the deduction for taxpayers whose adjusted gross income exceeds certain thresholds.

[35]S.3548 Coronavirus Aid Relief and Economic Security Act, Sec. 2104.

# DISCUSSION QUESTIONS

1. **LO1, 3, 4** Most expenditures that have a business purpose and meet the ordinary, necessary, and reasonable requirements are deductible. However, specific rules must be adhered to in determining the deductibility of many expenses that meet this test. Why are these specific rules necessary?
2. **LO1** What requirements must be met for meal expenses to be deductible?
3. **LO2** What problems does the taxpayer who uses an automobile for both business and personal purposes encounter? What option(s) does the taxpayer have regarding the automobile expense deduction?
4. **LO1, 3, 4** What records are necessary to properly document travel, entertainment, and gift expenses?
5. **LO4** Under what circumstances are business gifts deductible?
6. **LO4** Explain the criteria used to determine whether an educational expense is deductible or nondeductible, and how education expenses are deducted on a taxpayer's return.
7. **LO4** Can an education expense incurred by one taxpayer be deductible whereas the same expense incurred by another taxpayer is not deductible? Explain.
8. **LO4** Is all compensation paid to an employee deductible? Discuss the circumstances in which employee compensation cannot be deducted.
9. **LO5** Explain the difference in the tax treatment of business and nonbusiness bad debts.
10. **LO5** What accounting method must be used to account for bad debts that result from the sale of merchandise or the provision of services?
11. **LO5** Explain how the tax benefit rule may apply to bad debt deductions.
12. **LO6** What requirements must be met to deduct life insurance premiums paid on an employee's policy?

13. **LO6** Are sales taxes deductible? Explain.

14. **LO6** Are all legal fees paid by a taxpayer deductible? Explain.

15. **LO6** Why are deductions for adjusted gross income "better" than deductions from adjusted gross income?

16. **LO7** What is an accountable employee expense reimbursement plan? What is the significance of such a plan?

17. **LO8** Why are self-employed taxpayers allowed to deduct their medical insurance premiums and part of their self-employment tax for adjusted gross income?

18. **LO9** Are all taxpayers allowed a deduction for contributions to a conventional individual retirement account? Explain.

19. **LO9, 10** How does the tax treatment of a conventional IRA differ from a Roth IRA?

20. **LO10** Who is eligible to make and receive contributions to a Coverdell Education Savings Account?

21. **LO11** Is the interest on education loans always deductible? Explain.

## PROBLEMS

22. **LO1** A.J. is the vice president for Keane Products, a marketing consulting firm. On a business trip to New York City in 2021, he meets with three executives from Keane's top account. After the meeting, A.J. takes them to dinner and then to the theater. The theater tickets cost $350. The cost of the meal is $190, including sales tax of $17 and a tip of $34. Throughout the evening, A.J. pays $42 in cab fares. How much can A.J. deduct as a business expense?

23. **LO1** Karl is the vice president of finance for Wyatt Industries. In 2021, he met a client at an afternoon baseball game. The box-seat tickets cost Karl $30 each. Because the client had a plane flight after the game, Karl was unable to take her to dinner. During the game, Karl spent $15 on sodas and snacks. What amount can Karl deduct as a business expense?

24. **LO1** For each of the following situations, explain whether a deduction should be allowed as a business expense:
    a. Neil owns a real estate agency and has an annual Christmas party at his house. The party is only for employees of his firm, and costs $2,600.
    b. Carol is a personal financial planner. Over the years, she has made it a practice to invite her best clients to lunch on the client's birthday. At the lunch, she always makes it a point to ask about any major changes in the client's financial status that she should be aware of. However, most of the conversation relates to personal matters. During the year, Carol spends $850 on these lunches.
    c. Vijay is a doctor at a local hospital. Every month, he buys lunch at the hospital for the six residents and interns who assist him in surgery and caring for his patients. The lunches cost $640 for the year.
    d. Tom, Hillary, and George are friends from college who live and work in the Dallas metropolitan area. They are all stockbrokers for different firms and get together twice a month for lunch to exchange rumors concerning the stock market. In addition, they catch up on personal news and make plans to get together with their spouses and other friends. Last year, George made $50,000 for a client based on a tip he received from Hillary at one of their meetings. Each stockbroker pays for their own lunch, and during the year, George paid $480.

25. **LO1** For each of the following situations, explain whether a deduction should be allowed as a business expense:
    a. Gayle, a dentist, invites 50 of her best patients to her daughter's wedding reception. The cost of the reception related to the presence of her patients is $5,000.
    b. Stan is one of 5 shift supervisors responsible for 100 employees at Label House, Inc. He regularly meets with the other shift supervisors at the plant. In addition, Stan makes it a practice to go to lunch at least once a week with each of the other 4 shift supervisors in order to network. During the current year, Stan pays $1,500 for his and the other supervisors' lunches. Stan's job description does not require him to entertain the other supervisors.

c. Jan is a real estate broker who holds an open house for a different client each Sunday afternoon. During the open house, she provides cookies and soft drinks for whoever visits the house. Jan pays $2,000 for open house entertainment.
d. Felicia is vice president of sales for Drivitt, Inc. She invites the company's major clients and some of her coworkers from Drivitt to her annual Super Bowl party. Most guests attend with their spouses. The party is held in a separate room at a local sports bar and costs her $1,500.

Communication Skills

26. **LO1** You have just been hired as a tax accountant by a local public accounting firm. One partner is impressed by your writing skills and asks you to write a one-page memo to a client describing the general rules on the deductibility of meals. The client also needs to know under what circumstances the cost of its skybox (with 10 tickets) at Optus Park is deductible.
27. **LO2** In the current year, Pablo is a computer sales representative and spends only four days a month in the office. His office is 18 miles from home. Pablo spends three days a month traveling to his out-of-town clients.
    a. What portion of Pablo's travel is considered business?
    b. During the year, Pablo keeps the following record of his travel:

| | Miles |
|---|---|
| Home to office | 864 |
| Office to home | 864 |
| Home to local clients to home | 10,630 |
| Home to out-of-town clients to home | 2,650 |

    The company reimburses Pablo for all of his lodging, meals, and entertainment while he is on the road. If he uses the standard mileage rate, what amount can he deduct as a business expense?

28. **LO7** In the current year, Julianita is a sales representative for a food distributor and spends only one day of the week in the office. In this position, Julianita is included in her employer's accountable plan. Her office is 12 miles from home. She also has a part-time job as a bartender. Typically, she works 2 nights during the week and 1 night on the weekend. The restaurant where she works is 5 miles from her office and 10 miles from her home.
    a. What portion(s) of Julianita's travel is considered business?
    b. During the year, Julianita keeps the following record of her travel:

| | Miles |
|---|---|
| Home to office | 588 |
| Office to home | 353 |
| Office to restaurant | 150 |
| Restaurant to home | 1,500 |
| Home to restaurant | 500 |
| Home to clients to home | 8,850 |
| Clients to restaurant | 2,100 |

    If she uses the standard mileage rate, what amount can she deduct as a business expense?

29. **LO2** Cassandra owns her own business and drives her van 15,000 miles a year for business and 5,000 miles a year for commuting and personal use. She purchases a new van in 2021 and wants to claim the largest tax deduction possible for business use. Cassandra's total auto expenses for 2021 are as follows:

| | |
|---|---|
| Gas, oil, and maintenance | $ 6,560 |
| Insurance | 775 |
| Interest on car loan | 1,200 |
| Depreciation | 3,160 |
| License | 180 |
| Parking fees and tolls (all business) | 240 |

    Determine Cassandra's 2021 deduction for business use of the van.

30. **LO2** Mario owns his own business and drives his car 15,000 miles a year for business and 7,500 miles a year for commuting and personal use. He wants to claim the largest tax deduction possible for business use of his car. His total auto expenses for 2021 are as follows:

| | |
|---|---|
| Gas, oil, and maintenance | $ 8,900 |
| Insurance | 800 |
| Interest on car loan | 480 |
| Depreciation | 3,160 |
| License | 180 |
| Parking fees and tolls (all business) | 290 |

a. What is Mario's 2021 deduction using the standard mileage rate method?
b. What is Mario's 2021 deduction using the actual cost method?

31. **LO2** Nia is a recent college graduate who has taken a position with a real estate brokerage firm. Initially, Nia will be selling both residential and commercial property. She is thinking about buying a new car at a cost of $14,500. However, the salesperson is trying to sell her a car that costs $18,000. He has assured her that because she is now self-employed, the entire cost of the car is tax deductible. Nia comes to you, her tax accountant, for advice about the purchase of the car. She tells you she expects that 65 percent of her driving will be for business purposes. She asks you to write her a letter specifying whether she can deduct the entire cost of the car, which expenses she needs to keep track of, and how these expenses are used in computing the business deduction for her car. Communication Skills

32. **LO3** Juanita travels to San Francisco for seven days. The following facts are related to the trip:

| | |
|---|---|
| Round trip airfare | $475 |
| Hotel daily rate for single or double occupancy | 175 |
| Meals—$40 per day | 40 |
| Incidentals—$25 per day | 25 |

a. If she spends four days on business and three days sightseeing, what amount may she deduct as travel expense?
b. If she spends two days on business and five days sightseeing, what amount may she deduct as travel expense?
c. Assume the same facts as in part a, except that Juanita's husband Jorge accompanied her on the trip and that the hotel's single occupancy rate is $150. Jorge went sightseeing every day and attended business receptions with Juanita at night. Assume that Jorge's expenses are identical to Juanita's. What amount may Juanita and Jorge deduct as travel expense?

33. **LO3** Chai is self-employed and travels to New Orleans for a business conference. The following facts are related to the trip:

| | |
|---|---|
| Round trip airfare | $375 |
| Hotel daily rate for single | 120 |
| Conference registration fee | 190 |
| Meals—$54 per day | 54 |
| Incidentals—$27 per day | 27 |

a. If Chai spends four days at the conference and two days sightseeing, what amount may he deduct as travel expense?
b. If he spends two days at the conference and 4 days sightseeing, what amount may he deduct as travel expense?
c. Next year, Chai would like his wife, Li, who does not work outside their home, to go with him to the conference. Li's expenses would be similar to Chai's except that the room rate for double occupancy is $150. Li would probably attend one or two sessions and the receptions at night. What portion of her expenses can they deduct?

Communication Skills

34. **LO3** Olga has to travel to Philadelphia for two days on business. She enjoys history and is planning to visit the Liberty Bell and other historic sites in the city. If time permits, she would like to make a side trip to nearby Gettysburg. A friend of Olga's tells her, "The best part of traveling on business is that once the business is over, you can sightsee all you want and the cost is tax-deductible." Olga, who is self-employed, has scheduled her trip for the Labor Day weekend so that she can spend three days sightseeing. Write a letter to Olga in which you explain whether her friend's advice is correct.

35. **LO3** Marisa is an obstetrician. Every February, she attends a three-day conference on financial planning with Ester, her college roommate. Ester is self-employed and is Marisa's accountant and a certified financial planner. This year, the seminar was in San Diego, and each had a separate hotel room. The costs of attending the conference for Marisa and Ester are as follows:

| | Marisa | Ester |
|---|---|---|
| Airfare | $425 | $375 |
| Hotel daily rate | 120 | 120 |
| Meals—$35 per day | 35 | 35 |
| Incidentals—$20 per day | 20 | 20 |
| Registration | 170 | 170 |
| Rental car* | 90 | 90 |

*Marisa and Ester split the cost of the rental car.

How much of the trip costs can Marisa and Ester deduct?

36. **LO3** Floyd owns an antique shop. During the year, he and his wife, Amanda, who works as a real estate broker, attend a three-day antique show in Boston. The following facts are related to the trip:

| | |
|---|---|
| Train per person | $110 |
| Hotel daily rate—double occupancy* | 115 |
| Meals—$37 per day per person | 37 |
| Incidentals—$14 per day per person | 14 |

*The hotel rate for double occupancy is $20 more than the single occupancy rate.

What amount can Floyd and Amanda deduct as travel expense? Explain.

37. **LO1, 4** Jan owns the Mews Bar and Grill. Every year at Christmas, he has a party for his 20 employees and their families. This year's party cost $1,600. At the party, Jan presented each employee with a $50 gift certificate redeemable for merchandise at a local department store.
    a. How much can Jan deduct for business and gift expenses?
    b. Assume that the party is attended by 10 employees and 10 of the Mews's major suppliers. At the party each receives a holiday cheese basket that cost $30. How much can Jan deduct?

38. **LO4** For each of the following situations, determine whether the expenses are deductible as an education expense:
    a. Dorothy owns a real estate business. She is enrolled in a one-year weekend MBA program that meets in a city three hours away. She takes a train to and from the city. A one-year weekend pass for the train is $800. The fee for the MBA program, including lodging, meals, books, and tuition, is $25,000.
    b. Forest is employed as a production manager for a printing company. He is enrolled in a night course costing $350 at the local college. The course is not required by his employer but does improve his job skills.
    c. Elise is a recent graduate of law school and has been hired by a local firm. The firm expects her to pass the bar exam on her first try. To prepare for the bar exam, she is taking a law review course that costs $1,500.
    d. Simon is the managing partner of an accounting firm and is required to attend 30 hours of continuing education every year. State law requires that 5 hours

be in ethics training. The 5-hour ethics course costs $400; the remaining 25 hours of continuing education cost $1,800.

39. Paula is single and works as a high school science teacher. Each summer, she travels to a national conference on high school science curriculum. She also spends one week during the summer traveling to areas in the United States to further her science knowledge. This year, she spent one week exploring the caves and rock formations around Carlsbad, New Mexico. She plans on using the knowledge and information from this trip in her earth science class. The costs of each trip are as follows: Communication Skills

| | Science Conference | Carlsbad Trip |
|---|---|---|
| Airfare | $350 | $450 |
| Hotel | 200 | 375 |
| Meals | 120 | 250 |
| Incidentals | 40 | 110 |
| Rental car | 75 | 190 |
| Registration | 100 | ... |
| Tours | ... | 90 |

Paula has asked for your advice on the deductibility of these costs as a business expense. Write her a letter explaining her allowable deduction for these costs. If any of the costs are not deductible, explain why she cannot deduct them.

40. **LO4** Cory is the fourth-highest-paid officer of the Mast Corporation, a publicly traded corporation. The company pays Cory a salary of $1,100,000. What amount can it deduct as salary expense? Would your answer change if Mast is a closely held corporation and the payments are typical of other companies of similar size in the industry?

41. **LO4** Ping is an officer of the Branson Corporation, a publicly traded corporation. His salary for the year is $1,320,000, which is the sixth-highest salary at Branson. All of the top ten highest salaried employees at Branson have been with the company for the entire year. What amount can the corporation deduct as salary expense? How would your answer change if Ping's salary is the third-highest at Branson?

42. **LO5** Howard loaned $8,000 to Bud two years ago. The terms of the loan call for Bud to pay annual interest at 8 percent, with the principal amount due in three years. Until this year, Bud had been making the required interest payments. When Howard didn't receive this year's payment, he called Bud and found out that Bud had filed for bankruptcy. Bud's accountant estimated that only 40 percent of his debts would be paid after the bankruptcy proceeding. No payments were received. In the next year, Howard received $2,700 in full satisfaction of the debt under the bankruptcy proceeding. What deductions are allowed to Howard, assuming that the debt was:
    a. Related to Howard's business?
    b. Unrelated to Howard's business?
    c. How would your answers to parts a and b change if Howard received $3,300 in satisfaction of the debt in the next year?

43. **LO5** During the year, Grace, Inc., has total sales of $800,000. Based on total sales, the corporation estimates that its bad debts for the year are 2 percent of sales. As a result, the corporation deducts $16,000 in bad debts for financial accounting purposes. At the end of the year, the controller reviews the accounts receivable ledger to identify uncollectible accounts. She determines that $3,900 in accounts receivable cannot be collected. In addition, the accountant's analysis shows that the corporation has recovered $1,400 in accounts receivable written off as a bad debt for tax purposes in the previous year. How should this information be reported for tax purposes?

44. **LO5** The following information is from the financial records of the Adham Corporation at the end of the year:

| | |
|---|---|
| Accounts receivable | $450,000 |
| Allowance for bad debts account | (34,000) |
| Net accounts receivable | $416,000 |

The allowance for bad debts account is based on an aging of the corporation's accounts receivable. At the end of the year, the allowance for bad debts account was increased from $7,000 to $34,000. During the year, $8,000 of the accounts receivable was specifically identified by the company as uncollectible and written off.

a. If Adham's bad debts arise from the sale of merchandise, how should the adjustments to the allowance for bad debt accounts be reported for tax purposes?

b. If Adham uses the cash method of accounting and the bad debts expense arises from providing counseling advice, how should the adjustments to the allowance for bad debt accounts be reported for tax purposes?

45. **LO5** In addition to being an employee of Rock Hard Roofing Material, Lou owns 10 percent of the company's common stock. Rock Hard falls on hard times in 2020. To forestall bankruptcy, Rock Hard's employees and shareholders lend the company $1,000,000. Lou's share of the total loan is $50,000—$25,000 related to her position as an employee and $25,000 related to her ownership of stock. In early 2021, creditors force Rock Hard into bankruptcy. Lou loses her entire $50,000.

a. Is Lou's loss related to a trade or business or an investment?

b. Can Lou deduct her loss as a bad debt expense?

46. **LO4** Tom is single and operates a golf store as a sole proprietorship. In 2021, the store has $130,000 of net income. Tom does not itemize and has other income from interest and dividends of $2,000. What is Tom's QBI deduction for 2021? What is his taxable income?

a. Assume the same facts as above, except that Tom is a CPA and operates an accounting firm as a sole proprietorship, and his net income is $195,000. In addition, he has capital gains of $3,000. What is Tom's QBI deduction for 2021? What is his taxable income?

b. Assume the facts of the original problem except that Tom has itemized deductions of $25,000, but the QBI from the business is $510,000, W-2 wages are $120,000, and unadjusted depreciable property is $180,000. What is Tom's QBI deduction for 2021? What is his taxable income?

47. **LO4** Dan and Katlyn are married and operate a pizza restaurant as an S corporation. They are not eligible for any additional standard deduction amounts. In 2021, the store has qualified business income of $300,000. Their itemized deductions are $22,000, and they have other income from interest and dividends of $9,000.

a. What is their QBI deduction for 2021? What is their taxable income?

b. Assume the same facts as above, except that Dan and Katlyn are lawyers and jointly operate their law firm as a partnership. The income that flows to them from the partnership is $385,000. In addition, they have capital gains of $5,000. What is their QBI deduction for 2021? What is taxable income?

c. Assume the facts of the original problem except that their itemized deductions are $32,000, the QBI from the business is $510,000, it has W-2 wages of $160,000, and unadjusted depreciable property of $180,000. What is their QBI deduction for 2021? What is their taxable income?

48. **LO4** For the last three years, the JCR corporation has averaged annual gross receipts of $27 million. This year, JCR has EBITDA of $6,000,000, and it has incurred $2,100,000 in business interest expense. What can JCR deduct as business interest in the current year?

a. Assume that in the following year, JCR has EBITDA of $7,000,000, and it has incurred $1,500,000 in business interest expense. What can JCR deduct as business interest?

49. **LO6** KOM pays the following insurance premiums during 2021:

| | |
|---|---|
| Auto accident and liability insurance: | |
| Paid 1/1/21 Coverage period 1/1/21–12/31/21 | $ 3,500 |
| Fire, storm, and other casualty insurance: | |
| Paid 4/1/21 Coverage period 4/1/21–3/31/23 | $ 5,000 |
| Business liability insurance: | |
| Paid 5/1/21 Coverage period 5/1/21–4/30/22 | $ 3,000 |

a. If KOM uses the accrual method of accounting, what is the insurance expense deduction for 2021?
b. If KOM uses the cash method of accounting, what is the insurance expense deduction for 2021?

50. **LO6** For each of the following situations, state whether the expense related to the transaction can be deducted as an insurance expense:

Communication Skills

a. Baker Company pays the insurance premium to provide each of its employees with a $50,000 whole life insurance policy. Baker and the insurance company consider the employee the owner of the policy. As owner of the policy, the covered employee designates the beneficiary of the life insurance proceeds in the event of the employee's death. Each employee's policy costs $2,000 per year.
b. Baker Company has a nondiscriminatory self-insured medical reimbursement plan for the benefit of its employees. Once a mont h, Baker transfers $1,000 in cash from its general bank account to a special medical reimbursement checking account. The transfer is based on the premium an insurance company would demand to provide the same benefits to the employees.
c. The employees of Baker Company receive large sums of cash in the mail. To protect against loss, Baker pays a $500 annual insurance premium for an employees' fidelity bond.
d. Baker Company is owned by Ross. Baker pays a $1,500 annual premium for a sickness and disability income continuation insurance policy on Ross. The purpose of the policy is to give Ross $3,500 per month if he is unable to work for Baker because he is sick or disabled.

51. **LO6** State whether the following taxes are allowed as a current deduction for taxes paid by a business:

a. Sales tax on the purchase of a desk
b. State and local income, real estate, and personal property taxes
c. Federal income, estate, and gift taxes
d. An employer's payment to the IRS of federal income and Social Security taxes withheld from an employee's wages

52. **LO6** Martin receives the following tax bills, related to a rental dwelling, from the county treasurer:

| | |
|---|---|
| Special assessment for installing sidewalks and streets | $ 12,000 |
| Real property tax on dwelling for the 1/1/21–12/31/21 property tax year, due on 10/1/21 | $ 1,500 |

On May 1, 2021, Martin sells the dwelling for $70,000. His basis in the dwelling at the date of sale is $40,000. Martin's basis in the dwelling does not reflect the property tax bills. As part of the sale contract, the buyer agrees to pay the real property taxes when they come due on October 1, 2021, but Martin has to pay the special assessment before the sale closes. What is the proper tax treatment of the tax payments?

53. **LO6** The Kimpton Corporation pays the following taxes during 2021:

| | |
|---|---|
| Federal taxes withheld from employees | $ 26,000 |
| State taxes withheld from employees | 9,000 |
| Social Security withheld from employees | 4,850 |
| Kimpton's share of Social Security taxes | 4,850 |

| | |
|---|---:|
| Federal income tax paid in 2021 with 2020 tax return | 1,790 |
| Federal income tax paid in 2021 | 12,340 |
| Real estate taxes | 6,750 |
| State income taxes paid in 2021 | 5,720 |
| State income taxes paid in 2021 with 2020 return | 690 |
| State tax on capital acquisitions | 2,700 |
| Sales tax on supplies | 3,250 |

Also, the county treasurer notifies Kimpton that it is being assessed a special real estate tax of $64,000 for upgrading the sidewalks and sewer connections in the area. The special tax is payable in four yearly installments of $16,000. What amount can Kimpton deduct for taxes paid in 2021?

54. **LO6** Kuerten Manufacturers sues the Rafter Corporation for patent infringement. The court upholds Kuerten's claim and requires Rafter to pay Kuerten $2,000,000 in damages. However, the court does not allow Kuerten to recover its $100,000 in legal expenses from Rafter. Can Kuerten deduct the $100,000 in legal expenses? Would your answer change if Kuerten were allowed to collect the legal fees from Rafter?

55. **LO6** Can Joe Corporation deduct the following expenses related to its business?
    a. Legal fee paid ($40,000) to acquire a competing chain of stores
    b. Legal fee paid ($12,000) to determine whether it should become an S corporation
    c. Legal fee paid ($5,000) to defend the company's president in a lawsuit filed by a disgruntled customer
    d. Legal fee paid ($500) to defend title to a vacant lot Joe is holding for construction of a storage building for use in its business
    e. Legal fee paid ($2,500) to defend against damages suffered by a customer who was injured when he fell in the company's store

56. **LO7** Mona works for Leonardo Corporation as a sales representative. Leonardo gives her a travel allowance of $350 per month. During 2021, she spends the following amounts on valid travel expenses:

| | |
|---|---:|
| Transportation | $2,700 |
| Meals | 1,500 |
| Lodging | 1,800 |

How should Mona treat the $350 per month travel allowance and the travel costs she incurs if Leonardo's reimbursement plan is an accountable plan?

57. **LO7** Alvin is an employee of York Company. During 2021, he incurs the following employment-related expenses:

| | |
|---|---:|
| Travel | $4,000 |
| Meals | 3,500 |
| Lodging | 2,500 |

a. How should Alvin treat these expenses if York Company has an accountable employee business expense reimbursement plan and Alvin is reimbursed
   $9,000?
   $10,000?
   $11,000?

b. How would your answer to part a change if Alvin were self-employed (i.e., receiving no reimbursements)?

58. **LO7** The Ballaraat Corporation is cutting costs. The vice president of finance has asked the tax department to justify the company's continued use of an accountable employee expense reimbursement plan. You are the manager of the tax department. Prepare a letter to the vice president of finance explaining the tax consequences of not using an accountable employee expense reimbursement plan. Also discuss any nontax benefits of maintaining the plan. Communication Skills

59. **LO8** Evelyn is single and a self-employed engineer. During 2021, Evelyn's income from her engineering business is $55,000. Evelyn pays $3,100 for her medical insurance policy.
   a. How should the medical insurance policy payment be reflected on Evelyn's 2021 return?
   b. What is Evelyn's 2021 self-employment tax deduction?

60. **LO8** Thomas is single and a self-employed architect. During 2021, Thomas's income from his business is $170,000. He also pays $2,200 for a medical insurance policy.
   a. How should the medical insurance policy payment be reflected on his 2021 tax return?
   b. What is his 2021 self-employment tax deduction?
   c. Assume that Thomas's income from his business is $228,000. What in his 2021 self-employment tax deduction?
   d. Assume the same facts as in part a, except Thomas is married, his wife's salary is $30,000, and they are covered by a medical policy from her employer.

61. **LO9** Carlos and Angela are married, file a joint return, and are both 42 years old. During the current year, Carlos's salary is $70,000. Neither Carlos nor Angela is covered by an employer-sponsored pension plan. Determine the maximum IRA contribution and deduction amounts in each of the following cases:
   a. Angela earns $28,000, and their adjusted gross income is $110,000.
   b. Angela does not work outside the home, and their adjusted gross income is $75,000.
   c. Assume the same facts as in part a, except that Carlos is 52, Angela is 48, and both are covered by an employer-sponsored pension plan.
   d. Assume the same facts as in part a, except that Carlos is covered by an employer-sponsored pension plan.

62. **LO9** Lois and Shanice are married and file a joint return. Lois earns $64,500 and Shanice earns $40,000. Their adjusted gross income is $115,000. Determine the maximum IRA contribution and deduction in each of the following cases:
   a. Neither Lois nor Shanice is covered by an employee-sponsored pension plan.
   b. Both Shanice and Lois are covered by an employee-sponsored pension plan.
   c. Assume that only Shanice is covered by an employer-sponsored pension plan and that their adjusted gross income is $154,000.

63. **LO9** In the current year, Kathy, who is single and 25, inherited $7,000 from her grandmother. A coworker has suggested that Kathy open an individual retirement account with the $7,000. Her friend says that an IRA is a great way to save because you don't have to pay tax on the income from the investment and you get a tax deduction for your contribution. Write a letter to Kathy explaining whether her friend's advice is correct. To the extent her friend's information is inaccurate, provide Kathy with the correct tax treatment and explain how different facts may lead to different tax treatments. Communication Skills

64. **LO10** In the current year Chanda is 36, single, and an active participant in a qualified employee pension plan. Determine the maximum Roth IRA contribution that she can make in each of the following cases:
   a. Her adjusted gross income for the year is $66,000.
   b. Her adjusted gross income for the year is $126,000.
   c. Her adjusted gross income for the year is $150,000.
   d. Her adjusted gross income for the year is $65,000, and she makes a $3,500 contribution to a deductible IRA account.
65. **LO9, 10** In the current year Kevin and Jill are married and file a joint return. Kevin is 52 and is not an active participant in a qualified employee pension plan, while Jill is 48 and is an active participant in a qualified employee pension plan. Determine the maximum Roth IRA contribution that can be made in each of the following cases:
   a. Their adjusted gross income for the year is $125,000.
   b. Their adjusted gross income for the year is $199,000.
   c. Their adjusted gross income for the year is $215,000.
   d. How would your answers to parts a and b change if Kevin makes the maximum allowable contribution to his deductible IRA?
66. **LO10** Alex and Carmin are married and have two children, ages 6 and 3. Their adjusted gross income for the year is $123,000. What is the maximum amount they can contribute to each child's Coverdell Education Savings Account for the year? If their adjusted gross income is $208,000, what is the maximum contribution that can be made to each child's education saving account?
67. **LO10** Gary and Patricia are divorced and have three children, ages 9, 6, and 2. Patricia has custody of the children and is entitled to the dependency exemption for each child. Their adjusted gross incomes are $48,000 and $61,000, respectively. During the current year, Gary contributes $1,500 to each child's Coverdell Education Savings Account. What is the maximum amount that Patricia can contribute to her children's education savings account?
68. **LO11** Martha graduated from Tassle Tech and immediately started working as an accountant for Creedon Industries. To finance her college education, she borrowed $23,000 from a local bank, and pays $1,800 of interest expense during the year. Her adjusted gross income for the year is $39,000.
   a. What amount can Martha deduct as student loan interest?
   b. Assume that Martha borrowed $32,000 to finance her education and paid interest during the year of $2,700. What amount can she deduct as student loan interest?
   c. Assume the same facts as in part a, except that Martha's adjusted gross income is $75,000. What amount can she deduct as student loan interest?
69. **LO11** Simon graduated from Lessard University last year. He financed his education by working part-time and borrowing $16,000. During the current year, he pays $1,400 of interest on his student loan.
   a. What amount can Simon deduct as student loan interest if his adjusted gross income is $33,000?
   b. What amount can Simon deduct as student loan interest if his adjusted gross income is $82,000?

## ISSUE IDENTIFICATION PROBLEMS

In each of the following problems, identify the tax issue(s) posed by the facts presented. Determine the possible tax consequences of each issue that you identify.

70. Marjorie is an accountant and Alana is an attorney. They have been business acquaintances for about 10 years. They meet every Friday at 6 P.M. at a local tavern to socialize. As always happens with attorneys and accountants, they discuss what is

happening in their offices. They take turns paying the bar tab, which averages $30 for each meeting.

71. Salvador is an insurance representative for the Hendricken Insurance Company. Recently, he heard that the controller of his largest account, Gore Plastics, was asking other insurance representatives to submit quotes on the cost of providing workers' compensation insurance for the company. Hendricken's contract with Gore is due to expire in two months. Knowing that the controller of Gore is an avid golfer, Salvador sends him the new Big Whomper Driver. The golf club costs $350. Salvador submits the bill for the golf club to the company, and the expense is approved for reimbursement by the vice president of finance.

72. Jennifer is self-employed. At Christmas, she gives the elevator operator in the building where her office is located a pair of gloves. She makes similar gifts to the two parking lot attendants who park her car.

73. Carla has a B.S. degree in history and is employed as an administrative assistant for a public accounting firm. After work, she attends Wittman College, where she is enrolled in an accounting course. Her goal is to take the necessary courses to sit for the CPA exam. Her firm does not reimburse her for the cost of the course.

74. Vince is the third-highest-paid executive for Sensor Corporation, a publicly traded corporation. His salary is $1,250,000.

75. Jake loaned his cousin, Arnold, $10,000 in March 2019 to open a cybercafe in Santa Barbara. Arnold signed a loan agreement to pay Jake 7 percent interest annually, with the principal due in 2021. Jake received his 2019 interest payment but did not receive any interest payment in 2020. In March 2021, Jake's father informs him that his cousin has filed for bankruptcy.

76. Mei loaned $2,000 to her minister a year ago. The loan is not evidenced by a note and does not bear interest. The minister has moved out of town without paying her back. She doesn't want to embarrass him by asking him to repay the loan.

77. The Copeland Corporation acquires a machine for $5,000 and pays $250 in state sales tax. The machine has a tax life of seven years.

78. The town of Dinsmore passed a bill requiring that all homes be connected to the town sewer system. Baskin Ridge is the only section of town that does not have town sewers. Dinsmore will finance the project by assessing each homeowner in Baskin Ridge $10,000, payable over a 10-year period.

79. Scott is single and wants to maximize his retirement income. He contributes the maximum allowable to his company's qualified pension plan. His adjusted gross income for the year is $80,000.

# TECHNOLOGY APPLICATIONS

Tax Simulation

80. Sam, the owner of The Perfect Cut, a wholesale meat distributor, unexpectedly dies during the current year. In an effort to provide equally for his two children, Sam's will provides that the entire business less 40 percent of its accounts receivables be left to his daughter Helen. Sam's son, Phil, is to receive the other 40 percent of the business's receivables and the majority of Sam's other assets. The following year, after extensive legal action, Phil is unable to collect a $5,000 receivable from his father's business and the receivable is deemed worthless.

REQUIRED: Determine how Phil should treat the worthless receivable on his tax return. Search a tax research database and find the relevant authority(ies) that form the basis for your answer. Your answer should include the exact text of the authority(ies) and an explanation of the application of the authority to Phil's facts. If there is any uncertainty about the validity of your answer, indicate the cause for the uncertainty.

Research Skills

81. Pierre is a certified high school teacher in Kansas. During the year, his wife's employer transfers her to New Jersey. In applying for a job in New Jersey, Pierre is informed that he will be granted only a 6-month provisional teaching certificate unless he completes two additional math courses. During the summer, Pierre completes the two courses at a local university and receives his teaching certificate. Can he deduct the cost of the courses as an education expense?

Research Skills

82. Evander, an officer in the Marine Corps, was appointed commanding officer of the Marine training base in Beaufort, S.C. As is customary in connection with changes in command, he hosts a party at his home for officers and guests the night before he assumes command of the base. Can Evander deduct the cost of the party as an entertainment expense?

Tax Form

83. Stephanie Zane is the sole proprietor of Shear Madness, a hair salon. Her revenue comes from two sources, haircuts and the sale of hair products. Stephanie has three employees whose compensation consists of a weekly salary and a 40 percent commission on the services they provide to the customer. Stephanie uses a hybrid method of accounting—the cash method for haircuts and the accrual method for sales of hair products. For the current year she has the following revenue and expenses:

| | |
|---|---|
| Revenue from haircuts | $141,650 |
| Revenue from the sale of products | 36,240 |
| Beginning inventory of product | 1,756 |
| Ending inventory of product | 1,469 |
| Product purchased | 18,345 |
| Gross salaries (including commission) | 66,000 |
| Social Security taxes | 5,049 |
| Employee withholding: | |
| Social Security taxes | 5,049 |
| Federal taxes | 15,200 |
| State taxes | 4,200 |
| Other payroll taxes | 375 |
| Advertising | 1,200 |
| Rent | 12,100 |
| Utilities | 1,600 |
| Phone | 570 |
| Postage | 220 |
| Accounting fees | 1,200 |
| Legal fees | 625 |

Complete Form 1040 Schedule C (Profit or Loss From Business) and Form 1040 Schedule SE (Self-Employment Tax) using the above information. Stephanie's Social Security number is 123-62-7897, her employer ID number is 05-9987561, and her business address is 99 Fortin Lane, Metuchen, New Jersey 07865. Forms and instructions can be downloaded from the IRS website (www.irs.gov).

# INTEGRATIVE PROBLEM

84. Rufus and Rhonda are a married couple with three dependent children, all under 16 years of age. Rufus, 46, is an executive with Plowshare Corporation. Rhonda, 39, is a self-employed attorney.

Rufus receives an annual salary of $78,000. He participates in Plowshare's qualified pension plan by contributing 4 percent of his annual salary, which is matched by Plowshare. Rufus also receives group term life insurance at twice his annual salary. The coverage costs Plowshare $2,100. All employees are covered by a medical insurance policy. (Rufus's policy costs $2,300.) He also participates in the company's flexible benefits plan by paying $200 per month into the plan. During the year, Rufus submits claims totaling $1,800 to the plan. An additional benefit that only top-level executives such as Rufus enjoy is the payment of $2,300 in country club dues by Plowshare. Although Rufus occasionally entertains clients at the club, his primary use of the facility is personal.

Rhonda bills clients a total of $125,000 for services rendered during the current year. She receives $17,000 in payments from billings in prior years and $87,000 from current-year billings. Rhonda pays the following expenses related to her legal practice:

| | | |
|---|---|---|
| Office rent | | $14,400 |
| Secretary's salary | | 24,000 |
| Withholdings from secretary's salary: | | |
| Federal income taxes | $2,250 | |
| State income taxes | 520 | |
| Social Security taxes | 1,836 | 4,606 |
| Matching Social Security tax payment | | 1,836 |
| Cost of business meals in restaurants | | 4,000 |
| Seminar costs | | 1,155 |
| Insurance on building—2 years prepaid on August 1 | | 1,600 |
| Supplies | | 2,250 |
| Bar association dues | | 600 |
| State licensing fee | | 725 |
| Automobile costs | | 4,700 |
| Business gifts | | 850 |
| Salary paid to Rhonda | | 64,000 |
| Salary paid to Rhonda's son | | 2,500 |

In addition to these out-of-pocket costs, Rhonda determines that $2,400 in accounts receivable from previous years' billings are uncollectible.

Rhonda uses her automobile extensively in her business. She keeps a log to record business miles and related costs. Her records show that she drove 10,000 business miles and 3,000 personal miles during the current year. In past years, she had always kept track of her business miles but failed to keep an accurate record of her actual costs. Accordingly, her records indicate that she has never depreciated any of the $26,000 cost of the automobile she purchased two years ago—she has used the standard mileage rate method.

Every year, Rhonda gives her top eight clients a gift to thank them for their support of her practice. This year, she gives each client a marble paperweight engraved with the client's name. Each paperweight costs $75 plus $5 for engraving and $5 for gift wrapping.

The seminar costs relate to a three-day meeting in New York on a legal topic involving her biggest client. Because of a special airline promotion, she takes along her 16-year-old son free. However, she has to pay $200 per night for her hotel room instead of the $175 per night single rate. A summary of the seminar costs is as follows:

| | |
|---|---|
| Airfare | $325 |
| Lodging (3 nights @ $200 each) | 600 |
| Meals (including $80 for her son) | 200 |
| Taxi to and from the airport | 30 |

Rhonda pays the $2,500 salary to her son for cleaning up after the open house reception. Although she could hire a service to do the job for $400, he needs the money to buy a used motorcycle.

Rufus is hit by a car one morning while he is out jogging. The driver is at fault, and his insurance company pays Rufus $8,000 for his pain and suffering and $13,000 of his $15,500 medical expenses. The remaining medical expenses are paid by Plowshare's medical insurance policy. Rufus also receives $2,650 in disability pay from the Plowshare policy for the time he misses from work recovering from the injury.

Rufus and Rhonda have the following investment-related items during the current year:

| | |
|---|---|
| Interest on savings account | $ 1,900 |
| Interest on Puerto Rico development bonds | 7,000 |
| Cash dividends on stock | 3,200 |
| Stock dividend shares | |
| (300 shares received when the market value of the stock was $40 per share) | 12,000 |

Early in the year, Rhonda inherits 900 shares of stock from her grandmother. The total value of the shares is $16,000. Later in the year, the stock value begins to fall rapidly, and she sells the shares at a $4,500 loss.

Rufus and Rhonda own a cabin in the mountains. They use it on weekends and for short holidays and rent it out whenever they can. During the current year, they use the cabin 25 days and rent it out 75 days. The details on the cabin income and expenses are as follows:

| | |
|---|---|
| Rental income | $10,000 |
| Mortgage interest | 9,000 |
| Property taxes | 2,300 |
| Utilities and maintenance | 840 |
| Depreciation (unallocated) | 7,500 |

In addition, Rufus and Rhonda have $19,220 in other allowable itemized deductions. Based on the information provided, calculate Rufus and Rhonda's taxable income and their tax liability. Assume that they are cash basis taxpayers and want to be as aggressive as possible in taking their allowable deductions.

# DISCUSSION CASES

85. Norman was the sole shareholder and operator of two successful video arcades. While he was in the hospital with heart problems, his wife, Helen, filed for divorce and took a number of legal steps, including obtaining a temporary restraining order against him to gain control of his businesses. In addition, Helen and her boyfriend fired the two corporations' employees, and took cash and equipment from the businesses.

    When Norman got out of the hospital, he engaged a law firm to help him regain possession of his businesses and recover the assets his wife took, and to represent him in the divorce action. Norman incurred $65,000 in legal fees in trying to get back his business and the divorce action. Are his legal fees deductible?

86. Felix and Ismael were college roommates. Five years after they graduate, Ismael is a tax manager in a large public accounting firm, and Felix is still in his first job as an engineer for a construction company. Felix is not sure whether he wants to stay in engineering or change careers. Either way, he knows he will need to take some courses at the local university. While reading the Sunday paper, Felix notices an ad for the university: "Enroll now: The cost of post-baccalaureate courses is tax-deductible!" The small print advises, "Consult your tax adviser about the deductibility of each course."

    Felix calls Ismael the next day. After he explains that he may pursue a new career, Ismael explains to Felix under what circumstances education expenses are deductible. If you were Ismael, what would you have said to Felix?

# TAX PLANNING CASES

87. In 2019, Samantha loaned her friend Lo Ping $15,000. The loan required Lo Ping to pay interest at 8 percent per year and to pay back the $15,000 loan principal on July 31, 2021. Lo Ping used the loan to start a clothing store. Lo Ping paid Samantha interest on the loan in 2019 and 2020. Although her store appeared to be very successful, her accountant continued to inform her that her business was barely making a profit because of its "high cost structure." In early 2021, Lo Ping became suspicious of her accountant's claims and hired a local CPA firm to examine her accounting records. The CPA firm discovered that Lo Ping's accountant had embezzled $30,000. As a result, Lo Ping had to file for bankruptcy. It is estimated that Samantha will receive 30 percent of the amount she loaned Lo Ping and that the bankruptcy proceedings will conclude in either December 2021 or January 2022. Samantha also is considering whether to sell 200 shares of stock in late 2021 or early 2022. The shares are expected to generate a $2,500 loss. This is the only sale of stock Samantha anticipates making. Explain to Samantha why it is important to determine the date that the bankruptcy proceedings will be concluded before selling her 200 shares of stock.

88. Harold and Maude are both 55 years of age and have two married children. Harold is an engineer and is an active participant in his company's qualified pension plan. Maude is a retired school teacher and works for an educational nonprofit

organization. Harold and Maude plan to retire at age 60 and relocate to South Carolina. Because the nonprofit organization does not have a qualified pension plan for its employees, Maude must decide whether to set up a conventional deductible IRA or a Roth IRA. With either IRA, she plans on making the maximum allowable contribution for each of the next five years and does not anticipate making any contributions after retiring. Harold and Maude will not draw on the account until they are age 65. At that time, they plan to draw down the fund balance equally over a 10-year period to use for trips with their children and grandchildren. Determine whether Maude will have more funds available for her trips with a conventional deductible IRA or a Roth IRA. In making this determination, assume the following:

- Any current tax savings from a deductible IRA will be invested in a tax-free municipal bond fund that will earn 4 percent annually until age 65
- The earnings on either IRA account will be 6 percent annually until age 65
- Their marginal tax rate will be 22 percent while both are working and 12 percent when they retire
- Their adjusted gross income is expected to be less than $150,000 for each year that they are both working

# ETHICS DISCUSSION CASE

89. Tom is a CPA for a large regional firm. In preparing the tax return for Espresso Industries, he notices that the firm has an unusually high amount of travel and meal expenses. Therefore, he decides to examine the supporting documentation. In doing so, Tom notices that the business purpose for many of the meals is not provided. When Tom questions Frank, the company controller, Frank assures him that all the meal expenses are legitimate. After further examination, Tom finds that for every business day in June, July, and August, four of the corporation's senior officers have been reimbursed for their lunch and dinner costs. He confronts Frank and the assistant controller, Doug, with this information. He informs Frank that his firm will not prepare the return unless the meals that do not have a business purpose are omitted. Frank, angered by Tom's decision, tells Tom to prepare the return and that he will take it from there. The following Saturday, Tom is playing golf with Doug and asks him what Frank means by his remarks. Doug tells Tom that Frank will simply replace Tom's number with one that includes the entire meal expense. Can Tom prepare the tax return, knowing that the company will change the meal expense? If he does prepare the return, what ethical standards refer to Statements on Standards for Tax Services, which can be found at www.aicpa.org.com if any, has Tom violated? Assume that Tom prepares the return. If asked, should he prepare next year's return?

# Losses—Deductions and Limitations

7

Learning Objectives:

LO 1 Explain the difference between an annual loss and a transaction loss.

LO 2 Determine the tax treatment of annual net operating losses.

LO 3 Describe the general operation of a tax shelter.

LO 4 Explain the at-risk rules and how they limit annual loss deductions.

LO 5 Describe passive losses and how they limit annual loss deductions.

LO 6 Identify the limitations on the deductibility of passive losses incurred in nonreal estate activities.

LO 7 Explain the limitations on the deductibility of passive losses incurred in real estate activities.

LO 8 Determine the general tax treatment of transaction losses incurred in a trade or business.

LO 9 Explain the tax treatment of business casualty and theft losses.

LO 10 Explain the tax treatment of transaction losses incurred in production-of-income activities, including wash sales, small business stock, and related party sales.

LO 11 Determine the tax treatment of transaction losses incurred in a personal activity.

LO 12 Describe the tax treatment for personal casualty losses.

## concept review

### GENERAL CONCEPTS

**Ability to pay** A tax should be based on the amount that the taxpayer can afford to pay, relative to other taxpayers. pg. 2-2

**Administrative convenience** Those items for which the cost of compliance would exceed the revenue generated are not taxed. pg. 2-3

**Related party** Family members and corporations that are owned by family members are considered related parties, as are certain other relationships between entities in which the power to control the substance of a transaction is evidenced through majority ownership. pg. 2-4

### ACCOUNTING CONCEPTS

**Annual accounting period** All tax entities must report the results of their operations on an annual basis (the tax year). Each year stands on its own, apart from other tax years. pg. 2-9

**Entity** All items of income, deduction, and so on are traced to the tax unit responsible for the item. pg. 2-6

**Substance over form** Transactions are to be taxed according to their true intention rather than some form that may have been contrived. pg. 2-11

**Tax benefit rule** Any deduction taken in a prior year that is recovered in a subsequent year is income in the year of recovery, to the extent that a tax benefit was received from the deduction. pg. 2-10

### INCOME CONCEPTS

**Basis** This is the amount of unrecovered investment in an asset. As amounts are expended and/or recovered relative to an asset over time, the basis is adjusted in consideration of such changes. The **adjusted basis** of an asset is the original basis, plus or minus the changes in the amount of unrecovered investment. pgs. 2-13, 2-21

**Capital recovery** No income is realized until the taxpayer receives more than the amount invested to produce the income. The amount invested in an asset represents the maximum amount recoverable. pg. 2-13

**Realization** No income or loss is recognized until it has been realized. A realization involves a change in the form and/or substance of a taxpayer's property rights that results from an arm's-length transaction. pg. 2-14

### DEDUCTION CONCEPTS

**Business purpose** To be deductible, an expenditure or a loss must have a business or other economic purpose that exceeds any tax avoidance motive. The primary motive for the transaction must be to make a profit. pg. 2-18

**Legislative grace** Any tax relief provided is the result of a specific act of Congress that must be strictly applied and interpreted. All income received is taxable unless a specific provision in the tax law excludes the income from taxation. Deductions must be approached with the philosophy that nothing is deductible unless a provision in the tax law allows the deduction. pg. 2-12

## 7-1 INTRODUCTION

LO 1
Explain the difference between an annual loss and a transaction loss.

The tax law allows the deduction of certain types of losses in the calculation of taxable income. The deductibility of losses is a matter of legislative grace and is based on the ability-to-pay concept. The reasoning behind deductions and losses is similar. In fact, many classification rules for deductions also apply to losses.

How are losses different from deductions? Deductions are the current expenditures (and amortization or depreciation of capital expenditures) made for the production of current period income. Losses can result when an entity's deductions for the period exceed the income generated (i.e., a negative income for the period). This type of loss is referred to as an *annual loss*, or *activity loss.*

**Example 1** Emma owns a restaurant. During the current year, she has gross income of $74,000 and allowable deductions related to the business of $90,000. What is Emma's income from the restaurant?

**Discussion: Emma has suffered a business loss of $16,000 ($74,000 – $90,000). This loss is an annual loss created by an excess of allowable deductions over income.**

**Note that Emma can have more than one annual loss if she engages in multiple activities. Remember that the results of each entity must be kept separate from all other entities for recording and reporting purposes. In this case, Emma would combine the allowable loss from her restaurant business with her income and deductions from her other activities on her individual tax return.**

In contrast to an annual loss, a loss can also occur as a result of the disposition of an asset. An asset that is disposed of at less than its basis creates a loss that represents the taxpayer's unrecovered capital investment. This type of loss is referred to as a *transaction loss.*

**Example 2** Alfred purchases 50 shares of Inventor, Inc., common stock for $5,000 in 2020. He sells the 50 shares for $4,400 in 2021. What are the tax effects for Alfred of his investment in the Inventor, Inc., stock?

**Discussion: Alfred has a loss of $600 ($4,400 – $5,000) on the sale of the stock in 2021. The loss represents Alfred's basis in the stock that was not recovered when he disposed of the stock.**

Figure 7-1 outlines the general scheme for the treatment of losses. The first requirement is that a realization of the loss must have occurred. The realized loss may be either an annual loss or a transaction loss.

*Figure 7-1*

**General Scheme for Treatment of Losses**

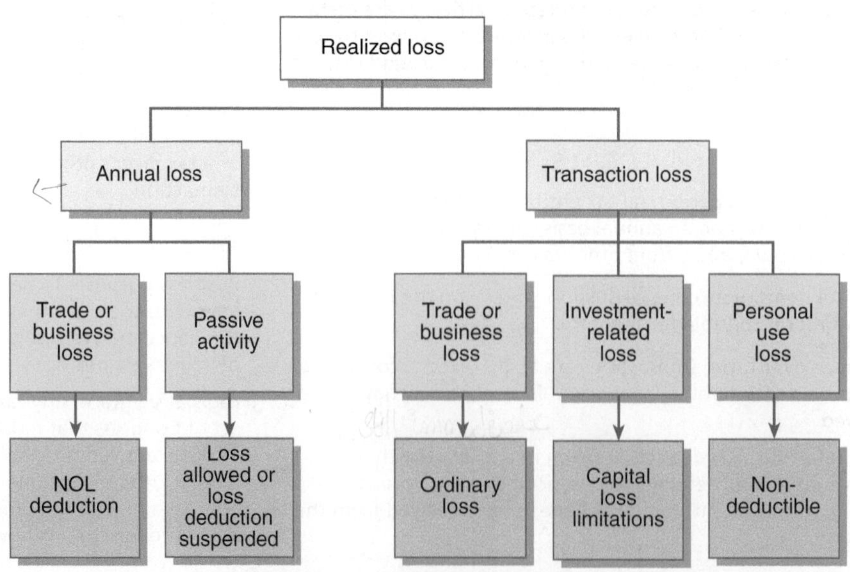

Under the business purpose concept, only losses that result from a profit-motivated transaction or venture are deductible. Thus, annual loss deductions are allowed only for activities that constitute a trade or business. Note in Figure 7-1 that an annual loss incurred in a passive activity is not generally allowed as a deduction. Thus, it is important to distinguish those activities that constitute a trade or business from those that are passive.

The tax treatment of transaction losses depends on the source of the loss. As a result, transaction losses are classified as related to a trade or business, an income-producing activity, or a personal use. Once a loss has been properly categorized, the rules for deductibility are applied by category, as with deductions. Figure 7-1 shows the general difference in treatments among the three categories of transaction losses. That is, all losses incurred in a trade or business are fully deductible. Losses incurred in an income-producing activity are subject to the capital loss limitations. Losses on personal use of property are generally disallowed. Thus, the general approach to the treatment of transaction losses is similar to the approach to deductions, as discussed in Chapter 5.

The purpose of this chapter is to discuss the tax treatment(s) of the most common types of losses. As with most areas of the tax law, there are exceptions to the general treatment of losses, which are outlined in Figure 7-1. The more important of these exceptions are discussed later in the chapter.

## 7-2 ANNUAL LOSSES

**Annual losses** result from an excess of deductions over income. The only deductions allowed for annual losses are for those incurred in a trade or business. Taxpayers who have annual activities with a significant personal use element (hobbies, vacation homes, home offices) are not allowed to deduct expenses in excess of income. As a result, the two primary types of annual losses are net operating losses (NOLs) and passive activity losses. Figure 7-2 outlines the treatment of annual losses. When an annual loss is realized, the key question is whether the taxpayer materially participates in the operation of the business. If the taxpayer does not materially participate in the business, the passive activity loss rules apply. If the taxpayer does materially participate in the business reporting the

*Figure 7-2*

### Treatment of Annual Losses

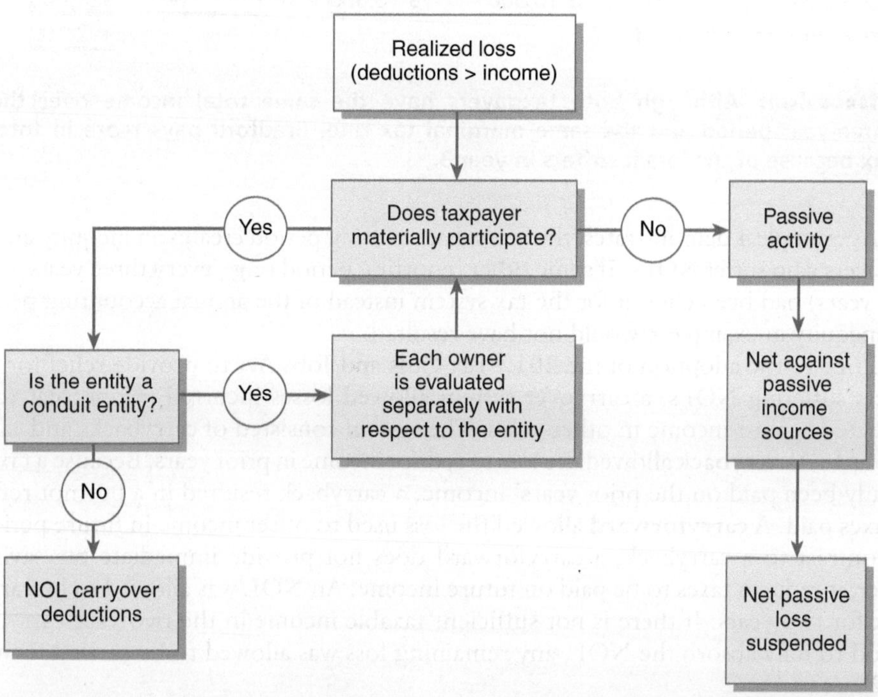

loss, a net operating loss deduction is usually allowed. However, if the entity that owns the activity is a conduit entity, the loss flows through to the owner(s) of the entity, and the material participation test is repeated with regard to each owner's share of the loss.

## 7-3 NET OPERATING LOSSES

LO 2 Determine the tax treatment of annual net operating losses.

A **net operating loss (NOL)** is an annual loss incurred in a trade or business in which the taxpayer materially participates. It results from an excess of allowable deductions over income for the accounting period.

**Example 3** Pete is the sole proprietor of Pete's Pizza Parlor. During the current year, the pizza parlor has income of $80,000 and deductions of $100,000, resulting in a net operating loss of $20,000. What is the treatment of the loss?

**Discussion: Although not a true conduit entity, the loss from the pizza parlor flows through to the owner, Pete, and is reported on his return. Pete is allowed to deduct the $20,000 loss from the pizza parlor against his other sources of income.**

What happens when a taxable entity has an NOL? Because a taxable entity (i.e., an individual or a corporation) pays tax on the income it generates, it would pay no tax for the year in which an NOL occurs. Taxable entities are not allowed to pass the loss through to their owners for deduction. With no relief from this situation, taxable entities are at a distinct disadvantage.

**Example 4** Consider the following taxable income (losses) for taxpayers Alston Company (Taxpayer A) and Bradford Company (Taxpayer B), both of whom are taxable entities for a 3-year period. The marginal tax rate for both entities is 21% over the three years.

| | Year 1 | Year 2 | Year 3 | Total |
|---|---|---|---|---|
| **Taxpayer A** | $ 30,000 | $ 30,000 | $ 30,000 | $90,000 |
| Tax rate | × 21% | × 21% | × 21% | |
| Taxes paid | $ 6,300 | $ 6,300 | $ 6,300 | $18,900 |
| **Taxpayer B** | $ 50,000 | $ 50,000 | $(10,000) | $90,000 |
| Tax rate | × 21% | × 21% | × 21% | |
| Taxes paid | $ 10,500 | $ 10,500 | $ -0- | $21,000 |
| **Difference in taxes paid** | | | | 2,100 |

**Discussion: Although both taxpayers have the same total income over the three-year period and the same marginal tax rate, Bradford pays more in total tax because of the loss it suffers in year 3.**

As example 4 demonstrates, the annual accounting period creates an inequity among taxpayers who suffer NOLs. If some other reporting period (e.g., every three years, every four years) had been chosen for the tax system instead of the annual accounting period, the inequity in example 4 would not have resulted.

Prior to the adoption of the 2017 Tax Cuts and Jobs Act to provide relief for taxpayers suffering NOLs, a carryover system allowed losses incurred in one year to be deducted against income in other years. The system consisted of carrybacks and carryforwards. A **carryback** allowed the loss to reduce income in prior years. Because a tax has already been paid on the prior years' income, a carryback resulted in a prompt refund of taxes paid. A **carryforward** allowed the loss used to offset income in future periods. In contrast to a carryback, a carryforward does not provide immediate tax savings; rather, it reduces taxes to be paid on future income. An NOL was allowed to be carried back for two years. If there is not sufficient taxable income in the two-year carryback period to fully absorb the NOL, any remaining loss was allowed to be carried forward for 20 years.[1]

**Example 5** What was the tax treatment of Bradford's $10,000 loss under prior law?

| | Year 1 | Year 2 | Year 3 | Total |
|---|---|---|---|---|
| Income | $50,000 | $50,000 | ($10,000) | $90,000 |
| Less: NOL | $(10,000) | | | |
| Tax rate | × 21% | × 21% | × 21% | |
| Income after NOL | $40,000 | | | |
| Tax rate | × 21% | | | |
| Taxes paid | $ 8,400 | $10,500 | $ -0- | $18,900 |

**Discussion: While Bradford initially paid taxes of $10,500 in year 1, when the loss occurred in year 3, it was allowed to carryback that loss to reduce its taxes to $8.400 and receive a tax refund of $2,100. The effect of the carryback of the NOL was to equalize the taxes paid by Alston and Bradford. After the carryback, Alston and Bradford paid the same tax over the 3-year period.**

However, with the adoption of the 2017 Tax Cuts and Jobs Act (TCJA), a taxpayer is no longer allowed to carryback an NOL and can only carry forward the loss. While the losses can now be carried forward indefinitely, the new law only allows a taxpayer to offset 80 percent of the current years' taxable income with the carryforward loss. The new NOL rules are effective for tax years beginning after December 31, 2017, and apply to all corporations except real estate investment trusts and property and casualty companies.

**Example 6** The Daffron Corporation, a calendar year taxpayer, was incorporated in 2020 and had operating income of $25,000. The company incurred a net operating loss of $35,000 in 2021 and had operating income in 2022 of $40,000. Assume that the tax rate for all 3 years is 21%. What is the treatment of the 2020 loss?

**Discussion: For tax years after December 31, 2017, a taxpayer that incurs an NOL is not permitted to carry that loss back to offset prior years' income but rather can only carry the NOL forward. In addition, the maximum amount of income that can be offset from that carryforward loss is limited to 80% of taxable income. Therefore, over the 3-year period, Daffron's total tax liability is $6,930, and it has an NOL carryforward of $3,000.**

| | 2020 | 2021 | 2022 |
|---|---|---|---|
| Income before limitation | $25,000 | $(35,000) | $40,000) |
| Less: NOL limited to 80% | - | - | (32,000) |
| Income after NOL | $25,000 | $ -0- | $ 8,000 |
| Tax rate | × 21% | × 21% | × 21% |
| Tax paid | $ 5,250 | $ -0- | $ 1,680 |
| NOL Carryforward to 2022 | | | $ 3,000 |

Under the prior law, Daffron would have been allowed to carryback $25,000 of the 2021 loss to 2020 and receive a refund of the $5,250 taxes paid in 2020. In addition, Daffron would have carried forward the remaining NOL of $10,000 ($35,000 – $25,000), to offset the $40,000 of income in 2022 and its tax liability would have been $6,300 ($30,000 × 21 percent). Daffron's tax liability under the new law is $630 ($6,930 – $6,300) more than under the prior law. It should be noted that the 2020 Cares Act created a special provision for NOLs arising in tax years beginning after December 31, 2017, but before January 1, 2021. The NOLs can be carried back to each of the five tax years preceding the tax year of such loss. In addition, the CARES Act temporarily removes the 80% limitation and allows 100% of the NOL to be used.

Several additional problems need to be considered in regard to NOLs. First, what happens when losses from a conduit entity cause an individual taxpayer to have a negative taxable income? The tax return of an individual contains a mixture of business-related and specifically allowed personal itemized deductions or a standard deduction. Because an NOL can be caused only by a business loss, a negative individual taxable income does not necessarily mean that the taxpayer has an NOL from a trade or business for the year. To determine whether an individual does have an NOL, a complex set of adjustments is made to the negative taxable income figure. The complexity of these adjustments is beyond the scope of this textbook and is omitted from the discussion.

**concept check**

To deduct an annual loss, the *business purpose concept* requires the activity to have a business or other economic purpose that exceeds any tax avoidance motive. In addition, the primary motive for the activity must be to make a profit. The *annual accounting period concept* requires all entities to report the results of operations on an annual basis. The problem with following this concept is that two companies could report the same total operating income over a 3-year period yet one could pay more in taxes during the period than the other. This would occur if one company reports operating income in all three years while the other reports a higher income in two of the years but a loss in the third. Under the *ability to pay concept*, an entity's tax liability should be based on the amount the taxpayer can afford to pay, relative to other taxpayers. Through the *legislative grace concept*, Congress specifically allows an entity to offset an annual business loss from 1 year against its business income indefinitely. However, a taxpayer can only offset 80 percent of the current years' taxable income.

## 7-4 TAX-SHELTER LOSSES: AN OVERVIEW

LO 3

Describe the general operation of a tax shelter.

In its broadest application, the term **tax shelter** refers to any investment activity that is designed to minimize the effect of the income tax on wealth accumulation. Under this definition, an investment in tax-exempt municipal bonds would be viewed as a tax shelter. However, in tax practice, the term is generally applied to investments that produce significant tax losses as a result of the allowable deductions associated with the investment. These losses are then used to offset taxable income from other income sources. The losses from the investment "shelter" a portion (or all) of the other sources of income from taxation. The taxpayer investing in such a shelter will have to pay a tax on the investment when it is sold. However, the deduction of losses from the shelter in tax years before the payment of tax on the gain presents a time value of money savings opportunity.

A taxpayer is allowed to take advantage of the provisions for deductions and losses to legitimately reduce taxable income (i.e., tax avoidance is legal). In the late 1960s and early 1970s, many high-income taxpayers made substantial investments in tax shelters to reduce their income from other sources. In a typical tax shelter, the taxpayer would invest an amount in the activity. In return, the taxpayer would be allowed to deduct a share of the losses generated by the activity on her or his individual return, reducing the tax paid on other forms of income such as salaries and investment income. The amount of the deduction provided by a tax shelter could vary from three to ten times the amount invested. For a $10,000 investment, the taxpayer could take loss deductions totaling $30,000 to $100,000. During this period, the highest marginal tax rate was 50 percent. Thus, a high marginal rate taxpayer making a $10,000 investment could be guaranteed a tax savings from the investment ranging from $15,000 to $50,000. Because of this return from saving taxes, taxpayers often made investments in tax shelters that had little or no hope of long-term economic success. The tax savings provided a high enough return that success of the venture was unimportant. Many tax shelters were activities that were not economically viable investments in the absence of the tax deductions.

In 1976 Congress reacted to this perceived abuse of tax shelters with several measures, including limitations on investment interest deductions (discussed in Chapter 8) and a set of at-risk rules to limit the amount of loss deductible. However, these limitations met with limited success, because promoters of tax shelters and their clever tax advisers found ways to work around them. As a result, offerings of publicly registered tax shelters doubled in the early 1980s.

In 1986 Congress took additional action against tax shelters by severely limiting the deductions on tax shelters through enactment of the passive activity loss rules. The basic passive loss rule disallows the deduction of current period passive losses against active and portfolio income sources (e.g., salaries, trade or business income, interest, dividends). These rules are in some cases unduly complex and in other cases have hindered investment in legitimate economic investments.

In the sections that follow, the at-risk rules, which limit the amount of any deductible loss to the amount that the taxpayer has at risk in the activity, are discussed first. Then, the basic operation of the passive loss rules is presented and discussed to provide an understanding of how these important limitations on losses affect investments made by taxpayers.

A few basic aspects of tax shelters should be clarified before proceeding. First, many tax advantages that allow such activities to generate losses are the result of a conscious effort by Congress to attract investment capital to activities with a high national priority and/or a high degree of risk. The basic intent of the generous tax laws is to provide incentive to taxpayers to engage in activities that they ordinarily would reject because of either low returns or high risk.

A limited partnership has many tax and nontax advantages that make it a preferred vehicle for tax shelters. The flow-through of the income and deductions of a partnership to the owners allows investment by many individuals who have no actual involvement in the tax shelter's business activities. In addition, it is often possible to make special allocations of income and expense items, which let the partnership confer many of the special tax deductions on the tax shelter's investors. A partnership also can be structured to accept investors as limited partners, so that their maximum loss from the activity is the amount of their investment in the property. Finally, a partner's tax basis in the investment includes the partner's share of its outstanding liabilities (discussed in Chapter 13). This can significantly increase the amount of loss that can be deducted by the partners under the at-risk rules.

## 7-4a The At-Risk Rules

LO 4 Explain the at-risk rules and how they limit annual loss deductions.

Congress enacted the at-risk rules to disallow the deduction of artificial losses generated by tax-shelter investments. The intention of the **at-risk rules** is to limit loss deductions by individuals and closely held corporations on business and investment-related activities to the amount of the taxpayer's actual economic investment. This is done by limiting the current year's loss deduction to the amount that the taxpayer has at risk in the activity.[2] The computation of the amount at risk is presented in Exhibit 7-1.

*Exhibit 7-1*

### Computation of Amount at Risk

| | |
|---|---|
| **Items That Increase Amount at Risk:** | |
| Cash invested by the taxpayer in the activity | $ XXX |
| Adjusted basis of property contributed to the activity | XXX |
| Amounts borrowed for use in the activity for which the taxpayer is personally liable | XXX |
| Amounts borrowed for use in the activity for which the taxpayer has pledged property not used in the activity as security | XXX |
| The taxpayer's share of any income produced by the activity | XXX |
| **Items That Decrease Amount at Risk:** | |
| The taxpayer's share of any loss produced by the activity | (XXX) |
| Withdrawals of assets from the activity | (XXX) |
| Equals: The amount at risk in the activity | $ XXX |

A brief review of Exhibit 7-1 clarifies what it means to "be at risk." From the computation, the at-risk amount is equal to cash or other assets that have been contributed to the activity. In addition, any debts of the activity for which the taxpayer would be responsible if the activity could not pay them are also considered to be at risk. Thus, the amount at risk in an activity is the maximum amount of personal funds (assets) that could be lost if the activity failed.

**Example 7** Jolene purchases a business for $200,000 by investing $20,000 of her own funds and borrowing $180,000 from State Bank. She is personally liable for repayment of the loan to State Bank. What is Jolene's at-risk amount in the business?

**Discussion: Jolene is at risk for $200,000. If the business is not successful, she stands to lose the $20,000 in cash she invested and would be liable for payment of the $180,000 loan. Thus, she can lose a maximum of $200,000 from her investment in the business.**

The amount at risk is also adjusted for the taxpayer's share of the income (loss) from the activity and reduced by withdrawals from the activity. That is, when an activity has income that is taxed to the taxpayer, the income becomes subject to loss. Similarly, losses from the activity that are deducted by the taxpayer reduce the amount that the taxpayer has to lose. Any amounts that are withdrawn from the activity by the taxpayer are no longer subject to loss and reduce the amount at risk in the activity.

**Example 8** During the first year, Jolene operates the business she purchased in example 7, she suffers a loss of $70,000. She also withdraws $40,000 from the business for her personal use. What is Jolene's at-risk amount in the business at the end of the first year of operation?

**Discussion: Jolene has a sufficient amount at risk to enable her to deduct the loss from the business. Therefore, she must reduce her amount at risk by the $70,000 loss. In addition, the $40,000 withdrawn from the business is no longer at risk. Thus, her amount at risk has declined to $90,000 ($200,000 − $70,000 − $40,000) at the end of the first year of operation.**

In many cases, a taxpayer's amount at risk in an activity is the same as the taxpayer's adjusted basis. A main difference between a taxpayer's adjusted basis in an activity and the amount at risk in an activity occurs when basis is financed by nonrecourse debt. A **nonrecourse debt** is a liability that is secured only by the underlying property. The borrower is not personally liable for the debt.

**Example 9** Assume that Jolene purchases $40,000 worth of equipment by borrowing from Local Bank. Local Bank makes the loan with the equipment as the security for the debt. Jolene is not personally liable for the debt. How are Jolene's basis and at-risk amount affected by the purchase of the equipment?

**Discussion: Jolene obtains a basis of $40,000 in the equipment. However, because she is not personally liable for the debt incurred to finance the purchase, she is not at risk with respect to the debt. That is, if her business fails, she will not be personally liable for repayment of the debt. Therefore, her at-risk amount does not increase.**

A major exception to the at-risk rules is made for nonrecourse financing of real estate operations. Before 1987, the at-risk rules did not apply to real estate activities. In 1986, the at-risk rules were extended to real estate activities to a limited extent. After 1987, nonrecourse financing is considered at risk if the taxpayer is either engaged in the trade or business of holding real property or is holding the real property for the production of income. In addition, the debt must be secured by the real property used in the activity and must be made on reasonably commercial terms. A business qualifies as holding real property if it owns personal property and provides services that are incidental to making the property available as living accommodations. For example, if the taxpayer owns an apartment building or a hotel, any nonrecourse debt that is secured by the apartment building or the hotel is considered to be at-risk. In most cases, this lets shelter activities acquire real estate with nonrecourse financing, which is considered at risk by the investors in the shelter.

**Example 10** Assume that in example 9, Jolene purchases a building for $40,000 with nonrecourse financing. Would the $40,000 be at risk?

**Discussion: The $40,000 is not considered to be at risk because Jolene is not in the trade or business of holding real property nor is she holding the real property for the production of income. Therefore, Jolene's at-risk amount is not increased by the debt.**

**Example 11** Ruben invests $10,000 in the Gold Partnership and receives a 10% interest in the partnership. Gold is a real estate development firm and uses the $50,000 in cash paid in by investors to purchase an apartment building that costs $1,000,000. The remaining $950,000 of the cost of the building is financed by a nonrecourse loan from State Insurance Company. The loan is made on terms comparable to other real estate loans in the area. What is Ruben's at-risk amount in the Gold Partnership?

**Discussion: Ruben's at-risk amount includes the $10,000 cash contribution and his share of the nonrecourse loan. His $95,000 share of the nonrecourse loan ($950,000 × 10%) is considered at risk, because the loan was used in an activity that is in the business of holding real property and was made on reasonably commercial terms. Thus, Ruben's at-risk amount is $105,000 ($10,000 cash investment + $95,000 share of real estate debt).**

Under the at-risk rules, taxpayers cannot deduct any losses in excess of the amount they have at risk in the activity. Any current period losses that are not deductible because they exceed the taxpayer's at-risk amount are carried forward to the next year and are deductible when the taxpayer has enough at risk to allow the deduction.[3]

**Example 12** Return to the facts of example 11. Assume that the Gold Partnership has a loss of $800,000 in the first year of operation and a loss of $600,000 in the second year. How much of the loss can Ruben deduct in each of the first two years?

**Discussion: Ruben's share of the year one loss is $80,000. Because his at-risk amount is $105,000, he can deduct the full $80,000. This will reduce his at-risk amount in the partnership to $25,000 ($105,000 − $80,000). His share of the year 2 loss is $60,000. However, he can deduct only the $25,000 he has at risk. The remaining $35,000 of the loss is carried forward to succeeding years until he has enough at risk to deduct the loss.**

**Although the loss is deductible per the at-risk rules, the passive activity rules still apply. That is, if Ruben's investment in the partnership is considered a passive activity, the $80,000 and $25,000 in losses allowed by the at-risk rules still are subject to restrictions under the passive loss rules.**

## 7-4b Passive Activity Losses

LO 5 Describe passive losses and how they limit annual loss deductions.

Although the at-risk rules provide some measure of protection against the deduction of artificial losses created by tax shelters, Congress felt that the rules still allowed too much room for abuse and promoted investment in ventures based on their tax characteristics rather than their economic potential. In 1986 Congress enacted the **passive activity loss (PAL) rules**, effective for tax years after 1986. The basic intent of these rules is to disallow the deduction of losses from passive activities against other forms of income. Thus, passive activity losses cannot generally be used to shelter other sources of income. Even the basic operation of the passive loss rules can be extremely complex, and the complexity of the rules increases as a taxpayer engages in more and more passive activities.

### Passive Activity Definition

A **passive activity** is defined as the conduct of any trade or business in which the taxpayer does not materially participate.[4] In general, to be a **material participant**, the taxpayer must be involved in the operations of the activity on a regular, continuous, and substantial basis. The purpose of the material participation standard is to limit the passive loss deductions of those taxpayers investing in tax shelters who do not participate in the operation of the business in any meaningful way. However, the definition provided by Congress caused severe problems. Consider the following:

**Example 13** Ling works for 20 years to build up her business. During the last 10 years, she reorganizes the business and takes on two partners to help her manage it. Ling retires this year and no longer is involved in the day-to-day operations of the business. In retirement, she will attend one or two meetings a year to discuss general strategy with her partners. She still maintains a 1/3 interest in the partnership. Is Ling's partnership interest a passive activity?

**Discussion: Ling no longer participates in the operation of the business in a material, substantial, and continuous manner. Therefore, under the general definition of material participation, her partnership interest would be considered passive.**

It is doubtful that Congress intended to subject the partnership interest in example 13 to the passive loss rules. In response to numerous other instances of perceived inequities in the definition of material participation, the IRS provided seven tests under which a taxpayer would be considered a material participant in an activity.[5] The two basic tests for **material participation** are that the individual (including the individual's spouse) participates in the activity for more than 500 hours per year, or the taxpayer spends more than 100 hours a year in the activity, and the time spent in the activity is more hours than any other owner or nonowner spends on the activity (known as the 100-hour test). The remaining five tests are based on lower levels of participation, combined with other factors about the operation of the business, that would indicate material participation and special rules to take care of situations such as that in example 13. Because most taxpayers would qualify under these two tests, this book does not discuss the remaining five tests in detail. The determination of material participation under these tests is best left to a tax professional.

Before 1995, Congress defined two particular types of activities as always being passive and two types of activities as never being passive. Rental activities and limited partnership interests were always passive. Today, only working interests in oil and gas deposits are active and not subject to the passive loss rules.

However, since 1995, taxpayers who are involved in real property as a trade or business are permitted, if they meet certain criteria, to treat rental real estate as an active activity. The criteria for and the definition of a *real property trade or business* are discussed later in the chapter. The law has no effect on the treatment of limited partnerships—they still are always considered a passive activity.

**Rental Activities** For purposes of the passive loss rules, a rental activity is always considered a passive activity, except for certain qualifying taxpayers. A **rental activity** is defined as one in which the payment received is primarily for the use of tangible property. Rentals that include significant services are not rental activities for the passive loss rules. The IRS has provided guidelines for determining when the provision of personal services is significant and does not constitute a rental activity for passive loss purposes.[6] Some of the more common forms of this type of rental include

| | |
|---|---|
| Hotel rooms | Hospital rooms |
| Car rentals | Video rentals |
| Clothing rentals | Golf course fees |
| Tool rentals | Automobiles rented by dealers while repair work is done |
| Cable television rentals | |

Although this list is not all-inclusive, it illustrates the basic intent—to exclude rental activities that also provide significant services from the passive loss rules. As long as the owner(s) of such activities meet the material participation standard, the activity is not considered passive. That is, even if the activity is not considered a rental activity, each owner of the activity still must meet the material participation standard for the activity to be considered active.

**Example 14** Toby owns a miniature golf course. He and his wife, Eve, are actively involved in the management of the business. Each devotes an average of 40 hours per week to working at the miniature golf course and performing other business functions (record keeping, bank deposits, etc.). Is the miniature golf course a passive activity for Toby and Eve?

**Discussion: The activity is not a rental activity, because it provides significant personal services. Toby and Eve participate in its operation more than 500 hours per year, making them material participants in the activity. Therefore, the activity is not a passive activity.**

Note that although the activity in example 14 is not a rental activity for purposes of the passive loss rules, Toby and Eve still must meet the material participation standard for their business to escape classification as a passive activity.

**Example 15** Assume that in example 14, the miniature golf course is organized as a partnership. Upon forming the business, Toby and Eve did not have enough capital. Their friend Alan invested $20,000 in the business for a 1/3 interest in the partnership. Toby and Eve run the business. Alan does not have any responsibilities for operating the business. He merely receives his annual share of the partnership's income. Is the miniature golf course a passive activity for Alan?

**Discussion: Although the activity is not considered a rental activity, Alan does not materially participate in it. Therefore, his partnership interest is considered a passive activity.**

**Note that the activity remains an active business interest for Toby and Eve. That is, each taxpayer involved in the activity is evaluated separately. This is a result of the entity concept.**

Given all the exceptions, what is a rental activity for purposes of the passive loss rules? The more common forms of passive activity rentals involve the rental of real property. This would include apartment buildings, rental houses, office building rentals, warehouse rentals, factory rentals, and so on. That is, these activities are all rentals of real property that include no significant provision of personal services.

**Example 16** Both Alf and Bart are lawyers. The two decide to purchase an apartment building in 2020 at a cost of $600,000. Each provides half of the $60,000 down payment. Both are busy practicing law, so they hire Chester to manage the building. Chester has full control over all management decisions (getting tenants, collecting rent, taking care of repairs, etc.). Alf and Bart agree to split the profits evenly after paying Chester's salary of $50,000. Is the building a passive activity for Alf and Bart?

**Discussion: The apartment building is a rental activity for passive loss purposes. It is a rental of tangible property with no significant services provided. Thus, it is a passive activity. This is true for both Alf and Bart.**

**Limited Partnership Interests** A limited partnership interest is generally considered passive. In a **limited partnership**, one general partner organizes the partnership and is usually responsible for the day-to-day operation of its business. Limited partners are investors who purchase their interest to provide capital for the partnership. They generally have no responsibilities for operating the partnership. They merely invest money and receive their share of partnership income or loss. The limited partnership is the most popular tax-shelter vehicle. As a conduit entity, investors in a limited partnership can share in the losses of the tax shelter without any involvement in its operation. Because Congress has specified that limited partnership interests are passive, the degree of participation by a limited partner or the type of activity does not change the passive activity classification. To determine whether the general partner's interest is passive or active, the general partner's participation must be evaluated using the rules for all taxpayers.

**Example 17** Jonah purchases a limited partnership interest for $40,000. Monica is the general partner, oversees the operation of the partnership, and is responsible for its day-to-day operations. Is the activity passive for Jonah? for Monica?

**Discussion: Because Jonah is a limited partner, the activity is passive for him. Monica is a general partner and must be evaluated according to the rules for all taxpayers to determine whether the activity is passive for her. She would appear to meet the material participation standard, making her interest active and not subject to the passive loss rules.**

**Working Interest in Oil and Gas** A working interest in an oil and gas deposit is always considered an active business for purposes of the passive activity rules. A working interest is an outright ownership interest held by the operator of the property. As such, a working interest has unlimited liability for all debts of the operation and is responsible for the costs of operating the property. Royalty interests in the property held by individuals who are not active in its operation are not considered working interests. However, royalty interests in an oil and gas operation would not be passive. They are considered portfolio income, because they share only revenue from the deposit, not expenses from the operation of the oil and gas deposit.

**Example 18** Whitney is the sole proprietor of an oil and gas drilling company. Brooke owns the mineral rights to some land on which Whitney would like to drill for oil. They enter into an agreement whereby Whitney can drill on Brooke's land; Whitney pays Brooke $2,000 for the right to drill and $^{1}/_{12}$ of the value of any oil and gas produced from the well. Whitney is responsible for the payment of all expenses of the operation and retains the remaining value of the oil and gas produced. Is this a passive activity for either Whitney or Brooke?

**Discussion: Because Whitney is the operator of the oil and gas deposit, her interest is a working interest and is always active. Although Brooke is not at all involved in the operation of the deposit, her royalty interest would not be passive because she does not share expenses of the operation. The royalties she receives would be portfolio income.**

**Real Estate Professional Exception** The tax law permits a taxpayer to treat rental real estate in which the taxpayer materially participates as an active activity and to use any losses to offset active and portfolio income. This lets a real estate professional use losses from rental property to offset active and portfolio income (see Figure 7-3). In essence, a taxpayer who qualifies as a real estate professional is permitted to treat the loss from the rental property as a loss from a trade or business (i.e., an active activity).

A taxpayer qualifies under the **real estate professional exception** if:

- More than 50 percent of the taxpayer's total personal services (work) are in real property trades or businesses in which the taxpayer materially participates.
- The taxpayer performs more than 750 hours a year of service in real property trades or businesses in which the taxpayer materially participates.
- The taxpayer materially participates in the rental activity.[7]

As discussed earlier in this chapter, to materially participate in an activity, the taxpayer generally must spend more than 500 hours a year working in that activity or meet the 100-hour test. A **real property trade or business** is any real property development, redevelopment, construction, acquisition, conversion, rental operation, management, leasing, or brokerage trade or business. In addition, an individual who is an employee of a business engaged in a real property trade or business qualifies for this exception only if the employee has an ownership interest in the business that is greater than 5 percent.

**Example 19** Return to the facts of example 16. In 2021, Bart decides to quit practicing law and take Chester's place as the manager of the building. Bart devotes all his personal services, 2,000 hours, to managing the apartments (getting tenants, collecting rent, taking care of repairs, etc.). Alf continues to work as a lawyer. Is the apartment building a passive activity for either of them?

**Discussion: In 2020 the rental activity is passive for both Alf and Bart. Under the real estate professional exception, Bart can treat the rental property as an active activity in 2021. More than 50% of his personal services are devoted to working in a real property trade or business in which he materially participates, the time he devotes to the real property trade or business is more than 750 hours, and he materially participates in the rental activity (spends more than 500 hours working in the activity or meets the 100-hour test). The rental property remains passive for Alf because he fails to meet any of the tests. In fact, Alf does not even materially participate in the rental activity. NOTE: Each individual in the activity is evaluated separately, and the individual must meet all three tests to qualify a rental as an active activity.**

**Example 20** Assume the same facts as in example 19, except that Alf is a real estate broker employed by a corporation in which he owns a 20% interest. He spends 1,800 hours a year as a broker and 200 hours a year helping Bart manage the apartment building.

*Figure 7-3*

## Determining Whether Rental Property Is Active or Passive

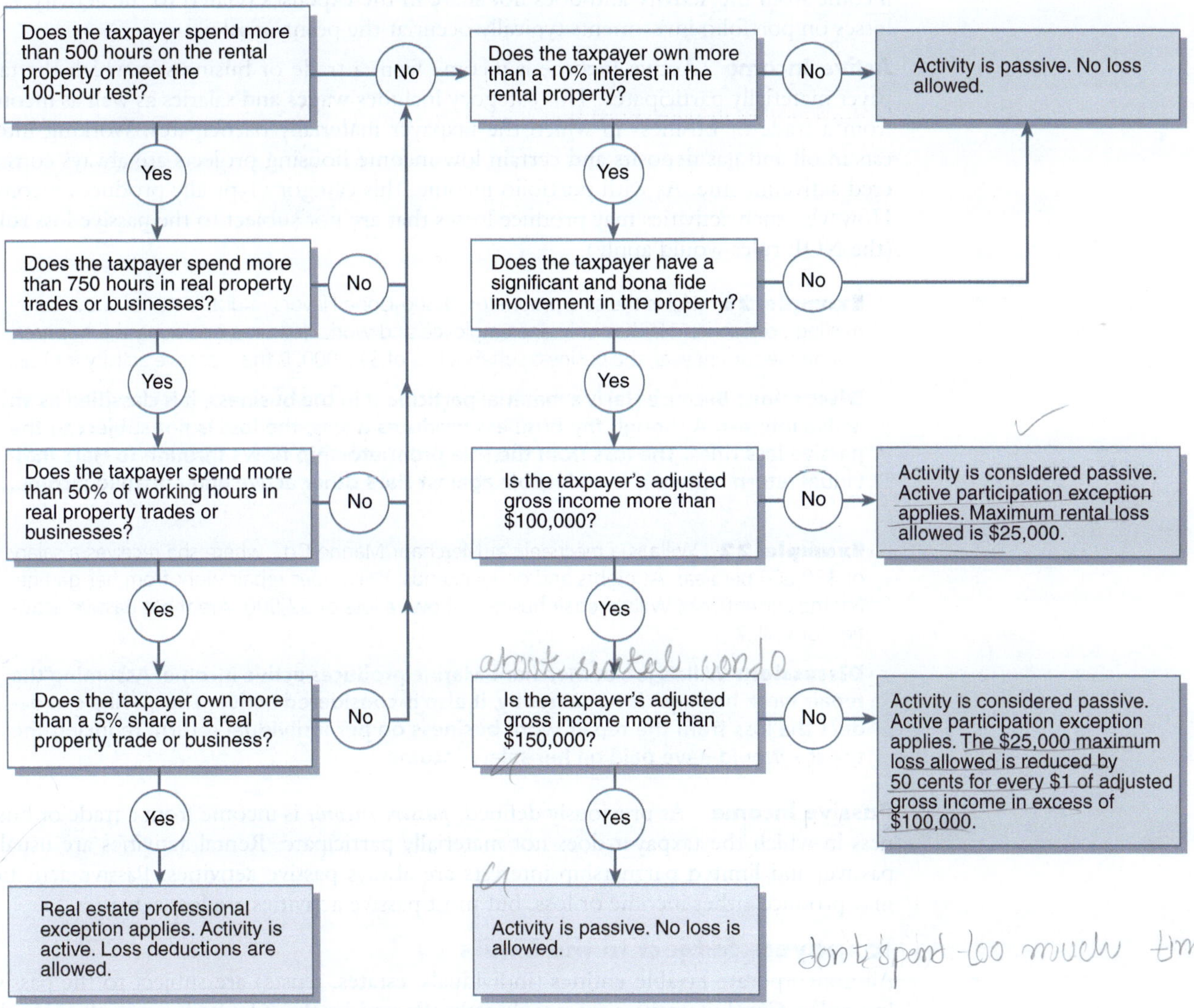


**Discussion: Again, Bart is permitted to treat the rental activity as active only if he meets the tests described earlier. Although Alf spends more than 50% of his working hours (1,800 hours ÷ 2,000 hours) in a real property trade or business in which he materially participates and the number of hours he spends in that activity is greater than 750, he fails to materially participate in the rental real estate activity. NOTE: If Alf had spent more than 500 hours helping Bart to manage the apartment complex, he would have been able to treat the rental activity as active. Although he spends more than 100 hours on the activity, he does not meet the 100-hour test because his time spent is not more than that of anyone else involved in the activity.**

### Types of Income

Under the passive activity loss rules, all income must be classified as active, passive, or portfolio income. Active and passive income result from activities considered trades or businesses. Portfolio income is income from investments. The first step is to separate portfolio income from active (i.e., activity-based) income.

**Portfolio Income** Portfolio income consists of unearned income from dividends, interest, royalties, annuities, and other assets held as investments. Portfolio income also includes income from the sale of the asset creating the portfolio income. The main characteristic of portfolio income is that such investments almost always produce positive income while the investment is held. In portfolio activities, the investor only receives income from the activity and does not share in the expenses related to the activity. Any losses on portfolio investments typically occur at the point of sale.

**Active Income** Active income is income from a trade or business in which the taxpayer materially participates. This category includes wages and salaries as well as income from a trade or business in which the taxpayer materially participates. Working interests in oil and gas deposits and certain low-income housing projects are always considered active income. As with portfolio income, this category typically produces income. However, such activities may produce losses that are not subject to the passive loss rules (the NOL rules would apply).

**Example 21** Hai is the sole proprietor of Sno-Cone Flavors, a distributor of snow cone-making accessories. Hai has only one employee and works full-time operating the business. During the current year, the business suffers a loss of $11,000. Is this a passive activity for Hai?

**Discussion: Because Hai is a material participant in the business, it is classified as an active interest. Although the business produces a loss, the loss is not subject to the passive loss rules. The loss from the sole proprietorship flows through to Hai's individual return, where it is deductible against Hai's other active and portfolio income.**

**Example 22** Willa is a mechanic at Merchant Marine Co., where she receives a salary of $30,000 per year. At nights and on weekends, Willa does repair work from her garage. For the current year, Willa's repair business shows a loss of $2,500. Are these passive activities for Willa?

**Discussion: Willa's job at Merchant Marine produces active income. Assuming the repair work business is not a hobby, it also is considered active. Thus, Willa can deduct the loss from the repair work business on her individual return, reducing the tax she would have paid on her salary income.**

**Passive Income** As previously defined, *passive income* is income from a trade or business in which the taxpayer does not materially participate. Rental activities are usually passive, and limited partnership interests are always passive activities. Passive activities may produce either income or loss, but most passive activities are loss activities.

## Taxpayers Subject to the Limits

All noncorporate taxable entities (individuals, estates, trusts) are subject to the passive loss rules. Conduit entities are not directly affected by these limits because their results are passed through and taxed to the owners. Note that in Figure 7-2, a conduit entity is usually a material participant in the operation of the business. However, the loss from the conduit flows through to the owners of the entity. Each owner must then determine whether they materially participate in the operation of the business to determine whether an NOL deduction is allowed or if their interest in the business is a passive activity. Thus, conduit entities must report the results of their operations to owners so that the owners may apply the applicable rules for the deduction of losses.

**Example 23** Harnads Department Store is organized as an S corporation and is owned equally by Able, Benito, and Charlene. During the current year, Harnads has a loss from operations. How does the loss affect Harnads, Able, Benito, and Charlene?

**Discussion: Harnads is a conduit entity, and the loss is passed through to Able, Benito, and Charlene. Able, Benito, and Charlene each must determine whether their participation in the operation of Harnads is material. If any (or all) of them do materially participate, they may deduct their share of the Harnads loss on their individual tax returns. Any who do not materially participate in the operation of Harnads are subject to the passive activity loss rules.**

Two classes of corporate taxpayers, publicly held and closely held corporations, are not subject to the passive loss limitations. Publicly held corporations can offset passive losses against both active and portfolio income, while a closely held corporation can offset passive losses only against active income.

For passive loss purposes, a corporation is a **closely held corporation** if five or fewer shareholders own 50 percent or more of the stock in the corporation during the last half of the tax year. This exception for closely held corporations gives owners of small businesses an opportunity to avoid the passive limits by incorporating their businesses. This tax-planning mechanism is discussed and illustrated in Chapter 14.

## General Rule for Passive Activities

LO 6 Identify the limitations on the deductibility of passive losses incurred in nonreal estate activities.

The purpose of the passive activity rules is to deny current loss deductions for tax-shelter activities. The general rule for implementing this intent is that passive losses may be deducted only to the extent of passive income. Under the general rule, passive losses cannot be deducted against income from portfolio or active income.

**Example 24** Harriet has a taxable income of $100,000 in 2021 from portfolio and active income sources. In addition, she owns two passive activities. Passive activity 1 (PA1) has a net loss of $20,000, and passive activity 2 (PA2) has a net income of $2,000 in 2021. What is the effect of the two passive activities on Harriet's 2021 income?

**Discussion: The $2,000 of income from PA2 is included in gross income. Under the passive activity loss rules, only $2,000 of the loss from PA1 is deductible in 2021. The net $18,000 ($20,000 − $2,000) passive loss in 2021 is not deductible against Harriet's $100,000 of taxable income from portfolio and active income sources. In essence, passive losses are deductible only up to the amount of passive income.**

Any passive activity loss that is not deductible in the current year is a **suspended loss**. A suspended loss is not permanently disallowed. Suspended losses are carried forward and may be deducted against passive income in subsequent years.

**Example 25** Assume that Harriet, in example 24, purchases passive activity 3 (PA3) in 2022. The results of the three passive activities in 2022 are as follows:

| | |
|---|---|
| PA1 | $(10,000) |
| PA2 | 3,000 |
| PA3 | 12,000 |

What is the effect of the passive activities on Harriet's 2022 taxable income?

**Discussion: Harriet's net passive loss of $18,000 from PA1 in 2021 is suspended and carried forward for deduction against 2022 passive income sources:**

| | 2021 | 2022 |
|---|---|---|
| PA1 | $(20,000) | $(10,000) |
| PA1 suspended loss | — | (18,000) |
| PA2 | 2,000 | 3,000 |
| PA3 | | 12,000 |
| Suspended loss carryforward | $(18,000) | $(13,000) |

**As you can see, the suspension and carryforward of the 2021 net passive loss result in Harriet being able to deduct $5,000 of the 2021 suspended loss against 2022 passive income. The $15,000 in income from PA2 and PA3 is included in Harriet's gross income. However, it would be offset by the $15,000 loss from PA1, leaving her 2022 taxable income unchanged. The $13,000 net passive loss is carried forward to 2023.**

LO 7 Explain the limitations on the deductibility of passive losses incurred in real estate activities.

**Active Participation Exception** The tax law allows a taxpayer who actively participates in rental real estate to deduct losses as great as $25,000 per year against portfolio and active sources of income (see Figure 7-3). An **active participant** must own at least a 10-percent interest in the activity and have significant and bona fide involvement in it. *Significant and bona fide involvement* requires that the individual be involved in some significant aspect of the rental (e.g., arranging financing, collecting rents, arranging for repairs and maintenance, keeping the activities records). In most cases, taxpayers eligible for this exception easily meet the significant involvement standard.

This exception, known as the **active participation exception**, is geared to individuals of more moderate means, because the $25,000 annual deduction amount is phased out when the individual's adjusted gross income exceeds $100,000. For every dollar of adjusted gross income in excess of $100,000, the taxpayer loses 50 cents of the $25,000 deduction. Thus, when adjusted gross income reaches $150,000 [($150,000 − $100,000) × $0.50 = $25,000], the deduction is no longer available.

**Example 26** Rory is a mechanic who owns an apartment building that has a net rental loss of $22,000 during the current year. His adjusted gross income is $120,000. If Rory owns no other passive activities, how much of the rental loss can he deduct?

**Discussion: Because the property is rental real estate, it always is considered a passive activity unless Rory is a real estate professional or he meets the active participation exception. Rory owns 100% of the property, and it is assumed that he is involved in the rental in some significant way. The special deduction for rental real estate is $25,000. However, because Rory's adjusted gross income exceeds $100,000, he must reduce the allowable deduction by $10,000 [($120,000 − $100,000) × $0.50] to $15,000. Rory can deduct $15,000 of the rental loss against his $120,000 of adjusted gross income. The remaining $7,000 is suspended and treated like any other passive loss.**

Any amount not deductible in one year is suspended as a passive loss and can be deducted in a subsequent year, either against passive income or under a subsequent year's $25,000 rental real estate limit.

**Example 27** Return to example 26. Assume that in the following year, Rory's rental property has a $20,000 loss and that his adjusted gross income is $90,000. How much of a rental real estate loss deduction is Rory allowed?

**Discussion: Because his adjusted gross income is less than $100,000, there is no phase-out of the $25,000 rental real estate deduction. However, Rory's current loss of $20,000 and his suspended loss of $7,000 exceed the $25,000 rental real estate limitation. Therefore, he is able to deduct only $25,000 under the special annual deduction, and the remaining $2,000 of suspended loss is carried forward.**

## Dispositions of Passive Activities

When a taxpayer disposes of a passive activity in a taxable transaction, any suspended loss in the activity must be accounted for. Deductions of suspended losses are allowed when passive activities are sold and when they are disposed of because the taxpayer dies.[8] However, disposition of a passive activity by gift does not result in a deduction. In each disposition case, you must calculate the amount of suspended passive loss attributable to the activity being sold to determine the proper deduction. In the previous examples, this was not a problem because the taxpayer had only one activity with a loss. Thus, the suspended loss was attributable to the one activity. However, if the taxpayer owns more than one passive activity that creates losses, the total suspended loss for the period must be allocated among the loss activities to keep track of the amount of suspended loss attributable to each activity. The allocation of suspended losses is made on the basis of the relative loss of each activity (including any suspended losses carried forward from the activity). Each loss activity is deemed to contribute proportionately to the total amount of suspended loss.

**Example 28** Recall from example 25 that Harriet has a 2022 suspended loss carryover attributable to PA1 of $13,000. Continuing with that example, assume that the three passive activities have the following results for 2023:

| | |
|---|---:|
| PA1 | $ (2,000) |
| PA1 suspended loss carryforward from 2022 | (13,000) |
| Total loss attributable to PA1 | $(15,000) |
| PA2 | 2,000 |
| PA3 | (5,000) |
| 2023 suspended loss | $(18,000) |

How much of the $18,000 suspended loss is attributed to PA1? PA3?

**Discussion:** **The total $18,000 suspended loss is allocated proportionately to the two loss activities based on their relative loss. That is, the two activities (including the $13,000 carried forward from PA1 for 2022) combine for a total loss of $20,000 ($15,000 + $5,000). Therefore, PA1 is responsible for $13,500 [$18,000 × ($15,000 ÷ $20,000)] of the suspended loss, and PA3 is responsible for $4,500 [$18,000 × ($5,000 ÷ $20,000)] of the suspended loss.**

**Disposition by Sale** When an entire interest in a passive activity is sold in a taxable transaction, any suspended loss on the activity is deductible in the year of sale against portfolio and active income.

**Example 29** Return to example 28. Assume that Harriet sells PA1 on January 2, 2024, for $42,000. Her basis in PA1 is $36,000. What is the effect of the sale of PA1 on Harriet's taxable income in 2024?

**Discussion:** **Harriet's gain of $6,000 ($42,000 − $36,000) on the sale of PA1 is included in her gross income for 2024. The $13,500 suspended loss is deductible against active and portfolio income sources. Thus, the net effect of the sale is a reduction in her taxable income of $7,500 ($6,000 − $13,500).**

From example 29, you can see that the passive activity loss rules do not permanently disallow deductions of losses. Rather, they operate as a deferral mechanism. During the period in which the passive activity is held, the entire economic loss is deductible. To see this, look at Harriet's actual losses from PA1 versus her actual loss deductions:

| | 2021 | 2022 | 2023 | 2024 | Total |
|---|---|---|---|---|---|
| Actual loss | $(20,000) | $(10,000) | $(2,000) | — | $(32,000) |
| Amount deducted | $ (2,000) | $(15,000) | $(1,500) | $(13,500) | $(32,000) |

One final note of caution on dispositions by sale: The gain or loss on the sale of the activity generally is a capital gain or a capital loss. Recall from Chapter 3 that gains and losses from the sale of capital assets are treated differently than other types of gains and losses. Briefly, net long-term capital gains are taxed at 0 percent, 15 percent, or 20 percent. Net capital losses are limited to a deduction of $3,000 per year. Thus, in example 29, the $6,000 capital gain Harriet had on the sale of PA1 would be subject to a 15 percent tax rate since her taxable income is greater than $40,000 (breakpoint for single taxpayers).

**Example 30** Assume the same facts as in example 29, except that Harriet sells PA1 for only $29,000, resulting in a loss of $7,000. What is the effect on Harriet's taxable income?

**Discussion:** **Harriet still is allowed the full deduction of the $13,500 suspended loss. However, the $7,000 loss on the sale of PA1 is a capital loss and subject to the limitations on capital losses. If this is Harriet's only capital asset sale during 2024, she is allowed to deduct only $3,000 of the capital loss in 2024, with the remaining $4,000 loss carried forward to 2025.**

**Disposition upon Death** When a taxpayer dies while holding passive activities, the passive activities become part of the estate and subject to the estate tax. For estate tax purposes, all assets are valued at the fair market value at the date of death. Heirs who receive property from an estate take as their basis the fair market value of the property at the date of death (the estate tax valuation). The result of this valuation process is that any unrealized gain on an asset is not subject to an income tax.

**Example 31** Felipe dies and leaves a piece of land to his son. Felipe had paid $12,000 for the land, which is worth $23,000 at the date of his death. Upon receiving the land, Felipe's son immediately sells it for $23,000. What are the income tax consequences of the sale of the land?

**Discussion:** **The land is valued at $23,000 for estate tax purposes. The $23,000 estate tax valuation becomes the son's basis in the land. Therefore, the son has neither gain nor loss on the sale of the land. The $11,000 in unrealized gain on the land was not subject to the income tax, because the fair market value of the land was assigned for estate tax purposes, with a corresponding increase in basis to fair market value for the son.**

Because the unrealized gains on property passing through an estate escape taxation, the passive loss rules limit the amount of the deduction for suspended losses on property held at death to the amount of the suspended loss in excess of any unrealized gain on the activity. The effect of this provision is to provide the same net loss deduction the decedent taxpayer would have received had that person sold the property.

**Example 32** Assume the same facts as in example 29, except that Harriet dies on January 2, 2024. PA1 has a fair market value of $42,000 and an adjusted basis of $36,000 as of that date. The suspended loss at that date is $13,500. How much of the suspended loss can be deducted on Harriet's 2024 income tax return?

**Discussion: If Harriet had sold PA1, she would have had a gain of $6,000 on the sale, and the $13,500 in suspended loss would have been deductible. This results in a net deduction of $7,500. Because she died, the $6,000 in gain is never subject to income tax. Therefore, the suspended loss deduction is limited to the $7,500 by which she would have been able to reduce her income had the property been sold. That is, $7,500 is the amount of suspended loss in excess of the unrealized gain on PA1.**

If a passive activity with a suspended loss has a basis greater than its fair market value (i.e., a loss property) at death, no deduction of the suspended loss is allowed. This is the unfortunate result of the statutory language that allows deductions only for the excess of suspended losses over unrealized gains. Under the legislative grace concept, the interpretation of the language is that because the statute is silent as to unrealized losses, no suspended loss deductions are allowed.

**Example 33** Assume the same facts as in example 29, except that Harriet dies on January 2, 2024. PA1 has a fair market value of $29,000 and an adjusted basis of $36,000 as of that date. The suspended loss at that date is $13,500. How much of the suspended loss can be deducted on Harriet's 2024 income tax return?

**Discussion: Because PA1 has an unrealized loss of $7,000 as of the date of death, there is no excess of suspended loss over unrealized gain. Therefore, no suspended loss deduction is allowed on Harriet's 2024 income tax return.**

**Disposition by Gift** When a taxpayer makes a **gift** of property to another taxpayer, there is no income tax effect for either party. The donor does not have to recognize an unrealized gain on the property, and the donee does not have income from the receipt of the gift. The donor's basis becomes the donee's basis. This is called a ***carryover basis*** and is necessary to ensure that any unrealized gains on the gift property do not go untaxed.

**Example 34** John owns property with a basis of $3,000 and a fair market value of $10,000. He gives the property to his daughter Nancy as a gift. Nancy immediately sells the property for $10,000. What are the tax effects of the gift and subsequent sale?

**Discussion: The transfer of the gift is not a taxable event for either John or Nancy. Nancy takes John's basis in the property. Her gain on the sale is $7,000 ($10,000 − $3,000). This treatment ensures that unrealized gains on gift property do not escape income taxation.**

Because making a gift is not a taxable event for the donor, the person who receives a gift cannot take a deduction for a suspended loss. Instead, the suspended loss is added to the basis of the donee. The effect of this treatment is to recognize that the donor does not realize (or recognize) a gain on the disposition of a gift property. Because the donor does not recognize the gain, the donor cannot take an offsetting suspended loss deduction. It is carried through to the donee and remains unrealized until the donee disposes of the property.

**Example 35** Assume that in example 34 the property John gives to Nancy is a passive activity that has a suspended loss of $20,000 at the date of the gift. What is the tax effect of the gift for John and Nancy?

**Discussion: The gift has no tax effect for either party. Because John has given the unrealized gain to Nancy (i.e., John will never be taxed on the gain), he is not**

**allowed any deductions for the suspended loss. The suspended loss becomes part of Nancy's basis in the asset, $23,000 ($3,000 + $20,000).**

**This treatment prevents a taxpayer from passing suspended losses to a related taxpayer who could benefit from the suspended passive losses. Nancy is not allowed to deduct John's suspended loss against any passive income she may have. Because the suspended loss is added to the basis of the donee, the only way Nancy can benefit from the suspended loss is by selling the passive activity.**

The 2017 Tax Cut and Jobs Act creates a new limitation on the amount a noncorporate taxpayer can deduct from a pass-through entity, such as an S corporation or partnership or a sole proprietorship. The new excess business loss (EBL) rule, which is indexed for inflation, effectively prevents net losses from a taxpayer's trade or business from offsetting nonbusiness income beyond $524,000 for married taxpayers or $262,000 for other taxpayers. The EBL limitation is applied after the application of the passive loss rules. These rules are extremely complex and due to the conceptual nature of this textbook are not discussed.

### concept check

The *legislative grace concept* requires any tax relief provided to be the result of a specific act of Congress that must be strictly applied and interpreted. Therefore, losses must be approached with the philosophy that the loss is not deductible unless a provision in the tax law allows it. Through this concept, Congress specifically limits the deduction for passive activity losses to taxpayers that are active participants in a rental activity and have an adjusted gross income of less than $150,000. In addition, Congress also specifically allows a taxpayer to deduct a loss from a working interest in an oil and gas deposit.

## 7-5 TRANSACTION LOSSES

A **transaction loss** results from a single disposition of property. Most transaction losses are the result of selling a property at less than its basis (i.e., incomplete capital recovery). However, other forms of disposition, such as exchanges of assets and involuntary conversions (e.g., casualties and thefts), may also produce losses.

The allowance of deductions for losses follows the same line of reasoning as for the allowance of deductions. That is, the loss must be categorized according to the activity producing the loss:

1. Trade or business losses
2. Investment-related losses
3. Personal use losses

Once categorized, the rules for deductibility of losses within each category are applied to determine the amount of deductible loss. These treatments are depicted in Figure 7-4. In general, transaction losses must have a business purpose to be deductible. Casualty losses and theft losses are the only loss deductions allowed for personal use losses.[9] If the loss is incurred in a trade or business, the taxpayer generally is allowed to take a **trade or business loss**. However, losses on sales to related parties are never allowed, regardless of their relation to a trade or business or investment activity. **Investment-related losses** involve dispositions of capital assets. Net capital loss deductions are limited for both individuals and corporations. The most important aspects of each of the three categories of transaction losses are discussed in turn.

### 7-5a Trade or Business Losses

LO 8 Determine the general tax treatment of transaction losses incurred in a trade or business.

In general, all transaction losses incurred in a trade or business are deductible. With one major exception, these losses are treated as ordinary losses in the period they are incurred and are deducted without limit against the income from the trade or business.[10] For an individual, a trade or business loss is deductible as a deduction for adjusted gross income.[11] An exception to this rule is for losses on exchanges of business and investment real property that must be deferred to a future period. This exception is covered in Chapter 12. The calculation of a transaction loss is straightforward—a loss results when the asset's basis is greater than the amount realized from the disposition.[12] One area that needs extra attention is the determination of the amount of loss from casualties and thefts.

*Figure 7-4*

**Treatment of Transaction Losses**

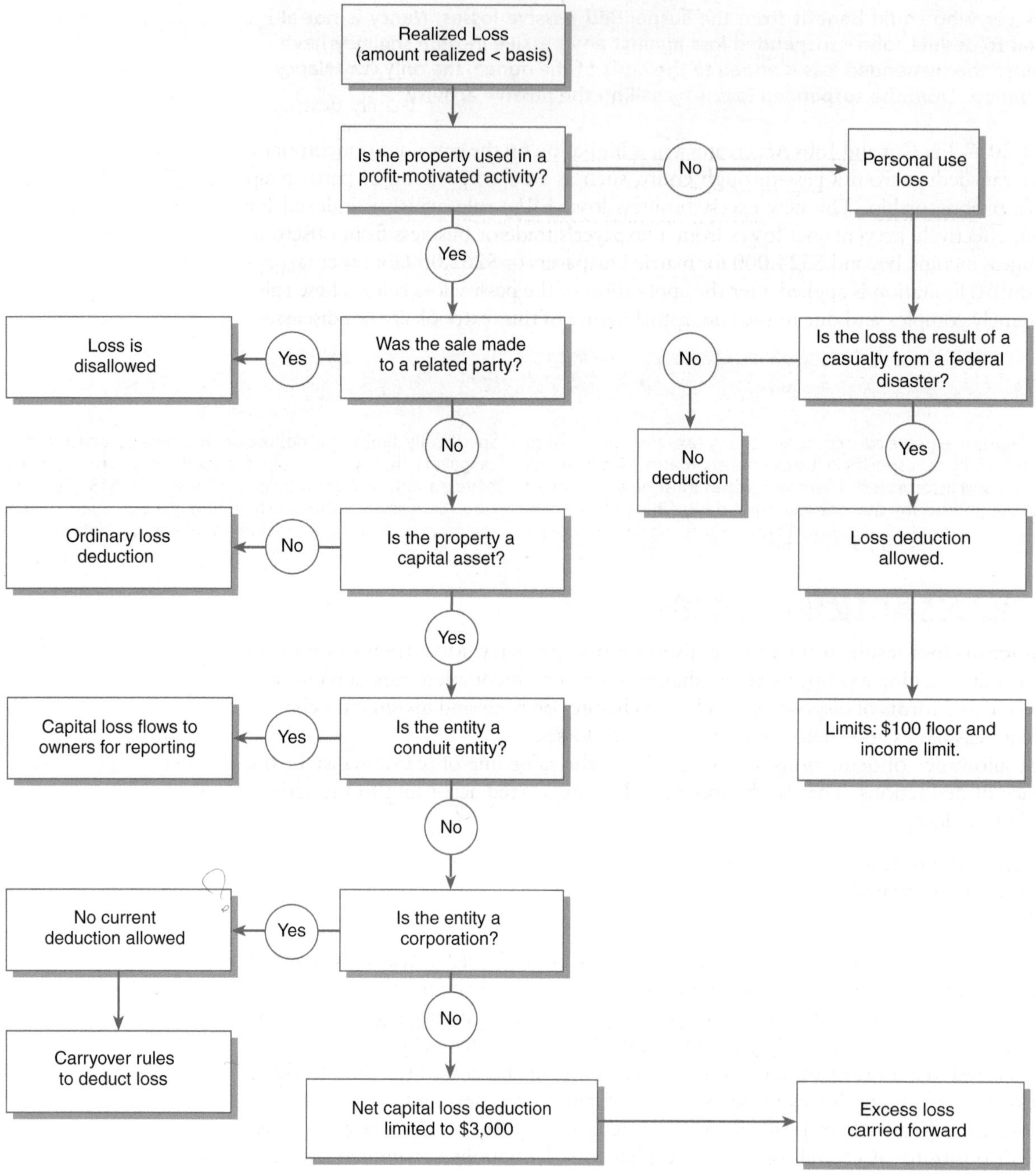


LO 9
Explain the tax treatment of business casualty and theft losses.

## Business Casualty and Theft Losses

A **casualty** is the result of some sudden, unexpected, or unusual event.[13] In addition to being sudden and unexpected, actual physical damage to property must occur to have a **casualty loss.**[14] If there is no physical damage to property but the property declines in value because of a sudden and unexpected event, the loss in value is not considered a casualty. The most common types of casualties include damage from fire, storms, earthquakes, and accidents. Losses that occur gradually over time do not constitute casualties. Examples of losses that are not casualties would include damage from termites, losses from insects or disease, and loss in value of land because of wind erosion.[15]

A **theft** is similar to a casualty in that it must be sudden and unexpected. A theft may occur as a result of a robbery, larceny, or embezzlement.[16] Misplacing or losing items does not constitute a theft. The damage caused by a theft is that the entire property is lost. As such, **theft losses** are treated in the same manner as casualty losses.

When a casualty occurs, one of two things can happen. The property may be fully destroyed and have no value, or it may be partially destroyed and have some remaining value. The calculation of the amount of loss depends on whether the property was fully or partially destroyed in the casualty.[17] A theft is treated as property fully destroyed (all value lost).

**Business Property Fully Destroyed** When a business property is fully destroyed (or stolen), the taxpayer's entire investment in the property has been lost. The capital recovery concept lets a taxpayer fully recover the investment in business property. The measure of a taxpayer's investment in a property is its basis. Therefore, the measure of a **business casualty loss** for fully destroyed business property is the property's basis.

**Example 36** A driver for Portable Phone Providers (PPP) is involved in an accident that totally destroys one of the company's vans. The van had been purchased for $26,000, and depreciation taken to date on the van is $8,000. What is the measure of the loss on the van?

**Discussion: Because the van was totally destroyed in the accident, the measure of the loss is the unrecovered investment in the van, its basis. Although the van cost $26,000, the company has recovered $8,000 of the cost through depreciation deductions. The unrecovered portion, $18,000 ($26,000 − $8,000), is the amount of the investment lost.**

Most business assets are covered by insurance. Any amounts received from insurance on property subject to a casualty are a capital recovery. Thus, the amount of the loss must be reduced by any insurance proceeds received from the casualty.

**Example 37** Assume that in example 36, PPP's van is covered by insurance and that PPP receives $15,000 from the insurance company for the accident. What is PPP's casualty loss?

**Discussion: PPP's loss is $3,000. Of the $18,000 of basis that was unrecovered at the date of the casualty, $15,000 was recovered from the insurance company. NOTE: When insurance proceeds are received, the loss is calculated as the difference between the amount realized (insurance proceeds) and the basis. Thus, the calculation of a casualty loss for business property fully destroyed is identical to the calculation of a loss from the sale of a property.**

At this point, we should note that all casualties do not result in losses. That is, if the insurance proceeds received from a casualty exceed the adjusted basis of the property, the result of the casualty would be a **casualty gain**.

**Example 38** Assume that in example 37, PPP receives $20,000 for the destruction of its van. What is PPP's casualty gain (loss)?

**Discussion: PPP has a gain of $2,000 ($20,000 − $18,000) from the casualty. PPP has recovered more than its remaining investment in the van. Therefore, under the capital recovery concept, PPP has a gain from the receipt of insurance proceeds in excess of adjusted basis.**

Gains from business casualties are subject to a special election under which a casualty gain may be deferred. Because the focus of this chapter is on losses, the discussion of this election is deferred until Chapter 12.

**Business Property Partially Destroyed** When a casualty occurs and property is not totally destroyed, an estimate of the amount lost because of the casualty must be made. The amount of the real loss from a partial destruction is the decrease in the taxpayer's wealth resulting from the casualty. This can be measured by the decline in the market value of the property that results from the casualty. The decline in the value of the property is

The fair market value of the property *before* the casualty
Less: The fair market value of the property *after* the casualty
Equals: The decline in value because of the casualty

In most cases, this is an adequate measurement of the loss the taxpayer has incurred as a result of the casualty. However, under the capital recovery concept, the maximum amount that can be recovered on any property is the amount invested in the property—

its basis. Thus, a loss deduction because of a casualty can never exceed the property's basis. This leads to the following rule for measuring a loss on partially destroyed business property:

The measure of the loss is equal to the lesser of

- The decline in the value of the property

or

- The adjusted basis of the property

The purpose of this measurement rule is to ensure that the amount of the loss deducted does not exceed the amount of unrecovered investment in the property.

**Example 39** This year, a hurricane damages a warehouse used by Sugar Exporters, Inc. (SEI), in its exporting operation. SEI had paid $200,000 for the warehouse and had taken $80,000 in depreciation before the hurricane. Appraisals indicate that the warehouse was worth $300,000 before the hurricane. In its damaged state, the warehouse can be sold for only $100,000. What is the amount of loss SEI suffered on the warehouse because of the hurricane?

**Discussion: The value of the warehouse declined $200,000 ($300,000 − $100,000) because of the hurricane damage. However, SEI's unrecovered investment in the warehouse is $120,000 ($200,000 − $80,000).**

**SEI's loss is the lesser of the decline in value because of the hurricane, $200,000, or its basis in the warehouse, $120,000. In this case, the maximum amount that SEI can recover through a loss deduction is the $120,000 basis.**

As with fully destroyed business property, the calculated loss must be reduced by any insurance proceeds received because of the casualty.

**Example 40** Assume that in example 39, SEI's warehouse is covered by insurance. SEI receives $100,000 from the insurance company for the hurricane damage. What is SEI's casualty loss?

**Discussion: The $120,000 loss must be reduced by the $100,000 of insurance proceeds. SEI's deductible loss is $20,000 ($120,000 − $100,000).**

In many instances, the measurement of the decline in the value of a property that results from a casualty poses formidable problems. That is, by definition a casualty is the result of a sudden and unexpected event. This makes it unlikely that the taxpayer had the foresight to have the property appraised shortly before the casualty. After a property has been damaged, assessing its true condition before being damaged is often difficult. Thus, the estimate of the decline in value of the property because of the casualty is difficult to obtain. For this reason, the IRS lets the taxpayer use the cost of repairing the property to estimate the decline in value of the property.

**Example 41** Mammoth Company operates ski resorts throughout the western United States. In February, an avalanche at one of its resorts damages a ski lift. The lift had cost $450,000, and Mammoth had taken depreciation of $200,000 before the casualty. It costs $160,000 to have the lift repaired. What is the amount of Mammoth's loss because of the avalanche?

**Discussion: Because of the difficulty of determining the value of the ski lift before the casualty (and after the casualty), the cost of repairing the lift can be used to estimate the decline in value because of the damage. This is a partial destruction of business property, and the amount of the loss is measured by the lesser of the decline in value, $160,000, or the basis of the ski lift, $250,000 ($450,000 − $200,000). In this case, the $160,000 cost of repairing the lift is lower than the basis and is used to measure the loss. Any insurance proceeds Mammoth receives would reduce the amount of the loss that is deductible.**

It should be noted that the 2020 Cares Act created a special provision for NOLs arising in tax years beginning after December 31, 2017, but before January 1, 2021. The NOLs can be carried back to each of the five tax years preceding the tax year of such loss. In addition, the CARES Act temporarily removes the 80 percent limitation and allows 100 percent of the NOL to be used.

LO 10

Explain the tax treatment of transaction losses incurred in production-of-income activities, including wash sales, small business stock, and related party sales.

## 7-5b Investment-Related Losses

Losses on transactions related to investment activities are generally allowed as deductions. However, in contrast to trade or business losses, which are always deductible in full, the amount of the current period deduction for an investment-related loss may be limited. This occurs because investment-related assets are capital assets. A **capital asset** is defined as any asset that is not a receivable, an inventory item, depreciable or real property used in a trade or business, or certain intangible assets such as copyrights.[18] Note that the items that are not capital assets are primarily assets used in a trade or business. Thus, assets that are not used in a trade or business are capital assets. This would include both investment assets and personal use assets. There are limits on the amount of loss from the sale of capital assets that is deductible in any one tax year. In addition, the tax law provides several other significant provisions related to losses on the sale of capital assets.

## Capital Losses

When a taxpayer suffers losses on the disposition of capital assets, the tax law provides a procedure for netting these losses against any gains from capital asset dispositions during the year. As discussed in Chapter 3, the purpose of this netting procedure is to produce a single position for net capital asset transactions for the entire year. The net transaction position can be either a gain or a loss. An overview of the netting procedure was presented in Chapter 3. More specific details of the treatment of capital gains and losses are covered in Chapter 11. At this juncture, the critical aspect is the treatment of net capital losses. A **net capital loss** occurs when a taxpayer's total capital losses exceed the taxpayer's total capital gains for a tax year. The treatment of a net capital loss for an individual is different than the treatment for a corporation.[19]

**Net Capital Losses of Individuals** An individual taxpayer is limited to a deduction of $3,000 in net capital losses per year. The capital loss deduction is a deduction for adjusted gross income. Any loss in excess of $3,000 2022? is carried forward and netted against capital gains in subsequent years. Thus, the capital loss limitation is a deferral-of-loss-recognition provision, not a total loss disallowance provision.

**Example 42** Mona has the following total capital gains and losses for 2021 and 2022. What is her deductible capital loss in 2021 and 2022?

| | 2021 | 2022 |
|---|---|---|
| Capital gains | $ 12,000 | $ 17,000 |
| Capital losses | (20,000) | (16,000) |

**Discussion: Mona has a net capital loss of $8,000 in 2021. Because of the capital loss limitations, she can deduct only $3,000 of this loss in 2022. The remaining $5,000 of 2021 loss is carried forward to 2022 and included in the 2022 netting:**

| | 2021 | 2022 |
|---|---|---|
| Capital gains | $ 12,000 | $ 17,000 |
| Capital losses | (20,000) | (16,000) |
| Net 2021 capital loss | $ (8,000) | |
| 2021 capital loss deduction | 3,000 | |
| 2021 capital loss carryforward | $ (5,000) | (5,000) |
| Net 2022 capital loss | | $ (4,000) |
| 2022 capital loss deduction | | 3,000 |
| 2022 capital loss carryforward | | $ (1,000) |

**As you can see, the carryforward of the $5,000 capital loss from 2021 to 2022 creates a net capital loss of $4,000 in 2022. Without the carryforward, Mona would have had a $1,000 ($17,000 − $16,000) net capital gain in 2022. However, when the $5,000 of 2021 loss is carried forward and included in the 2022 netting, the result is a $4,000 loss. Per the capital loss limitations, $3,000 of the net capital loss is deductible in 2022. The remaining $1,000 of net capital loss must be carried forward and included in Mona's capital gain-and-loss netting in 2023.**

**Net Capital Losses of Corporations** In contrast to individuals, corporations are not allowed to deduct net capital losses against noncapital gain income. Corporations can use capital losses only to offset capital gains. When a corporation incurs a net capital loss for a tax year, the net capital loss is carried back as a short-term capital loss and used to offset any net capital gains on which it paid tax in the preceding three years. Any net capital loss that is not used in the three-year carryback period is carried forward as a short-term capital loss to offset capital gains for five years.

**Example 43** El Fredo Corporation has the following net capital gains and losses for 2020 through 2023:

| 2020 | 2021 | 2022 | 2023 |
|---|---|---|---|
| $ 8,000 | $ 5,000 | $ 7,000 | $ (35,000) |

Assuming that El Fredo is in a 21% marginal tax rate bracket during each of these years, what is the effect of the $35,000 capital loss in 2023?

**Discussion: El Fredo cannot deduct any of the $35,000 capital loss against its 2023 income. It must carry the loss back 3 years and use the loss to reduce any capital gains during that period. For El Fredo, the loss would first be applied against the $8,000 in 2020 capital gain, resulting in a $1,680 (21% × $8,000) refund of the tax paid in 2020. Applying the remaining loss against the $5,000 and $7,000 of net capital gains in 2021 and 2022, respectively, would result in refunds of $1,050 and $1,470. The 3-year carryback uses up $20,000 of the $35,000 year 2023 net capital loss. The remaining $15,000 in loss would be carried forward and used to reduce capital gains in the next 5 years.**

## Specially Treated Investment Losses

Three provisions related to losses on investment assets deserve mention. Each of these provisions provides special treatment in certain transaction loss situations.

**Losses on Small Business Stock** To encourage individuals to invest in new companies, the tax law provides an exception to the $3,000 annual loss limitation on losses incurred on qualifying **small business stock**. This provision lets an individual taxpayer deduct up to $50,000 in losses on small business stock per year. The limit is raised to $100,000 for a married couple filing a joint return.[20] Any losses on small business stock in excess of $50,000 ($100,000 for married couples) are subject to the regular capital gain-and-loss netting procedure.

**Example 44** Linda is a single taxpayer whose only capital asset transaction for 2021 is a $70,000 capital loss on the sale of qualifying small business stock. How much of the $70,000 loss can Linda deduct in 2021?

**Discussion: Linda is allowed to deduct $50,000 of the loss under the special exception for losses on small business stock. The remaining $20,000 of the loss is a capital loss subject to the annual $3,000 limitation. Thus, she can deduct an additional $3,000. This gives Linda a total loss deduction of $53,000 in 2021. The remaining $17,000 in loss must be carried forward to 2022 and deducted under the regular capital gain-and-loss netting procedure. NOTE: If Linda had been married in 2021, she and her husband could have deducted the entire $70,000 loss in 2021.**

It should be stressed that the special deduction applies to losses incurred during a given tax year. Losses in excess of the allowable $50,000 ($100,000) deduction that are carried forward as a capital loss are subject to the capital loss limitation in later years, not the small business stock limitation.[21]

**Example 45** Assume that in example 44, Linda has one capital asset transaction in 2022 that results in a $5,000 capital gain. What is her 2022 capital loss deduction?

**Discussion: The $17,000 in net capital loss carries forward from 2021 to be netted against the $5,000 in capital gain in 2022, resulting in a net capital loss for 2022 of $12,000. Linda cannot use the small business stock deduction on this loss because it occurs in 2021. Therefore, only $3,000 of the $12,000 loss can be deducted in 2022. The $9,000 remaining loss must be carried forward to 2023 and included in Linda's capital gain-and-loss netting in 2023.**

To qualify as small business stock, the stock must be purchased directly from the corporation at original issue. That is, the stock cannot be acquired from another individual or other taxable entity. The corporation itself must satisfy several other requirements, the most important of which is that the contributed capital of the corporation at the time the stock is issued must be less than $1 million.

**Losses on Related Party Sales** To receive its intended income tax effect, a transaction must be entered into at arm's length. The tax law recognizes that related party transactions often lack the necessary bargaining to characterize the transactions as arm's length. The objective of the related party rules is to defer or disallow losses on transactions that are not made at arm's length. The primary provision regarding losses is that a loss on the sale of property to a **related party** is disallowed as a deduction.[22]

**Example 46** Rasheed sells 500 shares of ABC Corporation stock to his sister, Tawana, for $5,000. Rasheed had paid $7,500 for the stock. Can he deduct the $2,500 loss on the sale of the stock to his sister?

**Discussion: Rasheed cannot deduct the loss on the sale of the stock because Tawana is a related party. Losses on sales of property to related parties are disallowed.**

If the property subject to the related party sale disallowance is later sold to an unrelated party at a gain, the gain realized on the sale may be reduced by the amount of loss previously disallowed.[23]

**Example 47** Assume that in example 46, Tawana later sells the shares of ABC stock to an unrelated party for $9,000. How much gain does Tawana have to recognize from the sale?

**Discussion: Tawana's basis is the $5,000 she paid for the stock, giving her a gain on the sale of $4,000 ($9,000 − $5,000). She is allowed to reduce her $4,000 gain by Rasheed's $2,500 disallowed loss. She has to recognize only a $1,500 ($4,000 − $2,500) gain on the sale.**

The gain on a subsequent sale to an unrelated party may be reduced only to zero (no gain or loss recognized). A loss cannot be created on a subsequent sale by using the previously disallowed loss.

**Example 48** Assume that in example 47, Tawana sells the stock to an unrelated party for $6,000. How much gain does Tawana have to recognize on the sale?

**Discussion: Tawana realizes a gain of $1,000 ($6,000 − $5,000) on the sale. She may use Rasheed's $2,500 disallowed loss to reduce gain on the subsequent sale but only to zero. In this case, Tawana does not recognize any gain on the sale of the stock. However, note that the remaining $1,500 of Rasheed's previously disallowed loss is permanently lost in this case.**

If the subsequent sale to an unrelated party results in a loss, the disallowed loss may not be used to increase the loss on the subsequent sale.

**Example 49** Assume that in example 47, Tawana sells the stock to an unrelated party for $3,000. How much loss does Tawana recognize on the sale?

**Discussion: The loss on the sale is $2,000 ($3,000 − $5,000). Tawana is not allowed to use Rasheed's $2,500 disallowed loss to increase the loss on the sale and is permanently lost. She is allowed to recognize only the actual $2,000 loss.**

The related party disallowance rule also applies to the sale to a related party of property used in a trade or business.

**Example 50** Catherine, the CEO of the Adtech Corporation, owns 60% of the Adtech Corporation. She sells land with a basis of $35,000 to Adtech for $31,000. Can Catherine deduct the $4,000 loss?

**Discussion: Catherine cannot deduct any of the loss on the sale of the land. Because she owns more than 50% of Adtech, she and Adtech are related parties. The disallowed loss of $4,000 can be used only to reduce any gain Adtech might have when it sells the land.**

In summary, when property is sold at a loss to a related party, no loss is allowed. However, if the property is later sold to an unrelated party at a gain, the disallowed loss can be used to reduce the gain but not below zero (i.e., no loss allowed). Also, if the property is subsequently sold to an unrelated party at a loss, no portion of the disallowed loss from the related party sale is deductible.

The related party rules apply *only* to losses on sales to related parties. No comparable provisions restrict the reporting of gains on sales to related parties. Gains on sales to related parties are treated as any other type of gain would be treated.

**Wash Sales** A **wash sale** occurs when a security (stocks, bonds, options) is sold at a loss, and during the 30-day period before or after the loss sale date, the seller purchases substantially identical securities to replace the securities sold.[24] In a wash sale, a taxpayer's economic position with respect to the shares replaced remains unchanged. A wash sale loss lacks economic substance—in essence, it is an artificial loss created for tax purposes without any change in the taxpayer's underlying economic position. The wash sale provisions recognize the substance of the transaction rather than its form (substance-over-form doctrine) by disallowing recognition of all losses on wash sales. The disallowed loss is added to the basis of the replacement shares.[25]

**Example 51** Moses owns 400 shares of Nick Nack Corporation stock that he purchased for $20,000 several years ago. In December of the current year, Moses sells the 400 shares for $12,000. One week later, he purchases 400 shares of Nick Nack stock for $12,000. What are the tax consequences of the sale of the Nick Nack stock?

**Discussion: The $8,000 loss on the sale of the 400 shares of stock is a wash sale because Moses repurchases substantially identical shares within 30 days of the sale of the shares at a loss. The $8,000 loss is disallowed. However, the disallowance is not permanent—Moses adds the $8,000 loss to the basis of the replacement shares, giving him a basis of $20,000 in the replacement shares. He will be able to recover the $8,000 of disallowed loss when he disposes of the stock in a transaction that does not constitute a wash sale.**

The wash sale provisions do not apply to dispositions at a gain, to securities that are sold at a loss but not replaced, or to dealers in securities.

**Example 52** Assume that in example 51, Moses repurchases only 300 shares of the Nick Nack stock for $9,000 after the $12,000 sale. What are the tax consequences of the sale of the 400 shares of stock?

**Discussion: In this case, only the 300 shares of stock that are replaced are a wash sale. The loss on the 100 shares that are not replaced, $2,000 [(100 ÷ 400) × $8,000], is recognized. The $6,000 loss on the replaced shares is subject to the wash sale disallowance and is not deductible. The basis of the 300 replacement shares is $15,000 ($9,000 + $6,000).**

**Example 53** Assume that in example 51, Moses repurchases 600 shares of the Nick Nack stock for $18,000. What are the tax consequences of the sale of the Nick Nack stock?

**Discussion: The $8,000 loss on the sale of the 400 shares of stock is a wash sale because Moses repurchases substantially identical shares within 30 days of the sale of the shares at a loss. The $8,000 loss is disallowed. However, the disallowance is not permanent—Moses adds the $8,000 loss to the basis of the replacement shares, giving him a basis of $20,000 in the 400 replacement shares. The other 200 shares that he purchases have a basis of $6,000 ($18,000 ÷ 600 = $30 × 200 = $6,000).**

## Personal Use Losses

LO 11 Determine the tax treatment of transaction losses incurred in a personal activity.

Losses on the sale or other disposition of personal use assets are generally disallowed—losses on the sale of personal use items such as autos, jewelry, furniture, and clothing have no tax effect. Prior to January 1, 2018, the only personal use loss that the tax law allowed as a deduction was for losses from casualty or theft. Under the legislative grace concept, Congress placed several restrictions on the amount of a personal use casualty loss that may be deducted. One such restriction is that **personal casualty losses** and theft losses would only be deductible as personal itemized deductions. Thus, a taxpayer needed to itemize to deduct a personal casualty or theft loss. In addition, a per occurrence limitation and an annual limitation was imposed on personal casualty and theft losses. For tax years beginning after December 31, 2017, the personal casualty and theft loss deduction is suspended except for personal casualty losses incurred from a federally-declared disaster. However, if a taxpayer has personal casualty gains, the loss suspension doesn't apply to the extent that such loss doesn't exceed the gain.

LO 12
Describe the tax treatment for personal casualty losses.

**Measuring the Personal Casualty Loss** In contrast to business casualty losses, which have a measurement rule for fully destroyed property (basis) and a separate rule for partially destroyed property (the lesser of the decline in value or the basis), personal casualty and theft losses are always measured as the lesser of

- The decline in the value of the property

or

- The basis of the property

The effect of this measurement rule is to disallow losses in the value of property before the casualty that were attributable to everyday wear and tear from personal use. This is consistent with the general rule that losses from personal use are not deductible.

**Example 54** Naomee's car is destroyed when a tornado comes through her neighborhood. Her neighborhood is part of an area that is declared a federal disaster. She had purchased the auto several years ago for $30,000. A used car dealer tells her that a comparable car can be bought today for $10,000. What is the amount of Naomee's loss on the casualty?

**Discussion: The measure of the amount of loss is the lesser of the decline in value because of the casualty, $10,000, or the basis, $30,000. Thus, the amount of Naomee's loss is $10,000.**

**Note that the $20,000 loss in value between what Naomee paid for the auto, $30,000, and what the auto was worth before the tornado $10,000, is not a loss attributable to the casualty. The $20,000 loss in value occurred during Naomee's personal use of the auto and was not from the casualty. Thus, the loss in value from personal use is not deductible.**

**Discussion: If Naomee had used her car exclusively in a trade or business, the amount of loss would have been her $30,000 basis. The treatment is different because of the business purpose of the automobile. All expenses and losses incurred in a trade or business are deductible. Personal expenses and losses are generally not deductible.**

**Limitations on Personal Casualty Losses** As with any casualty loss, the amount of loss must be reduced by any insurance proceeds received. In addition, you must file a claim for any insurance due to claim a deduction. Personal use casualty losses are also reduced by $100 **statutory floor** per occurrence and 10 percent of adjusted gross income (AGI). The $100 statutory floor reduction is an element of administrative convenience. Because including $100 losses on individual returns adds cost and complexity to the tax system, the $100 floor eliminates the deduction of small personal casualty losses.

**Example 55** Assume that in example 54, Naomee receives $7,000 from her insurance company and her AGI is $40,000. What is her casualty loss?

**Discussion: The $10,000 loss must be reduced by the $7,000 insurance reimbursement and the $100 statutory floor. This results in a $2,900 ($10,000 – $7,000 – $100) loss on the casualty. Since 10% of her AGI, $4,000 ($40,000 x 10%) is greater than $2,900, she is not entitled to a casualty loss deduction.**

## concept check

The *capital recovery concept* allows the recovery of capital invested in an asset. The amount invested in an asset is the maximum amount recoverable under this concept. *Adjusted basis* represents a taxpayer's unrecovered investment in an asset. Therefore, the maximum loss that can be recognized from a casualty or theft is the asset's adjusted basis. An *arm's-length transaction* is one in which all parties to the transaction have bargained in good faith and for their individual benefit, not for the benefit of the transaction group. *Related party* transactions are usually subject to scrutiny by the IRS because the tax law assumes that related parties do not transact at arm's length. The *substance-over-form* doctrine taxes transactions according to their true intent rather than some (possibly) contrived form of the transaction. This concept prevents a taxpayer from recognizing a loss on the sale of stock if it is replaced within 30 days of (either before or after) the date of sale.

## CHAPTER SUMMARY

Losses result from either an excess of deductions over income for an entire tax year (annual loss) or an excess of basis over the amount realized from a disposition of property (transaction loss). Annual losses from a trade or business in which a taxpayer materially participates are carried forwarded indefinitely and cannot be carried back. A taxpayer can only offset 80 percent of the current years' taxable income with the carryforward. Such losses are deductible only to the extent that the taxpayer is at risk in the activity.

If the taxpayer does not materially participate in the operation of the trade or business generating the loss, the deduction of the loss is subject to the passive loss rules. These rules generally disallow the deduction of a net passive loss against active and portfolio income. Any loss not currently deductible is suspended and carried forward for deduction against future passive income. If an individual meets the real estate professional exception, the loss from the rental property is fully deductible against active and portfolio income. If an individual meets the active participation test, the individual is allowed to deduct against active and portfolio income up to $25,000 of loss per year incurred in the rental real estate activity. When a passive activity is disposed of, any suspended loss on the activity is deductible against active and portfolio income.

The treatment of transaction losses follows the general pattern for all deductions. Losses are classified as either personal or related to a profit-motivated transaction or venture. The only personal use losses that are deductible are casualty losses incurred from a federally-declared disaster. Personal casualty losses are subject to a $100 per occurrence statutory floor limitation, and are further limited to the amount of loss in excess of 10 percent of the taxpayer's adjusted gross income.

Transaction losses that are related to a trade or business are deductible in full. Investment-related losses are subject to the capital gain-and-loss netting procedure. Net capital loss deductions of individuals are limited to $3,000 per year, with any excess capital loss carried forward for use in subsequent years. Corporations incurring net capital losses are not allowed to deduct capital losses against other forms of income. Net capital losses may be carried back three years and forward five years as a short-term capital loss and used to reduce the tax on any net capital gains in the carryover years.

Several types of transaction losses are subject to special rules. Up to $50,000 ($100,000 married) in losses on qualified small business stock may be deducted as an ordinary loss. Losses on sales to related parties are specifically disallowed. If a security is sold at a loss and replaced within 30 days of the sale, the wash sale rules disallow the loss.

A summary of the reporting of losses discussed in this chapter for individuals is presented in Exhibit 7-2.

*Exhibit 7-2*

### Individual Tax Calculation Summary To Date

| | |
|---|---|
| Gross Income (Chapters 3 and 4) | $ XXX |
| Less: Deductions for adjusted gross income (AGI) | |
| Trade or business expenses (Chapters 5 and 6) | |
| Trade or business losses | |
| Net operating loss deductions | |
| Business transaction loss deductions | |
| Rental & royalty expenses (Chapters 5 and 6) | |
| Passive loss deductions | |
| Suspended losses freed by disposition | |
| Rental real estate losses | |
| Capital losses | (XXX) |
| Equals: Adjusted gross income | $ XXX |
| Less: Deductions from adjusted gross income | |
| Specifically allowable personal expenditures (Chapter 8) | |
| Production-of-income expenses (Chapters 5 and 6) | (XXX) |
| Equals: Taxable income | $ XXX |

# KEY TERMS



# PRIMARY TAX LAW SOURCES

[1]Sec. 172—Defines a *net operating loss* and provides the rules for deducting net operating losses.

[2]Sec. 465—Defines the amount at risk in an activity and limits loss deductions to the amount the taxpayer has at risk in the activity.

[3]Prop. Reg. Sec. 1.465-41—Provides examples of the application of the at-risk rules.

[4]Sec. 469—Defines *passive activities* and provides the rules for deducting passive activity losses.

[5]Reg. Sec. 1.469-5T—Provides the tests for material participation in an activity.

[6]Reg. Sec. 1.469-1T—States that suspended passive losses are carried forward to the following year, where they are treated as if they were incurred in that year; provides rules for distinguishing rental activities for purposes of the passive loss rules.

[7]Sec. 469(c)(7)—Provides the rules for the real estate professional exception for rental real estate.

[8]Reg. Sec. 1.469-2T—Provides rules for deducting suspended losses on passive activities when the activity is disposed of in a taxable transaction.

[9]Sec. 165—Specifies the allowable deductions for losses; limits the deductions of losses by individuals to those incurred in a trade or business, in a transaction entered into for profit, or resulting from storms, fires, shipwrecks, or other casualties.

[10]Sec. 65—Defines an *ordinary loss* as any loss that does not result from the sale or exchange of a capital asset.

[11]Sec. 62—Defines *adjusted gross income* for individual taxpayers and specifies the deductions allowed for adjusted gross income; allowable loss deductions include losses incurred in a trade or business, net operating losses, and capital losses.

[12]Sec. 1001—Prescribes the calculation of gains and losses on dispositions of property; defines *amount realized* for purposes of determining gain or loss on dispositions.

[13]Matheson v. Comm., 54 F.2d 537 (2d Cir. 1931)—held that a casualty is the result of some sudden, unexpected, or unusual event.

[14]Pulvers v. Comm., 407 F.2d 838 (9th Cir. 1969)—Held that for a casualty loss to be deductible, a casualty must damage a property; mere declines in value are not deductible.

[15]Rev. Rul. 63-232—States that a loss resulting from termite damage is not a casualty loss.

[16]Reg. Sec. 1.165-8—States that a theft includes larceny, embezzlement, and robbery.

[17]Reg. Sec. 1.165-7—Provides the rules for calculating casualty losses.

[18]Sec. 1221—Defines *capital assets.*

[19]Sec. 1211—Sets forth the limits on deductions of capital losses of corporations and individuals.

[20]Sec. 1244—Defines qualified *small business stock* and allows deductions for losses of up to $50,000 per year ($100,000 for married, filing jointly) on such stock.

[21]Reg. Sec. 1.1244(b)-1—Provides the limits on the deductibility of losses on small business stock; clarifies that any loss that is carried forward to a subsequent year is not eligible for that year's special loss deduction.

[22]Sec. 267—Defines *related parties* and disallows losses on sales to related parties.

[23]Reg. Sec. 1.267(d)-1—Provides the rules for deducting disallowed losses on related party sales on the subsequent sale to an unrelated party.

[24]Sec. 1091—Defines a *wash sale* and disallows current deductions for wash sale losses.

[25]Reg. Sec. 1.1091-1—States that the loss on a wash sale is disallowed on shares of stock that are actually replaced; provides basis adjustment rules for wash sale shares.

# DISCUSSION QUESTIONS

1. **LO1** How are deductions and losses different? How are they similar? Explain.
2. **LO1** Discuss the basic differences between annual losses and transaction losses.
3. **LO2** How are the new net operating loss rules different than the old rules? Are the rules better or worse for the taxpayer?
4. **LO3** What are the characteristics of a *tax shelter*, as the term is commonly used by tax practitioners?
5. **LO4** How is a taxpayer's amount at risk in an activity different from the taxpayer's basis in the same activity? What purpose does the amount at risk serve in regard to losses?
6. **LO4** What is a nonrecourse debt? How is financing using nonrecourse debt different from financing using recourse debt?
7. **LO5** What is the purpose of the passive loss rules?
8. **LO5** Are the passive loss rules disallowance-of-loss provisions or are they loss deferral provisions? Explain.
9. **LO6** For purposes of the passive loss rules, what is a closely held corporation? How is the tax treatment of passive losses incurred by a closely held corporation different from the tax treatment of passive losses incurred by
   a. Individuals?
   b. Corporations?
10. **LO9** When a business sustains a loss from a casualty, one of two measurement rules is used to determine the amount of the loss. Why is the use of two measurement rules necessary for determining a business casualty loss?
11. **LO8, 10** What are the limitations on the deductibility of capital losses by individuals? How do the limitations compare with those for corporations?
12. **LO10** Most sales of securities at a loss result in capital losses. Under what circumstances would a loss on the sale of a security be treated as an ordinary loss? Explain the rationale for this treatment.
13. **LO10** What is the purpose of the related party rules as they apply to sales of property?
14. **LO10** Losses incurred on the sale of business assets are generally deductible in full in the year the loss is realized. Describe a situation in which a realized loss on the sale of a business asset is not deductible in the current year, and explain why it would not be deductible.
15. **LO10** What is a wash sale? How is the treatment of a wash sale different from the treatment of other sales of securities?
16. **LO12** When is a taxpayer allowed to deduct a personal casualty loss, and how is it calculated?

# PROBLEMS

17. **LO2** The Graves Corporation was incorporated in 2020 and incurred a net operating loss of $35,000. The company's operating income in 2021 was $47,000. Because of a downturn in the local economy, the company suffers a net operating loss of $21,000 in 2022. What is the treatment of the 2022 loss? How would your answer change if Graves were an S corporation?
18. **LO2** Habiby, Inc., began operations in 2020 and has the following income and expenses for 2020 through 2023.

| | 2020 | 2021 | 2022 | 2023 |
|---|---|---|---|---|
| Income | $ 180,000 | $ 300,000 | $ 320,000 | $ 320,000 |
| Expenses | (280,000) | (150,000) | (400,000) | (220,000) |
| Taxable Income | $(100,000) | $ 150,000 | $ (80,000) | $ 100,000 |

What is the amount of tax that Habiby should pay each year?

19. **LO4** Marlene opens an outdoor sports complex that features batting cages, miniature golf, and a driving range. She invests $100,000 of her own money and borrows $750,000 from her bank. She uses $475,000 of the loan proceeds to acquire the land and construct the office building for the sports complex. The remaining

loan proceeds are used to acquire equipment and furnishings. The loan is secured by the land, building, and equipment. What is Marlene's amount at risk in the business if the $750,000 debt was obtained on reasonably commercial terms and is secured by:

a. The business assets purchased, and Marlene is personally liable if the business assets are insufficient to satisfy the debt?
b. The business assets purchased, and Marlene is not personally liable if the business assets are insufficient to satisfy the debt?
c. Assume the same facts as in part b, except that Marlene uses the $750,000 loan to purchase an apartment complex.

20. **LO4** Carlos opens a dry cleaning store during the year. He invests $30,000 of his own money and borrows $60,000 from a local bank. He uses $40,000 of the loan to buy a building and the remaining $20,000 for equipment. During the first year, the store has a loss of $24,000. How much of the loss can Carlos deduct if the loan from the bank is nonrecourse? How much does Carlos have at risk at the end of the first year?

21. **LO4** Return to the facts of problem 20. In the next year, Carlos has a loss from the dry cleaning store of $18,000. How much of the loss can Carlos deduct? Explain.

22. **LO4** Wayne owns 30 percent of Label Maker Corporation. Label Maker is organized as an S corporation. During 2021, Label Maker has a loss of $160,000. At the beginning of 2021, Wayne's at-risk amount in Label Maker is $30,000.
    a. Assuming that Wayne's investment in Label Maker is not a passive activity, what is his deductible loss in 2021?
    b. In 2022, Label Maker has a taxable income of $50,000. What is the effect on Wayne's 2022 income?

23. **LO5, 6, 7** A taxpayer has the following income (losses) for the current year:

| Active Income | Portfolio Income | Passive Income |
|---|---|---|
| $18,000 | $31,000 | $(35,000) |

What is the taxpayer's taxable income (loss) if
a. The taxpayer is a publicly held corporation?
b. The taxpayer is a closely held corporation?
c. The taxpayer is a single individual and the passive income is not from a rental activity?
d. The taxpayer is a single individual and the passive income is the result of a rental activity for which the taxpayer is a qualified real estate professional?
e. The taxpayer is a single individual and the passive income is the result of a rental activity for which the taxpayer fails to qualify as a real estate professional but does meet the active participation test?

24. **LO5, 6, 7** A taxpayer has the following income (losses) for the current year:

| Active Income | Portfolio Income | Passive Income |
|---|---|---|
| $43,000 | $29,000 | $(27,000) |

What is the taxpayer's taxable income (loss) if
a. The taxpayer is a single individual and the passive income is not from a rental activity?
b. The taxpayer is a single individual and the passive income results from a rental activity for which the taxpayer qualifies as a real estate professional?
c. The taxpayer is a single individual and the passive income results from a rental activity for which the taxpayer fails to qualify as a real estate professional but does meet the active participation test?

25. **LO6, 7** Which of the following would be a passive activity? Explain.
    a. Kevin is a limited partner in Marlin Bay Resort and owns a 15 percent interest in the partnership.
    b. Tom owns a 15 percent interest in a real estate development firm. He materially participates in the management and operation of the business.
    c. Jasmine owns and operates a bed-and-breakfast.
    d. Felicia owns a 25 percent working interest in an oil and gas deposit.
    e. Assume the same facts as in part d, except that Felicia owns a 25 percent interest in a partnership that owns a working interest in an oil and gas deposit. She does not materially participate in the management and operation of the partnership.

26. **LO6, 7** Which of the following are passive activities?
    a. Marvin is a limited partner in the Jayhawk Beach Club and owns a 20 percent interest in the partnership.
    b. Marcie owns a royalty interest in an oil and gas operation.
    c. Neil owns an 18-hole semiprivate golf course. He is a certified professional golfer and serves as the club pro. He provides lessons and is involved in the daily management of the business.
    d. Assume the same facts as in part c, except that Neil plays on the professional tour. When on break from the tour, he mingles with the members and conducts golf clinics. The club is managed by his brother and sister.
    e. Laura owns a commercial office building. She spends more than 500 hours a year managing the building. She also spends 1,700 hours working in her own real estate development firm.
    f. Assume the same facts as in part e, except that Laura hires a full-time manager for the commercial office building. She spends 75 hours meeting with the manager and reviewing the operations.

27. **LO4, 5** Sidney and Gertrude own 40 percent of Bearcave Bookstore, an S corporation. The remaining 60 percent is owned by their son Boris. Sidney and Gertrude do not participate in operating or managing the store, and they invested $19,000 in the business when it opened in 2018. The bookstore reported the following net income (loss) for the years 2018 through 2021:

| 2018 | 2019 | 2020 | 2021 |
|---|---|---|---|
| $(24,000) | $(14,000) | $(12,000) | $5,000 |

    a. How much do Sidney and Gertrude have at risk in Bearcave at the end of each year (2018–2021)?
    b. What amount can they recognize as income or loss from Bearcave for each year (2018–2021)?
    c. Assume that Sidney and Gertrude materially participate in Bearcave for each year (2018–2021). What amount can they recognize as income or loss from Bearcave for each year (2018–2021)?

28. **LO7** Aretha and Betina own a 10-unit apartment complex. Aretha owns a 60 percent interest in the apartment complex, and Betina has a 40 percent interest. Aretha is an investment banker and spends 120 hours helping to manage the apartment complex. Betina is the co-owner of a real estate agency where she works 1,600 hours a year. She also spends 520 hours managing the apartment complex. During the current year, the apartment complex generates a loss of $24,000. Aretha's adjusted gross income before considering the loss from the apartment complex is $175,000, and Betina's is $162,000.
    a. How much of the loss can Aretha deduct?
    b. How much of the loss can Betina deduct?

c. Assume the same facts except that Aretha's adjusted gross income before the rental loss is $145,000 and Betina's is $140,000. How much of the loss can Aretha deduct? How much of the loss can Betina deduct?

29. **LO7** Carlos is a 25 percent owner of CEBJ Builders, a company that specializes in residential construction. The other 75 percent of CEBJ is owned by his three brothers. During the year, Carlos spends 1,800 hours managing the operations of CEBJ. He also is the 100 percent owner of four rental properties and spends 125 hours a year maintaining the properties, more than any other individual. During the current year, the four properties generate a loss of $18,500. His adjusted gross income before considering the rental loss is $118,000.
   a. What amount of the loss can Carlos deduct in the current year?
   b. Assume that Carlos's ownership interest in CEBJ is 4 percent. What amount of the loss can he deduct?
   c. Assume that Carlos spends only 600 hours managing CEBJ Builders and 1,200 hours managing a microbrewery he acquired earlier in the year. What amount of the loss can he deduct?
   d. Assume that Carlos hires his brother-in-law to help him manage the properties. Carlos spends 125 hours and his brother-in-law spends 225 hours managing the rental properties. What amount of the loss can Carlos deduct?

30. **LO7** Mort is the sole owner of rental real estate that produces a net loss of $18,000 in 2020 and $20,000 in 2021 and income of $6,000 in 2022. His adjusted gross income, before considering the rental property for the years 2020 through 2022 is $120,000, $140,000, and $90,000, respectively.
   a. What is Mort's adjusted gross income for 2020, 2021, and 2022 if he qualifies as a real estate professional?
   b. What is Mort's adjusted gross income for 2020, 2021, and 2022 if he actively participates in the rental activity?

31. **LO7** Katrina is the sole owner of rental real estate that produces a net loss of $18,000 in 2020 and $22,000 in 2021 and income of $9,000 in 2022. Her adjusted gross income, before considering the rental property for the years 2020 through 2022, is $115,000, $137,000, and $88,000, respectively.
   a. What is Katrina's adjusted gross income for 2020, 2021, and 2022 if she qualifies as a real estate professional?
   b. What is Katrina's adjusted gross income for 2020, 2021, and 2022 if she actively participates in the rental activity?

32. **LO7** Ivan and Olga own a duplex. They collect the rents and make repairs to the property when necessary. That is, they are active participants in the rental property. During the current year, the duplex has gross rents of $16,000 and total allowable deductions of $31,000. What is the effect of the duplex rental on their taxable income if their adjusted gross income is
   a. $87,000?
   b. $122,000?
   c. $155,000?
   d. $139,000?

33. **LO7** Jacqueline is a 60 percent owner of a rental property and has a significant role in the management of the property. During the current year, the property has a rental loss of $21,500. What is the effect of the rental property on her taxable income, if her adjusted gross income is
   a. $71,000?
   b. $187,000?
   c. $129,000?
   d. $107,000?

34. **LO5** Janet has a taxable income of $54,000 from her salary and investment assets. She also owns 3 passive activities that have the following income (loss) for the year.

| | |
|---|---|
| Passive activity 1 | $ 12,000 |
| Passive activity 2 | $ (18,000) |
| Passive activity 3 | $ (9,000) |

a. What is the effect of the passive activities on Janet's income? Explain.
b. How much suspended loss does Janet have in each passive activity?

35. **LO5** Return to the facts of problem 34. In the next year, Janet has a taxable income from her salary and investment activities of $62,000. The results for her three passive activities are

| | |
|---|---|
| Passive activity 1 | $ 15,000 |
| Passive activity 2 | $ (8,000) |
| Passive activity 3 | $ (2,000) |

a. What is the effect of the passive activities on Janet's income? Explain.
b. How much suspended loss does Janet have in each passive activity?

36. **LO7** Mason owns a passive activity that generates a loss of $14,000 in 2020, $12,000 in 2021, and income of $4,000 in 2022. In 2021, Mason purchases a second passive activity that has passive income of $6,000 in 2021 and $10,000 in 2022. Discuss the effect of Mason's passive activity investments on his taxable income in 2020, 2021, and 2022. Assume that neither passive activity involves rental real estate.

37. **LO7** Return to the facts of problem 36. At the end of 2022, Mason sells the passive activity that generated the losses for $16,000. What is the effect on his taxable income if his basis in the activity sold is
a. $4,000?
b. $21,000?

38. **LO5** Jeremy owns a passive activity that has a basis of $30,000 and a suspended loss of $16,000. His taxable income from active and portfolio income is $81,000.
a. What is the effect on Jeremy's taxable income if he sells the passive activity for $37,000?
b. What is the effect on Jeremy's taxable income if he sells the passive activity for $25,000?

39. **LO5** Return to the facts of problem 38. Assume that Jeremy dies when the passive activity has a fair market value of $37,000. What is the effect on Jeremy's taxable income for the year he dies?

40. **LO5** Return to the facts of problem 38. Assume that Jeremy dies when the passive activity has a fair market value of $25,000. What is the effect on Jeremy's taxable income for the year he dies?

41. **LO5** Return to the facts of problem 38. Assume that Jeremy gives the property to his son Felipe when the property has a fair market value of $37,000. What is the effect of the gift on Jeremy's taxable income? Felipe's taxable income?

42. **LO5** Masaya owns a passive activity that has a basis of $32,000 and a suspended loss of $13,000. Masaya's taxable income from active and portfolio income is $73,000.
a. What is the effect on Masaya's taxable income if he sells the passive activity for $46,000?
b. What is the effect on Masaya's taxable income if he sells the passive activity for $26,000?
c. What is the effect on Masaya's taxable income if he dies this year while the fair market value of the passive activity is $40,000?
d. What is the effect on Masaya's taxable income if he dies this year while the fair market value of the passive activity is $22,000?

e. What is the effect on Masaya's taxable income if he gives the passive activity to his daughter Hideko when the fair market value of the passive activity is $40,000? What would the effect of this be on Hideko's taxable income?

43. **LO5** Claudio owns a passive activity that has a basis of $28,000 and a fair market value of $38,000. The activity has suspended losses of $16,000. To reduce their estate, every year Claudio and his wife give their son Anthony and his wife a gift of approximately $40,000. During the year, Anthony sells stock that results in a $10,000 short-term capital loss. A friend of Claudio's suggests that he give his passive activity to Anthony. The friend says that this will allow Claudio to avoid tax on the $10,000 capital gain and let his son offset his short-term capital loss with the $10,000 ($38,000 − $28,000) gain from the sale of the passive activity. In addition, Claudio can use the suspended loss from the passive activity to offset his other ordinary income. Write a letter to Claudio explaining the tax consequences of making the passive activity a gift to his son. Communication Skills

44. **LO8** ABC Company owns a chain of furniture stores. How much loss can ABC Company deduct in each of the following cases? Explain.
   a. ABC closes a store in a depressed part of the county. Rather than move furniture to other stores, ABC sells furniture that had cost $275,000 for $140,000.
   b. A fire severely damages one store. The cost of repairing the damage is $127,000. ABC's basis in the store building is $320,000. ABC's insurance company reimburses ABC $100,000 for the fire damage.
   c. ABC decides to begin replacing some of its older delivery vans. It sells for $4,200 one van that had a basis of $7,300.
   d. ABC discovers that one of its buildings is infested with termites. The building is old and has been fully depreciated for tax purposes. The cost of getting rid of the termites is $8,400, none of which is covered by insurance.
   e. Someone breaks into one store by destroying the security system. Cash of $9,000 is missing from a safe. In addition, televisions that had cost $17,500 and were marked to sell for $34,000 are gone. The security system has a basis of $10,800. Because the system is outdated, a security expert estimates it is worth only $2,700 at the time it is destroyed.

45. **LO8** The Goodson Company is a chain of retail electronics stores. How much of a loss can Goodson deduct in each of the following cases? Explain.
   a. An employee drops a 65-inch 3D television, cracking the plastic casing on the back. The television normally sells for $3,300. The cost of the set is $2,400, and Goodson sells the damaged set for $1,500.
   b. The company replaces its inventory system. The old system cost $45,000 and has a basis of $16,000. The company sells the old system for $7,500. The new system costs $75,000.
   c. A flood damages one of Goodson's retail stores. The building suffers extensive water damage. The basis of the building is $60,000, and the cost of repairing the damage is $72,000. The insurance company reimburses Goodson $50,000.
   d. The owner of Goodson sells a complete home entertainment center (e.g., projection TV, DVD, stereo system) to his sister for $7,000. The usual sales price is $8,500. The system costs $6,300.
   e. Assume the same facts as in part d, except that the owner sells the home entertainment center to his sister for $5,500.
   f. The owner of Goodson finds that the controller has embezzled $10,000 from the company. Before the owner can confront the controller, the controller leaves town and cannot be found.

g. Upon arriving at the company's headquarters, the vice president of sales finds that someone has broken in and stolen three computers. The damage to the outside door is extensive. The cost of repairing the door is $1,500, and the cost of replacing the three computers is $9,500. The original cost of the computers totals $10,500. Goodson's basis in the computers is $5,000. The thieves also stole $350 from the petty cash fund. Goodson files a claim with its insurance company and receives $4,800.

46. **LO9** Gordon is the sole proprietor of Fashion Flowers Florals (FFF). During the current year, one of FFF's delivery vans is involved in an automobile accident. The van has a basis of $6,000. What is FFF's allowable casualty loss deduction under each of the following situations?
    a. A comparable van sells for $4,000. FFF's van was totally destroyed in the accident. FFF's insurance pays $2,200 on the casualty.
    b. A comparable van sells for $8,400. FFF's van was totally destroyed in the accident. FFF's insurance pays $6,400 on the casualty.

47. **LO9** Assume the same facts as in problem 46. What is FFF's allowable casualty loss deduction under each of the following situations?
    a. A comparable van sells for $4,000. After the accident, the insurance adjuster estimates the van was worth $1,500. The insurance company pays FFF $1,200 on the casualty.
    b. A comparable van sells for $8,400. After the accident, the insurance adjuster estimates the value of the van at $1,500. The insurance company pays FFF $1,200 on the casualty.

Communication Skills

48. **LO9** Stella owns a taxicab company. During the year, two of her cabs are involved in accidents. One is totally destroyed; the other is heavily damaged. Stella is able to replace the destroyed cab with an identical model for $5,500. Her adjusted basis in the destroyed cab is $3,750, and the insurance company pays her $2,800. The adjusted basis of the damaged cab is $3,800. The insurance adjuster estimates that the damaged cab is worth $3,600. Although a comparable cab sells for $7,800, the insurance company gives Stella only $2,900. Write a letter to Stella explaining the amount of her deductible casualty loss.

49. **LO9** Rhoda owns an electronics store that is burglarized during the current year. The burglars destroy the point-of-sale terminal and steal $380 from the cash drawer. The point-of-sale terminal was purchased for $7,500, and its adjusted basis is $3,700. The insurance adjuster estimates that the fair market value of a similar point-of-sale terminal is $6,000. The burglars also steal stereo equipment costing $4,200 that has a retail value of $7,000. In breaking into the store, the burglars break a large glass door that costs Rhoda $540 to replace. What is Rhoda's deductible loss if the insurance company reimburses her $5,000?

50. **LO8** Wilbur owns a 25 percent interest in the Talking Horse Corporation, which is organized as an S corporation. His basis in the property is $15,000. For the year, Talking Horse reports an operating loss of $28,000 and a capital loss of $6,000. Wilbur's adjusted gross income is $72,000.
    a. What effect would these losses have on Wilbur's adjusted gross income if he does not materially participate in Talking Horse? Explain.
    b. What effect would these losses have on Wilbur's adjusted gross income if he materially participates in Talking Horse? Explain.

51. **LO10** During 2021, Yoko has total capital gains of $8,000 and total capital losses of $16,000.
    a. What is the effect of the capital gains and losses on Yoko's 2021 taxable income? Explain.
    b. Assume that in 2022 Yoko has total capital gains of $10,000 and total capital losses of $7,500. What is the effect of the capital gains and losses on Yoko's taxable income in 2022? Explain.
    c. How would your answer change if Yoko's total capital losses are $14,000 in 2022?

52. **LO10** Goldie sells 600 shares of Bear Corporation stock for $9,000 on December 14, 2021. She paid $27,000 for the stock in February 2018.
   a. Assuming that Goldie has no other capital asset transactions in 2021, what is the effect of the sale on her 2021 income?
   b. Assume that Goldie has no capital asset transactions in 2022. What is the effect of the Bear Corporation stock sale on her 2022 income?
   c. On July 2, 2023, Goldie sells 100 shares of Panda common stock for $12,400. Goldie purchased the stock on September 4, 2021, for $7,500. What is the effect of the sale on Goldie's 2023 income?
53. **LO8** Labrador Corporation has total capital gains of $18,000 and total capital losses of $35,000 in 2021. Randy owns 25 percent of Labrador's outstanding stock. What is the effect on Labrador's and Randy's 2021 taxable income if
   a. Labrador is a corporation? Explain how Labrador and Randy would treat the capital gains and losses.
   b. Labrador is an S corporation? Explain how Labrador and Randy would treat the capital gains and losses.
54. **LO8** Bongo Corporation was incorporated in 2019. It had no capital asset transactions in 2019. From 2020 through 2023, Bongo has the following capital gains and losses:

| | 2020 | 2021 | 2022 | 2023 |
|---|---|---|---|---|
| Capital gains | $ 14,000 | $ 12,000 | $ 9,000 | $ 30,000 |
| Capital losses | (8,000) | (26,000) | (22,000) | (11,000) |

Assuming that Bongo's marginal tax rate during each of these years is 21 percent, what is the effect of Bongo's capital gains and losses on the amount of tax due each year?

55. **LO8** Newcastle Corporation was incorporated in 2020. For the years 2020 through 2022, Newcastle has the following net capital gain or loss.

| | 2020 | 2021 | 2022 |
|---|---|---|---|
| Net capital gain (loss) | $6,000 | $(27,000) | $18,000 |

If Newcastle is in the 21 percent marginal tax bracket for each of these years, what effect do the net capital gains (losses) have on its tax liability for 2020, 2021, and 2022?

56. **LO10** Sonya, who is single, owns 20,000 shares of Malthouse Corporation stock. She acquired the stock in 2018 for $75,000. On August 12, 2021, Sonya's father tells her of a rumor that Malthouse will file for bankruptcy within the next week. The next day, Sonya sells all her shares of Malthouse for $20,000.
   a. How much of the loss can she deduct?
   b. Assume the same facts, except that the stock is qualifying small-business stock. How much of the loss can she deduct?
   c. Assume the same facts as in part b, except that Sonya is married. How much of the loss can she deduct?
57. **LO10** Rick, a single taxpayer, owns 30,000 shares of qualifying small business stock that he had purchased for $300,000. During the current year, he sells 10,000 of the shares for $25,000.
   a. What are the tax effects for Rick from selling the shares?
   b. Assume that Rick also sells other capital assets at a gain of $12,000. What are the tax effects of Rick's capital asset transactions?
   c. Assume the same facts as in part b. In the year after selling the 10,000 shares of qualified small business stock, Rick has total capital gains of $16,000 and total capital losses of $12,000. What are the effects of Rick's capital asset transactions on his taxable income?
58. **LO10** Evita sells two pieces of land during the current year. She had used the first piece as a parking lot for her pet store. (She owns the store as a sole proprietor.) Communication Skills

The land cost Evita $45,000, and she sells it for $28,000. The second piece is a building lot she had purchased as a speculative investment. Evita paid $45,000 for the lot and sells it for $28,000. Assume that Evita has no other dispositions during the year. Write a letter to Evita explaining the deductible loss from her two land transactions.

59. **LO10** Katelyn purchased 300 shares of Condine, Inc., stock in 2019 for $9,000. During 2021, she sells 200 shares of Condine to her brother, Jon, for $3,600 and the remaining 100 shares to an unrelated third party for $2,000.
   a. Assuming that these are her only stock sales during the year, what impact do these sales have on her 2021 taxable income?
   b. Assume that Jon sells the Condine stock in 2022 for $4,800. What impact does the sale have on his taxable income?
   c. Assume that Jon sells the shares in 2022 for $6,200. What impact does the sale have on his 2022 taxable income?
   d. Assume that Jon sells the shares in 2022 for $3,100. What impact does the sale have on his taxable income?

60. **LO10** Elliot sells some stock to his sister, Nancy, for $4,000. His basis in the stock is $6,000. Several years later, Nancy sells the stock for $7,000.
   a. What is the effect of the sales on Elliot and Nancy?
   b. Assume that the subsequent sale by Nancy is for $5,000.
   c. Assume that the subsequent sale by Nancy is for $2,000.

Communication Skills

61. **LO10** Howard Company is 100 percent owned by Rona. During the current year, Howard sells some land to Rona for $50,000 that had cost Howard $80,000 and that had a fair market value of $100,000. Write a letter to Rona explaining the tax effects of the sale.

62. **LO10** Darlene owns 500 shares of Sandmayor, Inc., common stock that she purchased several years ago for $20,000. During the current year, the Sandmayor stock declines in value. Darlene decides to sell the stock to realize the tax loss. On December 17, she sells the 500 shares for $12,000. Her investment adviser tells her she thinks the Sandmayor stock probably will begin to increase in value next year. On this advice, Darlene purchases 600 shares of Sandmayor common stock on January 10 of the next year for $15,000. The adviser turns out to be right—Darlene sells the 600 shares in May for $22,000. What are the effects of the sales on Darlene's taxable income in each year? Explain.

63. **LO10** Ed owns 500 shares of Northern Company for which he paid $15,000 several years ago. On November 24, he purchases an additional 350 shares for $6,300. Ed sells the original 500 shares for $10,000 on December 14. What are the effects of the December 14 sale? Explain.

64. **LO10** Leona owns 300 shares of Ross Industries. She acquired the shares on February 17, 2019, for $6,500. On September 17, 2021, she acquires another 200 shares of Ross for $4,800. Two weeks later, a lawsuit is filed against Ross for patent infringement, and its stock price drops to $19 per share. Unsure of the outcome of the lawsuit, Leona sells 300 shares of the stock for $5,400 on October 12, 2021. What is her recognized gain or loss on the sale of the Ross stock?

65. **LO12** Jorge and his spouse own a beachfront vacation home in Savannah, Georgia. During the year, high winds from a tropical storm shatter a sliding glass door and rain from the storm causes extensive water damage to the kitchen. The Savannah area qualified for federal disaster relief. Fortunately, during a calm in the storm, Jorge is able to board up the door, which limits the water damage to the kitchen. The items damaged in the storm are:

| | Cost | Value Before | Value After | Insurance Proceeds |
|---|---|---|---|---|
| Kitchen furniture | $2,100 | $1,400 | $400 | $650 |
| TV | 250 | 200 | -0- | 125 |
| Refrigerator | 1,000 | 950 | 100 | 800 |
| Linoleum flooring | 1,600 | 900 | -0- | 500 |

In addition, Jorge pays $625 to replace the sliding glass door. The insurance company will not reimburse him for the cost of the new door because the old sliding glass door did not meet the company's standards for a hurricane area. What is the amount of Jorge's casualty loss before considering any annual limitations that may apply?

66. **LO12** Ghon and Li own a home on Lake Gibran. During a heavy rainstorm, the lake overflows and floods the basement, which is used as their family room. The entire contents of the basement (rug, furniture, stereo, and so on) are destroyed. The flood qualified for federal disaster relief, and the insurance adjuster estimates that the damage to the basement and its contents is $13,500. Ghon and Li do not have flood insurance, so the insurance company will reimburse them only $2,700 for the damage. If their adjusted gross income for the year is $58,000, what is their deductible casualty loss?

67. **LO9, 12** Kevin is the sole proprietor of Murph's Golf Shop. During the current year, a hurricane hits the beach near Kevin's shop. His business building, which has a basis of $60,000, is damaged. In addition, his personal automobile, for which he paid $22,000, is damaged. Fair market values (FMV) before and after the hurricane are

| Case A | FMV Before | FMV After |
|---|---|---|
| Building | $130,000 | $85,000 |
| Automobile | 12,000 | 3,000 |
| **Case B** | | |
| Building | $130,000 | -0- |
| Automobile | 12,000 | -0- |

a. What is Kevin's gross loss in each of the above cases?
b. Assume that in case A, Kevin receives $36,000 from his insurance company for the building and $5,000 for his automobile. What is his allowable loss?
c. Assume that the insurance proceeds are $130,000 and $5,000 in case B. What is the tax effect of the casualty for Kevin?

68. **LO10, 11** Andy sells the following assets during the year.

| | Gain (Loss) |
|---|---|
| Personal automobile | $(2,000) |
| ABC stock | 4,800 |
| Personal furniture | 1,200 |
| BCCI bonds | (9,600) |

What is Andy's deductible loss? Explain.

69. **LO10, 11** Faith, who is single, sells the following assets during 2021:

- 20,000 shares of qualified small business stock at a loss of $62,000. Faith bought the stock in 2016.
- 1,200 shares of Geelong Industries at a gain of $4,500. Faith bought the stock in 2018.
- An XZ10 sailboat at a loss of $3,500. Faith acquired the boat, which she used in her leisure hours, in 2017.
- A 1973 Holden Deluxe automobile at a gain of $3,700. Faith never used the car for business.
- 50 shares of Fremantle, Inc., at a gain of $1,300. Faith bought the stock in 2021 and sells it to her brother.
- 75 shares of Fitzroy Corporation at a loss of $300. Faith bought the stock in 2017 and sells it to her sister.

Calculate Faith's net capital gain (loss) for 2021.

## ISSUE IDENTIFICATION PROBLEMS

In each of the following problems, identify the tax issue(s) posed by the facts presented. Determine the possible tax consequences of each issue that you identify.

70. The Readyhough Corporation was incorporated in 2013. During 2020, the corporation had operating income of $80,000. Because of a strike at its major supplier, the corporation had an operating loss of $60,000 in 2021. The corporation expects to rebound in 2022 forecasting operating income of $140,000. The current interest rate is 6 percent.
71. Celine opens a jewelry store during the current year. She invests $20,000 of her own money and receives a nonrecourse bank loan of $80,000. During the current year, the store has a loss of $24,000.
72. Anton is single and a self-employed plumber. His net income from his business is $56,000. He has dividend income of $6,000 and an $8,000 loss from a rental property in which he actively participates.
73. Rita is the sole owner of Video Plus, a local store that rents video games, software, and movies. She works 40 hours a week managing the store.
74. Margery owns a passive activity with a basis of $15,000. The activity has a $9,000 suspended loss. Margery sells the passive activity for $22,000.
75. Orlando owns a passive activity with a basis of $13,000 and a $6,000 suspended loss. He dies when the passive activity has a fair market value of $17,000.
76. Emma owns and operates Conway Camera. One night someone breaks into the store and steals cameras that cost $2,200. The retail price of the cameras is $3,500.
77. Mike's Pizza decides to replace one of its delivery vehicles. The vehicle has a basis of $2,700 and Mike's is able to sell it for $2,100.
78. Zoriana sells stock that she acquired in 2017 for $7,500. Her basis in the stock is $14,000. She has a $2,000 long-term capital loss carryover from 2020.
79. Alphonse sells stock with a basis of $5,500 to his brother, Conner, for $4,000. His brother sells it later in the year for $5,100.
80. On January 1, 2021, Brenda acquires 200 shares of Disney stock for $8,000. She sells the 200 shares on September 2, 2021, for $30 per share. On September 23, 2021, Brenda acquires 400 shares of Disney stock for $10,400.

## TECHNOLOGY APPLICATIONS

Tax Simulation

81. Alicia, Bob, and Carol are equal partners in Dunning Law Associates. In 2015, Alicia, in an attempt to maximize the firm's return on its investment portfolio, encourages her partners to acquire $90,000 of stock in a local Internet provider. The stock was acquired by the partnership from the issuing corporation and the corporation that issued the stock meets all the tests for the stock to be treated as small business stock. In 2021, when the stock is worth $20,000, Bob and Carol, who are upset with Alicia's investment choice, distribute all the shares of the small business stock to Alicia as part of her partnership distribution. The following year, Alicia sells the stock for $15,000.

    REQUIRED: Determine the tax treatment of Alicia's loss on the sale of the stock. Search a tax research database and find the relevant authority(ies) that forms the basis for your answer. Your answer should include the exact text of the authority (ies) and an explanation of the application of the authority to Alicia's facts. If there is any uncertainty about the validity of your answer, indicate the cause for the uncertainty.

Research Skills

82. Suzanne is married and is the sole owner of Laidlaw Corporation. When the corporation was established in 2010, she received 10,000 shares of qualified small

business stock in exchange for her $100,000 investment. On four occasions, Suzanne made loans totaling $50,000 to the corporation when it had trouble paying its bills. In March 2021, Suzanne cancels the $50,000 debt and receives 5,000 shares of qualified small business stock. In May, she sells all her stock in the corporation for $60,000. Is Suzanne allowed ordinary loss treatment on the sale of her small business stock?

83. Adela owns rental real estate that generated a $27,000 loss during the current year. Using the information below as a guide, prepare a spreadsheet calculating her adjusted gross income. It should be flexible enough to calculate Adela's adjusted gross income if she meets either the real estate professional exception or the active participant test. A template to assist the student in solving this problem can be found at www.cengage.com. Spreadsheet Skills

| | |
|---|---|
| Salary | $80,000 |
| Dividends | 22,000 |
| Interest | 12,500 |

84. Rick and Debbie Siravo own a beachfront home in Wrightsville Beach, N.C. During the year, they rent it for 20 weeks (140 days) at $1,100 per week and use it 10 days for personal purposes. Rick actively participates in the management of the property, but does not qualify as a real estate professional. Their adjusted gross income for the year is $137,200 and the costs of maintaining the home for the year are: Tax Form

| | |
|---|---|
| Mortgage interest | $15,500 |
| Real property taxes | 4,500 |
| Management fee | 1,085 |
| Insurance | 1,200 |
| Utilities | 2,200 |
| Cleaning service (only for rental period) | 1,500 |
| Repairs and maintenance | 700 |
| Depreciation (unallocated) | 8,500 |

Complete Form 1040 Schedule E and Form 8582 using the above information. Rick's Social Security number is 036-87-1458, Debbie's Social Security number is 035-11-4856, and the address of the home is 435 Beachway Lane, Wrightsville Beach, NC 28480. Forms and instructions can be downloaded from the IRS website (www.irs.gov).

# COMPREHENSIVE PROBLEM

85. Calzone Trucking Company is a corporation that is 100 percent owned by Fred Calzone. Before he incorporated in 2018, Fred had operated the business as a sole proprietorship. The taxable income (loss) of Calzone for 2018 through 2020 is as follows:

| | 2018 | 2019 | 2020 |
|---|---|---|---|
| Taxable income (loss) | $32,000 | $(64,000) | $18,000 |

The 2020 taxable income includes a net long-term capital gain of $4,000. Calzone Trucking's 2021 operating income is $43,300 before considering the following transactions:

a. A hailstorm caused part of the roof of the truck barn to collapse. A truck inside sustained damage from the falling debris. The truck barn had a fair market value of $59,000 before the damage and an adjusted basis of $35,000. Repairs to the roof cost $13,200, of which $9,700 was reimbursed by insurance. The truck, which had an adjusted basis of $35,000, was worth $62,000 before the damage and had a fair market value after the damage of $37,000. Calzone Trucking's insurance company paid $16,600 for the damages.

b. Another truck was totally destroyed when its brakes failed and it plunged off a cliff. Fortunately, the driver was able to jump from the truck and escaped unharmed. The truck, which had an adjusted basis of $24,000, was worth $30,000 before the accident. Calzone received $13,700 from its insurance company for the destruction of the truck. In addition, the company was cited for failure to properly maintain the truck and paid a $7,250 fine to the state trucking commission.

c. Calzone sold equipment that had become obsolete for $10,800. The equipment had cost $28,000, and depreciation of $15,400 had been taken on it before the sale.

d. Calzone sold stock it owned in two other companies. Retro Corporation stock, which had cost $21,400, sold for $36,200. Shares of Tread Corporation stock with a cost of $62,100 sold for $31,700. Both stocks had been purchased in 2017.

e. Fred's son wanted to start a delivery business. To help his son out, Fred sold him one of Calzone's used trucks for $8,000. The truck had a fair market value of $15,200 and an adjusted basis of $10,100 at the date of the sale.

Calculate Calzone Trucking's 2021 taxable income. Indicate the amount and the effect of any carryforwards or carrybacks on Calzone Trucking's current, past, or future income.

## DISCUSSION CASES

86. The enactment of the passive loss rules has generally diminished the attractiveness of tax shelters as investments. However, rental real estate continues to provide a viable tax shelter for certain taxpayers. Explain why this is true.

87. Exeter Savings and Loan is located in a two-story building in downtown Exeter. The building has a basement in which the heating system for the bank is located. The bank also uses the basement to store records and photocopying equipment. Last fall, the Saugutuxet River overflowed and flooded the basement. The flood destroyed all the bank's records and damaged all the equipment. The building suffered no serious structural damage.

This is the second time in ten years that the basement has flooded. The state and county conducted a flood control study after the first flood but adopted no formal flood control plans. Fearful of another flood, the bank now stores all its records on the first and second floors.

The bank has claimed a casualty loss for the damaged records and equipment, and the decline in the market value of the building. It contends that because the basement of the building can no longer be used for storage, it is entitled to a casualty loss equal to the difference between the fair market value of the building before the casualty and the fair market value after the casualty. Explain whether Exeter Savings and Loan can deduct as a casualty loss the building's decline in fair market value.

88. Jordan and her brother Jason agree to purchase a hardware store from a local bank, which acquired it through foreclosure. Because the bank wants to sell the business, Jordan and Jason can buy it for only $160,000. Jordan will invest $42,000 and own 70 percent of the business, and Jason will invest $18,000 and own the remaining 30 percent. The bank is financing the remaining $100,000 with a nonrecourse loan secured by the building ($40,000), inventory ($45,000), and equipment ($15,000). Although Jordan and Jason believe that the store will prove to be an excellent investment within a few years, they expect losses of $35,000, $20,000, and $14,000 in the first three years of operation. They anticipate turning a profit

of $16,000 in the fourth year. Jason and Jordan are unsure whether to operate the business as a corporation or an S corporation. Both will materially participate in running the hardware store. Explain to Jordan and Jason how the store's operating results will be taxed if they operate as a corporation versus an S corporation.

## TAX PLANNING CASES

89. Jay is single and works as a salesperson. In December of the current year, he is selected as the company's outstanding salesperson. In recognition of this honor, he receives a $75,000 bonus, which puts him in the 37 percent tax bracket. Jay owns 2,400 shares of stock in Amtrav Corporation, which qualifies as small business stock. His broker has advised him to sell most, if not all, of his Amtrav stock. If he sells all his shares in the current year, he will recognize a $25 per share loss on the stock. Unfortunately, even if he sells all his stock, he will remain in the 37 percent tax bracket. He expects his marginal tax rate will drop to 24 percent next year but will be 32 percent for the years after that. He does not anticipate any other capital gains or losses during the next three years. If Jay's goal is to maximize his net cash flow, develop a strategy for how many shares and in what year(s) he should sell his Amtrav stock. Assume that if he does not sell all his stock in the current year, his loss per share will remain constant and that the time value of money is 7 percent.
90. Tom has $40,000 to invest and seeks your advice. A partner at Global Investments has proposed two investment opportunities: a real estate limited partnership or a five-year investment contract that will pay interest of 8 percent annually and return his original investment at the end of the fifth year. Tom will invest the interest he receives from the investment contract each year in a savings account that will pay 5 percent per year. The limited partnership expects losses in the first two years of $8,000 and $6,000 but expects that its income in years three through five will be $4,000, $10,000, and $12,000. At the end of year five, Tom believes, he will be able to sell the limited partnership at a gain of $5,000. He expects that his marginal tax rate over the five-year period will be 32 percent. Write a letter to Tom explaining whether he should invest in the limited partnership or the investment contract. In your letter, discuss any other factors he should consider concerning the two investments.

## ETHICS DISCUSSION CASE

91. Anthony owned a 2019 Luxuro automobile that had a fair market value of $78,000. He uses the car 90 percent for business. His son James, who is 19, borrows the car without his father's knowledge and totals it in 2020. James has been involved in two car accidents, and his father is afraid that James will not be able to get insurance. Therefore, Anthony decides not to file an insurance claim and deducts the loss on his 2020 tax return. In 2021, Anthony decides to have his friend Brigid, a local CPA, prepare his tax return. In preparing his 2021 return, Brigid reviews Anthony's 2020 return and finds that Anthony took a casualty loss on the Luxuro. Aware that Anthony has insurance, she is perplexed as to why he deducted the loss. Anthony tells her of his son's fearsome driving record and his worry that James could not get insurance. What are Brigid's responsibilities (refer to the Statements on Standards for Tax Services, which can be found at www.aicpa.org), if any, concerning Anthony's 2020 tax return? What effect does the issue have on Brigid's preparation of Anthony's 2021 return?

# 8

# Taxation of Individuals

Learning Objectives:

LO 1 Explain the requirements and the effects of filing status on the income tax paid by individuals.

LO 2 Explain when taxpayers utilize the standard deduction in lieu of their itemized deductions.

LO 3 Explain each of the allowable itemized deductions (medical, taxes, interest, and charitable contributions) and determine how each affects an individual's total itemized deductions.

LO 4 Explain the requirements to be classified as a dependent.

LO 5 Calculate an individual's tax liability and the special provisions for the calculation of the tax liability of a dependent.

LO 6 Explain how tax credits affect a taxpayer's tax liability and explain how each tax credit is determined.

LO 7 Explain the general rules relating to filing requirements.

## concept review

### GENERAL CONCEPTS

**Ability to pay** A tax should be based on the amount that a taxpayer can afford to pay, relative to other taxpayers. pg. 2-2

**Administrative convenience** Those items for which the cost of compliance would exceed the revenue generated are not taxed. pg. 2-3

**Pay as you go** A tax should be collected as close as possible to the time in which the income is earned. pg. 2-5

### ACCOUNTING CONCEPTS

**Annual accounting period** All entities must report the results of their operations on an annual basis (the tax year). Each tax year stands on its own, apart from other tax years. pg. 2-9

**Entity** All transactions must be traced to a single tax entity for recording and reporting by that entity. pg. 2-6

**Tax benefit rule** Any deduction taken in a prior year that is recovered in a subsequent year is income in the year of recovery, to the extent that a tax benefit was received from the deduction. pg. 2-10

### DEDUCTION CONCEPTS

**Business purpose** To be deductible, an expenditure or a loss must have a business or other economic purpose that exceeds any tax avoidance motive. The primary motive for the transaction must be to make a profit. pg. 2-18

**Legislative grace** Any tax relief provided is the result of a specific act of Congress that must be strictly applied and interpreted. All income received is taxable unless a specific provision in the tax law excludes the income from taxation. Deductions must be approached with the philosophy that nothing is deductible unless a provision in the tax law allows the deduction. pg. 2-12

## 8-1 INTRODUCTION

Individuals are by far the biggest single group of taxpaying entities. During 2019, individuals filed 80.6 percent of all tax returns received by the IRS. These returns accounted for more than 76.5 percent of all income tax collected during 2019. Individuals are unique. Unlike corporations, which are formed to conduct a business, individuals engage in both business and personal transactions. As a result of this split for individuals, calculating the tax base of an individual requires consideration of deductions for both business-related expenditures and specifically allowable personal expenditures.

Individuals are taxable entities. Because all individuals who meet certain income requirements must file an annual tax return, they must adopt an accounting period. Although individuals may adopt a fiscal year if they keep a complete set of accounting records, most use a calendar year for convenience. Individuals must also choose an accounting method for reporting their various business and personal activities. Although individuals may use any method of accounting that clearly reflects their income (i.e., cash, accrual, hybrid), unless the individual sells inventories—which require use of the accrual or hybrid method—most individuals choose the simpler cash method.

Exhibit 8-1 presents the format for calculating an individual's taxable income, which generally is equal to gross income minus allowable deductions. The exhibit shows that the basic taxable income calculation involves splitting deductions into two distinct classes: deductions *for* adjusted gross income and deductions *from* adjusted gross income. This split creates the intermediate figure called **adjusted gross income (AGI)**.

In Chapter 6, we discussed those expenditures that are allowed as deductions for adjusted gross income. The basic difference between the two classes of deductions is that most for-AGI deductions either have a business purpose or are employment related, whereas most from-AGI deductions are personal expenditures. Congress, through legislative grace, allows some personal expenditures (e.g., interest on student loans) as a deduction for AGI.

In this chapter, we finish the discussion of deductions by focusing on those personal expenditures that are deductible. Because personal expenditure deductions are allowed through legislative grace, most of a taxpayer's personal expenditures are not deductible. A characteristic unique to individuals is that some minimal amount of personal expenditure is necessary to exist—money that is not available for paying taxes. Congress has recognized this characteristic by allowing all taxpayers to deduct a minimum amount of personal expenditures.

Because Congress has created limits that tie some allowable personal deductions to the adjusted gross income of the taxpayer (e.g., casualty losses), adjusted gross income is a key component for determining the amount of allowable from-AGI deductions.

*Exhibit 8-1*

### Individual Income Tax Calculation

| | |
|---|---|
| Gross income (all income received less exclusions) | $ XXX |
| Less: Deductions *for* adjusted gross income | (XXX) |
| Equals: Adjusted gross income (AGI) | $ XXX |
| Less: Deductions *from* adjusted gross income | |
| The greater of | |
| 1. Itemized deductions | |
| OR | |
| 2. Applicable standard deduction | (XXX) |
| Less: QBI deduction | (XXX) |
| Equals: Taxable income | $ XXX |
| Calculation of tax due (refund) | |
| Tax on taxable income (from rate schedule/table) | $ XXX |
| Add: Additional taxes | XXX |
| Less: Tax credits | (XXX) |
| Equals: Net tax | $ XXX |
| Less: Amounts withheld for payment of tax | (XXX) |
| Estimated tax payments | (XXX) |
| Equals: Tax due (refund of tax paid) | $ XXX |

The remainder of this chapter is divided into two parts. The first discusses the filing status of a taxpayer and the basic allowable deductions from adjusted gross income. The chapter concludes with a discussion of the calculation of an individual's income tax liability. The discussion focuses on the tax treatment of income earned by children younger than 18, individual tax credits, and the requirements for filing a tax return. Determining who can be a dependent and the filing status of the taxpayer are discussed first because they affect many of the topics discussed throughout the chapter.

## 8-2 FILING STATUS

LO 1 Explain the requirements and the effects of filing status on the income tax paid by individuals.

A basic concept of the income tax system is that taxpayers pay tax according to their ability to pay. The measure of ability to pay is straightforward for an entity such as a corporation—gross income minus business-related deductions provides a reasonable measure of a corporate entity's ability to pay tax. Although this same measure may be appropriate for measuring the ability to pay tax on an individual's business income, it does not take into account a basic fact of life—individuals must incur some minimum level of personal expenditure just to stay alive. The income tax law takes this into account by allowing standard deductions and setting tax rates. For example, by imposing a higher marginal tax rate at a lower level of income for an unmarried person than for a married couple, the unmarried person pays a higher average tax rate. Based on ability to pay, a single person with a taxable income of $30,000 can afford to pay more tax than a married couple with the same $30,000 in taxable income. The tax law recognizes this difference in ability to pay by basing standard deductions and average tax rates on the taxpayer's **filing status**.

Individuals are classified in two groups—married and unmarried. Married taxpayers may either commingle all their income and deductions and file one return (joint return), or they may each file a separate return. Unmarried taxpayers may be classified as single, or if they qualify, as a head of household. This results in four filing statuses:

- Married, filing jointly (including a surviving spouse)
- Married, filing separately
- Single
- Head of household

### 8-2a Married, Filing Jointly

To qualify for the status of **married, filing jointly**, the taxpayers must be legally married as of the last day of the tax year.[1] If a spouse dies during the year, filing status is determined as of the date of death of the spouse if the survivor did not remarry during the year. Taxpayers who are divorced during the year or who are legally separated at the end of the year are not considered married for tax purposes. As originally conceived, the joint return filing status was designed to divide the combined income of a married couple in half and tax each half at the same rate as a single individual. The income-splitting benefit of a joint return has eroded through the years as Congress has changed the basic rate schedules. However, a married couple filing jointly may still pay less tax than a single individual at the same level of income. For example, an examination of the 2021 tax rate schedules in Appendix B shows that a single individual begins paying a 12-percent marginal tax rate at $9,950, whereas a married couple does not enter the 12-percent rate bracket until their taxable income reaches $19,900. Thus, at incomes greater than $9,950, married couples filing jointly pay less total tax than a single taxpayer with the same taxable income. The effect is to assess a lower average tax rate on the joint return.

In 1954, Congress recognized that the death of a spouse usually works a hardship on the survivor when a dependent child is still living in the home. In recognition of this hardship, a **surviving spouse** who has at least one dependent child or stepchild living at home may use the joint return tax rates to compute the tax for two tax years after the year in which the spouse died. In the year of death, the surviving spouse also files a joint return.

**Example 1** Juan and Bonita are married and have two dependent children living at home. In 2021, Juan is killed in an avalanche while skiing. What is their filing status for 2021? How will Bonita file for subsequent years?

**Discussion: In the year of Juan's death, Bonita files a joint return. For 2022 and 2023, she files as surviving spouse and uses the joint return tax rates if at least one of her two children remains a dependent and continues to live at home. If Bonita remarries, she would either file a joint return with her new spouse or file separately as a married taxpayer.**

## 8-2b Married, Filing Separately

Although married taxpayers may file separate returns, there are very limited circumstances in which it is to a couple's advantage to choose this status. An examination of the tax rate schedules in Appendix B shows that married couples filing separately pay higher marginal tax rates at lower income levels than any other filing status category. As a result, the **married, filing separately**, status has the highest average tax rate for any income level greater than $314,150 in 2021. In addition, Congress has carefully crafted most other tax relief provisions to take away any advantage this filing status might offer. Its primary use is in situations of marital or financial disagreement in which the spouses cannot agree to file together and are not divorced or legally separated by year's end.

## 8-2c Single

A **single** taxpayer is a person who is not married on the last day of the tax year and does not have any dependents to support. Although single individuals pay more than a married couple filing jointly on the same taxable income, their taxes are less than those paid by a married couple filing separately. Historically, there existed a marriage penalty where married couples paid a higher tax on a joint return than they would have paid had they remained single. However, as the example below indicates, the 2017 Tax Cut and Jobs Act has mostly removed this penalty.

**Example 2** Harold and Sadie are a married couple with a taxable income of $170,000. If they had filed as single individuals, Harold's taxable income would have been $80,000 and Sadie's taxable income would have been $90,000. What is their "marriage penalty tax" for 2021?

**Discussion: The 2017 Tax Cut and Jobs Act has in most situations removed the marriage tax penalty and, as this example indicates, married filing joint results in a lower tax, by $73, than if the couple had both been single.**

| Using the 2021 Tax Rate Schedules | | |
|---|---|---|
| Tax on $170,000 for a Married Couple Filing a Joint Return | | |
| [$9,328 + 22% × ($170,000 − $81,050)] = | | $28,897 |
| Tax on $80,000 for a Single Individual | | |
| [$4,664+ 22% × ($80,000 – $40,525)] = | $13,349 | |
| Tax on $90,000 for a Single Individual | | |
| [$14,751 + 24% × ($90,000 – $86,375)] = | $15,621 | $28,970 |
| Tax difference between married filing joint and single | | $ 73 |

## 8-2d Head of Household

The head of household filing status recognizes that some single taxpayers share a characteristic of married taxpayers—the burden of extra living costs to support a relative. To qualify as a **head of household**, the unmarried taxpayer must pay more than half the cost of maintaining a home that is the principal residence for more than half the year of a qualifying child or an individual who qualifies as a dependent of the taxpayer. A qualifying child includes the taxpayer's children (including adopted children and foster children), siblings and step-siblings, and their descendants. Parents who qualify as dependents do not have to live in the taxpayer's home for the taxpayer to claim head of household status.[2]

**Example 3** Larry is legally divorced. His 4-year-old son lives with him for the entire year and Larry's son qualifies as a dependent. What is Larry's filing status?

**Discussion: Because Larry is unmarried and maintains a household for a dependent child for more than half the year, he is entitled to file as a head of household.**

**Example 4** Assume that in example 3, Larry's son is unmarried, 26, and does not qualify as a dependent. If the son lives in Larry's home for the entire year, what is Larry's filing status?

**Discussion: Because Larry's son is not his dependent, he cannot claim head of household.**

A related relief provision lets an abandoned spouse file as a head of household. A married person is treated as an **abandoned spouse** if a dependent child lives in the taxpayer's home for more than half the year and the taxpayer's spouse does not live in the home at any time during the last half of the year.[3] The benefit provided by this provision is that a married taxpayer is considered unmarried for the entire year.

**Example 5** Lily and Bob married in 2012. They have one child, Bobby, who is 7. During the current year, Bob leaves the state on March 3. Lily is unaware of Bob's whereabouts, and no formal divorce proceedings are initiated. What is Lily's filing status for the current year?

**Discussion: Because Lily has a child living with her who qualifies as a dependent and her husband does not live in the home during the last 6 months of the tax year, Lily is considered unmarried for the entire year. Therefore, she may file as a head of household.**

Note that if formal divorce proceedings had begun and Lily and Bob were legally separated, Lily would have been considered unmarried under the general rules and would have qualified as a head of household. The primary use of the abandoned spouse provision is in cases in which one spouse has left the household and no formal divorce proceedings have begun as of the end of the tax year.

## 8-3 DEDUCTIONS FROM ADJUSTED GROSS INCOME

LO 2
Explain when taxpayers utilize the standard deduction in lieu of their itemized deductions.

This class of deductions consists of expenditures that Congress has allowed for certain costs that individuals incur that reduce the amount available to pay taxes. There is a minimum deduction allowable to all taxpayers called the **standard deduction**. As a matter of legislative grace and under the administrative convenience concept, taxpayers who incur minimum levels of the allowable itemized deductions may choose to use the minimum deduction instead of incurring the cost necessary to substantiate itemized deductions.

### 8-3a Standard Deduction

The amount of the standard deduction is based on the filing status of the taxpayer. The deduction is based on a statutorily determined amount for each category of filing status. Because costs are affected by inflation, the standard deduction amounts are adjusted upward each year for inflation.[4] Standard deduction amounts for 2020 and 2021 are provided in Table 8-1.

*Table 8-1*

## Standard Deduction Amounts—2020 and 2021

| Filing Status | 2020 | 2021 |
|---|---|---|
| Single taxpayers | $12,400 | $12,550 |
| Married taxpayers, filing jointly | $24,800 | $25,100 |
| Married taxpayers, filing separately | $12,400 | $12,550 |
| Head of household | $18,650 | $18,800 |
| Surviving spouse | $24,800 | $25,100 |

In addition to the regular standard deductions allowed all taxpayers, taxpayers who are either blind (as defined by the tax law)[5] or who have attained age 65 by the end of the tax year are allowed additional standard deductions. Unmarried taxpayers are allowed an additional standard deduction of $1,700 in 2021 ($1,650 in 2020) for each condition. Married taxpayers and a surviving spouse are allowed an additional $1,350 in 2021 ($1,300 in 2020) for each condition.

**Example 6** Malcolm, a single taxpayer, is 62 and legally blind. What is his 2021 standard deduction?

**Discussion: Malcolm's standard deduction is equal to the sum of the $12,550 standard deduction for a single taxpayer and an additional standard deduction of $1,700 for his blindness, a total of $14,250.**

**If Malcolm is 65 as of December 31, 2021, he is entitled to an additional $1,700 standard deduction for age, bringing his total standard deduction to $15,950. This is the maximum standard deduction allowed a single taxpayer.**

**Example 7** Carl and Luis file a joint tax return for 2021. Carl is 67, and Luis is 59. In addition, Luis is legally blind. What is the amount of Carl and Luis' 2021 standard deduction?

**Discussion: Carl and Luis' standard deduction is equal to the sum of the married, filing jointly, standard deduction, $25,100, and 2 additional standard deductions of $1,350 each (total $2,700) for Carl's age and Luis' blindness, a total of $27,800.**

Note that the additional standard deductions allowed for age and blindness are added to the general standard deduction amount for comparison with the taxpayer's itemized deductions. The additional standard deduction amounts are not added to the taxpayer's itemized deductions.

**Example 8** Return to the facts of example 7. If Carl and Luis' allowable itemized deductions total $24,750, what is their deduction from adjusted gross income for 2021?

**Discussion: Carl and Luis deduct the greater of their itemized deductions ($24,750) or their allowable standard deduction ($27,800). In this case, the standard deduction is greater, and they will not itemize their deductions.**

**Example 9** Assume that in example 8, Carl and Luis' allowable itemized deductions total $28,000. What is their deduction from adjusted gross income in 2021?

**Discussion: Carl and Luis deduct the greater of their itemized deductions ($28,000) or their allowable standard deduction ($27,800). In this case, Carl and Luis should choose to itemize their deductions to get the $28,000 deduction. Note: The $2,700 additional standard deduction Carl and Luis receive for age and blindness is not added to the itemized deduction amount. In effect, taxpayers with such conditions**

**who itemize their deductions do not receive any additional benefit because of their condition.**

## 8-3b Itemized Deductions

Individuals are allowed to deduct certain personal expenditures as **deductions from adjusted gross income** in lieu of the standard deduction. That is, taxpayers itemize deductions only when the sum of their allowable deductions exceeds their standard deduction.

LO 3
Explain each of the allowable itemized deductions (medical, taxes, interest, and charitable contributions) and determine how each affects an individual's total itemized deductions.

**Example 10** Raymond is a single individual with total allowable itemized deductions in 2021 of $11,100. How much of a deduction from adjusted gross income is Raymond allowed on his 2021 return?

**Discussion: Because the standard deduction for a single taxpayer in 2021 is $12,550, Raymond uses the standard deduction amount to calculate his 2021 taxable income.**

**Example 11** Assume that Raymond's total allowable itemized deductions are $13,200 for 2021. How much can Raymond deduct on his 2021 return?

**Discussion: Because Raymond's allowable itemized deductions exceed the $12,550 standard deduction, he deducts the $13,200 in itemized deductions in calculating his 2021 taxable income.**

In allowing certain personal expenditures to be deducted, Congress has exercised its power under the legislative grace concept to restrict the amount of deductible expenditures. These restrictions limit deductions to amounts exceeding a stated percentage of the taxpayer's adjusted gross income. Only amounts in excess of the limit are deductible. Restricting these deductions provides an element of administrative convenience. That is, with these limitations, many taxpayers will not have sufficient amounts of deductions to itemize, choosing instead to use the standard deduction amount. The use of the standard deduction lowers compliance costs, both for the taxpayer, who does not have to keep records of small amounts of expenses, and the government, which does not have to audit the standard deduction. This chapter discusses in turn each general category of itemized deductions and any applicable limitations. Table 8-2 summarizes the categories of allowable itemized deductions and their limitations.

### Medical Expenses

Individuals are allowed a deduction for their unreimbursed medical costs as well as those of their spouse and any dependents. An individual does not have to meet the gross income test or the joint return test to qualify for medical expense purposes.[6] A person who meets the support, relative, and residency tests is considered a dependent for purposes of the medical expense deduction. This treatment recognizes situations in which taxpayers are expending significant amounts on behalf of relatives who, because they earn too much money or are married, are not technically dependents. In addition, note that the medical expense area is the only context in which you are allowed a deduction for the payment of expenses of another taxpayer.

**Medical expenses** are defined as those expenditures incurred for "diagnosis, cure, mitigation, treatment, or prevention of disease," as well as those that are incurred because of problems "affecting any structure or function of the body."[7] This definition encompasses most costs we usually think of as medical expenses—doctor bills, dentistry, optometry, surgery, medicine and drugs, hospital charges, and so on. Deductions for medicines and drugs are limited to prescription drugs and insulin. In addition to these typical costs, taxpayers can deduct the cost of health and accident insurance premiums and transportation costs of 16 cents per mile for travel to and from the place of medical care.[8] Exhibit 8-2 lists deductible and nondeductible medical costs.

Table 8-2

## Summary of Allowable Itemized Deductions

| Type of Expense | Allowable Expenses | Limitations |
|---|---|---|
| Medical expenses | Unreimbursed medical expenses—doctors, dentists, optometrists, eyeglasses, hearing aids, medical insurance premiums, travel to medical care | Only prescription medicine and drugs and insulin allowed as medical expenses<br>Total medical expenses limited to the excess of 7.5% of adjusted gross income |
| Taxes | State and local income taxes, property taxes | Property taxes must be ad valorem |
| Interest | Qualified home mortgage interest | Interest on up to $750,000 in acquisition debt on taxpayer's principal residence and 1 other residence |
| | Investment interest | Investment interest deduction cannot exceed net investment income |
| Charitable contributions | Cash and property contributed to qualifying educational, religious, charitable, scientific, or literary organizations | Total deduction cannot exceed 60% of adjusted gross income (100% for 2020 and 2021)<br>Contributions of long-term capital gain property deducted at fair market value cannot exceed 30% of adjusted gross income |
| Casualty losses | Losses on personal use property from casualty is permitted if the casualty occurs in a federal disaster area (see Chapter 7). | Amount of loss is the lesser of the decline in value of the property or its adjusted basis<br>$100 statutory floor per occurrence<br>10% of adjusted gross income limitation for all casualties |
| Miscellaneous | Gambling losses, disabled work-related expenses, unrecovered annuity investment | Fully deductible |

Exhibit 8-2

## Examples of Medical Expenses

| Deductible Items | Nondeductible Items |
|---|---|
| The cost of all medical drugs, special foods, and drinks your doctor prescribes for treatment of an illness; pills or other birth control items your doctor prescribes; vitamins, iron, etc. your doctor prescribes; insulin. | Toothpaste<br>Cosmetics<br>Vitamins for general health<br>Veterinarian's fees |
| Payments to or for a doctor, surgeon, dentist, osteopath, ophthalmologist, optometrist, psychiatrist, psychologist, hospital care, therapy, lab fees, diagnostic tests, X-ray examination or treatment, nursing care. | Illegal operations or drugs<br>Cosmetic surgery<br>Funeral or burial expenses |
| Special items or equipment such as false teeth, eyeglasses, hearing aids, crutches, prescribed elastic hose, artificial limbs, guide dogs for the blind or deaf, motorized wheelchair, hand controls on a car, special telephone for the deaf. | Maternity clothing<br>Diaper service |
| Transportation to get medical care—to and from doctor, dentist, hospital, etc.<br>Health and accident insurance premiums, Medicare premiums—Parts A and B. | Life insurance premiums<br>Loss-of-earnings insurance premiums<br>Automobile insurance premiums |

Unreimbursed medical costs are deductible only to the extent that they exceed 7.5 percent of adjusted gross income. That is, medical costs below this limit are effectively disallowed.[9] This limitation severely restricts the benefit of the medical expense deduction for taxpayers with high incomes and/or those covered by medical insurance. Although low-income taxpayers are more likely to have medical expenses that exceed the limitation, most low-income taxpayers use the standard deduction and therefore receive no benefit for the medical expenses incurred.

**Example 12** Ari is a single individual with an adjusted gross income of $100,000. During the current year, he incurs several medical expenses. What is his allowable deduction for the following expenses?

| | |
|---|---|
| Doctors | $2,500 |
| Dentist | 1,250 |
| Optometrist | 150 |
| Prescription drugs | 375 |
| Aspirin, cold pills | 45 |
| Contact lenses | 200 |
| Crutch rental for broken leg | 80 |
| Health insurance premiums | 2,300 |
| Transportation—100 miles to and from doctors, dentist, etc. | |
| Reimbursements for medical care | 2,800 |

**Discussion: All of these are allowable medical expenses, with the exception of the $45 for aspirin and cold pills, which are not prescription drugs. In addition, Ari is allowed a deduction of 16 cents per mile for the 100 miles of transportation costs. His total allowable medical expenses before reimbursement are $6,871 ($2,500 + $1,250 + $150 + $375 + $200 + $80 + $2,300 + $16). Unreimbursed medical expenses are $4,071 ($6,871 − $2,800). This is subject to the 7.5% of AGI limitation, which is $7,500 (7.5% × $100,000). Therefore, Ari is not entitled to a medical expense deduction because his unreimbursed expenses do not exceed the AGI limitation.**

## Taxes

The 2017 Tax Cut and Jobs Act limits the deduction paid for state and local income taxes, real estate taxes, and other personal property taxes to $10,000.[10] For tax years beginning after December 31, 2003, a taxpayer can elect to deduct the greater of the amount paid in state and local income taxes or the amount paid in state and local sales taxes. This change is particularly appealing to residents in states that do not impose a state income tax (Texas, Washington, Tennessee, New Hampshire, Florida, Wyoming, Nevada, South Dakota). In determining the amount of their state and local sales tax deduction, a taxpayer will have two options. The first is to accumulate through actual receipts the amount paid in sales taxes during the year. The second is to use the table amount provided by the IRS that approximates the amount of sales taxes a taxpayer paid during the year. If the taxpayer chooses to use the table amount, the taxpayer will be allowed to add to that amount the sales tax paid on motor vehicles, boats and other items specified by the IRS.

**Example 13** Andre is single and lives in Alabama, which imposes a state income tax. During the year, Andre has income of $89,000 and pays $1,950 in state and local income taxes. Based on the table amount in Exhibit 8-3, Andre's sales tax deduction is $630. In addition, Andre purchased a motor vehicle during the year and paid $1,538 in sales tax on the purchase. What amount can Andre deduct in taxes for the year?

**Discussion: Andre's tax deduction for the year is $2,168. Andre can elect to deduct the amount he paid during the year in sales tax $2,168 ($1,538 + $630) since it is greater than the $1,950 he paid during the year in state and local income taxes. In computing his sales tax deduction, Andre is allowed to add the sales tax he paid on the motor vehicle to the table amount provided by the IRS. Note: Generally, a taxpayer who lives in state with an income tax will elect to use the amount of state income taxed paid over the sales tax deduction. Only in a year in which the taxpayer makes a major purchase (e.g., motor vehicle, boat) will the sales taxes paid possibly exceed the amount paid in state income taxes.**

*Exhibit 8-3*

# Sales Tax Deduction

## 2020 Optional State Sales Tax Tables

| Income | | Family Size | | | | | | Family Size | | | | | | Family Size | | | | | |
|---|---|---|---|---|---|---|---|---|---|---|---|---|---|---|---|---|---|---|---|
| At least | But less than | 1 | 2 | 3 | 4 | 5 | Over 5 | 1 | 2 | 3 | 4 | 5 | Over 5 | 1 | 2 | 3 | 4 | 5 | Over 5 |
| | | **Alabama** | | | **1** | | **4.0000%** | **Arizona** | | | **2** | | **5.6000%** | **Arkansas** | | | **2** | | **6.5000%** |
| $0 | $20,000 | 282 | 327 | 358 | 382 | 401 | 429 | 280 | 304 | 318 | 329 | 338 | 350 | 359 | 389 | 407 | 421 | 432 | 446 |
| $20,000 | $30,000 | 393 | 456 | 498 | 530 | 557 | 594 | 419 | 453 | 475 | 491 | 505 | 522 | 536 | 580 | 608 | 628 | 644 | 666 |
| $30,000 | $40,000 | 448 | 519 | 567 | 603 | 634 | 676 | 491 | 531 | 557 | 576 | 591 | 612 | 628 | 679 | 712 | 735 | 755 | 780 |
| $40,000 | $50,000 | 495 | 573 | 625 | 665 | 698 | 745 | 552 | 598 | 626 | 648 | 665 | 688 | 707 | 764 | 801 | 828 | 849 | 878 |
| $50,000 | $60,000 | 536 | 620 | 676 | 719 | 755 | 805 | 607 | 657 | 688 | 712 | 730 | 756 | 777 | 840 | 880 | 910 | 933 | 965 |
| $60,000 | $70,000 | 572 | 661 | 721 | 767 | 805 | 858 | 657 | 710 | 744 | 769 | 790 | 817 | 840 | 908 | 952 | 983 | 1009 | 1044 |
| $70,000 | $80,000 | 605 | 699 | 762 | 810 | 850 | 906 | 702 | 759 | 796 | 823 | 844 | 874 | 897 | 971 | 1017 | 1051 | 1079 | 1116 |
| $80,000 | $90,000 | 636 | 734 | 800 | 850 | 892 | 951 | 744 | 805 | 843 | 872 | 895 | 926 | 951 | 1029 | 1078 | 1114 | 1143 | 1182 |
| $90,000 | $100,000 | 664 | 766 | 835 | 888 | 931 | 992 | 784 | 848 | 888 | 918 | 942 | 975 | 1002 | 1084 | 1135 | 1173 | 1204 | 1245 |
| $100,000 | $120,000 | 702 | 809 | 881 | 937 | 982 | 1047 | 837 | 905 | 948 | 980 | 1005 | 1040 | 1069 | 1156 | 1211 | 1252 | 1284 | 1328 |
| $120,000 | $140,000 | 750 | 864 | 940 | 999 | 1048 | 1116 | 905 | 979 | 1025 | 1059 | 1087 | 1125 | 1156 | 1251 | 1310 | 1354 | 1389 | 1437 |
| $140,000 | $160,000 | 794 | 914 | 995 | 1057 | 1109 | 1180 | 969 | 1047 | 1097 | 1134 | 1163 | 1203 | 1236 | 1338 | 1401 | 1448 | 1486 | 1537 |
| $160,000 | $180,000 | 834 | 960 | 1045 | 1110 | 1164 | 1239 | 1028 | 1111 | 1163 | 1202 | 1233 | 1276 | 1311 | 1418 | 1486 | 1535 | 1575 | 1629 |
| $180,000 | $200,000 | 872 | 1003 | 1091 | 1159 | 1215 | 1294 | 1083 | 1170 | 1225 | 1266 | 1299 | 1344 | 1381 | 1494 | 1565 | 1618 | 1660 | 1716 |
| $200,000 | $225,000 | 911 | 1048 | 1139 | 1210 | 1268 | 1350 | 1140 | 1232 | 1290 | 1333 | 1368 | 1415 | 1454 | 1573 | 1648 | 1703 | 1747 | 1807 |
| $225,000 | $250,000 | 953 | 1095 | 1190 | 1264 | 1325 | 1410 | 1202 | 1299 | 1359 | 1405 | 1441 | 1491 | 1532 | 1657 | 1736 | 1794 | 1841 | 1904 |
| $250,000 | $275,000 | 992 | 1139 | 1238 | 1314 | 1377 | 1466 | 1260 | 1361 | 1425 | 1472 | 1510 | 1562 | 1605 | 1737 | 1819 | 1880 | 1929 | 1995 |
| $275,000 | $300,000 | 1028 | 1181 | 1283 | 1362 | 1427 | 1518 | 1315 | 1421 | 1487 | 1537 | 1576 | 1630 | 1675 | 1812 | 1898 | 1962 | 2013 | 2082 |
| $300,000 | or more | 1242 | 1423 | 1544 | 1638 | 1716 | 1824 | 1641 | 1772 | 1854 | 1916 | 1965 | 2032 | 2087 | 2258 | 2365 | 2445 | 2508 | 2594 |

| Income | | **California** | | | **3** | | **7.2500%** | **Colorado** | | | **2** | | **2.9000%** | **Connecticut** | | | **4** | | **6.3500%** |
|---|---|---|---|---|---|---|---|---|---|---|---|---|---|---|---|---|---|---|---|
| $0 | $20,000 | 360 | 390 | 408 | 422 | 433 | 448 | 146 | 157 | 164 | 169 | 173 | 179 | 270 | 283 | 290 | 296 | 300 | 306 |
| $20,000 | $30,000 | 529 | 572 | 599 | 619 | 635 | 657 | 216 | 233 | 243 | 251 | 257 | 265 | 401 | 420 | 431 | 439 | 445 | 454 |
| $30,000 | $40,000 | 616 | 665 | 696 | 720 | 738 | 763 | 253 | 272 | 284 | 293 | 300 | 310 | 469 | 490 | 503 | 513 | 520 | 530 |
| $40,000 | $50,000 | 690 | 745 | 780 | 806 | 826 | 855 | 284 | 306 | 319 | 329 | 337 | 348 | 526 | 551 | 565 | 576 | 584 | 595 |
| $50,000 | $60,000 | 756 | 816 | 854 | 882 | 905 | 935 | 312 | 335 | 350 | 361 | 370 | 382 | 578 | 604 | 620 | 632 | 641 | 653 |
| $60,000 | $70,000 | 815 | 880 | 920 | 951 | 975 | 1008 | 337 | 362 | 378 | 390 | 399 | 412 | 624 | 652 | 670 | 682 | 692 | 706 |
| $70,000 | $80,000 | 869 | 938 | 981 | 1013 | 1039 | 1074 | 360 | 387 | 404 | 416 | 426 | 440 | 666 | 697 | 715 | 729 | 739 | 753 |
| $80,000 | $90,000 | 919 | 992 | 1038 | 1072 | 1099 | 1136 | 381 | 410 | 428 | 441 | 452 | 466 | 705 | 738 | 757 | 772 | 783 | 798 |
| $90,000 | $100,000 | 966 | 1043 | 1090 | 1126 | 1155 | 1193 | 401 | 431 | 450 | 464 | 475 | 490 | 742 | 776 | 797 | 812 | 824 | 839 |
| $100,000 | $120,000 | 1029 | 1110 | 1160 | 1198 | 1229 | 1270 | 428 | 460 | 480 | 495 | 506 | 523 | 791 | 827 | 849 | 865 | 878 | 895 |
| $120,000 | $140,000 | 1110 | 1197 | 1251 | 1292 | 1324 | 1369 | 462 | 497 | 518 | 534 | 547 | 564 | 854 | 893 | 917 | 934 | 948 | 966 |
| $140,000 | $160,000 | 1185 | 1277 | 1335 | 1378 | 1413 | 1460 | 494 | 531 | 554 | 571 | 585 | 603 | 913 | 955 | 980 | 999 | 1013 | 1032 |
| $160,000 | $180,000 | 1253 | 1351 | 1412 | 1458 | 1495 | 1544 | 524 | 563 | 587 | 605 | 619 | 639 | 967 | 1011 | 1038 | 1058 | 1073 | 1093 |
| $180,000 | $200,000 | 1318 | 1421 | 1485 | 1533 | 1571 | 1623 | 552 | 593 | 618 | 637 | 652 | 673 | 1018 | 1064 | 1093 | 1113 | 1129 | 1151 |
| $200,000 | $225,000 | 1386 | 1493 | 1560 | 1611 | 1651 | 1706 | 581 | 623 | 650 | 670 | 686 | 708 | 1070 | 1119 | 1149 | 1171 | 1188 | 1211 |
| $225,000 | $250,000 | 1458 | 1570 | 1641 | 1694 | 1736 | 1793 | 612 | 657 | 685 | 706 | 722 | 745 | 1127 | 1178 | 1210 | 1233 | 1251 | 1275 |
| $250,000 | $275,000 | 1525 | 1643 | 1717 | 1772 | 1816 | 1876 | 641 | 688 | 717 | 739 | 757 | 780 | 1180 | 1234 | 1267 | 1291 | 1309 | 1335 |
| $275,000 | $300,000 | 1590 | 1712 | 1789 | 1846 | 1892 | 1954 | 668 | 717 | 748 | 771 | 789 | 814 | 1230 | 1287 | 1321 | 1346 | 1366 | 1392 |
| $300,000 | or more | 1968 | 2118 | 2212 | 2282 | 2338 | 2415 | 832 | 892 | 930 | 958 | 981 | 1011 | 1527 | 1598 | 1640 | 1671 | 1695 | 1728 |

| Income | | **District of Columbia** | | | **4** | | **6.0000%** | **Florida** | | | **1** | | **6.0000%** | **Georgia** | | | **2** | | **4.0000%** |
|---|---|---|---|---|---|---|---|---|---|---|---|---|---|---|---|---|---|---|---|
| $0 | $20,000 | 241 | 250 | 255 | 258 | 261 | 265 | 307 | 329 | 342 | 352 | 360 | 370 | 199 | 215 | 226 | 233 | 239 | 247 |
| $20,000 | $30,000 | 360 | 372 | 380 | 385 | 389 | 395 | 463 | 495 | 515 | 529 | 541 | 557 | 298 | 321 | 336 | 347 | 356 | 368 |
| $30,000 | $40,000 | 422 | 436 | 445 | 451 | 456 | 462 | 543 | 581 | 604 | 622 | 635 | 654 | 349 | 376 | 394 | 407 | 417 | 431 |
| $40,000 | $50,000 | 475 | 491 | 500 | 507 | 513 | 520 | 613 | 655 | 682 | 701 | 717 | 738 | 392 | 423 | 443 | 457 | 469 | 485 |
| $50,000 | $60,000 | 522 | 539 | 550 | 557 | 563 | 571 | 675 | 721 | 750 | 772 | 789 | 812 | 431 | 465 | 487 | 503 | 515 | 533 |
| $60,000 | $70,000 | 564 | 583 | 594 | 602 | 609 | 617 | 731 | 781 | 813 | 836 | 854 | 879 | 466 | 503 | 526 | 543 | 557 | 576 |
| $70,000 | $80,000 | 603 | 623 | 635 | 644 | 651 | 660 | 782 | 836 | 870 | 895 | 914 | 941 | 498 | 538 | 562 | 581 | 595 | 615 |
| $80,000 | $90,000 | 639 | 660 | 673 | 682 | 690 | 699 | 830 | 887 | 923 | 949 | 970 | 999 | 528 | 570 | 596 | 615 | 631 | 652 |
| $90,000 | $100,000 | 673 | 695 | 709 | 719 | 726 | 736 | 875 | 935 | 973 | 1000 | 1023 | 1052 | 556 | 600 | 627 | 648 | 664 | 686 |
| $100,000 | $120,000 | 718 | 742 | 756 | 767 | 775 | 786 | 935 | 999 | 1039 | 1069 | 1092 | 1124 | 594 | 640 | 669 | 691 | 709 | 732 |
| $120,000 | $140,000 | 776 | 802 | 818 | 829 | 838 | 849 | 1013 | 1082 | 1125 | 1157 | 1183 | 1217 | 642 | 692 | 724 | 747 | 766 | 792 |
| $140,000 | $160,000 | 831 | 858 | 875 | 887 | 896 | 909 | 1085 | 1159 | 1206 | 1240 | 1267 | 1304 | 687 | 741 | 774 | 799 | 820 | 847 |
| $160,000 | $180,000 | 881 | 910 | 927 | 940 | 950 | 963 | 1152 | 1230 | 1279 | 1316 | 1345 | 1384 | 729 | 785 | 821 | 847 | 869 | 897 |
| $180,000 | $200,000 | 928 | 958 | 977 | 990 | 1001 | 1015 | 1215 | 1298 | 1349 | 1387 | 1418 | 1459 | 768 | 827 | 865 | 893 | 915 | 945 |
| $200,000 | $225,000 | 977 | 1009 | 1028 | 1043 | 1054 | 1068 | 1280 | 1367 | 1422 | 1462 | 1494 | 1538 | 809 | 871 | 911 | 940 | 963 | 995 |
| $225,000 | $250,000 | 1029 | 1063 | 1084 | 1098 | 1110 | 1126 | 1350 | 1442 | 1500 | 1542 | 1576 | 1622 | 852 | 918 | 959 | 990 | 1015 | 1048 |
| $250,000 | $275,000 | 1079 | 1114 | 1136 | 1151 | 1163 | 1179 | 1416 | 1513 | 1573 | 1617 | 1653 | 1701 | 893 | 962 | 1005 | 1038 | 1063 | 1099 |
| $275,000 | $300,000 | 1126 | 1163 | 1185 | 1201 | 1214 | 1231 | 1479 | 1580 | 1643 | 1689 | 1726 | 1776 | 932 | 1004 | 1049 | 1083 | 1110 | 1146 |
| $300,000 | or more | 1403 | 1449 | 1477 | 1497 | 1512 | 1533 | 1851 | 1977 | 2055 | 2113 | 2160 | 2222 | 1163 | 1252 | 1308 | 1349 | 1383 | 1428 |

| Income | | **Hawaii** | | | **1,6** | | **4.0000%** | **Idaho** | | | **1** | | **6.0000%** | **Illinois** | | | **2** | | **6.2500%** |
|---|---|---|---|---|---|---|---|---|---|---|---|---|---|---|---|---|---|---|---|
| $0 | $20,000 | 321 | 367 | 396 | 419 | 437 | 463 | 421 | 485 | 527 | 560 | 587 | 625 | 313 | 342 | 361 | 375 | 387 | 403 |
| $20,000 | $30,000 | 464 | 529 | 571 | 604 | 630 | 667 | 596 | 685 | 745 | 790 | 828 | 880 | 459 | 500 | 527 | 548 | 564 | 587 |
| $30,000 | $40,000 | 536 | 611 | 660 | 698 | 728 | 770 | 684 | 786 | 854 | 905 | 948 | 1008 | 534 | 582 | 613 | 636 | 655 | 682 |
| $40,000 | $50,000 | 598 | 681 | 736 | 777 | 811 | 858 | 759 | 871 | 945 | 1003 | 1050 | 1116 | 598 | 651 | 686 | 712 | 733 | 762 |
| $50,000 | $60,000 | 652 | 743 | 802 | 847 | 884 | 935 | 824 | 945 | 1026 | 1088 | 1139 | 1210 | 655 | 713 | 750 | 779 | 802 | 834 |
| $60,000 | $70,000 | 700 | 798 | 861 | 910 | 950 | 1005 | 883 | 1012 | 1098 | 1164 | 1218 | 1294 | 706 | 768 | 808 | 839 | 864 | 898 |
| $70,000 | $80,000 | 745 | 848 | 916 | 967 | 1009 | 1068 | 936 | 1073 | 1163 | 1233 | 1291 | 1371 | 753 | 819 | 862 | 894 | 920 | 956 |
| $80,000 | $90,000 | 785 | 894 | 966 | 1020 | 1064 | 1126 | 985 | 1128 | 1224 | 1297 | 1357 | 1441 | 797 | 866 | 911 | 945 | 972 | 1010 |
| $90,000 | $100,000 | 824 | 938 | 1012 | 1069 | 1116 | 1180 | 1031 | 1181 | 1280 | 1356 | 1419 | 1507 | 838 | 910 | 957 | 992 | 1021 | 1061 |
| $100,000 | $120,000 | 874 | 995 | 1074 | 1135 | 1184 | 1252 | 1091 | 1249 | 1354 | 1435 | 1501 | 1594 | 892 | 968 | 1018 | 1056 | 1086 | 1129 |
| $120,000 | $140,000 | 939 | 1069 | 1154 | 1219 | 1272 | 1345 | 1169 | 1338 | 1450 | 1536 | 1607 | 1705 | 962 | 1044 | 1097 | 1138 | 1170 | 1216 |
| $140,000 | $160,000 | 999 | 1137 | 1228 | 1296 | 1353 | 1431 | 1241 | 1419 | 1538 | 1629 | 1704 | 1808 | 1027 | 1114 | 1171 | 1213 | 1248 | 1296 |
| $160,000 | $180,000 | 1054 | 1200 | 1295 | 1368 | 1427 | 1509 | 1307 | 1494 | 1618 | 1714 | 1792 | 1902 | 1087 | 1179 | 1238 | 1283 | 1320 | 1370 |
| $180,000 | $200,000 | 1106 | 1258 | 1358 | 1434 | 1497 | 1583 | 1369 | 1564 | 1693 | 1793 | 1875 | 1990 | 1144 | 1239 | 1302 | 1349 | 1387 | 1440 |
| $200,000 | $225,000 | 1159 | 1319 | 1424 | 1504 | 1569 | 1659 | 1432 | 1636 | 1771 | 1875 | 1961 | 2080 | 1202 | 1302 | 1367 | 1417 | 1457 | 1512 |
| $225,000 | $250,000 | 1216 | 1384 | 1494 | 1577 | 1646 | 1740 | 1500 | 1713 | 1854 | 1963 | 2052 | 2177 | 1265 | 1370 | 1438 | 1489 | 1532 | 1590 |
| $250,000 | $275,000 | 1270 | 1444 | 1559 | 1646 | 1717 | 1816 | 1564 | 1785 | 1932 | 2045 | 2138 | 2267 | 1324 | 1433 | 1504 | 1558 | 1602 | 1662 |
| $275,000 | $300,000 | 1320 | 1502 | 1621 | 1712 | 1786 | 1888 | 1624 | 1853 | 2005 | 2122 | 2218 | 2353 | 1380 | 1493 | 1567 | 1623 | 1668 | 1731 |
| $300,000 | or more | 1616 | 1838 | 1983 | 2093 | 2184 | 2309 | 1975 | 2249 | 2432 | 2572 | 2688 | 2849 | 1710 | 1847 | 1937 | 2004 | 2060 | 2136 |

Because most individuals are cash basis taxpayers, the deduction allowed is for **taxes paid** during the year, not the ultimate total of the tax imposed. Thus, taxpayers who itemize deductions normally have an adjustment for state and local taxes paid in the year following the deduction. If the taxpayer obtains a state or local tax refund, the tax benefit rule requires that person to include the refund in the subsequent year's taxable income. Similarly, if the taxpayer pays additional taxes, these are added to the tax paid for the subsequent year to determine that year's deduction.

**Example 14** Alana's withholding for state income taxes totals $2,500 during 2021. She is single, and her itemized deductions—including state income taxes—total $13,000. In filing her state income tax return, Alana receives a refund of $300. What is the proper treatment of the refund?

**Discussion: Because Alana's 2021 deduction is recovered through the $300 refund in 2022, the $300 is included in her 2022 gross income. Note: The tax benefit rule applies only to taxpayers who itemize deductions. A taxpayer who elects to use the standard deduction has not claimed a deduction for taxes paid. Therefore, a taxpayer who uses the standard deduction and receives a refund of state income taxes has no income to recognize.**

**Example 15** Assume the same facts as in example 14, except that Alana's total itemized deductions, including state income taxes, are $12,600 ($2,500 in state taxes + $10,100 in other itemized deductions). What is the proper tax treatment of the refund?

**Discussion: Alana must include $50 of the refund as income. The actual amount of her state itemized deductions should have been $2,200 ($2,500 claimed minus the $300 refund). If Alana had deducted the actual amount of taxes ($2,200) in preparing her return, she would have had $12,300 in itemized deductions. Because the $12,300 is less than the standard deduction of $12,550, she would have prepared her return using the standard deduction. Under the tax benefit rule, only the $50 benefit she derived by claiming $12,600 of itemized deductions, instead of the standard deduction of $12,550, must be included on her 2022 income tax return.**

An individual cannot use any of the following in calculating itemized tax deductions: federal taxes, including income and Social Security taxes; water use and sewer taxes; excise taxes on alcohol, tobacco, or firearms; gasoline taxes; utility taxes; and assessments for local benefits such as sidewalks.[11] Note that assessments for local benefits are not considered taxes and would be added to the basis of property. It should be stressed that although these taxes are not deductible by individuals as itemized deductions, they may be deductible or capitalized as part of the cost when incurred in a trade or business (see Chapter 6).

## Interest Expense

Itemized deductions for interest payments have been severely restricted in recent years. Personal interest (e.g., credit cards and auto loans) is specifically disallowed. The only interest deductible as an itemized deduction is qualified home mortgage interest and investment interest.[12] Each type of interest is subject to several restrictions.

**Home Mortgage Interest** Only interest on debt that is secured by the taxpayer's principal residence and one other residence is deductible as **qualified home mortgage interest**. The second residence either must qualify as a vacation home (see Chapter 5 for vacation home requirements) if it is rented out during the year or is not rented at all during the year to qualify as a second residence. If a second home is considered rental property (i.e., a rental loss is allowed), the portion of the interest expense attributable to the personal use of the home is considered personal interest and is not deductible. A *residence* includes a house, cooperative apartments, condominiums, and mobile homes and boats that have living accommodations (living quarters, cooking facilities, etc.).

Qualified home mortgage interest includes both acquisition debt and home equity debt. **Acquisition debt** is any debt incurred to acquire, construct, or substantially improve a qualified residence of the taxpayer. The limit on acquisition debt is $750,000. **Home equity debt** is any debt that is secured by a personal residence that is not acquisition debt. However, there is a cap on the level of indebtedness for each type of qualified home mortgage interest.

Under the Tax Cuts and Jobs Act of 2017, interest on a home equity loan used to purchase, build or substantially renovate an existing home remains deductible, whereas interest on a similar loan used to pay personal living expenses, such as credit card debts, is not deductible. As under prior law, the loan must be secured by the taxpayer's main home or second home (known as a qualified residence).[13]

**Points** are prepaid interest amounts that must be paid to acquire financing. They are expressed as a percentage of the value of the loan and paid at loan acquisition. As such, they represent prepaid interest, which usually is capitalized and amortized over the term of the loan. A special provision in the tax law allows points paid to acquire an initial mortgage on a taxpayer's principal residence to be deducted in the year the points are paid.[14] However, points paid to refinance an existing mortgage must be capitalized and amortized as interest expense over the term of the loan. Loan origination fees that replace charges for services in obtaining the loan are not deductible as points. Prepayment penalties for the early payment of a mortgage are also deductible as qualified home mortgage interest.

**Example 16** Anita purchases a new home, borrowing $80,000 from Local Bank to finance the purchase. She also pays $1,600 in points and $1,000 in loan origination fees. Interest paid on the $80,000 mortgage totals $8,400. What is Anita's allowable interest deduction?

**Discussion: Assuming that the $80,000 debt is secured by the property, Anita can deduct the $8,400 in mortgage interest and the $1,600 in points paid to obtain the mortgage—$10,000 in all. The loan origination fees are not deductible interest.**

**Example 17** Zane's home is worth $250,000. He purchased the home 20 years ago using a $100,000 mortgage. During the current year, Zane pays $5,400 in interest on the original mortgage, which has a balance of $45,000. He also borrows $110,000 on a home equity loan and uses the proceeds to pay off personal debts, buy a new sports car, and take a trip around the world. Zane pays $11,000 in interest (i.e., a 10% interest rate) on the home equity loan. How much is his allowable interest deduction?

**Discussion: The $5,400 paid on the original mortgage is qualified home mortgage interest. The home equity loan was not used to buy, build, or substantially improve Zane's home the debt is not considered "acquisition debt" and the interest paid is nondeductible.**

## Charitable Contributions

Individuals are allowed to deduct contributions to organizations that are organized for religious, charitable, educational, scientific, or literary purposes.[15] Deductions are also allowed for contributions to organizations that work to prevent cruelty to animals or children and for contributions to government units. The top panel of Exhibit 8-4 contains examples of organizations that do and those that do not qualify as **charitable organizations**.

Most charitable contributions are made in cash or are out-of-pocket costs for performing charitable work. Examples of these expenses include the cost of uniforms and mileage at 14 cents per mile. Generally, these charitable contributions do not present valuation problems. However, when a taxpayer contributes property to a charitable organization, the type of property determines the amount of the contribution.[16] As indicated in the lower panel of Exhibit 8-4, the deduction for property of a type that would produce ordinary income or short-term capital gain if it were sold is limited to the lesser

Exhibit 8-4

## Summary of Charitable Contribution Rules

| Examples of Qualified Charities: | Examples of Nonqualifying Organizations: |
|---|---|
| Churches, mosques, synagogues | Chambers of Commerce and other business leagues or organizations |
| Salvation Army, Red Cross, CARE, Goodwill, United Way, Boy Scouts, Girl Scouts, Boys/Girls Club of America | Civic leagues |
| Fraternal orders (if gift used for charitable purpose) | Communist organizations |
| Nonprofit schools and hospitals | International organizations |
| Veterans' groups | Social clubs |
| Certain cultural groups | Country clubs |
| Federal, state, and local governments | |
| **Examples of Allowable Contribution Items:** | **Items That Are Not Deductible:** |
| Cash | Political contributions |
| Clothing | Raffle, bingo, or lottery tickets |
| Furniture | Tuition to a private school |
| Fixtures | The value of a person's time |
| Inventory | Value of blood donated to a blood bank or Red Cross |
| Real property | Gifts to individuals |
| Stocks, bonds | |
| Paintings, works of art | |
| Jewelry | |
| Automobiles | |
| Appliances | |
| Out-of-pocket costs for performing charitable work: special uniforms, mileage (at 14 cents per mile), etc. | |

| Type of Property: | Amount of Contribution: | Maximum Deduction (Limit): |
|---|---|---|
| Cash | Amount contributed | 60% of AGI (100% for 2020) |
| Ordinary income or Short-term capital gain property | The lesser of 1. the fair market value at the time of the contribution or | 60% of AGI (100% for 2020) |
| | 2. the adjusted basis of the property | 60% of AGI (100% for 2020) |
| Long-term capital gain property | Fair market value at the date of contribution | 30% of adjusted gross income |
| | An election can be made to reduce the amount of the contribution to the adjusted basis of the property. | 60% of AGI (100% for 2020) |

of (1) the fair market value of the property on the date of the contribution, or (2) the adjusted basis of the property. This limitation makes it an unwise tax-planning strategy to donate ordinary income property with a fair market value that is less than the adjusted basis (i.e., loss property).

**Example 18** Tomas owns 2 properties that are ordinary income properties. Each has a fair market value of $10,000. Property A has an adjusted basis of $6,000, and property B has an adjusted basis of $25,000. Which property would be the better to contribute to his alma mater?

**Discussion:** **If Tomas contributes property A, his deduction is only $6,000. (Fair market value is greater than adjusted basis.) A contribution of property B results in a deduction of $10,000. (Fair market value is less than adjusted basis.) However, if Tomas contributes property B, he loses the $15,000 ($10,000 − $25,000) in unrealized loss on the property. By contributing property A, his deduction is lower, but he avoids tax on the $4,000 ($10,000 − $6,000) in unrealized gain on the property.**

**If Tomas wishes to contribute property B, it would be better to sell the property, realize the ordinary loss of $15,000, and contribute the $10,000 in cash from the sale. The charitable contribution deduction would still be $10,000, and Tomas would have an ordinary loss deduction of $15,000 on the sale. Note that one big advantage of gifting property A is the avoidance of tax on the $4,000 in unrealized gain on property A.**

Taxpayers can deduct the fair market value of contributions of property that would result in a long-term capital gain if the property were sold. Long-term gain property includes property held more than 12 months, and collectibles gain property held more than 12 months. However, the taxpayer may elect to reduce the amount of the contribution to the adjusted basis of the property and use a higher contribution ceiling, as discussed next.

**Example 19** Assume that in example 18, both of Tomas's properties are long-term capital gain properties. Which is the better property to contribute?

**Discussion: Deductions for contributions of long-term capital gain property are allowed for the fair market value of the property. In this case, both properties would result in a deduction of $10,000. However, Tomas would be better off if he contributes property A and avoids the tax on the $4,000 in unrealized gain on the property.**

There are three major limitations on the deductible amount of charitable contributions. First, the overall amount of the charitable contribution deduction cannot exceed 60 percent of the taxpayer's adjusted gross income, (this limitation was suspended for 2020 by the CARES Act and extended to 2021 by the CAA of 2021 allowing charitable deductions up to 100 percent of AGI the examples in this text use the 60 percent limit which applies in 2022). Second, contributions of capital gain property that are deducted at fair market value cannot exceed 30 percent of adjusted gross income. But a taxpayer who is willing to give up the deduction related to the property's appreciation (i.e., use the adjusted basis as the deductible amount) is not subject to the 30 percent limit. In addition, contributions to certain nonoperating private foundations are subject to rather complex limitations that are beyond the scope of this discussion. Finally, any contributions in excess of the limitations are carried forward for deduction for five years.

**Example 20** Antonia owns stock for which she paid $20,000 several years ago; she would like to donate the stock to the Girl Scouts. The stock is worth $25,000, and Antonia's adjusted gross income is $40,000. Assuming that she has made no other charitable contributions, what is her allowable deduction?

**Discussion: Because the sale of the stock would produce a long-term capital gain if Antonia sold it, she is allowed to use the $25,000 fair market value as the amount of her contribution. However, deductions for contributions of property that are measured at fair market value are limited to 30% of adjusted gross income. In this case, Antonia's current deduction would be limited to $12,000 (30% × $40,000), with the $13,000 remainder carried forward for deduction in the subsequent 5 years.**

**Antonia has the option of measuring the amount of her contribution at her adjusted basis in the stock, $20,000. Property measured at the adjusted basis is subject to the general 60% (or 100% for 2020 and 2021) of adjusted gross income limit for charitable contributions. By valuing her contribution at $20,000 (her basis), she could deduct the entire $20,000 in the current year. However, she would have no remaining deduction carryforward under this election.**

## Miscellaneous Itemized Deductions

This category of deductions, miscellaneous itemized deductions, includes amounts expended for gambling losses (not to exceed the amount of gambling winnings), impairment-related work expenses of a disabled person, and the unrecovered investment in an annuity contract when the annuity ceases because of death (as discussed in Chapter 3).

**concept check**

The *annual accounting period concept* requires individuals to report their income and deductions on an annual basis. This concept also requires taxpayers to adopt a method of accounting that clearly reflects their income. Most individual taxpayers will use the cash method. To deduct an expense, the *business purpose concept* requires the expense to have a business or other economic purpose that exceeds any tax avoidance motive. Under this concept, personal expenditures are not deductible. However, Congress, through *legislative grace*, has specifically allowed individuals to deduct certain personal expenses (i.e., itemized deductions). The *administrative convenience concept* allows the omission of items for which the cost of compliance exceeds the tax revenue generated. Because of this concept, the tax law allows individuals to deduct a minimum amount of itemized deductions (i.e., the standard deduction). The *ability to pay concept* requires a taxpayer's tax liability to be based on the amount the taxpayer can afford to pay, relative to other taxpayers. The tax law recognizes the difference in a taxpayer's ability to pay by basing standard deduction amounts, and tax rate schedules on the taxpayer's filing status.

## 8-4 STANDARD DEDUCTION RESTRICTIONS ON DEPENDENTS

LO 4
Explain the requirements to be classified as a dependent.

An individual can qualify as a **dependent** of the taxpayer if they are a qualifying child or a qualifying relative. While the personal and dependency exemptions have been repealed by the Tax Cuts and Jobs Act, the qualification requirements remain important for other tax benefits such as filing status, the Child Tax Credit, and the Dependent Care Credit. To be considered a dependent as a **qualifying child**, the individual must meet all five tests. The five tests for a qualifying child are different from the five tests for a qualifying relative discussed later.

### 8-4a Qualifying Child Tests

**Age Test** To meet the **age test**, the individual must be either under the age of 19 at the end of the year, a full-time student under the age of 24 at the end of the year, or be permanently and totally disabled.[17]

**Non-Support Test** To meet the **non-support test**, the individual being claimed as a dependent must not have provided more than one-half of their support. For purposes of this test, scholarships are not considered support.

**Example 21** Peter is 22 and a college student. He spends $5,000 of the income he earns doing television commercials on his support and puts the remainder of his earnings in a money market account. His parents contribute $6,000 toward his support. Does Peter meet the non-support test?

**Discussion: Peter meets the non-support test because he does not pay more than one-half [$5,000 < ($5,000 + $6,000) ÷ 2] of his support. Note: The fact that Peter earned more than the amount his parents paid toward his support has no bearing on whether he meets the support test.**

**Relationship Test** Under the **relationship test**, an individual must be the taxpayer's son, daughter, stepson, stepdaughter, eligible foster child or descendant of such a child, or the taxpayer's brother, sister, stepbrother, stepsister, or any descendant of any such relative.

**Principal Residence Test** To meet the **principal residence test**, the individual must live with the taxpayer for more than one-half of the year. Temporary absences due to illness, vacation, education, military service or other special circumstances are not considered as time living away from the principal residence.

**Example 22** Continuing with example 21, assume that Peter is 22 and spends 9 months of the year away from home at Halvern College. He spends the remaining 3 months with his parents. Does Peter meet the principal residence test?

**Discussion: Peter meets the principal residence test because the time he spent at Halvern College is considered a temporary absence. Therefore, Peter is considered to have lived with his parents for 12 months.**

**Example 23** Assume that, in example 22, Peter is 22 and graduates from Halvern College in May. Upon graduation, he takes a job in the admissions office at Halvern. Does Peter meet the principal residence test?

**Discussion: Peter does not meet the principal residence test. Although the time (5 months) he spent at Halvern College is considered a temporary absence and is treated as time at his parent's principal residence, he fails to spend more than one-half of the year at their principal residence.**

**Example 24** Jerry's mother, Jolene, lives with him through all of 2021. Her only sources of income are $300 from a savings account, $4,100 in interest from tax-exempt municipal bonds, and $2,600 in Social Security benefits. Does Jolene pass the gross income test for dependency?

**Discussion: Although Jolene's economic income is $7,000, her gross income for tax purposes is only $300. Because this is less than the $4,300 exemption amount, she passes the gross income test. Note: Although Jolene has passed the gross income test, she also must satisfy the other four requirements before Jerry can claim her as a dependent under the qualifying relative rules.**

**Citizen or Residency Test** To meet the **citizen or residency test**, the child must be a citizen of the United States, or a resident of the United States, Canada, or Mexico.

**Qualifying Relative Tests** To be a **qualifying relative**, the individual must meet the five tests set forth below. Therefore, a qualifying relative is an individual who meets the following five tests but does not meet the definition of a qualifying child.

**Gross Income Test** The **gross income** test states that to be a dependent, an individual must have a gross income (as defined for tax return purposes) in 2021 less than $4,300. This amount will be indexed for inflation. Note that excludable forms of income do not count in determining gross income for purposes of this test.

**Support Test** The **support test** requires that the taxpayer who claims that an individual is a dependent must provide more than half the support of the dependent. Support is not necessarily related to the income of the dependent. This test simply requires a tallying up of amounts spent on support and determining whether the taxpayer seeking the dependency exemption has provided more than half of the entire amount spent on support.

**Example 25** Refer to example 24. Assume that Jolene spends all of her $7,000 in income to support herself. Jerry spends an additional $4,500 to support Jolene. Does Jolene meet the support test?

**Discussion: Jerry does not provide more than half of Jolene's total support of $11,500 ($7,000 + $4,500) in 2021. Therefore, Jolene does not meet the qualifying relative support test and does not qualify as a dependent. Note: The fact that $6,700 ($2,600 + $4,100) of the income is not taxable has no bearing on the support test.**

**Example 26** Assume that in example 25, Jolene spends only $3,000 of the income she-receives in 2021 on her own support. She puts the remaining $4,000 in a savings account. Does Jolene pass the support test?

**Discussion: Jerry provides more than half of Jolene's total support of $7,500 in 2021. Therefore, Jolene does pass the qualifying relative support test.**

**Example 27** Donna and Doug were divorced last year. Donna has custody of their son. Doug pays $3,800 in child support payments during the current year. The cost of supporting the son during the year is $5,000. Who is entitled to treat their son as a dependent?

**Discussion: Because Donna is the custodial parent, she is entitled to treat their son as a dependent, regardless of the amount of support Doug pays during the year. The only way that Doug will be able to treat their son as a dependent is if Donna agrees in writing that Doug can treat their son as a dependent. The written agreement must be attached to Doug's return.**

An additional support situation deals with support of children of divorced parents. In this case, the custodial parent is entitled to treat the individual as a dependent, regardless of actual support provided. For the noncustodial parent to consider the individual as a dependent, it must be stipulated as part of the divorce or separation agreement or the custodial parent must agree to sign a written declaration waiving their right to it.

**Relationship, or Member of Household, Test** Under the **relationship, or member of household, test** a dependent must either be a relative of the taxpayer or a member of the taxpayer's household for the entire year. *Relatives* are defined as ancestors (e.g., grandfather), lineal descendants (e.g., granddaughter, son), siblings (brother, sister), and blood relationships such as aunt, nephew, or niece. Once a relative relationship is established, it does not change with divorce or death of a spouse. Thus, a wife's nephew continues to qualify as a relative even if the wife dies or the wife and her spouse divorce. Note that individuals who are not relatives meet this test if they are members of the taxpayer's household for the entire tax year.

**Citizen or Residency Test** Under the *citizen or residency test*, a dependent must be either (a) a citizen of the United States, or (b) a resident of the United States, Canada, or Mexico. Undocumented children adopted by U.S. citizens and living with them in a foreign country qualify under this test.

**Joint Return Test** Dependents who are married may not file joint returns with their spouses for the exemption year in question. An exception to this test, which is known as the **joint return test**, is provided for married dependents who are not required to file a tax return (see the section on filing requirements) but file a return solely for the purpose of obtaining a refund.

The tax law provides several restrictions on the use of standard deductions by dependents. Dependents are subject to a restriction on the amount of the allowable standard deduction. A dependent's standard deduction is the greater of

- $1,100 ($1,100 in 2020)

  or
- The dependent's earned income plus $350 or the standard deduction amount for a single individual, whichever results in a smaller deduction

The intent of this provision is to deny the benefit of a full standard deduction to a dependent who has large amounts of unearned income. This takes away some of the incentive for high marginal tax rate taxpayers to shift significant amounts of unearned income to lower marginal tax rate dependents. However, dependents with earned sources of income are still allowed to use the standard deduction to reduce the tax on earned income.

**Example 28** Andreas, 20, is a full-time college student at City Tech. He earns $12,650 during 2021 that he uses to pay for living expenses. His father provides more than half of his support. What is Andreas' standard deduction amount for 2021?

**Discussion: Because Andreas has earned income of $12,650, he is allowed the full $12,550 single standard deduction. Assuming that Andreas has no deductions for AGI, his taxable income for 2021 is $100 ($12,650 − $12,550).**

**Example 29** Amy is a dependent of her parents; she earns $2,200 from a summer job and receives $1,200 in interest in 2021 from a savings account established by her grandfather. What is Amy's standard deduction?

**Discussion: Because Amy is a dependent, her standard deduction is the greater of $1,100 or her earned income plus $350,$2,550 ($2,200 + $350). Her standard deduction is $2,550 ($2,200 + $350). Note: Assuming that Amy has no deductions for AGI, her taxable income is $850. Thus, she is only able to shield $350 of her unearned income through use of the standard deduction.**

## 8-5 CALCULATING TAX LIABILITY

LO 5

Calculate an individual's tax liability and the special provisions for the calculation of the tax liability of a dependent.

After determining the taxpayer's taxable income, the tax is computed using the appropriate rate schedule for the taxpayer's filing status. Individuals with taxable incomes of less than $100,000 generally use the tax tables provided by the IRS. A 2020 tax table and tax rate schedules for 2021 can be found in Appendix B.

The next step in completing the tax liability calculation is to add any additional taxes due with the return and deduct any allowable tax credits to arrive at the next tax liability for the year (see Exhibit 8-1). The earned income tax credit and the child-care credit have been the most widely used individual tax credits. Most taxpayers qualify for at least one of the following tax credits: the child credit, the American Opportunity Tax Credit (AOTC), or the Lifetime Learning Tax Credit (LLTC).

Several other taxes are paid with an individual's income tax return. These include the self-employment tax, the alternative minimum tax (see Chapter 15), recapture taxes, and the Social Security tax on unreported tip income.

The net tax liability is then compared with amounts withheld from the taxpayer's salary and payments of estimated taxes to determine the amount of tax due (or the refund to be received) with the return.[18] If the amount of tax due is greater than $1,000 and more than 10 percent of the tax liability, the taxpayer may be penalized for the under-payment of estimated taxes.[19]

### 8-5a Tax on Unearned Income of a Minor Child

In 1986, Congress complicated the tax calculation for a minor child with significant amounts of unearned income (interest, dividends, royalties, etc.). The provision enacted was designed to eliminate the tax rate advantage that could have been gained under prior law by shifting unearned forms of income from the parents to a minor child. The basic thrust of the law is to tax the net unearned income of a child who has not attained the age of 18 or is a full-time student under the age of 24 at the rates applicable to the child's parents. Although not specifically stated, this treatment is an extension of the assignment-of-income doctrine for investment income. That is, the substance of giving minor children investment property is to make an assignment of the parents' unearned income to the children in an attempt to lower taxes. For purposes of this calculation,

Net unearned income = Unearned income

Less: $1,100

Less: The greater of $1,100 or the costs of producing the unearned income

Note that under this definition, any unearned income in excess of $2,200 ($1,100 + $1,100) is taxed at the parents' marginal tax rate. The remaining taxable income of the child is taxed at the child's marginal tax rate. This treatment has the effect of disallowing the assignment of unearned income in excess of $2,200 to a minor child.

**Example 30** Dan and Madeline are a married couple with a taxable income of $150,000 in 2021. Their daughter, Dawn, 10, has interest income of $2,450 in 2021. What is Dawn's tax liability?

**Discussion: Because Dawn is younger than 18 and has unearned income in excess of $2,200, the tax on unearned income of a minor child applies. Her net unearned income is $250 ($2,450 − $1,100 − $1,100), which is taxed at her parents' marginal tax rate. Her remaining taxable income of $1,100 ($2,450 − $1,100 − $250) is taxed per the single taxpayer schedule. At a taxable income of $150,000, her parents' marginal tax rate is 22%**

| Calculation of Dawn's Taxable Income | |
|---|---|
| Gross income | $ 2,450 |
| Less: Standard deduction | (1,100) |
| Exemption | —0— |
| Taxable income | $ 1,350 |
| Net Unearned Income Taxed at Parents' Rate | |
| $2,450 − $1,100 − $1,100 = | 250 |
| Remainder taxed at Dawn's rate ($1,350 − $250) | $ 1,100 |
| | |
| Tax Calculation | |
| Tax on income taxed at parents' rate | |
| ($250 × 22%) = | $55 |
| Tax on remaining income at Dawn's rate | |
| ($1,100 × 10%) = | $110 |
| Total tax on taxable income | $165 |

**NOTE: If a portion of the $2,450 had been dividend income, a portion of the dividend would be taxed at the parent's marginal dividend rate, and a portion at the child's marginal dividend rate. If a child's pro rata share of the dividend income exceeds the child's taxable income, the child's entire share of taxable income is treated as dividend income and taxed at the favorable 0% tax rate.**

## 8-5b Income Tax Credits

LO 6 Explain how tax credits affect a taxpayer's tax liability and explain how each tax credit is determined.

As discussed in Chapter 1, a **tax credit** is a direct reduction in the tax liability of the taxpayer receiving the credit. As such, tax credits are not part of the tax base used to compute the tax liability. Because they are not part of the base and reduce the tax liability dollar for dollar, tax credits are neutral with respect to the marginal tax rate of the taxpayer. That is, in contrast to tax deductions, a $100 tax credit is worth a $100 reduction in taxes to a taxpayer regardless of the taxpayer's marginal tax rate.

The tax credits available for individuals are generally intended to provide tax relief to certain classes of taxpayers. The neutrality of tax credits with respect to marginal tax rates lets Congress ensure that specific taxpayers receive the credit. The purposes of individual tax credits are to:

- Provide incentives for taxpayers to engage in specific activities (e.g., lifetime learning),
- Provide equitable treatment among taxpayers (e.g., child-care credit), and
- Provide tax relief for low-income taxpayers (e.g., earned income credit), taxpayers who are 65 years and older, and disabled taxpayers.

Congress has favored the use of credits (rather than deductions) in these situations because the amount of the relief is equal for taxpayers in different marginal tax brackets. Most individual tax credits are nonrefundable: if the amount of the credit exceeds the tax liability, the taxpayer is not entitled to a refund of the excess. However, the earned income tax credit and, in some cases, the child credit are refundable. A **refundable tax credit** means that the taxpayer is entitled to a refund of the excess credit (the amount of the credit that is left after the tax liability reaches zero). This is a form of negative income tax. The taxpayer does not pay a tax but receives a payment from the government based on the taxpayer's income.

Table 8-3

## Individual Tax Credits and Their Purpose

| Individual Tax Credit | Purpose of Credit |
|---|---|
| Child credit | To provide tax relief to taxpayers with children under the age of 17 |
| Earned income credit | To provide tax relief to low-income taxpayers |
| Child and dependent care credit | To provide tax relief to taxpayers who incur child and dependent care expenses so that they can be employed |
| American Opportunity Tax Credit | To provide tax relief to taxpayers for the first 4 years of higher education expenses |
| Lifetime Learning Tax Credit | To provide tax relief to taxpayers for undergraduate and graduate education expenses |
| Adoption credit | To provide tax relief as an incentive for taxpayers to adopt a child |
| Tax credit for the elderly and the disabled | To provide extra tax relief to low-income taxpayers who are either 65 years and older or retired because of a permanent and total disability |

Table 8-3 lists the tax credits available to individual taxpayers and the purpose of each credit. One characteristic of the individual tax credits is that they begin to phase-out (are reduced) when a taxpayer's income (e.g., earned income or adjusted gross income) reaches a predetermined level. The use of the phase-out rule gives a larger credit to lower income taxpayers and either reduces or eliminates the credit for taxpayers with higher incomes. The child credit, earned income credit, child care credit, American Opportunity Tax Credit (formerly the Hope Scholarship Tax Credit), and Lifetime Learning Tax Credit are discussed in the text.

### Child Credit

The **child credit** allows a $2,000 tax credit for each qualifying child under 17 years of age. The definition of a qualifying child is the same as the definition of a qualifying child for dependency purposes except that the child must be under age 17 at the end of the tax year and must be a U.S. citizen or a resident of the United States.[20]

**Example 31** Jack and Susan are married and have 2 children ages 12 and 10. Their adjusted gross income for the year is $75,000. What amount can Jack and Susan claim as a child credit for 2021?

**Discussion: Jack and Susan can claim a child credit of $4,000 ($2,000 × 2) for 2021.**

**Example 32** Assume the same facts as in example 31, except that Jack and Susan's adjusted gross income is $404,300. What amount can Jack and Susan claim as a child credit in 2021?

**Discussion: Because their adjusted gross income exceeds $400,000, Jack and Susan must reduce the $2,000 child credit by $50 for each $1,000 (or fraction thereof) that their adjusted gross income exceeds $400,000. Their excess income is $4,300, which rounds to 5 increments of $1,000. This results in a $250 reduction in their allowable child credit:**

$404,300 − $400,000 = $4,300 ÷ $1,000 = 4.3 (round to 5)
$50 × 5 = $250 reduction in credit

**Jack and Susan are allowed a child credit of $3,750 ($4,000 − $250).**

The 2017 Tax Cut and Jobs Act also allows a taxpayer to receive a $500 tax credit referred to as a family credit for other dependents. Unlike the child tax credit this credit is nonrefundable.

**Example 33** Rick and Chris have two children who are 16 and 18. In addition, Rick's mother lives with them and is considered a dependent. What is the amount of the child tax credit if their adjusted gross income is $85,000.

**Discussion: Rick and Chris can claim a child tax credit of $3,000 ($2,000 + $500 + $500). A $2,000 child tax credit for their 16-year-old, a family tax credit of $500 for their 18-year-old and a $500 tax credit for Rick's mother.**

For all families, a portion of the child credit may be refundable. The amount of the child credit that is refundable depends, is capped at $1,400 per child, and is calculated as follows:

$$\text{Maximum refundable credit} = 15\% \times (\text{earned income} - \$2{,}500)$$

Up to $1,400 per child of the child tax credit is refundable. This refundable amount is capped at 15 percent of your earned income. If earned income exceeds $13,833 the limit is the full $1,400.

**Example 34** Howard and Paula have 2 children under age 17, have earned income of $17,600. Their tax liability is $300 before the child credit. What amount can they claim as a child credit, and what portion of the credit is refundable?

**Discussion: Howard and Paula's child credit is $4,000 ($2,000 × 2), which is greater than their $300 income tax liability. The maximum amount of the credit that can be refunded is $2,265 [15% × ($17,600 − $2,500)]. The child credit of $4,000 will reduce their tax liability of $300 to zero, and they will receive a refund of $2,265 since it is less than $2,800 ($1,400 × 2).**

## Earned Income Credit

The **earned income credit (EIC)** provides tax relief to low-income taxpayers. Unlike the other individual tax credits, the EIC is refundable. That is, a taxpayer who has no tax liability can receive a refund equal to the amount of the credit. Because the amount of credit depends on the taxpayer's earned income and phases out after the taxpayer's income reaches a predetermined level, married taxpayers are required to file a joint return to take the EIC. This prevents taxpayers from filing separate returns and obtaining a credit based only on each spouse's income. By filing separate returns, the couple would be able to receive a higher credit or in some cases qualify for the credit when their combined income would exceed the maximum allowable earned income.

Another factor in determining the amount of the taxpayer's earned income credit is the number of qualifying children living in the taxpayer's home. A qualifying child is the same as previously discussed for a dependent with two exceptions. First, an individual can be a qualifying child for the earned income credit even if the qualifying child provides more than one-half of their support. Second, if the qualifying child would have been a dependent of the taxpayer except for the custodial parent releasing the dependency exemption through a separation agreement or divorcee decree, the child is considered a qualifying child for purposes of the earned income credit. To be eligible for the earned income credit, a taxpayer must meet all of the following requirements:

1. The taxpayer's principal place of abode for more than half the year must be in the United States.
2. The taxpayer or the taxpayer's spouse must be older than 24 but under age 65.
3. The taxpayer or taxpayer's spouse cannot be a dependent of another taxpayer.[21]

The IRS has simplified the calculation of the credit for taxpayers by providing a table that calculates the credit. The amount of the credit is based on the greater of the taxpayer's earned income or her/his adjusted gross income and varies based on the number of dependent children of the taxpayer(s). A portion of the 2020 earned income credit table is reproduced in Exhibit 8-5. The entire 2020 earned income credit table is in the appendix to this chapter.

## Exhibit 8-5

# 2020 Earned Income Tax Credit

**Earned Income Credit (EIC) Table** - *Continued* (**Caution.** This is **not** a tax table.)

| If the amount you are looking up from the worksheet is– | | And your filing status is– Single, head of household, or qualifying widow(er) and you have– | | | | Married filing jointly and you have– | | | |
|---|---|---|---|---|---|---|---|---|---|
| | | 0 | 1 | 2 | 3 | 0 | 1 | 2 | 3 |
| At least | But less than | Your credit is– | | | | Your credit is– | | | |
| 19,200 | 19,250 | 0 | 3,584 | 5,920 | 6,660 | 190 | 3,584 | 5,920 | 6,660 |
| 19,250 | 19,300 | 0 | 3,584 | 5,920 | 6,660 | 186 | 3,584 | 5,920 | 6,660 |
| 19,300 | 19,350 | 0 | 3,584 | 5,920 | 6,660 | 182 | 3,584 | 5,920 | 6,660 |
| 19,350 | 19,400 | 0 | 3,576 | 5,911 | 6,651 | 179 | 3,584 | 5,920 | 6,660 |
| 19,400 | 19,450 | 0 | 3,568 | 5,900 | 6,640 | 175 | 3,584 | 5,920 | 6,660 |
| 19,450 | 19,500 | 0 | 3,560 | 5,889 | 6,629 | 171 | 3,584 | 5,920 | 6,660 |
| 19,500 | 19,550 | 0 | 3,552 | 5,879 | 6,619 | 167 | 3,584 | 5,920 | 6,660 |
| 19,550 | 19,600 | 0 | 3,544 | 5,868 | 6,608 | 163 | 3,584 | 5,920 | 6,660 |
| 19,600 | 19,650 | 0 | 3,536 | 5,858 | 6,598 | 160 | 3,584 | 5,920 | 6,660 |
| 19,650 | 19,700 | 0 | 3,528 | 5,847 | 6,587 | 156 | 3,584 | 5,920 | 6,660 |
| 19,700 | 19,750 | 0 | 3,520 | 5,837 | 6,577 | 152 | 3,584 | 5,920 | 6,660 |
| 19,750 | 19,800 | 0 | 3,512 | 5,826 | 6,566 | 148 | 3,584 | 5,920 | 6,660 |
| 19,800 | 19,850 | 0 | 3,504 | 5,816 | 6,556 | 144 | 3,584 | 5,920 | 6,660 |
| 19,850 | 19,900 | 0 | 3,497 | 5,805 | 6,545 | 140 | 3,584 | 5,920 | 6,660 |
| 19,900 | 19,950 | 0 | 3,489 | 5,795 | 6,535 | 137 | 3,584 | 5,920 | 6,660 |
| 19,950 | 20,000 | 0 | 3,481 | 5,784 | 6,524 | 133 | 3,584 | 5,920 | 6,660 |
| 20,000 | 20,050 | 0 | 3,473 | 5,774 | 6,514 | 129 | 3,584 | 5,920 | 6,660 |
| 20,050 | 20,100 | 0 | 3,465 | 5,763 | 6,503 | 125 | 3,584 | 5,920 | 6,660 |
| 20,100 | 20,150 | 0 | 3,457 | 5,753 | 6,493 | 121 | 3,584 | 5,920 | 6,660 |
| 20,150 | 20,200 | 0 | 3,449 | 5,742 | 6,482 | 117 | 3,584 | 5,920 | 6,660 |
| 20,200 | 20,250 | 0 | 3,441 | 5,732 | 6,472 | 114 | 3,584 | 5,920 | 6,660 |
| 20,250 | 20,300 | 0 | 3,433 | 5,721 | 6,461 | 110 | 3,584 | 5,920 | 6,660 |
| 20,300 | 20,350 | 0 | 3,425 | 5,710 | 6,450 | 106 | 3,584 | 5,920 | 6,660 |
| 20,350 | 20,400 | 0 | 3,417 | 5,700 | 6,440 | 102 | 3,584 | 5,920 | 6,660 |
| 20,400 | 20,450 | 0 | 3,409 | 5,689 | 6,429 | 98 | 3,584 | 5,920 | 6,660 |
| 20,450 | 20,500 | 0 | 3,401 | 5,679 | 6,419 | 94 | 3,584 | 5,920 | 6,660 |
| 20,500 | 20,550 | 0 | 3,393 | 5,668 | 6,408 | 91 | 3,584 | 5,920 | 6,660 |
| 20,550 | 20,600 | 0 | 3,385 | 5,658 | 6,398 | 87 | 3,584 | 5,920 | 6,660 |
| 20,600 | 20,650 | 0 | 3,377 | 5,647 | 6,387 | 83 | 3,584 | 5,920 | 6,660 |
| 20,650 | 20,700 | 0 | 3,369 | 5,637 | 6,377 | 79 | 3,584 | 5,920 | 6,660 |
| 20,700 | 20,750 | 0 | 3,361 | 5,626 | 6,366 | 75 | 3,584 | 5,920 | 6,660 |
| 20,750 | 20,800 | 0 | 3,353 | 5,616 | 6,356 | 72 | 3,584 | 5,920 | 6,660 |
| 20,800 | 20,850 | 0 | 3,345 | 5,605 | 6,345 | 68 | 3,584 | 5,920 | 6,660 |
| 20,850 | 20,900 | 0 | 3,337 | 5,595 | 6,335 | 64 | 3,584 | 5,920 | 6,660 |
| 20,900 | 20,950 | 0 | 3,329 | 5,584 | 6,324 | 60 | 3,584 | 5,920 | 6,660 |
| 20,950 | 21,000 | 0 | 3,321 | 5,574 | 6,314 | 56 | 3,584 | 5,920 | 6,660 |
| 21,000 | 21,050 | 0 | 3,313 | 5,563 | 6,303 | 52 | 3,584 | 5,920 | 6,660 |
| 21,050 | 21,100 | 0 | 3,305 | 5,553 | 6,293 | 49 | 3,584 | 5,920 | 6,660 |
| 21,100 | 21,150 | 0 | 3,297 | 5,542 | 6,282 | 45 | 3,584 | 5,920 | 6,660 |
| 21,150 | 21,200 | 0 | 3,289 | 5,531 | 6,271 | 41 | 3,584 | 5,920 | 6,660 |
| 21,200 | 21,250 | 0 | 3,281 | 5,521 | 6,261 | 37 | 3,584 | 5,920 | 6,660 |
| 21,250 | 21,300 | 0 | 3,273 | 5,510 | 6,250 | 33 | 3,584 | 5,920 | 6,660 |
| 21,300 | 21,350 | 0 | 3,265 | 5,500 | 6,240 | 29 | 3,584 | 5,920 | 6,660 |
| 21,350 | 21,400 | 0 | 3,257 | 5,489 | 6,229 | 26 | 3,584 | 5,920 | 6,660 |
| 21,400 | 21,450 | 0 | 3,249 | 5,479 | 6,219 | 22 | 3,584 | 5,920 | 6,660 |
| 21,450 | 21,500 | 0 | 3,241 | 5,468 | 6,208 | 18 | 3,584 | 5,920 | 6,660 |
| 21,500 | 21,550 | 0 | 3,233 | 5,458 | 6,198 | 14 | 3,584 | 5,920 | 6,660 |
| 21,550 | 21,600 | 0 | 3,225 | 5,447 | 6,187 | 10 | 3,584 | 5,920 | 6,660 |
| 21,600 | 21,650 | 0 | 3,217 | 5,437 | 6,177 | 7 | 3,584 | 5,920 | 6,660 |
| 21,650 | 21,700 | 0 | 3,209 | 5,426 | 6,166 | 3 | 3,584 | 5,920 | 6,660 |
| 21,700 | 21,750 | 0 | 3,201 | 5,416 | 6,156 | * | 3,584 | 5,920 | 6,660 |
| 21,750 | 21,800 | 0 | 3,193 | 5,405 | 6,145 | 0 | 3,584 | 5,920 | 6,660 |
| 21,800 | 21,850 | 0 | 3,185 | 5,395 | 6,135 | 0 | 3,584 | 5,920 | 6,660 |
| 21,850 | 21,900 | 0 | 3,177 | 5,384 | 6,124 | 0 | 3,584 | 5,920 | 6,660 |
| 21,900 | 21,950 | 0 | 3,169 | 5,373 | 6,113 | 0 | 3,584 | 5,920 | 6,660 |
| 21,950 | 22,000 | 0 | 3,161 | 5,363 | 6,103 | 0 | 3,584 | 5,920 | 6,660 |
| 22,000 | 22,050 | 0 | 3,153 | 5,352 | 6,092 | 0 | 3,584 | 5,920 | 6,660 |
| 22,050 | 22,100 | 0 | 3,145 | 5,342 | 6,082 | 0 | 3,584 | 5,920 | 6,660 |
| 22,100 | 22,150 | 0 | 3,137 | 5,331 | 6,071 | 0 | 3,584 | 5,920 | 6,660 |
| 22,150 | 22,200 | 0 | 3,129 | 5,321 | 6,061 | 0 | 3,584 | 5,920 | 6,660 |
| 22,200 | 22,250 | 0 | 3,121 | 5,310 | 6,050 | 0 | 3,584 | 5,920 | 6,660 |
| 22,250 | 22,300 | 0 | 3,113 | 5,300 | 6,040 | 0 | 3,584 | 5,920 | 6,660 |
| 22,300 | 22,350 | 0 | 3,105 | 5,289 | 6,029 | 0 | 3,584 | 5,920 | 6,660 |
| 22,350 | 22,400 | 0 | 3,097 | 5,279 | 6,019 | 0 | 3,584 | 5,920 | 6,660 |

| If the amount you are looking up from the worksheet is– | | And your filing status is– Single, head of household, or qualifying widow(er) and you have– | | | | Married filing jointly and you have– | | | |
|---|---|---|---|---|---|---|---|---|---|
| | | 0 | 1 | 2 | 3 | 0 | 1 | 2 | 3 |
| At least | But less than | Your credit is– | | | | Your credit is– | | | |
| 22,400 | 22,450 | 0 | 3,089 | 5,268 | 6,008 | 0 | 3,584 | 5,920 | 6,660 |
| 22,450 | 22,500 | 0 | 3,081 | 5,258 | 5,998 | 0 | 3,584 | 5,920 | 6,660 |
| 22,500 | 22,550 | 0 | 3,073 | 5,247 | 5,987 | 0 | 3,584 | 5,920 | 6,660 |
| 22,550 | 22,600 | 0 | 3,065 | 5,237 | 5,977 | 0 | 3,584 | 5,920 | 6,660 |
| 22,600 | 22,650 | 0 | 3,057 | 5,226 | 5,966 | 0 | 3,584 | 5,920 | 6,660 |
| 22,650 | 22,700 | 0 | 3,049 | 5,216 | 5,956 | 0 | 3,584 | 5,920 | 6,660 |
| 22,700 | 22,750 | 0 | 3,041 | 5,205 | 5,945 | 0 | 3,584 | 5,920 | 6,660 |
| 22,750 | 22,800 | 0 | 3,033 | 5,194 | 5,934 | 0 | 3,584 | 5,920 | 6,660 |
| 22,800 | 22,850 | 0 | 3,025 | 5,184 | 5,924 | 0 | 3,584 | 5,920 | 6,660 |
| 22,850 | 22,900 | 0 | 3,017 | 5,173 | 5,913 | 0 | 3,584 | 5,920 | 6,660 |
| 22,900 | 22,950 | 0 | 3,009 | 5,163 | 5,903 | 0 | 3,584 | 5,920 | 6,660 |
| 22,950 | 23,000 | 0 | 3,001 | 5,152 | 5,892 | 0 | 3,584 | 5,920 | 6,660 |
| 23,000 | 23,050 | 0 | 2,993 | 5,142 | 5,882 | 0 | 3,584 | 5,920 | 6,660 |
| 23,050 | 23,100 | 0 | 2,985 | 5,131 | 5,871 | 0 | 3,584 | 5,920 | 6,660 |
| 23,100 | 23,150 | 0 | 2,977 | 5,121 | 5,861 | 0 | 3,584 | 5,920 | 6,660 |
| 23,150 | 23,200 | 0 | 2,969 | 5,110 | 5,850 | 0 | 3,584 | 5,920 | 6,660 |
| 23,200 | 23,250 | 0 | 2,961 | 5,100 | 5,840 | 0 | 3,584 | 5,920 | 6,660 |
| 23,250 | 23,300 | 0 | 2,953 | 5,089 | 5,829 | 0 | 3,584 | 5,920 | 6,660 |
| 23,300 | 23,350 | 0 | 2,945 | 5,079 | 5,819 | 0 | 3,584 | 5,920 | 6,660 |
| 23,350 | 23,400 | 0 | 2,937 | 5,068 | 5,808 | 0 | 3,584 | 5,920 | 6,660 |
| 23,400 | 23,450 | 0 | 2,929 | 5,058 | 5,798 | 0 | 3,584 | 5,920 | 6,660 |
| 23,450 | 23,500 | 0 | 2,921 | 5,047 | 5,787 | 0 | 3,584 | 5,920 | 6,660 |
| 23,500 | 23,550 | 0 | 2,913 | 5,037 | 5,777 | 0 | 3,584 | 5,920 | 6,660 |
| 23,550 | 23,600 | 0 | 2,905 | 5,026 | 5,766 | 0 | 3,584 | 5,920 | 6,660 |
| 23,600 | 23,650 | 0 | 2,897 | 5,015 | 5,755 | 0 | 3,584 | 5,920 | 6,660 |
| 23,650 | 23,700 | 0 | 2,889 | 5,005 | 5,745 | 0 | 3,584 | 5,920 | 6,660 |
| 23,700 | 23,750 | 0 | 2,881 | 4,994 | 5,734 | 0 | 3,584 | 5,920 | 6,660 |
| 23,750 | 23,800 | 0 | 2,873 | 4,984 | 5,724 | 0 | 3,584 | 5,920 | 6,660 |
| 23,800 | 23,850 | 0 | 2,865 | 4,973 | 5,713 | 0 | 3,584 | 5,920 | 6,660 |
| 23,850 | 23,900 | 0 | 2,857 | 4,963 | 5,703 | 0 | 3,584 | 5,920 | 6,660 |
| 23,900 | 23,950 | 0 | 2,849 | 4,952 | 5,692 | 0 | 3,584 | 5,920 | 6,660 |
| 23,950 | 24,000 | 0 | 2,841 | 4,942 | 5,682 | 0 | 3,584 | 5,920 | 6,660 |
| 24,000 | 24,050 | 0 | 2,833 | 4,931 | 5,671 | 0 | 3,584 | 5,920 | 6,660 |
| 24,050 | 24,100 | 0 | 2,825 | 4,921 | 5,661 | 0 | 3,584 | 5,920 | 6,660 |
| 24,100 | 24,150 | 0 | 2,817 | 4,910 | 5,650 | 0 | 3,584 | 5,920 | 6,660 |
| 24,150 | 24,200 | 0 | 2,809 | 4,900 | 5,640 | 0 | 3,584 | 5,920 | 6,660 |
| 24,200 | 24,250 | 0 | 2,801 | 4,889 | 5,629 | 0 | 3,584 | 5,920 | 6,660 |
| 24,250 | 24,300 | 0 | 2,793 | 4,879 | 5,619 | 0 | 3,584 | 5,920 | 6,660 |
| 24,300 | 24,350 | 0 | 2,785 | 4,868 | 5,608 | 0 | 3,584 | 5,920 | 6,660 |
| 24,350 | 24,400 | 0 | 2,777 | 4,858 | 5,598 | 0 | 3,584 | 5,920 | 6,660 |
| 24,400 | 24,450 | 0 | 2,769 | 4,847 | 5,587 | 0 | 3,584 | 5,920 | 6,660 |
| 24,450 | 24,500 | 0 | 2,761 | 4,836 | 5,576 | 0 | 3,584 | 5,920 | 6,660 |
| 24,500 | 24,550 | 0 | 2,753 | 4,826 | 5,566 | 0 | 3,584 | 5,920 | 6,660 |
| 24,550 | 24,600 | 0 | 2,745 | 4,815 | 5,555 | 0 | 3,584 | 5,920 | 6,660 |
| 24,600 | 24,650 | 0 | 2,737 | 4,805 | 5,545 | 0 | 3,584 | 5,920 | 6,660 |
| 24,650 | 24,700 | 0 | 2,729 | 4,794 | 5,534 | 0 | 3,584 | 5,920 | 6,660 |
| 24,700 | 24,750 | 0 | 2,721 | 4,784 | 5,524 | 0 | 3,584 | 5,920 | 6,660 |
| 24,750 | 24,800 | 0 | 2,713 | 4,773 | 5,513 | 0 | 3,584 | 5,920 | 6,660 |
| 24,800 | 24,850 | 0 | 2,705 | 4,763 | 5,503 | 0 | 3,584 | 5,920 | 6,660 |
| 24,850 | 24,900 | 0 | 2,698 | 4,752 | 5,492 | 0 | 3,584 | 5,920 | 6,660 |
| 24,900 | 24,950 | 0 | 2,690 | 4,742 | 5,482 | 0 | 3,584 | 5,920 | 6,660 |
| 24,950 | 25,000 | 0 | 2,682 | 4,731 | 5,471 | 0 | 3,584 | 5,920 | 6,660 |
| 25,000 | 25,050 | 0 | 2,674 | 4,721 | 5,461 | 0 | 3,584 | 5,920 | 6,660 |
| 25,050 | 25,100 | 0 | 2,666 | 4,710 | 5,450 | 0 | 3,584 | 5,920 | 6,660 |
| 25,100 | 25,150 | 0 | 2,658 | 4,700 | 5,440 | 0 | 3,584 | 5,920 | 6,660 |
| 25,150 | 25,200 | 0 | 2,650 | 4,689 | 5,429 | 0 | 3,584 | 5,920 | 6,660 |
| 25,200 | 25,250 | 0 | 2,642 | 4,679 | 5,419 | 0 | 3,584 | 5,920 | 6,660 |
| 25,250 | 25,300 | 0 | 2,634 | 4,668 | 5,408 | 0 | 3,575 | 5,908 | 6,648 |
| 25,300 | 25,350 | 0 | 2,626 | 4,657 | 5,397 | 0 | 3,567 | 5,898 | 6,638 |
| 25,350 | 25,400 | 0 | 2,618 | 4,647 | 5,387 | 0 | 3,559 | 5,887 | 6,627 |
| 25,400 | 25,450 | 0 | 2,610 | 4,636 | 5,376 | 0 | 3,551 | 5,877 | 6,617 |
| 25,450 | 25,500 | 0 | 2,602 | 4,626 | 5,366 | 0 | 3,543 | 5,866 | 6,606 |
| 25,500 | 25,550 | 0 | 2,594 | 4,615 | 5,355 | 0 | 3,535 | 5,856 | 6,596 |
| 25,550 | 25,600 | 0 | 2,586 | 4,605 | 5,345 | 0 | 3,527 | 5,845 | 6,585 |

**Example 35** Bo and April are married and have 1 dependent child who lives in their home during the entire tax year. Bo and April have earned income of $27,550 in 2020. They have no other sources of income or deductions. What are Bo and April's income tax liability and EIC for 2020?

**Discussion: Bo and April's 2020 taxable income is $2,750, and their tax liability, before considering the earned income credit and the child tax credit, is $275 ($2,750 × 10%). For purposes of the earned income credit, their earned income is equal to their adjusted gross income.**

| | |
|---|---|
| Gross income | $ 27,550 |
| Less: Standard deduction | ($24,800) |
| Taxable income | $ 2,750 |

**Using the first column of Exhibit 8-5, their earned income is at least $27,550 but less than $27,600. Reading over to the column labeled Married, One child, their earned income credit is $3,207. Although Bo and April owe $275, they are entitled to a refund of $2,932 ($3,207 – $275) and any amounts withheld from their income for the year.**

A taxpayer with portfolio or passive income in excess of $3,650 ($3,650 for 2020) is not eligible for the earned income credit. Recall from Chapter 7 that portfolio income consists of interest, dividends, and capital gains. For purposes of the earned income credit, tax-exempt interest and royalty income are also considered portfolio income.

**Example 36** Assume the same facts as in example 35, except that April sells 200 shares of stock purchased two years ago. Her gain on the sale of the stock is $5,000. What are Bo and April's income tax liability and EIC for 2020?

**Discussion: Bo and April's 2020 taxable income is $7,750 and their tax liability, before considering the earned income credit and the child tax credit, is $275 [($5,000 × 0%) + ($2,750 × 10%)]. The $5,000 gain on the sale of stock is consid ered portfolio income. Because their portfolio and passive income exceeds $3,600 for 2020, they do not qualify for the earned income credit.**

| | |
|---|---|
| Gross income ($27,550 + $5,000) | $ 32,550 |
| Less: Standard deduction | $ 24,800 |
| Taxable income | $ 7,750 |

## Child and Dependent Care Credit

Taxpayers who pay someone to care for their child and/or other dependent so the taxpayers can work are eligible for a credit based on the amount of their expenses and their earned income level. It is known as the **child and dependent care credit**. This credit is designed to encourage taxpayers who work and have children to provide them with adequate care while they are at work. It also provides tax relief to lower income working families who have children at home. The child and dependent care credit is a nonrefundable credit. To qualify for the credit, a taxpayer must meet two conditions:

1. The taxpayer must incur employment-related expenses.
2. The expenses must be for the care of qualified individuals.

An employment-related expense is one that must be paid to enable the taxpayer to work and must be paid for either household services or for the care of a qualified individual. Generally, the expenses must be incurred within the taxpayer's home, although out-of-the-home expenses for dependents younger than 13 and for a disabled dependent or spouse (if the disabled person has the same principal residence for more than one-half year) also qualify. The exception for the disabled encourages individuals to keep disabled dependents or a spouse in the home rather than institutionalize them.[22]

A qualifying individual includes any dependent younger than 13 or a dependent or a spouse of the taxpayer who is physically or mentally incapacitated. A taxpayer can claim the child and dependent care credit for a dependent who lives with the taxpayer for more than one-half of the year, even if the taxpayer does not provide more than one-half of the cost of maintaining the household.

**Example 37** Aria is a CPA, and her spouse is an auto mechanic. They employ a housekeeper who cleans the house, cooks, and takes care of their 6-year-old son. Are Aria and her spouse entitled to a credit for child and dependent care?

**Discussion: The expenditures for the housekeeper are eligible for the credit. They allow Aria and her spouse to be employed, are spent for household services, and their 6-year-old son is a qualifying individual because he is younger than 13.**

**Example 38** Assume the same facts as in example 37. Because her spouse's shop is open 7 days a week, he doesn't have time to take care of their yard. They hire a lawn service to fertilize and mow the lawn. Does the cost of the lawn service qualify for the child and dependent care credit?

**Discussion: The child care and lawn care services do allow Aria and her spouse to be employed. However, the lawn care services are not either household services or for the care of a qualifying dependent. Therefore, they are not eligible costs for the credit. However, the housekeeper costs are still eligible for the credit.**

**Example 39** Julie's husband, Paul, was injured in an accident at work several years ago and is confined to a wheelchair. Because he is unable to care for himself, Julie leaves Paul at a day-care center while she works. Is Julie eligible for the child and dependent care credit?

**Discussion: Because her husband is disabled, Julie may make arrangements for his care outside the home. She is eligible for the credit so long as Paul has the same principal residence for one-half of the year.**

The amount of the credit is generally 35 percent of the qualified expenditures incurred, limited to \$3,000 (\$6,000 with two or more qualifying individuals). The 35 percent rate is reduced by 1 percent for each \$2,000 (or portion thereof) of the taxpayer's adjusted gross income in excess of \$15,000. The maximum reduction is limited to 15 percent, leaving a minimum allowable credit of 20 percent. The 20 percent minimum credit limit is reached when the taxpayer's adjusted gross income exceeds \$43,000.[23]

**Example 40** Jorge is a single parent with 2 dependent children living with him. He has an adjusted gross income of $24,000 and pays $3,000 in qualified child care expenses. Assuming that both children are younger than 13, what is Jorge's child and dependent care credit?

**Discussion: Because his AGI is in excess of $15,000, Jorge must reduce the 35% general credit rate by 1% for each $2,000 (or portion thereof) of AGI in excess of $15,000. Jorge's credit is $900:**

| | | | |
|---|---|---|---|
| Amount of qualified child care expenses | | | $3,000 |
| Basic credit rate | | 35% | |
| Reduction for excess AGI: | | | |
| Jorge's AGI | $ 24,000 | | |
| Less: | (15,000) | | |
| Excess AGI | $ 9,000 | | |
| Divided by number of $2,000 increments (rounded up) | ÷ 2,000 | | |
| | 5 | | |
| Reduction % per increment | × 1% | 5% | × 30% |
| Child-care credit | | | $ 900 |

The expenditures qualifying for the credit cannot exceed the earned income of the taxpayer. For married taxpayers, the lower earned income of the two is used for the purpose of the limit. The purpose of the limit on expenditures is consistent with the purpose of the credit—to allow the taxpayer to be gainfully employed. If the expense of child care is in excess of the income earned by working, the employment does not provide a net gain to the household income.

**Example 41** Maria and Dorothy are married and have 2 dependent children younger than 13. Dorothy is an airline pilot who earns $150,000 per year. Maria is interested in art and is employed part-time at an art gallery. Maria earns $3,000 at the art gallery. Qualified child care expenses are $8,000. What is Maria and Dorothy's child and dependent care credit?

**Discussion: Qualifying child-care expenditures are limited to the earned income of the lesser paid spouse. In this case, Maria's earned income ($3,000) is less than the amount expended for child care ($8,000). Only the $3,000 is eligible for the credit. Because their AGI is in excess of $43,000, they are allowed the minimum 20% credit. This results in a child and dependent care credit of $600 ($3,000 × 20%).**

## Higher Education Tax Credits

Eligible taxpayers who incur expenses for higher education can elect to claim one of two tax credits: the American Opportunity Tax Credit or the Lifetime Learning Tax Credit (LLTC). Only one of the credits can be claimed for each qualifying student, and married taxpayers must file a joint return to claim either credit. A qualifying student must be enrolled on at least a half-time basis for at least one semester during the academic year.

For the American Opportunity Tax Credit, qualifying higher education expenses include tuition, related fees, and course materials (i.e., textbooks) required for enrollment at an eligible institution. Unlike the AOTC, course materials are not a qualifying expense in calculating the Lifetime Learning Tax Credit. Student activity fees and athletic fees do not qualify for either credit. In addition, tuition and related fees for sports, games, or hobbies (unless the course is part of the student's degree program) are also ineligible for the higher education credits. The credits are available only for out-of-pocket expenses. They cannot be claimed for expenses covered by an employer's educational assistance plan if the income is not included on either the taxpayer's tax return or the dependent's (i.e., student's) tax return. In addition, the amount of qualifying higher education expenses are reduced by the amount of any scholarships or fellowships received by the taxpayer or the dependent student.

The taxpayer can claim an education tax credit if the taxpayer receives a tax-free distribution from a Coverdell Education Savings Account. To prevent a taxpayer from receiving a double benefit, the educational expenses that are paid from the CESA cannot be used in determining the total education expenses for purposes of the AOTC or the LLTC. Recall from Chapter 6 that a tax-free distribution from a Coverdell Education Savings Account can be used to pay for up to $2,500 of room and board expenses. Therefore, a taxpayer can claim an education tax credit for tuition and fees while using a distribution from a Coverdell Education Savings Account to pay for up to $2,500 of room and board expenses.

The expenses must be incurred on behalf of the taxpayer, the taxpayer's spouse, or a dependent of the taxpayer. If a student is claimed as a dependent by another taxpayer, the student cannot claim the credit; it must be claimed by the taxpayer claiming the dependency exemption. Any qualifying expenses paid by the student are treated as being paid by the taxpayer claiming the dependency exemption.

**American Opportunity Tax Credit** The **American Opportunity Tax Credit (AOTC)** provides for a 100 percent tax credit on the first $2,000 of qualifying expenses and a 25 percent tax credit on the next $2,000 of qualifying expenses paid during the year for each qualifying student. Therefore, the maximum credit a taxpayer may claim per year for each qualifying student is $2,500 [($2,000 × 100%) + ($2,000 × 25%)]. The AOTC can be claimed for the first four years of undergraduate study.[24]

**Example 42** Shaw and Oriana are married and have 2 children. Sophia is a freshman in college and Jonas is in his fifth year at State University. Shaw and Oriana's adjusted gross income is $90,000. They pay $2,500 in tuition and fees for Sophia. They also pay $700 for textbooks and $3,800 for her room and board. Jonas's tuition and fees are $4,500, his room and board is $3,700, and they pay $425 for his textbooks. What amount can Shaw and Oriana claim for the American Opportunity Tax Credit?

**Discussion: Jonas's tuition and fees and textbooks do not qualify for the AOTC because he is in his fifth year of study. Only amounts paid for tuition and fees and textbooks are qualified higher education expenses for the AOTC. Shaw and Oriana incurred $3,200 ($2,500 + $700) of qualified expenses and can claim a 100% credit for the first $2,000 of expenses and a 25% credit on the next $1,200 of expenses. Their American Opportunity Tax Credit is $2,300 [($2,000 × 100%) + ($1,200 × 25%)].**

**Lifetime Learning Tax Credit** The **Lifetime Learning Tax Credit (LLTC)** provides a 20 percent credit for up to $10,000 of qualified higher education expenses. The LLTC is limited to a maximum amount of $2,000 ($10,000 × 20%) regardless of the number of qualifying individuals incurring higher education expenses.[25] However, while the AOTC can be claimed only for higher education expenses incurred for the first four years of undergraduate study, the LLTC can be claimed for qualifying expenses incurred each year for undergraduate or graduate education. In addition to being used by students enrolled on at least a half-time basis, the credit can be claimed for a student who is enrolled less than half-time in a course(s) that helps the student acquire or improve job skills.

**Example 43** Assume the same facts as in example 42. What amount can Shaw and Oriana claim in tax credits for the higher education expenses they pay?

**Discussion: Jonas's qualifying expenses are eligible for the Lifetime Learning Tax Credit. As with the AOTC, room and board expenses are not qualifying higher education expenses. However, unlike the AOTC, the cost of textbooks is not a qualifying expense. Shaw and Oriana can claim a 20% tax credit for $4,500 of Jonas's qualifying expenses (tuition and fees). Their LLTC is $900 ($4,500 × 20%). Shaw and Oriana's total higher education tax credit is $3,200 ($2,300 AOTC for Sophia + $900 LLTC for Jonas).**

**Phase-Out of Higher Education Tax Credits** The AOTC and the LLTC are both phased out ratably over the same base of $20,000 for married taxpayers and $10,000 for all other taxpayers. The education credits are phased out ratably for married taxpayers with adjusted gross income between $160,000 and $180,000 and for all other taxpayers with adjusted gross income between $80,000 and $90,000. The formula for calculating the percentage reduction of the education credits and computing the allowable amount of the credit for a married couple follows:

$$\text{Tax credit percentage} = \frac{\text{Adjusted gross income} - \$160{,}000}{\$20{,}000}$$

$$\text{Credit allowed} = \text{Calculated tax credit} \times (1 - \text{tax credit percentage})$$

**Example 44** Assume the same facts as in example 42, except that Shaw and Oriana's adjusted gross income is $166,000. What is their higher education tax credit?

**Discussion: Because Shaw and Oriana's adjusted gross income exceeds $160,000, the credits are phased out. They have to reduce their $2,300 AOTC and their $900 LLTC using the following formula:**

$$30\% = \frac{\$166{,}000 - \$160{,}000}{\$20{,}000}$$

$$\$2{,}240 = \$3{,}200 \times (1 - 30\%)$$

**Shaw and Oriana's total higher education tax credit is $2,240 ($1,610 AOTC for Sophia + $630 LLTC for Jonas).**

## 8-6 FILING REQUIREMENTS

LO 7 Explain the general rules relating to filing requirements.

Whether an individual is required to file a return depends on the taxpayer's gross income. General **filing requirements** for individuals are that they must file a return when their gross income exceeds their standard deduction amount. Married individuals must file a return if the individual's gross income, when combined with the individual's spouse's gross income, for the tax year is more than the standard deduction that applies for a joint return, as long as: (i) the individual and spouse, at the close of the tax year, had the same household as their home; (ii) the spouse does not file separately; and (iii) neither the individual nor the spouse is a dependent of another taxpayer who has income (other than earned income) in excess of the limited deduction allowed for dependents (for 2021, $1,100).

Of course, taxpayers with gross income less than the required filing level will want to file when they are entitled to a refund of taxes. The filing levels for various taxpayers are given in Table 8-4.

*Table 8-4*

**2020 & 2021 Filing Requirements**

| Filing Status | 2020 Gross Income | 2021 Gross Income |
|---|---|---|
| Single | $12,400 | $12,550 |
| Single—age 65 or older | $13,850 | $14,250 |
| Married, filing jointly | $24,800 | $25,100 |
| Married, filing jointly—one spouse 65 or older | $26,100 | $26,450 |
| Married, filing jointly—both 65 or older | $27,400 | $27,800 |
| Surviving spouse | $24,800 | $25,100 |
| Surviving spouse—age 65 or older | $26,100 | $26,450 |
| Married, filing separately | 0 | 0 |
| Head of household | $18,650 | 18,800 |
| Dependent with unearned income | 1,100 | 1,100 |

# CHAPTER SUMMARY

Calculating taxable income for an individual is complex because of several factors. First, unlike other income tax entities, individuals engage in both business and personal transactions. Congress has allowed individuals to take certain deductions for personal expenditures and has allowed for some element of convenience through use of the standard deduction. This causes a split of an individual's deductions into those for adjusted gross income and those from adjusted gross income. In addition, Congress has chosen to limit the availability and the amount of certain deductions to dependents and high-income taxpayers. Congress enacted the kiddie tax to prevent high-income taxpayers (parents) from shifting unearned income to low-income taxpayers (children). The earned income credit (EIC) and the child-care and dependent care credit are generally intended to provide tax relief to specific taxpayers. The neutrality of tax credits with respect to marginal tax rates lets Congress ensure that only certain taxpayers receive the credit. Generally, a taxpayer is required to file a tax return only if her or his gross income exceeds a certain threshold.

# KEY TERMS

# PRIMARY TAX LAW SOURCES

[1]Sec. 6013—Allows a married couple to file a joint return; specifies that marital status is determined on the last day of the tax year or at date of death of spouse.

[2]Sec. 2—Defines *surviving spouse* and *head of household*; allows an abandoned spouse to file as a head of household.

[3]Sec. 7703—Defines *abandoned spouse.*

[4]Sec. 63—Defines *taxable income;* allows individual taxpayers to deduct the greater of their allowable itemized deductions or the standard deduction; specifies standard deduction amounts and requires their annual adjustment for inflation.

[5]Reg. Sec. 1.151-1—Defines *blindness* for purposes of additional standard deduction amount; provides examples of items that constitute support for purposes of the dependency exemption.

[6]Reg. Sec. 1.213-1—States that a medical dependent does not have to pass the gross income and joint return tests.

[7]Sec. 213—Allows the deduction of medical expenses as an itemized deduction for individual taxpayers; defines *medical expenses* and prescribes limitations on the amount of the deduction.

[8]Notice 2019-2—Provides the standard mileage rates for use of an automobile for medical and charitable purposes.

[9]Sec. 213—See endnote 11.

[10]Sec. 164—Specifies the allowable deductions for taxes.

[11]Reg. Sec. 1.164-2—Lists taxes that individuals cannot deduct as itemized deductions.

[12]Sec. 163—Specifies the allowable deductions for interest; disallows personal interest other than qualified home mortgage interest and investment interest.

[13]News Release 2018-32—Explains how the interest on a home equity loan can still be deductible as home mortgage interest.

[14]Sec. 461—Allows a current deduction for points paid to acquire a home mortgage.

[15]Sec. 170—Allows a deduction for contributions to qualifying charities.

[16]Reg. Sec. 1.170A-1—Provides general rules for determining amounts of charitable contributions; disallows a deduction for the contribution of time or services to a qualifying organization.

[18] Sec. 152(c)(3)-Provides that an individual meets the age test if they are under 19, under 24 and a full time student or permanently and totally disabled.

[18]Sec. 31—Provides that amounts withheld as tax from salaries and wages are allowed as credits against that year's tax liability.

[19]Sec. 6654—Provides that all individuals must pay estimated taxes when their tax liability is expected to be greater than $1,000; imposes a penalty for not paying the proper amount of estimated tax.

[22]Sec. 24—Allows the child credit and prescribes the limitations and phase-outs for the credit.

[21]Sec. 32—Allows the earned income credit and prescribes the limitations on the amount of the credit.

[22]Reg. Sec. 1.44A-1—Discusses the general requirements and defines the terms applicable to the child-care credit.

[23]Sec. 21—Allows a tax credit for child-care and dependent-care expenses and prescribes the limits on the amount of the credit.

[24]Sec. 25A(b)—Allows the American Opportunity Tax Credit and prescribes the requirements for the credit.

[25]Sec. 25A(c)—Allows the Lifetime Learning Tax Credit and prescribes the requirements for the credit.

# DISCUSSION QUESTIONS

1. **LO1** What are the five tests that must be met for an individual to be considered a dependent as a qualifying child? as a qualifying relative? Briefly explain each test. After passage of the Tax Cuts and Jobs Act, why are these test still relevant?
2. **LO2** Why is a taxpayer's filing status important?
3. **LO2** What is a surviving spouse? Explain the tax benefit available to a surviving spouse.
4. **LO2** Under what circumstances can a married person file as a head of household?
5. **LO3** What is (are) the main difference(s) between deductions for AGI and deductions from AGI?
6. **LO3** What is the standard deduction? Explain its relationship to a taxpayer's itemized deductions.
7. **LO3** One general requirement for deduction is that the expense be the taxpayer's, not that of another. Is this always true? Explain.
8. **LO4** Explain the limitations placed on deductions for medical expenses.
9. **LO4** What is an ad valorem tax? What is the significance of an ad valorem tax?
10. **LO4** Which types of interest are deductible as itemized deductions? What limitations (if any) are imposed on the deduction?
11. **LO4** In what year(s) are points paid to acquire a loan deductible? Explain.
12. **LO4** Why is interest paid on a loan used to purchase municipal bonds not deductible?
13. **LO4** What limits are placed on deductions for charitable contributions?
14. **LO4** Explain how the deduction allowed for a charitable contribution of ordinary income property is different from the deduction for a donation of long-term capital gain property.

15. **LO5** What is the standard deduction amount for a dependent? Under what conditions can a dependent claim the same standard deduction as a single individual who is not a dependent?
16. **LO5** Why did Congress enact the "kiddie tax"?
17. **LO6** Can all taxpayers who claim a child as a dependent receive a child tax credit for that child? Explain.
18. **LO6** What are the general criteria for eligibility for the earned income credit?
19. **LO6** Is the child credit refundable? Explain.
20. **LO6** What are the general criteria for eligibility for the child- and dependent-care credit?
21. **LO6** Does the child-care credit help promote a progressive tax rate structure? Explain.
22. **LO6** Compare and contrast the Hope Scholarship Tax Credit with the Lifetime Learning Tax Credit.
23. **LO7** What determines who must file a tax return?

# PROBLEMS

24. **LO2** Determine the filing status in each of the following situations:
    a. Angela is single for most of the year. She marries Margot on December 30.
    b. An is divorced during the current year. Their son lives with An's former spouse. An lives alone.
    c. Rita is married to Bob, and they have two children, ages two and four, at home. Bob and Rita have a fight in March; Bob leaves and never returns. Rita has no idea where Bob is.
    d. Joe is single. He provides all the support for his parents, who live in a nursing home. Joe's parents' only source of income is Social Security.
    e. Sam's spouse died in February of last year. Their children are all of legal age and none lives in the household. Sam has not remarried.
    f. Would your answer to part e change if Sam has a dependent child who still lives in the home?
25. **LO2** Determine the 2021 filing status in each of the following situations:
    a. Michaela and Harrison decide to separate on October 12, 2021. Before filing their 2021 tax return on February 18, 2022, Michaela files for and is granted a formal separation agreement.
    b. Bernardo is single and owns a condominium in Florida. His father lives in the condominium, and Bernardo receives $1,000 per year from his father as rent. The total expenses of maintaining the condominium are $15,000. His father receives a pension of $25,000 and Social Security benefits of $8,000.
    c. Nick is 32 years old, single, and is a successful investment banker. Peter, Nick's cousin and friend, has fallen on hard times and lives with Nick. Peter works part-time, earns $3,000 and lives with Nick for the entire year. Nick pays the entire cost of maintaining the household and provides $5,000 toward Peter's support.
    d. Jamal's spouse died in 2019. He maintains a household for his twin daughters, who are seniors in high school.
    e. Kathy and Sven are married with two children, ages 14 and 12. In June, Kathy leaves Sven and their children. Sven has not heard from Kathy, but a former coworker of Kathy's tells Sven that Kathy wanted to move to Ireland.
26. **LO3** Determine the maximum deduction from AGI for 2021 for each of the following taxpayers:
    a. Pedro is single and maintains a household for his father. His father is not a dependent of Pedro's. Pedro's itemized deductions are $12,900.
    b. Jie and Ling are married. Jie is 66 years old, and Ling is 62. They have itemized deductions of $19,000.
    c. Myron and Samantha are married, and both are 38 years of age. Samantha is legally blind. They have itemized deductions of $24,500.

d. Joelynn is divorced and maintains a home for her 21-year-old son, who is a part-time student at the local university. He pays less than one-half of his support and his earned income for the year is $3,900. Her itemized deductions are $17,000.
e. Frank is 66 years of age. During the year, his spouse dies. His itemized deductions are $23,700.
f. Assume the same facts as in part e, except that Frank's spouse dies in 2019.

27. **LO3** Determine the maximum deduction from AGI for 2021 for each of the following taxpayers:
   a. Selen is single and has itemized deductions for the year of $12,900. In addition, Selen's mother lives with her, but she does not claim her mother as a dependent.
   b. Amanda and Adam are married. Amanda is 67 years old and is legally blind. Adam is 64 years old. They have itemized deductions of $25,800.
   c. Micah and Ilana are married and have two children. In April, they have an argument and Micah leaves Ilana. At year-end, Ilana is unaware of Micah's whereabouts, and no formal divorce proceedings have been initiated. Ilana's itemized deductions total $14,000.
   d. Constantino is divorced and maintains a home for his 25-year-old daughter, who is a graduate student at a local university and earns $6,800 during the year. His itemized deductions are $12,800.
   e. Helen is 69 and a widow. Her 20-year-old grandson, who is a full-time student at the local university, lives with her for the entire year. Her husband, Sam, dies in 2020 at the age of 71. Her itemized deductions are $14,000.
   f. Assume the same facts as in part e, except that Sam dies in 2021.

28. **LO3, 5** Hongtao is single and has a gross income of $89,000. His allowable deductions for adjusted gross income are $4,200, and his itemized deductions are $19,000.
   a. What is Hongtao's taxable income and tax liability for 2021?
   b. If Hongtao has $12,000 withheld from his salary during 2021, is he entitled to a refund or does he owe additional taxes?
   c. Assume the same facts as in parts a and b, except that Hongtao is married. His spouse's salary is $30,000, and she has $2,000 withheld from her paycheck. What is their taxable income and tax liability for 2021? Are they entitled to a refund, or do they owe additional taxes?

29. **LO3, 5** Arthur and Cora are married and have two dependent children. They have a gross income of $95,000. Their allowable deductions for adjusted gross income total $4,000, and they have total allowable itemized deductions of $26,250.
   a. What is Arthur and Cora's taxable income?
   b. What is Arthur and Cora's income tax?
   c. If Arthur has $3,900 and Cora has $3,600 withheld from their paychecks, are they entitled to a refund, or do they owe additional taxes?

30. **LO4** Rebecca and Irving incur the following medical expenses during the current year:

| | |
|---|---|
| Medical insurance premiums | $4,500 |
| Hospital | 950 |
| Doctors | 1,925 |
| Dentist | 575 |
| Veterinarian | 170 |
| Chiropractor | 220 |
| Cosmetic surgery | 1,450 |
| Over-the-counter drugs | 165 |
| Prescription drugs | 195 |
| Crutches | 105 |

They receive $4,000 in reimbursements from their insurance company of which $300 is for the cosmetic surgery. What is their medical expense deduction if

a. Their adjusted gross income is $59,500?

b. Their adjusted gross income is $65,000

31. **LO4** Lian is 56 years old and is injured in an automobile accident this year. She is hospitalized for four weeks and misses three months of work after getting out of the hospital. The costs related to her accident are:

| | |
|---|---|
| Hospitalization | $16,100 |
| Prescription drugs | 2,050 |
| Doctor's fees | 12,225 |
| Wheelchair rental | 380 |
| Visits by home nursing service | 2,400 |

Lian's employer-provided insurance policy pays $23,220 of the costs. She also receives $4,800 in disability pay from her employer while she is absent from work. By the end of the year, Lian is able to pay only $6,100 of the costs that aren't covered by her medical insurance. What is Lian's allowed itemized deduction for medical expenses if her adjusted gross income is $39,000 before considering any of this information?

32. Paula lives in Arkansas, which imposes a state income tax. During 2021, she pays the following taxes:

| | |
|---|---|
| Federal tax withheld | 5,125 |
| State income tax withheld | 1,900 |
| State sales tax – actual receipts | 370 |
| Real estate tax | 1,740 |
| Property tax on car (ad valoreum) | 215 |
| Social Security tax | 4,324 |
| Gasoline taxes | 124 |
| Excise taxes | 112 |

a. If Paula's adjusted gross income is $35,000 what is her allowable deduction for taxes?

b. Assume the same facts as in part a, except that Paula pays $1,600 in sales tax on a motor vehicle she purchased during the year. What is Paula's allowable deduction for taxes?

33. **LO4** Jesse is a resident of New Jersey who works in New York City. He also owns rental property in South Carolina. During 2021, he pays the following taxes:

| | |
|---|---|
| New Jersey state estimated tax payments | $ 850 |
| New York City income tax withheld | 440 |
| New York State income tax withheld | 1,375 |
| Federal income tax withheld | 6,310 |
| Property tax—New Jersey home | 2,110 |
| South Carolina income taxes paid when filing 2019 tax return | 220 |
| South Carolina estimated tax payments | 400 |
| Gasoline taxes | 190 |
| Excise taxes | 160 |

During 2021, Jesse's 2019 New York State and New York City tax returns are audited. Based on the audit, he pays an additional $250 in New York City taxes but receives a refund of $185 in New York State taxes. He also has to pay a $40 penalty and interest of $12 to New York City. However, he receives interest of $16 from New York State. What is Jesse's allowable deduction for taxes for 2021?

34. **LO4** Simon is single and a stockbroker for a large investment bank. During 2021, he has withheld from his paycheck $2,250 for state taxes and $400 for city taxes. In June 2022, Simon receives a state tax refund of $145. What is the proper tax treatment of the refund in 2022 if

a. Simon uses the standard deduction?
b. Simon has itemized deductions other than state and city income taxes of $10,350?
c. Simon has itemized deductions other than state and city income taxes of $9,850?

35. **LO4** Frank and Liz are married. During 2021, Frank has $2,800 in state income taxes withheld from his paycheck, and Liz makes estimated tax payments totaling $2,200. In May 2022, they receive a state tax refund of $465. What is the proper tax treatment of the refund in 2022 if
   a. They use the standard deduction?
   b. They have itemized deductions other than state income taxes of $21,000?
   c. They have itemized deductions other than state income taxes of $20,000?

36. **LO4** Rocco owns a piece of land as investment property. He acquired the land in 1995 for $18,000. On June 1, 2021, he sells the land for $80,000. As part of the sale, the buyer agrees to pay all of the property taxes ($3,600) for the year.
   a. What is Rocco's gain on the sale of the land?
   b. What amount of the property taxes can Rocco deduct? What amount can the buyer deduct?
   c. What is the buyer's basis in the land?

37. **LO4** Robin is single and purchases a new home for $80,000 in 2021. She pays $8,000 down and borrows the remaining $72,000 by securing a mortgage on the home. Robin pays $1,750 in closing costs, $1,600 in points to obtain the mortgage, and $4,440 in interest on the mortgage during the year. Her adjusted gross income is $78,000. What is Robin's allowable itemized deduction for interest paid?

38. **LO4** On March 1, Roxanne acquires a house for $160,000. She pays $20,000 down and borrows the remaining $140,000 by obtaining a 15-year mortgage. Roxanne pays $3,500 in closing costs and $2,500 in points in purchasing the house. During the year, she pays $10,300 of interest on her mortgage.
   a. What is her allowable interest deduction for the year?
   b. How would your answer to part a change if Roxanne already owned the house and the points paid on March 1 were for a 15-year mortgage to refinance her existing mortgage?

39. **LO4** Astrid originally borrowed $600,000 to acquire her home. When the balance on the original mortgage is $540,000, she purchases a ski chalet by borrowing $500,000, which is secured by a mortgage on the chalet. Astrid pays $45,000 in interest on her home mortgage and $32,000 in interest on the chalet's mortgage. What is Astrid's allowable itemized deduction for interest paid?

40. **LO4** Jana gives property worth $54,000 to her alma mater during the current year. She purchased the property several years ago for $38,000.
   a. What is Jana's maximum deduction if the property is ordinary income property?
   b. What is Jana's maximum deduction if the property is long-term capital gain property?
   c. How would your answers change if Jana's adjusted gross income were $60,000?

41. **LO4** Determine the allowable charitable contribution in each of the following situations:
   a. Karen attends a charity auction where she pays $250 for two tickets to a Broadway show. The tickets have a face value of $150.
   b. State University holds a raffle to benefit the football team. Each raffle ticket costs $100, and only 500 tickets are sold, with the winner receiving $10,000. Gary buys two raffle tickets but does not win the $10,000 prize.
   c. Peter is a nurse at a local hospital and earns $150 per day. One Saturday a month, he volunteers 8 hours of his time at a medical clinic in a neighboring town. The round-trip distance from Peter's home to the clinic is 25 miles.

d. Jordan donates stock with a fair market value of $36,000 to Caulfield College. She acquired the stock in 2004 for $13,000. Her adjusted gross income is $60,000.

Communication Skills

42. **LO4** Miguel is a successful businessman who has been approached by St. Kilda University to make a donation to its capital campaign. He agrees to contribute $75,000, but he is unsure which of the following assets he should contribute:

| Asset | Basis | Fair Market Value |
|---|---|---|
| Ordinary income property | $41,000 | $75,000 |
| Long-term capital gain property | 84,000 | 75,000 |
| Long-term capital gain property | 32,000 | 75,000 |

Write a letter to Miguel advising him which property he should contribute to St. Kilda's capital campaign.

43. **LO4** Heather makes cash contributions during the current year of $30,000 and donates property worth $40,000 to a local hospital. She purchased the property several years ago for $32,000. Her adjusted gross income is $100,000.
    a. What is Heather's maximum deduction if the property is ordinary income property?
    b. What is Heather's maximum deduction if the property is long-term capital gain property?

44. **LO5** Determine the taxable income of each of the following dependents for 2021:
    a. Louis is 12 and receives $1,250 in interest income.
    b. Jackson is 16. He earns $2,050 from his newspaper route and receives $700 in dividends on GCM stock.
    c. Loretta is 18 and a full time student. She earns $5,000 as a lifeguard during the summer. In addition, Loretta wins a rescue contest and receives a municipal bond worth $600. During the year, the bond pays $20 in interest.
    d. Eva is 15. Her income consists of municipal bond interest of $750, qualified dividend income of $1,400, and interest credited to her savings account of $900.
    e. Elaine is a college student. Her only income consists of $3,000 from her part-time job delivering pizzas. Her itemized deductions total $400.
    f. Greg is 2. He has certificates of deposit given to him by his grandparents that pay $2,500 in interest.

45. **LO5** For each of the dependents in problem 44, calculate the income tax on their taxable income. The parents' marginal tax rate is 24 percent and the dependent's is 10 percent in each part.

46. **LO5** Calculate the 2021 tax liability and the tax or refund due for each situation:
    a. Mark is single with no dependents and has a taxable income of $60,000. He has $9,200 withheld from his salary for the year.
    b. Harry and Linda are married and have taxable income of $60,000. Harry has $4,250 withheld from his salary. Linda makes estimated tax payments totaling $3,000.
    c. Aspra is single. His 20-year-old son, Calvin, lives with him throughout the year. Calvin pays for less than one-half of his support and his earned income for the year is $3,000. Aspra pays all costs of maintaining the household. His taxable income is $60,000. Aspra's withholdings total $7,800.
    d. Randy and Raina are married. Because of marital discord, they are not living together at the end of the year, although they are not legally separated or divorced. Randy's taxable income is $25,000, and Raina's is $60,000. Randy makes estimated tax payments of $3,500, and Raina has $7,500 in tax withheld from her salary.

47. **LO6** Anika and Jespar are married and have two children ages 16 and 14. Their adjusted gross income for the year is $98,000.
   a. What amount can they claim for the child credit?
   b. What amount can they claim for the child credit if their adjusted gross income is $417,600?
   c. What amount can they claim for the child credit if the children are ages 18 and 16 and their adjusted gross income is $96,000?

48. **LO6** Neville and Julie are married and have two children ages 19 and 14. Their adjusted gross income for the year is $85,000.
   a. What amount can they claim for the child credit?
   b. What amount can they claim for the child credit if their children are ages 16 and 13?
   c. Assume the same facts as in part a, except that their adjusted gross income is $416,400.

49. **LO6** Miguel and Katrina have two children under age 17, have earned income of $75,000. Miguel's father lives with them and is considered a dependent. What amount can they claim as a child credit?

50. **LO6** Determine the total allowable 2020 earned income credit in each of the following situations:
   a. Judy is single and earns $6,500 in salary for the year. In addition, she receives $3,500 in unemployment compensation during the year.
   b. Monica is a single parent with one dependent child. She earns $12,500 from her job as a taxicab driver. She also receives $4,700 in child support from her ex-spouse.
   c. Paul and Yvonne are married and have three dependent children. Their earned income is $21,300, and they receive $3,900 in interest income from their savings account.
   d. Hattie is married to Herbert, and they have two dependent children. During February, Herbert leaves and hasn't been seen or heard from since. Hattie earns $16,400 from her job. During January and February, Herbert earned $4,800, but Hattie has no idea how much he earned for the entire year.

51. **LO6** Determine the total allowable 2020 earned income credit in each of the following situations:
   a. Rina is single and earns $6,800 in salary for the year. In addition, she receives $2,200 in unemployment compensation during the year.
   b. Lachlan is single with one dependent child. During the year, he earns $8,000 as a waiter and receives alimony of $10,000 from a 2018 divorce decree and child support of $5,000.
   c. Zorica is a single parent with two dependent children. She earns $19,000 from her job as a mechanic. She also receives $3,000 in child support from her ex-spouse.
   d. Elliot and Pam are married and have three dependent children. Elliot and Pam earn $12,000 and $9,000 from their jobs, respectively. They receive $800 in interest and $1,000 in dividend income.

52. **LO6** Determine the amount of the child and dependent care credit to which each of the following taxpayers is entitled:
   a. Michael and Jermaine are married and have a seven-year-old child. Their adjusted gross income is $44,000, and they pay $3,300 in qualified child-care expenses during the year. Michael earns $12,000 and Jermaine earns $40,000 from their jobs.
   b. Jill is a single parent with an 11-year-old daughter. Her adjusted gross income is $24,500, and she pays $2,100 in qualified child-care expenses.

c. Cory is a single parent who earns $9,000 and receives other nontaxable government assistance totaling $5,700 during the year. She pays $1,600 in qualified child-care expenses during the year.
d. Roosevelt and Myrtle are married and have two children. Roosevelt earns $94,000, and Myrtle has a part-time job from which she earns $4,400 during the year. They pay $4,700 in qualified child-care expenses during the year.
e. Randy is single and earns $80,000 per year. He maintains a home for his father, who has been confined to a wheelchair since he had a stroke several years ago. Randy's father receives $6,000 in Social Security but has no other income. Because his father requires constant attention, Randy hires a helper to take care of his father while he is at work. Randy pays the helper $13,000 during the current year.

53. **LO6** Determine the amount of the child- and dependent-care credit to which each of the following taxpayers is entitled:
a. Caryle and Philip are married and have a four-year-old daughter. Their adjusted gross income is $48,000, and they pay $2,100 in qualified child-care expenses during the year. Caryle earns $18,000, and Philip earns $30,000 in salary.
b. Natalie is a single parent with an eight-year-old son. Her adjusted gross income is $27,000, and she pays $3,100 in qualified child-care expenses.
c. Leanne and Ross are married and have three children, ages six, four, and one. Their adjusted gross income is $78,000, and they pay $6,500 in qualified child-care expenses during the year. Leanne earns $48,000, and Ross earns $30,000 in salary.
d. Malcolm and Mirella are married and have two children. Mirella earns $55,000, and Malcolm has a part-time job from which he earns $4,000 during the year. They pay $4,800 in qualified child-care expenses during the year.
e. Andrew is a single parent with a 14-year-old son. Because he does not arrive home from work until 7 p.m., Andrew has hired someone to take care of his son after school and cook him supper. Andrew's adjusted gross income is $59,000, and he pays $3,400 in child-care expenses.
f. Assume the same facts as in part e, except that Andrew's son is 12 years old.

54. **LO6** Martina is single and has two children in college. Matthew is a sophomore and Christine is in her fifth year of college. Martina pays $3,600 in tuition and fees for Matthew, $700 for textbooks, and $2,000 for his room and board. Christine's tuition and fees are $4,800, her textbooks are $550, and her room and board expenses are $1,800. Martina's adjusted gross income is $63,000.
a. What amount can Martina claim as a tax credit for the higher education expenses she pays?
b. Assume that Martina's adjusted gross income is $83,000. What amount can she claim as a tax credit for the higher education expenses she pays?

55. **LO6** Brendan and Theresa are married and have three children in college. Their twin daughters, Christine and Katlyn, are freshmen and attend the same university. Their son, Kevin, is a graduate student. Brendan and Theresa pay $12,000 in tuition and fees ($6,000 each) and $1,100 in textbooks ($500 and $600, respectively) for their daughters and $4,200 in tuition and fees for Kevin and $400 in textbooks. The twins' room and board is $2,600, whereas Kevin's room and board is $1,400. Brendan and Theresa have an adjusted gross income of $77,000.
a. What amount can they claim as a tax credit for the higher education expenses they pay?
b. Assume that their adjusted gross income is $121,000. What amount can they claim as a tax credit for the higher education expenses they pay?
c. Assume the same facts as in part a, except that Kevin is a freshman and the twins are graduate students. What amount can Brendan and Theresa claim as a tax credit for the higher education expenses they pay?

56. **LO7** Determine whether each of the following taxpayers must file a return for 2021:
    a. Jamie is a dependent who has wages of $4,150.
    b. Joel is a dependent who has interest income of $1,200.
    c. Martin is self-employed. His gross business receipts are $24,000, and business expenses are $24,300. His only other income is $2,600 in dividends from stock he owns.
    d. Valerie is 68 and unmarried. Her income consists of $6,500 in Social Security benefits and $15,000 from a qualified employer-provided pension plan.
    e. Raul and Yvonne are married and have two dependent children. Their only income is Raul's $26,000 salary.
57. **LO7** Determine whether each of the following taxpayers must file a return for 2021:
    a. Felicia is a dependent who has wages of $6,350 and interest income of $225.
    b. Jason is a dependent who has interest income of $800.
    c. Jerry is self-employed. His gross business receipts are $43,000, and business expenses are $40,300. His only other income is $1,200 in interest from municipal bonds.
    d. Wayne and Florencia are married and have one dependent child. Wayne stays home and takes care of their child. Florencia's salary is $23,000.

# ISSUE IDENTIFICATION PROBLEMS

In each of the following problems, identify the tax issue(s) posed by the facts presented. Determine the possible tax consequences of each issue that you identify.

58. Kahn is 21 years old and a full-time student. He lives at home with his parents and pays less than half of his support. During the year, he earns $6,400 working as a sales clerk in a department store.
59. Lois is single. She provides more than 50 percent of the support for her mother, who lives in a nursing home. Her mother receives $4,000 from Social Security and $7,000 in dividends.
60. Hector is 66 years of age. During the year, his spouse dies.
61. Myrth is 67, single, and has poor hearing. She pays $300 for special equipment attached to her phones to amplify a caller's voice.
62. Jacqueline is single. In June 2021, she receives a refund of $250 from her 2020 state tax return. Her 2020 itemized deductions were $8,000. In October 2021, her 2019 state tax return is audited, and she has to pay an additional $340 in state taxes. During 2021, Jacqueline has $2,450 withheld from her paycheck for state income taxes.
63. Troy's 2019 tax return is audited. The auditor determines that Troy inadvertently understated his ending inventory in calculating his business income. The error creates an additional tax liability of $5,000. The IRS charges interest on the additional tax liability of $600.
64. Dwight purchases a new home costing $100,000 in the current year. He pays $15,000 down and borrows the remaining $85,000 by securing a mortgage on the home. He also pays $2,000 in closing costs and $1,700 in points to obtain the mortgage. He pays $7,500 in interest on the mortgage during the year.
65. Jose donates stock worth $20,000 to the United Way. He purchased the stock several years ago for $8,000. His adjusted gross income is $60,000.
66. Casandra and Hai are married and have a daughter who is a junior at State University. Their adjusted gross income for the year is $88,000, and they are in the 24 percent marginal tax bracket. They paid their daughter's $3,500 tuition, $450 for text-books, and $3,200 in room and board with $4,750 in savings and by withdrawing $2,400 from a Coverdell Education Savings Account.

# TECHNOLOGY APPLICATIONS

Tax Simulation

67. Ross and Jessica are married and have one child who is two years old. Ross is a recent college graduate and works as a software engineer. Jessica is a full-time student at Hendrick College, and attends classes in the Fall and Spring semesters. Ross earns $32,000 during the year and the couple incurred $2,200 in child-care expenses so that Jessica could attend class.

    REQUIRED: Determine the income tax treatment of the child care expenses. Search a tax research database and find the relevant authority(ies) that forms the basis for your answer. Your answer should include the exact text of the authority(ies) and an explanation of the application of the authority to Ross and Jessica's facts. If there is any uncertainty about the validity of your answer, indicate the cause for the uncertainty.

Research Skills

68. Ben is single and works as a lawyer. His mother lives in a nursing home that costs $30,000 per year. Ben pays $10,000, his mother pays $6,000, and her health insurance policy pays the remaining $14,000. His mother's only income for the year is $9,000 from Social Security. Can Ben claim his mother as a dependent on his tax return? Explain. Would your answer change if the $14,000 were not from a health insurance policy but from Medicare? Explain.

Research Skills

69. Amanda graduated summa cum laude in marketing from State University. As an honor student, she was a member of Beta Gamma Sigma, an honorary business fraternity. She has agreed to donate $250,000 to State University if it uses the proceeds to build a fraternity house for Beta Gamma Sigma. In addition, she has agreed to donate the money only if it is deductible as a charitable contribution. Determine whether Amanda's donation qualifies as a charitable contribution.

Research Skills

70. Using the information below, prepare a spreadsheet calculating the taxable income and tax liability for all taxpayers with adjusted gross income below $100,000. The spreadsheet should be flexible enough to calculate the taxable income if the taxpayer's filing status is single or married. A template to assist the student in solving this problem can be found at www.cengage.com.

| | |
|---|---|
| Salary | $80,000 |
| Interest | 10,000 |
| Deductions for adjusted gross income | 2,500 |
| Deductions from adjusted gross income | 26,000 |

Tax Form

71. Joe and Sharon Racca are married and have two children. Joe works as a sales manager for a national pharmaceutical company and Sharon is a nurse. They own a vacation home in New Hampshire that is used 30 percent for personal purposes. During the year they receive $800 in reimbursements from their medical plan and report $2,200 of investment income. They contributed stock with a fair market value of $4,000 that they acquired in 2010 at a cost of $1,700 to Stanton College.

    The Raccas' gambling winnings for the year were $1,000 and are included in their adjusted gross income. Their adjusted gross income for the year is $88,000 and they provide you with the following data:

| | |
|---|---|
| Automobile insurance | $1,450 |
| Homeowners' insurance | 625 |
| Life insurance | 980 |
| Disability insurance | 375 |
| Health insurance premiums | 1,420 |
| Country club dues | 1,800 |
| Health club dues | 750 |
| Hospital | 4,700 |
| Doctor | 1,275 |
| Chiropractor | 650 |

| | |
|---|---|
| Dentists | 3,750 |
| Prescription drugs | 275 |
| Over-the-counter drugs | 460 |
| State taxes withheld | 3,475 |
| Property taxes (ad valorem) | 320 |
| Investment interest | 1,600 |
| Mortgage interest (primary residence) | 6,850 |
| Real estate taxes (primary residence) | 2,240 |
| Mortgage interest (vacation residence—unallocated) | 3,000 |
| Real estate taxes (vacation residence—unallocated) | 1,350 |
| Charitable contributions (cash) | 8,435 |
| Charitable contribution (clothes at FMV) | 100 |
| Gambling losses | 650 |

Complete Form 1040 Schedule A. Joe's Social Security number is 063-79-4105 and Sharon's Social Security number is 530-22-6584. Forms and instructions can be downloaded from the IRS website (www.irs.gov).

## INTEGRATIVE PROBLEMS

72. Robert and Susan (both 39) are married and have two children. Their son, Dylan, is eight and their daughter, Harper, is three. Susan sells pharmaceuticals for the Bendigo Drug Company. Robert is a teacher at the local junior high school. In the summer, Robert earns extra money as a self-employed house painter. Their income from their jobs is as follows:

| | Salary | Federal Tax Withheld | State Tax Withheld |
|---|---|---|---|
| Susan | $85,000 | $6,500 | $5,400 |
| Robert | 45,000 | 6,100 | 3,150 |

Bendigo has a cafeteria benefits plan that lets employees select benefits equal to as much as 10 percent of their annual salary or receive the cash equivalent. Susan selects dental insurance, $170,000 in group term life insurance, disability insurance, and company-provided day care. The total cost to Bendigo of these benefits is $6,600. Susan takes the remaining benefits to which she is entitled in cash. Because Bendigo does not have an employee pension plan, Robert and Susan each contribute $5,500 to their individual retirement accounts.

The school district gives Robert medical insurance and group term life insurance equal to 100 percent of his annual salary. He pays an additional $125 a month to cover Susan and the children under his medical plan. The school district also has a qualified contributory pension plan to which it contributes 5 percent of Robert's annual salary; he is required to contribute 3 percent. Robert is allowed to make additional contributions of up to 2 percent of his salary, and he contributes the maximum.

In addition to the life insurance coverage provided by their employers, Robert and Susan purchase $100,000 in whole life insurance on each other, along with a disability insurance policy for Robert. The checkbook analysis that follows shows the costs of these policies.

Susan's job requires her to travel throughout her six-state region. Bendigo has an accountable reimbursement plan from which Susan receives $8,500 for the following expenses:

| | |
|---|---|
| Transportation | $4,100 |
| Lodging | 2,700 |
| Meals | 1,800 |

In April, Susan and Robert go the racetrack with Susan's client Annie and her spouse. After wagering $170 without winning, Susan wins $2,600 on the last race. The racetrack withholds $780 for federal income taxes and $260 for state income taxes.

Robert hires college students to help him paint houses. This year, he is able to hire eight students (two four-person crews). Robert shuttles between sites, supervising the jobs, talking to prospective clients, and painting. He treats the college students as independent contractors. His business generates the following income and expenses:

| | |
|---|---|
| Revenues | $112,000 |
| Paint | 33,100 |
| Other material | 6,100 |
| Insurance | 5,500 |
| Payments to student help | 48,400 |

During the year, Robert and Susan receive the following portfolio income:

| | |
|---|---|
| Interest on savings account | $1,900 |
| Interest on U.S. Treasury bills | 400 |
| Cash dividends on stock | 1,750 |
| Interest on city of Buffalo bonds | 600 |
| Interest on Puerto Rico government bonds | 400 |

Robert and Susan own 3,000 shares of qualified small business stock that they purchased in 2012 for $37,000. Early in 2021, they sell all the shares for $16,800. Robert and Susan also sell 100 shares of Sobey Corporation stock for a short-term capital gain of $3,500 and 250 shares of the Bristol Corporation for a long-term capital loss of $7,250. They pay investment interest of $550 during the year.

Robert and Susan own a 4 percent interest in a limited partnership. The limited partnership reports the following information to them:

| | |
|---|---|
| Ordinary loss | $2,100 |
| Long-term capital gain | 600 |
| Charitable contribution | 300 |
| Cash distribution | 2,400 |

During the year, the family spends 20 days at its summer home; they rent it to vacationers for 80 days. Information pertaining to the rental is as follows:

| | |
|---|---|
| Rental income | $6,500 |
| Interest on mortgage | 4,450 |
| Property taxes | 1,600 |
| Management fee | 380 |
| Repairs | 320 |
| Utilities | 650 |
| Insurance | 420 |
| Depreciation (unallocated) | 7,000 |

One night, while returning home from a parent-teacher conference at school, Robert is involved in an automobile accident and is hospitalized for seven days. He incurs $14,000 in medical expenses. His employer-provided policy reimburses him $11,800 of the costs. In addition, his disability policy pays him $3,200 for the time he misses from school.

The car is totally destroyed. It was purchased in 2018 for $19,500, and Robert finds a similar car selling for $8,000. The insurance company reimburses him $6,700.

An analysis of Susan and Robert's checkbook reveals the following payments in 2021:

| | |
|---|---|
| Automobile insurance | $1,200 |
| Homeowners' insurance | 420 |
| Life insurance | 750 |
| Disability insurance | 180 |

| | |
|---|---|
| Country club dues | 2,400 |
| Health club dues | 600 |
| Optometrist | 285 |
| Veterinarian | 275 |
| Prescription drugs | 175 |
| Over-the-counter medicine | 320 |
| Chamber of Commerce contribution | 150 |
| Contribution to candidate for Congress | 500 |
| United Way | 260 |
| St. Philip's Church | 750 |
| Randolph University | 520 |
| Auto registration on automobiles ($130 of which is a license fee) | 390 |
| Tax preparation fee | 375 |

During 2021, Robert and Susan take out a $33,000 home equity loan that they use to pay off $8,000 in credit card debt. The remaining loan proceeds go to renovating the house. Interest paid on this loan totals $1,950 during 2021. Robert and Susan purchased their current home by paying $16,000 down and signing a $160,000 mortgage note, secured by the home. The home is worth $225,000, and the balance on the original mortgage is $134,000. They pay interest on their home mortgage of $14,700 during 2021. They also pay $310 in interest on their personal credit cards and $1,720 in property taxes on their home during 2021.

Compute Robert and Susan's taxable income for 2021, the tax on this income, and the amount of any refund or additional tax due. You should provide a summary schedule of these calculations (in proper form) with a supplemental discussion of the treatment of each item given in the facts. If an item does not affect their taxable income calculation, you should discuss why it doesn't enter into the computation.

*If you are using tax forms to solve this problem*, you will need the following forms and schedules: Form 1040, Schedule A, Schedule B, Schedule C, Schedule D, Schedule E, Form 2106, Form 4684, and Form 8606. In addition, you should obtain a copy of the Form 1040 instructions to help you prepare the tax return.

73. In integrative problem 84 in Chapter 4, you were asked to calculate Carmin's gross income for 2021. This is the second phase, which provides the additional information necessary for you to calculate her taxable income, income tax liability, and additional tax (or refund due). Note: The gross income items from problem 84 still apply. However, some additional items might affect the amount of gross income that Carmin must report. That is, several items included in the gross income from integrative problem 84 are either not reported as gross income or need to be combined with the additional information in this problem to determine the correct treatment. Therefore, you should make the appropriate adjustments to gross income in integrative problem 84, and begin your tax calculation under the heading of Gross Income from Problem 84, as adjusted.

Communication Skills

From this point on, any items of gross income from the information in this problem should be listed to determine gross income for tax purposes. You do not need to list all the individual gross income items from integrative problem 84 in your solution. However, you should explain the adjustments made to the phase 1 gross income figure as part of your discussion of the solution.

Carmin has the following amounts withheld from her paycheck for the payment of state income taxes, federal taxes, and Social Security taxes:

| | |
|---|---|
| State income taxes | $4,768 |
| Federal income taxes | 9,723 |
| Social Security taxes | 6,120 |

In addition, Carmin makes timely federal estimated tax payments of $400 per quarter and estimated state tax payments of $150 per quarter. To minimize her tax liability, she makes her last estimated state tax payment on December 31, 2020.

Because of her busy work schedule, Carmin is unable to give her accountant the tax documents necessary for filing her 2020 state and federal income tax return by the due date (April 15, 2021). In filing her extension on April 15, 2021, she makes a state tax payment of $245 and a federal tax payment of $750. Her return is eventually filed on June 25, 2021. In August 2021, she receives a federal refund of $180 and a state tax refund of $60.

Carmin pays $1,980 in real estate taxes on her principal residence. The real estate tax is used to pay for town schools and other municipal services. The town also has 5 fire districts, which levy a separate tax (i.e., fire tax) to fund each district's fire department. The fire tax is based on the assessed value of the taxpayer's home. Carmin pays $170 in fire tax during the year.

Carmin drives a 2020 Tarago 919 Wagon. Her car registration costs $50 and covers the period 1/1/21 through 12/31/21. In addition, she pays $280 in property tax to the town, based on the book value of the car.

In addition to the medical costs presented in problem 84 in Chapter 4, Carmin incurs the following unreimbursed medical costs:

| | |
|---|---|
| Dentist | $310 |
| Doctor | 390 |
| Prescription drugs | 215 |
| Over-the-counter drugs | 140 |
| Optometrist | 125 |
| Emergency room charges | 440 |
| Chiropractor | 265 |

Carmin receives the following information on her investment in Grubstake Mining and Development:

| | |
|---|---|
| Ordinary income | $7,400 |
| Short-term capital gain | 300 |
| Long-term capital loss | 5,200 |
| Charitable contribution | 500 |

In May 2021, she contributes clothing to the Salvation Army. The original cost of the clothing was $740. She receives a statement from the Salvation Army valuing the donation at $360. In addition, she makes the following cash contributions:

| | |
|---|---|
| Larkin College | $850 |
| United Way | 125 |
| First Methodist Church | 790 |
| Amos House (homeless shelter) | 200 |
| Kappa Delta Delta Sorority | 150 |
| Local Chamber of Commerce | 100 |

Carmin sells real estate in the evenings and on weekends. She runs the business from a 600-square-foot office in her basement. She has been operating in a businesslike way since April 2013 and has always shown a profit. She has the following income and expenses from her business:

| | |
|---|---|
| Commissions | $24,230 |
| Advertising | 4,300 |
| Telephone | 550 |
| Real estate license | 160 |

Carmin has a separate telephone line to her office. The $550 telephone cost includes a $30 monthly fee and $190 in long-distance calls related to her business.

Carmin uses her car in her business and properly documents 8,000 business-related miles. The business and personal use of her car during the year total 20,000 miles. In 2021, Carmin elects to use the standard mileage method to calculate her car expenses. She spends $85 on tolls and $225 on parking related to her real estate business.

Carmin incurs the following expenses in operating her home:

| | |
|---|---|
| Water | $ 205 |
| Electricity | 980 |
| Gas | 630 |
| Insurance | 1,470 |

The living area of Carmin's house (not including the basement) measures 2,400 square feet. When she started her business in April 2013, the fair market value of the house was $100,000. Approximately 10 percent of the purchase price is attributable to the land. Depreciation on the house (unallocated) for 2021 would be $2,077.

Carmin's company has an accountable employee expense reimbursement plan from which Carmin receives $10,800 for the following expenses:

| | |
|---|---|
| Airfare | $4,700 |
| Hotels | 3,400 |
| Meals | 2,000 |
| Car rentals | 600 |
| Incidentals | 100 |

During the year, she also pays $295 for business publications and $775 for a local accountant to prepare her 2020 tax return. The bill from the accountant indicated that preparation of the business portion of Carmin's return cost $550.

In 2019, Carmin loaned $10,000 to her ex-husband Ray so he could start a new business. Their loan agreement requires Ray to pay Carmin 8 percent interest on the unpaid balance of the loan on December 31 of each year and to begin repaying the loan in $2,500 annual installments on July 1, 2021. Carmin receives the interest on the loan during 2019 and 2020. In March 2021, she receives a letter informing her that Ray has filed for bankruptcy. On February 22, 2021, the bankruptcy court awards all creditors 40 percent of their claims on Ray's assets.

Calculate Carmin's taxable income, income tax liability, and tax (or refund) due on her 2021 tax return. Then do one or both of the following, according to your professor's instructions:

a. Include a brief explanation of how you determined each deduction and any item you did not treat as a deduction. Your solution to the problem should contain a list of each deduction and its amount, with the explanations attached.

b. Write a letter to Carmin explaining how you determined each deduction and any items you did not treat as a deduction. You should include a list of each deduction and its amount.

# DISCUSSION CASES

74. Chapter 6 discusses expenditures of individuals that are deductible for adjusted gross income (e.g., student loan interest) and explains the advantage of having an expenditure classified as a deduction for adjusted gross income. Chapter 8 discusses expenditures that are deductible from adjusted gross income (e.g., medical expenses). Select an example of each type of deduction (i.e., for and from) and present an argument as to why that deduction is incorrectly classified. That is, why the expenditure that is a deduction for adjusted gross income should be reclassified as a deduction from adjusted gross income, and why the expenditure that is a deduction from adjusted gross income should be reclassified as a deduction for adjusted gross income.

75. Harold works for the Zanten Corporation. Ken is self-employed. Zanten pays all of Harold's medical insurance premiums, whereas Ken purchases medical insurance from his insurance agent. Explain how the payments of Ken's and Harold's medical insurance are treated for tax purposes. Does this treatment meet Adam Smith's equity criterion?

# TAX PLANNING CASES

Communication Skills

76. Lauren owns stock for which she paid $70,000 several years ago. She is considering donating the stock to the United Way. The fair market value of the stock is $80,000. Her adjusted gross income is $90,000. Lauren has $5,000 of other itemized deductions. She expects that her adjusted gross income will decrease by $10,000 a year and her itemized deductions will remain constant over the next four years. Assume a present value factor of 10 percent. Write a letter to Lauren explaining whether she should deduct the fair market value of the stock or reduce the amount of her contribution to the adjusted basis of the property.

Communication Skills

77. Reg and Rhonda are married and have two children, ages five and three. Rhonda has not worked outside the home since the birth of their first child. Now that the children are older, she would like to return to work and has a job offer that would pay her $27,000 per year. For her to take the job, the children will have to be put into a day-care center. The day-care center will cost $500 per month. Given the high cost of the day-care center, Reg and Rhonda are wondering whether it is worth it for Rhonda to take the job. They project their current-year taxable income (without considering Rhonda's job) as $50,000. Write a letter to Rhonda explaining how much additional cash (after taxes) she will earn if she accepts the job. You should include in your letter the nontax factors Rhonda should consider before taking the job.

Communication Skills

78. Beverly and Charlie are married and have one child, Carla, who is eight years old. With all the changes in the tax law concerning higher education expenses, Beverly and Charlie realize they need to plan for their daughter's college education. They intend to contribute $2,000 per year for the next 10 years to a Coverdell Education Savings Account for Carla. Their broker has advised them that the $20,000 they contribute to the Coverdell Education Savings Accounts will generate total income of $8,900. The total cost of tuition and fees for Carla's four years at the local university is expected to be $80,000. Beverly and Charlie expect to have $11,600 in savings and $28,900 from the Coverdell Education Savings Accounts available to pay for Carla's tuition costs. They plan on obtaining $14,500 in qualified student loans and selling stock for $25,000 to provide the additional money they need to pay Carla's tuition and fees. The amount of their savings is based on annual growth of 6 percent, and the gain on the stock is based on a growth rate of 8 percent per year. The payments on the student loans will not start until six months after Carla's graduation. The sale of the stock is expected to generate a gain of $12,000. The broker also estimates that when Carla starts school, the phase-out range for married taxpayers for the American Opportunity Tax Credit and the Lifetime Learning Tax Credit will be $180,000 to $200,000 and that the phase-out for student loan interest will be $85,000 to $100,000. The phase-outs will increase by $1,000 per year. The American Opportunity Tax Credit limits are expected to be 100 percent of the first $3,000 of expenses and 25 percent of the next $3,000 of expenses in 10 years. The Lifetime Learning Tax Credit will be limited to 20 percent of the first $15,000 of expenses. Beverly and Charlie's adjusted gross income when Carla starts college is expected to be $84,000 and will increase 5 percent per year. The tuition is constant over the four years ($20,000 per year), and Carla's $80,000 tuition can be paid using any combination of the funding sources. Write a letter to Beverly and Charlie suggesting one combination of the funding sources to pay for Carla's tuition. Your letter should also explain the tax savings from your proposed funding strategy and why other possible funding source combinations will not produce greater savings.

## ETHICS DISCUSSION CASE

79. Tom, an executive for a large corporation, enjoys the challenge of preparing his tax return. He is aggressive in preparing his return and searches through all the available publications to reduce his tax liability. In all the years Tom has completed his return, he has never been audited. However, in preparing his 2019 tax return, Tom misinterpreted a complex change in the law and is being audited. Aware that he probably should have an expert represent him before the IRS, Tom has hired Josephine, a local CPA. During the audit process, Josephine finds expenses that Tom had failed to deduct. However, the IRS also disallowed some of Tom's other deductions. During a meeting, Josephine and the IRS agent agree on Tom's revised taxable income. When Josephine receives the auditor's change letter, she checks the agent's calculation and finds that the agent has miscalculated the new tax liability by $750 in Tom's favor. In fact, Tom will now receive a refund. When Tom receives his copy of the letter, he leaves a message on Josephine's voice mail congratulating her on her work. You are Josephine's assistant. Josephine asks you to write a letter to Tom explaining the course of action she must take.

# Appendix to Chapter 8

## 8A-1 SCHEDULE EIC (EARNED INCOME CREDIT) 2020 EARNED INCOME CREDIT TABLE

## Worksheet A—2020 EIC—Line 27

*Keep for Your Records*

***Before you begin:*** √ Be sure you are using the correct worksheet. Use this worksheet only if you answered "No" to Step 5, question 2. Otherwise, use Worksheet B.

### Part 1

**All Filers Using Worksheet A**

**1.** Enter your earned income from Step 5. **1** ______

**2.** Look up the amount on line 1 above in the EIC Table (right after Worksheet B) to find the credit. Be sure you use the correct column for your filing status and the number of children you have. Enter the credit here. **2** ______

If line 2 is zero, STOP You can't take the credit.
Enter "No" on the dotted line next to Form 1040 or 1040-SR, line 27.

**3.** Enter the amount from Form 1040 or 1040-SR, line 11. **3** ______

**4.** Are the amounts on lines 3 and 1 the same?

☐ **Yes.** Skip line 5; enter the amount from line 2 on line 6.

☐ **No.** Go to line 5.

### Part 2

**Filers Who Answered "No" on Line 4**

**5.** If you have:

- No qualifying children, is the amount on line 3 less than $8,800 ($14,700 if married filing jointly)?
- 1 or more qualifying children, is the amount on line 3 less than $19,350 ($25,250 if married filing jointly)?

☐ **Yes.** Leave line 5 blank; enter the amount from line 2 on line 6.

☐ **No.** Look up the amount on line 3 in the EIC Table to find the credit. Be sure you use the correct column for your filing status and the number of children you have. Enter the credit here. **5** ______
Look at the amounts on lines 5 and 2.
Then, enter the **smaller** amount on line 6.

### Part 3

**Your Earned Income Credit**

**6. This is your earned income credit.** **6** ______

Enter this amount on Form 1040 or 1040-SR, line 27.

**Reminder—**

√ If you have a qualifying child, complete and attach Schedule EIC.

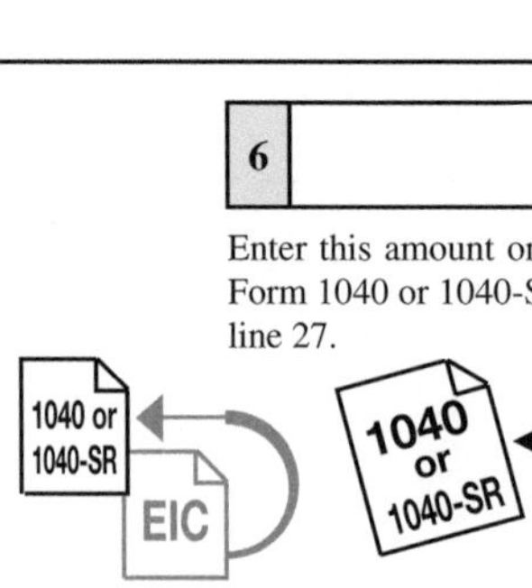


CAUTION *If your EIC for a year after 1996 was reduced or disallowed, see* Form 8862, who must file, *earlier, to find out if you must file Form 8862 to take the credit for 2020.*

## Worksheet B—2020 EIC—Line 27

*Keep for Your Records*

**Use this worksheet if you answered "Yes" to Step 5, question 2.**

√ Complete the parts below (Parts 1 through 3) that apply to you. Then, continue to Part 4.

√ If you are married filing a joint return, include your spouse's amounts, if any, with yours to figure the amounts to enter in Parts 1 through 3.

### Part 1

**Self-Employed, Members of the Clergy, and People With Church Employee Income Filing Schedule SE**

| | | | |
|---|---|---|---|
| **1a.** Enter the amount from Schedule SE, Part I, line 3. | | **1a** | |
| **b.** Enter any amount from Schedule SE, Part I, line 4b and line 5a. | + | **1b** | |
| **c.** Combine lines 1a and 1b. | = | **1c** | |
| **d.** Enter the amount from Schedule SE, Part I, line 13. | − | **1d** | |
| **e.** Subtract line 1d from line 1c. | = | **1e** | |

### Part 2

**Self-Employed NOT Required To File Schedule SE**

For example, your net earnings from self-employment were less than $400.

**2.** Don't include on these lines any statutory employee income, any net profit from services performed as a notary public, any amount exempt from self-employment tax as the result of the filing and approval of Form 4029 or Form 4361, or any other amounts exempt from self-employment tax.

| | | | |
|---|---|---|---|
| **a.** Enter any net farm profit or (loss) from Schedule F, line 34; and from farm partnerships, Schedule K-1 (Form 1065), box 14, code A*. | | **2a** | |
| **b.** Enter any net profit or (loss) from Schedule C, line 31; and Schedule K-1 (Form 1065), box 14, code A (other than farming)*. | + | **2b** | |
| **c.** Combine lines 2a and 2b. | = | **2c** | |

**If you have any Schedule K-1 amounts, complete the appropriate line(s) of Schedule SE, Part I. Reduce the Schedule K-1 amounts as described in the Partner's Instructions for Schedule K-1. Enter your name and social security number on Schedule SE and attach it to your return.*

### Part 3

**Statutory Employees Filing Schedule C**

| | | |
|---|---|---|
| **3.** Enter the amount from Schedule C, line 1, that you are filing as a statutory employee. | **3** | |

### Part 4

**All Filers Using Worksheet B**

**Note.** If line 4b includes income on which you should have paid self-employment tax but didn't, we may reduce your credit by the amount of self-employment tax not paid.

| | | |
|---|---|---|
| **4a.** Enter your earned income from Step 5. | **4a** | |
| **b.** Combine lines 1e, 2c, 3, and 4a. **This is your total earned income.** | **4b** | |

If line 4b is zero or less, STOP You can't take the credit. Enter "No" on the dotted line next to Form 1040 or 1040-SR, line 27.

**5.** If you have:

- 3 or more qualifying children, is line 4b less than $50,954 ($56,844 if married filing jointly)?
- 2 qualifying children, is line 4b less than $47,440 ($53,330 if married filing jointly)?
- 1 qualifying child, is line 4b less than $41,756 ($47,646 if married filing jointly)?
- No qualifying children, is line 4b less than $15,820 ($21,710 if married filing jointly)?

☐ **Yes.** If you want the IRS to figure your credit, see *Credit figured by the IRS*, earlier. If you want to figure the credit yourself, enter the amount from line 4b on line 6 of this worksheet.

☐ **No.** STOP You can't take the credit. Enter "No" on the dotted line next to Form 1040 or 1040-SR, line 27.

## Worksheet B—2020 EIC—Line 27—*Continued*

*Keep for Your Records*

**Part 5**

**All Filers Using Worksheet B**

6. Enter your total earned income from Part 4, line 4b. | 6 | |

7. Look up the amount on line 6 above in the EIC Table to find the credit. Be sure you use the correct column for your filing status and the number of children you have. Enter the credit here. | 7 | |

   If line 7 is zero, STOP You can't take the credit. Enter "No" on the dotted line next to Form 1040 or 1040-SR, line 27.

8. Enter the amount from Form 1040 or 1040-SR, line 11. | 8 | |

9. Are the amounts on lines 8 and 6 the same?

   ☐ **Yes.** Skip line 10; enter the amount from line 7 on line 11.

   ☐ **No.** Go to line 10.

**Part 6**

**Filers Who Answered "No" on Line 9**

10. If you have:
    - No qualifying children, is the amount on line 8 less than $8,800 ($14,700 if married filing jointly)?
    - 1 or more qualifying children, is the amount on line 8 less than $19,350 ($25,250 if married filing jointly)?

    ☐ **Yes.** Leave line 10 blank; enter the amount from line 7 on line 11.

    ☐ **No.** Look up the amount on line 8 in the EIC Table to find the credit. Be sure you use the correct column for your filing status and the number of children you have. Enter the credit here. | 10 | |

    Look at the amounts on lines 10 and 7. Then, enter the **smaller** amount on line 11.

**Part 7**

**Your Earned Income Credit**

11. **This is your earned income credit.** | 11 | |

Enter this amount on Form 1040 or 1040-SR, line 27.

**Reminder—**

√ If you have a qualifying child, complete and attach Schedule EIC.

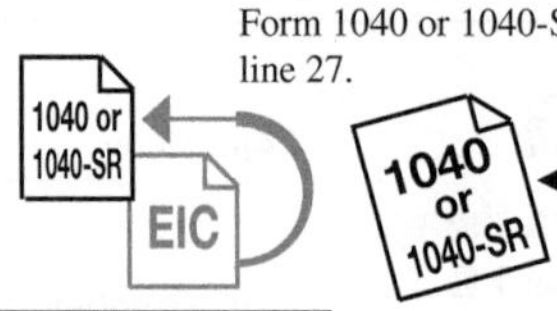


CAUTION *If your EIC for a year after 1996 was reduced or disallowed, see* Form 8862, who must file, *earlier, to find out if you must file Form 8862 to take the credit for 2020.*

# 2020 Earned Income Credit (EIC) Table

## Caution. This is **not** a tax table.

**1.** To find your credit, read down the "At least - But less than" columns and find the line that includes the amount you were told to look up from your EIC Worksheet.

**2.** Then, go to the column that includes your filing status and the number of qualifying children you have. Enter the credit from that column on your EIC Worksheet.

**Example.** If your filing status is single, you have one qualifying child, and the amount you are looking up from your EIC Worksheet is $2,455, you would enter $842.

| If the amount you are looking up from the worksheet is– | | And your filing status is– Single, head of household, or qualifying widow(er) and the number of children you have is– | | | |
|---|---|---|---|---|---|
| | | 0 | 1 | 2 | 3 |
| At least | But less than | Your credit is– | | | |
| 2,400 | 2,450 | 186 | 825 | 970 | 1,091 |
| 2,450 | 2,500 | 189 | 842 | 990 | 1,114 |

| If the amount you are looking up from the worksheet is– | | And your filing status is– Single, head of household, or qualifying widow(er) and you have– | | | | Married filing jointly and you have– | | | |
|---|---|---|---|---|---|---|---|---|---|
| | | 0 | 1 | 2 | 3 | 0 | 1 | 2 | 3 |
| At least | But less than | Your credit is– | | | | Your credit is– | | | |
| $1 | $50 | $2 | $9 | $10 | $11 | $2 | $9 | $10 | $11 |
| 50 | 100 | 6 | 26 | 30 | 34 | 6 | 26 | 30 | 34 |
| 100 | 150 | 10 | 43 | 50 | 56 | 10 | 43 | 50 | 56 |
| 150 | 200 | 13 | 60 | 70 | 79 | 13 | 60 | 70 | 79 |
| 200 | 250 | 17 | 77 | 90 | 101 | 17 | 77 | 90 | 101 |
| 250 | 300 | 21 | 94 | 110 | 124 | 21 | 94 | 110 | 124 |
| 300 | 350 | 25 | 111 | 130 | 146 | 25 | 111 | 130 | 146 |
| 350 | 400 | 29 | 128 | 150 | 169 | 29 | 128 | 150 | 169 |
| 400 | 450 | 33 | 145 | 170 | 191 | 33 | 145 | 170 | 191 |
| 450 | 500 | 36 | 162 | 190 | 214 | 36 | 162 | 190 | 214 |
| 500 | 550 | 40 | 179 | 210 | 236 | 40 | 179 | 210 | 236 |
| 550 | 600 | 44 | 196 | 230 | 259 | 44 | 196 | 230 | 259 |
| 600 | 650 | 48 | 213 | 250 | 281 | 48 | 213 | 250 | 281 |
| 650 | 700 | 52 | 230 | 270 | 304 | 52 | 230 | 270 | 304 |
| 700 | 750 | 55 | 247 | 290 | 326 | 55 | 247 | 290 | 326 |
| 750 | 800 | 59 | 264 | 310 | 349 | 59 | 264 | 310 | 349 |
| 800 | 850 | 63 | 281 | 330 | 371 | 63 | 281 | 330 | 371 |
| 850 | 900 | 67 | 298 | 350 | 394 | 67 | 298 | 350 | 394 |
| 900 | 950 | 71 | 315 | 370 | 416 | 71 | 315 | 370 | 416 |
| 950 | 1,000 | 75 | 332 | 390 | 439 | 75 | 332 | 390 | 439 |
| 1,000 | 1,050 | 78 | 349 | 410 | 461 | 78 | 349 | 410 | 461 |
| 1,050 | 1,100 | 82 | 366 | 430 | 484 | 82 | 366 | 430 | 484 |
| 1,100 | 1,150 | 86 | 383 | 450 | 506 | 86 | 383 | 450 | 506 |
| 1,150 | 1,200 | 90 | 400 | 470 | 529 | 90 | 400 | 470 | 529 |
| 1,200 | 1,250 | 94 | 417 | 490 | 551 | 94 | 417 | 490 | 551 |
| 1,250 | 1,300 | 98 | 434 | 510 | 574 | 98 | 434 | 510 | 574 |
| 1,300 | 1,350 | 101 | 451 | 530 | 596 | 101 | 451 | 530 | 596 |
| 1,350 | 1,400 | 105 | 468 | 550 | 619 | 105 | 468 | 550 | 619 |
| 1,400 | 1,450 | 109 | 485 | 570 | 641 | 109 | 485 | 570 | 641 |
| 1,450 | 1,500 | 113 | 502 | 590 | 664 | 113 | 502 | 590 | 664 |
| 1,500 | 1,550 | 117 | 519 | 610 | 686 | 117 | 519 | 610 | 686 |
| 1,550 | 1,600 | 120 | 536 | 630 | 709 | 120 | 536 | 630 | 709 |
| 1,600 | 1,650 | 124 | 553 | 650 | 731 | 124 | 553 | 650 | 731 |
| 1,650 | 1,700 | 128 | 570 | 670 | 754 | 128 | 570 | 670 | 754 |
| 1,700 | 1,750 | 132 | 587 | 690 | 776 | 132 | 587 | 690 | 776 |
| 1,750 | 1,800 | 136 | 604 | 710 | 799 | 136 | 604 | 710 | 799 |
| 1,800 | 1,850 | 140 | 621 | 730 | 821 | 140 | 621 | 730 | 821 |
| 1,850 | 1,900 | 143 | 638 | 750 | 844 | 143 | 638 | 750 | 844 |
| 1,900 | 1,950 | 147 | 655 | 770 | 866 | 147 | 655 | 770 | 866 |
| 1,950 | 2,000 | 151 | 672 | 790 | 889 | 151 | 672 | 790 | 889 |
| 2,000 | 2,050 | 155 | 689 | 810 | 911 | 155 | 689 | 810 | 911 |
| 2,050 | 2,100 | 159 | 706 | 830 | 934 | 159 | 706 | 830 | 934 |
| 2,100 | 2,150 | 163 | 723 | 850 | 956 | 163 | 723 | 850 | 956 |
| 2,150 | 2,200 | 166 | 740 | 870 | 979 | 166 | 740 | 870 | 979 |
| 2,200 | 2,250 | 170 | 757 | 890 | 1,001 | 170 | 757 | 890 | 1,001 |
| 2,250 | 2,300 | 174 | 774 | 910 | 1,024 | 174 | 774 | 910 | 1,024 |
| 2,300 | 2,350 | 178 | 791 | 930 | 1,046 | 178 | 791 | 930 | 1,046 |
| 2,350 | 2,400 | 182 | 808 | 950 | 1,069 | 182 | 808 | 950 | 1,069 |
| 2,400 | 2,450 | 186 | 825 | 970 | 1,091 | 186 | 825 | 970 | 1,091 |
| 2,450 | 2,500 | 189 | 842 | 990 | 1,114 | 189 | 842 | 990 | 1,114 |
| 2,500 | 2,550 | 193 | 859 | 1,010 | 1,136 | 193 | 859 | 1,010 | 1,136 |
| 2,550 | 2,600 | 197 | 876 | 1,030 | 1,159 | 197 | 876 | 1,030 | 1,159 |
| 2,600 | 2,650 | 201 | 893 | 1,050 | 1,181 | 201 | 893 | 1,050 | 1,181 |
| 2,650 | 2,700 | 205 | 910 | 1,070 | 1,204 | 205 | 910 | 1,070 | 1,204 |
| 2,700 | 2,750 | 208 | 927 | 1,090 | 1,226 | 208 | 927 | 1,090 | 1,226 |
| 2,750 | 2,800 | 212 | 944 | 1,110 | 1,249 | 212 | 944 | 1,110 | 1,249 |

| If the amount you are looking up from the worksheet is– | | And your filing status is– Single, head of household, or qualifying widow(er) and you have– | | | | Married filing jointly and you have– | | | |
|---|---|---|---|---|---|---|---|---|---|
| | | 0 | 1 | 2 | 3 | 0 | 1 | 2 | 3 |
| At least | But less than | Your credit is– | | | | Your credit is– | | | |
| 2,800 | 2,850 | 216 | 961 | 1,130 | 1,271 | 216 | 961 | 1,130 | 1,271 |
| 2,850 | 2,900 | 220 | 978 | 1,150 | 1,294 | 220 | 978 | 1,150 | 1,294 |
| 2,900 | 2,950 | 224 | 995 | 1,170 | 1,316 | 224 | 995 | 1,170 | 1,316 |
| 2,950 | 3,000 | 228 | 1,012 | 1,190 | 1,339 | 228 | 1,012 | 1,190 | 1,339 |
| 3,000 | 3,050 | 231 | 1,029 | 1,210 | 1,361 | 231 | 1,029 | 1,210 | 1,361 |
| 3,050 | 3,100 | 235 | 1,046 | 1,230 | 1,384 | 235 | 1,046 | 1,230 | 1,384 |
| 3,100 | 3,150 | 239 | 1,063 | 1,250 | 1,406 | 239 | 1,063 | 1,250 | 1,406 |
| 3,150 | 3,200 | 243 | 1,080 | 1,270 | 1,429 | 243 | 1,080 | 1,270 | 1,429 |
| 3,200 | 3,250 | 247 | 1,097 | 1,290 | 1,451 | 247 | 1,097 | 1,290 | 1,451 |
| 3,250 | 3,300 | 251 | 1,114 | 1,310 | 1,474 | 251 | 1,114 | 1,310 | 1,474 |
| 3,300 | 3,350 | 254 | 1,131 | 1,330 | 1,496 | 254 | 1,131 | 1,330 | 1,496 |
| 3,350 | 3,400 | 258 | 1,148 | 1,350 | 1,519 | 258 | 1,148 | 1,350 | 1,519 |
| 3,400 | 3,450 | 262 | 1,165 | 1,370 | 1,541 | 262 | 1,165 | 1,370 | 1,541 |
| 3,450 | 3,500 | 266 | 1,182 | 1,390 | 1,564 | 266 | 1,182 | 1,390 | 1,564 |
| 3,500 | 3,550 | 270 | 1,199 | 1,410 | 1,586 | 270 | 1,199 | 1,410 | 1,586 |
| 3,550 | 3,600 | 273 | 1,216 | 1,430 | 1,609 | 273 | 1,216 | 1,430 | 1,609 |
| 3,600 | 3,650 | 277 | 1,233 | 1,450 | 1,631 | 277 | 1,233 | 1,450 | 1,631 |
| 3,650 | 3,700 | 281 | 1,250 | 1,470 | 1,654 | 281 | 1,250 | 1,470 | 1,654 |
| 3,700 | 3,750 | 285 | 1,267 | 1,490 | 1,676 | 285 | 1,267 | 1,490 | 1,676 |
| 3,750 | 3,800 | 289 | 1,284 | 1,510 | 1,699 | 289 | 1,284 | 1,510 | 1,699 |
| 3,800 | 3,850 | 293 | 1,301 | 1,530 | 1,721 | 293 | 1,301 | 1,530 | 1,721 |
| 3,850 | 3,900 | 296 | 1,318 | 1,550 | 1,744 | 296 | 1,318 | 1,550 | 1,744 |
| 3,900 | 3,950 | 300 | 1,335 | 1,570 | 1,766 | 300 | 1,335 | 1,570 | 1,766 |
| 3,950 | 4,000 | 304 | 1,352 | 1,590 | 1,789 | 304 | 1,352 | 1,590 | 1,789 |
| 4,000 | 4,050 | 308 | 1,369 | 1,610 | 1,811 | 308 | 1,369 | 1,610 | 1,811 |
| 4,050 | 4,100 | 312 | 1,386 | 1,630 | 1,834 | 312 | 1,386 | 1,630 | 1,834 |
| 4,100 | 4,150 | 316 | 1,403 | 1,650 | 1,856 | 316 | 1,403 | 1,650 | 1,856 |
| 4,150 | 4,200 | 319 | 1,420 | 1,670 | 1,879 | 319 | 1,420 | 1,670 | 1,879 |
| 4,200 | 4,250 | 323 | 1,437 | 1,690 | 1,901 | 323 | 1,437 | 1,690 | 1,901 |
| 4,250 | 4,300 | 327 | 1,454 | 1,710 | 1,924 | 327 | 1,454 | 1,710 | 1,924 |
| 4,300 | 4,350 | 331 | 1,471 | 1,730 | 1,946 | 331 | 1,471 | 1,730 | 1,946 |
| 4,350 | 4,400 | 335 | 1,488 | 1,750 | 1,969 | 335 | 1,488 | 1,750 | 1,969 |
| 4,400 | 4,450 | 339 | 1,505 | 1,770 | 1,991 | 339 | 1,505 | 1,770 | 1,991 |
| 4,450 | 4,500 | 342 | 1,522 | 1,790 | 2,014 | 342 | 1,522 | 1,790 | 2,014 |
| 4,500 | 4,550 | 346 | 1,539 | 1,810 | 2,036 | 346 | 1,539 | 1,810 | 2,036 |
| 4,550 | 4,600 | 350 | 1,556 | 1,830 | 2,059 | 350 | 1,556 | 1,830 | 2,059 |
| 4,600 | 4,650 | 354 | 1,573 | 1,850 | 2,081 | 354 | 1,573 | 1,850 | 2,081 |
| 4,650 | 4,700 | 358 | 1,590 | 1,870 | 2,104 | 358 | 1,590 | 1,870 | 2,104 |
| 4,700 | 4,750 | 361 | 1,607 | 1,890 | 2,126 | 361 | 1,607 | 1,890 | 2,126 |
| 4,750 | 4,800 | 365 | 1,624 | 1,910 | 2,149 | 365 | 1,624 | 1,910 | 2,149 |
| 4,800 | 4,850 | 369 | 1,641 | 1,930 | 2,171 | 369 | 1,641 | 1,930 | 2,171 |
| 4,850 | 4,900 | 373 | 1,658 | 1,950 | 2,194 | 373 | 1,658 | 1,950 | 2,194 |
| 4,900 | 4,950 | 377 | 1,675 | 1,970 | 2,216 | 377 | 1,675 | 1,970 | 2,216 |
| 4,950 | 5,000 | 381 | 1,692 | 1,990 | 2,239 | 381 | 1,692 | 1,990 | 2,239 |
| 5,000 | 5,050 | 384 | 1,709 | 2,010 | 2,261 | 384 | 1,709 | 2,010 | 2,261 |
| 5,050 | 5,100 | 388 | 1,726 | 2,030 | 2,284 | 388 | 1,726 | 2,030 | 2,284 |
| 5,100 | 5,150 | 392 | 1,743 | 2,050 | 2,306 | 392 | 1,743 | 2,050 | 2,306 |
| 5,150 | 5,200 | 396 | 1,760 | 2,070 | 2,329 | 396 | 1,760 | 2,070 | 2,329 |
| 5,200 | 5,250 | 400 | 1,777 | 2,090 | 2,351 | 400 | 1,777 | 2,090 | 2,351 |
| 5,250 | 5,300 | 404 | 1,794 | 2,110 | 2,374 | 404 | 1,794 | 2,110 | 2,374 |
| 5,300 | 5,350 | 407 | 1,811 | 2,130 | 2,396 | 407 | 1,811 | 2,130 | 2,396 |
| 5,350 | 5,400 | 411 | 1,828 | 2,150 | 2,419 | 411 | 1,828 | 2,150 | 2,419 |
| 5,400 | 5,450 | 415 | 1,845 | 2,170 | 2,441 | 415 | 1,845 | 2,170 | 2,441 |
| 5,450 | 5,500 | 419 | 1,862 | 2,190 | 2,464 | 419 | 1,862 | 2,190 | 2,464 |
| 5,500 | 5,550 | 423 | 1,879 | 2,210 | 2,486 | 423 | 1,879 | 2,210 | 2,486 |
| 5,550 | 5,600 | 426 | 1,896 | 2,230 | 2,509 | 426 | 1,896 | 2,230 | 2,509 |

*(Continued)*

## Earned Income Credit (EIC) Table - *Continued*

(**Caution.** This is **not** a tax table.)

| If the amount you are looking up from the worksheet is– | | And your filing status is– Single, head of household, or qualifying widow(er) and you have– | | | | Married filing jointly and you have– | | | |
|---|---|---|---|---|---|---|---|---|---|
| | | 0 | 1 | 2 | 3 | 0 | 1 | 2 | 3 |
| At least | But less than | Your credit is– | | | | Your credit is– | | | |
| 5,600 | 5,650 | 430 | 1,913 | 2,250 | 2,531 | 430 | 1,913 | 2,250 | 2,531 |
| 5,650 | 5,700 | 434 | 1,930 | 2,270 | 2,554 | 434 | 1,930 | 2,270 | 2,554 |
| 5,700 | 5,750 | 438 | 1,947 | 2,290 | 2,576 | 438 | 1,947 | 2,290 | 2,576 |
| 5,750 | 5,800 | 442 | 1,964 | 2,310 | 2,599 | 442 | 1,964 | 2,310 | 2,599 |
| 5,800 | 5,850 | 446 | 1,981 | 2,330 | 2,621 | 446 | 1,981 | 2,330 | 2,621 |
| 5,850 | 5,900 | 449 | 1,998 | 2,350 | 2,644 | 449 | 1,998 | 2,350 | 2,644 |
| 5,900 | 5,950 | 453 | 2,015 | 2,370 | 2,666 | 453 | 2,015 | 2,370 | 2,666 |
| 5,950 | 6,000 | 457 | 2,032 | 2,390 | 2,689 | 457 | 2,032 | 2,390 | 2,689 |
| 6,000 | 6,050 | 461 | 2,049 | 2,410 | 2,711 | 461 | 2,049 | 2,410 | 2,711 |
| 6,050 | 6,100 | 465 | 2,066 | 2,430 | 2,734 | 465 | 2,066 | 2,430 | 2,734 |
| 6,100 | 6,150 | 469 | 2,083 | 2,450 | 2,756 | 469 | 2,083 | 2,450 | 2,756 |
| 6,150 | 6,200 | 472 | 2,100 | 2,470 | 2,779 | 472 | 2,100 | 2,470 | 2,779 |
| 6,200 | 6,250 | 476 | 2,117 | 2,490 | 2,801 | 476 | 2,117 | 2,490 | 2,801 |
| 6,250 | 6,300 | 480 | 2,134 | 2,510 | 2,824 | 480 | 2,134 | 2,510 | 2,824 |
| 6,300 | 6,350 | 484 | 2,151 | 2,530 | 2,846 | 484 | 2,151 | 2,530 | 2,846 |
| 6,350 | 6,400 | 488 | 2,168 | 2,550 | 2,869 | 488 | 2,168 | 2,550 | 2,869 |
| 6,400 | 6,450 | 492 | 2,185 | 2,570 | 2,891 | 492 | 2,185 | 2,570 | 2,891 |
| 6,450 | 6,500 | 495 | 2,202 | 2,590 | 2,914 | 495 | 2,202 | 2,590 | 2,914 |
| 6,500 | 6,550 | 499 | 2,219 | 2,610 | 2,936 | 499 | 2,219 | 2,610 | 2,936 |
| 6,550 | 6,600 | 503 | 2,236 | 2,630 | 2,959 | 503 | 2,236 | 2,630 | 2,959 |
| 6,600 | 6,650 | 507 | 2,253 | 2,650 | 2,981 | 507 | 2,253 | 2,650 | 2,981 |
| 6,650 | 6,700 | 511 | 2,270 | 2,670 | 3,004 | 511 | 2,270 | 2,670 | 3,004 |
| 6,700 | 6,750 | 514 | 2,287 | 2,690 | 3,026 | 514 | 2,287 | 2,690 | 3,026 |
| 6,750 | 6,800 | 518 | 2,304 | 2,710 | 3,049 | 518 | 2,304 | 2,710 | 3,049 |
| 6,800 | 6,850 | 522 | 2,321 | 2,730 | 3,071 | 522 | 2,321 | 2,730 | 3,071 |
| 6,850 | 6,900 | 526 | 2,338 | 2,750 | 3,094 | 526 | 2,338 | 2,750 | 3,094 |
| 6,900 | 6,950 | 530 | 2,355 | 2,770 | 3,116 | 530 | 2,355 | 2,770 | 3,116 |
| 6,950 | 7,000 | 534 | 2,372 | 2,790 | 3,139 | 534 | 2,372 | 2,790 | 3,139 |
| 7,000 | 7,050 | 538 | 2,389 | 2,810 | 3,161 | 538 | 2,389 | 2,810 | 3,161 |
| 7,050 | 7,100 | 538 | 2,406 | 2,830 | 3,184 | 538 | 2,406 | 2,830 | 3,184 |
| 7,100 | 7,150 | 538 | 2,423 | 2,850 | 3,206 | 538 | 2,423 | 2,850 | 3,206 |
| 7,150 | 7,200 | 538 | 2,440 | 2,870 | 3,229 | 538 | 2,440 | 2,870 | 3,229 |
| 7,200 | 7,250 | 538 | 2,457 | 2,890 | 3,251 | 538 | 2,457 | 2,890 | 3,251 |
| 7,250 | 7,300 | 538 | 2,474 | 2,910 | 3,274 | 538 | 2,474 | 2,910 | 3,274 |
| 7,300 | 7,350 | 538 | 2,491 | 2,930 | 3,296 | 538 | 2,491 | 2,930 | 3,296 |
| 7,350 | 7,400 | 538 | 2,508 | 2,950 | 3,319 | 538 | 2,508 | 2,950 | 3,319 |
| 7,400 | 7,450 | 538 | 2,525 | 2,970 | 3,341 | 538 | 2,525 | 2,970 | 3,341 |
| 7,450 | 7,500 | 538 | 2,542 | 2,990 | 3,364 | 538 | 2,542 | 2,990 | 3,364 |
| 7,500 | 7,550 | 538 | 2,559 | 3,010 | 3,386 | 538 | 2,559 | 3,010 | 3,386 |
| 7,550 | 7,600 | 538 | 2,576 | 3,030 | 3,409 | 538 | 2,576 | 3,030 | 3,409 |
| 7,600 | 7,650 | 538 | 2,593 | 3,050 | 3,431 | 538 | 2,593 | 3,050 | 3,431 |
| 7,650 | 7,700 | 538 | 2,610 | 3,070 | 3,454 | 538 | 2,610 | 3,070 | 3,454 |
| 7,700 | 7,750 | 538 | 2,627 | 3,090 | 3,476 | 538 | 2,627 | 3,090 | 3,476 |
| 7,750 | 7,800 | 538 | 2,644 | 3,110 | 3,499 | 538 | 2,644 | 3,110 | 3,499 |
| 7,800 | 7,850 | 538 | 2,661 | 3,130 | 3,521 | 538 | 2,661 | 3,130 | 3,521 |
| 7,850 | 7,900 | 538 | 2,678 | 3,150 | 3,544 | 538 | 2,678 | 3,150 | 3,544 |
| 7,900 | 7,950 | 538 | 2,695 | 3,170 | 3,566 | 538 | 2,695 | 3,170 | 3,566 |
| 7,950 | 8,000 | 538 | 2,712 | 3,190 | 3,589 | 538 | 2,712 | 3,190 | 3,589 |
| 8,000 | 8,050 | 538 | 2,729 | 3,210 | 3,611 | 538 | 2,729 | 3,210 | 3,611 |
| 8,050 | 8,100 | 538 | 2,746 | 3,230 | 3,634 | 538 | 2,746 | 3,230 | 3,634 |
| 8,100 | 8,150 | 538 | 2,763 | 3,250 | 3,656 | 538 | 2,763 | 3,250 | 3,656 |
| 8,150 | 8,200 | 538 | 2,780 | 3,270 | 3,679 | 538 | 2,780 | 3,270 | 3,679 |
| 8,200 | 8,250 | 538 | 2,797 | 3,290 | 3,701 | 538 | 2,797 | 3,290 | 3,701 |
| 8,250 | 8,300 | 538 | 2,814 | 3,310 | 3,724 | 538 | 2,814 | 3,310 | 3,724 |
| 8,300 | 8,350 | 538 | 2,831 | 3,330 | 3,746 | 538 | 2,831 | 3,330 | 3,746 |
| 8,350 | 8,400 | 538 | 2,848 | 3,350 | 3,769 | 538 | 2,848 | 3,350 | 3,769 |
| 8,400 | 8,450 | 538 | 2,865 | 3,370 | 3,791 | 538 | 2,865 | 3,370 | 3,791 |
| 8,450 | 8,500 | 538 | 2,882 | 3,390 | 3,814 | 538 | 2,882 | 3,390 | 3,814 |
| 8,500 | 8,550 | 538 | 2,899 | 3,410 | 3,836 | 538 | 2,899 | 3,410 | 3,836 |
| 8,550 | 8,600 | 538 | 2,916 | 3,430 | 3,859 | 538 | 2,916 | 3,430 | 3,859 |
| 8,600 | 8,650 | 538 | 2,933 | 3,450 | 3,881 | 538 | 2,933 | 3,450 | 3,881 |
| 8,650 | 8,700 | 538 | 2,950 | 3,470 | 3,904 | 538 | 2,950 | 3,470 | 3,904 |
| 8,700 | 8,750 | 538 | 2,967 | 3,490 | 3,926 | 538 | 2,967 | 3,490 | 3,926 |
| 8,750 | 8,800 | 538 | 2,984 | 3,510 | 3,949 | 538 | 2,984 | 3,510 | 3,949 |
| 8,800 | 8,850 | 535 | 3,001 | 3,530 | 3,971 | 538 | 3,001 | 3,530 | 3,971 |
| 8,850 | 8,900 | 531 | 3,018 | 3,550 | 3,994 | 538 | 3,018 | 3,550 | 3,994 |
| 8,900 | 8,950 | 527 | 3,035 | 3,570 | 4,016 | 538 | 3,035 | 3,570 | 4,016 |
| 8,950 | 9,000 | 524 | 3,052 | 3,590 | 4,039 | 538 | 3,052 | 3,590 | 4,039 |
| 9,000 | 9,050 | 520 | 3,069 | 3,610 | 4,061 | 538 | 3,069 | 3,610 | 4,061 |
| 9,050 | 9,100 | 516 | 3,086 | 3,630 | 4,084 | 538 | 3,086 | 3,630 | 4,084 |
| 9,100 | 9,150 | 512 | 3,103 | 3,650 | 4,106 | 538 | 3,103 | 3,650 | 4,106 |
| 9,150 | 9,200 | 508 | 3,120 | 3,670 | 4,129 | 538 | 3,120 | 3,670 | 4,129 |
| 9,200 | 9,250 | 505 | 3,137 | 3,690 | 4,151 | 538 | 3,137 | 3,690 | 4,151 |
| 9,250 | 9,300 | 501 | 3,154 | 3,710 | 4,174 | 538 | 3,154 | 3,710 | 4,174 |
| 9,300 | 9,350 | 497 | 3,171 | 3,730 | 4,196 | 538 | 3,171 | 3,730 | 4,196 |
| 9,350 | 9,400 | 493 | 3,188 | 3,750 | 4,219 | 538 | 3,188 | 3,750 | 4,219 |
| 9,400 | 9,450 | 489 | 3,205 | 3,770 | 4,241 | 538 | 3,205 | 3,770 | 4,241 |
| 9,450 | 9,500 | 485 | 3,222 | 3,790 | 4,264 | 538 | 3,222 | 3,790 | 4,264 |
| 9,500 | 9,550 | 482 | 3,239 | 3,810 | 4,286 | 538 | 3,239 | 3,810 | 4,286 |
| 9,550 | 9,600 | 478 | 3,256 | 3,830 | 4,309 | 538 | 3,256 | 3,830 | 4,309 |
| 9,600 | 9,650 | 474 | 3,273 | 3,850 | 4,331 | 538 | 3,273 | 3,850 | 4,331 |
| 9,650 | 9,700 | 470 | 3,290 | 3,870 | 4,354 | 538 | 3,290 | 3,870 | 4,354 |
| 9,700 | 9,750 | 466 | 3,307 | 3,890 | 4,376 | 538 | 3,307 | 3,890 | 4,376 |
| 9,750 | 9,800 | 462 | 3,324 | 3,910 | 4,399 | 538 | 3,324 | 3,910 | 4,399 |
| 9,800 | 9,850 | 459 | 3,341 | 3,930 | 4,421 | 538 | 3,341 | 3,930 | 4,421 |
| 9,850 | 9,900 | 455 | 3,358 | 3,950 | 4,444 | 538 | 3,358 | 3,950 | 4,444 |
| 9,900 | 9,950 | 451 | 3,375 | 3,970 | 4,466 | 538 | 3,375 | 3,970 | 4,466 |
| 9,950 | 10,000 | 447 | 3,392 | 3,990 | 4,489 | 538 | 3,392 | 3,990 | 4,489 |
| 10,000 | 10,050 | 443 | 3,409 | 4,010 | 4,511 | 538 | 3,409 | 4,010 | 4,511 |
| 10,050 | 10,100 | 439 | 3,426 | 4,030 | 4,534 | 538 | 3,426 | 4,030 | 4,534 |
| 10,100 | 10,150 | 436 | 3,443 | 4,050 | 4,556 | 538 | 3,443 | 4,050 | 4,556 |
| 10,150 | 10,200 | 432 | 3,460 | 4,070 | 4,579 | 538 | 3,460 | 4,070 | 4,579 |
| 10,200 | 10,250 | 428 | 3,477 | 4,090 | 4,601 | 538 | 3,477 | 4,090 | 4,601 |
| 10,250 | 10,300 | 424 | 3,494 | 4,110 | 4,624 | 538 | 3,494 | 4,110 | 4,624 |
| 10,300 | 10,350 | 420 | 3,511 | 4,130 | 4,646 | 538 | 3,511 | 4,130 | 4,646 |
| 10,350 | 10,400 | 417 | 3,528 | 4,150 | 4,669 | 538 | 3,528 | 4,150 | 4,669 |
| 10,400 | 10,450 | 413 | 3,545 | 4,170 | 4,691 | 538 | 3,545 | 4,170 | 4,691 |
| 10,450 | 10,500 | 409 | 3,562 | 4,190 | 4,714 | 538 | 3,562 | 4,190 | 4,714 |
| 10,500 | 10,550 | 405 | 3,584 | 4,210 | 4,736 | 538 | 3,584 | 4,210 | 4,736 |
| 10,550 | 10,600 | 401 | 3,584 | 4,230 | 4,759 | 538 | 3,584 | 4,230 | 4,759 |
| 10,600 | 10,650 | 397 | 3,584 | 4,250 | 4,781 | 538 | 3,584 | 4,250 | 4,781 |
| 10,650 | 10,700 | 394 | 3,584 | 4,270 | 4,804 | 538 | 3,584 | 4,270 | 4,804 |
| 10,700 | 10,750 | 390 | 3,584 | 4,290 | 4,826 | 538 | 3,584 | 4,290 | 4,826 |
| 10,750 | 10,800 | 386 | 3,584 | 4,310 | 4,849 | 538 | 3,584 | 4,310 | 4,849 |
| 10,800 | 10,850 | 382 | 3,584 | 4,330 | 4,871 | 538 | 3,584 | 4,330 | 4,871 |
| 10,850 | 10,900 | 378 | 3,584 | 4,350 | 4,894 | 538 | 3,584 | 4,350 | 4,894 |
| 10,900 | 10,950 | 374 | 3,584 | 4,370 | 4,916 | 538 | 3,584 | 4,370 | 4,916 |
| 10,950 | 11,000 | 371 | 3,584 | 4,390 | 4,939 | 538 | 3,584 | 4,390 | 4,939 |
| 11,000 | 11,050 | 367 | 3,584 | 4,410 | 4,961 | 538 | 3,584 | 4,410 | 4,961 |
| 11,050 | 11,100 | 363 | 3,584 | 4,430 | 4,984 | 538 | 3,584 | 4,430 | 4,984 |
| 11,100 | 11,150 | 359 | 3,584 | 4,450 | 5,006 | 538 | 3,584 | 4,450 | 5,006 |
| 11,150 | 11,200 | 355 | 3,584 | 4,470 | 5,029 | 538 | 3,584 | 4,470 | 5,029 |
| 11,200 | 11,250 | 352 | 3,584 | 4,490 | 5,051 | 538 | 3,584 | 4,490 | 5,051 |
| 11,250 | 11,300 | 348 | 3,584 | 4,510 | 5,074 | 538 | 3,584 | 4,510 | 5,074 |
| 11,300 | 11,350 | 344 | 3,584 | 4,530 | 5,096 | 538 | 3,584 | 4,530 | 5,096 |
| 11,350 | 11,400 | 340 | 3,584 | 4,550 | 5,119 | 538 | 3,584 | 4,550 | 5,119 |
| 11,400 | 11,450 | 336 | 3,584 | 4,570 | 5,141 | 538 | 3,584 | 4,570 | 5,141 |
| 11,450 | 11,500 | 332 | 3,584 | 4,590 | 5,164 | 538 | 3,584 | 4,590 | 5,164 |
| 11,500 | 11,550 | 329 | 3,584 | 4,610 | 5,186 | 538 | 3,584 | 4,610 | 5,186 |
| 11,550 | 11,600 | 325 | 3,584 | 4,630 | 5,209 | 538 | 3,584 | 4,630 | 5,209 |
| 11,600 | 11,650 | 321 | 3,584 | 4,650 | 5,231 | 538 | 3,584 | 4,650 | 5,231 |
| 11,650 | 11,700 | 317 | 3,584 | 4,670 | 5,254 | 538 | 3,584 | 4,670 | 5,254 |
| 11,700 | 11,750 | 313 | 3,584 | 4,690 | 5,276 | 538 | 3,584 | 4,690 | 5,276 |
| 11,750 | 11,800 | 309 | 3,584 | 4,710 | 5,299 | 538 | 3,584 | 4,710 | 5,299 |
| 11,800 | 11,850 | 306 | 3,584 | 4,730 | 5,321 | 538 | 3,584 | 4,730 | 5,321 |
| 11,850 | 11,900 | 302 | 3,584 | 4,750 | 5,344 | 538 | 3,584 | 4,750 | 5,344 |
| 11,900 | 11,950 | 298 | 3,584 | 4,770 | 5,366 | 538 | 3,584 | 4,770 | 5,366 |
| 11,950 | 12,000 | 294 | 3,584 | 4,790 | 5,389 | 538 | 3,584 | 4,790 | 5,389 |
| 12,000 | 12,050 | 290 | 3,584 | 4,810 | 5,411 | 538 | 3,584 | 4,810 | 5,411 |
| 12,050 | 12,100 | 286 | 3,584 | 4,830 | 5,434 | 538 | 3,584 | 4,830 | 5,434 |
| 12,100 | 12,150 | 283 | 3,584 | 4,850 | 5,456 | 538 | 3,584 | 4,850 | 5,456 |
| 12,150 | 12,200 | 279 | 3,584 | 4,870 | 5,479 | 538 | 3,584 | 4,870 | 5,479 |
| 12,200 | 12,250 | 275 | 3,584 | 4,890 | 5,501 | 538 | 3,584 | 4,890 | 5,501 |
| 12,250 | 12,300 | 271 | 3,584 | 4,910 | 5,524 | 538 | 3,584 | 4,910 | 5,524 |
| 12,300 | 12,350 | 267 | 3,584 | 4,930 | 5,546 | 538 | 3,584 | 4,930 | 5,546 |
| 12,350 | 12,400 | 264 | 3,584 | 4,950 | 5,569 | 538 | 3,584 | 4,950 | 5,569 |
| 12,400 | 12,450 | 260 | 3,584 | 4,970 | 5,591 | 538 | 3,584 | 4,970 | 5,591 |
| 12,450 | 12,500 | 256 | 3,584 | 4,990 | 5,614 | 538 | 3,584 | 4,990 | 5,614 |
| 12,500 | 12,550 | 252 | 3,584 | 5,010 | 5,636 | 538 | 3,584 | 5,010 | 5,636 |
| 12,550 | 12,600 | 248 | 3,584 | 5,030 | 5,659 | 538 | 3,584 | 5,030 | 5,659 |
| 12,600 | 12,650 | 244 | 3,584 | 5,050 | 5,681 | 538 | 3,584 | 5,050 | 5,681 |
| 12,650 | 12,700 | 241 | 3,584 | 5,070 | 5,704 | 538 | 3,584 | 5,070 | 5,704 |
| 12,700 | 12,750 | 237 | 3,584 | 5,090 | 5,726 | 538 | 3,584 | 5,090 | 5,726 |
| 12,750 | 12,800 | 233 | 3,584 | 5,110 | 5,749 | 538 | 3,584 | 5,110 | 5,749 |

*(Continued)*

**Earned Income Credit (EIC) Table** - *Continued* (**Caution.** This is **not** a tax table.)

| If the amount you are looking up from the worksheet is– | | And your filing status is– Single, head of household, or qualifying widow(er) and you have– | | | | Married filing jointly and you have– | | | |
|---|---|---|---|---|---|---|---|---|---|
| | | 0 | 1 | 2 | 3 | 0 | 1 | 2 | 3 |
| At least | But less than | Your credit is– | | | | Your credit is– | | | |
| 12,800 | 12,850 | 229 | 3,584 | 5,130 | 5,771 | 538 | 3,584 | 5,130 | 5,771 |
| 12,850 | 12,900 | 225 | 3,584 | 5,150 | 5,794 | 538 | 3,584 | 5,150 | 5,794 |
| 12,900 | 12,950 | 221 | 3,584 | 5,170 | 5,816 | 538 | 3,584 | 5,170 | 5,816 |
| 12,950 | 13,000 | 218 | 3,584 | 5,190 | 5,839 | 538 | 3,584 | 5,190 | 5,839 |
| 13,000 | 13,050 | 214 | 3,584 | 5,210 | 5,861 | 538 | 3,584 | 5,210 | 5,861 |
| 13,050 | 13,100 | 210 | 3,584 | 5,230 | 5,884 | 538 | 3,584 | 5,230 | 5,884 |
| 13,100 | 13,150 | 206 | 3,584 | 5,250 | 5,906 | 538 | 3,584 | 5,250 | 5,906 |
| 13,150 | 13,200 | 202 | 3,584 | 5,270 | 5,929 | 538 | 3,584 | 5,270 | 5,929 |
| 13,200 | 13,250 | 199 | 3,584 | 5,290 | 5,951 | 538 | 3,584 | 5,290 | 5,951 |
| 13,250 | 13,300 | 195 | 3,584 | 5,310 | 5,974 | 538 | 3,584 | 5,310 | 5,974 |
| 13,300 | 13,350 | 191 | 3,584 | 5,330 | 5,996 | 538 | 3,584 | 5,330 | 5,996 |
| 13,350 | 13,400 | 187 | 3,584 | 5,350 | 6,019 | 538 | 3,584 | 5,350 | 6,019 |
| 13,400 | 13,450 | 183 | 3,584 | 5,370 | 6,041 | 538 | 3,584 | 5,370 | 6,041 |
| 13,450 | 13,500 | 179 | 3,584 | 5,390 | 6,064 | 538 | 3,584 | 5,390 | 6,064 |
| 13,500 | 13,550 | 176 | 3,584 | 5,410 | 6,086 | 538 | 3,584 | 5,410 | 6,086 |
| 13,550 | 13,600 | 172 | 3,584 | 5,430 | 6,109 | 538 | 3,584 | 5,430 | 6,109 |
| 13,600 | 13,650 | 168 | 3,584 | 5,450 | 6,131 | 538 | 3,584 | 5,450 | 6,131 |
| 13,650 | 13,700 | 164 | 3,584 | 5,470 | 6,154 | 538 | 3,584 | 5,470 | 6,154 |
| 13,700 | 13,750 | 160 | 3,584 | 5,490 | 6,176 | 538 | 3,584 | 5,490 | 6,176 |
| 13,750 | 13,800 | 156 | 3,584 | 5,510 | 6,199 | 538 | 3,584 | 5,510 | 6,199 |
| 13,800 | 13,850 | 153 | 3,584 | 5,530 | 6,221 | 538 | 3,584 | 5,530 | 6,221 |
| 13,850 | 13,900 | 149 | 3,584 | 5,550 | 6,244 | 538 | 3,584 | 5,550 | 6,244 |
| 13,900 | 13,950 | 145 | 3,584 | 5,570 | 6,266 | 538 | 3,584 | 5,570 | 6,266 |
| 13,950 | 14,000 | 141 | 3,584 | 5,590 | 6,289 | 538 | 3,584 | 5,590 | 6,289 |
| 14,000 | 14,050 | 137 | 3,584 | 5,610 | 6,311 | 538 | 3,584 | 5,610 | 6,311 |
| 14,050 | 14,100 | 133 | 3,584 | 5,630 | 6,334 | 538 | 3,584 | 5,630 | 6,334 |
| 14,100 | 14,150 | 130 | 3,584 | 5,650 | 6,356 | 538 | 3,584 | 5,650 | 6,356 |
| 14,150 | 14,200 | 126 | 3,584 | 5,670 | 6,379 | 538 | 3,584 | 5,670 | 6,379 |
| 14,200 | 14,250 | 122 | 3,584 | 5,690 | 6,401 | 538 | 3,584 | 5,690 | 6,401 |
| 14,250 | 14,300 | 118 | 3,584 | 5,710 | 6,424 | 538 | 3,584 | 5,710 | 6,424 |
| 14,300 | 14,350 | 114 | 3,584 | 5,730 | 6,446 | 538 | 3,584 | 5,730 | 6,446 |
| 14,350 | 14,400 | 111 | 3,584 | 5,750 | 6,469 | 538 | 3,584 | 5,750 | 6,469 |
| 14,400 | 14,450 | 107 | 3,584 | 5,770 | 6,491 | 538 | 3,584 | 5,770 | 6,491 |
| 14,450 | 14,500 | 103 | 3,584 | 5,790 | 6,514 | 538 | 3,584 | 5,790 | 6,514 |
| 14,500 | 14,550 | 99 | 3,584 | 5,810 | 6,536 | 538 | 3,584 | 5,810 | 6,536 |
| 14,550 | 14,600 | 95 | 3,584 | 5,830 | 6,559 | 538 | 3,584 | 5,830 | 6,559 |
| 14,600 | 14,650 | 91 | 3,584 | 5,850 | 6,581 | 538 | 3,584 | 5,850 | 6,581 |
| 14,650 | 14,700 | 88 | 3,584 | 5,870 | 6,604 | 538 | 3,584 | 5,870 | 6,604 |
| 14,700 | 14,750 | 84 | 3,584 | 5,890 | 6,626 | 534 | 3,584 | 5,890 | 6,626 |
| 14,750 | 14,800 | 80 | 3,584 | 5,910 | 6,649 | 531 | 3,584 | 5,910 | 6,649 |
| 14,800 | 14,850 | 76 | 3,584 | 5,920 | 6,660 | 527 | 3,584 | 5,920 | 6,660 |
| 14,850 | 14,900 | 72 | 3,584 | 5,920 | 6,660 | 523 | 3,584 | 5,920 | 6,660 |
| 14,900 | 14,950 | 68 | 3,584 | 5,920 | 6,660 | 519 | 3,584 | 5,920 | 6,660 |
| 14,950 | 15,000 | 65 | 3,584 | 5,920 | 6,660 | 515 | 3,584 | 5,920 | 6,660 |
| 15,000 | 15,050 | 61 | 3,584 | 5,920 | 6,660 | 511 | 3,584 | 5,920 | 6,660 |
| 15,050 | 15,100 | 57 | 3,584 | 5,920 | 6,660 | 508 | 3,584 | 5,920 | 6,660 |
| 15,100 | 15,150 | 53 | 3,584 | 5,920 | 6,660 | 504 | 3,584 | 5,920 | 6,660 |
| 15,150 | 15,200 | 49 | 3,584 | 5,920 | 6,660 | 500 | 3,584 | 5,920 | 6,660 |
| 15,200 | 15,250 | 46 | 3,584 | 5,920 | 6,660 | 496 | 3,584 | 5,920 | 6,660 |
| 15,250 | 15,300 | 42 | 3,584 | 5,920 | 6,660 | 492 | 3,584 | 5,920 | 6,660 |
| 15,300 | 15,350 | 38 | 3,584 | 5,920 | 6,660 | 488 | 3,584 | 5,920 | 6,660 |
| 15,350 | 15,400 | 34 | 3,584 | 5,920 | 6,660 | 485 | 3,584 | 5,920 | 6,660 |
| 15,400 | 15,450 | 30 | 3,584 | 5,920 | 6,660 | 481 | 3,584 | 5,920 | 6,660 |
| 15,450 | 15,500 | 26 | 3,584 | 5,920 | 6,660 | 477 | 3,584 | 5,920 | 6,660 |
| 15,500 | 15,550 | 23 | 3,584 | 5,920 | 6,660 | 473 | 3,584 | 5,920 | 6,660 |
| 15,550 | 15,600 | 19 | 3,584 | 5,920 | 6,660 | 469 | 3,584 | 5,920 | 6,660 |
| 15,600 | 15,650 | 15 | 3,584 | 5,920 | 6,660 | 466 | 3,584 | 5,920 | 6,660 |
| 15,650 | 15,700 | 11 | 3,584 | 5,920 | 6,660 | 462 | 3,584 | 5,920 | 6,660 |
| 15,700 | 15,750 | 7 | 3,584 | 5,920 | 6,660 | 458 | 3,584 | 5,920 | 6,660 |
| 15,750 | 15,800 | 3 | 3,584 | 5,920 | 6,660 | 454 | 3,584 | 5,920 | 6,660 |
| 15,800 | 15,850 | * | 3,584 | 5,920 | 6,660 | 450 | 3,584 | 5,920 | 6,660 |
| 15,850 | 15,900 | 0 | 3,584 | 5,920 | 6,660 | 446 | 3,584 | 5,920 | 6,660 |
| 15,900 | 15,950 | 0 | 3,584 | 5,920 | 6,660 | 443 | 3,584 | 5,920 | 6,660 |
| 15,950 | 16,000 | 0 | 3,584 | 5,920 | 6,660 | 439 | 3,584 | 5,920 | 6,660 |
| 16,000 | 16,050 | 0 | 3,584 | 5,920 | 6,660 | 435 | 3,584 | 5,920 | 6,660 |
| 16,050 | 16,100 | 0 | 3,584 | 5,920 | 6,660 | 431 | 3,584 | 5,920 | 6,660 |
| 16,100 | 16,150 | 0 | 3,584 | 5,920 | 6,660 | 427 | 3,584 | 5,920 | 6,660 |
| 16,150 | 16,200 | 0 | 3,584 | 5,920 | 6,660 | 423 | 3,584 | 5,920 | 6,660 |
| 16,200 | 16,250 | 0 | 3,584 | 5,920 | 6,660 | 420 | 3,584 | 5,920 | 6,660 |
| 16,250 | 16,300 | 0 | 3,584 | 5,920 | 6,660 | 416 | 3,584 | 5,920 | 6,660 |
| 16,300 | 16,350 | 0 | 3,584 | 5,920 | 6,660 | 412 | 3,584 | 5,920 | 6,660 |
| 16,350 | 16,400 | 0 | 3,584 | 5,920 | 6,660 | 408 | 3,584 | 5,920 | 6,660 |
| 16,400 | 16,450 | 0 | 3,584 | 5,920 | 6,660 | 404 | 3,584 | 5,920 | 6,660 |
| 16,450 | 16,500 | 0 | 3,584 | 5,920 | 6,660 | 400 | 3,584 | 5,920 | 6,660 |
| 16,500 | 16,550 | 0 | 3,584 | 5,920 | 6,660 | 397 | 3,584 | 5,920 | 6,660 |
| 16,550 | 16,600 | 0 | 3,584 | 5,920 | 6,660 | 393 | 3,584 | 5,920 | 6,660 |
| 16,600 | 16,650 | 0 | 3,584 | 5,920 | 6,660 | 389 | 3,584 | 5,920 | 6,660 |
| 16,650 | 16,700 | 0 | 3,584 | 5,920 | 6,660 | 385 | 3,584 | 5,920 | 6,660 |
| 16,700 | 16,750 | 0 | 3,584 | 5,920 | 6,660 | 381 | 3,584 | 5,920 | 6,660 |
| 16,750 | 16,800 | 0 | 3,584 | 5,920 | 6,660 | 378 | 3,584 | 5,920 | 6,660 |
| 16,800 | 16,850 | 0 | 3,584 | 5,920 | 6,660 | 374 | 3,584 | 5,920 | 6,660 |
| 16,850 | 16,900 | 0 | 3,584 | 5,920 | 6,660 | 370 | 3,584 | 5,920 | 6,660 |
| 16,900 | 16,950 | 0 | 3,584 | 5,920 | 6,660 | 366 | 3,584 | 5,920 | 6,660 |
| 16,950 | 17,000 | 0 | 3,584 | 5,920 | 6,660 | 362 | 3,584 | 5,920 | 6,660 |
| 17,000 | 17,050 | 0 | 3,584 | 5,920 | 6,660 | 358 | 3,584 | 5,920 | 6,660 |
| 17,050 | 17,100 | 0 | 3,584 | 5,920 | 6,660 | 355 | 3,584 | 5,920 | 6,660 |
| 17,100 | 17,150 | 0 | 3,584 | 5,920 | 6,660 | 351 | 3,584 | 5,920 | 6,660 |
| 17,150 | 17,200 | 0 | 3,584 | 5,920 | 6,660 | 347 | 3,584 | 5,920 | 6,660 |
| 17,200 | 17,250 | 0 | 3,584 | 5,920 | 6,660 | 343 | 3,584 | 5,920 | 6,660 |
| 17,250 | 17,300 | 0 | 3,584 | 5,920 | 6,660 | 339 | 3,584 | 5,920 | 6,660 |
| 17,300 | 17,350 | 0 | 3,584 | 5,920 | 6,660 | 335 | 3,584 | 5,920 | 6,660 |
| 17,350 | 17,400 | 0 | 3,584 | 5,920 | 6,660 | 332 | 3,584 | 5,920 | 6,660 |
| 17,400 | 17,450 | 0 | 3,584 | 5,920 | 6,660 | 328 | 3,584 | 5,920 | 6,660 |
| 17,450 | 17,500 | 0 | 3,584 | 5,920 | 6,660 | 324 | 3,584 | 5,920 | 6,660 |
| 17,500 | 17,550 | 0 | 3,584 | 5,920 | 6,660 | 320 | 3,584 | 5,920 | 6,660 |
| 17,550 | 17,600 | 0 | 3,584 | 5,920 | 6,660 | 316 | 3,584 | 5,920 | 6,660 |
| 17,600 | 17,650 | 0 | 3,584 | 5,920 | 6,660 | 313 | 3,584 | 5,920 | 6,660 |
| 17,650 | 17,700 | 0 | 3,584 | 5,920 | 6,660 | 309 | 3,584 | 5,920 | 6,660 |
| 17,700 | 17,750 | 0 | 3,584 | 5,920 | 6,660 | 305 | 3,584 | 5,920 | 6,660 |
| 17,750 | 17,800 | 0 | 3,584 | 5,920 | 6,660 | 301 | 3,584 | 5,920 | 6,660 |
| 17,800 | 17,850 | 0 | 3,584 | 5,920 | 6,660 | 297 | 3,584 | 5,920 | 6,660 |
| 17,850 | 17,900 | 0 | 3,584 | 5,920 | 6,660 | 293 | 3,584 | 5,920 | 6,660 |
| 17,900 | 17,950 | 0 | 3,584 | 5,920 | 6,660 | 290 | 3,584 | 5,920 | 6,660 |
| 17,950 | 18,000 | 0 | 3,584 | 5,920 | 6,660 | 286 | 3,584 | 5,920 | 6,660 |
| 18,000 | 18,050 | 0 | 3,584 | 5,920 | 6,660 | 282 | 3,584 | 5,920 | 6,660 |
| 18,050 | 18,100 | 0 | 3,584 | 5,920 | 6,660 | 278 | 3,584 | 5,920 | 6,660 |
| 18,100 | 18,150 | 0 | 3,584 | 5,920 | 6,660 | 274 | 3,584 | 5,920 | 6,660 |
| 18,150 | 18,200 | 0 | 3,584 | 5,920 | 6,660 | 270 | 3,584 | 5,920 | 6,660 |
| 18,200 | 18,250 | 0 | 3,584 | 5,920 | 6,660 | 267 | 3,584 | 5,920 | 6,660 |
| 18,250 | 18,300 | 0 | 3,584 | 5,920 | 6,660 | 263 | 3,584 | 5,920 | 6,660 |
| 18,300 | 18,350 | 0 | 3,584 | 5,920 | 6,660 | 259 | 3,584 | 5,920 | 6,660 |
| 18,350 | 18,400 | 0 | 3,584 | 5,920 | 6,660 | 255 | 3,584 | 5,920 | 6,660 |
| 18,400 | 18,450 | 0 | 3,584 | 5,920 | 6,660 | 251 | 3,584 | 5,920 | 6,660 |
| 18,450 | 18,500 | 0 | 3,584 | 5,920 | 6,660 | 247 | 3,584 | 5,920 | 6,660 |
| 18,500 | 18,550 | 0 | 3,584 | 5,920 | 6,660 | 244 | 3,584 | 5,920 | 6,660 |
| 18,550 | 18,600 | 0 | 3,584 | 5,920 | 6,660 | 240 | 3,584 | 5,920 | 6,660 |
| 18,600 | 18,650 | 0 | 3,584 | 5,920 | 6,660 | 236 | 3,584 | 5,920 | 6,660 |
| 18,650 | 18,700 | 0 | 3,584 | 5,920 | 6,660 | 232 | 3,584 | 5,920 | 6,660 |
| 18,700 | 18,750 | 0 | 3,584 | 5,920 | 6,660 | 228 | 3,584 | 5,920 | 6,660 |
| 18,750 | 18,800 | 0 | 3,584 | 5,920 | 6,660 | 225 | 3,584 | 5,920 | 6,660 |
| 18,800 | 18,850 | 0 | 3,584 | 5,920 | 6,660 | 221 | 3,584 | 5,920 | 6,660 |
| 18,850 | 18,900 | 0 | 3,584 | 5,920 | 6,660 | 217 | 3,584 | 5,920 | 6,660 |
| 18,900 | 18,950 | 0 | 3,584 | 5,920 | 6,660 | 213 | 3,584 | 5,920 | 6,660 |
| 18,950 | 19,000 | 0 | 3,584 | 5,920 | 6,660 | 209 | 3,584 | 5,920 | 6,660 |
| 19,000 | 19,050 | 0 | 3,584 | 5,920 | 6,660 | 205 | 3,584 | 5,920 | 6,660 |
| 19,050 | 19,100 | 0 | 3,584 | 5,920 | 6,660 | 202 | 3,584 | 5,920 | 6,660 |
| 19,100 | 19,150 | 0 | 3,584 | 5,920 | 6,660 | 198 | 3,584 | 5,920 | 6,660 |
| 19,150 | 19,200 | 0 | 3,584 | 5,920 | 6,660 | 194 | 3,584 | 5,920 | 6,660 |

* If the amount you are looking up from the worksheet is at least $15,800 but less than $15,820, and you have no qualifying children, your credit is $1.
If the amount you are looking up from the worksheet is $15,820 or more, and you have no qualifying children, you can't take the credit.

*(Continued)*

## Earned Income Credit (EIC) Table - *Continued*

**(Caution.** This is **not** a tax table.)

| If the amount you are looking up from the worksheet is– | | And your filing status is– Single, head of household, or qualifying widow(er) and you have– | | | | Married filing jointly and you have– | | | |
|---|---|---|---|---|---|---|---|---|---|
| | | 0 | 1 | 2 | 3 | 0 | 1 | 2 | 3 |
| At least | But less than | Your credit is– | | | | Your credit is– | | | |
| 19,200 | 19,250 | 0 | 3,584 | 5,920 | 6,660 | 190 | 3,584 | 5,920 | 6,660 |
| 19,250 | 19,300 | 0 | 3,584 | 5,920 | 6,660 | 186 | 3,584 | 5,920 | 6,660 |
| 19,300 | 19,350 | 0 | 3,584 | 5,920 | 6,660 | 182 | 3,584 | 5,920 | 6,660 |
| 19,350 | 19,400 | 0 | 3,576 | 5,911 | 6,651 | 179 | 3,584 | 5,920 | 6,660 |
| 19,400 | 19,450 | 0 | 3,568 | 5,900 | 6,640 | 175 | 3,584 | 5,920 | 6,660 |
| 19,450 | 19,500 | 0 | 3,560 | 5,889 | 6,629 | 171 | 3,584 | 5,920 | 6,660 |
| 19,500 | 19,550 | 0 | 3,552 | 5,879 | 6,619 | 167 | 3,584 | 5,920 | 6,660 |
| 19,550 | 19,600 | 0 | 3,544 | 5,868 | 6,608 | 163 | 3,584 | 5,920 | 6,660 |
| 19,600 | 19,650 | 0 | 3,536 | 5,858 | 6,598 | 160 | 3,584 | 5,920 | 6,660 |
| 19,650 | 19,700 | 0 | 3,528 | 5,847 | 6,587 | 156 | 3,584 | 5,920 | 6,660 |
| 19,700 | 19,750 | 0 | 3,520 | 5,837 | 6,577 | 152 | 3,584 | 5,920 | 6,660 |
| 19,750 | 19,800 | 0 | 3,512 | 5,826 | 6,566 | 148 | 3,584 | 5,920 | 6,660 |
| 19,800 | 19,850 | 0 | 3,504 | 5,816 | 6,556 | 144 | 3,584 | 5,920 | 6,660 |
| 19,850 | 19,900 | 0 | 3,497 | 5,805 | 6,545 | 140 | 3,584 | 5,920 | 6,660 |
| 19,900 | 19,950 | 0 | 3,489 | 5,795 | 6,535 | 137 | 3,584 | 5,920 | 6,660 |
| 19,950 | 20,000 | 0 | 3,481 | 5,784 | 6,524 | 133 | 3,584 | 5,920 | 6,660 |
| 20,000 | 20,050 | 0 | 3,473 | 5,774 | 6,514 | 129 | 3,584 | 5,920 | 6,660 |
| 20,050 | 20,100 | 0 | 3,465 | 5,763 | 6,503 | 125 | 3,584 | 5,920 | 6,660 |
| 20,100 | 20,150 | 0 | 3,457 | 5,753 | 6,493 | 121 | 3,584 | 5,920 | 6,660 |
| 20,150 | 20,200 | 0 | 3,449 | 5,742 | 6,482 | 117 | 3,584 | 5,920 | 6,660 |
| 20,200 | 20,250 | 0 | 3,441 | 5,732 | 6,472 | 114 | 3,584 | 5,920 | 6,660 |
| 20,250 | 20,300 | 0 | 3,433 | 5,721 | 6,461 | 110 | 3,584 | 5,920 | 6,660 |
| 20,300 | 20,350 | 0 | 3,425 | 5,710 | 6,450 | 106 | 3,584 | 5,920 | 6,660 |
| 20,350 | 20,400 | 0 | 3,417 | 5,700 | 6,440 | 102 | 3,584 | 5,920 | 6,660 |
| 20,400 | 20,450 | 0 | 3,409 | 5,689 | 6,429 | 98 | 3,584 | 5,920 | 6,660 |
| 20,450 | 20,500 | 0 | 3,401 | 5,679 | 6,419 | 94 | 3,584 | 5,920 | 6,660 |
| 20,500 | 20,550 | 0 | 3,393 | 5,668 | 6,408 | 91 | 3,584 | 5,920 | 6,660 |
| 20,550 | 20,600 | 0 | 3,385 | 5,658 | 6,398 | 87 | 3,584 | 5,920 | 6,660 |
| 20,600 | 20,650 | 0 | 3,377 | 5,647 | 6,387 | 83 | 3,584 | 5,920 | 6,660 |
| 20,650 | 20,700 | 0 | 3,369 | 5,637 | 6,377 | 79 | 3,584 | 5,920 | 6,660 |
| 20,700 | 20,750 | 0 | 3,361 | 5,626 | 6,366 | 75 | 3,584 | 5,920 | 6,660 |
| 20,750 | 20,800 | 0 | 3,353 | 5,616 | 6,356 | 72 | 3,584 | 5,920 | 6,660 |
| 20,800 | 20,850 | 0 | 3,345 | 5,605 | 6,345 | 68 | 3,584 | 5,920 | 6,660 |
| 20,850 | 20,900 | 0 | 3,337 | 5,595 | 6,335 | 64 | 3,584 | 5,920 | 6,660 |
| 20,900 | 20,950 | 0 | 3,329 | 5,584 | 6,324 | 60 | 3,584 | 5,920 | 6,660 |
| 20,950 | 21,000 | 0 | 3,321 | 5,574 | 6,314 | 56 | 3,584 | 5,920 | 6,660 |
| 21,000 | 21,050 | 0 | 3,313 | 5,563 | 6,303 | 52 | 3,584 | 5,920 | 6,660 |
| 21,050 | 21,100 | 0 | 3,305 | 5,553 | 6,293 | 49 | 3,584 | 5,920 | 6,660 |
| 21,100 | 21,150 | 0 | 3,297 | 5,542 | 6,282 | 45 | 3,584 | 5,920 | 6,660 |
| 21,150 | 21,200 | 0 | 3,289 | 5,531 | 6,271 | 41 | 3,584 | 5,920 | 6,660 |
| 21,200 | 21,250 | 0 | 3,281 | 5,521 | 6,261 | 37 | 3,584 | 5,920 | 6,660 |
| 21,250 | 21,300 | 0 | 3,273 | 5,510 | 6,250 | 33 | 3,584 | 5,920 | 6,660 |
| 21,300 | 21,350 | 0 | 3,265 | 5,500 | 6,240 | 29 | 3,584 | 5,920 | 6,660 |
| 21,350 | 21,400 | 0 | 3,257 | 5,489 | 6,229 | 26 | 3,584 | 5,920 | 6,660 |
| 21,400 | 21,450 | 0 | 3,249 | 5,479 | 6,219 | 22 | 3,584 | 5,920 | 6,660 |
| 21,450 | 21,500 | 0 | 3,241 | 5,468 | 6,208 | 18 | 3,584 | 5,920 | 6,660 |
| 21,500 | 21,550 | 0 | 3,233 | 5,458 | 6,198 | 14 | 3,584 | 5,920 | 6,660 |
| 21,550 | 21,600 | 0 | 3,225 | 5,447 | 6,187 | 10 | 3,584 | 5,920 | 6,660 |
| 21,600 | 21,650 | 0 | 3,217 | 5,437 | 6,177 | 7 | 3,584 | 5,920 | 6,660 |
| 21,650 | 21,700 | 0 | 3,209 | 5,426 | 6,166 | 3 | 3,584 | 5,920 | 6,660 |
| 21,700 | 21,750 | 0 | 3,201 | 5,416 | 6,156 | * | 3,584 | 5,920 | 6,660 |
| 21,750 | 21,800 | 0 | 3,193 | 5,405 | 6,145 | 0 | 3,584 | 5,920 | 6,660 |
| 21,800 | 21,850 | 0 | 3,185 | 5,395 | 6,135 | 0 | 3,584 | 5,920 | 6,660 |
| 21,850 | 21,900 | 0 | 3,177 | 5,384 | 6,124 | 0 | 3,584 | 5,920 | 6,660 |
| 21,900 | 21,950 | 0 | 3,169 | 5,373 | 6,113 | 0 | 3,584 | 5,920 | 6,660 |
| 21,950 | 22,000 | 0 | 3,161 | 5,363 | 6,103 | 0 | 3,584 | 5,920 | 6,660 |
| 22,000 | 22,050 | 0 | 3,153 | 5,352 | 6,092 | 0 | 3,584 | 5,920 | 6,660 |
| 22,050 | 22,100 | 0 | 3,145 | 5,342 | 6,082 | 0 | 3,584 | 5,920 | 6,660 |
| 22,100 | 22,150 | 0 | 3,137 | 5,331 | 6,071 | 0 | 3,584 | 5,920 | 6,660 |
| 22,150 | 22,200 | 0 | 3,129 | 5,321 | 6,061 | 0 | 3,584 | 5,920 | 6,660 |
| 22,200 | 22,250 | 0 | 3,121 | 5,310 | 6,050 | 0 | 3,584 | 5,920 | 6,660 |
| 22,250 | 22,300 | 0 | 3,113 | 5,300 | 6,040 | 0 | 3,584 | 5,920 | 6,660 |
| 22,300 | 22,350 | 0 | 3,105 | 5,289 | 6,029 | 0 | 3,584 | 5,920 | 6,660 |
| 22,350 | 22,400 | 0 | 3,097 | 5,279 | 6,019 | 0 | 3,584 | 5,920 | 6,660 |
| 22,400 | 22,450 | 0 | 3,089 | 5,268 | 6,008 | 0 | 3,584 | 5,920 | 6,660 |
| 22,450 | 22,500 | 0 | 3,081 | 5,258 | 5,998 | 0 | 3,584 | 5,920 | 6,660 |
| 22,500 | 22,550 | 0 | 3,073 | 5,247 | 5,987 | 0 | 3,584 | 5,920 | 6,660 |
| 22,550 | 22,600 | 0 | 3,065 | 5,237 | 5,977 | 0 | 3,584 | 5,920 | 6,660 |
| 22,600 | 22,650 | 0 | 3,057 | 5,226 | 5,966 | 0 | 3,584 | 5,920 | 6,660 |
| 22,650 | 22,700 | 0 | 3,049 | 5,216 | 5,956 | 0 | 3,584 | 5,920 | 6,660 |
| 22,700 | 22,750 | 0 | 3,041 | 5,205 | 5,945 | 0 | 3,584 | 5,920 | 6,660 |
| 22,750 | 22,800 | 0 | 3,033 | 5,194 | 5,934 | 0 | 3,584 | 5,920 | 6,660 |
| 22,800 | 22,850 | 0 | 3,025 | 5,184 | 5,924 | 0 | 3,584 | 5,920 | 6,660 |
| 22,850 | 22,900 | 0 | 3,017 | 5,173 | 5,913 | 0 | 3,584 | 5,920 | 6,660 |
| 22,900 | 22,950 | 0 | 3,009 | 5,163 | 5,903 | 0 | 3,584 | 5,920 | 6,660 |
| 22,950 | 23,000 | 0 | 3,001 | 5,152 | 5,892 | 0 | 3,584 | 5,920 | 6,660 |
| 23,000 | 23,050 | 0 | 2,993 | 5,142 | 5,882 | 0 | 3,584 | 5,920 | 6,660 |
| 23,050 | 23,100 | 0 | 2,985 | 5,131 | 5,871 | 0 | 3,584 | 5,920 | 6,660 |
| 23,100 | 23,150 | 0 | 2,977 | 5,121 | 5,861 | 0 | 3,584 | 5,920 | 6,660 |
| 23,150 | 23,200 | 0 | 2,969 | 5,110 | 5,850 | 0 | 3,584 | 5,920 | 6,660 |
| 23,200 | 23,250 | 0 | 2,961 | 5,100 | 5,840 | 0 | 3,584 | 5,920 | 6,660 |
| 23,250 | 23,300 | 0 | 2,953 | 5,089 | 5,829 | 0 | 3,584 | 5,920 | 6,660 |
| 23,300 | 23,350 | 0 | 2,945 | 5,079 | 5,819 | 0 | 3,584 | 5,920 | 6,660 |
| 23,350 | 23,400 | 0 | 2,937 | 5,068 | 5,808 | 0 | 3,584 | 5,920 | 6,660 |
| 23,400 | 23,450 | 0 | 2,929 | 5,058 | 5,798 | 0 | 3,584 | 5,920 | 6,660 |
| 23,450 | 23,500 | 0 | 2,921 | 5,047 | 5,787 | 0 | 3,584 | 5,920 | 6,660 |
| 23,500 | 23,550 | 0 | 2,913 | 5,037 | 5,777 | 0 | 3,584 | 5,920 | 6,660 |
| 23,550 | 23,600 | 0 | 2,905 | 5,026 | 5,766 | 0 | 3,584 | 5,920 | 6,660 |
| 23,600 | 23,650 | 0 | 2,897 | 5,015 | 5,755 | 0 | 3,584 | 5,920 | 6,660 |
| 23,650 | 23,700 | 0 | 2,889 | 5,005 | 5,745 | 0 | 3,584 | 5,920 | 6,660 |
| 23,700 | 23,750 | 0 | 2,881 | 4,994 | 5,734 | 0 | 3,584 | 5,920 | 6,660 |
| 23,750 | 23,800 | 0 | 2,873 | 4,984 | 5,724 | 0 | 3,584 | 5,920 | 6,660 |
| 23,800 | 23,850 | 0 | 2,865 | 4,973 | 5,713 | 0 | 3,584 | 5,920 | 6,660 |
| 23,850 | 23,900 | 0 | 2,857 | 4,963 | 5,703 | 0 | 3,584 | 5,920 | 6,660 |
| 23,900 | 23,950 | 0 | 2,849 | 4,952 | 5,692 | 0 | 3,584 | 5,920 | 6,660 |
| 23,950 | 24,000 | 0 | 2,841 | 4,942 | 5,682 | 0 | 3,584 | 5,920 | 6,660 |
| 24,000 | 24,050 | 0 | 2,833 | 4,931 | 5,671 | 0 | 3,584 | 5,920 | 6,660 |
| 24,050 | 24,100 | 0 | 2,825 | 4,921 | 5,661 | 0 | 3,584 | 5,920 | 6,660 |
| 24,100 | 24,150 | 0 | 2,817 | 4,910 | 5,650 | 0 | 3,584 | 5,920 | 6,660 |
| 24,150 | 24,200 | 0 | 2,809 | 4,900 | 5,640 | 0 | 3,584 | 5,920 | 6,660 |
| 24,200 | 24,250 | 0 | 2,801 | 4,889 | 5,629 | 0 | 3,584 | 5,920 | 6,660 |
| 24,250 | 24,300 | 0 | 2,793 | 4,879 | 5,619 | 0 | 3,584 | 5,920 | 6,660 |
| 24,300 | 24,350 | 0 | 2,785 | 4,868 | 5,608 | 0 | 3,584 | 5,920 | 6,660 |
| 24,350 | 24,400 | 0 | 2,777 | 4,858 | 5,598 | 0 | 3,584 | 5,920 | 6,660 |
| 24,400 | 24,450 | 0 | 2,769 | 4,847 | 5,587 | 0 | 3,584 | 5,920 | 6,660 |
| 24,450 | 24,500 | 0 | 2,761 | 4,836 | 5,576 | 0 | 3,584 | 5,920 | 6,660 |
| 24,500 | 24,550 | 0 | 2,753 | 4,826 | 5,566 | 0 | 3,584 | 5,920 | 6,660 |
| 24,550 | 24,600 | 0 | 2,745 | 4,815 | 5,555 | 0 | 3,584 | 5,920 | 6,660 |
| 24,600 | 24,650 | 0 | 2,737 | 4,805 | 5,545 | 0 | 3,584 | 5,920 | 6,660 |
| 24,650 | 24,700 | 0 | 2,729 | 4,794 | 5,534 | 0 | 3,584 | 5,920 | 6,660 |
| 24,700 | 24,750 | 0 | 2,721 | 4,784 | 5,524 | 0 | 3,584 | 5,920 | 6,660 |
| 24,750 | 24,800 | 0 | 2,713 | 4,773 | 5,513 | 0 | 3,584 | 5,920 | 6,660 |
| 24,800 | 24,850 | 0 | 2,705 | 4,763 | 5,503 | 0 | 3,584 | 5,920 | 6,660 |
| 24,850 | 24,900 | 0 | 2,698 | 4,752 | 5,492 | 0 | 3,584 | 5,920 | 6,660 |
| 24,900 | 24,950 | 0 | 2,690 | 4,742 | 5,482 | 0 | 3,584 | 5,920 | 6,660 |
| 24,950 | 25,000 | 0 | 2,682 | 4,731 | 5,471 | 0 | 3,584 | 5,920 | 6,660 |
| 25,000 | 25,050 | 0 | 2,674 | 4,721 | 5,461 | 0 | 3,584 | 5,920 | 6,660 |
| 25,050 | 25,100 | 0 | 2,666 | 4,710 | 5,450 | 0 | 3,584 | 5,920 | 6,660 |
| 25,100 | 25,150 | 0 | 2,658 | 4,700 | 5,440 | 0 | 3,584 | 5,920 | 6,660 |
| 25,150 | 25,200 | 0 | 2,650 | 4,689 | 5,429 | 0 | 3,584 | 5,920 | 6,660 |
| 25,200 | 25,250 | 0 | 2,642 | 4,679 | 5,419 | 0 | 3,584 | 5,920 | 6,660 |
| 25,250 | 25,300 | 0 | 2,634 | 4,668 | 5,408 | 0 | 3,575 | 5,908 | 6,648 |
| 25,300 | 25,350 | 0 | 2,626 | 4,657 | 5,397 | 0 | 3,567 | 5,898 | 6,638 |
| 25,350 | 25,400 | 0 | 2,618 | 4,647 | 5,387 | 0 | 3,559 | 5,887 | 6,627 |
| 25,400 | 25,450 | 0 | 2,610 | 4,636 | 5,376 | 0 | 3,551 | 5,877 | 6,617 |
| 25,450 | 25,500 | 0 | 2,602 | 4,626 | 5,366 | 0 | 3,543 | 5,866 | 6,606 |
| 25,500 | 25,550 | 0 | 2,594 | 4,615 | 5,355 | 0 | 3,535 | 5,856 | 6,596 |
| 25,550 | 25,600 | 0 | 2,586 | 4,605 | 5,345 | 0 | 3,527 | 5,845 | 6,585 |

* If the amount you are looking up from the worksheet is at least $21,700 but less than $21,710, and you have no qualifying children, your credit is $0. If the amount you are looking up from the worksheet is $21,710 or more, and you have no qualifying children, you can't take the credit.

*(Continued)*

**Earned Income Credit (EIC) Table** - *Continued* (**Caution.** This is **not** a tax table.)

| If the amount you are looking up from the worksheet is– | | And your filing status is– Single, head of household, or qualifying widow(er) and you have– | | | | Married filing jointly and you have– | | | |
|---|---|---|---|---|---|---|---|---|---|
| | | 0 | 1 | 2 | 3 | 0 | 1 | 2 | 3 |
| At least | But less than | Your credit is– | | | | Your credit is– | | | |
| 25,600 | 25,650 | 0 | 2,578 | 4,594 | 5,334 | 0 | 3,519 | 5,835 | 6,575 |
| 25,650 | 25,700 | 0 | 2,570 | 4,584 | 5,324 | 0 | 3,511 | 5,824 | 6,564 |
| 25,700 | 25,750 | 0 | 2,562 | 4,573 | 5,313 | 0 | 3,503 | 5,814 | 6,554 |
| 25,750 | 25,800 | 0 | 2,554 | 4,563 | 5,303 | 0 | 3,495 | 5,803 | 6,543 |
| 25,800 | 25,850 | 0 | 2,546 | 4,552 | 5,292 | 0 | 3,487 | 5,793 | 6,533 |
| 25,850 | 25,900 | 0 | 2,538 | 4,542 | 5,282 | 0 | 3,479 | 5,782 | 6,522 |
| 25,900 | 25,950 | 0 | 2,530 | 4,531 | 5,271 | 0 | 3,471 | 5,772 | 6,512 |
| 25,950 | 26,000 | 0 | 2,522 | 4,521 | 5,261 | 0 | 3,463 | 5,761 | 6,501 |
| 26,000 | 26,050 | 0 | 2,514 | 4,510 | 5,250 | 0 | 3,455 | 5,750 | 6,490 |
| 26,050 | 26,100 | 0 | 2,506 | 4,500 | 5,240 | 0 | 3,447 | 5,740 | 6,480 |
| 26,100 | 26,150 | 0 | 2,498 | 4,489 | 5,229 | 0 | 3,439 | 5,729 | 6,469 |
| 26,150 | 26,200 | 0 | 2,490 | 4,478 | 5,218 | 0 | 3,431 | 5,719 | 6,459 |
| 26,200 | 26,250 | 0 | 2,482 | 4,468 | 5,208 | 0 | 3,423 | 5,708 | 6,448 |
| 26,250 | 26,300 | 0 | 2,474 | 4,457 | 5,197 | 0 | 3,415 | 5,698 | 6,438 |
| 26,300 | 26,350 | 0 | 2,466 | 4,447 | 5,187 | 0 | 3,407 | 5,687 | 6,427 |
| 26,350 | 26,400 | 0 | 2,458 | 4,436 | 5,176 | 0 | 3,399 | 5,677 | 6,417 |
| 26,400 | 26,450 | 0 | 2,450 | 4,426 | 5,166 | 0 | 3,391 | 5,666 | 6,406 |
| 26,450 | 26,500 | 0 | 2,442 | 4,415 | 5,155 | 0 | 3,383 | 5,656 | 6,396 |
| 26,500 | 26,550 | 0 | 2,434 | 4,405 | 5,145 | 0 | 3,375 | 5,645 | 6,385 |
| 26,550 | 26,600 | 0 | 2,426 | 4,394 | 5,134 | 0 | 3,367 | 5,635 | 6,375 |
| 26,600 | 26,650 | 0 | 2,418 | 4,384 | 5,124 | 0 | 3,359 | 5,624 | 6,364 |
| 26,650 | 26,700 | 0 | 2,410 | 4,373 | 5,113 | 0 | 3,351 | 5,614 | 6,354 |
| 26,700 | 26,750 | 0 | 2,402 | 4,363 | 5,103 | 0 | 3,343 | 5,603 | 6,343 |
| 26,750 | 26,800 | 0 | 2,394 | 4,352 | 5,092 | 0 | 3,335 | 5,593 | 6,333 |
| 26,800 | 26,850 | 0 | 2,386 | 4,342 | 5,082 | 0 | 3,327 | 5,582 | 6,322 |
| 26,850 | 26,900 | 0 | 2,378 | 4,331 | 5,071 | 0 | 3,319 | 5,571 | 6,311 |
| 26,900 | 26,950 | 0 | 2,370 | 4,320 | 5,060 | 0 | 3,311 | 5,561 | 6,301 |
| 26,950 | 27,000 | 0 | 2,362 | 4,310 | 5,050 | 0 | 3,303 | 5,550 | 6,290 |
| 27,000 | 27,050 | 0 | 2,354 | 4,299 | 5,039 | 0 | 3,295 | 5,540 | 6,280 |
| 27,050 | 27,100 | 0 | 2,346 | 4,289 | 5,029 | 0 | 3,287 | 5,529 | 6,269 |
| 27,100 | 27,150 | 0 | 2,338 | 4,278 | 5,018 | 0 | 3,279 | 5,519 | 6,259 |
| 27,150 | 27,200 | 0 | 2,330 | 4,268 | 5,008 | 0 | 3,271 | 5,508 | 6,248 |
| 27,200 | 27,250 | 0 | 2,322 | 4,257 | 4,997 | 0 | 3,263 | 5,498 | 6,238 |
| 27,250 | 27,300 | 0 | 2,314 | 4,247 | 4,987 | 0 | 3,255 | 5,487 | 6,227 |
| 27,300 | 27,350 | 0 | 2,306 | 4,236 | 4,976 | 0 | 3,247 | 5,477 | 6,217 |
| 27,350 | 27,400 | 0 | 2,298 | 4,226 | 4,966 | 0 | 3,239 | 5,466 | 6,206 |
| 27,400 | 27,450 | 0 | 2,290 | 4,215 | 4,955 | 0 | 3,231 | 5,456 | 6,196 |
| 27,450 | 27,500 | 0 | 2,282 | 4,205 | 4,945 | 0 | 3,223 | 5,445 | 6,185 |
| 27,500 | 27,550 | 0 | 2,274 | 4,194 | 4,934 | 0 | 3,215 | 5,435 | 6,175 |
| 27,550 | 27,600 | 0 | 2,266 | 4,184 | 4,924 | 0 | 3,207 | 5,424 | 6,164 |
| 27,600 | 27,650 | 0 | 2,258 | 4,173 | 4,913 | 0 | 3,199 | 5,414 | 6,154 |
| 27,650 | 27,700 | 0 | 2,250 | 4,163 | 4,903 | 0 | 3,191 | 5,403 | 6,143 |
| 27,700 | 27,750 | 0 | 2,242 | 4,152 | 4,892 | 0 | 3,183 | 5,392 | 6,132 |
| 27,750 | 27,800 | 0 | 2,234 | 4,141 | 4,881 | 0 | 3,175 | 5,382 | 6,122 |
| 27,800 | 27,850 | 0 | 2,226 | 4,131 | 4,871 | 0 | 3,167 | 5,371 | 6,111 |
| 27,850 | 27,900 | 0 | 2,218 | 4,120 | 4,860 | 0 | 3,159 | 5,361 | 6,101 |
| 27,900 | 27,950 | 0 | 2,210 | 4,110 | 4,850 | 0 | 3,151 | 5,350 | 6,090 |
| 27,950 | 28,000 | 0 | 2,202 | 4,099 | 4,839 | 0 | 3,143 | 5,340 | 6,080 |
| 28,000 | 28,050 | 0 | 2,194 | 4,089 | 4,829 | 0 | 3,135 | 5,329 | 6,069 |
| 28,050 | 28,100 | 0 | 2,186 | 4,078 | 4,818 | 0 | 3,127 | 5,319 | 6,059 |
| 28,100 | 28,150 | 0 | 2,178 | 4,068 | 4,808 | 0 | 3,119 | 5,308 | 6,048 |
| 28,150 | 28,200 | 0 | 2,170 | 4,057 | 4,797 | 0 | 3,111 | 5,298 | 6,038 |
| 28,200 | 28,250 | 0 | 2,162 | 4,047 | 4,787 | 0 | 3,103 | 5,287 | 6,027 |
| 28,250 | 28,300 | 0 | 2,154 | 4,036 | 4,776 | 0 | 3,095 | 5,277 | 6,017 |
| 28,300 | 28,350 | 0 | 2,146 | 4,026 | 4,766 | 0 | 3,087 | 5,266 | 6,006 |
| 28,350 | 28,400 | 0 | 2,138 | 4,015 | 4,755 | 0 | 3,079 | 5,256 | 5,996 |
| 28,400 | 28,450 | 0 | 2,130 | 4,005 | 4,745 | 0 | 3,071 | 5,245 | 5,985 |
| 28,450 | 28,500 | 0 | 2,122 | 3,994 | 4,734 | 0 | 3,063 | 5,234 | 5,974 |
| 28,500 | 28,550 | 0 | 2,114 | 3,984 | 4,724 | 0 | 3,055 | 5,224 | 5,964 |
| 28,550 | 28,600 | 0 | 2,106 | 3,973 | 4,713 | 0 | 3,047 | 5,213 | 5,953 |
| 28,600 | 28,650 | 0 | 2,098 | 3,962 | 4,702 | 0 | 3,039 | 5,203 | 5,943 |
| 28,650 | 28,700 | 0 | 2,090 | 3,952 | 4,692 | 0 | 3,031 | 5,192 | 5,932 |
| 28,700 | 28,750 | 0 | 2,082 | 3,941 | 4,681 | 0 | 3,024 | 5,182 | 5,922 |
| 28,750 | 28,800 | 0 | 2,074 | 3,931 | 4,671 | 0 | 3,016 | 5,171 | 5,911 |
| 28,800 | 28,850 | 0 | 2,066 | 3,920 | 4,660 | 0 | 3,008 | 5,161 | 5,901 |
| 28,850 | 28,900 | 0 | 2,058 | 3,910 | 4,650 | 0 | 3,000 | 5,150 | 5,890 |
| 28,900 | 28,950 | 0 | 2,050 | 3,899 | 4,639 | 0 | 2,992 | 5,140 | 5,880 |
| 28,950 | 29,000 | 0 | 2,042 | 3,889 | 4,629 | 0 | 2,984 | 5,129 | 5,869 |
| 29,000 | 29,050 | 0 | 2,034 | 3,878 | 4,618 | 0 | 2,976 | 5,119 | 5,859 |
| 29,050 | 29,100 | 0 | 2,026 | 3,868 | 4,608 | 0 | 2,968 | 5,108 | 5,848 |
| 29,100 | 29,150 | 0 | 2,018 | 3,857 | 4,597 | 0 | 2,960 | 5,098 | 5,838 |
| 29,150 | 29,200 | 0 | 2,010 | 3,847 | 4,587 | 0 | 2,952 | 5,087 | 5,827 |
| 29,200 | 29,250 | 0 | 2,002 | 3,836 | 4,576 | 0 | 2,944 | 5,077 | 5,817 |
| 29,250 | 29,300 | 0 | 1,994 | 3,826 | 4,566 | 0 | 2,936 | 5,066 | 5,806 |
| 29,300 | 29,350 | 0 | 1,986 | 3,815 | 4,555 | 0 | 2,928 | 5,055 | 5,795 |
| 29,350 | 29,400 | 0 | 1,978 | 3,805 | 4,545 | 0 | 2,920 | 5,045 | 5,785 |
| 29,400 | 29,450 | 0 | 1,970 | 3,794 | 4,534 | 0 | 2,912 | 5,034 | 5,774 |
| 29,450 | 29,500 | 0 | 1,962 | 3,783 | 4,523 | 0 | 2,904 | 5,024 | 5,764 |
| 29,500 | 29,550 | 0 | 1,954 | 3,773 | 4,513 | 0 | 2,896 | 5,013 | 5,753 |
| 29,550 | 29,600 | 0 | 1,946 | 3,762 | 4,502 | 0 | 2,888 | 5,003 | 5,743 |
| 29,600 | 29,650 | 0 | 1,938 | 3,752 | 4,492 | 0 | 2,880 | 4,992 | 5,732 |
| 29,650 | 29,700 | 0 | 1,930 | 3,741 | 4,481 | 0 | 2,872 | 4,982 | 5,722 |
| 29,700 | 29,750 | 0 | 1,922 | 3,731 | 4,471 | 0 | 2,864 | 4,971 | 5,711 |
| 29,750 | 29,800 | 0 | 1,914 | 3,720 | 4,460 | 0 | 2,856 | 4,961 | 5,701 |
| 29,800 | 29,850 | 0 | 1,906 | 3,710 | 4,450 | 0 | 2,848 | 4,950 | 5,690 |
| 29,850 | 29,900 | 0 | 1,899 | 3,699 | 4,439 | 0 | 2,840 | 4,940 | 5,680 |
| 29,900 | 29,950 | 0 | 1,891 | 3,689 | 4,429 | 0 | 2,832 | 4,929 | 5,669 |
| 29,950 | 30,000 | 0 | 1,883 | 3,678 | 4,418 | 0 | 2,824 | 4,919 | 5,659 |
| 30,000 | 30,050 | 0 | 1,875 | 3,668 | 4,408 | 0 | 2,816 | 4,908 | 5,648 |
| 30,050 | 30,100 | 0 | 1,867 | 3,657 | 4,397 | 0 | 2,808 | 4,898 | 5,638 |
| 30,100 | 30,150 | 0 | 1,859 | 3,647 | 4,387 | 0 | 2,800 | 4,887 | 5,627 |
| 30,150 | 30,200 | 0 | 1,851 | 3,636 | 4,376 | 0 | 2,792 | 4,876 | 5,616 |
| 30,200 | 30,250 | 0 | 1,843 | 3,626 | 4,366 | 0 | 2,784 | 4,866 | 5,606 |
| 30,250 | 30,300 | 0 | 1,835 | 3,615 | 4,355 | 0 | 2,776 | 4,855 | 5,595 |
| 30,300 | 30,350 | 0 | 1,827 | 3,604 | 4,344 | 0 | 2,768 | 4,845 | 5,585 |
| 30,350 | 30,400 | 0 | 1,819 | 3,594 | 4,334 | 0 | 2,760 | 4,834 | 5,574 |
| 30,400 | 30,450 | 0 | 1,811 | 3,583 | 4,323 | 0 | 2,752 | 4,824 | 5,564 |
| 30,450 | 30,500 | 0 | 1,803 | 3,573 | 4,313 | 0 | 2,744 | 4,813 | 5,553 |
| 30,500 | 30,550 | 0 | 1,795 | 3,562 | 4,302 | 0 | 2,736 | 4,803 | 5,543 |
| 30,550 | 30,600 | 0 | 1,787 | 3,552 | 4,292 | 0 | 2,728 | 4,792 | 5,532 |
| 30,600 | 30,650 | 0 | 1,779 | 3,541 | 4,281 | 0 | 2,720 | 4,782 | 5,522 |
| 30,650 | 30,700 | 0 | 1,771 | 3,531 | 4,271 | 0 | 2,712 | 4,771 | 5,511 |
| 30,700 | 30,750 | 0 | 1,763 | 3,520 | 4,260 | 0 | 2,704 | 4,761 | 5,501 |
| 30,750 | 30,800 | 0 | 1,755 | 3,510 | 4,250 | 0 | 2,696 | 4,750 | 5,490 |
| 30,800 | 30,850 | 0 | 1,747 | 3,499 | 4,239 | 0 | 2,688 | 4,740 | 5,480 |
| 30,850 | 30,900 | 0 | 1,739 | 3,489 | 4,229 | 0 | 2,680 | 4,729 | 5,469 |
| 30,900 | 30,950 | 0 | 1,731 | 3,478 | 4,218 | 0 | 2,672 | 4,719 | 5,459 |
| 30,950 | 31,000 | 0 | 1,723 | 3,468 | 4,208 | 0 | 2,664 | 4,708 | 5,448 |
| 31,000 | 31,050 | 0 | 1,715 | 3,457 | 4,197 | 0 | 2,656 | 4,697 | 5,437 |
| 31,050 | 31,100 | 0 | 1,707 | 3,447 | 4,187 | 0 | 2,648 | 4,687 | 5,427 |
| 31,100 | 31,150 | 0 | 1,699 | 3,436 | 4,176 | 0 | 2,640 | 4,676 | 5,416 |
| 31,150 | 31,200 | 0 | 1,691 | 3,425 | 4,165 | 0 | 2,632 | 4,666 | 5,406 |
| 31,200 | 31,250 | 0 | 1,683 | 3,415 | 4,155 | 0 | 2,624 | 4,655 | 5,395 |
| 31,250 | 31,300 | 0 | 1,675 | 3,404 | 4,144 | 0 | 2,616 | 4,645 | 5,385 |
| 31,300 | 31,350 | 0 | 1,667 | 3,394 | 4,134 | 0 | 2,608 | 4,634 | 5,374 |
| 31,350 | 31,400 | 0 | 1,659 | 3,383 | 4,123 | 0 | 2,600 | 4,624 | 5,364 |
| 31,400 | 31,450 | 0 | 1,651 | 3,373 | 4,113 | 0 | 2,592 | 4,613 | 5,353 |
| 31,450 | 31,500 | 0 | 1,643 | 3,362 | 4,102 | 0 | 2,584 | 4,603 | 5,343 |
| 31,500 | 31,550 | 0 | 1,635 | 3,352 | 4,092 | 0 | 2,576 | 4,592 | 5,332 |
| 31,550 | 31,600 | 0 | 1,627 | 3,341 | 4,081 | 0 | 2,568 | 4,582 | 5,322 |
| 31,600 | 31,650 | 0 | 1,619 | 3,331 | 4,071 | 0 | 2,560 | 4,571 | 5,311 |
| 31,650 | 31,700 | 0 | 1,611 | 3,320 | 4,060 | 0 | 2,552 | 4,561 | 5,301 |
| 31,700 | 31,750 | 0 | 1,603 | 3,310 | 4,050 | 0 | 2,544 | 4,550 | 5,290 |
| 31,750 | 31,800 | 0 | 1,595 | 3,299 | 4,039 | 0 | 2,536 | 4,540 | 5,280 |
| 31,800 | 31,850 | 0 | 1,587 | 3,289 | 4,029 | 0 | 2,528 | 4,529 | 5,269 |
| 31,850 | 31,900 | 0 | 1,579 | 3,278 | 4,018 | 0 | 2,520 | 4,518 | 5,258 |
| 31,900 | 31,950 | 0 | 1,571 | 3,267 | 4,007 | 0 | 2,512 | 4,508 | 5,248 |
| 31,950 | 32,000 | 0 | 1,563 | 3,257 | 3,997 | 0 | 2,504 | 4,497 | 5,237 |
| 32,000 | 32,050 | 0 | 1,555 | 3,246 | 3,986 | 0 | 2,496 | 4,487 | 5,227 |
| 32,050 | 32,100 | 0 | 1,547 | 3,236 | 3,976 | 0 | 2,488 | 4,476 | 5,216 |
| 32,100 | 32,150 | 0 | 1,539 | 3,225 | 3,965 | 0 | 2,480 | 4,466 | 5,206 |
| 32,150 | 32,200 | 0 | 1,531 | 3,215 | 3,955 | 0 | 2,472 | 4,455 | 5,195 |
| 32,200 | 32,250 | 0 | 1,523 | 3,204 | 3,944 | 0 | 2,464 | 4,445 | 5,185 |
| 32,250 | 32,300 | 0 | 1,515 | 3,194 | 3,934 | 0 | 2,456 | 4,434 | 5,174 |
| 32,300 | 32,350 | 0 | 1,507 | 3,183 | 3,923 | 0 | 2,448 | 4,424 | 5,164 |
| 32,350 | 32,400 | 0 | 1,499 | 3,173 | 3,913 | 0 | 2,440 | 4,413 | 5,153 |
| 32,400 | 32,450 | 0 | 1,491 | 3,162 | 3,902 | 0 | 2,432 | 4,403 | 5,143 |
| 32,450 | 32,500 | 0 | 1,483 | 3,152 | 3,892 | 0 | 2,424 | 4,392 | 5,132 |
| 32,500 | 32,550 | 0 | 1,475 | 3,141 | 3,881 | 0 | 2,416 | 4,382 | 5,122 |
| 32,550 | 32,600 | 0 | 1,467 | 3,131 | 3,871 | 0 | 2,408 | 4,371 | 5,111 |
| 32,600 | 32,650 | 0 | 1,459 | 3,120 | 3,860 | 0 | 2,400 | 4,361 | 5,101 |
| 32,650 | 32,700 | 0 | 1,451 | 3,110 | 3,850 | 0 | 2,392 | 4,350 | 5,090 |
| 32,700 | 32,750 | 0 | 1,443 | 3,099 | 3,839 | 0 | 2,384 | 4,339 | 5,079 |
| 32,750 | 32,800 | 0 | 1,435 | 3,088 | 3,828 | 0 | 2,376 | 4,329 | 5,069 |

*(Continued)*

## Earned Income Credit (EIC) Table - *Continued*

**(Caution.** This is **not** a tax table.)

| If the amount you are looking up from the worksheet is– | | And your filing status is– Single, head of household, or qualifying widow(er) and you have– | | | | Married filing jointly and you have– | | | |
|---|---|---|---|---|---|---|---|---|---|
| | | 0 | 1 | 2 | 3 | 0 | 1 | 2 | 3 |
| At least | But less than | Your credit is– | | | | Your credit is– | | | |
| 32,800 | 32,850 | 0 | 1,427 | 3,078 | 3,818 | 0 | 2,368 | 4,318 | 5,058 |
| 32,850 | 32,900 | 0 | 1,419 | 3,067 | 3,807 | 0 | 2,360 | 4,308 | 5,048 |
| 32,900 | 32,950 | 0 | 1,411 | 3,057 | 3,797 | 0 | 2,352 | 4,297 | 5,037 |
| 32,950 | 33,000 | 0 | 1,403 | 3,046 | 3,786 | 0 | 2,344 | 4,287 | 5,027 |
| 33,000 | 33,050 | 0 | 1,395 | 3,036 | 3,776 | 0 | 2,336 | 4,276 | 5,016 |
| 33,050 | 33,100 | 0 | 1,387 | 3,025 | 3,765 | 0 | 2,328 | 4,266 | 5,006 |
| 33,100 | 33,150 | 0 | 1,379 | 3,015 | 3,755 | 0 | 2,320 | 4,255 | 4,995 |
| 33,150 | 33,200 | 0 | 1,371 | 3,004 | 3,744 | 0 | 2,312 | 4,245 | 4,985 |
| 33,200 | 33,250 | 0 | 1,363 | 2,994 | 3,734 | 0 | 2,304 | 4,234 | 4,974 |
| 33,250 | 33,300 | 0 | 1,355 | 2,983 | 3,723 | 0 | 2,296 | 4,224 | 4,964 |
| 33,300 | 33,350 | 0 | 1,347 | 2,973 | 3,713 | 0 | 2,288 | 4,213 | 4,953 |
| 33,350 | 33,400 | 0 | 1,339 | 2,962 | 3,702 | 0 | 2,280 | 4,203 | 4,943 |
| 33,400 | 33,450 | 0 | 1,331 | 2,952 | 3,692 | 0 | 2,272 | 4,192 | 4,932 |
| 33,450 | 33,500 | 0 | 1,323 | 2,941 | 3,681 | 0 | 2,264 | 4,181 | 4,921 |
| 33,500 | 33,550 | 0 | 1,315 | 2,931 | 3,671 | 0 | 2,256 | 4,171 | 4,911 |
| 33,550 | 33,600 | 0 | 1,307 | 2,920 | 3,660 | 0 | 2,248 | 4,160 | 4,900 |
| 33,600 | 33,650 | 0 | 1,299 | 2,909 | 3,649 | 0 | 2,240 | 4,150 | 4,890 |
| 33,650 | 33,700 | 0 | 1,291 | 2,899 | 3,639 | 0 | 2,232 | 4,139 | 4,879 |
| 33,700 | 33,750 | 0 | 1,283 | 2,888 | 3,628 | 0 | 2,225 | 4,129 | 4,869 |
| 33,750 | 33,800 | 0 | 1,275 | 2,878 | 3,618 | 0 | 2,217 | 4,118 | 4,858 |
| 33,800 | 33,850 | 0 | 1,267 | 2,867 | 3,607 | 0 | 2,209 | 4,108 | 4,848 |
| 33,850 | 33,900 | 0 | 1,259 | 2,857 | 3,597 | 0 | 2,201 | 4,097 | 4,837 |
| 33,900 | 33,950 | 0 | 1,251 | 2,846 | 3,586 | 0 | 2,193 | 4,087 | 4,827 |
| 33,950 | 34,000 | 0 | 1,243 | 2,836 | 3,576 | 0 | 2,185 | 4,076 | 4,816 |
| 34,000 | 34,050 | 0 | 1,235 | 2,825 | 3,565 | 0 | 2,177 | 4,066 | 4,806 |
| 34,050 | 34,100 | 0 | 1,227 | 2,815 | 3,555 | 0 | 2,169 | 4,055 | 4,795 |
| 34,100 | 34,150 | 0 | 1,219 | 2,804 | 3,544 | 0 | 2,161 | 4,045 | 4,785 |
| 34,150 | 34,200 | 0 | 1,211 | 2,794 | 3,534 | 0 | 2,153 | 4,034 | 4,774 |
| 34,200 | 34,250 | 0 | 1,203 | 2,783 | 3,523 | 0 | 2,145 | 4,024 | 4,764 |
| 34,250 | 34,300 | 0 | 1,195 | 2,773 | 3,513 | 0 | 2,137 | 4,013 | 4,753 |
| 34,300 | 34,350 | 0 | 1,187 | 2,762 | 3,502 | 0 | 2,129 | 4,002 | 4,742 |
| 34,350 | 34,400 | 0 | 1,179 | 2,752 | 3,492 | 0 | 2,121 | 3,992 | 4,732 |
| 34,400 | 34,450 | 0 | 1,171 | 2,741 | 3,481 | 0 | 2,113 | 3,981 | 4,721 |
| 34,450 | 34,500 | 0 | 1,163 | 2,730 | 3,470 | 0 | 2,105 | 3,971 | 4,711 |
| 34,500 | 34,550 | 0 | 1,155 | 2,720 | 3,460 | 0 | 2,097 | 3,960 | 4,700 |
| 34,550 | 34,600 | 0 | 1,147 | 2,709 | 3,449 | 0 | 2,089 | 3,950 | 4,690 |
| 34,600 | 34,650 | 0 | 1,139 | 2,699 | 3,439 | 0 | 2,081 | 3,939 | 4,679 |
| 34,650 | 34,700 | 0 | 1,131 | 2,688 | 3,428 | 0 | 2,073 | 3,929 | 4,669 |
| 34,700 | 34,750 | 0 | 1,123 | 2,678 | 3,418 | 0 | 2,065 | 3,918 | 4,658 |
| 34,750 | 34,800 | 0 | 1,115 | 2,667 | 3,407 | 0 | 2,057 | 3,908 | 4,648 |
| 34,800 | 34,850 | 0 | 1,107 | 2,657 | 3,397 | 0 | 2,049 | 3,897 | 4,637 |
| 34,850 | 34,900 | 0 | 1,100 | 2,646 | 3,386 | 0 | 2,041 | 3,887 | 4,627 |
| 34,900 | 34,950 | 0 | 1,092 | 2,636 | 3,376 | 0 | 2,033 | 3,876 | 4,616 |
| 34,950 | 35,000 | 0 | 1,084 | 2,625 | 3,365 | 0 | 2,025 | 3,866 | 4,606 |
| 35,000 | 35,050 | 0 | 1,076 | 2,615 | 3,355 | 0 | 2,017 | 3,855 | 4,595 |
| 35,050 | 35,100 | 0 | 1,068 | 2,604 | 3,344 | 0 | 2,009 | 3,845 | 4,585 |
| 35,100 | 35,150 | 0 | 1,060 | 2,594 | 3,334 | 0 | 2,001 | 3,834 | 4,574 |
| 35,150 | 35,200 | 0 | 1,052 | 2,583 | 3,323 | 0 | 1,993 | 3,823 | 4,563 |
| 35,200 | 35,250 | 0 | 1,044 | 2,573 | 3,313 | 0 | 1,985 | 3,813 | 4,553 |
| 35,250 | 35,300 | 0 | 1,036 | 2,562 | 3,302 | 0 | 1,977 | 3,802 | 4,542 |
| 35,300 | 35,350 | 0 | 1,028 | 2,551 | 3,291 | 0 | 1,969 | 3,792 | 4,532 |
| 35,350 | 35,400 | 0 | 1,020 | 2,541 | 3,281 | 0 | 1,961 | 3,781 | 4,521 |
| 35,400 | 35,450 | 0 | 1,012 | 2,530 | 3,270 | 0 | 1,953 | 3,771 | 4,511 |
| 35,450 | 35,500 | 0 | 1,004 | 2,520 | 3,260 | 0 | 1,945 | 3,760 | 4,500 |
| 35,500 | 35,550 | 0 | 996 | 2,509 | 3,249 | 0 | 1,937 | 3,750 | 4,490 |
| 35,550 | 35,600 | 0 | 988 | 2,499 | 3,239 | 0 | 1,929 | 3,739 | 4,479 |
| 35,600 | 35,650 | 0 | 980 | 2,488 | 3,228 | 0 | 1,921 | 3,729 | 4,469 |
| 35,650 | 35,700 | 0 | 972 | 2,478 | 3,218 | 0 | 1,913 | 3,718 | 4,458 |
| 35,700 | 35,750 | 0 | 964 | 2,467 | 3,207 | 0 | 1,905 | 3,708 | 4,448 |
| 35,750 | 35,800 | 0 | 956 | 2,457 | 3,197 | 0 | 1,897 | 3,697 | 4,437 |
| 35,800 | 35,850 | 0 | 948 | 2,446 | 3,186 | 0 | 1,889 | 3,687 | 4,427 |
| 35,850 | 35,900 | 0 | 940 | 2,436 | 3,176 | 0 | 1,881 | 3,676 | 4,416 |
| 35,900 | 35,950 | 0 | 932 | 2,425 | 3,165 | 0 | 1,873 | 3,666 | 4,406 |
| 35,950 | 36,000 | 0 | 924 | 2,415 | 3,155 | 0 | 1,865 | 3,655 | 4,395 |
| 36,000 | 36,050 | 0 | 916 | 2,404 | 3,144 | 0 | 1,857 | 3,644 | 4,384 |
| 36,050 | 36,100 | 0 | 908 | 2,394 | 3,134 | 0 | 1,849 | 3,634 | 4,374 |
| 36,100 | 36,150 | 0 | 900 | 2,383 | 3,123 | 0 | 1,841 | 3,623 | 4,363 |
| 36,150 | 36,200 | 0 | 892 | 2,372 | 3,112 | 0 | 1,833 | 3,613 | 4,353 |
| 36,200 | 36,250 | 0 | 884 | 2,362 | 3,102 | 0 | 1,825 | 3,602 | 4,342 |
| 36,250 | 36,300 | 0 | 876 | 2,351 | 3,091 | 0 | 1,817 | 3,592 | 4,332 |
| 36,300 | 36,350 | 0 | 868 | 2,341 | 3,081 | 0 | 1,809 | 3,581 | 4,321 |
| 36,350 | 36,400 | 0 | 860 | 2,330 | 3,070 | 0 | 1,801 | 3,571 | 4,311 |
| 36,400 | 36,450 | 0 | 852 | 2,320 | 3,060 | 0 | 1,793 | 3,560 | 4,300 |
| 36,450 | 36,500 | 0 | 844 | 2,309 | 3,049 | 0 | 1,785 | 3,550 | 4,290 |
| 36,500 | 36,550 | 0 | 836 | 2,299 | 3,039 | 0 | 1,777 | 3,539 | 4,279 |
| 36,550 | 36,600 | 0 | 828 | 2,288 | 3,028 | 0 | 1,769 | 3,529 | 4,269 |
| 36,600 | 36,650 | 0 | 820 | 2,278 | 3,018 | 0 | 1,761 | 3,518 | 4,258 |
| 36,650 | 36,700 | 0 | 812 | 2,267 | 3,007 | 0 | 1,753 | 3,508 | 4,248 |
| 36,700 | 36,750 | 0 | 804 | 2,257 | 2,997 | 0 | 1,745 | 3,497 | 4,237 |
| 36,750 | 36,800 | 0 | 796 | 2,246 | 2,986 | 0 | 1,737 | 3,487 | 4,227 |
| 36,800 | 36,850 | 0 | 788 | 2,236 | 2,976 | 0 | 1,729 | 3,476 | 4,216 |
| 36,850 | 36,900 | 0 | 780 | 2,225 | 2,965 | 0 | 1,721 | 3,465 | 4,205 |
| 36,900 | 36,950 | 0 | 772 | 2,214 | 2,954 | 0 | 1,713 | 3,455 | 4,195 |
| 36,950 | 37,000 | 0 | 764 | 2,204 | 2,944 | 0 | 1,705 | 3,444 | 4,184 |
| 37,000 | 37,050 | 0 | 756 | 2,193 | 2,933 | 0 | 1,697 | 3,434 | 4,174 |
| 37,050 | 37,100 | 0 | 748 | 2,183 | 2,923 | 0 | 1,689 | 3,423 | 4,163 |
| 37,100 | 37,150 | 0 | 740 | 2,172 | 2,912 | 0 | 1,681 | 3,413 | 4,153 |
| 37,150 | 37,200 | 0 | 732 | 2,162 | 2,902 | 0 | 1,673 | 3,402 | 4,142 |
| 37,200 | 37,250 | 0 | 724 | 2,151 | 2,891 | 0 | 1,665 | 3,392 | 4,132 |
| 37,250 | 37,300 | 0 | 716 | 2,141 | 2,881 | 0 | 1,657 | 3,381 | 4,121 |
| 37,300 | 37,350 | 0 | 708 | 2,130 | 2,870 | 0 | 1,649 | 3,371 | 4,111 |
| 37,350 | 37,400 | 0 | 700 | 2,120 | 2,860 | 0 | 1,641 | 3,360 | 4,100 |
| 37,400 | 37,450 | 0 | 692 | 2,109 | 2,849 | 0 | 1,633 | 3,350 | 4,090 |
| 37,450 | 37,500 | 0 | 684 | 2,099 | 2,839 | 0 | 1,625 | 3,339 | 4,079 |
| 37,500 | 37,550 | 0 | 676 | 2,088 | 2,828 | 0 | 1,617 | 3,329 | 4,069 |
| 37,550 | 37,600 | 0 | 668 | 2,078 | 2,818 | 0 | 1,609 | 3,318 | 4,058 |
| 37,600 | 37,650 | 0 | 660 | 2,067 | 2,807 | 0 | 1,601 | 3,308 | 4,048 |
| 37,650 | 37,700 | 0 | 652 | 2,057 | 2,797 | 0 | 1,593 | 3,297 | 4,037 |
| 37,700 | 37,750 | 0 | 644 | 2,046 | 2,786 | 0 | 1,585 | 3,286 | 4,026 |
| 37,750 | 37,800 | 0 | 636 | 2,035 | 2,775 | 0 | 1,577 | 3,276 | 4,016 |
| 37,800 | 37,850 | 0 | 628 | 2,025 | 2,765 | 0 | 1,569 | 3,265 | 4,005 |
| 37,850 | 37,900 | 0 | 620 | 2,014 | 2,754 | 0 | 1,561 | 3,255 | 3,995 |
| 37,900 | 37,950 | 0 | 612 | 2,004 | 2,744 | 0 | 1,553 | 3,244 | 3,984 |
| 37,950 | 38,000 | 0 | 604 | 1,993 | 2,733 | 0 | 1,545 | 3,234 | 3,974 |
| 38,000 | 38,050 | 0 | 596 | 1,983 | 2,723 | 0 | 1,537 | 3,223 | 3,963 |
| 38,050 | 38,100 | 0 | 588 | 1,972 | 2,712 | 0 | 1,529 | 3,213 | 3,953 |
| 38,100 | 38,150 | 0 | 580 | 1,962 | 2,702 | 0 | 1,521 | 3,202 | 3,942 |
| 38,150 | 38,200 | 0 | 572 | 1,951 | 2,691 | 0 | 1,513 | 3,192 | 3,932 |
| 38,200 | 38,250 | 0 | 564 | 1,941 | 2,681 | 0 | 1,505 | 3,181 | 3,921 |
| 38,250 | 38,300 | 0 | 556 | 1,930 | 2,670 | 0 | 1,497 | 3,171 | 3,911 |
| 38,300 | 38,350 | 0 | 548 | 1,920 | 2,660 | 0 | 1,489 | 3,160 | 3,900 |
| 38,350 | 38,400 | 0 | 540 | 1,909 | 2,649 | 0 | 1,481 | 3,150 | 3,890 |
| 38,400 | 38,450 | 0 | 532 | 1,899 | 2,639 | 0 | 1,473 | 3,139 | 3,879 |
| 38,450 | 38,500 | 0 | 524 | 1,888 | 2,628 | 0 | 1,465 | 3,128 | 3,868 |
| 38,500 | 38,550 | 0 | 516 | 1,878 | 2,618 | 0 | 1,457 | 3,118 | 3,858 |
| 38,550 | 38,600 | 0 | 508 | 1,867 | 2,607 | 0 | 1,449 | 3,107 | 3,847 |
| 38,600 | 38,650 | 0 | 500 | 1,856 | 2,596 | 0 | 1,441 | 3,097 | 3,837 |
| 38,650 | 38,700 | 0 | 492 | 1,846 | 2,586 | 0 | 1,433 | 3,086 | 3,826 |
| 38,700 | 38,750 | 0 | 484 | 1,835 | 2,575 | 0 | 1,426 | 3,076 | 3,816 |
| 38,750 | 38,800 | 0 | 476 | 1,825 | 2,565 | 0 | 1,418 | 3,065 | 3,805 |
| 38,800 | 38,850 | 0 | 468 | 1,814 | 2,554 | 0 | 1,410 | 3,055 | 3,795 |
| 38,850 | 38,900 | 0 | 460 | 1,804 | 2,544 | 0 | 1,402 | 3,044 | 3,784 |
| 38,900 | 38,950 | 0 | 452 | 1,793 | 2,533 | 0 | 1,394 | 3,034 | 3,774 |
| 38,950 | 39,000 | 0 | 444 | 1,783 | 2,523 | 0 | 1,386 | 3,023 | 3,763 |
| 39,000 | 39,050 | 0 | 436 | 1,772 | 2,512 | 0 | 1,378 | 3,013 | 3,753 |
| 39,050 | 39,100 | 0 | 428 | 1,762 | 2,502 | 0 | 1,370 | 3,002 | 3,742 |
| 39,100 | 39,150 | 0 | 420 | 1,751 | 2,491 | 0 | 1,362 | 2,992 | 3,732 |
| 39,150 | 39,200 | 0 | 412 | 1,741 | 2,481 | 0 | 1,354 | 2,981 | 3,721 |
| 39,200 | 39,250 | 0 | 404 | 1,730 | 2,470 | 0 | 1,346 | 2,971 | 3,711 |
| 39,250 | 39,300 | 0 | 396 | 1,720 | 2,460 | 0 | 1,338 | 2,960 | 3,700 |
| 39,300 | 39,350 | 0 | 388 | 1,709 | 2,449 | 0 | 1,330 | 2,949 | 3,689 |
| 39,350 | 39,400 | 0 | 380 | 1,699 | 2,439 | 0 | 1,322 | 2,939 | 3,679 |
| 39,400 | 39,450 | 0 | 372 | 1,688 | 2,428 | 0 | 1,314 | 2,928 | 3,668 |
| 39,450 | 39,500 | 0 | 364 | 1,677 | 2,417 | 0 | 1,306 | 2,918 | 3,658 |
| 39,500 | 39,550 | 0 | 356 | 1,667 | 2,407 | 0 | 1,298 | 2,907 | 3,647 |
| 39,550 | 39,600 | 0 | 348 | 1,656 | 2,396 | 0 | 1,290 | 2,897 | 3,637 |
| 39,600 | 39,650 | 0 | 340 | 1,646 | 2,386 | 0 | 1,282 | 2,886 | 3,626 |
| 39,650 | 39,700 | 0 | 332 | 1,635 | 2,375 | 0 | 1,274 | 2,876 | 3,616 |
| 39,700 | 39,750 | 0 | 324 | 1,625 | 2,365 | 0 | 1,266 | 2,865 | 3,605 |
| 39,750 | 39,800 | 0 | 316 | 1,614 | 2,354 | 0 | 1,258 | 2,855 | 3,595 |
| 39,800 | 39,850 | 0 | 308 | 1,604 | 2,344 | 0 | 1,250 | 2,844 | 3,584 |
| 39,850 | 39,900 | 0 | 301 | 1,593 | 2,333 | 0 | 1,242 | 2,834 | 3,574 |
| 39,900 | 39,950 | 0 | 293 | 1,583 | 2,323 | 0 | 1,234 | 2,823 | 3,563 |
| 39,950 | 40,000 | 0 | 285 | 1,572 | 2,312 | 0 | 1,226 | 2,813 | 3,553 |

*(Continued)*

**Earned Income Credit (EIC) Table** - *Continued* **(Caution.** This is **not** a tax table.)

| If the amount you are looking up from the worksheet is– | | And your filing status is– Single, head of household, or qualifying widow(er) and you have– | | | | Married filing jointly and you have– | | | |
|---|---|---|---|---|---|---|---|---|---|
| | | 0 | 1 | 2 | 3 | 0 | 1 | 2 | 3 |
| At least | But less than | Your credit is– | | | | Your credit is– | | | |
| 40,000 | 40,050 | 0 | 277 | 1,562 | 2,302 | 0 | 1,218 | 2,802 | 3,542 |
| 40,050 | 40,100 | 0 | 269 | 1,551 | 2,291 | 0 | 1,210 | 2,792 | 3,532 |
| 40,100 | 40,150 | 0 | 261 | 1,541 | 2,281 | 0 | 1,202 | 2,781 | 3,521 |
| 40,150 | 40,200 | 0 | 253 | 1,530 | 2,270 | 0 | 1,194 | 2,770 | 3,510 |
| 40,200 | 40,250 | 0 | 245 | 1,520 | 2,260 | 0 | 1,186 | 2,760 | 3,500 |
| 40,250 | 40,300 | 0 | 237 | 1,509 | 2,249 | 0 | 1,178 | 2,749 | 3,489 |
| 40,300 | 40,350 | 0 | 229 | 1,498 | 2,238 | 0 | 1,170 | 2,739 | 3,479 |
| 40,350 | 40,400 | 0 | 221 | 1,488 | 2,228 | 0 | 1,162 | 2,728 | 3,468 |
| 40,400 | 40,450 | 0 | 213 | 1,477 | 2,217 | 0 | 1,154 | 2,718 | 3,458 |
| 40,450 | 40,500 | 0 | 205 | 1,467 | 2,207 | 0 | 1,146 | 2,707 | 3,447 |
| 40,500 | 40,550 | 0 | 197 | 1,456 | 2,196 | 0 | 1,138 | 2,697 | 3,437 |
| 40,550 | 40,600 | 0 | 189 | 1,446 | 2,186 | 0 | 1,130 | 2,686 | 3,426 |
| 40,600 | 40,650 | 0 | 181 | 1,435 | 2,175 | 0 | 1,122 | 2,676 | 3,416 |
| 40,650 | 40,700 | 0 | 173 | 1,425 | 2,165 | 0 | 1,114 | 2,665 | 3,405 |
| 40,700 | 40,750 | 0 | 165 | 1,414 | 2,154 | 0 | 1,106 | 2,655 | 3,395 |
| 40,750 | 40,800 | 0 | 157 | 1,404 | 2,144 | 0 | 1,098 | 2,644 | 3,384 |
| 40,800 | 40,850 | 0 | 149 | 1,393 | 2,133 | 0 | 1,090 | 2,634 | 3,374 |
| 40,850 | 40,900 | 0 | 141 | 1,383 | 2,123 | 0 | 1,082 | 2,623 | 3,363 |
| 40,900 | 40,950 | 0 | 133 | 1,372 | 2,112 | 0 | 1,074 | 2,613 | 3,353 |
| 40,950 | 41,000 | 0 | 125 | 1,362 | 2,102 | 0 | 1,066 | 2,602 | 3,342 |
| 41,000 | 41,050 | 0 | 117 | 1,351 | 2,091 | 0 | 1,058 | 2,591 | 3,331 |
| 41,050 | 41,100 | 0 | 109 | 1,341 | 2,081 | 0 | 1,050 | 2,581 | 3,321 |
| 41,100 | 41,150 | 0 | 101 | 1,330 | 2,070 | 0 | 1,042 | 2,570 | 3,310 |
| 41,150 | 41,200 | 0 | 93 | 1,319 | 2,059 | 0 | 1,034 | 2,560 | 3,300 |
| 41,200 | 41,250 | 0 | 85 | 1,309 | 2,049 | 0 | 1,026 | 2,549 | 3,289 |
| 41,250 | 41,300 | 0 | 77 | 1,298 | 2,038 | 0 | 1,018 | 2,539 | 3,279 |
| 41,300 | 41,350 | 0 | 69 | 1,288 | 2,028 | 0 | 1,010 | 2,528 | 3,268 |
| 41,350 | 41,400 | 0 | 61 | 1,277 | 2,017 | 0 | 1,002 | 2,518 | 3,258 |
| 41,400 | 41,450 | 0 | 53 | 1,267 | 2,007 | 0 | 994 | 2,507 | 3,247 |
| 41,450 | 41,500 | 0 | 45 | 1,256 | 1,996 | 0 | 986 | 2,497 | 3,237 |
| 41,500 | 41,550 | 0 | 37 | 1,246 | 1,986 | 0 | 978 | 2,486 | 3,226 |
| 41,550 | 41,600 | 0 | 29 | 1,235 | 1,975 | 0 | 970 | 2,476 | 3,216 |
| 41,600 | 41,650 | 0 | 21 | 1,225 | 1,965 | 0 | 962 | 2,465 | 3,205 |
| 41,650 | 41,700 | 0 | 13 | 1,214 | 1,954 | 0 | 954 | 2,455 | 3,195 |
| 41,700 | 41,750 | 0 | 5 | 1,204 | 1,944 | 0 | 946 | 2,444 | 3,184 |
| 41,750 | 41,800 | 0 | * | 1,193 | 1,933 | 0 | 938 | 2,434 | 3,174 |
| 41,800 | 41,850 | 0 | 0 | 1,183 | 1,923 | 0 | 930 | 2,423 | 3,163 |
| 41,850 | 41,900 | 0 | 0 | 1,172 | 1,912 | 0 | 922 | 2,412 | 3,152 |
| 41,900 | 41,950 | 0 | 0 | 1,161 | 1,901 | 0 | 914 | 2,402 | 3,142 |
| 41,950 | 42,000 | 0 | 0 | 1,151 | 1,891 | 0 | 906 | 2,391 | 3,131 |
| 42,000 | 42,050 | 0 | 0 | 1,140 | 1,880 | 0 | 898 | 2,381 | 3,121 |
| 42,050 | 42,100 | 0 | 0 | 1,130 | 1,870 | 0 | 890 | 2,370 | 3,110 |
| 42,100 | 42,150 | 0 | 0 | 1,119 | 1,859 | 0 | 882 | 2,360 | 3,100 |
| 42,150 | 42,200 | 0 | 0 | 1,109 | 1,849 | 0 | 874 | 2,349 | 3,089 |
| 42,200 | 42,250 | 0 | 0 | 1,098 | 1,838 | 0 | 866 | 2,339 | 3,079 |
| 42,250 | 42,300 | 0 | 0 | 1,088 | 1,828 | 0 | 858 | 2,328 | 3,068 |
| 42,300 | 42,350 | 0 | 0 | 1,077 | 1,817 | 0 | 850 | 2,318 | 3,058 |
| 42,350 | 42,400 | 0 | 0 | 1,067 | 1,807 | 0 | 842 | 2,307 | 3,047 |
| 42,400 | 42,450 | 0 | 0 | 1,056 | 1,796 | 0 | 834 | 2,297 | 3,037 |
| 42,450 | 42,500 | 0 | 0 | 1,046 | 1,786 | 0 | 826 | 2,286 | 3,026 |
| 42,500 | 42,550 | 0 | 0 | 1,035 | 1,775 | 0 | 818 | 2,276 | 3,016 |
| 42,550 | 42,600 | 0 | 0 | 1,025 | 1,765 | 0 | 810 | 2,265 | 3,005 |
| 42,600 | 42,650 | 0 | 0 | 1,014 | 1,754 | 0 | 802 | 2,255 | 2,995 |
| 42,650 | 42,700 | 0 | 0 | 1,004 | 1,744 | 0 | 794 | 2,244 | 2,984 |
| 42,700 | 42,750 | 0 | 0 | 993 | 1,733 | 0 | 786 | 2,233 | 2,973 |
| 42,750 | 42,800 | 0 | 0 | 982 | 1,722 | 0 | 778 | 2,223 | 2,963 |
| 42,800 | 42,850 | 0 | 0 | 972 | 1,712 | 0 | 770 | 2,212 | 2,952 |
| 42,850 | 42,900 | 0 | 0 | 961 | 1,701 | 0 | 762 | 2,202 | 2,942 |
| 42,900 | 42,950 | 0 | 0 | 951 | 1,691 | 0 | 754 | 2,191 | 2,931 |
| 42,950 | 43,000 | 0 | 0 | 940 | 1,680 | 0 | 746 | 2,181 | 2,921 |
| 43,000 | 43,050 | 0 | 0 | 930 | 1,670 | 0 | 738 | 2,170 | 2,910 |
| 43,050 | 43,100 | 0 | 0 | 919 | 1,659 | 0 | 730 | 2,160 | 2,900 |
| 43,100 | 43,150 | 0 | 0 | 909 | 1,649 | 0 | 722 | 2,149 | 2,889 |
| 43,150 | 43,200 | 0 | 0 | 898 | 1,638 | 0 | 714 | 2,139 | 2,879 |

| If the amount you are looking up from the worksheet is– | | And your filing status is– Single, head of household, or qualifying widow(er) and you have– | | | | Married filing jointly and you have– | | | |
|---|---|---|---|---|---|---|---|---|---|
| | | 0 | 1 | 2 | 3 | 0 | 1 | 2 | 3 |
| At least | But less than | Your credit is– | | | | Your credit is– | | | |
| 43,200 | 43,250 | 0 | 0 | 888 | 1,628 | 0 | 706 | 2,128 | 2,868 |
| 43,250 | 43,300 | 0 | 0 | 877 | 1,617 | 0 | 698 | 2,118 | 2,858 |
| 43,300 | 43,350 | 0 | 0 | 867 | 1,607 | 0 | 690 | 2,107 | 2,847 |
| 43,350 | 43,400 | 0 | 0 | 856 | 1,596 | 0 | 682 | 2,097 | 2,837 |
| 43,400 | 43,450 | 0 | 0 | 846 | 1,586 | 0 | 674 | 2,086 | 2,826 |
| 43,450 | 43,500 | 0 | 0 | 835 | 1,575 | 0 | 666 | 2,075 | 2,815 |
| 43,500 | 43,550 | 0 | 0 | 825 | 1,565 | 0 | 658 | 2,065 | 2,805 |
| 43,550 | 43,600 | 0 | 0 | 814 | 1,554 | 0 | 650 | 2,054 | 2,794 |
| 43,600 | 43,650 | 0 | 0 | 803 | 1,543 | 0 | 642 | 2,044 | 2,784 |
| 43,650 | 43,700 | 0 | 0 | 793 | 1,533 | 0 | 634 | 2,033 | 2,773 |
| 43,700 | 43,750 | 0 | 0 | 782 | 1,522 | 0 | 627 | 2,023 | 2,763 |
| 43,750 | 43,800 | 0 | 0 | 772 | 1,512 | 0 | 619 | 2,012 | 2,752 |
| 43,800 | 43,850 | 0 | 0 | 761 | 1,501 | 0 | 611 | 2,002 | 2,742 |
| 43,850 | 43,900 | 0 | 0 | 751 | 1,491 | 0 | 603 | 1,991 | 2,731 |
| 43,900 | 43,950 | 0 | 0 | 740 | 1,480 | 0 | 595 | 1,981 | 2,721 |
| 43,950 | 44,000 | 0 | 0 | 730 | 1,470 | 0 | 587 | 1,970 | 2,710 |
| 44,000 | 44,050 | 0 | 0 | 719 | 1,459 | 0 | 579 | 1,960 | 2,700 |
| 44,050 | 44,100 | 0 | 0 | 709 | 1,449 | 0 | 571 | 1,949 | 2,689 |
| 44,100 | 44,150 | 0 | 0 | 698 | 1,438 | 0 | 563 | 1,939 | 2,679 |
| 44,150 | 44,200 | 0 | 0 | 688 | 1,428 | 0 | 555 | 1,928 | 2,668 |
| 44,200 | 44,250 | 0 | 0 | 677 | 1,417 | 0 | 547 | 1,918 | 2,658 |
| 44,250 | 44,300 | 0 | 0 | 667 | 1,407 | 0 | 539 | 1,907 | 2,647 |
| 44,300 | 44,350 | 0 | 0 | 656 | 1,396 | 0 | 531 | 1,896 | 2,636 |
| 44,350 | 44,400 | 0 | 0 | 646 | 1,386 | 0 | 523 | 1,886 | 2,626 |
| 44,400 | 44,450 | 0 | 0 | 635 | 1,375 | 0 | 515 | 1,875 | 2,615 |
| 44,450 | 44,500 | 0 | 0 | 624 | 1,364 | 0 | 507 | 1,865 | 2,605 |
| 44,500 | 44,550 | 0 | 0 | 614 | 1,354 | 0 | 499 | 1,854 | 2,594 |
| 44,550 | 44,600 | 0 | 0 | 603 | 1,343 | 0 | 491 | 1,844 | 2,584 |
| 44,600 | 44,650 | 0 | 0 | 593 | 1,333 | 0 | 483 | 1,833 | 2,573 |
| 44,650 | 44,700 | 0 | 0 | 582 | 1,322 | 0 | 475 | 1,823 | 2,563 |
| 44,700 | 44,750 | 0 | 0 | 572 | 1,312 | 0 | 467 | 1,812 | 2,552 |
| 44,750 | 44,800 | 0 | 0 | 561 | 1,301 | 0 | 459 | 1,802 | 2,542 |
| 44,800 | 44,850 | 0 | 0 | 551 | 1,291 | 0 | 451 | 1,791 | 2,531 |
| 44,850 | 44,900 | 0 | 0 | 540 | 1,280 | 0 | 443 | 1,781 | 2,521 |
| 44,900 | 44,950 | 0 | 0 | 530 | 1,270 | 0 | 435 | 1,770 | 2,510 |
| 44,950 | 45,000 | 0 | 0 | 519 | 1,259 | 0 | 427 | 1,760 | 2,500 |
| 45,000 | 45,050 | 0 | 0 | 509 | 1,249 | 0 | 419 | 1,749 | 2,489 |
| 45,050 | 45,100 | 0 | 0 | 498 | 1,238 | 0 | 411 | 1,739 | 2,479 |
| 45,100 | 45,150 | 0 | 0 | 488 | 1,228 | 0 | 403 | 1,728 | 2,468 |
| 45,150 | 45,200 | 0 | 0 | 477 | 1,217 | 0 | 395 | 1,717 | 2,457 |
| 45,200 | 45,250 | 0 | 0 | 467 | 1,207 | 0 | 387 | 1,707 | 2,447 |
| 45,250 | 45,300 | 0 | 0 | 456 | 1,196 | 0 | 379 | 1,696 | 2,436 |
| 45,300 | 45,350 | 0 | 0 | 445 | 1,185 | 0 | 371 | 1,686 | 2,426 |
| 45,350 | 45,400 | 0 | 0 | 435 | 1,175 | 0 | 363 | 1,675 | 2,415 |
| 45,400 | 45,450 | 0 | 0 | 424 | 1,164 | 0 | 355 | 1,665 | 2,405 |
| 45,450 | 45,500 | 0 | 0 | 414 | 1,154 | 0 | 347 | 1,654 | 2,394 |
| 45,500 | 45,550 | 0 | 0 | 403 | 1,143 | 0 | 339 | 1,644 | 2,384 |
| 45,550 | 45,600 | 0 | 0 | 393 | 1,133 | 0 | 331 | 1,633 | 2,373 |
| 45,600 | 45,650 | 0 | 0 | 382 | 1,122 | 0 | 323 | 1,623 | 2,363 |
| 45,650 | 45,700 | 0 | 0 | 372 | 1,112 | 0 | 315 | 1,612 | 2,352 |
| 45,700 | 45,750 | 0 | 0 | 361 | 1,101 | 0 | 307 | 1,602 | 2,342 |
| 45,750 | 45,800 | 0 | 0 | 351 | 1,091 | 0 | 299 | 1,591 | 2,331 |
| 45,800 | 45,850 | 0 | 0 | 340 | 1,080 | 0 | 291 | 1,581 | 2,321 |
| 45,850 | 45,900 | 0 | 0 | 330 | 1,070 | 0 | 283 | 1,570 | 2,310 |
| 45,900 | 45,950 | 0 | 0 | 319 | 1,059 | 0 | 275 | 1,560 | 2,300 |
| 45,950 | 46,000 | 0 | 0 | 309 | 1,049 | 0 | 267 | 1,549 | 2,289 |
| 46,000 | 46,050 | 0 | 0 | 298 | 1,038 | 0 | 259 | 1,538 | 2,278 |
| 46,050 | 46,100 | 0 | 0 | 288 | 1,028 | 0 | 251 | 1,528 | 2,268 |
| 46,100 | 46,150 | 0 | 0 | 277 | 1,017 | 0 | 243 | 1,517 | 2,257 |
| 46,150 | 46,200 | 0 | 0 | 266 | 1,006 | 0 | 235 | 1,507 | 2,247 |
| 46,200 | 46,250 | 0 | 0 | 256 | 996 | 0 | 227 | 1,496 | 2,236 |
| 46,250 | 46,300 | 0 | 0 | 245 | 985 | 0 | 219 | 1,486 | 2,226 |
| 46,300 | 46,350 | 0 | 0 | 235 | 975 | 0 | 211 | 1,475 | 2,215 |
| 46,350 | 46,400 | 0 | 0 | 224 | 964 | 0 | 203 | 1,465 | 2,205 |

* If the amount you are looking up from the worksheet is at least $41,750 but less than $41,756, and you have one qualifying child, your credit is $0. If the amount you are looking up from the worksheet is $41,756 or more, and you have one qualifying child, you can't take the credit.

*(Continued)*

**Earned Income Credit (EIC) Table** - *Continued* (**Caution.** This is **not** a tax table.)

| If the amount you are looking up from the worksheet is– | | And your filing status is– Single, head of household, or qualifying widow(er) and you have– | | | | Married filing jointly and you have– | | | |
|---|---|---|---|---|---|---|---|---|---|
| | | 0 | 1 | 2 | 3 | 0 | 1 | 2 | 3 |
| At least | But less than | Your credit is– | | | | Your credit is– | | | |
| 46,400 | 46,450 | 0 | 0 | 214 | 954 | 0 | 195 | 1,454 | 2,194 |
| 46,450 | 46,500 | 0 | 0 | 203 | 943 | 0 | 187 | 1,444 | 2,184 |
| 46,500 | 46,550 | 0 | 0 | 193 | 933 | 0 | 179 | 1,433 | 2,173 |
| 46,550 | 46,600 | 0 | 0 | 182 | 922 | 0 | 171 | 1,423 | 2,163 |
| 46,600 | 46,650 | 0 | 0 | 172 | 912 | 0 | 163 | 1,412 | 2,152 |
| 46,650 | 46,700 | 0 | 0 | 161 | 901 | 0 | 155 | 1,402 | 2,142 |
| 46,700 | 46,750 | 0 | 0 | 151 | 891 | 0 | 147 | 1,391 | 2,131 |
| 46,750 | 46,800 | 0 | 0 | 140 | 880 | 0 | 139 | 1,381 | 2,121 |
| 46,800 | 46,850 | 0 | 0 | 130 | 870 | 0 | 131 | 1,370 | 2,110 |
| 46,850 | 46,900 | 0 | 0 | 119 | 859 | 0 | 123 | 1,359 | 2,099 |
| 46,900 | 46,950 | 0 | 0 | 108 | 848 | 0 | 115 | 1,349 | 2,089 |
| 46,950 | 47,000 | 0 | 0 | 98 | 838 | 0 | 107 | 1,338 | 2,078 |
| 47,000 | 47,050 | 0 | 0 | 87 | 827 | 0 | 99 | 1,328 | 2,068 |
| 47,050 | 47,100 | 0 | 0 | 77 | 817 | 0 | 91 | 1,317 | 2,057 |
| 47,100 | 47,150 | 0 | 0 | 66 | 806 | 0 | 83 | 1,307 | 2,047 |
| 47,150 | 47,200 | 0 | 0 | 56 | 796 | 0 | 75 | 1,296 | 2,036 |
| 47,200 | 47,250 | 0 | 0 | 45 | 785 | 0 | 67 | 1,286 | 2,026 |
| 47,250 | 47,300 | 0 | 0 | 35 | 775 | 0 | 59 | 1,275 | 2,015 |
| 47,300 | 47,350 | 0 | 0 | 24 | 764 | 0 | 51 | 1,265 | 2,005 |
| 47,350 | 47,400 | 0 | 0 | 14 | 754 | 0 | 43 | 1,254 | 1,994 |
| 47,400 | 47,450 | 0 | 0 | * | 743 | 0 | 35 | 1,244 | 1,984 |
| 47,450 | 47,500 | 0 | 0 | 0 | 733 | 0 | 27 | 1,233 | 1,973 |
| 47,500 | 47,550 | 0 | 0 | 0 | 722 | 0 | 19 | 1,223 | 1,963 |
| 47,550 | 47,600 | 0 | 0 | 0 | 712 | 0 | 11 | 1,212 | 1,952 |
| 47,600 | 47,650 | 0 | 0 | 0 | 701 | 0 | ** | 1,202 | 1,942 |
| 47,650 | 47,700 | 0 | 0 | 0 | 691 | 0 | 0 | 1,191 | 1,931 |
| 47,700 | 47,750 | 0 | 0 | 0 | 680 | 0 | 0 | 1,180 | 1,920 |
| 47,750 | 47,800 | 0 | 0 | 0 | 669 | 0 | 0 | 1,170 | 1,910 |
| 47,800 | 47,850 | 0 | 0 | 0 | 659 | 0 | 0 | 1,159 | 1,899 |
| 47,850 | 47,900 | 0 | 0 | 0 | 648 | 0 | 0 | 1,149 | 1,889 |
| 47,900 | 47,950 | 0 | 0 | 0 | 638 | 0 | 0 | 1,138 | 1,878 |
| 47,950 | 48,000 | 0 | 0 | 0 | 627 | 0 | 0 | 1,128 | 1,868 |
| 48,000 | 48,050 | 0 | 0 | 0 | 617 | 0 | 0 | 1,117 | 1,857 |
| 48,050 | 48,100 | 0 | 0 | 0 | 606 | 0 | 0 | 1,107 | 1,847 |
| 48,100 | 48,150 | 0 | 0 | 0 | 596 | 0 | 0 | 1,096 | 1,836 |
| 48,150 | 48,200 | 0 | 0 | 0 | 585 | 0 | 0 | 1,086 | 1,826 |
| 48,200 | 48,250 | 0 | 0 | 0 | 575 | 0 | 0 | 1,075 | 1,815 |
| 48,250 | 48,300 | 0 | 0 | 0 | 564 | 0 | 0 | 1,065 | 1,805 |
| 48,300 | 48,350 | 0 | 0 | 0 | 554 | 0 | 0 | 1,054 | 1,794 |
| 48,350 | 48,400 | 0 | 0 | 0 | 543 | 0 | 0 | 1,044 | 1,784 |
| 48,400 | 48,450 | 0 | 0 | 0 | 533 | 0 | 0 | 1,033 | 1,773 |
| 48,450 | 48,500 | 0 | 0 | 0 | 522 | 0 | 0 | 1,022 | 1,762 |
| 48,500 | 48,550 | 0 | 0 | 0 | 512 | 0 | 0 | 1,012 | 1,752 |
| 48,550 | 48,600 | 0 | 0 | 0 | 501 | 0 | 0 | 1,001 | 1,741 |
| 48,600 | 48,650 | 0 | 0 | 0 | 490 | 0 | 0 | 991 | 1,731 |
| 48,650 | 48,700 | 0 | 0 | 0 | 480 | 0 | 0 | 980 | 1,720 |
| 48,700 | 48,750 | 0 | 0 | 0 | 469 | 0 | 0 | 970 | 1,710 |
| 48,750 | 48,800 | 0 | 0 | 0 | 459 | 0 | 0 | 959 | 1,699 |
| 48,800 | 48,850 | 0 | 0 | 0 | 448 | 0 | 0 | 949 | 1,689 |
| 48,850 | 48,900 | 0 | 0 | 0 | 438 | 0 | 0 | 938 | 1,678 |
| 48,900 | 48,950 | 0 | 0 | 0 | 427 | 0 | 0 | 928 | 1,668 |
| 48,950 | 49,000 | 0 | 0 | 0 | 417 | 0 | 0 | 917 | 1,657 |
| 49,000 | 49,050 | 0 | 0 | 0 | 406 | 0 | 0 | 907 | 1,647 |
| 49,050 | 49,100 | 0 | 0 | 0 | 396 | 0 | 0 | 896 | 1,636 |
| 49,100 | 49,150 | 0 | 0 | 0 | 385 | 0 | 0 | 886 | 1,626 |
| 49,150 | 49,200 | 0 | 0 | 0 | 375 | 0 | 0 | 875 | 1,615 |

| If the amount you are looking up from the worksheet is– | | And your filing status is– Single, head of household, or qualifying widow(er) and you have– | | | | Married filing jointly and you have– | | | |
|---|---|---|---|---|---|---|---|---|---|
| | | 0 | 1 | 2 | 3 | 0 | 1 | 2 | 3 |
| At least | But less than | Your credit is– | | | | Your credit is– | | | |
| 49,200 | 49,250 | 0 | 0 | 0 | 364 | 0 | 0 | 865 | 1,605 |
| 49,250 | 49,300 | 0 | 0 | 0 | 354 | 0 | 0 | 854 | 1,594 |
| 49,300 | 49,350 | 0 | 0 | 0 | 343 | 0 | 0 | 843 | 1,583 |
| 49,350 | 49,400 | 0 | 0 | 0 | 333 | 0 | 0 | 833 | 1,573 |
| 49,400 | 49,450 | 0 | 0 | 0 | 322 | 0 | 0 | 822 | 1,562 |
| 49,450 | 49,500 | 0 | 0 | 0 | 311 | 0 | 0 | 812 | 1,552 |
| 49,500 | 49,550 | 0 | 0 | 0 | 301 | 0 | 0 | 801 | 1,541 |
| 49,550 | 49,600 | 0 | 0 | 0 | 290 | 0 | 0 | 791 | 1,531 |
| 49,600 | 49,650 | 0 | 0 | 0 | 280 | 0 | 0 | 780 | 1,520 |
| 49,650 | 49,700 | 0 | 0 | 0 | 269 | 0 | 0 | 770 | 1,510 |
| 49,700 | 49,750 | 0 | 0 | 0 | 259 | 0 | 0 | 759 | 1,499 |
| 49,750 | 49,800 | 0 | 0 | 0 | 248 | 0 | 0 | 749 | 1,489 |
| 49,800 | 49,850 | 0 | 0 | 0 | 238 | 0 | 0 | 738 | 1,478 |
| 49,850 | 49,900 | 0 | 0 | 0 | 227 | 0 | 0 | 728 | 1,468 |
| 49,900 | 49,950 | 0 | 0 | 0 | 217 | 0 | 0 | 717 | 1,457 |
| 49,950 | 50,000 | 0 | 0 | 0 | 206 | 0 | 0 | 707 | 1,447 |
| 50,000 | 50,050 | 0 | 0 | 0 | 196 | 0 | 0 | 696 | 1,436 |
| 50,050 | 50,100 | 0 | 0 | 0 | 185 | 0 | 0 | 686 | 1,426 |
| 50,100 | 50,150 | 0 | 0 | 0 | 175 | 0 | 0 | 675 | 1,415 |
| 50,150 | 50,200 | 0 | 0 | 0 | 164 | 0 | 0 | 664 | 1,404 |
| 50,200 | 50,250 | 0 | 0 | 0 | 154 | 0 | 0 | 654 | 1,394 |
| 50,250 | 50,300 | 0 | 0 | 0 | 143 | 0 | 0 | 643 | 1,383 |
| 50,300 | 50,350 | 0 | 0 | 0 | 132 | 0 | 0 | 633 | 1,373 |
| 50,350 | 50,400 | 0 | 0 | 0 | 122 | 0 | 0 | 622 | 1,362 |
| 50,400 | 50,450 | 0 | 0 | 0 | 111 | 0 | 0 | 612 | 1,352 |
| 50,450 | 50,500 | 0 | 0 | 0 | 101 | 0 | 0 | 601 | 1,341 |
| 50,500 | 50,550 | 0 | 0 | 0 | 90 | 0 | 0 | 591 | 1,331 |
| 50,550 | 50,600 | 0 | 0 | 0 | 80 | 0 | 0 | 580 | 1,320 |
| 50,600 | 50,650 | 0 | 0 | 0 | 69 | 0 | 0 | 570 | 1,310 |
| 50,650 | 50,700 | 0 | 0 | 0 | 59 | 0 | 0 | 559 | 1,299 |
| 50,700 | 50,750 | 0 | 0 | 0 | 48 | 0 | 0 | 549 | 1,289 |
| 50,750 | 50,800 | 0 | 0 | 0 | 38 | 0 | 0 | 538 | 1,278 |
| 50,800 | 50,850 | 0 | 0 | 0 | 27 | 0 | 0 | 528 | 1,268 |
| 50,850 | 50,900 | 0 | 0 | 0 | 17 | 0 | 0 | 517 | 1,257 |
| 50,900 | 50,950 | 0 | 0 | 0 | 6 | 0 | 0 | 507 | 1,247 |
| 50,950 | 51,000 | 0 | 0 | 0 | *** | 0 | 0 | 496 | 1,236 |
| 51,000 | 51,050 | 0 | 0 | 0 | 0 | 0 | 0 | 485 | 1,225 |
| 51,050 | 51,100 | 0 | 0 | 0 | 0 | 0 | 0 | 475 | 1,215 |
| 51,100 | 51,150 | 0 | 0 | 0 | 0 | 0 | 0 | 464 | 1,204 |
| 51,150 | 51,200 | 0 | 0 | 0 | 0 | 0 | 0 | 454 | 1,194 |
| 51,200 | 51,250 | 0 | 0 | 0 | 0 | 0 | 0 | 443 | 1,183 |
| 51,250 | 51,300 | 0 | 0 | 0 | 0 | 0 | 0 | 433 | 1,173 |
| 51,300 | 51,350 | 0 | 0 | 0 | 0 | 0 | 0 | 422 | 1,162 |
| 51,350 | 51,400 | 0 | 0 | 0 | 0 | 0 | 0 | 412 | 1,152 |
| 51,400 | 51,450 | 0 | 0 | 0 | 0 | 0 | 0 | 401 | 1,141 |
| 51,450 | 51,500 | 0 | 0 | 0 | 0 | 0 | 0 | 391 | 1,131 |
| 51,500 | 51,550 | 0 | 0 | 0 | 0 | 0 | 0 | 380 | 1,120 |
| 51,550 | 51,600 | 0 | 0 | 0 | 0 | 0 | 0 | 370 | 1,110 |
| 51,600 | 51,650 | 0 | 0 | 0 | 0 | 0 | 0 | 359 | 1,099 |
| 51,650 | 51,700 | 0 | 0 | 0 | 0 | 0 | 0 | 349 | 1,089 |
| 51,700 | 51,750 | 0 | 0 | 0 | 0 | 0 | 0 | 338 | 1,078 |
| 51,750 | 51,800 | 0 | 0 | 0 | 0 | 0 | 0 | 328 | 1,068 |
| 51,800 | 51,850 | 0 | 0 | 0 | 0 | 0 | 0 | 317 | 1,057 |
| 51,850 | 51,900 | 0 | 0 | 0 | 0 | 0 | 0 | 306 | 1,046 |
| 51,900 | 51,950 | 0 | 0 | 0 | 0 | 0 | 0 | 296 | 1,036 |
| 51,950 | 52,000 | 0 | 0 | 0 | 0 | 0 | 0 | 285 | 1,025 |

* If the amount you are looking up from the worksheet is at least $47,400 but less than $47,440, and you have two qualifying children, your credit is $4.
If the amount you are looking up from the worksheet is $47,440 or more, and you have two qualifying children, you can't take the credit.

** If the amount you are looking up from the worksheet is at least $47,600 but less than $476,46, and you have one qualifying child, your credit is $4.
If the amount you are looking up from the worksheet is $47,646 or more, and you have one qualifying child, you can't take the credit.

*** If the amount you are looking up from the worksheet is at least $50,950 but less than $50,954, and you have three qualifying children, your credit is $0.
If the amount you are looking up from the worksheet is $50,954 or more, and you have three qualifying children, you can't take the credit.

*(Continued)*

**Earned Income Credit (EIC) Table** - *Continued* (**Caution.** This is **not** a tax table.)

| If the amount you are looking up from the worksheet is– | | And your filing status is– Single, head of household, or qualifying widow(er) and you have– | | | | Married filing jointly and you have– | | | |
|---|---|---|---|---|---|---|---|---|---|
| | | 0 | 1 | 2 | 3 | 0 | 1 | 2 | 3 |
| At least | But less than | Your credit is– | | | | Your credit is– | | | |
| 52,000 | 52,050 | 0 | 0 | 0 | 0 | 0 | 0 | 275 | 1,015 |
| 52,050 | 52,100 | 0 | 0 | 0 | 0 | 0 | 0 | 264 | 1,004 |
| 52,100 | 52,150 | 0 | 0 | 0 | 0 | 0 | 0 | 254 | 994 |
| 52,150 | 52,200 | 0 | 0 | 0 | 0 | 0 | 0 | 243 | 983 |
| 52,200 | 52,250 | 0 | 0 | 0 | 0 | 0 | 0 | 233 | 973 |
| 52,250 | 52,300 | 0 | 0 | 0 | 0 | 0 | 0 | 222 | 962 |
| 52,300 | 52,350 | 0 | 0 | 0 | 0 | 0 | 0 | 212 | 952 |
| 52,350 | 52,400 | 0 | 0 | 0 | 0 | 0 | 0 | 201 | 941 |
| 52,400 | 52,450 | 0 | 0 | 0 | 0 | 0 | 0 | 191 | 931 |
| 52,450 | 52,500 | 0 | 0 | 0 | 0 | 0 | 0 | 180 | 920 |
| 52,500 | 52,550 | 0 | 0 | 0 | 0 | 0 | 0 | 170 | 910 |
| 52,550 | 52,600 | 0 | 0 | 0 | 0 | 0 | 0 | 159 | 899 |
| 52,600 | 52,650 | 0 | 0 | 0 | 0 | 0 | 0 | 149 | 889 |
| 52,650 | 52,700 | 0 | 0 | 0 | 0 | 0 | 0 | 138 | 878 |
| 52,700 | 52,750 | 0 | 0 | 0 | 0 | 0 | 0 | 127 | 867 |
| 52,750 | 52,800 | 0 | 0 | 0 | 0 | 0 | 0 | 117 | 857 |
| 52,800 | 52,850 | 0 | 0 | 0 | 0 | 0 | 0 | 106 | 846 |
| 52,850 | 52,900 | 0 | 0 | 0 | 0 | 0 | 0 | 96 | 836 |
| 52,900 | 52,950 | 0 | 0 | 0 | 0 | 0 | 0 | 85 | 825 |
| 52,950 | 53,000 | 0 | 0 | 0 | 0 | 0 | 0 | 75 | 815 |
| 53,000 | 53,050 | 0 | 0 | 0 | 0 | 0 | 0 | 64 | 804 |
| 53,050 | 53,100 | 0 | 0 | 0 | 0 | 0 | 0 | 54 | 794 |
| 53,100 | 53,150 | 0 | 0 | 0 | 0 | 0 | 0 | 43 | 783 |
| 53,150 | 53,200 | 0 | 0 | 0 | 0 | 0 | 0 | 33 | 773 |
| 53,200 | 53,250 | 0 | 0 | 0 | 0 | 0 | 0 | 22 | 762 |
| 53,250 | 53,300 | 0 | 0 | 0 | 0 | 0 | 0 | 12 | 752 |
| 53,300 | 53,350 | 0 | 0 | 0 | 0 | 0 | 0 | * | 741 |
| 53,350 | 53,400 | 0 | 0 | 0 | 0 | 0 | 0 | 0 | 731 |
| 53,400 | 53,450 | 0 | 0 | 0 | 0 | 0 | 0 | 0 | 720 |
| 53,450 | 53,500 | 0 | 0 | 0 | 0 | 0 | 0 | 0 | 709 |
| 53,500 | 53,550 | 0 | 0 | 0 | 0 | 0 | 0 | 0 | 699 |
| 53,550 | 53,600 | 0 | 0 | 0 | 0 | 0 | 0 | 0 | 688 |
| 53,600 | 53,650 | 0 | 0 | 0 | 0 | 0 | 0 | 0 | 678 |
| 53,650 | 53,700 | 0 | 0 | 0 | 0 | 0 | 0 | 0 | 667 |
| 53,700 | 53,750 | 0 | 0 | 0 | 0 | 0 | 0 | 0 | 657 |
| 53,750 | 53,800 | 0 | 0 | 0 | 0 | 0 | 0 | 0 | 646 |
| 53,800 | 53,850 | 0 | 0 | 0 | 0 | 0 | 0 | 0 | 636 |
| 53,850 | 53,900 | 0 | 0 | 0 | 0 | 0 | 0 | 0 | 625 |
| 53,900 | 53,950 | 0 | 0 | 0 | 0 | 0 | 0 | 0 | 615 |
| 53,950 | 54,000 | 0 | 0 | 0 | 0 | 0 | 0 | 0 | 604 |
| 54,000 | 54,050 | 0 | 0 | 0 | 0 | 0 | 0 | 0 | 594 |
| 54,050 | 54,100 | 0 | 0 | 0 | 0 | 0 | 0 | 0 | 583 |
| 54,100 | 54,150 | 0 | 0 | 0 | 0 | 0 | 0 | 0 | 573 |
| 54,150 | 54,200 | 0 | 0 | 0 | 0 | 0 | 0 | 0 | 562 |
| 54,200 | 54,250 | 0 | 0 | 0 | 0 | 0 | 0 | 0 | 552 |
| 54,250 | 54,300 | 0 | 0 | 0 | 0 | 0 | 0 | 0 | 541 |
| 54,300 | 54,350 | 0 | 0 | 0 | 0 | 0 | 0 | 0 | 530 |
| 54,350 | 54,400 | 0 | 0 | 0 | 0 | 0 | 0 | 0 | 520 |
| 54,400 | 54,450 | 0 | 0 | 0 | 0 | 0 | 0 | 0 | 509 |
| 54,450 | 54,500 | 0 | 0 | 0 | 0 | 0 | 0 | 0 | 499 |
| 54,500 | 54,550 | 0 | 0 | 0 | 0 | 0 | 0 | 0 | 488 |
| 54,550 | 54,600 | 0 | 0 | 0 | 0 | 0 | 0 | 0 | 478 |
| 54,600 | 54,650 | 0 | 0 | 0 | 0 | 0 | 0 | 0 | 467 |
| 54,650 | 54,700 | 0 | 0 | 0 | 0 | 0 | 0 | 0 | 457 |
| 54,700 | 54,750 | 0 | 0 | 0 | 0 | 0 | 0 | 0 | 446 |
| 54,750 | 54,800 | 0 | 0 | 0 | 0 | 0 | 0 | 0 | 436 |
| 54,800 | 54,850 | 0 | 0 | 0 | 0 | 0 | 0 | 0 | 425 |
| 54,850 | 54,900 | 0 | 0 | 0 | 0 | 0 | 0 | 0 | 415 |
| 54,900 | 54,950 | 0 | 0 | 0 | 0 | 0 | 0 | 0 | 404 |
| 54,950 | 55,000 | 0 | 0 | 0 | 0 | 0 | 0 | 0 | 394 |
| 55,000 | 55,050 | 0 | 0 | 0 | 0 | 0 | 0 | 0 | 383 |
| 55,050 | 55,100 | 0 | 0 | 0 | 0 | 0 | 0 | 0 | 373 |
| 55,100 | 55,150 | 0 | 0 | 0 | 0 | 0 | 0 | 0 | 362 |
| 55,150 | 55,200 | 0 | 0 | 0 | 0 | 0 | 0 | 0 | 351 |
| 55,200 | 55,250 | 0 | 0 | 0 | 0 | 0 | 0 | 0 | 341 |
| 55,250 | 55,300 | 0 | 0 | 0 | 0 | 0 | 0 | 0 | 330 |
| 55,300 | 55,350 | 0 | 0 | 0 | 0 | 0 | 0 | 0 | 320 |
| 55,350 | 55,400 | 0 | 0 | 0 | 0 | 0 | 0 | 0 | 309 |
| 55,400 | 55,450 | 0 | 0 | 0 | 0 | 0 | 0 | 0 | 299 |
| 55,450 | 55,500 | 0 | 0 | 0 | 0 | 0 | 0 | 0 | 288 |
| 55,500 | 55,550 | 0 | 0 | 0 | 0 | 0 | 0 | 0 | 278 |
| 55,550 | 55,600 | 0 | 0 | 0 | 0 | 0 | 0 | 0 | 267 |
| 55,600 | 55,650 | 0 | 0 | 0 | 0 | 0 | 0 | 0 | 257 |
| 55,650 | 55,700 | 0 | 0 | 0 | 0 | 0 | 0 | 0 | 246 |
| 55,700 | 55,750 | 0 | 0 | 0 | 0 | 0 | 0 | 0 | 236 |
| 55,750 | 55,800 | 0 | 0 | 0 | 0 | 0 | 0 | 0 | 225 |
| 55,800 | 55,850 | 0 | 0 | 0 | 0 | 0 | 0 | 0 | 215 |
| 55,850 | 55,900 | 0 | 0 | 0 | 0 | 0 | 0 | 0 | 204 |
| 55,900 | 55,950 | 0 | 0 | 0 | 0 | 0 | 0 | 0 | 194 |
| 55,950 | 56,000 | 0 | 0 | 0 | 0 | 0 | 0 | 0 | 183 |
| 56,000 | 56,050 | 0 | 0 | 0 | 0 | 0 | 0 | 0 | 172 |
| 56,050 | 56,100 | 0 | 0 | 0 | 0 | 0 | 0 | 0 | 162 |
| 56,100 | 56,150 | 0 | 0 | 0 | 0 | 0 | 0 | 0 | 151 |
| 56,150 | 56,200 | 0 | 0 | 0 | 0 | 0 | 0 | 0 | 141 |
| 56,200 | 56,250 | 0 | 0 | 0 | 0 | 0 | 0 | 0 | 130 |
| 56,250 | 56,300 | 0 | 0 | 0 | 0 | 0 | 0 | 0 | 120 |
| 56,300 | 56,350 | 0 | 0 | 0 | 0 | 0 | 0 | 0 | 109 |
| 56,350 | 56,400 | 0 | 0 | 0 | 0 | 0 | 0 | 0 | 99 |
| 56,400 | 56,450 | 0 | 0 | 0 | 0 | 0 | 0 | 0 | 88 |
| 56,450 | 56,500 | 0 | 0 | 0 | 0 | 0 | 0 | 0 | 78 |
| 56,500 | 56,550 | 0 | 0 | 0 | 0 | 0 | 0 | 0 | 67 |
| 56,550 | 56,600 | 0 | 0 | 0 | 0 | 0 | 0 | 0 | 57 |
| 56,600 | 56,650 | 0 | 0 | 0 | 0 | 0 | 0 | 0 | 46 |
| 56,650 | 56,700 | 0 | 0 | 0 | 0 | 0 | 0 | 0 | 36 |
| 56,700 | 56,750 | 0 | 0 | 0 | 0 | 0 | 0 | 0 | 25 |
| 56,750 | 56,800 | 0 | 0 | 0 | 0 | 0 | 0 | 0 | 15 |
| 56,800 | 56,844 | 0 | 0 | 0 | 0 | 0 | 0 | 0 | ** |

* If the amount you are looking up from the worksheet is at least $53,300 but less than $53,330, and you have two qualifying children, your credit is $3.
If the amount you are looking up from the worksheet is $53,330 or more, and you have two qualifying children, you can't take the credit.

** If the amount you are looking up from the worksheet is at least $56,800 but less than $56,844, and you have three qualifying children, your credit is $5.
If the amount you are looking up from the worksheet is $56,844 or more, and you have three qualifying children, you can't take the credit.

# Property Transactions



PART 4

Virtually all persons or objects in this country . . . may have tax problems. Every day the economy generates thousands of sales, loans, gifts, purchases, leases wills and the like, which suggests the possibility of tax problems for somebody. Our economy is tax relevant in almost every detail.

—Potter Stewart

# Acquisitions of Property

9

Learning Objectives:

LO 1 Define the different types and classes of property.

LO 2 Provide an overview of the property investment cycle from acquisition through disposition, and the tax problems encountered throughout the cycle.

LO 3 Explain the calculation of a property's adjusted basis.

LO 4 Differentiate between a realized and a recognized gain or loss on a disposition of property.

LO 5 Explain how to determine the initial basis of purchased property.

LO 6 Explain how taxes impact the various ways to purchase the assets of a business.

LO 7 Describe the rules for determining the initial basis of gift property, inherited property, and personal use property converted to business use property.

LO 8 Explain the tax problems associated with determining the initial basis of securities.

## concept review

### GENERAL CONCEPTS

**Arm's-length transaction** A transaction in which all parties have bargained in good faith and for their individual benefit, not for the benefit of the transaction group. pg. 2-4

**Related party** Family members and corporations that are owned by family members are considered related parties, as are certain other relationships between entities in which the power to control the substance of a transaction is evidenced through majority ownership. pg. 2-4

### ACCOUNTING CONCEPTS

**Accounting method** A taxpayer must adopt an accounting method that clearly reflects income. pg. 2-9

**Annual accounting period** All entities must report the results of their operations on an annual basis (the tax year). Each tax year stands on its own, apart from other tax years. pg. 2-9

**Conduit entity** An entity whose tax attributes flow through to its owners for tax purposes. pg. 2-6

**Entity** All items of income, deduction, and so on are traced to the tax unit responsible for the item. pg. 2-6

**Substance-over-form doctrine** Transactions are to be taxed according to their true intention rather than some form that may have been contrived. pg. 2-11

### INCOME CONCEPTS

**All-inclusive income** All income received is taxable unless a specific provision in the tax law either excludes the income from taxation or defers its recognition to a future tax year. pg. 2-12

**Capital recovery** No income is realized until the taxpayer receives more than the amount invested to produce the income. The amount invested in an asset represents the maximum amount recoverable. pg. 2-13

**Legislative grace** Any tax relief provided is the result of a specific act of Congress that must be strictly applied and interpreted. All income received is taxable unless a specific provision in the tax law excludes the income from taxation. Deductions must be approached with the philosophy that nothing is deductible unless a provision in the tax law allows the deduction. pg. 2-12

**Realization** No income or loss is recognized until it has been realized. A realization involves a change in the form and/or the substance of a taxpayer's property rights that results from an arm's-length transaction. pg. 2-14

### DEDUCTION CONCEPTS

**Basis** The amount of unrecovered investment in an asset. As amounts are expended and/or recovered relative to an asset over time, the basis is adjusted in consideration of such changes. The **adjusted basis** of an asset is the original basis, plus or minus the changes in the amount of unrecovered investment. pgs. 2-13, 2-21

**Business purpose** To be deductible, an expenditure or a loss must have a business or other economic purpose that exceeds any tax avoidance motive. The primary motive for the transaction must be to make a profit. pg. 2-18

## 9-1 INTRODUCTION

Chapter 5 discussed the general criteria for deducting expenses. Expenses incurred in a trade or business, for the production of income, and certain personal expenditures are deductible when they are paid or incurred. However, expenditures incurred in these activities that provide benefits that extend significantly beyond the end of the tax year cannot be deducted as a current expense. These expenditures, which provide long-lived benefits, are called *capital expenditures.* Thus, capital expenditures result in assets that provide economic or personal benefits that extend significantly beyond the end of the accounting period in which the expenditure is made. The term **property** is used in taxation to refer to long-lived assets that are owned by a taxpayer. Throughout the remaining chapters, the terms *property* and *asset* are used interchangeably to mean anything owned or possessed by a taxpayer.

The capital recovery concept provides the foundation for the tax accounting for property. According to this concept, the amount invested in an asset is recovered tax-free before the taxpayer realizes any taxable income from the property investment. The two basic methods of recovering the capital invested in an asset are by deducting a portion of the cost of the asset against income during the life of the asset (e.g., through depreciation deductions) and by offsetting the invested amount against any amounts realized from the disposition of the asset at the end of its period of use. The amount of investment in an asset is the asset's basis. An asset's basis establishes the initial amount of capital investment that can be recovered tax-free as a capital recovery. It is used to determine the amount of any annual deductions allowed for depreciation, and it represents the amount of unrecovered capital for determining gain or loss upon the disposition of the asset. Therefore, determining the correct basis of property is essential to properly account for the tax effects of investments in property.

The next four chapters discuss the tax aspects related to the acquisition, use, and disposition of property. This chapter begins with a discussion of the different classes of property and their characteristics. An overview of the property investment cycle is discussed next; it provides the framework for the study of Chapters 9 through 12. The remainder of the chapter deals with problems involved in determining the initial basis of property when it is acquired.

## 9-2 CLASSES OF PROPERTY

LO 1
Define the different types and classes of property.

For tax purposes, property is classified by both its use and its type. The use of property determines whether deductions are allowed for current-year expenditures (i.e., repairs, maintenance) relating to the property and for capital recovery deductions for depreciation, depletion, or amortization. To take any deductions relating to property, the property must have a business purpose: It must be used in a trade or business or held for the production of income. This is the general requirement for deductibility of expenses discussed in Chapter 5. Deductions for expenditures on property that is held for purely personal use are not generally allowed. Only those specifically allowed expenditures (discussed in Chapter 8) on **personal use property**, such as property taxes and home mortgage interest, are deductible. Thus, proper classification of the use of an asset is essential in determining the effect of the property on taxable income.

**Example 1** Ellen, a physician, purchases a television for her patients to watch while they wait for their appointments. What is the proper classification of the television for Ellen?

**Discussion: Because the television is used in relation to Ellen's business, it is classified as property used in a trade or business. She may deduct any annual expenditures made relative to the television as ordinary and necessary business expenses. In addition, Ellen may deduct the appropriate amount of depreciation on the television during its tax life.**

**Example 2** When Ellen purchased the television in example 1, she purchased another television that she put in her family room at home. What is the proper classification of the second television set?

**Discussion: The second television is used for personal purposes and therefore is a personal use asset. Ellen is not allowed any deductions for expenditures made relative to the second television, nor is she allowed to depreciate the television because it is a personal use asset.**

As these examples illustrate, the use of the property, not the type of property, is the key factor in determining deductibility. That is, any property can be used in any of the three basic categories: trade or business, production of income, or personal use. In addition, a single property may be used in more than one category. Such property is referred to as a **mixed-use property** (also called *mixed-use asset*). Proper accounting for mixed-use property requires a reasonable allocation of costs among the uses of the property.

**Example 3** Don purchases a duplex for $80,000. He lives in 1 unit and rents out the other. How should Don account for the duplex?

**Discussion: The duplex is mixed-use property. The unit Don lives in is a personal use asset and must be accounted for separately from the unit that is rented. Don is allowed an itemized deduction only for the interest and property taxes from the personal use unit. However, on the rental unit, he can deduct all ordinary and necessary expenses of maintaining the unit. For example, if Don pays the utility bill of both units, only the portion that is reasonably allocable to the rental unit is deductible. In addition, Don may take the allowed depreciation deductions on the rental unit but is not allowed any depreciation deduction on the personal unit.**

The type of property also affects the deductions allowed during the period the property is used. All property may be classified as tangible property or intangible property. **Tangible property** is any property that has a physical existence. That is, tangible property has form, shape, and substance. Land, buildings, machinery, equipment, automobiles, and furniture are all examples of tangible property. **Intangible property** lacks any physical characteristics and exists only because of economic rights the property possesses. Stocks, bonds, copyrights, trademarks, goodwill, and patents are examples of intangible property.

Tangible property is broken down further for tax purposes into real property and personal property. **Real property** consists of land and any structures permanently attached to land. A building and its structural components, such as the air-conditioning system, electrical wiring, and an elevator, are considered real property. Real property is often referred to as **real estate** or realty, and the terms are used interchangeably. **Personal property** is any tangible property that is not real property. Machinery, equipment, livestock, automobiles, computers, and paintings are all examples of personal property. Personal property is often referred to as personalty, and the terms are used interchangeably. Personal property is a *type* of property that is different from personal use property, which is a *use* of property. The type of property should not be confused with its use.

In contrast with the use of property, the type of property does not change from taxpayer to taxpayer. That is, land is always real property, and a computer is always personal property, regardless of the use of the property. The type of property determines such things as the amount of allowable depreciation on it. Personal property generally has a shorter useful life than real property, and the amount and timing of the depreciation deductions on the two properties are adjusted for the difference in useful lives. The allowable depreciation methods for different types of property are discussed in Chapter 10. Property type is also important in determining the tax effects of property dispositions. As will be discussed in Chapter 11, depreciable real property and depreciable personal property are subject to special rules that reclassify income from capital gain income to ordinary income at disposition. The type of property determines the amount of the gain that is reclassified. Table 9-1 provides a summary of the different types of property.

## 9-3 THE PROPERTY INVESTMENT CYCLE

LO 2
Provide an overview of the property investment cycle from acquisition through disposition, and the tax problems encountered throughout the cycle.

Generating income involves the acquisition and use of property to produce that income. That is, businesses acquire factories, equipment, supplies, and so on to produce products that are sold to generate income. Similarly, investors purchase stocks and bonds to produce dividend and interest income as well as appreciation in the value of the security. Individuals acquire homes, furniture, clothing, and automobiles that they use in their personal activities. Acquisition of property begins a property investment cycle that has income tax effects throughout the period in which the taxpayer uses the property.

*Table 9-1*

## Summary of Property Types

| Types of Property | Property Characteristics | Examples |
|---|---|---|
| Personal property (Personalty) | Property that has a physical existence and is not real estate or permanently attached to real estate. Personal property has form, shape, and substance. | Machinery, equipment, automobiles, trucks, computers, furniture, fixtures, telephone systems, works of art, livestock, video equipment. |
| Real property (Real estate) (Realty) | Land and any structures that are permanently attached to land. Real property has form, shape, and substance. | Land and land improvements such as landscaping, shrubbery, sidewalks, parking lots, and fences; buildings, barns, sheds. |
| Intangible property | Property that lacks a physical existence; the rights to the property exist only on paper. Intangible property does not have form, shape, or physical substance. | Patents, copyrights, trademarks, goodwill, covenants not to compete, stocks, bonds, and other securities. |
| Personal use property | Any property that is used by the taxpayer for purely personal purposes. Personal use property can be personal property, real property, or intangible property. | Personal residence, clothing, furniture, home computer, lawnmower, personal automobile. |

*Figure 9-1*

## Property Investment Cycle

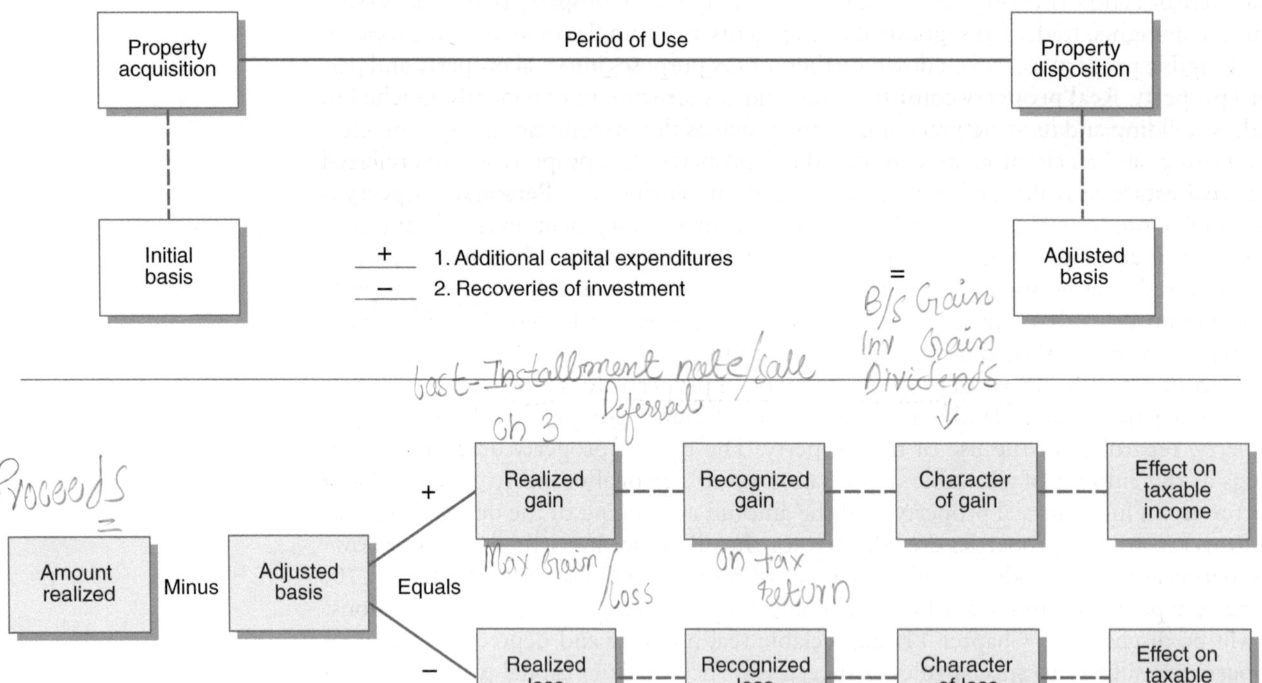


The property investment cycle and the tax accounting related to it are illustrated in Figure 9-1. In the top panel of Figure 9-1, the investment process begins with acquisition of the property. The most common method of acquiring property is by purchase. However, property may also be acquired through other means, such as by gift or inheritance. The initial basis of the property must be determined at acquisition.

Exhibit 9-1

## Computation of Adjusted Basis

| | |
|---|---|
| **Initial basis** | $ XXX |
| **Increases in basis from** | |
| • Additional investments | |
| • Capital invested | |
| • Costs of protecting ownership | |
| • Special property tax assessments for local benefits | XXX |
| • Reinvestment of income | |
| • Income taxed to owners of conduit entities | XXX |
| **Decreases in basis from** | |
| • Annual tax deductions resulting in a reduction of tax liability | |
| • Depreciation, depletion, and amortization | |
| • Losses from conduit entities | (XXX) |
| • Dispositions of all or part of interest in an asset | |
| • Casualty loss | |
| • Sale or gift of part of an asset | (XXX) |
| • Capital recovery resulting from excluded income | |
| • Nontaxable dividends | |
| • Easements | (XXX) |
| **Equals: Adjusted basis** | $ XXX* |

*Adjusted basis cannot be less than zero.

The **initial basis** of an asset is generally the cost of acquiring the asset and placing it into service. When assets are acquired by means other than purchase, special rules determine the initial basis to assign to the asset for tax purposes. The cost of acquiring an asset by purchase and the special rules for other methods of acquisition are discussed later in this chapter.

## 9-3a Adjusted Basis

LO 3 Explain the calculation of a property's adjusted basis.

Under the capital recovery concept, a taxpayer is allowed to recover the amount of capital invested in an asset tax-free. Thus, basis sets the limit on the maximum amount that can be recovered tax-free. As an asset is used to generate income, it may be necessary to adjust the initial basis to account for additional capital investments in the asset or for recoveries of capital investment.[1] As Figure 9-1 illustrates, these adjustments result in an amount that is referred to as the **adjusted basis**. Adjusted basis is equal to the initial basis, plus or minus the cumulative effects of the adjustments. Adjusted basis roughly corresponds to the book-value concept studied in financial accounting.

At any point in time, the remaining capital investment to be recovered is represented by an asset's adjusted basis. An asset's adjusted basis may never be less than zero (a negative number). For investments such as publicly traded corporate stocks, few, if any, adjustments to the initial basis are needed. But for other types of assets, such as depreciable assets used in a business, the adjusted basis calculation is made at least annually and on the date of an asset's disposition. Exhibit 9-1 presents a general format for computing an asset's adjusted basis.

### Increases in Basis

As Exhibit 9-1 indicates, there are two broad categories of increases in basis. An asset's basis is increased by expenditures that are an additional investment in the asset. Additional investments are expenditures made on behalf of the asset that cannot be deducted as a current period expense and must be capitalized as part of its basis.[2] Additional investments would include improvements to an asset that enlarge an asset (adding a room onto a building) or extend its useful life (putting a new roof on a building).

In addition, any costs of defending the ownership of the property and special assessments for such local benefits as widening the street in front of a building are capitalized as part of the cost of the property.

Basis is also increased by items that constitute taxable income but are not withdrawn from the asset for personal or other use. The taxable income of a conduit entity that is allocated to the owner of the entity is added to the basis of the investment in the entity, because the owner is taxed on the income yet does not necessarily receive income.[3,4] This category of basis addition includes the bargain element that is recognized as income in a bargain purchase of property.

**Example 4** Sasha is an employee of Shelf Road Development Company. The company recently subdivided some property and offered lots for sale at a price of $50,000 each. Shelf sells Sasha a lot for $20,000. The difference between the $50,000 fair market value and the $20,000 purchase price—$30,000—is taxable income to Sasha because the transaction is a bargain purchase. The purchase price is an attempt to compensate Sasha. How does Sasha's recognition of this income affect her basis in the property?

**Discussion: The bargain purchase difference, $30,000, is added to Sasha's purchase price of $20,000 to reflect the income recognition that results from the bargain purchase. Therefore, Sasha will have to recognize the income from the bargain purchase, $30,000, only once. The property's basis becomes $50,000, which may reduce her capital gain when she sells the property.**

### Decreases in Basis

Decreases in basis are grouped into three broad categories. The first group results from annual expense deductions that are allowed when the asset is used to earn income. The deduction of an expense is a capital recovery of an investment in an asset. The capital recovery results from reducing the taxable income for the year in which the deduction is claimed. In addition, any losses from a conduit entity that are allocated to the owner of the entity are subtracted from the basis of the investment, because the owner is entitled to the allowable loss deduction on the investment.

Basis is also reduced as a result of disposing of part of the asset. For example, a gift of half of a taxpayer's interest in an asset reduces the taxpayer's basis by half. If property is subject to a casualty, the asset's basis is reduced by the amount of loss deducted.

Special income items also reduce basis. For example, a payment received from a utility company for an easement for power lines does not constitute a realization, because the form or substance of the taxpayer's property rights does not change; such a payment is excluded from income. For tax purposes, the payment is treated as a capital recovery and a reduction in the basis of the land. Similarly, a shareholder who receives a nontaxable dividend from a corporation treats the payment as a recovery of the stock's basis. If the shareholder receives nontaxable dividends that ultimately reduce the stock's basis to zero, any additional nontaxable dividends mean the shareholder must recognize gain (from the "sale" of the asset).

**Example 5** In July of the current year, Cynthia buys 500 shares of Watkins common stock at $35 per share ($17,500 total cost). On December 31, Watkins pays a $4 per share cash distribution. Watkins reports that $3 per share is taxable as a dividend and $1 per share is a nontaxable dividend. What is Cynthia's adjusted basis in the Watkins stock?

**Discussion: Cynthia's adjusted basis in the Watkins stock after she receives the dividend is $34 per share. Cynthia must reduce her $17,500 initial basis by the $500 nontaxable dividend that is excluded from gross income ($1 × 500). Thus, Cynthia's adjusted basis on December 31 for the 500 shares is $17,000. The $3 per share taxable dividend is reported as gross income and does not affect the basis of the stock.**

**Example 6** James buys an office building in 2016. He pays $30,000 for the land and $170,000 for the building. Shortly after he acquires the property, the city imposes a $20,000 special property tax assessment to pave streets and install sidewalks. In addition, James pays $25,000 to remodel two rooms in the building to make them suitable for his use. When a dispute arises with a neighbor concerning property lines, James pays his attorney $2,000 to protect his interest in the land. Total depreciation deducted from 2016 through 2021 is $35,000. A fire in 2021 results in an $8,000 uninsured casualty loss to the building, which James deducts as a loss on his tax return. During 2021, he pays mortgage interest of $9,000, real estate taxes of $3,000, and maintenance service fees of $4,000 on the building. What is James's adjusted basis in the property on December 31, 2021?

**Discussion: James's adjusted basis in the building is $152,000 and in the land is $52,000, computed as follows:**

| Expenditure | Building | Land | Current Expenses |
|---|---|---|---|
| Initial basis | $170,000 | $30,000 | |
| Remodel offices | 25,000 | | |
| Special tax assessment for local benefits | | 20,000 | |
| Attorney's fee to defend title | | 2,000 | |
| Depreciation deducted | (35,000) | | |
| Casualty loss from fire | (8,000) | | |
| Mortgage interest | | | $(9,000) |
| Real estate taxes | | | (3,000) |
| Maintenance service fees | | | (4,000) |
| Adjusted basis | $152,000 | $52,000 | |

**The expenditures must be identified as adjustments to the basis of the land or the basis of the building or as current expenses. The $2,000 legal fee to defend title to the land increases the land's basis. The $20,000 in special tax assessments for local benefits is considered to attach to the basis of the land and also increases the land's basis. The $25,000 spent to remodel the building for James's use is added to its basis. The $35,000 deduction for depreciation and the $8,000 casualty loss deduction are capital recoveries that reduce the basis of the building. The $9,000 mortgage interest, the $3,000 in real estate taxes, and the $4,000 in maintenance service fees are current expenses. They do not affect the basis of the building or the land.**

The recovery of capital investment may occur at several different times. Assets that have definite useful lives may be recovered over the period of use through depreciation, depletion, or amortization deductions. To allocate the depreciation deduction to the correct accounting period, you must use tax accounting rules to correctly measure the basis subject to depreciation. If the basis of an asset is undervalued, depreciation deductions may be permanently lost. In addition, an asset's basis must be reduced by the larger of the depreciation allowable, based on tax accounting methods for computing depreciation, or the amount of depreciation actually deducted on the taxpayer's returns.[5] Therefore, claiming smaller deductions than those to which the taxpayer is entitled can result in lost basis and unused deductions. On the other hand, a taxpayer who claims inflated depreciation deductions may be subject to penalties. Thus, proper determination of the basis in business assets is crucial to computing annual deductions for depreciation, depletion, and amortization. The example that follows highlights the importance of properly reporting depreciation deductions. Do not be concerned with depreciation methods until Chapter 10.

**Example 7** Kalil Corporation uses a machine in its business that cost $10,000. Using tax depreciation methods, Kalil is entitled to total allowable depreciation on the machine of $9,000. However, because of clerical errors, Kalil actually deducted a total of $6,000 in allowed depreciation on its tax returns. Kalil sells the machine on July 1 for $5,000. What are the tax effects to Kalil of the clerical errors?

**Discussion: Kalil Corporation must report a gain of $4,000 from the sale of the asset [$5,000 – ($10,000 – $9,000 allowable depreciation)]. The tax law requires Kalil to reduce its basis in the machine by the larger of the depreciation that it actually deducted or the amount it should have deducted based on tax depreciation methods. As a result, Kalil has lost the benefit of $3,000 in depreciation to which it was entitled under the capital recovery concept ($9,000 allowable – $6,000 deducted). Kalil Corporation might be able to salvage some of the lost basis by filing amended tax returns to correct the error.**

Exhibit 9-2

## Conduit Entity Basis Computation

| | |
|---|---|
| **Initial basis in stock (cost) or basis of investment at the beginning of the current year** | $X,XXX |
| **Increases in basis:** | |
| • Additional capital invested during the year | |
| • Taxable and nontaxable income allocated to the owner for the current year | |
| • Liability adjustment | |
| – A partner's share of any increase in liabilities related to the partnership | XXX |
| **Decreases in basis:** | |
| • Cash received from the entity | |
| • Property received from the entity: | |
| – If a partnership, subtract the partnership's basis for the property | |
| – If an S corporation, subtract the fair market value of the property | |
| • Deductions, losses, and nondeductible expenses allocated to the owner for the current year | |
| • Liability adjustment | |
| – A partner's share of any decrease in liabilities related to the partnership | (XXX) |
| **Equals: Adjusted basis in the conduit entity** | $X,XXX |

## 9-3b Basis in Conduit Entities

Partnerships and S corporations are conduit entities. As a result, the income and deductions of these entities are passed through and included in the gross income of the owners of the entity. Ownership of an interest in a **conduit entity** creates an interesting tax accounting problem. Effectively, owners must determine the adjusted basis of their investment using an equity accounting method. Using the equity accounting method, the investor increases and decreases the basis of the investment for items that change the amount that may be excluded from income under the capital recovery concept. These adjustments are explained in detail in Chapter 14; Exhibit 9-2 presents the effect of these adjustments on adjusted basis.

The taxpayer's adjusted basis for the investment in the conduit entity can be zero, but it may not be a negative number, as explained in Chapter 14.

**Example 8** Tina owns a 25% interest in Quality Conduit Entity. At the beginning of the current year, Tina's adjusted basis for her investment is $75,000. For the current year, Quality reports the following pass-through tax information:

| | |
|---|---|
| Ordinary income | $100,000 |
| Capital losses | 10,000 |
| Nondeductible expenses | 5,000 |
| Charitable contributions | 1,600 |

During the year, Quality distributes $15,000 in cash to Tina. What is Tina's basis in Quality Conduit Entity at the end of the current year?

**Discussion: At the end of the year, Tina's basis in Quality is $80,850. The adjusted basis is computed as follows:**

| | |
|---|---|
| Adjusted basis at the beginning of year | $75,000 |
| Add: Share of current income | 25,000 |
| Deduct: Share of deductions and losses | |
| Capital losses | (2,500) |
| Nondeductible expenses | (1,250) |
| Charitable contributions | (400) |
| Deduct: Cash received | (15,000) |
| Adjusted basis at the end of year | $80,850 |

**The capital loss and charitable contribution limitations are applied on Tina's personal tax return to determine the amounts that she may deduct. Tina must reduce her basis in the Quality stock regardless of whether she can deduct the capital loss, the charitable contributions, or the nondeductible expenses on her personal tax return. These adjustments are illustrated in Chapter 14.**

If all or part of the taxpayer's interest in the partnership or S corporation is sold, the adjusted basis reduces the selling price as a capital recovery to compute the gain or loss on the sale. Thus, the equity accounting method requires an investor in a partnership or S corporation to continually record adjustments to the basis of the investment.

**Example 9** Using the adjusted basis computed in example 8, what would Tina's gain or loss be if she sells her interest at the end of the current year for $100,000? $50,000?

**Discussion: If Tina sells the investment in Quality for $100,000, she would report a $19,150 gain ($100,000 – $80,850) from the sale. If she sells the investment in Quality for $50,000, Tina would report a $30,850 loss. Tina's adjusted basis in the investment in Quality is subtracted from the sale price as a capital recovery.**

## 9-3c Property Dispositions

LO 4
Differentiate between a realized and a recognized gain or loss on a disposition of property.

The amount invested in an asset that has not been recovered through deductions related to its use for a business purpose is recovered at the date of its disposition. When an asset is sold, exchanged, abandoned, or otherwise disposed of, a realization of income occurs with respect to the **property disposition**. At this point, the tax effect of the realization must be determined. This process is illustrated in the lower panel of Figure 9-1. Capital is recovered upon disposition by offsetting the adjusted basis at the date of disposition with the amount realized from the disposition.[6] The **amount realized** from a disposition is the amount received from the disposition (generally the sale price of the property), less the expenses incurred to make the disposition. Thus, if the amount realized is greater than the adjusted basis, the taxpayer has a **realized gain** on the disposition. If the amount realized is less than the adjusted basis, the taxpayer has not fully recovered the capital investment and has a **realized loss** on the disposition. Calculating the amount realized and gains and losses realized on property dispositions is discussed in detail in Chapter 11.

As a general rule, taxpayers must recognize any gain realized on a property disposition under the all-inclusive income concept. *To recognize a gain* means to include it in the current year's taxable income calculation. However, gains from certain types of asset exchanges, involuntary conversions of property, and the sale of a principal residence may not be recognized in total in the year the disposition occurs. That is, provisions in the tax law allow gains from these transactions to be fully or partially deferred for recognition in a future tax year or excluded. Similarly, not all realized losses are recognized in the current year. Losses on certain types of transactions are disallowed (e.g., personal use losses) and therefore are never deductible, whereas other realized losses are deferred for future recognition (e.g., wash sale losses). Thus, after determining the amount of realized gain or loss from a disposition of property, you must determine the amount of gain or loss to be recognized in the current year. Chapter 12 discusses the tax treatments of commonly encountered transactions that are not recognized (nonrecognition transactions) in the year of realization.

The character of the recognized gain or loss determines its ultimate effect on taxable income for the current period. Thus far, all gains and losses have been characterized as being either ordinary (no special treatment) or capital. For individuals, long-term capital gains are taxed at a maximum 20 percent rate, whereas net capital loss deductions are limited to $3,000 per year. In addition to ordinary gains and capital gains, sales of certain business assets produce what are referred to as *Section 1231 gains and losses.* Net Section 1231 gains receive long-term capital gain treatment, whereas net Section 1231 losses are deductible as ordinary losses. Because of the differences in treatment for the different types of gains, it is important to properly characterize each gain or loss. Chapter 11 discusses how to characterize the different types of gains and losses and their effects on taxable income for the year.

To properly characterize the gain or loss from a disposition of property, the holding period must be determined. The term *holding period* means the length of time an asset is owned. An asset's holding period normally begins on the day after it is acquired and ends on the day of its disposition.[7] In determining the holding period, include the day the asset is sold and exclude the day it was bought. The holding period of an asset acquired on January 1, 2021, begins on January 2, 2021. If the asset is still held on January 3, 2021, it is held for more than one year. Another way to remember this rule is that an asset that is held for one calendar year plus one day from its acquisition date is held for more than one year.

**Example 10** Timothy purchases stock in Real Corporation on July 1, 2021. He sells the stock on July 3, 2022. What is Timothy's holding period?

**Discussion: Timothy's holding period begins on July 2, 2021, and ends on July 3, 2022. Thus, Timothy held the stock for 1 year and one day.**

In certain types of acquisition transactions, the basis of another taxpayer or another asset is carried over to the basis of the asset acquired. The term **carryover basis** refers to all or part of an asset's basis that transfers from one owner to another or from one asset to another. Transactions resulting in a carryover basis are subject to special rules for determining the holding period. These rules require an adding on (tacking on) of the holding period of the previous asset or of the previous owner. Situations that involve a carryover basis are discussed later in this chapter and in Chapter 12.

## concept check

According to the *capital recovery concept*, the amount invested in an asset is recovered tax-free before the taxpayer realizes any taxable income from the property investment. *Basis* is the original amount invested in an asset. The original basis is used to calculate depreciation deductions on depreciable assets. As additional amounts are invested in an asset and recoveries of investment are taken on the asset, the basis is adjusted to account for such changes in the amount of capital invested. This results in the *adjusted basis* of the asset. The adjusted basis is used to calculate gain or loss on the disposition of an asset. The *business purpose concept* is useful in classifying assets by use to determine if a cost recovery deduction is allowable.

## 9-4 INITIAL BASIS

LO 5
Explain how to determine the initial basis of purchased property.

Initial basis represents the taxpayer's total investment in an asset on its acquisition date. The initial basis of a purchased asset generally is the cost of acquiring the asset and placing it into service. If an asset is acquired by means other than a purchase, its initial basis may be more difficult to determine. As stated earlier, the initial basis of a property has tax effects throughout the period in which the asset is used. To properly account for the investment in an asset throughout its tax life, you must determine the initial basis correctly. The remainder of this chapter discusses the tax rules and problems associated with different types of property acquisitions.

## 9-5 PURCHASE OF ASSETS

When an asset is purchased, the amount invested must be determined to establish an initial basis in a transaction. Once the total investment is determined, it must be assigned to the specific asset(s) purchased. If one asset is purchased, the assignment of the amount invested is straightforward. But in many transactions, such as the purchase of multiple assets or a business, the taxpayer must use a reasonable method to allocate a single purchase price to multiple assets. In addition, self-constructed assets require allocation of costs to the constructed asset.

### 9-5a Determining the Amount Invested

In an arm's-length transaction, the amount paid for an asset is assumed to be its fair market value. But for practical business reasons (e.g., a forced sale in liquidation of a business), a taxpayer might pay more or less than the true fair market value for an asset. When an asset is purchased with cash, the initial basis of the asset is easy to identify and is the same as the amount of cash paid. Measuring the basis of an asset can become complex when other forms of value are used to pay for the asset. The initial basis (amount invested) in an asset is equal to the purchase price of the asset plus any cost incurred to get the asset ready for its intended use.[8]

The purchase price of an asset is the sum of the

- Cash paid
- Fair market value of other property given to another entity in the exchange
- Fair market value of the taxpayer's services given to another entity in the exchange
- Increases in the taxpayer's liabilities related to the purchase (i.e., increases in debts owed by the taxpayer)

The purchase of an asset by using debt financing (e.g., assuming the seller's debt on the property or obtaining a bank loan to purchase the asset) results in an initial basis equal to the total amount paid for the asset.[9] Effectively, these buyers are treated as if they had borrowed money and then used the cash to pay the seller for the asset. When the taxpayer pays off the debt, the asset's basis is not changed. The repayment of the debt merely reduces the lender's claims against the taxpayer. Depending on whether the asset is a business or personal use asset, interest paid on the loan may or may not yield an interest expense deduction, as discussed in Chapters 5 and 8. The payment of interest expense on the loan does not affect the asset's basis.

**Example 11** Lorenzo purchases a new car by paying the dealer $2,000 cash down and signing an installment note to be paid monthly for $15,000 with interest at 13%. What is the initial basis of the car?

**Discussion: Lorenzo's initial basis in the new car is $17,000. His basis includes the $2,000 cash plus the $15,000 note that increases his personal liability. The interest paid on the installment note does not affect the basis of the car. As he pays on the note each month, he reduces his indebtedness but does not affect the basis in the car.**

In addition to the purchase price of the property, any other costs incurred to get the property ready for its intended use are capitalized as part of the initial basis. Such costs would include commissions, sales tax paid on the purchase, legal fees, recording fees, accounting fees, transportation costs, installation and testing costs, licensing fees, title insurance, surveys, and any other cost that must be incurred to place the property in service.

**Example 12** Eve Corporation purchases an apartment building by paying $10,000 cash and borrowing $130,000 on a 12%, 30-year mortgage. Eve pays legal fees of $2,000 related to the purchase. Because the apartments are in a rundown condition, Eve spends $13,000 painting them and $20,000 in other repair work before it can rent out the apartments. This is a list of items related to the purchase:

| | |
|---|---:|
| Cash down payment | $ 10,000 |
| Mortgage | 130,000 |
| Legal fees | 2,000 |
| Painting | 13,000 |
| Repairs | 20,000 |
| Total | $175,000 |

What is Eve's initial basis in the apartment building?

**Discussion: The purchase price of the building is $140,000 ($10,000 cash + $130,000 increase in liabilities). Eve Corporation will also add the $2,000 in legal fees to its basis as an acquisition cost. Painting and repair work are usually expensed as ongoing maintenance. However, in this case, the painting and repair work had to be performed to get the apartments into condition to rent. Therefore, the costs are capitalized as a cost of getting the apartment building placed into service. The total initial basis in the apartment building is $175,000.**

**Example 13** Holly purchases a new home for $85,000. To complete the sale and obtain a mortgage to finance the purchase, Holly pays the following:

| | |
|---|---|
| Attorney fees for title opinion | $ 150 |
| Points to acquire mortgage | 2,000 |
| Title insurance | 250 |
| Survey | 125 |
| Fee to record the deed | 25 |
| Total additional costs | $2,550 |

What is Holly's basis in the home?

**Discussion: Holly's basis in her new home is $85,550. Her basis includes the $85,000 paid the seller plus $550 in costs paid to establish her ownership of the home. The $2,000 in points paid to acquire the mortgage is not related to the acquisition cost of the home. Points are prepaid interest charges on the mortgage that are deductible as interest in the year of acquisition (see Chapter 8).**

If property taxes are owed on an asset when it is acquired and the buyer agrees to pay the taxes for the seller, the payment of the seller's taxes must be added to the asset's basis as part of the acquisition cost.[10] Thus, in the year real estate is acquired, property taxes must be allocated between the buyer and the seller. The taxes should be allocated according to the number of days each owns the property during the period covered by the tax assessment. The period covered by the assessment is called the ***real property tax year***. For purposes of the allocation, the buyer's ownership period begins on the date of the sale.

**Example 14** On February 28 of the current year, Mark Corporation purchases a vacant city lot for $15,000 as an investment. The annual real estate tax on the lot is $120. The property tax year is a calendar year with the current year's tax payable on November 1. In the contract with the seller, Mark Corporation agrees to pay the $120 in real estate tax for the current year when the payment comes due on November 1. What is Mark's basis in the lot?

**Discussion: Mark's basis in the lot is increased by the $19 [(58 ÷ 365) × $120] in real estate tax that it pays on behalf of the seller. The $101 in property tax related to the part of the year that the lot is owned by Mark Corporation is deductible as a property tax. Thus, Mark's basis in the lot is $15,019.**

## 9-5b Basis of a Bargain Purchase

In Chapter 3, we applied the all-inclusive income concept to employee and shareholder **bargain purchases**. This concept requires recognition of income to the extent of the difference between the fair market value of an asset and its sale price. Because the bargain element (discount) is recognized as income, a basis is established in the asset. The asset's basis is equal to the amount paid plus the income recognized from the discount. Thus, the basis of an asset acquired in a bargain purchase is its fair market value on the date purchased. Likewise, a person who provides a service in exchange for an asset must recognize the fair market value of the asset received as income from services. The initial basis of the asset is its fair market value, and the fair market value of the asset is the amount of income recognized from the services. For these kinds of asset acquisitions, the asset's basis generally is the amount paid plus imputed income recognized for tax purposes. Again, the asset's basis usually is equal to its fair market value.

**Example 15** Jack is an employee of Charles Construction Company. Charles is a home builder that is developing a new subdivision. Charles has built five new houses that are priced to sell for $150,000. To get a family in the subdivision and to thank Jack for his efforts as an employee, Charles sells a house to him for $100,000. What are the tax effects of the purchase for Jack?

**Discussion: Jack has a $150,000 initial basis in his new home. Because of the bargain purchase rules, Jack has to recognize $50,000 in gross income. His basis in the new home is the sum of the $100,000 purchase price plus the $50,000 in income recognized from the bargain purchase.**

## 9-5c Purchase of Multiple Assets

When more than one asset is bought for a single price (called a **multiple asset purchase**), the cost must be allocated to the individual assets in proportion to their fair market value on the date purchased.[11] This allocation of the purchase price is necessary because one or more of the assets may be subject to depreciation or the assets may be disposed of in different accounting periods. If the taxpayer does not make a reasonable allocation of the purchase price to the individual assets purchased, the IRS may decide to reallocate the cost. An appraisal of the individual assets usually provides a reasonable basis for allocating the purchase price. As an alternative, the buyer and seller could agree, at arm's length, on an allocation of the purchase price. Another method that is commonly used to allocate the cost of real estate is based upon the property's tax-assessed value. As noted in Chapter 1, assessed values are usually less than actual fair market values. However, the assessed value does give a reasonable measure of the relative value of the assets (by ratio). Using this method, the purchase price is allocated to land and buildings according to the relative values placed on property by the tax assessor. The reasonable allocation of the purchase price of furniture and equipment is more complex and generally should be based on appraisals, not assessed values. Allocating the cost of furniture and equipment should take into account the age and condition of each item.

**Example 16** The Kay Partnership pays $150,000 for land and a building. At the date of purchase, the property tax valuations show that the land is assessed at $10,000 and the building at $40,000. What is the basis of the land? the building?

**Discussion: The basis in the land is $30,000, and the basis of the building is $120,000. The $150,000 purchase price should be allocated on a reasonable basis to the individual assets. Based on the property tax assessments, the purchase price should be allocated as follows:**

| Asset | Assessed Value | Percentage of Assessed Value | | Purchase Price | Cost Basis |
|---|---|---|---|---|---|
| Land | $10,000 | 20% | × | $150,000 | $ 30,000 |
| Building | 40,000 | 80% | × | 150,000 | 120,000 |
| Totals | $50,000 | 100% | | | $150,000 |

## 9-5d Purchase of a Business

LO 6 Explain how taxes impact the various ways to purchase the assets of a business.

A taxpayer who is interested in acquiring the assets of a business may purchase the assets directly from the owner. A purchase of assets results in the actual transfer of ownership of the assets to the purchaser. If the assets are owned by a corporation, the taxpayer may choose to buy the corporation's stock. The purchase of the corporation's stock results in ownership of the entity. Ownership of the entity results in indirect ownership of the corporation's assets. The tax effects of the two approaches for acquiring a business are explained in the discussion that follows.

### Purchase of the Assets of a Business

The purchase of the assets of a business results in a direct transfer of ownership of the assets. The main problem encountered in a direct purchase of assets is the allocation of the purchase price to the assets acquired. A taxpayer who purchases the assets of a business usually wants to allocate as much of the purchase price as possible to assets that will be subject to depreciation, amortization, or some other form of annual capital recovery and as little as possible to those assets that are not recoverable until they are sold. When the price paid exceeds the sum of the value of the individual assets, the excess price is considered **goodwill**. (Chapter 10 discusses amortization for goodwill and other intangible assets.)

One approach to allocating the purchase price is for the buyer and seller to agree to a written allocation of the purchase price to individual assets. If the buyer and seller do not agree to an allocation, the purchase price must be allocated to all the acquired assets according to their relative fair market values. To identify the amount paid for goodwill, the purchase price is allocated to identifiable assets based on their relative market values.

If the purchase price exceeds the total fair market value of the identifiable assets, the excess payment is considered goodwill.[12]

**Example 17** Sandra Corporation purchases the following business assets from Rafael:

| Identifiable Asset | Rafael's Adjusted Basis | Fair Market Value |
|---|---|---|
| Accounts receivable | $ 100 | $ 100 |
| Furniture and fixtures | 500 | 800 |
| Equipment | 300 | 600 |
| Building | 1,400 | 1,000 |
| Land | 100 | 300 |
| Totals | $2,400 | $2,800 |

Sandra Corporation pays $2,100 in cash and assumes $1,000 of Rafael's liabilities. Thus, Sandra's total cost for the assets is $3,100 ($2,100 cash + $1,000 increase in liabilities). What is Sandra's basis in the assets purchased?

**Discussion: Sandra Corporation should allocate the purchase price according to the relative fair market values of the acquired assets. Because the $3,100 purchase price exceeds the total fair market value of $2,800, Sandra is considered to have paid $300 for goodwill. Each identifiable asset will have a tax basis equal to its fair market value on the date acquired by Sandra. Rafael's adjusted basis for the assets does not affect Sandra's allocation of the purchase price to the assets acquired.**

**Example 18** Assume that in example 17, Sandra Corporation pays Rafael $2,100 for the assets and does not assume any of his liabilities. What is Sandra's basis in the assets purchased?

**Discussion: Sandra should allocate the $2,100 purchase price to the identifiable assets acquired in proportion to their relative fair market values on the date acquired:**

| Identifiable Asset | FMV | Relative FMV | × Purchase Price | = | Allocated Basis |
|---|---|---|---|---|---|
| Accounts receivable | $ 100 | $ 100/$2,800 × | $2,100 | = | $ 75 |
| Furniture and fixtures | 800 | 800/$2,800 × | $2,100 | = | 600 |
| Equipment | 600 | 600/$2,800 × | $2,100 | = | 450 |
| Building | 1,000 | 1,000/$2,800 × | $2,100 | = | 750 |
| Land | 300 | 300/$2,800 × | $2,100 | = | 225 |
| Totals | $2,800 | | | | $2,100 |

**Because the amount paid for the identifiable assets is less than their total fair market value, none of the purchase price is allocated to goodwill. Rafael's adjusted basis for the assets is not relevant to Sandra's allocation of the purchase price to the assets acquired.**

The relative market value allocation of the purchase price results in a reasonable assignment of a cost basis to each asset purchased. The use of a relative market value allocation is important for two reasons. First, the purchase price is objectively allocated among those assets subject to depreciation and amortization and those assets for which the cost is locked in until disposal of the asset. For example, the basis of accounts receivable is recovered as the accounts are collected. The cost of buildings, furniture, and equipment is recovered through depreciation. The land is locked in and is not recoverable until its disposition. Second, the amounts subject to capital recovery are based on current costs paid by the buyer instead of the seller's adjusted basis.

### Purchase of Corporate Stock

The purchase of a corporation's stock to gain control over its business assets has a completely different result than the direct purchase of the assets. Because the corporation is a separate and distinct tax entity, the taxpayer owns shares of stock instead of the corporation's assets. Thus, the new owner controls the assets through the ownership of the entity, rather than through direct ownership of the individual business assets. As a separate entity, the corporation retains control over the assets, and it is entitled to the tax deductions and benefits resulting from the business use of the assets. The shareholder is entitled to receive a return on the amount invested in the stock in the form of dividends. Because of the entity concept, the corporation's tax basis in its assets does not change to reflect the amount the shareholder paid to purchase stock.

**Example 19** Assume that in example 17, Sandra Corporation purchases 100% of Rafael Corporation's stock for $3,100 to gain control over its assets. The facts related to Rafael's assets are the same as in example 17. What is the tax effect of the stock purchase for Sandra?

**Discussion: Sandra Corporation owns 100% of Rafael Corporation's stock with a tax basis of $3,100. Sandra and Rafael Corporation are separate tax entities. Sandra should expect to receive dividend income from the investment in the stock. When Sandra Corporation sells the stock, it may reduce the sales price by the $3,100 basis to compute the gain or loss on the disposition.**

**Example 20** What are the tax effects of Sandra's purchase for Rafael Corporation?

**Discussion: Rafael Corporation's basis in its assets is not affected by the purchase of its stock by a shareholder. Rafael Corporation will continue to use its assets in its business, and it will continue to compute depreciation and other capital recovery deductions according to the corporation's basis in the assets. The corporation is indifferent about who owns its stock and does not revalue its assets when ownership shares change hands.**

The purchase of a corporation's stock instead of its assets has several pitfalls. The basis of the corporation's assets is not affected by the amount paid for its stock by a shareholder. Thus, there is a potential loss of depreciation deductions based on current values of the company's assets. The corporation keeps its tax history even though its controlling shareholders (owners) may change. As a result, the corporation must continue to use accounting methods adopted by previous owners. An additional serious problem with buying a corporation is that all the tax problems created by previous owners continue and could result in unexpected liabilities for the new owner.

## 9-5e Constructed Assets

Taxpayers who construct property for their own use must capitalize both the direct and indirect construction costs.[13] **Direct construction costs** are those actually incurred to physically construct the asset. Examples of direct costs include materials, labor, supplies, architectural fees, and payments to subcontractors. **Indirect construction costs** are other general costs of the business that indirectly support the construction project. Indirect costs include interest on funds to finance the construction, taxes, general administrative costs, depreciation on equipment, and pension costs for workers on the project. Because all the indirect costs are costs that are normally expensed in the period incurred, the effect of capitalizing them as part of the asset's cost is to delay the tax deduction for the costs. The value of the time the taxpayer devotes to the construction of the asset is not included in the property's basis.

**Example 21** Fred is constructing a building for use in his business. The land costs $20,000, direct labor costs are $40,000, and the cost of construction materials totals $35,000. Fred pays architects, subcontractors, and permit fees totaling $85,000. The interest on his construction loan is $10,000. In addition, Fred considers his allocation of $7,000 in indirect administrative costs to the construction activity to be reasonable. The value of Fred's time related to the building's construction is $4,000. Fred's income taxes for the year are $40,000. What is Fred's basis in the building?

**Discussion: Fred's cost basis in the land is $20,000 and is $177,000 in the building. His cost basis in the building includes direct labor, direct materials, other costs directly related to the construction of the building, and a reasonable allocation of indirect costs. The building's cost does not include the $4,000 value of Fred's time.**

**The income taxes are not related to the construction and are not allocated to the building. Fred's cost basis in the building consists of the following:**

| | |
|---|---|
| Direct labor | $ 40,000 |
| Direct materials | 35,000 |
| Other direct costs | 85,000 |
| Construction interest | 10,000 |
| Allocated indirect costs | 7,000 |
| Cost basis in building | $177,000 |

**Note that the effect of the requirement that indirect costs be allocated to the building is to reduce the current year's deductions by the $17,000 in interest and allocated indirect costs that are not allowed as current-year deductions. These costs will have to be recovered over the life of the building through depreciation deductions.**

## 9-6 SPECIALLY VALUED PROPERTY ACQUISITIONS

Although the general rule is that the initial basis of property is its cost as measured by the amount paid by the taxpayer to acquire and place the property in service, several situations require the use of a different basis. In the transfers considered next, the property's initial basis may be its fair market value, the adjusted basis in the hands of a prior owner, or a basis determined by referring to the basis in a related asset. The discussion that follows explains special valuation rules that apply when property has been acquired by means other than an arm's-length transaction.

## 9-7 BASIS OF PROPERTY ACQUIRED BY GIFT

In Chapter 4, a **gift** was defined as a transfer of property proceeding from a "detached and disinterested generosity . . . out of affection, respect, admiration, charity, or like impulses."[14] Thus, by definition, a transfer of property from a donor to a donee is not a profit-motivated, arm's-length transaction. Neither the donor nor the donee recognizes any income or pays income tax on the transfer of gift property. However, the donor may be subject to a gift tax imposed on the transfer, based on the fair market value of the gift. Whether the donor must pay a gift tax depends on several factors, including the fair market value of the gift, total gifts made during the year, and exclusions and credits that the donor may use to reduce or eliminate the gift tax. Although computation of the gift tax is a topic that is beyond the scope of this discussion, considering the effect of the gift tax on the basis of an asset is necessary.

The receipt of property by gift and the payment of gift tax on the transfer ultimately have an income tax effect. The donee may have to determine the property's income tax basis on the date of gift to compute depreciation, depletion, or amortization deductions. In addition, the property's adjusted basis must be calculated upon disposition of the property to determine the income tax effect of the disposition. Depending on the property's adjusted basis in the hands of the donor, the fair market value of the asset on the date of gift, the amount of gift tax paid, and the amount received upon disposition of the property, the appropriate basis could be any one of three different amounts.

### 9-7a General Rule for Gift Basis

LO 7
Describe the rules for determining the initial basis of gift property, inherited property, and personal use property converted to business use property.

Because there is no realization upon the transfer of property from one taxpayer to another as a gift, the general rule for gift property is that the basis of the donor carries over to the donee. This result holds as long as the fair market value of the property on the date of gift is greater than the donor's adjusted basis for the property (i.e., the property has appreciated in value). Thus, the tax law allows the transfer of unrealized gains from one taxpayer to another through the use of gifts.

**Example 22** Sanh owns stock worth $10,000 for which he paid $2,000 this year. He is a 32% marginal tax rate payer. Sanh's son needs $10,000 to pay for college tuition next year. Sanh must sell the stock to come up with the cash necessary to pay his son's college expenses. Sanh's son is a 12% marginal tax rate payer. Should Sanh sell the stock or gift it to his son to sell?

**Discussion: Sanh should gift the stock and have his son sell it. If Sanh sells the stock, the $8,000 gain will result in a tax of $2,560 ($8,000 × 32%). By gifting the stock to his son, the $8,000 gain is effectively transferred to the son through the carryover of basis. His son will pay a tax of only $960 ($8,000 × 12%) on the $8,000 gain. Thus, Sanh will save $1,600 ($2,560 – $960) by gifting the stock to his son to sell.**

In addition to the carryover of basis, any gift tax paid by the donor on the net appreciation in the value of the property is treated as a capital expenditure and is added to the donee's basis. The donee's basis in gift property received is the donor's adjusted basis plus the gift tax paid on the asset's net appreciation (i.e., the increase in the asset's value while it was owned by the donor).[15] The pattern of the values in the transaction can be represented as follows:

| Date Determined | Value Pattern | Basis |
|---|---|---|
| On the date of gift | Fair market value of gift *is greater than* donor's adjusted basis. | Donor's adjusted basis plus gift tax on net appreciation is used to compute gain, loss, and depreciation. |

The calculation to determine the donee's basis on the date of the gift is

Donor's adjusted basis on date of gift $X,XXX

Plus: Gift tax paid by donor on net appreciation

$$\frac{\text{FMV of gift} - \text{Donor's adjusted basis}}{\text{FMV of gift}} \times \text{Gift tax paid} = XXX$$

Equals: Donee's basis on date of gift $X,XXX

The sum of the donor's adjusted basis on the date of gift plus the gift tax related to the net appreciation in value may not be greater than the asset's fair market value on the date of gift. The application of this formula automatically imposes the fair market value limitation.

**Example 23** Elena purchased 10 acres of land 10 years ago for $40,000. On January 20 of the current year, she gives the land to her son, Demetri. Elena pays $5,000 in gift tax on the transfer based on the land's $50,000 fair market value. What is Demetri's basis in the land received from Elena?

**Discussion: Demetri has a basis of $41,000 in the land he receives from his mother. Demetri's basis is Elena's adjusted basis of $40,000 plus the $1,000 in gift tax paid on the appreciation in the value of the asset. The gift tax on the net appreciation while the land was owned by Elena is added to Demetri's basis [$1,000 = ($10,000 appreciation ÷ $50,000 fair market value of gift) × $5,000 gift tax paid].**

## 9-7b Split Basis Rule for Loss Property

Although the general rule for gifts allows the transfer of unrealized gains from one taxpayer to another, the result does not hold true for loss transfers. If the fair market value of the property at the date of the gift is less than the donor's basis, a split basis rule applies. A **split basis rule for gifts** means that the property has one basis for determining gains and a separate basis for determining losses upon disposition. Thus, the basis of a gift of a loss property depends on the sale price of the asset upon its disposition. The basis for determining gains is the donor's adjusted basis.[16] The basis for determining losses is the fair market value on the date of the gift. Generally, the basis for depreciation is the gain basis (i.e., donor's adjusted basis).[17] However, if the donor had used the property for personal use and the donee converts the property to business use, then the fair market value at the date of the gift is the depreciable basis.[18]

The use of the split basis rule for gifts effectively eliminates the transfer of unrealized losses from one taxpayer to another by gift. The pattern of the gift values that invoke the special rules can be represented as follows:

| Date Determined | Value Pattern | Basis |
|---|---|---|
| On the date of gift | Donor's adjusted basis *is greater than* fair market value of gift. | Donor's adjusted basis is used to compute gain. Fair market value is used to compute a loss. |

If the property is sold for an amount between the basis for gain and the basis for loss, the basis is assumed to be equal to the selling price (i.e., no gain or loss is realized).

Whenever the fair market value is less than the donor's basis at the date of the gift, any gift tax paid by the donor is not capitalized as part of the donee's basis in the gift property, because the property has not appreciated. Remember that only gift tax paid on net appreciation can be added to the donor's basis. As a result of not adding gift tax on a loss property, the donee's basis can never be more than the donor's adjusted basis.

**Example 24** Assume that in example 23, Elena's adjusted basis is $40,000, the fair market value of the land on the date of gift is $28,000, and Elena paid $3,000 in gift tax on the transfer based on the land's $28,000 fair market value. What is Demetri's basis in the land if he sells the land for $46,000? for $24,000?

**Discussion: Demetri's gain basis in the land is his mother's $40,000 adjusted basis. Because the fair market value of the property at the date of gift is less than Elena's adjusted basis, none of the gift tax can be added to basis. Demetri will report a $6,000 ($46,000 − $40,000) gain on the sale of the land.**

**If Demetri sells the land for $24,000, his basis for computing a loss on the sale of the land is the $28,000 fair market value on the date of the gift. Demetri has a loss on the sale of $4,000 ($24,000 − $28,000).**

### Special Sale Price Basis

At this point, the donee has a dilemma if the property is sold for less than its adjusted basis but more than its fair market value on the date of gift. In this special situation, the donee should not report a gain or a loss. The property's basis is considered to be the same as the sale price.

**Example 25** Refer to example 24. Assume that Demetri sells the land for $33,000.

**Discussion: Demetri's gain basis is Elena's $40,000 adjusted basis. However, use of his gain basis produces a loss. His loss basis is the $28,000 fair market value on the date of gift. Here, use of the loss basis produces a gain. As a result, Demetri will not report gain or loss on the sale of the land. His basis ($33,000) will be the same as the sale price ($33,000).**

## 9-7c Holding Period

The holding period for gifts follows the general rules for determining holding period. Whenever the donor's adjusted basis is used to compute a gain or loss on the donee's disposition of property received by gift, the donee's holding period includes the period of time the property was owned by both the donor and the donee.[19] As stated earlier, whenever a carryover basis is used, the holding period of the previous owner carries over to the new owner. However, if fair market value is used as the gift's basis, the donee's holding period begins on the date of gift. When fair market value is used, there is no carryover of basis and thus no carryover of holding period.

# 9-8 BASIS OF PROPERTY ACQUIRED BY INHERITANCE

LO 7
Describe the rules for determining the initial basis of gift property, inherited property, and personal use property converted to business use property.

When a person dies (decedent), a personal representative (executor) is appointed to determine the value of property owned by the person on the date of death, pay estate taxes, and distribute the remaining assets to the heirs of the estate. The property owned on the date of death is normally valued at its fair market value at the date of death,[20] or the executor may elect to use the fair market value on the alternate valuation date. The total value of the assets may be subject to a transfer tax called the *estate tax*. Whether an estate tax is paid depends on the size of the estate and the dollar amount of estate tax exemptions and credits that the estate can use to reduce the tax.

Generally, property passing from a decedent to an heir receives a fair market value basis. The property's new basis is stepped up or stepped down from the decedent's adjusted basis to its fair market value. Because of elections available to an executor, the executor can use one of three dates to establish the fair market value of assets owned on the date of death. These dates are the date of death, an alternate valuation date, and the distribution date. Because the assets owned at the date of the decedent's death are valued per the estate tax rules, the heirs have no control over the valuation of the assets.

## 9-8a Primary Valuation Date

The general rule for the initial basis of inherited property is its fair market value on the date of the deceased owner's death. The date of death is called the **primary valuation date**. Absent any special elections by the executor of the estate, the date of death is used to value the assets of the estate. The adjusted basis of the decedent does not carry over to an heir. Because fair market value establishes the heirs' basis, none of the estate tax paid may be used to increase the basis of inherited property. Under the holding period rules, **inherited property** is always treated as being held long-term, even if the decedent bought it the day before dying and the heir sold it the day after the deceased's death.

**Example 26** Sam dies on January 1 of the current year. On the date of his death, he owns 100 shares of Dandy common stock. He purchased the stock 5 years ago for $500. The stock trades for $50 per share on January 1, $75 per share on April 15, and $45 per share on July 1. The Dandy stock is inherited by Betty, Sam's daughter. What is Betty's basis in the stock?

**Discussion: Betty's initial basis for the stock is its $5,000 fair market value on the day of Sam's death (100 shares × $50). If Betty sells the stock on the day after she receives it from Sam's estate, she reports it as having been held long-term.**

## 9-8b Alternate Valuation Date

The executor of the estate may elect not to use the primary valuation date to value the assets of the estate. The **alternate valuation date** is six months after the date of the decedent's death. The alternate valuation date may be used only if *all three* of the following conditions are met:

- The alternate value of the total estate is less than the value on the date of death.
- The total estate tax based on the alternate value of the estate's assets is less than the tax due based on the date of death asset valuation.
- The executor of the estate uses the alternate valuation date to compute the estate tax.[21]

**Example 27** Refer to example 26. Assume that the executor elects to value Sam's estate on the alternate valuation date. The election reduces the amount of Sam's gross estate and the estate taxes. What is Betty's basis in the stock?

**Discussion: Betty's basis for gain or loss on disposition of the stock is $4,500, its fair market value on July 1 (100 shares × $45). If Betty sells the stock on the day after she receives it from Sam's estate, she reports it as being held long term.**

## 9-8c Distribution Date

Although an executor may elect to use the alternate valuation date for the estate, specific assets may be distributed to beneficiaries before the end of the six-month period.

When the alternate valuation date has been elected and property is distributed before the six-month valuation date, its basis is its fair market value on the date it is distributed from the estate. The assets still held by the estate on the alternate valuation date are assigned a basis equal to their fair market value on the alternate date. Assets may not be valued at a date later than the alternate valuation date.

Alternate Valuation Date
Six Months after Date

| 1/1 | Distribution Date | 7/1 |
|---|---|---|
| Fair market value at death | Fair market value of an asset distributed before alternate valuation date | Fair market value at alternate date |

**Example 28** Refer to example 26. Assume that the executor elects the alternate valuation date. Also assume that the executor transfers the stock to Betty on April 15 of the current year. The alternate valuation date election reduces the amount of Sam's gross estate and the estate taxes. What is Betty's basis in the stock?

**Discussion: Betty's initial basis for gain or loss on disposition of the stock is its $7,500 fair market value on April 15 (100 shares × $75). The stock is valued in Sam's estate at $75 per share. Other assets still held by the estate at the end of the 6-month period have a basis equal to their fair market value on the alternate valuation date.**

**Example 29** Refer to example 26. Assume that the executor elects the alternate valuation date. Also assume that the executor transfers the stock to Betty on October 15 of the current year, when the shares are trading for $85. The alternate valuation date election reduces the amount of Sam's gross estate and the estate taxes. What is Betty's basis in the stock?

**Discussion: Betty's basis for gain or loss on disposition of the stock is $4,500, its fair market value on July 1 (100 shares × $45). The latest that assets can be valued is the alternate valuation date. The value on the date of distribution applies only when the alternate date is elected and property is distributed before the alternate date.**

## 9-8d Other Considerations

Any unrealized gain on property held by a decedent on the date of death escapes income taxation. However, unrealized losses at the date of death will never be allowed as an income tax deduction. If a taxpayer sells an appreciated asset and then dies before the sales proceeds are spent or given away, the gain is subject to income tax and the sales proceeds still held on the date of death are subject to the estate tax. If possible, a taxpayer should continue to own appreciated assets and let them pass through the estate to step up their basis to fair market value. When the estate or an heir sells the appreciated asset after the date of death, no income tax is paid on the appreciation in value during the time the decedent held the property. On the other hand, if a loss asset is sold before death, the loss can be deducted for income tax, whereas the fair market value of the asset (i.e., the sale proceeds) is subject to estate tax. Thus, the taxpayer can receive the benefit of a loss deduction for income tax purposes that would be lost if the property is held at death. The estate tax value would be about the same amount because it is assessed on a stepped-down basis.

**Example 30** Frank has a serious heart problem and is near death. He owns stock that has a cost basis of $10,000 and a fair market value of $90,000. Should Frank sell the stock?

**Discussion: If Frank sells the stock, he must report $80,000 in gain on the sale. Unless he can find a way to get the $90,000 in sale proceeds out of his estate, the full $90,000 may also be subject to estate tax. Thus, the appreciation on the stock is subject to both income and estate tax. If Frank continues to hold the stock, no income tax will be paid on the $80,000 unrealized appreciation in the value of the stock. Frank should not sell the stock.**

**Example 31** Based on the information in example 30, should Frank sell the stock if its fair market value is only $1,000?

**Discussion: If the stock is worth only $1,000, Frank could sell the stock and recognize a $9,000 loss on the sale. If the sale proceeds are still held on the day he dies, only $1,000 would be included in his gross estate. Frank benefits by the amount of the income tax savings on the $9,000 tax loss if he sells the stock before he dies.**

# 9-9 PERSONAL USE PROPERTY CONVERTED TO BUSINESS USE

When property held for personal use is changed to property held for a business purpose, a split basis problem similar to the special valuation rule for gifts may develop. The split basis problem arises from the legislative grace concept's disallowance of personal deductions. Depending on the facts at the time the asset is changed to business use, the asset may have a basis equal to its adjusted basis, its fair market value, or its value on disposition. Because the asset may be subject to depreciation, depletion, or amortization while it is used in the business activity, the correct basis must be identified to compute the annual deduction.

## 9-9a General Rule for Basis

If the fair market value of personal use property is more than its adjusted basis on the date business use begins, the general basis rule applies. The asset's adjusted basis is used to compute depreciation and gain or loss on its disposition. As the asset is used in the business, its basis must be further reduced by depreciation allowed or allowable in computing taxable income.

**Example 32** Five years ago, Mary purchased her home for $100,000. The purchase price is properly allocated as $90,000 to the structure and $10,000 to the land. Because of tremendous growth in her business, she needs office space for her employees and herself. In the current year, she pays a contractor $15,000 to convert her home into suitable office space. At the date the home is changed to business property, the house is appraised at $130,000 and the land at $20,000. What is Mary's basis in the building for business purposes?

**Discussion: Mary's basis in the office building is $105,000 ($90,000 + $15,000). Her business basis is her adjusted basis of $90,000 plus the $15,000 cost of improvements to prepare it for business use. The $10,000 basis of the land also carries over to the business.**

**The $105,000 basis also is used to compute depreciation on the building. If Mary deducts depreciation totaling $8,000 and then sells the property, her adjusted basis is $107,000 ($105,000 building less $8,000 depreciation plus $10,000 basis of the land). Her gain or loss on the sale is computed by comparing the sale price to her $107,000 adjusted basis.**

## 9-9b Split Basis Rule

If the fair market value of personal use property is less than its adjusted basis on the date it is changed to business use, it will have one basis for gain and a different basis for loss and depreciation.[22] An expense must be incurred for a business purpose to be deductible. The legislative grace concept prohibits the deduction of personal living expenses or losses related to a personal use asset. Because the property's loss of value occurred while it was held for personal use, the lost value cannot be deducted. The **split basis rules for business property** prevent the deduction of the disallowed personal loss through depreciation or as a loss from the sale of a business asset. The following basis rules apply when the personal use asset's fair market value is less than its adjusted basis on the date it changes to business property:

- The initial basis for gain is the property's adjusted basis on the conversion date.
- The initial basis for loss and depreciation is the property's fair market value on the conversion date.
- If the property is later sold for an amount that falls between the adjusted basis for gain and the adjusted basis for loss, the adjusted basis for the sale is the sale price.

The pattern of the values involved in this situation can be diagrammed as follows:

| Date Determined | Value Pattern | Basis |
|---|---|---|
| At the date business use begins | Adjusted basis *is greater than* fair market value of property. | Adjusted basis is used to compute a gain. Fair market value is used to compute a loss and depreciation. |

If the property is sold for an amount between the basis for gain and the basis for loss, the basis is assumed to be equal to the sale price.

**Example 33** Latoya owns a personal use asset that cost her $50,000 5 years ago. During the current year, when the asset's fair market value is $30,000, she starts using it in her business. What is Latoya's basis in the asset for business purposes?

**Discussion: The nondeductible loss in value related to personal use is $20,000 ($50,000 − $30,000 fair market value). Because the fair market value is less than the adjusted basis, depreciation is calculated using the $30,000 fair market value. Using the lower value avoids deduction of the loss of value attributable to personal use. The basis for determining gain is the $50,000 adjusted basis before conversion to business use.**

**Example 34** Refer to example 33. Assume that after deducting $7,000 in depreciation on the asset, Latoya sells it for $60,000. What is her gain or loss on the sale?

**Discussion: To determine the appropriate basis, Latoya must subtract the $7,000 in depreciation from both the gain basis and the loss basis to arrive at the adjusted basis for gain and for loss. Latoya's adjusted basis on the date of sale is calculated as follows:**

| | Gain Basis | Loss Basis |
|---|---|---|
| Initial basis at date converted | $50,000 | $30,000 |
| Less: Depreciation deducted while used in business (based on FMV) | (7,000) | (7,000) |
| Adjusted basis at date of sale | $43,000 | $23,000 |

**The $60,000 sale price means that the asset was sold at a gain. Therefore, the $43,000 adjusted basis for computing gain is used to determine that Latoya has a $17,000 gain on the sale.**

**Example 35** Assume the same facts as in example 34, except that Latoya sells the asset for $20,000. What is her gain or loss on the sale?

**Discussion: The $20,000 sale price means that the asset is sold at a loss. Therefore, the $23,000 adjusted basis for determining loss is used to determine that Latoya has realized a loss of $3,000 on the sale.**

**Example 36** Assume the same facts as in example 34, except that Latoya sells the asset for $35,000. What is her gain or loss on the sale?

**Discussion: When the $35,000 sale price is compared with the $43,000 gain basis, a loss results. Similarly, comparison with the $23,000 loss basis results in a gain. Therefore, the adjusted basis is equal to the selling price, and neither gain nor loss is realized on the sale.**

Example 35 illustrates that any loss related to the period of personal use is not allowed as a deduction because of the split basis rule. The use of fair market value for computing depreciation also prevents taxpayers from recovering personal use losses through depreciation deductions.

## 9-10 BASIS IN SECURITIES

LO 8 Explain the tax problems associated with determining the initial basis of securities.

Acquiring securities is usually straightforward. The initial basis is equal to the cost paid to acquire the security. The cost of a security includes the purchase price and any commissions paid on the purchase.[23] In certain circumstances, a taxpayer acquires securities subject to special rules or does so without paying a purchase price. These situations include the receipt of stock dividend shares and shares acquired in a wash sale.

### 9-10a Stock Dividends

Most **stock dividends** are nontaxable. When additional shares of a corporation's stock are received as a nontaxable dividend, part of the basis of the original stock must be allocated to the new stock received as a dividend.[24] Because the basis of the new shares is made by referring to the basis of the old shares, the holding period for the new shares of stock includes the holding period of the old shares. If the stock received as a dividend is the same class as the original stock, the allocation is made by using the following formula:

$$\text{Basis per share} = \text{Original cost} \div \text{Total shares held after dividend}$$

**Example 37** Reginald owns 200 shares of Arko common stock for which he paid $22,000 on December 14, 2017. On July 8, 2021, Arko declares and distributes a 10% stock dividend. Reginald receives 20 additional shares of Arko common stock from the dividend. What is his basis in the 220 shares of stock he owns?

**Discussion: Reginald must allocate part of the $22,000 original basis of the 200 shares to the basis of the 20 new shares. The total basis of the 220 shares remains at $22,000. However, the basis per share of the 220 shares is now $100. All 220 shares are deemed to have been held since December 15, 2017.**

Basis before dividend = $22,000 ÷ 200 = $110 per share
Basis after dividend = $22,000 ÷ 220 = $100 per share

If the dividend shares are of a different class of stock than the original stock, the original basis is allocated according to the relative fair market values of the original stock and the stock received as a dividend.[25] Fair market values are determined on the date the new shares are distributed by the corporation. If, for example, preferred stock is distributed as a dividend to common stockholders, the allocation of the original basis is made by using the following formulas:

$$\begin{array}{c}\text{Basis of}\\ \text{preferred stock}\end{array} = \frac{\text{FMV of preferred stock}}{\left\{\begin{array}{c}\text{FMV of preferred stock}\\ +\\ \text{FMV of common stock}\end{array}\right\}} \times \begin{array}{c}\text{Original}\\ \text{common stock}\\ \text{basis}\end{array}$$

$$\begin{array}{c}\text{Basis of}\\ \text{common stock}\end{array} = \frac{\text{FMV of common stock}}{\left\{\begin{array}{c}\text{FMV of preferred stock}\\ +\\ \text{FMV of common stock}\end{array}\right\}} \times \begin{array}{c}\text{Original}\\ \text{common stock}\\ \text{basis}\end{array}$$

**Example 38** Mac Corporation distributes to its common shareholders 1 share of preferred stock for each share of common stock they hold on the record date. The common stock has a $50 per share market value, and the preferred stock has a $20 per share market value on the stock dividend distribution date. Asha, a Mac Corporation shareholder, owns 100 shares of common stock on the record date. She had purchased the stock on March 9, 2013, for $3,000. Asha receives 100 shares of preferred stock as a dividend. What is her basis in the stock?

**Discussion: Asha's $3,000 basis in the common stock must be allocated between the common and preferred stock in proportion to their relative market values on the date the stock dividend is distributed. Asha's basis in the preferred stock is $857, and her basis in the common stock is $2,143. The basis of each type of stock is determined as follows:**

| | |
|---|---|
| Market value of preferred stock = 100 × $20 = | $2,000 |
| Market value of common stock = 100 × $50 = | 5,000 |
| Total market value | $7,000 |

**Allocation of $3,000 original cost:**

Preferred = ($2,000 ÷ $7,000) × $3,000 = $857 or $8.57 per share
Common = ($5,000 ÷ $7,000) × $3,000 = $2,143 or $21.43 per share

**The holding period for both the common and preferred stock begins on March 10, 2013, the day after Asha originally purchased the common shares.**

### Taxable Stock Dividends

Whenever the shareholder has the option of receiving cash or stock as a dividend, the dividend is taxable even if the shareholder elects to receive the stock. The amount of taxable income from the dividend is the fair market value of the shares on the date of distribution. In the case of a taxable stock dividend, the shareholder has a basis equal to the amount of income recognized.[26] The inclusion of the income recognized in the basis of the shares is necessary to ensure that the income is not taxed twice. Because the basis of the dividend is made by reference to the fair market value, the holding period of the shares begins on the date of distribution.

**Example 39** Tanya purchases 500 shares of Upubco common stock on January 18, 2016, at a total cost of $4,600. On April 12, 2021, Upubco declares a 10% stock dividend with the option to receive $8 cash in lieu of taking the dividend shares. The dividend is distributed on June 15, 2021, when the fair market value of the stock is $8 per share. What are the tax effects for Tanya if she elects to take the cash option?

**Discussion: Tanya recognizes the $400 [(500 × 10%) × $8] in cash received as income when she receives the cash. The basis of her original 500 shares is unaffected by the dividend.**

**Example 40** Assume that in example 39, Tanya elects to receive the stock instead of taking the cash option. What are the tax effects for Tanya?

**Discussion: Because a cash option is available, Tanya must recognize the fair market value of the stock received on the date of distribution. Her taxable income is $400 [(500 × 10%) × $8]. Her basis in the 50 dividend shares is the $400 in income recognized. The holding period for the new shares begins on June 16, 2021. The basis of the original 500 shares is unaffected by the dividend.**

## 9-10b Wash Sale Stock Basis

A **wash sale** occurs when a security (stock, bond, option, etc.) is sold at a loss and is replaced within 30 days *before or after* the sale date with a substantially identical security.[27] Because the taxpayer's ownership interest has not changed as a result of the sale and repurchase of the stock, the transaction lacks economic substance. Thus, the form of a transaction has been used to create a paper tax loss. As a result, the substance-overform doctrine applies to the artificial loss. The wash sale loss is not allowed as a current deduction. Deductions for wash sale losses were discussed in Chapter 7.

Because a wash sale loss cannot be used as a current deduction, the taxpayer still has an unrecovered investment in the stock sold. The capital recovery concept permits the unrecovered investment to be added to the basis of the new stock.

**Example 41** Tracy purchases 100 shares of DHI stock for $20,000 in 2015. On December 29, 2021, Tracy sells all 100 shares for $15,000 so she can use the $5,000 capital loss to offset capital gains from other transactions. When the stock market reopens on January 2, 2022, Tracy repurchases 100 shares of DHI for $16,000. What are the tax effects for Tracy of the sale and repurchase of the DHI stock?

**Discussion: Because the stock sold at a loss was replaced within 30 days of the sale date, the $5,000 wash sale loss cannot be deducted. The wash sale loss is added to Tracy's basis in the stock purchased on January 2, 2022. Tracy's basis in the DHI stock bought on January 2, 2022, is the sum of the $16,000 cost plus the $5,000 wash sale loss, a total basis of $21,000.**

**Example 42** On November 30, 2022, Tracy sells the 100 shares of DHI stock purchased on January 2, 2021, for $29,000. What is Tracy's gain on the sale?

**Discussion: Tracy has a gain on the sale of $8,000 ($29,000 − $21,000). Note that the effect of adding the $5,000 in disallowed wash sale loss to the basis of the acquired shares is to decrease the gain on the subsequent sale by the $5,000 loss previously disallowed. That is, Tracy had a gain of $13,000 ($29,000 − $16,000) based on the actual purchase price of the shares. However, the wash sale loss basis adjustment brings the gain down to $8,000.**

Example 42 illustrates that a loss from a wash sale is not disallowed forever. The loss is merely deferred until the taxpayer's interest in the replacement stock is disposed of in a taxable transaction. When the replacement stock is sold, the deferred loss is included in the amount subject to capital recovery. As a result, the deferred loss either decreases the gain or increases the loss that would otherwise have been recognized on the sale of the replacement stock.

Frequently, a taxpayer sells shares of stock and then repurchases either a larger or smaller number of replacement shares. If so, the wash sale rule applies on a first-in, first-out basis only to the extent the loss stock is replaced. As a result, a loss on shares of stock not replaced is deductible. Likewise, the basis of the shares of stock purchased in excess of the number of shares sold is not affected by the wash sale.

**Example 43** Assume that in example 41, Tracy repurchases 150 shares of DHI for $24,000 on January 2, 2022. What is her basis in the replacement stock?

**Discussion: The wash sale disallowance rule applies only to the shares sold at a loss that are replaced. Thus, the loss on the 100 shares sold is added to the basis of the first 100 shares repurchased during the 30 days before or after the wash sale date. The basis of the 50 shares that are not replacement stock under the wash sale rule is not affected. Tracy's basis is as follows:**

| | |
|---|---|
| Cost of 100 replacement shares | $16,000 |
| Add: Deferred wash sale loss on 100 shares | 5,000 |
| Basis of 100 shares reacquired on 1/2/22 | $21,000 |
| Basis of extra 50 shares acquired 1/2/22 ($24,000 ÷ 150 = $160 × 50) | $ 8,000 |

**Example 44** Assume that in example 41, Tracy repurchases only 50 shares of DHI for $8,000. What is her basis in the replacement stock?

**Discussion: Because she repurchases only 50 of the 100 shares, the loss on the 50 shares replaced is disallowed and is added to the basis of the replacement shares. Tracy can deduct the loss on the 50 shares she does not replace. Tracy's basis in the 50 replacement shares is the sum of the $8,000 replacement cost plus $2,500 [(50 ÷ 100) × $5,000] in deferred loss from the wash sale, $10,500.**

## concept check

The *capital recovery concept* allows the recovery of capital invested in an asset. Therefore, capital recovery is an important concept throughout the tax life of an asset—from determining its initial basis through annual recoveries of capital until its disposition. Bargain purchases deserve special treatment because of the *substance-over-form doctrine*. The income that is recognized on a bargain purchase because of the *all-inclusive income concept* is added to the basis of the asset purchased to prevent double taxation of the income. Because a gift of property does not result in a realization of income, the donee is generally allowed to carry over the donor's basis to ensure capital recovery on the property. However, when gift property has an unrealized loss, a split-basis rule is used to ensure that losses are not passed to *related parties* by gifting the property. Mixed-use assets or property converted from personal to business use are subject to the *business purpose concept*, which disallows deductions on personal use property. *Substance over form* is considered in the treatment of stock dividends and wash sales.

# CHAPTER SUMMARY

An asset owned by a taxpayer may be classified according to its business, investment, personal, or mixed use. Because deductions are permitted by legislative grace, a deduction for expenses and losses related to personal and mixed-use assets may be limited. Also, assets may be classified as real property, personal property, or intangible property. Personal property, as used in this classification scheme, refers to any tangible property that is not real estate; it does not refer to property held for personal use by the taxpayer.

Amounts allowed as a capital recovery for tax purposes reduce the amount of income that must be recognized under the all-inclusive income concept. If an asset is used for a business purpose, the full amount of the investment will usually be subject to capital recovery, either as the asset is used to earn income or upon its disposition.

The tax law requires that a capital recovery be reported in the proper annual accounting period based on the taxpayer's accounting method.

An asset's initial basis on the date acquired must be adjusted over time for amounts that represent additional capital investments and recoveries. The adjusted investment amount is called the asset's *adjusted basis.* Adjusted basis represents the unrecovered capital investment in an asset.

The adjusted basis of an investment in a conduit entity is determined by using an equity accounting method. Thus, increases and decreases in the owner's investment in the conduit entity are reflected in the owner's accounting records and tax returns as the changes take place.

The initial basis of a purchased asset is its cost. Cost includes the purchase price of the asset plus any other costs incurred to acquire the asset and place it into service. The purchase price is the sum of any amount paid for the asset in cash, the fair market value of property or services given to the seller, and the assumption of a liability by the buyer. If the purchase price includes more than one asset, it must be reasonably allocated to the individual assets acquired. If goodwill is among the purchased assets, a portion of the purchase price must be allocated to goodwill. The basis of a self-constructed asset includes all direct and indirect costs related to construction of the asset.

When property is received as a gift, the general rule provides that the donee receives a carryover of the donor's basis. If the fair market value of the gift is greater than the donor's basis, the gift tax paid by the donor on the net appreciation in the value of the asset is added to the donee's basis. When the fair market value of the gift is less than the donor's basis (the property has an unrealized loss), the split basis rule applies. The split basis rule provides that the donee's basis for gain is the donor's basis and the basis for loss is the fair market value of the gift. If the asset is sold for a price that falls between the special gain basis and loss basis, the basis is equal to the selling price, and no gain or loss results from the disposition.

Inherited property generally has a basis equal to the asset's fair market value on the date of the original owner's death. As an alternative, the executor of the estate may elect to value the estate's assets six months later, on the alternate valuation date.

When property is converted from personal to business use, a split basis problem can result. The tax treatment is similar to the split basis rule for gifts. The basis for gain is the property's adjusted basis, and the basis for loss (and depreciation) is the lower of the property's adjusted basis or fair market value. As with gifts, if the sale price falls between the gain basis and the loss basis, the basis is equal to the selling price.

The basis of a taxable stock dividend is the fair market value of the stock on the date it is distributed by the corporation. However, the basis of a nontaxable stock dividend is determined by allocating the taxpayer's investment in the original stock to the old shares and to the new shares received as a dividend. A loss on a wash sale is added to the basis of the replacement securities.

Table 9-2 summarizes the basis rules discussed in this chapter. The table briefly states how the asset's basis is determined according to how an asset was acquired.

*Table 9-2*

## Summary of Basis Rules

| How Asset Was Acquired | Basis of Asset Acquired |
|---|---|
| Purchase of a single asset | Cost—Generally, the asset's fair market value on the date purchased plus any other costs incurred to obtain the asset and place it into service. |
| Purchase of several assets for a single price | Cost—The single purchase price is allocated to individual assets according to their relative fair market values on the date purchased. |
| Purchase of the assets of a business | Cost—The single purchase price is allocated to individual assets according to their relative fair market values on the date purchased. If the purchase price exceeds the total fair market value of the identifiable assets, the excess is allocated to goodwill. |
| Purchase of the stock of a corporation | Cost—Purchase price plus any other costs incurred to obtain the stock, such as commissions and legal fees. |
| Self-constructed assets | Cost—Total direct and indirect construction costs. |
| Gift: | |
| Fair market value on date of gift greater than donor's adjusted basis | Donor's adjusted basis plus gift tax on net appreciation. |
| Fair market value on donor's date of gift less than donor's adjusted basis | Gain—Donor's adjusted basis. (Gift tax cannot be added to basis.)<br>Loss—Fair market value on gift date.<br>If asset is sold for an amount between the gain basis and the loss basis, the basis is deemed to be equal to the selling price. |

| How Asset Was Acquired | Basis of Asset Acquired |
|---|---|
| Inheritance | Fair market value of the asset on the date of death or alternate valuation date. |
| Conversion of personal use property to business use | Gain—Adjusted basis.<br>Loss and depreciation—Lesser of the adjusted basis or the fair market value when put into business use.<br>If asset is sold for an amount between the gain basis and the loss basis, the basis is deemed to be equal to the selling price. |
| Conduit entity | Initial basis determined by how interest in entity was acquired; initial basis is adjusted for investments and recoveries of capital, using an equity accounting method. |
| Stock dividend: | |
| Taxable | Fair market value of stock on distribution date. |
| Nontaxable | A part of old stock's basis is allocated to the new stock. |
| Wash sale stock | Cost of replacement stock plus deferred loss on wash sale. |

# KEY TERMS

adjusted basis (p. 9-7)
alternate valuation date (p. 9-21)
amount realized (p. 9-11)
bargain purchases (p. 9-14)
carryover basis (p. 9-12)
conduit entity (p. 9-10)
direct construction costs (p. 9-17)
gift (p. 9-18)
goodwill (p. 9-15)
indirect construction costs (p. 9-17)
inherited property (p. 9-21)
initial basis (p. 9-7)
intangible property (p. 9-5)
mixed-use property (p. 9-5)
multiple asset purchase (p. 9-15)
personal property (p. 9-5)
personal use property (p. 9-4)
primary valuation date (p. 9-21)
property (p. 9-4)
property disposition (p. 9-11)
real estate (p. 9-5)
real property (p. 9-5)
realized gain (p. 9-11)
realized loss (p. 9-11)
split basis rule for gifts (p. 9-19)
split basis rules for business property (p. 9-23)
stock dividends (p. 9-24)
tangible property (p. 9-5)
wash sale (p. 9-26)

# PRIMARY TAX LAW SOURCES

[1]Sec. 1016—Prescribes the adjustments that must be made to the basis of property.

[2]Reg. Sec. 1.1016-2—Gives examples of items that are added to basis as adjustments.

[3]Sec. 705—Prescribes the adjustments that must be made to a partner's basis.

[4]Sec. 1367—Prescribes the adjustments that must be made to an S corporation shareholder's basis.

[5]Reg. Sec. 1.1016-3—Requires adjustment of the basis of a depreciable asset even if depreciation was not claimed on the asset.

[6]Sec. 1001—Prescribes the computation of gain or loss on the disposition of property.

[7]Reg. Sec. 1.1223-1—Explains the rules for determining the holding period of assets in different circumstances.

[8]Sec. 1012—States the general rule that the initial basis of a property is the property's cost.

[9]Crane v. Comm., 331 U.S. 1 (1947)—Held that mortgage debt must be included in the basis of property to properly reflect the economic cost of the property.

[10]Reg. Sec. 1.1001-1—Requires adjustment of the selling price (and therefore basis of the buyer) to account for property taxes paid as part of a sales agreement.

[11]Reg. Sec. 1.61-6(a)—Requires a reasonable apportionment of the cost of properties sold to the individual properties.

[12]Sec. 1060—Requires an allocation of the purchase price of the identifiable assets of a business, either by agreement with the seller or by the use of relative fair market values.

[13]Reg. Sec. 1.263A-1—Discusses the uniform capitalization rules as they apply to property constructed by taxpayers for their own use.

[14]Comm. v. Duberstein, 363 U.S. 278 at 283 (1960)—Held that a Cadillac received by a taxpayer from a businessman to whom he occasionally gave names of potential customers was not a tax-free gift.

[15]Sec. 1015—States the general rule that the basis of property received by gift is the donor's adjusted basis.

[16]Reg. Sec. 1.1015-1—Explains the split basis rule for gifts and gives examples of the application of the rule.

[17]Sec. 167(c)(1) and Reg. Sec. 1.167(g)-1—The basis upon which the allowance for depreciation is to be computed with respect to any property shall be the adjusted basis for the purpose of determining gain on the sale or disposition of such property.

[18]Perkins v. Comm., 125 F.2d 150 (6th Cir. 1942)—Held that the basis amount for depreciation on real property that is converted to business use by the donee is the value of the property as of the gift transfer date when fair market value is less than the adjusted basis.

[19]Sec. 1223—Provides the rules for determining the holding period of property.

[20]Sec. 1014—States that the basis of property acquired from a decedent is its fair market value at the date of death, unless the executor elects to value the estate assets on the alternate valuation date.

[21]Sec. 2032—Provides the rules for an executor to elect to value the estate assets at the alternate valuation date.

[22]Reg. Sec. 1.167(g)-1—States that the basis for computing depreciation on personal use property that has been converted to business

use is the lesser of the fair market value or the adjusted basis of the property at the date of the conversion.

[23]Reg. Sec. 1.263(a)—Gives examples of capital expenditures; specifically states that the commissions paid on the purchase of securities are capital expenditures.

[24]Sec. 307—Requires the allocation of the adjusted basis of securities to nontaxable dividend shares received.

[25]Reg. Sec. 1.307-1—Requires the allocation of adjusted basis using relative market values when stock of a different class is received in a nontaxable stock dividend.

[26]Sec. 301—States that the basis of stock received in a taxable stock dividend is its fair market value on the date of distribution.

[27]Sec. 1091—Defines a *wash sale* and prescribes the rules for treatment of disallowed losses on wash sales.

# DISCUSSION QUESTIONS

1. **LO1** What effect does a property's use have on the cost recovery allowable on the property?
2. **LO1** What is the difference between a property's use and its type?
3. **LO1** Explain the difference between tangible property and intangible property.
4. **LO1** How is personal property different from personal use property?
5. **LO4** Explain the role an asset's initial basis plays in determining the income to be recognized upon disposal of the asset.
6. **LO3, 5** Explain the difference between a property's initial basis and its adjusted basis.
7. **LO6** Larry is interested in acquiring a business owned by Jane. If Jane's business is organized as a corporation, what options are available to Larry in acquiring the business? Explain to Larry the difference in the options.
8. **LO5** What tax problems does a taxpayer encounter when purchasing more than one asset for a single price? Explain.
9. **LO5** What are the tax implications of a taxpayer's self-construction of assets for use in the taxpayer's trade or business?
10. **LO5** List some costs that are normally expensed that must be capitalized when a taxpayer self-constructs an asset for use in a trade or business.
11. **LO7** Why are gifts of property not income to the person receiving the gift?
12. **LO7** A person who receives property as a gift makes no investment to receive the property. Why is a basis assignment to the gift property necessary even though the donee has no investment in the property?
13. **LO7** What is the general rule for determining the basis of gift property?
14. **LO7** Janine is planning to make a gift of 50 shares of Acran, Inc., stock to her nephew to help with his college tuition. The stock cost Janine $5,000, and its current value is $4,000. Explain to Janine why the gift might not be the best way to achieve her goal.
15. **LO7** What is the general rule for determining when the holding period of an asset begins?
16. **LO7** What type(s) of asset acquisitions do not follow the general rule for determining when the holding period of the asset begins?
17. **LO7** When is the primary valuation date for valuing inherited property? Does the executor of the estate have to do anything to use the primary valuation date?
18. **LO7** When is the alternate valuation date for valuing inherited property? When elected, are all assets valued on the alternate date? Explain.
19. **LO8** Are commissions paid to acquire securities a deductible expense? If not, are they ever deductible?

# PROBLEMS

20. **LO1** For each of the following assets, determine whether it is personal property, real property, intangible property, or personal use property:
    a. Reagan gave her mother a new set of golf clubs for Christmas.
    b. Roberta bought a whistle and uniform for use in her job as a referee.
    c. Rochelle purchased a building and furnishings to use as a pet shop.
    d. Graham secured a copyright on a novel that he wrote.
    e. Farmer Brown installed an air-conditioning unit in the building that houses his chickens.
    f. Alonzo traded his truck for cows for his dairy farm.

21. **LO1** For each of the following assets, determine whether it is personal property, real property, intangible property, or personal use property:
    a. Woodrow spent $5,380 on trees and shrubs for use in his landscaping business.
    b. Woodrow spent $12,100 on a new tennis court for the backyard of his personal residence.
    c. Woodrow purchased the trade name Green Gopher Landscaping for $3,400 from the owner of a defunct business.
    d. Woodrow purchased an acre of land with the idea of eventually using it to grow shrubs for resale.
    e. Woodrow purchased an alarm system for the fences surrounding his landscaping business.
    f. Woodrow spent $2,600 on lights for the backyard of his residence.
22. **LO3** Determine the adjusted basis of each of the following assets:
    a. Leineia purchased an automobile two years ago for $30,000. She uses it 75 percent in her business and 25 percent for personal use. To date, she has deducted $4,209 in allowable depreciation on the business use portion of the automobile.
    b. Three years ago, Quon purchased an office building for $330,000. The purchase price was properly allocated as $250,000 to the building and $80,000 to the land. Building remodeling cost $8,000. He paid $12,000 for the installation of a parking lot and sidewalks. Insurance premiums on the building are $5,000 per year. Quon has deducted total allowable depreciation on the building of $70,620 and $1,000 on the land improvements for the three years.
23. **LO3** Determine the adjusted basis of each of the following assets:
    a. André purchased a parcel of land three years ago for $17,000. In the current year, the adjoining property owner sues him, claiming that part of André's property belongs to him under the right of adverse possession. André incurs $4,000 in legal fees successfully defending against the lawsuit. He pays annual property taxes of $300 on the land and has paid $3,700 in interest on the loan he took out to acquire the property.
    b. René purchases 1,000 shares of Cramdem Company common stock for $8 per share on October 13, 2020. In 2021, Cramdem pays a taxable cash dividend of 30 cents per share. René sells 300 shares on August 22, 2022, for $3 per share. On December 2, 2022, Cramdem pays a nontaxable cash dividend of 10 cents per share.
    c. Rufus owns 12 acres of land he purchased as an investment for $5,000. He spent an additional $37,000 subdividing the land into residential parcels and having utility lines run to the property. After the subdividing and utility lines had been completed, he gifted two acres of the land to his sister as a wedding present.
24. **LO3** Alberta owns 5 acres of land she purchased several years ago for $6,500. A new housing development is being built on the north side of her property. The owner of the development needs part of Alberta's land to run utility and sewer lines to the new development. The owner offers Alberta $13,000 for half of her land, but Alberta decides to wait to see if the land will appreciate further after the development is built. She agrees to grant the developers an easement to run the utility and sewer lines through her property for $3,000. Write a letter to Alberta explaining the tax consequences of granting the easement. Communication Skills
25. **LO3** Luana pays $40 per share for 100 shares of Manano Corporation common stock. At the end of the year, the market price of the stock is $60 per share. During the year, she receives a cash dividend of $4 per share. Manano reports that $3 per share is taxable and $1 per share is a nontaxable dividend. What are the tax effects of these events?
26. **LO3** Carl Corporation acquires a business use warehouse for $200,000 on January 2, 2014. From 2014 through 2019, Carl Corporation properly deducts a total of $30,000 in depreciation. Carl incurs a net operating loss and deducts no depreciation in 2020, even though $12,500 could have been claimed. Kelsa Company has offered to buy the warehouse for $185,000. The sale will be completed on Communication Skills

January 1, 2021, if Carl accepts the offer. You are asked to review the proposed sale. Write a memorandum explaining the tax results of the proposed transaction.

27. **LO3** Han owns a farm. He purchases a tractor in 2017 at a cost of $25,000. Because 2017 is a bad year, he does not deduct any depreciation on the tractor in 2017. He sells the tractor in 2021 for $16,000. He takes straight-line depreciation on the tractor of $12,500 for the years 2018 to 2021. The total allowable straight-line depreciation for the tractor for 2017 to 2021 is $15,000. What is Han's gain or loss on the sale of the tractor? Explain.

28. **LO3** Determine whether each of the following transactions would result in an increase in basis, a decrease in basis, or no effect on basis:
    a. Dolly pays $3,000 for a survey to disprove her neighbor's claim that the boundaries dividing their properties are in error.
    b. Dolly pays a $500 street improvement assessment.
    c. Dolly receives $1,000 from the county for a portion of her property that was needed to widen the street.
    d. Dolly's property tax bill totals $1,200 for the year.

29. **LO3** During the current year, Horace's personal residence is damaged by a tornado. Horace's entire county was declared a federal disaster area. The residence had an adjusted basis of $80,000 before the tornado. The cost of repairing the damage is $30,000. Horace's insurance company reimburses him $22,000 for the repairs. Horace itemizes his deductions and has an adjusted gross income of $57,000 for the year. What is his adjusted basis in the residence after the tornado?

30. **LO3** Amos and Thomas form the Show Corporation during the current year. Amos owns 40 percent of Show's stock, Thomas owns 20 percent, and Arthur owns the remaining 40 percent. Amos paid $50,000 for his interest, and Thomas paid $25,000. Amos and Thomas are responsible for Show's daily operations and serve as cochief executive officers. During the current year, Show Corporation has an operating income of $60,000 and pays out $10,000 in dividends. What are Amos's and Thomas's adjusted bases in the Show Corporation stock if
    a. Show Corporation is organized as a corporation?
    b. Show Corporation is organized as an S corporation?

31. **LO3** Return to the facts of problem 30. Assume that Show Corporation is organized as an S corporation. In its second year of operations, Show has an operating loss of $40,000 and pays out $20,000 in dividends. On December 31, Amos gives a 10 percent interest in Show (i.e., ¼ of his interest) to his son, Buddy. What is Amos's adjusted basis in the Show stock? What is Buddy's adjusted basis in the Show stock?

32. **LO3** Paula purchases a 40 percent interest in Dancer Enterprises for $52,000 on January 2 of the current year. Dancer is organized as a partnership and has an income of $50,000 in the current year. Dancer also distributes a total of $15,000 to the partners in the current year. What are the tax effects to Paula of her investment in Dancer? What is her adjusted basis in the partnership at the end of the current year?

33. **LO3** Troy owns 600 of the 1,000 outstanding shares of Oiler Corporation. His adjusted basis in the Oiler stock at the beginning of the current year is $88,000. Oiler Corporation is organized as an S corporation and reports the following results for the current year:

| | |
|---|---|
| Operating income before special items | $58,000 |
| Charitable contributions | 8,000 |
| Nondeductible expenses | 9,000 |
| Cash dividends paid | 22,000 |

    a. What is Troy's adjusted basis in the Oiler corporation stock at the end of the current year?
    b. What is Troy's gain or loss if he sells the 600 shares for $100,000 to an unrelated person at the beginning of next year?

34. **LO3, 5** Erin purchases two acres of land in 2021 by paying $4,000 in cash at closing and borrowing $40,000 to be repaid at $8,000 per year for the next five years with interest on the unpaid balance at 10 percent. In addition, Erin agrees to let the seller store farm equipment on the land for two years (rental value of $1,000 per year). In return, the seller agrees to pay the $800 in points required to obtain the $40,000 loan. Erin also pays legal and abstracting fees of $700 on the purchase.
    a. In 2022, Erin pays $250 in property tax on the land. In addition, the county paves the road that runs by the land and assesses each taxpayer $1,300 for the paving. What is Erin's adjusted basis in the land at the end of 2022?
    b. In 2023, Erin sells one acre of the land to her brother for $18,000. What is her gain or loss on the sale of the land? What is her basis in the remaining acre of land?

35. **LO3, 5** Florian Corporation purchases a piece of land for investment purposes on April 1. Florian pays the seller $2,000 cash and agrees to pay the seller $3,000 per year for the next five years plus interest at 9 percent per year on the outstanding balance. As part of the purchase agreement, Florian agrees to pay all property taxes for the year, a total of $360. In addition, Florian pays legal fees of $500 connected with the purchase and gives the seller a car worth $4,000 (Florian's basis is $11,000). What is Florian Corporation's basis in the land?

36. **LO5** Alphonse purchases a store and a warehouse. The asking price includes $150,000 for the store, $50,000 for the warehouse, and $90,000 for the land. Alphonse agrees to this price even though he does not want to buy the warehouse because it does not meet his needs. He sells the warehouse building for $15,000 but has to pay $10,000 to have the warehouse moved. What is Alphonse's basis in the land and store?

37. **LO5** Barbara wanted to go into the long-distance trucking business. She bought a used tractor and trailer for $102,000. However, the trailer wasn't suitable for Barbara's needs, so she sold it for $24,000 and purchased the trailer she needed for $30,000. What is Barbara's basis in the tractor? What is Barbara's basis in the trailer?

38. **LO4, 5** On October 1, 2021, Mitzo Realty Partnership purchases a lot for future development for $60,000 from the Elm Trust. The trust's adjusted basis in the lot is $20,000. Real estate taxes attributable to the property are $1,000. The city in which the lot is located operates on a calendar year, and taxes are due on April 1 of the following year. The sales agreement provides that Mitzo will pay the property tax bill in 2022.
    a. What is Mitzo's initial basis in the lot?
    b. What is Elm Trust's gain on the sale?
    c. Assume that the sales agreement provides that Elm Trust will pay its portion of the real estate taxes. The sales price remains at $60,000. On April 1, 2022, Mitzo Realty Partnership pays the $1,000 property tax bill. What is Mitzo's initial basis in the lot? What is Elm Trust's gain on the sale?

39. **LO5** Fala is the sole shareholder of Campbell, Inc. During the current year, Campbell sells Fala land that has a fair market value of $40,000 for $28,000. Campbell had paid $30,000 for the land. What are the tax effects of the sale for Fala and Campbell? What is Fala's basis in the land?

40. **LO5** Izzy is an employee of Kosmo's Kustom Kars, Inc. The company rebuilds classic automobiles for resale. Last year, Izzy bought a rebuilt 1958 Thunderbird for $15,000 from the company. A car like Izzy's Thunderbird generally sells for $28,000. On December 20 of the current year, Izzy receives an offer of $25,000 for the car. What are the tax results if Izzy completes the sale?

41. **LO5** Nathaniel purchases a house by paying $25,000 in cash and securing a home mortgage for $75,000. He also incurs $3,000 in legal fees, title search, and closing costs. He agrees to pay the property taxes for the entire year ($6,000), even though his share would be $1,000. A neighbor pays Nathaniel $50 for a playhouse located

Communication Skills

in the backyard. As the neighbor is moving the playhouse from the property, he accidentally damages Nathaniel's fence. The neighbor is unaware of the damage. Not wanting to cause trouble in a new neighborhood, Nathaniel pays $100 to have the fence repaired. Write a letter to Nathaniel explaining his basis in the house.

42. **LO5** Hester Corporation purchases a building by giving stock with a fair market value of $30,000 (original cost was $21,000) and borrowing $210,000. Hester pays closing costs of $10,000 on the purchase. For property tax purposes, the land is assessed at $10,000 and the building at $40,000. Before buying the property, Hester hires an independent appraiser and receives appraisals of $21,000 on the land and $279,000 on the building. Compare initial bases of the properties using different allocation methods. What initial basis amounts should Hester use? Explain. Is there any other way to determine initial basis?

43. **LO6** Earl purchases all the assets and assumes the liabilities of Buddy's Market Shop. The details concerning the adjusted basis and fair market value of Buddy's assets and liabilities are as follows:

| Asset | Adjusted Basis | Fair Market Value |
|---|---|---|
| Inventory | $ 30,000 | $ 40,000 |
| Equipment | 22,000 | 70,000 |
| Land | 10,000 | 15,000 |
| Building | 118,000 | 155,000 |
| Liabilities | (60,000) | (60,000) |

a. If Earl pays $250,000 for Buddy's net assets, what is Earl's basis in the assets purchased?

b. Assume that Buddy's Market Shop is a closely held corporation and that Earl pays $250,000 for all the stock. What is Earl's basis, and what is the basis of the assets of the corporation?

44. **LO6** ABC Company purchases all the assets of John's Saw Shop. The details on basis and fair market values of John's Saw Shop's assets are as follows:

| Asset | Adjusted Basis | Fair Market Value |
|---|---|---|
| Inventory | $10,000 | $27,000 |
| Machinery & equipment | 2,000 | 12,000 |
| Land | 8,000 | 15,000 |
| Building | 20,000 | 6,000 |

a. What is ABC's basis in the assets purchased if ABC pays $40,000 for them?

b. What is ABC's basis in the assets purchased if ABC pays $70,000 for them?

c. What is ABC's basis if John's Saw Shop is a corporation and ABC purchases all John's stock for $60,000?

45. **LO6** Kieu Corporation constructs a new warehouse. It pays $100,000 for materials and $70,000 to the general contractor. Architectural fees total $18,000. The corporation pays $13,000 in interest on its loan to finance construction. The land costs $15,000, and the real estate taxes paid on the land during construction amount to $1,000. What is Kieu's initial basis in the warehouse?

46. **LO6** Latham Corporation constructs a new factory building. The materials cost $300,000. Other costs include direct labor of $150,000, worker pension costs of $5,000, architectural fees of $15,000, and depreciation on equipment of $25,000. The land was purchased for $30,000. A loan of $500,000 is needed to finance the construction, and interest of $40,000 is paid during the year. What is Latham's basis in the building?

47. **LO7** Julia receives 1,000 shares of Cookery Corporation stock from her grandfather as a wedding present. The shares are selling for $24 per share on the date of the gift. Grandfather paid $8,000 for them four years earlier. He pays $3,000 in gift tax on the transfer of the shares to Julia.

a. What is Julia's basis in the Cookery Corporation shares?
b. Two months after her wedding, Julia wants to take a trip to Europe. To get the money for the trip, she sells 400 Cookery shares at $17 per share and pays a $500 commission on the sale. What is Julia's gain or loss on the sale of the 400 shares? What is her holding period for the shares?

48. **LO7** Calculate the basis for gain and basis for loss and the taxable gain or deductible loss for the following gifts which are received and sold in the current year:

| | Donor's Adjusted Basis | FMV at Time of Gift | Gift Tax Paid | Selling Price |
|---|---|---|---|---|
| a. | $100,000 | $400,000 | $40,000 | $350,000 |
| b. | 100,000 | 80,000 | 8,000 | 70,000 |
| c. | 100,000 | 30,000 | 6,000 | 40,000 |

49. **LO7** For his birthday, Moose gives his son, Babe, a valuable basketball card. Moose paid $100 for the card 12 years earlier. On Babe's birthday, the card is valued in a basketball card guidebook at $90. What is Babe's basis in the card? Explain.
a. Assume that Babe sells the card two months after his birthday for $80. What is Babe's gain or loss on the sale of the card? What is the holding period?
b. Assume that Babe sells the card two months after his birthday for $125. What is Babe's gain or loss on the sale of the card? What is the holding period?
c. Assume that Babe sells the card two months after his birthday for $95. What is Babe's gain or loss on the sale of the card?

50. **LO7** Stockton pays $10,000 for 1,000 shares of Megacron, Inc., common stock on the day his niece Chama is born. Stockton's plan is to give the stock to Chama when she is ready to go to college. Eighteen years later, Chama is ready to leave for Eastern Private University. She needs the money for tuition. However, the market value of the stock is $6,500. Stockton's marginal tax rate is 28 percent. Chama's marginal tax rate is 15 percent.
a. What alternative course(s) of action does the situation offer?
b. Should Stockton sell the shares and give the proceeds to Chama? Explain.

51. **LO7** Florence's daughter, Eunice, needs $5,000 to start a business. Florence agrees to give her the money but will have to sell some securities to raise that much cash. Florence has 1,200 shares of Tom Corporation common stock, which is selling for $5 per share. Florence purchased the shares six months ago for $4 per share. Florence is in the 28 percent marginal tax rate bracket, and Eunice is in the 10 percent marginal tax rate bracket. Should Florence sell the shares and give the proceeds to her daughter? Write a memorandum to Florence explaining the tax results. Communication Skills

52. **LO7** Mikel's daughter, Liudmila, is planning to go to law school in the fall. Mikel has promised her that he will pay her tuition, fees, and book costs. Mikel has 1,000 shares of Konrad Corporation stock that he bought four years ago for $50 per share plus commissions. He would like to use the stock to finance Liudmila's law school costs. The Konrad Corporation stock is selling for $40 per share. If Mikel is in the 28 percent marginal tax rate bracket, should he sell the shares or gift them to Liudmila? Explain the difference in the tax consequences of each option.

53. **LO7** Alex begins using his automobile for business purposes in his new job. The automobile cost $25,000 and has a fair market value of $9,000 on the date of the conversion to business use.
a. What is Alex's initial basis in the automobile? Explain.
b. What is Alex's basis for computing depreciation on the automobile? Explain.

54. **LO7** Refer to problem 53. Alex uses the automobile for three years and then sells it. During this period, he properly deducts a total of $3,600 in depreciation. What is Alex's gain or loss on the automobile if he sells it for
a. $4,000?
b. $23,000?
c. $9,000?

55. **LO7** Yohanse's aunt Millie gives him a storage warehouse valued at $250,000 to use in his delivery business. The warehouse has been vacant since Millie inherited it from her grandfather several years ago. At that time, the warehouse had a value of $300,000 and a basis of $50,000.
   a. What is Yohanse's initial basis in the warehouse? Explain.
   b. What is Yohanse's depreciable basis for the warehouse? Explain.
   c. Determine the holding period for Yohanse's warehouse.

56. **LO7** Refer to problem 55. Yohanse uses the warehouse for four years and sells it. During this period, he properly deducts a total of $25,000 in depreciation. What is Yohanse's gain or loss on the warehouse if he sells it for
   a. $285,000?
   b. $215,000?
   c. $245,000?

57. **LO7** Chanetra inherits land from her aunt, Tameka. Tameka's adjusted basis in the land was $150,000, and the fair market value at the date of her death was $200,000. Six months after Tameka's death, the land is appraised at $225,000. Plans for a nearby shopping mall are announced, and the fair market value skyrockets to $400,000 when the land is transferred to Chanetra nine months after her aunt's death. The total value of all Tameka's assets is $850,000 at date of death and $860,000 six months after death.
   a. Can the executor elect the alternate valuation date? Explain.
   b. What is Chanetra's basis?

58. **LO7** Jesse's grandfather dies on April 13 of the current year. Jesse inherits the following property:

| Property | Basis | FMV—April 13 | FMV—Oct. 13 |
|---|---|---|---|
| Land | $ 5,000 | $20,000 | $13,000 |
| Stock | 14,000 | 10,000 | 12,000 |
| Watch | 50 | 500 | 500 |

   a. What is Jesse's basis in the inherited property?
   b. What is Jesse's basis in the property if the executor of the estate elects the alternate valuation date?
   c. Assume that the executor elects the alternate valuation date and distributes title to the land to Jesse on June 23 of the current year, when the fair market value of the land is $17,000. What is Jesse's basis in her inherited property?
   d. Assume that the executor elects the alternate valuation date and distributes the property to Jesse on December 2 of the current year, when the fair market values are $15,000 for the land, $11,500 for the stock, and $500 for the watch. What is Jesse's basis in her inherited property?

59. **LO7** Taylor dies on February 19 of the current year. Among the assets in his estate are 500 shares of Dane Company preferred stock. Ten years earlier, Taylor paid $14 per share for the stock. Market values per share for Dane preferred stock on various dates in the current year are as follows:

| | |
|---|---|
| February 19 | $12 |
| April 1 | $18 |
| August 19 | $10 |
| November 21 | $16 |

Taylor's will provides that his niece Sherry is to receive the Dane shares. What is Sherry's basis in the shares in each of the following circumstances?
   a. No elections are made by the executor, and the shares are given to Sherry on April 1.
   b. The executor validly elects the alternate valuation date, and Sherry receives the shares on November 21.
   c. The executor validly elects the alternate valuation date, and Sherry receives the shares on April 1.

60. **LO7** Phong would like to begin planning her estate. She owns marketable securities that cost $10,000 twelve years ago. The market value is $40,000. She wonders whether she should sell her securities and distribute the proceeds to her son before she dies or just give the securities directly to him. Phong's marginal tax rate is 33 percent; her son's marginal tax rate is 12 percent. Write a letter to Phong explaining an optimal tax strategy for transferring assets to her son. Communication Skills

61. **LO7** Return to the facts in problem 60. Assume that the securities have a fair market value of $2,000. What positive tax strategy exists in this situation? Explain.

62. **LO7** Demetri starts a public accounting practice during the current year. He converts 10 percent of his home into an office. Demetri purchased the property four years ago for $100,000. The portion of the purchase price allocated to the house was $80,000. The house (exclusive of the land) is worth $120,000 when he begins operating his practice in his home. What is Demetri's basis in the home office?

63. **LO7** Alexis purchases a duplex by paying $18,000 cash and assuming the seller's $80,000 mortgage. She pays legal fees of $3,000 and spends $9,000 on painting and carpeting the 2 units before renting out 1 unit and moving into the other (i.e., 1 unit is her personal residence). Three years later, Alexis purchases a house and moves out of the duplex unit and rents it out. She had taken $4,800 in depreciation on the rental unit and had her unit repainted at a cost of $900 before renting it out. Because of a general decline in property values, the duplex is worth only $60,000 when she moves out of it. What is her adjusted basis in the duplex?

64. **LO7** Phoebe opens a bait delivery service during the current year. In starting up the business, she decides to use her personal truck as a delivery vehicle. She had paid $16,000 for the truck, which was worth $10,000 when she turned it into a delivery truck. Communication Skills
    a. What is her initial basis in the truck? What is her basis for depreciation on the truck? Explain.
    b. After using the truck for two years, Phoebe sells it and uses the $5,300 in proceeds as a down payment on a new delivery van. She had correctly deducted $2,700 in straight-line depreciation on the truck during the two years of business use. Write a letter to Phoebe explaining the amount of gain or loss resulting from the sale and why that is the result.

65. **LO8** On January 5, 2021, Henry purchases 500 shares of Wichmann, Inc., common stock at a cost of $24,700. On April 1, 2021, he purchases an additional 300 shares for $19,500. On November 13, 2021, Wichmann, Inc., declares and distributes a 30 percent stock dividend. On December 23, 2021, Wichmann distributes a cash dividend of 50 cents per share. On February 19, 2022, Henry sells 800 shares of the Wichmann, Inc., stock for $45 per share.
    a. How much income or loss does Henry recognize in 2021 and 2022 on his Wichmann, Inc. stock?
    b. Explain how Henry can improve the tax results of the 2022 sale.

66. **LO8** On September 5 of last year, Edwina purchased 100 shares of Atlantis Corporation common stock for $5,000. In December of the current year, she receives a nontaxable stock dividend of 10 shares of preferred stock from Atlantis. At the date of the dividend, the fair market value of the preferred stock is $20 per share, and the fair market value of the common stock is $30 per share. What is the basis of the preferred and common shares owned by Edwina?

67. **LO8** Clarece has the option of receiving 2 shares of common stock as a stock dividend on the 10 shares of Ramble Company common stock that she owns. She paid $30 per share for her 10 shares. The common stock is now selling for $20 per share. In lieu of receiving the 2 shares, Clarece may elect to receive $40 in cash. Write a memo explaining the tax consequences of Clarece's options. Communication Skills

68. **LO8** Eric owns 600 shares of Razor, Inc., stock for which he paid $3,500 in 2016. On December 14, 2021, he sells the 600 shares for $4 per share and pays a commission of $200 on the sale. On January 3, 2022, Eric purchases 500 shares of

Razor, Inc., for $3 per share and pays a $150 commission on the purchase. What is Eric's recognized gain or loss on the sale of the 600 shares? What is his basis in the 500 shares purchased in 2022?

69. **LO8** On November 14, 2021, Noel sells 2,000 shares of Marker, Inc., stock for $6,000. He had purchased the stock two years earlier for $10,000. Because the price of the stock continued to drop, Noel purchases additional shares of Marker stock on December 10, 2021. What are the tax effects of the sale of the stock and the basis in the new shares if Noel
    a. Repurchases 2,000 shares for $5,000?
    b. Repurchases 800 shares for $2,000?
    c. Repurchases 4,000 shares for $9,000?
70. **LO8** Lynn bought 100 shares of Filidelphia Corporation stock for $10,000 three years ago. On December 24, she sells 50 shares for $4,000. She plans to buy 100 more shares of Filidelphia stock for $7,000 on January 17. Explain the tax treatment of these transactions. Include a discussion of the underlying concepts that govern the results. What could Lynn do to change the results?

## ISSUE IDENTIFICATION PROBLEMS

In each of the following problems, identify the tax issue(s) posed by the facts presented. Determine the possible tax consequences of each issue that you identify.

71. Leineia owns 1,000 shares of Serous Corporation common stock. She paid $26 per share several years ago. On December 31 of the current year, Serous distributes a $5 per share cash dividend. It reports that $3 per share is taxable and $2 is a nontaxable dividend.
72. During the current year, Horace's business warehouse is damaged by a tornado. It had an adjusted basis of $40,000 before the tornado. The cost of repairing the damage is $11,000. Horace's insurance company reimburses him $8,000 for the repairs.
73. Jolene owns a dry-cleaning business. During the current year, a rainstorm causes a roof leak that shorts out a dry-cleaning machine. The cost of repairing the machine is $300, none of which is compensated by Jolene's insurance. The adjusted basis of the machine before it shorted was $14,000.
74. Charles buys a car for $15,000 that has a fair market value of $10,000.
75. Kendrick pays a construction company $20,000 to remodel a house.
76. The Lester Partnership wants to develop a shopping mall on a former farm. The farmer wanted $260,000 for the land, $80,000 for the farm buildings, and $130,000 for the farmhouse. Although it wanted only the land, Lester agreed to the farmer's terms. It then paid Ace Wrecking Company $20,000 to tear down the buildings. Lester was able to sell the scrap lumber from the buildings for $12,000.
77. Carter wants to retire from his florist business, and his long-time employee, Howard, would like to take over the business.
78. For his 18th birthday, Kevin gave his son, Gabe, 5 gold coins for which he paid $500 each two years earlier. On Gabe's birthday, coins were selling for $450. One month after his birthday, Gabe sells two of the coins for $525 each and uses the money to buy a motorcycle.
79. Tommi inherits Dierhopf Corporation common stock from her uncle, Norvel. Norvel's adjusted basis in the stock is $200,000, and the fair market value is $380,000. Six months after Norvel's death, the stock's value is $420,000. Nine months after his death, when the stock's value is $350,000, Tommi receives the stock from her uncle's estate.

80. On September 14 of last year, Wenona purchased 1,000 shares of Campbell Corporation common stock at a total cost of $8,000. In December of the current year, Campbell pays a nontaxable stock dividend of 1 share of preferred stock for every 10 shares of common. On the date of the dividend announcement, Campbell's common stock is selling for $14 per share and its preferred stock for $20 per share.

81. Monica owns 1,400 shares of Northeast Utilities common stock. In August of this year, when its stock was selling for $10 per share, Northeast announced a 20 percent stock dividend. In lieu of receiving the dividend shares, stockholders have the option of receiving $2 per share in cash.

# TECHNOLOGY APPLICATIONS

82. **RIA RESEARCH EXERCISE** Use the RIA Checkpoint database to answer the following questions. Cut and paste the relevant Internal Revenue Code and Treasury Regulation section(s) into your solution and explain how the authority answers the tax issue in question. Give the most specific citation applicable [e.g., Sec. 168(a)(1)] that answers the question. Note: If the answer can be found in both the code and regulations, you must provide both authorities.

the answer company™ THOMSON REUTERS®

Research Skills

a. On March 1, Angela sells land that cost $20,000 for $32,000. To make the sale, Angela agrees to pay the property taxes on the land for the entire year. What code section and/or regulation provides the tax treatment of the payment of the property taxes on the sale of the property?
b. Miguel receives stock with a fair market value of $30,000 from his grandfather as a wedding present. His grandfather's basis is the stock is $5,000. A gift tax of $2,000 is paid by the grandfather on the transfer. What code section and/or regulation provides the tax treatment of the gift taxes paid by the grandfather?
c. Gloria exchanges her interest in the Amling Partnership for an interest in the Staten Partnership. What code section and/or regulation denies like-kind exchange treatment on Gloria's exchange?
d. Melvin's apartment building is condemned by the City of Lacy. To compensate Melvin, the city gives him a comparable apartment building in another part of the city. Melvin had paid $80,000 for the apartment building. The replacement building is worth $125,000. What code section and/or regulation allows Melvin to defer recognition of the gain he realizes on his apartment building?

83. **RIA RESEARCH EXERCISE** Use the RIA Checkpoint database to answer the following questions. Cut and paste the relevant Internal Revenue Code and Treasury Regulation section(s) into your solution and explain how the authority answers the tax issue in question. Give the most specific citation applicable [e.g., Sec. 168(a)(1)] that answers the question. NOTE: If the answer can be found in both the code and regulations, you must provide both authorities.

the answer company™ THOMSON REUTERS®

Research Skills

Jerry and Jane are married on March 18, 2021. They use Jane's house as their residence and sell Jerry's house on April 27, 2021 for $420,000. Jerry had purchased the house in 2014 for $120,000.

a. What code section and/or regulation allows the exclusion of gain from the sale of a taxpayer's residence?
b. What code section and/or regulation provides the general limit on the amount of gain that can be excluded?
c. What code section and/or regulation further limits the amount of gain that Jerry and Jane can exclude on their joint return?

84. Blair and Britain divorce in the current year. Blair agrees to transfer her interest in their principal residence to Britain. They had purchased the home for $80,000 four years before the divorce. At the time of the divorce, the house is worth $120,000.

Tax Simulation

REQUIRED: Determine the income tax consequences of this transfer of property for Blair and Britain. Search a tax research database and find the relevant authority(ies) that forms the basis for your answer. Your answer should include the exact text of the authority(ies) and an explanation of the application of the authority to Britain and Blair's facts. If there is any uncertainty about the validity of your answer, indicate the cause for the uncertainty.

Research Skills

85. Several years ago, Steve gave his nephew Rashan his coin collection valued at $12,000 with a basis of $3,000. Steve's intent was to ensure that Rashan has money for college. Rashan is now a senior in high school, and the coins are worth $16,000. Rashan is considering selling some of the coins to put toward his first semester's tuition. His marginal tax rate is 15 percent and will remain at that rate throughout his college years because of part-time work. Steve asks Rashan to give the coins back to him and tells Rashan not to worry about it. Steve is older, and his will states that Rashan gets the coin collection. Rashan is confused. He can cover his tuition, fees, and other expenses for the first two years from savings and student loans. But he does not understand what Steve is trying to accomplish by asking for the coins. Research this situation and explain all the tax ramifications to Rashan.

Research Skills

86. Harry and Freddi, a married couple, purchased 100 shares of Opaque Mutual Fund in 2006 for $2,800 as joint tenants with the right of survivorship. Freddi dies during the current year. The fair market value of the shares is $5,000 on the date of death. Six months later, the value is $5,100. Determine Harry's basis in the 100 shares.

# INTEGRATIVE PROBLEM

87. Emelio and Charita are married taxpayers with two dependent children. Emelio starts a computer consulting business in 2021. Charita works as a real estate broker. During 2021, they have the following property transactions:
    a. Emelio purchases an office building on March 15, 2021, to use in his computer consulting business. The price of the property is $120,000. He pays $15,000 in cash and signs a 30-year, 10 percent mortgage for the remainder. For property tax purposes, the land is assessed at $10,000 and the building at $30,000. Emelio pays $3,000 for a new roof for the building.
    b. Emelio was employed by Computer Corporation as a consultant before starting his own business. Computer Corporation lets Emelio purchase the computer equipment in his office for use in his business. He makes the purchase on April 3, 2021. The fair market value of the equipment is $20,000, but Emelio pays $16,000 to Computer Corporation. Computer Corporation's original basis in the equipment was $36,000, and its adjusted basis at the time of the transfer to Emelio is $8,000.
    c. Emelio takes the color printer that the children have been using at home to use in the office in his consulting business. The original price of the printer was $8,000, but it is worth $4,000 when converted to business use on April 1, 2021.
    d. On March 30, 2021, Emelio buys office furniture to use in his business for $2,200.
    e. In January, Charita purchases a new car to use in her real estate business. She pays $19,500 for the car and $1,500 to have a sunroof installed in it. During the year, she drives the car 6,800 miles for business and 3,200 for personal use.

f. Charita uses a room in their home exclusively and regularly as an office. The room is 12 feet by 12 feet. The total area in the home is 2,400 square feet. Charita purchased office furniture for $800 when she started using the office in the home in June 2016. She and Emelio paid $140,000 for the property in 2011, of which $20,000 is allocated to the land.

g. Emelio and Charita own a rental house. Charita acquired the house from her former husband in 2013 as part of their divorce settlement. Charita and her former husband paid $50,000 for the house (which is her basis in the property) in 2004. Charita estimates that the property increased in value to $80,000 ($70,000 for the house, $10,000 for the land) when it was converted to rental property in October 2013.

h. Charita inherits 200 shares of stock in Desmond, Inc., from her uncle, who paid $700 for it in 1988. At the date of the uncle's death, the stock is worth $14,000. The executor of the estate elects to use the alternate valuation date, at which time the stock is worth $13,300. Charita receives the stock two months later when it is worth $14,500.

i. Emelio and Charita own stock in Software Corporation. They purchased 1,000 shares for $20 per share in July 2014. They paid $400 in brokerage commissions. On July 21, 2021, Software Corporation distributed a 2-for-1 stock split. The fair market value at the time of the split was $100 per share.

j. On July 21, 2016, Emelio's father gave him 100 shares of stock in Flex Corporation. His father paid $35 per share in June 2007. The fair market value at the date of the gift was $45 per share.

Based on the information provided, determine the initial basis of each of Emelio and Charita's assets. If more than one basis is possible, list the alternatives and explain when each basis would apply.

# DISCUSSION CASES

88. Monica is planning to start her own accounting, tax, and financial planning business. Her uncle Gus has given her file cabinets, a desk, computer equipment, and bookcases that were in his den until he sold his house. Gus recently moved to a lakefront cottage and no longer needs the furniture and equipment. Gus's adjusted basis for all the items is $3,500, and the fair market value is $2,000. Monica will convert 20 percent of her personal residence into her office and will use it exclusively for her business. Monica's residence has a fair market value of $150,000 and an adjusted basis of $80,000 (10 percent is allocated to the land). What are the tax ramifications of the gifts and the conversion? What will be the depreciable basis of the property? Explain your answers in terms of the underlying concepts that govern the result.

89. Terry purchased stock in Yippee Corporation for $10,000 in May 1986. He bought stock in Zapper Corporation for $20,000 in June 1989. The Yippee Corporation stock is currently worth $90,000, and the Zapper Corporation stock is worth $15,000. Terry is in very poor health, and he comes to you for tax advice. What advice would you give him regarding his stock holdings? Is there any additional information you would like to ask him for before giving him tax advice?

# TAX PLANNING CASES

Communication Skills

90. Luther, 72, is a lifelong bachelor who has been very successful in his business and investment endeavors. He realizes that he should begin to do some tax planning for his death. Although he intends to leave the bulk of his $200,000,000 estate to the Northern State Technical University School of Accounting, he does have a few nieces and nephews for whom he would like to provide (although not too lavishly). Listed here is a selection of assets he is thinking of giving to his nephews and nieces:

| Asset | Fair Market Value | Basis | Suspended Loss |
|---|---|---|---|
| Keating S&L stock | $ 10,000 | $ 200,000 | |
| Impressionist painting | 5,000,000 | –0– | |
| Land held as an investment | 2,000,000 | 1,500,000 | |
| Limited partnership interest | 100,000 | 400,000 | $1,300,000 |
| Rental property | 4,000,000 | 1,000,000 | 2,500,000 |
| General Motors stock | 2,000,000 | 1,000,000 | |

1. Consider each of the following questions from Luther's point of view (what is best from the standpoint of his tax situation). Explain.
   a. Which of these properties would be best to give away to his favorite nephew? Why?
   b. Which of these properties would be the worst to give away? Why?
   c. Which property(ies) should Luther definitely retain? Why?
   d. Which property(ies) should Luther consider selling? Why?
2. Luther comes to your accounting firm for advice. Write a memorandum explaining your recommendations for optimizing Luther's tax situation in regard to assets listed.

Communication Skills

91. Your client, Dale, is the president and sole stockholder of a steel fabrication company. He has been planning to buy a new piece of equipment for $500,000. He is upset to learn that the $500,000 cost would have to be depreciated over seven years. He comes to you with an idea from his son, Dale Jr., who is taking an introductory accounting course at the local college. Dale Jr. tells his father that self-constructed assets are accounted for differently from purchased assets and that the company could be better off if it constructed the needed new equipment. Dale figures his regular employees could indeed build the new equipment using the company's idle capacity. For several years, the company has operated at 80 percent of capacity, and that level of production is used as the denominator level for allocation of overhead. Overhead is currently charged to production at a rate of 150 percent of direct labor cost, but Dale Jr. says the new equipment will not have to bear any overhead costs because the company has idle capacity and all overhead costs are already being absorbed by regular production. Dale expects to incur the following incremental costs if his regular employees construct the new equipment:

| | |
|---|---|
| Direct labor | $300,000 |
| Direct materials | 120,000 |
| Other direct costs | 30,000 |
| Interest on construction loan | 50,000 |
| | $500,000 |

Although the cost will be the same regardless of whether Dale makes or buys the equipment, he feels he would be better off under the construction alternative because the interest is deductible in the year incurred. As a result, the depreciable cost would be only $450,000.

Do you agree or disagree with Dale's analysis? Write a memorandum to Dale explaining your recommendations for optimizing his tax situation.

# ETHICS DISCUSSION CASE

92. Assume you are a CPA. A new client, Mark, a local chiropractor, has brought you the financial information for his business at the close of the past year. Previously, Mark prepared his own tax returns and had them reviewed by Blacke & Co. You find the information to be organized and fairly straightforward. Mark does bring one recent transaction to your attention. He sold an x-ray machine for $10,000 near the end of the past year. The machine cost $25,000 three years earlier. Mark did not deduct depreciation expense in the year of acquisition. His business incurred an operating loss that year. Therefore, Mark "saved" some of his basis and did not report a loss as big as he could have. For the following year and for this year, Mark recorded depreciation of $5,000 annually. He tells you that he would like to "reclaim" the depreciation he did not deduct in the year of acquisition. He insists there will not be a problem because he could have taken the depreciation three years ago. Also, by applying it to the adjusted basis for the sales transaction, he will not report a loss. So the recognized loss will not be used to offset other income. Advise Mark on the propriety of this transaction. You may wish to consult the Statements on Standards for Tax Services (which can be found at www.aicpa.org). Write Mark a letter explaining his situation. Communication Skills

10

# Cost Recovery on Property: Depreciation, Depletion, and Amortization

## Learning Objectives:

LO 1 Explain how taxpayers recover the cost of long-lived assets and the general criteria for taking deductions for depreciation, depletion, or amortization on an investment in a long-lived asset.

LO 2 Illustrate how the timing of the cost-recovery deduction affects the real after-tax return on an investment property.

LO 3 Identify the factors involved in and the general approach to calculating depreciation on assets acquired before 1981.

LO 4 Explain the general changes in the approach to calculating depreciation on assets acquired after 1980 under the Accelerated Cost Recovery System (ACRS).

LO 5 Explain Section 179's Election to Expense and its limitations on the deduction.

LO 6 Explain how to determine the amount of cost recovery on various classes of assets under the Modified Accelerated Cost Recovery System (MACRS).

LO 7 Calculate cost recovery using the Alternative Depreciation System (ADS).

LO 8 Describe the limitations on depreciation deductions for listed property in general and the specific limitation on depreciation of automobiles.

LO 9 Explain the deduction for depletion and how to calculate depletion using the cost method and the statutory percentage method.

LO 10 Describe how taxpayers deduct amortization on intangible assets.

## concept review

### GENERAL CONCEPTS

**Administrative convenience** Those items for which the cost of compliance would exceed the revenue generated are not taxed. pg. 2-3

**Related party** Family members and corporations that are owned by family members are considered related parties, as are certain other relationships between entities in which the power to control the substance of a transaction is evidenced through majority ownership. pg. 2-4

### ACCOUNTING CONCEPTS

**Accounting method** A taxpayer must adopt an accounting method that clearly reflects income. pg. 2-9

**Annual accounting period** All entities must report the results of their operations on an annual basis (the tax year). Each tax year stands on its own, apart from other tax years. pg. 2-9

**Conduit entity** An entity whose tax attributes flow through to its owners for tax purposes. pg. 2-6

**Entity** All items of income, deduction, and so on are traced to the tax unit responsible for the item. pg. 2-6

### DEDUCTION CONCEPTS

**Basis** The amount of unrecovered investment in an asset. As amounts are expended and/or recovered relative to an asset over time, the basis is adjusted in consideration of such changes. The **adjusted basis** of an asset is the original basis, plus or minus the changes in the amount of unrecovered investment. pgs. 2-13, 2-21

**Business purpose** To be deductible, an expenditure or a loss must have a business or other economic purpose that exceeds any tax avoidance motive. The primary motive for the transaction must be to make a profit. pg. 2-18

**Capital recovery** No income is realized until the taxpayer receives more than the amount invested to produce the income. The amount invested in an asset represents the maximum amount recoverable. pg. 2-13

**Legislative grace** Any tax relief provided is the result of a specific act of Congress that must be strictly applied and interpreted. All income received is taxable unless a specific provision in the tax law excludes the income from taxation. Deductions must be approached with the philosophy that nothing is deductible unless a provision in the tax law allows the deduction. pg. 2-12

# 10-1 INTRODUCTION

LO 1

Explain how taxpayers recover the cost of long-lived assets and the general criteria for taking deductions for depreciation, depletion, or amortization on an investment in a long-lived asset.

LO 2

Illustrate how the timing of the cost-recovery deduction affects the real after-tax return on an investment property.

Based on the legislative grace concept, business expenses are classified as related either to a trade or business or to a production-of-income activity. To be deductible, an expense must have a business purpose and be related to the current tax year. If an expenditure results in a long-lived asset that benefits several annual accounting periods, its cost is generally allocated on a reasonable basis to the tax years in which it is used to produce income. According to the capital recovery concept, a taxpayer does not realize taxable income until after the capital used to produce the income is recovered. An asset's basis is the maximum amount of investment in an asset that can be subtracted from income as a capital recovery. Tax **depreciation**, amortization, and depletion are tax accounting methods used to periodically recover the investment in assets. These accounting methods provide a reasonable allocation of bases to the annual accounting periods benefited by the use of the assets. The text first discusses the concept of capital recovery through depreciation. Then, it turns to tax accounting for depreciation, amortization, and depletion.

This chapter considers several depreciation methods. Generally, a taxpayer can choose among three alternative depreciation methods. The method chosen determines the timing and the amount of the annual depreciation deduction. The timing and the amount of the depreciation expense affect the present value of the tax savings from the deduction (the time value of money effect). As a general rule, the earlier the taxpayer can claim a depreciation deduction, the greater its present value is.

**Example 1** Angelo has $100,000 to invest in an asset. The cost of asset A will be deductible immediately. The cost of asset B cannot be deducted until it is sold. Both assets produce the same annual revenue and cost flows and will be held for 10 years. If Angelo is in a 32% marginal tax rate bracket during the 10-year period and the cost of capital is 10%, which asset will provide the greater real after-tax return?

**Discussion: The deduction for both assets provides a $32,000 ($100,000 × 32%) tax savings. However, because asset A's tax savings occur in the first year, it results in real tax savings of $32,000. The present value of the future deduction for asset B is only $12,352 [$32,000 × 0.386 (the present value of $1 at 10% for 10 years)]. As a result of deferring the capital recovery on asset B for 10 years, its present value to Angelo is decreased by $19,648 ($32,000 − $12,352), compared to the immediate tax savings resulting from asset A.**

**More likely, a taxpayer will be faced with a situation in which the investment can be recovered as the asset is used to earn income.**

**Example 2** Tawana purchases an apartment building for $100,000 at the beginning of 2021 for use as rental property. Assume that she is in the 24% marginal tax bracket, her cost of capital is 10%, and she sells the building at the end of 10 years for $100,000, its original cost. To determine the effect of depreciation on the transaction, ignore the cost of the land, which is not included in the $100,000 cost basis of the building. Also, assume that the 15% net long-term capital gains rate applies. What are the tax effects of the purchase, use, and disposition of the building?

**Discussion: The $100,000 cost of the building is depreciated using the MACRS depreciation system (explained later in this chapter). The depreciation calculations and the annual tax savings at a 24% marginal tax rate discounted at 10% are as follows:**

| Year | MACRS Depreciation Rate | Annual Depreciation Deduction | 24% Tax Rate Savings | 10% PV Factor | PV of Tax Savings |
|---|---|---|---|---|---|
| 2021 | 3.485 | $ 3,485 | $ 836 | 0.909 | $ 760 |
| 2022 | 3.636 | 3,636 | 873 | 0.826 | 721 |
| 2023 | 3.636 | 3,636 | 873 | 0.751 | 656 |
| 2024 | 3.636 | 3,636 | 873 | 0.683 | 596 |
| 2025 | 3.636 | 3,636 | 873 | 0.621 | 542 |
| 2026 | 3.636 | 3,636 | 873 | 0.564 | 492 |
| 2027 | 3.636 | 3,636 | 873 | 0.513 | 448 |
| 2028 | 3.636 | 3,636 | 873 | 0.467 | 408 |
| 2029 | 3.636 | 3,636 | 873 | 0.424 | 370 |
| 2030 | 3.636 | 3,636 | 873 | 0.386 | 337 |
| **Totals** | | $36,209 | $8,693 | | $5,330 |

| **Present value of tax savings on building** | | | $ 5,330 |
|---|---|---|---|
| **Sale of Building:** | | | |
| Sales price | | $100,000 | |
| Less: Adjusted basis: | | | |
| Building—cost | $100,000 | | |
| Less: Depreciation | (36,209) | (63,791) | |
| Gain on sale of property | | $ 36,209 | |
| Tax on gain at capital gain rate (15% × $36,209) | | $ 5,431 | |
| Present value factor | | × .386 | |
| Present value of tax cost of gain on sale | | | (2,096) |
| Net tax savings from depreciation deduction | | | $ 3,234 |

**The present value of Tawana's tax savings related to depreciation on the building is $3,234 (effectively a cash inflow resulting from reducing taxes that would have been paid out). When Tawana sells the building at the end of 10 years, she realizes and recognizes a $36,209 gain. The gain recognized stems from the depreciation deducted over the 10-year period in which the building was used. The gain on the sale of the building is taxed at the 15% capital gains rate for an individual. The present value of the tax to be paid on the gain from the sale of the building is $2,096 (a cash outflow). Thus, Tawana has been able to earn a $3,234 profit. The profit results from the timing differences in the present value (depreciation deductions versus gain on the sale) and from marginal tax rate differences (ordinary tax rates versus capital gains tax rate).**

In example 2, note the following points:

- The earlier the depreciation deduction is taken, the greater will be the present value of the tax savings to the taxpayer.
- A taxpayer can receive an economic benefit by accelerating the recovery of basis and deferring income related to the property. In example 2, the property is sold for its original purchase price. Yet, the effect of depreciation is to provide the taxpayer with a positive present value.
- The taxpayer benefits when deductions can be claimed at regular tax rates and any gain from the sale of the property is taxed at a lower rate. The depreciation deductions in example 2 reduce ordinary income subject to tax at 24 percent. However, the gain on the sale of the building is subject to tax at the 15 percent long-term capital gains rate. Limitations on this effect are explained in Chapter 11.

### concept check

The *business purpose concept* allows a deduction for expenses that have a business or other profit-making purpose that exceeds any tax avoidance motive. If an expenditure results in a long-lived asset that benefits several accounting periods, its cost is generally allocated on a reasonable basis to the tax years in which it is used to produce income in accordance with the *annual accounting period concept*. The cost is allocated using depreciation, amortization, and depletion methods that fully recover the cost per the *capital recovery concept*.

## 10-2 CAPITAL RECOVERY FROM DEPRECIATION OR COST RECOVERY

LO 3

Identify the factors involved in and the general approach to calculating depreciation on assets acquired before 1981.

The depreciation rules in effect when an asset is placed in service determine the depreciation method to be used during the life of the asset. An asset is placed in service when it is set up and ready for its intended use for a business purpose.[1] This general rule provides certainty and consistency when computing the depreciation deduction for a specific asset. However, frequent changes in the tax laws make the depreciation rules seem complex when computing depreciation for assets acquired over several years. As the time line in Figure 10-1 shows, depreciation methods have undergone three major changes since 1980. In addition, Congress has made several important but less dramatic changes in nearly every session. Taxpayers and tax advisers alike face significant difficulty in coping with the frequent changes in the depreciation rules.

Figure 10-1

## Major Changes in Depreciation Methods Since 1980

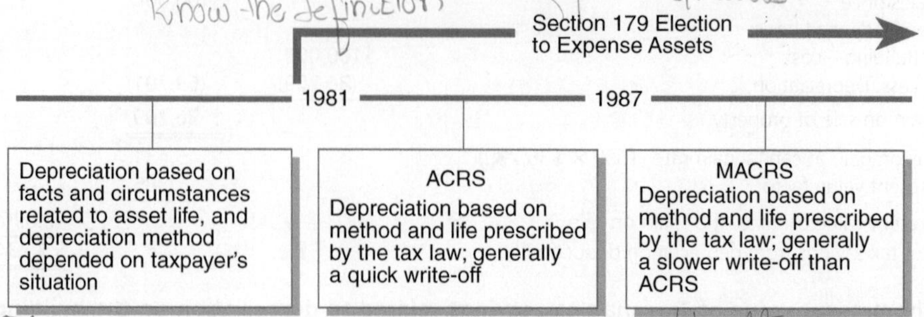


Congress has established four different depreciation systems since the mid-1960s. Two systems, facts and circumstances and the Asset Depreciation Range (ADR), apply to assets placed in service before 1981. These systems were derived from financial accounting and required taxpayers to depreciate an asset's net cost over its estimated useful life in the business. Taxpayers had considerable freedom in selecting the actual computational method. Most taxpayers used one of the methods commonly taught in financial accounting—straight-line, sum-of-the-year's digits, or declining balance—all of which were appropriate for facts and circumstances depreciation systems. These methods require taxpayers to estimate an asset's useful life and its salvage value and to determine a method of allocating depreciation to the first and last year of the asset's life. The ADR system differed from facts and circumstances because it had specific classes for depreciable assets. For each class, the IRS specified the average life of assets in the class. Taxpayers did not have to determine their useful life. Also, ADR required the adoption of a convention for depreciating assets in their first year of use. That is, taxpayers did not have to be concerned with the actual date assets were placed in service. The convention stated the percentage of depreciation allowed in the year assets were placed in service. Although the ADR system helped minimize conflicts between taxpayers and the IRS over useful life estimates, record-keeping complexities and other factors beyond the scope of this discussion doomed this system. These disputes continued because of computational errors and the estimates taxpayers were using under the facts and circumstances system.

LO 4

Explain the general changes in the approach to calculating depreciation on assets acquired after 1980 under the Accelerated Cost Recovery System (ACRS).

In 1981, Congress mandated the **Accelerated Cost Recovery System (ACRS)** in an effort to provide incentives for capital investment—and effectively eliminated the use of the facts and circumstances and ADR systems for assets placed in service after 1980. As part of the Economic Recovery Tax Act of 1981, this radically new approach to calculating depreciation was an attempt to influence the economy through tax legislation.[2] Unlike the facts and circumstances system and ADR, ACRS did not attempt to match an asset's depreciation to the annual accounting period that benefits from its use. Rather, the primary purpose of ACRS was to accelerate the capital recovery (i.e., present value of tax savings) that taxpayers receive from depreciating property. In fact, ACRS and the current system, MACRS, both use the term *cost recovery* instead of *depreciation* to identify the deduction. Accordingly, in the discussion that follows, depreciation and cost recovery are used interchangeably to mean depreciation as it is generally understood.

Another factor that influenced the switch to ACRS from traditional depreciation methods was the concern over the complexity of the tax law. ACRS enhanced administrative convenience by standardizing the depreciation rules to help reduce the continuing conflict between the IRS and taxpayers over estimated useful life and salvage value. This was accomplished by having only five useful lives, by not subtracting an estimate of salvage value from an asset's depreciable basis, and by standardizing the conventions for depreciation in the years of an asset's acquisition and disposition.

The current depreciation system, the **Modified Accelerated Cost Recovery System (MACRS)**, is used for assets placed in service after 1986. As its name indicates, MACRS is a modification of ACRS and operates in a similar manner. The primary difference between the two systems is that MACRS specifies longer recovery periods for depreciable assets, which result in slower depreciation than allowed by ACRS. Congress made these modifications because it was more concerned with raising revenue than stimulating the economy. The 1986 tax act reduced individual tax rates to 28 percent from a high of 50 percent and corporate tax rates to 34 percent from a high of 46 percent. To minimize the loss of revenue from tax rate reductions, Congress had to broaden the tax base. One way it did this was by specifying longer recovery periods for depreciable assets, which would result in slower depreciation than allowed by ACRS. However, MACRS continues the use of a standardized depreciation calculation that reduces the complexity of the calculation.[3]

The Alternative Depreciation System (ADS) is an alternative to regular MACRS. Its primary use is for calculating the alternative minimum tax (discussed in Chapter 15). However, taxpayers may elect ADS for determining regular taxable income when there is no need for the greater MACRS deductions. A discussion of ADS follows the discussion of MACRS later in this chapter.

In addition to accelerating the recovery of an investment through ACRS and MACRS, Congress introduced the Section 179 election to expense certain depreciable assets placed in service after 1981. The Section 179 election replaces the deduction for additional first-year depreciation that was allowed before 1981. Initially, Section 179 allowed an expense deduction of as much as $5,000 in the year of acquisition on qualifying property. However, the 1986 act increased the limit to $10,000 for years after 1986. This limit has been increased numerous times. The Protecting Americans from Tax Hikes Act of 2015 increased the limit to $500,000. The 2017 Tax Cuts and Jobs Act increases the limit to $1,000,000. Table 10-1 shows the limitations for recent years.

## 10-3 SECTION 179 ELECTION TO EXPENSE ASSETS

**Section 179** allows an annual current expense deduction for the cost of qualifying depreciable property purchased for use in a trade or business. The deduction for expensed assets is treated as a depreciation deduction. This election allows many small businesses to expense assets as they are purchased instead of depreciating them over several years. The immediate deduction promotes administrative convenience by eliminating the need for extensive depreciation schedules for small purchases.

### 10-3a Qualified Taxpayers

LO 5
Explain Section 179's Election to Expense and its limitations on the deduction.

Individuals, corporations, S corporations, and partnerships may elect to deduct as an expense up to $1,050,000 in 2021 in investment in qualified property to be used in an active trade or business.[4] A married couple is considered one entity for purposes of the election to expense. Although the phrase "active trade or business" is not defined in the tax law, it appears to have the same meaning as the phrase "trade or business" (Chapter 5). The elements of profit motivation, regularity, and continuity of the taxpayer's involvement in the activity and the absence of hobby, amusement, and similar

*Table 10-1*

**Limitation on Section 179 Election to Expense**

| For Tax Years Beginning In | Dollar Limitation | Investment Limitation |
|---|---|---|
| 2010–2015 | 500,000 | 2,000,000 |
| 2016 | 500,000 | 2,010,000 |
| 2017 | 510,000 | 2,030,000 |
| 2018 | 1,000,000 | 2,500,000 |
| 2019 | 1,020,000 | 2,550,000 |
| 2020 | 1,040,000 | 2,590,000 |
| 2021 | 1,050,000 | 2,620,000 |

motivations are important factors to consider when determining whether an activity qualifies for the Section 179 election. This interpretation is supported by the fact that the deduction is not allowed for assets purchased for use in an activity related to the production of income (an investment activity). However, the portion of a mixed-use asset that is used in a trade or business does qualify for immediate deduction under Section 179. Estates and trusts cannot use the Section 179 election to expense assets. The election is not available to these entities because they are formed to protect and conserve the entity's assets for the benefit of the beneficiaries and not to operate an active trade or business.

## 10-3b Qualified Property

The Section 179 expense deduction is allowed only on depreciable, tangible, personal property used in a trade or business. Examples of eligible property are trucks, machinery, furniture, computers, and store shelving. In general, real property, such as buildings, does not qualify for the special election to expense. Although certain building improvements, such as roofs, heating/cooling, and security systems, do qualify. Also excluded from the deduction are land and improvements made directly to the land, such as a parking lot, sidewalks, or a swimming pool. In addition, qualifying property does not include intangible assets such as patents, copyrights, and goodwill.

**Example 3** Kelly purchases a new computer and a new telephone system and installs a new roof and a fire alarm system in her office building. Which of the expenditures qualify for the election to expense?

**Discussion: The computer and the telephone system are depreciable, tangible, personal property and therefore qualify under Section 179. The roof and the fire alarm system are building components and qualify for immediate expensing.**

## 10-3c Limitations on Deduction

The Section 179 election-to-expense deduction is subject to three limitations in 2021:

**Dollar Limitation:** A taxpayer's annual Section 179 deduction cannot exceed the maximum annual limitation ($1,050,000).

**Investment Limitation:** If the taxpayer's investment in Section 179 property exceeds $2,620,000 for the tax year, the annual deduction limit is reduced by one dollar for each dollar of investment over $2,620,000. A taxpayer who purchases more than $3,670,000 of qualifying property may not take any election-to-expense deduction for any of the purchases.

**Taxable Income Limitation:** The Section 179 deduction allowed for a tax year cannot exceed the taxable income from the active conduct of all the taxpayer's trade or business activities.

### Annual Deduction Limit

The annual deduction limit does not have to be prorated according to the length of time an asset is used during the year. The annual deduction limit applies to all tax entities entitled to use Section 179. Thus, the annual limit applies separately to a partnership and to its individual partners. The annual limit also applies separately to an S corporation and to its shareholders.[5] Because the partnership and S corporation are conduit entities, a portion of the entity's total deduction is allocated to each owner, who subtracts it as an expense on the owner's personal tax return. However, the Section 179 deduction allocated to the taxpayer from the conduit entity plus the taxpayer's Section 179 deduction from all other sources cannot exceed the annual limit. Any excess Section 179 election resulting from allocations from several entities must be carried forward to be used in subsequent years.

**Example 4** Roberto is a 50% shareholder and full-time employee of an S corporation. During 2021, the S corporation invests $1,230,000 in equipment qualifying for the Section 179 deduction. Roberto also owns a sole proprietorship that constructs kitchen cabinets. The cabinet business qualifies as an active business for Roberto. During 2021, he purchases

$546,000 worth of equipment to use in his cabinet business. What is the maximum amount that Roberto can deduct as a Section 179 expense for 2021?

**Discussion:** **Roberto's deductible Section 179 expenditures are limited to $1,050,000. The S corporation can elect to deduct $1,050,000 of its $1,230,000 in capital expenditures. The remaining $180,000 is subject to regular depreciation. The S corporation allocates $525,000 (50% × $1,050,000) of its Section 179 deduction to Roberto. Thus, Roberto's qualified Section 179 expenditures total $1,071,000 ($525,000 from the S corporation + $546,000 from the cabinet business). However, the $1,050,000 annual deduction limit applies at the shareholder level as well as at the S corporation level. Therefore, Roberto may elect to deduct only $1,050,000 as a Section 179 expense.**

A taxpayer may choose to use all, part, or none of the annual deduction. By electing to expense less than the limit for a tax year, the taxpayer can avoid a Section 179 deduction carryforward resulting from either the annual limitation or the trade or business income limitation.

**Example 5** Based on the information in example 4, how should Roberto allocate his Section 179 deduction in 2021?

**Discussion:** **Roberto should claim as a Section 179 deduction the $525,000 allocated to him from the S corporation plus $525,000 of the cost of the equipment purchased for use in the cabinet business. The remaining $21,000 cost of the equipment used in his cabinet business is depreciated using regular depreciation methods.**

**If Roberto expenses the $546,000 worth of equipment he purchased for the cabinet business, he will lose $21,000 of the deduction allocated to him from the S corporation by exceeding the $1,050,000 annual limitation by $21,000 ($525,000 + $546,000 = $1,071,000) this year. The $21,000 carries forward to be used in subsequent years. Any amounts that flow to a taxpayer from a conduit entity should always be expensed under Section 179 before any amount is elected from another trade or business of the taxpayer.**

After an asset's basis is reduced by the amount expensed under Section 179, the remaining basis is subject to regular depreciation under any valid method.

**Example 6** Devra Corporation purchases a machine costing $1,052,000 for use in its business. Devra wants to expense $1,050,000 of the asset's cost under Section 179. If Devra makes the Section 179 election to expense $1,050,000 of the asset's cost, what is its depreciable basis in the machine?

**Discussion:** **Devra's depreciable basis for regular depreciation is $2,000. The depreciable basis of the machine is its $1,052,000, less the $1,050,000 it elects to expense under Section 179. The reduction of depreciable basis by amounts expensed under Section 179 is necessary to ensure that the total capital recovery on the machine does not exceed the $1,052,000 invested.**

The Section 179 deduction can be allocated to reduce the basis of qualifying assets in any manner the taxpayer chooses. This allows the deduction to be allocated equally to all assets acquired during the year or to specific assets. This option is important. Two general rules apply to choosing assets to expense. First, do not use the Section 179 election to expense automobiles. As discussed later, automobiles are subject to annual depreciation deduction limits. For purposes of this annual limitation, the Section 179 expense is treated as a depreciation deduction. Because MACRS depreciation on most automobiles exceeds the first-year annual limitation amount, using the election to expense on an automobile does not result in additional tax savings. Second, based on time value of money concepts, taxpayers should take the depreciation deduction as early as possible. This is accomplished by expensing the assets with the longest life and using regular depreciation methods to depreciate assets with the shortest life.

**Example 7** Gwendolyn purchases equipment costing $1,050,000 and a computer system that also costs $1,050,000 for use in her business in 2021. Under MACRS, the equipment is 7-year property, and the computer is 5-year property. How should Gwendolyn allocate her $1,050,000 Section 179 expense deduction?

**Discussion: If Gwendolyn wants to deduct the $1,050,000 maximum election to expense, she should elect to expense the $1,050,000 cost of the equipment. The $1,050,000 cost of the computer system will be deducted over its 5-year life, resulting in greater deductions sooner than if she elected to expense the computer.**

**Gwendolyn could elect to deduct less than the full $1,050,000 Section 179 limit. Because Section 179 is elective, Gwendolyn can decide how much to deduct and the specific assets to expense. This allows taxpayers who do not want or need the extra deductions in the current year to spread the deductions out through depreciation charges.**

## Annual Investment Limit

The annual deduction limit is reduced dollar for dollar by the amount of the investment in qualifying property in excess of $2,620,000 in 2021. As a result of this limitation, a taxpayer who purchases $3,670,000 or more of qualified property cannot expense any amount under Section 179 in 2021.

**Example 8** During 2021, the Allen Partnership places $2,643,000 of Section 179 property in service for use in its business. What is Allen's maximum Section 179 deduction?

**Discussion: Allen's election to expense is reduced to $1,027,000 by the $2,620,000 annual investment limit. Because the partnership invested $23,000 more than the $2,620,000 annual investment limitation ($2,643,000 − $2,620,000), it must reduce the annual deduction limit dollar for dollar by the excess ($1,050,000 − $23,000 = $1,027,000). Note: The $23,000 lost through the annual investment limit is not carried forward to future years. It is lost forever.**

## Active Trade or Business Income Limit

The Section 179 deduction is limited to the total taxable income from the taxpayer's active conduct of any trade or business during the year. Total taxable income is the amount of taxable income computed before deducting the Section 179 expense. For purposes of the income limit, the taxpayer includes salaries and wages, income from a proprietorship, and any trade or business income allocated to the taxpayer from a partnership or S corporation in which the taxpayer actively participates (i.e., passive activities do not enter into the calculation). If the taxable income from the active conduct of a trade or business is less than the allowable Section 179 deduction, any expense election that is over the limit carries forward for use in subsequent years.

**Example 9** During 2021, Michael has a $5,000 net loss in his cabinet-making business. To supplement the family's income, Serena, Michael's wife, earns $7,000 working part-time as a cashier at a local grocery. In addition, they earn $1,000 in interest income on their savings account. Michael also purchases $14,000 worth of equipment for use in his business. For 2021, what is Serena and Michael's maximum Section 179 deduction?

**Discussion: Their maximum deduction is $2,000 because Michael and Serena's taxable business income is only $2,000 ($7,000 salary − $5,000 business loss). The interest income cannot be counted because it is from an investment. Thus, the business income limitation applies, and they can deduct only $2,000 for 2021. They can still elect to expense the full $14,000 Michael paid for the equipment. The $12,000 that they cannot deduct in 2021 carries forward, to be deducted as a Section 179 expense in subsequent years.**

Any Section 179 deduction that is elected and not used because of the taxable income limit can be carried forward and used in a later year. The deductions are carried forward and used on a first-in, first-out basis against the annual limit after current-year deductions. All or part of the deferred deduction can be used in a year in which the investment in qualifying property is less than the annual limits. The basis of an expensed asset for regular depreciation is reduced by the amount expensed under Section 179, even though the deduction cannot be used in the current year and is carried forward.[6] As stated earlier, a taxpayer does not have to use the full expense deduction limit or expense the full cost of an asset. Instead of claiming the full deduction, the taxpayer can elect to expense an amount equal to the income limitation and avoid the carryover.

This alternative is desirable if the taxpayer continually invests in qualified property and would not expect to use the carryforward in the next tax year. The portion of an asset's basis not expensed remains subject to regular depreciation.

**Example 10** Assume that in example 9, Michael purchases $36,000 worth of equipment in 2022. During 2022, Michael has $30,000 in taxable income from his business, and Serena earns a salary of $10,000. What is their maximum Section 179 deduction in 2022?

**Discussion: Michael and Serena may elect to expense up to $40,000 as a Section 179 expense because their taxable business income is $40,000 ($30,000 + $10,000). Michael's current-year purchases of qualified property are less than $40,000, so the amount they can expense depends on the amount elected in 2021. If they elected to expense only the $2,000 income limit amount, they have no deduction to carry forward from 2021, and they can expense only the $36,000 in 2022 purchases. If they had elected to expense the full $14,000 purchase in 2021, they could also expense $4,000 ($40,000 − $36,000 current-year purchases) of the 2021 carryforward. This leaves $8,000 ($12,000 carryforward − $4,000 expensed) of the 2021 carryforward for use in 2023.**

**In this case, if they had anticipated continuing qualifying purchases of at least $40,000 in 2022, they should have elected to expense only the $2,000 limit in 2021. This would have allowed them to depreciate the remaining $12,000 worth of equipment rather than take it slowly over what may be a longer period.**

Note the similarity to the loss limitations discussed in Chapter 7. The effect of the taxable active trade or business income limit is to prevent the Section 179 deduction from creating business losses that offset income from investment income sources.

## Additional First-Year (Bonus) Depreciation

Taxpayers are allowed to claim 100 percent of the cost of qualified property acquired and placed in service after September 27, 2017, and before January 1, 2023, for use in a trade or business or for the production of income. The additional depreciation phases out as follows: 80 percent in 2023, 60 percent in 2024, 40 percent in 2025, 20 percent in 2026, and 0 percent after 2026. Qualifying property is new and used MACRS property with a recovery period of 20 years or less and certain other property. Property that must be depreciated using the alternative depreciation system (ADS) does not qualify.

To ensure that the capital recovery concept is not violated, the depreciable basis of the property is reduced by the bonus depreciation for purposes of computing the regular MACRS depreciation deduction.

**Example 11** Omer Corporation purchases $600,000 of new machinery on February 19, 2021. The machinery is 5-year MACRS property. What is the depreciable basis in the machinery?

**Discussion: MACRS property with a recovery period of 20 years or less qualifies for the 100 percent additional depreciation deduction. Accordingly, Omer deducts $600,000 ($600,000 × 100%) in bonus depreciation. Its depreciable basis in the machinery is reduced to $0 ($600,000 − $600,000).**

The additional first-year depreciation must be claimed on all eligible property unless a taxpayer makes an election not to claim the deduction. The election is made on a class-by-class basis.

**Example 12** Assume that in example 11, Omer Corporation does not want to claim the additional first-year depreciation on the machinery. What is Omer's depreciable basis in the machinery?

**Discussion: Omer must make an election not to claim the additional first-year depreciation deduction. The election applies to all 5-year MACRS property that Omer acquires in 2021. Omer's depreciable basis in the machinery is $600,000 if it elects not to claim bonus depreciation on the machinery.**

Bonus depreciation and the Section 179 election to expense provide for writing off the cost of an asset in the year of acquisition. However, Section 179 has more limitations, primarily the income and investment limits.

**Example 13** Bomhoff Inc. purchases office equipment costing $1,000,000 on April 1, 2021. What are Bomhoff's options for claiming cost recovery on the office equipment in the year of acquisition?

**Discussion: Bomhoff could elect to expense $1,000,000 of the cost of the office equipment. This reduces the adjusted basis (and depreciable basis) of the equipment to $0 ($1,000,000 − $1,000,000). Office equipment is 7-year MACRS property and is eligible for the bonus depreciation deduction. Thus, another option is that Bomhoff deducts $1,000,000 ($1,000,000 × 100%) in additional first-year depreciation. The depreciable basis is reduced to $0 ($1,000,000 − $1,000,000). The choice between the two options will depend on several factors, such as the acquisition of other assets and the income and investment limits of Section 179.**

Important points to remember about additional first-year depreciation:

- The 20 year or less recovery period requirement for qualifying property eliminates residential rental property and nonresidential real property from receiving additional first-year depreciation.
- If a qualifying property is purchased, bonus depreciation must be claimed unless an election not to claim the bonus depreciation is made. The election is made on a class by class basis. Therefore, a taxpayer can claim the bonus depreciation on one or more classes of property (e.g., 10-year property) and not claim the bonus depreciation on other classes of property (e.g., three-year property) acquired during the applicable period.
- The depreciable basis must be reduced by any allowable bonus depreciation.
- Unlike the Section 179 election to expense, there is no dollar or investment limit nor is there an annual income limit. That is, additional first-year depreciation can be deducted even if it causes the business to have a net operating loss. Also, additional first-year depreciation may be taken on property used for the production of income in addition to trade or business property.

For illustrative purposes, unless otherwise noted, the following examples assume that the taxpayer has elected not to claim additional first-year (i.e., bonus) depreciation.

## 10-4 MODIFIED ACCELERATED COST RECOVERY SYSTEM (MACRS)

LO 6

Explain how to determine the amount of cost recovery on various classes of assets under the Modified Accelerated Cost Recovery System (MACRS).

MACRS took effect on January 1, 1987, after six years of ACRS rules. MACRS retains the basic straightforward ACRS approach to calculating the depreciation deduction. The computation is straightforward because the tax law specifies the recovery period, depreciation method, and the acquisition- and disposition-year conventions to be used. To simplify depreciation calculations, the IRS has developed tables incorporating these factors. Under MACRS, an asset's depreciable basis is multiplied by a percentage obtained from an IRS table to determine the depreciation deduction. Therefore, the taxpayer's primary objective is to decide the right table to use. To make that determination, a taxpayer must answer several questions:

- Does the property qualify for MACRS treatment?
- What is the asset's depreciable basis?
- What is the depreciable asset's recovery period?
- What is the appropriate first-year and last-year convention?
- Is an accelerated or a slower cost-recovery method desirable?

These decisions lead a taxpayer to the appropriate IRS percentage tables. Then the depreciation deduction is calculated by multiplying the depreciable basis by the correct percentage from the table.

Table 10-2

## Assets Owned by Individuals

| Depreciable Asset | Nondepreciable Asset |
|---|---|
| House held for rent to others | House used as taxpayer's personal residence |
| Auto used for a *business purpose* (e.g., if 60% of the miles an auto is driven relates to business use, 60% of the auto is a business asset subject to depreciation) | Auto used for commuting to and from work and for other personal uses |
| Furniture in business office | Furniture in taxpayer's personal residence |
| Computer used in a business | Computer used by members of the family for personal record keeping and educational purposes |

## 10-4a Property Subject to MACRS

MACRS applies to new and used tangible depreciable property. Tangible depreciable property includes buildings, land improvements, and equipment. Tangible property can be depreciated only if it is used in a trade or business or held for the production of income and has a determinable useful life.[7] Therefore, land, intangible assets, and personal use assets cannot be depreciated under MACRS.

A taxpayer may not take a deduction for the periodic capital recovery of the basis of an asset held for personal use. A taxpayer can depreciate the business basis of a mixed-use asset but not the personal use part. An intangible asset used for both business and personal purposes, such as an extended (repair) warranty agreement on a car, can be amortized and deducted to the extent the asset is used for a business purpose. Table 10-2 illustrates examples of depreciable and nondepreciable assets that an individual might own.

**Example 14** On January 1 of the current year, Melody buys a new car that she plans to use 80% of the time in her business and 20% of the time for personal transportation. She also buys a 5-year extended warranty on her new car for $500. Can Melody deduct the cost of the extended warranty as an expense?

**Discussion: The $500 paid for the extended warranty is not a current expense. The extended warranty is an intangible long-lived asset that provides benefits for 5 tax years. Because the asset provides business benefits, its cost is subject to amortization. The annual amortization is $100 ($500 ÷ 5 years). However, Melody is allowed a deduction of only $80 for the expense related to business use of the car (80% business use × $100). She cannot deduct the $20 expense related to personal use of the car.**

A typical business asset that is not subject to depreciation is inventory. When inventory is sold, its cost basis is subtracted from sales as a deduction for the cost of goods sold.

**Example 15** Mitch uses the following assets in his corner grocery:

| | |
|---|---|
| Inventory | Store building |
| Shelving | Land |
| Black-topped parking lot | Shopping carts |

Which of the assets are subject to depreciation?

**Discussion: Mitch may depreciate the shelving, store building, black-topped parking lot, and the shopping carts. These assets are used to conduct the grocery business, and they have a limited useful life in Mitch's business. The land cannot be depreciated because it has an indefinite useful life. The sale of inventory results in a deduction for the cost of goods sold.**

MACRS does not apply to any property that the taxpayer elects to depreciate using an accounting method that is based on units of production or any basis other than years of use. A taxpayer who uses the standard mileage rate method to compute an auto expense deduction has elected a special depreciation method. The auto is depreciated using a standard depreciation rate per mile (e.g., 25 cents per mile in 2017 and 2018, 26 cents per mile in 2019, 27 cents per mile in 2020 and 26 cents per mile in 2021) and is not subject to MACRS. Therefore, a taxpayer can avoid the use of MACRS by electing to depreciate an asset using an alternative depreciation method not base on years of use. To be valid, the election must be made in the first year the asset is placed in service.

## 10-4b Basis Subject to Cost Recovery

**Depreciable basis** is the asset's original basis for depreciation less any amounts deducted under the Section 179 election to expense assets. Therefore, the basis rules discussed in Chapter 9 provide the starting point for computing the capital recovery deduction. An asset's basis for depreciation does not have to be reduced by its salvage value. The depreciable basis of an asset is the amount of basis that is subject to depreciation and is the amount used to determine the annual depreciation deduction.[8] The depreciable basis does not change during an asset's tax life unless additional capital expenditures are made for the asset. The total capital recovered as a depreciation deduction over an asset's useful life may never be more than its depreciable basis. Do not confuse the term *depreciable basis* with *adjusted basis.* **Adjusted basis** refers to the unrecovered capital of an asset at any point in time. An asset's adjusted basis decreases as cost-recovery deductions are taken. The capital recovery under MACRS does not necessarily relate to the true remaining useful life and salvage value of the asset. That is, an asset's depreciable basis can be fully recovered, even though the asset remains in service and salvage value exists.

**Example 16** In 2021, Estelle Corporation purchases office equipment costing $27,000 for use in its repair business. Because equipment is eligible to be expensed under Section 179, Estelle elects to expense $25,000 of the cost of the equipment. What is Estelle Corporation's depreciable basis in the equipment?

**Discussion: Estelle's initial basis in the equipment is $27,000. The election to expense reduces the depreciable basis to $2,000 ($27,000 − $25,000). The corporation recovers its $27,000 investment in the equipment through expensing $25,000 in the year of purchase, and $2,000 in depreciation expense deductions over the life of the equipment.**

**If the office equipment had cost only $22,000 and Estelle elected to expense the entire $22,000 cost under Section 179, the corporation would fully recover its capital investment in 2021. The depreciable basis in the equipment then is zero, and the corporation is allowed no further capital recovery deductions on its initial $22,000 investment. However, the equipment remains in service and may provide several years of quality use.**

## 10-4c MACRS Recovery Period

Each asset subject to MACRS must be placed in a MACRS class according to its **class life**. Table A10-1 (in the appendix to this chapter and partially reproduced here in Table 10-3) is an excerpt from IRS Revenue Procedure 87–56, which specifies the class lives used to place assets in MACRS classes and determines recovery periods.[9] Revenue Procedure 87–56 gives the recovery periods for both MACRS (under the column labeled *General Depreciation System*) and ADS (under the column labeled *Alternative Depreciation System*) for broad classes of assets and industry groups. Specifying the recovery periods standardizes the depreciation calculation. Thus, MACRS eliminates several sources of potential conflict between the IRS and taxpayers concerning an asset's useful life and the calculation of the depreciation deduction.

MACRS provides 3-, 5-, 7-, 10-, 15-, and 20-year recovery periods for property other than real estate. Most personal property is in the 3-, 5-, or 7-year class. The 10-, 15-, and 20-year classes generally include land improvements and specialized types of buildings and other property. In addition, residential rental real estate is given a 27.5-year recovery period, whereas nonresidential real estate placed in service before May 13, 1993, is assigned a 31.5-year recovery period. The recovery period for nonresidential real estate placed in service after May 12, 1993, has been increased to 39 years. If personal property is not listed in a specific asset class or identified with a specific industry in the revenue procedure, it is assigned a 7-year recovery period for MACRS and a 12-year recovery period for ADS.

**Example 17** Refer to the office equipment Estelle Corporation purchased in example 16. Using Table A10-1, what is the class life of the equipment and what are its recovery periods under MACRS and ADS?

Table 10-3

## IRS Table of MACRS Classes *(Partial Table)*

| Asset Class | Description of Assets Included | Class Life (in years) | General Depreciation System | Alternative Depreciation System |
|---|---|---|---|---|
| | | | Recovery Periods (in years) | |
| **Specific Depreciable Assets Used in All Business Activities, Except as Noted:** | | | | |
| 00.11 | Office Furniture, Fixtures, and Equipment: Includes furniture and fixtures that are not a structural component of a building. Includes such assets as desks, files, safes, and communications equipment. Does not include communications equipment that is included in other classes | 10 | 7 | 10 |
| 00.22 | Automobiles, Taxis | 3 | 5 | 5 |
| 00.23 | Buses | 9 | 5 | 9 |
| 00.241 | Light General Purpose Trucks: Includes trucks for use over the road (actual unloaded weight less than 13,000 pounds) | 4 | 5 | 5 |
| 00.242 | Heavy General Purpose Trucks: Includes heavy general purpose trucks, concrete ready mix-trucks, and ore trucks, for use over the road (actual unloaded weight 13,000 pounds or more) | 6 | 5 | 6 |
| 00.25 | Railroad Cars and Locomotives, except those owned by railroad transportation companies | 15 | 7 | 15 |
| 00.26 | Tractor Units for Use Over-the-Road | 4 | 3 | 4 |
| 00.27 | Trailers and Trailer-Mounted Containers | 6 | 5 | 6 |
| 00.28 | Vessels, Barges, Tugs, and Similar Water Transportation Equipment, except those used in marine construction | 18 | 10 | 18 |
| **Certain Property for Which Recovery Periods Assigned:** | | | | |
| | A. Personal Property with No Class Life | | 7 | 12 |
| | Section 1245 Real Property with No Class Life | | 7 | 40 |

**Discussion:** According to Table A10-1, this equipment has a class life of 10 years, a MACRS recovery period of 7 years, and an ADS recovery period of 10 years. Therefore, Estelle's depreciable basis must be recovered over either 7 years or 10 years. If Estelle chooses to maximize cost recovery with MACRS, the recovery period is 7 years (found under the *Recovery Period* column labeled *General Depreciation System*). If Estelle chooses to minimize cost recovery, she elects ADS, and the recovery period is 10 years.

**Example 18** Drake purchases the following assets for use in his business:

| Purchase Date | Asset | Cost |
|---|---|---|
| 1/7 | Truck (light) | $ 8,000 |
| 2/11 | Machinery | 5,000 |
| 4/5 | Computer | 6,000 |
| 5/11 | Land | 50,000 |
| 6/1 | Sidewalks | 10,000 |
| 8/3 | Warehouse | 150,000 |
| 9/4 | Office furniture | 25,000 |

What are the MACRS and ADS recovery periods for each asset Drake purchases?

**Discussion:** Using Table A10-1, the recovery periods for MACRS (*General Depreciation System* column) and ADS (*Alternative Depreciation System* column) are as follows:

| Asset | Recovery Period MACRS | Recovery Period ADS |
|---|---|---|
| Truck (light) | 5 | 5 |
| Machinery | 7 | 10 |
| Computer | 5 | 5 |
| Land | not depreciable | |
| Sidewalks | 15 | 20 |
| Warehouse | 39 | 40 |
| Office furniture | 7 | 10 |

## 10-4d MACRS Conventions

To avoid difficulties associated with computing depreciation for fractions of a year, Congress used the concept of administrative convenience and adopted three **depreciation conventions** for use under MACRS: a mid-year, mid-month, and mid-quarter convention.[10] All IRS percentage tables incorporate the appropriate convention for the first year. Generally, the mid-year convention applies to all classes of property except real estate.[11] The **mid-year convention** assumes that personal property is placed in service (and disposed of) in the middle of the year. Under this convention, a half-year of depreciation is allowed in both the first and last years of use. As a result, it takes four tax years to fully depreciate a three-year asset, six years to depreciate a five-year asset, and so forth for the other categories of property. Note that the IRS depreciation percentages listed in Table 10-4 incorporate the mid-year convention. In recovery year 1, the depreciation rate is significantly less than the rate for recovery year 2, even though an accelerated method of depreciation is in use. This happens because the year 1 rate is for only a half-year.

The **mid-month convention** is used only for real estate. This convention allocates depreciation according to the number of months the real estate is in service. The mid-month convention assumes that real estate is placed in service (and disposed of) in the middle of the month. Therefore, the months of acquisition and disposition are counted only as half months. A taxpayer is never allowed a full year's depreciation in the year of acquisition or disposition under the mid-month convention.

The **mid-quarter convention** applies to personal property and assumes that all property is placed in service and disposed of in the middle of the quarter of the year of acquisition and disposition. Assets placed in service during the first quarter of the year are depreciated from the middle of the first quarter to the end of the year, or 10.5 months ÷ 12 of a full year's depreciation. The details of this convention are discussed later in this section.

Determining the appropriate convention to use to allocate first and last years' depreciation is one nuance of MACRS. However, note that each IRS table specifies the convention being used by that particular class life. The most important point underlying all

*Table 10-4*

### MACRS Depreciation for Property Other Than Real Estate

Applicable convention: mid-year *(applicable methods: 200% or 150% declining balance, switching to straight-line)*

| If the recovery year is | And the recovery period is 3 Years | 5 Years | 7 Years | 10 Years | 15 Years | 20 Years |
|---|---|---|---|---|---|---|
| | The depreciation rate is | | | | | |
| 1 | 33.33 | 20.00 | 14.29 | 10.00 | 5.00 | 3.750 |
| 2 | 44.45 | 32.00 | 24.49 | 18.00 | 9.50 | 7.219 |
| 3 | 14.81 | 19.20 | 17.49 | 14.40 | 8.55 | 6.677 |
| 4 | 7.41 | 11.52 | 12.49 | 11.52 | 7.70 | 6.177 |
| 5 | | 11.52 | 8.93 | 9.22 | 6.93 | 5.713 |
| 6 | | 5.76 | 8.92 | 7.37 | 6.23 | 5.285 |
| 7 | | | 8.93 | 6.55 | 5.90 | 4.888 |
| 8 | | | 4.46 | 6.55 | 5.90 | 4.522 |
| 9 | | | | 6.56 | 5.91 | 4.462 |
| 10 | | | | 6.55 | 5.90 | 4.461 |
| 11 | | | | 3.28 | 5.91 | 4.462 |
| 12 | | | | | 5.90 | 4.461 |
| 13 | | | | | 5.91 | 4.462 |
| 14 | | | | | 5.90 | 4.461 |
| 15 | | | | | 5.91 | 4.462 |
| 16 | | | | | 2.95 | 4.461 |
| 17 | | | | | | 4.462 |
| 18 | | | | | | 4.461 |
| 19 | | | | | | 4.462 |
| 20 | | | | | | 4.461 |
| 21 | | | | | | 2.231 |

the conventions is that the precise date of acquisition or disposition is not crucial in making the allocation, as was the case in computing depreciation under the facts and circumstances method.

**Example 19** On March 10, 2021, Quynh purchases and places into service office furniture costing $20,000. Quynh does not elect to expense any of the furniture under Section 179. What is the correct convention for this property?

**Discussion: The mid-year convention applies in this case because the office furniture is personal property. It is 7-year MACRS recovery property. (See Table A10-1.) The mid-year convention assumes the property is placed in service on July 1. The IRS depreciation percentage table that incorporates the mid-year convention for 7-year property is Table 10-4. The depreciation rate for year 1 is 14.29%. Multiplying this rate by the furniture's depreciable basis gives the first-year depreciation of $2,858 ($20,000 × 14.29%). Note that the 14.29% is based upon the 200% declining balance depreciation method and uses the mid-year convention. Thus, the MACRS depreciation can also be calculated without the percentage table: $2,857 = ($20,000 ÷ 7 years × 200% declining balance × 1/2 year). The $1 difference is the result of rounding. Using IRS percentage tables that incorporate the mid-year convention saves work and chance of errors.**

The IRS tables provide the percentage for a full year of depreciation for each class of property. Therefore, the tables' percentages must be adjusted for the last year's depreciation if an asset is disposed of before the end of its recovery period.

**Example 20** Assume that Quynh sells the office furniture in example 19 on December 14, 2023. How does the mid-year convention affect the allowable 2023 depreciation deduction on the office furniture?

**Discussion: The 2023 depreciation deduction for the office furniture is $1,749. From Table 10-4, the depreciation percentage for 7-year property for the third year (2023) is 17.49%. A full year's depreciation would be $3,498 ($20,000 × 17.49%). However, under the mid-year convention only half the annual depreciation is allowed in the year of disposition—$1,749 ($3,498 × ½). The mid-year convention is built into the percentage tables only for property held for its total recovery period. Note that the adjusted basis of Quynh's office furniture is $10,495 [$20,000 – ($2,858 + $4,898 + $1,749)] at the sale date.**

The mid-month convention applies only to real estate. It allocates depreciation according to the number of months the real estate is in service. However, the month of acquisition is counted as only a half month. Table 10-5 incorporates the mid-month convention for 39-year nonresidential real estate.

**Example 21** Tomas Corporation's depreciable basis in a store building it purchased on May 31, 2015, is $100,000. What is the correct convention for this property, and how does it affect the first-year depreciation?

**Discussion: Real estate always uses the mid-month convention. Accordingly, only one-half of the depreciation for May is allowed, regardless of the day in the month the building was actually placed in service. The building is considered to have been in service for 7.5 months (June through December plus one half-month for May) in 2015. Depreciation using the first-year depreciation rate of 1.605% is $1,605 ($100,000 × 1.605%). This rate is found in Table 10-5, reading across year 1 to column 5. Alternatively, the depreciation deduction can be calculated by using the straight-line method over 39 years and applying the mid-month convention. The deduction for 12 months in year 1 is $2,564 ($100,000 ÷ 39 years). Because Tomas placed the building in service in May, it is necessary to adjust the depreciation for the 7.5 months of service in 2015. Remember that the mid-month convention allows only one half-month of depreciation in the first month. So, $1,603 [$2,564 × (7.5 ÷ 12)] is the calculation for depreciation for 2015. (The $2 difference between this calculation and the amount in the table is the result of rounding.)**

If real estate is disposed of during the year, the percentages in the IRS tables must be adjusted to the month of disposition using the mid-month convention.

*Table 10-5*

## MACRS Depreciation for Nonresidential Real Estate Placed in Service After May 12, 1993

Applicable convention: mid-month *(applicable recovery period: 39 years)*

| If the recovery year is | And the month in the first recovery year the property is placed in service is | | | | | | | | | | | |
|---|---|---|---|---|---|---|---|---|---|---|---|---|
| | 1 | 2 | 3 | 4 | 5 | 6 | 7 | 8 | 9 | 10 | 11 | 12 |
| | The depreciation rate is | | | | | | | | | | | |
| 1 | 2.461 | 2.247 | 2.033 | 1.819 | 1.605 | 1.391 | 1.177 | 0.963 | 0.749 | 0.535 | 0.321 | 0.107 |
| 2–39 | 2.564 | 2.564 | 2.564 | 2.564 | 2.564 | 2.564 | 2.564 | 2.564 | 2.564 | 2.564 | 2.564 | 2.564 |
| 40 | 0.107 | 0.321 | 0.535 | 0.749 | 0.963 | 1.177 | 1.391 | 1.605 | 1.819 | 2.033 | 2.247 | 2.461 |

**Example 22** Return to example 21. If Tomas sells the store building on March 1, 2021, how does the mid-month convention affect the 2021 depreciation deduction?

**Discussion: The property is 39-year nonresidential rental property that was placed into service in the fifth month of Tomas's tax year. Therefore, the MACRS percentages from Table 10-5, column 5, are the depreciation schedule for the property. The asset is used in 2021, its seventh year. To determine the deduction for 2021, read across year 7 to column 5 to find 2.564%. The deduction for 12 months in year 7 is $2,564 ($100,000 × 2.564%). Because Tomas sold the asset in March, it has to adjust the annual table's deduction to claim 2.5 months' depreciation using the mid-month convention (January + February + 1/2 month for March). Tomas Corporation deducts $534 in depreciation [$2,564 × (2.5 months ÷ 12 months)] in 2021.**

### Mid-Quarter Convention

If more than 40 percent of the depreciable basis of personal property is placed in service during the last three months of the tax year, the taxpayer must use the mid-quarter convention. The mid-quarter convention applies only to personal property placed in service during the year. Real estate is never subject to the mid-quarter convention; it is always depreciated using the mid-month convention. This convention requires the calculation of depreciation from the middle of the quarter in which an asset is placed in service through the end of the year.

The first year's depreciation using the mid-quarter convention is computed by multiplying the depreciation on the asset for the full year by the applicable percentage for the quarter of acquisition:

| Property Placed in Service During | Months Used | Percentage |
|---|---|---|
| 1st quarter | 10.5 ÷ 12 | 87.5 |
| 2nd quarter | 7.5 ÷ 12 | 62.5 |
| 3rd quarter | 4.5 ÷ 12 | 37.5 |
| 4th quarter | 1.5 ÷ 12 | 12.5 |

Fortunately, MACRS percentage tables (see the appendix to this chapter, Tables A10-3 through A10-6) with appropriate depreciation percentages for the quarter of acquisition are available for computing the depreciation deduction. Thus, the major problem is identifying those situations in which more than 40 percent of the personal property acquired during a year is placed in service in the last three months of the year.

**Example 23** On February 2 of the current year, the Rogers Partnership purchases a computer for $3,500. It buys office furniture for $6,000 on November 15 of the current year. No other personal property is placed in service in the current year. Rogers does not elect to expense any of the property under Section 179. How much depreciation may the partnership deduct for the current year?

**Discussion: Because more than 40% {63% = [$6,000 ÷ ($6,000 + $3,500)]} of the depreciable basis of personal property was placed in service during the last 3 months of the year, Rogers must use the mid-quarter convention. Rogers can use the mid-quarter convention MACRS percentage tables in the appendix to this chapter to calculate its depreciation. From Table A10-3, the depreciation on the computer placed in service in the first quarter is $1,225 ($3,500 × 35% for 5-year property). From Table A10-6, the depreciation on the office furniture placed in service in the fourth quarter is $214 ($6,000 × 3.57% for 7-year property). The partnership's current-year depreciation deduction is $1,439 ($1,225 + $214).**

The use of the mid-quarter convention generally results in a smaller depreciation deduction than the mid-year convention because of the small portion of the first-year depreciation allowed on the fourth-quarter purchases. Therefore, taxpayers wishing to maximize deductions should plan their personal property purchases to avoid making more than 40 percent of such purchases during the last three months of the tax year. In certain situations, the Section 179 election can be used to avoid the mid-quarter convention by expensing assets purchased in the fourth quarter.[12]

**Example 24** Ari Enterprises purchases 5-year property costing $280,000 on April 4 of the current year. The company purchases other 5-year property costing $1,061,000 on November 3 of the current year. No other personal property is placed in service in 2021. What is Ari's maximum depreciation deduction?

**Discussion: Ari's fourth-quarter purchases are 79% [$1,061,000 ÷ ($1,061,000 + $280,000)] of the total purchases during the year. Therefore, the mid-quarter convention applies. However, the 40% rule is based on the depreciable basis placed in service during the fourth quarter. Because the Section 179 election reduces the depreciable basis of assets expensed, Ari can reduce the depreciable basis placed in service during the fourth quarter by expensing $1,050,000 of the $1,061,000 worth of property purchased on November 3. This reduces the depreciable basis of the property to $11,000 and the percentage placed in service during the fourth quarter to 7% [$11,000 ÷ ($280,000 + $11,000)]. Ari is not subject to the mid-quarter convention and uses the general mid-year convention for personal property. The overall result is to give Ari a greater depreciation deduction on the property purchases:**

| | Mid-quarter | Mid-year |
|---|---|---|
| April 4 property basis | $ 280,000 | $ 280,000 |
| Depreciation % (Table A10-4) | × 25% | × 20% (Table 10-4) |
| MACRS depreciation | $ 70,000 | $ 56,000 |
| November 3 property basis | $1,061,000 | $1,061,000 |
| Less: Section 179 expense | -0- | (1,050,000) |
| Depreciable basis | $1,061,000 | $ 11,000 |
| Depreciation % (Table A10-6) | × 5% | × 20% (Table 10-4) |
| MACRS depreciation | $ 53,050 | $ 2,200 |
| Totals ($70,000 + $53,050) = | $ 123,050 | |
| ($56,000 + $1,050,000 + $2,200) = | | $1,108,200 |

## 10-4e Depreciation Method Alternatives

Under current tax law, taxpayers have three alternatives for calculating depreciation:

- Regular MACRS
- Straight-line over the MACRS recovery period
- Straight-line over the Alternative Depreciation System (ADS) recovery period

Figure 10-2 illustrates these choices for depreciating personal property. A taxpayer decides which to use by first choosing whether to maximize or minimize the depreciation deduction in the year of acquisition. The taxpayer would maximize by using the

*Figure 10-2*

**Taxpayer's Choices for Depreciation: To Maximize or Minimize (in Year of Acquisition)**

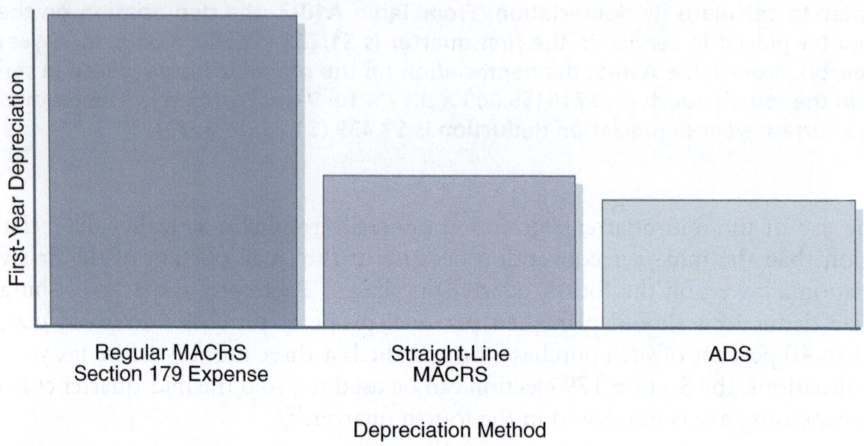


additional first-year depreciation or the Section 179 election, and using regular MACRS for the remaining depreciable basis. Regular MACRS depreciates property in the 3-, 5-, 7-, and 10-year classes using the 200-percent declining balance method with an optimal, automatic switch to straight-line in the IRS percentage tables. Assets in the 15- and 20-year classes are depreciated using the 150-percent declining balance method. The taxpayer who needs a slower depreciation rate can minimize the deduction by using straight-line (S-L) MACRS or ADS. Because of the longer recovery period, ADS produces the smallest depreciation deduction.

**Example 25** On March 14, 2021, Lorange Mining company purchases a fleet of buses costing $1,058,000 to transport its employees from the parking area to the mines. What should Lorange do if it wants to recover its cost as quickly as possible (i.e., maximize the cost recovery)?

**Discussion: To maximize cost recovery, Lorange could claim 100% bonus depreciation and expense $1,058,000. If bonus depreciation is not claimed, Lorange should elect to expense $1,050,000 of cost under Section 179, leaving a depreciable basis of $8,000 ($1,058,000 − $1,050,000), which would be recovered using the regular MACRS 200% declining balance method over the 5-year recovery period for buses. The recovery period is found in Table A10-1 under the column labeled *General Depreciation System*. The regular MACRS method (using Table 10-4) provides the fastest depreciation write-off for the property's depreciable basis:**

| | |
|---|---|
| Initial basis | $ 1,058,000 |
| Section 179 election | $1,050,000 |
| Depreciable basis | $ 8,000 |
| MACRS % (Table 10-4) | × 20% |
| Year 1 depreciation | $ 1,600 |
| Maximum cost recovery | $1,051,600 ($1,050,000 + $1,600) |

**Example 26** Assume that in example 25, Lorange wants to recover the $1,058,000 cost as slowly as possible (i.e., minimize the cost recovery). Which options should Lorange elect?

**Discussion: The slowest cost recovery is obtained by not using Section 179 and electing to use straight-line depreciation over the ADS life of the property. The ADS recovery period is always greater than or equal to the MACRS recovery period. Table A10-1 shows that the ADS recovery period is 9 years for buses. Remember that the MACRS recovery period is 5 years. Thus, the use of the ADS life**

**generally stretches the depreciation deductions over a longer period, thereby diminishing the deduction amounts for each year in the recovery period:**

| | |
|---|---|
| Depreciable basis | $1,058,000 |
| Full-year S-L deduction ($1,058,000 ÷ 9) | $ 117,556 |
| Mid-year convention | × ½ |
| First-year depreciation | $ 58,778 |

**Lorange could also elect an intermediate recovery scheme by using the straight-line method over the MACRS life. This method depreciates the property more slowly than the regular MACRS 200% declining balance method but more rapidly than straight-line during the ADS life:**

| | |
|---|---|
| Depreciable basis | $1,058,000 |
| MACRS S-L 5-year rate (Table A10-11) | × 10% |
| Depreciation deduction | $ 105,800 |

**As the following comparison of depreciation methods for Lorange shows, using the ADS life instead of the regular MACRS method has the effect of stretching out the recovery period:**

| Year | Maximum Section 179 + MACRS | Intermediate MACRS S-L | Minimum ADS |
|---|---|---|---|
| 1 | $1,051,600 | $ 105,800 | $ 58,778 |
| 2 | 2,560 | 211,600 | 117,556 |
| 3 | 1,536 | 211,600 | 117,556 |
| 4 | 922 | 211,600 | 117,556 |
| 5 | 922 | 211,600 | 117,556 |
| 6 | 460 | $ 105,800 | 117,556 |
| 7 | | | 117,556 |
| 8 | | | 117,556 |
| 9 | | | 117,556 |
| 10 | | | 58,778 |
| Total | $1,058,000 | $1,058,000 | $1,058,000 |

Under MACRS, real property is depreciated using the straight-line method. However, taxpayers may choose either MACRS straight-line or ADS. MACRS straight-line uses a 27.5-year recovery period for residential rental real estate and a 39-year recovery period for nonresidential real estate placed in service after May 12, 1993. For nonresidential real estate placed in service before May 13, 1993, the MACRS recovery period is 31.5 years. ADS generally uses a 40-year recovery period for real estate. The 2017 Tax Cut and Jobs Act decreased the ADS recovery period for residential rental property placed in service after December 31, 2017, to 30 years.

## 10-4f Using MACRS Percentage Tables

Once an asset's depreciable basis, recovery period, and appropriate convention are known, and the taxpayer has decided whether to use regular MACRS or to elect a straight-line depreciation method, percentage tables published by the IRS provide the depreciation rate. The asset's depreciable basis is multiplied by the depreciation rate to determine the annual deduction. All of the relevant IRS percentage tables are reproduced in the appendix to this chapter. The MACRS percentage table for property other than real estate appears in Table 10-4. The percentage tables are constructed to permit full capital recovery of an asset's basis over its recovery period. In addition, the percentage tables incorporate the proper first-year convention, and they make the switch from the declining balance to the straight-line method to optimize the deduction. In effect, the columns of the percentage tables are the depreciation schedule for each recovery period of an asset. Using the tables standardizes the depreciation calculation and minimizes the possibility of error in the depreciation calculation—a taxpayer does not have to perform the mechanics of declining balance depreciation to benefit from the method.

**Example 27** Kwan Corporation purchases an asset in the 3-year MACRS recovery class on January 5, 2021, for $45,000. Assume that Kwan elects not to expense under Section 179 or claim bonus depreciation. What amount may Kwan deduct as depreciation expense for each year of the asset's recovery period?

**Discussion: Kwan may deduct a total of $45,000 over the machine's 3-year recovery period. Because the machine qualifies as 3-year property, it should use the 3-year column of Table 10-4. The deduction is determined each year by multiplying the $45,000 depreciable basis by the appropriate percentage for the year being calculated. This is the depreciation schedule for the asset:**

| Year | MACRS % | Depreciable Basis | Depreciation |
|---|---|---|---|
| 2021 | 33.33 | $45,000 | $14,999 |
| 2022 | 44.45 | 45,000 | 20,003 |
| 2023 | 14.81 | 45,000 | 6,665 |
| 2024 | 7.41 | 45,000 | 3,333 |
| Total depreciation | | | $45,000 |

**Note that although the machine is 3-year class property, it takes 4 years to fully depreciate its cost. The mid-year convention used by MACRS assumes that assets are placed in service in the middle of the year and disposed of in the middle of the year. Thus, the first year and the fourth year are each allowed only a half-year of depreciation.**

Real estate depreciation begins with the selection of the correct IRS table for the type of real estate being depreciated (i.e., residential rental or nonresidential). Table A10-7 provides percentages for residential rental real estate (27.5-year property). Table A10-8 provides percentages for nonresidential real estate placed in service before May 13, 1993 (31.5-year property), and Table A10-9 provides percentages for nonresidential real estate placed in service after May 12, 1993 (39-year property). The mid-month convention for depreciable real estate requires determining the month the property is placed in service and finding that month among the twelve columns in the appropriate percentage table. The column chosen becomes the depreciation schedule for the property. The rates in the table are percentages. If a column is added up, it will total 100 percent—representing complete cost recovery. Each row of the column is the depreciation year. For example, the year of acquisition is recovery year 1.

**Example 28** On February 5 of the current year, Pauline acquires an apartment building that costs $120,000. The basis allocated to the building is $100,000, and the basis of the land is $20,000. What is Pauline's depreciation deduction for the property for the current year?

**Discussion: The land is not depreciable. The $100,000 building cost is depreciated using the schedule for 27.5-year residential real property. Pauline should use the IRS percentages in Table A10-7, reading across the row labeled *year 1* and down the column labeled *month 2* to find the first-year percentage, 3.182%. Pauline should deduct $3,182 ($100,000 × 3.182%) in depreciation on the building for the current year. The month-2 column of the table becomes the depreciation schedule for the building for the rest of its period of use.**

## 10-4g MACRS Straight-Line Election

Taxpayers may depreciate personal property at a slower rate than the 200-percent declining balance method of MACRS by making the MACRS straight-line election. Taxpayers may desire the smaller straight-line deductions because of current low income or loss. This election provides an intermediate recovery scheme by using the straight-line method over the MACRS life. This method does not stretch out the recovery period as long as the ADS straight-line method does. Table A10-11 provides the rate schedules under this election.

*Table 10-6*

## MACRS Depreciation for Residential Rental Real Estate

Applicable convention: mid-month *(applicable recovery period: 27.5 years)*

| If the recovery year is | And the month in the first recovery year the property is placed in service is: 1 | 2 | 3 | 4 | 5 | 6 | 7 | 8 | 9 | 10 | 11 | 12 |
|---|---|---|---|---|---|---|---|---|---|---|---|---|
| | The depreciation rate is | | | | | | | | | | | |
| 1 | 3.485 | 3.182 | 2.879 | 2.576 | 2.273 | 1.970 | 1.667 | 1.364 | 1.061 | 0.758 | 0.455 | 0.152 |
| 2 | 3.636 | 3.636 | 3.636 | 3.636 | 3.636 | 3.636 | 3.636 | 3.636 | 3.636 | 3.636 | 3.636 | 3.636 |
| 3 | 3.636 | 3.636 | 3.636 | 3.636 | 3.636 | 3.636 | 3.636 | 3.636 | 3.636 | 3.636 | 3.636 | 3.636 |
| 4 | 3.636 | 3.636 | 3.636 | 3.636 | 3.636 | 3.636 | 3.636 | 3.636 | 3.636 | 3.636 | 3.636 | 3.636 |
| 5 | 3.636 | 3.636 | 3.636 | 3.636 | 3.636 | 3.636 | 3.636 | 3.636 | 3.636 | 3.636 | 3.636 | 3.636 |
| 6 | 3.636 | 3.636 | 3.636 | 3.636 | 3.636 | 3.636 | 3.636 | 3.636 | 3.636 | 3.636 | 3.636 | 3.636 |
| 7 | 3.636 | 3.636 | 3.636 | 3.636 | 3.636 | 3.636 | 3.636 | 3.636 | 3.636 | 3.636 | 3.636 | 3.636 |
| 8 | 3.636 | 3.636 | 3.636 | 3.636 | 3.636 | 3.636 | 3.636 | 3.636 | 3.636 | 3.636 | 3.636 | 3.636 |
| 9 | 3.636 | 3.636 | 3.636 | 3.636 | 3.636 | 3.636 | 3.636 | 3.636 | 3.636 | 3.636 | 3.636 | 3.636 |
| 10 | 3.637 | 3.637 | 3.637 | 3.637 | 3.637 | 3.637 | 3.636 | 3.636 | 3.636 | 3.636 | 3.636 | 3.636 |
| 11 | 3.636 | 3.636 | 3.636 | 3.636 | 3.636 | 3.636 | 3.637 | 3.637 | 3.637 | 3.637 | 3.637 | 3.637 |
| 12 | 3.637 | 3.637 | 3.637 | 3.637 | 3.637 | 3.637 | 3.636 | 3.636 | 3.636 | 3.636 | 3.636 | 3.636 |
| 13 | 3.636 | 3.636 | 3.636 | 3.636 | 3.636 | 3.636 | 3.637 | 3.637 | 3.637 | 3.637 | 3.637 | 3.637 |
| 14 | 3.637 | 3.637 | 3.637 | 3.637 | 3.637 | 3.637 | 3.636 | 3.636 | 3.636 | 3.636 | 3.636 | 3.636 |
| 15 | 3.636 | 3.636 | 3.636 | 3.636 | 3.636 | 3.636 | 3.637 | 3.637 | 3.637 | 3.637 | 3.637 | 3.637 |
| 16 | 3.637 | 3.637 | 3.637 | 3.637 | 3.637 | 3.637 | 3.636 | 3.636 | 3.636 | 3.636 | 3.636 | 3.636 |
| 17 | 3.636 | 3.636 | 3.636 | 3.636 | 3.636 | 3.636 | 3.637 | 3.637 | 3.637 | 3.637 | 3.637 | 3.637 |
| 18 | 3.637 | 3.637 | 3.637 | 3.637 | 3.637 | 3.637 | 3.636 | 3.636 | 3.636 | 3.636 | 3.636 | 3.636 |
| 19 | 3.636 | 3.636 | 3.636 | 3.636 | 3.636 | 3.636 | 3.637 | 3.637 | 3.637 | 3.637 | 3.637 | 3.637 |
| 20 | 3.637 | 3.637 | 3.637 | 3.637 | 3.637 | 3.637 | 3.636 | 3.636 | 3.636 | 3.636 | 3.636 | 3.636 |
| 21 | 3.636 | 3.636 | 3.636 | 3.636 | 3.636 | 3.636 | 3.637 | 3.637 | 3.637 | 3.637 | 3.637 | 3.637 |
| 22 | 3.637 | 3.637 | 3.637 | 3.637 | 3.637 | 3.637 | 3.636 | 3.636 | 3.636 | 3.636 | 3.636 | 3.636 |
| 23 | 3.636 | 3.636 | 3.636 | 3.636 | 3.636 | 3.636 | 3.637 | 3.637 | 3.637 | 3.637 | 3.637 | 3.637 |
| 24 | 3.637 | 3.637 | 3.637 | 3.637 | 3.637 | 3.637 | 3.636 | 3.636 | 3.636 | 3.636 | 3.636 | 3.636 |
| 25 | 3.636 | 3.636 | 3.636 | 3.636 | 3.636 | 3.636 | 3.637 | 3.637 | 3.637 | 3.637 | 3.637 | 3.637 |
| 26 | 3.637 | 3.637 | 3.637 | 3.637 | 3.637 | 3.637 | 3.636 | 3.636 | 3.636 | 3.636 | 3.636 | 3.636 |
| 27 | 3.636 | 3.636 | 3.636 | 3.636 | 3.636 | 3.636 | 3.637 | 3.637 | 3.637 | 3.637 | 3.637 | 3.637 |
| 28 | 1.970 | 2.273 | 2.576 | 2.879 | 3.182 | 3.485 | 3.636 | 3.636 | 3.636 | 3.636 | 3.636 | 3.636 |
| 29 | 0.000 | 0.000 | 0.000 | 0.000 | 0.000 | 0.000 | 0.152 | 0.455 | 0.758 | 1.061 | 1.364 | 1.667 |

Note that the MACRS mid-year convention for both recovery year 1 and the final year of service is built into each depreciation schedule. For example, an asset with a five-year life is depreciated at a rate of one-half of the regular straight-line rate, or 10 percent (½ × 20%), in the year of acquisition. Also, note that depreciation is deducted over six years.

**Example 29** On March 9 of the current year, Antonia Stables Corporation places in service a 4-year-old racehorse that costs $50,000 (3-year MACRS class) and a mower for its hay field that costs $15,000 (7-year MACRS class). Antonia does not need the accelerated depreciation deductions provided under MACRS and would like to spread out the deductions on the assets without using the recovery periods provided by the ADS election. What is Antonia's depreciation deduction for these two assets for the current year?

**Discussion: Antonia's total depreciation deduction for the current year is $9,406 ($8,335 + $1,071). The first-year depreciation for the horse is determined by using the straight-line method with the mid-year convention for the 3-year MACRS recovery period for racehorses older than two (Table A10-1). This results in a deduction of $8,335 [$50,000 × 16.67% from Table A10-11 or ($50,000 ÷ 3) × ½]. The first-year depreciation for the mower is determined by using the straight-line method with the mid-year convention for the 7-year MACRS recovery period for agricultural machinery (Table A10-1). This results in a deduction of $1,071 [$15,000 × 7.14% from Table A10-11, or ($15,000 ÷ 7) × ½].**

**Note that this straight-line MACRS election lowers the first-year depreciation by $9,403 ($18,809 − $9,406) when compared with regular MACRS. Regular MACRS depreciation for the racehorse (3-year MACRS class) is $16,665 ($50,000 × 33.33% from Table 10-4), and regular MACRS for the mower (7-year MACRS class) is $2,144 ($15,000 × 14.29% from Table 10-4). Antonia's total first-year depreciation would be $18,809 ($16,665 + $2,144) if regular MACRS is used without a Section 179 election.**

## 10-4h Alternative Depreciation System (ADS)

LO 7
Describe the Alternative Depreciation System (ADS) and explain the calculation of cost recovery using the ADS.

The **Alternative Depreciation System (ADS)** generally spreads depreciation deductions over longer recovery periods than MACRS. Taxpayers may elect ADS for determination of regular taxable income. However, it is mandatory for calculation of the alternative minimum tax (discussed in Chapter 15).

A taxpayer may elect to use ADS for several reasons. First, the taxpayer may be experiencing a low income (or loss) period and not need the greater MACRS deductions this year. By electing ADS, the taxpayer effectively defers the deduction to a future tax year when income is expected to be greater. A second reason for electing to use ADS is to avoid the alternative minimum tax. Taxpayers with large purchases of depreciable assets may become subject to the alternative minimum tax because of the greater MACRS depreciation deductions, which are not allowed in computing the alternative minimum tax. In some cases, by electing to take smaller depreciation deductions, the taxpayer could reduce their final tax bill.

The election to use ADS is made on a class-by-class, year-by-year basis for property other than real estate. For real estate, ADS is elected on a property-by-property basis in the year of acquisition.

If a taxpayer elects to use the Alternative Depreciation System, the depreciation is generally computed using the straight-line method over the specified, longer alternative recovery period. However, tangible personal property with a class life of 3, 5, 7, or 10 years that uses regular MACRS depreciation must use 150 percent declining balance depreciation with optimal switch to straight-line over the MACRS class life for alternative minimum tax purposes. If a straight-line election is made for regular

**Example 30** Alvarez purchases a heavy-duty ore truck for $200,000 on March 15 of the current year. Alvarez uses regular MACRS depreciation on the ore truck, but does not elect to expense any of its cost under Section 179 or claim bonus depreciation. What is Alvarez's depreciation deduction for regular tax and alternative minimum tax purposes over its tax life?

**Discussion: A heavy-duty ore truck is in asset class 00.242 and has a MACRS life of 5 years and an ADS life of 6 years. Because Alvarez uses regular MACRS depreciation, he must use the 150% declining balance method for alternative minimum tax purposes over the 5-year MACRS life. The depreciation for the 6-year tax life of the ore truck for regular and alternative minimum tax purposes follows:**

| Year | Depreciable Basis | MACRS Percentage | MACRS Depreciation | ADS Percentage | ADS Depreciation |
|---|---|---|---|---|---|
| 1 | $200,000 | 20.00 | $ 40,000 | 15.00 | $ 30,000 |
| 2 | $200,000 | 32.00 | 64,000 | 25.50 | 51,000 |
| 3 | $200,000 | 19.20 | 38,400 | 17.85 | 35,700 |
| 4 | $200,000 | 11.52 | 23,040 | 16.66 | 33,320 |
| 5 | $200,000 | 11.52 | 23,040 | 16.66 | 33,320 |
| 6 | $200,000 | 5.76 | 11,520 | 8.33 | 16,660 |
| Total | | | $200,000 | | $200,000 |

Table 10-7

## Alternative Minimum Tax Depreciation

Applicable convention: mid-year *(applicable method: 150% declining balance, switching to straight-line)*

| If the recovery year is | And the recovery period is | | | |
|---|---|---|---|---|
| | 3 Years | 5 Years | 7 Years | 10 Years |
| | The depreciation rate is | | | |
| 1 | 25.00 | 15.00 | 10.71 | 7.50 |
| 2 | 37.50 | 25.50 | 19.13 | 13.88 |
| 3 | 25.00 | 17.85 | 15.03 | 11.79 |
| 4 | 12.50 | 16.66 | 12.25 | 10.02 |
| 5 | | 16.66 | 12.25 | 8.74 |
| 6 | | 8.33 | 12.25 | 8.74 |
| 7 | | | 12.25 | 8.74 |
| 8 | | | 6.13 | 8.74 |
| 9 | | | | 8.74 |
| 10 | | | | 8.74 |
| 11 | | | | 4.37 |

tax purposes, the same depreciation method and recovery period must be used for alternative minimum tax purposes. Table 10-7 provides the depreciation percentages using the 150 percent declining balance method for MACRS property with a class life of 3, 5, 7, and 10 years.

For computing the ADS deduction, an asset's life is determined by using the column for the Alternative Depreciation System in Table A10-1. For example, office fixtures have a regular MACRS (general depreciation system) recovery period of 7 years. Under ADS, the recovery period is 10 years. Residential rental real estate has a 27.5-year MACRS recovery period and a 40-year recovery period for ADS purposes. For property placed in service after December 31, 2017, the ADS recovery period is 30 years. Nonresidential real estate has a 31.5-year or 39-year MACRS recovery period (depending on whether it was placed in service before or after May 13, 1993) and a 40-year recovery period for ADS purposes. However, automobiles have a 5-year recovery period under both MACRS and ADS. The deduction for the first and last years of an asset's recovery period must be calculated using the applicable mid-year, mid-quarter, or mid-month convention.

Table 10-8 summarizes the steps to follow in calculating MACRS depreciation.

Table 10-8

## Steps for Calculating MACRS Depreciation

1. Determine depreciable basis of asset.
2. Subtract Section 179 expense from basis of asset, (if elected for that asset) and additional first-year depreciation (if claimed).
3. Determine recovery period. (Use Table A10-1 in appendix to this chapter.)
4. Identify appropriate MACRS convention: mid-year, mid-month, or mid-quarter.
5. Select the depreciation method: regular MACRS, straight-line over the MACRS recovery period, or straight-line over the ADS recovery period.
6. Find the appropriate percentage from the IRS table and multiply it by the depreciable basis (as determined in step 2 after subtracting the Section 179 expense).

## 10-4i Limitations on Listed Property

LO 8

Describe the limitations on depreciation deductions for listed property in general and the specific limitation on depreciation of automobiles.

Because taxpayers abused the opportunity to claim depreciation deductions for mixed-use property, Congress enacted listed property rules in 1984. The **listed property rules** require taxpayers to adequately substantiate the extent of an asset's business use.[13] If listed property is not predominantly used in a trade or business, the business portion of the asset must be depreciated under the Alternative Depreciation System. Another important aspect of the listed property rules is that an annual dollar limitation is placed on the depreciation deduction for automobiles.[14] Some examples of **listed property** are passenger autos, trucks, boats, and motorcycles. Computers and peripheral equipment are no longer listed property effective in 2018.

If more than 50 percent of an asset's total use for each year of its tax life is related to the taxpayer's trade or business, the asset is considered to be predominantly used in a trade or business and is treated the same as any other business asset. Using the asset in an investment activity (i.e., production-of-income use) is not counted as business use to satisfy the 50-percent test. When listed property is used 50 percent or less in the taxpayer's business, the asset is not considered predominantly used in a trade or business, and depreciation deductions are limited. The Section 179 expense election does not apply to the asset, and the annual depreciation deduction must be calculated using the Alternative Depreciation System (ADS).[15]

### Limitation on Passenger Autos

Passenger autos are subject to a limitation on the annual amount of the deductible depreciation. The annual depreciation deduction for a passenger automobile cannot exceed a specified amount, which is based on the year a car is placed in service. Any depreciation that is disallowed because of the annual limitations may be deducted when the auto's recovery period ends. If an auto is not used wholly for a business purpose, the amount of the annual **passenger automobile limitation** must be reduced by multiplying it by the business use percentage.[16] The depreciation subject to the first-year annual limitation includes any amount that is expensed using Section 179. As mentioned earlier, the annual limitation on the auto depreciation deduction makes it impractical to deduct any of the cost of an auto under Section 179.

The 2020 maximum first-year depreciation deduction (including bonus depreciation) on passenger automobiles, trucks, and vans is $18,100 ($10,100 if bonus depreciation is not claimed). At the time this book went to press, the 2021 annual limitation had not been issued, so the 2020 limitation is used here and in Chapter 6.

**Example 31** On July 5, 2020, Oscar purchases a new car for $60,000. Based on his mileage records, Oscar uses the car 80% of the time for a qualified business use. What is his depreciation deduction on the car for 2020?

**Discussion: Automobiles are 5-year MACRS property. Because he uses the automobile more than 50% of the time for business, his allowable depreciation is the lesser of the regular MACRS depreciation or the passenger automobile limitation. Oscar's 2020 depreciation is limited to $14,480:**

| Regular MACRS Depreciation | |
|---|---|
| Initial basis | $ 60,000 |
| Business use percentage | × 80% |
| Business depreciable basis | $ 48,000 |
| Bonus depreciation percentage | × 100% |
| Total first-year MACRS depreciation | $ 48,000 |

| Passenger Automobile Limitation | |
|---|---|
| Annual depreciation limit for an automobile placed in service in 2020 | $ 18,100 |
| Business use percentage | × 80% |
| Oscar's maximum 2020 depreciation on the auto | $ 14,480 |

**Although the computed depreciation using MACRS is $48,000, Oscar's deduction cannot exceed the annual limitation, adjusted for the percentage of business use, $14,480. Note that the effect of the auto depreciation limit is to make the Section 179 election a poor choice for an automobile, because the Section 179 election is considered depreciation for purposes of applying the auto limit.**

**Discussion: If Oscar elects not to claim bonus depreciation, his 2020 depreciation is limited to $8,080:**

| Regular MACRS Depreciation | |
|---|---|
| Initial basis | $60,000 |
| Business use percentage | × 80% |
| Business depreciable basis | $48,000 |
| MACRS table percentage | × 20% |
| Total first year MACRS depreciation | $ 9,600 |

| Passenger Automobile Limitation | |
|---|---|
| Annual depreciation limit for an automobile placed in service in 2020 | $10,100 |
| Business use percentage | × 80% |
| Oscar's maximum 2020 depreciation on the auto | $ 8,080 |

## Adequate Record Keeping

Listed property is subject to special record-keeping requirements for documenting business use and amounts expended. To substantiate deductions, the taxpayer must be able to prove the

- Amount of each expenditure related to the property, such as the cost of the property, repairs, insurance, and other expenses
- Use of the asset, including documentation of the amount of business, investment, and other use of the asset
- Date of the expenditure or use of the asset
- Business purpose for the expenditure or the use of the asset

The best proof is written records that show the business use of the listed property. The records should contain receipts when possible and any other documentation necessary to prove the existence of these items. The most common method of substantiation is a diary or a log book in which the taxpayer records the necessary information as the expense is incurred.

### concept check

The *administrative convenience concept's* focus on reducing the cost of compliance explains much of the evolution of tax depreciation methods. Traditional depreciation methods have been replaced by MACRS to standardize and simplify tax depreciation calculations. This reduces disputes between taxpayers and the IRS as well as promoting fewer errors in the depreciation calculations. The Section 179 election to expense simplifies record-keeping for small businesses which can write off the bulk of their fixed assets purchases rather than capitalizing the cost and calculating depreciation deductions.

# 10-5 DEPLETION

LO 1

Discuss the recovery of the cost of long-lived assets and the general criteria for taking deductions for depreciation, depletion, or amortization on an investment in a long-lived asset.

A taxpayer who owns an economic interest in a natural resource that wastes away through use is entitled to a capital recovery deduction for depletion. Minerals, oil and gas, other natural deposits, and timber are subject to depletion. **Depletion** is an accounting method used to recover the basis of an investment in a natural resource as it is used up to earn income. An investment in personal or real property (e.g., machinery, equipment, and buildings) related to recovering the natural resource remains subject to the depreciation rules and not depletion.

A taxpayer has an economic interest in a natural resource if two basic requirements are met. First, the investment in the natural resource must still be in place. *In place* means that the mineral deposit has not been removed from its original source (i.e., is still underground). Second, capital recovery of the taxpayer's investment depends on the amount of income the taxpayer derives from the extraction of the natural resource.[17]

**Example 32** DeWayne invests $90,000 in a coal mine. The investment is allocated as follows: $25,000 as the basis in machinery and equipment, $50,000 as the basis in the coal deposit still in place below ground, and $15,000 as the basis of the residual value of the land. How should DeWayne recover his investment?

**Discussion: DeWayne's $50,000 investment in the coal deposit in place is subject to depletion. The $25,000 investment in the machinery and equipment used to recover the coal is subject to depreciation. The basis of the land is not subject to depletion or depreciation. The basis of the land will be recovered at disposition.**

## 10-5a Depletion Methods

LO 9
Explain the deduction for depletion and how to calculate depletion using the cost method and the statutory percentage method.

Two methods are used to compute depletion of natural resources: the cost depletion method and the percentage (statutory) depletion method. Each year, the taxpayer is allowed to deduct the greater figure yielded by the two methods. Therefore, a taxpayer may use the cost method in one year and the percentage method in another. Regardless of which depletion method is used, the deduction reduces the adjusted basis of the natural resource. A deduction for cost depletion is allowed until the depletable basis has been fully recovered.

In most cases, the taxpayer may continue to use percentage (statutory) depletion after the initial basis has been fully recovered. This use of percentage depletion violates the capital recovery concept by permitting total depletion deductions over the life of the natural resource to exceed the property's depletable basis. As a result, the taxpayer's depletion deduction can exceed the cost of the depletable asset. Although this is clearly a benefit for regular tax purposes, the depletion in excess of cost is not allowed for alternative minimum tax purposes.[18] As with the use of MACRS depreciation, taking depletion deductions in excess of cost could trigger the alternative minimum tax and make the use of percentage depletion undesirable.

**Example 33** Assume that the coal mine in example 32 has operated for several years and that before deducting depletion for the current year DeWayne's adjusted basis for depletion of the coal deposit is $2,000. Further, assume that DeWayne's cost depletion for the current year is $2,000 and his percentage depletion is $2,500. What is DeWayne's current depletion deduction, and how does it affect his depletable basis?

**Discussion: DeWayne is allowed to deduct the $2,500 in percentage depletion because it is greater than the $2,000 cost depletion. His $2,000 adjusted basis in the coal deposit is reduced to zero by the percentage depletion deduction. At this point, DeWayne has claimed $500 more in capital recovery deductions than he had invested in the coal deposit ($2,500 deduction − $2,000 basis). Because DeWayne has fully recovered his basis, he cannot claim cost depletion in future years. However, he may continue to claim percentage depletion so long as he has gross income from the sale of the coal.**

## 10-5b Cost Depletion

To compute **cost depletion**, you must know the basis subject to depletion, the recoverable quantity of the natural resource, and the quantity of the natural resource sold during the year. The basis of the natural resource subject to depletion is the basis that would be used to compute a gain on its sale.[19] For other assets, the basis construct has been used to describe the amount subject to capital recovery. For natural resources, *unrecovered basis* better describes the amount being recovered through depletion, because the estimate of the quantity of the resource to which the basis relates is subject to change each year. Cost depletion is calculated using a units-of-production method.

The following computation is the general framework for calculating cost depletion using the units-of-production method:

$$\text{Cost depletion} = \frac{\text{Basis of natural resource subject to capital recovery (unrecovered basis)}}{\text{Estimated number of mineral units to be recovered (e.g., tons of mineral, barrels of liquid)}} \times \text{Number of units sold during tax year}$$

The cost depletion computation allocates the unrecovered basis over the number of mineral units of the natural resource (useful life of the resource) to which the investment relates.

**Example 34** In example 33, DeWayne estimates that his $50,000 investment in the coal deposit will result in 350,000 recoverable tons of coal. During 2021, he mines and sells 40,000 tons of coal. What is DeWayne's cost depletion deduction for 2021?

**Discussion: DeWayne's cost depletion deduction for 2021 is $5,714 [($50,000 basis ÷ 350,000 tons of coal) × 40,000 tons sold]. His unrecovered basis of the coal deposit after deducting $5,714 for depletion is $44,286 ($50,000 − $5,714).**

Because an estimate of the remaining recoverable units at the end of each year is used to make the computation, the cost depletion per unit will probably change for each tax year. Based on the annual accounting period concept, depletion deductions for prior years are not corrected because of a change in the estimate of recoverable units remaining. The adjustment related to a change in the estimate is allocated to current and future years by incorporating the new estimate in the formula.

**Example 35** Assume that during 2022, DeWayne in example 34 sells 105,000 tons of coal. Based on mining reports, he increases his estimate of recoverable coal by 5,000 tons. What is DeWayne's cost depletion deduction for 2022?

**Discussion: DeWayne's cost depletion deduction for 2022 is $14,762. His unrecovered basis in the coal deposit after deducting $14,762 for depletion is $29,524 ($44,286 − $14,762).**

**At the end of 2021, the estimated coal to be mined and sold is 310,000 tons (350,000 original estimate − 40,000 tons sold). The 5,000-ton revision in DeWayne's estimate increases the recoverable coal to 315,000 tons. The increase in the number of recoverable mineral units in 2022 affects 2022 and later years. DeWayne's 2022 cost depletion is $14,762 [($44,286 unrecovered basis ÷ 315,000 tons of coal) × 105,000 tons sold]. Based on the annual accounting period concept, the 2021 depletion deduction is not revised for the change in the estimate of recoverable mineral units in 2022.**

## 10-5c Percentage Depletion

**Percentage depletion** (also called statutory depletion) is calculated by multiplying gross income from the sale of the natural resource by a statutory percentage.[20] The statutory percentage is the depletion rate specified by the tax law. For example, depletion (by percentage) is allowed for:

| | |
|---|---|
| Sulphur, uranium | 22% |
| Gold, copper, silver, iron ore | 15% |
| Asbestos, brucite, coal | 10% |
| Gravel, peat, sand | 5% |

In addition, the tax law specifies a statutory depletion rate for many other natural resources, including oil and gas. The maximum allowable percentage depletion deduction for the tax year is limited to 50 percent of the taxable income from the natural resource before subtracting the depletion deduction.[21]

**Example 36** In example 34, DeWayne sells the 40,000 tons of coal in 2021 for $1.20 per ton. After deducting operating expenses, his taxable income from the property (before deducting percentage depletion) is $10,000. What is DeWayne's maximum depletion deduction for 2021?

**Discussion: DeWayne's percentage depletion deduction is $4,800 (40,000 tons × $1.20 × 10% depletion rate for coal). Because 50% of the taxable income from the property, $5,000 ($10,000 × 50%), is greater than the computed percentage depletion, $4,800, the taxable income limit does not apply. Because the cost depletion computed in example 34 is greater than the percentage depletion, DeWayne should deduct cost depletion for 2021. His maximum 2021 depletion deduction is $5,714, using the cost depletion method. Note: Cost depletion is not subject to the 50% taxable income limit.**

**Example 37** In example 35, DeWayne sells the 105,000 tons of coal in 2022 for $1.50 per ton. After deducting operating expenses, his taxable income from the property (before deducting percentage depletion) is $30,000. What is DeWayne's maximum depletion deduction for 2022?

**Discussion: Based on the taxable income limitation, DeWayne's maximum allowable percentage depletion deduction is $15,000 ($30,000 × 50%). The tentative percentage depletion deduction is $15,750 (105,000 tons × $1.50 × 10% depletion). From example 35, cost depletion is $14,762, which is less than percentage depletion. However, the $15,000 taxable income limitation applies, because it is less than the $15,750 tentative percentage depletion deduction. Thus, the allowable percentage depletion is $15,000.**

**For 2022, DeWayne should deduct the $15,000 in percentage depletion because it is greater than the $14,762 in cost depletion computed in example 35. As a result, he reduces his recoverable basis in the coal deposit by the percentage depletion deduction instead of the cost depletion deduction. DeWayne's recoverable basis in the coal deposit at the end of 2022 is $29,286 ($44,286 − $15,000 percentage depletion).**

## 10-6 INTANGIBLE ASSETS

LO 10
Describe how taxpayers deduct amortization on intangible assets.

Patents, copyrights, agreements not to compete, franchises, and goodwill are all **intangible property**.[22] Capital recovery of the investment in an intangible asset is allowed as an expense deduction through amortization. The basis of an intangible is allocated on a straight-line basis over its useful life. To qualify for **amortization**, the intangible asset must be used for a business purpose and must have a limited useful life that can be estimated with reasonable accuracy.

As a result of the limited life requirement, determining whether a specific intangible asset qualifies for amortization has required an analysis of the facts related to the taxpayer. Because goodwill does not have a useful life that can be estimated with reasonable accuracy, goodwill generally is not subject to amortization. However, Congress enacted Section 197 in 1993, which requires goodwill and other intangibles purchased after August 9, 1993, to be amortized over 15 years. This section is a step toward simplifying tax law and offers an element of administrative convenience to the task of determining useful lives of intangibles. Also, through legislative grace, Congress now allows the amortization of goodwill that has been purchased.

Not all intangible assets are subject to the 15-year amortization period. Generally, intangibles subject to the 15-year amortization period are those that are acquired in connection with the purchase of assets constituting a trade or business. Exhibit 10-1 provides a list of qualifying intangible assets.

**Example 38** Natasha is a partner in Future Designs. She has decided to leave the partnership and move to a different state. In the current year, Future and Natasha enter an agreement not to compete. Future pays Natasha $50,000 for Natasha's agreement not to compete or interfere with Future's conduct of business within 250 miles of Future's home office for 5 years. The agreement is effective September 1 of the current year. What is the tax effect of the transaction for Future and Natasha?

**Discussion: Future can amortize the $50,000 investment in the agreement not to compete by using straight-line amortization over 15 years. For the current year, Future can deduct $1,111 for 4 months' amortization of the investment in the agreement [($50,000 ÷ 15) × (4 ÷ 12)]. Based on the claim-of-right doctrine, Natasha**

Exhibit 10-1

## Intangible Assets Subject to 15-Year Amortization

- Goodwill and going concern value
- Certain types of intangible property that generally relate to workforce, information base, know-how, customers, suppliers, or other similar items
- Any license, permit, or other right granted by a government unit or agency
- Any covenant not to compete (or other similar arrangement) entered into in connection with the acquisition of a trade or business (including a stock acquisition) or an interest in a trade or business
- Any franchise, trademark, or trade name

Examples of intangible assets covered include customer lists, subscription lists, insurance expirations, patient or client files, and lists of newspaper, magazine, radio, or television advertisers.

**must report the entire $50,000 payment she receives in the current year as ordinary income related to services. Note that because the agreement not to compete is acquired in connection with the purchase of a trade or business, it must be amortized over the 15-year statutory period, not the 5-year term of the agreement.**

**Example 39** On January 1 of the current year, Nisalke Company sells all assets used in its business to Layden Company. The assets consist of real estate, a customer list, goodwill, a patent, and a covenant not to compete. The values allocated to each asset are as follows:

| | |
|---|---:|
| Real estate | $10,000,000 |
| Customer list | 800,000 |
| Goodwill | 500,000 |
| Patent | 1,000,000 |
| Covenant | 900,000 |
| Total purchase price | $13,200,000 |

The real estate is subject to a recovery period of 39 years. The customer list has a 6-year useful life, the covenant not to compete lasts 3 years, and the patent has 10 years remaining on its useful life. What is Layden's intangible amortization amount for the current year?

**Discussion: The four intangible assets must be amortized over 15 years. Total amortization for the current year is $213,333 ($3,200,000 ÷ 15). Although the company receives the benefit of amortizing the $500,000 of goodwill now, the other intangibles are amortized for a period longer than their useful lives. If Section 197 had not been enacted, the total amortization for the current year would have been $533,333 [$300,000 ($900,000 ÷ 3) from the covenant; $133,333 ($800,000 ÷ 6) from the customer list; $100,000 ($1,000,000 ÷ 10) from the patent; and zero from goodwill]. Layden reports $320,000 ($533,333 − $213,333) more in taxable income for the current tax year as a result of the 15-year amortization rule.**

Certain intangible assets, such as sports franchises, are specifically excluded from the 15-year amortization period. Prior law continues to apply to the excluded assets, which are listed in Exhibit 10-2. For example, patents and copyrights not acquired in the purchase of a trade or business are generally amortized over periods of 20 years and 70 years plus the author's life, respectively. These amortization periods are useful lives that are set by statute.

**Example 40** On July 2 of the current year, Conroy Company purchases from Technical Process Company, Inc., the patent to a process for extruding certain plastic forms. Conroy pays $170,000 for the newly developed patent process. The purchase does not represent an acquisition of Technical Process Company. What is the amount of patent amortization in the current year?

Exhibit 10-2

## Intangible Assets Specifically Excluded from 15-Year Amortization

- Interests in notional principal contracts and other similar financial instruments
- Stock, partnership interests
- Interests in land
- Certain computer software
- Interests in films, videotapes, books, and other like property, unless acquired in an acquisition of a trade or business
- Patents and copyrights, unless acquired in an acquisition of a trade or business
- Professional sports franchises
- Certain purchased mortgage service rights
- Interests under an existing lease of tangible property

**Discussion: Because the patent was not acquired as part of the purchase of a trade or business, the amortization period is 20 years (the legal life set by the government). Therefore, Conroy's deduction for amortization is $4,250 [($170,000 ÷ 20) × 6/12].**

# CHAPTER SUMMARY

The deduction for depreciation demonstrates the application of many concepts discussed in earlier chapters. It is well established that an annual deduction is allowed for the recovery of capital invested in a long-lived asset that is used up to earn income. The problem over the years has been how to determine the deduction for the capital recovery. The central concern of taxpayers is to recover their investment as quickly as possible to maximize the present value of depreciation deductions. However, Congress and the IRS have generally been concerned with protecting the collection of revenue. In addition, Congress has varied the amount of allowable depreciation as a method of stimulating capital investment.

Tangible real and personal property with a limited useful life used in a trade or business or in a production-of-income activity is subject to depreciation. An asset's depreciable basis is generally determined using the basis rules discussed in Chapter 9. Assets are depreciated according to the tax law in effect when the asset is placed in service. Before 1981, taxpayers usually used the facts and circumstances method to compute depreciation. This method was a source of continuing controversy between taxpayers and the IRS because the depreciation computation used a variety of estimates (e.g., estimated life and salvage value) and taxpayers had a wide variety of choices in regard to depreciation methods and acquisition- and disposition-year conventions.

ACRS was a revolutionary approach to depreciation that was introduced in 1981. Because ACRS more precisely prescribed how depreciation was to be calculated, it eliminated several areas of controversy that existed under the old system. Under ACRS, the tax law determined the recovery period, depreciation method, salvage value (none considered), and the first- and last-year conventions for real estate and personal property.

As ACRS was being introduced, Congress added to the tax law the Section 179 election to expense assets. This election, which applies to personal property, primarily benefits small businesses. This election allows taxpayers to expense $1,050,000 in 2021 in qualified investment in Section 179 property, subject to two limitations. The annual election to expense under Section 179 is reduced dollar for dollar when the taxpayer places more than $2,620,000 for 2021 in qualified property in service during the year. In addition, the annual deduction is limited to the taxpayer's taxable active business income for the year. The Section 179 expense deduction is treated as regular depreciation. Therefore, any amount expensed under Section 179 reduces an asset's depreciable basis.

After 1986, MACRS is used to depreciate personal property and real estate. MACRS is a modification of ACRS that generally spreads the depreciation deduction over a longer time period. Table 10-9 presents an overview of MACRS. To depreciate property using MACRS, you need to know:

- The property's depreciable basis
- The MACRS recovery period
- Whether regular MACRS or straight-line depreciation is to be used
- The applicable convention

*Table 10-9*

## Overview of the Modified Accelerated Cost Recovery System

| MACRS Recovery Period Class | MACRS Method | MACRS Convention | Straight-line Election | ADS |
|---|---|---|---|---|
| 3-, 5-, 7-, 10-year | 200% DB | Half-year<br>Mid-quarter | SL over MACRS recovery period | 150% DB over MACRS recovery period if regular MACRS used |
| 15-, 20-year | 150% DB | Half-year<br>Mid-quarter | SL over MACRS recovery period | SL over alternate MACRS recovery period |
| 27.5-year residential rental real estate | SL | Mid-month | SL over MACRS recovery period | SL over alternate MACRS recovery period (30 years) |
| 31.5-year nonresidential real estate | SL | Mid-month | SL over MACRS recovery period | SL over alternate MACRS recovery period (40 years) |
| 39-year nonresidential real estate | SL | Mid-month | SL over MACRS recovery period | SL over alternate MACRS recovery period (40 years) |

With this information, depreciation is calculated by multiplying the asset's depreciable basis by a prescribed percentage obtained from an IRS table. If an asset is disposed of before the end of its recovery period, the table's percentages have to be adjusted according to the applicable convention to claim depreciation for the fractional part of the last year in which the asset was used. Instead of using the declining balance method prescribed by MACRS, a taxpayer may elect to use the straight-line method with the same first- and last-year conventions as under regular MACRS. Listed property is subject to special record-keeping requirements and limitations. The depreciation deduction for automobiles is subject to an annual limit based on the year of acquisition and use.

A deduction for depletion is allowed when a taxpayer has an economic interest in a natural resource in place. The investment must be recovered from income received from its removal and sale. The depletion deduction is determined by using the cost or percentage depletion methods. A straight-line amortization deduction is allowed for intangible assets that have a useful life that can be estimated with reasonable accuracy. To lessen the difficulty of estimating useful lives, Congress enacted Section 197 in 1993. This provision allows certain purchased intangibles, including goodwill, to be amortized over 15 years.

# KEY TERMS

Accelerated Cost Recovery System (ACRS) (p. 10-4)
adjusted basis (p. 10-12)
Alternative Depreciation System (ADS) (p. 10-22)
amortization (p. 10-28)
class life (p. 10-12)
cost depletion (p. 10-26)
depletion (p. 10-25)
depreciable basis (p. 10-12)
depreciation (p. 10-2)
depreciation conventions (p. 10-14)
intangible property (p. 10-28)
listed property (p. 10-24)
listed property rules (p. 10-24)
mid-month convention (p. 10-14)
mid-quarter convention (p. 10-14)
mid-year convention (p. 10-14)
Modified Accelerated Cost Recovery System (MACRS) (p. 10-4)
passenger automobile limitation (p. 10-24)
percentage depletion (statutory depletion) (p. 10-27)
Section 179 (p. 10-5)

# PRIMARY TAX LAW SOURCES

[1]Reg. Sec. 1.167(a)-2—Specifies the requirements that must be met to depreciate a property.

[2]S. Rep. No. 144, 97th Cong., 1st Sess., 47 (1981)—States congressional motives in enacting ACRS—that Congress felt that the old depreciation rules were unnecessarily complicated and did not provide "the investment stimulus necessary that is essential for economic expansion."

[3]Sec. 168—Prescribes the calculations necessary for determining depreciation using cost recovery (ACRS and MACRS).

[4]Reg. Sec. 1.179-3—Provides definitions related to the Section 179 election to expense deduction.

[5]Reg. Sec. 1.179-2—Discusses dollar limitations on the Section 179 expense deduction and the application of the limitations to partnerships (and their partners) and S corporations (and their shareholders).

[6]Reg. Sec. 1.179-1—Requires the reduction of the unadjusted basis of an asset for any amounts expensed under Section 179.

[7]U.S. v. Ludley, 274 U.S. 295 (1927)—Stated the original depreciation theory: By using up a depreciable asset, a gradual sale is made of the asset.

[8]Prop. Reg. Sec. 1.168-2—Requires the use of a property's unadjusted basis to compute depreciation under the cost-recovery system.

[9]Rev. Proc. 87-56—Provides the class lives of property that are necessary to compute depreciation deductions.

[10]Reg. Sec. 1.168(d)-1—Explains and gives examples of MACRS conventions.

[11]Sec. 168(d)(4)(A)—Describes the convention as half-year. For consistency, this text uses the term *mid-year.*

[12]Reg. Sec. 1.168(d)-1(b)(4)(i)—Specifies that depreciable basis for purposes of the 40-percent test reflect a reduction for any Sec. 179 expensing.

[13]Reg. Sec. 1.274-5—Explains the substantiation requirements for various types of listed property.

[14]Sec. 280F—Defines listed property and provides limits on the deduction of depreciation when listed property is used 50 percent or less in a taxpayer's trade or business.

[15]Reg. Sec. 1.280F-3T—Explains the calculation of depreciation deductions on listed property when the trade or business use of the property is 50 percent or less.

[16]Reg. Sec. 1.280F-2T—Explains the limitations on depreciation deductions for passenger automobiles.

[17]Sec. 611—Specifies the requirements for a depletion deduction for natural resources.

[18]Sec. 57—States that the percentage depletion deduction in excess of the cost of the property is an addition to a taxpayer's alternative minimum taxable income.

[19]Sec. 612—Requires the use of basis for computing gain in the cost depletion calculation.

[20]Sec. 613—Specifies the calculation of percentage depletion and provides statutory rates for various types of depletable property.

[21]Reg. Sec. 1.613-2—Provides examples of the 50 percent of taxable income limit on percentage depletion deductions.

[22]Reg. Sec. 1.167(a)-3—Defines *intangible assets* for which a periodic expense deduction (through amortization) may be taken; specifically disallows any periodic deductions for goodwill.

# DISCUSSION QUESTIONS

1. **LO2** How does the allowable capital recovery period affect the potential return on the investment in an asset?
2. **LO1** Which two tests must be met to claim a periodic recovery deduction on a capital expenditure?
3. **LO1** What types of capital expenditures are not deductible over time (i.e., their cost is recovered upon disposition of the asset)?
4. **LO1** What is the depreciable basis of an asset? What role does depreciable basis play in determining the annual cost recovery on a depreciable asset?
5. **LO3** What was the purpose of changing from the facts and circumstances depreciation method to the ACRS method?
6. **LO5** In general, which types of property may be expensed under Section 179, and what is the current maximum limit on the deduction?
7. **LO5** What limitations are placed on the maximum amount to be expensed under Section 179?
8. **LO5** Is the Section 179 election to expense an incentive to all businesses to invest in qualifying property?
9. **LO2** In general, taxpayers want to depreciate property as rapidly as possible. Under what circumstances might a taxpayer not want to use accelerated depreciation? How can this be done under MACRS?
10. **LO6** What is the purpose of the acquisition- and disposition-year convention?
11. **LO6** What acquisition- and disposition-year conventions are used in MACRS and to what types of property does each of the conventions apply?
12. **LO6** Why is the calculation of depreciation using MACRS generally considered easier and more efficient than the calculation using the facts and circumstances method?
13. **LO7** What is the Alternative Depreciation System (ADS)? How is it different from a straight-line election under MACRS?
14. **LO7** Why might a taxpayer elect to depreciate assets using the Alternative Depreciation System?
15. **LO8** Why are restrictions placed on the cost recovery of listed property?
16. **LO8** When a taxpayer purchases an automobile for use in a trade or business, what limits are placed on the cost recovery on the automobile?
17. **LO9** Which types of property are allowed a deduction for depletion?
18. **LO9** How is cost depletion different from percentage depletion?
19. **LO9** Which income tax concepts might taxpayers who take depletion deductions be violating?
20. **LO10** How are the costs of intangible assets recovered?

# PROBLEMS

21. **LO1** Peter Corporation purchases the following assets during the current year. Identify which assets are not subject to cost recovery using depreciation, and state why that is so.
   a. Land
   b. Copyright
   c. Building
   d. Goodwill
   e. Inventory for sale in its store
   f. 500 shares of Excellent common stock
   g. A house to be rented out
   h. Equipment for use in its business
   i. An interest in an oil well
   j. A car that will be used 60 percent for business and 40 percent for personal use

22. **LO1** State whether each of the following expenditures incurred during the current year should be treated as a repair expense or capitalized and depreciated using MACRS:
   a. Replacement of the carpeting in a rental apartment
   b. Replacement of the drill bit on a gas-powered post-hole digger
   c. Replacement of the water in the ponds of a catfish farm
   d. Replacement of spark plugs in a delivery truck
   e. Repainting the exterior of a personal use auto

23. **LO1** For each of the following expenditures incurred during the current year, indicate whether it should be treated as a repair expense or capitalized and depreciated using MACRS:
   a. Replacement of the roof on an apartment building
   b. Replacement of the condenser in a central air conditioning unit
   c. Replacement of the tires on a delivery truck
   d. Addition of 10 tons of gravel to a parking lot to restore its surface
   e. Repainting of the interior and exterior of an apartment building

24. **LO5** A taxpayer purchases $507,000 worth of property that qualifies for the Section 179 deduction during the current year. The taxpayer would like to deduct the greatest depreciation expense possible (including the Section 179 deduction) on the property. Indicate how the depreciation expense should be determined:
   a. An individual
   b. A corporation
   c. An S corporation
   d. A partnership

25. **LO5** Firefly, Inc., acquires business equipment in July 2021 for $2,605,000. Assume that Firefly elects not to claim bonus depreciation.
   a. What is Firefly's maximum Section 179 deduction for 2021? Explain.
   b. What happens to any portion of the annual limit not deducted in 2021? Explain.
   c. What is the depreciable basis of the equipment? Explain.

26. **LO5** In 2021, Terrell, Inc., purchases machinery costing $2,618,000. Its 2021 taxable income before considering the Section 179 deduction is $1,100,000. Assume that Terrell elects not to claim bonus depreciation.
   a. What is Terrell's maximum Section 179 deduction in 2021? Explain.
   b. What is the depreciable basis of the equipment?

27. **LO5** In 2021, Theo purchases $16,000 of Section 179 property for use in his delivery business. During 2021, he has $12,000 in taxable income from his business. Assume that Theo elects not to claim bonus depreciation.
   a. What is Theo's maximum Section 179 deduction in 2021? Explain.
   b. Theo's business taxable income for 2021 is $5,000. He purchases $1,000 of new Section 179 property in 2021. What is Theo's maximum Section 179 deduction for 2021?

28. **LO5** During 2021, Belk Corporation purchases $70,000 worth of equipment for use in its business. Belk's current taxable income before considering the Section 179 deduction is $26,000. Assume that Belk elects not to claim bonus depreciation.
    a. What is Belk's maximum Section 179 deduction in 2021? Explain.
    b. Belk's 2021 business taxable income—before a Section 179 deduction—is $50,000. What is Belk's maximum Section 179 deduction in 2021? Explain.

29. **LO5** Brad is a shareholder and full-time employee of an S corporation. During 2021, he earns a $50,000 salary from the S corporation and is allocated $12,000 as his share of its net operating loss. In addition, Brad owns a limited partnership interest from which he earns $12,000 during 2021. Kanika, Brad's wife, operates a small business as a sole proprietorship. During 2021, she spends $65,000 on equipment for use in her business, which has a taxable income of $17,000 before the Section 179 deduction.
    a. What is Brad and Kanika's maximum Section 179 deduction for 2021?
    b. Assume that Brad is allocated $12,000 in Section 179 expense from the S corporation for 2021 and Kanika spends an additional $14,000 on equipment for use in her business. Also, assume that their taxable active business income is $35,000 for 2021. What is Brad and Kanika's maximum Section 179 deduction for 2021?

Communication Skills

30. **LO5** Jennifer owns a 40 percent interest in the Thomas Partnership. She also owns and operates an architectural consulting business. During the current year, the partnership purchases $1,536,000 worth of property qualifying under Section 179 and elects to expense $1,040,000. Jennifer purchases $625,200 worth of qualifying Section 179 property for use in her architectural consulting business. Write a letter to Jennifer explaining what she should do to maximize her cost recovery.

31. **LO6** In each of the following situations, determine the depreciable basis of the asset:
    a. Rudy inherits his father's pickup truck. The truck is immediately placed in service in Rudy's delivery business. The fair market value of the truck at the date of Rudy's father's death is $8,000, and the value on the alternate valuation date is $8,500. The executor of the estate does not make any special elections. The truck originally cost Rudy's father $15,000.
    b. Maline purchases an office building to use as the main office of her mail order business. She pays the seller $100,000 in cash. In addition, she gives the seller her personal note for $250,000 plus 10 acres of real estate. At the date of the transaction, the real estate, which cost $20,000, is worth $50,000. Property tax records show the land is assessed at $10,000 and the building is assessed at $40,000.
    c. Steve owns a computer that he bought for $3,000. The computer was used for personal family activities. When he starts his business, Steve takes the computer to his new office. The computer is worth $500 when he begins using it in his business.
    d. Martha's aunt Mabel gives her a used table, which had been stored in Mabel's garage, to use in the conference room in Martha's office. Mabel paid $1,200 for the table several years ago, and it is worth only $700 at the date of the gift. Mabel does not pay any gift tax on the transfer.

32. **LO6** In each of the following situations, determine the depreciable basis of each asset:
    a. Melissa purchases furniture and fixtures from the estate of the owner of a business for $45,000. She plans to use these assets in her business.
    b. Quang purchased a computer from his employer for $4,000. He plans to use it in his consulting practice, which he conducts in the evenings and on weekends. The fair market value of the computer is $7,000.
    c. Jenny begins using her personal computer equipment in her business. She purchased the equipment for $19,000 in 2018, and it is currently worth $13,000.

d. Fletcher inherits a collectible car from his grandfather's estate. The grandfather's basis in the car was $5,000. The executor of the estate does not make any special elections and values the car at its appraised fair market value of $25,000. Fletcher plans to use the car in his business.

33. **LO6** Determine the class life, MACRS recovery period, and ADS recovery period of each of the following assets:

a. Barge
b. Computer
c. Automobile
d. Breeding sheep
e. Breeding horses
f. Barn
g. Office furniture
h. Land improvements

34. **LO6** Determine the class life, MACRS recovery period, and ADS recovery period of each of the following assets acquired for a sports bar:

a. Pool table
b. Safe
c. Photocopying machines
d. Pickup truck
e. Electronic video games
f. Brewing tanks for the bar's microbrewery
g. Four-year-old racehorse named Goforthe Brew purchased by the bar owners and raced locally
h. Point-of-sale computerized cash registers

35. **LO6** For each asset in problem 34, determine the correct IRS percentage table, recovery period, and applicable convention.

36. **LO6** Determine the correct IRS percentage table, recovery period, and applicable convention for each of the following assets:

a. Helicopter
b. 68-unit apartment building
c. The new Wings Field baseball stadium in Buffalo
d. Automobile
e. Commercial office building
f. Farm equipment storage building

37. **LO6** The United Express Company begins business in August 2021 by purchasing the assets listed in the table below. If United Express elects not to claim bonus depreciation, calculate the maximum MACRS depreciation on the assets.

| Asset | Cost |
|---|---|
| Trucks | $588,000 |
| Tractor units | 55,000 |
| Office equipment | $506,000 |

38. **LO6** Assume that in problem 37, the United Express Company sells a truck that cost $50,000 in 2021 for $15,000 in June 2024. Assume that none of the truck was expensed in 2021. Compute the adjusted basis of the truck and the gain or loss from the sale.

39. **LO6** The Browser Company purchases a computer in August 2021 for $12,000. Browser elects not to claim bonus depreciation and does not elect to expense the asset but wants to claim the maximum depreciation. In May 2024, the company sells the computer. Calculate the adjusted basis of the computer at the date of sale.

40. **LO6** The Browser Company purchases a computer in December 2021 for $12,000. This is the only depreciable personal property acquired during the year. Browser elects not to claim bonus depreciation and does not elect to expense the asset but wants to claim the maximum depreciation. In May 2024, the company sells the computer. Calculate the adjusted basis of the computer at the date of sale.

41. **LO6** Larry purchases machinery for his business (7-year MACRS property) on April 1 at a cost of $1,057,000. On June 1, he spends $84,000 for equipment (5-year MACRS property). Larry does not want to claim bonus depreciation.
    a. What is the maximum deduction allowable?
    b. What is the minimum deduction allowable?
42. **LO6** Kris starts a new business in 2021. She purchases 7-year MACRS property costing $12,000. Her business income before any cost-recovery deductions is $8,000. Kris does not want to claim bonus depreciation.
    a. What is the maximum cost-recovery deduction allowable for 2021?
    b. How does your answer change if Kris informs you that she plans to make significant investments in personal property over the next three years?
43. **LO6** Dikembe purchases 1,000 breeding hogs for $1,124,000 in April 2021.
    a. What is his maximum 2021 cost-recovery deduction for the hogs?
    b. Dikembe's farming operation incurs a net loss this year and probably will next year before taking the cost recovery into consideration. What should Dikembe do in regard to his cost-recovery deductions?
44. **LO6** Rograin Corporation purchases turning lathes costing $1,643,000 and buses costing $975,000 in June of the current year. The lathes are 7-year MACRS property, and the buses are 5-year MACRS property. Rograin does not want to claim bonus depreciation.
    a. What is Rograin's maximum Section 179 deduction?
    b. Assuming that Rograin deducts the maximum Section 179 expense, what are the depreciable basis of the lathes and the buses?
    c. If Rograin wants to maximize its cost recovery this year, how much first-year depreciation may it deduct?
45. **LO6** Baker, Inc., purchases office furniture (7-year MACRS property) costing $1,051,000 and a computer system (5-year MACRS property) costing $1,051,000 in 2021. Assuming that Baker elects not to claim bonus depreciation, what is the maximum cost-recovery deduction in 2021? (Hint: Maximixe the Section 179 election effect.)
46. **LO6** Chen Corporation purchases the following business assets during the current year:

| Asset | Date Purchased | Cost | Recovery Period |
|---|---|---|---|
| Office furniture | 1/15/21 | $480,000 | 7 |
| Computer | 4/1/21 | $ 60,000 | 5 |
| Boat | 7/21/21 | $ 1,053,000 | 10 |

    Assuming that Chen elects not to claim bonus depreciation, what is the maximum current year cost-recovery deduction on the assets purchased? (Hint: Maximize the Section 179 election effect.)
47. **LO6** Harold purchases the following business assets on the dates indicated:

| Asset | Date Purchased | Cost | Recovery Period |
|---|---|---|---|
| Photocopy equipment | 2/14/21 | $50,000 | 5 |
| Dump truck | 7/16/21 | $ 300,000 | 5 |
| Bus | 12/24/21 | $ 1,051,000 | 5 |

    a. What is Harold's 2021 cost-recovery deduction if he elects not to claim bonus depreciation and does not elect to expense any of the assets under Section 179?
    b. What could Harold do to maximize his 2021 deduction?
48. **LO6** The Gladys Corporation buys office equipment costing $1,124,000 on May 12, 2021. In 2024, new and improved models of the equipment make it obsolete, and Gladys sells the old equipment for $34,000 on December 27, 2024.

a. What is Gladys Corporation's gain or loss on the sale assuming that Gladys takes the maximum cost-recovery deduction allowable on the equipment but does not want to claim bonus depreciation?
b. What is Gladys Corporation's gain or loss on the equipment assuming that Gladys takes the minimum cost-recovery deduction allowable on the equipment?

49. **LO6** In June 2021, Copper Kettle, Inc., purchases duplicating equipment for $541,000.
 a. Compare cost-recovery deductions using maximum, minimum, and intermediate methods over the recovery period of the equipment.
 b. Explain why Copper Kettle, Inc. would elect to use each of these methods.

50. **LO6** In July 2021, Surecut Sawmills buys office furniture for $1,100,000. Assume that Surecut elects not to claim bonus depreciation.
 a. Compare cost-recovery deductions using maximum, minimum, and intermediate methods over the recovery period of the equipment.
 b. Explain why Surecut would elect to use each of these methods.

51. **LO7** Stan purchases machinery costing $100,000 for use in his business in 2021. The machinery is 7-year MACRS property and has an ADS life of 12 years. Complete a depreciation schedule using the regular MACRS method and ADS depreciation assuming that Stan does not make a Section 179 election and elects not to claim bonus depreciation. Round depreciation percentages to two decimal places. Round your final answer to the nearest dollar. For ADS, use mid-year convention. For MACRS, adjust the amount of depreciation in 2028 (the last year) so the total depreciation equals $100,000.

52. **LO6** Guadalupe purchases an office building to use in her business at a cost of $520,000. She properly allocates $20,000 of the cost to the land and $500,000 to the building. Assuming that Guadalupe would like to deduct the maximum depreciation on the building, what is her first-year depreciation on the building if she purchases the building on
 a. June 30, 1992?
 b. June 30, 1994?

53. **LO6** Refer to problem 52. Guadalupe sells the building on October 26, 2021. What is her 2021 depreciation deduction if she purchased the building on
 a. June 30, 1992?
 b. June 30, 1994?

54. **LO6** Anton purchases a building on May 4, 2004, at a cost of $270,000. The land is properly allocated $30,000 of the cost. Anton sells the building on October 18, 2021, for $270,000. What is his gain or loss on the sale if he uses the regular MACRS system and the building is
 a. An apartment building?
 b. An office building?
 c. How would your answers to parts a and b change if Anton makes a straight-line election on the building? Explain.

55. **LO6** On March 1, 2021, Babar Inc., pays $1,200,000 for a store building, moves into the building, and begins business on April 1. Babar properly allocates $1,000,000 of its cost to the building and $200,000 to the land. On May 21, 2021, it installs $1,073,000 worth of new display shelving. Babar wants to claim the maximum allowable depreciation on the property it purchased but does not want to claim bonus depreciation. On January 2, 2024, Babar sells the land and building for $1,400,000 and the display shelving for $45,000.
 a. What is Babar's maximum depreciation deduction for 2021?
 b. What is Babar's maximum depreciation deduction for 2024?
 c. What is Babar's gain or loss on the sale of the land and building?
 d. What is Babar's gain or loss on the sale of the shelving?

56. **LO8** On June 1, 2021, Kirsten buys an automobile for $60,000. Her mileage log for the year reveals the following: 20,000 miles for business purposes; 7,000 miles

for personal reasons; and 3,000 miles commuting to and from work. What is Kirsten's maximum cost-recovery deduction for 2021?

57. **LO8** On May 15, 2021, Lurlene buys a used automobile for $20,000. She drives it 9,000 miles for business and 3,000 miles for personal trips during the year. What is Lurlene's maximum cost recovery for 2021?

58. **LO9** On July 4 of the current year, Lawrence invests $240,000 in a mineral property. He estimates that he will recover 800,000 units of the mineral from the deposit. During the current year, Lawrence recovers and sells 100,000 units of the mineral for $3.50 per unit.
    a. What are Lawrence's cost depletion deduction for the current year and his adjusted basis for the mineral deposit after deducting depletion?
    b. If the percentage depletion rate for the mineral is 10 percent, what are his depletion deduction for the current year and his adjusted basis for the mineral deposit after deducting depletion?
    c. If the statutory percentage depletion rate for the mineral is 10 percent and Lawrence's income from the mineral before the depletion deduction is $9,200, what are his depletion deduction for the current year and his adjusted basis for the mineral deposit after deducting depletion?

Communication Skills

59. **LO9** Isidro purchases an interest in an oil-producing property for $100,000 on November 3. His geologist estimates 15,000 barrels of oil are recoverable. The entity sells 1,000 barrels for $20,000 during November and December of the year of acquisition. Assume the percentage depletion rate for oil is 15 percent. Operating expenses related to the revenues are $3,000.
    a. Advise Isidro on the amount of depletion he should deduct in the year of acquisition.
    b. At the end of the second year, the geologist estimates the remaining number of recoverable barrels is 18,000. Isidro has an offer of $190,000 for his investment. In the second year, the entity sold only 3,000 barrels of oil. Gross revenues were $50,000 and operating expenses totaled $4,000. If Isidro sells the property, what is the amount of his realized gain?
    c. Write a memorandum explaining the details of Isidro's gain. Include a recommendation about whether he should accept the offer.

60. **LO10** On June 2, 2021, Lokar Corporation purchases a patent for $68,000 from the inventor of a new extrusion process. The patent has 12 years remaining on its legal life. Also, Lokar purchases substantially all the assets of the Barrios Corporation for $750,000 on September 8, 2021. The values of the assets listed in the purchase agreement are as follows:

| | |
|---|---|
| Inventory | $ 250,000 |
| Manufacturing equipment | 1,186,000 |
| Patent on compression process | 105,000 |
| Goodwill | 95,000 |

Determine the maximum 2021 cost-recovery deductions for the assets purchased.

61. **LO10** On April 18, 2021, Petros buys all the assets of Brigid's Muffler Shop. Included in the purchase price of $295,000 is a payment of $20,000 to Brigid not to open a competing shop in the state for a period of five years. Brigid's assets at the date of sale are as follows:

| Asset | Adjusted Basis | Fair Market Value |
|---|---|---|
| Inventory | $ 8,500 | $ 10,000 |
| Equipment | 3,500 | 30,000 |
| Building | 80,000 | 120,000 |
| Patent | 500 | 15,000 |
| Land | 5,000 | 10,000 |

The patent is on a special muffler that Brigid developed and patented five years ago. Petros would like to know the maximum amount of the deduction he will be allowed on the purchase of Brigid's assets for 2021.

62. **LO10** On October 1 of the current year, Lee Corporation enters negotiations with Kay Corporation to acquire a patent. The patent has 10 years remaining on its legal life.
   a. If Lee Corporation purchases the patent for $36,000, how much amortization expense may Lee Corporation deduct in the current year?
   b. Assume that Lee Corporation purchases all of the assets of Kay Corporation for $510,000. All of the identifiable assets of Kay Corporation have a fair market value of $420,000, including the patent, which has a fair market value of $36,000. Also, a covenant not to compete for three years costing $72,000 is included in the purchase agreement. How much amortization expense may Lee Corporation deduct in the current year?

# ISSUE IDENTIFICATION PROBLEMS

In each of the following problems, identify the tax issue(s) posed by the facts presented. Determine the possible tax consequences of each issue that you identify.

63. Bailey Construction Company purchases a bulldozer on December 20, 2021. An ice storm delays delivery until December 24. Because of the holidays, the equipment is not used until January 2.
64. Jason is transferred to another city to work and is unable to sell his house. He rents out the house until it is sold.
65. Gates, Inc., purchases a painting by a 16th-century Italian artist and displays it in the corporate headquarters.
66. During 2021, Schottenheim Corporation buys laptop computers and desktop computers to use in its general sales offices. Schottenheim buys laptops for $42,000 on March 29, additional laptops for $18,000 on September 26, and the desktop computers for $1,070,000 on October 5. The Corporation makes no other capital expenditures this year.
67. GM Corporation purchases equipment costing $18,000 and wants to claim the maximum deduction possible for this expenditure.
68. Oliver Company obtains a patent by paying $15,000 on June 21 of this year.

# TECHNOLOGY APPLICATIONS

69. Dawkins Logging Company buys 400 acres of forest land for $50,000. The purchase price is allocated as follows: $10,000 to the land and the remaining $40,000 to the timber. At the time of purchase, there was an estimated 400,000 board feet of timber on the land. During the first year, Dawkins cuts and sells 100,000 board feet of timber off the land.

    REQUIRED: Determine the depletion deduction that Dawkins will be allowed to claim for the first year. Search a tax research database and find the relevant authority(ies) that forms the basis for your answer. Your answer should include the exact text of the authority(ies) and an explanation of the application of the authority to Dawkins's facts. If there is any uncertainty about the validity of your answer, indicate the cause for the uncertainty.
70. Your client purchases land that has been severely eroded. He plans to fill the holes caused by the erosion with waste material. Prepare a memorandum discussing any cost recovery deductions that can be claimed on this property. Research Skills
71. Your client, Stone Mining Company, comes to you with a tax planning idea. This year's mining revenues are disappointing, but the company is very optimistic that next year's mining revenues will increase dramatically. To avoid concern among shareholders, Stone Mining wants to minimize expenses this year to make its income appear higher. Therefore, it plans to claim no depletion expense this year and to claim depletion next year under both the percentage Research Skills

and cost depletion methods. Another alternative it is considering is to claim cost depletion this year because it is lower than the percentage method. Prepare a written memorandum discussing whether either of these plans will succeed.

## INTEGRATIVE PROBLEMS

72. In problem 87 of Chapter 9, you were asked to determine the initial basis of Emelio and Charita's business, investment, and personal use assets. In this problem, you are to determine the adjusted basis of the assets as of December 31, 2021. You should disclose all calculations made to arrive at the December 31, 2021, basis values. For depreciable assets and amortizable assets, present the basis in the following form:

    Asset: ______________________________
    Date acquired: _______________________
    Initial basis: _________________________
    Depreciation/Amortization life: ________
    Depreciation/Amortization deducted to December 31, 2021: __________
    (per the schedule here)
    Basis on December 31, 2021: ____________
    Depreciation/Amortization Schedule:

| Year | Depreciable Basis | Depreciation Percentage | Depreciation |
|---|---|---|---|

    Assume that Emelio and Charita have always deducted the maximum depreciation allowable. However, in 2021, because their income is less as a result of the opening of Charita's new business, they do not wish to expense any eligible amounts or claim bonus depreciation.

Communication Skills

73. Joy opened a shop to sell concrete yard ornaments in 2017. In June of 2018, she converted a building in front of her residence into a store. The fair market value of the building when she opened the store was $50,000. The land, her house, and the store building cost $100,000 when she purchased them in 2011. The appraised values in 2011 were as follows: $10,000 for the store building, $15,000 for the land, and $25,000 for the house.

    In 2018, Joy began traveling to craft shows in her van to sell her ornaments. The van cost $12,000 in 2014 and had a fair market value of $5,000 in 2018 when she began using it in the business. She paid $1,000 in 2018 to modify the van so that it could carry the heavy loads. Her business mileage has remained at 60 percent of her total mileage since 2018, and she has always used the standard mileage deduction. In 2021, she travels 12,000 miles to craft shows.

    In January 2021, the manufacturer from whom she purchases her concrete ornaments tells Joy he wants to retire and asks if she is interested in buying his business. Joy believes she can increase her profits by making her own products, and agrees to purchase the business. The negotiated purchase price of the assets is as follows:

| Asset | Adjusted Basis | Fair Market Value |
|---|---|---|
| Inventory | $ 5,000 | $ 7,500 |
| Equipment | 12,000 | 18,000 |

    When Joy starts to manufacture the concrete ornaments during the winter of 2021, she finds that she needs a structure in which to work to protect her and the concrete mixture from the cold. She purchases the materials for a barn for $6,000 and hires laborers to build it for $4,000.

a. Determine Joy's maximum 2021 cost-recovery deduction on her business assets. Assume that she has always taken the maximum allowable cost-recovery deduction on her business assets but has never had enough business income to elect to expense assets under Section 179. In 2021, Joy estimates that her net business income before any cost-recovery deductions will be at least $30,000, and she would like to take the maximum allowable deduction in 2021.

b. Write a letter to Joy explaining the results of maximizing her 2021 allowable cost-recovery deductions.

# DISCUSSION CASES

74. Fiona is a professional bass violinist with the St. Paul Symphony Orchestra. In February of the current year, she purchases at auction for $200,000 an eighteenth-century bass violin built by the renowned Asa Santavar. Fiona is thrilled by her acquisition. The violin is a treasured artwork and a quality investment. Also, it is an asset she will use almost daily in her profession. May Fiona deduct part of her expenditure this year? Explain.

75. The tax law provides four methods of cost recovery for assets: (1) immediate deduction of the total cost when paid or incurred; (2) deferral of cost until the property is sold or otherwise disposed of; (3) deduction based on a percentage of income from the property over its life; and (4) deduction over a period of years, beginning at date of acquisition, using a consistent method. Discuss each cost recovery method. Provide examples of each and explain the reasoning underlying each method.

# TAX PLANNING CASES

76. You are the resident tax expert for Wetzel's Pretzels, an international producer of snack food. The controller has come to you with the company's capital expenditures budget for next year. The budget shows that Wetzel's Pretzels plans to spend $1,050,000 next year on personal property. The largest single item in the budget is the purchase of new, high-tech pretzel twisters costing $473,000. The pretzel twisters are on order, but because of high demand for the technology, Wetzel's Pretzels will not receive the new twisters until November. The remaining $577,000 is for company automobiles, delivery trucks, personal computers, and office furniture. These items will be purchased throughout the year as needed. Communication Skills

The controller asks your advice on the tax aspects of these purchases. She is particularly interested in making sure that Wetzel's Pretzels can deduct the maximum amount regarding these purchases in the year of purchase.

How would you advise the controller? That is, are there any tax problems associated with these purchases? If so, suggest one or more ways in which Wetzel's can take advantage of the situation. Write a memorandum to the controller explaining your suggestions.

77. Joan is interested in buying a special diagnostic machine for use in her medical practice. The machine will cost her $16,000 and will have a $2,000 salvage value at the end of its eight-year life. Joan would like to know the actual cost of the machine after considering the effect of the present value of tax savings from depreciation. If she buys the machine, she will place it in service on April 1, 2021. Based on the following assumptions, what is Joan's after-tax cost? Assume that Joan is in the Communication Skills

32 percent marginal tax rate bracket and that the time value of money is worth 10 percent. Write a letter to Joan explaining the following options:

a. Joan will depreciate the machine over five years using MACRS.
b. Joan will depreciate the machine using the straight-line method over the seven-year ADS life.
c. Joan will deduct the $16,000 investment as an expense in 2021.

# ETHICS DISCUSSION CASE

Communication Skills

78. Steem Advertising Corporation acquires 100 laptop computers in 2020 for its account executives to use. Steem pays $300,000 for the computers. You are the newly hired CPA and you expect to advise Steem on tax issues regarding tax years 2021 and 2021. Upon examining the firm's records for 2020, you find that each computer was expensed and deducted in 2020. Later, when examining one of the computers, you notice it has several games loaded on the hard drive. Also, you find several items of personal correspondence saved in a subdirectory of the word-processing software package.
    a. What should you do? What are your obligations under the Statements on Standards for Tax Services (found at www.aicpa.org)?
    b. Write a memorandum to your supervisor in the CPA firm explaining your observations and suggestions.

# Appendix to Chapter 10

## 10A-1 MACRS CLASS LIVES AND MACRS DEPRECIATION SCHEDULES

### 10A-1a REV. PROC. 87-56

#### Section 1. Purpose

The purpose of this revenue procedure is to set forth the class lives of property that are necessary to compute the depreciation allowances available under section 168 of the Internal Revenue Code, as amended by section 201(a) of the Tax Reform Act of 1986 (Act), 1986-3 (Vol. 1) C.B. 38. Rev. Proc. 87-57, page 17, this Bulletin, describes the applicable depreciation methods, applicable recovery periods, and applicable conventions that must be used in computing depreciation allowances under section 168.

#### Section 2. General Rules of Application

**.01 In General** This revenue procedure specifies class lives and recovery periods for property subject to depreciation under the general depreciation system provided in section 168(a) of the Code or the alternative depreciation system provided in section 168(g).

**.02 Definition of Class Life** Except with respect to certain assigned property described in section 3 of this revenue procedure, for purposes of both the general depreciation system and the alternative depreciation system, the term "class life" means the class life that would be applicable for any property as of January 1, 1986, under section 167(m) of the Code (determined without regard to paragraph 4 thereof and determined as if the taxpayer had made an election under section 167(m)). The class life that would be applicable for any property as of January 1, 1986, under section 167(m), is the asset guideline period (midpoint class life) for the asset guideline class in which such property is classified under Rev. Proc. 83-35, 1983-1 C.B. 745. However, for purposes of the alternative depreciation system, section 168(g)(3)(B) assigns a class life to certain property that is taken into account under section 168 rather than the class life that would be applicable as of January 1, 1986. The class life of property that is either determined as of January 1, 1986, under Rev. Proc. 83-35 or assigned under section 168(g)(3)(B) may be modified by the Secretary pursuant to authority granted under section 168(i)(1). See section 4 of this revenue procedure.

**.03 Rev. Proc. 83-35** Rev. Proc. 83-35 sets out the asset guideline classes, asset guideline periods and ranges, and annual asset guideline repair allowance percentages for the Class Life Asset Depreciation Range System. The asset guideline periods (midpoint class lives) set out in Rev. Proc. 83-35 are also used in defining the classes of recovery property under the Accelerated Cost Recovery System (that is, section 168 of the Code as in effect prior to amendment by section 201 of the Act). Rev. Proc. 83-35 remains effective for property subject to depreciation under those systems. Rev. Proc. 83-35 does not apply to property subject to depreciation under section 168, other than as a basis for determining the class lives of such property under section 2.02 of this revenue procedure.

**.04 Property with No Class Life** Property that is neither described in an asset guideline class listed in section 5 of this revenue procedure nor assigned a class life under section 168(g)(3)(B) of the Code is treated as property having no class life for purposes of section 168 unless and until a class life is prescribed by the Secretary pursuant to the authority granted under section 168(i)(1). See section 4 of this revenue procedure.

The general and alternative depreciation systems contain separate rules for classifying property that does not have a class life.

## Section 5. Tables of Class Lives and Recovery Periods

**.01** Except for property described in section 5.02, below, the class lives (if any) and recovery periods for property subject to depreciation under section 168 of the Code appear in the tables below. These tables are based on the definition of class life in section 2.02 of this revenue procedure and the assigned items described in section 3 of this revenue procedure.

**.02** For purposes of depreciation under the general depreciation system; residential rental property has a recovery period of 27.5 years and nonresidential real property has a recovery period of 31.5 years. For purposes of the alternative depreciation system, residential rental and nonresidential real property each have a recovery period of 40 years.

**.04** In addition to specifying class lives for each asset guideline class, the tables list certain property for which a recovery period is assigned, notwithstanding such property's class life (if any). See section 3 of this revenue procedure. The listed assigned property classes (denoted A–E) generally do not correspond to asset guideline classes for which class lives are specified in the tables. The class life (if any) of an item of assigned property described in classes A–E is determined by reference to the asset guideline class (if any) containing such item of property. If an item of assigned property described in classes A–E is not contained in any asset guideline class, such item of property has no class life.

**Examples** Qualified technological equipment as defined in section 168(i)(2) (class B) is assigned a recovery period of five years for both the general and alternative depreciation systems, notwithstanding such property's class life (if any). Property that is a computer or peripheral equipment, high technology telephone station equipment installed on the customer's premises, or high technology medical equipment within the meaning of section 168(i)(2), may be described in asset guideline class 00.12 (class life six years), 48.13 (class life 10 years), or 57.0 (class life nine years), respectively. Property used in connection with research and experimentation referred to in section 168(e)(3)(B) (class C) is assigned a recovery period of 5 years for the general depreciation system, notwithstanding its class life (if any). Such property's recovery period for the alternative depreciation system is based on its class life (if any). An item of property used in connection with research and experimentation has a class life if such property is contained in an asset guideline class.

**.05** The following special rules are incorporated from Rev. Proc. 83-35, sections 2.02 (iii) and (iv):

1 Asset guideline class 00.3, "Land Improvements," includes "other tangible property" that qualifies under section 1.48-1(d) of the Income Tax Regulations. However, a structure that is essentially an item of machinery or equipment or a structure that houses property used as an integral part of an activity specified in section 48(a)(1)(B)(i) of the Code, if the use of the structure is so closely related to the use of the property that the structure clearly can be expected to be replaced when the property it initially houses is replaced, is included in the asset guideline class appropriate to the equipment to which it is related.

Table A10-1

## IRS Table of MACRS Classes *(Partial Table)*

| Asset Class | Description of Assets Included | Class Life (in years) | Recovery Periods (in years): General Depreciation System | Recovery Periods (in years): Alternative Depreciation System |
|---|---|---|---|---|
| **Specific Depreciable Assets Used in All Business Activities, Except as Noted:** | | | | |
| 00.11 | Office Furniture, Fixtures, and Equipment: Includes furniture and fixtures that are not a structural component of a building. Includes such assets as desks, files, safes, and communications equipment. Does not include communications equipment that is included in other classes | 10 | 7 | 10 |
| 00.12 | Information Systems: Includes computers and their peripheral equipment used in administering normal business transactions and the maintenance of business records, their retrieval and analysis. Information systems are defined as: 1. Computers: A computer is a programmable electronically activated device capable of accepting information, applying prescribed processes to the information, and supplying the results of these processes with or without human intervention. It usually consists of a central processing unit containing extensive storage, logic, arithmetic, and control capabilities. Excluded from this category are adding machines, electronic desk calculators, etc., and other equipment described in class 00.13. 2. Peripheral equipment consists of the auxiliary machines that are designed to be placed under control of the central processing unit. Nonlimiting examples are: Card readers, card punches, magnetic tape feeds, high-speed printers, optical character readers, tape cassettes, mass storage units, paper tape equipment, keypunches, data entry devices, teleprinters, terminals, tape drives, disc drives, disc files, disc packs, visual image projector tubes, card sorters, plotters, and collators. Peripheral equipment may be used on-line or off-line. Does not include equipment that is an integral part of other capital equipment that is included in other classes of economic activity, i.e., computers used primarily for process or production control, switching, channeling, and automating distributive trades and services such as point of sale (POS) computer systems. Also, does not include equipment of a kind used primarily for amusement or entertainment of the user | 6 | 5* | 5* |
| 00.13 | Data Handling Equipment, except Computers: Includes only typewriters, calculators, adding and accounting machines, copiers, and duplicating equipment | 6 | 5 | 6 |
| 00.21 | Airplanes (airframes and engines), except those used in commercial or contract carrying of passengers or freight, and all helicopters (airframes and engines) | 6 | 5 | 6 |
| 00.22 | Automobiles, Taxis | 3 | 5 | 5 |
| 00.23 | Buses | 9 | 5 | 9 |
| 00.241 | Light General Purpose Trucks: Includes trucks for use over the road (actual unloaded weight less than 13,000 pounds) | 4 | 5 | 5 |
| 00.242 | Heavy General Purpose Trucks: Includes heavy general purpose trucks, concrete ready mix-trucks, and ore trucks, for use over the road (actual unloaded weight 13,000 pounds or more) | 6 | 5 | 6 |
| 00.25 | Railroad Cars and Locomotives, except those owned by railroad transportation companies | 15 | 7 | 15 |
| 00.26 | Tractor Units for Use Over-the-Road | 4 | 3 | 4 |
| 00.27 | Trailers and Trailer-Mounted Containers | 6 | 5 | 6 |
| 00.28 | Vessels, Barges, Tugs, and Similar Water Transportation Equipment, except those used in marine construction | 18 | 10 | 18 |

*(Continued on next page)*

*Table A10-1*

## IRS Table of MACRS Classes *(Partial Table) (continued)*

| Asset Class | Description of Assets Included | Class Life (in years) | Recovery Periods (in years): General Depreciation System | Recovery Periods (in years): Alternative Depreciation System |
|---|---|---|---|---|
| 00.3 | Land Improvements: Includes improvements directly to or added to land, whether such improvements are section 1245 property or section 1250 property, provided such improvements are depreciable. Examples of such assets might include sidewalks, roads, canals, waterways, drainage facilities, sewers (not including municipal sewers in Class 51), wharves and docks, bridges, fences, landscaping, shrubbery, or radio and television transmitting towers. Does not include land improvements that are explicitly included in any other class, and buildings and structural components as defined in section 1.48-1(e) of the regulations. Excludes public utility initial clearing and grading land improvements as specified in Rev. Rul. 72-403, 1972-2 C.B. 102 | 20 | 15 | 20 |
| 00.4 | Industrial Steam and Electric Generation and/or Distribution Systems: Includes assets, whether such assets are section 1245 property or 1250 property, providing such assets are depreciable, used in the production and/or distribution of electricity with rated total capacity in excess of 500 Kilowatts and/or assets used in the production and/or distribution of steam with rated total capacity in excess of 12,500 pounds per hour for use by the taxpayer in its industrial manufacturing process or plant activity and not ordinarily available for sale to others. Does not include buildings and structural components as defined in section 1.48-1(e) of the regulations. Assets used to generate and/or distribute electricity or steam of the type described above but of lesser rated capacity are not included, but are included in the appropriate manufacturing equipment classes elsewhere specified. Also includes electric generating and steam distribution assets, which may utilize steam produced by a waste reduction and resource recovery plant, used by the taxpayer in its industrial manufacturing process or plant activity. Steam and chemical recovery boiler systems used for the recovery and regeneration of chemicals used in manufacturing, with rated capacity in excess of that described above, with specifically related distribution and return systems are not included, but are included in appropriate manufacturing equipment classes elsewhere specified. An example of an excluded steam and chemical recovery boiler system is that used in the pulp and paper manufacturing industry | 22 | 15 | 22 |
| **Depreciable Assets Used in the Following Activities:** | | | | |
| 01.1 | Agriculture: Includes machinery and equipment, grain bins, and fences but no other land improvements, that are used in the production of crops or plants, vines, and trees; livestock; the operation of farm dairies, nurseries, greenhouses, sod farms, mushroom cellars, cranberry bogs, apiaries, and fur farms; the performance of agriculture, animal husbandry, and horticultural services | 10 | 7 | 10 |
| 01.11 | Cotton Ginning Assets | 12 | 7 | 12 |
| 01.21 | Cattle, Breeding or Dairy | 7 | 5 | 7 |
| 01.22 | Horses, Breeding or Work | 10 | 7 | 10 |
| **Specific Depreciable Assets Used in All Business Activities, Except as Noted:** | | | | |
| 01.221 | Any breeding or work horse that is 12 years old or less at the time it is placed in service | 10 | 7 | 10 |
| 01.222 | Any breeding or work horse that is more than 12 years old at the time it is placed in service | 10 | 3 | 10 |
| 01.223 | Any race horse that is more than 2 years old at the time it is placed in service | * | 3 | 12 |
| 01.224 | Any horse that is more than 12 years old at the time it is placed in service and that is neither a race horse nor a horse described in class 01.222 | * | 3 | 12 |
| 01.225 | Any horse not described in classes 01.221, 01.222, 01.223, or 01.224 | * | 7 | 12 |
| 01.23 | Hogs, Breeding | 3 | 3 | 3 |
| 01.24 | Sheep and Goats, Breeding | 5 | 5 | 5 |
| 01.3 | Farm buildings except structures included in Class 01.4 | 25 | 20 | 25 |
| 01.4 | Single purpose agricultural or horticultural structures (within the meaning of section 48(p) of the Code) | 15 | 7 | 15 |

*Table A10-1*

# IRS Table of MACRS Classes *(Partial Table) (continued)*

| Asset Class | Description of Assets Included | Class Life (in years) | General Depreciation System | Alternative Depreciation System |
|---|---|---|---|---|
| | | Recovery Periods (in years) | | |
| 10.0 | Mining: Includes assets used in the mining and quarrying of metallic and nonmetallic minerals (including sand, gravel, stone, and clay) and the milling, beneficiation, and other primary preparation of such materials | 10 | 7 | 10 |
| 13.1 | Drilling of Oil and Gas Wells: Includes assets used in the drilling of onshore oil and gas wells and the provision of geophysical and other exploration services; and the provision of such oil and gas field services as chemical treatment, plugging and abandoning of wells, and cementing or perforating well casings. Does not include assets used in the performance of any of these activities and services by integrated petroleum and natural gas producers for their own account | 6 | 5 | 6 |
| 15.0 | Construction: Includes assets used in construction by general building, special trade, heavy and marine construction contractors, operative and investment builders, real estate subdividers and developers, and others except railroads | 6 | 5 | 6 |
| 20.1 | Manufacture of Grain and Grain Mill Products: Includes assets used in the production of flours, cereals, livestock feeds, and other grain and grain mill products | 17 | 10 | 17 |
| 57.0 | Distributive Trades and Services: Includes assets used in wholesale and retail trade, and personal and professional services. Includes section 1245 assets used in marketing petroleum and petroleum products | 9 | 5 | 9** |
| 57.1 | Distributive Trades and Services—Billboard, Service Station Buildings, and Petroleum Marketing Land Improvements: Includes section 1250 assets, including service station buildings and depreciable land improvements, whether section 1245 property or section 1250 property, used in the marketing of petroleum and petroleum products, but not including any of these facilities related to petroleum and natural gas trunk pipelines. Includes car wash buildings and related land improvements. Includes billboards, whether such assets are section 1245 property or section 1250 property. Excludes all other land improvements, buildings, and structural components as defined in section 1.48-1(e) of the regulations | 20 | 15 | 20 |
| 79.0 | Recreation: Includes assets used in the provision of entertainment services on payment of a fee or admission charge, as in the operation of bowling alleys, billiard and pool establishments, theaters, concert halls, and miniature golf courses. Does not include amusement and theme parks and assets that consist primarily of specialized land improvements or structures, such as golf courses, sports stadia, race tracks, ski slopes, and buildings that house the assets used in entertainment services | 10 | 7 | 10 |
| 80.0 | Theme and Amusement Parks: Includes assets used in the provision of rides, attractions, and amusements in activities defined as theme and amusement parks, and includes appurtenances associated with a ride, attraction, amusement, or theme setting within the park such as ticket booths, facades, shop interiors, and props, special purpose structures, and buildings other than warehouses, administration buildings, hotels, and motels. Includes all land improvements for or in support of park activities (e.g., parking lots, sidewalks, waterways, bridges, fences, landscaping) and support functions (e.g., food and beverage retailing, souvenir vending and other nonlodging accommodations) if owned by the park and provided exclusively for the benefit of park patrons. Theme and amusement parks are defined as combinations of amusements, rides, and attractions that are permanently situated on park land and open to the public for the price of admission. This guideline class is a composite of all assets used in this industry except transportation equipment (general purpose trucks, cars, airplanes, etc., that are included in asset guideline classes with the prefix 00.2), assets used in the provision of administrative services (asset classes with the prefix 00.1), and warehouses, administration buildings, hotels, and motels | 12.5 | 7 | 12.5 |

*(Continued on next page)*

Table A10-1

## IRS Table of MACRS Classes *(Partial Table) (continued)*

| Asset Class | Description of Assets Included | Class Life (in years) | General Depreciation System | Alternative Depreciation System |
|---|---|---|---|---|
| | | Recovery Periods (in years) | | |
| **Certain Property for Which Recovery Periods Assigned:** | | | | |
| | A. Personal Property with No Class Life | | 7 | 12 |
| | Section 1245 Real Property with No Class Life | | 7 | 40 |
| | B. Qualified Technological Equipment, as defined in section 168(i)(2). | ++ | 5 | 5 |
| | C. Property Used in Connection with Research and Experimentation referred to in section 168(e)(3)(B) | ++ | 5 | class life if no class life—12 |
| | D. Alternative Energy Propert described in sections 48(l)(3)(viii) or (iv), or section 48(l)(4) of the Code. | ++ | 5 | class life if no class life—12 |
| | E. Biomass property described in section 48(l)(15) and is a qualifying small production facility within the meaning of section 3(17)(c) of the Federal Power Act (16 U.S.C. 796(17)(C)), as in effect on September 1, 1986 | ++ | 5 | class life if no class life—12 |

*Property described in asset class 00.12 that is qualified technological equipment as defined in section 168(i)(2) is assigned a recovery period of 5 years notwithstanding its class life. See section 3 of the revenue procedure.

**Any high-technology medical equipment as defined in section 168(i)(2)(C) which is described in asset guideline class 57.0 is assigned a 5-year recovery period for the alternative depreciation system.

++The class life (if any) of property described in classes B, C, D, or E is determined by reference to the asset guideline classes in this revenue procedure. If an item of property described in paragraphs B, C, D, or E is not described in any asset guideline class, such item of property has no class life.

Table A10-2

## MACRS Depreciation for Property Other Than Real Estate

Applicable convention: mid-year *(applicable methods: 200% or 150% declining balance, switching to straight-line)*

| If the recovery year is | And the recovery period is | | | | | |
|---|---|---|---|---|---|---|
| | 3 Years | 5 Years | 7 Years | 10 Years | 15 Years | 20 Years |
| | The depreciation rate is | | | | | |
| 1 | 33.33 | 20.00 | 14.29 | 10.00 | 5.00 | 3.750 |
| 2 | 44.45 | 32.00 | 24.49 | 18.00 | 9.50 | 7.219 |
| 3 | 14.81 | 19.20 | 17.49 | 14.40 | 8.55 | 6.677 |
| 4 | 7.41 | 11.52 | 12.49 | 11.52 | 7.70 | 6.177 |
| 5 | | 11.52 | 8.93 | 9.22 | 6.93 | 5.713 |
| 6 | | 5.76 | 8.92 | 7.37 | 6.23 | 5.285 |
| 7 | | | 8.93 | 6.55 | 5.90 | 4.888 |
| 8 | | | 4.46 | 6.55 | 5.90 | 4.522 |
| 9 | | | | 6.56 | 5.91 | 4.462 |
| 10 | | | | 6.55 | 5.90 | 4.461 |
| 11 | | | | 3.28 | 5.91 | 4.462 |
| 12 | | | | | 5.90 | 4.461 |
| 13 | | | | | 5.91 | 4.462 |
| 14 | | | | | 5.90 | 4.461 |
| 15 | | | | | 5.91 | 4.462 |
| 16 | | | | | 2.95 | 4.461 |
| 17 | | | | | | 4.462 |
| 18 | | | | | | 4.461 |
| 19 | | | | | | 4.462 |
| 20 | | | | | | 4.461 |
| 21 | | | | | | 2.231 |

*Table A10-3*

# MACRS Depreciation for Property Other Than Real Estate

Applicable convention: mid-quarter; property placed in service in first quarter
*(applicable methods: 200% or 150% declining balance, switching to straight-line)*

| If the recovery year is | And the recovery period is | | | | | |
|---|---|---|---|---|---|---|
| | 3 Years | 5 Years | 7 Years | 10 Years | 15 Years | 20 Years |
| | The depreciation rate is | | | | | |
| 1 | 58.33 | 35.00 | 25.00 | 17.50 | 8.75 | 6.563 |
| 2 | 27.78 | 26.00 | 21.43 | 16.50 | 9.13 | 7.000 |
| 3 | 12.35 | 15.60 | 15.31 | 13.20 | 8.21 | 6.482 |
| 4 | 1.54 | 11.01 | 10.93 | 10.56 | 7.39 | 5.996 |
| 5 | | 11.01 | 8.75 | 8.45 | 6.65 | 5.546 |
| 6 | | 1.38 | 8.74 | 6.76 | 5.99 | 5.130 |
| 7 | | | 8.75 | 6.55 | 5.90 | 4.746 |
| 8 | | | 1.09 | 6.55 | 5.91 | 4.459 |
| 9 | | | | 6.56 | 5.90 | 4.459 |
| 10 | | | | 6.55 | 5.91 | 4.459 |
| 11 | | | | 0.82 | 5.90 | 4.459 |
| 12 | | | | | 5.91 | 4.460 |
| 13 | | | | | 5.90 | 4.459 |
| 14 | | | | | 5.91 | 4.460 |
| 15 | | | | | 5.90 | 4.459 |
| 16 | | | | | 0.74 | 4.460 |
| 17 | | | | | | 4.459 |
| 18 | | | | | | 4.460 |
| 19 | | | | | | 4.459 |
| 20 | | | | | | 4.460 |
| 21 | | | | | | 0.557 |

Table A10-4

# MACRS Depreciation for Property Other Than Real Estate

Applicable convention: mid-quarter; property placed in service in second quarter
*(applicable methods: 200% or 150% declining balance, switching to straight-line)*

| If the recovery year is | And the recovery period is | | | | | |
|---|---|---|---|---|---|---|
| | 3 Years | 5 Years | 7 Years | 10 Years | 15 Years | 20 Years |
| | The depreciation rate is | | | | | |
| 1 | 41.67 | 25.00 | 17.85 | 12.50 | 6.25 | 4.688 |
| 2 | 38.89 | 30.00 | 23.47 | 17.50 | 9.38 | 7.148 |
| 3 | 14.14 | 18.00 | 16.76 | 14.00 | 8.44 | 6.612 |
| 4 | 5.30 | 11.37 | 11.97 | 11.20 | 7.59 | 6.116 |
| 5 | | 11.37 | 8.87 | 8.96 | 6.83 | 5.658 |
| 6 | | 4.26 | 8.87 | 7.17 | 6.15 | 5.233 |
| 7 | | | 8.87 | 6.55 | 5.91 | 4.841 |
| 8 | | | 3.33 | 6.55 | 5.90 | 4.478 |
| 9 | | | | 6.56 | 5.91 | 4.463 |
| 10 | | | | 6.55 | 5.90 | 4.463 |
| 11 | | | | 2.46 | 5.91 | 4.463 |
| 12 | | | | | 5.90 | 4.463 |
| 13 | | | | | 5.91 | 4.463 |
| 14 | | | | | 5.90 | 4.463 |
| 15 | | | | | 5.91 | 4.462 |
| 16 | | | | | 2.21 | 4.463 |
| 17 | | | | | | 4.462 |
| 18 | | | | | | 4.463 |
| 19 | | | | | | 4.462 |
| 20 | | | | | | 4.463 |
| 21 | | | | | | 1.673 |

Table A10-5

## MACRS Depreciation for Property Other Than Real Estate

Applicable convention: mid-quarter; property placed in service in third quarter
*(applicable methods: 200% or 150% declining balance, switching to straight-line)*

| If the recovery year is | And the recovery period is | | | | | |
|---|---|---|---|---|---|---|
| | 3 Years | 5 Years | 7 Years | 10 Years | 15 Years | 20 Years |
| | The depreciation rate is | | | | | |
| 1 | 25.00 | 15.00 | 10.71 | 7.50 | 3.75 | 2.813 |
| 2 | 50.00 | 34.00 | 25.51 | 18.50 | 9.63 | 7.289 |
| 3 | 16.67 | 20.40 | 18.22 | 14.80 | 8.66 | 6.742 |
| 4 | 8.33 | 12.24 | 13.02 | 11.84 | 7.80 | 6.237 |
| 5 | | 11.30 | 9.30 | 9.47 | 7.02 | 5.769 |
| 6 | | 7.06 | 8.85 | 7.58 | 6.31 | 5.336 |
| 7 | | | 8.86 | 6.55 | 5.90 | 4.936 |
| 8 | | | 5.53 | 6.55 | 5.90 | 4.566 |
| 9 | | | | 6.56 | 5.91 | 4.460 |
| 10 | | | | 6.55 | 5.90 | 4.460 |
| 11 | | | | 4.10 | 5.91 | 4.460 |
| 12 | | | | | 5.90 | 4.460 |
| 13 | | | | | 5.91 | 4.461 |
| 14 | | | | | 5.90 | 4.460 |
| 15 | | | | | 5.91 | 4.461 |
| 16 | | | | | 3.69 | 4.460 |
| 17 | | | | | | 4.461 |
| 18 | | | | | | 4.460 |
| 19 | | | | | | 4.461 |
| 20 | | | | | | 4.460 |
| 21 | | | | | | 2.788 |

Table A10-6

## MACRS Depreciation for Property Other Than Real Estate

Applicable convention: mid-quarter; property placed in service in fourth quarter
*(applicable methods: 200% or 150% declining balance, switching to straight-line)*

| If the recovery year is | And the recovery period is | | | | | |
|---|---|---|---|---|---|---|
| | 3 Years | 5 Years | 7 Years | 10 Years | 15 Years | 20 Years |
| | The depreciation rate is | | | | | |
| 1 | 8.33 | 5.00 | 3.57 | 2.50 | 1.25 | 0.938 |
| 2 | 61.11 | 38.00 | 27.55 | 19.50 | 9.88 | 7.430 |
| 3 | 20.37 | 22.80 | 19.68 | 15.60 | 8.89 | 6.872 |
| 4 | 10.19 | 13.68 | 14.06 | 12.48 | 8.00 | 6.357 |
| 5 | | 10.94 | 10.04 | 9.98 | 7.20 | 5.880 |
| 6 | | 9.58 | 8.73 | 7.99 | 6.48 | 5.439 |
| 7 | | | 8.73 | 6.55 | 5.90 | 5.031 |
| 8 | | | 7.64 | 6.55 | 5.90 | 4.654 |
| 9 | | | | 6.56 | 5.90 | 4.458 |
| 10 | | | | 6.55 | 5.91 | 4.458 |
| 11 | | | | 5.74 | 5.90 | 4.458 |
| 12 | | | | | 5.91 | 4.458 |
| 13 | | | | | 5.90 | 4.458 |
| 14 | | | | | 5.91 | 4.458 |
| 15 | | | | | 5.90 | 4.458 |
| 16 | | | | | 5.17 | 4.458 |
| 17 | | | | | | 4.458 |
| 18 | | | | | | 4.459 |
| 19 | | | | | | 4.458 |
| 20 | | | | | | 4.459 |
| 21 | | | | | | 3.901 |

Table A10-7

## MACRS Depreciation for Residential Rental Real Estate

Applicable convention: mid-month *(applicable recovery period: 27.5 years)*

| If the recovery year is | And the month in the first recovery year the property is placed in service is | | | | | | | | | | | |
|---|---|---|---|---|---|---|---|---|---|---|---|---|
| | 1 | 2 | 3 | 4 | 5 | 6 | 7 | 8 | 9 | 10 | 11 | 12 |
| | The depreciation rate is | | | | | | | | | | | |
| 1 | 3.485 | 3.182 | 2.879 | 2.576 | 2.273 | 1.970 | 1.667 | 1.364 | 1.061 | 0.758 | 0.455 | 0.152 |
| 2 | 3.636 | 3.636 | 3.636 | 3.636 | 3.636 | 3.636 | 3.636 | 3.636 | 3.636 | 3.636 | 3.636 | 3.636 |
| 3 | 3.636 | 3.636 | 3.636 | 3.636 | 3.636 | 3.636 | 3.636 | 3.636 | 3.636 | 3.636 | 3.636 | 3.636 |
| 4 | 3.636 | 3.636 | 3.636 | 3.636 | 3.636 | 3.636 | 3.636 | 3.636 | 3.636 | 3.636 | 3.636 | 3.636 |
| 5 | 3.636 | 3.636 | 3.636 | 3.636 | 3.636 | 3.636 | 3.636 | 3.636 | 3.636 | 3.636 | 3.636 | 3.636 |
| 6 | 3.636 | 3.636 | 3.636 | 3.636 | 3.636 | 3.636 | 3.636 | 3.636 | 3.636 | 3.636 | 3.636 | 3.636 |
| 7 | 3.636 | 3.636 | 3.636 | 3.636 | 3.636 | 3.636 | 3.636 | 3.636 | 3.636 | 3.636 | 3.636 | 3.636 |
| 8 | 3.636 | 3.636 | 3.636 | 3.636 | 3.636 | 3.636 | 3.636 | 3.636 | 3.636 | 3.636 | 3.636 | 3.636 |
| 9 | 3.636 | 3.636 | 3.636 | 3.636 | 3.636 | 3.636 | 3.636 | 3.636 | 3.636 | 3.636 | 3.636 | 3.636 |
| 10 | 3.637 | 3.637 | 3.637 | 3.637 | 3.637 | 3.637 | 3.636 | 3.636 | 3.636 | 3.636 | 3.636 | 3.636 |
| 11 | 3.636 | 3.636 | 3.636 | 3.636 | 3.636 | 3.636 | 3.637 | 3.637 | 3.637 | 3.637 | 3.637 | 3.637 |
| 12 | 3.637 | 3.637 | 3.637 | 3.637 | 3.637 | 3.637 | 3.636 | 3.636 | 3.636 | 3.636 | 3.636 | 3.636 |
| 13 | 3.636 | 3.636 | 3.636 | 3.636 | 3.636 | 3.636 | 3.637 | 3.637 | 3.637 | 3.637 | 3.637 | 3.637 |
| 14 | 3.637 | 3.637 | 3.637 | 3.637 | 3.637 | 3.637 | 3.636 | 3.636 | 3.636 | 3.636 | 3.636 | 3.636 |
| 15 | 3.636 | 3.636 | 3.636 | 3.636 | 3.636 | 3.636 | 3.637 | 3.637 | 3.637 | 3.637 | 3.637 | 3.637 |
| 16 | 3.637 | 3.637 | 3.637 | 3.637 | 3.637 | 3.637 | 3.636 | 3.636 | 3.636 | 3.636 | 3.636 | 3.636 |
| 17 | 3.636 | 3.636 | 3.636 | 3.636 | 3.636 | 3.636 | 3.637 | 3.637 | 3.637 | 3.637 | 3.637 | 3.637 |
| 18 | 3.637 | 3.637 | 3.637 | 3.637 | 3.637 | 3.637 | 3.636 | 3.636 | 3.636 | 3.636 | 3.636 | 3.636 |
| 19 | 3.636 | 3.636 | 3.636 | 3.636 | 3.636 | 3.636 | 3.637 | 3.637 | 3.637 | 3.637 | 3.637 | 3.637 |
| 20 | 3.637 | 3.637 | 3.637 | 3.637 | 3.637 | 3.637 | 3.636 | 3.636 | 3.636 | 3.636 | 3.636 | 3.636 |
| 21 | 3.636 | 3.636 | 3.636 | 3.636 | 3.636 | 3.636 | 3.637 | 3.637 | 3.637 | 3.637 | 3.637 | 3.637 |
| 22 | 3.637 | 3.637 | 3.637 | 3.637 | 3.637 | 3.637 | 3.636 | 3.636 | 3.636 | 3.636 | 3.636 | 3.636 |
| 23 | 3.636 | 3.636 | 3.636 | 3.636 | 3.636 | 3.636 | 3.637 | 3.637 | 3.637 | 3.637 | 3.637 | 3.637 |
| 24 | 3.637 | 3.637 | 3.637 | 3.637 | 3.637 | 3.637 | 3.636 | 3.636 | 3.636 | 3.636 | 3.636 | 3.636 |
| 25 | 3.636 | 3.636 | 3.636 | 3.636 | 3.636 | 3.636 | 3.637 | 3.637 | 3.637 | 3.637 | 3.637 | 3.637 |
| 26 | 3.637 | 3.637 | 3.637 | 3.637 | 3.637 | 3.637 | 3.636 | 3.636 | 3.636 | 3.636 | 3.636 | 3.636 |
| 27 | 3.636 | 3.636 | 3.636 | 3.636 | 3.636 | 3.636 | 3.637 | 3.637 | 3.637 | 3.637 | 3.637 | 3.637 |
| 28 | 1.970 | 2.273 | 2.576 | 2.879 | 3.182 | 3.485 | 3.636 | 3.636 | 3.636 | 3.636 | 3.636 | 3.636 |
| 29 | 0.000 | 0.000 | 0.000 | 0.000 | 0.000 | 0.000 | 0.152 | 0.455 | 0.758 | 1.061 | 1.364 | 1.667 |

*Table A10-8*

## MACRS Depreciation for Nonresidential Real Estate Placed in Service before May 13, 1993

Applicable convention: mid-month *(applicable recovery period: 31.5 years)*

| If the recovery year is | And the month in the first recovery year the property is placed in service is | | | | | | | | | | | |
|---|---|---|---|---|---|---|---|---|---|---|---|---|
| | 1 | 2 | 3 | 4 | 5 | 6 | 7 | 8 | 9 | 10 | 11 | 12 |
| | The depreciation rate is | | | | | | | | | | | |
| 1 | 3.042 | 2.778 | 2.513 | 2.249 | 1.984 | 1.720 | 1.455 | 1.190 | 0.926 | 0.661 | 0.397 | 0.132 |
| 2 | 3.175 | 3.175 | 3.175 | 3.175 | 3.175 | 3.175 | 3.175 | 3.175 | 3.175 | 3.175 | 3.175 | 3.175 |
| 3 | 3.175 | 3.175 | 3.175 | 3.175 | 3.175 | 3.175 | 3.175 | 3.175 | 3.175 | 3.175 | 3.175 | 3.175 |
| 4 | 3.175 | 3.175 | 3.175 | 3.175 | 3.175 | 3.175 | 3.175 | 3.175 | 3.175 | 3.175 | 3.175 | 3.175 |
| 5 | 3.175 | 3.175 | 3.175 | 3.175 | 3.175 | 3.175 | 3.175 | 3.175 | 3.175 | 3.175 | 3.175 | 3.175 |
| 6 | 3.175 | 3.175 | 3.175 | 3.175 | 3.175 | 3.175 | 3.175 | 3.175 | 3.175 | 3.175 | 3.175 | 3.175 |
| 7 | 3.175 | 3.175 | 3.175 | 3.175 | 3.175 | 3.175 | 3.175 | 3.175 | 3.175 | 3.175 | 3.175 | 3.175 |
| 8 | 3.175 | 3.174 | 3.175 | 3.174 | 3.175 | 3.174 | 3.175 | 3.175 | 3.175 | 3.175 | 3.175 | 3.175 |
| 9 | 3.174 | 3.175 | 3.174 | 3.175 | 3.174 | 3.175 | 3.174 | 3.175 | 3.174 | 3.175 | 3.174 | 3.175 |
| 10 | 3.175 | 3.174 | 3.175 | 3.174 | 3.175 | 3.174 | 3.175 | 3.174 | 3.175 | 3.174 | 3.175 | 3.174 |
| 11 | 3.174 | 3.175 | 3.174 | 3.175 | 3.174 | 3.175 | 3.174 | 3.175 | 3.174 | 3.175 | 3.174 | 3.175 |
| 12 | 3.175 | 3.174 | 3.175 | 3.174 | 3.175 | 3.174 | 3.175 | 3.174 | 3.175 | 3.174 | 3.175 | 3.174 |
| 13 | 3.174 | 3.175 | 3.174 | 3.175 | 3.174 | 3.175 | 3.174 | 3.175 | 3.174 | 3.175 | 3.174 | 3.175 |
| 14 | 3.175 | 3.174 | 3.175 | 3.174 | 3.175 | 3.174 | 3.175 | 3.174 | 3.175 | 3.174 | 3.175 | 3.174 |
| 15 | 3.174 | 3.175 | 3.174 | 3.175 | 3.174 | 3.175 | 3.174 | 3.175 | 3.174 | 3.175 | 3.174 | 3.175 |
| 16 | 3.175 | 3.174 | 3.175 | 3.174 | 3.175 | 3.174 | 3.175 | 3.174 | 3.175 | 3.174 | 3.175 | 3.174 |
| 17 | 3.174 | 3.175 | 3.174 | 3.175 | 3.174 | 3.175 | 3.174 | 3.175 | 3.174 | 3.175 | 3.174 | 3.175 |
| 18 | 3.175 | 3.174 | 3.175 | 3.174 | 3.175 | 3.174 | 3.175 | 3.174 | 3.175 | 3.174 | 3.175 | 3.174 |
| 19 | 3.174 | 3.175 | 3.174 | 3.175 | 3.174 | 3.175 | 3.174 | 3.175 | 3.174 | 3.175 | 3.174 | 3.175 |
| 20 | 3.175 | 3.174 | 3.175 | 3.174 | 3.175 | 3.174 | 3.175 | 3.174 | 3.175 | 3.174 | 3.175 | 3.174 |
| 21 | 3.174 | 3.175 | 3.174 | 3.175 | 3.174 | 3.175 | 3.174 | 3.175 | 3.174 | 3.175 | 3.174 | 3.175 |
| 22 | 3.175 | 3.174 | 3.175 | 3.174 | 3.175 | 3.174 | 3.175 | 3.174 | 3.175 | 3.174 | 3.175 | 3.174 |
| 23 | 3.174 | 3.175 | 3.174 | 3.175 | 3.174 | 3.175 | 3.174 | 3.175 | 3.174 | 3.175 | 3.174 | 3.175 |
| 24 | 3.175 | 3.174 | 3.175 | 3.174 | 3.175 | 3.174 | 3.175 | 3.174 | 3.175 | 3.174 | 3.175 | 3.174 |
| 25 | 3.174 | 3.175 | 3.174 | 3.175 | 3.174 | 3.175 | 3.174 | 3.175 | 3.174 | 3.175 | 3.174 | 3.175 |
| 26 | 3.175 | 3.174 | 3.175 | 3.174 | 3.175 | 3.174 | 3.175 | 3.174 | 3.175 | 3.174 | 3.175 | 3.174 |
| 27 | 3.174 | 3.175 | 3.174 | 3.175 | 3.174 | 3.175 | 3.174 | 3.175 | 3.174 | 3.175 | 3.174 | 3.175 |
| 28 | 3.175 | 3.174 | 3.175 | 3.174 | 3.175 | 3.174 | 3.175 | 3.174 | 3.175 | 3.174 | 3.175 | 3.174 |
| 29 | 3.174 | 3.175 | 3.174 | 3.175 | 3.174 | 3.175 | 3.174 | 3.175 | 3.174 | 3.175 | 3.174 | 3.175 |
| 30 | 3.175 | 3.174 | 3.175 | 3.174 | 3.175 | 3.174 | 3.175 | 3.174 | 3.175 | 3.174 | 3.175 | 3.174 |
| 31 | 3.174 | 3.175 | 3.174 | 3.175 | 3.174 | 3.175 | 3.174 | 3.175 | 3.174 | 3.175 | 3.174 | 3.175 |
| 32 | 1.720 | 1.984 | 2.249 | 2.513 | 2.778 | 3.042 | 3.175 | 3.174 | 3.175 | 3.174 | 3.175 | 3.174 |
| 33 | 0.000 | 0.000 | 0.000 | 0.000 | 0.000 | 0.000 | 0.132 | 0.397 | 0.661 | 0.926 | 1.190 | 1.455 |

*Table A10-9*

## MACRS Depreciation for Nonresidential Real Estate Placed in Service after May 12, 1993

Applicable convention: mid-month *(applicable recovery period: 39 years)*

| If the recovery year is | And the month in the first recovery year the property is placed in service is | | | | | | | | | | | |
|---|---|---|---|---|---|---|---|---|---|---|---|---|
| | 1 | 2 | 3 | 4 | 5 | 6 | 7 | 8 | 9 | 10 | 11 | 12 |
| | The depreciation rate is | | | | | | | | | | | |
| 1 | 2.461 | 2.247 | 2.033 | 1.819 | 1.605 | 1.391 | 1.177 | 0.963 | 0.749 | 0.535 | 0.321 | 0.107 |
| 2–39 | 2.564 | 2.564 | 2.564 | 2.564 | 2.564 | 2.564 | 2.564 | 2.564 | 2.564 | 2.564 | 2.564 | 2.564 |
| 40 | 0.107 | 0.321 | 0.535 | 0.749 | 0.963 | 1.177 | 1.391 | 1.605 | 1.819 | 2.033 | 2.247 | 2.461 |

Table A10-10

## MACRS Depreciation for a Car Placed in Service in 2020, 200% Declining Balance Method

| Recovery Year | Mid-Year Convention | Maximum Depreciation Limit (without Bonus Depreciation)* Passenger Automobiles, Trucks and Vans |
|---|---|---|
| 1 | 20.00% | $10,100* |
| 2 | 32.00% | $16,100 |
| 3 | 19.20% | $ 9,700 |
| 4 | 11.52% | $ 5,760 |
| 5 | 11.52% | $ 5,760 |
| 6+ | 5.76% | $ 5,760 |

*If additional first-year depreciation is claimed this amount is increased by $8,000 to $18,100.

Table A10-11

## Optional Straight-Line Macrs Depreciation for Property Other Than Real Estate

Applicable convention: mid-year

| If the recovery year is | And the recovery period is 3 Years | 5 Years | 7 Years | 10 Years | 15 Years | 20 Years |
|---|---|---|---|---|---|---|
| | The depreciation rate is | | | | | |
| 1 | 16.67 | 10.00 | 7.14 | 5.00 | 3.33 | 2.50 |
| 2 | 33.33 | 20.00 | 14.29 | 10.00 | 6.67 | 5.00 |
| 3 | 33.33 | 20.00 | 14.29 | 10.00 | 6.67 | 5.00 |
| 4 | 16.67 | 20.00 | 14.29 | 10.00 | 6.67 | 5.00 |
| 5 | | 20.00 | 14.29 | 10.00 | 6.67 | 5.00 |
| 6 | | 10.00 | 14.29 | 10.00 | 6.67 | 5.00 |
| 7 | | | 14.29 | 10.00 | 6.67 | 5.00 |
| 8 | | | 7.14 | 10.00 | 6.67 | 5.00 |
| 9 | | | | 10.00 | 6.67 | 5.00 |
| 10 | | | | 10.00 | 6.67 | 5.00 |
| 11 | | | | 5.00 | 6.67 | 5.00 |
| 12 | | | | | 6.67 | 5.00 |
| 13 | | | | | 6.67 | 5.00 |
| 14 | | | | | 6.67 | 5.00 |
| 15 | | | | | 6.67 | 5.00 |
| 16 | | | | | 3.33 | 5.00 |
| 17 | | | | | | 5.00 |
| 18 | | | | | | 5.00 |
| 19 | | | | | | 5.00 |
| 20 | | | | | | 5.00 |
| 21 | | | | | | 2.50 |

# Property Dispositions

11

Learning Objectives:

LO 1 Explain the calculation of realized gain or loss from the sale or other disposition of property.

LO 2 Differentiate between a realized gain or loss from a property disposition and the amount of gain or loss that is recognized in the tax year of the disposition.

LO 3 Discuss what constitutes the amount realized from a disposition of property.

LO 4 Explain capital assets and the year-end netting procedure used to determine the effect of capital asset transactions on taxable income.

LO 5 Explain how year-end tax-planning strategies can take advantage of the capital asset netting procedure.

LO 6 Describe Section 1231 assets and the year-end netting procedure used to determine the effect of Section 1231 transactions on taxable income.

LO 7 Explain the reclassification of gain on the sale of depreciable assets as ordinary income under the depreciation recapture provisions.

LO 8 Identify Section 1245 and Section 1250 assets and the depreciation recapture rule applicable to each type.

LO 9 Explain the treatment of unrecaptured Section 1250 gains.

LO 10 Identify a framework for analyzing the effect of a variety of different asset dispositions on taxable income for the year.

## concept review

### GENERAL CONCEPTS

**Arm's-length transaction** A transaction in which all parties to the transaction have bargained in good faith and for their individual benefit, not for the benefit of the transaction group. pg. 2-4

### ACCOUNTING CONCEPTS

**Annual accounting period** All entities must report the results of their operations on an annual basis (the tax year). Each tax year stands on its own, apart from other tax years. pg. 2-9

### INCOME CONCEPTS

**All-inclusive income** All income received is taxable unless a specific provision in the tax law either excludes the income from taxation or defers its recognition to a future tax year. pg. 2-12

**Capital recovery** No income is realized until the taxpayer receives more than the amount invested to produce the income. The amount invested in an asset represents the maximum amount recoverable. pg. 2-13

**Legislative grace** Any tax relief provided is the result of a specific act of Congress that must be strictly applied and interpreted. All income received is taxable unless a specific provision in the tax law excludes the income from taxation. Deductions must be approached with the philosophy that nothing is deductible unless a provision in the tax law allows the deduction. pg. 2-12

**Realization** No income or loss is recognized until it has been realized. A realization involves a change in the form and/or the substance of a taxpayer's property rights that results from an arm's-length transaction. pg. 2-14

**Wherewithal to pay** Income is recognized in the period in which the taxpayer has the means to pay the tax on the income. pg. 2-16

### DEDUCTION CONCEPTS

**Basis** The amount of unrecovered investment in an asset. As amounts are expended and/or recovered relative to an asset over time, the basis is adjusted in consideration of such changes. The **adjusted basis** of an asset is the original basis, plus or minus the changes in the amount of unrecovered investment. pgs. 2-13, 2-21

**Business purpose** To be deductible, an expenditure or a loss must have a business or other economic purpose that exceeds any tax avoidance motive. The primary motive for the transaction must be to make a profit. pg. 2-18

## 11-1 INTRODUCTION

LO 1
Explain the calculation of realized gain or loss from the sale or other disposition of property.

A taxpayer realizes gain or loss on property when the form or substance of the property or its underlying property rights changes as a result of an arm's-length transaction. Realization of gain or loss typically occurs upon disposition of property in a transaction with another entity. The most common way to dispose of an asset is by sale. However, property is also disposed of through exchanges, casualties, and abandonments or retirements.

Figure 11-1 presents an overview of the steps involved in analyzing a disposition of property. The first step is to calculate the amount realized from the disposition. Under the capital recovery concept, taxpayers do not recognize gain until they have recovered all capital invested in the property. The amount of unrecovered investment in the property is measured by the property's basis. As Chapter 9 explained, many properties are subject to adjustments to account for additional investment and deductions for cost recoveries throughout their lives. These adjustments give the property an adjusted basis at the date of disposition.

The second step is to calculate the gain or loss realized on the disposition. This is the difference between the amount realized from the disposition of the property and its adjusted basis.

A gain on the disposition of a property represents an amount realized in excess of the unrecovered investment in the property. A gain is taxable under the all-inclusive income concept. On the other hand, a loss on a disposition represents a loss of capital invested in the property. As Figure 11-1 shows, some realized gains and losses are not recognized for tax purposes. Realized gains from certain types of transactions (e.g., like-kind exchanges, casualties and thefts) have been granted tax relief. Because these sale-and-replacement transactions require the reinvestment of the amount realized from the disposition, the taxpayer lacks the necessary wherewithal to pay. As a result, gains from these transactions are deferred for recognition in a future accounting period. Because these deferrals are a matter of

*Figure 11-1*

**Property Disposition Procedure**

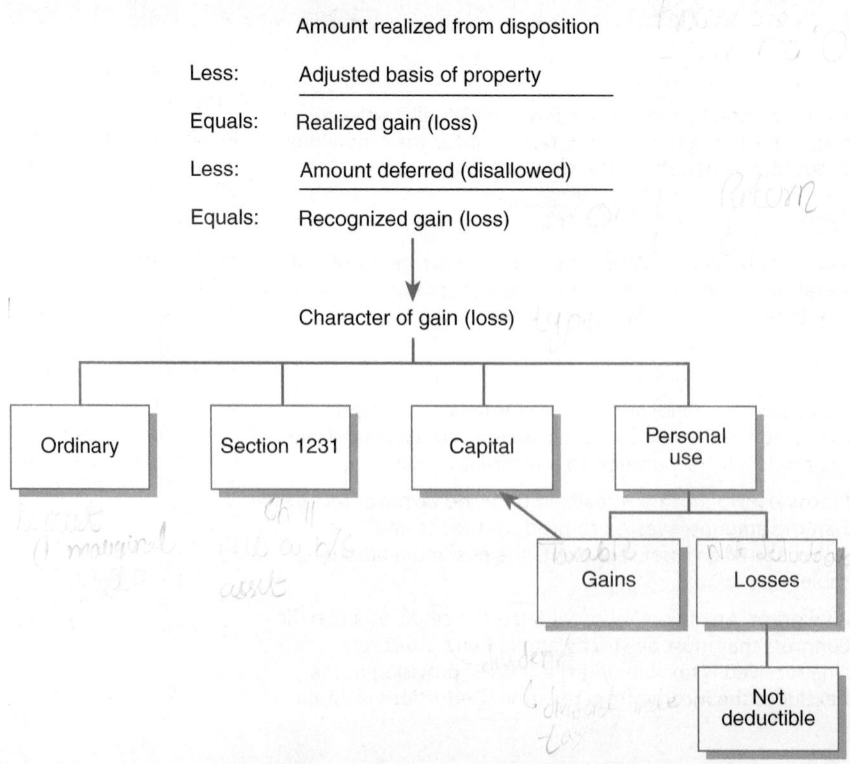

legislative grace, few transactions qualify for this special relief. The most common nontaxable transactions and their unique characteristics are discussed in Chapter 12. Deductions for losses on dispositions are also subject to the legislative grace concept. Therefore, certain types of realized losses are deferred (e.g., like-kind exchanges, wash sales), whereas others are specifically disallowed (e.g., losses on sales of personal use property). Thus, the third step in the analysis of the disposition of property is to determine the amount of gain or loss that is to be recognized in the current tax year. A **recognized gain** or a **recognized loss** is one that is included in the calculation of the current year's taxable income.

LO 2

Differentiate between a realized gain or loss from a property disposition and the amount of gain or loss that is recognized in the tax year of the disposition.

**Example 1** Ramona sells 600 shares of Barcelona stock to her father, Hermano, for $9,000. The stock had cost Ramona $15,000. One year later, Hermano sells the 600 shares for $12,000. What are Ramona's and Hermano's realized and recognized gains or losses on the sales of the Barcelona stock?

**Discussion: Ramona has realized a loss of $6,000 ($9,000 − $15,000) on the sale of the stock. However, the loss is disallowed because the sale is to a related party. Thus, Ramona has a nondeductible loss from the sale of the stock.**

**Her father realizes a gain of $3,000 ($12,000 − $9,000) on his sale of the stock. However, under the related party rules, Hermano can use Ramona's disallowed loss to reduce his gain to zero. (As discussed in Chapter 7, the disallowed loss cannot be used to create a loss on the second sale.) Hermano has realized a gain on the sale of the stock, but it is not recognized because of the related party rules.**

**Example 2** Michael exchanges a building he uses in his dental practice with a fair market value (FMV) of $65,000 and a basis of $45,000 for a new building. He pays $25,000 in cash for the new building, which has a FMV of $90,000. Has Michael realized a gain from the exchange of the buildings?

**Discussion: The exchange of the buildings is a disposition of the old building. Michael has realized a gain of $20,000 ($65,000 − $45,000) on the exchange. The substance of the transaction is a sale of his old building for $65,000 and the purchase of the new building for $90,000.**

**In this case Michael would not recognize any gain on the exchange in the current period. This is an exchange of business property for like-kind business property that can be deferred under the wherewithal-to-pay-concept. Although Michael has realized a gain on the transaction, the net effect is that he pays out $25,000 in cash to effect the exchange. Michael has no assets remaining after the exchange with which to pay the tax on the realized gain. The definition of like-kind property and other rules regarding exchanges are discussed in Chapter 12.**

After calculating the amount of gain or loss to be recognized, you must determine the character of the gain or loss. The tax law provides different treatments for gains and losses from different categories of property. As Figure 11-1 shows, all recognized gains and losses are categorized as one of the following:

1. Ordinary gains and losses
2. Capital gains and losses
3. Section 1231 gains and losses
4. Personal use gains and losses

Different procedures and rules apply to each category of gains and losses in determining their effect on current taxable income. Exhibit 11-1 contains a representative list of assets in each of the four categories.

This chapter presents and discusses the basic treatments of dispositions of property. The first topic is how the amount of realized gain or loss is determined, followed by ways to characterize recognized gains and losses as ordinary, capital, or Section 1231. The final, and perhaps the most complex, topic is reclassifying gains from the sale of depreciable property as ordinary income under the depreciation recapture rules. The detailed discussion of determining gains and losses deferred under the wherewithal-to-pay concept appears in Chapter 12.

*Exhibit 11-1*

## Classification of Assets

| **Ordinary Income Assets** | **Capital Assets** |
|---|---|
| Inventories, receivables | Stocks, bonds, options |
| Gains from depreciation | Rental property (if not considered a trade or business) |
| Losses on small business stock | Investments in conduit entities |
| Depreciable property held ≤12 months | Investments in passive activities |
| Sales of copyrights, artistic compositions, etc., by the person creating the property | Personal use property sold at a gain (but not at a loss) |
| **Section 1231 Assets** | **Personal Use Assets** |
| Property used in a trade or business and held for more than 12 months | Residence, automobile, clothing, furniture, etc. |
| Land, buildings, equipment, machinery, automobiles, computers, furniture, etc. | Any asset used for personal purposes (e.g., a computer used at home solely for personal purposes) |
| Unharvested crops, timber, coal, domestic iron ore | |
| Livestock used for draft, breeding, dairy, or sporting purposes | |

## 11-2 REALIZED GAIN OR LOSS

LO 3

Discuss what constitutes the amount realized from a disposition of property.

Whenever a property disposition occurs, the taxpayer must calculate the realized gain or loss. Realized gain or loss is equal to the difference between the amount realized and the adjusted basis of the property.[1] The rules for determining a property's basis and the common adjustments to basis were discussed in Chapters 9 and 10. Thus, the primary focus of this section is on determining the amount realized from a disposition of property.

### 11-2a Amount Realized

The **amount realized** from a disposition must be calculated to determine whether the taxpayer has realized a gain or a loss. The amount realized is the gross sales price less all expenses incurred to complete the sale (selling expenses). The **gross sales price** is the price agreed upon by the seller and the buyer. In an arm's-length transaction, the gross sales price is equal to the fair market value of the property. Selling expenses include commissions, legal fees, title costs, advertising, and any other costs incurred to complete the disposition transaction. When the property sold has an objectively determined market value, this is a straightforward computation.

**Example 3** Alvah sells 200 shares of Brett Company stock for $25 per share. He pays $300 in commissions to his stockbroker for making the sale. Alvah had purchased the stock for $18 per share plus a $200 commission. What is his realized gain on the sale of the stock?

**Discussion: The realized gain on the sale is $900, determined as follows:**

| | |
|---|---|
| Amount realized from sale ($5,000 − $300) | $ 4,700 |
| Adjusted basis of shares sold ($3,600 + $200) | (3,800) |
| Realized gain on sale | $ 900 |

**Note the effect of the commissions Alvah paid on the gain from the sale. Commissions paid to buy or sell property are never deducted as current expenses. When Alvah bought the stock, the $200 in commissions became part of the stock's basis (i.e., he had to pay the commissions to acquire the stock). When Alvah sold the stock, the commissions reduced the amount realized from the sale (i.e., they are a selling expense). On both sides of the transaction, the effect of the commissions is to reduce the amount of gain that Alvah realizes from the stock investment.**

The gross sales price of a property that does not have an objectively determined market value is any value received from the buyer less any value given back to the buyer. More formally, the gross selling price includes the following:

Amounts received by the seller from the buyer

- Cash
- Fair market value of property received

- Fair market value of services received
- Amount of the seller's expenses paid by the buyer
- Amount of the seller's debt assumed by the buyer

LESS:

Amounts given by the seller to the buyer

- Amount of the buyer's expenses paid by the seller
- Amount of the buyer's debt assumed by the seller

As you can see, the gross selling price is not always obvious. The terms of the sales agreement must be carefully analyzed to determine how much the buyer actually paid the seller for the property. In analyzing more complex situations, keep in mind that what you are determining is what the buyer actually paid the seller for the property.

**Example 4** Arnold has a tractor that Jack wants to buy. Jack has $300 in cash. Arnold agrees to sell Jack the tractor for the $300 in cash if Jack agrees to mow Arnold's field for 1 year. Arnold usually pays a neighbor $1,000 per year to mow the field. What is the gross selling price of the tractor?

**Discussion: The gross selling price is equal to the $300 in cash plus the $1,000 value of the mowing services Jack agreed to provide as part of the sale. Thus, Arnold sold the tractor to Jack for $1,300.**

**Example 5** On April 1, Blake Corporation sells Zeke some land that it had bought for $8,000. Under the terms of the sale, Zeke is to pay Blake $13,000 in cash. In addition, Zeke has to pay property taxes of $1,000 on the land for the entire year. Blake incurs commissions and legal fees of $1,600 related to the sale. What are the gross selling price, the amount realized, and Blake Corporation's gain or loss on the sale of the land to Zeke?

**Discussion: From Chapter 3, the payment of another's expenses in a business setting constitutes income to the person whose expenses are being paid. Therefore, the payment of Blake Corporation's share of the property taxes by Zeke is part of the sales price of the property. The gross selling price is equal to the $13,000 cash payment plus the $250 payment of Blake's property tax obligation ($1,000 × 3/12 for January, February, and March). Blake's amount realized is $11,650 ($13,250 − $1,600), resulting in a gain of $3,650 ($11,650 − $8,000) on the sale of the land.**

| | |
|---|---|
| Cash paid | $13,000 |
| Blake's property taxes paid ($1,000 × 3/12) | 250 |
| Gross selling price | $13,250 |
| Commissions and legal fees paid | (1,600) |
| Amount realized | $11,650 |
| Adjusted basis of land sold | (8,000) |
| Gain realized | $ 3,650 |

## 11-2b Effect of Debt Assumptions

A buyer's assumption of the seller's debt increases the gross sales price.[2] Conversely, any debt of the buyer assumed by the seller in the transaction reduces the gross sales price. To understand why the assumption of debt by the buyer constitutes a realization of income for the seller, consider the following examples:

**Example 6** Lydia Partnership owns land with a fair market value of $70,000 on which it owes a debt of $40,000. The partnership sells the land to Kerry for $70,000 in cash (with no debt assumption as part of the sales agreement). What is the gross selling price of the land? How much cash does the partnership have after the sale of the land?

**Discussion: The gross selling price is the $70,000 in cash that Kerry paid to Lydia Partnership. After receiving the $70,000, the partnership will have to pay off the $40,000 debt on the land, and it will have only $30,000 in cash remaining.**

**Example 7** Assume in example 6 that Kerry agrees to assume Lydia's debt on the land as part of the sales agreement. How much cash will Kerry pay to the partnership to purchase the land?

**Discussion: Because the agreed-upon fair market value of the land is $70,000, Kerry will pay Lydia Partnership only $30,000 in cash if she assumes the $40,000 debt on the land. From Lydia's point of view, the transaction is equivalent to the transaction in example 6. In either case, the partnership receives $30,000 in cash from the sale after subtracting the debt on the property.**

As these examples demonstrate, assuming another's debt is the same as paying cash to the debtor, who then uses it to pay off the debt. Therefore, any debt of the seller that is assumed by the buyer is always included in the amount realized by the seller.

In exchanges of property, parties often trade the debts they have on their properties. Trading debt along with the property often eliminates the need for the parties to obtain additional financing for the transaction.

**Example 8** Doris and Cory both own land that they would like to trade. The fair market values and the debts of each are as follows:

| | Doris | Cory |
|---|---|---|
| Fair market value | $15,000 | $ 25,000 |
| Mortgage debt on land | (5,000) | (20,000) |
| Equity in land | $10,000 | $ 5,000 |

Doris and Cory agree to exchange their land and assume each other's debt, with any difference paid in cash. Who will have to pay cash, and how much will that person have to pay?

**Discussion: Cory will have to pay Doris $5,000. Although Cory's land is worth $10,000 more than Doris's land, Doris's land has a net of mortgage cash value of $10,000 ($15,000 – $5,000). Therefore, in a sale of her land with an assumption of her mortgage, she would expect to receive $10,000 in cash. On the other hand, Cory's net of mortgage cash value is only $5,000 ($25,000 – $20,000). Therefore, if Cory sold the land with the assumption of his mortgage, he would expect to receive $5,000. Because they are exchanging their land and their mortgages, they are really exchanging net mortgage value. Thus, Cory must pay Doris $5,000 to effect the exchange.**

**Example 9** What are the gross selling prices of Doris's and Cory's properties from the exchange in example 8?

**Discussion: The gross selling prices realized by Doris and Cory will be the fair market values of their properties.**

| | |
|---|---|
| Doris realizes a gross selling price equal to $15,000: | |
| Cash received from Cory | $ 5,000 |
| Fair market value of land received | 25,000 |
| Mortgage assumed by Cory | 5,000 |
| Less: Assumption of Cory's mortgage | (20,000) |
| Gross selling price | $ 15,000 |
| Cory realizes a gross selling price equal to $25,000: | |
| Fair market value of land received | $ 15,000 |
| Mortgage assumed by Doris | 20,000 |
| Less: Assumption of Doris's mortgage | (5,000) |
| Less: Cash paid to Doris | (5,000) |
| Gross selling price | $ 25,000 |

## 11-3 CHARACTER OF GAIN OR LOSS

After determining the amount of realized gain or loss to be recognized in the current period, you must classify the recognized gain or loss according to the character of the asset creating the gain or loss. Characterizing gains and losses from property dispositions follows the general classification scheme outlined for deductions and losses in Chapters 5 through 7. In general, gains and losses on the sale of property used in a trade or business are considered ordinary gains and losses. However, gains on the sale of certain types of business assets, referred to as *Section 1231 property*, can be treated as capital gains under certain circumstances. This treatment is different from gains and losses from production-of-income activities, which are always considered capital gains and losses. Gains from the sale of personal use assets are capital gains, whereas losses on dispositions of personal use assets (other than casualty losses in a declared federal disaster area) are specifically disallowed. Each asset type and the treatment of its gains and losses are discussed in turn.

**concept check**

The *realization concept* states that no income or loss is recognized until it is realized. A realization occurs when there is a change in the form and/or the substance of a taxpayer's property or property rights in an *arm's-length transaction*. The *capital recovery concept* allows the recovery of capital invested in an asset when there is a realization. The *adjusted basis* represents the amount of capital invested in an asset (original basis adjusted for additional capital investments and deductions taken on the asset). A gain results when the amount realized is greater than the capital invested in a property. A loss results when the capital invested in an asset is not fully recovered upon its disposition. Recognized gains or losses must be categorized according to the character of the asset producing the gain or loss. Assets are categorized as being ordinary, capital, Section 1231, or personal. This categorization determines the ultimate tax treatment of the recognized gain or loss.

## 11-4 CAPITAL GAINS AND LOSSES

LO 4 Explain capital assets and the year-end netting procedure used to determine the effect of capital asset transactions on taxable income.

Capital gains and losses result from the disposition of capital assets. Historically, net capital gains have received preferential treatment over other types of income, whereas deductions for capital losses have been limited. The preferences and limitations applicable to capital gains have varied throughout the years, depending on the economic and political climate. For example, before 1988, 60 percent of an individual's net long-term capital gains was allowed as a deduction for adjusted gross income. Thus, only 40 percent of a net long-term capital gain was subject to tax. During this period, the top marginal tax rate was 50 percent. This meant that the actual maximum marginal tax rate on a long-term capital gain was only 20 percent (40 percent × 50 percent). For a taxpayer in the 50-percent marginal tax rate bracket, classifying a gain as a capital gain produced significant tax savings. From 1988 through May 6, 1988, long-term capital gains of individuals were taxed at a maximum rate of 28 percent. Under this law, taxpayers did not receive any tax benefit from capital gains until their marginal tax rate exceeded 28 percent. From 1999 through May 5, 2004, the rate on long-term capital gains was 20 percent (10 percent for 15-percent marginal tax rate taxpayers). The Jobs and Growth Tax Relief Reconciliation Act of 2003 lowered the rate on long-term capital gains to 15 percent (zero percent for taxpayers in the 10-percent or 15-percent marginal tax rate bracket). The American Taxpayer Relief Act of 2012 reinstated the 20 percent rate for taxpayers in the 39.6 percent marginal tax rate bracket.

The 2017 Tax Cut and Jobs Act retains the maximum rates on net capital gains and qualified dividends; however, it sets the point at which the rates (15 percent and 20 percent) change based on the 2018 tax rate schedule and indexes them for inflation using C-CPI-U for tax years after December 31, 2017. For 2021, the 15 percent breakpoint is $80,800 for joint returns and surviving spouses (half this amount for married taxpayers filing separately), $54,100 for heads of household, $2,700 for trusts and estates, and $40,400 for single taxpayers. The 20 percent breakpoint is $501,600 for joint returns and surviving spouses (half this amount for married taxpayers filing separately), $473,750 for heads of household, $13,250 for trusts and estates, and $445,850 for single taxpayers.

The 2017 Tax Cuts and Jobs Act (TCJA) amended the types of assets that are excluded from being capital assets to include patents, inventions, models or designs (whether or not patented), and secret formulas or processes that are held either by the taxpayer who created the property or by a taxpayer with a substituted or transferred basis from the taxpayer who created the property.

The basic economic rationale for extending favorable treatment to long-term gains on capital assets is that such gains result from holding the property for a long time. During this holding period, inflation acts to reduce the purchasing power of the gains realized. The reduction of the gain subject to tax is often justified as necessary to offset the inflationary effects, which have less impact on assets held for a short time. Although this is true for assets held for lengthy periods, it is not necessarily true for the more than 12 months holding period that qualifies a disposition for long-term capital gain treatment. A better justification for a differential rate of tax for long-term capital gains is that it gives investors incentives to provide capital to companies on a more permanent basis, thereby expanding the amount of capital available to companies and lowering the cost of capital.

## 11-4a Capital Asset Definition

A **capital asset** is defined as any asset that is not

1. An inventory item
2. A receivable
3. Real or depreciable property used in a trade or business
4. A copyright, literary, musical, or artistic composition, letter or memorandum, or similar property held by the person creating the property or held by a person who received the property as a gift from its creator
5. Patents, inventions, models or designs (whether or not patented), and secret formulas or processes that are held either by the taxpayer who created the property or by a taxpayer with a substituted or transferred basis from the taxpayer who created the property (or for whom the property was created)
6. Certain U.S. government publications[3]

A cursory examination of the list of properties that are not capital assets reveals that most trade or business assets are not capital assets. The first three categories excluded from capital asset status form the asset core of any business.

The fourth category consists of assets that are essentially inventories for their creators and are thus excluded from capital asset status. For example, an artist is in the trade or business of creating paintings. Artists who sell their paintings are like merchants who sell inventory. The exclusion of such property for anyone who receives it as a gift from its creator is intended to stop the conversion of ordinary income to capital gain income through gifts of the property. However, note that not all sales of paintings would constitute inventory sales. For example, a collector of art may purchase a painting for long-term appreciation. For the collector, the painting is a capital asset that creates a capital gain or loss upon disposition. The fifth category was created by the 2017 Tax Cuts and Jobs Act and in essence broadens the number of self-created assets that are excluded from capital gain treatment.

The last category of assets was added to the list of noncapital assets to stop former presidents of the United States from obtaining large charitable contribution deductions for giving their papers to nonprofit organizations after they left office. As such, it is not of concern to most taxpayers.

## 11-4b Long-Term versus Short-Term Classification

Preferential treatment for capital gains has always been limited to net long-term capital gains. All capital gains and losses must be classified as being held short-term or long-term. To be a long-term gain or loss, the property must be held for more than 12 months. Gains and losses from property held exactly 12 months or less are short-term gains and losses.[4]

The **holding period** of an asset is generally the length of time the taxpayer actually owns the property. However, situations arise that do not fit this rule and that are inequitable if the law were strictly applied.

**Example 10** Heidi receives 100 shares of stock from her Uncle Guiseppi as a graduation present. Guiseppi paid $600 for the shares 5 years earlier. On the date of the gift, the shares are worth $2,000. One month after receiving the shares, Heidi sells them for $2,100, net of commissions. What is her gain on the sale of the stock? Is the gain short-term or long-term?

**Discussion: Heidi's gain on the sale is $1,500 ($2,100 − $600). Because the fair market value of the shares on the date of the gift was greater than her uncle's basis, Heidi's basis is equal to her uncle's basis. Although Heidi has personally held the stock for only 1 month, the gain on the stock is the result of holding the shares for more than 5 years. Therefore, the gain on the sale of the stock is a long-term capital gain.**

Example 10 illustrates the basic rule for determining the holding period of a property: Whenever a taxpayer's basis is determined, either in whole or in part, by reference to another asset's basis, the holding period of the other asset is included in the taxpayer's holding period. Under this rule, the prior holding period of any property with a carryover basis (see Chapter 9) is added to the current holding period. However, if the taxpayer's basis is made by reference to a market value at the date of acquisition, the holding period begins at the date of acquisition. The primary exception to the market value rule is for inherited property, which is always considered long term.[5]

**Example 11** Rolf receives a gift of stock from his mother, Sheila, as a graduation present. Sheila paid $500 for the stock 5 years earlier. On the date of the gift, the stock is worth $400. Six months later, Rolf sells it for $350. What is Rolf's gain or loss on the sale of the stock? Is the gain or loss short-term or long-term?

**Discussion: Because the fair market value of the stock at the date of the gift was less than Sheila's basis, the split basis rule for gifts applies. Rolf's basis for computing losses is equal to the fair market value of the stock on the date of the gift. Rolf has a loss of $50 ($350 − $400) on the sale. The loss is a short-term capital loss because he held the stock for only 6 months. Rolf does not get his mother's holding period because his basis is the fair market value at the date of acquisition.**

**Example 12** Assume the same facts as in example 11, except that Rolf sells the stock 6 months later for $600. What is his gain or loss on the sale? Is the gain or loss short-term or long-term?

**Discussion: Under the split basis rule for gifts, Rolf's basis for determining gain is his mother's basis. He has a gain of $100 ($600 − $500) on the sale of the stock. Because Rolf's basis is Sheila's basis, he receives his mother's holding period. Thus, Rolf has a $100 long-term capital gain on the sale.**

## 11-4c Capital Gain-and-Loss Netting Procedure

Exhibit 11-2 presents the procedure for determining the net capital gain or loss for a tax year.[6] The first step in the process is to identify all gains and losses from the sale of capital assets during the year. The gains and losses are then separated into short-term and long-term gains and losses per the holding period of the property sold. In addition, gains and losses on the sale of collectibles, gains from the sale of qualified small business stock, and unrecaptured Section 1250 gains must be identified at this point. Sales of collectibles that are held for more than 12 months produce collectibles gains and collectibles losses.[7] Collectibles include works of art, rugs, antiques, metals, gems, stamps, coins, and alcoholic beverages. Gains on qualified small business stock and unrecaptured Section 1250 gains are defined and discussed later in this chapter. Distinguishing among the various types of gains and losses is important because each category is accorded different treatment in determining the income tax liability of a taxpayer.

The second step is to combine all the capital gains and losses for the year into a single position. That is, the taxpayer has either gained in total from capital asset dispositions during the year or has lost in total during the year. This is accomplished by first netting together all short-term gains and losses to produce a single net short-term gain or loss amount for the year. The long-term gains and losses are also netted together to produce a net long-term gain or loss amount for the year. Collectibles gains and losses, gains from the sale of qualified small business stock, and unrecaptured Section 1250 gains are treated as long-term gains and losses in the capital gain and loss netting procedure. If the result of these two nettings is the same—both are losses or both are gains—no further netting is required; a single position of gain or loss has been achieved. However, if the results of the first netting are opposite—one is a gain and one is a loss—a second netting is necessary to obtain a single position for the year, either a gain or a loss. In doing the capital gain-and-loss nettings, keep in mind that the ultimate goal of the netting is to reduce all capital gains and losses for the year to a single net position—the taxpayer has either gained or lost on the whole for the year, and that is the position that ultimately affects the taxpayer's taxable income.

*Exhibit 11-2*

## Capital Gain-and-Loss Netting Procedure

1. Identify capital gains and losses occurring during the year: short-term gains and losses, long-term gains and losses, collectibles gains and losses, gains on qualified small business stock, and unrecaptured Section 1250 gains.

   Classify as short-term or long-term based on holding period:
   - Short-term—held ≤ 12 months
   - Long-term—held > 12 months

2. Net short-term and long-term gains and losses to obtain a net short-term and a net long-term position for the year. Collectibles gains and losses, gains on qualified small business stock, and unrecaptured Section 1250 gains are treated as long-term gains and losses in the netting procedure.

| | | | |
|---|---|---|---|
| Short-term capital gain | $ XX | | |
| Short-term capital loss | (XX) | | |
| Net short-term gain (loss) | | → | Short-term capital gain or loss |
| Long-term capital gain | $ XX | | |
| Long-term capital loss | (XX) | | |
| Net long-term gain (loss) | | → | Long-term capital gain or loss |

3. If long-term and short-term positions are the same (both gains, both losses), no further netting is done.

   Short-term capital gain | Long-term capital gain — or — Short-term capital loss | Long-term capital loss

4. If long-term and short-term positions are opposite (1 gain, 1 loss), net again to produce either a gain or loss.

   Short-term capital gain ↘ Long-term capital loss — or — Short-term capital loss ↙ Long-term capital gain

   Long-term capital gain ‖ Short-term capital loss — or — Long-term capital loss ‖ Short-term capital gain

   or — or

   Long-term capital gain — Long-term capital loss

**Example 13** Johanna has the following capital gains and losses for the current tax year:

| | |
|---|---|
| Short-term capital gain | $ 4,000 |
| Collectibles gain | 7,000 |
| Long-term capital gain | 3,000 |
| Short-term capital loss | (6,000) |
| Collectibles loss | (6,000) |
| Long-term capital loss | (8,000) |

What is Johanna's net capital gain or loss position for the year?

**Discussion: The collectibles gain and the collectibles loss are included in the long-term capital gain and loss netting. Johanna has a net short-term capital loss of $2,000 and a net long-term capital loss of $4,000:**

| | | |
|---|---|---|
| Short-term capital gain | $ 4,000 | |
| Short-term capital loss | (6,000) | |
| Net short-term capital loss | | $(2,000) |
| Long-term capital gain | $ 3,000 | |
| Collectibles gain | 7,000 | |
| Collectibles loss | (6,000) | |
| Long-term capital loss | (8,000) | |
| Net long-term capital loss | | $(4,000) |

**Because the short- and long-term positions are both losses, no further netting is necessary. Johanna's capital asset transactions for the year have produced a loss.**

**Example 14** Assume the same facts as in example 13, except that Johanna's long-term capital gain for the year is $13,000 instead of $3,000. What is her net capital gain or loss position for the year?

**Discussion: Johanna has a net long-term capital gain of $4,000 for the year:**

| | | |
|---|---|---|
| Short-term capital gain | $ 4,000 | |
| Short-term capital loss | (6,000) | |
| Net short-term capital loss | | $(2,000) |
| Long-term capital gain | $13,000 | |
| Collectibles gain | 7,000 | |
| Collectibles loss | (6,000) | |
| Long-term capital loss | (8,000) | |
| Net long-term capital gain | | 6,000 |
| Net long-term capital gain | | $ 4,000 |

**Because the short-term position was a $2,000 loss and the long-term position was a $6,000 gain, the short-term and long-term positions are netted again to produce a single position for the year, which is a $4,000 long-term capital gain.**

The tax law prescribes the treatment of the gain or loss after the position for the year has been determined. Table 11-1 summarizes these treatments for individuals and corporations.

In calculating taxable income, net capital gains are added to gross income. A review of Table 11-1 reveals that net short-term capital gains of individuals and all corporate capital gains are treated as ordinary income. Only capital gains of individuals are accorded any tax relief. In addition, the provisions for collectibles gains and losses, gains on qualified small business stock, and unrecaptured Section 1250 gains do not apply to corporations.

*Table 11-1*

## Treatment of Capital Gains and Losses

| Capital Gain/Loss Position | Individual Treatment | Corporate Treatment |
|---|---|---|
| Short-term capital gain | Ordinary income. | Ordinary income. |
| Adjusted net capital gain | Taxed 0%, 15%, and 20% based on the breakpoints discussed above. | Ordinary income. |
| Unrecaptured Section 1250 gain | Taxed at a maximum rate of 25%. | Not applicable. |
| Net collectibles gain | Taxed at a maximum rate of 28%. | Not applicable. |
| Gain on qualified small business stock | 50% of gain is excluded. 75% for stock acquired after February 17, 2009, and before September 27, 2010. 100% for stock acquired after September 27, 2010. Remaining gain is taxed at a maximum rate of 28%. | Not applicable. |
| Short-term capital loss | Deductible loss for AGI; limited to $3,000 per year with indefinite carryforward of excess loss to future year's netting. | No current deduction; may carry back 3 years and forward 5 years to offset capital gains. |
| Long-term capital loss | Deductible loss for AGI; limited to $3,000 per year with indefinite carryforward of excess loss to future year's netting. Any short-term losses are applied against the $3,000 limit before long-term losses are deducted. | No current deduction; may carry back 3 years and forward 5 years as a short-term capital loss to offset capital gains. |

The tax relief provided for the various types of capital gains is applied in the calculation of the individual's income tax liability. *Adjusted net capital gains* are taxed at 15 percent. The rate is reduced to zero percent if the taxpayer is in the 10 percent or 15 percent marginal tax rate bracket and increased to 20 percent if the taxpayer is in the 37 percent marginal tax rate bracket. *Unrecaptured Section 1250 gains* are taxed at a maximum rate of 25 percent. **Net collectibles gains** are taxed at a maximum rate of 28 percent. One-half of the gain on *qualified small business stock* is excluded from income. The remaining gain is taxed at a maximum rate of 28 percent. The exclusion percentage is increased to 75 percent for stock acquired after February 17, 2009, and before September 27, 2010. The Tax Relief Act of 2010 increased the exclusion percentage to 100 percent for qualifying small business stock acquired after September 27, 2010, and before January 1, 2012, and was extended by The American Taxpayer Relief Act of 2012 to stock acquired before January 1, 2014. Finally, the 100 percent exclusion was made permanent by the Protecting Americans from Tax Hikes Act of 2015.

To calculate the capital gains tax, a series of nettings is done to determine the composition of the net long-term capital gain. **Adjusted net capital gain** is defined as the net long-term gain from the netting procedure minus the 28-percent rate gain and the unrecaptured Section 1250 gain plus *eligible dividend income*. Adjusted net capital gain cannot be negative. The 28-percent rate gain is equal to the sum of the net collectibles gain (loss), and gain on qualified small business stock reduced by net short-term capital losses and any long-term capital loss carryover from previous years. If the 28-percent rate gain is negative, the remaining loss is netted against the unrecaptured Section 1250 gain.[8] The practical effect is that net long-term capital gains are accorded the most favorable rates first. That is, the net long-term capital gain from the netting procedure is first allocated to the gain taxed at 15 percent (adjusted net capital gain), then to the gain taxed at 25 percent (unrecaptured Section 1250 gain), and last to the gain taxed at 28 percent (net collectibles gain and gain on qualified small business stock).

**Example 15** Return to the facts of example 14. Johanna has a net long-term capital gain of $4,000 for the current year. Assuming that she is a single individual whose taxable income from all other sources is $100,000 during the current year, what amount of tax relief does Johanna receive on her $4,000 net long-term capital gain?

**Discussion: Johanna adds the $4,000 net long-term capital gain to her gross income, increasing taxable income to $104,000. Her $4,000 net long-term capital gain consists of a net long-term capital gain of $5,000 ($13,000 − $8,000), a $1,000 ($7,000 − $6,000) net collectibles gain, and a net short-term capital loss of $2,000. In computing her tax liability, the 28% rate gain is a negative $1,000 ($1,000 net collectibles gain − $2,000 net short-term capital loss). The $1,000 negative 28% rate gain reduces the net long-term capital gain to $4,000, which is her adjusted net capital gain. Note that the effect of the netting is to allocate the net long-term capital gain from the capital gain and loss netting procedure to the lowest rate categories first. The adjusted net capital gain is taxed at 15%.**

**Example 16** Norman has the following capital gains and losses for the current year:

| | |
|---|---:|
| Short-term capital loss | $(3,000) |
| Long-term capital loss carryover from previous year | (2,000) |
| Long-term capital loss | (1,000) |
| Collectibles gain | 8,000 |
| Long-term capital gain | 7,000 |

Norman is single and has a taxable income of $180,000 without considering his capital gains and losses. What is Norman's taxable income and his income tax liability?

**Discussion: Norman has a $3,000 net short-term capital loss and a $12,000 long-term capital gain. The short-term loss and the long-term gain are netted, resulting in a $9,000 net long-term capital gain:**

| | | |
|---|---|---|
| Net short-term capital loss | | $ (3,000) |
| Long-term capital gain | $ 7,000 | |
| Collectibles gain | 8,000 | |
| Long-term capital loss carryover | (2,000) | |
| Long-term capital loss | (1,000) | |
| Net long-term capital gain | | 12,000 |
| Net long-term capital gain | | $ 9,000 |

**The $9,000 net long-term capital gain is added to Norman's taxable income, increasing it to $189,000. In calculating his tax, Norman has a $6,000 ($7,000 − $1,000) net long-term capital gain, an $8,000 collectibles gain, a $2,000 long-term capital loss carryover, and a $3,000 short-term capital loss. The 28% rate gain is $3,000 ($8,000 − $2,000 − $3,000). The adjusted net capital gain is $6,000 ($9,000 − $3,000). The $9,000 net long-term capital gain is composed of a $6,000 adjusted net capital gain and a $3,000 collectibles gain. Note that the netting procedure is equivalent to allocating the net long-term capital gain to the 15% rate category first, with the additional gain allocated to the 28% rate category. Because his marginal tax rate is 32%, the collectibles gain is taxed at the 28% maximum rate. Norman's tax liability is $40,167:**

| | |
|---|---|
| Tax on $180,000 − $33,603.00 + [32% × (180,000 − $164,925)] | $38,427 |
| Tax on adjusted net capital gain − $6,000 × 15% | 900 |
| Tax on collectibles gain − $3,000 × 28% | 840 |
| Income tax liability | $40,167 |

**Without the capital gains rate relief, Norman's tax on the $9,000 net long-term capital gain would have been $2,880 ($9,000 × 32%). Norman saves $1,140 ($2,880 − $900 − $840) because of the lower capital gains rates.**

Because short-term capital gains of individuals and all net capital gains of corporations are treated as ordinary income, it would seem that these capital gains and losses have no tax significance. Although this is true whenever an individual or a corporation has a net capital gain position for the year, the primary benefit of these gains is through the capital gain-and-loss netting procedure. That is, these gains can be used to offset and reduce capital losses occurring during the year. As shown in Table 11-1 (and covered in Chapter 7), capital loss deductions for both individuals and corporations are limited. Therefore, a tax benefit does result to the extent that a net short-term gain is used to off-set a capital loss in the netting procedure. The loss treatments in Table 11-1 are the same treatments studied in Chapter 7.

**Example 17** Return to the facts of example 13 in which Johanna has a net short-term capital loss of $2,000 and a net long-term capital loss of $4,000 during the current year. How much of the losses can Johanna deduct in the current year, and how much is carried forward to subsequent years?

**Discussion: Johanna is allowed to deduct a maximum of $3,000 in capital losses per year with any excess loss carried forward to subsequent years. Johanna's total capital loss for the year is $6,000. Her $3,000 deduction is composed of the $2,000 short-term capital loss and $1,000 of the long-term capital loss. The remaining $3,000 of the net long-term capital loss is carried forward and used in the next year's netting as a $3,000 long-term capital loss carryforward.**

## Capital Gain Exclusion on Qualified Small Business Stock

To stimulate investment in certain small businesses, 50 percent of the gain (not reduced by any capital losses) from **qualified small business stock** that is held for more than five years is excluded from taxation.[9] The exclusion percentage is increased to 75 percent for stock acquired after February 17, 2009, and before September 28, 2010. The exclusion percentage is further increased to 100 percent for stock acquired after September 27, 2010. The gain remaining after the exclusion is taxed at a maximum rate of 28 percent; it is not eligible for the 15-percent long-term capital gains rate. The effect of the provision is to limit the marginal tax rate on such gains to a maximum of 14 percent

(50 percent × 28 percent maximum rate, 7 percent for 75 percent exclusion, zero percent for 100 percent exclusion). This provision prevents a taxpayer from reaping a double benefit from the sale of qualified small business stock (i.e., 50 percent exclusion and the 15-percent capital gains rate). However, if small business stock is sold before the required five-year holding period, the gain would not be eligible for exclusion but would be taxed at the 15-percent adjusted net capital gains rate. The maximum gain that can be excluded in a year is limited to the greater of 10 times the investor's basis in the stock or $10 million for each qualified small business. Seven percent of the exclusion amount is treated as a tax preference under the individual alternative minimum tax provisions (discussed in Chapter 15). This incentive provision is in addition to the loss deduction rules for certain qualifying small business stock discussed in Chapter 7. Thus, Congress has again used tax law to try to stimulate investment in small businesses.

**Example 18** Isabel purchases 1,000 shares of qualified small business stock on November 19, 2008. On December 20, 2021, she sells the 1,000 shares at a gain of $120,000. What is the effect of the sale of the stock on Isabel's tax liability, assuming that she has no other capital asset transactions and is in the 32% marginal tax bracket?

**Discussion: Because the stock is qualified small business stock that Isabel held for more than 5 years, she excludes 50% of the gain, $60,000, from her capital gain income. Because she has no other capital gains or losses, her net capital gain position is a net long-term capital gain of $60,000 ($120,000 gain − $60,000 exclusion). The gain is taxed at the 28% maximum tax rate for gains on qualified small business stock, resulting in a tax liability of $16,800 ($60,000 × 28%). Note that tax on the gain is 14% of the total gain ($16,800 ÷ $120,000 = 14%).**

**Discussion: If Isabel had purchased the stock on November 19, 2009, and sold it on December 20, 2021, she excludes 75% of the gain, $90,000, from her capital gain income. For qualified small business stock held for more than 5 years and acquired after February 17, 2009, and before September 27, 2010, the exclusion increases to 75% of the gain. Because she has no other capital gains, her net capital gain position is a net long-term capital gain of $30,000 ($120,000 − $90,000). The gain is taxed at the 28% maximum rate for gains on qualified small business stock, resulting in a tax liability of $8,400 ($30,000 × 28%). Note that the tax on the gain is 7% of the total gain ($8,400 ÷ $120,000 = 7%).**

**Discussion: If Isabel had purchased the stock on October 23, 2013, and sold it on February 17, 2021, she excludes 100% of the gain from her capital gain income and she is not taxed on the gain. For qualified small business stock held for more than 5 years and acquired after September 27, 2010, the exclusion increases to 100% and none of the gain is taxable.**

**Example 19** Assume the same facts as in example 18, except that Isabel has a net capital loss of $20,000 from her other capital asset transactions. What is the effect of the sale of the stock on Isabel's tax liability?

**Discussion: The 50% exclusion is taken before the capital gain-and-loss netting. Therefore, Isabel is entitled to an exclusion of $60,000. The $60,000 long-term capital gain that remains after the exclusion is netted against the $20,000 capital loss, resulting in a net long-term capital gain of $40,000. Isabel's tax on the $40,000 net long-term capital gain is $11,200 ($40,000 × 28%).**

Qualifying small business stock is stock originally issued after August 10, 1993, by a corporation that did not have gross assets in excess of $50 million after August 10, 1993, and before the stock issuance. The stock must be purchased at its original issue directly from the corporation or through its underwriter. That is, the stock cannot be acquired from another individual or entity. The small business issuing the stock must generally be an active corporation that uses substantially all its assets (at least 80 percent of the value) in the active conduct of a trade or business during the five-year holding period. Generally, only stock in manufacturing, retailing, and wholesaling businesses qualifies for the exclusion. Banking, leasing, real estate, farming, mineral extraction, and hotels, motels, restaurants, or similar businesses are specifically denied treatment as qualified small business stock. In addition, the stock of certain service corporations does not qualify. Nonqualifying service corporations include those in the fields of health, law, engineering, accounting, architecture, performing arts, athletics, and financial and brokerage services.

Only noncorporate investors are eligible to claim the exclusion. Conduit entities, such as partnerships and S corporations, may hold qualified small business stock and may be able to pass the gain through to a partner or shareholder eligible for the exclusion.

**Example 20** GARS Partnership was organized by 4 equal owners: 3 individuals (Garth, Adam, and Rachelle) and Solide Corporation. The partnership purchased 10,000 shares of Mystuk Corporation stock directly from the corporation for $100,000 at its original issue on December 11, 2014. Mystuk is a pharmaceutical manufacturing enterprise, the gross assets of which have never exceeded $35 million. GARS held the stock until December 30, 2021, when it was sold for $220,000. What are the tax implications of the sale for GARS Partnership and the partners?

**Discussion: Mystuk Corporation stock qualifies as small business stock. Its gross assets did not exceed $50 million after August 10, 1993, and before the stock was issued. Mystuk is an active manufacturer, and the original issue of the stock was after August 10, 1993. GARS realized a $120,000 gain ($220,000 – $100,000) on the stock sale. Because GARS is a conduit entity, the gain passes through to the partners. Each partner is allocated 25%, or $30,000, of the gain. Garth, Adam, and Rachelle can exclude their $30,000 individual shares of the gain. However, Solide Corporation must recognize all $30,000 of its share of the partnership's realized gain. Corporations are not allowed the benefits of the qualified small business stock exclusion.**

An individual may elect to roll over (defer recognition of) gain from the sale of qualified small business stock held for more than six months if other qualified small business stock is purchased within 60 days of the sale. Gain is recognized to the extent that the amount realized on the sale exceeds the cost of the replacement stock. The basis of the replacement stock is reduced by any gain not recognized on the sale. If more than one qualifying small business stock is purchased, the basis adjustment is applied to the stocks in the order each is acquired. The holding period of the replacement stock includes the holding period of the stock sold.

**Example 21** Jenny purchases qualified small business stock in Thomas Company for $100,000 on September 14, 2019. She sells the stock for $150,000 on December 10, 2021. On January 22, 2022, she purchases qualified small business stock in MS Corporation for $130,000. How much gain must Jenny recognize on the sale of the Thomas Company stock, and what is her basis in the MS Corporation stock?

**Discussion: Because Jenny has held the Thomas Company stock more than 6 months and purchases the MS Corporation stock within 60 days of the Thomas Company sale, she can elect to roll over the $50,000 ($150,000 − $100,000) gain on the sale. Because she did not reinvest the entire $150,000 proceeds in acquiring the MS Corporation stock, she must recognize a gain of $20,000 ($150,000 amount realized − $130,000 cost of replacement stock) on the sale. The $20,000 gain is a long-term capital gain and is taxed at 15%. The $30,000 gain that is not recognized reduces Jenny's basis in the MS Corporation stock to $100,000 ($130,000 − $30,000). Jenny's holding period for the MS Corporation stock begins on September 14, 2019 the date she acquired the Thomas Company stock. Note: This is an election, and Jenny does not have to defer the gain. She can include the $50,000 in income and be taxed on the gain at the 15% long-term capital gain rate (since the stock was held more than 12 months) if she does not want to defer the gain.**

**Example 22** Assume that in example 21, Jenny also purchases qualifying small business stock in Bryan, Inc., for $30,000 on January 25, 2022. How much gain must she recognize on the sale of the Thomas Company stock, and what is her basis in the MS Corporation stock and the Bryan, Inc., stock?

**Discussion: The Bryan, Inc., stock is purchased within 60 days of the Thomas Company sale and can be used to reduce the gain on the sale. The entire gain can be deferred because the cost of the replacement stocks ($130,000 + $30,000) exceeds the amount realized on the sale. The basis of the MS Corporation stock is reduced to $80,000 ($130,000 − $50,000) by the deferred gain. The Bryan, Inc., stock basis is $30,000. The holding period of both stocks begins on September 14, 2019.**

LO 5

Explain how year-end tax-planning strategies can take advantage of the capital asset netting procedure.

## 11-4d Capital Gains and Losses—Planning Strategies

Before the end of any tax year, taxpayers should analyze their net capital gain or loss position for the year and determine whether there are any actions they might take to use the capital gain-and-loss netting procedures to their advantage. In this regard, the taxpayer may be in either a net capital gain position or a net capital loss position before the end of the year.

### Net Capital Gain Position

A taxpayer with a net capital gain position will have to pay tax on the net capital gains for the year. Therefore, the taxpayer should consider reducing the net capital gain by selling capital assets on which there is an unrealized loss. To obtain the maximum tax benefit, the taxpayer should take losses that cancel out the net capital gain to date. In addition, individuals can take $3,000 in losses over and above the net capital gain to take advantage of the net capital loss deduction provisions.

**Example 23** Before the end of the current year, Ramsey has a net long-term capital gain of $20,000 on all capital asset transactions during the year. What is Ramsey's optimal year-end tax-planning strategy for capital gains and losses?

**Discussion: Any capital losses Ramsey realizes before the end of the year will reduce the $20,000 net long-term capital gain. Optimally, Ramsey will sell capital assets with unrealized losses to produce additional capital losses of $23,000. This will change his capital gain/loss position to a net loss of $3,000 ($20,000 − $23,000) for the year. He will then be able to deduct the entire $3,000 of the net capital loss.**

**STRATEGY PITFALL: If Ramsey sells stock to create the $23,000 loss, he will not be able to repurchase any shares of the same company for 30 days. If he repurchases shares in the same company within 30 days, the wash sale rules disallow the loss on the shares replaced. Therefore, this strategy is contingent upon the taxpayer either not desiring to remain a shareholder in the loss shares or being willing to wait more than 30 days to replace the shares.**

### Net Capital Loss Position

A taxpayer with a net capital loss position before the end of the year should act to avoid the limitations on capital loss deductions. For individuals, the optimal action is to take unrealized capital gains to reduce the net capital loss for the year to the $3,000 maximum deduction amount.

**Example 24** Golda has a net capital loss of $15,000 before the end of the current tax year. What is her optimal year-end tax-planning strategy for capital gains and capital losses?

**Discussion: Because Golda can deduct only $3,000 of her $15,000 net capital loss, she should sell capital assets with unrealized gains to produce a capital gain of $12,000. The effect of the strategy is to fully use the net capital loss within the current period by offsetting the loss with a capital gain.**

**Note that if Golda sells securities to produce the desired capital gain, nothing prevents her from repurchasing the shares because there is no gain equivalent to the rules that disallow wash sale losses.**

Example 24 illustrates the previously mentioned benefit of capital gains under current tax law—the ability to deduct capital gains against capital losses that would otherwise be nondeductible in the current period. Taxpayers in net capital loss situations may take capital gains that are essentially tax-free in the current period and take advantage of the capital gain-and-loss netting procedure.

### Worthless Securities

When a security becomes worthless, a technical disposition does not take place. However, the tax law recognizes the loss of investment suffered by the taxpayer in such situations; taxpayers with **worthless securities** are deemed to have realized the loss on the last day of the tax year in which the security is determined to be worthless. The realized loss is equal to the basis of the worthless security. The last day of the tax year is the date of realization in determining the holding period of the security for classification of the loss as short-term or long-term.[10]

**Example 25** Zev owns 500 shares of Newstart Company that he purchased on November 4, 2020, for $20,000. In April 2021, Newstart declares bankruptcy, and Zev is unable to sell his shares. The bankruptcy court liquidates the company, and the shareholders receive no cash for their stock. How should Zev treat the loss on his Newstart stock?

**Discussion: The Newstart stock is deemed to be worthless on December 31, 2021, which is when Zev realizes the loss of his $20,000 basis. The loss is a long-term capital loss, because Zev has held the stock for more than 12 months (November 4, 2020 to December 31, 2021). Note: If the stock in Newstart were qualified small business stock, Zev could deduct the loss as an ordinary loss. (See Chapter 7.)**

## Basis of Securities Sold

When taxpayers sell only some of the securities they hold, the shares being sold must be identified if the securities were purchased at different times and at different prices. Because securities are generic, it is often difficult to precisely identify specific shares as being from a specific purchase. The tax law provides that, in the absence of a specific identification of the shares sold, the shares are sold in a first-in, first-out (FIFO) order.[11]

**Example 26** On December 10, 2021, DeWitt sells 400 shares of Rubble, Inc., common stock for $8,000 and pays a $500 commission on the sale. DeWitt had purchased his Rubble shares as follows:

| Purchase Date | Number of Shares | Cost |
|---|---|---|
| February 10, 2020 | 200 | $3,000 |
| December 19, 2020 | 300 | $3,000 |

What is DeWitt's gain or loss on the sale of the 400 shares?

**Discussion: DeWitt's amount realized on the sale of the 400 shares is $7,500 ($8,000 − $500). Because he purchased the 500 shares at two different times and at different prices, he must either specifically identify the shares sold or determine the basis of the 400 shares in first-in, first-out order. Assuming that DeWitt does not specifically identify the 400 shares, his basis would be $5,000:**

| | |
|---|---|
| Basis of 200 shares from February purchase | $3,000 |
| Basis of 200 shares from December purchase | |
| $3,000 ÷ 300 = $10 per share × 200 shares | 2,000 |
| Basis of 400 shares | $5,000 |

**DeWitt realizes a gain of $750 ($3,750 − $3,000) on the shares purchased in February. The $750 gain is a long-term capital gain (because the stock was held more than 12 months). He realizes a $1,750 ($3,750 − $2,000) gain on the sale of the shares purchased in December. The $1,750 gain is a short-term capital gain (because the shares were held 12 months or less).**

The first-in, first-out rule for the sale of securities can be overridden by directing in writing that certain lots of securities are to be sold. Thus, a taxpayer who has purchased shares at different times and at different prices can determine the amount of gain or loss to be recognized on a particular sale of shares.

**Example 27** Cathi owns 600 shares of Wetzel's Pretzels common stock. She purchased the 600 shares as follows:

| Purchase Date | Number of Shares | Cost |
|---|---|---|
| October 2017 | 200 | $ 6,000 |
| May 2018 | 200 | $ 9,000 |
| December 2019 | 200 | $14,000 |

Before December 28, 2021, Cathi has a net capital gain of $7,000. On December 28, 2021, Wetzel's Pretzels' stock is trading for $60 per share. If Cathi wants to sell some Wetzel's Pretzels stock to decrease her 2021 taxable income, what should she do?

**Discussion: The optimal strategy in a net capital gain situation is to take capital losses to reduce capital gain income. In this case, Cathi should direct her broker, in writing, to sell the 200 shares purchased in December 2019. Ignoring sales commissions, the sale would result in a $2,000 [(200 × $60) − $14,000] capital loss, reducing her net capital gain to $5,000.**

**If Cathi does not specify in writing the precise shares to be sold, the October 2017 shares would be sold under the FIFO rule, resulting in a $6,000 ($12,000 − $6,000) long-term capital gain. However, by specifying that the loss shares be sold, Cathi can control whether she has a gain or a loss on the sale.**

## concept check

The *legislative grace concept* requires any tax relief provided to be the result of a specific act of Congress that must be strictly applied and interpreted. Under this concept, individuals are accorded tax relief on net long-term capital gains. For 2021 taxpayers below the 15% breakpoint are not taxed on their capital gains and the 15% breakpoint is $80,800 for joint returns and $40,400 for single individuals. The 20% breakpoint is $501,600 for joint returns and $445,850 for single individuals. In providing this relief, Congress has also limited the deduction of capital losses of individuals to $3,000 per year. Capital gains of corporations are not provided any tax relief. Corporate capital losses are deductible only against capital gains, providing no current period relief for a net capital loss. However, corporations are allowed to carry a net capital loss back three years and forward five years to offset capital gains in the carryback and carryforward years. To encourage investment in small businesses, half (100% if acquired after September 27, 2010) the gain on qualified small business stock is excluded from income. To avoid a double benefit, any remaining gain is taxed at a maximum rate of 28%, instead of the 15% long-term capital gains rate.

# 11-5 SECTION 1231 GAINS AND LOSSES

The discussion of capital assets noted that most business assets do not receive capital gain or loss treatment. Therefore, dispositions of assets used in a trade or business would generally produce ordinary gains and losses. However, Congress has provided capital gain relief for certain long-lived business assets. The rationale for this treatment is that long-lived assets sold at a gain have characteristics common to capital assets and deserve the same treatment to negate inflationary gains and promote capital investment in long-lived business assets. The assets accorded this special relief are referred to as *Section 1231 property*. The basic intention of Section 1231 is to provide long-term capital gain status to net **Section 1231 gains** for a tax year while preserving the ordinary loss deduction for years in which a business has net **Section 1231 losses**. Therefore, this provision provides the best of both worlds—preferential capital gain treatment for net gains and ordinary loss deductions for net losses.

## 11-5a Definition of Section 1231 Property

LO 6

Describe Section 1231 assets and the year-end netting procedure used to determine the effect of Section 1231 transactions on taxable income.

Assets eligible for the preferential treatment under Section 1231 include:

1. Property used in a trade or business that is held for more than 12 months and that is depreciable property or real property
2. Timber, coal, and domestic iron ore
3. Cattle and horses held for draft, breeding, dairy, or sporting purposes that are held for 24 months or more
4. Other livestock held for draft, breeding, dairy, or sporting purposes that are held for 12 months or more
5. Unharvested crops

The assets qualifying for Section 1231 treatment must be held for more than 12 months. Assets that are held 12 months or less are never given Section 1231 treatment and always produce ordinary income. The first category affects most businesses, because it includes all fixed assets of a business. Note that **Section 1231 property** is used primarily to operate the business. Property such as inventory that is sold to produce the income of the business generally is not Section 1231 property. However, the last four categories are inventory-type items for which Congress has applied the legislative grace concept to grant the special treatment provided by Section 1231.

## 11-5b Section 1231 Netting Procedure

As with capital gains and losses, the tax treatments accorded Section 1231 property apply to the net gain or loss on all Section 1231 transactions occurring during a tax year. The netting procedure involves two separate nettings of transactions occurring during the current tax year and a separate netting of any net Section 1231 gains in the current year against net 1231 loss deductions taken during the previous five years. Figure 11-2 outlines the netting procedure.[12]

The first step in the **Section 1231 netting procedure** is to net together all casualty and theft gains and losses on Section 1231 property to produce a single net casualty gain or loss for the year. If the result of the first netting is a loss, all casualty gains and losses for the year are considered ordinary losses. This results in a net ordinary casualty loss deduction for the year. If the result of the first netting is a gain, the net casualty gain is carried into the second netting. The purpose of this separate netting of casualty and theft losses is to provide the maximum benefit possible for casualty and theft losses—ordinary loss deductions for net casualty losses and capital gain treatment of net casualty gains.

In the second netting, all other Section 1231 gains and losses occurring during the year are netted together with any net casualty gain from the first netting. As in the first netting, if the result of the second netting is a loss, all gains and losses for the year are considered ordinary. This results in a net ordinary loss deduction for Section 1231 transactions for the year.

*Figure 11-2*

**Section 1231 Netting**

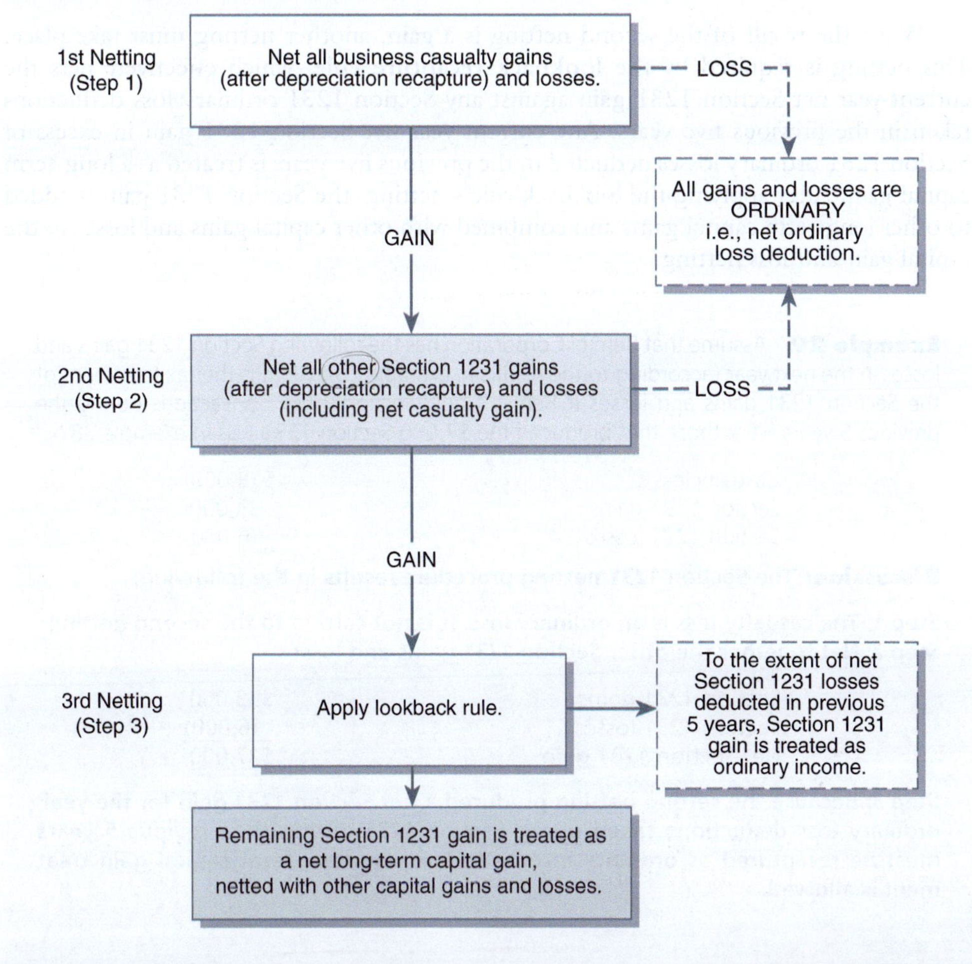

**Example 28** After summarizing the results of all its transactions for the year, Bemigi Corporation has the following gains and losses from Section 1231 property:

| | |
|---|---|
| Casualty gains | $ 23,000 |
| Casualty losses | (5,000) |
| Section 1231 gains | 35,000 |
| Section 1231 losses | (60,000) |

What is the effect of the Section 1231 transactions on Bemigi's taxable income for the current year?

**Discussion: To determine the tax effect, Bemigi must go through the Section 1231 netting procedure:**

**Step 1: Net all casualty gains and losses.**

| | |
|---|---|
| Casualty gains | $23,000 |
| Casualty losses | (5,000) |
| Net casualty gain | $18,000 |

**Because this netting results in a gain, the net gain is carried to the second netting.**

**Step 2: Net all other Section 1231 gains and losses with the net casualty gain.**

| | |
|---|---|
| Net casualty gain | $ 18,000 |
| Section 1231 gains | 35,000 |
| Section 1231 losses | (60,000) |
| Net Section 1231 loss | $ (7,000) |

**Because the Section 1231 netting produced a loss, all Section 1231 gains and losses for the year are considered ordinary gains and losses. The result is that the Section 1231 transactions reduce Bemigi's taxable income by $7,000. This is a favorable result because there are no restrictions on the deductibility of an ordinary loss.**

When the result of the second netting is a gain, another netting must take place. This netting is required by the **lookback recapture rule**, which effectively nets the current-year net Section 1231 gain against any Section 1231 ordinary loss deductions taken in the previous five years. Any current-year net Section 1231 gain in excess of Section 1231 ordinary losses deducted in the previous five years is treated as a long-term capital gain. After applying the lookback rule's netting, the Section 1231 gain is added to other long-term capital gains and combined with other capital gains and losses in the capital gain-and-loss netting.

**Example 29** Assume that Bemigi Corporation has the following Section 1231 gains and losses in the next year (according to the results in example 28). What is the tax treatment of the Section 1231 gains and losses if Bemigi's only Section 1231 transactions during the previous 5 years were those that produced the $7,000 Section 1231 loss in example 28?

| | |
|---|---|
| Casualty loss | $ (8,000) |
| Section 1231 gains | 33,000 |
| Section 1231 losses | (6,000) |

**Discussion: The Section 1231 netting procedure results in the following:**

**Step 1: The casualty loss is an ordinary loss. It is not carried to the second netting.**
**Step 2: Net together the other Section 1231 gains and losses.**

| | |
|---|---|
| Section 1231 gains | $33,000 |
| Section 1231 losses | (6,000) |
| Net Section 1231 gain | $27,000 |

**Step 3: Because the second netting produced a net Section 1231 gain for the year, ordinary loss deductions taken under Section 1231 during the previous 5 years must be recaptured as ordinary income before any long-term capital gain treatment is allowed.**

| | |
|---|---|
| Net Section 1231 gain | $27,000 |
| Section 1231 loss deduction from last year | (7,000) |
| Long-term capital gain | $20,000 |

**The results of the Section 1231 netting are summarized as follows:**

| | |
|---|---|
| Ordinary casualty loss deduction | $ (8,000) |
| Ordinary income under lookback rule | 7,000 |
| Long-term capital gain | 20,000 |

**The ordinary income from the lookback recapture rule and the ordinary loss from the casualty are combined (added or subtracted) in the calculation of Bemigi's taxable income. The $20,000 long-term capital gain is combined with any other capital gains and losses in the capital gain-and-loss netting procedure to determine its effect on taxable income.**

Once ordinary Section 1231 loss deductions have been recaptured as ordinary income, they do not have to be recaptured again. The intent of the lookback rule is to net together ordinary loss deductions against the net Section 1231 gains to equalize the characterization of gains and losses over the five-year lookback period. Once an ordinary loss deduction of one year has been offset by Section 1231 gain of a later year, there is no need for further recapture.

**Example 30** Assume that in the year after that described in example 29, Bemigi Corporation has the following Section 1231 gains and losses:

| | |
|---|---|
| Section 1231 gains | $40,000 |
| Section 1231 losses | (12,000) |

What is the effect of the Section 1231 gains and losses on Bemigi's taxable income?

**Discussion: Bemigi has a net Section 1231 gain of $28,000 ($40,000 − $12,000) for the year. Because Bemigi recaptured all of its Section 1231 ordinary loss deductions last year, the entire $28,000 gain is a long-term capital gain. The $28,000 long-term capital gain is combined with other capital gains and capital losses in the capital gain-and-loss netting procedure.**

Given that the current treatment of long-term capital gains is not of great benefit to corporate taxpayers (see Table 11-1), why is the Section 1231 capital gain relief important? As with any net capital gain, one benefit under current law is the reduction of otherwise currently nondeductible capital losses. Without the Section 1231 provisions, many taxpayers would pay tax on their gains from selling business assets while realizing little or no current relief from net capital losses.

**Example 31** Assume that in example 29, which produced a net long-term capital gain of $20,000 from the Section 1231 netting, Bemigi also has the following capital gains and losses for the year. What is the treatment of the capital gains and losses?

| | |
|---|---|
| Short-term capital gains | $ 13,000 |
| Long-term capital losses | (30,000) |

**Discussion: The capital gain-and-loss netting procedure produces a net short-term capital gain of $3,000:**

| | | |
|---|---|---|
| Short-term capital gain | | $ 13,000 |
| Long-term capital gain from Section 1231 | $ 20,000 | |
| Long-term capital loss | (30,000) | |
| Net long-term capital loss | | (10,000) |
| Net short-term capital gain | | $ 3,000 |

**Note that without the long-term capital gain from the Section 1231 netting, Bemigi would have a long-term capital loss of $17,000 ($13,000 – $30,000) for the year. As a corporation, Bemigi would not be allowed to deduct any of the capital loss in the current year. The capital loss would be carried back 3 years and used to offset net capital gains. If Bemigi has no capital gains in the carryback period, it could carry the capital loss forward for 5 years. Because the Section 1231 netting produced a capital gain, Bemigi has effectively deducted the $17,000 loss in the current year.**

## 11-6 DEPRECIATION RECAPTURE

LO 7
Explain the reclassification of gain on the sale of depreciable assets as ordinary income under the depreciation recapture provisions.

In extending capital gain relief through the capital gain and Section 1231 provisions, Congress was concerned that only gains derived from appreciation in the value of a property were granted tax relief. In many instances, the entire gain on the disposition of a property is derived from appreciation.

**Example 32** Raquel purchases 300 shares of Houston Company stock on September 4, 2020 at a cost of $4,500. On April 5, 2021, she sells the 300 shares of stock for $8,500. Is Raquel's $4,000 gain on the sale derived from appreciation in the value of the stock?

**Discussion: Raquel's $4,000 gain is totally derived from appreciation in the price of the Houston Company stock. Because she is not allowed to recover any of her $4,500 investment in the stock until it is sold, any gain on the sale of the stock is attributable solely to price appreciation.**

We can conclude from example 32 that when the investment in the asset is recovered only at disposition, any gain on the sale is derived from price appreciation. However, through depreciation deductions, taxable entities recover capital investments in many assets while the asset is used to produce income. As an asset is depreciated, the basis in the asset is reduced. When the asset is disposed of, the gain or loss is measured as the difference between the amount realized and the adjusted basis of the asset. As a result, some—and perhaps all—of the gain on the sale of a depreciable asset derives from depreciation previously deducted on the asset.

**Example 33** In 2019, Latifa Corporation purchases a computer to be used solely in its trade or business at a cost of $15,000. Latifa elects to use straight-line depreciation on the computer. In 2021, when the adjusted basis of the computer is $9,000, the corporation sells the computer for $10,000. How much of Latifa's $1,000 gain on the sale derives from the depreciation it took on the computer?

**Discussion: The entire $1,000 gain is attributable to depreciation. That is, the computer has not appreciated in value from its original acquisition cost. It has actually lost $5,000 in value since Latifa purchased it. Only because Latifa took $6,000 in depreciation on the computer (reducing its basis) did the corporation have a gain.**

Example 33 illustrates the basic rationale for disallowing long-term capital gain treatment for gains from depreciation deductions. Although the computer has lost $5,000 in value, the $6,000 in depreciation taken on it has resulted in a gain of $1,000 on the sale of the computer. This gain is created by the depreciation that was deducted as an ordinary expense for the business, reducing the tax on ordinary income. Allowing long-term capital gain treatment on the sale of the computer would allow an ordinary deduction to create a capital gain on the disposition. As previously discussed, one purpose of the preferential treatment for capital gains and Section 1231 property is that the gains have been artificially increased by inflation. However, with depreciable assets, a portion of the gain is created through ordinary deductions. The purpose of the depreciation recapture rules is to reclassify gains from depreciation as ordinary income.

Recapture can be seen as giving back the ordinary deduction that created the gain. Only the gain remaining in excess of the recaptured amount is accorded capital gain or Section 1231 treatment. Thus, **depreciation recapture** is the reclassification as ordinary income of all or part of a gain on the disposition of a capital asset or a Section 1231 asset. The recaptured amount does not receive preferential treatment in the calculation of taxable income.

There are two primary recapture provisions, referred to as *Section 1245 recapture* and *Section 1250 recapture*. All depreciable assets must be classified as either a Section 1245 property or a Section 1250 property and the appropriate recapture rule applied when the asset is disposed of at a gain. In studying these provisions, keep in mind that their intent is to reclassify gains from depreciation as ordinary income. Depreciation deductions do not create losses. Therefore, the depreciation recapture provisions do not apply to depreciable assets sold at a loss.

## 11-6a Section 1245 Recapture Rule

LO 8 Identify Section 1245 and Section 1250 assets and the depreciation recapture rule applicable to each type.

Section 1245 property is subject to a full recapture of all depreciation taken as ordinary income.[13] The practical effect of this provision is to deny capital gain or Section 1231 treatment on any Section 1245 property that is disposed of at less than its original cost.

**Example 34** Reactor Tractor Company purchases machinery in 2020 at a cost of $40,000. In 2021, when the adjusted basis of the machinery is $15,000, Reactor sells it for $26,000. The machinery is Section 1245 property. What is the character of the $11,000 gain on the sale of the machinery?

**Discussion: Machinery used in a trade or business is Section 1231 property. However, Reactor is required to recapture as ordinary income any gain on the sale that derives from depreciation before any of the gain is considered Section 1231 gain. In this case, the $11,000 gain is totally derived from the $25,000 ($40,000 − $15,000) in depreciation taken on the machinery. Therefore, all gain on the sale is ordinary income. None of the gain is eligible for treatment under the Section 1231 netting procedure.**

**Example 35** Assume the same facts as in example 34, except that the machinery is sold for $47,000, resulting in a gain on the sale of $32,000. What is the character of the $32,000 gain on the sale of the machinery?

**Discussion: Of the total gain on the sale, $25,000 derives from the reduction in basis for depreciation and is recaptured as ordinary income. The remaining $7,000 of gain derives from price appreciation in the machinery and is characterized as gain from the sale of a Section 1231 asset.**

| | |
|---|---|
| Amount realized | $ 47,000 |
| Adjusted basis ($40,000 − $25,000) | (15,000) |
| Gain on sale | $ 32,000 |
| Gain from depreciation—ordinary income | (25,000) |
| Gain from price appreciation—Section 1231 gain | $ 7,000 |

These two examples illustrate a basic result of the **Section 1245 recapture rule**: No capital gain or Section 1231 treatment results from the sale of a Section 1245 property unless it is sold for more than its original cost. Note that the $7,000 in Section 1231 gain in example 35 is the appreciation in price from the $40,000 original cost to the $47,000 selling price. This result always holds for a Section 1245 property.

## 11-6b Section 1250 Recapture Rule

The recapture rule for gains on the sale of Section 1250 assets is more generous than under Section 1245. Under the **Section 1250 recapture rule**, only gains that are attributable to excess depreciation are recaptured as ordinary income. *Excess depreciation* is defined as the total depreciation taken to date, less the allowable straight-line depreciation on the asset.[14] Note that if a Section 1250 asset has been depreciated using the straight-line method, no recapture of depreciation occurs, because no excess depreciation has been deducted on the asset.

**Example 36** Ragwood Company purchases an apartment building in 1985 at a cost of $800,000. The apartment building is sold in 2021 for $700,000. The maximum allowable depreciation on the building as of the date of sale is $600,000. Straight-line depreciation for the same period would be $400,000. The building is a Section 1250 property. What is the character of the gain on the sale of the building if Ragwood takes the maximum allowable depreciation deduction on the building?

**Discussion: The gain on the sale of the building is $500,000. The apartment building is a Section 1231 property. However, before any of the gain is Section 1231 gain, the excess depreciation of $200,000 must be recaptured as ordinary income. This leaves $300,000 of Section 1231 gain:**

| | |
|---|---|
| Amount realized on sale | $ 700,000 |
| Adjusted basis ($800,000 – $600,000) | (200,000) |
| Gain on sale | $ 500,000 |
| Depreciation recapture—ordinary income ($600,000 – $400,000) | (200,000) |
| Section 1231 gain | $ 300,000 |

**Example 37** Assume that in example 36, Ragwood had deducted straight-line depreciation while it held the apartment building. What is the character of the gain on the sale of the building?

**Discussion: Using straight-line depreciation, the gain on the sale of the building would have been $300,000 [$700,000 – ($800,000 – $400,000)]. Because Ragwood used the straight-line method to depreciate the building, there is no excess depreciation to recapture. Thus, the entire $300,000 gain is Section 1231 gain.**

A comparison of these examples reveals the basic result of the Section 1250 recapture rule: The Section 1231 gain (or capital gain) is always equal to the gain that would have occurred had straight-line depreciation been used. The gain remaining after depreciation recapture on a Section 1250 property is equal to the sum of the straight-line depreciation plus any price appreciation in the property. Note that this recapture result is more generous than that under Section 1245, which allows only true price appreciation to result in Section 1231 or capital gain.

**Example 38** A depreciable asset used in a trade or business that was purchased for $80,000 is sold for $95,000. Actual depreciation deducted on the asset totals $35,000. Allowable straight-line depreciation for the same period would be $20,000. What is the character of the gain if the asset is a Section 1245 property? a Section 1250 property?

**Discussion: The gain on the sale of the asset is $50,000 [$95,000 – ($80,000 – $35,000)]. The character of the gain under Section 1245 and Section 1250 is calculated as follows:**

| | Section 1245 | Section 1250 |
|---|---|---|
| Gain on sale | $ 50,000 | $ 50,000 |
| Depreciation recapture—ordinary income | | |
| Section 1245—all depreciation | (35,000) | |
| Section 1250—excess depreciation ($35,000 – $20,000) | | (15,000) |
| Section 1231 gain | $ 15,000 | $ 35,000 |

**Under Section 1245, the Section 1231 gain is equal to the price appreciation in the asset ($95,000 – $80,000). Under Section 1250, the Section 1231 gain is equal to the sum of the $15,000 price appreciation and the $20,000 straight-line depreciation deduction that is not recaptured under Section 1250.**

The depreciation recapture rules apply to all depreciable assets.[15] There are no exceptions in the tax law that override the depreciation recapture rules. Whenever a gain is recognized on a depreciable asset, the applicable recapture rule must be applied to determine the character of the gain. In applying the recapture rules, any amounts expensed under Section 179 are considered depreciation. As a final reminder, the depreciation recapture rules apply only to gains caused by depreciation; losses are not subject to recapture.

## 11-6c Section 1245 and Section 1250 Properties

To apply the proper recapture rule, you must determine the type of depreciable property. Depreciable assets fall into two basic categories: tangible personal property and real property. (See Chapter 10.) Historically, the distinction between **Section 1245 property** and **Section 1250 property** was between these two basic classes of property. All depreciable tangible personal property was Section 1245 property, and all depreciable real property was Section 1250 property. Note that assets that are not depreciable because (1) they have indefinite lives (e.g., land) or (2) they are capital assets or Section 1231 assets that are not depreciable, are not subject to depreciation recapture. In 1981, the ACRS depreciation system drastically increased the allowable depreciation deductions on real property by allowing accelerated depreciation over a 15-year life. In allowing this rapid acceleration of depreciation on real property, Congress took back some of the benefit by reclassifying most real property using the accelerated ACRS method as Section 1245 property.

Table 11-2 compares the asset classifications for assets purchased before 1981 and those purchased after 1980. The key difference in classification of assets acquired from 1981 through 1986 is for real property. Note that only four types of real property purchased from 1981 through 1986 qualify for the more-generous Section 1250 treatment:

- Residential rental property
- Low-income housing
- Any real property that is depreciated using the straight-line method
- Real property used predominantly outside the United States

The third general category causes most of the confusion. For example, a factory building purchased in 1977 (before 1981) is always a Section 1250 property, regardless of the depreciation method used. The same factory building purchased in 1983 would be a Section 1245 property if the regular ACRS (accelerated) method was used. However, if the owner of the factory building had elected to use the straight-line method, the building would be a Section 1250 property. On the other hand, an apartment building is always considered Section 1250 property, regardless of when it is purchased or which depreciation method is used.

*Table 11-2*

### Section 1245 and 1250 Properties

| | Section 1245 | Section 1250 |
|---|---|---|
| **Assets acquired before 1981** | Depreciable personal property:<br>Autos, trucks, equipment<br>Machinery, computers<br>Greenhouses, grain silos<br>Patents, copyrights<br>Leaseholds<br>Livestock | Depreciable real property:<br>Office buildings<br>Apartment buildings<br>Warehouses<br>Factory buildings<br>Low-income housing |
| **Assets acquired 1981–1986** | Depreciable personal property<br>Depreciable real property that does not qualify as Section 1250 property | Residential rental property<br>Low-income housing<br>Any real property that has been depreciated using the straight-line method<br>Real property used predominantly outside the United States |
| **Assets acquired after 1986** | Depreciable personal property:<br>Autos, trucks, equipment<br>Machinery, computers<br>Greenhouses, grain silos<br>Patents, copyrights<br>Leaseholds<br>Livestock | Depreciable real property:<br>Office buildings<br>Apartment buildings<br>Warehouses<br>Factory buildings<br>Low-income housing |

You should note, in the last row of Table 11-2, that any real property purchased after 1986 is Section 1250 property. This result occurs because all real property purchased after 1986 is subject to the MACRS depreciation system. Under MACRS, all real property is depreciated using the straight-line method. Thus, all real property purchased after 1986 is once again Section 1250 property, and the original distinction between Section 1245 and Section 1250 properties is restored. The practical effect of this reclassification and the use of straight-line depreciation for real property under MACRS is that there is no excess depreciation to recapture on real property purchased after 1986.

## 11-6d Unrecaptured Section 1250 Gain

LO 9 Explain the treatment of unrecaptured Section 1250 gains.

Unrecaptured Section 1250 gain on the sale of real property by individuals is taxed at a maximum rate of 25 percent. **Unrecaptured Section 1250 gain** is the amount of gain not otherwise treated as ordinary income that would be ordinary income if the property were Section 1245 property.[16]

**Example 39** Ryan bought an apartment building in 1985 for $800,000. The building is sold in the current year for $700,000. Ryan deducts $600,000 in depreciation on the building. Straight-line depreciation for the same period would have been $400,000. What is the character of the gain on the sale of the building?

**Discussion: The gain on the sale of the building is $500,000. The apartment building is a Section 1231 property. The $200,000 of excess depreciation is recaptured as ordinary income, leaving a $300,000 Section 1231 gain:**

| | |
|---|---|
| Amount realized on sale | $ 700,000 |
| Adjusted basis ($800,000 − $600,000) | (200,000) |
| Gain on sale | $ 500,000 |
| Depreciation recapture—ordinary income ($600,000 − $400,000) | (200,000) |
| Section 1231 gain | $ 300,000 |

**If the building had been Section 1245 property, the $500,000 gain would have been recaptured as ordinary income ($500,000 gain < $600,000 depreciation). The unrecaptured Section 1250 gain is $300,000 ($500,000 − $200,000). The $300,000 Section 1231 gain is subject to the Section 1231 netting.**

The amount of unrecaptured Section 1250 gain taxed at 25 percent cannot exceed the net Section 1231 gain (Section 1231 gain after applying the lookback recapture rule) for the year.

**Example 40** Assume that in example 39, Ryan also has a $100,000 Section 1231 loss in the current year. What is the character of the gain on the sale of the building?

**Discussion: Ryan's $300,000 Section 1231 gain is netted with the $100,000 Section 1231 loss, resulting in a $200,000 net Section 1231 gain. The $200,000 net Section 1231 gain is Ryan's unrecaptured Section 1250 gain.**

**Example 41** Assume that in example 40, Ryan has the following capital gains and losses in the current year:

| | |
|---|---|
| Short-term capital loss | $(20,000) |
| Long-term capital loss carryover | (15,000) |
| Long-term capital gain | 30,000 |

If Ryan's marginal tax rate is 32%, what is the effect of the sale of the office building on his taxable income and his income tax liability?

**Discussion: In the capital gain and loss netting procedure, the $200,000 unrecaptured Section 1250 gain is a long-term capital gain. Ryan has a $20,000 net short-term capital loss and a $215,000 net long-term capital gain. This results in a $195,000 net long-term capital gain:**

| | | |
|---|---|---|
| Short-term capital loss | | $ (20,000) |
| Long-term capital gain | $ 30,000 | |
| Long-term capital loss carryover | (15,000) | |
| Unrecaptured Section 1250 gain | 200,000 | |
| Net long-term capital gain | | 215,000 |
| Net long-term capital gain | | $195,000 |

**The net long-term capital gain is added to Ryan's gross income, increasing his taxable income by $195,000. In calculating his tax liability, there is no 28% tax rate gain, and the $35,000 of capital losses reduces the unrecaptured Section 1250 gain to $165,000 ($200,000 − $20,000 − $15,000). Ryan's adjusted net capital gain is $30,000 ($195,000 − $165,000). The adjusted net capital gain is taxed at 15%. Because his marginal tax rate is greater than 25%, the $165,000 unrecaptured Section 1250 gain is taxed at 25%. Ryan's income tax liability increases by $45,750:**

| | |
|---|---|
| Tax on adjusted net capital gain—$30,000 × 15% | $ 4,500 |
| Tax on unrecaptured Section 1250 gain—$165,000 × 25% | 41,250 |
| Increase in tax liability | $45,750 |

## concept check

Through the *legislative grace concept*, gains on certain business assets are taxed as long-term capital gains while losses on such assets retain their ordinary loss character. In providing this relief, Congress has limited the relief to the net Section 1231 gain that exceeds the net Section 1231 losses that were deducted in the previous five years. In addition, this relief is not available on gain that is attributable to the depreciation taken on a Section 1245 asset or gain attributable to depreciation in excess of straight-line on a Section 1250 asset, both of which are recaptured as ordinary income. Individuals are further limited on Section 1250 gains by taxing the unrecaptured Section 1250 gain (the gain that would have been ordinary income if the property were Section 1245 property) at a 25% maximum tax rate rather than the 15% long-term capital gains rate.

# CHAPTER SUMMARY

Whenever property is disposed of, the realized gain or loss from the disposition must be calculated. Dispositions of property occur as a result of sales, exchanges, casualties and thefts, and abandonments and retirements. The realized gain or loss is equal to the amount realized less the adjusted basis of the property. The amount realized from a disposition is the gross selling price less the costs incurred in making the disposition. The gross selling price is equal to the net value received by the taxpayer for the property.

All realized gains and losses are not recognized in the period in which they are realized. Gains from certain types of transactions (as discussed in Chapter 12) are deferred for future recognition. Losses from other types of transactions (wash sales, related party sales) are also deferred. Losses on the sale of personal use assets are never deductible. Thus, after the realized gain or loss on a disposition has been calculated, the amount that must be recognized in the current period must be determined.

Recognized gains and losses are then categorized according to the use of the property creating the gain or loss. All property can be categorized as ordinary income property, capital gain property, Section 1231 property, or personal use property. Once categorized, gains and losses are treated according to the rules for the particular category of property.

Ordinary gains and losses receive no special treatment in the calculation of taxable income. Losses on the sale of personal use property are not deductible, whereas gains on personal use property are subject to tax as capital gains. Thus, the primary distinction as to the effect on income involves ordinary income property, capital gain property, and Section 1231 property.

Before any gain on the sale of a depreciable asset is characterized as a capital gain or a Section 1231 gain, the appropriate depreciation recapture rule must be applied. Thus, gains on disposition of depreciable capital assets and Section 1231 property will produce ordinary income to the extent required by the depreciation recapture rules. This requires that the appropriate depreciation recapture be calculated before proceeding with the capital asset and Section 1231 netting. In addition, because the ultimate result of the Section 1231 netting is to tax net Section 1231 gains as long-term capital gains, the Section 1231 netting must be performed before the capital gain-and-loss netting. The year-end process for property dispositions is charted in Exhibit 11-3.

Section 1231 netting is done after applying the applicable depreciation recapture rules. If the netting results in a loss, all Section 1231 gains and losses for the year are considered ordinary gains and losses. If the Section 1231 netting results in a gain, the resulting gain is treated as a long-term capital gain that is combined with other capital gains and losses in the capital gain-and-loss netting procedure.

The goal of the capital gain-and-loss netting procedure is to reduce all gains and losses for the year to a net position that is either a gain or a loss. This is accomplished by determining a net short-term gain or loss for the year and a net long-term gain or loss for the year. If the short-term and long-term positions are the same, no further netting is required. If the two positions are opposite, a second netting of the short-term and long-term positions is required to reduce the transactions to one net position for the year, either a gain or loss.

Only individuals receive preferential treatment for net capital gains; net capital gains of corporations are ordinary income. Individuals are taxed at 0%, 15%, and 20% based on the breakpoints. The breakpoint for 15% is $40,400 (single) and $80,800 (married) taxpayers. The 20% breakpoint is $445,850 (single) and $501,600 (married) on adjusted net capital gains. Unrecaptured Section 1250 gains are taxed at a maximum rate of 25 percent. Net collectibles gains and gains on qualified small business stock are taxed at a maximum rate of 28 percent. Net capital loss deductions are limited. For individuals, only $3,000 in net capital losses is deductible, with any remaining loss carried forward indefinitely. Corporations can deduct capital losses only against capital gains. Thus, a current-year capital loss can be deducted only against capital gains from the previous three years (carryback period) and in the succeeding five years (carryforward period).

Because of the different treatments accorded various types of gains and losses, the proper characterization of gains and losses on dispositions is crucial to the proper calculation of taxable income.

*Exhibit 11-3*

## Summary of the Property Disposition Process

LO 10
Identify a framework for analyzing the effect of a variety of different asset dispositions on taxable income for the year.

1. Determine the amount of realized and recognized gain or loss from each property disposition occurring during the year.
2. Classify all recognized gains and losses as
   a. Ordinary income property
   b. Capital gain property
   c. Section 1231 property
   d. Personal use property
3. All depreciable property sold at a gain is classified as either Section 1245 or Section 1250 property, and the appropriate depreciation recapture rule is applied. On real property, individuals must determine the unrecaptured Section 1250 gain. Any gain remaining is either a capital gain or a Section 1231 gain, according to the classification made in step 2. *Depreciable property sold at a loss is not subject to recapture.*
4. Perform the Section 1231 netting procedure. If the netting results in a loss, the loss is ordinary. If the netting process results in a gain, the net Section 1231 gain is a long-term capital gain.
5. Perform the capital gain-and-loss netting procedure. Include in the netting any long-term capital gain from the Section 1231 netting.
6. Apply the treatment rules for capital gains and losses to the results of the capital gain-and-loss netting.
   a. Net long-term capital gains of individuals are given preferential treatment:
      1. Adjusted net capital gains are taxed at 15%.
      2. Unrecaptured Section 1250 gains are taxed at a maximum rate of 25%.
      3. Net collectibles gains and gains on qualified small business stock are taxed at a maximum rate of 28%.
   b. Deductions for net long-term capital losses are limited:
      1. Individuals can deduct only $3,000 in net capital losses per year.
      2. Corporations can deduct net capital losses only against capital gains. This is done by allowing a 3-year carryback and 5-year carryforward for deduction of a current-year net capital loss.

# KEY TERMS

adjusted net capital gain (p. 11-12)
amount realized (p. 11-4)
capital asset (p. 11-8)
depreciation recapture (p. 11-22)
gross sales price (p. 11-4)
holding period (p. 11-8)
lookback recapture rule (p. 11-20)
net collectibles gains (p. 11-12)
qualified small business stock (p. 11-13)
recognized gain (p. 11-3)
recognized loss (p. 11-3)
Section 1231 gains (p. 11-18)
Section 1231 losses (p. 11-18)
Section 1231 netting procedure (p. 11-19)
Section 1231 property (p. 11-18)

Reinforce this chapter's concepts by going to **www.cengage.com**

# PRIMARY TAX LAW SOURCES

[1]Sec. 1001—Defines gain or loss on the sale or other disposition of property.

[2]Reg. Sec. 1.001-2—Discusses the effect of discharges of liabilities on the amount realized from the sale or other disposition of property.

[3]Sec. 1221—Defines *capital assets.*

[4]Sec. 1222—Defines *holding periods for short-term and long-term capital gains and losses.*

[5]Sec. 1223—Provides rules for determining the holding period of property in different circumstances.

[6]Reg. Sec. 1.1222-1—Defines the *capital gain-and-loss netting procedure.*

[7]Sec. 1(h)—Defines *collectibles gains and losses* and *unrecaptured Section 1250 gain.* Prescribes the tax rates to be paid on capital gains.

[8]IRS Restructuring and Reform Act of 1998, Sec. 5000—Provides the netting rules for capital gains and losses in calculating the tax on capital gains.

[9]Sec. 1202—Defines *qualified small business stock.* Provides for a 50 percent exclusion of gain on the sale of qualified small business stock. The exclusion percentage is increased to 75 percent for stock acquired after February 17, 2009, and before September 27, 2010. The exclusion percentage is further increased to 100 percent for stock acquired after September 27, 2010.

[10]Sec. 165—Treats losses from worthless securities as occurring on the last day of the tax year in which the security becomes worthless.

[11]Reg. Sec. 1.1012-1—Provides rules for identifying securities sold, including what constitutes specific identification of a security sold.

[12]Reg. Sec. 1.1231-1—Explains the Section 1231 netting procedure and gives examples of its application.

[13]Reg. Sec. 1.1245-1—Explains the general operation of Section 1245 and gives examples of the application of Section 1245 in various situations.

[14]Reg. Sec. 1.1250-2—Defines *excess depreciation* and gives examples of the calculation of excess depreciation for purposes of recapture under Section 1250.

[15]Reg. Sec. 1.1245-6—States that all other nonrecognition provisions of the tax law are overridden by Section 1245. A similar provision is found in Section 1.1250-1 of the Treasury regulations relating to Section 1250 recapture.

[16]Notice 97-59—Clarifies that unrecaptured Section 1250 gain does not include gain recaptured as ordinary income under Section 1250.

# DISCUSSION QUESTIONS

1. **LO2** In determining the amount of a realized gain or loss to be recognized in the current year, certain types of gains and losses are deferred, whereas others are disallowed. What is the difference between deferring a gain or loss realized in the current period and disallowing the recognition of a current period loss? Give at least one example of each that has been studied to date in this course.
2. **LO3** What effect does the assumption of a seller's debt have on the amount realized from the disposition of a property?
3. **LO3** Are brokerage commissions paid on the sale of stock a current period expense? Explain.
4. **LO3** In a transaction in which the seller of property agrees to take other property from the buyer as part of the sales price, why is the buyer's adjusted basis unimportant in determining the amount realized by the seller?
5. **LO4** What is the purpose of the capital gain-and-loss netting procedure?
6. **LO4** Why is a distinction made between long-term capital gain (loss) property and short-term capital gain (loss) property?
7. **LO4** What is (are) the current tax advantage(s) of selling an asset at a long-term capital gain?
8. **LO4** Evaluate the following statement: Corporations can never deduct net capital losses.
9. **LO4** Under what conditions may a taxpayer exclude a portion of a realized capital gain?
10. **LO5** What basic tax-planning strategy should a taxpayer with a large net capital gain for the year pursue before the end of the year?
11. **LO4** How should taxpayers determine the basis of securities sold when their portfolios contain several purchases of the same stock at different prices? Explain.
12. **LO4** When does a taxpayer realize a loss on a worthless security? What is the amount of realized loss? What rules govern the recognition of a loss on a worthless security? Explain.
13. **LO6** What is Section 1231 property?
14. **LO6** What is the tax advantage of selling a Section 1231 property at a gain?
15. **LO4, 6** One primary problem in properly accounting for property dispositions is differentiating capital assets and Section 1231 property. Why is it important to correctly identify as either a capital asset or a Section 1231 property an asset that has been disposed of? Explain.
16. **LO6** Explain the lookback rule as it applies to the Section 1231 netting procedure.

17. **LO7** The chapter noted that all depreciable property is subject to the depreciation recapture rules. What is the intent of the depreciation recapture rules?

18. **LO8** How are the recapture provisions for Section 1245 and Section 1250 property different?

19. **LO8** Are buildings always Section 1250 property? If not, explain the circumstances under which a building would not be Section 1250 property.

20. **LO8** Some tax theorists have noted that in most cases, a sale of a depreciable asset will not be accorded capital gain treatment. What would prompt tax theorists to make this statement?

21. **LO9** What is unrecaptured Section 1250 gain, and how is the gain taxed?

## PROBLEMS

22. **LO3** Determine the amount realized in each of the following property dispositions:
    a. Herbert sells some land he owns to Elroy in exchange for $23,000 in cash and two breeding hogs worth $1,500 each (adjusted basis of $500 each). In closing the sale, Herbert incurs legal fees of $600, title search costs of $250, and document filing fees of $50.
    b. Saada Corporation sells a building it owned to Paris, who finances the purchase by obtaining a $200,000 loan and paying an additional $20,000 in cash. As part of the sales agreement, Saada agrees to pay the $4,000 in points that Paris had to pay to obtain the loan. The corporation incurs commission costs of $12,000 and $5,000 in legal fees in making the sale.
    c. Andrew and Sandra agree to exchange land that each owns. Andrew's land is worth $46,000, and Sandra's land is worth $51,000. Therefore, in the exchange of the land, Andrew has to pay Sandra $5,000.
    d. Artworld, Inc., sells its building to Paula for $22,000 in cash. As part of the sales agreement, Paula agrees to assume Artworld's $90,000 mortgage on the property.

23. **LO3** Determine the amount realized in each of the following property dispositions:
    a. Umberto wants to buy Kevin's truck. Because Umberto has no cash and cannot obtain a loan to finance the purchase, Kevin agrees to let Umberto pay him $320 a month for six months. In addition, Umberto agrees to put a new roof on Kevin's house as part of the truck purchase. Umberto estimates that his cost of reroofing the house will be $750, although he would have charged Kevin $2,500 if Kevin were a paying customer.
    b. During the current year, a tornado totally destroys a warehouse that Ajax, Inc., uses in its manufacturing operation. The warehouse has a fair market value of $195,000. Ajax's insurance company pays $170,000 on the destruction of the warehouse. The president of Ajax is upset that the insurance company will not pay full fair market value, because Ajax had paid annual insurance premiums of $10,000 for the last 10 years on the warehouse.
    c. Paloma Pitchfork Company sells an apartment complex it owns to Greedy Investors, Inc. The terms of the sale call for Greedy to pay $40,000 cash, assume Paloma's $520,000 mortgage debt on the property, and give Paloma 10,000 shares of Horticulture, Inc., common stock. Greedy had paid $16 per share for the Horticulture stock, which is currently trading for $5 per share.
    d. Melinda and Nancy agree to exchange apartment buildings and the related mortgage debt on each building. Melinda's apartment building is worth $250,000 and is encumbered by a mortgage of $100,000. Nancy's building is worth $300,000 and has a $200,000 mortgage. In addition to exchanging the properties and the underlying debt, Nancy pays Melinda $50,000 cash to complete the exchange.

24. **LO3** Tuyen is negotiating the sale of her lakefront property near Wabasha. Nils is offering the following: Communication Skills

- Cash of $10,000
- A parcel of land near Red Wing valued at $5,000 with an adjusted basis of $3,000
- A ski boat valued at $9,000 with an adjusted basis of $15,000
- Installation of new heating and air conditioning in Tuyen's Rochester residence (Nils's labor and equipment costs are valued at $4,500)
- Payment of $2,000 in real estate taxes due on the property
- Assumption of the $120,000 balance of the mortgage on the property
- Payment of the $900 in attorney fees and $50 in filing fees to complete the transaction

In addition, Tuyen is offering to transfer her pontoon boat and outboard motor to Nils. The boat and motor have a fair market value of $8,500 and an adjusted basis of $10,000. Also, she would assume the $3,000 mortgage balance on the Red Wing real estate.

Tuyen's brother tells her she should not accept an offer of less than $150,000 for the Wabasha property. Write a letter to Tuyen explaining how much she would realize if she accepts Nils's offer as presented.

25. **LO3** Determine the amount of gain or loss realized and the amount of gain or loss to be recognized in each of the following dispositions:
    a. On October 1, Rufus Partnership sells land to Gerald for which it had paid $32,000. Gerald agrees to pay Rufus $15,000 and to assume Rufus's $13,000 mortgage on the land. In addition, Gerald agrees to pay $1,000 in property taxes on the land for the entire year.
    b. Carrie sells to her brother Dolph for $4,000 stock that had cost her $9,000. Several years later, Dolph sells the stock for $13,000.
    c. Jill wants to refurnish her new home. As part of her refurnishing plan, she sells all her old living room furniture for $1,800; it had cost her $4,200. She uses the $1,800 as a down payment on new furniture costing $6,000.
    d. Upon obtaining a job in New City, Gary sells his house for $130,000. He pays selling expenses of $12,000. Gary had paid $60,000 for the house and had added a den at a cost of $22,000 and a swimming pool costing $16,000.

26. **LO3** Determine the amount of gain or loss realized and the amount of gain or loss to be recognized in each of the following dispositions:
    a. Jorge owns 800 shares of Archer Company stock. He had purchased 300 of the shares for $9,000 and 500 of the shares for $10,000. During the current year, Jorge instructs his broker to sell 400 of the shares when their market value hits $29. He pays a $300 commission on the sale.
    b. Alana owns 300 shares of Courtney common stock that had cost her $6,000. On February 1, she sells the 300 shares for $4,800 and pays a $300 commission on the sale. On February 19, Alana purchases 500 shares of Courtney common stock for $5,300 plus a $400 commission.
    c. Janet goes to the local flea market on Saturday morning and purchases a painting for $20. Although she doesn't really want the painting, she feels that the frame alone is worth $20. When she returns home, she takes the old painting out of the frame and finds another painting hidden in the back. She takes the new painting to a local art dealer who tells her it is almost certainly a Pistachio and worth at least $20,000. Janet decides that she will wait a couple of years, get another expert's opinion, and see if she can sell the painting for more than $20,000.
    d. Enrique owns some land that he is holding as an investment. A local developer wants to build a housing project on the north side of his land. The local utility company wants to run utility lines along the east side of Enrique's land. Enrique had paid $8,000 for the land but does not want to sell it yet because he thinks the housing project will greatly enhance its value. He agrees to accept $2,000 from the utility company for an easement to run its lines along the edge of his property. Enrique estimates that the lines will use up about 1/50 of his land.

Communication Skills

27. **LO3** During the current year, James sells some land he purchased in 2016 as an investment. He had paid $4,000 in cash and borrowed $22,000 to buy the land. He had paid legal fees of $440 and commissions of $560 on the purchase. He sells the land on October 1 to DeWayne, who gives James 200 shares of Aardvark common stock with a fair market value of $9,600 (DeWayne had paid $3,700 for the stock) and assumes James's debt on the land, which is $20,800 at the time of sale. James pays legal fees of $400 and $1,800 of commissions on the sale. DeWayne pays legal fees of $575 and commissions of $980 related to the purchase. In addition, DeWayne agrees to pay the property taxes of $800 on the land for the entire year.

    Assume you are a staff accountant in a CPA firm. Write a memorandum to your supervisor explaining James's gain or loss on the land sale, James's basis in the common stock received, DeWayne's gain or loss on the transaction, and DeWayne's basis in the land.

Communication Skills

28. **LO3** Elvira owns an office building, and Jared Partnership owns an apartment building. Each property is encumbered by a mortgage. Elvira and Jared Partnership agree to exchange their properties and mortgages, with any difference to be paid in cash. The fair market values, mortgages, and adjusted bases for the properties are as follows:

| | Elvira's Building | Jared Partnership Building |
|---|---|---|
| Fair market value | $220,000 | $250,000 |
| Mortgage debt | 80,000 | 150,000 |
| Adjusted basis | 100,000 | 175,000 |

    a. Write a letter to Elvira explaining who will have to pay cash to complete the exchange, the amount of her gross selling price, and the amount of gain or loss she will realize on the exchange.
    b. Write a letter to Jared Partnership explaining who will have to pay cash to complete the exchange, the amount of the gross selling price of its property, and the amount of gain or loss it will realize on the exchange.

29. **LO3** Guerda owns 1,500 shares of Ditchdirt common stock. During the current year, she sells 500 shares of the stock for $15 per share and pays a commission of $300 on the sale. Guerda had purchased the 1,500 shares as follows:

| Purchase Date | No. of Shares | Purchase Price | Commissions Paid |
|---|---|---|---|
| 1/18/19 | 200 | $1,600 | $200 |
| 5/12/19 | 100 | 1,100 | 100 |
| 9/11/19 | 300 | 3,000 | 300 |
| 2/15/20 | 400 | 5,500 | 500 |
| 12/31/20 | 500 | 2,700 | 300 |

    What is Guerda's gain or loss on the sale of the stock?

30. **LO3** Return to the facts of problem 29. Assume that Guerda later sells an additional 200 shares of the Ditchdirt stock for $20 per share, paying a commission of $600 on the sale. What is her gain or loss on the sale of the stock?

31. **LO3** Return to the facts of problem 29. Assume that Guerda sells the remaining 800 shares of Ditchdirt stock for $10 per share and pays a commission of $400 on the sale. What is her gain or loss on the sale?

32. **LO3** Return to the facts of problem 29. What tax-planning strategy can be used to achieve more favorable tax results? Use this strategy to determine Guerda's gain or loss on the sale.

33. **LO4, 6** Classify each of the following assets as ordinary income property, capital asset property, Section 1231 property, or personal use property. If more than one classification is possible, explain the circumstances that would determine the proper classification.

a. Sarah is a sculptor. During the current year, she gives one of her statues to her niece as a gift.
b. Petros sells facsimiles of Greek artifacts in a store he owns. Because of a cash-flow problem, he sells some accounts receivable to a discounter for 75 percent of face value.
c. Lana is a college professor. She owns an apartment building and rents apartments to students.
d. Ryan uses his automobile 75 percent of the time in his job as a real estate salesperson. The remaining use of the automobile is for personal purposes.
e. Fred owns a used car business. During the current year, he purchases a piece of land across the street from his used car business. Fred intends to expand his business and feels that he will ultimately need the space for the extra inventory he wants to purchase over the next few years.
f. Althea gets a tip from a friend that a new golf course is going to be developed south of town. Because she thinks the surrounding land is sure to appreciate in value after the golf course is built, Althea purchases several plots of land near where her friend tells her the golf course is to be built.

34. **LO4, 6** Classify each of the following assets as ordinary income property, capital asset property, Section 1231 property, or personal use property. If more than one classification is possible, explain the circumstances that would determine the proper classification.
    a. Letters written by then-Vice President Harry Truman to Helena Desponsa on the day Franklin Delano Roosevelt died. Desponsa still holds the letters.
    b. Ritva is a home-building contractor. She built her own principal residence.
    c. Domingos, a real estate broker, owns undeveloped land as an investment.
    d. Chas Automobile Plaza, Inc., owns cars held for resale to customers.
    e. Arcie, Inc., buys a utility van from Chas Automotive Plaza to use in its concrete installation business.
    f. Anne Marie Arcie, the president of Arcie, Inc., buys a car to use for commuting to the corporate offices from her home.

35. **LO4** Spencer purchases 100 shares of Reality Virtual Corporation common stock for $1,200 on July 30, 2021. He sells 75 shares of this stock for $525 on December 27, 2021. On January 12, 2022, Spencer purchases 300 shares of Reality Virtual stock for $2 per share.
    a. What are the tax effects of these transactions?
    b. What is the adjusted basis of Spencer's stock on April 15, 2022, when the FMV of the stock is $9 per share?

36. **LO4** Mort begins investing in stocks in 2020. Listed here are his stock transactions for 2020 and 2021. Determine Mort's gain or loss on his stock transactions for 2020 and 2021. In addition, for each sale of stock, determine whether the gain or loss is short-term or long-term.

| Stock | Transaction Date | Transaction | Price per Share | Commissions Paid |
|---|---|---|---|---|
| Pepper Farm | 5/24/20 | Purchased 50 shares | $ 8 | $ 50 |
| Acala Steel | 10/5/20 | Purchased 200 shares | 14 | 200 |
| Horton, Inc. | 12/10/20 | Purchased 300 shares | 3 | 100 |
| Acala Steel | 12/28/20 | Sold 50 shares | 18 | 70 |
| Horton, Inc. | 2/4/21 | Purchased 200 shares | 2 | 30 |
| Pepper Farm | 2/15/21 | Sold 25 shares | 12 | 25 |
| Horton, Inc. | 3/1/21 | Sold 100 shares | 2 | 20 |
| Pepper Farm | 8/13/21 | Sold 25 shares | 13 | 35 |
| Angor Mills | 11/11/21 | Purchased 800 shares | 6 | 400 |
| Angor Mills | 12/4/21 | Sold 300 shares | 9 | 250 |
| Horton, Inc. | 12/19/21 | Sold 400 shares | 7 | 250 |

37. **LO4** For each of the following capital asset dispositions, determine whether the taxpayer has realized a gain or loss on the disposition and whether that gain or loss is short-term or long-term.
   a. Ari receives some stock from his grandfather Stephan for Christmas. Stephan paid $4,300 for the stock three years earlier. The stock has a fair market value of $7,000 on December 24. Ari sells it on December 28 for $7,100 and pays a commission of $500 on the sale.
   b. Joan owns 600 shares of Archibald common stock that she purchased in 2017 for $7,920. On July 1, 2021, Archibald declares and distributes a 10 percent stock dividend. Joan sells the 660 shares of Archibald stock on November 14, 2021, for $13,400 and pays a $700 commission on the sale.
   c. On April 1, 2021, LeRoy sells to his son for $3,000 shares of stock for which he had paid $8,000 two years earlier. His son sells the shares for $11,000 on June 14, 2021.
   d. Lee owns 800 shares of Bolstead, Inc., stock that she purchased for $20,000 on October 11, 2020. On July 5, 2021, she sells 400 shares of Bolstead stock for $7,000. On July 27, 2021, Lee purchases an additional 600 shares of Bolstead stock for $6,000. On December 3, 2021, she sells the remaining 1,000 shares of Bolstead stock for $12,000.

38. **LO4** For each of the following capital asset dispositions, determine whether the taxpayer has realized a gain or loss and whether that gain or loss is short-term or long-term:
   a. Larry's aunt June dies on May 4, 2021. He inherits some land that she purchased in 2021 for $2,000. On May 4, 2021, the land is worth $40,000. Larry receives title to the land on October 15, 2021, and sells it on November 27, 2021, for $40,000. He pays $3,000 in commissions and other selling expenses.
   b. Sterling receives 4,000 shares of Suburb Corporation stock as a birthday present from his mother-in-law on May 6, 2021. His mother-in-law had paid $18,000 for the stock eight years earlier. On May 6, 2021, the stock has a fair market value of $4,000. On June 18, 2021, Sterling sells 1,000 shares of the stock for $800.
   c. Assume the same facts as in part b. Suburb Corporation becomes the target of a takeover attempt in July, and its stock soars. Sterling sells the remaining 3,000 shares for $19,000 on August 6, 2021.
   d. Bert owns 1,000 shares of Crooner Capital Corporation common stock for which he paid $8,000 in 2014 On March 13, 2020, Crooner declares a dividend of 1 share of preferred stock for each 10 shares of common stock owned. On the date the preferred shares are distributed, Crooner's common shares are selling for $7 per share, and its preferred shares are selling for $10 per share. On November 14, 2021, Bert sells the 100 preferred shares for $1,100.

39. **LO4** Rudy has the following capital gains and losses for the current year. What is the effect of the capital asset transactions on his taxable income? Explain and show any calculations.

| | |
|---|---|
| Short-term capital loss | $15,500 |
| Long-term capital gain | 11,600 |
| Long-term capital loss | 4,500 |

40. **LO4** Judith Corporation has the following gains and losses from sales of capital assets during the current year. What is the effect of the capital asset transactions on Judith's taxable income? Explain and show any calculations.

| | |
|---|---|
| Short-term capital gain | $2,700 |
| Short-term capital loss | 5,600 |
| Long-term capital loss | 200 |

41. **LO4** Return to the facts of problem 40. Assume that Judith is an individual taxpayer. What is the effect of the capital asset transactions on Judith's taxable income? Compare this result with the result in problem 40.

42. **LO4** Tate has the following gains and losses from sales of capital assets during the current year. What is the effect of the capital asset transactions on Tate's taxable income? Explain, and show any calculations.

| | |
|---|---|
| Short-term capital gain | $3,600 |
| Long-term capital gain | 8,400 |
| Long-term capital loss | 5,200 |

43. **LO4** Troy has the following gains and losses from sales of capital assets during the current year. What is the effect of the capital asset transactions on his taxable income? Explain, and show any calculations.

| | |
|---|---|
| Short-term capital gain | $7,800 |
| Short-term capital loss | 9,000 |
| Long-term capital gain | 5,400 |
| Long-term capital loss | 2,100 |

44. **LO4** Rollie has the following capital gains and losses during the current year:

| | |
|---|---|
| Short-term capital gain | $ 3,000 |
| Collectibles gain | 4,000 |
| Long-term capital gain | 11,000 |
| Long-term capital loss | 6,000 |

Rollie is married and has a taxable income of $75,000 before considering the effect of his capital gains and losses. What is the effect of Rollie's capital gains and losses on his taxable income and his income tax liability?

45. **LO4** Loretta has the following capital gains and losses during the current year:

| | |
|---|---|
| Short-term capital loss | $ 4,000 |
| Collectibles gain | 10,000 |
| Long-term capital gain | 8,000 |
| Long-term capital loss carryover | 2,000 |

Loretta is single and has a taxable income of $200,000 before considering the effect of her capital gains and losses. What is the effect of Loretta's capital gains and losses on her taxable income and her income tax liability?

46. **LO4** Samantha has the following capital gains and losses during the current year:

| | |
|---|---|
| Short-term capital loss | $ 7,000 |
| Short-term capital gain | 5,000 |
| Collectibles loss | 11,000 |
| Long-term capital gain | 8,000 |
| Long-term capital loss | 4,000 |

Samantha is married and has a taxable income of $119,000 before considering the effect of her capital gains and losses. What is the effect of Samantha's capital gains and losses on her taxable income and her income tax liability?

47. **LO4** Jie has the following capital gains and losses during the current year:

| | |
|---|---|
| Short-term capital loss | $ 2,000 |
| Collectibles gain | 3,000 |
| Unrecaptured Section 1250 gain | 8,000 |
| Long-term capital gain | 12,000 |
| Long-term capital loss carryover | 7,000 |

Jie is married, files jointly, and has a taxable income of $520,000 before considering the effect of her capital gains and losses. What is the effect of Jie's capital gains and losses on her taxable income and her income tax liability?

48. **LO4** Yorgi purchases qualified small business stock in Gnu Company, Inc., on September 15, 2008, for $50,000. She sells the shares for $400,000 on December 30, 2021. The stock retains its qualified small business status through the date of the sale.
   a. Determine the amount of realized and recognized gain on the sale.
   b. What is Yorgi's effective tax rate on this transaction? (Assume her marginal tax rate is 35 percent.)

49. **LO4** Return to the facts of problem 48. Assume that Yorgi has a net capital loss of $80,000 from her other capital asset transactions in 2021. What is the effect of the sale of the stock on Yorgi's tax liability if her marginal tax rate is 35 percent?

50. **LO4** Return to the facts of problem 48. Assume that Yorgi purchased the qualified small business stock in Gnu Company, Inc., on September 15, 2009, and sells the shares for $400,000 on December 30, 2021.
   a. Determine the amount of realized and recognized gain on the sale.
   b. What is Yorgi's effective tax rate on this transaction? (Assume her marginal tax rate is 35 percent.)

51. **LO4** Return to the facts of problem 50. How would your answer change if Yorgi purchased the qualified small business stock in Gnu Company, Inc., on September 15, 2012, and sells the shares for $400,000 on December 30, 2021?

Communication Skills

52. **LO4** During August 2016, Madeline invests $400,000 in Qual Company, Inc., buying 100,000 shares of stock. Her broker tells her this will be an excellent investment because the securities are qualified small business stock. He predicts the stock will triple in value over the next three years. At the end of 2020, Madeline's shares are valued at $700,000. Madeline is encouraged. She decides that she will cash out of the investment sometime in 2021 if the stock continues to appreciate. Madeline comes to you for advice. Write a letter advising her what she should do.

53. **LO4** In 2010, RAD Partnership was organized by three equal partners: two individuals (Rachael and Adam) and Depesh Corporation. On January 10, 2011, RAD Partnership purchases 18,000 shares of qualified small business stock in Miltown Corporation for $36,000. On December 2, 2021, RAD sells all of the Miltown Corporation stock for $180,000. Rachael, Adam, and Depesh Corporation each have a net capital loss from other transactions of $10,000. What are the tax implications of the sale for:
   a. RAD Partnership
   b. Rachael
   c. Adam
   d. Depesh Corporation

54. **LO4** Marnie buys 500 shares of qualified small business stock in H.R. Pizza, Inc., on September 10, 2008, for $20,000. She sells the 500 shares for $120,000 on October 2, 2021. Marnie's other capital asset transactions consist of a $7,000 short-term capital loss, a $25,000 long-term capital gain, and an $8,000 long-term capital loss carryover from 2020. Marnie is single, and her taxable income is $110,000 without considering her capital asset transactions. What is the effect of the sale of the stock on Marnie's 2021 income tax liability?

Communication Skills

55. **LO5** Neila sells 500 shares of Bolero Corporation stock for $10,500 and pays $500 in sales commissions on September 23 of the current year. She acquired the stock for $4,700 plus $300 in commissions five years ago. Neila owns the following securities in December of the current year.

| Security | Number of Shares | Purchase Date | Basis | Market Value |
|---|---|---|---|---|
| Rondo Corporation | 200 | 2/13/18 | $ 3,000 | $ 6,000 |
| Harley, Inc. | 300 | 4/11/20 | 11,000 | 5,000 |
| Flescher Company | 400 | 7/18/21 | 24,000 | 20,000 |

Write a memorandum to Neila recommending an optimal year-end tax-planning strategy for her capital gains and losses.

56. **LO5** Ansel sells 400 shares of Sharpe, Inc., common stock on October 12, 2021, for $11,800 and pays $600 in commissions on the sale. He acquired the stock for $18,400 plus $800 in commissions on July 8, 2020. Ansel owns the following securities in December 2021:

| Security | Number of Shares | Purchase Date | Basis | Market Value |
|---|---|---|---|---|
| Telio Corporation | 400 | 2/13/18 | $ 2,000 | $ 7,000 |
| Perry, Inc. | 300 | 8/11/19 | 12,000 | 27,000 |
| Header Company | 600 | 4/13/20 | 14,000 | 20,000 |

What actions should Ansel take to optimize his capital gains and losses for 2021?

57. **LO4** Opal's neighbor, Jilian, persuades her to invest in Schaake Corporation, a new venture, on March 4, 2020. Opal pays $15,000 for 3,000 shares of common stock. On February 6, 2021, Schaake Corporation declares bankruptcy and closes its doors forever. Opal never receives a return on her investment or a reimbursement of her original investment. What are the tax consequences to Opal?

58. **LO6** Fred's Foam Foundations (FFF) is a sole proprietorship that Fred started in 2016. Before the current year, FFF had not disposed of any property it owned. During the current year, FFF has the following gains and losses:

| | |
|---|---|
| Casualty loss on foam truck | $3,200 |
| Section 1231 gains | 9,400 |
| Section 1231 losses | 3,000 |

What is the effect of these transactions on Fred's taxable income? Explain, and show the calculations.

59. **LO6** Refer to the facts in problem 58. In the following year, FFF has these gains and losses:

| | |
|---|---|
| Casualty gain on building | $ 5,000 |
| Section 1231 gains | 3,000 |
| Section 1231 losses | 17,000 |

What is the effect of these transactions on Fred's taxable income? Explain, and show the required calculations.

60. **LO6** In 2021, Sondra Corporation recognizes $18,000 in Section 1231 gains and 10,000 in Section 1231 losses. In 2016, Sondra reported $12,000 in Section 1231 losses and no Section 1231 gains. No other Section 1231 gains or losses were recognized by Sondra during the 2016–2020 period. What is the tax treatment of Sondra's 2021 Section 1231 gains and losses?

61. **LO6** Dawn started her own rock band on January 2, 2019. She acquired all her equipment on January 2, 2019, and did not dispose of any of it before 2021. On April 15, 2021, the band's amplifiers, speakers, and other electronic equipment are stolen after a concert. The stolen equipment's basis is $15,000, and its fair market value before the theft is $23,000. The insurance company reimburses Dawn $23,000. Her road bus runs off the highway on September 13, 2021. The basis of the bus is $60,000. Its fair market value before the accident is $80,000, and the fair market value after the accident is $70,000. The insurance company reimburses Dawn $4,000 for the bus accident. Dawn's other -financial gains and losses during 2021 are:

| | |
|---|---|
| Section 1231 gains | $8,000 |
| Section 1231 losses | 9,000 |

What is the effect of these transactions on Dawn's 2021 taxable income? Explain, and show your calculations.

62. **LO6** Rhinelander Corporation has the following net Section 1231 gains and losses for 2016 through 2020:

| | |
|---|---|
| 2016 | $ 8,000 |
| 2017 | (6,000) |
| 2018 | (13,000) |
| 2019 | 11,000 |
| 2020 | 15,000 |

a. What is the proper characterization of the net Section 1231 gains and losses for 2016–2020 for Rhinelander Corporation?

b. Assume that in 2021, Rhinelander has a net Section 1231 gain of $9,000. What is the proper characterization of the $9,000 gain?

63. **LO8** The Gladys Corporation buys office equipment costing $1,114,000 on May 12, 2021. In 2024, new and improved models of the equipment make it obsolete, and Gladys sells the old equipment for $34,000 on December 27, 2024.

a. What is the character of Gladys Corporation's gain or loss on the sale assuming that it takes the maximum cost-recovery deductions allowable on the equipment?
b. What is the character of Gladys Corporation's gain or loss on the equipment assuming that it takes the minimum cost-recovery deduction allowable on the equipment?

Note: The depreciation calculations were done for problem 48, Chapter 10.

64. **LO8** Avalon, Inc., buys equipment costing $150,000 in 2018, and sells it in 2021. Avalon deducts $94,000 in depreciation on the equipment before the sale. What is the character of the gain or loss on the sale of the equipment if the selling price is
a. $90,000? b. $155,000? c. $40,000?

Communication Skills

65. **LO8** Maria sells the automobile she uses in her job as a marketing representative for $3,000. The car cost $15,000 four years earlier. Maria uses the automobile 80 percent of the time in her job and 20 percent of the time for personal purposes. At the date of sale, Maria had taken $10,000 in depreciation on the automobile. Write a letter to Maria explaining the amount and character of her realized gain or loss from the sale and how much she must recognize for tax purposes.

66. **LO8, 9** Alex purchases a building in 1986 at a cost of $500,000. ACRS depreciation on the building totals $320,000, whereas straight-line depreciation would be $260,000 for the same period. Alex sells the building for $620,000.
a. What is Alex's gain on the sale if he deducts the ACRS depreciation on the building?
b. If the building is an apartment building that Alex rents to individuals, what is the character of the gain? Assume that Alex holds the building as an investment.
c. How would your answer to part b change if the building were sold for $105,000?
d. What is Alex's gain on the sale if he deducts the straight-line depreciation on the building?
e. If Alex deducts straight-line depreciation on the building, what is the character of the gain? Assume that Alex holds the building as an investment.

67. **LO8, 9** Manuel is negotiating the sale of two of his rental properties. He has an offer of $500,000 for each condo. Manuel bought one condo in 1986 for $400,000 and has deducted depreciation of $185,000 using ACRS (accelerated depreciation). Straight-line depreciation would have been $125,000 if he had elected to use it. Manuel paid $300,000 for the condo he bought in 1995, and he has deducted depreciation of $81,800 using the MACRS rates for residential real estate. Compare the realized gains or losses and the recognized gains or losses of the two properties, assuming Manuel sells both. Explain the differences.

68. **LO8, 9** Anton purchases a building on May 4, 2003, at a cost of $270,000. The land is properly allocated $30,000 of the cost. Anton sells the building on October 18, 2021, for $270,000. What is the character of Anton's gain or loss on the sale if he uses the regular MACRS system and the building is
a. An apartment building?
b. An office building?

Note: The depreciation calculations for this problem were done for problem 54, Chapter 10.

69. **LO4, 8, 9** Assume that the building in problem 68 is an apartment building held for investment. In addition to the sale of the building, Anton has the following capital gains and losses during 2021:

| | |
|---|---|
| Short-term capital loss | $ 4,000 |
| Collectibles gain | 7,000 |
| Long-term capital gain | 15,000 |
| Long-term capital loss carryover from 2020 | 6,000 |

Anton is single and has a taxable income of $175,000 without considering his capital gains and losses. What is his taxable income and income tax liability?

70. **LO4, 8, 9** Thuy bought a rental house in 2013 for $75,000. In 2021, she sells it for $86,000. Thuy properly deducted $22,000 in depreciation on the house before its sale.
   a. What is the amount and character of the gain on the sale?
   b. Thuy also sells the following securities:

| Security | Purchase Date | Sales Date | Basis | Sales Price |
|---|---|---|---|---|
| Delphi Corporation | 4/13/18 | 4/08/21 | $ 3,000 | $ 7,000 |
| Mondo, Inc. | 6/11/20 | 7/15/21 | 12,000 | 10,000 |
| Horace Company | 4/13/21 | 8/13/21 | 14,000 | 19,000 |

   Determine the amount of tax that Thuy will pay on her capital asset transactions. Assume that she is in the 35 percent marginal tax rate bracket.

## ISSUE IDENTIFICATION PROBLEMS

In each of the following problems, identify the tax issue(s) posed by the facts presented. Determine the possible tax consequences of each issue that you identify.

71. Nadia sells land for $4,000 and the buyer assumes her $13,000 mortgage. She pays $1,000 in real estate commissions on the sale.
72. Luke trades his baseball card collection for an automobile. The automobile is worth $11,000, and Luke assumes the $3,000 loan on the car. Luke has $3,500 invested in his baseball card collection.
73. Marino inherits antique pottery from the estate of his grandmother on March 10, 2021. He immediately sells the pottery for $15,000 to a collector who had made the offer to the executor of the estate several weeks before. The estate valuation of the pottery is $13,000. Marino's grandmother paid $20,000 for the pottery during an October 2019 visit to a flea market, convinced it was a valuable investment—that she was getting a "steal" and the pottery would substantially appreciate over time.
74. Jackie receives 100 shares of stock as a birthday gift from her Uncle Horace. Horace acquired the shares 22 years ago for $4 each. The stock's value on Jackie's birthday is $36 per share. She sells half her shares for $1,500 five months after her birthday and pays a broker $50 to complete the sale.
75. While snorkeling on spring break in Cancun, Melody finds a small bag containing several jewels lodged between some rocks about 25 yards offshore. She reports the find to the local authorities. However, no one has reported a loss of jewels, and Melody is allowed to keep them. Upon returning home, she takes the jewels to an appraiser, who sets their value at $18,000. Because she needs money to pay for her college tuition, dormitory room and board, and books, Melody sells the jewels to a local jewelry store for $16,000.
76. Carter owns 1,200 shares of Echo Corporation stock. He purchased 400 shares of the stock on December 23, 2019, for $48,000, and the other 800 shares on October 31, 2020, for $84,000. On August 14, 2021, he sells 500 shares of the stock for $15,000 and pays a $900 commission on the sale.
77. Martina purchases 10,000 shares of Monrovia Corporation stock for $90,000 on November 14, 2020. On June 18, 2021, Monrovia declares bankruptcy. Because the corporation's assets are less than its liabilities, the stock is determined to be worthless on October 16, 2021.
78. Deskjet Corporation sells equipment with an adjusted basis of $22,000 for $3,000. The corporation paid $43,000 for the equipment three years ago.
79. Bostian Company reports a net Section 1231 gain of $31,000 during the current year.
80. Jammer, Inc., sells a building for $180,000. The company paid $135,000 for the building four years earlier and had taken $12,000 in depreciation on it up to the date of the sale.

81. Bernadero Corporation sells a construction crane with an adjusted basis of $32,000 for $37,000. The corporation paid $50,000 for the crane.
82. Harry sells the automobile he has used in his job as a salesman for $2,000. It cost $15,000 four years earlier. Harry used the automobile 70 percent of the time in his job and 30 percent of the time for personal purposes. At the date of sale, Harry had taken $10,000 in depreciation on the car.
83. Tawana purchased real property in 2019 at a cost of $200,000. In 2021, she is experiencing cash-flow problems and sells the property for $220,000. The adjusted basis of the property is $185,000.

## TECHNOLOGY APPLICATIONS

Tax Simulation

84. In 2020 Nuts & Seeds Inc., purchased a new "high-tech" shelling machine from Soft-Core Corporation. Nuts and Seeds paid $1,000 in cash and gave Soft-Core a $29,000 note. The note is nonrecourse and Soft-Core's only recourse in the event of default by Nuts & Seeds is to take back the shelling machine. The sales agreement allows Nuts & Seeds to transfer ownership of the machine back to Soft-Core at any time to satisfy payment of the remaining indebtedness on the note. Nuts & Seeds elects to expense the $30,000 cost of the machine in 2020. The shelling machine doesn't live up to expectations, and in 2021, Nuts & Seeds transfers ownership of the machine back to Soft-Core, thereby satisfying the indebtedness on the note. At the time of the transfer, the fair market value of the shelling machine is $16,000 and the remaining principal balance on the note is $28,000.

    REQUIRED: Determine the income tax treatment of Nuts & Seeds Inc.'s transfer of the ownership of the shelling machine in satisfaction of the outstanding debt on the machine. Use a tax research database and find the relevant authority(ies) that form the basis for your answer. Your answer should include the exact text of the authority(ies) and an explanation of the application of the authority to the sale. If there is any uncertainty regarding the tax treatment of the sale, explain what is uncertain and what you need to know to resolve the uncertainty.

Research Skills

85. On April 3, 2020, Arlene sells land that she holds as an investment to a construction company. The deed conveying the land to the construction company contains a covenant restricting construction on the land to single-family residences. The market for apartment buildings picks up in 2021, and the construction company pays Arlene $5,000 on August 10, 2021, to release the restrictive covenant so that it can build apartments on the land. Determine the income tax treatment of the $5,000 payment Arlene receives for the release of the restrictive covenant.

Research Skills

86. Jeremiah owns farm land that he paid $20,000 for in 2009. In 2020, he planted a winter wheat crop on the land, incurring $35,000 of expenses. Jeremiah deducted the $20,000 of planting expenses that he paid in 2020. He pays the remaining $15,000 of expenses in 2021. Jeremiah sells the land together with the unharvested wheat crop for $110,000 in 2021. Determine the tax consequences of the sale of the land.

## INTEGRATIVE PROBLEMS

87. In problem 87 in Chapter 9 and problem 72 in Chapter 10, the initial basis and the adjusted basis of Emelio and Charita's assets were determined as of December 31, 2021. During 2022, they have the following transactions related to the assets:
    a. In June, an electrical connection shorts out and starts a fire in Emelio's building. The cost of repairing the damage caused by the fire is $11,500. Emelio's insurance policy reimburses him $5,500 for the fire damage.
    b. The real estate market begins to deteriorate in 2022. Emelio and Charita decide to sell their rental house before it loses any more value. They sell the house for $76,000 on October 16, 2022. They pay $325 to advertise the property for sale. In addition, they pay $5,200 in brokerage commissions and $1,045

in legal fees on the sale. Because their renters had a one-year rental agreement, Emelio and Charita have to pay the renters $900 to vacate the lease.

c. Emelio's office building is next to a new industrial park development project. The developer needs to run utility lines through Emelio's property. The developer agrees to pay Emelio $2,000 for an easement to run the utility lines along one side of Emelio's property.

d. While assessing the damage caused by the fire, the contractor Emelio hired to repair the damage finds an antique chair that had been sealed behind one wall. Emelio sells the chair to a local dealer for $1,200.

e. Emelio raises the additional cash he needs to complete the building repairs by selling 100 shares of Software Corporation stock for $24 per share. (He pays brokerage commissions of $140.) He also sells 100 shares of Flex Corporation stock for $40 per share. (Brokerage commissions are $200.)

f. Charita decides to upgrade her home office by purchasing new furniture costing $1,300. She gives the old office furniture to her gardener, who agrees to exchange eight weeks of gardening services for the furniture. The gardener normally charges $50 per week.

g. In addition to these transactions, Charita tells you that a company in which she and Emelio had invested went bankrupt in 2020. They had purchased the stock from Charita's father for $24,000 in 2015. The company was dissolved in 2020, and the shareholders received nothing from the bankruptcy proceeding. Emelio and Charita had no other capital asset transactions in 2020 and 2021.

For each of these transactions, determine the realized and recognized gain or loss and the character of the gain or loss. Do the appropriate year-end netting procedures and determine the effect of the transactions on Emelio and Charita's 2022 adjusted gross income and their income tax liability. Assume that Emelio and Charita's adjusted gross income before considering these transactions is $120,000.

88. Duke Plumbing and Wallpaper Company is a corporation that has been in business since 2021. During the current year, it has the following property transactions:

a. A warehouse purchased in 2010 for $200,000 is sold for $180,000. Depreciation taken on the building to date of sale totals $62,000.

b. Wallpaper that cost $60,000 becomes obsolete when a new type of wallpaper is developed. Duke is unable to sell the wallpaper and ends up throwing it in the trash.

c. Two of Duke's service trucks collide in the parking lot, destroying both trucks. The older truck cost $18,000 and had an adjusted basis of $5,000. Its fair market value of $9,000 is reimbursed by Duke's insurance company. The newer truck was purchased three months earlier for $22,000. It has a fair market value of $18,000, which is reimbursed by Duke's insurance company.

d. Plumbing equipment purchased in January for $6,000 is sold in November for $4,000. The equipment was advertised as being the easiest of its kind to use in installing new plumbing fixtures. However, it is so complicated to operate that none of Duke's employees can figure out how to use it, and Duke decides it is easier to do the work the old-fashioned way.

e. Duke's computer system becomes obsolete and is sold for $1,500. Duke paid $15,000 for the system four years earlier and has taken $11,500 in depreciation on the system as of the date of sale.

f. Because the two service trucks that were destroyed (in part c) have to be replaced, Duke decides to sell its other service truck and buy three new trucks. The third service truck cost $19,000 two years earlier and has an adjusted basis of $14,000. Duke receives $15,000 from the sale of the truck.

g. An antique plumbing plunger for which Duke had paid $4,000 and which was fully depreciated is sold for $7,000.

h. Duke decides not to replace the warehouse it sold in part a. The office building it erected in 2013 at a cost of $140,000 to service the warehouse is no longer of any use and is sold for $162,000. The office building has an adjusted basis of $122,000.

For each of these transactions, determine the gain or loss that must be recognized on the transaction and the character of the gain or loss. Determine the effect of all the transactions on Duke's taxable income for the year.

Communication Skills

89. Barney is a farmer who has the following transactions during 2021:
   a. A barn that cost $36,000 in 2013 with an adjusted basis of $16,000 is destroyed by a tornado. Barney's insurance pays him $26,000 for the casualty.
   b. Barney's prize bull, for which he paid $22,000 and which has an adjusted basis of $14,000, is in the barn when the tornado hits. Although the bull is not killed, he is injured severely enough that he can no longer breed. The bull is worth only $2,000 after the casualty (at stud, he was valued at more than $30,000), but he is such a favorite of Barney's that Barney keeps him and puts him out to pasture. Barney's insurance company refuses to pay anything for the bull's injuries.
   c. Breeding cattle that cost $19,500 in 2018 with an adjusted basis of $7,200 are sold for $21,000.
   d. A tractor that cost $20,000 and has an adjusted basis of $12,000 is sold for $7,000.
   e. Stock in Old Mill Company that Barney purchased on November 13, 2020, for $20,000 becomes worthless when Old Mill goes out of business on April 1, 2021.
   f. A horse Barney purchased in February for $8,000 as a gift for his daughter comes up lame and has to be sold for $2,000.
   g. Barney sells 80 acres of farmland for $42,000. He had received the land as a gift from his uncle when he first went into farming. Barney's uncle paid $8,000 for the land, which was worth $30,000 at the time of the gift.

   What is the effect of these transactions on Barney's taxable income for 2021? In solving this problem, first determine the amount and character of gain or loss on each of the transactions. Then, perform the appropriate netting procedures. Your answer should summarize the gains and losses as they would appear on Barney's tax return. Write a letter to Barney explaining the tax results of his transactions.

## DISCUSSION CASES

90. As a gift for her granddaughter Ella's 13th birthday, Melanie bought 500 shares of Soft'n Sales Corporation stock on September 25, 2016. Melanie bought the stock directly from the underwriter for $20,000. Soft'n Sales had just gone public, and Melanie believes the stock will be a good investment for Ella's college education. Melanie tells Ella that she will receive control of the stock on her 18th birthday so long as Ella maintains an A average in high school.

   Soft'n Sales is a software development enterprise in San Diego. At the date of the public offering, its gross assets total $10 million. These assets include mostly intangibles, equipment, and raw materials for product development. The company owns no real estate and holds no investment securities. All capital is reinvested in the enterprise.

   When Ella begins college in September 2021, the Soft'n Sales stock is worth $50,000. Explain Melanie's options for transferring the stock to Ella to use for college expenses. What are the tax implications of each option?

91. Christoffe sells 1,000 shares of HoTech Corporation preferred stock for $37 per share on August 3 of the current year. Sales commissions total $300. The stock's price has been falling since HoTech's management was sued for patent infringement four months ago. The price is expected to keep falling until the lawsuit is settled. Christoffe received the stock as a Christmas gift from his wife last year. She paid $48 per share plus a $400 commission. The year-end is approaching, and he wants to optimize his tax position. Christoffe's current portfolio contains the following corporate stock:

| Stock | Number of Shares | Date Acquired | Adjusted Basis per Share | FMV |
|---|---|---|---|---|
| MURF Corp. | 1,000 | 1/12/18 | $11 | $30 |
| Tellics, Inc. | 2,000 | 8/4/20 | 15 | 18 |
| HIGG Corp. | 600 | 2/9/21 | 41 | 48 |

   Make recommendations to Christoffe.

## TAX PLANNING CASES

92. At the beginning of 2021, Heather owns the following stocks:

| Stock | Date Purchased | Number of Shares | Per Share Price | Commissions |
|---|---|---|---|---|
| Clutch common | 11/30/20 | 250 | $40 | $ 500 |
| Pauley preferred | 4/13/20 | 100 | 10 | 100 |
| Leines common | 10/14/20 | 1,000 | 35 | 2,000 |

In addition to these stocks, Heather received 400 shares of Poor Boy preferred stock from her grandfather as a gift on December 25, 2020. The shares were selling for $25 per share on December 24, 2020. No gift tax was paid on the transfer of the stock. Her grandfather had purchased the shares for $5 per share in 2005.

During 2021, Heather has the following stock transactions:

| Stock | Transaction | Date | Sales Price | Commissions Paid |
|---|---|---|---|---|
| Poor Boy | Sold 100 shares | 3/13 | $ 2,200 | $200 |
| Leines | Sold 400 shares | 6/9 | 5,300 | 300 |
| Clutch | Sold 200 shares | 10/19 | 4,700 | 270 |
| Ragtop common | Purchased 2,000 | 12/19 | 20,000 | 600 |
| Leines | Purchased 200 | 12/25 | 3,550 | 450 |

a. What is Heather's net capital gain or loss for 2021?

b. On December 28, 2021, Heather's stocks have the following fair market value:

| | |
|---|---|
| Pauley | $13 per share |
| Clutch | 28 per share |
| Leines | 23 per share |
| Poor Boy | 37 per share |
| Ragtop | 4 per share |

Assuming that the commission paid on any sale is equal to 5 percent of the selling price, what action(s) would you recommend to Heather to minimize her 2021 tax? Discuss the potential tax effects of selling each of the stocks Heather owns at the end of the year.

c. Assume that in addition to the stock sales, Heather sells some land she inherited from her father. Her father paid $5,000 for the land in 2006. He died on April 14, 2015, when the land was worth $12,000. Heather sells the land on May 21, 2021, for $50,000. Legal fees and commissions of $5,500 are paid on the sale. What is Heather's net capital gain or loss for 2021?

d. Given the fair market values, what action would you recommend Heather take to minimize her 2021 tax? Explain.

93. Rosie has owned a successful luncheonette for several years. Tired of the long hours and eager to try another way of life, she decides to buy a fishing boat and start a charter service near Key West. The only obstacle is the sale of the following assets of the luncheonette to fund her fishing boat endeavor: Communication Skills

| Asset | Date Acquired | Adjusted Basis | Original Cost |
|---|---|---|---|
| Building | 1/12/86 | $ 5,000 ($6,600 if S-L depreciation used) | $50,000 |
| Land | 1/12/86 | 10,000 | 10,000 |
| Equipment | 2/9/17 | 7,800 | 25,000 |
| Supplies | Current year | 5,000 | 5,000 |

Hank, Rosie's part-time cook, offers her $175,000 for the luncheonette, which Rosie believes is a fair price. However, she is concerned about the tax consequences of the sale. For example, she wonders how to allocate the sales price among the assets to receive the most advantageous tax results. Write a letter to Rosie about the best way to make the allocations and explaining the tax effects of your recommendations.

94. Twenty years ago, Consuela Guererro invented and patented a high-speed burrito-stuffing machine. Through the years, she has guarded her invention, al-lowing its use only in El Consuela's, a chain of restaurants in which she owns 60 percent of the stock. (Her basis in the stock is $200,000.) On the advice of her accountant, the patent is owned and manufacturing of the burrito stuffer is done exclusively by Consuela's wholly owned corporation, Stuff, Inc. (Consuela's basis in the Stuff, Inc., stock is $250,000.)

    Consuela has been approached by the Frijoles Company about acquiring her burrito-stuffing operation. Specifically, Frijoles would like to acquire Stuff, Inc.'s patent and burrito-stuffer manufacturing operation. Consuela is tired after spending so many years fighting off the competition, and she agrees to sell to Frijoles. Consuela feels that the patent and manufacturing equipment are worth at least $2,000,000, although they are carried on Stuff, Inc.'s books at their adjusted basis of $100,000. Consuela wants your advice on how best to structure her exit from the burrito-stuffing business. She intends to retain her ownership interest in El Consuela's.

    a. From Consuela's point of view, should she sell the burrito-stuffer assets owned by Stuff, Inc., directly to Frijoles, or should she sell her stock in Stuff, Inc.? Consider not only the tax aspects of the alternatives but also how each alternative could influence the proposed $2,000,000 purchase price.
    b. Consider part a from Frijoles's point of view.

# ETHICS DISCUSSION CASE

Communication Skills

95. You are a CPA who works for a local accounting firm. While having lunch at Willie's Diner last Thursday, you overheard Beth Murray describe how Bart (her spouse) was able to get a $2,000 business loss, free car maintenance for two years, and $4,000 cash to spend on their vacation in exchange for an old truck. You didn't think too much about the conversation until you returned to your office. While you were at lunch, Bart Murray dropped off the tax information for his business, Bart's Mobile Glass Service, for the past year. Your curiosity gets the best of you. You open the packet of information and immediately look for the truck sale information. The only documentation you find is a handwritten memo stating, "2016 Dodge truck sold for $4,000 and loss on sale = $2,000." The memo is initialed by Bart Murray. Attached to it is a photocopy of a check from Haroldene Harvey's Auto Castle, Inc., for $4,000. Haroldene Harvey is also your client. You know that Haroldene and Bart are neighbors and good friends. Your review of Bart Murray's asset and depreciation schedules confirms that the truck had an adjusted basis of $6,000 as of the sale date. What are your obligations under the Statements on Standards for Tax Services (found at www.aicpa.org)? Write a memorandum to the managing partner explaining what should be done about the situation involving Bart Murray.

# Nonrecognition Transactions

12

## Learning Objectives:

LO 1 Identify the commonly encountered classes of property transactions for which the nonrecognition (deferral) of gains is allowed.

LO 2 Explain the rationale for nonrecognition (deferral) of gain on the two classes of property transactions.

LO 3 Identify the common characteristics of the two classes of nonrecognition transactions and how the characteristics affect the nonrecognition of gain calculations and adjustments.

LO 4 Determine the basic nonrecognition rules for like-kind exchanges of property and the calculation of the basis of property received in a like-kind exchange.

LO 5 Identify properties that qualify as like-kind for the deferral of gains and losses on exchanges.

LO 6 Explain the effects of boot paid and received in like-kind exchanges.

LO 7 Describe how involuntary conversions of property occur and how gains (but not losses) may be deferred when a qualified replacement property is purchased.

LO 8 Determine what constitutes a qualified replacement property for property that is involuntarily converted.

LO 9 Explain the provisions for excluding gain on the sale of a taxpayer's principal residence.

## concept review

### GENERAL CONCEPTS

**Related party** Family members and corporations that are owned by family members are considered related parties, as are certain other relationships between entities in which the power to control the substance of a transaction is evidenced through majority ownership. pg. 2-4

### ACCOUNTING CONCEPTS

**Annual accounting period** All entities must report the results of their operations on an annual basis (the tax year). Each tax year stands on its own, apart from other tax years. pg. 2-9

**Substance-over-form doctrine** Transactions are to be taxed according to their true intention rather than some form that may have been contrived. pg. 2-11

### INCOME CONCEPTS

**All-inclusive income** All income received is taxable unless a specific provision in the tax law either excludes the income from taxation or defers its recognition to a future tax year. pg. 2-12

**Realization** No income or loss is recognized until it has been realized. A realization involves a change in the form and/or the substance of a taxpayer's property rights that results from an arm's-length transaction. pg. 2-14

**Wherewithal to pay** Income is recognized in the period in which the taxpayer has the means to pay the tax on the income. pg. 2-16

### DEDUCTION CONCEPTS

**Basis** The amount of unrecovered investment in an asset. As amounts are expended and/or recovered relative to an asset over time, the basis is adjusted in consideration of such changes. The **adjusted basis** of an asset is the original basis, plus or minus the changes in the amount of unrecovered investment. pgs. 2-13, 2-21

**Legislative grace** Any tax relief provided is the result of a specific act of Congress that must be strictly applied and interpreted. All income received is taxable unless a specific provision in the tax law excludes the income from taxation. Deductions must be approached with the philosophy that nothing is deductible unless a provision in the tax law allows the deduction. pg. 2-12

## 12-1 INTRODUCTION

LO 1
Identify the commonly encountered classes of property transactions for which the nonrecognition (deferral) of gains is allowed.

Chapter 11 noted that a gain or a loss realized on a disposition of property may not be recognized in the year the transaction takes place. Earlier discussions of nonrecognition focused on realized losses that are permanently disallowed (e.g., personal use losses) and those that are deferred (e.g., wash sales) for recognition. In addition, gains on certain types of dispositions are not recognized in the period in which they are realized.

Under the all-inclusive income concept, any gain realized on a disposition of property is taxable (i.e., recognized in the period of realization). However, Congress has granted tax relief for certain types of transactions. These are referred to as **nonrecognition transactions**. It should be noted that these transactions are not nontaxable in the sense that tax will never be paid on the realized gain. Rather, recognition of these gains is deferred until a future period. Two commonly encountered nonrecognition transactions discussed in this chapter are exchanges of like-kind property and involuntary conversions of property.

The tax law also lets a taxpayer exclude from taxation $250,000 of gain on the sale of a principal residence. The exclusion is increased to $500,000 for married taxpayers who file a joint return. Unlike the nonrecognition provisions, which only provide for a deferral of the gain, the amount of gain excluded on the sale of a principal residence is never subject to tax.

Although each type of nonrecognition transaction is distinct, the underlying rationale for deferral of gains is the same. In addition, these transactions share characteristics and mechanisms for deferring gains and losses upon their disposition.

## 12-2 RATIONALE FOR NONRECOGNITION

LO 2
Explain the rationale for nonrecognition (deferral) of gain on the two classes of property transactions.

There are two interrelated reasons that the two types of transactions have been granted tax relief. First, in each transaction, the initial realization is considered part of a continuing investment process. That is, although one asset has been disposed of, another asset with similar characteristics has taken its place. Under the substance-over-form doctrine, the new property acquired in the transaction is viewed as a continuation of the original investment. This view represents a refinement of the realization concept, which postpones recognition of appreciation in value until the taxpayer disposes of a property. In effect, the nonrecognition provisions mandate deferral of the tax consequences if a disposition and its timely replacement provide the taxpayer with a continuing interest in a similar property.

**Example 1** Archibald, Inc.'s warehouse is destroyed by a fire. The warehouse has an adjusted basis of $100,000 and a fair market value before the fire of $325,000. Archibald receives $300,000 from its insurance company for the loss of the warehouse. Archibald uses the $300,000 to purchase another warehouse costing $400,000. What is Archibald's realized gain or loss on the casualty?

**Discussion: Archibald has realized a gain of $200,000 ($300,000 − $100,000) on the casualty. The loss on business property fully destroyed is the adjusted basis of the property, $100,000. However, the receipt of the $300,000 in insurance proceeds results in a gain of $200,000 on the casualty:**

| | |
|---|---|
| Amount realized from insurance | $ 300,000 |
| Adjusted basis of warehouse | (100,000) |
| Realized gain on the casualty | $ 200,000 |
| Recognized gain | -0- |
| Deferred gain | $ 200,000 |

**A casualty loss on business property is an involuntary conversion. Because the warehouse is critical to Archibald's business, it was replaced. Thus, the new warehouse is a continuation of the investment in the original warehouse, and Archibald may defer the gain on the involuntary conversion. In effect, the tax law views the destruction of the warehouse and its replacement as not constituting a realization of the appreciation in the value of the warehouse.**

The second rationale for not recognizing these transactions is that the taxpayer lacks the wherewithal to pay the tax on the realized gain because the amount realized on the transaction is reinvested in the replacement asset. A primary requirement for total deferral of gain in both types of transactions is that any amounts realized from the disposition must be fully reinvested in a replacement asset.

**Example 2** In example 1, does Archibald have the wherewithal to pay tax on the $200,000 realized gain on the warehouse?

**Discussion: In acquiring the replacement warehouse, Archibald reinvested the entire $300,000 it received from its insurance company. It does not have any cash remaining to pay the tax on the $200,000 gain. Archibald does not have the wherewithal to pay tax on the gain because all the insurance proceeds were used to replace the warehouse.**

## 12-3 COMMONALITIES OF NONRECOGNITION TRANSACTIONS

LO 3
Identify the common characteristics of the two classes of nonrecognition transactions and how the characteristics affect the nonrecognition of gain calculations and adjustments.

The continuity of investment criteria and lack of wherewithal to pay for both types of nontaxable transactions provide five distinctive commonalities in the tax treatment of these transactions. Figure 12-1 illustrates these factors. First, the wherewithal-to-pay concept provides the rationale for deferring gain. Thus, both nonrecognition

*Figure 12-1*

### Commonalities of Nonrecognition Transactions

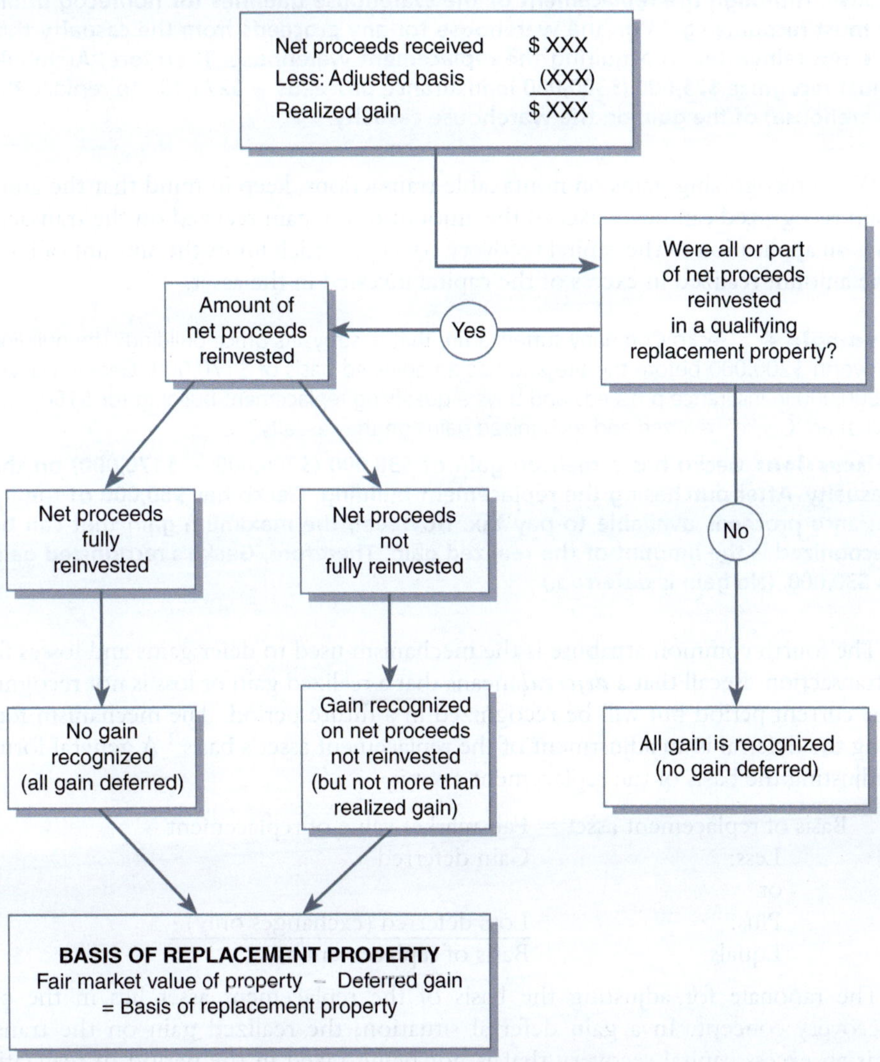

transactions provide for the deferral of realized gains. Deferring gains is mandatory for like-kind exchanges but is generally elective for involuntary conversions. On the loss side, deferring realized losses on like-kind exchanges is mandatory. Losses on involuntary conversions are never deferred and are recognized in the period of realization.

Second, classification of a nonrecognition transaction as a continuation of an investment requires a replacement asset. Each type of nonrecognition transaction requires the purchase of a qualified replacement asset within a specified time period. The time allowed for the qualified replacement varies with each type of non-recognition transaction. As you can see in Figure 12-1, the transaction is taxable and treated as any other disposition of property if a qualified replacement property is not purchased within the allowable time period.

The third factor common to these transactions also is a result of the wherewithal-to-pay concept. Although the transactions qualify for nonrecognition, gains on all the transactions must be recognized when the taxpayer has the wherewithal to pay the tax on part of the realized gain. As depicted in Figure 12-1, no gain is recognized as long as the entire proceeds received in the nonrecognition transaction are reinvested in a qualified replacement asset. However, if all the proceeds are not reinvested, the taxpayer has the wherewithal to pay tax in the amount of those proceeds not reinvested. In general, the amount of gain to be recognized is the portion of the amount realized that the taxpayer has not reinvested in a replacement asset.

**Example 3** Assume that in example 1, Archibald purchases a qualifying replacement warehouse at a cost of $275,000. What amount of gain must Archibald recognize on the casualty?

**Discussion: Archibald realizes a gain of $200,000 on the destruction of the warehouse. Although the replacement of the warehouse qualifies for nonrecognition, it must recognize gain on the warehouse for any proceeds from the casualty that are not reinvested in acquiring the replacement warehouse. Therefore, Archibald must recognize $25,000 ($300,000 in insurance proceeds − $275,000 to replace the warehouse) of the gain on the warehouse casualty.**

When recognizing gains on nontaxable transactions, keep in mind that the amount of gain recognized can never exceed the amount of the gain realized on the transaction. This is an application of the capital recovery concept, which limits the amount of income to the amount realized in excess of the capital invested in the asset.

**Example 4** Gecko Company suffers a fire that destroys its office building. The building is worth $200,000 before the fire and has an adjusted basis of $170,000. Gecko receives $200,000 in insurance proceeds and buys a qualifying replacement building for $150,000. What are Gecko's realized and recognized gains on the casualty?

**Discussion: Gecko has a realized gain of $30,000 ($200,000 − $170,000) on the casualty. After purchasing the replacement building, Gecko has $50,000 of the insurance proceeds available to pay tax. However, the maximum gain that can be recognized is the amount of the realized gain. Therefore, Gecko's recognized gain is $30,000. (No gain is deferred.)**

The fourth common attribute is the mechanism used to defer gains and losses from the transaction. Recall that a *deferral* means that a realized gain or loss is not recognized in the current period but will be recognized in a future period. The mechanism for effecting the deferral is an adjustment of the replacement asset's basis.[1] A general formula for adjusting the basis of the replacement asset is

| | |
|---|---|
| Basis of replacement asset = | Fair market value of replacement |
| Less: | Gain deferred |
| or | |
| Plus: | Loss deferred (exchanges only) |
| Equals: | Basis of replacement asset |

The rationale for adjusting the basis of the replacement asset lies in the capital recovery concept. In a gain deferral situation, the realized gain on the transaction is an excess capital recovery that is not being taxed in the period of realization.

Moreover, without the basis adjustment, the deferred gain would never be recognized. As a continuation of investment, the amount of capital recovery allowed on the replacement asset must be reduced by the amount of any gain deferred. In subsequent periods, the amount of capital recovery taken on the replacement asset through depreciation and at disposition of the replacement asset will be reduced by the amount of the gain deferred. While the replacement asset is being used, taxable income will increase by the amount of the gain deferred in calculating the replacement asset's basis.

**Example 5** Jordan owns land with a fair market value of $10,000. He had purchased the land as an investment in 2015 for $6,000. In 2020, he trades the land in a qualifying like-kind exchange for another parcel of land that is worth $10,000. What are Jordan's realized and recognized gains on the like-kind exchange and the basis in the new parcel of land?

**Discussion: Jordan has realized a gain of $4,000 on the exchange of the land. However, all of it is deferred because Jordan has no wherewithal to pay the tax on the $4,000 gain. The basis of the new parcel of land is $6,000:**

| | |
|---|---|
| Amount realized (fair market value of land received) | $10,000 |
| Adjusted basis of land exchanged | (6,000) |
| Realized gain on exchange | $ 4,000 |
| Recognized gain on exchange | -0- |
| Deferred gain on exchange | $ 4,000 |

Basis of new parcel = $10,000 − $4,000 = $6,000

**By reducing the basis in the second parcel, Jordan will not be able to recover the deferred gain tax-free when he disposes of the second parcel in a taxable transaction. When Jordan disposes of the second parcel in a taxable transaction, his realized gain or loss will be a combination of the $4,000 in gain deferred on the exchange and any subsequent gain or loss in value of the second parcel.**

**Example 6** In 2021, Jordan sells the second parcel of land for $13,000. What are his realized and recognized gains on the sale?

**Discussion: Jordan has realized a gain of $7,000 ($13,000 − $6,000) on the sale of the land. The sale of the land is a taxable transaction, and he must recognize the entire $7,000 gain.**

**The $7,000 recognized gain is composed of two separate gains on the individual parcels. The first parcel yielded a $4,000 gain, which was not recognized on the exchange for the second parcel. The second parcel was worth $10,000 when Jordan received it in the exchange. It appreciated in value by $3,000 while Jordan held it. Thus, Jordan's $7,000 gain is the result of a $4,000 gain on his initial land investment and a $3,000 gain on the subsequent investment acquired in the like-kind exchange. Over the 2-year period, the same amount of gain is recognized for the exchange deferral as would have been recognized if no deferral had been allowed on the exchange:**

| | Gain Recognized | | |
|---|---|---|---|
| | 2020 | 2021 | Total |
| No gain deferral allowed | $4,000 | $3,000 | $7,000 |
| With exchange deferral | -0- | $7,000 | $7,000 |

Note in examples 5 and 6 that Jordan's basis in the new parcel of land is equal to his basis in the parcel of land exchanged (carryover basis). This reflects the fact that Jordan made no additional investment to obtain the second parcel of land. The amount of his investment has not changed by continuing his investment in land, resulting in a carryover of his initial $6,000 investment to the investment in the second parcel. However, the general basis adjustment takes into account any additional investment made to acquire the replacement asset.

**Example 7** Assume that in example 5, Jordan exchanges his land for another parcel of land that is worth $12,000. Because his land is worth only $10,000, Jordan has to pay $2,000 to make the exchange. What are Jordan's realized and recognized gains on the exchange and his basis in the new parcel of land?

**Discussion: Jordan realizes a gain of $4,000 on the exchange of the land. However, all gain from the like-kind exchange is deferred because Jordan has no wherewithal to pay the tax on the $4,000 gain. The basis of the new parcel of land is $8,000:**

| | |
|---|---|
| Amount realized ($12,000 – $2,000) | $10,000 |
| Adjusted basis | (6,000) |
| Realized gain on exchange | $ 4,000 |
| Recognized gain on exchange | -0- |
| Deferred gain on exchange | $ 4,000 |

Basis of new parcel = $12,000 – $4,000 = $8,000

**The $8,000 basis in the second parcel of land is the $6,000 invested in the first parcel (which remains unrealized) and the additional $2,000 Jordan paid to acquire the second parcel.**

**Example 8** Assume that in example 5, Jordan exchanges his land for another parcel of land that is worth $7,000. Because his land is worth $10,000, Jordan receives $3,000 in the exchange. What are Jordan's realized and recognized gains on the exchange and his basis in the new parcel of land?

**Discussion: Jordan has realized a $4,000 gain on the exchange. However, Jordan has $3,000 in cash after the exchange that is available to pay tax. Therefore, he must recognize $3,000 of the $4,000 gain, leaving only $1,000 of the gain to be deferred. His basis in the new land is $6,000:**

| | |
|---|---|
| Amount realized ($7,000 + $3,000) | $10,000 |
| Adjusted basis | (6,000) |
| Realized gain on exchange | $ 4,000 |
| Recognized gain on exchange (cash received) | 3,000 |
| Deferred gain on exchange | $ 1,000 |

Basis of new parcel = $7,000 – $1,000 = $6,000

The final commonality is the carryover of the tax attributes of the first asset to the replacement asset to reflect the replacement asset's status as a continuation of the investment in the first asset. These attributes include the holding period of the first asset and any unrecognized depreciation recapture on the first asset.[2,3] These carryovers are essential to give full effect to the second asset as the continuation of the investment in the first asset.

**Example 9** Kolby Company purchases a building in 2003 at a cost of $300,000. In the current year, Kolby exchanges the building for another building with a fair market value of $200,000. MACRS depreciation on the building was $141,000. The exchange qualifies as a like-kind exchange. What are Kolby's realized gain, recognized gain, and basis in the new building?

**Discussion: Kolby has a realized gain of $31,000 on the exchange. Because Kolby has no wherewithal to pay after the exchange, the entire gain is deferred. The basis of the new building is $169,000:**

| | |
|---|---|
| Amount realized (FMV of new building) | $ 200,000 |
| Adjusted basis ($300,000 – $141,000) | (169,000) |
| Realized gain on exchange | $ 31,000 |
| Recognized gain on exchange | -0- |
| Deferred gain on exchange | $ 31,000 |

Basis of new building = $200,000 – $31,000 = $169,000

**Example 10** Assume that Kolby immediately sells the building received in the exchange in example 9 for $200,000. What are the amount of recognized gain on the sale and the character of the gain on the sale?

**Discussion: Kolby's realized and recognized gain on the sale is $31,000 ($200,000 – $131,000). A building used in a trade or business is Section 1231 property.**

**Because the building is depreciable property, it is subject to the depreciation recapture rules under Section 1250. (See Chapter 11.)**

**Although Kolby has taken no depreciation on the building sold, the tax attributes of the initial building attach to the building sold. As a continuation of the original investment in the building, the building sold is considered to have been held since 2003 when the initial purchase took place. In addition, characterization of any gain on a taxable disposition of the building must view the $141,000 in depreciation taken on the initial building as taken on the building sold. Recall from Chapter 11 that 1250 recapture occurs only when there is excess depreciation (MACRS exceeds straight-line). Since the property was placed in service in 2003, there is no excess depreciation.**

Carrying over the depreciation recapture for nonrecognition transactions gives the gain from disposition of the replacement the attributes of the original asset. This effectively eliminates the use of nonrecognition transactions to avoid the depreciation recapture rules.

## 12-4 LIKE-KIND EXCHANGES

LO 4 Determine the basic nonrecognition rules for like-kind exchanges of property and the calculation of the basis of property received in a like-kind exchange.

A realized gain or loss is never recognized on an exchange of business or investment property for other like-kind property for business or investment use. Realized gain or loss on a transaction that qualifies as an exchange of like-kind property for other like-kind property must always be deferred.[4] However, gains on like-kind exchanges must be recognized when the taxpayer has the wherewithal to pay the tax after the exchange is completed. The wherewithal to pay is evidenced by the receipt of other nonqualifying property with the like-kind property. (In tax jargon, other nonqualifying property is called **boot**, so named because, along with the like-kind property, one party has received nonqualified property "to boot.") Thus, gains are recognized to the extent that boot is received in the exchange. However, realized losses on like-kind exchanges are never recognized, even when boot is received in the deal.

### 12-4a Exchange Requirement

To qualify for nonrecognition, a direct exchange of like-kind property must occur. Thus, a sale of property and a purchase of like-kind property from another would not be considered an exchange unless the two transactions were interdependent. If the sale and purchase transactions are interdependent, the transactions are treated as an exchange under the substance-over-form doctrine.

**Example 11** Sarah sells land to Angelica for $20,000. The land has an adjusted basis of $25,000 at the date of sale. Sarah uses the $20,000 as a down payment on new property she purchases from Alpha Real Estate for $28,000. What are the tax effects for Sarah of the sale and purchase of the autos?

**Discussion: Because the two transactions are not interdependent, an exchange of like-kind property has not occurred. Sarah realizes and recognizes a loss on the sale of the land of $5,000 ($20,000 − $25,000). Her basis in the new land is the $28,000 purchase price.**

Classifying the transaction in example 11 as a sale has important tax implications. As a sale, Sarah can deduct the loss she realizes on the transaction. However, if the transaction had been characterized as an exchange, Sarah would not be allowed to recognize the loss. Nonrecognition of gains and losses on exchanges of like-kind property is mandatory. Thus, a taxpayer wishing to recognize a loss on the disposition of an asset that is to be replaced must be careful not to make the sale and purchase transactions interdependent. Sale and repurchase from a dealer in property usually collapse under IRS scrutiny and are treated as an exchange of property.

**Example 12** Assume that in example 11, Sarah sells her land to Alpha Real Estate for $20,000. She deposits the check in the bank and writes a separate check to Alpha for $28,000 to purchase the land. What are the tax effects for Sarah of the sale and purchase of the land?

**Discussion: Because the sale and purchase transactions were made with the same dealer in property, the IRS would collapse the two transactions and treat them as a**

**direct exchange of property. That is, although the form of the transaction is a sale and a purchase, the substance of the transaction is an exchange of land between Sarah and Alpha Real Estate.**

**Because the transaction is an exchange of like-kind business property for like-kind business property, Sarah is not allowed to recognize the $5,000 loss on the exchange. The loss is added to the basis of the land. Thus, instead of recognizing a $5,000 loss and having land with a basis of $28,000 (example 11), Sarah has no recognized loss and her basis in the land is $33,000 ($28,000 + $5,000).**

The direct exchange of property requirement does not mean that the exchange must be simultaneous. Taxpayers are allowed to structure transactions through third parties that qualify as exchanges if they meet certain time requirements for identifying properties and closing the transaction.

**Example 13** Percy Corporation would like to obtain land owned by Olivia. Olivia does not want to sell the land because she would have to recognize a large gain, but she is willing to trade for land owned by Bake. Under a binding contract, Olivia delivers title to her land to Percy, and Percy agrees to purchase the land from Bake and deliver title to the land to Olivia. Percy purchases the land from Bake and delivers title to Olivia. Does the transaction qualify as an exchange?

**Discussion: The transaction between Percy Corporation and Olivia qualifies as a direct exchange of property if the transaction meets the time requirements for completing it.**

**The transaction between Percy Corporation and Bake is not an exchange. It is a sale of property by Bake to Percy and is not part of the exchange transaction.**

The exchange illustrated in example 13 is referred to as a **deferred (third-party) exchange**. The deferred exchange rules let a transaction be structured as an exchange when the two parties do not have property that they want to exchange directly.[5] The basic rules for structuring such exchanges require that the property to be exchanged be identified within 45 days of the date of the first property transfer. In addition, the exchange must be completed within 180 days of the first property transfer. In example 13, the land owned by Bake would have to be identified as being part of the exchange within 45 days of the transfer of land from Olivia to Percy Corporation. In addition, Percy would have 180 days to purchase the land from Bake and transfer title to the land to Olivia to qualify the transaction as an exchange. Application of the deferred exchange rules can be quite complex in practice and is beyond the scope of this text. However, you should know that exchanges can still be made when one party does not own the property the other party desires to receive in the exchange.

## 12-4b Like-Kind Property Requirements

LO 5
Identify properties that qualify as like-kind for the deferral of gains and losses on exchanges.

The **like-kind exchange rules** require that the property being transferred be used either in a trade or business or held as an investment. This excludes personal use property (residences, personal automobiles, etc.) from the nonrecognition rules for like-kind exchanges. In addition, stock-in-trade (inventories); other property held primarily for sale; stocks, bonds, notes, other securities; partnership interests; and intangible assets are specifically excluded from the exchange nonrecognition rules. Exchanges of these assets generally result in recognized gains and losses.

The property received in the exchange must be like-kind property and be held for business or investment use. This is interpreted as meaning that the property is of like kind in the taxpayer's hands, not the prior owner's. Thus, a taxpayer can make a like-kind exchange with a dealer in property even though the dealer does not hold the property for business or investment use. In addition, the requirement that both the property exchanged and the property received be held for business or investment use is interpreted as meaning that business use property can be exchanged for property to be held as an investment and vice versa, so long as the two properties are of like kind.

**Example 14** Ace Trucking Company owns a parcel of land it acquired several years earlier as an investment. Ace needs more land to park its trucking fleet, so it exchanges the investment land for a parcel of land next to its truck barn. Is the exchange of land eligible for treatment as a like-kind exchange?

**Discussion: Exchanging land held for investment purposes for land to be used in a trade or business is a like-kind exchange. Investment property can be exchanged for business use property so long as both properties are of like kind. In this case, the two parcels of land are of like kind.**

The 2017 Tax Cuts and Jobs Act limits the type of property that qualifies for like-kind exchange treatment. Effective January 1, 2018, no gain or loss is recognized only if the exchange of real property is held for productive use in a trade or business or for investment and that property is exchanged solely for real property of like kind which is to be held either for productive use in a trade or business or for investment.[6] The new law no longer allows tangible personal property used in a trade or business or held for investment to qualify for like-kind exchange treatment. Therefore, the exchange of like-kind and like-class business machinery is no longer permitted.

Central to the exchange nonrecognition provisions is that the properties exchanged are like kind. The Treasury regulations on like-kind exchanges give the following interpretation of what constitutes **like-kind property**:

> The words "like kind" have reference to the nature or character of the property and not to its grade or quality. The fact that any real estate involved is improved or unimproved is not material, for that fact relates only to the grade or quality of the property and not to its kind or class.[7]

The exchange requirement lets any real property be exchanged for any other real property in a like-kind exchange. For example, unimproved land exchanged for an office building is a like-kind exchange because both properties are real property.

**Example 15** Miguel exchanges a parcel of land he holds as an investment for an office building to be used in his business. Are the two properties of like kind?

**Discussion: An exchange of real property for other real property is a like-kind exchange. It does not matter that the land is unimproved property and the building is improved property. Miguel's exchange is a like-kind exchange.**

The following exchanges never qualify for like-kind exchange treatment:

- Exchanges involving personal use property
- Exchanges of stocks, bonds, and inventories
- Exchanges of intangible property
- Exchanges of tangible personal property for real property
- Exchanges of partnership interests
- Exchanges of real property located in the United States for real property located outside the United States

## 12-4c Effect of Boot

LO 6 Explain the effects of boot paid and received in like-kind exchanges.

When properties of different values are exchanged, the party with the lower-valued property must equalize the transaction by transferring cash, securities, or other property not of like kind (boot). Boot does not taint the like-kind nature of the exchange. However, any gain or loss realized on the transfer of the nonqualifying property must be recognized.

**Example 16** Geraldine trades unimproved land, which is worth $30,000, for a building with a fair market value of $45,000. In obtaining the building, she gives the owner $5,000 in cash and stock with a fair market value of $10,000. Geraldine has adjusted bases of $20,000 in the unimproved land and $4,000 in the stock. What are the tax consequences of the exchange?

**Discussion: The exchange of unimproved land for a building is a like-kind exchange for Geraldine. Her realized gain on the exchange is $10,000, none of which is recognized. Her basis in the building is $35,000:**

| | |
|---|---|
| Amount realized (trade-in value) | $30,000 |
| Adjusted basis | (20,000) |
| Realized gain | $ 10,000 |
| Recognized gain (no boot received) | -0- |
| Deferred gain | $ 10,000 |

Basis in the building = $45,000 − $10,000 = $35,000

**Although the exchange of unimproved land for the building is tax-free, stock is not like-kind property, and its disposition as part of the exchange transaction is a taxable transaction. Geraldine has a gain, realized and recognized, of $6,000 ($10,000 − $4,000) on the transfer of the stock.**

## Receipt of Boot

The receiver of boot in a like-kind exchange has the wherewithal to pay tax on the exchange to the extent of the boot received. Therefore, a gain on a like-kind exchange is recognized to the extent of any boot received (but never more than the realized gain on the exchange). Losses on like-kind exchanges are never recognized, even when boot is received. The most common form of boot payment is cash. However, anything of value can be used to equalize the exchange. Therefore, receipts of other assets, services, and assumptions of debt constitute boot.[8]

**Example 17** Endorra Corporation owns a building with a fair market value of $70,000 and an adjusted basis of $40,000. It exchanges the building for land with a fair market value of $45,000 and receives $25,000 in cash. Both properties are investment properties for Endorra. What are Endorra Corporation's realized gain, recognized gain, and basis in the land?

**Discussion: The exchange of a building for land is a like-kind exchange. Endorra Corporation realizes a gain of $30,000 on the building. Because it receives $25,000 in cash boot, the corporation must recognize $25,000 of the gain. Endorra's basis in the land is $40,000:**

| | |
|---|---|
| Amount realized ($45,000 + $25,000) | $ 70,000 |
| Adjusted basis | (40,000) |
| Realized gain | $ 30,000 |
| Recognized gain (cash boot received) | (25,000) |
| Deferred gain | $ 5,000 |

Basis in land = $45,000 − $5,000 = $40,000

**Example 18** Assume that Endorra has a $10,000 mortgage on the building. As part of the exchange, the owner of the land agrees to assume the mortgage and pay the corporation $15,000 in cash. What are Endorra's realized gain, recognized gain, and basis in the land?

**Discussion: Endorra realizes a gain of $30,000 on the building. The corporation receives $25,000 in boot from the $10,000 mortgage assumption and the $15,000 in cash. Therefore, it must recognize a gain of $25,000. Endorra Corporation's basis in the land is $40,000:**

| | |
|---|---|
| Amount realized ($45,000 + $10,000 + $15,000) | $ 70,000 |
| Adjusted basis | (40,000) |
| Realized gain | $ 30,000 |
| Recognized gain (liability assumed + cash received) | (25,000) |
| Deferred gain | $ 5,000 |

Basis in land = $45,000 − $5,000 = $40,000

Example 18 illustrates that the assumption of a liability is considered boot received and therefore subject to current taxation. This occurs because a buyer who assumes a mortgage in essence gives cash to the seller, which the seller uses to pay off the existing mortgage. In example 18, the owner of the land could have paid Endorra $25,000 in cash to effect the exchange. Endorra would then have used $10,000 of the cash to pay off its mortgage, leaving the corporation with $15,000 in cash. This treatment of debt assumptions makes the taxation of exchanges neutral with respect to debt. That is, the same result is obtained regardless of whether the property being exchanged includes the assumption of debt on the property. However, if a mortgage is assumed and boot is paid in the transaction, the boot paid is offset by the boot received in the mortgage assumption.[9]

**Example 19** Assume that in example 17, Endorra's mortgage on the building is $30,000. To make the exchange for the land, the corporation has to pay $5,000. What are Endorra's realized gain, recognized gain, and basis in the land?

**Discussion: Endorra realizes a gain of $30,000 on the building. The corporation receives mortgage boot of $30,000 but it is allowed to offset the mortgage boot with the $5,000 cash boot it paid to make the exchange. Thus, Endorra recognizes a gain of $25,000 on the exchange. The corporation's basis in the land is $40,000:**

| | |
|---|---|
| Amount realized ($45,000 + $30,000 − $5,000) | $ 70,000 |
| Adjusted basis | (40,000) |
| Realized gain | $ 30,000 |
| Recognized gain (liability assumed − cash boot paid) | (25,000) |
| Deferred gain | $ 5,000 |

Basis in land = $45,000 − $5,000 = $40,000

**Note that the amount by which the cash boot offsets the mortgage is equal to the amount by which Endorra could have reduced its mortgage ($25,000) and then traded the mortgaged building for the land in an even exchange.**

The tax law does not allow the receiver of money or other boot property to use liabilities assumed in the exchange to offset the boot received.

**Example 20** Raul owns land with a fair market value of $30,000 and an adjusted basis of $8,000. He trades the land for another parcel of land with a fair market value of $35,000 and a $10,000 mortgage. In the exchange, Raul assumes the $10,000 mortgage and receives $5,000 in cash. What are Raul's realized gain, recognized gain, and his basis in the land acquired in the exchange?

**Discussion: Raul has realized a gain of $22,000 on the exchange of the land. He must recognize a gain equal to the $5,000 in cash boot. He cannot offset the $5,000 cash boot with the $10,000 he paid in mortgage boot. His basis in the new land is $18,000:**

| | |
|---|---|
| Amount realized ($35,000 + $5,000 − $10,000) | $30,000 |
| Adjusted basis | (8,000) |
| Realized gain | $22,000 |
| Recognized gain (cash boot received) | (5,000) |
| Deferred gain | $17,000 |

Basis in land = $35,000 − $17,000 = $18,000

**The $18,000 basis in the land consists of the $8,000 basis in the original parcel of land plus the extra $10,000 in debt Raul took on in the exchange.**

When both properties being exchanged are encumbered by mortgages and the mortgages on the properties are exchanged, the mortgages are netted out. Only the party with the larger mortgage is considered to have received mortgage boot. The party with the smaller mortgage is a net payer of mortgage boot and does not recognize gain from the net mortgage boot paid.

**Example 21** Tara owns an office building and the Barney Partnership owns an apartment building. Each property is encumbered by a mortgage. They agree to exchange their properties and their mortgages, with any difference to be paid in cash. The fair market values (FMV), mortgages, and adjusted bases for each property are listed here. Who must pay the cash to make the exchange, and how much must that taxpayer pay? What are the tax effects of the exchange for Tara and the Barney Partnership?

| | Tara's Office Building | Barney's Apartment Building |
|---|---|---|
| FMV | $220,000 | $250,000 |
| Mortgage | 80,000 | 150,000 |
| Adjusted basis | 100,000 | 175,000 |

**Discussion: The partnership must pay Tara $40,000 to make the exchange. Tara's property has a net of mortgage value of $140,000 ($220,000 – $80,000), and Barney's net of mortgage value is $100,000 ($250,000 – $150,000). Therefore, the partnership must pay the $40,000 difference in the net value being exchanged.**

**Tara realizes a gain of $120,000 on her office building. She will have to recognize the $40,000 in cash boot she receives, but she is not allowed to offset the $40,000 with the $70,000 ($80,000 – $150,000) of net mortgage boot she pays on the exchange. Her basis in the apartment building is $170,000:**

| | |
|---|---|
| Amount realized ($250,000 + $40,000 + $80,000 – $150,000) | $ 220,000 |
| Adjusted basis | (100,000) |
| Realized gain | $ 120,000 |
| Recognized gain (cash boot received) | (40,000) |
| Deferred gain | $ 80,000 |

Basis in apartments = $250,000 – $80,000 = $170,000

**Tara's basis in the apartment building is her $100,000 basis in the office building plus the additional $70,000 ($150,000 – $80,000) of debt she takes on in the exchange.**

**Barney realizes a gain of $75,000 on its apartment building. The partnership receives net mortgage boot of $70,000 ($150,000 – $80,000). However, it is allowed to use the $40,000 cash boot paid to Tara to offset the mortgage boot paid to Tara. Therefore, the partnership will recognize a gain of only $30,000. Barney's basis in the office building is $175,000:**

| | | |
|---|---|---|
| Amount realized ($220,000 + $150,000 – $80,000 – $40,000) | | $ 250,000 |
| Adjusted basis | | (175,000) |
| Realized gain | | $ 75,000 |
| Recognized gain – net mortgage boot: | | |
| Barney's mortgage assumed by Tara | $150,000 | |
| Tara's mortgage assumed by Barney | (80,000) | |
| Net mortgage boot received | $ 70,000 | |
| Less: Cash boot paid | (40,000) | |
| Net boot received | | (30,000) |
| Deferred gain | | $ 45,000 |

Basis in office building = $220,000 – $45,000 = $175,000

The recognition of gains on like-kind exchanges to the extent of any boot received is based on the wherewithal-to-pay concept. However, this concept is not applicable to losses—losses do not require that resources be available for payment of tax on the transaction. Therefore, losses on like-kind exchanges are never recognized, even when boot is received in the exchange.

**Example 22** Genevieve exchanges an apartment building held as an investment for a parcel of land. The apartment building has a fair market value of $43,000 and an adjusted basis of $65,000. Because the land is worth only $30,000, Genevieve receives $13,000 in cash in the exchange. What are Genevieve's realized and recognized gain or loss on the exchange and her basis in the land?

**Discussion: Genevieve has a realized loss of $22,000 on the exchange. Losses on like-kind exchanges are never recognized. Her basis in the land is $52,000:**

| | |
|---|---|
| Amount realized ($30,000 + $13,000) | $ 43,000 |
| Adjusted basis | (65,000) |
| Realized loss | $(22,000) |
| Recognized loss | -0- |
| Deferred loss | $(22,000) |

Basis in land = $30,000 + $22,000 = $52,000

**Note that in this case, Genevieve's basis in the land is not equal to the basis she had in the building because she has recovered $13,000 of her investment with no tax consequences. Thus, her unrecovered investment is $52,000 ($65,000 − $13,000).**

## 12-4d Related Party Exchanges

Tax law subjects transactions involving related parties to careful scrutiny. Many transactions between related parties are either disallowed or subject to special limitations. Like-kind exchange treatment is allowed for qualifying exchanges between related parties. However, for related party exchanges, each party must hold the property received in the exchange for two years to qualify as a like-kind exchange. If either party disposes of the property received in the exchange sooner than two years, both parties must immediately recognize the tax effects of the initial exchange. Note that the recognition takes place in the year of the disposition. The year in which the original exchange occurred is not amended under the annual accounting period concept.

**Example 23** Fred owns land with a fair market value of $85,000 and an adjusted basis of $5,000. Nance Corporation, which is wholly owned by Fred, owns an apartment building with a fair market value of $85,000 and an adjusted basis of $70,000. In December 2021, Fred exchanges his land for Nance Corporation's apartment building. What are the tax consequences to Fred and Nance Corporation?

**Discussion: An exchange of land for an apartment building is a like-kind exchange. The fact that Fred and Nance are related parties will not affect the nonrecognition of the exchange transaction in 2021. Fred has a realized gain of $80,000 ($85,000 − $5,000), none of which is recognized in 2021. Fred's basis in the apartments is $5,000. Nance has a realized gain of $15,000 ($85,000 − $70,000), none of which is recognized in 2021. Nance's basis in the land is $70,000. So long as both Fred and Nance hold the properties for two full years from the date of the exchange, no gains will be recognized from the exchange.**

| | Fred | Nance Corporation |
|---|---|---|
| Amount realized | $85,000 | $ 85,000 |
| Adjusted basis | (5,000) | (70,000) |
| Realized gain | $80,000 | $ 15,000 |
| Recognized gain | -0- | -0- |
| Deferred gain | $80,000 | $ 15,000 |
| Basis in property received | $5,000 ($85,000 − $80,000) | $70,000 ($85,000 − $15,000) |

**Example 24** In January 2022, Nance Corporation sells the land acquired from Fred to Dan for $85,000. What are the tax consequences to Fred and Nance Corporation of the sale to Dan?

**Discussion: Because Nance sold the land acquired from Fred without holding it for two full years, the original exchange no longer qualifies as a like-kind exchange. Fred must recognize his $80,000 in realized gain on the land in 2022. This gives him a basis in the apartment buildings of $85,000. Nance must recognize the $15,000 gain realized on the apartment building in 2022, leaving Nance with a basis of $85,000 in the land. The sale of the land to Dan results in no realization of gain ($85,000 − $85,000).**

| | Fred | Nance Corporation |
|---|---|---|
| Amount realized | $ 85,000 | $ 85,000 |
| Adjusted basis | (5,000) | (70,000) |
| Realized gain | $ 80,000 | $ 15,000 |
| Recognized gain | (80,000) | (15,000) |
| Deferred gain | -0- | -0- |
| Basis in property received (FMV) | $ 85,000 | $ 85,000 |

## 12-4e Carryover of Tax Attributes

As discussed earlier in the chapter and set forth in examples 9 and 10, when property is exchanged in a qualifying like-kind exchange, the tax attributes of the asset carry over and are attributed to the new asset acquired in the exchange. As a continuation of investment, the holding period of the new asset includes the period during which the initial asset was held. More important, if the asset being exchanged is a depreciable asset, the recapture potential of the first asset carries to the second asset. The recapture potential of an asset is the maximum amount of recapture on the asset at the time of the exchange. The recapture potential of a Section 1250 asset is the excess depreciation, if any, taken on the asset as of the date of the exchange.

### concept check

The *realization concept* states that income is not recognized until it is realized. A realization involves a change in the form and/or the substance of a taxpayer's property in an *arm's-length transaction*. When like-kind assets are exchanged, the property acquired in the exchange is viewed as a continuation of the investment in the original asset, and a realization is not generally deemed to take place. Therefore, gains on like-kind exchanges are generally not recognized. However, when boot is received in a like-kind exchange, the *wherewithal-to-pay concept* requires recognition of the gain to the extent of the boot received. Because wherewithal to pay is an income recognition concept, losses on like-kind exchanges are never recognized for tax purposes. When gains and losses from like-kind exchanges are not recognized in the current period, an adjustment of the new asset's *basis* is necessary to ensure that the gain or loss will be properly recognized when the new asset is subsequently disposed of in a taxable transaction. Losses represent incomplete capital recovery on the original asset, and therefore, any deferred loss must be added to the basis of the new asset to ensure that it will be recovered in the future. Gains are excess capital recoveries and require a reduction in the new asset's basis to ensure that the gain will be taxed on a future disposition of the replacement asset.

## 12-5 INVOLUNTARY CONVERSIONS

An **involuntary conversion** occurs whenever a gain or loss is realized from a transaction that occurs against the taxpayer's will. That is, an involuntary conversion is a disposition of property that is beyond the control of the taxpayer. Involuntary conversions result when property is destroyed or damaged in a casualty or theft, when a government unit condemns property under its power of eminent domain, or when a foreign government seizes or nationalizes property. Property that is sold under a threat or imminence of a condemnation or seizure is considered an involuntary conversion. In addition, the selling of livestock because of disease, drought, flood, or other weather-related conditions is treated as an involuntary conversion.

## 12-5a Treatment of Involuntary Conversion Gains and Losses

LO 7

Describe how involuntary conversions of property occur and how gains (but not losses) may be deferred when a qualified replacement property is purchased.

The key to understanding the tax treatment of involuntary conversions is that the disposition of the property was not within the taxpayer's control. Although the taxpayer may have been fully insured and realized a gain on the conversion, replacement of the income-producing capacity of an asset involuntarily converted may take months or years. This puts the business at a distinct disadvantage. Because of the detrimental nature of involuntary conversions, the tax law provides the maximum relief possible.

To provide tax relief, losses on involuntary conversions of business or investment property are always recognized in full. However, a condemnation loss on a personal use asset is not deductible.

When an involuntary conversion results in a gain, taxpayers may elect to defer the gain if they purchase qualified replacement property. This provision allows taxpayers who suffer an involuntary conversion the maximum allowable relief. Under the wherewithal-to-pay concept, any involuntary conversion proceeds that are not reinvested in a qualified replacement property must be recognized.[10] However, the amount of gain recognized can never exceed the gain realized on the involuntary conversion.

**Example 25** Bolder Company's truck storage shed is destroyed by an avalanche. The shed cost $160,000 and has an adjusted basis of $70,000 when it is destroyed. The shed is worth $200,000, and Bolder receives $180,000 from its insurance company for the casualty. What is the minimum amount of gain Bolder must recognize in each of the following cases? What is the basis of the replacement shed in each case?

Case A

Bolder purchases a qualified replacement shed for $230,000.

**Discussion: Bolder has realized a gain of $110,000 on the casualty. Because Bolder used all the insurance proceeds to replace the shed, it has no wherewithal to pay tax on the gain. None of the gain must be recognized. Bolder's basis in the new shed is $120,000:**

| | | |
|---|---|---|
| Amount realized (insurance proceeds) | | $180,000 |
| Adjusted basis | | (70,000) |
| Realized gain | | $110,000 |
| Recognized gain: | | |
| Insurance proceeds received | $180,000 | |
| Amount reinvested in new shed | 230,000 | |
| Insurance proceeds remaining after replacement | | -0- |
| Deferred gain | | $110,000 |

Basis of new shed = $230,000 − $110,000 = $120,000

**Note that the basis of the new shed ($120,000) is equal to the $70,000 basis of the old shed plus the additional $50,000 ($230,000 − $180,000) of out-of-pocket cost of purchasing the replacement shed.**

Case B

Bolder purchases a qualified replacement shed costing $150,000.

**Discussion: After replacing the shed, Bolder has $30,000 of the insurance proceeds remaining. It must recognize $30,000 of the $110,000 gain on the shed. Bolder's basis in the new shed is $70,000:**

| | | |
|---|---|---|
| Realized gain | | $110,000 |
| Recognized gain: | | |
| Insurance proceeds received | $ 180,000 | |
| Amount reinvested in new shed | (150,000) | |
| Insurance proceeds remaining after replacement | | (30,000) |
| Deferred gain | | $ 80,000 |

Basis of new shed = $150,000 − $80,000 = $70,000

In an involuntary conversion, the taxpayer typically receives insurance proceeds or a cash payment for the property from the government condemning or seizing the property. In the rare case of a direct conversion to another piece of property (no cash payment received), no gain on the conversion is recognized. Direct conversions are analogous to like-kind exchanges. Therefore, tax law treats direct conversions as such. The basis of the property converted is carried over to the basis of the property received.[11] If the direct conversion results in a loss, the loss on the conversion is recognized.

**Example 26** Kari's warehouse is condemned by the city development authority so the land can be used as a site for low-income housing. Her adjusted basis in the warehouse is $130,000. In consideration for her old warehouse, the development authority transfers to Kari title to a warehouse with a fair market value of $400,000 in a new industrial park. What are Kari's tax consequences of the involuntary conversion?

**Discussion: Kari's realized gain on the involuntary conversion is $270,000 ($400,000 − $130,000). Because this is a direct conversion, she must defer the gain. The basis in her replacement warehouse is $130,000 ($400,000 − $270,000).**

| | |
|---|---|
| Amount realized | $ 400,000 |
| Adjusted basis | (130,000) |
| Realized gain | $ 270,000 |
| Recognized gain | -0- |
| Deferred gain | $ 270,000 |

Basis of the replacement property = $400,000 − $270,000 = $130,000

The deferral of gain realized on an involuntary conversion is not mandatory. A taxpayer may choose to recognize the entire gain on an involuntary conversion. A gain deferral provides a time value of money savings on the income tax deferred and is usually the preferred alternative. However, situations do arise in which a gain on an involuntary conversion can be recognized without paying additional tax. For example, a taxpayer with a large net capital loss that could not otherwise be deducted in the current year may elect to recognize gain if the property involuntarily converted produces either a capital gain or a Section 1231 gain (which is treated as a long-term capital gain). In such cases, the recognized gain is offset by the capital loss, with no additional tax required of the taxpayer. Because the gain is fully recognized, the basis of the replacement property is not reduced, resulting in larger deductions on the property in future tax years.

**Example 27** A rental property Cecilia holds as an investment is destroyed by a flood in the current year. Cecilia purchased the property 7 years ago, and it has an adjusted basis of $95,000 when it is destroyed. Cecilia receives $115,000 in insurance proceeds, which she uses to buy a qualifying rental property costing $140,000. Cecilia has a net capital loss of $33,000 from her other capital asset transactions during the year. What are the tax consequences if Cecilia recognizes the $20,000 gain on the involuntary conversion?

**Discussion: The $20,000 realized gain ($115,000 − $95,000) is a capital gain. Because the property was depreciated using the MACRS system, there is no excess depreciation to recapture if the gain is recognized. The entire gain would be a long-term capital gain that would be netted against the $33,000 net capital loss. Cecilia would then have a net capital loss of $13,000. If she elects to recognize the gain, she pays no additional tax. In addition, her basis in the replacement property would be $140,000, versus a basis of $120,000 if she elects to defer the gain. The election to recognize the gain does not increase her tax liability, and she may deduct the additional $20,000 of basis in the new property through depreciation over the life of the new property.**

| | |
|---|---|
| Amount realized | $115,000 |
| Adjusted basis | (95,000) |
| Realized gain | $ 20,000 |
| Recognized long-term capital gain | (20,000) |
| Deferred gain | -0- |
| Basis in the new purchased property | $140,000 |
| Net capital losses | $ (33,000) |
| Long-term capital gain | 20,000 |
| Net capital loss | $ (13,000) |

Example 27 illustrates a case in which an election to recognize a gain on an involuntary conversion can prove beneficial. However, don't forget that the depreciation recapture rules may reclassify most, if not all, of the gain as ordinary income. Under such circumstances, recognition of the gain may not provide the desired offset of the net capital loss. The important point is that by making the deferral of a gain on an involuntary conversion elective rather than mandatory (as in like-kind exchanges), the taxpayer is given maximum flexibility in obtaining the optimal tax result for the particular situation. Combined with the recognition of losses on involuntary conversions, the tax law provides taxpayers who suffer an involuntary conversion the maximum tax relief possible.

## 12-5b Qualified Replacement Property

LO 8 Determine what constitutes a qualified replacement property for property that is involuntarily converted.

Taxpayers may defer gains on involuntary conversions only if they purchase qualified replacement property within two years of the close of the tax year in which the involuntary conversion occurred; this time limit is referred to as the involuntary conversion replacement period. Qualified replacement property must be "property similar or related in service or use."[12] This requirement is referred to as the *functional use test*. It requires that the replacement property perform the same function or have the same use to the taxpayer as the property involuntarily converted. The functional use test applies to all business and investment property—other than a condemnation of real property—that is subject to an involuntary conversion. The replacement requirement for condemned business or investment real property is that the taxpayer must purchase like-kind property.[13] As discussed earlier, *like-kind* means that the taxpayer can purchase any other type of real property. Thus, the replacement requirements for condemnations of real property are more generous than for other types of conversions.

**Example 28** One of Sno-Cone, Inc.'s ice-making factories is destroyed by a fire. Sno-Cone uses the insurance proceeds from the fire to purchase another ice-making factory. Is the new ice-making factory a qualified replacement property?

**Discussion: Sno-Cone must replace the factory with property that has the same functional use. Because the new ice-making facility performs the same function as the factory involuntarily converted, it is a qualified replacement property.**

**Example 29** Assume that Sno-Cone does not need to purchase another ice-making facility to maintain its production capacity and uses the insurance proceeds to purchase a lollipop factory. Is the lollipop factory a qualified replacement property?

**Discussion: The lollipop factory does not perform the same function in Sno-Cone, Inc.'s business as the ice-making factory. It is not a qualified replacement property.**

**Example 30** Assume the same facts as in example 29, except that the ice-making factory is condemned and bought by the local government. Is the purchase of the lollipop factory a qualified replacement property?

**Discussion: Sno-Cone must replace the condemned business real property with like-kind property. Because a lollipop factory is real property, it is like-kind property that is a qualified replacement property for condemned real property.**

In general, qualified replacement property must be purchased within two years after the close of the tax year in which the involuntary conversion occurred. If a property is sold under a threat of condemnation, the replacement period begins at the date of the threat of condemnation. In addition, the replacement period for condemned business or investment real property is extended to three years.

### concept check

The *legislative grace concept* requires any tax relief provided to be the result of a specific act of Congress that must be strictly applied and interpreted. Because the nature of an involuntary conversion is such that the taxpayer could not have anticipated the event causing the conversion, Congress provides tax relief in two ways. First, losses on involuntary conversions of business or investment use property are always deductible. Individuals are only allowed to deduct personal casualty losses subject to the event and gross income limitations if they occur in a federal disaster area. However, in exercising its power of legislative grace, Congress did not extend the relief to condemnation losses on personal use property. The second form of tax relief provided is the deferral of realized gains on involuntary conversions of business or investment use property when a qualifying replacement property is purchased. If the taxpayer has the wherewithal to pay after a qualifying replacement property is purchased, gain must be recognized to the extent that proceeds received from the conversion are not reinvested. To provide maximum relief, the deferral of gains on involuntary conversions is not mandatory; taxpayers who can benefit from inclusion of an involuntary conversion gain in their taxable income calculation are allowed to recognize the gain.

## 12-6 SALE OF A PRINCIPAL RESIDENCE

LO 9

Explain the provisions for excluding gain on the sale of a taxpayer's principal residence.

A realized loss on the sale or exchange of a taxpayer's personal residence is not deductible because of the restrictions on loss deductions for personal use assets. On the other hand, a realized gain from the sale or exchange of a personal residence is taxable under the all-inclusive income concept. Individuals can elect to exclude up to $250,000 ($500,000 if married) of gain on the sale or exchange of a principal residence. Because this is an exclusion provision, the taxpayer is not required to purchase another residence. If the taxpayer does acquire a new residence, there is no adjustment to the basis of the new residence for the amount of gain excluded. Any gain in excess of the exclusion amount cannot be deferred and is treated as a capital gain.

**Example 31** Muhammad sells his principal residence on June 6, 2021 for $133,000 and pays a commission of $8,000. He acquired the residence on May 8, 2012, for $60,000 and made $20,000 of improvements to it. He purchases a new residence on August 18, 2021, for $140,000. How much gain must Muhammad recognize on the sale of his residence, and what is the basis of his new residence if he is single?

**Discussion: Muhammad's amount realized is $125,000 ($133,000 − $8,000), and he realizes a gain of $45,000 [$125,000 − $80,000 ($60,000 + $20,000)] on the sale. Muhammad should elect to exclude the $45,000 gain. Because he excludes the gain on the sale of the residence, no basis adjustment is necessary on the new residence. The basis of the new residence is its $140,000 cost.**

**Example 32** Assume the same facts as in example 31, except that Muhammad sells his principal residence on June 6, 2021, for $350,000 net of commissions and purchases a new residence for $400,000. How much gain must Muhammad recognize on the sale of his residence, and what is the basis of his new residence?

**Discussion: Muhammad's realized gain is $270,000 ($350,000 − $80,000), and his recognized gain is $20,000 ($270,000 − $250,000). He should elect to exclude $250,000 of the gain. Even though he reinvests more than the selling price in the new residence, Muhammad cannot defer the $20,000 of gain in excess of the $250,000 exclusion. The basis of the new residence is $400,000.**

## 12-6a Requirements for Exclusion

To be eligible for the exclusion, the residence sold must be used as the principal residence of the taxpayer. A **principal residence** is where the taxpayer lives most of the time. A taxpayer can have only one principal residence at a time. A principal residence can be a house, mobile home, cooperative apartment, condominium, or a houseboat, provided it is where the taxpayer lives. Ordinarily, it is not difficult to determine whether the property sold constitutes the taxpayer's principal residence. However, the distinction is crucial, because the exclusion provision does not apply to the sale of a vacation home.

**Example 33** Althea owns a cabin in the mountains that she uses on weekends and during a few weeks in the summer. The remaining time, the property is rented and for tax purposes is classified as a vacation home. Althea lives in an apartment in the city that she rents from an unrelated party. She sells the cabin at a gain of $120,000 and uses the proceeds to purchase a condominium that she will use as her principal residence. Can Althea exclude the gain on the sale of the cabin?

**Discussion: Althea is taxed on the $120,000 gain she realizes on the sale of the cabin. Although the proceeds will be used to acquire a principal residence, to be eligible for the exclusion, the residence sold must have been Althea's principal residence.**

The taxpayer must have owned and occupied the property as a principal residence for an aggregate of at least two of the previous five years before the sale or exchange. That is, the taxpayer must own the property for at least two years of the five preceding the sale (ownership test), and the property must be used as a principal residence for two of the five years (use test). When the property was acquired in a like-kind exchange, the property must be owned for five years to receive the exclusion. The exclusion applies to only one sale or exchange every two years.[14]

**Example 34** On July 2, 2016, Saanvi buys a condominium for $100,000. On August 15, 2021 she sells it for $140,000 and uses the proceeds to purchase a house for $155,000 on September 15, 2021. How much of the $40,000 gain on the sale of the condominium can Saanvi exclude?

**Discussion: Saanvi has owned the condominium for more than 2 years and has used it as a principal residence for more than 2 years. Therefore, she meets the ownership and use tests and can exclude the $40,000 gain on the sale.**

If a taxpayer does not meet the ownership and use tests or the one sale every two years requirement, a pro rata amount of the exclusion is allowed if the sale is due to a change in employment, health, or unforeseen circumstances. In such cases, the amount of the exclusion is equal to $250,000 ($500,000 if married) multiplied by the fraction of the two-year period in which the tests were met. The numerator of the fraction is:

the shorter of

(1) the aggregate periods in which the ownership and use tests were met during the five-year period ending on the date of the sale,

or

(2) the period after the date of the most recent sale or exchange to which the exclusion applied.[15]

**Example 35** Assume that in example 34, Saanvi's employer transfers her to another state and she sells the house on June 15, 2022, for $165,000. How much of the $10,000 gain on the sale of the house can Saanvi exclude?

**Discussion: Saanvi does not meet the ownership and use tests and cannot use the full $250,000 exclusion. However, since the sale was due to a change in employment, a pro rata amount of the $250,000 exclusion is allowed. The numerator of the fraction she can exclude is the lesser of (1) the 9 months she owned and used the property as a principal residence, or (2) the 10 months from the sale of the condominium. Saanvi's exclusion is based on the ratio of the 9 months she met the ownership and use tests to the required 24 months. Her maximum exclusion is $93,750 [$250,000 × (9 ÷ 24)], and she can exclude the entire $10,000 gain on the sale of the house. Note that the amount excluded is a pro rata portion of the $250,000 exclusion, not a pro rata portion of the realized gain.**

**Example 36** Assume that in example 34, Saanvi quits her job to attend law school. On June 15, 2022, she sells her house for $165,000 and relocates to another state. How much of the $10,000 gain on the sale of the house can Saanvi exclude?

**Discussion: Saanvi does not meet the ownership and use tests and cannot elect the $250,000 exclusion. Because the sale was not due to a change in employment, health, or unforeseen circumstances, she must include the $10,000 in income as a short-term capital gain (because the holding period is less than 12 months).**

The amount of excludable gain is increased to $500,000 for married taxpayers filing a joint return if: (1) either spouse meets the ownership test, (2) both spouses meet the use test, and (3) neither spouse is ineligible for the exclusion by virtue of a sale or exchange of a residence within the last two years.

**Example 37** Henry and Louis were married in 2016. On June 15, 2017, they bought a residence costing $80,000. They live in the residence until October 10, 2021, when they sell it for $400,000 and purchase another residence costing $500,000. How much gain must Henry and Louis recognize on the sale, and what is the basis of the new residence?

**Discussion: Henry and Louis realize a gain of $320,000 ($400,000 − $80,000) on the sale. They can exclude up to $500,000 of gain on the sale of the residence because they both meet the ownership (June 15, 2017, to October 10, 2021 > 2 years) and use tests (used as a principal residence more than 2 years), and neither has used the exclusion within the last 2 years. Therefore, they can exclude the $320,000 gain. Their basis in the new residence is $500,000.**

The exclusion is determined on an individual basis. If a married couple does not share a principal residence but files a joint return, a $250,000 exclusion is available for a qualifying sale or exchange of each spouse's residence. The provision limiting the exclusion to once every two years does not prevent a husband and wife from filing a joint return and each excluding up to $250,000 of gain from the sale of each spouse's principal residence. Also, the fact that an individual's spouse has used the exclusion within the previous two years does not prevent the individual from claiming their $250,000 exclusion.

**Example 38** Jorge bought a house that he used as his principal residence on April 1, 2019, for $90,000. Amelia bought a house costing $120,000 that she used as her principal residence on September 16, 2019. Jorge and Amelia are married on April 15, 2021, and they use Amelia's home as their principal residence. Jorge sells his house on May 30, 2021, for $160,000. How much of the gain must he recognize on the sale of his house?

**Discussion: Jorge can elect to exclude the $70,000 ($160,000 − $90,000) gain on the sale of his house. Even though he and Amelia file a joint return for 2021, Jorge is entitled to a $250,000 exclusion on the sale of his principal residence because he meets the ownership and use tests on it and has not taken the exclusion during the previous 2 years.**

**Example 39** Assume the same facts as in example 38. On February 19, 2022, Jorge and Amelia sell their principal residence for $400,000. How much of the gain on the sale must Jorge and Amelia recognize?

**Discussion: Jorge has not met the use test with respect to the residence and has used the exclusion within the previous 2 years. Therefore, he cannot claim a $250,000 exclusion on the sale. Amelia meets all the tests and can exclude $250,000 of the $280,000 ($400,000 − $120,000) gain. Each spouse is entitled to a $250,000 exclusion every 2 years. The fact that Jorge used his exclusion on the sale of his residence does not prevent Amelia from claiming her $250,000 exclusion. The $30,000 ($280,000 − $250,000) recognized gain is a long-term capital gain.**

In addition to the rules discussed above, several special rules determine the period of ownership and use of the property as a residence. A detailed discussion of the rules set forth below is beyond the scope of this text.

- Taxpayers may include periods of ownership and use of all prior residences with respect to which gain was deferred under prior law.
- If an individual becomes physically or mentally incapable of self-care, the time in which the individual owns the residence and resides in a licensed care facility is considered to be use as a principal residence. To qualify for this treatment, the taxpayer must have owned the residence and used it as a principal residence for at least one year during the five years preceding its sale.
- A taxpayer who receives a residence incident to a divorce is deemed to have used it during the time the taxpayer's spouse owned the property and used it as a residence. A taxpayer who owns a residence that is occupied by the taxpayer's spouse or former spouse under a divorce or separation agreement is deemed to use it as a principal residence during the period of such use.
- A taxpayer's period of ownership includes the period during which the taxpayer's deceased spouse owned the residence.
- An involuntary conversion of a principal residence that results in a gain is treated as a sale of a principal residence. Thus, taxpayers are allowed to use the $250,000 gain exclusion on an involuntary conversion of a principal residence.

# CHAPTER SUMMARY

The all-inclusive income concept requires that all gains are subject to tax when they are realized in an arm's-length transaction. However, Congress has provided current period tax relief for gains from like-kind exchanges and involuntary conversions. Although each nonrecognition transaction has unique characteristics, the two classes of transactions have five distinctive commonalities. First, the rationale for nonrecognition of these transactions comes from the wherewithal-to-pay concept. Because this concept is a basis for not recognizing gains, both transactions allow for the deferral of gains. The deferral is mandatory for like-kind exchanges. Gains on involuntary conversions are deferred at the election of the taxpayer. Losses on like-kind exchanges must be deferred. Involuntary conversion losses are deducted in the period of realization. Realized losses on a principal residence cannot be deducted or deferred.

Each nonrecognition transaction is viewed as the continuation of an ongoing investment in the asset disposed of in the transaction. Therefore, each nonrecognition transaction requires the acquisition of a qualified replacement property within a prescribed period for gain to be deferred.

Gains are fully deferred when the entire proceeds of the realization are reinvested in a replacement property. However, any amount realized on a nonrecognition disposition that is not reinvested in a qualifying replacement property is subject to tax under the wherewithal-to-pay concept. The amount of gain to be recognized cannot exceed the gain realized on the transaction.

The deferral of gains (and losses on like-kind exchanges) is effected through an adjustment of the basis of the replacement property. The basis of the replacement property is reduced for any gain deferred on the nonrecognition transaction. Losses on like-kind exchanges are deferred by increasing the basis of the replacement property.

As a continuation of the original investment in the property on which gain has been realized, the tax attributes of the original property attach to the replacement property. Under this attribution, the holding period of the replacement property includes the holding period of the original property. In addition, any depreciation recapture potential on the original property is attributed to the replacement. Recall from Chapter 11 that 1250 recapture only occurs when there is excess depreciation (MACRS exceeds straight-line).

The tax law allows a taxpayer to exclude from taxation $250,000 of gain on the sale of a principal residence. This exclusion is increased to $500,000 for married taxpayers who file a joint return. Unlike the nonrecognition provisions, which only provide for a deferral of the gain, the amount of gain excluded on the sale of a principal residence is never subject to tax.

In addition to being the taxpayer's principal residence, the property must have been owned by the taxpayer for at least two of the five years preceding the sale (ownership test) and must have been used as a principal residence by the taxpayer for two of the five years (use test). The exclusion applies to only one sale or exchange every two years. A realized loss on the sale or exchange of a taxpayer's personal residence is not deductible.

Table 12-1 compares and summarizes the characteristics and requirements for nonrecognition in each of the nonrecognition transactions.

*Table 12-1*

**Characteristics of Nonrecognition Transactions**

| Characteristic | Like-Kind Exchanges | Involuntary Conversions | Sale of Principal Residence |
|---|---|---|---|
| Property eligible for nonrecognition | Real property is held for productive use in a trade or business or for investment. | Property used in a trade or business or business or held for investment. | Principal residence of the taxpayer. |
| Replacement property requirement | Like-kind business or investment property. | Property must have the same functional use to the taxpayer as the property converted. Condemned real property must be replaced with like-kind property. | No property purchase required. |
| Replacement period | Property to be received in the exchange must be identified within 45 days and transaction completed within 180 days of first transfer of property. | Two years from the end of the tax year of the conversion. Taxpayer has 3 years to replace condemned real property. | No property purchase required. |
| Realized gains | Deferral of gains is mandatory. Gains are recognized to the extent of boot received in the exchange. | Deferral of gains is elective. If deferral is elected, any proceeds not reinvested must be recognized. | Single taxpayers can exclude up to $250,000 of gain every 2 years. Married taxpayers can exclude up to $500,000 of gain every 2 years. |
| Realized losses | Deferral of losses is mandatory. | Losses are recognized. | Losses are not deductible. |
| Basis of replacement property | Gains: reduce by deferred gain. Losses: increase by deferred loss. | Reduce basis by deferred gain. | Property purchase is not required. |

# KEY TERMS

boot (p. 12-7)
deferred (third-party) exchange (p. 12-8)
involuntary conversion (p. 12-14)
like-kind exchange rules (p. 12-8)
like-kind property (p. 12-9)
nonrecognition transaction (p. 12-2)
principal residence (p. 12-19)

# PRIMARY TAX LAW SOURCES

[1]Reg. Sec. 1.1031(c)-1—Requires adjustment of the basis of property acquired in a nontaxable exchange. Similar provisions are found in Reg. Sec. 1.1033(b)-1 for involuntarily converted property.

[2]Sec. 1223—The general rule for holding period requires a carryover of holding period when a carryover basis is used.

[3]Reg. Sec. 1.1250-3—Requires the carryover of excess depreciation on any Section 1250 property acquired in a tax-free transaction.

[4]Sec. 1031—Provides rules for like-kind exchanges of property.

[5]Reg. Sec. 1.1031(k)-1—Provides the rules for deferred exchanges and gives examples of qualifying exchanges.

[6]Code Sec. 1031—Amended by Act Sec 13303 of the 2017 Tax Cut and Jobs Act.

[7]Reg. Sec. 1.1031(a)-1—Gives the general definition of *like-kind property* for purposes of Section 1031.

[8]Reg. Sec. 1.1031(b)-1—Discusses the treatment of boot in like-kind exchanges.

[9]Reg. Sec. 1.1031(d)-2—Provides rules for treatment of mortgage assumptions in like-kind exchanges.

[10]Sec. 1033—Provides rules for deferring gains on involuntary conversions.

[11]Reg. Sec. 1.1033(a)-2—Provides the rules for direct conversions of property.

Reinforce this chapter's concepts by going to **www.cengage.com**

[12]Sec. 1033—See footnote 10.

[13]Reg. Sec. 1.1033(g)-1—Allows condemned real property used in a trade or business or for the production of income to be replaced with like-kind property.

[14]Sec. 121(b)—Allows taxpayers to exclude up to $250,000 of gain ($500,000 if married, filing a joint return) on the sale of a principal residence.

[15]Sec. 121(c)—Allows a taxpayer to claim a pro rata share of the exclusion when the ownership and use tests or the one sale every two years requirement are not met due to a change in employment or health, or unforeseen circumstances.

# DISCUSSION QUESTIONS

1. **LO2** How does the wherewithal-to-pay concept affect the recognition of gains on asset dispositions? What else is necessary for nonrecognition of a gain upon disposition of an asset?
2. **LO2** How is the tax treatment of a deferred gain similar to and different from the treatment of an excluded gain?
3. **LO3** When a gain on a property disposition is deferred, the basis of the replacement property is reduced by the amount of gain deferred. Which concept supports this treatment? Explain.
4. **LO6** What is boot? How does boot affect the recognition of gains or losses on like-kind exchanges?
5. **LO4** What constitutes an exchange of assets?
6. **LO4** Does an exchange have to occur simultaneously to qualify for nonrecognition? Explain.
7. **LO4** Define what qualifies as a like-kind exchange.
8. **LO6** Why does the assumption of a mortgage when exchanging related assets constitute boot?
9. **LO5** Discuss the restrictions placed on like-kind exchanges between related parties. Include the reasoning behind the restriction in your discussion.
10. **LO4** What is the recapture potential of an asset?
11. **LO7** The rules for loss recognition on involuntary conversions are more liberal than those for exchanges. What features of an involuntary conversion contribute to the difference in treatments for the two types of transactions?
12. **LO7** How long does a taxpayer who suffers an involuntary conversion of an asset have to replace the asset to qualify for nonrecognition? Explain.
13. **LO8** What is a principal residence of a taxpayer?
14. **LO8, 9** Losses on exchanges must be deferred. A loss on an involuntary conversion is never deferred. In contrast, a loss on the sale of a principal residence is never recognized. Explain why losses on the sale of a principal residence are treated differently from losses on exchanges and involuntary conversions.
15. **LO9** What are the requirements for excluding gain on the sale of a principal residence?
16. **LO9** In general, a taxpayer can exclude up to $250,000 of gain on the sale of a principal residence. However, this exclusion is only available every two years. Explain the circumstances under which the two-year restriction is modified and the tax treatment when the restriction is modified.

# PROBLEMS

17. **LO2, 3** Honre Corporation's warehouse and Filip Company's office building were located side by side until a fire raced through both structures, completely destroying them. The warehouse has an adjusted basis of $250,000 and a fair market value (FMV) before the fire of $500,000. Honre Corporation's fire insurance policy covers the FMV and pays $500,000. Honre decides not to replace the warehouse because it already has adequate storage space. Filip Company's office building has an adjusted basis of $400,000 and an FMV before the fire of $750,000. Filip's fire insurance covers a maximum structural loss of only $650,000 and pays that amount. Filip uses the $650,000 to build a new office building on its old site.

    Honre Corporation has a taxable transaction. Filip Company does not. Compare these tax results using only the attributes and commonalities of nonrecognition transactions. (Do not use the specific rules of involuntary conversions.)

18. **LO5** Which of the following transfers meet the exchange requirement for deferral under like-kind exchange provisions?
    a. Bonita sells her rental condominium in Park City and uses the proceeds as a down payment to buy a rental condominium in Breckenridge.
    b. Enrique Corporation sells its old pasta machine to Angelo Distributing Company and after shopping around for a few days, purchases a new Angelo Model 5 Pasta Machine from Angelo Distributing Company.
    c. Louise owns an apartment building in Milwaukee, which Rebecca offers to purchase. Louise is willing to part with the property but does not want to recognize the substantial gain on the sale. She is willing to exchange the apartment for a lakefront resort lodge in Minnesota. Rebecca finds such a property and buys it from Ole. Then Rebecca exchanges the lodge for Louise's apartment building.
19. **LO5** Which of the following exchanges of property are like-kind exchanges?
    a. Land traded for an airplane.
    b. A warehouse used in a trade or business exchanged for land to be used as a personal residence.
    c. Land in Greece held as an investment for a hotel in Rome.
    d. A business computer for a business computer.
20. **LO5** Which of the following exchanges of property are like-kind exchanges?
    a. Horace trades his personal use auto for another personal use auto.
    b. Lian trades an office building she rents out for a warehouse to use in her business.
    c. Ace Construction Company trades a used pile driving hammer for a rock crusher.
21. **LO4, 6** Beaver Corporation owns a parcel of land with a fair market value (FMV) of \$75,000 and a basis of \$40,000. Beaver exchanges the land for a building with an FMV of \$65,000. The corporation also receives \$10,000 in cash. Both properties are investment properties for Beaver.
    a. What is Beaver's amount realized on the exchange?
    b. What is Beaver's realized gain or loss on the exchange?
    c. How much of the realized gain or loss must Beaver recognize?
    d. What is the character of the recognized gain or loss?
    e. What is Beaver's basis in the building it acquired?
22. **LO4, 6** Leon exchanges an office building which he held as investment property for a bowling alley. His office building has a basis of \$175,000 and a fair market value of \$160,000, and it is subject to a mortgage of \$40,000. The fair market value of the bowling alley is \$120,000. The owner of the bowling alley will assume Leon's debt on the office building.
    a. Is this a like-kind exchange? Explain.
    b. What is Leon's realized gain or loss on the office building?
    c. How much of the realized gain or loss is recognized on the exchange?
    d. What is the character of the recognized gain or loss?
    e. How much of the realized gain or loss is deferred?
    f. What is the basis of the bowling alley acquired in the exchange?
23. **LO4, 5, 6** Jose owns a warehouse in Mexico City with a basis of \$430,000 and a fair market value of \$700,000. Lucien owns a warehouse in Boulder, Colorado, with a basis of \$200,000 and a fair market value of \$700,000. Jose and Lucien agree to exchange the warehouses.
    a. Does this transaction qualify as a like-kind exchange?
    b. Will Lucien recognize a gain or a loss? How much?
    c. What is Lucien's basis in his Mexico City warehouse?
24. **LO4, 6** Maya exchanges an office building with a fair market value of \$200,000 and a basis of \$110,000 for \$20,000 cash and a warehouse with a fair market value of \$300,000. In the exchange, she assumes the \$120,000 mortgage on the warehouse.
    a. Has Maya given or received boot? Explain.

b. Does Maya recognize any gain or loss on this exchange?
c. What is Maya's basis in the warehouse that she acquires in the exchange?

25. **LO4, 6** Oscar and Harriet agree to exchange apartment buildings and the mortgages on the buildings, with any difference in value to be paid in cash. Particulars of their respective buildings are as follows:

| | Oscar | Harriet |
|---|---|---|
| Fair market value | $120,000 | $112,000 |
| Mortgage | 70,000 | 52,000 |
| Adjusted basis | 40,000 | 55,000 |

a. How much cash must be paid, and who must pay the cash to equalize the exchange?
b. What are Oscar's realized and recognized gains on the exchange and his basis in the apartment building acquired in the exchange?
c. What are Harriet's realized and recognized gains on the exchange and her basis in the apartment building acquired in the exchange?

26. **LO4, 5, 6** On July 8, 2021, Cynthia and her daughter Constance agree to exchange land they held for investment. Both tracts are worth $18,000. Cynthia acquired her land four years earlier for $9,000. Constance paid $16,000 for her land the previous year.
a. What are the tax effects of the exchange for Cynthia and Constance?
b. On February 15, 2023, Constance sells the land acquired in the exchange for $21,000. What are the tax effects of the sale? Explain.

27. **LO8** Which of the following are qualified replacement properties for properties involuntarily converted? Explain.
a. The insurance proceeds from a warehouse destroyed by a fire are used to purchase a manufacturing plant. The warehouse and the plant are both used in the taxpayer's manufacturing business.
b. Assume the same facts as in part a, except that the warehouse is held as an investment and rented out to businesses. The plant will also be rented out to a manufacturing business.
c. An office building used in a trade or business is condemned. The proceeds are used to buy an apartment complex that will be used as an investment activity.
d. The insurance proceeds from the destruction of a construction crane are used to buy a fleet of forklifts. The crane and the forklifts are used in the taxpayer's construction business.
e. An antique vase is stolen from the lobby of a business. The insurance proceeds are used to buy a painting that is hung in the same lobby.

28. **LO8** Which of the following are qualified replacement properties for properties involuntarily converted? Explain.
a. The city of Marble River announces plans to condemn Heima's rental apartment complex on July 2, 2021. On August 7, 2021, Heima purchases a warehouse to use as a rental. The city pays Heima $890,000 on November 1, 2021, as the condemnation proceedings come to a close.
b. The city of Marble River also announces plans to condemn Heima's principal residence on July 2, 2021. He receives a check for $350,000 on the November 1, 2021, condemnation closing date. On March 29, 2022, Heima purchases a new residence for $375,000. His basis in the condemned residence is $60,000.
c. Lila uses the insurance proceeds from the destruction of her commercial fishing boat by Hurricane Fredd to buy new fishing equipment and nets for her other fishing boat.
d. Milo uses the insurance proceeds from a fire that totally destroys his warehouse to buy 100 percent of the common stock of Storage Space Corporation, a company that owns and operates three warehouses.

29. **LO7** A fire in the factory of Franny's Famous Frankfurters destroys several stuffing machines. The machines have an adjusted basis of $125,000 and a fair market value of $225,000. Franny's insurance company reimburses Franny's $100,000 for the destruction of the machines. Franny's uses the insurance proceeds to buy second-hand stuffers costing $175,000. What are Franny's realized and recognized gains or losses on the fire and the basis in the replacement stuffers?

30. **LO7** Grant Industries' warehouse is condemned by the city on August 18, 2021. Because of widespread publicity leading up to the condemnation, Grant anticipates it and purchases a replacement warehouse on April 15, 2021, for $670,000. The city pays Grant $430,000 for the condemned property, which has an adjusted basis to Grant of $220,000.
   a. What is Grant's realized gain or loss on the condemnation?
   b. What is the minimum amount of gain Grant must recognize on the condemnation?
   c. If Grant elects to recognize the minimum amount of gain on the condemnation, what is the basis in the new warehouse?

Communication Skills

31. **LO7** Refer to the facts of problem 30. Write a letter to Grant Industries explaining why it might want to recognize the entire gain on the condemnation.

32. **LO7** One of Reddy's Fancy Dog Food factories is destroyed by a tornado. The factory has an adjusted basis of $375,000. Reddy's receives $540,000 from its insurance company to cover the loss. What is the minimum amount of gain that must be recognized in each of the following situations and the basis of any property purchased with the insurance proceeds?
   a. Reddy's decides that the lost production could be made up by its other factories and uses the proceeds to pay a cash dividend to its shareholders.
   b. Reddy's purchases another factory for $590,000.
   c. Reddy's purchases another factory for $480,000.
   d. Reddy's purchases another factory for $350,000.

33. **LO7** A fire totally destroys a manufacturing plant owned by Ansel Corporation. The plant, located in Louisiana, has been used for more than 30 years and is fully depreciated. Ansel's insurance pays $500,000 for the destruction. In analyzing qualified replacement properties, Ansel can buy a qualified replacement manufacturing plant in Oklahoma for $460,000. What is the minimum amount of gain Ansel must recognize on the insurance proceeds? What is the basis of the Oklahoma plant? Explain.

34. **LO7** MacKenzie owns a boat rental business. During the current year, a tidal wave sweeps through the harbor where she keeps her boats anchored. Four boats are totally destroyed, but the rest of the rental fleet escapes serious damage. MacKenzie replaces the four boats within six months of the tidal wave. The details on each boat destroyed and the cost of its replacement are as follows:

| Boat | Insurance Proceeds | Adjusted Basis | Replacement Cost |
|---|---|---|---|
| Sailboat | $ 50,000 | $ 18,000 | $ 48,000 |
| Yacht | $136,000 | $ 75,000 | $150,000 |
| Speedboat | $ 82,000 | $102,000 | $ 95,000 |
| Fishing boat | $142,000 | $112,000 | $ 80,000 |

   a. What is the realized gain or loss on each of the boats?
   b. What is the minimum amount of gain or loss that must be recognized on each of the boats?
   c. Assuming that MacKenzie elects to recognize the minimum amount of gain or loss on each boat, what is the basis of each replacement boat?

Communication Skills

35. **LO7** Alley's automobile dealership, which has an adjusted basis of $400,000, is destroyed by a hurricane in the current year. Alley's receives $600,000 from its

insurance company to cover the loss. Alley's has begun to rebuild the dealership at an estimated cost of $750,000. Assume that the rebuilding costs at least $750,000.

a. What is the minimum gain Alley's must recognize on the hurricane damage?
b. Alley's is organized as a corporation. Because of a slump in the automobile industry, Alley's has net operating losses totaling $400,000 that it is carrying forward from the previous five years. Alley's expects to have another operating loss in the current year. Write a letter to Alley's explaining how to account for the involuntary conversion results and why you advise taking those measures.

36. **LO9** In each of the following cases, determine the amount of realized gain or loss and the recognized gain or loss:

a. Chen sells her house for $73,000 and pays $4,000 in commissions on the sale. She paid $83,000 for the house four years earlier.
b. In July 2021, Alexandra, who is single, is transferred to San Diego. She had purchased a new home the previous month for $50,000, and had contracted to make $25,000 of improvements to the house. After the improvements are completed in November, Alexandra sells the house for $97,000 and pays a $3,000 commission on the sale.
c. Oswald is single and sells his principal residence for $340,000. He pays selling expenses of $20,000. Oswald purchased the house for $75,000 in 2006.
d. Ushi was transferred to North Carolina in September 2018 and was unable to sell her home in Texas before moving. She acquired the home in October 2016 for $110,000. She rents out the Texas house on a six-month lease. In March 2020, Ushi purchases a new residence in North Carolina at a cost of $150,000. She continues to rent out the Texas property on a six-month lease. The Texas house finally sells in December 2021 for $130,000. Ushi pays $10,000 in commissions on the sale.

37. **LO9** Aretha sells her house on June 9, 2021, for $220,000 and pays commissions of $10,000 on the sale. She had purchased the house for $60,000 and made capital improvements costing $15,000. What are Aretha's realized and recognized gains in each of the following cases?

a. Aretha is single and acquired the house on September 15, 2013.
b. Assume the same facts as in part a, except that Aretha sells the house for $375,000 and pays commissions of $30,000 on the sale.
c. Aretha is single and acquired the house on September 1, 2020. She sells the house because her company transfers her to Phoenix.
d. Assume the same facts as in part c, except that Aretha moves to Phoenix to enter medical school.

38. **LO9** Mai, a single taxpayer, sells her residence in the suburbs for $300,000. She bought the house twelve years ago for $60,000 and made $30,000 of improvements to it. Mai buys a new downtown condominium for $155,000 a few weeks after she sells her suburban residence.

a. What are Mai's realized gain and recognized gain on the sale? What is her basis in the condominium?
b. Assume that Mai sells the property for $350,000. What are her realized gain and recognized gain on the sale? What is her basis in the condominium?

39. **LO9** Manuel and Rita sell their home in Minneapolis for $495,000, incurring selling expenses of $25,000. They had purchased the residence for $85,000 and made capital improvements totaling $20,000 during the 20 years they lived there. They buy a new residence in Tampa for $225,000.

a. What are Manuel and Rita's realized gain and recognized gain on the sale? What is their basis in the Tampa house?
b. Assume that Manuel and Rita sell the Minneapolis home for $675,000. What are their realized gain and recognized gain on the sale? What is their basis in the Tampa house?

40. **LO9** Kerri and John are married. On May 12, 2021, they sell their home for $190,000 and purchase another residence costing $225,000. What are Kerri and John's realized gain and recognized gain in each of the following cases?
    a. They purchased the residence for $85,000 on February 8, 2019.
    b. Kerri purchased the residence for $85,000 on August 15, 2018. They are married on June 13, 2019, and use Kerri's house as their principal residence.
    c. Assume the same facts as in part b, except that they sell the house for $390,000.

41. **LO9** Gary and Gertrude are married on April 8, 2020. They use Gertrude's home as their residence. Gertrude purchased the home on November 14, 2018, for $60,000. On February 19, 2021, Gertrude is killed in an automobile accident. Gary is distraught and sells their residence on May 14, 2021, for $110,000 and moves to Portugal. How much of the gain on the sale of the residence is taxable?

# ISSUE IDENTIFICATION PROBLEMS

In each of the following problems, identify the tax issue(s) posed by the facts presented. Determine the possible tax consequences of each issue that you identify.

42. Bonnie wants to trade her Snow Bird, Utah, condominium, which she has held for investment, for investment property in Steamboat Springs or Crested Butte, Colo. On April 20, 2021, she transfers title to the Snow Bird property to Thanh/Hao Partnership, which transfers $300,000 cash to a real estate broker to hold in escrow until Bonnie finds a replacement property. The broker is commissioned to find suitable property for Bonnie.

43. Erica owns A-1 Landscaping Services. She trades a lawn tractor with a basis of $200 for a powered post hole digger worth $300.

44. Rollie exchanges a parking lot used in his business for a tract of land worth $20,000 and $4,000 in cash. He plans to subdivide and sell the land as residential lots. The adjusted basis of the parking lot is $30,000.

45. Johann exchanges an apartment building for an office building worth $100,000. The apartment building has an adjusted basis of $80,000 and is encumbered by a $30,000 mortgage, which the owner of the office building assumes in the exchange.

46. Stephanie owns 75 percent of the Gould Corporation. She exchanges land that she owns as an investment for an office building owned by Gould that has a fair market value of $130,000. In the exchange, Stephanie gives Gould Corporation stock with a fair market value of $20,000. Stephanie's basis in the land is $60,000, and her basis in the stock is $28,000. Gould's basis in the office building is $90,000.

47. Festus Farmers Cooperative truck barn, which has a $50,000 adjusted basis, is destroyed by a fire. Festus receives $80,000 from its insurance company for the barn and uses the proceeds as a down payment on a new grain silo costing $160,000.

48. Raylene's personal automobile is destroyed by a tornado and occurred in a federal disaster area. Her insurance company paid her $5,000, which she used to purchase a new automobile costing $10,000. Raylene received the automobile that was destroyed as a graduation present from her uncle Earl. Earl's basis in the automobile was $2,000. The automobile was worth $8,000 when Raylene received it.

49. Inez is a freelance artist. She purchased 10 acres of land in 2016 for $5,000. On July 15, 2021, the land is condemned by the county government to build a new courthouse and jail facility. The county awards Inez $35,000 for the condemnation of the land. Inez uses the proceeds to purchase a building that she will use as a production studio for her artwork.

50. Laurie bought a home in 2018 for $65,000. On November 2, 2021, she sells it for $114,000. Laurie uses the proceeds to purchase a duplex costing $200,000. She uses one unit in the duplex as her principal residence.
51. Harvey sells his personal residence on March 18, 2021, for $78,000. He paid $86,000 for it on April 22, 2019.
52. Eva and Mario are married on June 14, 2020. They use Eva's home as their principal residence. Eva purchased the home for $97,000 in 2017. On January 13, 2021, Eva and Mario are divorced. As part of the settlement, Mario receives the home. He sells it on March 30, 2021, for $119,000.

# TECHNOLOGY APPLICATIONS

53. Will owns residential rental property that is destroyed by a tornado in March 2020. He files a claim with his insurance company and receives $90,000 for the property. The building is fully depreciated, and the adjusted basis of the land is $3,000. The area around the property is being developed into a high-priced residential subdivi sion, and Will does not have the cash to build a replacement unit consistent with the quality of the new homes being built. In April 2021, he sells the land for $75,000, and in December 2021, he finds a suitable replacement rental property that costs $170,000. Before Will acquires the replacement property, he would like you to determine whether the sale of the land will be considered part of the involuntary conversion and eligible for gain deferral. Research Skills
54. Orley, Goutam, and Serena each own undivided one-third interests as tenants in common in three parcels of land held as an investment. One of the parcels is mortgaged for $60,000, for which each is personally liable. They would like to rearrange their interests in the properties so that each becomes a 100 percent owner of one property. Orley has agreed to take the mortgaged parcel and assume the $60,000 liability. Goutam and Serena will each issue Orley a $20,000 note to compensate him for taking the mortgaged parcel. Each parcel is worth $75,000 and has a basis of $30,000. Determine the tax consequences of the proposed transaction.

# COMPREHENSIVE PROBLEM

55. During the current year, the Harlow Corporation, which specializes in commercial construction, has the following property transactions. Determine the realized and recognized gain or loss on each of Harlow's property transactions and the basis of any property acquired in each transaction: Research Skills
    a. In April, a tornado damages a crane and a dump truck at one of its construction sites. The crane was acquired in 2018 for $120,000 and has an adjusted basis of $39,650. The dump truck was acquired in 2016 for $70,000 and has an adjusted basis of $33,880. The insurance company reimburses Harlow $35,000 for the crane and $42,000 for the dump truck. The company decides not to replace the dump truck and uses the insurance proceeds to purchase a new crane for $110,000.
    b. A fire destroys the company's supply warehouse. The warehouse originally cost $300,000 and has an adjusted basis of $200,000. Its fair market value before the fire was $250,000. The insurance company pays Harlow $230,000, which it uses to acquire a warehouse costing $280,000.
    c. The city of PeaceDale condemns land that Harlow had acquired in 1985 for $22,000 and held as an investment. The city pays Harlow the $195,000 fair market value of the land. Harlow uses the proceeds to acquire a commercial office park for $350,000.

# DISCUSSION CASES

56. On July 8, 2019, Joe and Mateo sell their principal residence for $650,000. Their adjusted basis in the property is $275,000. To complete the sale, Joe and Mateo have to take back a second mortgage for $120,000. The buyers borrow $465,000 from a local bank and put down $65,000 in cash.

    In December 2021, Joe and Mateo are notified that the buyers have defaulted on the second mortgage and filed for bankruptcy. A large manufacturing plant near the house has closed, and the housing market is overstocked; the value of the house has dropped significantly—below the amount remaining on the bank's mortgage. Joe and Mateo want to deduct the loss on the second mortgage. The IRS Hot Line adviser tells them the loss is not recognizable because they have no basis in the mortgage debt. Joe and Mateo never reported as income the payments they received on the second mortgage. Advise Joe and Mateo on the deductibility of the defaulted mortgage.

57. The city of Stillcreek decides to expand the runway at the local airport. To get the land for the expansion, it condemns the property it needs and pays the owners the current appraised value. Buster's house is condemned, and he is paid $340,000 for his property. Buster, who is single, had purchased the property for $70,000 and had made $30,000 in improvements to it. He plans to use the proceeds to purchase a new residence but is unsure how much he should reinvest in the new home. In addition to the condemnation, 1,000 shares of stock that Buster owns in Cantmis Corporation become worthless during the year. His loss on the stock is $22,000, and he does not anticipate any large capital gains in the next few years. Buster has heard that there have been changes in the tax law concerning principal residences, and seeks your advice. Discuss Buster's options concerning the condemnation of his property.

# TAX PLANNING CASES

58. In October 2021, fire completely destroys the principal residence of Olaf, who is 63 and single, and lives in Bemidji, Minnesota. He owned the home for 16 years; his adjusted basis is $58,000. Olaf receives insurance proceeds of $200,000.

    Olaf plans to move to Scottsdale, Arizona, to be near his daughter no later than 2024, when she plans to return there after finishing a five-year tour of duty with the U.S. Foreign Service. Olaf also owns a condominium in Hilton Head, South Carolina, which he paid $120,000 for in February 2020. Write a letter to Olaf advising him on his options and their tax consequences.

Communication Skills

59. Ken and Helen own a bed and breakfast in Vermont. They acquired the property in 2005 for $190,000, and their adjusted basis in it is $95,000. The property is worth $260,000, and they have a mortgage of $100,000. Both are tired of the cold winters and eventually would like to retire in the Southwestern United States. However, Ken and Helen feel that they need to work another seven or eight years first. A friend has suggested that they could move now if they can find another bed and breakfast or a small motel in the Southwest and do a like-kind exchange. However, their friend warns them: "If you do a like-kind exchange, you better get some tax help and don't make the same mistake I made." After consulting with a regional real estate firm, they find three properties that they are interested in pursuing. Before they go to the expense of visiting the properties, Ken and Helen have come to you for tax advice. They tell you that any cash needed to acquire the new property would come from the sale of stock. The long-term capital gain on the sale would be 70 percent of the sale proceeds. They are in the 32 percent marginal tax bracket. Using the information on the three properties below, determine which property will minimize the tax consequences of the exchange.

| Type of Property | Fair Market Value | Mortgage | Cash Received (Paid) |
|---|---|---|---|
| Bed and Breakfast | $300,000 | $150,000 | $ 10,000 |
| Motel | $320,000 | $140,000 | $(20,000) |
| Bed and Breakfast | $250,000 | $125,000 | $ 35,000 |

# ETHICS DISCUSSION CASE

60. Claude is a CPA and a partner with SKH and Associates, a regional public accounting firm. In September 2019, Brokaw Technologies approached one of his clients, Walter Fenner, about acquiring 100 acres of land that Walter owned next to the company's headquarters. To minimize its tax liability, Brokaw was interested in doing a like-kind exchange to obtain the property. Walter was not interested in a like-kind exchange because he wanted to recognize the capital gain from the sale of the land to offset losses he had incurred in the stock market. In November 2018, Brokaw Technology was approached by Simmons Corporation about buying land that Brokaw owned in a neighboring town. Brokaw informed Simmons that it would be interested in doing a like-kind exchange if the corporation could acquire Walter Fenner's property. Because Walter was anxious to recognize the capital gain in 2019, Simmons Corporation bought the property from him on December 15, 2019, with the intention of making the exchange with Brokaw Technology. Because of a legal problem with the title on the Brokaw property, the exchange did not take place until July 1, 2020.

In June 2021, Brokaw Technology becomes a client of SKH and Associates, and Claude is named the partner-in-charge on the engagement. While reviewing the prior year audit workpapers and tax return, he notices that Brokaw acquired the land for its new warehouse in a like-kind exchange. Because the address and description of the property are familiar, Claude obtains the supporting documentation on the transaction from the previous auditors. The documentation confirms that Claude's client, Walter Fenner, did previously own the land acquired in the like-kind exchange. Since Brokaw did not acquire the property within 180 days of Walter's sale of the property, Claude is unsure of Brokaw's treatment of the transaction as a like-kind exchange. A closer look at the supporting document shows the date Simmons Corporation acquired the property from Walter as January 15, 2020. The chief financial officer of Brokaw tells Claude: "I remember it took a little longer than we expected because of some legal issues concerning title to the property we owned. As to when Simmons acquired the property, that is documentation Simmons provided to us." Claude is sure that the CFO is not telling him the whole story. However, he is unsure how to proceed. What is Claude's obligation under the Statements on Standards for Tax Services (which can be found at www.aicpa.org) concerning Brokaw's 2020 return and the preparation of its 2021 return?

# Income Tax Entities

PART 5



The hardest thing in the world to understand is the Income Tax.

—Albert Einstein

iStock.com/davidf

# Choice of Business Entity—General Tax and Nontax Factors/Formation

13

Learning Objectives:

LO 1 Describe the nontax characteristics that affect the choice of business entity.

LO 2 Compare the nontax characteristics of sole proprietorships, partnerships, corporations, S corporations, limited liability companies, and limited liability partnerships, and explain the effects of their characteristics on the choice of business entity.

LO 3 Explain the general income tax characteristics of the various entities, including the incidence of taxation, double taxation, and the status of an owner as an employee of the entity.

LO 4 Show how general income tax provisions can affect the choice of business entity.

LO 5 Explain the differences in treatment of items that occur at the formation of an entity, including transfers to the entity and how they affect the basis of the entity and its owners.

LO 6 Explain the treatment of start-up and organizational costs.

LO 7 Compare accounting method and accounting period choices among the various entities.

## concept review

### GENERAL CONCEPTS

**Related party** Family members and corporations that are owned by family members are considered related parties, as are certain other relationships between entities in which the power to control the substance of a transaction is evidenced through majority ownership. pg. 2-4

### ACCOUNTING CONCEPTS

**Accounting method** A taxpayer must adopt an accounting method that clearly reflects income. pg. 2-9

**Annual accounting period** All entities must report the results of their operations on an annual basis (the tax year). Each tax year stands on its own, apart from other tax years. pg. 2-9

**Conduit entity** An entity for which the tax attributes flow through to its owners for tax purposes. pg. 2-6

**Entity** All items of income, deduction, and so on are traced to the tax unit responsible for the item. pg. 2-6

**Substance-over-form doctrine** Transactions are to be taxed according to their true intention rather than some form that may have been contrived. pg. 2-11

### INCOME CONCEPTS

**Basis** This is the amount of unrecovered investment in an asset. As amounts are expended and/or recovered relative to an asset over time, the basis is adjusted in consideration of such changes. The **adjusted basis** of an asset is the original basis, plus or minus the changes in the amount of unrecovered investment. pgs. 2-13, 2-21

**Capital recovery** No income is realized until the taxpayer receives more than the amount invested to produce the income. The amount invested in an asset represents the maximum amount recoverable. pg. 2-13

**Legislative grace** Any tax relief provided is the result of a specific act of Congress that must be strictly applied and interpreted. All income received is taxable unless a specific provision in the tax law excludes the income from taxation. Deductions must be approached with the philosophy that nothing is deductible unless a provision in the tax law allows the deduction. pg. 2-12

**Realization** No income or loss is recognized until it has been realized. A realization involves a change in the form and/or the substance of a taxpayer's property rights that results from an arm's-length transaction. pg. 2-14

### DEDUCTION CONCEPTS

**Business purpose** To be deductible, an expenditure or a loss must have a business or other economic purpose that exceeds any tax avoidance motive. The primary motive for the transaction must be to make a profit. pg. 2-18

## 13-1 INTRODUCTION

Although individuals are the largest group of taxpaying entities (as discussed in Chapter 8) and generally the principal focus of an entry-level tax course, many different legal, natural, economic, social, and cultural entities exist. Not all entities pay income tax. Because of legislative grace, only three types of entities are taxed on their income: individuals, corporations, and fiduciaries (trusts and estates). All other entities are either exempt or are considered conduit entities. Whether an entity is taxable, tax-exempt, or a conduit can depend on practical considerations or the theoretical foundation of the entity. For example, organizations whose primary function is charity are not required to pay tax on the income generated by their charitable function. This exemption from tax is based on the premise that such organizations are not formed for a business purpose and that the proceeds are to be used to promote the charitable function. Because most of these organizations perform functions that would fall to the government if they did not exist, extracting revenue from these entities is neither practical nor desirable.

Taxpayers often need to choose a form for a business entity. Because simple formulas for deciding the correct form for conducting a business do not exist, this chapter and Chapters 14 and 15 address many factors that affect the choice of business entity. Both tax and nontax factors must be considered. Accordingly, these three chapters compare the consequences of events during an entity's life cycle from the viewpoints of sole proprietors, partnerships, corporations, and S corporations.

These chapters do not discuss trusts and estates. Their purpose generally is to preserve assets rather than to conduct a trade or business. Therefore, they are not a consideration in choosing a business entity.

This chapter begins with a discussion of the nontax factors that can affect the choice of business entity. It then reviews each entity in relation to these factors and compares the general income tax factors for each business form. A discussion of issues that arise at the formation of an entity begins the life-cycle explanation of factors that affect the choice of business entity.

Chapter 14 concludes the life cycle entity discussion by examining the differences in the calculation of taxable income for the various entity forms, the effects of income calculations on an owner's basis, and the tax treatment of distributions received from an entity. Chapter 15 discusses special topics affecting the various entity forms. These topics include types of compensation plans available to owners of various entity types, tax credits available for businesses, the effect of the alternative minimum tax on individual owners, and the impact of multinational operations on the choice of business entity.

## 13-2 NONTAX FACTORS

LO 1
Describe the nontax characteristics that affect the choice of business entity.

Income taxation is only one factor to consider when an economic decision must be made. Often, taxation is not as significant as nontax factors in the choice of business form. The number of owners, limiting personal liability, freedom to choose how to transfer ownership, anticipated life of the enterprise, ability to participate in business management, costs of organizing the entity, and ability to raise capital are some of the nontax factors.

The number of owners can restrict the choice of entity. For example, a one-owner business cannot use the partnership form of ownership because a partnership must have more than one owner. Similarly, if the number of owners is large, use of an S corporation may be prohibited. Therefore, the number of current and potential future owners affects the choice of entity used to conduct a business.

**Limited liability** means that investors are not risking more of their personal assets than the amount they paid for their investment interest. That is, an investor's personal assets are not at risk to cover liabilities incurred by the entity. Limiting personal liability is often the most important factor for investors choosing a legal form for operating their businesses.

The **transferability of ownership interest** refers to the ease with which ownership can be transferred. In certain situations, restricting the buying and selling of an ownership interest may be desirable. Common restrictions include those that keep an investor from selling to anyone other than a current owner and/or require the ownership group to vote on the acceptance of any new owners. Such restrictions generally occur with closely held businesses. In contrast, companies trading on the major public stock exchanges offer free transferability of ownership interests. The ability to restrict the transfer of ownership interests is often an important factor in choosing the form for doing business.

Businesses that have frequent changes in ownership must consider the continuity of an entity's life when choosing a business form. **Continuity of life** refers to whether an entity continues to operate or technically dissolves and ceases to exist in its present form when a change occurs in the ownership structure. State law dictates whether an entity continues or technically dissolves if its ownership structure changes. Continuity of life is an attribute of corporations that ensures that a corporate business will continue to exist, regardless of which shareholders trade their stock. Under most state laws, partnerships technically dissolve when ownership changes.

The degree of management control also can vary across entities. Corporations use **centralized management** structures, which ensure the existence of a corporation even when managers and owners come and go. General partnerships allow broad-based management: All partners have the right to participate in management decisions. However, the nature of a partnership lets the partners define each partner's role in managing the business.

The cost of organizing each entity varies according to legal requirements. In general, corporations are more costly to organize than are sole proprietorships; partnerships cost more than sole proprietorships but less than corporations. In addition, each entity has legal characteristics that can affect the ability of the entity to raise additional capital should the need arise.

**Example 1** Barbara is planning to open a travel agency. Her father died recently, and she inherited property and cash worth several hundred thousand dollars. Barbara has spent the past 18 years as a high school social studies teacher and wants to change careers. She is single and has 3 children: Catrina, 23; Niki, 21; and Patrick, 19. Barbara wants to know the proper form for her business entity. Should she incorporate her new business?

**Discussion: The initial answer is, "It depends. . . ." There is no simple cookie-cutter answer to this question. Many factors, both tax and nontax, affect the choice. Barbara should conduct a comparative analysis of forming a sole proprietorship, partnership, corporation, and S corporation and focus on the nontax and tax factors of each entity.**

This section discusses the nontax factors associated with each of the four types of entity. Special entities such as limited liability companies, limited liability partnerships, and personal service corporations are also addressed.

The nontax factors arise primarily because of the legal differences in the various entity forms. This section also discusses the legal aspects and their effect on the nontax factors for each entity.

## 13-2a Sole Proprietorship

A **sole proprietorship** is a business owned by one individual. It is the most common business form in the United States. Individuals need do nothing formal to establish a sole proprietorship. A sole proprietorship is easy to form because the business is not separate from the individual owner from both a legal and a tax perspective. The only restriction is that the business can have only one owner, who must be an individual. This makes the sole proprietorship the least costly form of business to organize.

LO 2

Compare the nontax characteristics of sole proprietorships, partnerships, corporations, S corporations, limited liability companies, and limited liability partnerships, and explain the effects of their characteristics on the choice of business entity.

State law does not treat the sole proprietorship as an entity that owns property separately from the individual entrepreneur. Business debts are directly attributable to the individual business owner. Thus, the sole proprietor is personally liable for all debts of the business. This factor often discourages use of the sole proprietorship in a business that has a substantial risk of lawsuits involving product liability or malpractice.

Sometimes the separation issue becomes blurred because of financial accounting rules that require proprietors to exclude reporting of nonbusiness items (e.g., personal expenses or nonbusiness income) from proprietorship financial reports. Schedule C of Form 1040 is the vehicle for reporting the proprietorship income and expenses. This reporting mechanism appears to separate the proprietor from the proprietor's business.

Yet, this reporting procedure reinforces the conduit nature of the sole proprietorship. The net operating income flows directly to the individual proprietor's Form 1040 as an item of gross income.

**Example 2** Refer to the facts in example 1. Assume that Barbara wants to use the sole proprietorship for her business. What are the legal effects of running her travel agency as a sole proprietorship?

**Discussion: There are no formal requirements to meet when starting a business that will operate as a sole proprietorship. Barbara will not have to spend a great deal of money to organize the business. However, any business debts resulting from either contractual obligations of the business (e.g., loans or accounts payable) or tort claims resulting from operating malfeasance can be collected from her family's personal assets, which are fairly extensive. Barbara needs to assess the vulnerability of her personal assets, given the level of risk in operating a travel agency. For example, she could have liability exposure if she books tickets for clients on an airplane that subsequently has an accident or for a vacation tour to Hawaii that is ruined by a hurricane. Purchasing insurance can mitigate some of her liability, but it may not be economically feasible to purchase insurance that will adequately cover all her personal wealth.**

As the only owner of the business, the sole proprietor has the freedom to transfer ownership at any time and in any manner. When a sole proprietor dies, the business becomes part of the owner's estate and can be passed on to a spouse, children, or others, according to the owner's desires. The sole proprietorship also enjoys complete management control. One limitation of being the sole owner is that it is often difficult to raise large amounts of capital if the need arises.

## 13-2b Partnership

Most states declare that a **partnership** exists when two or more individuals engage collectively in an activity with the expectation of generating profits. A partnership is a flexible business form because the arrangement is purely consensual. Any individual owner in the partnership may dissolve the partnership at any time and depart with her or his share of the assets. Partnerships, like sole proprietorships, usually have no special state reporting requirements other than tax returns that report the results of operations.

Each general partner is personally responsible for any partnership obligations that arise during the existence of the partnership—similar to a sole proprietorship. Also, general partners legally have equal abilities to contribute to management decision making.

Although partnerships are considered conduits for the purpose of income taxation, they are treated as separate entities under local law. Thus, partnerships can transact business and own property in their names, separate from the partners. This characteristic is a major difference between sole proprietorships and partnerships. The legal characteristics of partnerships are common and similar to those for other statutory business forms, such as corporations.

Partnerships give owners the ability to raise capital more easily than a sole proprietor because of the greater number of owners. Also, the costs of raising additional capital are relatively low when compared with those of corporations, which have fairly high costs for issuing stocks and bonds. However, the inability to issue stocks and bonds to the general public limits the amount of capital a partnership can raise. Even though it is relatively easy to form a partnership, the costs of ending the partnership and winding up its affairs may be costly. A tax is borne by the partners in the form of liquidating distributions that may have built up over the years as a profitable partnership. The partners will pay a tax on the difference between their basis in the partnership and the value of the partnership interest. Some of this difference may be treated as ordinary income, and some may be treated as capital gain. Liquidating distributions are covered in more detail in Chapter 14.

Certain types of partnerships can take on the corporate characteristic of limited liability to make the acquisition of capital easier. A **limited partnership** has at least one partner whose liability is limited to the amount of their investment in the partnership. This attribute provides a measure of safety for a limited partner's personal assets. To obtain the limited liability attribute, a limited partner gives up any right to participate in the management of the business. Management is left to at least one general partner, whose liability is not limited and who is responsible for the ongoing activities of the business. The limited partnership has been a popular medium for investors in risky activities, such as mining or oil and gas exploration.

**Example 3** Refer to example 1. Can Barbara operate the travel agency as a partnership?

**Discussion: Barbara's business is hers alone. She needs at least one other person as an owner to establish a partnership. Because Barbara apparently does not need additional capital for her business, she does not need partners as additional investors. Barbara could bring one or more of her children into the business and form a partnership if she determined that it was the best form after considering all other factors. She might want to form a partnership if she needed additional capital or expertise. In that case, Barbara could offer either general or limited partnership ownership interests in her travel agency to obtain these assets. Transactions costs for exchanges like these are minimal. Preparation of a partnership agreement is generally the only expense. Barbara is not constrained to a maximum number of partners. She can add any number of partners to the ownership group and still maintain her individual management role by creating limited partnership interests. Only general partners are allowed to participate in day-to-day business decisions. Unlike limited partnership interests, adding general partnership interests spreads the business liability risks among more people. Of course, Barbara can offer a mixture of general and limited partnership interests in exchange for additional capital.**

## 13-2c Corporation

A **corporation** is an artificial entity created under the auspices of state law. As a separate statutory entity, a corporation can enter into contracts in its name, own property, and be sued, and it must pay income tax based on its taxable income.

Attaining corporate status is fairly simple. Articles of incorporation are drafted and filed with the appropriate state agency (e.g., the Division of Corporations and Commercial Code of the state of Utah). Then the state grants a charter, and the corporation issues stock to shareholders. Once the corporation is formed and operating, it must follow a myriad of formal rules. The corporation must hold stockholder meetings and record the minutes of each meeting. Also, it must maintain stock transfer records and file annual reports with the appropriate state agency. All these requirements are costly, both in terms of time and actual money spent. For example, legal fees, charter and franchise fees, underwriter fees, and other organizational costs can be extensive.

Adhering to all the rules required by the state of incorporation gives the entity a separate legal identity that has the nontax attributes of limited liability, unlimited life, free transferability of ownership, and centralized management. These nontax factors are often the impetus for operating a business in the corporate form.

The attribute of limited liability can be misleading for small-business owners. That is, most shareholders of closely held corporations are required to personally guarantee loans to the corporation. Bankers and other creditors want assurance that the corporate debts are secured. Therefore, shareholders of closely held corporations often have only partial limited liability. However, this attribute still protects the personal assets of corporate shareholders from product liability or malpractice judgments brought against the business.

Limited liability is not available in most states for professional service (e.g., accounting, law, health care, and architecture) corporations. This incorporated entity loses the traditional corporate protection for shareholders' personal assets. Customers and clients retain recourse against professionals when malpractice is a factor.

**Example 4** Return to example 1. If Barbara incorporates her business, what will be its legal characteristics?

**Discussion: Barbara is not constrained by a number-of-owners requirement if she chooses the corporate form of business. One shareholder is generally enough to form a corporation. However, some states require a minimum of 2 or 3 members for the board of directors. Barbara can attain this by naming as a director the attorney who helps her with the filing requirements or by using 1 or more of her children as**

**directors without effectively diluting her ownership control. If she needs additional equity in the future, she can have her corporation sell more shares of stock. The corporate attribute of free transferability of ownership interests permits the corporation or the shareholders to transfer ownership interests without jeopardizing the existence of the entity. Corporate status for Barbara's business will give her the key attribute of limited liability. This characteristic will shield her personal assets from creditors' claims. Given Barbara's financial position, limited liability is a characteristic that should be important to her and her family.**

## 13-2d S Corporation

An **S corporation** is a regular corporation with special tax attributes. Corporations, chartered under the laws of one of the 50 states, may obtain conduit entity tax status by making a valid election per Subchapter S of the Internal Revenue Code of 1986.[1] The S corporation retains the legal characteristics of the corporate form (limited liability, free transferability of interests, continuity of life, and centralized management) while obtaining taxation characteristics similar to those of a partnership.

S corporation status is attained when a qualified corporation elects this status. The election is effective for the current tax year if the election is filed at any time during the preceding year or on or before the 15th day of the third month of the current year. Therefore, a calendar-year corporate taxpayer desiring S corporation status for 2021 must file the election at any time from January 1, 2020, through March 15, 2021. To qualify as an S corporation, a corporation:

- Must be a domestic corporation
- May not have more than 100 shareholders (All family members can elect to be treated as one shareholder for purposes of the 100-shareholder limit.)
- Must have as its shareholders only individuals, estates, tax-exempt organizations, and certain trusts
- Cannot have a nonresident alien as a shareholder
- Must have only one class of stock outstanding
- Must have the consent of all shareholders to the election of S corporation status[2]

Unlike partnerships and regular corporations, the number and type of owners in an S corporation are limited. No more than 100 shareholders may participate in ownership, and only individuals, estates, and certain trusts can be shareholders. The election is only for federal tax purposes. Certain states do not recognize this election for state income tax purposes. You should consult the state taxing authority to determine whether the S corporation election is valid for your state's income tax system.

**Example 5** Refer to example 4. Barbara wants to incorporate her business to get limited liability while retaining the benefits of conduit tax treatment. What are the key entity attributes if she makes the S corporation election?

**Discussion: If Barbara incorporates her business and elects S corporation status, she converts a taxable entity to a conduit entity. Operating losses often result in the early years of a new business, and flow-through tax treatment lets Barbara deduct the losses on her personal tax return. Barbara's corporation retains the corporate characteristics of limited liability, free transferability of interests, continuity of life, and centralized management.**

Every qualifying requirement must be met at the time of the election and at all times thereafter. The S corporation election terminates immediately when one or more of the qualifying characteristics ceases to exist. As of the date of termination, the corporation becomes a taxable corporate entity.

**Example 6** Assume that Barbara makes a valid S corporation election in 2020. On April 1, 2022, she sells 100 shares of her stock to Holder LTD, a limited partnership. Does this transaction affect the status of Barbara's corporation?

**Discussion: Barbara's S corporation election terminates on April 1, 2022. Partnerships may not be shareholders in S corporations. Therefore, Barbara's corporation is**

**an S corporation through March 31 and a taxable corporation from April 1 through December 31. Note: If the termination of the election is inadvertent, the S status may continue uninterrupted if the corporation corrects the disqualifying action. Therefore, if Barbara becomes aware of the implications of her action and can revoke the sale of the stock to the limited partnership, her corporation will not lose S corporation status.**

An S corporation may forfeit its election voluntarily. If holders of more than 50 percent of the total shares of stock consent to revoke the S status, the revocation is effective for the current year if made on or before the 15th day of the third month of the year.

**Example 7** Assume that Barbara owns 70% of the S corporation and that each of her 3 children owns a 10% interest. In 2023, Barbara no longer desires S status, and on June 30, she files an intent to terminate. Is the termination valid? If it is, when is it effective?

**Discussion: The termination is valid because Barbara owns more than 50% of the shares of the S corporation. The earliest effective date for the termination of S status is January 1 of the next tax year because the termination was not made on or before the 15th day of March during the current year.**

Once an election is terminated, the corporation may not make a new election for five years without special consent of the commissioner of the IRS.[3]

## 13-2e Limited Liability Company

The limited liability company is a relatively new and unique form of business organization created under state laws. The **limited liability company (LLC)** combines the corporate characteristic of limited liability with the conduit tax treatment of partnerships. This form of business organization developed because of the growth of international trade. U.S. businesses were dealing with German and Latin American entities with management and earnings-sharing agreements that were more flexible than those afforded U.S. corporations. These foreign organizations had the basic corporate attributes of limited liability and recognition as a separate legal entity, as well as the partnership characteristics of dissolution on an owner's death and controlled admission of new owners. To satisfy the need of these foreign entities to know whether they would be treated as conduits or taxable entities, the IRS followed the tests contained in the regulations for determining whether an entity is a corporation or a partnership.[4]

When they saw the advantages of LLC entities, U.S. businesses began lobbying state legislatures to enact laws allowing similar structures. Today all states legally recognize or are considering recognition of LLCs. Although an LLC resembles a corporation in many respects, it accommodates more flexible business arrangements. Like a corporation, an LLC is created by following the requirements of state law. It is treated as a legal entity, separate from its individual owners, and is recognized as the owner of the trade or business property. The members of an LLC, like shareholders of a corporation, have limited liability: Members' personal assets are not at risk for the entity's liabilities. Owners of noncorporate entities will choose whether to be taxed as a corporation or to receive conduit tax treatment, without regard to the corporate attribute test.[5] This will greatly enhance the ability of a business to limit its liability without resorting to the use of a corporation.

Although corporations are created by filing articles of incorporation, LLCs file articles of organization. The entity must have two or more members, have an objective to carry on a business, and establish a specific method for dividing the profits and losses from the business. The ability to create special allocations of profits and losses is an attribute of partnerships and LLCs not permitted to corporations. Corporate shareholders receive their shares of an entity's earnings based on the percentage of stock owned. Also, similar to a partnership, LLC members are allowed to control who owns an interest; the corporate characteristic of free transferability of interests does not exist for these conduit entities.

LLC members have great flexibility in organizing the entity's management structure. Unlike a limited partnership, all members of an LLC may be involved in the enterprise's operating decisions. For example, members can choose a centralized management group while retaining the right to contribute to company decision making in a manner similar to a corporate board of directors.

**Example 8** Recalling the facts in example 1, Barbara is planning to open a travel agency with money that she inherited from her father. She has three children and would like to change careers from being a high school teacher to running the business full-time. Is a limited liability company an appropriate business form for Barbara?

**Discussion: Unless Barbara acquires at least one coowner, the choice of an LLC will not provide the conduit tax treatment of a partnership. Although some state laws allow single-member LLCs, the IRS regulations classify these entities as either a corporation or a sole proprietorship. At best, the travel agency would be considered a separate entity with limited liability for Barbara, and she would gain nothing over using the corporate form.**

## 13-2f Limited Liability Partnership

Another new form of organization that is growing in popularity is the limited liability partnership. The **limited liability partnership (LLP)** is a general partnership with the added characteristic of limited liability for owners. States allowing this type of entity are responding to concerns about the traditional concepts of partner liability: General partners are unconditionally liable for partnership debts. Accordingly, an LLP permits the usual partnership conduit tax treatment but limits the liabilities of partners. Under state partnership laws, partners in an LLP are liable for their acts and acts of individuals under their direction and control but not for negligence or misconduct by other partners. This characteristic differentiates an LLP from an LLC. In an LLC, no single owner has unlimited liability. A partner in an LLP has limited liability for business contractual obligations but can have unlimited liability for personal acts of malfeasance. Thus, an organization that seeks conduit tax treatment and limited personal liability for business obligations for all owners has two options that provide virtually the same tax treatment—LLPs and LLCs.

Certain states restrict the types of business entities that can choose either LLP or LLC status. For example, certain states allow professional service businesses (i.e., law firms, accounting firms, and health care businesses) only LLP status; they cannot elect LLC status. Because the LLC and the LLP have identical tax results, nontax factors determine whether the entity should be an LLC or an LLP.

**Example 9** Refer to example 8. Is a limited liability partnership an appropriate business form for Barbara?

**Discussion: Barbara cannot qualify for LLP status because she is the sole owner of her business. Like any partnership, at least 2 owners are necessary for this special type of limited liability entity. If Barbara brings in at least 1 partner and organizes her business as an LLP, her liability is limited for the contractual legal obligations of her business. However, she remains liable for any personal acts. Because her travel agency is not a professional service business, state law does not require her to choose an LLP if she desires a limited liability entity.**

## 13-2g Planning Commentary

Table 13-1 summarizes the nontax factors for each entity type. Ease of formation and low organizational costs are the primary nontax attributes of sole proprietorships. In addition, sole proprietors can freely transfer their interests and have complete management control. However, the proprietor is personally liable for all the liabilities of the business entity and has limited ability to raise additional capital. The lack of limited liability is the main factor discouraging the use of the sole proprietorship.

At least two owners are necessary to form a partnership. General partners have the ability to determine the management structure and can restrict the transfer of ownership interests. General partners are personally liable for the obligations of the entity. Limited partners bring in capital without being exposed to the liabilities of the business. If the business creates high liability exposure for the owners, using an LLC or LLP can limit personal liability while retaining the desirable conduit entity characteristics.

The primary advantage of the corporate form is limited liability for the owners. Corporations also have the greatest ability to raise additional capital, although incorporating

Table 13-1

## Comparison of Nontax Factors Among Business Forms

| Factor | Sole Proprietorship | Partnership | Limited Liability Company | Limited Liability Partnership | Corporation | S Corporation |
|---|---|---|---|---|---|---|
| Number of owners is restricted | Yes, restricted to 1 | No, except there must be more than 1 | No, generally more than 1 | No, except there must be more than 1 | No, certain states may have minimums | Yes, 100 owners maximum |
| Entity recognized as separate | No | Yes | Yes | Yes | Yes | Yes |
| Owners have limited liability | No | No, except for limited partners | Yes | Yes, except for personal acts of malfeasance by an individual partner | Yes, except for professional service corporations | Yes |
| Owners have the right to direct participation in management | Yes | Yes for general partners; no for limited partners | Yes | Yes | No | No |
| Entity continues regardless of ownership changes | No | No | No | No | Yes | Yes |
| Free transferability of ownership interests | Yes | No | No | No | Yes | Yes |
| Level of difficulty to form | Low | Low | Low | Low | Relatively high | Relatively high |
| Organizational costs | None | Moderate | Moderate | Moderate | Relatively high | Relatively high |
| Ability to raise capital | Limited | Good, better for limited partnerships | Good | Good | Excellent | Excellent |

and raising capital are more costly than with the other entity forms. Continuity of life of the entity and free transferability of ownership are attributes that can be positive or negative, depending on the owner's desires.

The S corporation is an income tax election. It is useful when owners desire the limited liability protection of the corporate form and the taxation characteristics of a conduit entity. However, the limited liability protection may be reduced initially because creditors may require the owners to provide personal assets as collateral for loans to the business.

# 13-3 GENERAL INCOME TAX FACTORS

The main income tax item of interest in choosing a business form is the total tax liability (entity tax plus owner's tax). This section discusses general income tax factors that affect the total tax liability of an entity. Differences in total tax liability are due to the incidence of taxation, double taxation of corporate dividends, and the question of whether an owner can be an employee of the entity.

## 13-3a Incidence of Income Taxation

LO 3

Explain the general income tax characteristics of the various entities, including the incidence of taxation, double taxation, and the status of an owner as an employee of the entity.

Corporations and individuals are the two primary taxpaying entities. Conduit entities do not pay tax; their income flows through to the owners of the entity for taxation. Therefore, the **incidence of taxation** rests with either incorporated taxable entities or owners of conduit entities. Because the tax rate schedules differ for individuals and corporations, proper entity selection offers opportunities to minimize income taxes. However, the tax law contains provisions that limit this ability when the corporation's primary income source is the personal service of the owner(s) or consists primarily of passive forms of income. The incidence of taxation for each entity form is the starting point for determining the entity that provides the most favorable income tax treatment in a given situation. This section provides an overview of the taxation of each entity.

## Sole Proprietorship

Sole proprietorships operate as conduits and tax the individual owner on the income of the business. The net operating income of a trade or business flows directly into the individual proprietor's gross income. The mechanism for accomplishing this is Schedule C of Form 1040. Individuals are subject to four tax rate schedules.[6] Each schedule is based on filing status. The schedules for all taxable entities appear in Appendix B. Each individual schedule has a seven-step progression for taxing taxable income. The seven rates are 10 percent, 12 percent, 22 percent, 24 percent, 32 percent, 35 percent, and 37 percent. The amounts of taxable income at which the tax rates change (i.e., from 10 percent to 12 percent) vary according to the individual's filing status.

Because sole proprietorships are not separate taxable entities, they may not deduct owner-employee salaries and owner-employee fringe benefits. In addition, a cash withdrawal from a sole proprietorship has no tax consequences because the only entity involved is the individual. Proprietorship cash draws are analogous to taking money from one pocket and putting it into another pocket in the same pair of pants.

For tax years beginning after December 31, 2017, Code Sec. 199A provides a 20 percent deduction for taxpayers other than C corporations, who have qualified business income (QBI) from a partnership, S corporation, or sole proprietorship. The 20 percent deduction applies to any income from a business so long as that income is effectively connected with the conduct of a U.S. business. The deduction applies to rental income (if the rental operations constitute a business). But, the deduction does not apply to certain types of investment income generated by a pass-through entity.

Qualified business income generally does not include compensation paid to owners of pass-through entities. The deduction does not apply to (i) reasonable compensation paid to the taxpayer by any qualified business of the taxpayer for services rendered with respect to the business, (ii) any guaranteed payment paid to a partner (or member) for services rendered with respect to the business, or (iii) to the extent provided in regulations, certain other payments to partners for services rendered with respect to the business. The owners of specific types of service businesses are only able to use the deduction if their income is below certain levels. A specified service business is any business involving the performance of services in the fields of health, law, actuarial sciences, accounting, performing arts, consulting, athletics, financial services, brokerage services, or any trade or business where the principal asset of such business is the reputation or skill of one or more of its employees or owners.

A recipient of pass-through income from a specified service business can use the full 20 percent deduction if the taxpayer's taxable income is less than $164,900 (if single) or $329,800 (if married). As taxable income increases, the deduction is gradually phased out. There is no deduction for married taxpayers whose taxable income exceeds $429,800 or for single taxpayers whose taxable income exceeds $214,900. "Taxable income" for limitation purposes is determined without regard to the 20 percent deduction.

Other types of pass-through businesses, including nonservice businesses (e.g. a manufacturing business or even a rental real estate business), can benefit from the 20 percent deduction. Owners of such pass-through entities can utilize the 20 percent deduction without regard to their asset or employment levels so long as their taxable income is less than $164,900 (if single) or $329,800 (if married) (with phase-out occurring over the next $50,000 [if single] or $100,000 [if married] of taxable income).

These pass-through businesses may also use the deduction even when their taxable income exceeds such limits. The owners of these pass-through businesses may use the deduction up to the greater of (a) 50 percent of the W-2 wages paid by the business (including to the owners) or (b) the sum of (i) 25 percent of W-2 wages paid by the business and (ii) 2.5 percent of the business's capital.[7]

As discussed in Chapter 6, the calculation of the QBI deduction is very complex. The purpose of this section of the book is to illustrate how taxes impact the choice of entity. Therefore, to better illustrate this concept, the QBI deduction is simplified and calculated as 20 percent of QBI.

**Example 10** Monte, who is married and has 3 children, owns and operates a chain of gas stations. In 2021, he draws a salary of $60,000. The net income from the gas stations before payment of the salary has consistently been $160,000 a year. What is Monte's income tax liability in 2021 if he operates the business as a sole proprietorship? For illustrative purposes, assume that Monte and his spouse have other income that exactly offsets their allowable deductions.

**Discussion: The taxable income for the business is $160,000. Monte's salary is not a deductible expense of the sole proprietorship. He is taxed on the earnings of the business, $128,000 [$160,000 – $32,000 ($160,000 × 20% QBI deduction)]. Because Monte is married, his filing status is married, filing jointly, giving him a tax liability of $19,657 {$9,328 + [22% × ($128,000 – $81,050)]} in 2021.**

## Partnership

Like sole proprietors, partners pay tax on their share of the partnership income. A partnership is a conduit entity that does not pay tax.[8] Income is taxed at the owner level rather than at the entity level. However, partnerships are still required to annually report the results of their operations. Form 1065 for partnerships is analogous to an individual taxpayer's Schedule C of Form 1040.

As discussed in Chapters 3 and 5, because taxation takes place at the partner level, any items that receive special treatment at the individual level (e.g., capital gains, investment expenses) must be reported separately to each partner. Therefore, partners must be provided with the items and amounts to be reported on their individual tax returns. This is accomplished by Schedule K-1 of Form 1065.

Partners generally have significant flexibility when allocating percentages of income, gains, losses, expenses, and credits. Unlike other entity forms, partnerships can specially allocate certain types and amounts of income, gains, losses, and the like among partners. As long as the allocations are economically realistic, partners with different marginal tax rates can receive allocations that provide relatively advantageous benefits.

Partners may take cash withdrawals from their businesses, but, as with a sole proprietorship, these payments are not going from one taxable entity to another. Unless the withdrawals represent guaranteed payments, the partnership may not deduct them and they are not taxable to the partner. They are nontaxable returns of capital. Therefore, partners are not subject to double taxation when earnings are distributed as cash withdrawals.

**Example 11** Assume the same facts as in example 10, except that Monte's cousin Beau manages one station and receives a salary of $40,000. Monte and Beau organize the gas station enterprise as a partnership called M&B Company. Monte owns an 80% interest and Beau owns a 20% interest. Monte is paid a salary of $60,000. Beau is single and has other income equal to his allowable deductions. How does this affect the total tax liability of the business income?

**Discussion: The partnership cannot deduct the salaries paid to Monte and Beau, resulting in partnership income of $160,000. The salaries are considered guaranteed payments and reduce the partnership's QBI. The QBI deduction is $12,000 [20% × ($160,000 – $60,000 – $40,000)]. Monte's share of the partnership income, $128,000 ($160,000 × 80%), flows through to him for inclusion on his personal tax return but is reduced by his 80% share of the QBI deduction (80% × $12,000 = $9,600). His taxable income is $118,400 ($128,000 – $9,600). His income tax liability is $17,545 {$9,328 + [22% × ($118,400 – $81,050)]}. Beau's share of income, $32,000 ($160,000 × 20%), flows to him, and, after deducting his $2,400 QBI deduction, he pays $3,353 {$995 + [12% × ($29,600 – $9,950)]} of tax. The total tax liability of both partners is $20,898. Bringing in Beau as a partner and splitting the business income between Monte and Beau increases the total tax liability by $1,241 ($20,898 – $19,657) compared with operating the business as a sole proprietorship. This is caused by the reduced QBI resulting from the guaranteed payments.**

General partnerships, limited partnerships, limited liability companies, and limited liability partnerships are treated as partnerships for tax purposes. Therefore, the results discussed in example 11 would be the same for those entity types.

## Corporation

Corporations are taxable entities that are separate and distinct from their owners. A corporation pays tax on its income.[9] Corporations are not eligible for the 20 percent QBI deduction. The results of corporate operations are reported on Form 1120, which is analogous to an individual's Form 1040. The owners (shareholders) are taxed on distributions of money (dividends), which are reported on their individual returns. For example, individual taxpayers report their dividend income on Schedule B of Form 1040.

Because the corporation is separate from its shareholders, it can employ shareholders and pay them salaries or wages. The ability to pay deductible salaries to owners, combined with the differences in the individual and corporate tax rate schedules, provides an opportunity to lower the total tax liability of the business.

For tax years beginning after December 31, 2017, the Tax Cuts and Jobs Act imposes a flat 21 percent tax on corporate taxable income. The higher individual income tax rates allow business owners who file single to use a corporation to shelter income when taxable income exceeds $40,525. Also, when taxable income is less than $81,050, a corporation is taxed at a higher rate than a married couple filing jointly. Therefore, under the right circumstances, business owners can lower their income tax liabilities by incorporating. However, if the corporation distributes dividends to the individual owner-shareholder, the individual incurs additional income taxes. This situation is a classic case of double taxation, which may mitigate the tax advantage of incorporating.

**Example 12** Recall the facts from example 11 in which Monte's cousin Beau manages one of the gas stations and is paid a salary of $40,000. Monte is to get a salary of $60,000. Assume Monte and Beau incorporate the business as M&B Company. Monte owns 80% of the stock of the corporation, and Beau owns 20%. Monte and Beau are employees of the business. The business has operating income of $160,000 before considering salary payments to Monte ($60,000) and Beau ($40,000). What is the total tax liability using the corporate form of business operation?

**Discussion: Because Monte and Beau can be employees of their corporation, their salaries are deductible in calculating taxable income. M&B's taxable income is $60,000 ($160,000 − $60,000 − $40,000), and it pays a tax of $12,600 ($60,000 × 21%). Monte pays a tax of $6,802 {$1,990 + [12% × ($60,000 − $19,900)]} on his $60,000 salary, and Beau pays a tax of $4,601 {$995 + [12% × ($40,000 − $9,950)]} on his $40,000 salary. The total tax liability is $24,003 compared with $20,898 when the business is operated as a partnership, an additional tax cost of $3,105. At Monte and Beau's income level, shifting $60,000 of Monte and Beau's partnership income, which was taxed at 12%, to the corporation, where it is taxed at 21%, does not result in any tax savings.**

**Example 13** Assume the same facts as in examples 11 and 12 except that the business is an accounting firm with income of $960,000. Under the partnership structure, neither Monte nor Beau will be eligible for QBI. The tax paid by Monte is $220,683 {$172,250 + 37% × ($768,000 − $628,300)}, and the tax paid by Beau is $42,267 {$33,603 + 32% × ($192,000 − $164,900)}. The total tax paid under the partnership structure is $262,950.

**Discussion: Under the corporate structure, assume Monte is paid a salary of $320,000 and Beau is paid a salary of $140,000; $500,000 is retained as corporate taxable income. The tax paid by the corporation is $105,000 ($500,000 × 21%). Monte's tax is $64,962 {$29,502 + 24% × ($320,000 − $172,250)}. Beau's tax is $27,621 {$14,751 + 24% × ($140,000 − $86,375)}. The total tax paid under the corporate structure is $197,583 ($105,000 + $64,962 + $27,621). This represents a savings of $65,367 ($262,950 − $197,583) over a partnership. This savings is accomplished by shifting $500,000 of Monte and Beau's partnership income, which was taxed at 37% and 32%, to the corporation where it is taxed at 21%.**

## S Corporation

An S corporation is a corporation with tax characteristics similar to those of a partnership. S corporations are conduit entities that do not pay tax.[10] Form 1120S is used to report operating results to the government. The income of an S corporation flows through to its shareholders for taxation. As with a partnership, taxation at the individual owner level requires that items that receive special treatment at the individual level be reported separately so that shareholders can prepare their returns properly. Schedule K-1 of Form 1120S provides shareholders with their proportionate share of entity income, deductions, and credits to include on their personal tax return. As with partnerships, distributions (dividends) paid to shareholders are nontaxable recoveries of capital. Because of the separate entity status of the corporation, S corporation shareholders can be employees of the business entity.

**Example 14** Assume the same facts as in example 12, except that Monte and Beau make the election to have M&B Company treated as an S corporation. What is the total tax liability?

**Discussion: Because Monte and Beau can be employees of the S corporation, their salaries are deductible in calculating taxable income. M&B's taxable income is $60,000 ($160,000 – $60,000 – $40,000). Monte is taxed on his $48,000 ($60,000 × 80%) share of the S corporation income and his $60,000 salary. His taxable income is $98,400 ($108,000 – $9,600 QBI deduction), and his tax liability is $13,145 {$9,328 + [22% × ($98,400 – $81,050)]}. Beau's taxable income is $49,600 ($40,000 salary + $12,000 S corporation income – $2,400 QBI deduction), and Beau pays a tax of $6,661 {$4,664 + [22% × ($49,600 – $40,525)]}. The total tax liability of $19,806 is less than the $24,003 tax on a corporation because the $60,000 in corporate income is taxed at the lower individual rates. The S corporation tax is $1,092 ($20,898 – $19,806) less than the partnership.**

## 13-3b Double Taxation

Obtaining cash or other property distributions is generally the ultimate objective of corporate owners. In addition to paying salaries to shareholder-employees, corporations distribute cash to shareholders via dividends. Salaries are deductible expenses; dividend payments are not. Dividends are considered distributions of corporate earnings (which have already been taxed). When shareholders receive the dividends, the dividends are taxed again at the long-term capital gains rate. Because the corporation and its shareholders are recognized as separate taxpaying entities, corporate earnings are subject to **double taxation** when paid to shareholders as dividends.

**Example 15** Assume that in example 12, M&B Company distributes the $60,000 in corporate earnings as a dividend. What is the effect of paying dividends on the total tax liability?

**Discussion: Dividends are not a deductible expense. Therefore, M&B pays a tax of $12,600 (example 12) on its $60,000 taxable income. Monte receives $48,000 of the dividend, which increases his tax liability to $14,002 [$6,802 + ($48,000 × 15%)]. Beau receives a $12,000 dividend and pays a tax of $6,401 [$4,601 + ($12,000 × 15%)]. The total tax liability of $33,004 is $9,000 ($33,003 – $24,003 from example 12) more than when no dividends are paid. This occurs because the $60,000 in corporate earnings is taxed twice: first at the corporate level and again at the individual stockholder level ($60,000 × 15% = $9,000 tax on the dividend).**

Double taxation occurs only with the use of a corporation. One way to avoid double taxation is to pay salaries to owner-employees equal to the corporate income. This eliminates taxation at the corporate level but negates the tax savings that can be obtained from income splitting. In addition, if the salary amounts are not reasonable, the portion of the salary that isn't reasonable will be recast as a dividend, and no savings will result. Choosing a conduit entity rather than an incorporated taxable entity eliminates the double taxation problem when reasonable salaries cannot be paid to achieve the desired tax result.

**Example 16** Assume that in example 15, Monte and Beau make a valid S corporation election for M&B Company, effective for the current year. How does this affect the total tax liability?

**Discussion: As a conduit entity, M&B pays no income tax. The $60,000 in corporate income passes through to Monte and Beau, who include it in their taxable income. The S corporation election eliminates the $12,600 corporate tax. Distributions paid to S corporation shareholders are nontaxable returns of capital and do not affect**

**Monte and Beau's taxable income. Their tax liabilities remain at $13,145 and $6,661, respectively, for a total tax liability of $19,806. By using a conduit entity, Monte and Beau have eliminated the double taxation of the earnings of the corporation without increasing their salaries to a point that may be considered unreasonable and also benefit from the QBI deduction.**

## 13-3c Employee versus Owner

Owners participating in the operation of their entity may or may not be treated as employees for tax purposes, depending on the business entity. If an owner is classified as an employee, the owner can receive a salary and fringe benefits, and can have access to company retirement plans (discussed in Chapter 15). These types of compensation potentially reduce the entity's taxable income and can minimize the effects of double taxation on corporations and their shareholders. The payment of tax-deductible salaries to owner-employees can be a planning tool for income splitting, which is used to decrease the total tax liability of the entity and its owners. The ability to provide nontaxable fringe benefits to owner-employees also reduces the total tax liability and can be an important factor in the choice of entity.

Unincorporated entities cannot have owner-employees. Because a sole proprietor is not legally an entity separate and apart from the business, the sole proprietor cannot be an employee of the business. (Individuals cannot hire themselves.) Therefore, the tax benefits of salaries or fringe benefits are not available to sole proprietors. The business is not allowed a deduction for these items, and fringe-benefit recipients are not permitted exclusions for the value of fringe benefits received.

**Example 17** Recall the facts in example 10, in which Monte owns and operates a chain of gas stations. He draws a salary of $60,000. The net income from the gas stations before payment of the salary has been consistently $160,000 a year. Assume that Monte's business provides him with $10,000 in otherwise-nontaxable fringe benefits. How are the salary and fringe benefits treated for tax purposes, and what is the total tax liability when the business is operated as a sole proprietorship?

**Discussion: Monte and his business are not considered separate entities. The business cannot deduct Monte's salary and fringe-benefit payments. The $160,000 taxable income is reported on Monte's individual return, resulting in a tax of $19,657 (see example 10).**

As with sole proprietorships, partnerships are not considered entities separate from their owners (partners), and the partners cannot be employees of the entity. Partners cannot receive deductible salaries. Partners often receive guaranteed payments for rendering services to or on behalf of the business. A **guaranteed payment** is a payment made to a partner for specific services performed by the partner and is made without regard to the income of the partnership. These payments are compensation to the partner but are treated as though they are paid to a self-employed individual, separate from the partnership. Unlike other payments made to partners, a guaranteed payment is deductible in determining a partnership's operating income.

**Example 18** Recall from the facts in example 11 that Monte and Beau formed a partnership with Monte owning an 80% interest and Beau owning a 20% interest. Monte is paid a salary of $60,000, and Beau is paid a salary of $40,000. Assume that the salaries paid to Monte and Beau are guaranteed payments. How does this affect the total tax liability?

**Discussion: The guaranteed payments are deductible by the partnership, reducing operating income to $60,000. Monte includes in his taxable income the $60,000 guaranteed payment and his $48,000 ($60,000 × 80%) share of partnership income. His taxable income is $108,000. Beau's $52,000 of taxable income consists of his $40,000 guaranteed payment and his $12,000 ($60,000 × 20%) share of partnership income. Monte's tax liability is $13,145 (example 14), and Beau's tax liability is $6,661 (example 14). Note that the total tax liability with the guaranteed payments is the same as that for an S corporation (example 14).**

Partners can receive certain fringe benefits from the partnership. The cost of the fringe benefits is considered a guaranteed payment to the partner. As a guaranteed payment, the cost of the fringe benefits received is taxable to the partner and deductible by the partnership.

**Example 19** Assume that M&B Company is operated as a partnership. Monte owns an 80% interest, and Beau owns a 20% interest. M&B provides Monte and Beau with $10,000 each in nontaxable fringe benefits. Partnership income is $160,000 before consideration of Monte and Beau's salaries (which are not guaranteed payments) and fringe benefits. How does this affect the total tax liability?

**Discussion: Because partners cannot be employees of the partnership, M&B cannot deduct the salary it pays to the partners. The partnership can deduct the fringe benefit payments it makes to the partners, but the partners must include the fringe benefit payments in their gross income. Partnership taxable income is reduced to $140,000 by the fringe benefit payments. Monte must include his share of the partnership income, $112,000 ($140,000 × 80%), on his individual return. In addition, the fringe benefit payments are included in his taxable income. Monte's taxable income is $122,000 ($112,000 + $10,000), and he pays $18,337 {$9,328 + [22% × ($122,000 − $81,050)]} in income tax. Beau's taxable income is $38,000 [($140,000 × 20%) + $10,000], and he pays $4,361 {$995 + [12% × ($38,000 − $9,950)]} in income tax. Note: To better illustrate the concept we did not recalculate the QBI deduction.**

The entity concept drives the ability of owners to be corporate employees for income tax purposes. Corporations are deemed separate entities, taxable on their income. Accordingly, corporate owners (shareholders) can be employees of their corporation(s). As described in Chapter 6, attempts to reduce corporate taxable income through the use of the owner-employee status can have pitfalls. The substance-over-form doctrine, dealing with the issues of lack of business purpose, unreasonableness of salary, and discriminatory fringe benefits, is the usual focus of IRS scrutiny. Closely held businesses are often objects of concern on these issues. Yet, when these pitfalls are avoided, benefits do accrue to owner-employees who take advantage of the corporate form of business.

**Example 20** Assume the same facts as in example 19, except that M&B Company is organized as a corporation. The salaries are reasonable based on the services performed for the corporation, and the fringe benefits do not discriminate in favor of Monte or Beau. How does this affect the total tax liability?

**Discussion: Because the corporation is viewed as a separate legal entity, it can employ Monte and Beau, pay them tax-deductible salaries, and provide them with nontaxable fringe benefits. After deduction of the salaries and the cost of the fringe benefits, the corporation's taxable income is $40,000 ($160,000 − $100,000 − $20,000), and it pays $8,400 ($40,000 × 21%) in income tax. Monte and Beau include their salaries in their taxable income and pay $6,802 and $4,601 (example 12), respectively, for a total tax of $19,803 ($8,400 + $6,802 + $4,601). In addition, the provision of nontaxable fringe benefits has lowered the overall tax liability by $4,200 through deduction by the corporation and exclusion from Monte and Beau's income tax.**

Because corporate entities can have owner-employees, an S corporation can pay tax-deductible salaries to its owners. However, the S corporation election generally results in the treatment of owner-employees as partners for fringe benefit purposes. Although certain fringe benefits can be provided to partners and S corporation owner-employees, the value of the fringe benefits is included in the owner's taxable income. The corporation can deduct the cost of the fringe benefits.

**Example 21** Assume the same facts as in example 20, except that M&B Company makes a valid S corporation election for the current year. How does the S corporation election affect the total tax liability?

**Discussion: M&B Company deducts the salary payments and the cost of the fringe benefits provided to Monte and Beau, reducing its income to $40,000. Monte's taxable income consists of his $60,000 salary, his $32,000 share of M&B income, and the $10,000 in fringe benefits. The tax on his $102,000 of income is $13,937. Beau's tax on his $58,000 ($40,000 + $8,000 + $10,000) in income is $8,509. The total tax**

**liability of $22,446 is greater than that of a corporation ($19,803 from example 20) because the $40,000 of corporate income is taxed at Monte and Beau's higher marginal tax rates and Monte and Beau cannot exclude the fringe benefits from taxation. Note: To be consistent with example 19, we did not recalculate the QBI deduction.**

## 13-3d Fringe Benefits

LO 4

Show how general income tax provisions can affect the choice of business entity.

Another consideration in choosing the appropriate entity for conducting business is the tax treatment of fringe benefits paid to employees. This is especially important for an individual who is also an owner of the business. These owners generally participate in the day-to-day activities of the business and have owner-employee status. Because a corporation is considered a separate entity and its income is taxable, the corporate owners (shareholders) can be employees of the corporation. Recall from the discussion in Chapter 4 that, because of legislative grace, certain employee benefits are excluded from taxation. The provision of tax-free fringe benefits is a key element in designing a compensation plan to attract and retain qualified employees. The following benefits are generally not included in an employee's gross income.

- Employer-provided term life insurance up to $50,000 coverage
- Employer-sponsored accident and health-care plans
- Meals and lodging furnished for the convenience of the employer
- Cafeteria plans
- Employer-provided educational assistance
- Dependent-care programs
- No additional-cost services
- Qualified employee discounts
- Working-condition fringe benefits
- De minimis fringe benefits

Because of related party concerns with owner-employees and the legislative grace afforded fringe benefits, Congress has established a set of nondiscriminatory rules. That is, historically some employers have provided tax-free fringe benefits to only a few highly compensated employees or to corporate officers. Therefore, companies must offer most types of fringe benefits of at least equal value to nonshareholder employees to retain the exclusion status for the recipients.

A corporation can deduct the cost of providing these fringe benefits to an employee, although the value of these benefits is not income to the employee. Thus, fringe benefits are an excellent compensation and tax savings tool for an owner-employee.

**Example 22** The Golic Group, a corporation, has a company health-care plan for all employees. Miguel, an employee, owns 15% of the corporate stock, and Roberto, also an employee, owns 1%. The cost of Miguel's health plan is $4,800, and Roberto's plan costs $4,200. How are the costs of these benefits treated by each shareholder-employee and by the corporation?

**Discussion: The cost of the health benefits provided to Miguel and Roberto is excluded from their gross income. The $9,000 cost of the health benefits is a deductible business expense for the corporation.**

A sole proprietorship is not a separate taxable entity. Because sole proprietors cannot be employees of their business, the salaries paid and fringe benefits provided to the owner are not deductible by the business. Likewise, the theoretical construct of the conduit entity provides that an employer-employee relationship cannot exist between a partnership and its partners. Unlike pension plans, which require that a partner own more than a 10-percent interest in the partnership to be considered an owner-partner, all partners are treated as owner-partners for fringe-benefit purposes. The partnership is allowed to deduct the cost of certain fringe benefits as a guaranteed payment, and the partners are required to include the guaranteed payment as income on their tax return. Only employer-provided group term life insurance coverage, employer-sponsored accident and health care plans, cafeteria plans, and meals and lodging furnished for the convenience of the employer are subject to this treatment. Because the tax law mentions only these fringe benefits, all other fringe benefits appear to be deductible by the partnership as an ordinary business expense and are not income to the partner. As a self-employed taxpayer, a partner can deduct the cost of health-care premiums for adjusted gross income.

**Example 23** Return to example 22. Assume that the Golic Group is a partnership and that both Miguel and Roberto are partners, owning 15% and 1%, respectively, in the partnership. How is the cost of the health-care plan treated by each partner and by the partnership?

**Discussion: The cost of both health plans is deductible as a guaranteed payment from the partnership to the partner. Both Miguel and Roberto must include in their income the cost of the health plan provided to them. Each is allowed a deduction for adjusted gross income for the cost of the health plan.**

Generally, shareholder-employees of an S corporation are treated the same as employees of regular corporations. Shareholder-employees must include their salary in gross income, and the S corporation can deduct the salary expense and the related payroll taxes. However, the tax treatment of fringe benefits paid by an S corporation to an employee-shareholder depends on the employee's ownership percentage. If an employee-shareholder owns 2 percent or less of an S corporation, the fringe benefits are deductible by the corporation and are not included in the employee's gross income. If a shareholder owns more than 2 percent of the S corporation stock, the tax treatment of the fringe benefits is similar to the tax treatment for a partner. The cost of the fringe benefit is deductible by the S corporation as salary expense, and the owner-employee must include the cost of the fringe benefit as income. The owner-employee can deduct the cost of health care premiums for adjusted gross income. As with a partnership, only employer-provided term life insurance coverage, employer-sponsored accident and health-care plans, cafeteria plans, and meals and lodging furnished for the convenience of the employer are subject to this treatment. As with a partnership, because the tax law mentions only these fringe benefits, all other fringe benefits appear to be deductible by an S corporation as an ordinary business expense and are not income to the owner-employee.

**Example 24** Return to example 22. Assume that Golic Group is an S corporation. How is the cost of the health-care plan treated by each shareholder-employee and by the S corporation?

**Discussion: Because Roberto owns less than 2% of Golic, the corporation can take as a deductible business expense the $4,200 paid for his health-care plan, and the cost is excluded from his gross income. Because Miguel owns more than 2% of the corporate stock, the corporation can deduct the $4,800 paid for his health plan, but Miguel must include it in his gross income. Miguel is allowed a deduction for adjusted gross income for the $4,800 cost of the medical premiums.**

Finally, in determining the total value of fringe benefits provided to an employee, a business needs to consider the cost of employment taxes. The two major employment taxes are Social Security and federal and state unemployment compensation (FUTA and SUTA). All entities are liable for the payment of these taxes on the salaries of their employees. Therefore, a business pays up to an additional 13.85 percent (7.65 percent for Social Security and a maximum 6.2 percent for FUTA and SUTA) of an employee's salary for these taxes.

## 13-3e Social Security Taxes

The Social Security tax is imposed on the wages of employees and the net self-employment income of self-employed individuals. For self-employed individuals, the Social Security tax is referred to as the **self-employment tax**. These terms are used interchangeably throughout the rest of this chapter. Employers are required to match the amount contributed by the employee. Employees pay 7.65 percent of their salary into the Social Security system. This percentage has two components: Old Age, Survivors, and

Disability Insurance (OASDI) at a rate of 6.2 percent, and Medical Health Insurance (MHI) at a rate of 1.45 percent of an individual's wages. For 2021, the maximum amount of earnings subject to the OASDI tax is $142,800. The MHI tax is levied on all wages or net self-employment income. The net operating income earned by a sole proprietor or a partner is considered self-employment income. A guaranteed payment to a partner is also self-employment income. A self-employed individual is considered both an employee and the employer and must pay 15.3 percent (7.65% × 2) in self-employment tax. To reduce this additional tax burden, a self-employed individual can deduct for adjusted gross income one-half of the amount of self-employment taxes paid. In determining self-employment income, the net earnings from self-employment are reduced by one-half of the self-employment tax paid. The effect of this provision is that only 92.35 percent [100% – (50% × 15.3%)] of the net earnings from self-employment are subject to self-employment tax.

**Example 25** Yari and Sven are partners in the Coffee Bean, a local cafe. Yari owns 80% of the business, and Sven owns 20%. The net operating income from the business is $200,000. Who is responsible for paying the Social Security taxes on the income Yari and Sven receive? Who is allowed a deduction for the Social Security taxes paid?

**Discussion: Because the Coffee Bean is a partnership, the individual partners cannot be employees of the entity. Therefore, each partner, and not the Coffee Bean, must pay the self-employment tax on his pro rata share of the income. Each is allowed a deduction for AGI for one-half of the self-employment taxes paid. Yari reports $160,000 ($200,000 × 80%) as self-employment income, and his net self-employment income is $147,760 ($160,000 × 92.35%). Sven reports $40,000 ($200,000 × 20%) as self-employment income, and his net self-employment income is $36,940 ($40,000 × 92.35%). Yari and Sven's self-employment tax and their deduction for self-employment taxes are as follows:**

| | |
|---|---|
| **Yari:** | |
| OASDI on $142,800 of net self-employment income: | |
| $142,800 × 12.4% | $17,707 |
| MHI on $147,760 of net self-employment income: | |
| $147,760 × 2.9% | 4,285 |
| Self-employment tax | $21,992 |
| Deduction for one-half of self-employment taxes paid | $10,996 |
| **Sven:** | |
| Tax on $36,940 of net self-employment income: | |
| $36,940 × 15.3% | $ 5,652 |
| Deduction for one-half of self-employment taxes paid | $ 2,826 |

**The total amount of self-employment taxes paid by Yari and Sven is $27,644 ($21,992 + $5,652).**

A corporation is a separate taxable entity. As a result, it can employ shareholders and deduct the salary or wages paid to them in arriving at the corporation's taxable income. The corporation must match the amount of Social Security taxes paid by an employee. The corporation is allowed to deduct its share of the Social Security taxes paid in calculating its taxable income.

**Example 26** Assume the same facts as in example 25, except that the Coffee Bean is a corporation and pays Yari and Sven salaries of $160,000 and $40,000, respectively. Who is responsible for paying the Social Security taxes on the salaries paid to Yari and Sven? Who is allowed a deduction for the Social Security taxes paid?

**Discussion: Each employee is responsible for paying Social Security taxes on her or his salary. Because Yari's salary exceeds the 2021 maximum of $142,800, he will pay a tax of 6.20% on the first $142,800 of his salary and 1.45% on his entire $160,000 salary. Because Sven's salary is below the maximum amount, he pays Social Security tax at a rate of 7.65% on his salary of $40,000. The Coffee Bean is responsible for matching the amount of the Social Security taxes paid by each employee.**

**The company can deduct the amount it pays in Social Security taxes. The amount Yari and Sven pay in Social Security taxes is not deductible.**

| | |
|---|---|
| Yari: | |
| OASDI on $142,800 of salary income: | |
| $142,800 × 6.2% | $ 8,854 |
| MHI on $160,000 of salary income: | |
| $160,000 × 1.45% | 2,320 |
| Social Security tax | $11,174 |
| Sven: | |
| Tax on $40,000 of salary income: | |
| $40,000 × 7.65% | $ 3,060 |
| Coffee Bean: ($11,174 + $3,060) | $14,234 |

**The total amount of Social Security tax paid by the Coffee Bean, Yari, and Sven is $28,468 ($14,234 + $11,174 + $3,060). The total Social Security tax paid using the corporate form of organization is $824 ($28,468 − $27,644) more than the tax paid using a partnership.**

Although an S corporation is a conduit entity, it can employ shareholders and deduct the salary or wages paid to them in determining the corporation's ordinary income. Unlike a partnership, the income that flows through to the owner of an S corporation is not subject to Social Security tax. Only the wages received by an owner-employee of an S corporation are subject to Social Security tax. An S corporation is required to match the amount contributed by the employee and receives a deduction for the amount paid.

**Example 27** Assume the same facts as in example 25, except that the Coffee Bean is an S corporation. Who is responsible for paying the Social Security taxes on the income Yari and Sven receive? Who is allowed a deduction for the Social Security taxes paid?

**Discussion: The amount of income that flows through to Yari and Sven is not subject to self-employment tax. Therefore, neither Yari nor Sven pays Social Security tax on his income. The use of an S corporation represents a tax savings of $27,644 ($27,644 − $0) over the partnership form and a savings of $28,468 ($28,468 − $0) over the corporate form.**

As the examples in this section illustrate, the use of an S corporation saves a substantial amount in Social Security taxes over other forms of organization. However, caution should be exercised in adopting the no-salary, all-flow-through approach used in example 27. The IRS would probably argue that the salary paid to Yari and Sven is not reasonable (i.e., the amount is too low). Therefore, a conservative yet effective tax-planning technique is to pay each owner-employee a moderate salary commensurate with the work performed.

In deciding whether to operate a business as a partnership, corporation, or S corporation, the employee-owner needs to consider the total tax liability of operating the business. Therefore, the employee-owner must combine the tax on the entity and the employee-owner's individual tax liabilities with the Social Security and self-employment taxes to determine the entity's total tax liability.

**Example 28** Return to the facts of example 25. Compare the total tax liability of operating the Coffee Bean as a partnership, corporation, or an S corporation. Assume that Yari and Sven are both single and have other income that exactly offsets their itemized deductions.

**Discussion: The total tax liability of operating the business includes the tax on the entity, the individual tax liability of the employee-owner, and the Social Security and any self-employment tax liability on the entity and the employee-owner.**

Partnership:
Because a partnership is a conduit entity, it pays no tax. In calculating his individual tax liability, each partner can deduct one-half of the self-employment taxes paid. Yari's taxable income is $149,004 ($160,000 − $10,996 from example 25) and Sven's taxable

income is $37,174 ($40,000 – $2,826 from example 25). The total tax liability of operating the business is $61,764:

| | | |
|---|---|---|
| Yari's income tax liability: $14,751 + [($149,320 – $86,375) × 24%] | = | $29,858 |
| Sven's income tax liability: $995 + [($37,174 – $9,950) × 12%] | = | $4,262 |
| Social Security tax (from example 25) | | $27,644 |
| Total tax liability | | $61,764 |

Corporation:
Because all of the corporation's revenue is paid to Yari and Sven in salary, the corporation has no tax liability. In fact, the corporation has a net operating loss carryforward of $13,620—the amount of Social Security taxes paid by the corporation. Yari and Sven cannot deduct the Social Security taxes they have paid; therefore their taxable income is equal to their salary.

| | | |
|---|---|---|
| Yari's income tax liability: $14,751 + [($160,000 – $86,375) × 24%] | = | $32,421 |
| Sven's income tax liability: $995 + [($40,000 – $9,950) × 12%] | = | $4,601 |
| Social Security tax (from example 26) | | $28,468 |
| Total tax liability | | $65,490 |

S Corporation:
Because an S corporation is a flow-through entity, it pays no tax. In addition, because the income that flows through to the individual owners is not subject to self-employment tax, neither the corporation nor the owner-employees pay Social Security taxes. As with the corporate form of organization, the taxable income of the owner-employees is equal to their salary.

| | | |
|---|---|---|
| Yari's income tax liability: $14,751 + [($160,000 – $86,375) × 24%] | = | $32,421 |
| Sven's income tax liability: $995 + [($40,000 – $9,950) × 12%] | = | $4,601 |
| Social Security tax (from example 27) | | -0- |
| Total tax liability | | $37,022 |

Using an S corporation represents a total tax savings of $24,742 ($61,764 – $37,022) over the partnership form and a savings of $28,468 ($65,490 – $37,022) over the corporate form. Note: To better illustrate the concept we have ignored the impact of the QBI deduction.

**concept check**

The tax treatment of fringe benefits provided to employees and employee/owners of entities is based on the *legislative grace concept*. With the exception of a sole proprietorship, all entities may deduct certain fringe benefits in arriving at the entities' taxable income. The *entity concept* requires each entity to report the income and deductions applicable to that entity. Because an owner may be an employee in either a corporation or an S corporation, the value of the fringe benefits is generally excluded from the recipient's income. However, partners and more than 2-percent S corporation shareholders are not separate entities and therefore must include the value of fringe benefits in income under the *conduit entity* construct.

## 13-3f Planning Commentary

Even at a basic level, the total tax liability of a particular entity form is the result of a complex interaction between the incidence of taxation and how payments to or on behalf of an owner-employee are treated for tax purposes. The choice of an entity form that minimizes the total tax liability in a given situation may conflict with other objectives of the owner(s). For example, the owner(s) of a business often need the limited liability feature of the corporation. However, the corporate form does not minimize the total tax liability in all cases. Therefore, other options, such as the use of an S corporation, LLC, or LLP, must be considered. Often these alternate forms can give equivalent tax results. In other situations, higher total taxes may have to be paid to achieve the nontax objectives of the owner(s). No two business situations are alike, and all factors, tax and nontax, must be analyzed carefully to determine the best entity form in a given situation.

Generally, the fringe benefits paid to an employee of a corporation are deductible by the corporation and are not taxable income for the employee. This is true even if the employee is an owner of the corporation. However, an individual who is a partner or an employee of an S corporation who owns more than 2 percent of the entity must include the cost of certain fringe benefits as income: employer-provided term life insurance coverage, employer-sponsored accident and health care plans, cafeteria plans, and meals and lodging furnished for the convenience of the employer. Both a partnership and an S corporation can deduct the cost of the fringe benefits as compensation expenses. The fringe benefits paid to an owner of a sole proprietorship are not deductible. However, the cost of health insurance premiums paid by a sole proprietor, partner, or an owner-employee of an S corporation who holds more than 2 percent of the entity are deductible for AGI on the individual's tax return.

A sole proprietor is subject to self-employment taxes on the net income of the business. Partners are subject to self-employment taxes on their pro rata share of the ordinary income of the partnership. Guaranteed payments received by a partner also are subject to self-employment tax. Because sole proprietors and partners are deemed to be both an employee and an employer for Social Security/self-employment tax purposes, each is responsible for both the employer's share (7.65 percent) and the employee's share (7.65 percent) of self-employment taxes. To offset this additional tax liability, sole proprietors and partners are allowed a deduction for adjusted gross income for one-half of the self-employment taxes paid.

An owner-employee of a corporation is responsible for Social Security taxes on only the amount of salary received. Dividends paid to an owner-employee are not subject to Social Security taxes. However, the dividends are subject to double taxation (i.e., at the corporate and individual levels). As a separate taxpaying entity, the corporation is required to match the Social Security tax paid by the owner-employee and receives a deduction for the amount of Social Security tax it pays.

The income from an S corporation that flows through to an owner-employee is not subject to self-employment tax. Only the salary received by an owner-employee is subject to Social Security tax. The S corporation must match the amount of Social Security tax paid by the employee and receives a deduction for the amount of Social Security tax it pays. Therefore, because the income that flows through to an owner-employee of an S corporation is not subject to Social Security tax, the use of this form of organization can significantly reduce an owner-employee's total tax liability.

# 13-4 FORMATION

A number of tax issues arise at the formation of a business entity. In forming the entity, the owner(s) typically contribute cash or other assets in exchange for an ownership interest. The entity incurs costs before it begins operations. Once the entity begins operations, it must select an accounting period and an accounting method. The taxability of transfers of property to an entity and the effects on the bases of the owner and the entity are important factors that can affect the choice of entity. The proper treatment of costs incurred before the business begins operations and the selection of accounting periods and methods are important tax issues that must be resolved at the beginning. This section discusses each of these factors and how they differ for each entity.

## 13-4a Transfers to an Entity

LO 5

Explain the differences in treatment of items that occur at the formation of an entity, including transfers to the entity and how they affect the basis of the entity and its owners.

In general, any exchange of property is a taxable event. As described in Chapter 11, when the amount realized from an exchange is greater than the adjusted basis of the property exchanged, a gain is realized on the transaction. Absent legislative grace, realized gains are recognized.

Congress has granted tax deferral status to certain transfers of property in exchange for an ownership interest in a business entity. In general, no gain or loss is recognized when taxpayers contribute property solely in exchange for an ownership interest in a business. The underlying rationale for this treatment is that the transferors are merely exchanging direct ownership of property for indirect ownership through their ownership interest in the entity. This is an application of the substance-over-form doctrine. In addition, even though a gain may be realized on such exchanges, such transfers do not provide the transferors with the wherewithal to pay the tax on the gain. Therefore, the tax treatment of the transfers parallels the tax treatment of like-kind exchanges. Consistent with the taxation of gains on like-kind exchanges, gains on exchanges of property for ownership interests are recognized to the extent that the transferor receives boot in the transaction.

## Sole Proprietorship

A sole proprietorship is not an entity that is separate from the owner. Transferring property to a sole proprietorship does not result in a realization because a second party is not involved in the transaction. Therefore, no tax effects arise when an individual contributes property to be used in a sole proprietorship.

## Partnership

No gain or loss is recognized when property is contributed to a partnership solely in exchange for a partnership ownership interest.[11] Direct ownership of the property is being replaced by an ownership interest in the property. The tax law permits partners to defer taxes on contributions associated with formation of a partnership and on contributions throughout the life of the entity. Services rendered are not considered property. Services exchanged for a partnership ownership interest do not represent a transformation of the ownership of property from direct to indirect. Under the all-inclusive income concept, the receipt of an ownership interest in exchange for services rendered to a partnership constitutes gross income.

**Example 29** Bonita and Chin plan to open a restaurant near the new airport in their community. Bonita owns a parcel of land that she inherited from her uncle when it was worth $100,000. She will contribute the land, now valued at $180,000, cash of $75,000, and her management skills to the business and receive a 90% ownership interest in Bonchin Restaurant. In return for her part of the ownership interest, Bonita will provide services valued at $15,000 while the business is in its developmental stage (e.g., negotiating loans, arranging for suppliers, and hiring employees). Chin will contribute $20,000 in cash and his personal recipe collection with an agreed-upon value of $10,000, and he will be the head chef for the restaurant. He will receive a 10% ownership interest in the restaurant. Both owners will receive $50,000 annually for the services they will contribute to the business operations. Bonita and Chin agree to form a partnership and share business profits and losses in a 90:10 ratio. What are the tax consequences of the transfers to the business in exchange for ownership interests in the partnership?

**Discussion: Neither the partners nor the partnership will recognize a gain or loss on the transfer of property solely in exchange for ownership in the restaurant. Both partners will provide services to the business in the future. They will recognize the income received for those services when they receive it. Bonita is to provide $15,000 in services for the entity while it is being organized. The value of those services is income to Bonita in the year rendered.**

## Corporation

Deferral provisions for contributions of property to a corporation in exchange for ownership interest are more restrictive than for a partnership. The exchange of property must be solely for stock of the corporation, and the shareholder(s) must control the corporation immediately after the transfer.[12] For deferral purposes, the shareholders must own at least 80 percent of the stock to control the corporation. Transfers qualifying for deferral may be made to existing corporations as well as newly created corporations. The shareholder recognizes as income stock received for services rendered to the corporation. Because the S corporation election relates primarily to the incidence of taxation, transfers to S corporations follow the same rules as for contributions of property to corporations.

**Example 30** Assume the same facts as in example 29, except that the two owners want to incorporate their business to limit their liability. Bonita will receive 900 shares of stock for her contributions to the business, and Chin will receive 100 shares of stock for his contributions. What are the tax consequences of the exchange?

**Discussion: Because Bonita will own at least 80% of the stock of the entity (actually, 90%), she will control the corporation immediately after the exchange of**

**her property for the corporate stock. She recognizes no gain. Bonita will include in her gross income for the year the $15,000 she receives for her services. Chin's exchange also qualifies for deferral because it is concurrent with Bonita's, and he will not recognize any gain on the exchange transaction. All that is necessary to satisfy the control requirement is that the transferor-shareholders together own at least 80% of the stock. Note: The same result occurs even if Bonita and Chin make an S corporation election.**

## 13-4b Basis Considerations

In forming an entity or purchasing an interest in an entity, the owner(s) obtain a basis for their investment. Basis is established when an investor purchases an ownership interest (e.g., shares of corporate stock or a partnership interest). The cost of the investment is the initial basis amount.[13] When an owner contributes property in exchange for an ownership interest, two assets are created. The owner has a basis in her or his investment, and the entity has a basis in the property it receives. Following the underlying rationale for gain deferral—that in substance, nothing is changed regarding ownership of property—the adjusted basis of the property exchanged is substituted for the basis of the ownership interest received. The entity receiving the property has a basis in the property equal to the owner's adjusted basis. If gain recognition occurs, the basis of the ownership interest and the entity's basis are increased by the gain recognized. The usual result is that both bases are equal to fair market value. An exception occurs when personal use property is contributed to the business entity. In this situation, the split-basis rule for personal property converted to business use applies (see Chapter 9), and the entity's basis in the property is the lower of the fair market value or the adjusted basis as of the contribution date.

### Sole Proprietorship

Because the ownership of property contributed to a sole proprietorship does not change hands, the sole proprietor remains the owner of the property. The owner's basis remains unchanged unless the property is personal use property converted to business.

**Example 31** Assume that in example 29, Bonita will be the sole owner of the restaurant. The restaurant will purchase Chin's recipes for $10,000, and Chin will lend $20,000 to the business. What is the basis of the property Bonita contributes to the business?

**Discussion: Bonita's sole proprietorship will use the land she contributes to the business operation. She still owns the land as an individual because she is not separate from her business, and her ownership interest does not change. The land retains the $100,000 basis established when Bonita inherited it from her uncle. Bonita also obtains a $10,000 basis in the recipe collection she purchases from Chin.**

**Example 32** Return to example 31, and assume that the land's value at the date it is placed in service of the business is $180,000 and Bonita's basis is $200,000. What is the basis of the land?

**Discussion: Because the value of the land is less than Bonita's basis at the date it is converted to business use, the split-basis rules apply. The land is not depreciable. Therefore, basis will not be determined until the land is sold. Bonita's gain basis is her $200,000 basis. Her loss basis is the $180,000 fair market value at the date of conversion to business use.**

### Partnership

Basis in a conduit entity may be the most critical attribute for owners. Basis establishes the amount of unrecovered investment in the conduit entity. Basis does more than establish the realized gain or loss upon disposition of the investment through application of the capital recovery concept; it also determines the taxability of distributions from the conduit entity to owners. Also, an owner must have an adequate amount of basis before the owner can recognize losses flowing from the conduit entity.

When a partner contributes property in exchange for a partnership interest, the general basis rules apply. The partner's basis in the partnership interest is equal to the basis of the property contributed.[14] The partnership's basis in the property is equal to the contributing partner's basis in the property.[15] When a partnership interest is received in exchange for services, the income recognized by the partner is added to the basis of the partnership interest. The partnership either deducts the cost of the services, if they are for current period expenses, or capitalizes the costs if they have a benefit that extends substantially beyond the end of the tax year (capital expenditure).

**Example 33** Recall the original facts from example 29 in which Bonita and Chin agree to form a partnership. Bonita contributes land worth $180,000, cash of $75,000, and services valued at $15,000 for a 90% interest in the partnership. Chin will contribute $20,000 in cash and a recipe collection valued at $10,000 for a 10% interest in the partnership. The land has a basis of $100,000 to Bonita. Both owners will receive $50,000 annually for the services they will contribute toward the business operation. What are Bonita's and Chin's bases in the partnership? What is the partnership's basis in the property contributed by Bonita and Chin?

**Discussion: Because the contribution of property was tax-free, Bonita and Chin will have bases in the partnership equal to the basis in the property each contributed. Bonita's basis is $190,000, consisting of her $100,000 basis in the land, the $75,000 in cash she contributed, and the $15,000 in fees received for organizing the partnership. Because she received part of her ownership for organizing the partnership, the income she recognizes becomes part of her ownership basis. Chin's basis is limited to his $20,000 cash contribution. Because he does not have a basis in the recipe collection, there is no basis to transfer to his ownership interest. The partnership has $95,000 in cash, and its basis in the land is equal to Bonita's $100,000 basis. Because Chin had no basis in the recipes, the partnership has a zero basis in the recipes. The partnership must also capitalize the $15,000 Bonita receives for services in organizing the partnership. (See the discussion of organization costs later in this chapter.)**

**Partnership Debt Effects** Recall that basis begins with a person's contribution of assets or services in exchange for an ownership interest. However, doing business as a partnership adds a unique complexity to basis calculations. Unlike corporate shareholders, partners are liable for the debts of the partnership. Because of this liability feature, **partnership debt** assumed by a partner and the partner's share of partnership debt are deemed to be additional cash contributions to the partnership by the partner.[16] Accordingly, any partnership debt assumed by the partner and the partner's share of partnership liabilities increase the partner's basis. Decreases in debts of a partner or a partnership are deemed cash distributions to partners.[17] Therefore, any partner's debt that is assumed by the partnership and any decreases in the partner's share of partnership liabilities decrease the partner's basis.

**Example 34** Assume the same facts as in example 33, except that Bonita's land is encumbered by a $20,000 mortgage that the partnership assumes. What effect does this have on Bonita's and Chin's bases?

**Discussion: Bonita adds her $18,000 ($20,000 × 90%) share of mortgage debt to her basis and subtracts the $20,000 in debt relief that she receives when the partnership assumes the mortgage on her land. Chin adds his $2,000 ($20,000 × 10%) share of the mortgage debt to his basis. Bonita's basis is $188,000, and Chin's basis is $22,000:**

| | Bonita | Chin |
|---|---|---|
| Basis of property or cash contributed | $190,000 | $20,000 |
| Plus: Debt assumed by partnership | | |
| Mortgage loan | 18,000 | 2,000 |
| Less: Debt relief | (20,000) | |
| Basis of ownership interest | $188,000 | $22,000 |

**Recourse and Nonrecourse Loans** Chapter 7 introduced the at-risk potential of loans. A **recourse debt** is a loan for which the debtor remains liable until repayment occurs. If the borrower defaults on repayment, the creditor has recourse; the creditor may obtain a judgment against the borrower, who must personally make up the amount of default. Because partners are liable for the liabilities of the partnership, individual partners have a potential risk of loss from partnership debts. Accordingly, partners are permitted to increase the basis of their partnership interest by their share of the potential loss from partnership debts. Partnership debt created before January 30, 1989, is allocated to partners by using the loss-sharing percentage.[18] Partnership debt created after January 29, 1989, is allocated by using what is called the economic risk of loss scenario.[19] The basic thrust of this approach is to determine the cash contribution each partner would have to make to pay off partnership liabilities if all the partnership assets became worthless. This can result in partners' allocations of liabilities in ratios different than their loss-sharing ratios. The rules for this approach are very complex and beyond the scope of this text. However, in many instances, the application of these rules provides results similar to those obtained by using the old liability-sharing rules. Therefore, to make it easier to understand adjustments to bases that are made for partnership debts, in our examples, we use the approach for debts created before January 30, 1989.

**Example 35** Return to example 33, and assume that Bonita and Chin agree to share profits and losses differently. Bonita will have a 90% interest in entity profits and an 80% interest in entity losses. Chin's ownership interests are 10% in profits and 20% in losses. The partnership obtains a loan to use for operating expenses. The loan is a $50,000, 3-year, 10% recourse loan with only the interest payable until maturity. What are the partners' bases in their ownership interests?

**Discussion: Bonita and Chin will add their respective shares of the loan to the bases they receive for their contributions of cash and other property. Because the loan is a recourse loan, the loss-sharing percentage is used to determine each partner's share of the debt. Bonita's basis is increased to $230,000 by her $40,000 ($50,000 × 80%) share of the partnership debt. Chin's $10,000 ($50,000 × 20%) share of the debt increases his basis to $30,000.**

| | Bonita | Chin |
|---|---|---|
| Basis of property or cash contributed | $190,000 | $20,000 |
| Plus: Recourse debt assumed by partnership | | |
| 80% | 40,000 | |
| 20% | | 10,000 |
| Basis of ownership interest | $230,000 | $30,000 |

A **nonrecourse debt** is a liability that is secured only by the underlying property; the borrower is not personally liable for the debt. In the case of a loan default, the creditor has no recourse against the borrower for liability amounts greater than the value of the property that secures the debt instrument. Nonrecourse debts are common when financing real estate and the creditor expects the property to increase in value. Borrowers repay nonrecourse loans from entity profits, and the property securing the loans aids in earning these profits. Therefore, partnerships with nonrecourse liabilities have the risk of losing profits if the property is lost in a loan default judgment. Accordingly, partners are allowed to increase the bases of their partnership interests by their share of nonrecourse partnership debt. As with recourse debt, the rules for allocating nonrecourse debt created before January 30, 1989, are straightforward: Nonrecourse debt is allocated by using the partners' profit-sharing percentages.[20] Nonrecourse debt created after January 29, 1989, also uses a complex set of rules to determine each partner's share of the debt; discussion of those rules is beyond the scope of this text.[21] As with the new rules for recourse debt, applying the new rules for nonrecourse debts often provides results similar to the old rules, and we use the rules for nonrecourse debt created before January 30, 1989, to illustrate the adjustments made to partners' bases for nonrecourse debt.

**Example 36** Assume the same facts as in example 35. To construct the restaurant building, the partnership obtains a $200,000, 15-year nonrecourse mortgage loan. How does the loan affect the partners' bases?

**Discussion: Bonita and Chin will add their respective shares of the loan liability to their bases. Because the loan is nonrecourse, the profit-sharing percentage is used to**

**determine each partner's share of the debt. Bonita adds $180,000 ($200,000 × 90%) to her basis, and Chin adds $20,000 ($200,000 × 10%) to his basis. Bonita's basis is $410,000, and Chin's basis is $50,000:**

| | Bonita | Chin |
|---|---|---|
| Basis of property or cash contributed | $190,000 | $20,000 |
| Plus: Debt assumed by partnership | | |
| Operating loan | 40,000 | 10,000 |
| Mortgage loan | 180,000 | 20,000 |
| Basis of ownership interest | $410,000 | $50,000 |

Note that the overall effect of a partnership's incurring debt is to increase the partners' basis in the partnership. When partnership operating losses flow through to the partners, the partners cannot deduct losses in excess of their bases. The increase in basis for debt of the partnership makes the partnership a desirable entity form for business ventures that finance their operations with substantial amounts of debt, thus allowing greater loss deductions by the partners.

## Corporation

When shareholders contribute property solely in exchange for stock in a tax-free transaction, the shareholders' bases in the property become their bases in the stock received.[22] The corporation uses the shareholders' bases in the property as its basis in the property.[23] As discussed earlier, receipt of stock for services constitutes income to a shareholder. The income recognized from such services is added to the shareholder's basis. The corporation either expenses the cost of the services or capitalizes the cost, depending on the life of the asset created by the services.

**Example 37** Return to example 30. Recall that Bonita and Chin wish to incorporate the business and contribute property in exchange for stock. What is the basis of the corporate stock in the hands of shareholders, and what is the basis of the property for the corporation?

**Discussion: Because the exchange of property for stock does not result in gain or loss recognition, Bonita's basis is $190,000 ($100,000 land basis + $75,000 cash + $15,000 for services) for her 900 shares of stock. Chin's basis is $20,000 ($20,000 cash + zero basis for the recipes) for his 100 shares of stock. The corporation has land with a basis of $100,000; the services provided by Bonita are capitalized at their $15,000 cost; and the recipes have a zero basis.**

Consistent with the wherewithal-to-pay concept and parallel to the treatment of like-kind exchanges, if the shareholder receives boot in a property-for-stock transaction, any gain realized on the exchange is recognized to the extent of the boot received. In recognizing gains on transfers of property to a corporation, a liability of the shareholder assumed by the corporation is not considered boot, and the shareholder is not taxed on the liability assumption.[24] To avoid double taxation of any gains recognized, the shareholder and the corporation increase their bases by the amount of gain recognized by the shareholder. Any liability of the shareholder assumed by the corporation reduces the shareholder's basis.

**Example 38** Bonita and Chin incorporate their restaurant business. Assume that Bonita's land is encumbered by a $20,000 mortgage that the corporation assumes. How does the assumption of the $20,000 mortgage on Bonita's land affect the taxability of the transaction and the bases of Bonita and Chin?

**Discussion: Because the corporation's assumption of Bonita's $20,000 mortgage is not considered boot received for purposes of the property-for-stock deferral, Bonita does not recognize a gain on the transaction. Since she has received debt relief without income recognition, Bonita must reduce the basis in her stock by the $20,000 mortgage assumption. Bonita's basis is $170,000 ($100,000 + $75,000 + $15,000 − $20,000). The corporation's basis in the land is $100,000, and it has a liability with a basis of $20,000.**

Because of the 80-percent control requirement, taxpayers contributing appreciated property to a corporation after formation usually recognize gains.

**Example 39** Assume that after several years of operating their business as a corporation, Bonita and Chin decide to expand their restaurant business by adding a delivery service. Reggie will manage the operation of the new service. He owns three delivery vans worth $30,000 that have an adjusted basis of $12,000. Reggie exchanges the delivery vans for 100 shares of corporate stock. What are the tax effects of this transaction?

**Discussion: Although the transfer is solely in exchange for stock in the corporation, Reggie does not control the corporation immediately after the transfer, and he cannot defer gain on the transaction. Reggie must recognize an $18,000 gain ($30,000 − $12,000) on the exchange. His basis in the stock is $30,000 ($12,000 basis + $18,000 gain recognized). The corporation's basis in the delivery vans is $30,000.**

**Corporation Debt Effects** Shareholders of corporations do not adjust their basis for increases and decreases in the liabilities of the corporation. A corporation is an entity that is separate from its owners, and therefore it is liable for its debts. Because the shareholders do not have any personal liability for corporate debts, they are not at risk, and a basis adjustment is not necessary.

**Example 40** Assume the same facts as in example 38, except that the corporation obtains a loan of $50,000 to use for operating expenses. What is the effect on Bonita and Chin's bases of the corporation's $50,000 loan?

**Discussion: Shareholders do not adjust their basis when the corporation borrows money or incurs other liabilities. Bonita and Chin's bases are unaffected by the corporation's $50,000 loan.**

As with the requirements for a tax-free exchange of property between a corporation and a shareholder, an S corporation is subject to the same basis rules as a corporation. Even though the incidence of taxation of an S corporation is similar to that of a partnership, S corporation shareholders are not allowed to add debt of the corporation to their basis. This follows from the limited liability feature of the corporation, which is retained by an S corporation.

**Example 41** Assume that in example 40, Bonita and Chin make an S corporation election for their business. How will this affect Bonita's and Chin's bases?

**Discussion: S corporation shareholders do not adjust their basis when the corporation borrows money or incurs liabilities. Bonita's and Chin's bases are unaffected by the corporation's $50,000 loan.**

## concept check

The tax law allows tax-free transfers of property solely in exchange for an ownership interest. This is in part because of the *wherewithal-to-pay concept*. The transferor is giving up direct control of assets in exchange for an ownership interest that provides indirect control of the same assets. Economically, the transferor is still in the same position as before the exchange. Further, if the transferor receives something in addition to the ownership interest (e.g., cash), the transferor must recognize gain to the extent of the additional amount received. When an entity assumes debt of a transferor, gain or loss is generally not recognized because of the *wherewithal-to-pay concept*. A partner's share of partnership debt increases the partner's basis to reflect the personal exposure to the liability that partners face. Corporate shareholders are not personally liable for the debt, and therefore, their basis in the stock they hold is not increased for debt. The *capital recovery concept* allows the recovery of capital investment before gain is recognized on a disposition. Because partners and S corporation shareholders pay tax on their share of the entity's income, the owners' basis is increased to avoid double taxation of the earnings. Similarly, partnership and S corporation losses and withdrawals from the entity reduce the owner's basis in the partnership interest to prevent a double tax benefit. These adjustments ensure that proper capital recovery is achieved when a partnership or S corporation interest is sold or otherwise disposed of. Because corporations and shareholders are separate entities, adjustments for the income of the corporation and dividends received from the corporation are not made to the shareholders' basis.

## 13-4c Organizational Costs

LO 6 Explain the treatment of start-up and organizational costs.

The business purpose concept allows deduction of the ordinary and necessary expenses of a business. A business cannot expense immediately those business expenditures with a life that extends substantially beyond the end of the tax year. These expenses are capitalized and deducted over their useful or statutory life. A business incurs **start-up costs** (as discussed in Chapter 5) before it begins operations. Other costs that pertain to getting the entity ready to operate are referred to as **organizational costs**. Typical organizational costs include the following:

- Legal services relating to drafting organizational documents and agreements
- Accounting services incident to the organization of the business
- Fees paid to the state in which the business is organized
- Expenses of temporary directors or management team

Costs that are incurred before the entity starts its business activities do not have a business purpose and cannot be deducted as operating expenses. Therefore, start-up and organizational costs must be capitalized. An election can be made to deduct up to $5,000 of organizational costs in the year in which the business begins operations. The $5,000 is phased out when total expenditures exceed $50,000 (i.e., no deduction allowed when expenditures total $55,000 or more). Any remaining organizational costs must be amortized over 180 months, beginning in the month the business begins operations.[25] If an election to amortize is not made, the entity cannot deduct start-up and/or organizational expenditures until it is liquidated or sold. The treatment of start-up and organizational costs applies to all business entities.

**Example 42** Return to example 29. How should the partnership account for the $15,000 interest Bonita receives for management services related to the organization of the partnership? Assume that the partnership begins operation on September 1, 2021.

**Discussion: Because the management services are performed before the business begins operations, the partnership must capitalize the $15,000 as an organizational cost. It can elect to deduct $5,000 of the expenditures in 2021. The remaining $10,000 of organizational costs must be amortized over 180 months, beginning in September 2021. The maximum 2021 deduction is $5,222 {$5,000 + [($10,000 ÷ 180) × 4 months]}.**

Expenses that are not considered organizational expenditures include those for the issue, or sale, of shares of corporate stock (e.g., commissions, printing costs).[26] These are selling expenses and reduce the amount of stockholders' equity that results from the sale of the stock.

**Example 43** Return to example 30. In addition to the stock issued for Bonita's services in organizing the corporation, the corporation pays $4,200 to attorneys, accountants, and state regulatory agencies to organize the corporation. Commissions and printing costs related to the stock issuance are $200. How should the corporation treat these costs? Assume that the corporation begins business operations on September 1, 2021.

**Discussion: The value of the stock Bonita receives for organizing the corporation and the $4,200 paid to organize the corporation must be capitalized. If an election to amortize is made, the maximum 2021 deduction is $5,315 {$5,222 + [($4,200 ÷ 180) × 4 months]}. The $200 in costs related to the issuance of the stock is not an organizational cost. It is treated as a reduction of stockholders' equity from the issuance of the shares.**

## 13-4d Accounting Periods

LO 7
Compare accounting method and accounting period choices among the various entities.

The annual accounting period concept requires all entities to report the results of operations on an annual basis. The period for which an entity reports is referred to as the **taxable year**. A taxable year may be either a calendar year (ending on December 31) or a fiscal year.[27] A **fiscal year** is defined as:

1. A period of 12 months ending on the last day of any month other than December.
2. A 52- to 53-week taxable year. The 52- to 53-week fiscal year ends on the same day of the week each year. The year must end either the last time a particular day occurs during the month (e.g., the last Wednesday in October) or the day that occurs closest to the end of a particular month (e.g., the Friday closest to March 31, even if that Friday happens to be April 2).

An entity establishes a taxable year by keeping its books on the basis of that year and filing its first tax return based on that taxable year.[28] This requires the entity to formally close its books on that date and file a timely tax return for the tax year selected. If the entity does not close its books on that date or if it does not keep formal books, it must use a calendar year. In addition, if the entity closes its books on a date that does not qualify as a fiscal year (e.g., November 15), it must use a calendar year for tax purposes.

Taxpayers are generally free to choose which accounting period they will use as their taxable year. However, the tax law limits the choices for partnerships and S corporations. A sole proprictorship is not an entity separate and apart from its owner and therefore must use the same tax year as its owner. Because of the record-keeping requirement, most individuals (who do not keep formal books for personal income and expenses) use calendar years. Corporations are separate legal and taxable entities and have extensive flexibility in their choice of accounting periods. Without any restrictions on the selection of a taxable year, owners of conduit entities could obtain a tax deferral benefit by having the entity select a taxable year different from that of the owners.

**Example 44** Mark, Suzanne, and Tim own Driveway Barbequers. Driveway is organized as a partnership and keeps its books on the basis of a fiscal year ending March 31. The owners, who receive the bulk of their income from the partnership, use a calendar year to report their incomes. What tax benefit will Mark, Tim, and Suzanne receive if the partnership is allowed to report its results to the government using the March 31 fiscal year?

**Discussion: If Driveway were allowed to use a March 31 fiscal year, Mark, Suzanne, and Tim would receive a 9-month deferral on the reporting of their income from Driveway. This would happen because income from a conduit entity is deemed to be earned on the last day of the entity's tax year. Because the owners would receive their income from Driveway on March 31, they would not report it on their individual returns until December 31, resulting in a 9-month deferral of income.**

Because of this potential deferral, the tax law contains a set of rules that limits the choice of taxable years for partnerships and S corporations.

## Partnership

A partnership tax year is selected on a hierarchical basis that attempts to match the tax year of the partnership to those of the partners.[29] First, the partnership must use the tax year used by those partners having a majority interest (more than 50 percent) in partnership profits and capital, called the **majority-interest tax year**.

**Example 45** Return to the facts of example 44, and assume that all the partners use calendar years. What taxable year must Driveway use?

**Discussion: Because more than 50% of the partnership interests use a calendar year, Driveway must also use a calendar year. The effect of this rule is to have the partnership's taxable year end match the year end of the majority of the partners.**

**Example 46** Assume that in example 45, Mark owns 60% of Driveway and Suzanne and Tim each own a 20% interest. Mark validly establishes a January 31 fiscal year. What taxable year must Driveway use?

**Discussion: Because Mark owns more than 50% of Driveway, Driveway must use the same fiscal year as Mark, January 31. As with example 45, the effect of this rule is to match 60% of the partnership's profits to Mark's taxable year, with only 40% subject to deferral.**

If the majority-interest partners do not have the same tax year, the partnership must use the tax year of its principal partners, referred to as the **principal partner tax year**. A principal partner is a partner with at least a 5-percent interest.[30]

**Example 47** Assume that in example 45, Driveway Barbequers is operated as a limited partnership with 38 limited partners each owning a 2% interest. The remaining 24% is owned equally by Mark, Suzanne, and Tim, each of whom uses a March 31 fiscal year. The tax years of the 38 limited partners are diverse; there is no majority-interest tax year. What tax year must Driveway use?

**Discussion: Because there is no majority-interest tax year, the partnership must use the tax year of the principal partners. In this case, none of the limited partners qualifies as a principal partner because each owns less than 5% of the partnership. Mark, Suzanne, and Tim are the only principal partners. Because the three principal partners have the same tax year, the partnership must use that tax year—a fiscal year ending March 31.**

When the principal partners do not have the same tax year, the partnership must use the tax year that results in the least aggregate deferral of income for the partners.[31] Because the purpose of the partnership limitations is to effect the least amount of deferral, under this rule, a partnership will always use the tax year of at least one partner. The rules for applying this technique are beyond the scope of this text.

A partnership can use a taxable year other than that prescribed by the hierarchical rules if it can establish to the IRS's satisfaction that a valid business purpose exists for having a different tax year.[32] To establish a **business purpose tax year** the partnership must obtain permission from the IRS by proving that the year selected does not create for either the partnership or its partners significant deferral of income or shifting of deductions. The type of business purpose tax year granted most frequently is the natural business tax year. The natural business year test (discussed next) also applies to S corporations.

## S Corporation

In general, an S corporation must use a calendar year.[33] However, it can choose an alternate year under the ownership tax year or the natural business year exceptions. An **ownership tax year** is the tax year of more than 50 percent of the owners of the corporation.[34] Thus, the ownership tax year is similar in concept to the majority-interest tax year of a partnership.

**Example 48** Assume that Mark, Suzanne, and Tim incorporate Driveway Barbequers with Mark owning 45%, Suzanne owning 35%, and Tim owning 20% of the stock. Mark uses a fiscal year that ends July 31. Suzanne and Tim use a fiscal year ending October 31. They make a valid S corporation election. What is the ownership tax year?

**Discussion: Suzanne and Tim have the same tax year and own more than 50% of the corporation. Therefore, the ownership tax year is Suzanne and Tim's tax year—the fiscal year ending October 31. Driveway can use either a calendar year or a fiscal year ending October 31.**

A **natural business year** is defined as "the annual accounting period encompassing all related income and expenses."[35] To establish a natural business year, an S corporation (or a partnership) must have peak and off-peak business periods. The natural business year is the end of the peak business period. A mechanical test determines a natural business year.[36] Under this test, an annual accounting period qualifies as a natural business year if the gross receipts from sales or services for the final two months of the current year and each of the two preceding years equal or exceed 25 percent of the gross receipts for the entire 12-month period.

**Example 49** Assume the same facts as in example 48. Driveway's heaviest sales period occurs during July and August, when demand is greatest for carryout barbecue. Gross sales for July and August and the 12-month period ending on August 31 of the current year and each of the 2 preceding years are as follows:

| | July and August | 12-Month Period |
|---|---|---|
| Current year | $35,000 | $125,000 |
| Preceding year 1 | 31,250 | 120,000 |
| Preceding year 2 | 25,000 | 100,000 |

Does August 31 qualify as a natural business year under the gross receipts test?

**Discussion: To qualify under the gross receipts test, the gross receipts for the last 2 months of the fiscal year (July and August) must equal or exceed 25% of the**

**gross receipts of the current year and the 2 preceding years. Here is the calculation of the gross receipt percentages for the 3 applicable periods:**

| | |
|---|---|
| Current year | $35,000 ÷ $125,000 = 28% |
| Preceding year 1 | $31,250 ÷ $120,000 = 26% |
| Preceding year 2 | $25,000 ÷ $100,000 = 25% |

**Because the gross receipts for July and August for the current year and the 2 preceding years equal or exceed 25% in each of those years, August 31 qualifies as a natural business year.**

## 13-4e Accounting Methods

Taxpayers are required to maintain the accounting records necessary to enable them to file their annual tax returns. To properly characterize income and deduction items, taxpayers must select an accounting method. The three acceptable accounting methods are the cash method, the accrual method, and the hybrid method.

In selecting a method of accounting, taxpayers are required to use for taxable income computation the method of accounting that they regularly use for their books. The method must be used consistently from period to period and must clearly reflect the income of the taxpayer. Once adopted, the taxpayer must use the accounting method consistently from one period to the next.

We have already discussed the general application of the accounting methods and applications of the methods to income and deductions. This section discusses the selection of an accounting method by the various entities. As with accounting periods, entities have a significant degree of latitude in selecting their accounting method. However, certain provisions restrict the choice for certain types of taxpayers. For example, a basic restriction imposed on entities that have inventories of goods is that they must use the accrual method to account for sales and cost of goods sold. This requires entities with inventories to select either the accrual or hybrid method to compute taxable income.

### Partnership

A partnership can generally elect to use any accounting method. The election is made at the partnership level and is independent of the method(s) of accounting used by the partners. For example, a partnership electing the accrual method forces its partners to report income of the partnership on the accrual method, even if the partners use the cash method.[37]

A partnership that has at least one corporate partner must use the accrual method. This restriction is an extension of the corporate restriction (discussed next) to prevent using a partnership to defer taxes through use of the cash method.

**Example 50** Jackamani Company is organized as a partnership. Jack owns a 20% interest, and Aman owns 60%. IM Corporation owns the remaining 20%. What accounting methods may Jackamani select if Jackamani is in the financial consulting business and does not have inventories?

**Discussion: Because a corporation is a partner, Jackamani must use the accrual method of accounting, unless one of the exceptions (discussed next) applies.**

### Corporation

A large corporation is generally required to use the accrual method of accounting.[38] Any method that accounts for some but not all items on the cash basis (i.e., the hybrid method) is considered a cash method. The restriction on the use of the cash method is designed to prevent a corporation from manipulating its cash receipt-and-disbursement policies to obtain a tax advantage.

Corporations and partnerships in which a corporation is a partner may still elect to use the cash method (if they are otherwise eligible to do so) if the average gross receipts for the three previous years are $25 million or less.

**Example 51** Assume the same facts as in example 50, except that Jackamani Company's average sales for the previous 3 years are $23,600,000. What accounting methods may Jackamani select?

**Discussion: Because Jackamani's average annual gross receipts for the previous 3 years are less than $25,000,000, Jackamani is exempted from the restriction on accounting methods that applies to a partnership with a corporation as a partner. Therefore, Jackamani can use either the cash method or the accrual method. Note: If Jackamani were organized as a corporation, the exception would also apply and Jackamani could use either method.**

A second exception allows a corporation or a partnership with a corporate partner that is engaged in farming to use the cash method, regardless of the amount of its gross receipts. However, if the entity is also engaged in a separate nonfarming business, it must account for that portion of its business by using the accrual method, unless the exception for average annual gross receipts applies.

### S Corporation

An S corporation is allowed to use either the cash method or the accrual method. No restrictions on the use of the cash method apply to S corporations, other than the general restriction regarding inventories.

**Example 52** Return to the facts of example 50. Assume that Jackamani is organized as a corporation and makes an S corporation election. If average annual sales for the last 3 years total $28,000,000, what methods of accounting may Jackamani select?

**Discussion: As an S corporation, Jackamani is not subject to the corporate restriction on the use of the cash method. It may elect to use either the cash or accrual method in accounting for its operations.**

## 13-4f Planning Commentary

Table 13-2 summarizes the major tax aspects to consider at the formation of a business entity. Although many tax treatments are identical for all entity forms, significant differences do exist. These differences should be considered when choosing an entity. As with the nontax and tax factors discussed earlier, no one factor will drive the choice of entity. All factors must be considered in determining the appropriate entity to use in a given situation.

All entities are allowed tax-free transfers of property solely in exchange for an ownership interest. Whenever an owner provides services or receives boot in the ownership exchange, the owner must recognize income. The corporate deferral provisions require that the transferors control the corporation immediately after the transfer. Thus, it is important that all owners of a new corporate entity make their transfers to the entity simultaneously to meet this requirement. Piecemeal transfers to a corporation may result in taxation of any unrealized gain on the property being transferred.

The most significant difference is the basis treatment of entity liabilities. Partners are allowed to add their share of partnership debt to their basis. This treatment allows a greater deduction of losses to flow from the partnership to the partners. This makes a partnership a desirable entity to use in a business that expects large operating losses in the early years of operations. This choice is enhanced when the business also uses large amounts of debt to finance its operations.

Partnerships and S corporations are restricted in their choice of an accounting period. These restrictions are intended to reduce the deferral advantage that can be

Table 13-2

## Tax Factors at Formation of a Business Entity

| Factor | Sole Proprietorship | Partnership | Corporation | S Corporation |
|---|---|---|---|---|
| Contribution of property to the entity | Not a taxable transaction | Generally, not a taxable transaction | A taxable transaction unless the transferors control the corporation immediately after the transfer | A taxable transaction unless the transferors control the corporation immediately after the transfer |
| Basis of ownership interest | Adjusted basis of property contributed | Adjusted basis of property contributed plus gain recognized plus share of partnership liabilities minus liabilities assumed by the partnership | Adjusted basis of property contributed plus gain recognized | Adjusted basis of property contributed plus gain recognized |
| Basis of property contributed to the entity | Adjusted basis of property contributed | Adjusted basis of property contributed plus gain recognized | Adjusted basis of property contributed plus gain recognized | Adjusted basis of property contributed plus gain recognized |
| Basis treatment of entity liabilities | Not applicable | Included in partners' bases | Cannot be included in shareholders' bases | Cannot be included in shareholders' bases |
| Start-up and organizational costs | Deduct $5,000. Remainder amortizable over 180 months | Deduct $5,000. Remainder amortizable over 180 months | Deduct $5,000. Remainder amortizable over 180 months | Deduct $5,000. Remainder amortizable over 180 months |
| Accounting periods | Same tax year as owner's | Restricted to tax year of majority-interest partner, principal partners, least aggregate deferral of partners' income, or natural business year | Unrestricted | Must use a calendar year or ownership tax year unless qualified for a natural business year |
| Accounting methods | Same accounting method as owner's | Generally unrestricted; cash method not available if a corporation is a partner unless the partnership's average annual gross receipts for last 3 years are $25 million or less, or it is engaged in farming | Restricted to accrual method unless average annual gross receipts for last 3 years are $25 million or less, or it is engaged in farming | Unrestricted |

obtained by a conduit entity that selects a tax year different from that of its owners. Partnerships that have a corporate partner are generally restricted to the accrual method of accounting, as are corporations. S corporations may select any method of accounting.

# CHAPTER SUMMARY

This chapter introduced the basic factors that must be considered when choosing a business entity. Many factors affect the choice of entity. Nontax factors, such as limited liability, transferability of interest, continuity of life, centralized management, and the cost of organizing various entity forms, are often more important than the income tax factors in determining the appropriate entity for a given business. Even so, the tax aspects of an entity are an important consideration in choosing a business entity.

Basic income tax factors that affect the choice of business entity are the incidence of taxation (who pays the tax), double taxation of corporate dividends, and the status of an owner as an employee (the deductibility of salaries paid to owner employees). The owners of sole proprietorships, partnerships, and S corporations pay tax on the income of the entity. A corporation pays tax on its income, and shareholders pay tax on dividends received from a corporation. This allows taxpayers to use a corporation to split income between the corporation and owner-employees but also results in double taxation of dividends. A sole proprietor or a partner cannot be an employee of the business. Owners of corporations and S corporations can be employed by the corporation.

Partnerships and S corporations can deduct the cost of fringe benefits provided to owner-employees or owner-partners. However, the payment of these benefits is treated as compensation to the recipient. Only employer-provided group term life insurance coverage, employer-sponsored accident and health-care plans, cafeteria plans, and meals and lodging furnished for the convenience of the employer are subject to this treatment. Employees of a corporation or an S corporation are required to pay Social Security tax on their compensation. The corporation matches the amount paid by the employee. Partners must pay self-employment tax on their net self-employment income. A guaranteed payment from a partnership is also treated as self-employment income. The net income from a sole proprietorship is subject to self-employment tax. Both a partner and a sole proprietor can deduct one-half of the self-employment taxes paid as a deduction for adjusted gross income. Unlike a partnership, the income that flows through to the individual owner of an S corporation is not subject to self-employment tax.

Several tax issues arise at the formation of an entity. The transfer of property in exchange for an ownership interest is generally nontaxable, although the requirements for a tax-free transfer to a corporation (and S corporation) are more restrictive than those for a partnership. When property is transferred to an entity in a nontaxable transaction, the owner and the entity receiving the property receive a basis equal to the adjusted basis of the property transferred. Because partners are liable for debts of a partnership, they are allowed to add their proportionate share of any partnership debt to their basis in the partnership.

All entities can deduct up to $5,000 of start-up and organizational costs. Any remaining costs must be amortized over 180 months. At formation, an entity must select an accounting period and an accounting method. Partnerships and S corporations face restrictions on the selection of their annual accounting period.

## KEY TERMS

business purpose tax year (p. 13-32)
centralized management (p. 13-5)
continuity of life (p. 13-5)
corporation (p. 13-7)
double taxation (p. 13-15)
fiscal year (p. 13-30)
guaranteed payment (p. 13-16)
incidence of taxation (p. 13-11)
limited liability (p. 13-4)
limited liability company (LLC) (p. 13-9)
limited liability partnership (LLP) (p. 13-10)
limited partnership (p. 13-6)
majority-interest tax year (p. 13-31)
natural business year (p. 13-32)
nonrecourse debt (p. 13-27)
organizational costs (p. 13-30)
ownership tax year (p. 13-32)
partnership (p. 13-6)
partnership debt (p. 13-26)
principal partner tax year (p. 13-31)
recourse debt (p. 13-26)
S corporation (p. 13-8)
self-employment tax (p. 13-19)
sole proprietorship (p. 13-5)
start-up costs (p. 13-30)
taxable year (p. 13-30)
transferability of ownership interest (p. 13-4)

## PRIMARY TAX LAW SOURCES

[1]Sec. 1362—Discusses the rules for election, disqualification, and revocation of S status.

[2]Sec. 1361—Provides the qualifying characteristics of corporations making the S election.

[3]Reg. Sec. 1.1372-5—Provides the circumstances under which an S corporation may retain that status without a five-year wait once that election is terminated.

[4]Reg. Sec. 301.7701-2—Lists the characteristics that are determinative in defining whether an entity is considered a corporation for tax purposes.

[5]Reg. Sec. 301.7701-1—Permits most noncorporate entities to elect whether to be treated as a corporation or a partnership for federal income tax purposes.

[6]Sec. 1—Imposes income tax on all individuals and other noncorporate entities; provides the tax rate schedules for noncorporate taxpayers.

[7]Sec. 199A—Allows a noncorporate taxpayer a deduction from Qualified Business Income (QBI) from a partnership, S corporation, or sole proprietorship.

[8]Sec. 701—States that a partnership is not subject to income tax and that partners are liable for taxes only on their individual shares.

[9]Sec. 11—Imposes income tax on corporate entities and provides the tax rates.

[10]Sec. 1363—Explains that S corporations are not subject to income tax and states that the S corporation computes its taxable income in a manner similar to that used by an individual taxpayer, except for the items that are subject to separate statement.

[11]Sec. 721—States that no gain or loss is recognized by the contributing partner or by the partnership upon the contribution of property to a partnership solely in exchange for a partnership interest.

[12]Sec. 351—States that no gain or loss is recognized on the transfer of property to a corporation solely in exchange for stock of the corporation if the transferees control the corporation immediately after the exchange.

[13]Sec. 1012—Defines *basis* of property: The general rule for the initial basis of a property is its cost.

[14]Sec. 722—States that partners' basis in their partnership interest is the adjusted basis of the property contributed to attain the partnership interest.

[15]Sec. 723—States that the basis of property contributed to a partnership by a partner is the adjusted basis of the property at the time of the contribution.

[16]Sec. 752—Describes the effect of partnership debt on a partner's basis.

[17]Reg. Sec. 1.752-1—Details how liabilities affect the basis of a partner's interest in a partnership.

[18]Reg. Sec. 1.752-1(e) before removal by TD 8237, 12/29/88—Partnership recourse debts incurred before January 30, 1989, are allocated among the partners according to the partners' loss-sharing percentages.

[19]Reg. Sec. 1.752-2—Describes the allocation to partners of partnership recourse debt incurred after January 29, 1989.

[20]Reg. Sec. 1.752-1(e) before removal by TD 8237, 12/29/88—Nonrecourse debt of a partnership incurred before January 30, 1989, is allocated among the partners according to the partners' profit-sharing percentages.

[21]Reg. Sec. 1.752-3—Provides the procedure for allocating to the partners any partnership nonrecourse debt incurred after January 29, 1989.

[22]Sec. 358(a)—States that the basis of a shareholder in stock received in exchange for property in a nontaxable exchange is equal to the basis of the property given in the exchange.

[23]Sec. 362(a)—States that the basis of property received by a corporation for stock of the corporation in a nontaxable exchange is equal to the transferor's basis in the property.

[24]Sec. 357(a)—Provides that liabilities of a shareholder assumed by a corporation in a nontaxable exchange of stock for property are not treated as boot received by the shareholder.

[25]Sec. 248(a)—Permits the deduction of up to $5,000 of organizational expenses in the year in which the business begins operations. Any remaining expenditures must be amortized over 180 months.

[26]Reg. Sec. 1.248-1—Gives examples of items that are considered organizational expenditures and examples of items that are not considered organizational expenditures

[27]Sec. 441—Allows taxpayers to use either a calendar year or a fiscal year to compute taxable income. Defines *fiscal year.*

[28]Reg. Sec. 1.441-1—Explains how to establish a tax year.

[29]Sec. 706—Provides the rules for selecting a partnership tax year.

[30]Reg. Sec. 1.706-1—Defines a *principal partner* for purposes of selecting a partnership tax year and illustrates the *principal partner tax year.*

[31]Reg. Sec. 1.706-1—Explains the computation of the *least aggregate deferral tax year* for a partnership.

[32]Rev. Rul. 87-57—Explains the factors necessary for a partnership to establish a business purpose tax year.

[33]Sec. 1378—Defines the tax years that an S corporation can use.

[34]Rev. Proc. 87-32—Explains the ownership tax year test and how to adopt an ownership tax year.

[35]Reg. Sec. 1.706-1—Defines *natural business year.*

[36]Rev. Proc. 87-32—Provides examples of the test for a natural business year.

[37]Sec. 703—States that elections related to the computation and reporting of partnership items are made at the partnership level and not by the individual partners.

[38]Sec. 448—Disallows the use of the cash method of accounting by corporations and partnerships in which a corporation is a partner. Provides exceptions for corporations and partnerships with a corporate partner with average annual gross receipts of $25 million or less for the last three years and for corporations and partnerships with a corporate partner engaged in farming activities.

# DISCUSSION QUESTIONS

1. **LO1** What are the primary nontax factors to consider when choosing a form for doing business?
2. **LO2** Compare and contrast the characteristics of sole proprietorships, partnerships, corporations, S corporations, limited liability companies, and limited liability partnerships.
3. **LO2** Discuss the comparative advantages and disadvantages of general partnerships and limited partnerships.
4. **LO2** Limiting the liability of the owner(s) of a business is often the primary motive for using the corporate form. Under what circumstances may the use of a corporation not shield the owner(s) from all liabilities of the business?
5. **LO2** What are the nontax differences between a corporation and an S corporation?
6. **LO2** What are the requirements to qualify for the S corporation election?
7. **LO2** How is a limited liability company different from a corporation?
8. **LO2** How is a limited liability partnership different from a partnership?
9. **LO3** Compare the incidence of taxation for each of the following entities:
   a. Sole proprietorship
   b. Partnership
   c. Corporation
   d. S corporation
10. **LO3** What type of entities are allowed a deduction for Qualified Business Income (QBI), and are there any limitations and/or restrictions on the deduction?
11. **LO3** Armand is an owner of Content Company. During the current year, he receives a $15,000 cash distribution from Content. What is the tax effect of the receipt of the $15,000 if Content is organized as
    a. A partnership?
    b. A limited liability company?
    c. A corporation?
    d. An S corporation?
12. **LO3** Which entity(ies) is/are subject to double taxation?
13. **LO3** Why is it important for an owner to also be classified as an employee of the business for tax purposes?

14. **LO3** Which entity form(s) recognize owners as employees of the business?
15. **LO3** What is the tax treatment for a guaranteed payment?
16. **LO4** Compare the tax treatment of fringe benefits provided to an owner of a corporation with the treatment of fringe benefits provided to an owner of
    a. A sole proprietorship.
    b. A partnership.
    c. An S corporation.
17. **LO4** Is all compensation that is paid to an employee deductible? Discuss the circumstances in which employee compensation cannot be deducted.
18. **LO4** What is the tax treatment of health insurance premiums paid on behalf of
    a. A sole proprietor?
    b. A partner?
    c. An owner-employee of a corporation?
    d. An owner-employee of an S corporation?
19. **LO5** What is the rationale for not taxing transfers of property in exchange for an ownership interest?
20. **LO5** What are the tax consequences of receiving an ownership interest in an entity in exchange for services rendered to the entity?
21. **LO5** Compare the requirements for a tax-free exchange of property for an ownership interest in a partnership with the requirements for a corporation.
22. **LO5** Discuss the basis of an ownership interest received in exchange for property and the basis of the property received in exchange for an ownership interest in the hands of the entity.
23. **LO5** How do liabilities affect the basis of a partner's interest in a partnership?
24. **LO5** Explain the difference between a recourse debt and a nonrecourse debt.
25. **LO5** Why are partners allowed to add their share of partnership debts to their bases?
26. **LO5** What is the tax effect of a corporation's assuming the debt of a shareholder on property that is exchanged for an ownership interest in the corporation?
27. **LO5** Why might a shareholder recognize a gain on an exchange of property for an ownership interest when a partner making the same exchange with a partnership would not recognize a gain?
28. **LO5** How do S corporation liabilities affect the basis of an S corporation shareholder's stock?
29. **LO6** Which of the following are organizational costs?
    a. State fees for incorporation
    b. Legal and accounting fees incident to organization
    c. Expenses for the sale of stock
    d. Organizational meeting expenses
30. **LO7** What is the difference between a calendar year and a fiscal year?
31. **LO7** Why are restrictions placed on the selection of a tax year by partnerships and S corporations?
32. **LO7** Which types of tax entities generally cannot elect to use the cash method of accounting?

## PROBLEMS

Communication Skills

33. **LO2** Herman, who is unmarried and has two dependent children, owns and operates a used car lot as a sole proprietorship. The net income from the business is consistently $120,000 annually. Herman's friends have told him that he should incorporate his business, but he does not understand how this would give him any advantage. He has come to you for advice. Write Herman a letter explaining the advantages and disadvantages of incorporating his business.
34. **LO2** Lydia and Paulo agree to become equal owners in a pizza delivery business. Lydia will manage the delivery side of the business, and Paulo will be in charge of kitchen operations. They will borrow most of the money they need to get the business started. Considering only the nontax factors associated with the business, what business entity(ies) would be appropriate for the new business? Discuss the positive and negative factors of each business entity that would be appropriate.
35. **LO3** Rollo and Andrea are equal owners of Gosney Company. During the current year, Gosney's taxable income before considering salaries paid to Andrea and Rollo is $140,000. Rollo is single, his salary is $30,000, and he has net taxable income of $20,000 from other sources. Andrea is also single, her salary is $40,000, and she

has net taxable income of $30,000 from other sources. What is the total income tax liability if Gosney is organized as

a. A partnership?
b. A corporation?
c. An S corporation?

36. **LO3** Return to the facts of problem 33. Compare the total income tax liability of Herman's incorporating his business versus operating it as a sole proprietorship. Assume that he is paid a $60,000 salary and has income from other sources that is $14,000 more than his allowable deductions.

37. **LO3** Polly is married and owns CopyEdit, a sole proprietorship. The net income from CopyEdit is consistently around $200,000. Polly is considering making Kevin, one of her employees, an owner of the business. He would continue to be paid his $40,000 salary and own a 25 percent interest in the business. Polly would receive a salary of $100,000 from the new entity. She has asked you to determine the total income tax liability for each of the entities listed below. Assume that both Polly and Kevin have income from other sources that offset their allowable deductions, and that they are both single.

a. Partnership
b. Corporation
c. S corporation

38. **LO3** Return to the facts of problem 37. Upon giving your tax calculation results to Polly, you learn that CopyEdit is acquiring a similar business and that its net income is expected to be $480,000. Write a letter to Polly explaining the effect of this information on the calculations you performed in problem 37. Communication Skills

39. **LO3** Kelly, Gwen, and Tuoi own 40 percent, 30 percent, and 30 percent, respectively, of an accounting business. During the current year, the income is $300,000 after deducting salaries of $60,000 for each shareholder-employee. Assume all three owners are single and that each of them has other income that offsets their allowable deductions. What is Kelly, Gwen, and Tuoi's income tax liability?

40. **LO3** Drew is the sole owner of Morris, Inc., a corporation. Morris's net income for the current year is $150,000 before considering Drew's $85,000 salary. Assume Drew is single and has income from other sources that is $30,000 more than his allowable deductions. What is the total income tax liability if Morris is

a. A corporation?
b. An S corporation?

41. **LO3** Return to the facts of problem 40. Assume that late in the year, Drew needs extra cash to pay off gambling debts and has the corporation declare a $25,000 dividend to provide the cash. What is the effect of the dividend payment on the total income tax liability if Morris is

a. A corporation?
b. An S corporation?

42. **LO3** In January of the current year, Josh purchases all the stock of Ballpark Corporation for $100,000. Ballpark's taxable income for the current year is $200,000, and it pays $42,000 in income tax. None of the earnings is distributed as dividends. Josh believes that if he sells his stock two years later for $238,750, he will avoid double taxation. Write a memo to Josh explaining why he is not avoiding double taxation just because he receives no dividends. Communication Skills

43. **LO3** Antonio and Michaela are equal partners in A&M Booking Services. Antonio manages the business and receives $40,000 per year for his management services. He and Michaela each withdraw $30,000 in cash during the current year. A&M's ordinary income is $80,000 before considering any payments to the partners. How much income do Michaela and Antonio have from A&M during the current year?

44. **LO3** Estel and Raymond own the GoalLine Partnership. Estel owns 70 percent of the business. She provided the capital for it and consults with Raymond on overall business strategy. Raymond is responsible for the daily operation of the business Communication Skills

and owns the remaining 30 percent. The business consistently produces net income of $200,000 per year. Each year, Estel withdraws $30,000 from the partnership and Raymond withdraws $70,000. Although Estel believes that Raymond is entitled to receive more cash each year because of his daily involvement in the business, she is concerned that she is taxed on 70 percent of the income. Estel has come to your firm for advice on how to improve their situation. Leonard, your supervisor, has assigned you the task of coming up with a strategy that will result in Estel's having less income from GoalLine. Write Leonard a memorandum explaining a strategy that GoalLine can use to reduce the income taxed to Estel without altering the current profit-sharing ratio.

45. **LO3** Artis owns 40 percent of the Rhode Island Chile Parlor (RICP). During the current year, Rhode Island gives Artis fringe benefits worth $4,000 in addition to his $30,000 salary. RICP's net taxable income before considering the payments to Artis is $160,000. Assume Artis is single and has income from other sources that offsets his allowable deductions. What are Artis's taxable income and income tax liability if RICP is organized as
    a. A partnership, and the salary is a guaranteed payment?
    b. A partnership, and the salary is not a guaranteed payment?
    c. A corporation?
    d. An S corporation?

46. **LO3, 4** Enterprise Business Systems pays the $5,000 health and accident insurance policy of its owner, Gena. The business's net operating income for the year is $60,000 before considering Gena's benefit. Determine the business's net income for the year and the tax effects for Gena for each of the following entities:
    a. A sole proprietorship
    b. A partnership
    c. A corporation
    d. An S corporation

47. **LO3, 4** Colleen, Rosemary, and Suzanne own a software development firm. Colleen owns 45 percent of the business, Rosemary 30 percent, and Suzanne 25 percent. The net operating income from the business is $220,000. Assume Suzanne is paid a salary of $45,000. For each of the following situations, determine who is responsible for paying the Social Security and self-employment taxes on the income from the business and who is allowed a deduction for the Social Security and self-employment taxes paid:
    a. The business is formed as a partnership. Suzanne's salary is not a guaranteed payment.
    b. The business is formed as a corporation.
    c. The business is formed as an S corporation.

Communication Skills

48. **LO4** Natalie operates her bookkeeping service as a corporation. She is the sole shareholder and is an employee functioning as the chief operating officer. The corporation employs several other individuals and offers them good fringe benefits: group term life insurance, health insurance, disability insurance, and a 12 percent qualified pension plan. Natalie's good friend, Ricci, operates a custom software development company. The business is an S corporation, and Ricci is the sole shareholder. She is also an employee who serves as the manager. Upon Natalie's recommendation, Ricci copies the fringe benefit package of Natalie's corporation. Assume both businesses are quite profitable.
    a. How do the employee benefits affect the tax bills of Natalie and her corporation?
    b. How do the employee benefits affect the tax bills of Ricci and her corporation?
    c. Write letters to both Natalie and Ricci explaining these tax ramifications.

49. **LO4** Billy Bob is employed by Pony Ranch Corporation and owns 1 percent of the corporation's stock. The corporation provides excludable meals and lodging for Billy Bob at a cost of $12,000 annually.

a. Can Pony Ranch Corporation deduct the costs of the meals and lodging provided to Billy Bob?
b. How are the meals and lodging treated for tax purposes if Pony Ranch is an S corporation?
c. Assume the same facts as in part b, except that Billy Bob owns 5 percent of Pony Ranch Corporation.

50. **LO5** Miko and Mona form M&M Beverages in the current year. Miko contributes $20,000 in cash and delivery trucks worth $70,000 for 30 percent interest. Miko's basis in the delivery trucks is $80,000. Mona contributes $30,000 and land worth $130,000 (basis = $100,000) and provides services in organizing the business worth $20,000 in exchange for her 70 percent interest. What are the tax effects of the transfers and the bases of the owners and the entity if M&M is organized as
a. A partnership?
b. A corporation?
c. An S corporation?

51. **LO5** John and Katerina form JK Enterprises in the current year. John contributes $200,000 in cash for a 40 percent interest. Katerina contributes real estate valued at $480,000 and encumbered by a mortgage of $180,000 that is assumed by the business. Katerina's basis in the real estate is $100,000. She receives a 60 percent interest in the business. What is each owner's basis in their interest and the entity's basis in the assets acquired if JK Enterprises is organized as
a. A partnership?
b. A corporation?
c. An S corporation?

52. **LO5** Emmon and Darcy are equal owners of Golf Instruction Academy (GIF). The business has been profitable, and they would like to expand their operations. Tiger owns Power Golf. Emmon and Darcy will make Tiger an equal owner of GIF (i.e., each will have a ⅓ interest) in exchange for Tiger's business assets. Tiger's business assets are worth $100,000 and have an adjusted basis of $70,000. What are the tax effects of Tiger's exchange of assets for the ownership interest if GIF is organized as
a. A partnership?
b. A corporation?

53. **LO5** Toby exchanges property worth $80,000 (basis of $55,000) for a 20 percent interest in Landscape Developers. What are the tax effects of the exchange if Landscape is organized as
a. A partnership?
b. A corporation?
c. An S corporation?

54. **LO5** Return to the facts of problem 53. Assume that the property Toby contributes is encumbered by a $20,000 mortgage that is assumed by Landscape Developers. How does this affect the tax results for each of the entity forms?

55. **LO5** Myron, Al, and Janda make the following transfers from their sole proprietorships to a newly formed business, each receiving a ⅓ ownership interest.

| Owner | Asset Transfers | Basis of Property Transferred | Fair Market Value of Property/Services Transferred | Liabilities Assumed by Business |
|---|---|---|---|---|
| Myron | Building | $60,000 | $110,000 | $30,000 |
| Al | Equipment | 90,000 | 80,000 | -0- |
| Janda | Vehicles | 30,000 | 60,000 | 10,000 |
| | Legal services | | 30,000 | |

In addition, the business borrows $60,000 from a local bank for working capital. The loan is a nonrecourse debt. Determine the gain or loss the owners must recognize from the transfers and their basis in the ownership interest received under the assumptions set forth here. Also, determine any gain or loss recognized by the business entity from the transfers and its basis in the property received:

a. The business is organized as a partnership.
b. The business is organized as a corporation.
c. The business is organized as an S corporation.

Communication Skills

56. **LO6** Big C Corporation, a calendar-year corporation, is formed during the current year and begins business operations on September 1. Big C pays $8,000 to attorneys, accountants, and state regulatory agencies to organize the corporation. Big C also pays $6,000 in commissions on the sale of corporate stock. Write a letter to Big C Corporation's controller explaining how much of the $14,000 expenditure is deductible.

57. **LO6** Shree is considering opening a travel agency. She spends $47,000 investigating the profitability of the business and potential locations and $5,000 for legal and other fees incident to the organization of the business. Although the costs are high, Shree believes that she will recover them quickly.
   a. What is the proper treatment of the costs?
   b. Will the treatment be different if she organizes the business as a sole proprietorship or a corporation?

58. **LO7** What tax year must each of the following taxpayers use? Explain.
   a. Brayanth works for Gippsland Corporation. His income for the year includes salary, interest, dividend income, and a long-term capital gain. Although he itemizes his deductions, he keeps no formal books or records, relying instead on his wage statement, canceled checks, and other formal documents furnished to him for preparing his tax return.
   b. Assume the same facts as in part a, except that Brayanth is self-employed as a plumber and keeps meticulous books and records.
   c. Cindy and Derek are partners in a pet shop. Cindy owns 55 percent, and Derek owns 45 percent. Cindy reports her income using a July 31 fiscal year, whereas Derek uses a calendar year.
   d. Syme, Inc., is an S corporation wholly owned by Jeremiah. He uses a calendar year to report his income.
   e. Assume the same facts as in part d, except that Syme, Inc., is a corporation.

59. **LO7** Determine the tax year(s) each of the following S corporations must use. Explain.
   a. Will, Dan, and Tom are equal owners of Rheen Corporation, and each has a different fiscal year. Will has a fiscal year that ends April 30, Dan's ends May 31, and Tom's ends November 30.
   b. Assume the same facts as in part a, except that Tom and Dan each own a 20 percent interest in Rheen and Will owns the remaining 60 percent.
   c. Assume the same facts as in part b. Rheen's business is seasonal; the heaviest revenue months are July and August. Revenues for three years are as follows:

| | July and August | 12-Month Period |
|---|---|---|
| Current year | $90,000 | $300,000 |
| Preceding year 1 | 80,000 | 260,000 |
| Preceding year 2 | 60,000 | 230,000 |

60. **LO7** Which accounting method must each of the following taxpayers use?
   a. Fax, Inc., is an S corporation wholly owned by Helena. She uses a calendar year to report her income.
   b. Assume the same facts as in part a, except that Fax, Inc., is a corporation. Its annual revenues have never exceeded $1,000,000.

c. Assume the same facts as in part b, except that Fax's annual revenues usually are between $27,000,000 and $28,000,000.
d. Spoke and Pedal Cyclery is organized as a partnership. It is owned by John and Gloria as equal partners.

61. **LO7** Kim and Brendan, who are longtime friends, have decided to buy a golf equipment store and go into business together as equal partners. Kim reports his income by calendar year, and Brendan uses a fiscal year that ends September 30. One attraction of owning the golf equipment store is that the business is seasonal and will let them take long vacations. The peak revenue months are June and July. The owner gives them the following information: Communication Skills

| | June and July 12 | 12-Month Period |
|---|---|---|
| Current year | $200,000 | $500,000 |
| Preceding year 1 | 280,000 | 700,000 |
| Preceding year 2 | 325,000 | 850,000 |

Write a memo to Kim and Brendan discussing each alternative below:
a. If Kim and Brendan form a corporation, what options, if any, do they have in choosing their tax year and method of accounting?
b. If Kim and Brendan form a partnership, what options, if any, do they have in choosing their tax year and method of accounting?
c. If Kim and Brendan form an S corporation, what options, if any, do they have in choosing their tax year and method of accounting?

# ISSUE IDENTIFICATION PROBLEMS

In each of the following problems, identify the tax issue(s) posed by the facts presented. Determine the possible tax consequences of each issue that you identify.

62. A former clergyman with a degree in counseling decides to go into business for himself. He contracts with four large corporations to provide alcohol, drug, and psychological analysis for their employees. The contracts require him to be available on a weekly basis to see employees who need help. He also contracts with other organizations to provide therapy for patients in hospitals and members of churches and other nonprofit organizations. He anticipates that he will need two offices and will need to hire staff to help with phone calls, appointments, and other administrative functions.
63. Raquel is an employee of Jones Company and owns a 30 percent interest in the company. Her salary is $44,000. She also receives a $10,000 cash distribution from Jones. During the current year, Jones's operating income is $130,000.
64. Rolf owns 20 percent of Chaminade Corporation. During the current year, Chaminade reports operating income of $240,000 and pays $60,000 in cash dividends.
65. Miriam is a self-employed computer consultant. Her business nets $120,000 annually and she takes $85,000 of the earnings in salary. Miriam is considering making her computer consulting business an S corporation.
66. Robbie is the vice president of Mailer Corporation. He owns 40 percent of Mailer, which is organized as an S corporation. Robbie's salary is $75,000, and he receives group-term life insurance and health and accident insurance that costs $3,000. Mailer's operating income without considering any payments or benefits that Robbie receives is $180,000.
67. Rikki and Rhonda are equal owners of LilMark Corporation. To expand their operations, Marsha will contribute a building worth $80,000 for which she will receive a one-third ownership interest in the corporation. Marsha's basis in the building is $30,000.

68. Ben and Pete form a corporation to run a real estate investment management company. Ben contributes cash of $40,000 to the corporation in exchange for 50 percent of its stock. Pete obtains his 50 percent ownership interest by contributing land with a fair market value of $40,000 and a basis of $60,000. The land has the potential to be more valuable to the business in the future. Ben is aware of the nonrecognition rules for contributions to corporations and wants to use the corporate form. Pete realizes that if he contributes the land, he will not be able to recognize the unrealized loss.
69. Ariel and Mia agree to combine their business assets to form the A&M corporation. Ariel's business assets are worth $135,000 and have a basis of $80,000. Mia's business assets are worth $200,000, have a basis of $165,000, and are encumbered by a $90,000 mortgage, which A&M will assume. Mia will also contribute $25,000 in cash to equalize their contributions.

# TECHNOLOGY APPLICATIONS

Research Skills

70. Ruiz and his two brothers founded a social club called the Last Snake Inn in 1999. They want to take advantage of a new state law that lets them serve beer, liquor, and wine to their patrons on Sundays. To do so, the club must obtain a special liquor license that is required of all retail businesses wishing to serve alcohol on Sundays. Ruiz and his brothers want to incorporate the club specifically to acquire the special license. The club will continue to be operated by the three brothers as before, with each paying for supplies and other materials as needed out of his own pocket. The three brothers will serve as the corporation's officers. Ruiz is designated as the president. He has learned that to form a corporation, it must have a clear business purpose, and wonders whether forming a corporation merely to acquire a special liquor license satisfies the business purpose requirement. Write a letter to Ruiz that addresses his concern about having sufficient business purpose for his planned incorporation of the club.

Research Skills

71. Shirley and Roseann form Rosa Corporation with each contributing assets and cash in exchange for all of the corporation's stock. Shirley and Roseann each own 50 percent of the stock immediately after the exchange. Shortly thereafter, Shirley sells all her stock to Don per a written agreement executed before the formation of Rosa Corporation. Prepare a memorandum discussing the effect of this prearranged agreement.

# DISCUSSION CASES

72. Jacqui and Joanne plan to buy a bed-and-breakfast inn for $200,000. Jacqui will contribute $20,000 toward the purchase and operate the enterprise. Joanne's primary role is that of investor. She will contribute $100,000. However, she will be an active participant because of her involvement in management decisions. They will borrow the balance of the purchase price from a local bank. Advise Jacqui and Joanne on a choice of business form. Consider that the enterprise is expected to realize operating losses of $50,000 annually for the first three years. During the 4th year, the inn should realize a meager profit.
73. Nan wants to incorporate her sole proprietorship and will transfer cash of $5,000 and property with a fair market value of $60,000 and a basis of $20,000. The corporation will assume the $55,000 mortgage on the property. Nan will be paid a salary of $40,000. She has been advised by her cousin that she might want to be

a corporation for tax purposes because its income is taxed at a lower rate and her salary can be deducted as a business expense to lower overall taxes. However, she recently read an article in a small business owners' journal extolling the virtues of using an S corporation. Discuss the income tax consequences for Nan if she structures her business as an S corporation versus a corporation.

## TAX PLANNING CASES

74. Tony and Susan are starting a retail business selling formal wear for men and women. They estimate profits and losses for the next five years to be: ($20,000), ($10,000), ($5,000), $10,000, and $50,000, respectively. Susan will work full time in the store while Tony will be involved in managing the operations. Susan is married to Tom and is in the 24 percent marginal tax bracket. Tony is single and has other sources of income that put him in the 24 percent marginal tax bracket. Susan will be paid a salary of $30,000 for the first five years, after which her compensation will be reviewed. Tony and Susan each contribute $50,000 to get the business started. The remaining question facing Tony and Susan is which business form to use for the business. They believe they should operate as a partnership but have been informed that forming a corporation might be a better option since it would limit their liability. Prepare an analysis to determine whether Tony and Susan should operate their business as a partnership or a corporation.

75. Tory, Becky, Hal, and Jere form TBHJ Partnership as equal owners. TBJH Partnership rents heavy tools and equipment. Becky and Hal are married to each other while Tory and Jere are brothers but are not related to Becky or Hal. Because Becky and Hal have other jobs, Tory and Jere are to be the full-time managers of the business. Although Tory and Jere will run the business full-time, Becky will help in the store on weekends and some evenings. Hal will lend his financial expertise to the firm by doing the bookkeeping and preparing the tax returns. Even though the four have equal ownership interests, it is not clear how each owner is to be compensated so that there is equity among the partners yet rewards for those engaged in specific tasks. Hal has told the others that they cannot receive deductible salaries. However, he suggests that guaranteed payments be made to each partner/employee for an agreed-upon amount based on the value of the services each provides and/or the time spent at the store. Discuss the ramifications of employing this plan and whether this is an equitable way to allocate compensation among the partners. What are the implications of this arrangement for the partners and the partnership?

## ETHICS DISCUSSION CASE

76. Assume that you are a CPA and a tax specialist. Your clients include Ale and Grains, Inc., an S corporation, and Gustav and Heidi Lager, a married couple who are shareholders and the operators of Ale and Grains. The S corporation has expanded to include 100 qualified shareholders this year. Gustav and Heidi have told you that they have just obtained a divorce. Both individuals will continue to operate Ale and Grains for the ownership group, and neither party plans to dispose of her or his ownership interest. They know that certain rules govern the number of shareholders allowed in an S corporation, but they tell you not to be concerned because only their mailing addresses will change. They refer to the doctrine of substance over form and how it fits this situation. Write a letter to Gustav, Heidi, and the other shareholders offering your advice. Refer to the AICPA Code of Professional Conduct and the Statements on Standards for Tax Services (which can be found at www.aicpa.org) where necessary.

Communication Skills

# Choice of Business Entity—Operations and Distributions

14

Learning Objectives:

LO 1 Elaborate on the calculation of taxable income from operations of the various entities, and explain differences in the treatment of items across entities.

LO 2 Explain the effects of operating items on the basis of the owners of the various entity types.

LO 3 Explain the treatment of current distributions and liquidation distributions from the perspective of both an entity and an owner.

LO 4 Create tax-planning opportunities using different forms of organization.

## concept review

### GENERAL CONCEPTS

**Ability to pay** A tax should be based on the amount that the taxpayer can afford to pay, relative to other taxpayers. pg. 2-2

**Administrative convenience** Those items for which the cost of enforcing compliance would exceed the revenue generated are not taxed. pg. 2-3

**Related party** Family members and corporations that are owned by family members are considered related parties, as are certain other relationships between entities in which the power to control the substance of a transaction is evidenced through majority ownership. pg. 2-4

### ACCOUNTING CONCEPTS

**Conduit entity** An entity for which the tax attributes flow through to its owners for tax purposes. pg. 2-6

**Entity** All items of income, deductions, and so on are traced to the tax unit responsible for the item. pg. 2-6

**Substance-over-form doctrine** Transactions are to be taxed according to their true intention rather than some form that may have been contrived. pg. 2-11

### INCOME CONCEPTS

**Capital recovery** No income is realized until the taxpayer receives more than the amount invested to produce the income. The amount invested in an asset represents the maximum amount recoverable. pg. 2-13

**Legislative grace** Any tax relief provided is the result of a specific act of Congress that must be strictly applied and interpreted. All income received is taxable unless a specific provision in the tax law excludes the income from taxation. Deductions must be approached with the philosophy that nothing is deductible unless a provision in the tax law allows the deduction. pg. 2-12

**Realization** No income or loss is recognized until it has been realized. A realization involves a change in the form and/or the substance of a taxpayer's property rights that results from an arm's-length transaction. pg. 2-14

### DEDUCTION CONCEPTS

**Basis** The amount of unrecovered investment in an asset. As amounts are expended and/or recovered relative to an asset over time, the basis is adjusted in consideration of such changes. The **adjusted basis** of an asset is the original basis, plus or minus the changes in the amount of unrecovered investment. pgs. 2-13, 2-21

**Business purpose** To be deductible, an expenditure or a loss must have a business or other economic purpose that exceeds any tax avoidance motive. The primary motive for the transaction must be to make a profit. pg. 2-18

## 14-1 INTRODUCTION

This chapter continues the discussion started in Chapter 13 about choosing a business entity. Continuing with the life-cycle approach, the chapter focuses on operational areas in which tax issues play a role in deciding the business form for an organization. This area begins with a presentation of differences in the calculation of taxable income for the various entity forms and a discussion of the effects of income calculations on the owner's basis.

The discussion of the life cycle of the entity concludes with an examination of the tax consequences of distributions made during the entity's life (current distributions) and upon the liquidation of the entity. Finally, the chapter presents tax-planning opportunities based on the organizational form of the business.

## 14-2 OPERATIONS

LO 1

Elaborate on the calculation of taxable income from operations of the various entities, and explain differences in the treatment of items across entities.

After an entity begins its business activity, it must report the results of its operations to the government. Exhibit 14-1 reproduces the income tax computational framework introduced in Chapter 1. This framework provides the starting point for the calculation of each entity's taxable income. However, the nature of each entity causes deviations in the basic calculation. The remainder of this chapter discusses the basic differences in the calculation of taxable income for each entity.

### 14-2a Sole Proprietorship

Because a sole proprietorship is not an entity separate from its owner, the results of the sole proprietorship are reported on the owner's tax return. Certain income and deduction items of individuals are treated differently on an individual tax return and cannot be included in the calculation of taxable income. This means that the sole proprietorship's taxable income is an operating income (business income – business expenses) calculation. Certain items are not included in the sole proprietorship's taxable income.

#### Investment Income and Interest Expense

Because individuals may deduct investment interest as itemized deductions subject to limitations (see Chapter 8), the calculation of the entity's taxable income does not include deduction of investment interest related to a sole proprietor's business. In addition, the limitation on the deduction of investment interest requires that any investment income (dividends, interest, royalties) earned by the sole proprietor's business not be included in calculating the entity's taxable income.

#### Capital Gains and Losses

All entities must segregate their capital gains and losses from other forms of income and net their capital gains and losses. Individuals receive the benefit of the 15-percent tax rate (0 percent for 10 percent and 15 percent marginal tax rate taxpayers, 20 percent for 37 percent marginal tax rate taxpayers) on net long-term capital gains and can deduct up to $3,000 per year in net capital losses. Therefore, capital gains and losses from a sole

*Exhibit 14-1*

**Income Tax Computational Framework**

| | |
|---|---|
| | Gross income |
| Minus: | Deductions |
| Equals: | Taxable income |
| × | Tax rate (schedule of rates) |
| Equals: | Income tax |
| Minus: | Tax prepayments |
| Minus: | Tax credits |
| Equals: | Tax (refund) due with return |

proprietorship are not reported as part of the business's taxable income. Rather, they must be combined with the owner's other capital gains and losses and treated according to the rules for individuals.

### Section 1231 Gains and Losses

Net Section 1231 gains are capital gains and must be included in the individual's capital gain-and-loss netting. The sole proprietorship does not include Section 1231 gains and losses in its taxable income calculation. Similarly, Section 1245 and Section 1250 gains are not included in the entity's taxable income calculation.

### Passive Activity Items

Individuals are subject to the passive activity loss rules (see Chapter 7). Therefore, if the sole proprietorship owns any passive activities, the results of the passive activities are reported on the proprietor's return, not in the calculation of the sole proprietorship's taxable income.

### Charitable Contributions

Individuals can deduct charitable contributions only as an itemized deduction subject to the 60-percent and 30-percent contribution limits (see Chapter 8). Therefore, charitable contributions of a sole proprietorship are not deductible in calculating the business's taxable income. They must be combined with the owner's other charitable contributions and deducted as an itemized deduction.

### Personal Expenses

Any of the owner's personal expenses paid by the business are not deductible in calculating the entity's taxable income. If the expenses are deductible by an individual (e.g., alimony, medical expenses, dental expenses), sole proprietors must deduct them on their return, subject to any limitations imposed on the deduction.

### Tax Credits

Sole proprietors include the taxable income from the entity on their individual returns and pay a tax on their taxable income. (The sole proprietorship itself does not pay tax.) Any tax credits from the sole proprietorship are credited against the sole proprietor's tax liability.

### Net Operating Losses

If the sole proprietorship has a net operating loss for the current period, the loss can only be used to offset other business income (e.g., salary) in the current year. Any current loss that is not deductible can be carried back two years and forward 20 years and used to offset business income in those years.

**Example 1** Thuy is a self-employed Internet development consultant. She operates the business, TID Consulting, as a sole proprietorship. During the current year, TID's records show the following income and expense items:

| | |
|---|---|
| Consulting fees | $170,000 |
| Interest | 2,000 |
| Long-term capital gain | 12,000 |
| Assistant's salary | 20,000 |
| Thuy's salary | 80,000 |
| Payroll taxes on assistant | 1,500 |
| Rent and utilities | 26,000 |
| Supplies, repairs | 13,000 |
| Charitable contributions | 3,000 |
| Medical insurance: | |
| Assistant | 2,500 |
| Thuy | 2,500 |

Thuy also sells stock that is not part of her business at a loss of $5,000. What is the income from Thuy's consulting business?

**Discussion: TID Consulting cannot include in its taxable income calculation any items of income or expense that must be treated separately by an individual. TID's taxable income is $107,000:**

| | |
|---|---|
| Consulting fees | $170,000 |
| Assistant's salary | (20,000) |
| Payroll taxes on assistant | (1,500) |
| Rent and utilities | (26,000) |
| Supplies, repairs | (13,000) |
| Medical insurance: | |
| Assistant | (2,500) |
| TID taxable income | $107,000 |

**The $12,000 long-term capital gain is netted against her $5,000 capital loss, resulting in a $7,000 long-term capital gain. The long-term capital gain is subject to a 15% marginal tax rate. Sole proprietors cannot deduct salaries they pay to themselves. The sole proprietor is taxed on the income from the business. The charitable contributions are deductible as an itemized deduction. Thuy can deduct her $2,500 medical insurance as a deduction for adjusted gross income.**

## 14-2b Partnership

A partnership is a conduit entity and does not pay tax on its income. It must report the results of its operations to the government and provide each partner with her or his individual share of the partnership income. The conduit aspect requires adjustments in the reporting of income, deduction, and credit items to the partners. Losses incurred by a partnership flow through to the partners for deduction. However, limitations on the deductibility of partnership net operating losses may result in the loss of all or part of the deduction in the year of the loss. In addition, transactions between the partners and the partnership may be subject to the related party rules. This section discusses each of these aspects.

### Income Reporting

Individuals, corporations, estates, trusts, or other partnerships may be members of a partnership. Each of these entities is subject to different rules for reporting and deducting items. To allow each partner to properly account for these items, the items are segregated and reported separately from the ordinary income of the partnership.[1] Items that partnerships are required to report separately include the following:

- Investment income (including tax-exempt income)
- Capital gains and losses
- Section 1231 gains and losses
- Passive activity items
- Charitable contributions
- Amounts expensed under Section 179
- Recovery of items previously deducted (tax benefit rule items)
- Alternative minimum tax (AMT) preference and adjustment items
- Nondeductible expenses and personal expenses of partners
- Tax credits[2]

Items that only individuals may deduct, such as the standard deduction, are not deductible by a partnership. In addition, if a partnership makes a payment on behalf of a partner that could be an itemized deduction (e.g., medical expenses), the partnership treats the payment either as a distribution or as a guaranteed payment to the partner. The partner must then determine the appropriate deduction on her or his return.

**Example 2** Alan and Melissa are partners in Orts Security. Alan owns a 70% interest, and Melissa owns the remaining 30%. Orts has the following transactions for the current year:

| | |
|---|---|
| Sales | $345,000 |
| Dividends received | 20,000 |
| Municipal bond interest | 8,000 |
| Short-term capital gain | 3,000 |
| Long-term capital loss | 12,000 |
| Salaries paid to employees | 135,000 |
| Other operating expenses | 110,000 |
| Section 179 expense | 10,000 |
| Charitable contributions | 2,000 |
| Alan's medical expenses | 1,000 |

What is the proper treatment of these transactions?

**Discussion: The partnership must segregate those items that must be stated separately in calculating its ordinary income. Partners will then receive their shares of the partnership's ordinary income and the separately stated items. The partnership's ordinary income is $100,000:**

| | |
|---|---|
| Sales | $ 345,000 |
| Salaries paid to employees | (135,000) |
| Other operating expenses | (110,000) |
| Ordinary income | $ 100,000 |

**Alan is taxed on $70,000, and Melissa is taxed on $30,000 in ordinary income. In addition, each partner receives the appropriate share of the separately stated items. These items must be included on the individual partner's tax return, subject to the rules applicable to individuals:**

| | Total | 70% Alan | 30% Melissa |
|---|---|---|---|
| Dividends received | $20,000 | $14,000 | $6,000 |
| Municipal bond interest | 8,000 | 5,600 | 2,400 |
| Short-term capital gain | 3,000 | 2,100 | 900 |
| Long-term capital loss | 12,000 | 8,400 | 3,600 |
| Section 179 expense | 10,000 | 7,000 | 3,000 |
| Charitable contributions | 2,000 | 1,400 | 600 |
| Alan's medical expenses | 1,000 | 1,000 | -0- |

**Alan and Melissa report as income their shares of the dividends received and must disclose the amount of the tax-exempt municipal bond interest on their individual returns. They must net their capital gains and losses with any other capital gains and losses that they have and apply the rules for capital gains and losses of individuals to the net results. For example, if Alan has no other capital gains and losses for the year, he has a $6,300 ($2,100 − $8,400) net long-term capital loss. Because of the limitation on capital losses of individuals, he can deduct only $3,000 of the loss in the current year. The Section 179 expense election is combined with any other Section 179 expense elections from other sources; the maximum deduction limitation (i.e., $1,050,000 in 2021) is applied to each partner's qualifying elections. The charitable contributions are deductible as itemized deductions. Alan must include in his gross income the $1,000 in medical expenses paid by the partnership (expense paid by another). He can claim the medical expenses paid by the partnership as a medical expense in calculating his allowable itemized deduction for medical expenses.**

As example 2 illustrates, the segregation and separate reporting of the specific partnership items to the partners is an essential element of conduit entity taxation. Because the owners of the partnership are taxed on its income, separate reporting ensures that the incidence of taxation properly falls on the partners and that the partnership cannot be a vehicle to disguise income and deductions that would otherwise be limited when taxed to the partners.

## Net Operating Losses

A net operating loss flows through to the partners for deduction on their returns. Three limitations apply to the deduction of partnership net operating losses by the partners. The first limits the deductions to the amount of a partner's basis.[3] This is an application of the capital recovery concept that limits deductions to the amount invested in the partnership. A partner's basis represents the amount of that person's unrecovered capital investment and therefore establishes the maximum deduction permissible for losses from the partnership. Any losses that are in excess of a partner's basis are suspended and can be deducted when the partner has an adequate amount of basis to deduct the loss.

**Example 3** Jose contributes undeveloped land with a basis of $10,000 and a fair market value of $50,000 to the JKL Partnership for a 20% interest. The partnership reports a net operating loss of $80,000 for the current year. How much of the loss can Jose deduct?

**Discussion: Jose's initial basis in JKL is $10,000. His share of the current net operating loss is $16,000 ($80,000 × 20%). Jose's loss deduction is limited to his $10,000 basis. The remaining $6,000 of loss is suspended until his basis increases enough to absorb it. Note: The $10,000 loss is deductible only if Jose meets the two additional limitations discussed next.**

A partner's basis is reduced by the amount of the deductible loss that flows through from the partnership. Other adjustments to a partner's basis are discussed later in this section. The basis limitation on the deduction of losses establishes that a partner's basis can never go below zero.

The second limitation on the deduction of partnership losses is that a partner cannot deduct more than the amount that the partner has at risk in the activity. Under the **at-risk rules** (as discussed in Chapter 7), a partner cannot deduct any losses in excess of the amount that they have at risk in the activity. For a partner, the amount at risk parallels the basis computation. The only significant difference between the two is the treatment of nonrecourse debt. A partner's basis includes the partner's share of any partnership nonrecourse debt. The at-risk rules allow only the addition of nonrecourse debt related to real estate.

**Example 4** Assume the same facts as in example 3, except that Jose's share of JKL's recourse liabilities is $4,000. How does this affect Jose's basis, his at-risk amount, and the amount of his deductible loss?

**Discussion: As discussed earlier, a partner's share of partnership liabilities increases the partner's basis. Jose's basis increases to $14,000 after the debt adjustment. Because partners are liable for the recourse debts of a partnership, a partner's share of partnership recourse liabilities is considered at risk. This increases Jose's at-risk amount to $14,000 ($10,000 basis of property contributed to the partnership + $4,000 share of liabilities). The increase in Jose's basis and at-risk amounts for the partnership debt allows him to deduct $14,000 of his $16,000 share of the current year's operating loss.**

**Example 5** Assume the same facts as in example 4, except that the partnership liabilities are nonrecourse and are not related to the financing of real estate. What is Jose's deductible loss?

**Discussion: Jose's basis remains at $14,000. However, because the partnership liabilities are nonrecourse and are not related to the financing of real estate, Jose's $4,000 share is not at risk. Jose's deductible loss is limited to $10,000 by the at-risk rules. Note: The general basis limit is applied before the at-risk limitation. Jose must reduce his basis by the $14,000 in loss allowed under the general basis limitation, leaving $2,000 disallowed under this limit. The additional $4,000 in disallowed loss is suspended under the at-risk rules and cannot be deducted until Jose's at-risk amount increases to absorb part or all of the loss.**

The third limitation on the deduction of partnership losses stems from the application of the *passive activity loss rules* (as discussed in Chapter 7). The partners must individually determine whether their investments in the partnership are passive activities or an active trade or business. An activity is passive if the taxpayer does not materially participate in the activity. The basic test for material participation is that the partner participates in the operations of the partnership for more than 500 hours per year. Six other tests that allow lower levels of participation based on the facts of the situation are provided in the Treasury regulations that define material participation. A limited partnership interest is generally considered a passive activity interest.

If a partner's interest is passive, the loss that has passed through the basis and at-risk limitations is combined with other passive gains and losses, and the passive activity limitations are applied. The general rule for passive activities is that passive losses can only be deducted against passive income.

**Example 6** Assume the same facts as in example 5. Jose manages a portion of JKL's product distribution system, a job that requires a minimum of 10 hours per week. How much of his $16,000 share of the partnership loss can he deduct?

**Discussion: Because Jose works more than 500 hours per year for the partnership, he is a material participant, and the passive loss rules do not apply. As a participant in an active trade or business, Jose can deduct the $10,000 loss allowable under the at-risk rules.**

**Example 7** Assume the same facts as in example 4, except that Jose is a limited partner in the JKL partnership. How does this affect the deductibility of his share of the partnership loss?

**Discussion: Limited partnership interests are passive activities. Jose's $10,000 loss allowable under the at-risk rules is a passive loss. He can deduct the loss only to the extent that he has other passive activities that produce income. Any portion of the loss that is not deductible is suspended under the passive loss rules and is carried forward to future years for deduction against passive income.**

As the examples in this section illustrate, the three limitations are applied in the order presented here. Losses that are disallowed by one of the limits are suspended under that limitation until adequate basis, at-risk amounts, or passive income is generated.

A partner can use the passive loss rules to advantage in certain circumstances. If an individual has passive activities that produce losses, buying a passive interest in a partnership that produces income will let the individual deduct the losses. This makes the passive income from the partnership essentially tax-free.

**Example 8** Assume that Jose's 20% interest in JKL is a limited partnership interest. Further assume that Jose owns other passive activities that produce $18,000 in losses and that JKL has ordinary income of $60,000 in the current year. What is the treatment of Jose's share of JKL's income?

**Discussion: None of the loss limitations applies. Jose's $12,000 ($60,000 × 20%) share of the partnership income is passive activity income. Jose nets the $12,000 in passive income against the $18,000 in passive losses, resulting in a $6,000 net passive loss for the year. The deduction of $12,000 in passive loss has resulted in $12,000 of tax-free partnership income in the current year.**

## Transactions Between Partners and Partnerships

Partners are generally subject to the *related party rules.* A partner and a partnership are related parties if the partner directly or indirectly owns more than 50 percent of the partnership.[4] The related party rules disallow losses on sales of property between related parties. Any disallowed loss on a related party sale can be used to offset subsequent gain on the sale of the property.

**Example 9** Judy owns 70% of the Schlimpert Partnership. She sells land with an adjusted basis of $35,000 to Schlimpert for $20,000. What are the tax consequences of the sale?

**Discussion: Judy and Schlimpert are related parties. The $15,000 ($20,000 − $35,000) loss on the sale is disallowed. The partnership has a $20,000 basis in the land. If the partnership subsequently sells the property and realizes a gain on the sale, it can reduce the gain by Judy's $15,000 disallowed loss.**

Gains are not subject to the related party rules. However, any gain realized on a related party sale between a partner and a partnership must be recognized as ordinary income unless the property is a capital asset to both the seller and the purchaser.[5]

**Example 10** Return to the facts of example 9. Assume that Judy sells the property to Schlimpert for $40,000. She had held the land for investment. The partnership is a real estate developer. What are the tax consequences of the sale?

**Discussion: Judy realizes a $5,000 gain on the sale. The land is a capital asset for Judy because she held it for investment purposes. It is inventory for the partnership and is not a capital asset. Therefore, Judy must recognize the $5,000 gain as ordinary income. Note: If the partnership were not in the real estate development business and its use of the property constituted a capital asset, Judy's gain would be characterized as a capital gain.**

Sales of property between a partner and a partnership that are not related parties are treated as being made at arm's length and given their full tax effect. Loan transactions and rental payments made between a partner and a partnership are also generally treated as being made at arm's length. Payments for services provided by a partner are also considered arm's length if the partner is not acting as a partner in providing the services.[6] This is generally interpreted to mean that the partner provides the services to other parties.

**Example 11** Assume the same facts as in example 9, except that Judy owns a 40% interest in the Schlimpert Partnership. Can she deduct the loss on the sale of the land?

**Discussion: Judy and Schlimpert are not related parties. Her sale of the property is considered to have been made at arm's length, letting her recognize the $15,000 loss on the sale.**

**Example 12** Return to the facts of example 9. Because Judy cannot deduct the loss on the sale of the property, she agrees to lease the land to Schlimpert for $10,000 per year. What are the tax effects of the lease agreement?

**Discussion: Even though Judy and Schlimpert are related parties, she can lease property to the partnership in an arm's-length transaction. Judy will recognize the $10,000 as rental income. Schlimpert can deduct the $10,000 payment as a rental expense.**

## Basis Considerations

LO 2

Explain the effects of operating items on the basis of the owners of the various entity types.

During the operation of a partnership, numerous adjustments are made to a partner's basis to reflect changes in the partner's investment in the partnership. That is, as additional investments are made in the partnership, the partner's basis increases. Similarly, returns of investment received by a partner reduce the partner's basis. Exhibit 14-2 provides a general formula for determining a partner's basis.[7]

*Exhibit 14-2*

### General Formula for Determining a Partner's Basis

| | |
|---|---|
| Initial basis | $ XXX |
| Add: Additional investments | |
| Share of partnership income (including separately stated income items) | XXX |
| Contribution of assets | XXX |
| Share of nontaxable income | XXX |
| Share of any increase in partnership liabilities | XXX |
| Deduct: Returns of investment | |
| Share of partnership losses (including separately stated deductions and capital losses) | (XXX) |
| Cash withdrawals | (XXX) |
| Share of nondeductible expenses | (XXX) |
| Share of any decrease in partnership liabilities | (XXX) |
| Equals: Partner's adjusted basis | $ XXX |

The additions to a partner's basis reflect the correct amount of capital recovery upon sale of the partnership interest and prevent double taxation. For example, when partners recognize their shares of partnership income, an addition to basis is necessary to avoid taxing the income a second time when the partnership interest is sold. Also, the addition to basis for income recognized provides a basis for recovering future losses of the partnership. Similarly, the addition of a partner's share of any tax-exempt income is necessary to ensure that the income is not taxed when the partner sells her or his interest.

Reductions in basis reflect recoveries of capital investment. Withdrawals of cash by a partner are not taxable to the partner and are a true capital recovery. Reducing basis for deductions and losses reflects the capital recovery that the partner receives from the reduction in taxable income. In addition, reducing the basis is necessary to ensure that a current deduction is not taken again when the partnership interest is sold. Similarly, the basis reduction for nondeductible expenses is necessary to prevent the deduction (by decreasing a gain or increasing a loss) in the future when the interest is sold.

**Example 13** Return to the facts of example 2. Alan's basis at the beginning of the year is $23,000. Melissa's basis is $27,000. Alan withdraws $45,000 and Melissa withdraws $33,000 from the partnership during the year. What are Alan's and Melissa's bases at the end of the year?

**Discussion: Each partner adds the appropriate share of the $100,000 in ordinary income to her or his basis. All the separately reported income items are also added to basis. The cash withdrawals reduce each partner's basis, as do the separately stated losses and expenses. Alan's and Melissa's bases are $51,900 and $26,100, respectively:**

| | Alan | Melissa |
|---|---|---|
| Basis at beginning of year | $ 23,000 | $ 27,000 |
| Add: Additional investments | | |
| Share of income | 70,000 | 30,000 |
| Dividends received | 14,000 | 6,000 |
| Municipal bond interest | 5,600 | 2,400 |
| Short-term capital gain | 2,100 | 900 |
| Deduct: Returns of investment | | |
| Partner withdrawals | (45,000) | (33,000) |
| Long-term capital loss | (8,400) | (3,600) |
| Section 179 expense | (7,000) | (3,000) |
| Charitable contributions | (1,400) | (600) |
| Alan's medical expenses | (1,000) | -0- |
| Basis at end of year | $ 51,900 | $ 26,100 |

**The separately stated deductions and losses reduce basis in full. The actual amount of current period deduction that the partner gets from these items is irrelevant to the basis adjustment.**

As discussed earlier, a partner's deduction for partnership losses is limited to the partner's basis. The limitation is based on the partner's basis at the end of the partnership's tax year. In determining the deductibility of losses, partner contributions, income items, and withdrawals are factored into the basis before considering any losses for the year.[8] This order of computation can affect the amount of loss that is deductible under the basis limitation.

**Example 14** Return to the facts of example 3. In the following year, the JKL Partnership has ordinary income of $45,000. Jose withdraws $7,000 from the partnership. Assuming that he is a material participant in the partnership, what is the tax effect of the partnership's income and Jose's withdrawal?

**Discussion: Jose began the year with a zero basis and a $6,000 suspended loss from the basis limitation. In determining the deductibility of the suspended loss, his basis is first adjusted for the current year's income and withdrawals. His $9,000 share ($45,000 × 20%) of JKL's income increases his basis. The $7,000 cash withdrawal reduces his basis to $2,000. This frees $2,000 of the suspended loss for deduction. Jose's at-risk amount is also increased by $2,000. Jose will report net partnership income of $7,000 ($9,000 income − $2,000 suspended loss deduction). His basis is reduced to zero by the loss deduction.**

The ordering rules for determining basis affect the amount of loss that is deductible. In example 14, if Jose had been able to determine his basis for loss deduction purposes before considering the effect of his withdrawals, he would have been able to deduct the entire $6,000 in suspended loss. Subsequent reduction for the cash withdrawals would have resulted in Jose's having a negative capital balance. Thus, the ordering rules eliminate the possibility of a partner's having a negative basis because of the deduction of a net operating loss.

## concept check

A partner is taxed on the distributive share of partnership income whether or not the amount is actually received by the partner. The *capital recovery concept* requires adjustments to a partner's basis to ensure that the partner is not taxed twice on income recognized by the partner. Adjustments are made to increase the basis in a partnership interest for income recognized by a partner. Similarly, operating losses of a partnership flow through to the partners for deduction. Withdrawals by a partner are not taxed. This requires decreasing a partner's basis for operating losses and withdrawals to avoid allowing a double tax benefit. The adjustments made to a partner's basis ensure that correct capital recovery occurs when a partnership interest is sold or otherwise disposed of.

## 14-2c Corporation

A corporation is a legal entity that is separate and apart from its owners. Therefore, a corporation must pay income tax on its taxable income. Shareholders are taxed on dividends received from the corporation. Because dividends paid to shareholders are distributions of corporate earnings, they are not deductible business expenses. The calculation of a corporation's taxable income follows the general formula for all entities. However, several notable exceptions are unique to the corporate computation, which is provided in Exhibit 14-3. Corporate treatment of capital gains and losses, passive losses, and charitable contributions differs from the rules for individuals. Corporations are subject to an additional depreciation recapture on Section 1250 property and receive a special deduction for dividends received from other corporations. This section discusses these and other factors affecting the tax liability of a corporation.

### Capital Gains and Losses

As discussed in Chapters 7 and 11, net capital gains and losses of corporations are treated differently from the capital gains and losses of individuals. Corporations receive no preferential treatment for net capital gains, which are added in calculating gross income. Corporations are allowed to deduct capital losses only against capital gains. Net capital losses provide no current period tax relief. However, net capital losses may be carried back three years and forward five years and used to offset capital gains in the carryback and carryforward years.

*Exhibit 14-3*

**Corporate Taxable Income Computation**

| | |
|---|---|
| Gross income (all income less exclusions) | $ XXX |
| Plus: Corporate depreciation recapture | XXX |
| Minus: Trade or business expenses | (XXX) |
| Minus: Special deductions | |
| Dividends received | (XXX) |
| Passive losses | (XXX) |
| Charitable contributions | (XXX) |
| Equals: Taxable income | $ XXX |
| Times: Tax rate (21%) | × XX |
| Equals: Income tax | $ XXX |
| Minus: Tax prepayments | (XXX) |
| Minus: Tax credits | (XXX) |
| Equals: Tax (refund) due with return | $ XXX |

Exhibit 14-4

## Corporate Depreciation Recapture Calculation

| | |
|---|---|
| Ordinary income if Section 1245 property | $ XXX |
| Less: Ordinary income under Section 1250 | (XXX) |
| Equals: Excess of ordinary income under Section 1245 over ordinary income under Section 1250 | $ XXX |
| Multiplied by: | × 20% |
| Equals: Corporate depreciation recapture (ordinary income) | $ XXX |

**Depreciation Recapture** All taxable entities are subject to the recapture of gains on Section 1245 and Section 1250 property. As discussed in Chapter 11, Section 1245 recaptures all depreciation taken on a property as ordinary income, whereas Section 1250 recaptures only excess depreciation (actual depreciation minus straight-line depreciation). Also, recall that the use of straight-line depreciation under the modified accelerated cost recovery system (MACRS) results in no Section 1250 recapture on real property acquired after 1986. Corporations that sell depreciable real property that is Section 1250 property are subject to an additional depreciation recapture provision. This **corporate depreciation recapture** provision requires corporations to recapture as ordinary income 20 percent of the difference between the amount that would be ordinary income if the property were classified as Section 1245 property and the amount that would be ordinary income if it were classified as Section 1250 property.[9] Therefore, even though there is no Section 1250 recapture on real property purchased after 1986, a corporation will always have recapture on Section 1250 property because of the corporate depreciation recapture provision. Exhibit 14-4 provides the formula for this calculation.

**Example 15** In 2013, Penelope purchased a building for $150,000 to use in her business. She sells it in 2021 for $175,000. MACRS depreciation on the building totals $47,500 up to the date of sale. What is the amount and character of Penelope's gain?

**Discussion: The building is depreciable real property used in a trade or business. It is Section 1231 and Section 1250 property. Penelope has a gain on the sale of $72,500. The building is depreciated under MACRS. Because MACRS uses straight-line depreciation, there is no Section 1250 recapture, and all of Penelope's gain is Section 1231 gain:**

| | |
|---|---|
| Amount realized | $175,000 |
| Less: Adjusted basis ($150,000 – $47,500) | 102,500 |
| Gain on sale | $ 72,500 |
| Section 1250 recapture | -0- |
| Section 1231 gain | $ 72,500 |

**[Note: Penelope must characterize $47,500 of the gain as Unrecaptured Section 1250 gain for purposes of computing the tax on the gain.]**

**Example 16** Assume the same facts as in example 15, except that the building is owned by Penelope Corporation. What is the character of the $72,500 gain?

**Discussion: As with an individual, the corporation has no Section 1250 gain on the sale. However, because the property is Section 1250 property, the corporation must apply the corporate recapture provision. If the property had been Section 1245 property, the $47,500 in depreciation would have been recaptured as ordinary income. With no Section 1250 recapture, the excess is $47,500 and the corporate recapture is $9,500:**

| | |
|---|---|
| Section 1245 ordinary income | $47,500 |
| Section 1250 ordinary income | -0- |
| Excess of Section 1245 over Section 1250 | $47,500 |
| Recapture percentage | × 20% |
| Corporate depreciation recapture | $ 9,500 |

**The corporation reports $9,500 in ordinary income and a $63,000 Section 1231 gain on the sale of the building:**

| | |
|---|---|
| Gain on sale | $72,500 |
| Corporate depreciation ordinary income | 9,500 |
| Section 1231 gain | $63,000 |

## Dividends-Received Deduction

Double taxation occurs when corporate after-tax profits are distributed as dividends to shareholders. The corporation is not allowed a tax deduction for dividends paid, and the individual shareholders include the dividends in their gross income. Accordingly, if one corporation is a shareholder in another corporation, triple taxation results. To rectify this problem, legislative grace provides corporations with a deduction for dividends received.[10]

The **dividends-received deduction (DRD)** generally provides only partial relief of the triple taxation problem. However, the actual amount of the DRD depends on the percentage of ownership held in the distributing corporation by the recipient shareholder. Generally, the DRD is 50 percent of the dividends received from U.S. taxable corporations. (Dividends from foreign corporations are not eligible for the DRD.) Table 14-1 presents the three deduction rates and the related ownership percentages for dividend recipients.

The 50-percent and 65-percent DRDs are subject to certain limitations:

- The taxable income limitation creates a ceiling (maximum value) for the DRD. It is limited to 50 percent or 65 percent, respectively, of taxable income computed without the deductions for dividends received and any net operating loss (NOL) carryovers to the current year.
- The taxable income limitation is disregarded if an NOL results after deducting the DRD, using the general rules.[11]

**Example 17** Hershal Corporation has the following income and expense items for the current tax year:

| | |
|---|---|
| Dividend income received from less than 20%-owned domestic corporations | $100,000 |
| Net income from operations | 30,000 |

What is the amount of Hershal's DRD?

**Discussion: Because Hershal owns less than 20% of the distributing corporations, the 50% deduction percentage applies. Under the general rule, the DRD is $50,000 (50% × $100,000 dividends). The taxable income limitation is $65,000 (50% × $130,000 taxable income before DRD). Because $50,000 is less than $65,000, the taxable income limitation does not apply, and Hershal Corporation may take the full 50% DRD.**

**Example 18** Assume the same facts as in example 17, except that Hershal Corporation has a $20,000 loss from operations for the current year. What are the amounts of the DRD and the actual taxable income calculated for tax purposes?

*Table 14-1*

### Dividends-Received Deduction Rates

| Percent Ownership | Deduction Percentage |
|---|---|
| <20% | 50% |
| 20% up to 80% | 65% |
| 80% or more | 100% |

**Discussion: The taxable income limitation is $56,000:**

| | |
|---|---|
| Net loss from operations | $ (20,000) |
| Dividend income | 100,000 |
| Taxable income without the DRD | $ 80,000 |
| DRD rate | × 50% |
| Taxable income limitation | $ 40,000 |

**A loss does not result after deducting the DRD under the general rule ($80,000 − $50,000 = $30,000); therefore, the taxable income limitation applies. The DRD is limited to $40,000, and the actual amount of the taxable income is $40,000:**

| | |
|---|---|
| Net loss from operations | $ (20,000) |
| Dividend income | 100,000 |
| DRD (taxable income limit) | (40,000) |
| Taxable income | $ 40,000 |

The taxable income limitation applies only to dividends received that are allowed the 50-percent or 65-percent DRD. Dividends received that qualify for the 100-percent DRD are not subject to the income limitation; they are fully deductible.

When the taxable income limitation applies, taxable income should be calculated using the general rule DRD. If this produces a loss, the taxable income limitation is disregarded and the general rule DRD is deductible.

**Example 19** Assume the same facts as in example 18, except that Hershal Corporation's net operating loss for the current year is $60,000, resulting in taxable income before the DRD of $40,000. What are the amounts of the DRD and the actual taxable income calculated for tax purposes?

**Discussion: From example 18, the general rule DRD is $50,000. The taxable income limitation is $20,000 (50% × $40,000). The taxable income limitation does not apply in this case because an NOL would result after the DRD (computed under the general rule) is subtracted from the operating loss and the dividend income:**

| | |
|---|---|
| Net loss from operations | $ (60,000) |
| Dividend income | 100,000 |
| General rule DRD | (50,000) |
| Net operating loss | $ (10,000) |

**Therefore, the $50,000 general rule DRD is allowed, and Hershal has a $10,000 net operating loss in the current year.**

As example 19 demonstrates, legislative grace permits income (dividends) to create a net operating loss by applying the dividends-received deduction. Hershal Corporation reports an NOL of $10,000 by deducting the full $50,000 DRD. If the taxable income limit were in effect, Hershal would report a taxable income of $20,000 ($40,000 − $20,000).

## Passive Activity Losses

Generally, regular corporate taxpayers are not subject to the passive loss limitations discussed in Chapter 7.

**Example 20** T&M, Inc., is a corporation formed by ten dentists who own all its stock. The corporation is a wholesale supplier of dental products. The corporation acquires a limited partnership interest in an oil exploration venture. T&M has the following results for the current year:

| | |
|---|---|
| Net income from dental services | $ 20,000 |
| Interest income | 18,000 |
| Limited partnership loss | (32,000) |

What is T&M's taxable income for the current year?

**Discussion: T&M Inc., is a corporation and is allowed to deduct the loss from the limited partnership. The corporation's taxable income for the year is $6,000 ($20,000 + $18,000 – $32,000).**

Closely held corporations are allowed to offset net passive losses against active income of the business. However, they cannot use passive losses to offset portfolio income.[12] For passive loss purposes, a corporation is a **closely held corporation** if five or fewer shareholders own 50 percent or more of its stock during the last half of the tax year.

**Example 21** Assume the same facts as in example 20, except that T&M, Inc., is owned by three individuals. What is T&M's taxable income?

**Discussion: T&M is a closely held corporation for purposes of the passive loss rules. Therefore, T&M can use the $32,000 passive loss to offset the $20,000 in active corporate income but cannot deduct the passive loss against the interest income. T&M's taxable income is $18,000:**

| | |
|---|---|
| Net income from dental product sales | $ 20,000 |
| Passive loss deduction | (20,000) |
| Interest income | 18,000 |
| Taxable income | $ 18,000 |

## Charitable Contributions

Like individuals, corporations face limitations on the deductibility of **charitable contributions**. Generally, the rules governing charitable contributions by corporations are the same as those pertaining to contributions by individuals. However, there are certain differences. For example, annual corporate charitable deductions are limited to 10 percent of taxable income computed without regard to the charitable contribution deduction, NOL carrybacks, capital loss carrybacks, or the dividends-received deduction.[13] Excess contributions may be carried forward for five years. Current-year contributions must be deducted against the limit before any carryover contributions may be deducted.

**Example 22** King Corporation has the following items on its books for 2021:

| | |
|---|---|
| Net income from operations | $125,000 |
| Dividends received (50% rule) | 10,000 |
| Charitable contributions made in current year | 15,000 |
| Charitable contribution carryover from 2020 | 3,000 |

What is King's 2021 charitable contribution deduction?

**Discussion: The charitable contribution deduction is limited to $13,500. For purposes of the 10% limitation only, King's taxable income is $135,000:**

| | |
|---|---|
| Net income from operations | $125,000 |
| Dividends received | 10,000 |
| Taxable income without the dividends-received and charitable contribution deduction | $135,000 |
| Charitable contribution limit | × 10% |
| Maximum charitable contribution deduction | $ 13,500 |

**Taxable income for 2021 is $116,500:**

| | |
|---|---|
| Net income from operations | $125,000 |
| Dividends received | 10,000 |
| | $135,000 |
| Less: Special deductions | |
| Charitable contributions | (13,500) |
| Dividends-received deduction (50% × $10,000) | (5,000) |
| Taxable income | $116,500 |

**The current year's excess charitable contribution of $1,500 ($15,000 − $13,500) and the $3,000 excess contribution from the previous year are carried over to the next tax year. They are subject to that year's limitation rules. The $3,000 carryover from the previous year will be deducted first if there is room under the next year's limit.**

**Example 23** King Corporation has the following items on its books for 2022:

| | |
|---|---|
| Net income from operations | $220,000 |
| Dividends received (50% rule) | 20,000 |
| Charitable contributions made in current year | 20,000 |

What is King's charitable contribution deduction for 2022?

**Discussion: The charitable contribution deduction limit is $24,000 (10% × $240,000 taxable income without the dividends-received and charitable contributions deductions). The current year's contributions and $4,500 of the carryover contributions are deductible. In determining the carryover deduction, the $3,000 carryover from 2020 is deducted first, followed by $1,000 of the $1,500 carryover from 2021. The taxable income is $206,000:**

| | |
|---|---|
| Net income from operations | $220,000 |
| Dividends received | 20,000 |
| | $240,000 |
| Less: Special deductions | |
| Charitable contributions | (24,000) |
| Dividends-received deduction (50% × $20,000) | (10,000) |
| Taxable income | $206,000 |

Another difference concerns donated inventory items. Generally, the amount of the contribution of **donated inventory** is limited to the adjusted basis of the inventory. However, an exception is provided for a corporate taxpayer that donates inventory for any of three types of uses:

- Items given solely for the care of the ill, needy, or infants
- Items donated to a university or qualified research organization to be used for research, experimentation, or research training in the biological or physical sciences
- Certain gifts to schools (grades K–12) of computer technology, equipment, and software

The amount of the deduction under this exception is the inventory's fair market value less 50 percent of the income that would be recognized if the inventory were sold at its fair market value. However, there is a ceiling, or maximum amount of deduction, which is twice the basis of the donated inventory items.[14]

**Example 24** Tech Corporation contributes some of its scientific software to the Department of Biophysics Research at Northwest University during the current year. As of the date of the contribution, the inventory has a fair market value of $50,000. Tech's basis in the software is $20,000. What is the amount of the charitable contribution?

**Discussion: The transaction qualifies under the exception for certain corporate inventory. The amount of Tech's contribution is $35,000:**

| | | |
|---|---|---|
| Fair market value | | $ 50,000 |
| Less: | | |
| Income if sold at fair market value ($50,000 − $20,000) | $ 30,000 | |
| Reduction percentage | × 50% | |
| | | (15,000) |
| Amount of charitable contribution | | $ 35,000 |

**Example 25** Assume the same facts as in example 24, except that the basis of the inventory is $10,000. What is the amount of the charitable contribution?

**Discussion:** The amount of Tech's contribution (before any limitations) is $30,000 [$50,000 – (50% × $40,000)]. However, the actual amount of the contribution deduction is limited to $20,000 (2 × $10,000), the ceiling of twice the basis of the inventory.

### Net Operating Losses

As a separate taxable entity, a corporation that suffers a net operating loss cannot distribute the loss to its shareholders for deduction. However, as discussed in Chapter 7, a corporation is allowed to carryforward losses indefinitely, but the loss can only offset 80 percent of taxable income for the year.

### Tax Credits

Chapter 15 discusses in detail the tax credits available to businesses. At this point, it is important to note that, as a separate taxpaying entity, a corporation uses tax credits to reduce its tax liability. In general, tax credits cannot reduce the tax liability below zero. Any unused credits are carried forward and used to reduce the tax liability in subsequent years.

### Basis Considerations

The nature of the relationship between a shareholder and a corporation requires few, if any, adjustments to the shareholder's basis. Because the corporation pays tax on its income, no adjustment to a shareholder's basis is necessary to avoid taxing the shareholder twice on the corporate income. Similarly, the receipt of a taxable dividend by a shareholder does not require a basis adjustment because the income has already been subject to tax. However, some cases do require a basis adjustment. Chapter 9 discusses basis adjustments to individual shares of stock for the receipt of a stock dividend and a stock split. At times, a shareholder may receive a nontaxable distribution of money or property from a corporation. The capital recovery concept requires basis to be reduced for a tax-free return of capital. If a shareholder receives a nontaxable distribution in excess of the basis of the stock (excess capital recovery), the shareholder recognizes a capital gain.

**Example 26** ABC Corporation distributes $200,000 in cash ($2 per share) to its shareholders in the current year. Only $50,000 of the distribution is taxable. What is the effect of the distribution on Zerenda, who owns 500 shares of ABC stock for which she paid $900?

**Discussion:** The first 25% ($50,000 ÷ $200,000) of the distribution is a taxable distribution. Zerenda will include $250 [25% × ($2 × 500 shares)] in dividend income in her gross income. The remainder of Zerenda's $1,000 distribution is not taxable and reduces the basis of her stock to $150 ($900 – $750).

**Example 27** Assume the same facts as in example 26, except that the entire distribution is nontaxable. What is the effect of the distribution on Zerenda?

**Discussion:** The $1,000 Zerenda receives is nontaxable to the extent of her basis in the stock. Because the distribution is greater than her basis, Zerenda must recognize the $100 ($1,000 – $900) distribution in excess of her basis as a capital gain. The basis of her stock then becomes zero.

## 14-2d S Corporation

As a conduit entity, an S corporation's incidence of taxation rests with the shareholders. Therefore, as with a partnership, the income of the S corporation must be segregated into ordinary income and those items that require separate reporting to shareholders.[15] Shareholders must include their individual shares of the S corporation's ordinary income and the separately stated items on their individual tax return. The rationale for stating these items separately is the same as for partnership—to get the correct taxation at the shareholder level. Therefore, the separately stated items are generally the same as those for a partnership. Items that S corporations are required to report separately include:

- Investment income (including tax-exempt income)
- Capital gains and losses

- Section 1231 gains and losses
- Passive activity items
- Charitable contributions
- Amounts expensed under Section 179
- Recovery of items previously deducted (tax benefit rule items)
- AMT preference and adjustment items
- Nondeductible expenses
- Tax credits

## Corporate Depreciation Recapture

S corporation status is an income tax election to be taxed as a conduit entity. As a corporation, an S corporation must follow the provisions for corporations unless specifically exempted from a particular provision. Therefore, an S corporation is subject to the corporate depreciation recapture rules for Section 1250 property. The ordinary income from the recapture is included in the S corporation's ordinary income. (It is not a separately stated item.) The Section 1231 gain must be stated separately.

**Example 28** Return to the facts of example 16. Recall that Penelope Corporation sells a building used in its trade or business that generates a Section 1231 gain subject to recapture under Section 1250. Assume that Penelope makes a valid S corporation election. What is the proper treatment of the $72,500 gain on the sale of the building?

**Discussion: Penelope must include in its ordinary income the $9,500 in corporate depreciation recapture on the building. The $63,000 Section 1231 gain is a separately stated item that is allocated to its shareholders according to their ownership interests.**

## Dividends-Received Deduction

The purpose of the special corporate dividends-received deduction is to alleviate the double taxation effect that occurs when a corporation distributes its earnings to shareholders. Because an S corporation is not taxed on dividends it receives, there is no double taxation of earnings of an S corporation. Therefore, the special dividends-received deduction for corporations does not apply to S corporations. The shareholders are allocated their proportionate shares of dividends received by the S corporation but are not allowed a deduction for dividends received.

## Net Operating Losses

The ability of shareholders to deduct operating losses of an S corporation is a major advantage over the corporate entity form. However, a shareholder's deductions for operating losses are limited in the same manner as the deductions for the operating losses of a partnership. That is, the shareholder cannot deduct losses in excess of basis.

**Example 29** Ali owns a 30% interest in Ono Company, an S corporation. Ono reports an operating loss of $80,000 in the current year. Ali's basis in the Ono stock is $20,000. How much of the loss can Ali deduct?

**Discussion: Ali's share of the loss is $24,000 (30% × $80,000). Her loss deduction is limited to her $20,000 basis, which is reduced to zero by the deduction. The $4,000 of loss is suspended until she has adequate basis to deduct the loss.**

Recall that a shareholder's basis is not adjusted for debts of an S corporation. However, a shareholder with insufficient basis is allowed to deduct losses to the extent of the basis of any loan that the shareholder made directly to the corporation.[16]

**Example 30** Assume the same facts as in example 29, except that Ono owes Ali $10,000 from a loan she made to the corporation several years ago. What is Ali's loss deduction?

**Discussion: Because Ali has insufficient basis to absorb the entire $24,000 loss, she is allowed to deduct the $4,000 to the extent of the $10,000 basis she has in**

**the loan to Ono Company. This provision lets her deduct the entire $24,000 loss. Because she receives a capital recovery from the $4,000 loss deduction, she must reduce the basis in the loan by the amount of the loss she deducts under this provision, leaving her a $6,000 basis in the loan.**

When a shareholder has deducted losses for loans to the corporation, the subsequent year's net increases in basis (resulting from all increases and decreases to basis) are applied first to restore the debt to its basis before the loss deduction.[17]

**Example 31** Return to the facts of example 30. Assume that in the following year, Ono Company has $40,000 in operating income and pays $10,000 in dividends to shareholders. What are the tax effects for Ali?

**Discussion: Ali must include her $12,000 (30% × $40,000) share of the income in her gross income. The $3,000 in dividends (30% × $10,000) she receives is a nontaxable recovery of capital. Ali has a net increase in basis of $9,000 ($12,000 – $3,000) from the income and dividends. She must use $4,000 of the net increase to restore the basis in the loan to the corporation to $10,000. The remaining $5,000 increases the basis of her stock.**

In addition to the basis limitation, operating loss deductions are subject to the at-risk and passive activity loss rules. As with partners, shareholders can deduct losses only to the extent that they are at risk in the activity. In addition, shareholders individually must determine whether their interest in the S corporation is a passive activity. If a shareholder's interest is passive, the deduction of losses is subject to the passive activity loss rules.

## Basis Considerations

After obtaining an initial basis in S corporation stock, a shareholder's basis in the stock is adjusted for items affecting the shareholder's capital recovery.[18] The basis adjustments generally parallel the adjustments made to a partner's basis, with the exception of the adjustments for debt. Exhibit 14-5 provides a general formula for calculating the basis in S corporation stock.

**Example 32** Herman owns 25% of Gordon, Inc., an S corporation. Herman's initial basis in the corporation is $20,000. During the current year, Gordon's ordinary income is $60,000, and the corporation pays a $40,000 cash dividend to shareholders. In addition, Gordon reports a $20,000 Section 1231 gain and pays a $16,000 nondeductible expense. What is Herman's adjusted basis in Gordon, Inc., at the end of the current year?

**Discussion: Herman adds his $15,000 share (25% × $60,000) of the ordinary income and his $5,000 share of the Section 1231 gain to his basis. He reduces his basis for his $4,000 share of the nondeductible expense and the $10,000 in cash dividends he receives. His adjusted basis is $26,000:**

*Exhibit 14-5*

## General Formula for Determining S Corporation Shareholder's Basis

| | |
|---|---|
| Initial basis | $ XXX |
| Add: Additional investments: | |
| Additional stock purchases | XXX |
| Capital contributions | XXX |
| Share of ordinary income | XXX |
| Share of separately stated income items (including nontaxable income) | XXX |
| Deduct: Returns of investment: | |
| Share of nondeductible expenses | (XXX) |
| Share of operating loss | (XXX) |
| Share of separately stated loss and deduction items | (XXX) |
| Nontaxable distributions received | (XXX) |
| Equals: Shareholder's adjusted basis | $ XXX |

| | |
|---|---|
| Initial basis | $ 20,000 |
| Add: Additional investments | |
| Share of ordinary income | 15,000 |
| Share of Section 1231 gain | 5,000 |
| Deduct: Returns of investment | |
| Share of nondeductible expense | (4,000) |
| Cash dividends received | (10,000) |
| Adjusted basis at end of year | $ 26,000 |

As discussed earlier, net operating losses are deductible only to the extent of the shareholder's basis plus any loans the shareholder has made to the corporation. Determining a shareholder's basis for purposes of deducting losses occurs at the end of the year. The order in which items are taken into account is the same as the order for partners: All items affecting a shareholder's basis are factored into the basis before considering any losses for the year.[19]

**Example 33** Assume the same facts as in example 32, except that Gordon, Inc., has a $100,000 operating loss. Assume that Herman is an active participant in Gordon's operations. What are the tax effects for Herman?

**Discussion: Herman must include his $5,000 share of the Section 1231 gain in his income. He can deduct his $25,000 share of the operating loss to the extent of his basis. To determine his basis for loss deduction purposes, the Section 1231 gain is added, and the nondeductible expenses and dividends are subtracted first, leaving Herman with a basis of $11,000:**

| | |
|---|---|
| Initial basis | $ 20,000 |
| Add: Section 1231 gain | 5,000 |
| Deduct: Nondeductible expenses | (4,000) |
| Deduct: Cash dividends received | (10,000) |
| Basis for deducting losses | $ 11,000 |

**Herman deducts $11,000 of the operating loss, reducing his basis to zero. The remaining $14,000 of loss is suspended until Herman's basis increases.**

## 14-2e Planning Commentary

After an entity begins operations, it must report the results of its operations on an annual basis to the government. Income for sole proprietorships, partnerships, and S corporations is taxed to the owners of the entities. This requires separate reporting of income and deduction items that have special treatments on individual tax returns. In addition, tax credits are taken on the owner's returns and used to reduce the owner's tax liabilities. A corporation is taxed on its taxable income. Shareholders are taxed on dividends received from a corporation. The differences in income reporting and the incidence of taxation give rise to basis adjustments that vary among the entities. Table 14-2 summarizes the treatment of various items from the operation of an entity.

The treatments of these items provide opportunities for owners of businesses to reduce their taxes. For example, the dividends-received deduction gives small-business owners who incorporate an opportunity to partially shield from federal taxation the dividends they obtain from their invested capital.

**Example 34** Conchita, a single taxpayer, operates Kapow Company, a garlic-packaging business, as a sole proprietorship. During the current year, the operating income is $100,000, and Conchita's taxable income from other sources is $20,000. Conchita annually invests any excess cash in common stock of Tortilla, Inc., a U.S. corporation. Tortilla pays Kapow $20,000 in dividends as of the end of the current year. What are the tax effects of the dividend income?

**Discussion: Because the business operates as a sole proprietorship, the dividends are included on Conchita's individual return and taxed at the long-term capital gains rate, 15%. Therefore, Conchita pays additional income tax of $3,000**

Table 14-2

# Operating Items of Entities

| Tax Consideration | Sole Proprietorship | Partnership | Corporation | S Corporation |
|---|---|---|---|---|
| Who is taxed on the income? | Owner | Partners are taxed on their share of the income. | Corporation. Shareholders are taxed on dividends received. | Shareholders are taxed on their share of the income. |
| Is a separate statement of income and deduction items required? | No, but certain items are part of the owner's income and deductions and are not included in operating income. | Yes | No | Yes |
| How are capital gains and losses handled? | Not included in operating income. Combined with owner's other capital gains and losses. | Separately stated item. Partners combine them with their other capital gains and losses. | Capital gains are ordinary income. Capital losses are deductible only against capital gains. Three-year carryback and 5-year carryforward of losses. | Separately stated item. Shareholders combine them with their other capital gains and losses. |
| Is corporate depreciation recapture required? | No | No | Yes, additional recapture on Section 1250 property. | Yes, additional recapture on Section 1250 property. |
| Is the dividends received deduction allowed? | No | No | Yes, 50% to 100% deduction for dividends from domestic corporations, subject to limitations. | No |
| Are net operating losses deductible? | Can deduct only against other business income of the owner. 20-year carryforward of losses. | Separately stated item. Deduction limited to partner's basis and at-risk amount. Loss may be subject to passive loss rules if partner does not materially participate. | Loss can be carried forward indefinitely, but the loss can only offset 80% of taxable income for the year. | Separately stated item. Deduction limited to shareholder's basis plus loans to the corporation and at-risk amount. Loss may be subject to passive loss rules if shareholder does not materially participate. |
| Is basis adjusted? | Not applicable | Partner's basis is adjusted for operating items, withdrawals, and liabilities of the partnership. | Shareholder's basis is generally not adjusted unless stock dividend or nontaxable cash dividend received. | Shareholder's basis is adjusted for operating items, dividends received. No adjustment for liabilities of the corporation. |
| Are passive losses deductible? | Not deductible in calculating operating income. Deductible per rules for individuals. | Separately stated item. Partners deduct per rules for individuals. | Passive loss rules generally not applicable to corporations. | Separately stated item. Shareholders deduct per rules for individuals. |
| Are charitable contributions deductible? | Not deductible in calculating operating income. Must be deducted on owner's return as itemized deduction. | Separately stated item. Partners deduct as itemized deductions. | Deductible, subject to 10% of taxable income limitation. Special rules for certain donated inventory. | Separately stated item. Shareholders deduct as itemized deduction. |

**($20,000 × 15%), leaving her with after-tax dividend income of $17,000 ($20,000 − $3,000). If Conchita incorporates her business, she can partially shield the dividend income from taxation because of the dividends-received deduction. Assuming that Kapow Company becomes the owner of the Tortilla stock, 50% of the dividends received by Kapow is deductible in determining corporate taxable income. Accordingly, only $10,000 [$20,000 − ($20,000 × 50%)] in dividend income is included in Kapow's taxable income. The $10,000 in additional income results in increased taxes of $2,100 ($10,000 × 21%). The after-tax dividend income is $17,900 ($20,000 − $2,100), resulting in a tax savings of $900 ($17,900 − $17,000) when the corporate form is used. However, if Conchita has the dividends received paid to her as a dividend, an additional tax of $3,000 ($20,000 × 15%) will be paid.**

An individual who owns a business operated as a sole proprietorship and also has passive activity losses cannot offset the operating (active) income with passive losses. Yet, if the individual incorporates the business and transfers the business assets and the passive activity investment assets to the corporation, the passive activity loss can shield the active income.

In starting a new business, owners who anticipate losses in the early years of the business will probably benefit from using the partnership or S corporation form. This allows the entity losses to flow through for deduction by the owners instead of being carried forward for future deduction by a corporation. However, the owners must take care that losses flowing from the conduit entity are not limited by the basis, at-risk, or passive loss limitations. When it appears that one or more of the owners will have a basis problem with loss deductions, actions can be taken to increase the owner's basis.

Examples of actions that an owner could take to avoid the basis limitation include making additional capital contributions to the entity and purchasing additional interests in the entity from owners with adequate basis. If the partnership form is used, the partnership could take on additional debt to increase the partners' interests, or the partner with a basis problem could reduce the amount of any withdrawals from the partnership. An S corporation shareholder could make a loan to the corporation for the amount of the net operating loss that is limited by the basis limitation. The corporation could reduce the amount of dividends it pays when shareholders face limitations on losses.

As with all the planning ideas presented in this chapter, no single strategy will work in every situation. Tax avoidance plans cannot be considered in isolation. The effects of all factors must be taken into consideration in every aspect of tax planning. For example, the decision to incorporate to shield dividends through the dividends-received deduction cannot be evaluated without considering the effects of all other facets of the corporate form. The incidence of taxation, double taxation of dividends, limitations on capital losses, and the disallowance of flow-through operating losses may negate the benefit from the dividends-received deduction. When choosing a particular entity form, a business must consider all factors of the form and assess how those factors will affect its operation.

## 14-3 ENTITY DISTRIBUTIONS

LO 3

Explain the treatment of current distributions and liquidation distributions from the perspective of both an entity and an owner.

Another major part of the life cycle of an entity is the tax treatment of distributions from an entity to its owners. A distribution can be made in cash or property. The tax treatment of the distribution to the shareholder can be classified as ordinary income, a capital gain, or a nontaxable return of capital, depending on the amount of the distribution and the entity making the distribution. A distribution made from a continuing entity is called a **nonliquidating distribution**; a distribution made upon the termination and liquidation of the entity is called a **liquidating distribution**. This section discusses each distribution and its effect on the shareholder-partner and the distributing entity.

### 14-3a Sole Proprietorship

A sole proprietorship is not considered a separate taxable entity. However, the entity concept does require that the business keep its records separate from the owner's personal records. Sole proprietors report the net income from the business on Schedule C of Form 1040 and include it as gross income on their individual tax return. As with a conduit entity, because the income has already been taxed to the individual owner, any distribution of cash or property from the business to the owner is not taxable. The distribution is viewed as a movement of the cash or property from the owner's business account to the owner's personal account.

Because a sole proprietorship is not a separate entity, the liquidation or termination of the business is not viewed as the sale of one asset but rather a sale of the individual assets of the business. Therefore, the gain or loss and its character (i.e., ordinary, capital) depends on the assets sold. If a business sells inventory and land, it will recognize ordinary income and capital gain income, respectively. As discussed in Chapter 9, when a basket of assets is acquired or sold, the total purchase price must be allocated among the individual assets.[20] For planning purposes, the seller will want to allocate more of the purchase price to the assets that will produce capital gain treatment.

**Example 35** Ali operates a bookstore as a sole proprietorship. During the year, he sells the business to Carla for $300,000. The assets sold and the allocation of the purchase price are as follows:

| | Adjusted Basis | Purchase Price |
|---|---|---|
| Inventory | $120,000 | $120,000 |
| Building | 60,000 | 90,000 |
| Land | 20,000 | 30,000 |
| Equipment | -0- | 20,000 |
| Goodwill | -0- | 40,000 |
| Total Assets | $200,000 | $300,000 |

Ali acquired the building in 2014 for $100,000 and paid $30,000 for the equipment. What are the tax consequences of the liquidation for Ali?

**Discussion: Ali will recognize a Section 1231 gain of $40,000 [($90,000 – $60,000) + ($30,000 – $20,000)] on the sale of the building and land. The $30,000 gain on the sale of the building is an unrecaptured Section 1250 gain. The sale of the fully depreciated equipment results in Ali's recognizing $20,000 in ordinary income (because of Section 1245 recapture). The remaining $40,000 represents goodwill and is treated as a capital gain. Because the amount of the purchase price allocated to inventory is equal to its cost, Ali has no gain or loss to recognize. Note: If the amount allocated to the inventory is greater or less than its basis, the taxpayer recognizes ordinary income or loss.**

## 14-3b Partnership

Recall that partners must include their pro rata share of the partnership's income or loss on their individual tax return. In addition, the amount of the income or loss increases or decreases their basis in the partnership. As a result, a nonliquidating distribution of cash from a partnership to the partner, which is known as a **partnership distribution**, is generally tax-free. This result is consistent with the capital recovery concept. That is, partners recognize no income until they have recovered their basis in the partnership. A partner will recognize a gain on a cash distribution only if the amount of cash distributed exceeds the partner's basis.[21]

**Example 36** Edna and Lucille have been equal partners in the KAK Partnership for several years. At the close of the current year, Edna's basis in her ownership interest is $10,000, and Lucille's basis is $4,000. At that time, the partnership distributes cash in the amount of $5,000 to each partner. What are the tax and basis effects of these cash distributions?

**Discussion: Edna receives her $5,000 tax-free; it is merely a recovery of capital. Her basis is reduced to $5,000 ($10,000 – $5,000). Lucille receives $4,000 tax-free as a recovery of capital. However, she must recognize the $1,000 excess capital recovery as a capital gain. Lucille's basis is now zero.**

| | Edna | Lucille |
|---|---|---|
| Initial basis | $10,000 | $ 4,000 |
| Cash distribution | (5,000) | (5,000) |
| Remaining basis | $ 5,000 | $ -0- |
| Taxable gain | $ -0- | $ 1,000 |

As with a distribution of cash, a distribution of property from a partnership is tax-free. Neither the partners nor the partnership recognizes a gain or loss on the distribution. If a partner receives a nonliquidating distribution of property, the partner's basis in the partnership is reduced by the basis of the property received.

**Example 37** The Beckman Group consists of two equal partners, Judy and Bill. At the close of the current year, Judy's basis in the partnership is $22,000, and Bill's basis is $19,000. At that time, the partnership distributes property with a basis of $13,000 and a fair market value of $15,000 to Bill. What are the tax and basis effects of the property distribution?

**Discussion: Bill does not recognize a gain or loss on the distribution of the property. His basis in the partnership is reduced by the adjusted basis of the property distributed to him. Bill's basis in the property is $13,000.**

| | |
|---|---|
| Initial basis | $ 19,000 |
| Property distribution | (13,000) |
| Remaining basis | $ 6,000 |
| Taxable gain | $ -0- |

If a partner receives a nonliquidating distribution of cash and property, the partner's basis in the partnership is first reduced by the cash distributed and then by the adjusted basis of the property distributed. Remember, a partner's basis in the partnership can never be reduced below zero. If the basis of the property distributed is greater than the partners' basis in the partnership, the partners must reduce their basis in the distributed property by the excess.

**Example 38** Return to the facts of example 37, except that Bill also receives a $12,000 cash distribution.

**Discussion: Bill does not recognize a gain or loss on the distribution of the cash and property. The cash distribution of $12,000 reduces his basis in the partnership to $7,000 ($19,000 − $12,000). Bill then reduces his basis in the partnership by the adjusted basis of the property distributed. The adjusted basis of the property distributed ($13,000) is greater than his remaining basis in the partnership ($7,000). Because Bill's basis in the partnership cannot be reduced below zero, the excess of the property's basis over Bill's remaining basis, $6,000 ($13,000 − $7,000), reduces his basis in the distributed property to $7,000 ($13,000 − $6,000).**

| | |
|---|---|
| Initial basis | $ 19,000 |
| Cash distribution | (12,000) |
| Remaining basis | $ 7,000 |
| Property distribution—limited to remaining basis | (7,000) |
| Partnership basis | $ -0- |
| Taxable gain | $ -0- |
| Partnership's basis in property | $ 13,000 |
| Reduction in basis | (6,000) |
| Bill's basis in the property | $ 7,000 |

A distribution of cash and/or property in complete liquidation of the partnership may result in the partners' recognizing a gain or loss. The rules for recognizing a gain upon the liquidation of a partnership interest are the same as those for a nonliquidating distribution. Gain is recognized only to the extent that the amount of cash distributed exceeds the partner's basis in the partnership. Unlike the situation with a nonliquidating cash distribution, a loss can be recognized on the complete liquidation of a partner's interest, but only if certain assets are distributed. The rules concerning the calculation of a loss are complex and beyond the scope of this text. However, as a general rule, if only cash is distributed and the amount of cash distributed is less than the partner's basis in the partnership, the partner can recognize a loss on the liquidation of the partnership. The partner does not recognize a gain or loss when only property is distributed.

**Example 39** Refer to example 36. Assume that Edna and Lucille receive liquidating distributions in cash of $8,000 and $4,000, respectively. What is the tax effect of the liquidating cash distributions?

**Discussion: Edna and Lucille have capital losses of $2,000 and $1,000, respectively. Under the capital recovery concept, Edna and Lucille can recognize a capital loss for the unrecovered portion of their investment. Whether the capital loss is long-term or short-term depends on how long Edna and Lucille held their partnership interest.**

| | Edna | Lucille |
|---|---|---|
| Liquidating cash distribution | $ (8,000) | $(4,000) |
| Initial basis | 10,000 | 5,000 |
| Capital loss | $ (2,000) | $(1,000) |

## 14-3c Corporation

A cash distribution to a noncorporate shareholder is generally taxable to the shareholder and is not deductible by the distributing corporation.[22] As a result, the dividend is subject to double taxation.

**Example 40** Linh, who is single, owns all the stock in the Jacaranda Corporation, which reports taxable income of $50,000 in the current year. The corporation distributes the $50,000 in earnings as a qualified dividend. Assuming that Linh's marginal tax rate on ordinary income is 22%, how much income tax do the Jacaranda Corporation and Linh pay?

**Discussion: The total income tax liability resulting from the $50,000 income and the distribution of the dividend is $18,000 ($10,500 + $7,500). The corporate income tax is $10,500 ($50,000 × 21%). Linh includes the dividend in his individual taxable income and pays $7,500 ($50,000 × 15%) in income tax on the qualified dividend amount. The corporate earnings are taxed twice—first at the corporate level and again at the individual stockholder level. Dividend payments are not deductible expenses.**

The tax definition of a **dividend** is a distribution by a corporation from its current or accumulated earnings and profits. The term *earnings and profits* is not technically defined in the tax law. Yet the law uses it as a measure of a corporation's economic ability to pay dividends without impairing capital. Although several differences exist, the definition of earnings and profits is conceptually analogous to the financial accounting term *retained earnings*. Earnings and profits generally represent undistributed, previously taxed corporate profits. Current earnings and profits must be distributed first, followed by accumulated earnings and profits, if necessary.[23]

**Example 41** Assume that Paige Corporation distributes a total of $100,000 to its shareholders during the current year. At the beginning of the year, the corporation has a deficit in its accumulated earnings and profits of $350,000. Current earnings and profits for the year are $300,000. How do the shareholders treat the $100,000 distribution?

**Discussion: The amount of current earnings and profits is sufficient to classify the $100,000 as dividend income to the shareholders. A year-end deficit in accumulated earnings and profits of Paige Corporation will not change the outcome because dividends are assumed to be paid out of the current year's earnings and profits first.**

If a **corporate distribution** exceeds both the current and accumulated earnings and profits, the capital recovery concept dictates that the distribution is tax-free to shareholders. Therefore, the amount of the tax-free return of capital reduces the basis in the stock held by shareholders. If a shareholder receives a distribution in excess of the basis of the stock (excess capital recovery), the shareholder recognizes a capital gain.

**Example 42** Return to the facts of example 41. Assume that Paige Corporation distributes \$200,000 in cash (\$2 per share) when its current and cumulative earnings and profits are \$50,000. What is the effect of the distribution on Won, who owns 500 shares of Paige stock for which he paid \$10,000?

**Discussion: The first 25% (\$50,000 ÷ \$200,000) of the distribution is a taxable dividend for Won of \$250 [25% × (\$2 × 500 shares)]. The remainder of Won's \$1,000 distribution is deemed a recovery of capital to the extent of his basis in the shares of stock. Because Won's basis is \$10,000, the remaining \$750 of the dividend (\$1,000 − \$250) reduces the basis of his stock to \$9,250 (\$10,000 − \$750). Note: If Won's basis had been less than \$750, the distribution in excess of the basis would cause him to recognize a capital gain. The stock's basis then becomes zero.**

A property distribution from a corporation has the same tax consequences to the shareholder as a cash dividend. Assuming that the corporation makes the distribution from earnings and profits, the shareholder recognizes income equal to the fair market value of the property. However, the tax treatment for the distributing corporation is different. The corporation will recognize gain if the fair market value of the property distributed exceeds its basis. However, if the fair market value of the property distributed is less than its basis, the corporation does not recognize a loss.[24]

**Example 43** In the current year, Farley Corporation distributes land with a fair market value of \$25,000 and a basis of \$5,000 to Lou, who is a shareholder. Farley's earnings and profits are \$150,000. What is the effect of the property distribution for Lou and Farley Corporation?

**Discussion: Lou will report dividend income of \$25,000, and Farley will recognize a gain of \$20,000 (\$25,000 − \$5,000). Lou's basis in the land is \$25,000. Note: If Farley's basis in the property is \$28,000, it does not recognize a loss. However, Lou still recognizes dividend income of \$25,000.**

The tax consequences of a distribution to a shareholder in complete liquidation of a corporation are the same whether the shareholder receives cash or property. The tax law treats shareholders as having sold their stock to the corporation for the amount of cash distributed or property received. If property is distributed, the amount received is equal to the fair market value of the property. Therefore, to the extent that the distribution is greater than the shareholder's basis in the stock, the stockholder recognizes gain. Conversely, if the shareholder's basis is less than the amount received, the shareholder recognizes a loss.

**Example 44** Return to the facts of example 43. Assume that instead of a property distribution, Farley makes a cash distribution of \$25,000 to Lou in complete liquidation of the corporation. Lou's basis in Farley stock is \$12,000. What is the tax treatment of the cash distribution to Lou?

**Discussion: Lou will recognize a capital gain of \$13,000 (\$25,000 − \$12,000). Whether the gain is long-term or short-term depends on how long Lou owned the Farley stock. Note: If Lou's basis in the stock is \$30,000, he will recognize a capital loss of \$5,000.**

Technically, a corporation will not recognize income on the distribution of cash in a complete liquidation. However, to have the cash to distribute, the corporation will need to convert (i.e., sell) all its noncash assets to cash. In that process, the corporation will recognize gain or loss on the sale of the assets. In essence, this makes the corporation recognize income on the cash distribution. Whether the income or loss is capital or ordinary will depend on the type of property sold (e.g., inventory or equipment).

If a corporation distributes property in a complete liquidation instead of selling it and then distributing the cash, the corporation will recognize gain to the extent that the fair market value of the property exceeds its basis. Generally, unlike the situation in a nonliquidating distribution of property, the corporation is allowed to recognize a loss if the fair market value of the property is less than its basis.[25]

**Example 45** Assume the same facts as in example 43, except that Farley distributes the land in complete liquidation of the corporation. What are the tax consequences for Lou and Farley Corporation?

**Discussion: Because the fair market value of the land distributed exceeds Lou's basis in the stock, he will recognize a capital gain of $13,000 ($25,000 − $12,000). His basis in the land is $25,000. The corporation will recognize a gain of $20,000 ($25,000 − $5,000).**

**Example 46** Assume the same facts as in example 45, except that Farley's basis in the land is $28,000 and Lou's basis in the stock is $30,000. What are the tax consequences to Lou and Farley Corporation if the property distribution is made in complete liquidation of the corporation?

**Discussion: Because the fair market value of the property distributed is less than Lou's basis in the stock, he will recognize a capital loss of $5,000 ($25,000 − $30,000). The corporation will recognize a loss of $3,000 ($25,000 − $28,000).**

## concept check

The *entity concept* requires each entity to separately report the results of its operations. Because a corporation and its owners are separate legal entities, distributions of earnings (dividends) to shareholders constitute income. Because dividends are not expenses incurred to produce income, they are not deductible under the *business purpose concept*. Under the *all-inclusive income concept*, distributions of cash or property are taxable to shareholders. The earnings and profits of a corporation consist of corporate earnings that have not been distributed to shareholders, and are a measure of a corporation's *ability to pay* dividends. The *capital recovery concept* allows the recovery of invested capital before income is recognized. Therefore, distributions that exceed earnings and profits are not taxable—they are returns of capital investment that reduce the shareholder's basis. A corporation recognizes gain, but not loss, on property distributed to a shareholder in a nonliquidating distribution. However, a corporation recognizes loss on liquidating distributions and can use the loss to offset other gains from the sale or exchange of appreciated property.

## 14-3d S Corporation

Like a partnership, an S corporation is a conduit entity with the income from the corporation flowing through and being taxed at the shareholder level. As a result, the rules for a nonliquidating cash distribution from S corporations are similar to those for partnerships. Recall from the discussion of partnerships that the capital recovery concept governs the treatment of distributions. Cash distributions from an S corporation to its shareholders are generally tax-free and reduce the shareholders' basis in the corporate stock.[26] If the distributions exceed a shareholder's basis, the excess amount is treated as a capital gain. A distribution of cash has no tax consequences for the S corporation.

**Example 47** Julio owns all the shares of Leysin Corporation, which operates as an S corporation. His basis in the stock is $35,000. During the year, he receives a cash distribution of $18,000 from the S corporation. What is the effect of this distribution on Julio and Leysin?

**Discussion: The $18,000 is a recovery of capital to the extent of Julio's basis. His basis is reduced by the amount of the cash distribution. After the tax-free receipt of the $18,000, Julio's adjusted basis is $17,000 ($35,000 − $18,000). There are no tax consequences for Leysin.**

**Example 48** Assume the same facts as in example 47, except that Julio receives a distribution of $40,000 instead of $18,000. How does that change the tax effects of the distribution for Julio and Leysin Corporation?

**Discussion: Applying the capital recovery concept, the first $35,000 (Julio's basis) of the distribution is tax-free. The excess $5,000 ($40,000 – $35,000) is a capital gain and reduces Julio's basis in the S corporation to zero. The distribution does not affect the taxable income of Leysin.**

If property is distributed to shareholders of an S corporation, the tax treatment for shareholders is similar to the treatment of a cash dividend. Shareholders will not recognize income to the extent the fair market value of the property received is less than their basis in the corporation. Because an S corporation possesses some characteristics of a conduit and some characteristics of a corporation, the tax treatment for an S corporation is similar to a property distribution from a corporation. The S corporation will recognize gain if the fair market value of the property distributed exceeds its basis. As with a corporation, an S corporation cannot recognize loss on the distribution of property.[27]

**Example 49** Return to the facts of example 47. Assume that Julio receives a nonliquidating distribution of land with a fair market value of $18,000 and that Leysin's basis in the property is $5,000. What is the effect of this distribution for Julio and Leysin?

**Discussion: As with a cash distribution, the distribution of land is a recovery of capital and reduces Julio's basis in the S corporation to $17,000 ($35,000 − $18,000). His basis in the land is $18,000. However, Leysin must recognize a gain on the distribution of $13,000 ($18,000 − $5,000). The recognition of gain by Leysin, that passes through to Julio, increases Julio's basis in the S corporation to $30,000 ($17,000 + $13,000).**

In a complete liquidation of a shareholder's interest in an S corporation, the tax treatment for the shareholder is the same whether the distribution is cash or property. Shareholders will recognize gain or loss depending on whether the distribution is more or less than their basis in the stock. The gain or loss is either short-term or long-term depending on how long the shareholder has held the stock. Although the liquidating S corporation does not recognize a gain or loss on the distribution of cash, the S corporation will need to convert its noncash assets to cash to make the distribution. In doing so, the S corporation will recognize income or loss, and the nature of the assets sold will determine the gain (i.e., capital or ordinary).

**Example 50** Return to the facts of example 47. Assume that Julio receives a cash distribution of $18,000 in complete liquidation of his interest in the S corporation. What is the effect of this distribution for Julio and Leysin?

**Discussion: The $18,000 is a recovery of capital to the extent of Julio's basis. His basis is reduced by the amount of the cash distribution. After the tax-free receipt of the $18,000, Julio's adjusted basis is $17,000 ($35,000 − $18,000). Under the capital recovery concept, Julio has a capital loss of $17,000 because he has not recovered his basis in the S corporation stock. Assuming that Julio has no other capital gains or losses, he can deduct $3,000 of the loss in the current year. The distribution has no tax consequences for Leysin.**

If the S corporation distributes property to shareholders in complete liquidation of their interest, the corporation will recognize gain or loss on the distribution. The tax treatment for the S corporation is identical to that for a corporation.

**Example 51** Assume the same facts as in example 49, except that the land Julio receives is in complete liquidation of his interest in the S corporation. What is the effect of this distribution for Leysin and Julio?

**Discussion: The distribution of the property by Leysin to Julio is treated as if Leysin sold the property to Julio. The corporation must recognize a gain of $13,000 ($18,000 − $5,000) on the distribution of the property to Julio. Because he is the sole owner of the corporation, the $13,000 gain increases his basis in Leysin to $48,000 ($35,000 + $13,000). The property distributed to Julio is tax-free and reduces his basis in Leysin to $30,000 ($48,000 − $18,000). Under the capital recovery concept, because Julio has not recovered his basis in the S corporation stock, he has a capital loss of $30,000. Assuming that Julio has no other capital gains or losses, he can deduct $3,000 of the loss in the current year.**

Tables 14-3 and 14-4 summarize the tax treatment of distributions for the recipient and the distributing entity.

Table 14-3

## Nonliquidating Distributions

| | Recipient | Distributing Entity |
|---|---|---|
| **Proprietorship** | | |
| Cash | No tax consequences. | No tax consequences. |
| Property | No gain or loss is recognized until the sole proprietor sells the distributed property. | No tax consequences. |
| **Partnership** | | |
| Cash | No gain is recognized unless the amount of cash distributed exceeds the partner's basis in the partnership. The excess is capital gain. | No tax consequences. |
| Property | No gain or loss is recognized. If the adjusted basis of the property exceeds the partner's basis, the basis of the property is reduced. | No tax consequences. |
| **Corporation** | | |
| Cash | Taxable as dividend income to the extent of earnings and profits. Any amount in excess of earnings and profit is a return of capital to the extent of basis in stock. An amount in excess of basis is capital gain. | No tax consequences. |
| Property | Same as for cash. Amount of dividend is the fair market value (FMV) of the property received. | Gain is recognized to the extent FMV exceeds basis of property. No loss is recognized. |
| **S Corporation** | | |
| Cash | No income is recognized unless the distribution exceeds the shareholder's basis in the corporation. The excess is capital gain. | No tax consequences. |
| Property | Same as for cash. Amount of distribution is FMV of the property received. | Gain is recognized to the extent FMV exceeds basis of property. No loss is recognized. |

Table 14-4

## Liquidating Distributions

| | Recipient | Distributing Entity |
|---|---|---|
| **Proprietorship** | | |
| Cash | No tax consequences. | No tax consequences. |
| Property | Gain or loss is recognized as assets are sold by the owner. | No tax consequences. |
| **Partnership** | | |
| Cash | No gain is recognized unless the amount of cash distributed exceeds the partner's basis in the partnership. The excess is capital gain. If only cash is distributed, loss can be recognized. | No tax consequences. |
| Property | Generally, no gain or loss is recognized. If the adjusted basis of the property exceeds the partner's basis, the basis of the property is reduced. | No tax consequences. |
| **Corporation** | | |
| Cash | If amount received exceeds basis in stock, capital gain is recognized. If amount received is less than basis in stock, loss is recognized. | No tax consequences. |
| Property | Same as for cash. Amount of dividend is FMV of the property received. | Gain is recognized to the extent FMV exceeds basis of property. Loss is recognized if FMV is less than basis. |
| **S Corporation** | | |
| Cash | If amount received exceeds basis in stock, capital gain recognized. If amount received is less than basis is in stock, loss is recognized. | No tax consequences. |
| Property | Same as for cash. Amount of dividend is FMV of the property received. | Gain is recognized to the extent FMV exceeds basis of property. Loss is recognized if FMV is less than basis. |

## 14-3e Planning Commentary

A nonliquidating distribution of cash or property from a sole proprietorship is tax-free because the sole proprietor and the business are not considered separate taxable entities. Rather, the two are viewed as one taxpaying entity. Although a distribution of property is treated the same as cash, the sole proprietor recognizes a gain or loss when the distributed property is later sold. However, the sole proprietor's recognition of loss is limited to the business use of the property. The same tax treatment occurs if a sole proprietorship makes a liquidating distribution of cash or property. Because the proprietor and the sole proprietorship are one taxpaying entity, nonliquidating and liquidating distributions of cash or property have no tax consequences for the sole proprietor or the sole proprietorship.

Generally, a partner does not recognize gain on a nonliquidating distribution of cash or property. Because a partnership is a conduit entity, a distribution to a partner is usually either a return of original investment or a distribution of previously taxed income. The partner recognizes gain only if the amount of cash received exceeds the partner's basis. A partner never recognizes a loss on a nonliquidating distribution of cash or property.

If property is distributed, the adjusted basis of the property distributed reduces a partner's basis in the partnership. When both cash and property are distributed, the partner's basis is reduced first by the cash received and then by the adjusted basis of the property. A partner's basis can never be reduced below zero. When the adjusted basis of property distributed exceeds the partner's remaining basis in the partnership, the partner's basis in the property received is reduced (but not below zero) by the amount the property's basis exceeds the partner's remaining basis in the partnership. With one exception, the tax treatment of a liquidating distribution of cash or property is the same as the tax treatment for a nonliquidating distribution. A partner can recognize a capital loss only if cash is distributed and the amount distributed is less than the taxpayer's basis in the partnership.

A nonliquidating cash distribution (i.e., dividend) from a corporation is taxable to the shareholder if the distribution comes from the corporation's current or accumulated earnings and profits. This results in double taxation of the dividend. Any amount distributed in excess of the corporation's current and accumulated earnings and profits is a tax-free return of capital to the extent of the shareholder's basis in the stock. If the amount distributed exceeds the shareholder's basis, the excess is a capital gain. There are no tax consequences for the corporation on the distribution.

The amount of the dividend on a nonliquidating corporate distribution of property is the fair market value of the property distributed. The tax treatment for the shareholder is the same as for a cash distribution. A corporation must recognize gain on a nonliquidating property distribution if the fair market value of the property distributed exceeds the adjusted basis of the property. However, it cannot recognize a loss on the distribution of property.

When a corporation makes a liquidating distribution of cash, the shareholder is treated as having sold stock to the corporation for cash. The shareholder recognizes a capital gain to the extent the cash received exceeds the stockholder's basis in the stock. The shareholder recognizes a capital loss if the amount received is less than the shareholder's basis. Unlike the situation with a nonliquidating distribution, the corporation's earnings and profits have no effect on the tax treatment of the distribution. A liquidating distribution of cash has no tax consequences for the corporation. A shareholder treats a liquidating distribution of property the same as a liquidating distribution of cash. If the fair market value of the property received is greater than the shareholder's basis, the shareholder recognizes a capital gain. If the fair market value of the property received is less than the shareholder's basis, the shareholder recognizes a capital loss. With one exception, the tax consequences for a corporation for a liquidating distribution of property are the same as those for a nonliquidating distribution. The exception is that a corporation is allowed to recognize a loss on a liquidating distribution of property.

The tax treatment of distributions by an S corporation is a combination of the tax treatment afforded partnerships and partners and that for corporations and shareholders. This combination of treatments occurs because an S corporation has tax attributes of both a conduit entity and a corporation. For both nonliquidating and liquidating distributions of cash, the tax treatment is similar to that for a partnership. The distribution is tax-free, and shareholders recognize gain only if the amount distributed exceeds the shareholders' basis in the stock. A loss is never recognized. As with a partnership, a cash distribution has no tax consequences for an S corporation.

For a nonliquidating or liquidating distribution of property, the shareholder will recognize gain to the extent that the amount distributed exceeds the shareholder's basis. As with a corporation, the amount of the distribution is the fair market value of the property. Shareholders can recognize a loss on a liquidating distribution of property. For an S corporation, the tax treatment for liquidating and nonliquidating distributions mirrors that for a corporation. The S corporation can only recognize gain on a nonliquidating distribution of property, whereas it can recognize both a gain and a loss on a liquidating distribution of property.

## 14-4 TAX PLANNING

LO 4
Create tax-planning opportunities using different forms of organization.

This section discusses various tax-planning techniques that can reduce the tax liability of an individual owner or the overall tax liability of a family. With proper tax planning, owners of a corporation can minimize their overall tax liability by ensuring that the income earned by the entity takes full advantage of the flat corporate tax rate. A technique for reducing the overall tax liability of a family that owns a business is to employ the children of the family in the business. Finally, a tax-planning technique that reduces a family's overall tax liability but requires the transfer of an ownership interest in the business is the creation of a family partnership or S corporation.

### 14-4a Income Splitting

One basic tax-planning use of entities involves splitting income among two or more taxable entities. Income splitting can provide tax savings because of the progressive tax rate structure for individuals versus the flat tax rate (21 percent) of a corporation. That is, shifting income to the entity with the lowest marginal tax rate can reduce net tax liabilities. For example, if one entity has a marginal rate of 35 percent and a second entity has a marginal rate of 21 percent, every dollar of income shifted from the first entity to the second saves 14 cents (35 percent – 21 percent) in taxes.

**Example 52** During the current year, Kam and Juanita operate a jewelry store as a sole proprietorship. They have one child, Darianne, who is 15. The business earns $170,000 annually. Kam must pay self-employment tax on the net self-employment income from the business. Kam's net self-employment income is $156,995 ($170,000 × 92.35%), and his self-employment tax is $22,260 [($142,800 × 12.40%) + ($156,995 × 2.90%)]. One-half of the self-employment taxes paid, $11,130 ($22,260 × 50%), is a deduction for AGI. The couple has taxable income of $133,770 ($170,000 – $11,130 – $25,100) and a joint income tax liability of $20,926 {$9,328 + [22% × ($133,770 – $81,050)]}. Their total tax liability is $43,186 (20,926 + $22,260). Can the couple decrease their income tax liability by shifting business income to a corporate entity (i.e., by incorporating their business)?

**Discussion: If the income shifted is taxed at a marginal rate lower than their individual marginal tax rate, their total tax liability will decrease. Incorporation decreases the marginal tax rate from 22% to 21%. By incorporating the business, Kam is no longer subject to self-employment tax. However, both Kam and the corporation must pay Social Security tax on his salary. If Kam and Juanita incorporate their business and pay Kam a salary of $120,000, they shift $50,000 of their individual income to the corporation. In addition, by paying only Kam a salary (instead of paying salary to both Kam and Juanita), they minimize their Social Security tax liability. Kam will pay $9,180 ($120,000 × 7.65%) in Social Security taxes, and the corporation is required to match this amount. Only the Social Security taxes paid by the corporation are deductible. Therefore, the corporate taxable income is $40,820 ($170,000 – $120,000 salary – $9,180 Social Security), and its tax liability is $8,572 ($40,820 × 21%). Kam and Juanita's joint taxable income is $94,900 ($120,000 – $25,100). Their joint income tax liability is $12,375 {$9,328 + [22% × ($94,900 – $81,050)]}. The total tax liability of Kam, Juanita, and the corporation is $39,307 ($12,375 + $8,572 + $9,180 + $9,180). Therefore, Kam and Juanita will save $3,879 ($43,186 – $39,307) by incorporating their business. If Kam and Juanita were in a higher individual marginal tax rate, the tax savings would be greater. Note: To better illustrate the concept, the solution does not include the QBI deduction.**

## 14-4b Children as Employees

Another tax-planning strategy for reducing the taxable income of a sole proprietorship, partnership, S corporation, or a corporation is the valid employment of an owner-employee's children in the business. This strategy lets the entity deduct the wages or salaries as expenses, lowering the net income, and it may permit the child to receive income tax-free. That is, the child can earn as much as $12,550 in 2021 with no income tax liability because of the standard deduction amount for single individuals. Therefore, employing children in a business can allow a transfer of cash from parents to children free of income tax.

**Example 53** Return to the facts of example 52. Assume that Kam and Juanita operate the jewelry store as a corporation. They employ their daughter, Darianne, to answer the telephone, take messages, prepare invoice forms, and do light cleanup. During the year, she works 500 hours after school and during summer vacation and is paid $10 per hour, an amount reasonable for the tasks performed. Kam and Juanita are the only stockholders of the corporation. If this is Darianne's only income, what is her tax liability for the year? What effect does employing Darianne have on the corporation's tax liability?

**Discussion: The $5,000 ($10 × 500 hours) Darianne earns is taxable income. Because she is allowed a standard deduction amount of $5,350 (the lower of her earned income plus $350 or $12,550), Darianne's taxable income is zero and she has no tax liability. However, she must pay Social Security tax of $383 ($5,000 × 7.65%) on the salary she receives. The corporation also must pay $383 in Social Security tax. The salary paid to Darianne and the Social Security tax paid reduce the corporation's taxable income to $35,437 ($40,820 − $5,000 − $383) and result in a tax savings of $1,130 ($5,383 × 21% marginal tax rate).**

Negative aspects of using children as employees include the incidence of payroll taxes and the possibility that the IRS will assert that this related party transaction fails the test for reasonable compensation. Related parties often face scrutiny of their transactions for reasonableness. Therefore, wages paid to children who are employees of their parents' business must be comparable to wages paid to any other employee for comparable services.

**Example 54** Return to the facts of example 53. Assume that Darianne is paid $50 per hour. Will her salary pass IRS scrutiny?

**Discussion: Because the wages appear to be excessive for the tasks performed, the IRS would probably find that her compensation is unreasonable. The IRS would deny the corporation a deduction for $20,000 [($50 − $10) × 500 hours] of the wages paid to Darianne. The additional $20,000 would be treated as a dividend from the corporation to her parents and a nontaxable gift from her parents to her. The tax effect of disallowing the $20,000 in salary paid to Darianne is to increase the family's tax liability. Because the $20,000 is dividend income to her parents, the family's tax liability increases by $1,125 ($7,500 × 15%).**

A benefit of operating a business as a sole proprietorship is that the owner's child is not subject to Social Security taxes when validly employed in the business. The wages paid are deductible expenses of the business, and the parent-proprietor also saves 7.65 percent (employer's share of Social Security) of the child's wages. This procedure lets the parent-proprietor put cash into the hands of children with positive results. In addition, if the child's earned income is less than $12,550, the child pays no income tax.[28]

**Example 55** Assume the same facts as in example 53, except that Kam and Juanita operate the business as a sole proprietorship. Assume that Darianne is paid $5,000 to answer telephone calls, take messages, prepare invoice forms, and do light cleanup. What amount must the sole proprietorship and Darianne pay in Social Security taxes?

**Discussion: Because Darianne is employed by her parents in their business, the sole proprietorship is not required to pay Social Security taxes on her salary. By using a sole proprietorship instead of a corporation, the business is able to save $383 ($5,000 × 7.65%) in Social Security taxes.**

## 14-4c Family Entities

Another form of income splitting is the creation of a family partnership or family S corporation. Both techniques involve the use of family members as partners or shareholders of the business. Generally, from a tax-planning perspective, a family partnership and a family S corporation achieve identical results. Therefore, we discuss the two entities as one tax-planning technique and refer to it as a *family entity*.

A **family entity** combines the tax-planning aspects of the progressive tax rate schedule with the use of the owner's children or relatives to minimize the overall family tax liability. With a family entity, the children or relatives become owners (partners) in the business. Because the income from a family entity flows through to each owner, the net income from the business is taxed at the owner's marginal tax rate regardless of whether the children are employed by the business.

**Example 56** Return to the facts of example 52. Assume that the business is operated as an S corporation and that Kam and Juanita each own 50% of the corporation. How is the $170,000 in income earned by the S corporation taxed?

**Discussion: Because an S corporation is a conduit entity, the corporation is not subject to tax. In addition, the income received by Kam and Juanita is not subject to Social Security and/or self-employment tax. Kam and Juanita will each report $85,000 in income, and their joint taxable income is $144,900 ($170,000 − $25,100 standard deduction). Their joint individual income tax liability is $23,375 {$9,328 + [22% × ($144,900 − $81,050)]}. The income tax with an S corporation is slightly higher than with a sole proprietorship because of the tax deduction a sole proprietor receives for paying self-employment taxes. However, Kam and Juanita's total tax liability is $19,811 less ($43,186 − $23,375) than with a sole proprietorship because they do not have to pay self-employment taxes. Their tax liability is $15,932 less ($39,307 − $23,375) than if they used the corporate form of organization.**

**Example 57** Assume the same facts as in example 56, except that only Kam works for the business but he is not paid a salary. Kam and Juanita each own 40% of the corporation, and their daughter, Darianne, owns the remaining 20%. What are the tax savings associated with operating the business as a family entity?

**Discussion: Kam and Juanita will each report $68,000 ($170,000 × 40%) in income, and Darianne will report $34,000 ($170,000 × 20%) in income. Kam and Juanita's joint taxable income is $110,900 [($68,000 × 2) − $25,100 standard deduction]. Their joint individual income tax liability is $15,895 {$9,328 + [22% × ($110,900 − $81,050)]}. Darianne's taxable income is $32,900 ($34,000 − $1,100 standard deduction), and her tax liability is $3,749 {$995 + [12% × ($32,900 − $9,950)]}. Her standard deduction is limited to $1,100 because the income from the S corporation is unearned. By using a family entity, the total tax liability for the family is $19,644 ($15,895 + $3,749), resulting in a tax savings of $3,731 ($23,375 − $19,644). Again, no family member pays Social Security and/or self-employment taxes.**

Examples 56 and 57 show that the use of a family entity is most effective when the income is diverted to someone other than the owner's spouse. However, to minimize the overall tax liability of the family, the owner(s) must agree to share a portion of the income and agree to transfer an ownership interest in the entity. The use of a family entity arrangement is not without risk. In addition to the potential for causing family disputes in the future, these entities often face challenges from the IRS. First, if the owner-employees are not paid a salary or are paid a minimal salary, the IRS could argue that the salary of the owner-employee is unreasonably low and that this low salary is an attempt to avoid Social Security taxes. As discussed in Chapter 13, by not paying a salary to an owner-employee, both the corporation and the employee are able to avoid the payment of Social Security taxes. Because the S corporation does not pay Social Security taxes, this increases the amount available for distribution to the owners. From the owner-employees' perspective, not paying Social Security tax on their pro rata share of the income increases their after-tax cash flow.

**Example 58** Assume the same facts as in example 57, except that Kam is paid a salary of $30,000. What is the total income tax paid by the owners of the family entity?

**Discussion: Because Kam receives a salary, he must pay Social Security taxes of $2,295 ($30,000 × 7.65%). The corporation must match this amount. By deducting the salary paid to Kam and the corporation's share of the Social Security tax, the amount of income that will flow through to the owners is reduced to $137,705 ($170,000 − $30,000 − $2,295). Because Kam and Juanita each own 40% of the S corporation, their share of the income is $110,164 ($137,705 × 40% × 2). Kam and Juanita have a joint taxable income of $115,064 ($110,164 + $30,000 − $25,100 standard deduction), and their joint individual income tax liability is $16,811 {$9,328 + [22% × ($115,064 − $81,050)]}. Darianne's share of the income is $27,541 ($137,705 × 20%). Her taxable income is $26,441 ($27,541 − $1,100 standard deduction), and her tax liability is $2,974 {$995 + [12% × ($26,441 − $9,950)]}. The total tax liability for the family, including the Social Security tax paid by Kam and the corporation, is $24,375 ($16,811 + $2,974 + $2,295 + $2,295). This results in an increase of $4,731 ($24,375 − $19,644) over the tax liability calculated in example 57 when no salary is paid.**

Even if the corporation pays an owner-employee a salary to avoid being accused of trying to avoid Social Security taxes, the IRS might question whether the compensation paid to the owner-employee is reasonable. If the IRS determines that the compensation is not reasonable (too low) for the duties and responsibilities of that position, the IRS has the authority to determine the appropriate amount of compensation that should be paid.

## 14-4d Planning Commentary

A simple formula that lets individuals select the best entity, or combination of entities, to meet their tax-planning objectives does not exist. Each taxpayer has a unique set of objectives, and these are intertwined with a unique set of personal and business attributes. All the information must be weighed and considered in developing a sound tax plan regarding the choice of entity. The corporate entity may reduce corporate taxable income by deducting owner-employee salaries and fringe benefits. However, this advantage must be weighed against the double taxation of dividends. Generally, S corporations and partnerships offer many similar advantages and disadvantages. Primarily, the flow-through nature of their tax attributes makes these two forms of business quite popular. However, these flow-through entities restrict the ability of owner (partner)-employees to receive tax-free some of the employee fringe benefits available to employees of a corporation. In addition to protecting the personal wealth of owners, the limited liability afforded by S corporation status makes capital acquisition easier. To obtain these S corporation benefits, owners are subject to many of the disadvantages of the corporate form. For example, state franchise fees, organizational costs, filing fees, and costs of record keeping can be substantial.

A sole proprietorship is the least expensive entity from an administrative standpoint and provides some important tax benefits when taxpayers employ their children. However, a sole proprietorship also has many of the disadvantages associated with S corporations and partnerships. Only by examining both the tax and nontax issues (as discussed in Chapter 13) related to using each type of entity can an owner decide the proper organizational form of the business.

# CHAPTER SUMMARY

This chapter continues the discussion of factors affecting the choice of business entity by examining factors associated with the operation of and distributions by various entities. The discussion involving operations focuses on factors affecting the computation of tax liability for each type of entity. The tax consequences of taking earnings out of an entity are examined in the section on distributions. Both of these topics greatly influence the choice of business entity.

After an entity starts doing business, it must report the results of its operations to the government. Sole proprietorships, partnerships, and S corporations must separately state those items of income that receive special tax treatment at the ownership level. In addition, the deductibility of losses flowing from a partnership or an S corporation may be limited in three ways. First, losses are deductible only to the extent of a partner's or S corporation shareholder's basis. Second, losses are limited to a partner's or S corporation shareholder's amount at risk in the activity. Third, if the partner's or S corporation shareholder's interest in the entity is a passive activity, the loss is deductible only to the extent allowed by the passive activity loss rules.

A corporation is subject to several special provisions that affect its taxable income. Net capital gains receive no special treatment, and capital losses are deductible only against capital gains. Net capital losses are carried back three years and forward five years and used to offset capital gains. Corporations are subject to an additional 20 percent depreciation recapture on gains from the sale of Section 1250 property. To avoid triple taxation, corporations receive a deduction for dividends received from domestic corporations. The passive activity loss rules do not generally apply to corporations. A closely held corporation is allowed to deduct passive losses only against active business income. A corporation is allowed to deduct charitable contributions up to a maximum of 10 percent of taxable income. A net operating loss can be carried forward indefinitely, but the loss can only offset 80 percent of taxable income for the year.

Partners and S corporation shareholders must adjust their basis for additional capital investments and capital recoveries. Although the basis adjustments are similar, partners are allowed to add their share of the debts of the partnership to their basis, whereas an S corporation shareholder cannot add debt to basis. All other things being equal, this allows a partner a larger basis for deducting losses than an S corporation shareholder.

A nonliquidating distribution of cash or property from a partnership is tax-free unless the cash distributed exceeds the partner's basis. In that case, the excess is treated as a capital gain. The distribution has no effect on the partnership. Generally, the tax treatment in complete liquidation of a partnership is the same as the tax treatment for a nonliquidating distribution, except that a loss can be recognized if cash is the only asset distributed.

However, a nonliquidating cash distribution from a corporate entity to a shareholder is subject to tax. Because the corporation previously paid tax on the distribution, the distribution to the owner results in double taxation. A distribution of appreciated property is income to both the shareholder and the corporation. The shareholder is taxed on the fair market value of the property received, and the corporation is taxed on the difference between the fair market value of the property distributed and its basis in the property. A corporation cannot recognize loss on a nonliquidating distribution of property. The rules for a liquidating distribution are the same except that both the shareholder and the corporation can recognize a loss on the distribution of cash or property.

Generally, a nonliquidating cash or property distribution from an S corporation is tax-free. If the amount of distribution exceeds the shareholder's basis, the shareholder will recognize a capital gain. A cash distribution has no tax consequences for the S corporation. However, a property distribution is taxable to an S corporation to the extent that the fair market value of the property exceeds its basis. The S corporation cannot recognize a loss on the distribution of the property. The rules for a liquidating distribution are the same except that both the shareholder and the S corporation can recognize a loss on the distribution of cash or property.

Innumerable tax-planning opportunities exist when all the various entities are considered. For example, proper use of income splitting for a family entity can provide substantial tax savings. However, a simple formula that lets individuals select the best entity, or entities, for meeting their objectives does not exist. All the taxpayer's objectives and characteristics need to be analyzed in conjunction with the attributes of the various entities.

# KEY TERMS

at-risk rules (p. 14-6)
charitable contribution (p. 14-14)
closely held corporation (p. 14-14)
corporate depreciation recapture (p. 14-11)
corporate distribution (p. 14-24)
dividend (p. 14-24)
dividends-received deduction (DRD) (p. 14-12)
donated inventory (p. 14-15)
family entity (p. 14-32)
liquidating distribution (p. 14-21)
nonliquidating distribution (p. 14-21)
partnership distribution (p. 14-22)

# PRIMARY TAX LAW SOURCES

[1]Sec. 703—Requires a partnership to state separately the items of income, gain, losses, deductions, and credits provided in Sec. 702 in computing its taxable income.

[2]Reg. Sec. 1.702-1—Describes the items that must be separately reported to partners by a partnership.

[3]Sec. 704(d)—Allows deduction of partnership losses to the extent of each partner's basis. Provides for the carryover of any disallowed loss until the partner's basis is restored.

[4]Sec. 707(b)(1)—Provides that a partner who owns more than a 50 percent interest in a partnership is subject to the related party rules of Sec. 267.

[5]Sec. 707(b)(2)—Provides that any gain on a sale between a partner and a partnership in which the partner owns more than a 50 percent interest is ordinary income if the property is ordinary income property for either the partner or the partnership.

[6]Reg. Sec. 1.707-1—Describes transactions between a partner and a partnership that are treated as being made at arm's length.

[7]Sec. 705—Sets forth the rules for determining the basis of a partner's investment in a partnership.

[8]Reg. Sec. 1.704-(1)(d)(2)—Prescribes the calculation of a partner's adjusted basis for purposes of deducting losses.

[9]Sec. 291—Requires corporations to recapture an additional 20 percent of the depreciation on Section 1250 property.

[10]Sec. 243—Allows corporations a deduction for dividends received from domestic corporations. Describes the procedures for calculating and determining the limitations on the dividends-received deduction.

[11]Reg. Sec. 1.246-2—Describes the limitations on the dividends-received deduction.

[12]Reg. Sec. 1.469-1T(g)—Describes the limitations on the deductions of passive activity losses by closely held corporations. Defines a closely held corporation for purposes of the passive activity loss rules.

[13]Sec. 170—Provides the rules for the deduction of charitable contributions of individuals and corporations.

[14]Sec. 170(e)(3)—Prescribes the treatment of inventory given to certain qualified charities by a corporation.

[15]Sec. 1366(a)—Requires separate statement of S corporation items that could affect the tax liability of any shareholder.

[16]Sec. 1366(d)—Allows deduction of S corporation losses to the extent of a shareholder's adjusted basis in a debt owed by the corporation to the shareholder.

[17]Sec. 1367(b)(2)—Requires any net increase in an S corporation shareholder's basis to be applied to restore the basis of any debt that was reduced for the deduction of a loss before the shareholder's basis in the S corporation stock is increased.

[18]Sec. 1367(a)—Provides the rules for the adjustment of the basis of stock in an S corporation.

[19]Sec. 1366(d)—Prescribes the order in which an S corporation shareholder's basis is adjusted in determining the deductibility of losses.

[20]Sec. 1060—Requires an allocation of the purchase price of the identifiable assets of a business, either by agreement with the seller or by use of the relative fair market values.

[21]Sec. 731—Describes the situations in which partners recognize gain or loss on the distribution of partnership assets; provides that the partnership does not recognize any gain or loss upon the distribution of assets to a partner.

[22]Sec. 301—Provides the tax treatment of corporate dividend distributions.

[23]Sec. 316—Provides that distributions are made out of earnings and profits of the current year first and that a distribution is a taxable dividend if paid out of current or accumulated earnings and profits.

[24]Sec. 311(b)—Provides that a corporation cannot recognize a loss on the distribution of property but that gain is recognized on the distribution of appreciated property.

[25]Sec. 336—Provides that a corporation can recognize a loss on the distribution of property in complete liquidation.

[26]Sec. 1368—Describes the tax effects of distributions by S corporations to their shareholders.

[27]Sec. 1367—Describes the rules for adjusting the basis of a shareholder's stock in an S corporation to account for income, losses, distributions, and expenses of the corporation.

[28]Sec. 3121(b)(3)—Excludes from Social Security tax wages earned by children younger than 18 who are employed in their parents' business.

# DISCUSSION QUESTIONS

1. **LO1** Why do sole proprietors not include all the items of income and deductions related to their business in the calculation of the business's operating income?
2. **LO1** Why must a partnership separately state certain items in reporting its income to the partners?
3. **LO1** Partners can generally deduct losses from the partnership. What are the three limitations on the deduction of partnership losses?
4. **LO2** Explain how a partner's basis in a partnership can differ from the partner's at-risk amount.
5. **LO1** Under what circumstances can a partner transact with a partnership at arm's length?
6. **LO2** Explain the general rationale for adjusting the basis of partners and S corporation shareholders.
7. **LO1** Explain the general difference in the treatment of each of the following items for a corporation:
   a. Capital gains and losses
   b. Passive losses
   c. Charitable contributions
   d. Dividends received
8. **LO1** Are passive losses treated the same for all types of entities?
9. **LO1** How does the recapture of depreciation on a Section 1250 property for a corporation differ from that of other entities?

10. **LO1** What is the purpose of the dividends-received deduction?

11. **LO1, 2** What are the similarities and differences in the income tax treatment of a partnership and an S corporation?

12. **LO3** Compare the tax treatment of a nonliquidating distribution of cash or property and a liquidating distribution of cash or property for each of the following entities:
    a. Sole proprietorship
    b. Partnership
    c. Corporation
    d. S corporation

13. **LO4** Explain the advantages to taxpayers of hiring their children to work in their businesses.

# PROBLEMS

The following information is to be used for problems 14–17:
Wrigley Juice has the following income, expense, and loss items for the current year:

| | |
|---|---|
| Sales | $850,000 |
| Tax-exempt interest | 40,000 |
| Long-term capital gain | 85,000 |
| Short-term capital loss | 35,000 |
| Passive activity loss | 20,000 |
| Cost of goods sold | 480,000 |
| Depreciation | 40,000 |
| Section 179 expense | 25,000 |
| Other operating expenses | 200,000 |
| Net operating loss (from preceding year) | 24,000 |

14. **LO1** Assume that Wrigley Juice is owned by Calvin as a sole proprietorship. Explain the effect of Wrigley's results on Calvin's tax return.

15. **LO1** Assume that Wrigley Juice is a partnership owned equally by Vinnie and Chandra. Explain the effect of Wrigley's results on Vinnie's and Chandra's tax returns.

16. **LO1** Assume that Wrigley Juice is a corporation owned by Cora. Explain the effect of Wrigley's results on Cora's tax return.

Communication Skills

17. **LO1** Assume that Wrigley Juice is an S corporation owned equally by Henry, Iris, and Jasmine. Prepare a memo explaining the effect of Wrigley's results on Henry's, Iris's, and Jasmine's tax returns.

18. **LO1** EndLand Company reports the following results for the current year:

| | |
|---|---|
| Gross profit from sales | $350,000 |
| Dividends received (less than 20 percent ownership) | 40,000 |
| Long-term capital loss | 60,000 |
| Salaries paid to employees | 70,000 |
| Salaries paid to owners | 130,000 |
| Investment expenses | 10,000 |
| Depreciation (including $10,000 expensed under Section 179) | 60,000 |
| Charitable contributions | 30,000 |

    a. Assume that EndLand is a partnership owned by Kira (60 percent) and Justin (40 percent). Kira receives a salary of $70,000, and Justin receives a salary of $60,000. The salaries are not guaranteed payments. Determine the tax treatment of EndLand's operating results and the effects of the results on Kira and Justin.
    b. Assume the same facts as in part a, except that EndLand is a corporation. Determine the tax treatment of EndLand's operating results and the effect of the results on Kira and Justin.
    c. Assume the same facts as in part b, except that EndLand is an S corporation. Determine the tax treatment of EndLand's operating results and the effect of the results on Kira and Justin.

19. **LO1** Return to the facts of problem 18. Determine the total tax liability for EndLand, Kira, and Justin for parts a, b, and c. Assume that Kira has net taxable income from other sources of $50,000, which includes a $30,000 long-term capital gain. Justin's net taxable income from other sources is $20,000. Assume Kira and Justin are both single and that both have income from other sources that offset their allowable deductions.

20. **LO1, 2** Fawn contributes undeveloped land with a basis of $15,000 and a fair market value of $90,000 to the Deer Partnership for a 25 percent interest in the partnership. What is Fawn's share of the partnership's operating income or loss, and how does the share affect Fawn's basis in each of the following situations? Assume that Fawn is a material participant in the partnership.
   a. Deer Partnership reports an operating loss of $40,000 for the current year.
   b. Deer Partnership reports operating income of $25,000 for the current year.
   c. Deer Partnership reports an operating loss of $80,000 for the current year.

21. **LO1, 2** Binh has a 50 percent interest in the Lamonica Partnership with a basis of $10,000 at the end of the year before accounting for his share of the current year's losses. The partnership suffers ordinary losses of $60,000. Assume that Binh is a material participant in the partnership.
   a. How much of the partnership's losses may Binh deduct? What is Binh's adjusted basis at the end of the year?
   b. Assume that next year, Binh makes additional capital contributions to Lamonica Partnership of $16,000, the partnership incurs $9,000 in additional debt, and the partnership realizes operating income of $2,000. How do these items affect Binh's adjusted basis?

22. **LO1, 2** Return to the facts of problem 21. How would your answers change if Binh is not a material participant in the Lamonica Partnership? Assume Binh has no other passive income in either year. Write a memo to Binh explaining what he must do to achieve mutual participation. Communication Skills

23. **LO1, 2** Annabell and Eva own and manage Purity Forms Development. Annabell's and Eva's bases in Purity at the beginning of the year are $18,000 and $24,000, respectively. During the current year, Purity suffers a $90,000 net operating loss. Purity's only debt is a $45,000 nonrecourse debt on its office building (incurred during the current year). Determine the deductibility of the net operating loss under each of the following assumptions:
   a. Purity is a partnership. Annabell owns one-third interest, and Eva owns two-thirds interest in the partnership.
   b. Purity is a corporation. Annabell owns one-third of the stock, and Eva owns two-thirds of the Purity stock.
   c. Purity is an S corporation. Annabell owns one-third of the stock, and Eva owns two-thirds of the Purity stock.

24. **LO1, 2** Assume the same facts as in problem 23, except that the $45,000 debt is a loan that Annabell made to Purity. How would your answers to parts a and c change? Assume that the beginning basis numbers do not reflect the debt to Annabell.

25. **LO1** Lanny is an owner of the Chasteen Partnership. He sells land to the partnership for $40,000 for which he had paid $52,000. Discuss the treatment of the sale under the following assumptions:
   a. Lanny owns a 30 percent interest in the partnership.
   b. Lanny owns a 60 percent interest in the partnership.
   c. Assume the same facts as in part b. Several years later, Chasteen sells the land for $60,000. What is Chasteen's recognized gain on the sale?

26. **LO1** Assume the same facts as in problem 25, except that Lanny sells the land to the partnership for $60,000. He held the land for investment. Chasteen is a real estate company. How would your answers to parts a and b change?

27. **LO1** Louis is the president and 40 percent owner of Adams Company. His basis in Adams at the beginning of the year is $8,000. Adams suffers a net operating loss of $15,000 during the current year. Louis receives a $5,000 cash distribution from Adams during the year. Determine the effect of the company's results on Louis under each of the following assumptions:
    a. Adams Company is a partnership.
    b. Adams Company is a corporation.
    c. Adams Company is an S corporation.

Communication Skills

28. **LO1, 2** Natrone pays $35,000 for stock in an S corporation and receives shares equal to a 20 percent interest in the corporation in the current year. At the same time, he pays $35,000 for a 20 percent interest in a general partnership. Both entities incur mortgage debt of $60,000 during the current year, and both report ordinary taxable income of $20,000. What is the maximum cash distribution each entity can make to Natrone this year without causing him to recognize income? Write a memo to Natrone explaining your answers in terms of the underlying concepts and facts that support your calculations.
29. **LO1** The Boo-Ball Corporation receives dividend income of $200,000 from Flew-Ball, a domestic corporation. Boo-Ball owns 70 percent of Flew-Ball. Boo-Ball's net income from operations is $50,000. What is Boo-Ball's dividends-received deduction?
30. **LO1** The John Corporation suffers a $22,000 net loss from operations for the current year but receives $150,000 in dividend income from corporations in which it owns 50 percent of the stock. What are the dividends-received deduction and the corporation's actual taxable income for the current year?
31. **LO1** The Bat-Ball Corporation incurs a net loss from operations of $62,000 for the current year. Bat-Ball receives $175,000 in cash dividends from 30 percent-owned domestic corporations. What are the dividends-received deduction and the actual taxable income for the current tax year?
32. **LO1** Adele owns 60 percent of Trouble, Inc., a corporation. During the current annual accounting period, Trouble has an operating income of $19,000, dividend income from investments in stock of other corporations of $2,800, interest income from First National of $2,200, and a loss from an investment in a limited partnership of $24,000. How much of the passive activity loss can Trouble use to offset other income?
33. **LO1** Elvira owns 100 percent of the stock of Midnite Corporation, a manufacturer of galobnotites. During the current year, Midnite has operating income of $50,000, dividend income of $16,000 from investments in other corporations, and losses from investments in limited partnerships of $46,000. It pays $20,000 in dividends.
    a. What are the amounts of taxable income and tax liability reported by Midnite for the current year?
    b. Assume that Midnite Corporation is operated as an S corporation. Explain why the amount of taxable income resulting from the items reported by both Midnite Corporation and Elvira are different from your answers in part a.
34. **LO1** Lulu Enterprises sells a building with an adjusted basis of $40,000 for $85,000. Lulu paid $60,000 for the building five years ago. What is the treatment of the gain on the sale of the building if
    a. Lulu is a sole proprietorship owned by Horace?
    b. Lulu is a partnership owned equally by Doreen and Fatima?
    c. Lulu is a corporation owned equally by Doreen and Fatima?
    d. Lulu is an S corporation owned equally by Doreen and Fatima?
35. **LO1** Lacy Corporation sells equipment and a building during the current year. The equipment, which cost $14,000 in 2018, is sold for $9,000. The equipment was expensed using the Section 179 election in 2018. The building, purchased in 2013 for $130,000, is sold for $180,000. The adjusted basis of the building at the date of sale is $95,000. How should Lacy report the gains on the sale of the equipment and the building?

36. **LO1** Assume the same facts as in problem 35, except that Lacy is an S corporation equally owned by Jorge and Gloria. How should Lacy report the gains on the sale of the equipment and the building?

37. **LO1** The Baker Corporation has the following entries on its books for the current tax year:

| | |
|---|---|
| Net income from operations | $120,000 |
| Dividends received (50 percent rules) | 14,000 |
| Charitable contributions made in current year | 13,000 |
| Charitable contribution carryover from the previous year | 1,900 |

What is the maximum charitable contribution deduction for the current year? What is Baker's taxable income for the current year?

38. **LO1** Fairplay Corporation has gross income of $150,000 and taxable income of $50,000. The company includes no special deductions in the calculation of its taxable income. While reviewing the tax return, Fairplay's accountant finds $20,000 in charitable contributions improperly classified as advertising and promotion expense. He sends the return back to the tax department for correction. Write a letter to Fairplay's accountant explaining why a correction to taxable income must be made. Communication Skills

39. **LO1** The New Tech Corporation contributes some of its inventory of scientific equipment to the computer department of Great University during the current year. At the date of the contribution, the equipment has a fair market value of $38,000. New Tech's basis in the equipment is $12,000.
   a. How much can New Tech deduct as a charitable contribution?
   b. Would your answer change if New Tech's basis in the equipment were $16,000?

40. **LO1** Mel's Super Groceries, Inc., donates $70,000 worth of canned food with a basis of $50,000 to St. Rebecca's Homeless Shelter, a qualified charitable organization. How much may Mel's deduct for the charitable contribution of the canned food?

41. **LO1** Tarhari Enterprises, Inc., donates $70,000 worth of computer equipment and related software to Northwest Gifford High School. The property's basis is $30,000. How much may Tarhari deduct for the charitable contribution of the computer equipment and related software?

42. **LO1** The Viking Corporation has the following items of income for 2021:

| | |
|---|---|
| Operating income | $350,000 |
| Dividend income (12 percent-owned corporations) | 15,000 |
| Long-term capital gains | 9,000 |
| Short-term capital gains | 3,000 |
| Capital loss carryover from 2020 | 8,000 |
| Charitable cash contributions | 12,000 |
| Net operating loss carryover from 2020 | 35,000 |

   a. Calculate the corporation's 2021 taxable income and its tax liability.
   b. Assume that Viking is, and always has been, an S corporation wholly owned by Fran, a single taxpayer with no other income or deductions. Will either Viking Corporation or Fran realize any tax savings, given the income and liability determined in part a? Explain.

43. **LO1** Charger, Inc., has the following items for the current year: Communication Skills

| | |
|---|---|
| Net operating income | $150,000 |
| Dividend income (50 percent-owned corporation) | 40,000 |
| Charitable cash contributions | 20,000 |
| Net operating loss carryover | 10,000 |

a. What are the corporation's taxable income and tax liability?
b. Assume that Charger is, and always has been, an S corporation wholly owned by Suzanne, a married taxpayer with no dependents and no other income or deductions. What are the tax liabilities of Charger and Suzanne?
c. Write a memo explaining why the answers in parts a and b are different.

44. **LO1** Myrna operates a plumbing business as a sole proprietorship. During the year, she sells the business to Tonya for $175,000. The assets sold and the allocation of the purchase price are as follows:

| | Adjusted Basis | Purchase Price |
|---|---|---|
| Plumbing parts | $ 6,000 | $ 8,000 |
| Building | 42,500 | 93,900 |
| Land | 10,000 | 15,100 |
| Equipment | 6,500 | 30,600 |
| Goodwill | -0- | 27,400 |
| Total assets | $65,000 | $175,000 |

Myrna acquired the building 10 years ago for $70,000. She acquired the equipment on various dates, paying a total of $30,000 for it. What are the tax consequences of the sale for Myrna?

45. **LO2, 3** Maurice, Lawrence, and Kerwin own and operate a chain of sandwich shops as a partnership. Maurice owns 40 percent, and his basis in the partnership is $80,000. Lawrence, a 35 percent owner, has a basis of $50,000, and Kerwin, who owns 25 percent, has a basis in the partnership of $15,000. What are the tax consequences and basis effects for each partner if the partnership's ordinary income is $70,000 and each receives a cash distribution of $30,000?

46. **LO3** The Boyle brothers own and operate a microbrewery. The partnership has 2 equal partners, Ed and John. At the close of the current year, John's basis in the partnership is $42,000, and Ed's basis is $31,000. What are the tax and basis effects if at year end, the partnership distributes to Ed
a. Property with a basis of $15,000 and a fair market value of $18,000?
b. Property with a basis of $12,000 and a fair market value of $35,000 along with $10,000 in cash?

Communication Skills

47. **LO3** The Hartford Group is a partnership owned and operated by June and Joyce. June owns a 60 percent interest, and her basis in the partnership is $33,000. Joyce owns a 40 percent interest, and her basis is $18,000. At the end of the year, both June and Joyce decide to retire and liquidate the business. Write a memo discussing the consequences for each partner if June and Joyce receive cash distributions of $455,000 and $28,000, respectively.

48. **LO3** Machela, a single individual, owns all the stock in Gordon Corporation, which reports taxable income of $55,000. The corporation distributes the $55,000 in earnings as a dividend. Machela also receives a salary from the company of $67,000. She has itemized deductions for the year of $21,000. What are Machela's and Gordon Corporation's tax liabilities for the year?

49. **LO3** Dance Corporation distributes $150,000 in cash to its shareholders during the current year. Accumulated earnings and profits are $25,000 at the beginning of the year. Current earnings and profits are $75,000. Jack, the sole shareholder of Dance Corporation, has a basis of $40,000 in the stock. What is the tax effect of this distribution for Jack?

Communication Skills

50. **LO3** Toy Corporation distributes $175,000 in cash ($1.75 per share) when its current and accumulated earnings and profits are $40,000. What is the effect of the distribution for Bernice, who owns 500 shares of Toy stock for which she paid $8,000? Write a letter to Bernice explaining the tax results using the income tax concepts discussed in the text.

51. **LO3** During the current year, Snowden Corporation distributes $600,000 in cash ($2 per share) to its shareholders. Yong owns 300 shares of Snowden stock with a basis of $9,000. What are the tax consequences for Yong if Snowden's current and accumulated earnings and profits are
   a. $300,000?
   b. $720,000?
52. **LO3** In the current year, Penelope receives a nonliquidating distribution of land from Royal Corporation. The corporation has earnings and profits of $300,000. What is the tax effect of the distribution for Royal and for Penelope if
   a. The land has a fair market value of $30,000 and a basis of $18,000?
   b. The land has a fair market value of $25,000 and a basis of $35,000?
53. **LO3** In the current year, Simon receives a liquidating cash distribution of $32,000 from Torborg Corporation. What is the tax effect of the distribution for Torborg and for Simon if
   a. Simon has a basis in his stock of $42,000?
   b. Simon has a basis in his stock of $19,000?
   c. Assume the same facts as in parts a and b, except that Torborg is an S corporation. What is the tax effect for Torborg and Simon?
54. **LO3** In the current year, Jose receives a liquidating property distribution from Valenzuela Corporation. The basis of the property distributed is $25,000. What is the tax effect of the distribution for Valenzuela and for Jose if
   a. The property distributed has a fair market value of $30,000, and Jose has a basis in his stock of $38,000?
   b. The property distributed has a fair market value of $20,000, and Jose has a basis in his stock of $18,000?
   c. Assume the same facts as in parts a and b, except that Valenzuela is an S corporation and Jose owns 20 percent of the stock. What is the tax effect of the distribution for Valenzuela and for Jose?
55. **LO3** Marco owns all the shares of Craig Corporation, which operates as an S corporation. His basis in the stock is $47,000. What are the tax consequences for Marco and the Craig Corporation if
   a. Marco receives a nonliquidating cash distribution of $18,000 from the S corporation?
   b. Marco receives a nonliquidating cash distribution of $50,000 from the S corporation?
   c. Marco receives a nonliquidating property distribution from the S corporation? The property distributed has a fair market value of $24,000 and a basis of $14,000.
   d. Marco receives a nonliquidating property distribution from the S corporation? The property distributed has a fair market value of $14,000 and a basis of $22,000.
56. **LO3** Michelle owns all the shares of Lockett Corporation, which operates as an S corporation. Her basis in the stock is $41,000. What are the tax consequences for Michelle and Lockett Corporation if
   a. Michelle receives a liquidating cash distribution of $24,500 from the S corporation?
   b. Michelle receives a liquidating cash distribution of $41,200 from the S corporation?
   c. Michelle receives a liquidating property distribution from the S corporation? The property distributed has a fair market value of $16,400 and a basis of $4,400.
   d. Michelle receives a liquidating property distribution from the S corporation? The property distributed has a fair market value of $9,500 and a basis of $17,200.

# ISSUE IDENTIFICATION PROBLEMS

In each of the following problems, identify the tax issue(s) posed by the facts presented. Determine the possible tax consequences of each issue that you identify.

57. Lydia owns 75 percent of Flower Farms, a partnership. She also owns land that she leases to Flower Farms for $6,000 per month.
58. Michael buys a piece of property from JFK Partnership for $60,000 that has a $70,000 basis. Michael owns 80 percent of JFK partnership.
59. Irene contributes land to Micro Development Partnership for a 30 percent interest. The land's basis is $20,000, and it has a fair market value of $80,000. Micro reports a net operating loss of $100,000 for the year. Irene devotes at least 12 hours a week to managing the partnership operations.
60. Powell owns a 20 percent interest in Cooke Partnership. At the beginning of 2020, Powell's basis is $22,000. Cooke reports a $90,000 operating loss in 2020, and Powell withdraws $10,000 from the partnership. Cooke's 2021 operating income is $70,000, and Powell withdraws $10,000 from the partnership.
61. Ramrod, Inc., sells a warehouse for $350,000. It purchased the warehouse 10 years ago for $250,000 and had taken $75,000 in depreciation on the building to the date of sale.
62. Myrtle Coast Corporation has a $35,000 operating loss during the current year. Not included in the loss is a $40,000 dividend it received from a corporation in which it owns a 15 percent interest.
63. LMC, Inc., is equally owned by Larry, Maurice, and Charles. The owners are sports agents. LMC's income consists solely of fees from the owners' clients. During the current year, LMC's net income from operations is $380,000, and it receives $20,000 in interest income. The corporation owns an interest in a limited partnership that generates a $24,000 loss in the current year.
64. Assume the same facts as in problem 63, except that LMC, Inc., is an electing S corporation.
65. Kummell Corporation reports a $200,000 taxable income in the current year. Included in the taxable income calculation are $20,000 in dividends received from less-than-20 percent-owned corporations, and $30,000 in charitable contributions.
66. Milena owns a 25 percent interest in Davis Company, an S corporation. Her basis in the Davis stock is $40,000. Davis reports an operating loss of $200,000 in the current year. Davis owes Milena $25,000 on a loan she made to the company several years ago.
67. Charlene owns a 70 percent interest in Maupin Mopeds, which is organized as a partnership. She wants to open another business and needs office space for it. She has Maupin distribute a building worth $150,000 to her in lieu of her normal cash distribution. Maupin's basis in the building is $55,000. Charlene's basis in Maupin is $80,000.
68. Ballou Corporation distributes $200,000 in cash to its shareholders during the current year. Accumulated earnings and profits at the beginning of the year are $45,000, and current year earnings and profits are $105,000. Buddy owns 80 percent of Ballou and has a basis of $60,000 at the beginning of the year.

# TECHNOLOGY APPLICATIONS

Research Skills

69. Tim and his daughter, Mary, own and operate Tamar Corporation. Tim is nearing retirement and would like to transfer ownership of the corporation to Mary but would like to stay on as a paid consultant providing retirement planning for the corporation's other employees. Tamar redeems all of Tim's common

stock and gives him a contract to provide employee retirement counseling. The contract states that Tim is to be paid a flat $60,000 for his services. Tamar will provide an office in the plant where he can interact with employees who take advantage of his services. Prepare a memo to Tim and Mary outlining the likely tax outcomes associated with the redemption of Tim's stock and subsequent contractual services.

70. ADC, Inc., is a corporation that was formerly a three-person partnership. It is in the business of acquiring software and distributing it to accounting firms that need specialized software in their operations. ADC, Inc., is still owned and operated by the original three owners, who own 100 percent of its stock. ADC decides to invest in a limited partnership that buys old office buildings and converts them into condominiums. ADC reports net income from its business of $400,000 and interest on investments of $12,000. ADC's share of the limited partnership's loss for the year is $100,000. Prepare a memo to ADC's president discussing the proper tax treatment of the loss from the limited partnership investment and the impact on the closely held business. Research Skills

## DISCUSSION CASES

71. Astrid, who is single, is a sales representative for several sporting goods manufacturers. She operates her enterprise as a sole proprietorship. Astrid has one employee, Melvin, who serves as office manager for the business. Gross revenues are $250,000 annually. Annual operating expenses are:

| | |
|---|---|
| Astrid's $50,000 term life insurance policy | $ 3,000 |
| Melvin's salary | 30,000 |
| Payroll taxes and fees | 3,000 |
| Utilities | 1,200 |
| Rent | 4,800 |
| Selling expenses | 8,000 |
| Premiums paid for Melvin: | |
| $50,000 term life insurance policy | 3,000 |
| Health insurance policy | 2,700 |

Astrid takes an annual draw of $2,700 to pay for health insurance coverage equal to Melvin's. Assume Astrid is paid a salary of $100,000 and has income from other sources that offset her allowable deductions. Astrid is considering incorporating her business. Discuss the benefits that will accrue to Astrid by incorporating. Recommend any alternative courses of action. (Hint: Don't forget Social Security/self-employment tax.)

72. Bert founded Sambert Corporation a little over a year ago. He believes that his company, which sells specialized computer toys, will be very profitable over the next several years, as evidenced by its $400,000 of earnings in the current year. Although Bert does not need the income, he is interested in getting the earnings out of the company while paying the least amount of tax possible. Bert intends to work actively in the company and be paid a reasonable salary for the next five years. At the end of that time, he expects his oldest son to take over the company after finishing college. Bert knows that the salary he draws will reduce the corporation's taxable income and that he will be taxed at ordinary rates on that income. However, he is interested in the tax implications of property distributions the company might make to him either in redemption of his shares or, if something prevents his son from taking over the business, in the liquidation of the corporation. Discuss the types of distributions that a shareholder might encounter over the life cycle of the corporation and the tax implications of each type of distribution.

# TAX PLANNING CASES

73. John and Joanne have two children, Joe, 16, and Jamie, 4. John is self-employed, and Joanne works as a swimming coach for Local University. John's business is manufacturing Jaugernauts. Through the years, JoJo's Jaugernauts has been fairly successful, providing a before-tax income of approximately $100,000 per year. The business has several employees, including a secretary-receptionist, two salespeople, four production workers, and two truck drivers.

    Last year, Joanne entered a contest and won a sizable block of stock in a computer company. This stock is expected to produce approximately $10,000 per year in taxable dividends. Other than this stock, their investment assets consist mainly of savings accounts and certificates of deposits. However, in 1982, John invested in a tax shelter that provided them with tax write-offs until the Tax Reform Act of 1986 curtailed the loss deduction from the shelter (i.e., the losses are considered passive losses).

    John and Joanne have come to you for advice. They would like to rearrange their business and personal affairs to obtain a better tax situation. Discuss at least three actions (don't feel limited if you can think of more) that John and Joanne could take, and state the advantages and disadvantages of each. Specific numerical calculations are not required, but if you think such an example would help explain your point, please feel free to use it.

74. For a number of years, Nina was a mechanical engineer for a chemical company. She always enjoyed working around her home in her spare time, doing necessary repairs and maintenance. However, she was always frustrated by the multitude of tools she had to carry around to do her tasks. One evening, she designed a gizmo that could do the work of 12 common home repair tools. At first, she made a few gizmos by hand and gave them to friends as gag gifts. Their reaction to the gizmo was so enthusiastic that Nina took out a patent on it, got a loan from a friend at Local Bank, quit her job, and began a small-scale manufacturing operation.

    In setting up her business, Nina took most of her advice from her brother-in-law, an assistant district attorney. Accordingly, she organized the business as a corporation and pays salaries to herself, her husband, Stan, and their three children (ages 2, 9, and 13). In addition, she put her investment portfolio inside the corporation.

    After the first year of business, the corporate books show a loss of $25,000 after paying salaries of $30,000 to Nina, $20,000 to Stan (who continues to earn $18,000 from his full-time job), and $5,000 to each child.

    a. What tax-related mistakes has Nina made regarding the business? Be specific. State any negative effects that could arise from this arrangement.
    b. Is there anything Nina can do to rectify the problems you identified? Explain, and state how each solution you propose cures or mitigates the problem.

# ETHICS DISCUSSION CASE

Communication Skills

75. Waldo Corporation has recently retained your accounting firm to prepare its income tax return. Art, the partner in charge of the engagement, has assigned you the job of reviewing last year's return and making recommendations on the preparation of this year's return. The only item of concern on the return is a $26,000 dividends received deduction that Waldo claimed on $40,000 in dividends it received from a Swiss corporation in which it owns a 30 percent interest. Write a memorandum to Art with your recommendation on the course of action your firm should take regarding the dividends received deduction.

# Choice of Business Entity—Other Considerations

15

Learning Objectives:

LO 1 Explain the difference between defined benefit plans and defined contribution plans and the limits on the contributions associated with these plans.

LO 2 Compare and contrast Keogh, SEP, IRA, Roth, and Simple pension plans and the limits on the contributions associated with these plans.

LO 3 Explain the requirements and tax treatment of distributions from pension plans as well as the penalties that ensure the responsible administration of these plans.

LO 4 Compare and contrast the treatment of nonqualified and incentive stock options.

LO 5 Explain the issue of reasonable compensation and its tax impact on different entity forms.

LO 6 Describe how tax credits are used to achieve various policy goals and explain the tax rules applicable to the most commonly used business tax credits.

LO 7 Explain the purpose of the alternative minimum tax and how to determine an individual's alternative minimum tax liability.

LO 8 Describe common tax transactions subject to multi-national tax jurisdiction.

## concept review

### GENERAL CONCEPTS

**Administrative convenience** Those items for which the cost of compliance would exceed the revenue generated are not taxed. pg. 2-3

**Arm's-length transaction** A transaction in which all parties have bargained in good faith and for their individual benefit, not for the benefit of the transaction group. pg. 2-4

**Pay as you go** A tax should be collected as close as possible to the time in which the income is earned. pg. 2-5

**Related party** Family members and corporations that are owned by family members are considered related parties, as are certain other relationships between entities in which the power to control the substance of a transaction is evidenced through majority ownership. pg. 2-4

### ACCOUNTING CONCEPTS

**Conduit entity** An entity for which the tax attributes flow through to its owners for tax purposes. pg. 2-6

**Entity** All items of income, deductions, and so on are traced to the tax unit responsible for the item. pg. 2-6

**Substance-over-form doctrine** Transactions are to be taxed according to their true intention rather than some form that may have been contrived. pg. 2-11

### INCOME CONCEPTS

**Basis** The amount of unrecovered investment in an asset. As amounts are expended and/or recovered relative to an asset over time, the basis is adjusted in consideration of such changes. The **adjusted basis** of an asset is the original basis, plus or minus the changes in the amount of unrecovered investment. pgs. 2-13, 2-21

**Capital recovery** No income is realized until the taxpayer receives more than the amount invested to produce the income. The amount invested in an asset represents the maximum amount recoverable. pg. 2-13

**Wherewithal to pay** Income is recognized in the period in which the taxpayer has the means to pay the tax on the income. pg. 2-16

### DEDUCTION CONCEPTS

**Business purpose** To be deductible, an expenditure or a loss must have a business or other economic purpose that exceeds any tax avoidance motive. The primary motive for the transaction must be to make a profit. pg. 2-18

**Legislative grace** Any tax relief provided is the result of a specific act of Congress that must be strictly applied and interpreted. All income received is taxable unless a specific provision in the tax law excludes the income from taxation. Deductions must be approached with the philosophy that nothing is deductible unless a provision in the tax law allows the deduction. pg. 2-12

## 15-1 INTRODUCTION

This chapter completes the discussion started in Chapter 13 about choosing a business entity. Continuing with the life-cycle approach, the chapter focuses on additional operational areas in which tax issues play a role in deciding the business form for an organization. One major area in which tax law plays a critical role is employee compensation. Although many employees consider only the amount they receive in their paycheck as compensation, an individual's total compensation package often includes many other benefits. In fact, some employers pay as much as an additional 35 percent of an employee's salary in fringe benefits. How these items are treated for tax purposes for an owner-employee is critical to how a business should be organized.

This chapter first discusses different types of pension plans available to an entity and the requirements and restrictions associated with each type of plan. A discussion of stock options follows. By definition, stock options are not available to all entities. Nonqualified stock options and incentive stock options are effective compensation tools but are subject to different rules and requirements.

The chapter then discusses the effect that a tax liability can have on the choice of the organizational form. Individuals are required to pay a minimum amount of tax on their income, which is called the *alternative minimum tax.* Finally, a discussion of the tax concepts associated with foreign tax transactions affecting U.S. taxpayers is presented.

## 15-2 COMPENSATION PLANS

In today's competitive business environment, organizations must provide compensation packages that will attract and retain competent and qualified employees. A typical employee compensation package might include salary, a contribution to an employer-provided pension plan, the right to acquire stock options, and fringe benefits such as medical coverage and dependent care. However, the tax consequences associated with a compensation package can differ according to the business entity that provides the compensation, the type of pension plan offered, and whether the employee is also an owner of the entity.

### 15-2a Qualified and Nonqualified Pension Plans

LO 1
Explain the difference between defined benefit plans and defined contribution plans and the limits on the contributions associated with these plans.

A pension plan is designed to provide an employee with a source of income after retirement. A qualified pension plan offers two major advantages. First, if the taxpayer elects, contributions to the pension plan are not subject to income tax. Second, the income earned on these contributions can accumulate tax-free, and it is not taxed until it is withdrawn from the pension plan.

A pension plan can be either contributory or noncontributory. A **contributory pension plan** requires the employee to make a contribution in addition to the contribution made by the employer. In many cases the employee's contribution is a percentage (i.e., 50 percent or 100 percent) of the employer's contribution. A **noncontributory pension plan** does not require the employee to contribute but in most cases allows the employee to make a contribution to the plan. Typically, upon retirement, employees will receive an annuity of payments over their lifetime; some plans provide married employees with benefits that extend over the lifetimes of both spouses. A pension plan and Social Security income usually provide the greatest source of a retired person's income. Therefore, the earlier people begin to plan for retirement, the more savings they will have at retirement.

**Example 1** Betty, 25, is an employee of the Fossil Corporation. Wilma, 45, is an employee of the Fredstone Corporation. Both participate in a contributory pension plan that requires them to match their employers' \$50 per month contribution. If both retire at age 65 and their \$100 a month (\$50 employee + \$50 employer) contribution earns 8% compounded annually, how much will each have available upon retirement?

**Discussion: According to Table 15-1, Betty will have accumulated \$310,867 [\$1,200 per year × 259.056 (40 years at 8%)] in her pension account, whereas Wilma will**

Table 15-1

## Future Value of an Ordinary Annuity of $1 per Period

| Period (n) | 4% | 5% | 6% | 7% | 8% | 9% | 10% | 12% |
|---|---|---|---|---|---|---|---|---|
| 1 | 1.00000 | 1.00000 | 1.00000 | 1.00000 | 1.00000 | 1.00000 | 1.00000 | 1.00000 |
| 5 | 5.41632 | 5.52563 | 5.63709 | 5.75074 | 5.86660 | 5.98471 | 6.10510 | 6.35285 |
| 10 | 12.00611 | 12.57789 | 13.18079 | 13.81645 | 14.48656 | 15.19293 | 15.93742 | 17.54874 |
| 15 | 20.02359 | 21.57856 | 23.27597 | 25.12902 | 27.15211 | 29.36092 | 31.77248 | 37.27971 |
| 20 | 29.77808 | 33.06595 | 36.78559 | 40.99549 | 45.76196 | 51.16012 | 57.27500 | 72.05244 |
| 25 | 41.64591 | 47.72710 | 54.86451 | 63.24904 | 73.10594 | 84.70090 | 98.34706 | 133.33387 |
| 30 | 56.08494 | 66.43885 | 79.05819 | 94.46079 | 113.28321 | 136.30754 | 164.49402 | 241.33268 |
| 35 | 73.65222 | 90.32031 | 111.43478 | 138.23688 | 172.31680 | 215.71076 | 271.02437 | 431.66350 |
| 40 | 95.02552 | 120.79977 | 154.76197 | 199.63511 | 259.05652 | 337.88245 | 442.59256 | 767.09142 |

**have only $54,914 [$1,200 per year × 45.762 (20 years at 8%)] in her pension account. Because Betty begins to provide for her retirement earlier than Wilma, the additional contributions to the account plus the earnings accumulating and compounding tax-free mean that Betty has $255,953 ($310,867 − $54,914) more than Wilma at retirement.**

For tax purposes, pension plans are classified as qualified or nonqualified. Under a **qualified pension plan**, neither the employee's nor the employer's contribution to the plan is treated as taxable income to the employee. In addition, the earnings on these contributions are not subject to tax until the employee makes a withdrawal from the pension plan. A nonqualified pension plan produces a tax treatment that is exactly opposite. The employee's contribution to a **nonqualified pension plan** cannot be deferred, and the employer is not allowed a tax deduction for the contribution unless the taxpayer includes the contribution in taxable income. In addition, the income earned on the contributions is subject to tax. Another important difference between these plans is that a qualified pension plan cannot discriminate in favor of highly compensated employees. Although the detailed tests for determining whether a pension plan discriminates in favor of highly compensated individuals are beyond the scope of this text, generally an individual who owns more than 5 percent of the entity or an individual who earns more than $130,000 is considered highly compensated.[1]

**Example 2** Assume the same facts as in example 1, except that Betty participates in a nonqualified pension plan. Her marginal tax rate is 24%, and the tax rate on the pension plan (i.e., the trust) is 25%. How much will Betty accumulate in her pension account from ages 25 to 65?

**Discussion: Because Betty participates in a nonqualified pension plan, both her contribution and her employer's contribution are subject to tax. Therefore, Betty's contribution, less the tax on her retirement fund, will be only $76 per month [$100 × (100% − 24%)] or $912 per year. In addition, because the income earned in the pension account is taxed at 25%, her yield on the investment income is only 6% [8% × (1 − 25%)]. Betty will accumulate $141,143 [$912 per year × 154.762 (40 years at 6%)] in her pension account. Because she is in a nonqualified pension plan and must pay tax on both her contributions and the income she earns on the contributions, Betty's accumulations are $169,724 ($310,867 − $141,143) less than with the qualified plan. Note: Betty will have to pay tax on any distributions she receives from the qualified plan, whereas any distributions from the nonqualified plan are tax-free. (The income has already been taxed.) However, even if Betty is taxed on the distributions from her qualified plan at the highest marginal tax rate (37%), her pension accumulations, less taxes, are $195,846 [$310,867 × (100% − 37%)], which is $54,703 ($195,846 − $141,143) more than with the nonqualified plan. This difference is due to the build-up of the tax-deferred earnings over the 40-year period prior to withdrawal.**

Qualified pension plans are available to employees of corporations, S corporations, and partnerships. However, an individual who is an owner-partner in a partnership or who is self-employed (sole proprietor) cannot be covered by the same qualified pension plan. A taxpayer who owns more than a 10 percent interest in a partnership is considered an owner-partner.[2] These individuals must use another retirement vehicle such as a *Keogh* plan, a simplified employee pension plan (SEP), an individual retirement account (IRA), or a savings incentive match plan for employees (SIMPLE). This section discusses each type of retirement plan.

For a pension plan to be treated as a qualified plan, it must meet certain requirements. Generally, the plan must cover all employees who are 21 years of age or older and who have worked for the company for at least two years. These are commonly referred to as the ***age and service requirements.*** The age and service requirements cannot be increased. However, the company can lower the requirements.

**Example 3** Carmen and Jose are employed by the Saco Company. Carmen has worked for Saco for 3 years, whereas Jose has worked for the company for only 18 months. Both are 25 years old. Are both Carmen and Jose eligible to be covered under Saco's pension plan?

**Discussion: Both Carmen and Jose meet the age requirement. However, only Carmen has worked for Saco long enough to be eligible for the plan. Therefore, only Carmen is eligible to participate. The company could decide to cover all employees who are 21 or older regardless of the number of years of service, or it could lower the number of years of service required.[3]**

A qualified pension plan must also meet the following requirements:

- The plan must be in writing.
- The contributions must be made to a trust.
- The plan must be for the exclusive benefit of the employees or their beneficiaries.
- The plan cannot discriminate in favor of highly paid employees.
- The plan must limit the amount of contributions that can be made to the plan and/or the benefits received from the plan.[4]

Qualified pension plans can be further classified as defined contribution plans or defined benefit plans. Retirement benefits for a **defined contribution plan** are based on the total contributions (from both employee and employer) made to the plan along with the gains and losses (net of expenses) earned by the assets in the plan.[5] As example 1 illustrates, the amount of retirement income Betty will receive is based on her contributions, those of her employer, and the investment income from these contributions. The two most common types of defined contribution plans are the money purchase plan and the profit-sharing plan.

In a defined contribution **money purchase plan**, the company and the employee (if it is a contributory plan) contribute a fixed percentage of the employee's salary to the pension plan. For example, the plan might require the employer to contribute 10 percent of the employee's salary and the employee to contribute 4 percent. This plan requires the employer to contribute a fixed amount every year, which can be a major drawback for a new and growing business.

Another type of defined contribution plan is a **profit-sharing plan**. This provides more flexibility than a money purchase plan because it does not require a fixed annual contribution. However, it must specify a formula for allocating the contributions among each of the plan's participants. All defined contribution plans are required to maintain a separate account for each employee.

**Example 4** Marcus is an employee of the Watch Hill Corporation and has a salary of $50,000. Watch Hill has a qualified pension plan that requires the company to contribute 6% of an employee's salary to the plan and the employee to contribute 2%. How much are Watch Hill and Marcus required to contribute to the plan?

**Discussion: Watch Hill is required to contribute $3,000 ($50,000 × 6%) to the pension plan, and Marcus is required to contribute $1,000 ($50,000 × 2%). The total contribution to the plan on behalf of Marcus is $4,000 ($3,000 + $1,000). Because the plan is qualified, Marcus can elect to defer the tax on his contribution. In doing so, only $49,000 ($50,000 − $1,000) of his salary is subject to tax. Note: If Watch**

**Hill's pension plan is a profit-sharing pension plan, it is not required to contribute to the pension plan every year. In addition, it can make contributions of less than the 6% maximum contribution. However, it must contribute on a regular basis and adopt a formula to allocate contributions to each employee.**

A **defined benefit plan** bases retirement benefits on the number of years an employee has worked for the company and the employee's annual salary.[6] However, unlike a defined contribution plan, the defined benefit plan does not require the employer to maintain a separate account for each employee. For example, the plan might allow an employee who has reached the plan's minimum retirement age and minimum number of years of service with the company to retire at 50 percent of the average of the employee's three highest consecutive years' salaries. With a defined benefit plan, no direct relationship exists between the amount contributed on behalf of the employee and the benefits paid to the employee.

**Example 5** Hong is an employee of the Paria Corporation and has worked for the company for 25 years. Employees are not required to contribute to the company's defined benefit plan. Based on the plan, Hong can retire at 30% of the average of his 3 highest consecutive years' salaries. His average salary over these 3 years is $60,000. What is Hong's retirement income from the Paria Corporation pension plan?

**Discussion: Hong will receive $18,000 ($60,000 × 30%) per year in retirement income. Because Hong did not contribute to the pension plan, the entire $18,000 he receives each year is taxable. Note: Hong's highest salaries do not have to be the salaries of the 3 most recent years, but the years must be consecutive.**

As you can see, the defined contribution plan and the defined benefit plan are dramatically different. A defined contribution plan is a forward-looking pension plan that is based on a fixed percentage of each year's salary, with the contributions and income accumulating over time. A defined benefit plan is a backward-looking pension plan that focuses on historical information, that is, years of service and highest salaries. Therefore, actuarial assumptions serve as the basis for the amount actually contributed on behalf of an individual. Because of the uncertainty of the benefits under a defined benefit plan, most companies use defined contribution plans.

Another difference between qualified defined contribution plans and qualified defined benefit plans is the maximum contribution a company can make to the plan (or the maximum amount of benefits it can pay from the plan). The contribution limit for defined contribution plans is the lesser of $58,000 or 25 percent of the employee's taxable compensation.[7,8,9]

**Example 6** The Conway Group has a qualified defined contribution plan. Keeley, a marketing manager for the company, receives an annual salary of $240,000. What is the maximum deductible contribution the company can make to the pension plan on her behalf?

**Discussion: The maximum deductible contribution is $58,000. Conway is allowed to contribute and deduct the lesser of $58,000 or $60,000 (25% × $240,000), Keeley's taxable compensation).**

The benefits paid to an employee from a defined benefit plan cannot exceed the lesser amount of $230,000 or 100 percent of the average of the employee's highest three consecutive years' compensation.[10] An employee who has 10 years of service with a company must receive a minimum benefit of $10,000.

**Example 7** Assume that in example 6, Keeley has worked for the Conway Group for 20 years. Conway has a defined benefit plan that lets employees retire at 80% of the average of their 3 highest consecutive years' salaries. Keeley's average salary for these 3 years is $300,000. What is the maximum benefit Keeley can receive from the pension plan?

**Discussion: The maximum benefit that Conway can pay Keeley is $230,000. Although the calculation of her benefit is $240,000 ($300,000 × 80%), Conway is limited to the $230,000 maximum.**

If an employee has less than ten years of service with the company, both the minimum benefit and the maximum benefit are reduced proportionately. Therefore, an individual with nine years of service can receive only 90 percent of the calculated benefits.[11]

**Example 8** Assume in example 7 that Keeley has worked for Conway for 7 years. What is the maximum benefit Keeley can receive from the pension plan?

**Discussion: Because Keeley has worked less than 10 years for the Conway Group, the maximum benefit she receives must be reduced proportionately. Therefore, her maximum pension benefit of $230,000 is reduced to $161,000 ($230,000 × 70%).**

The maximum amount a corporation can deduct with either a defined contribution plan or a defined benefit plan is limited to the actual amount it contributed to the plan. However, the deduction cannot exceed the maximum allowable contribution. Any contributions in excess of the maximum amount are subject to a 10 percent penalty (discussed later in this section).

**concept check**

The tax treatment of qualified pension plans reflects the *legislative grace concept* and the *wherewithal-to-pay concept*. To encourage savings for retirement, a current deduction is allowed for employer contributions, and the employee is not taxed on contributions to the plan. Under the *wherewithal-to-pay concept*, income is taxed in the period in which the taxpayer has the resources to pay the taxes. Because contributions to a qualified pension plan and earnings on the plan's assets are not available to pay tax when paid in or earned, income is not recognized until the contributions and the earnings are withdrawn from the plan.

## 15-2b Other Pension Plans

LO 2

Compare and contrast Keogh, SEP, IRA, Roth, and Simple pension plans and the limits on the contributions associated with these plans.

Although an individual can be both an owner and an employee of a corporation, sole proprietors and owner-partners are considered owners and not employees. Because only employees are allowed to participate in qualified pension plans, these individuals must use a Keogh plan (sometimes referred to as an *H.R. 10 plan*), an individual retirement account (IRA), a simplified employee pension (SEP) plan, or a savings incentive match plan for employees (SIMPLE) as their retirement vehicle. Generally, sole proprietors and partners use Keogh plans. Although a Keogh plan has greater administrative costs than a SEP or an IRA, it lets these entities make a larger contribution for employees covered by the plan than is available under a SEP plan.

### Keogh Plan

Before enactment of the Tax Equity and Fiscal Responsibility Act of 1982, Keogh plans were subject to more restrictive pension rules than the qualified plans that cover employees of corporations. In an effort to provide equity with the qualified plans, Congress modified the rules governing Keogh plans so that they would be similar to the rules governing qualified pension plans. As with a qualified plan, a Keogh plan can be either a defined contribution plan (i.e., a money purchase plan or a profit-sharing plan) or a defined benefit plan. In addition, the same eligibility rules for employee participation in a qualified plan and the discrimination rules that apply to highly compensated individuals (i.e., owner or owner-partner) apply to Keogh plans. A Keogh plan can have both employees and self-employed individuals as participants. The contribution limits for an employee covered by a Keogh plan are the same as those for a qualified plan.

**Example 9** In example 6, the Conway Group has a qualified defined contribution plan. Keeley is a marketing manager for the company and receives an annual salary of $320,000. Assume that the Conway Group is a partnership and that Keeley is not an owner-partner. What is the maximum deductible contribution the company can make to the pension plan on her behalf?

**Discussion: The maximum deductible contribution is the same as for an employee of a qualified pension plan. Because Keeley's salary exceeds $290,000, the**

**company can contribute only $72,500 ($290,000 × 25%) to a profit-sharing plan. However, the allowable contribution of $72,500 ($290,000 × 25%) is limited to the $58,000 maximum for defined contribution plans.**

Self-employed individuals and owner-partners use net self-employment income as the basis for determining their Keogh contribution. An individual's net self-employment income is calculated after subtracting the deduction for one-half of self-employment taxes and his or her Keogh contribution. The maximum contribution percentage to a Keogh plan for an individual who is a sole proprietor or owner-partner (referred to as *owners*) is lower than the amount for employees covered by the same plan to account for the individual's deductions for self-employment tax and Keogh plan contribution. The maximum contribution to a Keogh plan is the lesser of $58,000 or 20 percent of net self-employment income. For 2021, the maximum amount of net self-employment income that can be used in calculating the Keogh contribution is $290,000 ($58,000 ÷ 20%).

**Example 10** Return to the facts of example 9. Assume that the Conway Group is a partnership and that Keeley is a partner who owns an 18% interest in the partnership. Her net self-employment income is $210,000. What is the maximum contribution that Keeley can make to a Keogh plan?

**Discussion: Because Keeley owns more than a 10% interest, she is considered an owner-partner. Her maximum contribution to the plan is limited to the lesser of $58,000 or 20% of her net self-employment income. Therefore, the maximum contribution that she can make is $42,000 ($210,000 × 20%).**

If the Keogh plan is established as a defined benefit plan, the maximum benefit paid cannot exceed the lesser of $230,000 or 100 percent of the average of the employee's highest three consecutive years of compensation. These limits apply to both employees and owners and are the same as for employees of qualified pension plans.

## Individual Retirement Accounts

Similar to other pension plans, an **individual retirement account (IRA)** is an individual trust account maintained for the exclusive benefit of an individual or beneficiary. For tax years ending before December 31, 2019, a taxpayer was not allowed to make a contribution to their IRA after they reached 70½. The 2019 Setting Every Community Up for Retirement Enhancement (SECURE) Act repealed the age limit. Therefore, all taxpayers are allowed to contribute up to $6,000 per year of their earned income to an IRA. The limit is increased annually for inflation. In addition, taxpayers who are age 50 or over are allowed additional "catch-up contributions" to their IRA accounts during this period.

If a husband and wife both have earned income, each may contribute the $6,000 maximum amount to separate IRA accounts. Generally, a taxpayer who has no earned income is not eligible to establish an IRA. However, an IRA can be established for a nonworking spouse. The tax law permits a nonworking spouse to contribute up to $6,000 to an IRA if the earned income from the working spouse exceeds $12,000.

Unmarried taxpayers who are not **active participants** in a pension plan are allowed to deduct their entire contribution to an IRA regardless of the amount of their adjusted gross income. This is also the case for a married taxpayer if both spouses are not active participants in a pension plan.

Unmarried taxpayers who participate in an employer-sponsored plan must reduce the amount of an IRA deduction proportionately when their adjusted gross income reaches $66,000 ($65,000 in 2020). The entire deduction must be reduced to zero when adjusted gross income reaches $76,000 ($75,000 in 2020).[12] For married taxpayers filing a joint return, the phase-out range in 2021 is between $105,000 and $125,000 ($104,000 and $124,000 in 2020). The general formula for calculating the IRA percentage reduction and for computing the maximum deduction for an unmarried taxpayer in 2021 is:

$$\text{IRA percentage reduction} = \frac{(\text{Adjusted Gross Income} - \$66{,}000)}{\$10{,}000}$$

$$\text{Maximum IRA deduction} = \text{Maximum contribution} \times (100\% - \text{IRA percentage reduction})$$

**Example 11** Harry Salvo is a single taxpayer with an adjusted gross income of $70,000 who is covered by his employer's qualified pension plan. He makes a $6,000 contribution to his IRA in the current year. How much of the contribution will Harry be able to deduct?

**Discussion: Harry will not be able to deduct the entire amount of the contribution because his adjusted gross income is greater than the beginning of the phase-out range ($66,000). Harry's adjusted gross income exceeds the minimum threshold for the maximum $6,000 deduction by $4,000 ($70,000 − $66,000). The exclusion percentage is arrived at by dividing $4,000 by $10,000 (range of phase-out) to get 40%. Therefore, 40% of the $6,000 contributions will not be deductible. Harry will be able to deduct only $3,600 of the $6,000 contribution:**

$$\text{IRA percentage reduction} = \frac{(\$70{,}000 - \$66{,}000)}{\$10{,}000} = 40\%$$

$$\text{Maximum IRA deduction} = \$6{,}000 \times (100\% - 40\%) = \$3{,}600$$

A separate phase-out limitation exists for individuals who are not active participants in a pension plan but whose spouses are active participants. This lets the nonparticipant spouse make a full $6,000 deductible contribution to an IRA even if the spouse is an active participant. However, the $6,000 deduction limit is phased out over a $10,000 range when adjusted gross income reaches $198,000.

**Example 12** Jose is covered under an employer-sponsored plan where he works. His wife, Jana, is a full-time homemaker. They file a joint return with adjusted gross income of $130,000 before considering any IRA deduction. Can either taxpayer or both make a deductible IRA contribution?

**Discussion: Jana can make a deductible IRA contribution of $6,000 because she is not an active participant and the couple's adjusted gross income is below the $198,000 threshold. However, Jose cannot make a deductible contribution because he exceeds the income threshold for active participants ($125,000).**

**Example 13** Assume the same facts as in example 12, except that Jose and Jana's adjusted gross income is $250,000. Can Jose, Jana, or both make a deductible IRA contribution?

**Discussion: Neither Jose nor Jana is eligible to make a deductible contribution to an IRA because they exceed the income threshold $208,000.**

## Roth IRAs

Another vehicle that lets a taxpayer make nondeductible contributions is a **Roth IRA**.[13] The tax advantage of a Roth IRA is that distributions from the plan are generally tax-free. Taxpayers have always been allowed to make a contribution to their Roth IRA regardless of their age. Contributions are limited to a maximum of $6,000 a year. However, the total contribution an individual can make to all IRAs is limited to $6,000. The maximum annual contribution to a Roth IRA is phased out for unmarried taxpayers with adjusted gross income between $125,000 and $140,000 and for married taxpayers filing jointly between $198,000 and $208,000. Qualified distributions from a Roth IRA are not included in the taxpayer's gross income. To be a qualified distribution, the plan must have been established for five years and one of the following four requirements must be met:

- Must be made on or after the date on which the individual attains age 59½;
- Must be made to a beneficiary (or the individual's estate) after the individual's death;
- Is attributable to the individual's disability; or
- Is a distribution for "qualified first-time-homebuyer expenses."

A nonqualified distribution from a Roth IRA is subject to a 10 percent early withdrawal penalty.

**Example 14** Trinny establishes a Roth IRA at age 42 and contributes $6,000 per year for the next 20 years. He meets the income limits during the 20-year period. The account balance is now $170,000 ($100,000 in contributions and $70,000 in earnings), and Trinny wants to withdraw the entire amount this year. How much of the distribution will be taxable to Trinny?

**Discussion: Trinny may withdraw all of the Roth IRA funds tax-free because he has held them for more than 5 years and is over age 59½ at the date of the distribution.**

Amounts in traditional IRAs (both deductible and nondeductible) can be rolled over into a Roth IRA. However, a rollover from a deductible IRA to a Roth IRA is a taxable distribution.[14]

## Simplified Employee Pension Plan

A **simplified employee pension plan (SEP)** is a unique type of pension plan that any entity can use. The major advantage of a SEP is that it is administratively more convenient and economical than other qualified pension plans. Like a Keogh plan, a SEP can have both employees and self-employed individuals as participants. However, a SEP is unlike other qualified pension plans in that contributions to it are made to an IRA owned by the employee.

A simplified employee pension plan must meet many of the requirements for other pension plans. The plan must be in writing, it must establish a separate account for each employee, and it cannot discriminate in favor of highly compensated employees. In addition, a SEP must cover all employees who:

- Are at least 21 years of age
- Have performed services for the business during the year and at least three of the previous five years
- Have received at least $650 (2021) in compensation[15]

The maximum SEP contribution on behalf of an employee is the lesser of 25 percent of the employee's compensation or $58,000. The maximum contribution for owner-employees or owner-partners is 20 percent of their net self-employment income.[16] The contribution limits are the same as for a Keogh plan. Therefore, if in examples 9 and 10, the Conway Group had established a SEP instead of a Keogh plan, the amounts contributed on behalf of Keeley would be the same.

## Savings Incentive Match Plan for Employees

To encourage small businesses to establish retirement plans for their employees, Congress created the **savings incentive match plan for employees (SIMPLE)**. Employers that do not have a qualified pension plan and have fewer than 100 employees can establish a SIMPLE. To determine the number of employees in a business, the company considers only those paid at least $5,000 a year. All employees with compensation of at least $5,000 in each of the two previous years must be invited to participate if the employer establishes a SIMPLE. Owner-employees are also eligible to participate.

As with other pension plans, the employee's contribution to the plan can be tax deferred (i.e., not currently subject to income tax), and the business may deduct its contribution. An added advantage of establishing a SIMPLE is that it is not subject to the discrimination rules regarding highly compensated employees or other complex administrative requirements applicable to other qualified plans. This feature lowers the administrative costs of maintaining a SIMPLE and makes it an attractive alternative for a small business.

An employer can choose to establish either a SIMPLE-IRA or a SIMPLE-401(k). A 401(k) plan is a special type of profit-sharing pension plan. Both a SIMPLE-IRA and a SIMPLE-401(k) must allow employees to have the option of either receiving cash or having the employer make a contribution on their behalf to the SIMPLE. If an employee elects the cash option, the cash received is included in the employee's gross income.

Under a SIMPLE-IRA, eligible employees can choose to have a percentage of their salary, up to a maximum of $13,500, contributed to the plan. The employer's contribution must be made using one of the following funding formulas:

1. Match an employee's contribution up to a maximum of 3 percent of the employee's compensation. Under this option, the employer can elect to match a lower percentage but no less than 1 percent of each employee's compensation. Within a five-year period, the employer can twice elect to contribute less than 3 percent of each employee's compensation.

2. Contribute 2 percent of an employee's compensation. Under this option, employees do not have to contribute to the plan but can elect to make a contribution. The employer's contribution of 2 percent of an employee's compensation is mandatory even if the employee does not contribute. The maximum employee compensation that can be used in determining the employer's contribution in 2021 is $290,000 (i.e., the maximum employer contribution is $5,800).[17]

**Example 15** The Moran Corporation employs 80 individuals, each of whose annual compensation exceeds $5,000. In November 2020, Moran establishes a SIMPLE-IRA for its employees. Until then, the company did not have a retirement plan. The company has notified its employees that for 2021, it will fund the SIMPLE-IRA by matching an employee's contribution up to a maximum of 3% of the employee's salary (funding option 1). Carla is an employee of Moran with a salary in 2021 of $60,000. What is the maximum amount she can contribute to the SIMPLE-IRA? What amount must Moran contribute on Carla's behalf?

**Discussion: The maximum amount Carla can contribute to the SIMPLE-IRA is $13,500. Moran must contribute $1,800 ($60,000 × 3%) to the SIMPLE-IRA on Carla's behalf. Although the company must match Carla's contribution, the amount it contributes cannot exceed 3% of Carla's salary.**

**Example 16** Assume the same facts as in example 15, except that Moran contributes 2% of each employee's salary to the SIMPLE-IRA (funding option 2). What amounts must Carla and Moran contribute to the plan?

**Discussion: Carla is not required to make a contribution to the SIMPLE-IRA. However, she can elect to contribute up to $13,500 to the plan. Moran is required to contribute $1,200 ($60,000 × 2%) to the SIMPLE-IRA. Moran must make this contribution regardless of the amount Carla contributes to the plan.**

The employer is allowed to elect which of the two methods it will use to fund the SIMPLE-IRA on a year-by-year basis. To let employees properly plan their SIMPLE contributions, the employer is required to notify employees, 60 days before January 1, which funding method it will use for the coming year.

If the employer chooses to establish a SIMPLE-401(k), the maximum amount an employee can contribute to the plan is $13,500. The employer must contribute to the plan using the two general funding options available for a SIMPLE-IRA. However, the employer funding requirements for a SIMPLE-401(k) and a SIMPLE-IRA have two major differences. First, the maximum amount of an employee's compensation that can be used in determining the employer's contribution under either funding option is limited to $290,000 in 2021. For highly paid employees this reduces the maximum employer contribution under the 3 percent option from $13,500 to $8,700 (3% × $290,000). Second, the employer cannot elect to match the employee's contribution at a rate lower than 3 percent of the employee's salary. Therefore, establishing a SIMPLE-401(k) gives the employer less flexibility in funding the plan than the employer would have with a SIMPLE-IRA.

**Example 17** Assume the same facts as in example 15, except that Moran establishes a SIMPLE-401(k) and Carla's salary is $300,000. What is the maximum amount that Carla can contribute to the SIMPLE-401(k) plan? What amount is Moran required to contribute on her behalf?

**Discussion: The maximum amount that Carla can contribute to the SIMPLE-401(k) is $13,500. Moran is required to match Carla's contribution up to a maximum of 3% of her salary. However, the maximum amount of compensation that Moran can consider in determining its contribution under a SIMPLE-401(k) is $290,000. Therefore, Moran's required contribution is limited to $8,700 ($290,000 × 3%).**

Example 17 illustrates the two major funding differences between the two types of SIMPLE plans. First, Moran must make the 3 percent matching contribution to the SIMPLE-401(k). It does not have the option of reducing the contribution to 1 percent in two of every five years. Second, because of the compensation limit, the employer's matching contribution is lower for a SIMPLE-401(k). If Moran had established a SIMPLE-IRA in example 17, the maximum matching contribution would have been \$9,000 (\$300,000 × 3%).

## 15-2c Distributions

LO 3
Explain the requirements and tax treatment of distributions from pension plans as well as the penalties that ensure the responsible administration of these plans.

Distributions from a qualified pension plan, a Keogh plan, SEP, IRA, Roth IRA, or a SIMPLE can begin without penalty after a taxpayer reaches age 59½. The distributions from a pension plan, a Keogh plan, or a Roth IRA can be a lump sum or an annuity. Most taxpayers choose to receive the distributions as an annuity. Distributions from a SEP, IRA, or SIMPLE can only be in the form of an annuity. Prior to the enactment of the SECURE Act, a taxpayer had to either withdraw all the assets from the plan (a lump-sum distribution) or begin to receive an annuity no later than April 1 of the tax year after the taxpayer reaches age 70½ or the year the taxpayer retires. However, this rule does not apply to Roth IRA qualified distributions. If the taxpayer receives an annuity, all the assets of the plan must be distributed over the life expectancy of the taxpayer. For taxpayers who have not reached 70½ by December 31, 2020, the Secure Act now allows a taxpayer to wait begin to receive a distribution by April 1 of the tax year after the taxpayer reaches age 72 or the year the taxpayer retires.

The Treasury Department rules governing the **required minimum distribution (RMD)** amount are based on taxpayers' life expectancies and the determination of the taxpayer's designated beneficiaries. These rules simplify the required calculations through use of a uniform table for all taxpayers to calculate minimum distributions. The rules are designed to make it easier for taxpayers to change beneficiaries and do not require the taxpayer to immediately designate a beneficiary before or at the expected start date of distributions. In addition, the rules provide that a beneficiary can be named up to one year after the year of the taxpayer's death. They also provide for postmortem flexibility in estate planning and result in the taxpayer's being able to name a beneficiary after the required start date without increasing the RMD.

Another change made by the SECURE Act is if the taxpayer dies either before or after they start their RMD the inherited value of the plan must be distributed by the end of the tenth calendar year following the year of death. For example, if Simon who is single, dies in October of 2021, the remaining value of his pension plan must be distributed to his beneficiaries by the end of calendar year 2031.

An exception to this rule is for:

(1) the surviving spouse
(2) a child who has not reached majority
(3) a chronically ill individual
(4) any other individual who is not more than 10 years younger then the deceased

The RMD is determined by dividing the account balance as of the last valuation date in the calendar year immediately preceding the distribution calendar year by the applicable life expectancy. Table 15-2 provides the life expectancy factor used in the RMD calculation. The table factor is based on a taxpayer's age at the start date and assumes that the spouse is ten years younger than the taxpayer. The table begins with taxpayers age 72 and extends to taxpayers age 120. Generally, the new table is to be used by all taxpayers, eliminating the use of joint life expectancy tables. However, one exception lets taxpayers use the joint life expectancy tables if the taxpayer's spouse is more than ten years younger than the taxpayer.[18]

Table 15-2

## Uniform Lifetime Table Required Minimum Distributions

| Age of Employee | Distribution Period | Age of Employee | Distribution Period |
|---|---|---|---|
| 72 | 27.4 | 97 | 7.8 |
| 73 | 26.5 | 98 | 7.3 |
| 74 | 25.5 | 99 | 6.8 |
| 75 | 24.6 | 100 | 6.4 |
| 76 | 23.7 | 101 | 6.0 |
| 77 | 22.9 | 102 | 5.6 |
| 78 | 22.0 | 103 | 5.2 |
| 79 | 21.1 | 104 | 4.9 |
| 80 | 20.2 | 105 | 4.6 |
| 81 | 19.4 | 106 | 4.3 |
| 82 | 18.5 | 107 | 4.1 |
| 83 | 17.7 | 108 | 3.9 |
| 84 | 16.8 | 109 | 3.7 |
| 85 | 16.0 | 110 | 3.5 |
| 86 | 15.2 | 111 | 3.4 |
| 87 | 14.4 | 112 | 3.3 |
| 88 | 13.7 | 113 | 3.1 |
| 89 | 12.9 | 114 | 3.0 |
| 90 | 12.2 | 115 | 2.9 |
| 91 | 11.5 | 116 | 2.8 |
| 92 | 10.8 | 117 | 2.7 |
| 93 | 10.1 | 118 | 2.5 |
| 94 | 9.5 | 119 | 2.3 |
| 95 | 8.9 | 120 | 2.0 |
| 96 | 8.4 | | |

The plan account balance on the last day of the preceding calendar year is used as the beginning basis for computing the RMD for a particular year. In succeeding years, the account balance is reduced by the RMD amount before determining the next year's RMD.

**Example 18** Jason is a married taxpayer who retired from his job at Metacomet Industries. During 2021, he turned 72 and began withdrawing the $180,000 in assets (balance as of December 31, 2020) in his pension account on April 1, 2022 (the latest possible withdrawal date). The pension plan was noncontributory. What is Jason's RMD?

**Discussion: From Table 15-2, the factor for a taxpayer beginning distributions at age 72 is 27.4. Dividing the $180,000 plan balance as of December 31, 2020, by 27.4 gives Jason a $6,569 RMD for 2021, which must be distributed on or before April 1, 2022.**

The RMD after the first year depends on the earnings of the assets remaining in the plan and the previous year's calculated RMD. If the return on the assets is positive (i.e., income is earned), the RMD in the following year will likely be greater than the previous year's; if it is negative (i.e., a loss), the RMD will likely be less than the previous year's distribution.

**Example 19** Assume the same facts as in example 18. If the plan assets increase in value to $185,500 on December 31, 2021, what is Jason's RMD for 2022?

**Discussion: The plan balance used to calculate the RMD for 2020 is based on the December 31, 2021, account balance adjusted for earnings and the previous year's distribution. For Jason, the amount that must be used to determine the 2022 RMD is $178,931 ($185,500 − $6,569). The table factor for Jason is 26.5 (age 73 in 2022), and his RMD is $6,752 ($178,931 ÷ 26.5).**

The taxable amount of the distribution depends on whether the taxpayer has a basis in the pension plan account. Individuals can have a basis in their pension account only if their contributions to the account were not tax deferred. That is, the contributions were made with after-tax dollars. Under the capital recovery concept, the taxpayer includes as income only the portion of the distribution that exceeds the basis. Determining the taxable amount of a lump-sum distribution is straightforward. Only the amount of assets in the plan in excess of the employee's after-tax contributions is taxable as income. However, determining the actual tax liability due on a lump-sum distribution is rather complex and beyond the scope of this text. For an annuity, the tax law does not follow a strict interpretation of the capital recovery concept.

Recall from Chapter 3 that the tax law views a distribution from an annuity partly as return of capital and partly as income. Therefore, a portion of each annuity payment is treated as a return of capital and a portion is treated as taxable income.[19]

## 15-2d Penalties

The tax law has three major penalty provisions to ensure that the entities responsible for the administration of a pension plan comply with the rules and requirements established for qualified pension plans, Keogh plans, SEPs, IRAs, Roth IRAs, and SIMPLEs. The first penalty applies to excess contributions. An **excess contribution** is a contribution made to a qualified pension plan, Keogh plan, SEP, or a SIMPLE in excess of the maximum allowable amount. Excess contributions are subject to a 10 percent penalty.[20]

**Example 20** Phoebe is an employee of the Kobe Corporation with a yearly salary of \$80,000. The company maintains a noncontributory profit-sharing plan. During the year, the company contributed \$25,000 to the plan on her behalf in recognition of her outstanding work. Is the Kobe Corporation subject to a penalty for making an excess contribution?

**Discussion: The maximum that Kobe can contribute to a profit-sharing plan on behalf of Phoebe is \$20,000 (\$80,000 × 25%). Therefore, the excess contribution of \$5,000 (\$25,000 − \$20,000) is subject to a penalty of \$500 (\$5,000 × 10%).**

Excess contributions to an IRA or Roth IRA are subject to a 6-percent penalty on the amount in excess of \$6,000 or the value of the individual's IRA at the close of the tax year, whichever is less. The taxpayer can avoid the penalty by withdrawing the excess contribution from the IRA before the due date of the tax return.[21]

**Example 21** In addition to her pension plan, Phoebe maintains an IRA. During the year, she receives a \$7,000 inheritance from her aunt. Because she did not expect to receive the money, she decides to contribute it to her IRA. She does not take a deduction for the contribution. At the end of 2021, the total assets in the account are \$14,300. Is Phoebe subject to a penalty on her contribution?

**Discussion: Even though Phoebe is not allowed to take a deduction for her contribution, her maximum contribution is limited to \$6,000. Assuming that Phoebe does not withdraw the \$1,000 excess contribution from her account before April 15, 2022 (the due date of her return), she must pay a penalty of \$60. This is the lesser of \$858 (\$14,300 × 6%) or \$60 [6% × \$1,000 (\$7,000 − \$6,000)].**

A second tax law provision imposes a 10-percent penalty on early withdrawals. An **early withdrawal** occurs when a taxpayer takes money from a qualified pension plan, Keogh plan, SEP, IRA, Roth IRA, or a SIMPLE before reaching age 59½.[22]

The penalty is waived if the distribution is:

- Due to death or disability,
- Made in the form of certain periodic payments for the life of the individual or the individual's spouse,
- Used to pay medical expenses in excess of 10 percent of adjusted gross income,
- Used to purchase health insurance of an unemployed individual,
- Used to pay up to \$10,000 of expenses incurred by qualified first-time homebuyers,
- Used to pay birth or adoption expenses up to \$5,000.

 or
- Used to pay "qualified higher education expenses" of the taxpayer, the taxpayer's spouse, or any child or grandchild of the taxpayer or the taxpayer's spouse.[23]

Qualified first-time-homebuyer distributions are withdrawals that are used within 120 days of withdrawal to buy, build, or rebuild a "first" home that is the principal residence of the individual, the individual's spouse, or any child, grandchild, or ancestor of the individual or spouse. Acquisition costs include any usual or reasonable settlement, financing, or other closing costs. A first-time homebuyer is defined as one who has not had any ownership interest in a principal residence during a two-year period ending on the date the new home is acquired.

**Example 22** In 2019, Marie and Martin, ages 50 and 51, respectively, sold the home in which they lived and moved into an apartment. In 2021, Marie and Martin take an $18,000 distribution from their IRA to use as a down payment for the purchase of a new home. Is the distribution subject to the 10% early withdrawal penalty?

**Discussion: Because Marie and Martin have not had an ownership interest in a principal residence in the preceding 2 years, they are qualified first-time homebuyers. The early withdrawal penalty only applies to the $8,000 withdrawal in excess of the allowable $10,000. The penalty is $800 ($8,000 × 10%). In addition, the $18,000 distribution is subject to inclusion in their gross income under the usual IRA rules.**

Qualified higher education expenses include tuition, fees, books, supplies, and equipment required for enrollment or attendance at a post-secondary educational institution, including expenses associated with graduate-level courses. The amount of qualified expenses is reduced by other types of financial aid that the individual may exclude from income such as scholarships and educational assistance allowances.

**Example 23** Robby incurs $10,500 in tuition, fees, and book costs to take several graduate-level art courses at Boot University. He was awarded a $3,000 nontaxable scholarship from the local arts foundation and withdraws $7,500 from his IRA to pay for the remaining expenses. How much of the IRA distribution is subject to the early withdrawal penalty?

**Discussion: None of the IRA distribution is subject to the early withdrawal penalty because the $7,500 withdrawal was used to pay qualified education expenses. Robby's $10,500 in total expenses are reduced by the $3,000 scholarship, leaving $7,500 of expenses that can be paid without penalty from an IRA distribution. Robby must include the $7,500 in income using the usual IRA rules; the penalty is the only amount that Robby escapes, not the income tax.**

Roth IRA distributions are not subject to the 10 percent early withdrawal penalty if a five-year holding period is met, and the distribution is:

- Made to a beneficiary (or the individual's estate) after the individual's death,
- Attributable to the individual's becoming disabled,
- A distribution to pay for "qualified first-time-homebuyer expenses," or
- A distribution to pay for qualified education expenses.

These requirements are similar to those that apply to regular IRA distributions. In addition, individuals are always allowed to make contributions to a Roth IRA without penalty and are not required to take a distribution.

For distributions from plans other than Roth IRAs, the tax law imposes a 50 percent penalty on the difference between the required minimum distribution and the actual distribution for a taxpayer who fails to begin receiving a distribution in the year after reaching age 72 or the year of retirement, whichever is later.[24]

## 15-2e Planning Commentary

Table 15-3 summarizes the different types of retirement plans an entity can use classified by key attributes. As the table shows, all entities can establish a money purchase plan, profit-sharing plan, or defined benefit plan. Only businesses with 100 or fewer employees can establish a SIMPLE-IRA or a SIMPLE-401(k). The only distinction is that a partnership and a sole proprietorship must use either a Keogh plan, SEP, or SIMPLE. The reason for this is to restrict the amount that the owner-employee (partner) can contribute, which is less than the amount allowed for an employee. The biggest and probably most overlooked distinction between the different types of pension plans is that, with a money purchase plan, the taxpayer must make a fixed contribution to the plan every year. This can be a major issue for a new business or a business that has a long business cycle (i.e., greater than a year) and experiences temporary cash-flow problems.

Table 15-3

## Comparison of Pension Plan Attributes

| | Types of Retirement Plan | | | | | | | |
|---|---|---|---|---|---|---|---|---|
| **Attribute** | **Money Purchase** | **Profit Sharing** | **Defined Benefit** | **IRA** | **Roth IRA** | **SEP/IRA** | **SIMPLE-IRA** | **SIMPLE 401(k)** |
| Eligibility to use plan | All entities | All entities | All entities | All individuals eligible | All individuals eligible | Sole proprietor and partners | All entities with fewer than 100 employees | All entities with fewer than 100 employees |
| Maximum contribution for employee | $58,000 or 25% of employee's taxable compensation | $58,000 or 25% of employee's taxable compensation | $230,000 or 100% of employee's average of highest 3 consecutive years taxable compensation | Lesser of $6,000 or taxable compensation | Lesser of $6,000 or taxable compensation | $58,000 or 25% of employee's taxable compensation | Maximum of $13,500[a] | Maximum of $13,500[b] |
| Maximum contribution for owner-employee | $58,000 or 20% of employee's net self-employment income | $58,000 or 20% of employee's net self-employment income | Same as employee | The lower of the amount of the contribution or $6,000 | The lower of the amount of the contribution or $6,000 | Same as employee | Same as employee | Same as employee |
| Maximum deductible | Amount of contribution | Amount of contribution | Amount of contribution | If not a member of a qualified pension plan, the lower of the amount of the contribution or $6,000[c] | Contributions are not deductible | Amount of contribution | Amount of contribution | Amount of contribution |
| Date of last deductible contribution | No restriction | No restriction | The tax year the individual reaches age 72 | No restriction | No restriction | No restriction | No restriction | April 15 of tax year before the individual reaches age 72 or retires |
| Penalties: | | | | | | | | |
| Excess contributions | 10% of excess contribution | 10% of excess contribution | 10% of excess contribution | Lower of 6% of excess contribution or value of plan assets | Lower of 6% of excess contribution or value of plan assets | 10% of excess contribution | 10% of excess contribution | 10% of excess contribution |
| Early withdrawal | 10% of amount received | 10% of amount received | 10% of amount received | 10% of amount received | 10% of amount received | 10% of amount received | 10% of amount received | 10% of amount received |
| Failure to receive minimum distributed by age 72 | 50% of the difference between minimum distribution and amount received | 50% of the difference between minimum distribution and amount received | 50% of the difference between minimum distribution and amount received | 50% of the difference between minimum distribution and amount received | No restriction | 50% of the difference between minimum distribution and amount received | 50% of the difference between minimum distribution and amount received | 50% of the difference between minimum distribution and amount received |

[a]Employer must match 3% of the employee's compensation up to a maximum of $13,500 or contribute 2% of employee's compensation up to a maximum of $5,800. An employer can elect to contribute a minimum of 1% twice within a 5-year period.

[b]Employer must match 3% of the employee's compensation up to a maximum of $13,500 or contribute 2% of employee's compensation up to a maximum of $8,700.

[c]If the taxpayer is unmarried and a member of a qualified pension plan, the taxpayer can deduct the $6,000 maximum if adjusted gross income is less than $65,000. The deduction is phased out proportionately when adjusted gross income is between $66,000 and $76,000 in 2021. For married taxpayers the deduction is phased out proportionately when adjusted gross income is between $105,000 and $125,000 in 2021.

All entities are allowed to establish a SEP. The advantages of establishing a SEP are that the plan is administratively convenient and economical. However, using a SEP limits the amount the entity can contribute on behalf of the employee and the owner-employee (partner). Generally, this is a disadvantage only for the owner-employee (partner). The date that distributions must begin and penalties imposed for failure to comply with the IRS requirements are consistent for all plans except for Roth IRAs. The tax attributes associated with choosing a pension plan are just one of the many considerations in deciding the organizational form of operating a business. The organization must also consider the compliance costs, the ability to retain and attract quality employees, the cost of the pension contributions, and the entity's earnings in deciding which type of pension plan to adopt.

## 15-2f Stock Options

LO 4
Compare and contrast the treatment of nonqualified and incentive stock options.

Stock options are another compensation tool that corporations use to attract and retain key personnel. A **stock option** is a right to buy a share of stock at a fixed price (referred to as the *exercise price*) within a specified period of time. The two types of stock options are nonqualified stock options and incentive stock options. These options are sometimes referred to as *nonstatutory* and *statutory options.* An *incentive stock option (ISO)* is called a statutory option because the option must meet certain requirements set forth in the Internal Revenue Code (i.e., the statute). Although incentive stock options are typically used to compensate upper management, nonqualified stock options are designed to compensate a wide array of employees. Because a stock option gives the employee an equity share of the business, it is not a compensation tool that a sole proprietorship or partnership can use. An S corporation can use either a nonqualified stock option or an incentive stock option to compensate employees.

### Nonqualified Stock Options

A **nonqualified stock option (NQSO)** lets the employee acquire stock of the employer at a specified price beginning on a specified date. The option is generally not transferable. The tax consequences for the employee of a nonqualified stock option depend on whether the stock option has a readily ascertainable fair market value. If it does, the employee recognizes as income an amount equal to the fair market value of the option.[25] Because the employee recognizes income at the date of grant, the employer is entitled to a corresponding deduction. Because the option has a readily ascertainable fair market value, the employee does not have a basis in the stock of the company but in the option.

**Example 24** On April 14, 2021, Cranston Corporation grants Jiang an option to acquire 1,000 shares of the company's stock for $10 per share. The fair market price of the stock on the date of grant is $20. The fair market value of the option is $5. What are the tax consequences to Jiang and Cranston Corporation?

**Discussion: Jiang recognizes $5,000 ($5 × 1,000) of ordinary income on the date of the grant. Cranston Corporation is entitled to a compensation deduction of $5,000. Jiang's basis in the option is $5,000.**

When an employee exercises a stock option with a readily ascertainable fair market value, the employee does not recognize income, and the employer is not entitled to a deduction. However, the exercise of the option does affect the employee's basis in the stock. The employee's basis is equal to the amount of income recognized at the date of the grant plus the cash paid to exercise the option. The holding period for the stock begins at the exercise date.[26]

**Example 25** Return to the facts of example 24. Assume that Jiang exercises the option on May 15, 2021, when the fair market value of the stock is $22 per share. What are the tax consequences for Jiang and Cranston Corporation? What is Jiang's basis in the stock?

**Discussion: Jiang does not recognize any income on the exercise of the stock option, and the corporation does not receive a tax deduction. Jiang's basis in the stock is $15,000 [($10 + $5) × 1,000]. This represents the $5,000 ($5 × 1,000) in ordinary income he recognized on the date of grant plus the $10,000 ($10 × 1,000) he paid to exercise the option. His holding period for determining whether the gain or loss is short-term or long-term begins on May 15, 2021.**

Upon the sale of stock acquired through a nonqualified stock option, the employee will recognize a capital gain or loss equal to the difference between the fair market value of the stock at the date of sale and the employee's basis in the stock.

**Example 26** Return to the facts of example 25. What are the tax consequences for Jiang and Cranston Corporation if Jiang sells the stock on August 1, 2023, when the fair market value of the stock is $30?

**Discussion: When Jiang sells the stock, he will recognize a long-term capital gain (May 15, 2021, through August 1, 2023) of $15,000 [($30 − $15) × 1,000]. Cranston Corporation is not entitled to a deduction for the capital gain recognized by Jiang.**

Table 15-4 summarizes the tax treatment to the individual and the corporation of nonqualified stock options with a readily ascertainable fair market value.

Most companies that issue NQSOs do not have options with a readily ascertainable fair market value. Therefore, the employee does not recognize income at the date of grant but rather at the date of exercise. The amount of income the employee must recognize is the difference between the option price and the fair market value of the stock at the date of exercise.[27]

**Example 27** Return to the facts of example 24. Assume that the stock option does not have a readily ascertainable fair market value. What are the tax consequences for Jiang and Cranston Corporation?

**Discussion: Because the stock does not have a readily ascertainable fair market value, Jiang does not recognize income at the date of grant. As a result, Cranston is not entitled to a compensation deduction.**

**Example 28** Return to the facts of example 25. Assume that the stock option does not have a readily ascertainable fair market value and that Jiang exercises the option on May 15, 2021, when the fair market value of the stock is $22 per share. What are the tax consequences for Jiang and Cranston Corporation?

**Discussion: Because the stock does not have a readily ascertainable fair market value, Jiang does not recognize income until the date of exercise. At the date of exercise, he must report the difference between the exercise price and the fair market value as income. Jiang has compensation income of $12,000 [($22 − $10) × 1,000]. Cranston Corporation is entitled to a compensation deduction of $12,000. Jiang's basis in the stock is $22,000 [($10 + $12) × 1,000]. This represents the $10,000 ($10 × 1,000) he paid to exercise the option price plus the $12,000 ($12 × 1,000) in ordinary income he recognized on the date of exercise.**

*Table 15-4*

## Nonqualified Stock Options with Readily Ascertainable Fair Market Value

| Tax Attribute | Date of Grant | Date of Exercise | Date of Sale |
|---|---|---|---|
| Income recognition | The fair market value of the option is recognized as ordinary income. | No income is recognized. | The difference between the sales price and basis is a capital gain. |
| Basis | Amount of ordinary income recognized. | Amount of ordinary income recognized at date of grant plus the amount paid to exercise the option. | Basis does not change from exercise date. |
| Holding period/Character of gain | The holding period of the option begins at date of grant. | The holding period of the stock begins on date of exercise. | The character of the gain (short-term or long-term) depends on the holding period of the stock. |
| Corporate deduction | Equal to the amount of ordinary income recognized. | No deduction. | No deduction. |

**Example 29** Return to the facts of example 28. What are the tax consequences to Jiang and Cranston Corporation if Jiang sells the stock on August 1, 2023, when the fair market value of the stock is $30?

**Discussion: When Jiang sells the stock, he will recognize a long-term capital gain of $8,000 [($30 – $22) × 1,000]. Cranston Corporation is not entitled to a deduction for the capital gain income recognized by Jiang.**

Regardless of whether the stock option has a readily ascertainable fair market value, the total income Jiang recognizes is $20,000 [($5,000 + $15,000) or ($12,000 + $8,000)]. However, the character of the income recognized is different. If the option has a readily ascertainable fair market value, Jiang recognizes $7,000 ($12,000 – $5,000) less in ordinary income. In addition, the corporation receives a smaller compensation deduction. The character of the gain is important if the holding period of the stock is greater than 12 months. Table 15-5 summarizes the tax treatment to the individual and the corporation of nonqualified stock options with a fair market value that is not readily ascertainable.

As discussed earlier, virtually all stock options are nontransferable. In some cases a nonqualified stock option is subject to substantial risk of forfeiture. An option is considered subject to **substantial risk of forfeiture** if the employee must meet certain conditions or requirements before being eligible to receive the option.[28] For example, if an employee must remain with the company for two years after the date of exercise, the stock option is considered subject to substantial risk of forfeiture. If the stock option is subject to substantial risk of forfeiture and is nontransferable, the employee is not taxed until the restriction on the option has lapsed because the employee does not have a claim of right to the stock until then. In addition, the corporation does not receive a compensation deduction until the employee recognizes income.

**Example 30** Return to the facts of example 24. Assume that Jiang must remain with the company for 2 years after the date that he exercises the option. On May 15, 2021, when the fair market value of the stock is $22, Jiang exercises the option. What are the tax consequences for Jiang and Cranston Corporation?

**Discussion: Jiang does not recognize income at the date of grant or at the date of exercise because the option is subject to substantial risk of forfeiture. However, Jiang's basis in the stock is $10,000 ($10 × 1,000), the amount paid to exercise the option. Cranston Corporation is not entitled to a compensation deduction at either the date of grant or the date of exercise.**

When the restrictions lapse, the employee is taxed on the difference between the exercise price and the fair market value of the stock. This is true even if the stock option has a readily ascertainable fair market value. The employer is entitled to a compensation

*Table 15-5*

## Nonqualified Stock Options with Fair Market Value That Is Not Readily Ascertainable

| Tax Attribute | Date of Grant | Date of Exercise | Date of Sale |
|---|---|---|---|
| Income recognition | No income is recognized. | The difference between the fair market value of the stock and the exercise price is recognized as ordinary income. | The difference between the sales price and basis is a capital gain. |
| Basis | No income is recognized, so there is no basis in the stock. | Amount of ordinary income recognized at date of exercise plus the amount paid to exercise the option. | Basis does not change from exercise date. |
| Holding period/Character of gain | Not applicable. | Begins on date of exercise. | The character of the gain (short-term or long-term) depends on the holding period of the stock. |
| Corporate deduction | No deduction. | Equal to the amount of ordinary income recognized. | No deduction. |

deduction for the amount recognized as income by the employee. In addition, the employee's holding period begins on the date the restrictions lapse.[29]

**Example 31** Return to the facts of example 30. Assume that Jiang is an employee of Cranston Corporation on May 16, 2023, when the fair market value of the stock is $27. What are the tax consequences for Jiang and Cranston Corporation?

**Discussion: The $17,000 [($27 − $10) × 1,000] difference between the fair market value of the stock on the date the restrictions lapse and the exercise price is income to Jiang. At the exercise date, Jiang's basis in the stock is $27,000 ($17,000 + $10,000). This represents the amount paid for the stock at the exercise date ($10,000) plus the income recognized ($17,000). Cranston Corporation is entitled to a compensation deduction of $17,000. The holding period begins on the date (May 16, 2023) that the restrictions lapse.**

When the employee sells the stock, the employee will recognize a capital gain or loss equal to the difference between the fair market value of the stock at the date of sale and the employee's basis in the stock. The employee's basis in the stock is the amount paid for the shares on the exercise date plus the income recognized on the date that the restrictions lapse.

**Example 32** Return to the facts of example 31. What are the tax consequences for Jiang and Cranston Corporation if Jiang sells the stock on August 1, 2023, when the fair market value of the stock is $30?

**Discussion: When Jiang sells the stock, he will recognize a short-term capital gain of $3,000 [($30 − $27) × 1,000]. Jiang's basis in the stock is $27,000. Because he held the stock for less than 12 months (May 16, 2023, until August 1, 2023), the gain is short term. Cranston Corporation is not entitled to a deduction for the capital gain income recognized by Jiang.**

Table 15-6 summarizes the tax treatment to the individual and the corporation of nonqualified stock options that are substantially restricted.

The tax law allows an employee who receives nonqualified stock options that are nontransferable and subject to substantial restrictions to make a special election (known as a *Section 83(b) election*) at the date of exercise. By making this election, the taxpayer treats as ordinary income the difference between the exercise price and the fair market value of the stock at the date of exercise.[30] The employer is allowed a deduction for the amount of income recognized by the employee. This election lets the employee lock in the ordinary income (i.e., compensation) portion of the option. By locking in the

Table 15-6

## Nonqualified Stock Options That Are Substantially Restricted

| Tax Attribute | Date of Grant | Date Restrictions Lapse | Date of Sale |
|---|---|---|---|
| Income recognition | No income is recognized. | No income is recognized until the restrictions lapse. At that time, the difference between the fair market value of the stock and the exercise price is recognized as ordinary income. | The difference between the sales price and basis is a capital gain. |
| Basis | No income is recognized, so there is no basis in the stock. | Amount of ordinary income recognized at date the restrictions lapse plus the amount paid to exercise the option. | Basis does not change from when restrictions lapse. |
| Holding period/Character of gain | Not applicable. | Begins on date restrictions lapse. | The character of the gain (short-term or long-term) depends on the holding period of the stock. |
| Corporate deduction | No deduction. | Equal to the amount of ordinary income recognized when the restrictions lapse. | No deduction. |

ordinary income portion of the option, any subsequent appreciation in the value of the stock is treated as capital gain to the taxpayer. However, the taxpayer runs a risk by doing this. If the stock does not increase in value, the taxpayer will have recognized ordinary income but can deduct as a capital loss only the amount paid for the stock option. In addition, even though the taxpayer elects to be taxed at the date of exercise, the holding period of the stock does not begin until the date that the restrictions lapse.

**Example 33** Return to the facts of example 30. Assume that Jiang elects to be taxed on the option at the date of exercise. What are the tax consequences for Jiang and Cranston Corporation?

**Discussion: Because Jiang has made an election to be taxed at the date of exercise, he will recognize ordinary income of $12,000 [($22 – $10) × 1,000]. Cranston Corporation is entitled to a compensation deduction of $12,000. Jiang's basis at the date of exercise is $22,000 ($12,000 + $10,000), the amount of income recognized plus the cost of exercising the options.**

**Example 34** Return to the facts of example 33. Assume that the restrictions lapse on May 16, 2023, when the fair market value of the stock is $27. What are the tax consequences for Jiang and Cranston Corporation on May 16, 2023?

**Discussion: Because Jiang elected to be taxed at the date of exercise, he does not report income at the date the restrictions lapse, and Cranston Corporation is not entitled to a compensation deduction.**

**Example 35** Return to the facts of example 34. What are the tax consequences for Jiang if he sells the stock on August 1, 2023, for $30?

**Discussion: When Jiang sells the stock, he will recognize a short-term capital gain of $8,000 [($30 – $22) × 1,000]. Jiang's basis in the stock is $22,000. This represents the $10,000 he paid to exercise the option plus the $12,000 in ordinary income he recognized on the date of grant. The gain is short-term because Jiang's holding period begins on the date the restrictions lapse. Cranston Corporation is not entitled to a deduction for the capital gain income recognized by Jiang.**

**In comparing the tax results in examples 31 and 33, note that by making the special election, Jiang is able to lock in the ordinary income portion of the option and is able to convert $5,000 ($17,000 – $12,000) in ordinary income into capital gain income.**

Table 15-7 summarizes the tax treatment to the individual and the corporation of nonqualified stock options that are substantially restricted when the individual makes a Section 83(b) election.

*Table 15-7*

## Nonqualified Stock Options That Are Substantially Restricted, Section 83(b) Election

| Tax Attribute | Date of Grant | Date of Exercise | Date of Sale |
|---|---|---|---|
| Income recognition | No income is recognized. | The difference between the fair market value of the stock and the exercise price is recognized as ordinary income. | The difference between the sales price and basis is a capital gain. |
| Basis | No income is recognized, so there is no basis in the stock. | Amount of ordinary income recognized at date of the election plus the amount paid to exercise the option. | Basis does not change from exercise date. |
| Holding period/Character of gain | Begins on date restrictions lapse. | Begins on date restrictions lapse. | The character of the gain (short-term or long-term) depends on the holding period of the stock. |
| Corporate deduction | No deduction. | Equal to the amount of ordinary income recognized. | No deduction. |

## Incentive Stock Options

An incentive stock option is generally considered a better compensation tool than an NQSO because the stock is eligible for special tax treatment. Unlike a nonqualified stock option, an **incentive stock option (ISO)** is not taxable when the option is granted or when it is exercised.[31] Rather, the taxpayer is allowed capital gain treatment on the difference between the sales price of the stock and the price paid for the option (i.e., exercise price). However, this difference is a tax adjustment item in computing an individual's alternative minimum tax liability (discussed later). Because the employee receives special tax treatment, the employer is not entitled to a compensation deduction for the difference between the option price and the fair market value of the stock.

For a stock option to be treated as an ISO, the option must be part of a qualified stock plan approved by the shareholders. In addition, the plan must meet the following general requirements:

- The option must be exercised within ten years of the date of grant.
- The option price must be equal to or exceed the fair market value of the stock at the date of grant.
- The option can be exercised only by the employee to whom the option is granted (i.e., it is nontransferable).
- The fair market value of the ISOs granted in a year (number of ISOs granted multiplied by the fair market value of the stock) cannot exceed $100,000.[32]

**Example 36** On March 9, 2021, Li receives the right to acquire 500 shares of Gibran Corporation for $18 per share through an incentive stock option plan. The current fair market value of the stock is $10. What are the tax consequences for Li and Gibran Corporation?

**Discussion: Li does not recognize any income on the date of grant. Because she does not recognize any ordinary income, Gibran is not entitled to a compensation deduction.**

**Example 37** Return to the facts of example 36. On April 6, 2022, when the fair market value of the stock is $20 per share, Li exercises her right to purchase the stock. What are the tax consequences for Li and Gibran Corporation?

**Discussion: Li does not recognize any income on the date of exercise, and Gibran is not entitled to a compensation deduction. However, the difference between the fair market value of the shares at the date of grant ($20) and the exercise price ($18) is a tax adjustment for computing Li's alternative minimum tax liability. Li's tax adjustment is $1,000 [($20 − $18) × 500].**

**Example 38** Return to the facts of example 37. If Li sells the stock on October 31, 2023, when the price is $40 per share, what are the tax consequences for her and Gibran Corporation?

**Discussion: Li will recognize a long-term capital gain of $11,000 [($40 − $18) × 500] on the sale of the stock. The gain is long-term because she has held the stock more than 12 months from the date of exercise. Gibran is not entitled to a compensation deduction.**

To receive this special tax treatment, the employee must meet the following three requirements:

- The ISO stock cannot be sold within two years from the date of grant.
- The ISO stock cannot be sold within one year after the exercise date.
- The employee must be an employee of the company or have been employed within three months of the exercise date of the option.

If an employee fails to meet any of the requirements that qualify the stock option as an ISO, the option is no longer considered an ISO, and its tax treatment is the same as for a nonqualified stock option.

Table 15-8

**Incentive Stock Options**

| Tax Attribute | Date of Grant | Date of Exercise | Date of Sale |
|---|---|---|---|
| Income recognition | No income is recognized. | No income is recognized. The difference between the fair market value of the stock and the option price is a tax adjustment for alternative minimum tax purposes. | The difference between the sales price and basis is a capital gain, assuming that the stock is held 1 year from date of exercise and 2 years from the date of grant. |
| Basis | No income is recognized, so there is no basis in the stock. | Amount paid for stock on date of exercise. | Basis does not change from exercise date. |
| Corporate deduction | No deduction. | No deduction. | No deduction. |

**Example 39** Assume the same facts as in example 38, except that Li needs cash to purchase a new home and sells the shares for $35 per share on February 21, 2023. What are the tax consequences for Li and Gibran Corporation?

**Discussion: Because Li did not hold the stock for 2 years from the date of grant (March 9, 2021, until February 21, 2023), the stock does not receive the favorable tax treatment of an ISO. Li also failed to hold the stock more than 1 year from the date of exercise. For tax purposes, the stock is treated as a nonqualified stock option. Li must recognize $1,000 [($20 − $18) × 500] in ordinary income. She will recognize a short-term capital gain of $7,500 [($35 − $20) × 500] on the sale of the stock. The gain is short-term because she held the stock less than 12 months from the date of exercise (April 6, 2022 until February 21, 2023). Because Li recognizes ordinary income on the stock option, Gibran is entitled to a compensation deduction of $1,000.**

Table 15-8 summarizes the tax treatment to the individual and the corporation of incentive stock options.

## 15-2g Reasonableness of Compensation

LO 5
Explain the issue of reasonable compensation and its tax impact on different entity forms.

Attempts to reduce corporate taxable income through excess compensation are an issue of concern for both closely held and publicly traded corporations. However, the reasons for concern are different. For a closely held business, the substance-over-form doctrine, dealing with the issues of lack of business purpose and unreasonableness of salary, is the usual focus of IRS scrutiny. The tax law provides for the deduction of reasonable compensation paid to employees. This compensation is subject to two basic tests for deductibility: the payments must be for services actually performed by the employee, and the total payment for services of the employee must be reasonable in amount. The determination of whether total compensation is excessive is made for each employee. If the IRS disallows a deduction for salary paid to an individual who is an owner of the corporation, the payment is usually treated as dividend income to that individual.

**Example 40** Miles and his son Marvin each own 50% of Dinsmore, Inc. Miles is the president and chief financial officer of the corporation and receives a salary of $150,000. Other individuals with responsibilities that are similar to Miles's are paid approximately the same salary. Marvin, who is vice president of the corporation, is paid a salary of $75,000. However, Marvin is not involved in the business decisions and rarely visits the office. How should the payments to Marvin and Miles be treated for tax purposes?

**Discussion: The $150,000 salary to Miles should be deductible. The amount he is paid is similar to the pay received by other individuals functioning in the same capacity. However, the $75,000 paid to Marvin would not be a deductible expense of the corporation because it lacks a business purpose. The payment to Marvin would be treated as a dividend and included as income on his tax return. The corporation cannot deduct the payment of a dividend.**

For an S corporation, the issue of reasonable compensation can take a different approach. Because the salary received by an owner-employee of an S corporation is subject to Social Security tax, owner-employees would rather receive a minimal amount of salary and report a larger portion of the S corporation's profits as ordinary income. The IRS often challenges the compensation paid because the salary is unreasonably low.

**Example 41** Return to example 40. Assume the same facts except that Dinsmore is an S corporation and neither Miles nor Marvin receives a salary. What are the tax consequences for Miles and Marvin?

**Discussion: The IRS would probably assert that Miles should receive a salary commensurate with the salary paid to individuals in similar positions. Therefore, the IRS could argue that Miles's salary should be $150,000. By not receiving any compensation, Miles avoids paying $11,029 ($142,800 × 6.2%) + ($150,000 × 1.45%)] in Social Security taxes. In addition, the corporation does not have to make the matching Social Security payment of $11,029. This leaves the company with $11,029 more to distribute to Miles and Marvin. The lack of compensation to Marvin is probably justified because Marvin does not perform any meaningful tasks for the company.**

Although not paying a salary to an owner-employee of an S corporation might escape notice by the IRS, this technique does not work for sole proprietors and partnerships because the net income from these entities is treated as self-employment income. As discussed in Chapter 6, self-employment income in 2021 is subject to a tax of 15.3 percent on the first $142,800 of self-employment income and 2.9 percent on the excess. However, a self-employed individual can deduct one-half of the self-employment taxes paid as a deduction for AGI.

## 15-2h Planning Commentary

In deciding the organizational form of a business, careful consideration should be given to how the owners and employees of the business will be compensated. Only corporations can use nonqualified stock options and incentive stock options. Since the number of owners of an S corporation cannot exceed 100 individuals, S corporations must be careful not to issue so many stock options that they are likely to exceed the 100-owner limitation. An incentive stock option plan provides the greatest tax benefits to an employee because any appreciation in the value of stock over the grant price is treated as a capital gain. However, there is a tax cost to the corporation. Because the employee does not recognize ordinary income on the receipt, exercise, or sale of the incentive stock option, the corporation is not allowed a tax deduction. Employees who want the special tax treatment from an incentive stock option must meet certain requirements.

The amount of compensation paid to an employee must be reasonable for the services provided. Whether the compensation is reasonable is determined by examining several factors, including the individual's duties, responsibilities, and accomplishments, the relationship of the individual's pay to peers' pay at other organizations, and the relationship between compensation and the profitability of the entity. The issue of reasonable compensation is usually a problem for a closely held business.

Reasonableness of compensation also is important for S corporations. However, unlike in a closely held corporation, where the issue is excessive compensation, owner-employees of an S corporation might attempt to minimize their salary to avoid Social Security tax. As a conduit entity, the net income of an S corporation flows through to the individual owners and is subject to income tax on the individual's tax return. Because the income received is not subject to Social Security tax (i.e., self-employment tax), a controversial, yet often used, tax-planning technique is to minimize the amount of salary paid to an owner-employee and maximize the amount that flows through to the owner.

A partnership cannot avoid the payment of Social Security and self-employment taxes by minimizing a partner's salary and maximizing the amount of ordinary income that flows through to the partner. Both the salary received by a partner as a guaranteed payment and the income that flows through to the individual partner are subject to self-employment tax.

The owner of a sole proprietorship cannot be an employee of the entity. Therefore, any cash payments from the entity to the owner are treated as a nontaxable transfer of cash and are not a deduction for the business.

# 15-3 OTHER TAX LIABILITY CONSIDERATIONS

As discussed in the preceding chapters, deciding which business entity to use often begins by comparing the income tax liabilities for the different entities. However, income taxes are just one component in determining an entity's total tax liability. The effects of tax credits and the alternative minimum tax on the total tax liability of the entity and its owners must be considered.

## 15-3a Income Tax Credits

LO 6
Describe how tax credits are used to achieve various policy goals and explain the tax rules applicable to the most commonly used business tax credits.

A **tax credit** is a direct reduction in the tax liability of the taxpayer receiving the credit. As such, tax credits are not part of the tax base used to compute the tax liability. Because they are not part of the base and reduce the tax liability dollar for dollar, tax credits are neutral with respect to the marginal tax rate of the taxpaying entity (i.e., individual or corporation). That is, in contrast to tax deductions, a $100 tax credit is worth a $100 reduction in taxes to a taxpayer, regardless of the marginal tax rate.

Numerous tax credits are available to those who engage in certain types of business activities. These credits, unless noted, are available regardless of the entity the taxpayer chooses for conducting business. The list is extensive; this chapter discusses some of the more important ones. Table 15-9 provides a list of business tax credits and a summary of their purposes.

### Research and Experimental Credit

The purpose of the **research and experimental (R&E) tax credit** is to encourage research and development of new technologies and processes. The tax law allows two separate credits. The first credit is for incremental research expenditures and is available to all entities. The second credit, the basic research credit, is available only to corporations. The incremental credit is equal to 20 percent of the qualified research expenditures in the current year in excess of the base amount.[33]

Qualified expenditures must be technical in nature, intended to be useful in the development of a new or improved business component of the taxpayer, or be elements of a process of experimentation for a functional purpose.[34] Obviously, this characterization of qualified expenditures leads to numerous interpretations that are beyond the scope of this text. The basic point is that the credit is meant to encourage expenditures for new technology and for experimentation leading to new technology, not for fine-tuning existing processes or custom orders of a particular product.

Table 15-9

**Business Tax Credits and Their Purposes**

| Business Tax Credit | Purpose of Credit |
|---|---|
| Foreign tax credit | To provide relief from double taxation of income from foreign sources |
| Research and experimental credit | To encourage research in new technology which will strengthen the country's technological base |
| Targeted jobs credit | To encourage employers to hire unemployed workers from disadvantaged groups |
| Rehabilitation tax credit | To encourage the rehabilitation of older buildings and structures to preserve them for future generations |
| Child care cost credit | To encourage small and middle-sized businesses to provide child care for their employees |
| Credit for pension plan startup costs of small employers | To encourage small businesses to start and maintain pension plans for employees |
| Business energy credits | To encourage energy conservation and promote the use of alternative fuels |
| Low-income housing credit | To encourage construction of low-income housing |
| Disabled access credit | To encourage small businesses to provide access for disabled people |
| Alcohol fuels credit | To encourage the use of fuels with an alcohol base |
| Oil recovery credit | To encourage domestic production of oil through use of tertiary recovery methods |
| Reforestation credit | To provide relief to commercial timber products businesses for replanting and seeding trees |
| Welfare-to-work credit | To encourage employment of long-term family assistance recipients |
| Employer-Paid Family and Medical Leave | To encourage employers to better compensate workers who need to take family and/or medical leave |

The base amount for computing the credit is equal to the product of (1) the fixed base percentage, which is the ratio of the taxpayer's total qualified research expenses for the base period of 1985 to 1989 to its total gross receipts for the same period (limited to a maximum of 16 percent), and (2) the taxpayer's average annual gross receipts for the four previous years. The minimum base amount may not be less than 50 percent of the current year's expenditures.[35]

**Example 42** Creator Corporation spent $400,000 on qualified research activities during the current year. Its fixed base percentage is 13%, and average annual gross receipts for the previous 4 years were $1,300,000. What is Creator's base amount for computing the incremental research credit?

**Discussion: The base amount is the fixed base percentage multiplied by the average annual gross receipts for the 4 previous years. Creator's base amount for the current year is $169,000 ($1,300,000 × 13%) according to this calculation. However, the minimum base amount is 50% of current-year expenditures, $200,000 ($400,000 × 50%). Therefore, for purposes of computing the incremental research credit, Creator's base amount is $200,000, the minimum amount allowable.**

**Example 43** Refer to example 42. What is Creator's current-year incremental research expenditure credit?

**Discussion: The incremental research expenditure credit is equal to 20% of the excess of the current year's expenditures, minus the base amount. Creator's credit is $40,000 [20% × ($400,000 + $200,000)].**

The deduction for research and experimental expenditures must be reduced by the amount of the credit.

**Example 44** Refer to examples 42 and 43. What is Creator Corporation's allowable deduction for research and experimental expenditures?

**Discussion: The $400,000 in qualified expenditures must be reduced by the $40,000 tax credit. Therefore, Creator can deduct only $360,000 of the qualified expenditures in calculating its taxable income.**

The second component of the R&E credit is the basic research credit. This credit is equal to 20 percent of qualified expenditures for research that is intended to advance scientific knowledge without a specific commercial objective. For an expenditure to qualify, two conditions must be met: The payments must be made in cash under a written agreement, and the research must be performed or controlled by a university, college, or other nonprofit scientific research organization. Amounts expended for the basic research credit cannot be used in the calculation of the incremental research credit.

## Rehabilitation Tax Credit

Congress felt that some incentive was needed for rejuvenating inner cities and historic structures; it created two types of **rehabilitation tax credits**: a 10 percent older buildings credit and a 20-percent historic structures credit.[36] The older buildings credit applies to structures placed in service before 1936. To qualify for the historic structures credit, a building must be certified as historic by the Treasury Department and must be located in a registered historic district or listed on the National Register of Historic Places. The 2017 Tax Cut and Jobs Act repealed the 10 percent tax credit for buildings built before 1936. There are transition rules for taxpayers who owned or leased property eligible for the 10 percent credit but this is beyond the scope of this text. To avoid a double tax benefit from the tax credit, the basis of the building or structure must be reduced by the amount of the credit taken.

To qualify for the historic structures credit the structure must be "substantially rehabilitated." A substantial rehabilitation means that the rehabilitation expenditures exceed the greater of the property's adjusted basis or $5,000. In addition, at least 75 percent of the external walls (including at least 50 percent being used as external walls) and at least 75 percent of the internal structural framework must remain in place.

**Example 45** Eskimo Joe's purchases a building in downtown Stillwater at a cost of $100,000 and is certified as a historic building. The building was originally placed in service in 1929. Joe's spends $250,000 to rehabilitate the building for use as a restaurant. Do the expenditures qualify for the rehabilitation tax credit?

**Discussion: The expenditures qualify for the 20% historic rehabilitation credit because the building is used in Eskimo Joe's trade or business, the property is registered with the Treasury department as a historic structure. The $250,000 in rehabilitation expenditures exceed Eskimo Joe's $100,000 basis [the greater amount of Eskimo Joe's adjusted basis ($100,000) in the property or $5,000], and the property meets the 75% tests for external walls and internal structural framework. Eskimo Joe's tax credit is $50,000 ($250,000 × 20%). Joe's adjusted basis in the building is $300,000 ($100,000 + $250,000 − $50,000).**

To retain the full benefit of the tax credit, the owner must hold the property for five full years. If a rehabilitated structure is sold before the end of the five-year period, the credit is recaptured (added to the tax liability) in proportion to the number of years (or portions thereof) that the actual holding period fell short of the five-year holding period.

**Example 46** Assume that the building in example 45 is rehabilitated on June 4, 2021. Eskimo Joe's takes the proper credit on its 2021 tax return. On February 4, 2024, Eskimo Joe's sells the building. How much of the $25,000 rehabilitation tax credit must be recaptured in 2024?

**Discussion: Eskimo Joe's has not held the building 5 full years. Eskimo Joe's must recapture the credit attributable to the portion of the 5-year holding period requirement that it did not meet. In this case, the building was held for 2 years and 8 months. Therefore, Eskimo Joe's held the property for only 2 full years, leaving 3 years (2 full years plus a portion of year 3) subject to recapture. Eskimo Joe's must recapture $30,000 ($50,000 ×$^3/_5$) of the credit by adding it to its tax liability in 2024.**

## Child Care Cost Credit

The **child care cost credit** is designed to provide an incentive for employers to provide child care for their employees, either on the workplace premises or in a qualified facility. The credit is the sum of 25 percent of the qualified child care expenses the employer incurs plus 10 percent of qualified child care resources and referral expenditures associated with providing such services. The credit is limited to a maximum of $150,000 in any year. Qualified child care expenditures includes items used to acquire, construct, or expand property and any costs associated with training, compensating, or educating employees of the facility. The cost of contracting with an outside qualified child care facility is included in qualified child care expenses. Qualified child care and referral expenditures are costs incurred by an employer in contracting for qualified child care resources and referral services for its employees.[37]

**Example 47** Smith Company provides child care for its employees. The facility for child care costs $60,000 to operate for the year. Smith spends $3,600 for materials and resources for the facility and $2,500 training the employees on the use of the facility. In addition, Smith incurred $8,000 of qualified referral expenses. What is Smith Company's child care cost credit?

**Discussion: Smith is entitled to a child care cost credit for the sum of 25% of qualified child care expenditures and 10% of qualified child care resources and referral expenditures. During the year Smith incurs $66,100 ($60,000 + $3,600 + $2,500) of child care expenses that qualify for the 25% tax credit and $8,000 of referral expenditures that qualify for the 10% tax credit. Smith's total child care cost credit for the year is $17,325 [($66,100 × 25%) + ($8,000 × 10%)].**

## General Business Credit

The general business credit applies only to a taxpayer that has a tax credit carryover or can claim more than one general business credit during the year. The following are the major tax credits that make up the general business credit:

- Jobs credit
- Alcohol fuels credit
- Research credit
- Low-income housing credit
- Empowerment zone employment credit
- Disabled access credit
- Child care cost credit

The purpose of the **general business credit (GBC)** is to limit the amount of tax credits that can be used to reduce an individual's or a corporation's tax liability. Remember, for a conduit entity, the tax credits claimed by the entity flow through to the partner or shareholder and are deducted on the individual's tax return. The general business credit is limited to a taxpayer's net regular tax liability minus the greater of

The taxpayer's tentative alternative minimum tax (discussed in the next section)

or

Twenty-five percent of the taxpayer's net regular tax liability in excess of $25,000

A taxpayer's net regular tax liability is defined as a taxpayer's regular tax liability minus certain credits (e.g., child-care credit, foreign tax credit). In essence, the regular tax liability can be reduced by all tax credits other than the general business credits. The adoption of the 2017 Tax Cuts and Jobs Act eliminated the alternative minimum tax for corporations. Therefore, for a corporation, the taxpayer's tentative alternative minimum tax is always zero.

**Example 48** The Danmark Corporation has total general business credits of $30,000. It has a net regular tax liability of $27,000. What can Danmark deduct as its general business credit?

**Discussion: Danmark's general business tax credit is $26,500. The credit is limited to the net regular tax of $27,000 minus the greater of the tentative minimum tax, always zero for a corporation, or $500 [($27,000 − $25,000) × 25%]—25% of the excess of its net regular tax liability over $25,000.**

| | | |
|---|---|---|
| Net regular tax | | $27,000 |
| Less: the greater of | | |
| Tentative alternative minimum tax | $ 0 | |
| or | | |
| [25% × ($27,000 − $25,000)] | 500 | 500 |
| General business credit | | $26,500 |

## Reporting of Tax Credits

With the exception of the basic research tax credit, available only to corporations, the tax credits discussed thus far are available to all entities. Because only a corporation is a taxpaying entity, the other organizational forms of business do not receive a direct benefit for the tax credits. Rather, each owner-partner receives an individual statement (called a *K-1*) that states each owner-partner's pro rata share of the credit. As with a sole proprietor, owner-partners can use the credit amount to offset their individual tax liability. However, the amount each owner-partner can use to reduce his or her tax liability varies according to the taxpayer's other income or deductions for the year. A corporation must report the tax credits on Schedule J of Form 1120. Unless the corporation is subject to the general business credit, the amount of the tax credit will reduce its tax liability dollar for dollar. If a corporation or an individual has tax credit carryovers or has more than one general business credit during the year, the amount of tax credit that can be used to reduce the taxpayer's tax liability is limited by the general business credit. Taxpayers are required to use a one-year carryback and a 20-year carryforward period when the current year's general business credit exceeds the allowable limit.

LO 7

Explain the purpose of the alternative minimum tax and how to determine an individual's alternative minimum tax liability.

## 15-3b The Alternative Minimum Tax

In exercising its power of legislative grace, Congress in many instances has chosen to use the tax system to encourage taxpayers to engage in various transactions that it deems socially or economically desirable. This text has discussed many provisions that provide tax relief on transactions that depart from the treatment prescribed by the general concepts of taxation. As the number of such relief provisions proliferated through the years, Congress became increasingly aware that many taxpayers were carefully planning their affairs to take maximum advantage of these provisions. As a result of this planning, documented in various reports by the Treasury Department and academic studies, a large number of corporations and individuals with large economic incomes were paying little or no taxes.

Because Congress was hesitant to single out any one incentive by repealing its relief provisions, the legislators decided to impose an additional tax on those taxpayers who take too much advantage of a specified set of tax incentives. The tax incentives that became subject to this tax are called *tax preference items.* Tax preference items are provisions in the tax law that give certain items of income or deduction special treatment. In addition, to be considered a tax preference item, Congress must specify the item as such (i.e., all items that depart from the general concepts of taxation are not tax preference items).

In 1969, Congress enacted the first tax on preference items. This initial tax was called the *add-on minimum tax*, because the tax on preference items was paid in addition to the regular income tax liability. So as not to completely discourage taxpayers from engaging in tax preference activities, the first tax was 10 percent of tax preference items in excess of $30,000 (i.e., the first $30,000 of tax preference items was exempt from the tax). With minor adjustments, this system remained in effect until 1978. However, studies showed that the tax was not reaching its goal of assuring that all taxpayers paid their fair share of taxes. A new system of taxing preference items, initiated in 1978, was called the **alternative minimum tax (AMT)**. As its name implies, this tax is an alternative calculation of the tax liability that results in the minimum amount of tax that the taxpayer must pay. In effect, the AMT is a separate, parallel tax system. Within this system many preference items allowed in the calculation of the regular tax liability either are not allowed or the amount of tax relief provided is greatly diminished.

We need to point out two aspects of the AMT system before we discuss its mechanics. First, using a parallel system of tax rules requires individual taxpayers to keep a separate set of accounting records to compute the tax. Second, changes in the system in 1986, 1989, 1993, and 2003 have greatly increased the number of taxpayers subject to the tax. For example, the top **alternative minimum tax rate** paid by individual taxpayers has increased to 28 percent, compared with a top marginal regular tax rate of 37 percent. The relatively narrow spread between the two rates has subjected individual taxpayers with fairly minimal amounts of preference items to the tax. Thus, the AMT has become an increasingly important aspect of taxation in recent years. Therefore, to mitigate its impact, the 2017 Tax Cut and Jobs Act repealed the alternative minimum tax for corporations and increased the exemption amounts for individual taxpayers. The system is extremely complex. The discussion that follows provides an overview of the system and the effects it can have on individual taxpayers.

## 15-3c Basic Alternative Minimum Tax Computation

As a separate tax system, the AMT is calculated by applying a tax rate to a tax base.[38] The tax base is called **alternative minimum taxable income (AMTI)**. Exhibit 15-1 provides the general calculation of the AMT. The starting point for the calculation of AMTI is regular taxable income, the taxable income as computed under the general tax system discussed throughout the text. As shown in Exhibit 15-1, AMTI is determined by making two separate categories of modifications to the regular taxable income. The first modification is for adjustments and the second is for preferences. Adjustments are generally made to items that are treated differently in the current period but that will reverse themselves in future periods. As such, adjustments may be either positive or negative (generally positive in the first period and negative in future periods as the difference in treatment reverses itself). Preferences are items that are never allowed for AMT purposes. Because they are never allowed, they do not reverse over time and thus are always positive adjustments in calculating AMTI.

Exhibit 15-1

## Basic Alternative Minimum Tax (AMT) Calculation

| | |
|---|---|
| Regular taxable income | $ XXX |
| Add (Subtract): Adjustments | XXX |
| Add: Preferences | XXX |
| Equals: Tentative alternative minimum taxable income | $ XXX |
| Subtract: Applicable exemption amount | (XXX) |
| Equals: Alternative minimum taxable income | $ XXX |
| Times: Tax rate (26% and 28% for individuals) | × XX% |
| Equals: Tentative alternative minimum tax before allowable tax credits | $ XXX |
| Subtract: Allowable tax credits | (XXX) |
| Equals: Tentative minimum tax | $ XXX |
| Subtract: Regular tax liability | (XXX) |
| Equals: Alternative minimum tax (if positive) | $ XXX |

The AMT uses exemption amounts to recognize that some level of preference items should be allowed. However, these exemption amounts phase out at varying levels of tentative AMTI, resulting in reduced or eliminated exemption amounts for taxpayers with large amounts of tax preference items. Subtraction of the applicable exemption amount yields the tax base, AMTI. The tentative tax is calculated by applying a flat rate to AMTI. Individuals are subject to an AMT rate of 26 percent on the first $199,900 ($99,950 for married filing separately) of AMTI and 28 percent on AMTI in excess of $199,900 ($99,950 for married filing separately). These amounts will be adjusted annually for inflation. Multiplication of the AMTI by the AMT rate yields the tentative minimum tax amount before allowable tax credits. The tentative minimum tax is reduced by the foreign tax credit and individual nonrefundable tax credits. Subtraction of the allowable tax credits provides what is referred to as the *tentative minimum tax liability*. It is tentative because it must be compared with the regular tax liability to determine whether the AMT is applicable. Because the AMT is the minimum amount of tax that the taxpayer must pay, if the regular tax liability is greater than the tentative minimum tax, the AMT is not applicable and the taxpayer pays the regular tax liability. On the other hand, if the tentative minimum tax is greater than the regular tax, the taxpayer is subject to the AMT. Although the taxpayer pays the full amount of the tentative AMT, the tax law views the taxpayer as paying the tax in two components: the regular tax liability and the additional tax imposed because of the AMT. Thus, as a definition, the AMT is equal to the tentative minimum tax in excess of the regular tax liability.

The remainder of this section discusses the specific components of the AMT calculation. Because of the technical complexity of many of the adjustments and preferences, this book makes no attempt to present every detail of every item that affects the AMT. The purpose of the discussion is to provide a basic understanding of the approach the AMT uses to tax those taxpayers whose use of tax incentives is excessive (as defined by the AMT).

### Alternative Minimum Tax Adjustments

The purpose of the AMT adjustments is to account for the effect of items that must be determined using either alternative calculations or alternative accounting methods for AMT purposes. Many of these adjustments are extremely technical. Table 15-10 provides a brief description of the AMT adjustments by type of taxpayer affected.[39]

In general, the use of the AMT calculation method results in acceleration of income items or deferral of deduction items. The net effect of either is a higher taxable income in the initial period(s) of difference. However, most **alternative minimum tax adjustment** items are not disallowed for AMT purposes; they are merely spread out (in the case of deductions) or accelerated (in the case of income items), with the difference in the two calculations being temporary, not permanent. That is, the initial differences reverse themselves over time and therefore have the opposite effect on AMTI. Thus, adjustments can be either positive or negative in the calculation of AMTI.

Table 15-10

## Alternative Minimum Tax Adjustment Items

| Adjustment Item | General Description |
|---|---|
| Depreciation on property placed in service after 12/31/86 | AMT depreciation calculated using alternative depreciation system (longer life). |
| Mining exploration and development costs | Must be amortized over 10 years for AMT purposes. |
| Long-term contracts | Taxpayers using completed contract method must use percentage-of-completed-contract method for AMT purposes. |
| Amortization of pollution control facilities | Must be amortized over a longer period for AMT. |
| Gains deferred on installment sales | Gains may not be deferred on installment sales for AMT purposes. |
| Gain/loss on properties subject to AMT rules that affect basis | Any AMT adjustments that affect the basis of property must be reflected in the gain/loss on the property when it is disposed of. |
| Limitation on deductions from AGI | Most deductions from AGI disallowed or reduced; no standard deduction. |
| Exercise of incentive stock options | Excess of fair market value over exercise price at date of exercise is included in AMTI. |
| Research and development expenditures | Amounts expensed in excess of 10-year amortization are added back. |
| Certain tax shelter farming activities | Losses not deductible against current period passive losses; can only deduct against future period income from farming activities. |

The most common adjustments required of individual taxpayers are deductions from adjusted gross income that must be modified or are not allowed for AMT purposes. The only itemized deductions allowed from AGI for AMT purposes are:

- Medical expenses in excess of 7.5 percent of AGI
- Charitable contributions
- Qualified housing interest
- Investment interest
- Gambling losses (in excess of gambling winnings) and premature cessation of annuities

Therefore, individuals must add back all taxes. In addition, the standard deduction is not allowed and is added back by taxpayers who do not itemize.

Recall that one advantage of an incentive stock option is that the taxpayer does not recognize income on the exercise of the option. However, in computing the taxpayer's AMTI, the difference between the exercise price and the fair market value of the stock at the date of exercise is treated as a positive tax adjustment.

While the difference is a positive tax adjustment to AMTI in the year of exercise, for AMT purposes the amount is added to the taxpayer's basis in the stock for computing the AMT gain or loss on the sale of the stock. Therefore, the positive tax adjustment is a timing difference for AMT purposes.

**Example 49** On January 7, 2020, Maureen receives the right to acquire 400 shares of Rehoboth Corporation stock for $12 per share through an incentive stock option plan. The current fair market value of the stock is $8. She exercises her right to purchase the stock on September 9, 2021, when the fair market value of the stock is $15 per share. What amount must Maureen include as a tax adjustment on the exercise of the incentive stock option?

**Discussion: Maureen does not recognize income on the exercise of the option. However, the difference between the fair market value of the shares at the date of exercise ($15) and the exercise price ($12) is a tax adjustment in computing her alternative minimum tax liability. Maureen's AMT adjustment is $1,200 [($15 − $12) × 400].**

Table 15-11

## Alternative Minimum Tax (AMT) Preference Items

| Preference Item | General Description |
|---|---|
| Percentage depletion in excess of basis | Percentage depletion deductions in excess of the basis of the property are disallowed. |
| Intangible drilling costs on oil and gas properties | Limited to 65% of the net income from each property. |
| Excess depreciation on property placed in service before 1987 | Depreciation in excess of straight-line depreciation is not allowed for AMT purposes. |
| Exclusion of gain on qualified small business stock | Must include 7% of the gain excluded from income. |
| Reserves for bad debts of financial institutions | Financial institutions must use the specific write-off method for bad debts. |

**Example 50** Assume the same facts as in example 49. On October 23, 2023, Maureen sells the stock for $25. What is her gain for regular tax and AMT purposes?

**Discussion: Maureen's basis in the stock for regular tax purposes is $12 per share and her gain is $5,200 [($25 − $12) × 400]. However, for AMT purposes, Maureen adds the $3 per share ($1,200 ÷ 400 shares) tax preference amount included in her AMT calculation in 2020 to the basis of the stock. Her basis in the stock is $15 ($12 + $3) and Maureen's gain for AMT purposes is $4,000 [($25 − $15) × 400]. This results in a $1,200 ($4,000 − $5,200) negative AMT adjustment in 2023.**

### Alternative Minimum Tax Preferences

Preferences are always added in the computation of AMTI. Although the preference items reflect differences in how the two systems treat such items, preference items either do not reverse or Congress has determined that the taxpayer should not have the benefit of a reversal. Because preference reversals are not allowed, there is no correlative adjustment to the basis of the property for AMT purposes. The list of preference items is much shorter than the list of adjustment items. Table 15-11 lists the preference items and briefly describes the AMT treatment of the item.[40]

An example of a preference item is the capital gain on qualified small business stock. Recall from Chapter 11 that 50 percent of the gain on qualified small business stock acquired after August 10, 1993, and held for more than five years is excluded from taxation. However, in computing an individual's alternative minimum tax, seven percent of the excluded gain is treated as a tax preference.

**Example 51** Jagruti purchased 1,000 shares of qualified small business stock on October 27, 2016. On November 3, 2021, she sells the 1,000 shares at a gain of $150,000. What amount of the gain does Jagruti include as a tax preference?

**Discussion: In determining her taxable income, Jagruti can exclude $75,000 ($150,000 × $50%) of the gain from gross income. In computing her alternative minimum taxable income, she must include 7% of the exclusion, $5,250 ($75,000 × 7%), as a tax preference.**

### Alternative Minimum Tax Exemptions

After making all the required adjustments and adding the preference items to taxable income, the result is the tentative alternative minimum taxable income. In determining the AMTI tax base, an exemption amount is allowed as a reduction of the tentative AMTI. The exemption amount is designed to eliminate taxpayers with relatively moderate amounts of taxable income who do not have significant amounts of adjustments and/or preferences from the AMT. These amounts are indexed for inflation. The exemption amount starts at a tentative amount based on the type of taxpayer and is then reduced by 25 percent of every dollar by which the tentative AMTI exceeds a specified level. Table 15-12 provides the exemption amounts and their phase-out ranges by the taxpayer's filing status. Note that the effect of the phase-out is to deny exemption amounts to taxpayers whose AMTI exceeds the amounts in the last column of the table.

Table 15-12

## Alternative Minimum Tax (AMT) Exemption Amounts and Phase-Outs

| Type of Entity | Filing Status | Initial Exemption | Phase-Out Begins at AMTI of: | No Exemption if AMTI Exceeds: |
|---|---|---|---|---|
| Individual | Single | $ 73,600 | $ 523,600 | $ 818,000 |
| | Head of household | $ 73,600 | $ 523,600 | $ 818,000 |
| | Married filing jointly | $114,600 | $1,047,200 | $1,505,600 |
| | Married filing separately | $ 57,300 | $ 523,600 | $ 752,800 |

The practical effect of the exemption is that average individual taxpayers may ignore the AMT with little risk of its applying to them. However, individuals with more substantial incomes need to be aware of what could happen when they engage in transactions that result in AMT adjustments and preferences. Because of the complexity of the AMT calculation, the aid of a tax specialist is virtually a necessity for high-income individuals.

### Alternative Minimum Tax Credits

In general, the only tax credits allowed against the tentative AMT are the foreign tax credit and individual's nonrefundable tax credits.[41] Individual nonrefundable credits include the child tax credit, the child-and dependent-care credit, the adoption credit, the credit for the elderly and disabled, and the higher education tax credits.

### Alternative Minimum Tax Credit Against the Regular Tax

Most adjustments made in calculating AMTI are merely timing differences. The AMT calculation for these items accelerates income for AMT purposes so that it is reported earlier than it would be for regular tax purposes. This creates a form of double jeopardy when a taxpayer is subject to the AMT in earlier years and the regular tax in later years when the timing difference reverses. That is, the accelerated income is taxed first under the AMT and again later, when the timing difference reverses for regular tax purposes.

To avoid double taxation of reversal items, Congress enacted a minimum tax credit that can only be used to reduce the regular tax liability in later years when the regular tax exceeds the alternative minimum tax. The **AMT minimum tax credit** is calculated each year in which the AMT applies. The amount of the credit is the difference between the actual AMT for the year and a recomputed AMT. The recomputed AMT is the AMT that would have been paid if the reversal adjustments did not enter into the AMTI calculation. That is, the AMT is recalculated using only preference items and those adjustments that do not reverse. The credit is carried forward and used to reduce the regular tax liability in those years in which the regular tax is greater than the AMT. The credit may be used only to reduce the regular tax to the tentative AMT amount.[42]

### Tax Planning and the Alternative Minimum Tax

The relatively narrow gap between the 28 percent top AMT individual rate and the 37 percent maximum tax rate for individuals makes it easy to trigger the AMT. Thus, it is important for tax-planning purposes to consider AMT implications along with the regular tax. Although the overall goal of tax planning remains the maximization of wealth via the minimization of taxes, too great a reduction in the regular tax may trigger the AMT. When an individual expects the AMT to apply, a strategy opposite to that for regular tax purposes is often appropriate. A rule of thumb to follow for regular tax-planning purposes is to defer income and accelerate deductions. Because the AMT tax rate for individuals is lower than that for the regular tax, a taxpayer subject to the AMT would generally be better off to accelerate income into the AMT year and defer deductions to a regular tax year.

**Example 52** Eve is a financial consultant with several large clients. Her contract with her large clients lets her bill them for services monthly or quarterly, at her option. In reviewing her current-year tax situation, Eve determines that she will be subject to the alternative minimum tax at the 26% rate. Because of several reversing adjustments, Eve does not think that she will be subject to the AMT next year, but she will be in the 32% marginal tax rate bracket. If Eve submits monthly bills for November to her large clients, she estimates that she will receive $40,000 before the end of the year. What is Eve's tax savings on the $40,000 in income if she submits the monthly bills?

**Discussion: Because Eve is subject to the AMT, she will pay $10,400 ($40,000 × 26%) in tax. Delaying the billing to next year will result in a tax of $12,800 ($40,000 × 32%). Billing this year saves $2,400 ($12,800 − $10,400) in taxes. However, because she will have to pay the tax a year earlier, Eve should also consider the time value of money effect. Assuming a 10% time value of money, the present value of paying the tax next year is $11,635 ($12,800 × 0.909 present value factor). Eve's real tax savings by billing in the current year is $1,235 ($11,635 − $10,400).**

Although the planning result in example 52 is a straightforward application of the basic strategy, the complexity of the AMT calculation makes it difficult to apply the basic strategy in most situations. For example, should a taxpayer operating as a sole proprietorship and eligible to use the completed contract method of accounting for long-term contracts elect to use the percentage-of-completed-contract method to avoid paying the AMT? General answers to such questions do not usually hold up. The only reliable way for taxpayers to make such decisions is through the use of long-term planning projections that show the effects of all alternative courses of action. To make such long-term projections, taxpayers need to be aware of the adjustments and preferences that can trigger the AMT and consider them when evaluating investment opportunities.

### 15-3d Planning Commentary

A partnership and an S corporation must separately report to each partner-shareholder her or his share of the foreign tax credit, the historic rehabilitation tax credit, and the research and experimental tax credit. The incremental research credit is not available to partnerships or sole proprietorships. The amount of credits available to a partner-shareholder depends on the taxpayer's other income and deductions for the year. Therefore, tax planning at the entity level is difficult.

The alternative minimum tax ensures that an individual pays a minimum amount of tax each year. Because the income from a partnership or an S corporation flows through to each individual partner-owner, tax planning for the AMT is not done at the partnership or S corporation level but must be done at the individual partner-owner level. Further, because most of the adjustments and tax preferences affect individual taxpayers, the AMT is usually of greater concern for partners and shareholders of S corporations than for corporations.

## 15-4 INTERNATIONAL TAX ASPECTS

LO 8
Describe common tax transactions subject to multi-national tax jurisdiction.

One of the cornerstones of the tax law is that U.S. citizens, resident aliens, and domestic corporations are subject to U.S. tax on their worldwide income. Thus, a U.S. citizen working in England is taxed on the income earned in England. As the world continues to move toward a global economy, understanding how the U.S. income tax laws apply to individuals who have income in a foreign country or to corporations with foreign operations has become increasingly important. The remaining section of this chapter consists of two parts. The first deals with the tax treatment of foreign transactions by U.S. taxpayers, with the primary emphasis on how these transactions affect corporate taxpayers. The second part is an overview of the taxation of foreign persons and foreign corporations that generate income in the United States. Although a comprehensive study of international taxation is beyond the scope of this text, the discussion will provide a general understanding of the laws governing the taxation of foreign income and the U.S. taxation of foreign entities operating in the United States.

## 15-4a Taxpayers Subject to U.S. Taxation

United States citizens, resident aliens, and domestic corporations are subject to U.S. tax on their worldwide income. A **resident alien** is an individual who has established a legal residence in the United States but is not a citizen of the United States.[43] There are two general methods of establishing residency. Under the first, a non-U.S. citizen (commonly referred to as an alien) can become a resident alien by obtaining a permanent status card (referred to as a green card) from the U.S. Immigration and Naturalization Service. Residency also can be established by meeting the "substantial presence" test. This generally requires a non-U.S. citizen to be present in the United States for more than 183 days during the current year.[44]

A **nonresident alien** is an individual who is a resident of another country and is not a citizen or resident of the United States. Nonresident aliens and corporations or other legal entities not formed under U.S. laws are only subject to tax on income earned in the United States and not on their worldwide income. Therefore, the distinction between being classified as a resident alien or U.S. corporation and a nonresident alien or foreign corporation plays an important role in calculating an individual's or an entity's U.S. tax liability.

## 15-4b Tax Treaties

A **tax treaty** is an agreement between two countries that explains how a citizen or corporation of one country is taxed when working or conducting business in the other country. The primary objective of a tax treaty is to prevent income from being taxed in both countries (i.e., double taxation). The United States achieves this objective by allowing a foreign tax credit for foreign taxes paid. The details of the foreign tax credit are discussed later in the chapter. Another objective of a tax treaty is to promote cooperation and compliance with the tax laws of the treaty nations. In addition, treaties are usually designed to foster economic or social objectives between the countries or to resolve controversial issues. Currently, the United States has entered into tax treaty agreements with all the major industrialized nations. The starting point for the United States in negotiating a treaty with another country is a document referred to as the model tax treaty. Through negotiations, the model tax treaty is modified to reflect specific political, social, and tax objectives of the countries. As a result, treaties often contain provisions that exempt certain income from taxation or tax that income at a lower rate. For example, a treaty may contain a provision that the income earned by students, teachers, or doctors who are working in the country for a short period of time is exempt from tax. Provisions that clarify the residency status of an individual or corporation if the taxpayer qualifies for residency in both countries are also commonly found in a tax treaty.

## 15-4c Organizational Structure of Foreign Operations

The following section discusses several of the common organizational forms a corporation might use to conduct business outside the United States, and the general tax rules associated with establishing and operating these business forms.

### Foreign Subsidiary (Controlled Foreign Corporation)

Prior to the adoption of the 2017 Tax Cut and Jobs Act, the most common organizational structure U.S. corporations used in conducting foreign operations was a foreign subsidiary corporation established under the laws of the foreign country with the U.S. parent owning at least 50 percent of the foreign corporation. A **controlled foreign corporation (CFC)** is a foreign corporation that was more than 50 percent-owned by U.S. shareholders. The 50 percent ownership test was met if, on any day during the year, U.S. shareholders owned more than 50 percent of the voting stock or more than 50 percent of the total value of the corporate stock.[45]

**Example 53** Riopelle Corporation forms Imperato Corporation in the country of Gansed. Riopelle owns 80% of the voting stock and 40% of Imperato's preferred stock. The remaining stock is owned by citizens of Gansed. The preferred shares represent 25% of the fair market value of the company. All of Riopelle's shareholders are U.S. citizens. Is Imperato Corporation a controlled foreign corporation?

**Discussion: Because Riopelle owns more than 50% of the voting stock of Imperato, which is a foreign corporation, it is a CFC. Riopelle does not have to own more than 50% of all classes of stock, only more than 50% of the voting stock. In addition, Riopelle also meets the more-than-50%-of-fair-market-value test [70% = (80% × 75%) + (40% × 25%)].**

The major tax benefit associated with a CFC was that the U.S. parent was generally not taxed on the foreign corporation's income until the earnings were repatriated (i.e., paid) to the parent as a dividend. When the earnings were paid to the U.S. parent (income was recognized), the parent was allowed a foreign tax credit for foreign taxes paid by the CFC on the income.

**Example 54** In example 53, assume that Imperato has $2.5 million of taxable income from its manufacturing operations and that no dividend distributions are made during the year. The tax rate in Gansed is 22%, and Riopelle's marginal tax rate is 34%. What is the tax treatment of the income to Imperato and Riopelle?

**Discussion: Imperato will pay $550,000 ($2.5 million × 22%) of tax to Gansed. Because none of the earnings are paid to Riopelle, the $2.5 million is not subject to U.S. taxation. When the earnings are paid to Riopelle, it can claim a foreign tax credit for the taxes paid to Gansed on the income it recognizes.**

Although the general rule was that U.S. shareholders are not taxed on the foreign earnings of a CFC until a dividend is paid to the U.S. parent, certain income (referred to as *Subpart F income*) is taxed before being paid to the parent.

Historically, a U.S. corporation would establish a foreign subsidiary in a tax haven (i.e., a country with no tax or a minimal tax) to conduct its foreign operations. The foreign subsidiary would serve as a conduit through which the goods would pass on their way to the final customer. The tax savings from the arrangement offset the additional cost of operating the subsidiary. In fact, some companies actually shipped the goods from the U.S. parent directly to the customer and only had the documentation (e.g., sales invoices, payments) flow through the foreign subsidiary. To prevent this abuse, Congress established the Subpart F rules, which tax the Subpart F income when it is earned rather than when paid to the parent as a dividend.[46] **Subpart F income** consists primarily of interest, dividends, rents, royalties, and foreign base company income. Foreign base company income includes foreign personal holding company income, foreign base company sales income, foreign base company services income, foreign base company shipping income, and foreign base company oil-related income. The definitions of the various types of foreign base company income are extremely complex. For example, foreign base company sales income is income derived from the purchase of personal property from or on behalf of a related party, or from the sale of personal property to or on behalf of a related person.

The tax treatment of Subpart F income was similar to that of a conduit entity (i.e., partnership or S corporation) in that it is taxed whether or not it was actually distributed to the shareholder. Because the U.S. parent reports Subpart F income when it is earned, the parent is not taxed when the foreign subsidiary pays out the income as a dividend. Consistent with conduit entity accounting, the parent corporation's basis in the CFC stock is increased when Subpart F income is recognized and decreased when a nontaxable dividend is received.

**Example 55** Rosenburg, Inc., a U.S. corporation, owns 100% of Tourney, a foreign corporation operating in Bermuda, which has no income tax. Rosenburg ships its goods directly to its foreign customers from its manufacturing plant in Dallas. All sales invoices and receipts are processed by Tourney in Bermuda. Therefore, Tourney's income is foreign base company sales income. Tourney reports $3 million of income and does not pay any foreign taxes or distribute any dividends during the year. Rosenburg's marginal tax rate is 34%. What are the tax effects of this arrangement for Rosenburg?

**Discussion: Tourney is a CFC because Rosenburg owns more than 50% of its stock. The $3 million of foreign base company sales income is Subpart F income that is taxed to Rosenburg even though it was not actually distributed during the year. Rosenburg's basis in Tourney stock increases by the $3 million income recognition.**

**Example 56** Assume that, in example 55, Tourney pays a $500,000 dividend to Rosenburg in the following year from the $3 million of previously taxed income. Is Rosenburg taxed on the dividend?

**Discussion: Because Rosenburg included the $500,000 in income the previous year, the dividend is not included in the current year. Rosenburg's basis in the Tourney stock is decreased by the $500,000 nontaxable dividend. This treatment is similar to that of a distribution from a partnership or S corporation.**

The 2017 Tax Cut and Jobs Act changes the current tax treatment of foreign income from a controlled foreign corporation (a U.S. corporation owns more than 10 percent). Under the new law for tax years of foreign corporations that begin after December 31, 2017, the tax law provides an exemption (known as a deduction for dividends received or DRD) for certain foreign income. A DRD provides a 100 percent deduction for the foreign-source portion of dividends received from the foreign corporation. The foreign-source portion of a dividend is the ratio of post-1986 undistributed U.S. earnings to the total post-1986 undistributed earnings of the foreign corporation.

$$\text{Foreign Sourced Dividend Received} \times \frac{\text{Post-1986 Undistributed U.S. earnings}}{\text{Total Post-1986 Undistributed earnings}}$$

**Example 57** The Logo Corporation, a domestic corporation, owns 70% of TAG, a foreign corporation. During the current year, Logo receives $80,000 in dividends. Tag's post-1986 undistributed U.S. earnings are $2,000,000, and its post-1986 undistributed earnings are $8,000,000. What is Logo's dividend received deduction for the current year?

**Discussion: Logo is entitled to 100% DRD for the pro rata share of the dividend received from Tag. Logo's dividend received deduction is $20,000 [$80,000 × ($2,000,000 ÷ $8,000,000)].**

Under the new law, a U.S. company owning at least 10 percent of a foreign subsidiary must include in income the shareholder's pro-rata share of the undistributed, non-previously-taxed post-1986 foreign earnings and profits (E&P) of the foreign subsidiary. The amount included is net of any aggregate foreign earnings and profits deficits. The new law applies for the subsidiary's last tax year beginning before 2018. The portion of the E&P that is cash or cash equivalents is taxed at a reduced rate of 15.5 percent while any remaining E&P is taxed at 8 percent.

**Example 58** The Hanscom Corporation, a domestic corporation, owns 60% of Porano, a foreign corporation. Hanscom's pro rata share of post-1986 undistributed U.S. earnings is $3,000,000 of which $2,500,000 is cash or cash equivalents. How much will Hanscom pay in tax in the current year?

**Discussion: Hanscom will pay $387,500 ($2,500,000 × 15.5%) of tax on the E&P from cash and cash equivalents and $40,000 ($500,000 × 8%) on the other undistributed E&P. Hanscom's total tax will be $427,500 ($387,500 + $40,000).**

Under the new law, the U.S. shareholder can elect to pay the tax liability over a period of eight years. The payments for each of the first five years is 8 percent of the total tax liability. The amount in year six is 15 percent, year seven is 20 percent, and year eight is 25 percent.

**Example 59** Assume that, in example 58, Hanscom elects to pay its tax liability over 8 years, what amount would it owe each year?

**Discussion: Hanscom will pay $34,200 ($427,500 × 8%) in each of the first 5 years. It would pay $64,125 ($427,500 x 15%) in year 6, $85,500 ($427,500 x 20%) in year 7, and $106,875 ($427,500 x 25%) in year 8.**

**Transfer Pricing** Transfer pricing issues arise on the sale or exchange of goods and services between related entities. Tax avoidance may occur because of the ability of the related parties to control the timing, amount, and the location of the sale price. By manipulating the sale price, a U.S. parent could minimize its U.S. tax liability by selling its product at cost to a CFC located in a country with a lower marginal tax rate than the United States or in a country that does not impose a tax. To prevent this, Congress has established **transfer pricing** methods that set the sale price between related entities. One method, called cost plus, requires the parent to sell its goods to the foreign subsidiary at a price equal to its cost plus a markup.[47] Typically, the markup is stated as a percentage of the cost (e.g., 130 percent). However, the markup cannot be lower than the amount the parent would mark up the goods if it were selling them to an unrelated third party.

**Example 60** Whittman Corporation manufactures fiberglass insulation at a cost of $2.00 per linear foot. It sells the goods to wholesalers for $3.00 per linear foot. Whittman uses a 100%-owned CFC in Portugal to sell its insulation in Europe. Whittman sells the insulation to the CFC for $3.10 per linear foot. Is Whittman selling the insulation at a valid transfer price?

**Discussion: The $3.10 sale price is a valid transfer price under the cost plus method. There is no requirement that the price at which it sells the insulation to the CFC be the same as the wholesale price. The only requirement is that it not sell the insulation for less than $3.00 per linear foot (the price charged to unrelated parties). Note: The IRS still has the authority to set the transfer price if it feels that the price Whittman charges its CFC (e.g., $2.50 per linear foot) does not properly reflect its income.**

## concept check

Under the *arm's length transaction concept*, transactions that are not made at arm's-length are generally not accorded their intended tax effect. To prevent taxpayers from avoiding payment of the appropriate U.S. tax on transactions between related entities, transfer pricing rules are used to set prices on related party sales. If the IRS determines that the price being used in a sale to a related entity does not properly reflect the income from the transaction, it can set the transfer price at an amount it feels is appropriate in the circumstances.

## 15-4d Taxation of Nonresident Aliens and Foreign Corporations

The discussion above was limited to taxpayers who were citizens, resident aliens, or domestic corporations conducting business overseas. A very different tax treatment results if a nonresident alien or foreign corporation is doing business in the United States. The income earned by a nonresident alien or a foreign corporation is classified into three categories: U.S. trade or business income, U.S. nonbusiness income, and non-U.S. trade or business income. If the source of income is connected to a U.S. trade or business (referred to as effectively connected trade or business income), a nonresident alien or foreign corporation is taxed similarly to a U.S. citizen or corporation. U.S. nonbusiness income, which includes dividends, interest, royalties, and rents, is generally taxed at a flat rate of 30 percent. Trade or business income that is not effectively connected to the United States generally is not subject to U.S. tax.

## U.S. Trade or Business Income

Foreign corporations doing business in the United States are subject to U.S. tax on their effectively connected trade or business income at rates that apply to any domestic corporation.[48] Effectively connected trade or business income is determined by applying two tests: the asset use test and the business activities test.[49] Both of these tests are designed to aid in determining if the income should be subject to U.S. tax in the same manner as any U.S. corporation or if it should be treated as nonbusiness income subject to the flat 30 percent tax. The distinction is important because trade or business income is reported net of expenses, while no deductions are allowed against nonbusiness income.

The asset use test is met if income is derived from assets used in or held for use in the active conduct of a U.S. business. The business activities test is met if the U.S. business activities of the foreign corporation are a material factor in the realization of income or gain and loss. The two tests may be applied together or individually to determine if the resulting income or gain or loss is effectively connected trade or business income or nonbusiness income. Generally, if a nonresident alien or a foreign corporation is conducting a profit-oriented activity within the United States that is carried on in a regular, substantial, and continuous manner, income derived from the activity is deemed to be effectively connected trade or business income.

**Example 61** Konjo Corporation is a Japanese corporation that manufactures children's toys in a plant in Dayton, Ohio. Konjo sells all its toys to customers outside the U.S. and performs all warranty work on returned goods in Dayton. In the current year, Konjo's gross revenue from toy sales is $2 million. Cost of goods sold and other operating expenses total $1.5 million. What is the tax treatment of the income and expenses?

**Discussion: Because Konjo's manufacturing operation is located in the United States and the plant is a material factor in producing the income, it meets both the asset use test and the business activities test. Konjo deducts its cost of goods sold and related expenses in arriving at its taxable income of $500,000 ($2,000,000 – $1,500,000) and is taxed on the income at the same rate as a U.S. corporation.**

**Example 62** Assume the same facts as in example 61 except that Konjo also earns $300,000 in dividend income from investments made with the profits from its Dayton manufacturing operations. What is the tax treatment of the investment income?

**Discussion: Because Konjo acquired the investment assets with the profits from its manufacturing operations, the business activities test is met and the $300,000 of investment income is considered trade or business income. The dividend income increases Konjo's taxable income to $800,000 ($500,000 + $300,000).**

## Taxation of Nonbusiness Income from U.S. Sources

Nonbusiness income received by a foreign person or entity is not taxable unless the income is received from a U.S. source. For example, interest income paid by a U.S. bank or dividends paid by a U.S. corporation are considered U.S.-sourced nonbusiness income. Other taxable U.S. sources of nonbusiness income include rents and royalties. Because a foreign taxpayer may not be physically present in the United States, the payor of the income is required to withhold the tax when the income is paid. Therefore, it is referred to as a withholding tax. Generally, these sources of income are subject to a flat withholding tax of 30 percent, and the foreign taxpayer is not allowed any deductions against the income tax.[50] The withholding allows for the collection of tax on amounts that may otherwise go untaxed and is administratively convenient for both the taxpayer and the government. Although the tax rate on nonbusiness income is 30 percent, many tax treaties provide for lower tax withholding rates on certain types of income (e.g., interest).

**Example 63** Moby is a citizen and resident of Xarbu, a newly formed Eastern European country. Moby receives a $10,000 dividend from Finglass, a U.S. corporation, and $5,000 in interest income from the Bank of Xarbu. What is the tax treatment of Moby's dividend and interest income?

**Discussion: The dividend is received from a U.S. source, and a 30% tax is levied on the dividend. Finglass is required to withhold the $3,000 ($10,000 × 30%) tax from the dividend and pays Moby $7,000 ($10,000 − $3,000). If Xarbu has a tax treaty with the United States, the withholding rate might be less than the 30% rate. The interest income is not from a U.S. source, and Moby does not pay any U.S. tax on the $5,000 of interest income.**

If a nonresident alien or a foreign corporation is not conducting business in the United States, there is generally no withholding tax on the sale or exchange of U.S. personal property. One reason for the nontaxability of personal property transactions is the difficulty the IRS would have in correctly measuring the gain on the sale and collecting the appropriate tax. Consider the following situation. Two foreign corporations, the Maltise Corporation and the Congdon Corporation, own property in the United States. During the year, each sells its property for $200,000. Maltise acquired its property for $100,000 while Congdon paid $300,000 for its property. If both were assessed the 30 percent withholding tax on the sale price, each would pay a tax of $60,000 ($200,000 × 30%). Maltise's $60,000 tax on its $100,000 ($200,000 − $100,000) gain would produce an effective tax rate of 60 percent ($60,000 ÷ 100,000), or double the intended rate. The tax consequences to Congdon would be much worse. Congdon would pay a tax of $60,000 on a loss of $100,000 ($200,000 − $300,000). By exempting the sale of property from the 30 percent withholding tax, the tax law ensures that foreign taxpayers are not adversely affected by the tax.

## concept check

The withholding tax on nonbusiness income foreign taxpayers receive from U.S. sources reflects the *administrative convenience concept*. The U.S. tax law generally follows the *pay-as-you-go concept* with amounts withheld for taxes as income is earned. Tax returns are filed later that calculate the tax on the income, which is offset by such withholdings. Because it would be administratively difficult to require foreign individuals to file tax returns solely for the purpose of taxing nonbusiness income, a flat 30 percent withholding rate is used to tax nonbusiness income of foreign taxpayers.

# CHAPTER SUMMARY

Contributions to a qualified pension plan let an individual accumulate tax-free a substantial nest egg for retirement. Pension plans can be contributory or noncontributory. Qualified pension plans can be further classified as defined contribution plans or defined benefit plans. A defined contribution plan bases retirement benefits on the contributions to the plan and the growth in its assets. A defined benefit plan bases retirement benefits on the employee's salary and years of service. The two most common types of defined contribution plans are the money purchase plan and the profit-sharing plan. A drawback of the money purchase plan is that a fixed amount must be contributed to the plan each year. The maximum contribution to a money purchase plan is the lower of 25 percent of the employee's salary (up to $290,000) or $58,000. For a profit-sharing plan, the contribution is limited to 25 percent of the employee's salary (up to $290,000) or $58,000. The maximum yearly benefit that a retiree can receive under a defined benefit plan is $230,000.

Self-employed individuals and owner-partners of a partnership can establish either a Keogh plan, a simplified employee pension plan (SEP), or a savings incentive match plan for employees (SIMPLE). The maximum contribution to a Keogh plan is 20 percent of the owner's net self-employment income (up to $290,000) or $58,000. A single taxpayer can contribute up to $6,000 ($12,000 if married) of earned income to an individual retirement account (IRA). Taxpayers who are not participants in a qualified pension plan, including a Keogh plan, SEP, or a savings incentive match plan for employees (SIMPLE), can deduct the amount they contribute to an IRA. Unmarried taxpayers who are members of a pension plan can make a deductible contribution to an IRA if their adjusted gross income is less than $66,000 ($105,000 if married). The deductible amount of the contribution is phased out proportionately for adjusted gross incomes between $66,000 and $76,000 ($105,000 to $125,000) if married). Under a SIMPLE-IRA, eligible employees can choose to have a percentage of their salary, up to a maximum of $13,500, contributed to the plan. The employer has the option of either matching the employee's contribution up to a maximum of 3 percent of the employee's compensation, or contributing 2 percent of an employee's compensation regardless of the amount the employee contributes to the plan. Under the first option, the employer can elect to match a lower percentage but must match at least 1 percent of the employee's compensation. This election can be made only twice within a five-year period. Employee and employer contributions with a SIMPLE-401(k) are similar except that the employer cannot elect to match the employee's contribution at a lower percentage.

Whether a distribution from a qualified pension plan or an IRA is taxable depends on whether the taxpayer contributed to the plan with before-or after-tax dollars. Only the portion of the distribution that is from after-tax contributions is nontaxable (except for Roth IRAs, which are fully excludable). The IRS has established penalties to ensure that the entity or taxpayer responsible for the administration of the pension plan complies with the rules and requirements.

The two types of stock options are nonqualified stock options (NQSO) and incentive stock options (ISO). For an NQSO, the amount recognized as ordinary income and the date the income is recognized depend on whether the option has a readily ascertainable fair market value. If the option has a readily ascertainable fair market value, the taxpayer recognizes the income equal to the market value of the option at the date of grant. If the option does not have a readily ascertainable fair market value, the taxpayer recognizes as ordinary income the difference between the exercise price and the fair market value of the stock at date of exercise. Incentive stock options receive more-favorable tax treatment because no ordinary income is recognized either at the date of grant or date of exercise. Further, the difference between the amount paid for the ISO at the date of exercise and the price of the stock when it is sold is treated as a capital gain.

Tax credits are used to provide incentives for taxpayers to engage in specific activities, or provide equitable treatment among taxpayers.

The alternative minimum tax (AMT) is a parallel tax system that ensures that individuals pay a minimum amount of federal income taxes. The starting point for calculating an individual's AMT is regular taxable income. In calculating AMT, income and deductions are adjusted from the treatment provided under the regular tax system. These adjustments may be positive or negative. Adjustments are generally positive in the first period and negative in future periods as the difference in treatment reverses itself. Preferences are items that are never allowed in calculating the alternative minimum tax.

Individuals and corporations are taxed on their worldwide income. Resident aliens are taxed the same as U.S. citizens. Corporations doing business abroad may use several business forms to minimize U.S. tax on their foreign income. Each of these forms has special features that let them meet the firm's economic and/or tax objectives. Income from a controlled foreign corporation (CFC) is generally not taxed until it is paid to the parent as a dividend.

Foreign individuals and foreign corporations are taxed depending on the source and nature of the income. Trade or business income that is effectively connected to a U.S. trade or business is taxed just like trade or business income for any domestic entity. The asset use test and the business activities test are used to determine whether income is effectively connected to a U.S. trade or business. Nonbusiness income such as rent, royalties, interest, and dividends are generally subject to a 30 percent withholding rate without the benefit of being able to take any deductions against income.

# KEY TERMS

active participant (p. 15-7)
alternative minimum tax (AMT) (p. 15-28)
alternative minimum taxable income (AMTI) (p. 15-28)
alternative minimum tax adjustment (p. 15-29)
alternative minimum tax rate (p. 15-28)
AMT minimum tax credit (p. 15-32)
child care cost credit (p. 15-26)
contributory pension plan (p. 15-2)
controlled foreign corporation (CFC) (p. 15-34)
defined benefit plan (p. 15-5)
defined contribution plan (p. 15-4)
early withdrawal (p. 15-13)
excess contribution (p. 15-12)
general business credit (GBC) (p. 15-27)
incentive stock option (ISO) (p. 15-21)
individual retirement account (IRA) (p. 15-7)
money purchase plan (p. 15-4)
noncontributory pension plan (p. 15-2)
nonqualified pension plan (p. 15-3)
nonqualified stock option (NQSO) (p. 15-16)
nonresident alien (p. 15-34)
profit-sharing plan (p. 15-4)
qualified pension plan (p. 15-3)
rehabilitation tax credit (p. 15-25)
required minimum distribution (RMD) (p. 15-11)
research and experimental (R&E) tax credit (p. 15-24)
resident alien (p. 15-34)
Roth IRA (p. 15-8)
savings incentive match plan for employees (SIMPLE) (p. 15-9)
simplified employee pension plan (SEP) (p. 15-9)
stock option (p. 15-16)
Subpart F income (p. 15-35)
substantial risk of forfeiture (p. 15-18)
tax credit (p. 15-24)
tax treaty (p. 15-34)
transfer pricing (p. 15-37)

# PRIMARY TAX LAW SOURCES

[1]Sec. 414(q)—Defines *highly compensated employee.*

[2]Sec. 401(c)(3)—Defines an *owner-employee* as a partner who owns more than a 10 percent interest in either the capital or profits of the partnership.

[3]Sec. 410(a)(1)(A) and (B)—Sets forth the minimum standards employees must meet to participate in a qualified pension plan.

[4]Sec. 410(a)—Sets forth the requirements for a qualified pension plan.

[5]Sec. 414(i)—Provides the requirements for a pension plan that is a defined contribution plan.

[6]Sec. 414(j)—Provides the requirements for a pension plan that is a defined benefit plan.

[7]Sec. 415(c)—Limits the amount of contributions from a money purchase plan to the lower of 25 percent of compensation or $58,000.

[8]Sec. 404(l)—Limits the amount of compensation that determines the maximum contribution to a qualified money purchase plan.

[9]Sec. 404(a)(3)—Limits the amount of contributions to a profit sharing plan to the lower of 25 percent of compensation or $58,000.

[10]Sec. 415(b)—Limits the amount of benefits that can be paid under a defined benefit plan to the average of the employee's three highest consecutive years' salaries or $230,000, whichever amount is less. The $230,000 is indexed for inflation.

[11]Sec. 415(b)(5)—Limits the amount of benefits paid under a defined benefits plan when the employee has less than ten years of service.

[12]Sec. 219—Allows a deduction for contributions to an individual retirement account; prescribes the maximum amounts deductible and limitations on deductions for active participants in other pension plans.

[13]Sec. 408A—Provides the general rules applicable for establishing a nondeductible Roth IRA.

[14]Sec. 408(d)(3)(A)—Requires inclusion of income on the conversion of a deductible IRA to a Roth IRA.

[15]Sec. 408(k)—Prescribes the participation requirements for a simplified employee pension plan.

[16]Sec. 402(h)—Sets forth the contribution limits for a simplified employee pension plan.

[17]Sec. 408(p)(2)—Prescribes the contribution formulas a company must choose from in funding a SIMPLE.

[18]Reg. Sec. 1.401(a)(9)-5—Provides the rules for determining the required minimum distribution from qualified pension plans.

[19]Sec. 72(b)—Provides the formula for determining the taxable portion of an annuity payment from a qualified pension plan.

[20]Reg. Sec. 54-4973-1(f)—Provides an example illustrating how a taxpayer can avoid the 6 percent excess contributions penalty by withdrawing the excess contribution before the due date of the tax return.

[21]Sec. 4973—Imposes an excise tax of 6 percent on a contribution to an individual retirement account in excess of the maximum allowable amount.

[22]Sec. 72(t)(1)—Unless an exception is met, the tax law imposes a 10 percent penalty if a taxpayer receives a distribution from a qualified pension plan before age 59½.

[23]Sec. 72(t)(7)—The tax law imposes a 10 percent penalty unless the distribution qualifies for an exception for qualified first time home-buyer distributions or qualified education expenses spelled out in this provision.

[24]Sec. 4974—Imposes an excise tax of 50 percent on the difference between the minimum expected distribution and the actual distribution from a qualified pension plan.

[25]Reg. Sec. 1.83-7(b)—A taxpayer must include as ordinary income from a stock option the fair market value of the option at the date of grant as determined under Reg. Sec. 20.2031-2.

[26]Sec. 83(f)—States that the holding period of the stock received through a stock option plan begins on the date the stock is no longer subject to substantial risk of forfeiture.

[27]Sec. 83(f)—Provides the general rule for determining the amount of gross income recognized upon the exercise of a nonqualified stock option.

[28]Sec. 83(c)—Explains when a stock option is subject to substantial risk of forfeiture.

[29]Reg. Sec. 1.83-4(a)—States that the holding period of stock acquired through a stock option plan begins on the date the stock is transferred to the taxpayer.

[30]Sec. 83(b)—Allows a taxpayer to elect to include in gross income the difference between the exercise price of the stock and the fair market value of the stock at the date of exercise rather than when the restrictions lapse.

[31]Sec. 421(a)—Provides that no income is recognized on the transfer of an incentive stock option.

[32]Sec. 422—Sets forth the requirements that must be met for a stock option to qualify as an incentive stock option.

[33]Sec. 41—Allows a tax credit for increasing research activities.

[34]Reg. Sec. 1.41-2—Defines *qualified research expenses.*

[35]Sec. 41(c)(2)—Provides that the minimum base amount cannot be less than 50 percent of the qualified research expenses for the credit year.

[36]Sec. 47—Allows a tax credit for qualified rehabilitation expenditures.

[37]Sec. 45F—Allows a tax credit for employer-provided child care expenses.

[38]Sec. 55—Requires the calculation of the alternative minimum tax and defines its calculation.

[39]Sec. 56—Prescribes the adjustment items that must be taken into account in calculating the alternative minimum tax.

[40]Sec. 57—Prescribes the preference items that must be added in calculating alternative minimum taxable income.

[41]Sec. 59—Allows a credit for foreign taxes paid (subject to limitations) against the tentative alternative minimum tax.

[42]Sec. 53—Allows the alternative minimum tax credit against the regular tax and defines the calculation of the credit.

[43]Sec. 7701(b)—Defines a *resident alien* and a *nonresident alien.*

[44]Sec. 7701(b)—Sets forth the requirements for determining whether an individual meets the physical presence test.

[45]Sec. 957(a)—Defines a *controlled foreign corporation.*

[46]Sec. 952(a)—Defines what is included as Subpart F income.

[47]Reg. Sec. 1.482-3(d)—Sets forth the rules for the cost-plus method for transfers of goods between related entities.

[48]Sec. 882—Explains when income is considered effectively connected with a U.S. trade or business.

[49]Reg. Sec. 1.864-4(c)—Describes and explains the asset use test and the business activities test.

[50]Sec. 871(a)—Sets forth the taxation of nonbusiness income for a nonresident alien.

# DISCUSSION QUESTIONS

1. **LO1** What is the difference between a contributory and a noncontributory pension plan?
2. **LO1** What are the tax advantages of using a qualified pension plan instead of a nonqualified pension plan?
3. **LO1** What requirements must be met for a pension plan to be treated as a qualified pension plan?
4. **LO1** Are all entities allowed to establish the same type of qualified pension plan?
5. **LO1** Explain the difference between a defined benefit plan and a defined contribution plan.
6. **LO1** What is the maximum amount that can be contributed to a defined contribution pension plan?
7. **LO1** What is the maximum benefit that can be paid to an individual under a defined benefit plan?
8. **LO2** How does a Keogh plan differ from other qualified pension plans?
9. **LO2** What is meant by the term owner-partner?
10. **LO2** How does being an owner-partner affect the amount that can be contributed to a Keogh plan?
11. **LO2** Are all taxpayers (including spouses of active participants) allowed a deduction for a contribution to an individual retirement account? Explain.
12. **LO2** How does a simplified employee pension plan differ from a Keogh plan? From a qualified pension plan?
13. **LO2** What requirements must a taxpayer meet to establish a simplified employee pension plan?
14. **LO2** Compare the different funding options available to an employer under a SIMPLE-IRA and a SIMPLE-401(k). Discuss how these funding options affect the amount the employee and employer can contribute to the plan.
15. **LO3** How is the required minimum distribution (RMD) from a pension plan determined?
16. **LO3** Generally, at what age can pension plan distributions begin? When must they begin? Explain any exceptions to these general rules.
17. **LO3** Discuss the penalty provisions associated with qualified pension plans, Keogh plans, and IRAs.
18. **LO3** Discuss the penalty provisions associated with Roth IRAs.
19. **LO4** Explain the differences between a nonqualified stock option plan and an incentive stock option plan.
20. **LO4** Explain the difference in the tax treatment of a nonqualified stock option that has a readily ascertainable fair market value and one that does not have a readily ascertainable fair market value.
21. **LO4** How is a nonqualified stock option taxed if it is subject to substantial risk of forfeiture?
22. **LO4** What is the advantage of making a Section 83(b) election?
23. **LO4** What requirements must a stock option meet to qualify as an incentive stock option?
24. **LO4** What is the tax treatment of a stock option that qualifies as an incentive stock option? What is the treatment if the requirements are not met?
25. **LO6** Why are tax credits rather than a deduction used to provide tax relief?
26. **LO6** Why are business credits allowed to be carried forward to future tax years?
27. **LO6** What is Congress trying to accomplish with the use of tax credits? Provide an example of a tax credit and Congress's purpose for creating it.
28. **LO6** What is the purpose of the research and experimental tax credit?
29. **LO6** What types of expenditures qualify for the rehabilitation tax credit?
30. **LO6** What restrictions are placed on the rehabilitation tax credit?
31. **LO6** What is the purpose of the general business tax credit?
32. **LO7** What is the purpose of the alternative minimum tax?
33. **LO7** What is the tax base for the alternative minimum tax? Explain the general computation of the base.
34. **LO7** What is the basic difference between an AMT adjustment and a preference?
35. **LO7** Why can AMT adjustments be negative?
36. **LO7** What is the AMT exemption amount? Is it available to all taxpayers?
37. **LO7** What tax credits are allowed for AMT purposes?
38. **LO7** What is the purpose of the AMT credit against the regular tax?
39. **LO8** Compare and contrast how the United States taxes a U.S. citizen, a nonresident alien, a domestic corporation, and a foreign corporation.
40. **LO8** Why does the United States establish a tax treaty with a foreign country?
41. **LO8** Discuss how a controlled foreign corporation (U.S. corporation owns more than 10 percent) is taxed.
42. **LO8** What is the purpose of the transfer pricing rules?
43. **LO8** Explain how foreign corporations conducting business in the United States are taxed on their business and nonbusiness income.
44. **LO8** Why is the sale of property by a foreign corporation not subject to the withholding tax on nonbusiness income?

## PROBLEMS

45. **LO1** Salvadore, 35, is an employee of Malthouse Corporation. Henrique, 40, is an employee of the Sheedy Corporation. Both belong to a contributory pension plan that requires them to match their employers' contributions of $70 per month. Each plans to retire at 65. They expect that their $140 a month ($70 employee + $70 employer) contribution will earn 8 percent interest, compounded annually.
    a. How much will each have available upon retirement?
    b. Assume the same facts, except that Salvadore belongs to a nonqualified pension plan and that his marginal tax rate and the pension plan's (i.e., the trust's) marginal tax rate is 24 percent. Assume that the actual yield on Salvadore's investment is 6 percent. How much will he have in his pension account upon retirement?

46. **LO1** Manuel is an employee of Etowah Corporation and has worked for the company for 22 years. Employees are not required to contribute to the company's defined benefit plan. Based on the plan, Manuel can retire at 40 percent of the average of his three highest years' salaries. Determine the amount Etowah will pay Manuel in pension benefits in each of the following situations:
    a. His average salary for these three years is $50,000.
    b. His average salary for these three years is $625,000.

47. **LO1** Sarah is vice president of production for Fenner, Inc., a corporation, which maintains a money purchase pension plan for its employees. She owns 8 percent of Fenner's stock. Determine the maximum deductible contribution the company can make to the pension plan in each of the following situations:
    a. Sarah's salary is $95,000.
    b. Sarah's salary is $320,000.

48. **LO1** Warren is a partner in Baines Brothers, a consulting firm specializing in the design of Intranets. Baines maintains a profit-sharing Keogh plan for its partners and employees. Warren owns a 10 percent partnership interest in Baines Brothers. Determine the maximum deductible contribution the partnership can make to the pension plan in each of the following situations:
    a. The partnership's ordinary income is $1,350,000, and it has no income or deductions that require separate reporting.
    b. The partnership's ordinary income is $4,000,000, and it has no income or deductions that require separate reporting.

49. **LO2** Ferris and Jody are married and file a joint return. During the current year, Ferris has a salary of $45,000. Neither Ferris nor Jody is covered by an employer-sponsored pension plan. Determine the maximum IRA contribution and deduction amounts in each of the following cases:
    a. Jody earns $28,000, and their adjusted gross income is $132,000.
    b. Jody does not work outside the home, and their adjusted gross income is $70,000.
    c. Assume the same facts as in part a, except that Ferris is covered by an employer-sponsored pension plan.
    d. Assume the same facts as in part a, except that Ferris and Jody are covered by an employer-sponsored pension plan.

50. **LO2** Zorica and Pierre are married and file a joint return. Zorica earns $59,500, and Pierre earns $45,000. Their adjusted gross income is in 2021 $111,000. Determine the maximum IRA contribution and deduction in each of the following cases:
    a. Neither Zorica nor Pierre is covered by an employer-sponsored pension plan.
    b. Only Zorica is covered by an employer-sponsored pension plan.
    c. Assume the same facts as in part b, except that Pierre has no income, and their adjusted gross income is $128,000.

51. **LO2** Lenore, a single taxpayer with an adjusted gross income of $70,000 in 2021, is covered by her employer's pension plan. She makes a $6,000 contribution to her IRA during the current year.
    a. How much of the contribution can Lenore deduct?
    b. Assume the same facts as above, except that Lenore's adjusted gross income is $78,000.
    c. Assume that Lenore is married to Lathrop, who has no income, and their combined adjusted gross income is $130,000. Lathrop is not covered by any retirement plan. What are Lenore and Lathrop's maximum deductible IRA contributions?
52. **LO2** In October 2019, Clark Corporation decides to establish a SIMPLE-401(k) for its employees. Clark meets all requirements for establishing a SIMPLE. The company has notified its employees that in 2021, it will fund the SIMPLE-401(k) by contributing 2 percent of each employee's salary to the plan. Determine the maximum employee and employer contribution for Lei, an employee, in each of the following cases:
    a. Lei's salary is $62,000.
    b. Lei's salary is $295,000.
    c. Assume the same facts as in part b, except that Clark funds the plan by matching employees' contributions up to a maximum of 3 percent of each employee's com pensation. Lei contributes the maximum.
    d. Assume the same facts as in part b, except that Clark establishes a SIMPLE-IRA and Lei contributes the maximum.
    e. Assume the same facts as in part d, except that Clark funds the plan by matching an employee's contributions up to a maximum of 3 percent of each employee's compensation. Lei contributes the maximum.
53. **LO3** Ghon is a married taxpayer who retired from his job at Smithfield Printing in 2021. During 2022, he turns 72, and begins withdrawing the $215,000 (balance as of December 31, 2021) in assets in his pension account. Smithfield maintains a noncontributory pension plan. Determine the required minimum distribution that Ghon must take.
54. **LO3** Felicia is a single taxpayer who retired from her job as a sales executive with Waynesville Associates, LLC. During 2022, she turns 72 and begins withdrawing the $320,000 in assets (balance as of December 31, 2021) in her pension account. Her pension plan is a qualified noncontributory plan.
    a. What is the required minimum distribution that Felicia must take?
    b. Assume that the pension plan account balance on December 31, 2022, is $301,000. What is Felicia's minimum required distribution for 2023?

Communication Skills

55. **LO3** Suresh is a sales representative for Swinley Manufacturing. The corporation maintains a defined contribution profit-sharing plan on behalf of its employees. It contributes 15 percent of each employee's salary. Suresh's salary for 2021 is $200,000. Because of his record sales achievement during the year, the company decides to pay Suresh a bonus of $95,000. He is aware of the tax benefits associated with pension plans and has asked the controller of the company to pay him $35,000 of the bonus in cash and to contribute the remaining $60,000 ($95,000 – $35,000) to his pension. Prepare a letter to Suresh explaining the tax consequences of his proposal.
56. **LO2** Hector is a single taxpayer with adjusted gross income of $129,000. What is the maximum contribution that he can make to a Roth IRA for the current year?

Communication Skills

57. **LO3** Ross is single and maintains an IRA. During a trip to Las Vegas in 2021, he wins $15,000 at the roulette wheel. He decides to put half his earnings in his IRA and spend the other half on a trip to Europe. At the end of 2021, the total assets in his IRA are $29,000. Because he is covered by his employer's pension plan, Ross does not deduct any portion of his $7,500 IRA contribution. His salary for the year is $71,000. Write a letter to Ross advising him of the tax consequences of his actions.

58. **LO3** During the current year, Kyung purchases a boat for $70,000. Because she has only $7,000 of the necessary $14,000 down payment, Kyung makes a $7,000 withdrawal from her IRA. Immediately before the withdrawal, the balance in her account consists of $9,000 in deductible contributions, $13,000 in nondeductible contributions, and $3,000 in earnings on the plan's assets. What are the tax consequences of Kyung's making the $7,000 withdrawal from her IRA?
   a. Assume that the withdrawal is made for a down payment on Kyung's first home. What are the tax consequences of Kyung's $7,000 withdrawal from her IRA account?

59. **LO3** Glenna is retired from Cherry Hills Corporation. When she retired at age 72, she decided to take her pension as a lump-sum distribution and roll over the proceeds tax-free into her IRA. On January 1, 2022, she began to receive the required $22,000 distribution from her IRA. During the current year, she has a $40,000 gain on the sale of land that she inherits from her brother. Because of this gain, she decides to reduce her withdrawal from her IRA from the required $22,000 to $6,000. Explain to Glenna the tax consequences of her decision.

60. **LO2** Juan and Angel, ages 56 and 54, respectively, decide to establish Roth IRAs. Juan and Angel are married, and both are covered by pension plans where they work. Their adjusted gross income in 2021 is $125,000. They want to make the maximum contribution to the Roth IRAs. Communication Skills
   a. What is the maximum amount they may contribute to a Roth IRA?
   b. Assume that Juan and Angel's adjusted gross income for the year is $202,000. What is the maximum contribution they may make?
   c. Assume that Juan and Angel are now ages 62 and 60, respectively, and want to withdraw $10,000 to purchase a new car. What are the tax implications of the withdrawal from the Roth IRA?
   d. Assume the same facts as in part c, except that Juan is 60 and Angel is 58.
   e. Assume the same facts as in part a, except that Juan and Angel have a regular IRA they want to roll over to a Roth IRA. The balance in the IRA is $20,000. Write a memo describing the tax factors that Juan and Angel should consider before deciding to roll over the IRA to a Roth IRA.

61. **LO4** On September 1, 2021, Beaconsfield Corporation grants Albert a nonqualified stock option to acquire 500 shares of the company's stock for $8 per share. The fair market value of the stock on the date of grant is $14. Determine the tax consequences to both Albert and Beaconsfield Corporation in each of the following situations:
   a. The option has a readily ascertainable fair market value of $3 per share, and Albert exercises the option on February 15, 2022, when the FMV of the stock is $16.
   b. The option does not have a readily ascertainable fair market value, and Albert exercises the option on February 15, 2022, when the FMV of the stock is $16.
   c. The option has a readily ascertainable fair market value of $3 per share but is subject to a substantial risk of forfeiture, and Albert does not make a Section 83(b) election. When the restrictions lapse on September 30, 2022, the fair market value of the stock is $20 per share.
   d. The option has a readily ascertainable fair market value of $3 per share but is subject to substantial risk of forfeiture, and Albert makes a Section 83(b) election.

62. **LO4** Return to the facts of problem 61. On November 30, 2022, when the fair market value of the stock is $30, Albert sells the stock. Determine the tax consequences to both Albert and Beaconsfield Corporation in each situation presented in problem 61.

63. **LO4** On May 10, 2021, Somerton, Inc., grants Louise a nonqualified stock option to acquire 700 shares of the company's stock for $11 per share. The fair market value of the stock on the date of grant is $13. The option does not have a readily

ascertainable fair market value. On June 1, 2021, when the fair market value of the stock is $15, Louise exercises the stock option. Determine the tax consequences for Louise and Somerton on the grant date of the option and the exercise date.

64. **LO4** Return to the facts of problem 63. If the stock is subject to substantial restrictions, what are the tax consequences for both Louise and Somerton on the date Louise is granted the stock option and the date she exercises the option, assuming that she does not make a Section 83(b) election? How would your answer change if she makes a Section 83(b) election and the fair market value of the stock when the restrictions lapse on March 31, 2022, is $22?

65. **LO4** Return to the facts of problem 64. Assume that Louise sells the stock on October 31, 2022, for $35 per share. Determine the tax consequences for Louise and Somerton on the date of sale.

66. **LO4** On July 1, 2021, Howard is granted the right to acquire 500 shares of Matoney Corporation stock for $15 per share. The option qualifies under the company's incentive stock option plan. The current fair market value of the stock is $12. On August 18, 2022, when the stock is selling for $18 per share, Howard exercises his option to purchase the stock. He sells the shares on September 15, 2023, for $29 per share. Determine the tax consequences for Howard and Matoney Corporation on the
    a. Date of grant
    b. Date of exercise
    c. Date of sale

    Assume that Howard sells the stock on August 15, 2023, for $27 per share. What are the tax consequences to Howard and Matoney Corporation?

67. **LO5** Sonya owns 60 percent and her sister Karen owns 40 percent of the Tanglewood Group. They inherited their ownership from their mother, who died in 2020. Sonya is the president and chief financial officer of the corporation and receives a salary of $140,000, which is reasonable given her duties and responsibilities. Karen, who is vice president, is paid a salary of $60,000. She is not actively involved in the business and views her ownership as an investment. Discuss how the payments to Sonya and Karen are treated for tax purposes if
    a. Tanglewood is a corporation.
    b. Tanglewood is an S corporation.

68. **LO6** Clinton Corporation spends $800,000 on qualified research activities during the current year. Clinton's fixed base percentage is 10 percent, and the average of its annual gross receipts for the four preceding years is $2,000,000.
    a. What is Clinton's allowable incremental research and experimental tax credit?
    b. Assume that the average of Clinton's annual gross receipts for the preceding four years is $10,000,000. What is Clinton's allowable incremental research tax credit?

69. **LO6** Lavinia owns an advertising agency. In February 2021, she purchases a building for $125,000. Lavinia spends $275,000 rehabilitating the building for use as her advertising agency office. The rehabilitation is completed in November 2021.
    a. What criteria must Lavinia meet to qualify for the historic structures credit?
    b. Assume that Lavinia meets the criteria in part a and that the building qualifies for the credit. What is the tax credit for 2021? What is the basis of the building?

70. **LO6** Return to the facts of problem 69. Assume that Lavinia sells the building in April 2024. How much of the tax credit must Lavinia recapture?

71. **LO6** Hurst Corporation wants to provide child care for its employees. Because Hurst does not have a suitable facility on its premises, it rents a building for the center. The rent for the year totals $60,000. In addition, Hurst hires a qualified director to run the facility and spends an additional $5,000 in training costs for the director. Hurst incurs $20,000 in referral expenditures. What is Hurst Corporation's child care cost credit?

72. **LO7** Willtem Corporation has total general business credits of $25,000. It has a net regular tax liability of $17,000. What can Willtem deduct as its general business credit?

73. **LO7** Determine the total amount of tax due and the amount of the alternative minimum tax in each of the following situations:
    a. Wilbur's regular tax liability is $180,000, and his tentative alternative minimum tax is $150,000.
    b. Gene's regular tax liability is $27,000, and her tentative alternative minimum tax is $42,000.

74. **LO7** Alice and Frank have the following items on their 2021 tax return:

| | | | |
|---|---|---|---|
| Adjusted gross income | | | $ 140,000 |
| Less: Deductions from adjusted gross income: | | | |
| Medical expenses | $ 17,950 | | |
| Less: 7.5% × $140,000 | (10,500) | $7,450 | |
| Home mortgage interest | | 6,300 | |
| State income taxes | | 3,525 | |
| Property taxes | | 950 | |
| Charitable contributions (cash) | | 575 | |

Determine the amount of the adjustments that Alice and Frank will have to make in computing their alternative minimum tax.

75. **LO7** Joan and Matthew are married, have two children, and report the following items on their 2021 tax return: Communication Skills

| | | | |
|---|---|---|---|
| Adjusted gross income | | | $ 248,000 |
| Less: Deductions from adjusted gross income: | | | |
| Medical expenses | $ 26,150 | | |
| Less: 7.5% × $248,000 | (18,600) | $7,550 | |
| Home mortgage interest | | 13,500 | |
| State income taxes | | 4,000 | |
| Property taxes | | 5,700 | |
| Charitable contributions | | 7,000 | |
| Total itemized deductions | | | (37,750) |

Determine Joan and Matthew's regular tax liability and, if applicable, the amount of their alternative minimum tax. Write a memo to Joan and Matthew explaining the adjustments they will have to make in computing their alternative minimum tax.

76. **LO7** Pauline is considering investing in bonds. Her broker has given her two options to consider. The first is to invest in city bonds with an interest rate of 6 percent. The second option is the purchase of High-Flier Utility bonds yielding 9 percent interest. Assuming that Pauline's marginal tax rate is 32 percent, write a letter to her explaining which option she should choose. In your letter, be sure to consider all circumstances that could affect the after-tax return on the bonds. Communication Skills

77. **LO7** Determine the AMT exemption amount for each of the following taxpayers:
    a. Janine is a single individual with an alternative minimum taxable income of $165,000.
    b. Peter and Wendy have an alternative minimum taxable income of $1,140,000
    c. Samantha is single individual with an alternative minimum taxable income of $775,000.

78. **LO8** Bivona Corporation forms Jarvis Corporation in the country of Simants. Bivona owns 20 percent of Jarvis's voting stock and 30 percent of its preferred stock. The remaining Jarvis stock is owned by citizens of Simants. The preferred

shares represent 20 percent of the fair market value of the company. All Bivona shareholders are U.S. citizens. Is Jarvis a controlled foreign corporation? Explain.

79. **LO8** Smile Corporation invests $2 million for a 49 percent interest in Irehoe, Inc., a newly formed Irish corporation that manufactures farm equipment. Jim, a U.S. resident, owns 10 percent of Irehoe. Jim owns no stock in Smile Corporation. An Irish corporation owns the remaining Irehoe shares. Irehoe reports a profit for the current year of $150,000 and pays no dividends. Irehoe pays no income tax in Ireland because of a tax holiday for newly formed corporations with significant foreign ownership. Discuss the tax implications for Smile, Irehoe, and Jim.

80. **LO8** The Collins Corporation, a domestic corporation, owns 65 percent of O'Dwyer, a foreign corporation. During the current year, Logo receives $120,000 in dividends. O'Dwyer's post-1986 undistributed U.S. earnings are $1,500,000, and its post-1986 undistributed earnings are $5,000,000. What is Collins' dividend received deduction for the current year?

81. **LO8** The Duncan Corporation, a domestic corporation, owns 70 percent of Wildflower, a foreign corporation. Duncan's pro rata share of post-1986 undistributed U.S. earnings is $2,500,000 of which $1,000,000 is cash or cash equivalents.
    a. How much will Duncan pay in tax in the current year?
    b. Assume that Duncan elects to pay its tax liability over eight years, what amount will it owe each year?

82. **LO8** Taverez is a foreign corporation that operates a manufacturing plant in Lubbock, Texas. Taverez sells its products to customers outside the United States. In 2021 Taverez's gross revenue is $4 million. Cost of goods sold and other operating expenses total $2.8 million. Is Taverez taxed on the income? Explain.

83. **LO8** Conrad is a citizen and resident of Trinidad. He receives an $8,000 dividend from Sturino Industries, a U.S. domestic corporation.
    a. What is the tax treatment of the dividend?
    b. Under what circumstances would the dividend not be taxable?

# ISSUE IDENTIFICATION PROBLEMS

In each of the following problems, identify the tax issue(s) posed by the facts presented. Determine the possible tax consequences of each issue that you identify.

84. John is single and has $78,000 income from his job at Lawndale Ice Cream Company. He wants to invest $150 a month in an IRA but is not sure which type he qualifies for and whether this would be a better investment than putting the money in a money market account earning 3 percent interest per year.

85. Lisa works full-time at the Snowden Corporation as a manager in quality control. She is trying to get her employer to initiate a retirement program for all Snowden employees who make more than $80,000 a year.

86. The Schwarzbach Corporation manufactures metal fasteners at a cost of 55 cents per fastener and sells them to wholesalers for 60 cents each. During the year, it establishes a 100 percent-owned CFC in Portugal to sell the fasteners in Europe. Schwarzbach sells the fasteners to its CFC for 58 cents each.

# TECHNOLOGY APPLICATIONS

Research Skills

87. Genco Company is a small manufacturing company that makes metal presses for larger manufacturing companies. Genco is located in a large city and desires to expand its operations, which will require it to hire more workers. Some of the workers need to be highly skilled machinists, while others need little prior training or experience. Genco would like to hire employees from the economically

depressed neighborhoods near its plant. The plant manager has heard that there are income tax credits for providing work opportunities for certain targeted groups of individuals. He comes to you for information about who he could hire that would qualify for this credit. Prepare a memo for the plant manager that identifies the qualifying targeted groups and explain the tax benefits associated with employing individuals in these groups.

88. The United States and the country of Bersia are about to enter into a tax treaty. The United States is especially interested in establishing a treaty because many U.S. students attend medical school in Bersia and work while getting their medical degrees. In addition, many U.S. citizens are moving to Bersia to retire. Find the Model Income Tax Treaty. How many articles are included in the Model Treaty? Which article deals with the income tax treatment of students? List at least three other articles and the topics they cover. Research Skills

## DISCUSSION CASES

89. Alex and Jeff have differing views on the current tax system. Alex believes that any tax system that has two tax structures, a regular tax and an alternative minimum tax, is inefficient and inequitable. In fact, the system violates all canons of taxation espoused by Adam Smith. Jeff, however, feels that Congress should use the tax code as a vehicle for encouraging taxpayers to engage in various social and economic transactions. Therefore, he argues that the alternative minimum tax is necessary to ensure that each taxpayer pays some amount of tax. With whom do you agree? Why?

90. Lynn and Alicia are equal partners in a local bookstore. They have operated the bookstore for two years but have reported only a small profit. This year they anticipate that the bookstore will generate a profit that will allow each of them to contribute to a pension plan. They sought the advice of two local accountants on the type of pension plan they should adopt but received conflicting advice. They have come to your firm to help resolve the conflict. Explain the type of pension plans available to Lynn and Alicia and advise them on which type of plan they should adopt.

## TAX PLANNING CASES

91. William, Daniel, and Thomas are brothers who have decided to form an engineering firm. Although Thomas has an MBA degree and will function primarily as the firm's financial expert, he has no formal tax knowledge. William and Daniel are bringing clients from their former firm, but Thomas anticipates that the new firm's client base will not be large enough to avoid a tax loss for three years. After year 3, the firm's profits should increase rapidly. By year six, he anticipates that the firm will generate a substantial profit and employ 25 people. Because Thomas is unsure whether the firm should operate as an S corporation, partnership, or corporation, he has hired your accounting firm to guide him. Thomas is particularly concerned with how the form of organization would affect the: Communication Skills

- Pension plan the firm will adopt
- Firm's ability to compensate current owners and employees and attract new owners or employees
- Total tax liability of the owners
- Firm's ability to distribute cash and/or property

Write a letter to Thomas explaining how the organizational form of the business affects each of the items he has mentioned.

92. Fred, age 50, plans to retire when he reaches age 65. He is considering investing in either an IRA or a Roth IRA. He plans to contribute $7,000 per year until he retires. Fred expects his marginal tax rate to be 32 percent until he retires, when

he expects his marginal tax rate to drop to 12 percent. He anticipates that the rate of return on either IRA will be 8 percent before considering any tax effects. Prepare a memo analyzing the tax effects of investing in a regular IRA versus a Roth IRA. Discuss factors that might influence Fred's decision to choose either an IRA or a Roth IRA. Assume that Fred meets the income limits for making the maximum annual contribution.

## ETHICS DISCUSSION CASE

93. Nina is the auditor for Geiger Construction, a local builder. Geiger recently renovated a historic building in downtown Kingston. The building, which consists of five shops, is owned by the Restoring Historic Kingston Partnership (RHKP). Nina is also the tax accountant for Merlin, a limited partner in RHKP. In preparing Merlin's 2021 return, the K-1 of RHKP (which Nina did not prepare) shows that Merlin is entitled to a historic structures credit. Nina properly deducts the credit. Later that year, Nina is conducting the audit of Geiger Construction, and she compliments the owner on the wonderful job the company did in restoring the building while meeting the requirements necessary for the building to qualify for the historic rehabilitation credits. Marshall, the owner of Geiger Construction, informs Nina that because of an unforeseen structural problem, the company was not able to meet the historic rehabilitation requirements. The company could preserve only 50 percent, not the required 75 percent, of the external walls. What is Nina's obligation (refer to Statements on Standards for Tax Services, which can be found at www.aicpa.org), if any, with respect to Merlin's filed tax return? Does she have any obligation to Merlin's other partners? To the preparer of the partnership return?

PART 6

# Tax Research



Taxation, in reality, is life. If you know the position a person takes on taxes, you can tell their whole philosophy. The tax code, once you get to know it, embodies all the essence of life: greed, politics, power, goodness, charity.

—Sheldon S. Cohen

iStock.com/michaelmjc

# Tax Research

16

## Learning Objectives:

LO 1 Explain the difference between primary and secondary tax authorities.

LO 2 Identify the different types of legislative, administrative, and judicial primary authorities.

LO 3 Describe the hierarchy or different levels of importance attributable to each of the primary authorities.

LO 4 Prepare citations to each of the primary authorities.

LO 5 Identify the purpose of the different types of secondary authorities.

LO 6 Describe computer-assisted tax research (CATR).

LO 7 Explain the difference between tax planning and tax compliance.

LO 8 Describe the basic steps involved in tax research.

LO 9 Apply the tax research process to a comprehensive problem.

## 16-1 INTRODUCTION

LO 1
Explain the difference between primary and secondary tax authorities.

Tax research is the process by which the tax consequences of a completed or proposed transaction are determined. The tax treatment of any transaction must be based on some supporting authority. Indeed, all the rules in this text originate in some supporting authoritative pronouncement. Tax research is simply the means by which these authoritative pronouncements are located, evaluated, and applied to a specific set of facts.

All tax authorities fall into one of two classes: primary and secondary. **Primary authorities** relate to the three principal functions of government: legislative, executive/administrative, and judicial. The legislative authorities include the Constitution, tax treaties, the law as enacted by Congress (i.e., Internal Revenue Code), and the meaning of the law as described by the various congressional committee reports that accompany enactment of the law.

The tax law as enacted by Congress contains general language, so interpretations are necessary. The administrative authorities are the official interpretations of the law prepared by the Department of the Treasury and the Internal Revenue Service (IRS). These sources consist of regulations, revenue rulings, revenue procedures, and other miscellaneous pronouncements. Whenever the IRS and a taxpayer disagree about the interpretation and application of a specific Code provision, the courts may be called upon to decide the matter. Decisions by trial and appellate courts are the judicial authorities. All legislative, administrative, and judicial primary authorities are commonly referred to as the *tax law*. Figure 16-1 summarizes these primary sources of authority.

**Secondary authorities** serve primarily as tools for locating the relevant primary authorities. They also provide information that leads to better understanding, interpretation, and application of the primary authorities. Secondary authorities include all other statements, pronouncements, explanations, or interpretations of the law that are not primary; they consist chiefly of tax services, citators, research tax databases, and tax journals and newsletters.

This chapter first examines more closely the different types of primary and secondary authorities and the hierarchy, or different levels of importance, attributable to each type. This is followed by a step-by-step discussion of how these authorities are used to determine the tax consequences related to a specific set of facts.

*Figure 16-1*

**Primary Sources of Tax Law Authority**

**LEGISLATIVE AUTHORITY**

- U.S. Constitution
- Tax treaties
- Internal Revenue Code
  —Statutory language
- Internal Revenue Code
  —Legislative intent
  - House Ways and Means Committee reports
  - Senate Finance Committee reports
  - Joint Conference Committee reports

**ADMINISTRATIVE AUTHORITY**

- Regulations:
  Proposed, temporary, final
- Revenue rulings
- Revenue procedures
- Acquiescence/nonacquiescence
- Letter rulings: LTR, TAM
- Chief Counsel's Memoranda:
  TM, GCM, AOD
- Other IRS pronouncements:
  Notices, announcements, publications, tax return instructions

**JUDICIAL AUTHORITY**

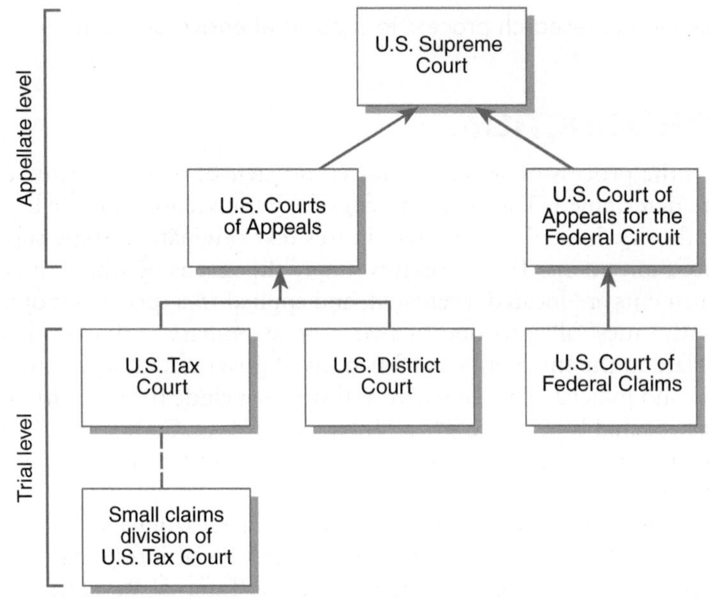


# 16-2 PRIMARY SOURCES OF FEDERAL INCOME TAX LAW

## 16-2a Legislative Sources

LO 2
Identify the different types of legislative, administrative, and judicial primary authorities.

The legislative primary authorities consist of the U.S. Constitution, new tax laws enacted by Congress and incorporated in the Internal Revenue Code, reports issued by congressional committees as new laws are enacted, and treaties with other countries, which are negotiated by the president with the advice and consent of the Senate. Collectively, these authorities are sometimes referred to as *statutory authorities*. They are generally accorded a higher level of authority than administrative or judicial primary authorities.

### The U.S. Constitution

The authority for the imposition of the federal income tax is found in Article I, Section 7, of the U.S. Constitution. It grants Congress the authority to impose taxes to pay debts and provide for the common defense and general welfare of the United States. It also requires that all tax legislation originate in the House of Representatives. Early attempts at an income tax were frustrated by additional requirements in Article I that direct taxes be apportioned among the states in proportion to the Census. As a result, most early attempts to raise revenue for the federal government were in the form of an excise tax. A tax based on income became an integral source of federal revenue with ratification of the Sixteenth Amendment to the Constitution in 1913. The Sixteenth Amendment permits a tax on income, from whatever source derived, without apportionment among the states and without regard to the Census.

Although the constitutional authority for an income tax is clear, tax protesters frequently have challenged it on the ground that it violates other constitutional rights. For example, protesters have claimed that their right to due process is violated, that they have religious or conscientious objections to military expenditures, and that the filing of tax returns violates their protection against self-incrimination. Tax protesters' activities include filing incomplete tax returns, modifying return forms in such a way that they cannot be processed by the IRS, or claiming deductions for items clearly not allowed. The various methods are intended to hinder the administration of the tax law or frustrate the collection of the tax due. Tax protesters have not been successful in the courts and are subject to substantial penalties for failure to file a proper return and pay the tax due.

## Internal Revenue Code of 1986

The most important source of current federal income tax law is the Internal Revenue Code of 1986, as amended (the Code, or I.R.C.). What is commonly referred to as the *Internal Revenue Code*, or simply *the Code*, is actually Title 26 of the *United States Code*. The *U.S. Code* is a consolidated and coordinated compilation of all laws enacted by Congress. All laws dealing with the same subject are brought together under one title. Other titles of the *U.S. Code* include, for instance, Title 10, dealing with the armed forces, and Title 28, dealing with the judiciary and judicial procedure.

Whenever Congress enacts a new tax law, the amendments are integrated into the I.R.C. The Code has been amended almost annually since it was comprehensively overhauled in 1986. The Code was comprehensively reorganized and amended in 1954, and from that time until 1986, it was referred to as the *Internal Revenue Code of* 1954. The first time the tax laws were codified was in the Internal Revenue Code of 1939.

**Structure** The Code has many subdivisions, each with a different designation. For example, there are subtitles, chapters, subchapters, parts, and subparts. The contents of the Code can be broadly defined by examining the names of its nine subtitles, which appear in Exhibit 16-1.

Each subtitle is further subdivided into chapters. Exhibit 16-2 shows that Subtitle A, which deals with income taxes, has chapters numbered 1 through 6 and that two chapters have been repealed. Each chapter may again be subdivided into numerous subchapters. Exhibit 16-3 lists some of the more-often-applied subchapters of Chapter 1, which

*Exhibit 16-1*

## Subtitles of the Internal Revenue Code

| Subtitle | Name | Beginning Code Section Number |
|---|---|---|
| A | Income Taxes | Sec. 1 |
| B | Estate and Gift Taxes | Sec. 2001 |
| C | Employment Taxes | Sec. 3101 |
| D | Miscellaneous Excise Taxes | Sec. 4001 |
| E | Alcohol, Tobacco, and Certain Other Excise Taxes | Sec. 5001 |
| F | Procedure and Administration | Sec. 6001 |
| G | The Joint Committee on Taxation | Sec. 8001 |
| H | Financing of Presidential Election Campaigns | Sec. 9001 |
| I | Trust Fund Code | Sec. 9501 |

Exhibit 16-2

## Chapters of Subtitle A

| Chapter | Name | Beginning Code Section Number |
|---|---|---|
| 1 | Normal Taxes and Surtaxes | Sec. 1 |
| 2 | Tax on Self-Employment Income | Sec. 1401 |
| 2A | Unearned income Medicare Contribution | Sec. 1411 |
| 3 | Withholding of Tax on Nonresident Aliens and Foreign Corporations | Sec. 1441 |
| 4 | [Repealed] | |
| 5 | Tax on Transfers to Avoid Income Tax [Repealed] | Sec. 1491 |
| 6 | Consolidated Returns | Sec. 1501 |

Exhibit 16-3

## Partial List of Subchapters of Chapter 1 of Subtitle A

| Subchapter | Name | Beginning Code Section Number |
|---|---|---|
| A | Determination of Tax Liability | Sec. 1 |
| B | Computation of Taxable Income | Sec. 61 |
| C | Corporate Distributions and Adjustments | Sec. 301 |
| D | Deferred Compensation | Sec. 401 |
| E | Accounting Periods and Methods of Accounting | Sec. 441 |
| I | Natural Resources | Sec. 611 |
| J | Estates, Trusts, Beneficiaries, and Decedents | Sec. 641 |
| K | Partners and Partnerships | Sec. 701 |
| N | Tax Based on Income from Sources within or without the United States | Sec. 861 |
| O | Gain or Loss on Disposition of Property | Sec. 1001 |
| P | Capital Gain or Loss | Sec. 1201 |
| S | Tax Treatment of S Corporations and Their Shareholders | Sec. 1361 |

deals with normal taxes and surtaxes. Each subchapter may also be subdivided into parts and subparts.

The basic reference to a particular part of the Code is typically by section number. Reference to larger divisions, such as subtitles and chapters, is generally omitted. The section numbers run consecutively from 1 to 9834, although many numbers in the sequence are missing to allow for further expansion of the tax law. Each section of the Code may be further subdivided into subsections, paragraphs, subparagraphs, and clauses. Exhibit 16-4 provides a comprehensive example of the arrangement for Section 170(b)(1)(A) dealing with percentage limitations on charitable contributions.

Some words of caution about reading the Code are warranted. You must always read the entire section, not just the smallest subdivision that may contain the apparent answer to a tax question. Frequently, other divisions of the section contain special rules or definitions that could apply.

For example, Section 170(a) generally allows a deduction for any charitable contribution to a qualified organization, including an educational institution. However, Section 170(l) provides that no deduction shall be allowed if the contribution entitles the donor to purchase tickets for seating at an athletic event in an athletic stadium of the educational institution (so-called donor seating).

Similarly, you must review other sections within the subpart, part, or other larger division that contains the particular section for similar limitations or cross-references to other parts of the Code that may be relevant. Section 168, for example, provides the general rules for computing the accelerated cost recovery deduction for depreciable property, including automobiles. It is located in Part VI, entitled "Itemized Deductions for Individuals

Exhibit 16-4

## Subdivisions of Section 170

| | |
|---|---|
| Title 26: | Internal Revenue Code |
| Subtitle A: | Income Tax |
| Chapter 1: | Normal Taxes and Surtaxes |
| Subchapter B: | Computation of Taxable Income |
| Part VI: | Itemized Deductions for Individuals and Corporations |
| Section: | Sec. 170 CHARITABLE, ETC., CONTRIBUTIONS AND GIFTS |
| Subsection: | (a) ALLOWANCE OF DEDUCTION |
| Paragraph: | (1) GENERAL RULE—There shall be allowed as a deduction any charitable contribution.…only if verified under regulations prescribed by the Secretary. |
| | …. |
| Subsection: | (b) PERCENTAGE LIMITATIONS |
| Paragraph: | (1) INDIVIDUALS—In the case of an individual, the deduction provided in subsection (a) shall be limited as provided in the succeeding subparagraphs. |
| Subparagraph: | (A) GENERAL RULE—Any charitable contribution to a [church]…shall be allowed to the extent that the aggregate of such contributions does not exceed 50 percent of the taxpayer's contribution base for the taxable year. |
| | (G) Increased limitation for cash contributions |
| | (i) In general<br>In the case of any contribution of cash ... the total amount of such contributions which may be taken into account under subsection (a) for any taxable year beginning after December 31, 2017, and before January 1, 2026, shall not exceed 60 percent of the taxpayer's contribution base for such year. |
| | …. |

and Corporations," of Subchapter A. Section 280F, however, which is located in Part IX, entitled "Items Not Deductible," limits the depreciation deduction in cases in which expensive cars are purchased or are not used at least 50 percent of the time in a trade or business.

Occasionally, the Code will specify that certain conditions must be met before the ultimate treatment can be determined. Under these circumstances, it is important to understand, for example, whether conditions 1, 2, *and* 3 must be satisfied or whether condition 1, 2, *or* 3 will satisfy. Obviously, the ultimate treatment can be drastically different, depending on which interpretation is applicable. Other small words, such as "a" and "the," can also make a difference. "A" implies one of many, while "the" usually relates to one specific item.

**The Legislative Process** Figure 16-2 diagrams the process by which amendments to the Code are enacted. Typically, amendments to the Code are initiated by the president or a member of Congress as a *bill*. In accordance with the constitutional requirements, the bill is introduced in the House of Representatives, where it is referred to the Ways and Means Committee, which has jurisdiction over all tax matters. After hearings and deliberations, a bill approved by the committee is sent to the full House. Under what is referred to as the *closed rule*, the House can only approve or disapprove the bill as written by the Ways and Means Committee. Bills approved by the House are sent to the Senate.

The bill follows a similar path in the Senate. It is first referred to the Finance Committee, which has jurisdiction over all tax matters in the Senate. The Senate Finance Committee may accept the bill as approved by the House, make amendments to it, or make so many amendments that the resulting bill is really a substitute. After the committee approves the bill, it is referred to the full Senate. In contrast with the House's closed rule procedure, any senator may propose changes to the bill when it is being considered by the full Senate. Usually, the versions passed by the House and Senate are not the same, and any differences are resolved by a joint conference committee. Members of the joint conference committee are the most senior, or ranking, members of the House Ways and Means Committee and the Senate Finance Committee.

Figure 16-2

## The Legislative Process for a Tax Law

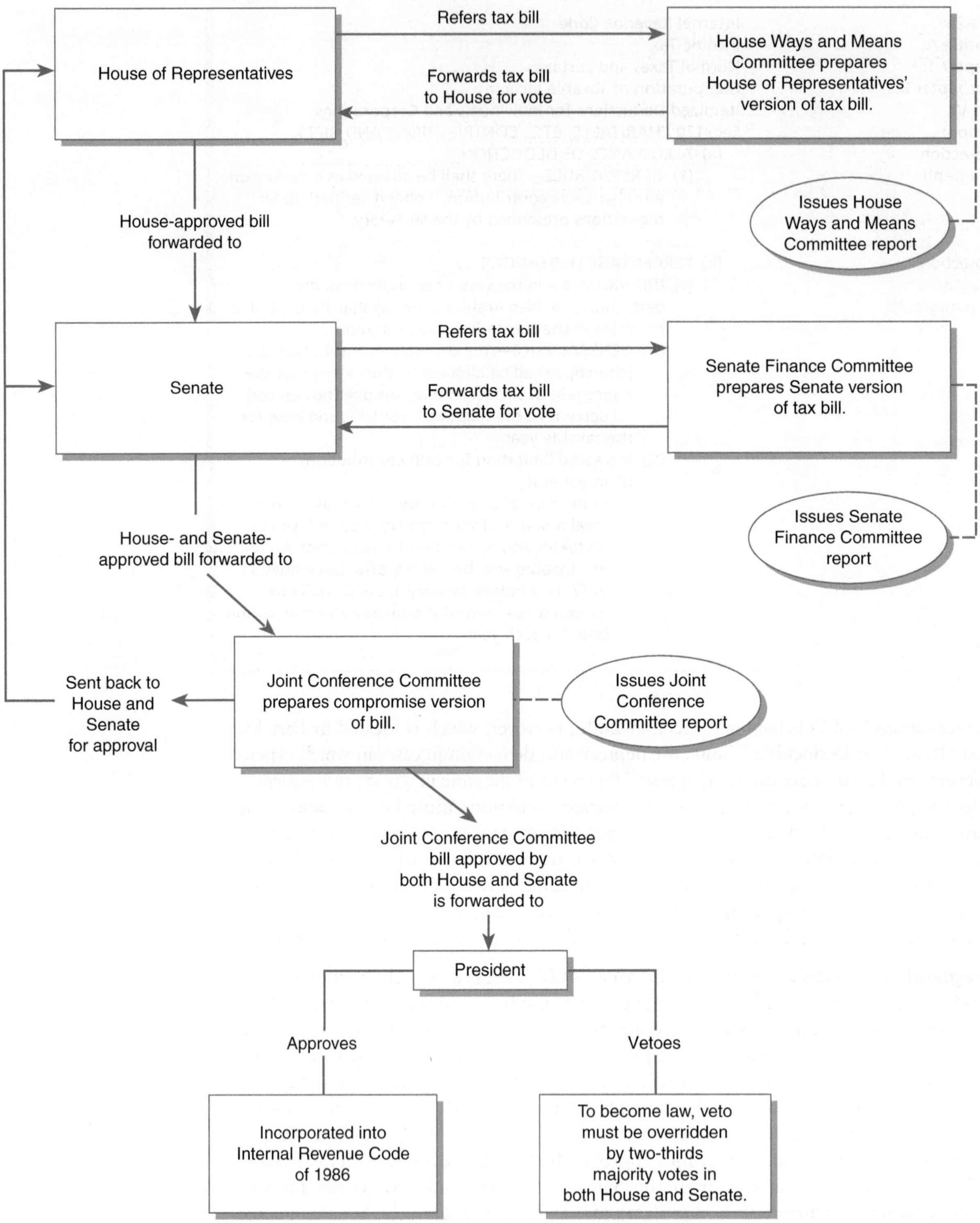


After the conference committee negotiates a resolution of the differences in the House and Senate versions of a bill, it is sent back to both the House and the Senate, where it can only be approved or disapproved. If the bill is passed by both the House and Senate, it is sent to the president. The president may approve the bill by signing it, or veto it. A veto can be overridden by a two-thirds majority of both the House and Senate.

Several documents that accompany a bill through the legislative process provide insight into Congress' intent in enacting the legislation. As each committee approves a bill, it writes a report that describes why the change in the law was considered necessary, explains each change, and often provides examples of how a particular rule is to be applied. Accordingly, the House Ways and Means Committee report, Senate Finance Committee report, and Joint Conference Committee report provide information that helps the IRS, taxpayers, and the courts understand and interpret the bill as it was approved at each stage of the process.

After a bill is enacted, the Joint Committee on Taxation prepares a general explanation of the bill as approved by the president. This report is commonly referred to as the *blue book* because of the color of its binding. The Joint Committee on Taxation should not be confused with the Joint Conference Committee. The Joint Conference Committee is an integral part of the legislative process that develops a new bill.[1] The Joint Committee on Taxation's primary responsibility is to oversee the operation and administration of the tax system as a whole. It is not directly involved in the legislative process of enacting a bill.

### Tax Treaties

Although the Code is the primary source of tax law in the United States, Congress also enters into tax treaties with other countries. Tax treaties are separate laws that define how residents of the two countries are to be taxed on income derived from working or investing in the other country. As such, they are important for individuals and corporations that do business in foreign countries. At times, the provisions of a tax treaty may override provisions of the Code.[2] Because of their variety and complexity, details of specific tax treaties are beyond the scope of this text.

## 16-2b Administrative Sources

The agency within the administrative branch of government with overall responsibility for the administration of the Internal Revenue Code is the Treasury Department.[3] This responsibility is fulfilled by the Internal Revenue Service, a branch of the Treasury Department that is directly responsible for interpreting, administering, and enforcing the tax laws. The official in charge of the IRS is called the *commissioner* and is given general legal assistance by the Office of the Chief Counsel.[4]

The Treasury Department provides overall interpretive guidance by issuing Treasury regulations. In fulfilling its function, the IRS issues revenue rulings, revenue procedures, and a variety of other pronouncements.[5] It is important to keep in mind that regulations, rulings, and other pronouncements have different levels of authority, or weight. This is analogous to saying that a Supreme Court decision is more important than a decision of a lower court. These varying levels of authority play an important role in the tax research process described later in the chapter.

### Treasury Regulations

LO 3
Describe the hierarchy or different levels of importance attributable to each of the primary authorities.

A Treasury regulation is the Treasury Department's official explanation of a related provision in the Internal Revenue Code. Regulations are the only administrative interpretations that require an intensive review and public comment process before they can be issued in final form. Regulations may be classified as interpretive or legislative. An **interpretive regulation** is issued under the general authority of the Treasury Department to provide official interpretations of I.R.C. provisions. A **legislative regulation** is issued when Congress specifically delegates the authority to the Treasury Department to write the specific rules for a designated Code section. For example, Section 469(l) specifically requires the Treasury Department to prescribe such regulations as may be necessary or appropriate to carry out all the provisions of Section 469. Prior to a 2011 Supreme Court ruling,[6] legislative regulations had a higher level of authority than interpretative regulations, but now they are equal.

A regulation may be issued in a proposed, temporary, or final form. **Proposed regulations** are issued to let the public know what the IRS believes is the proper interpretation of a related Code provision and to provide an opportunity for the public to comment before it is issued in final form. Proposed regulations are not binding on taxpayers or the IRS until they are issued as **final regulations**. **Temporary regulations** are issued to give taxpayers guidance until a final regulation is issued. Section 7805(e), added in 1988, requires all temporary regulations to also be issued as proposed regulations and specifies that the regulation will expire if it is not amended or issued as a final regulation within three years. A regulation issued in its final form represents the Treasury Department's official interpretation and may differ from the position taken in a proposed or temporary regulation.

## Revenue Rulings and Procedures

Although regulations provide valuable interpretative information, they include only statements of general principles and cannot address every situation that could arise under a given Code section. **Revenue rulings** are interpretations by the IRS of the Code and regulations as they apply to specific factual situations. They represent official policy of the IRS and are binding on the IRS until they are revoked, amended, or otherwise changed. They do not, however, carry the same force and effect as a regulation and will be held invalid by a court if they are found to conflict with the intent of the regulation or I.R.C. provision to which they relate.

**Revenue procedures** are issued to explain internal IRS administrative practices and procedures. For example, a revenue procedure may explain the means by which employers may submit withholding information on computer files instead of paper documents. Familiarity with these pronouncements facilitates the processing of the taxpayer's returns and assures compliance with other administrative matters when dealing with the IRS.

The IRS issues hundreds of revenue rulings and procedures every year. Because of the great volume, they are not subject to as extensive a review process as regulations. Because of the lower level of review, revenue rulings and revenue procedures are given less weight than regulations as an authoritative source of the tax law.

Notices and announcements issued by the IRS and published in the Internal Revenue Bulletin are considered authority and may be relied upon to the same extent as a revenue ruling or revenue procedure. Notices offer guidance before revenue rulings and regulations are available. Announcements provide information in a less formal manner than revenue rulings, revenue procedures, and notices. Notices and announcements are numbered by year.

## Acquiescence and Nonacquiescence

If the IRS loses in a court proceeding, it may issue an announcement as to whether it will follow the decision by issuing an acquiescence (acq.) or a nonacquiescence (nonacq.). **Acquiescence** indicates that the IRS accepts the decision of the court and will follow the holding in handling cases with similar facts and circumstances. An announcement of acquiescence does not necessarily mean that the IRS approves or disapproves of the reasons given by the court for its conclusions. The IRS may issue an acquiescence in result only, which indicates disagreement or concern with some or all of the court's reasoning, but means that the IRS will not appeal the decision. A **nonacquiescence** means that the IRS will not follow the decision in similar cases. An acquiescence or nonacquiescence may be withdrawn, modified, or reversed at any time and may be applied retroactively. An announcement of acquiescence may not be cited as precedent. A taxpayer in a situation similar to a case in which the IRS has issued a nonacquiescence will have to decide whether to follow the position favored by the IRS or be prepared to face a challenge by the IRS.

Under its current policy, the IRS may issue announcements of acquiescence or nonacquiescence on unappealed issues decided against the government in selected regular Tax Court opinions, Tax Court memorandum opinions, and opinions of U.S. District Courts, the U.S. Court of Federal Claims, and the Circuit Court of Appeals. Prior to 1991, the IRS issued announcements of acquiescence or nonacquiescence only for regular decisions of the Tax Court.[7]

## Other Pronouncements

The IRS issues various other interpretive pronouncements to aid taxpayers in complying with the tax law. A **private letter ruling (LTR)** is issued by the National Office of the IRS in response to specific questions raised by taxpayers and typically deals with prospective transactions. By issuing revenue procedures, the IRS restricts the areas in which it will issue private letter rulings. An LTR applies only to the taxpayer requesting the ruling and does not bind the IRS to take the same position when dealing with a different taxpayer. If the IRS believes that the transaction represented in an LTR may be of importance to taxpayers in general, it may issue a revenue ruling.

A **technical advice memorandum (TAM)** may be thought of as an LTR for a completed transaction.[8] A TAM originates as a request for assistance by a local office of the IRS and typically arises as part of an ongoing audit. Like the LTR, the TAM is issued by the National Office of the IRS and is not binding on the IRS. LTRs and TAMs are generically referred to as **letter rulings**, and although they are not officially published by the government, they are unofficially made available to the public by many private publishers such as Commerce Clearing House and Research Institute of America. Although they are accorded a lower level of authority, letter rulings are a useful source in determining the current position of the IRS on an issue.

Chief counsel's memoranda are issued by the Office of Chief Counsel of the IRS and include technical memoranda, general counsel's memoranda, and actions on decisions. These documents originate in the process of preparing other authoritative pronouncements and are frequently relied on by IRS personnel in disputes with taxpayers. **Technical memoranda (TM)** are used to explain Treasury regulations. The use of TM has decreased and been replaced with what is referred to as the *preamble* to Treasury regulations. **General counsel's memoranda (GCM)** explain the authority and reasoning used to prepare revenue rulings, private letter rulings, and technical advice memoranda. **Actions on decisions (AOD)** explain whether the Chief Counsel's Office believes that an adverse court decision should be appealed. The AOD may suggest that an acquiescence or nonacquiescence be issued. Like letter rulings, these documents are not binding on the service and are not officially published by the government. Nevertheless, they help in understanding the position of the IRS and are made unofficially available by private publishers.

The IRS does publish a variety of other documents designed to help taxpayers comply with the tax law. These include notices, announcements, IRS publications, and tax return instructions. For example, IRS Publication 17, entitled "Your Federal Income Tax," explains how to prepare an individual income tax return. Caution is warranted, however, because these publications are sometimes incomplete and misleading. And, although they are published by the IRS, the taxpayer may not rely on them as an authoritative source for a position taken on a tax return.

## 16-2c Judicial Sources

If a taxpayer and the IRS disagree on the interpretation and application of the Code, the matter may have to be resolved in court. Court decisions are official interpretations and applications of the Code by the judicial branch of government and therefore represent the third source of primary authority. All litigation must start in a trial court. It is the trial court's responsibility to determine the facts and then interpret and apply the law. Either the taxpayer or the IRS, when it loses at the trial level, may appeal the decision to a higher court. No appellate court, including the Supreme Court, holds another trial. (Lawyers' arguments must be based on the record of the original trial.) These courts' primary responsibility is to determine whether the law was correctly applied to the facts. Only rarely will an appellate court disturb the findings of fact by the trial court. Losses at the first appellate level may be further appealed to the Supreme Court, decisions of which are final and binding on all lower courts.

### Trial Courts

Taxpayers may choose one of the following three courts in which to initiate litigation: U.S. District Court, U.S. Court of Federal Claims, and U.S. Tax Court. These courts of original jurisdiction are referred to as the **trial courts**. Taxpayers willing to pay the tax in dispute and then sue for a refund can take their case to a U.S. District Court or the U.S. Court of Federal Claims. Each **U.S. District Court** hears cases on legal issues involving the entire *United States Code*, of which the Internal Revenue Code is but one small part. Therefore, district court judges must be generalists in matters of federal law and are not specialists in federal tax law. District courts are located throughout the country—each is assigned to serve a specific geographic area. To have a jury trial, taxpayers must file in district court. The **U.S. Court of Federal Claims** hears cases concerning any monetary claim against the federal government. Because income tax refunds are only one type of claim that can be filed against the federal government, claims court judges are not specialists in federal tax law. Unlike the district courts, the claims court does not allow jury trials.

As an alternative, taxpayers may choose not to pay the additional tax and then file a petition for relief in **U.S. Tax Court**. There are two distinct advantages in choosing the Tax Court. First, as indicated, the case can be taken to the Tax Court without first paying the tax. This is why the Tax Court is often referred to as the "poor person's court." Second, the Tax Court offers an opportunity for the issues to be decided by a court that specializes in tax matters.

The Tax Court has traditionally issued two types of decisions: regular and memorandum. **Tax Court regular decisions** are those that are presumed to have value as precedents or involve issues that have not previously been considered. All other decisions are **Tax Court memorandum decisions**. Regular decisions are generally regarded as stronger authorities than memorandum decisions, although the distinction has become somewhat blurred over the years.

In cases in which the amount of tax in dispute is less than $50,000, a taxpayer may elect to use the small claims division of the Tax Court. The purpose of the small claims division is to let taxpayers obtain a ruling on their case with a minimal amount of formality, delay, and expense. Caution is warranted, however, because small claims cases cannot be appealed, and the decisions are not published and cannot be used as precedents in other courts.

Both the Tax Court and the Court of Federal Claims are referred to as *national courts* because they hear cases from taxpayers living anywhere in the United States. A district court can hear cases only from taxpayers who live within the specific geographical area over which the court presides.[9] Taxpayers must consider these jurisdictional differences, whether to pay first, whether the technical expertise of the Tax Court is desirable, the advantages of a jury, and prior decisions on similar issues when selecting a trial court.

## Appellate Courts

Decisions of the district courts and Tax Court are appealed to one of 12 regional **U.S. Courts of Appeals** (previously the U.S. Circuit Courts of Appeals and occasionally still referred to as such). Each circuit court has a specific geographical area over which it has sole jurisdiction. Decisions of the U.S. Court of Federal Claims must be appealed to the **U.S. Court of Appeals for the Federal Circuit** in Washington, D.C. Decisions by appellate courts have precedence over trial court decisions. For example, if a circuit court has previously ruled on an issue, all the district courts within that circuit must follow that decision in any future cases.

The Tax Court will follow the holdings of a circuit court only for taxpayers residing within the specific geographical jurisdiction of the appellate court. Outside that circuit, the Tax Court may hold differently on exactly the same facts and issues. This so-called *Golsen*[10] rule has been justified by the Tax Court on the ground that it is a trial court with national jurisdiction. The Court of Federal Claims is bound to follow only decisions of the U.S. Court of Appeals for the Federal Circuit.

Although trial courts are bound only by the decisions of their own circuit courts, they frequently look to other circuit court decisions as well as decisions of other trial courts in forming their opinions. Similarly, each circuit court does not need to follow decisions of other circuit courts but does look to those decisions for guidance.

## Supreme Court

All decisions of appellate courts may be further appealed to the **U.S. Supreme Court**. Unlike the circuit courts, which must rule on every case that is appealed from the trial courts, the Supreme Court does not have to accept every case that is appealed from the circuit courts. The Supreme Court decides which cases it wants to review by granting a writ of certiorari. Granting the writ of certiorari simply means that at least four of the nine justices on the Court feel the case is important enough for them to review it.

Conversely, denying a writ of certiorari means only that the Court does not think the case is important enough for it to review at that time. It does not reverse or in any other way directly affect the decision of the lower court. Review will, however, strengthen the authority or importance of the case in the hierarchy of primary authorities. The Court limits its review of tax cases to those of major importance or to those in which the decisions of the circuit courts conflict.

If the Supreme Court agrees to review a decision, its interpretation and application of the law are the final authority, and all lower courts, taxpayers, and the IRS must follow its decision. If Congress is unhappy with the Court's interpretation and application of the law, its only recourse is to follow the legislative process described earlier and seek to amend the Code.

## 16-2d Citations to Primary Authorities

LO 4 Prepare citations to each of the primary authorities.

Whenever a reference is made to any primary authority, it is important to include a citation indicating where the full text of the document may be found. This is an especially crucial part of the tax research process described later in this chapter. Although it is beyond the scope of this text to discuss citation formats in any great depth, a brief review is necessary. Exhibit 16-5 illustrates citations to most of the primary authorities previously discussed and provides the basis for the discussion that follows.

### Committee Reports

All reports issued by the House Ways and Means Committee, the Senate Finance Committee, and the Joint Conference Committee are cited in the same general manner. The example in Exhibit 16-5 is for a House Ways and Means Committee report and tells the reader that it is the 432nd report issued by the House of Representatives during the second session of the 98th Congress and was issued on March 5, 1984. The name of the committee frequently is omitted from the citation. This generally occurs when reference to the committee that issued the report is made in a related text discussion.

*Exhibit 16-5*

### Citations to Primary Authorities

| Primary Authority | Citation |
|---|---|
| Committee report | HOUSE COMMITTEE ON WAYS AND MEANS, H. Rep. No. 432, 98th Cong., 2d Sess. (March 5,1984). |
| Internal Revenue Code | Sec. 469(e)(1)(A). |
| Treasury regulation—final | Reg. Sec. 1.269-1(a)(3). |
| Treasury regulation—proposed | Prop. Reg. Sec. 1.704-3(c). |
| Treasury regulation—temporary | Temp. Reg. Sec. 1.441-1T(a)(2). |
| Revenue ruling—temporary citation | Rev. Rul. 84-101, 1984-28 I.R.B. 5. |
| Revenue ruling—permanent citation | Rev. Rul. 54-56, 1954-2 C.B. 108. |
| Revenue procedure—temporary citation | Rev. Proc. 93-15, 1993-3 I.R.B. 12. |
| Revenue procedure—permanent citation | Rev. Proc. 88-12, 1988-1 C.B. 17. |
| Announcement—temporary citation | Ann. 2001-77, 2001-30 I.R.B. 83. |
| Announcement—permanent citation | Ann. 2001-77, 2001-2 C.B. 83. |
| Notice—temporary citation | Notice 2002-64, 2002-41 I.R.B. 690. |
| Notice—permanent citation | Notice 2002-64, 2002-2 C.B. 690. |
| Private letter ruling | LTR 8450056 (PLR) or LTR 200343030 (PLR). |
| U.S. Tax Court—regular decision | *J.B. Linderman*, 60 T.C. 609 (1973). |
| U.S. Tax Court—memorandum decision | *Thomas E. Lesslie*, 36 TCM 495 (1977), T.C. Memo ¶1977–111. |
| Acquiescence | *Phillip G. Larson*, 66 T.C. 159 (1976), *acq.* 1979-1 C.B. 1. |
| U.S. District Court | *Arnold v. U.S.*, 289 F. Supp. 206, 68-2 USTC ¶9590, 22 A.F.T.R.2d 5661 (E.D. N.Y., 1968). |
| U.S. Court of Federal Claims | *Zuchman v. U.S.*, 524 F.2d 729, 75-2 USTC ¶9778, 36 A.F.T.R.2d 75-6193 (Cl.Ct., 1975). |
| U.S. Courts of Appeals | *Comm. v. Percy W. Phillips*, 275 F.2d 33, 60-1 USTC ¶9294, 5 A.F.T.R.2d 855 (4th Cir.,1960). |
| U.S. Supreme Court | *Commissioner v. Duberstein*, 363 U.S. 278, 80 S. Ct. 1190, 60-2 USTC ¶9515, 5 A.F.T.R.2d 1626 (1960). |

## Code and Regulations

References to the Code have been introduced previously. Spelling out *Internal Revenue Code* or inserting *I.R.C.* is usually omitted in practice, because it is understood that the reference is to the Internal Revenue Code of 1986, as amended. The last group of numbers in any Code citation should reflect the smallest subdivision of a section that relates to the tax issue under consideration.

Treasury regulations follow a similar citation pattern, but they are preceded by a number that specifies the general area of tax to which the regulation relates. Most regulations start with *1*, signifying that they deal with income taxes. Other common numbers are *20*, relating to estate taxes; *25*, involving gift taxes; and *301* or *601*, dealing with administrative rules. The first numbers after the period state the related Code section. The Code section number is followed by a hyphen and the number of the regulation. Several regulations may be issued under the same Code section. The last group of numbers gives the smallest subdivision of the regulation that is appropriate. Proposed and temporary regulations follow the same format, except that they are preceded by *Prop.* or *Temp.* In addition—and only for temporary regulations—a *T* follows the regulation number. Again, spelling out *Treasury* or inserting *Treas.* is usually omitted in practice; common practice is to abbreviate *Section* as *Sec.*, instead of using the symbol for *section*, §.

## Other IRS Pronouncements

All other pronouncements of the IRS are initially published weekly by the U.S. Government Printing Office in the ***Internal Revenue Bulletin* (I.R.B.)**. Semiannually, the last six months of the I.R.B. are reorganized and published in a permanent document called the ***Cumulative Bulletin* (C.B.)**. Citations to most IRS documents should be to the C.B. Whenever the latest C.B. does not include the referenced document, a temporary citation is made to the I.R.B.

As Exhibit 16-5 illustrates, revenue rulings and procedures are cited similarly. The numbers following *Rev. Rul.* provide the reader with the following information: The ruling was the 56th ruling issued in 1954 and can be found on page 108 of the second volume of the 1954 *Cumulative Bulletin*. The temporary citation yields this information: The ruling is the 101st ruling issued in 1984 and can be found on page 5 of the 28th weekly issue of the *Internal Revenue Bulletin*. Revenue procedures read the same way.

Letter rulings, including private letter rulings and technical advice memoranda, are given an official seven-digit number. The first two digits provide the year the ruling was issued, the next two indicate the week, and the final three digits are the number assigned to that ruling for that week. Letter rulings issued after 2000 use four-digit years (e.g., LTR 200343030), whereas most letter rulings before 2000 used only two-digit years (e.g., LTR 8450056). The citation in Exhibit 16-5 tells the reader that the ruling was issued in 1984, during the 50th week, and was the 56th ruling issued that week. Sometimes, the citation includes a designation after the number that tells the reader which type of letter ruling is being cited (i.e., either a private letter ruling (PLR) or a technical advice memorandum [TAM]).

## Court Decisions

All judicial citations follow the same format: case name, volume number of the reporter in which the case is published, name of the reporter, and the page of the reporter on which the case begins. Case names should be underlined or italicized in text, but not in a footnote. Sometimes, the year of the decision or the name of the court is added in parentheses at the end. A **reporter** is a series of books published by the federal government or by a private publishing company that provides the full text of court decisions. The two biggest private publishers of reporters are the Research Institute of America (RIA, formerly Prentice Hall) and Commerce Clearing House (CCH). Complete citations typically include one citation to a government reporter and at least one additional citation to a CCH or RIA reporter. Different reporters are cited for each court that renders a decision.

**Tax Court** Regular decisions of the U.S. Tax Court are published by the Government Printing Office (GPO) in a reporter called ***Reports of the United States Tax Court* (T.C.)**.

CCH and RIA also publish regular Tax Court decisions in separate special decision reporters. Both are called *Tax Court Reporter*. However, common tax practice is to cite only T.C., the official GPO reporter. The citation for the *Linderman* case in Exhibit 16-5 provides the information that the case can be found on page 609 of volume 60 of *Reports of the United States Tax Court* and that it was decided in 1973.

Memorandum decisions of the U.S. Tax Court are not published in any government reporter. They are, however, published by both RIA *(T.C. Memorandum Decision)* and CCH *(Tax Court Memorandum Decisions)*. Common practice is to cite RIA's reporter as *T.C. Memo* and CCH's as *TCM*. As Exhibit 16-5 illustrates, citations for both services follow exactly the same format. For example, the *Lesslie* case can be found on page 495 of volume 36 of *Tax Court Memorandum Decisions* (TCM) and in the 1977 volume of T.C. Memo, at paragraph 77, 111. A complete citation would include citations to both reporters.

**All Other Courts Except the U.S. Supreme Court** The U.S. government does not officially publish the decisions of the district courts, claims court, or the appellate courts in any reporter. West Publishing Co., however, is treated as the official publisher, and any citation to decisions from these courts should include a citation to one of its reporters. This includes the ***Federal Supplement* (F. Supp.)** for all district court cases and the ***Federal Reporter*, second or third series (F.2d or F.3d)** for claims court and appellate court cases.

These decisions are also reported by RIA in *American Federal Tax Reports* (A.F.T.R. and A.F.T.R.2d) and by Commerce Clearing House in *U.S. Tax Cases* (USTC). The CCH and RIA reporters include only tax cases, whereas the West reporters include all cases decided by the respective courts. A complete citation should cite all three reporters. For example, the citation for the *Arnold* case in Exhibit 16-5 provides the following information: The case can be found on page 206 of volume 289 of the *Federal Supplement;* it is a case decided by the U.S. District Court for the eastern district of New York in 1968; it can also be found at paragraph 9590 of volume 68-2 of *U.S. Tax Cases* and on page 5661 of volume 22 of *American Federal Tax Reports,* second series. Decisions of the appellate courts and the claims courts are cited the same way.

**Acquiescence** Whenever the IRS issues an acquiescence (*acq.*) or nonacquiescence (*nonacq.*) to an unfavorable court decision, it should be included in the citation, as it is for the *Larson* case in Exhibit 16–5. This informs the reader that the acquiescence can be found on page 1 of volume 1 of the 1979 *Cumulative Bulletin*.

**Supreme Court** Decisions of the United States Supreme Court are officially printed by the government in the ***United States Reports* (U.S.)** reporter. Because of their importance, these decisions are also published by West Publishing in ***Supreme Court Reports* (S. Ct.)** and are included in the A.F.T.R. and *U.S. Tax Cases* series. A complete citation should include reference to either the S. Ct. or U.S. reporters and both the A.F.T.R. and USTC reporters. The *Duberstein* case in Exhibit 16-5 is an example of a citation that provides references to all four sources.

# 16-3 SECONDARY SOURCES OF FEDERAL INCOME TAX LAW

Answers to federal tax questions must be based on the primary authorities. However, as we have discussed, the number of these authorities is vast, they are constantly changing, and they are not indexed or coordinated in any logical fashion. The most important role of secondary authorities is to help in locating the legislative, administrative, or judicial primary authorities that provide the answers about the tax consequences related to a specific factual situation. Tax services, and citators are secondary authorities that are used for this purpose. Other secondary authorities, including textbooks, journals, and editorial comments in tax services, may also be used to help understand and interpret the law. These are unofficial interpretations only and have no legal authority.

## 16-3a Tax Services

LO 5

Identify the purpose of the different types of secondary authorities.

**Tax services**, one type of secondary authority, principally are tools for locating the primary authorities related to various factual circumstances. Tax services fall into two major categories, based on the amount of editorial discussion provided by the publisher. The first category consists of those services with limited editorial discussion and numerous brief interpretations and citations to the primary authorities (other than the Code and regulations, which are provided in full text). These abridged interpretations, or annotations consist chiefly of brief interpretations of revenue rulings and procedures, court cases, letter rulings, and other miscellaneous pronouncements. Services in this category include *Standard Federal Tax Reporter (CCH)* and *United States Tax Reporter (RIA)*. It is important to remember that the researcher using these services should not rely on the synopses given in the annotations because they represent only the editors' interpretations of the related authority. The researcher should always read the full text of the appropriate primary authority before reaching any conclusions.

The second category of tax services contains extensive editorial discussion and interpretation of the law, with citations to the primary authorities provided in the footnotes. These services also provide full text of the Code and regulations but are arranged by topical headings determined by the editor. Services in this category include the *Federal Tax Coordinator 2d* (published by RIA), *Tax Management Portfolios* (published by the Bloomberg BNA), and *Federal Tax Service* (published by CCH). The researcher should always read the entire text of the authority cited in the footnotes to be sure that the analysis and interpretation provided in the editorial discussion are proper.

In addition, the publishers of most services provide paperback versions of the Code and regulations, which are convenient and may answer some basic questions. Abridged paperback versions of most tax services, called *tax guides*, are also available from the publishers. Examples of tax guides are the *Master Tax Guide* (CCH) and the *Federal Tax Manual* (RIA). Because the coverage of tax guides is limited, they should be used only for orientation purposes and not for research.

## 16-3b Computer-Assisted Tax Research

LO 6

Describe computer-assisted tax research (CATR).

To reduce costs and improve efficiency, tax practitioners have shifted their use of tax services printed on paper to **computer-assisted tax research (CATR)** tools. All the major tax publishers now offer their primary and secondary authorities in CATR systems. CATR systems utilize powerful electronic search engines that let a researcher search an entire database and retrieve the full text of desired documents in a few seconds. The researcher can search by using keywords, Code section numbers, dates, topics, type of authority, or other criteria. The search returns a list of documents that fit the specified criteria. The researcher can scan the hits and retrieve the full text of documents that appear relevant. If too many hits are retrieved, the search can be refined by specifying additional criteria.

The major publishers of subscription-based CATR systems are Research Institute of America (RIA), Commerce Clearing House (CCH), Bloomberg BNA, Tax Analysts, Westlaw, and LEXIS. These services offer the most comprehensive collections of primary and secondary authorities and are updated daily.

Some tax authorities are available free on Internet sites, such as those listed in Exhibit 16-6. These tax directories contain links to other sites, sponsored by universities, government agencies, law firms, and public accounting firms, that contain the full text of some primary and secondary authorities.

The free Internet sites contain a limited selection of tax authorities but are gradually expanding their coverage. The available legislative authorities on free Internet sites include the full text of the current Internal Revenue Code and more recent congressional committee reports. The available administrative authorities include the full text of regulations and IRS publications but only a limited selection of other IRS pronouncements. Various law libraries are putting the full text of some judicial authorities on free Internet sites. Secondary tax authorities on the Internet include tax newsletters issued by tax-practice firms and publishers. Searches on the free Internet sites are less efficient than

Exhibit 16-6

## Tax Directories on the Internet

| Site and Author | Uniform Resource Locator (URL) |
|---|---|
| Income Tax Materials, Cornell Legal Information Institute | http://www.law.cornell.edu/uscode/text/26 |
| Internal Revenue Service, U.S. Treasury Department | http://www.irs.gov |
| Internet Law Library—Taxation, U.S. House Information Services | http://uscode.house.gov |
| Tax Information Worldwide Tax Analysts | http://www.taxanalysts.com |
| Tax Resources on the Web Alan G. Kalman | http://taxtopics.net |
| Tax Sites Directory | http://www.taxsites.com |
| Tax World, Tom Omer | http://www.taxworld.org |

those available on subscription services. Researchers are advised that these results may not have been updated for the most recent changes.

### 16-3c Citators

**Citators** are used primarily to determine the history of a judicial decision and how that decision has been criticized, approved, or otherwise commented upon in other court decisions. This type of information also is available for revenue rulings, revenue procedures, and certain other administrative pronouncements. Citators are a valuable tool in the "validation" step of tax research, described later in this chapter. Citators refer to the case being evaluated as the **cited case**, and any cases discussing that case are called the **citing cases**. Cited cases are listed alphabetically, followed by the citing cases and rulings.

The history of a cited case refers to all other decisions by higher or lower courts in the same case. For example, if the cited case has been appealed to a higher court, the citator provides the name of the appellate court and whether it affirmed, reversed, or modified the decision of the cited case. Similarly, if the cited case is an appellate court decision, the citator provides the name of the trial court and states whether the cited case affirmed, reversed, or otherwise modified the decision of the lower court. For revenue rulings, citators provide historical citations to related rulings that revoke, modify, or supersede the cited ruling and to any earlier rulings affected by the cited ruling. Citators further provide *citing references*, which provide other rulings or court cases that have discussed the cited ruling.

The citator also gives information about how the decision of the cited case has been interpreted by other courts. These courts can, in their decisions, agree or disagree with the cited case, differentiate the facts or law in their case from the cited case, or simply refer to the cited case without comment. Some citators use abbreviations to indicate which of these reasons are specified by the citing court. These notations are most useful when the citing cases are numerous. The tax citators most frequently used are Research Institute of America's ***Federal Tax Citator*** and Commerce Clearing House's *Citator*, which are available as part of their subscription tax services.

### 16-3d Tax Periodicals

Numerous publications, law school journals, and newsletters dealing with tax matters also serve as secondary authorities and sources of tax information. These are especially valuable for planning and notification of new developments. Examples of these sources include *Journal of Taxation, TAXES—The Tax Magazine, Tax Adviser, Tax Notes,* and *Daily Tax Report.*

## 16-4 TAX RESEARCH

LO 7 Explain the difference between tax planning and tax compliance.

Tax research is simply the process by which the answers to tax questions are determined. From an initial set of facts, the researcher identifies the tax issues to be resolved, then must locate the governing Code section and any administrative or judicial interpretations and evaluate and apply them to the facts. The researcher must draw conclusions and communicate the results and recommendations to the interested parties.

## 16-4a Tax Compliance Versus Tax Planning

Tax research usually becomes important for either a transaction that has already been completed or for one that is being contemplated. Finding the answer to a completed transaction is commonly referred to as *compliance work* (after-the-fact) and typically arises during the preparation of a tax return. Determining the tax consequence of transactions that have not yet been completed is called *tax planning* (or before-the-fact research). In planning situations, tax research is undertaken to find the "best" way to accomplish a desired result. Frequently, the best method depends on both tax and nontax considerations.

**Example 1** Edna, a client, tells you she would like to give her son some apartment buildings that she owns. She wants to know the best way to transfer this property to him.

**Discussion: The alternatives might include a sale, a gift, or transferring the property to a trust, with Edna's son as beneficiary. Each method has different tax consequences. You also know that Edna does not really trust her son and is worried that he will simply take all the profits and let the building deteriorate. This nontax factor may lead you to conclude that the "best" method would be to set up a trust, even if the tax consequences are not the most favorable.**

Whether tax research is for compliance or planning, it is important to use a systematic procedure for your research. The basic steps involved in this process are as follows:

1. Establish the facts and determine the issues.
2. Locate the relevant authorities.
3. Assess the importance of the authorities.
4. Reach conclusions, make recommendations, and communicate the results.

## 16-4b Step 1: Establish the Facts and Determine the Issues

LO 8
Describe the basic steps involved in tax research.

All tax research begins with determining the facts. The facts help define the initial tax issues and the apparently applicable Code provisions and any administrative or judicial interpretations. Reviewing these authorities most likely leads to the need for more information. Such additional information may yield citations of other applicable authorities, which again may require the researcher to track down further factual information. Following the trail of facts and authorities is an inherent part of the tax research process.

**Example 2** Let us return to your client, Edna. Assume she sells the property to her son and that the sale results in a loss. Is the loss deductible?

**Discussion: The applicable statutory provision is Sec. 267 of the Code. Sec. 267(a)(1) disallows losses between persons specified in Sec. 267(b), which includes members of family, as defined in Sec. 267(c)(4). Sec. 267(c)(4) specifies that members of a family include the taxpayer's brothers and sisters, spouse, ancestors, and lineal descendants. Your initial conclusion is that the loss will be disallowed as a deduction. But further discussion with the taxpayer yields the information that the son is really a stepson who was never legally adopted. This additional fact changes your conclusion. Under the authority of Reg. Sec. 1.267(c)-1(a)(4), only legally adopted lineal descendants are members of the family. Edna may take the loss as a deduction.**

Facts relevant to a tax situation include the taxpayer's method of accounting, the marital status of the taxpayer, whether the parties to a transaction are related, the domicile and citizenship of the taxpayer, and whether the taxpayer is a partner or S corporation shareholder. When the taxpayer is a corporation, relevant tax facts include whether it is an S or C corporation, whether it is tax exempt, and whether it is a financial institution, insurance company, or personal holding company. In some cases, the facts are well established, and the only issue is how the tax law is interpreted and how that interpretation applies to the facts. These are generally referred to as *questions of law*, in contrast with questions of fact.

## 16-4c Step 2: Locate the Relevant Authorities

Secondary authorities are most useful for locating the applicable primary authorities. Usually, this means that research begins with the index to or a keyword search of one of the tax services. This provides a reference to the part of the service that contains the full text of the relevant Code section and regulations, as well as annotations of court decisions and administrative pronouncements. Remember that any editorial commentary included in the tax services is secondary authority only. All conclusions and recommendations must be based on primary authorities. Further, conclusions should never be based on the annotations provided by the editorial staff of the publishers of the tax services. You must examine and evaluate the full text of the court case, revenue ruling, or other primary authority, as indicated in step 3.

## 16-4d Step 3: Assess the Importance of the Authorities

Once you have located the apparently applicable authorities, you must evaluate them to determine whether they actually apply to the facts and issues and to assess their importance. Determining whether the authority is relevant to the tax issues under consideration is accomplished by reading the full text of the document. Determining the importance, or relative weight, of the authorities is more difficult. In many cases, the Code and regulations do not provide a conclusive answer to the issues involved in a specific set of facts. You may have to rely on other administrative or judicial authorities, and these are frequently in conflict. To determine the inherent strength or weakness of these authorities, you need a general understanding of the hierarchy of the authorities and how to use a citator.

### Code and Regulations

Sometimes, simply reading the applicable Code section yields the answer to a tax question. More often, however, the statutory language is ambiguous or does not directly address the issues identified. Under these circumstances, the secondary authorities—especially the citators and annotations in the tax services—are useful for finding other primary authorities that may help in evaluating and applying the statute. In relatively rare circumstances, you will find no other regulations, IRS pronouncements, or court decisions that conclusively deal with the issue. When this occurs, you must examine the legislative history of the provision, as provided by the committee reports, for congressional intent. One other point bears repeating. Compliance work frequently requires determining the answer concerning a transaction that occurred some years earlier. Accordingly, it is important to be sure that the version of the Code or Treasury regulation you are using applies to the period in which the transaction occurred.

The Code is generally considered the highest authority, because it is the law as enacted by Congress. If the issue deals with international tax matters, treaties as enacted by Congress may supersede provisions in the Code. The courts can invalidate a section of the Code or a treaty only if it violates the U.S. Constitution.

Treasury regulations, representing the official interpretation of the law by the Treasury Department, are often referred to as having *the force and effect of the law*. The courts can invalidate them only by determining that they are inconsistent with the statute to which they relate. In assessing the importance of Treasury regulations, it is important to remember that there are different types of regulations. Temporary regulations are accorded the same weight as final regulations. Proposed regulations carry no authority because they are only indications of what the Treasury Department may decide. They are not binding on either the taxpayer or the IRS.

### Pronouncements

Revenue rulings, issued by the IRS, represent agency policy and are binding on the IRS and its personnel until they are revoked, modified, superseded, or withdrawn. Although they are accorded considerable importance, they do not have the force and effect of a Treasury regulation, primarily because they are subjected to only a limited review before they are issued. The courts frequently find that a ruling is inconsistent with the Code section or regulation it is interpreting. It is important to use a citator to determine not only the current status of the ruling but also *how* the ruling has been evaluated by the courts. Because an acquiescence or nonacquiescence by the IRS to an adverse court decision is tantamount to a revenue ruling, acquiescenses and nonacquiescenses are accorded the same weight as revenue rulings. This procedure should be followed in assessing the importance of any other IRS pronouncement.

### Court Decisions

Numerous factors affect the strength of a court decision. One factor is whether the decision was issued by a trial or appellate court. A decision by the U.S. Court of Appeals for the Third Circuit would be more authoritative than a trial court decision. An opinion by the Supreme Court would be the highest authority.

Another important factor is whether the decision was issued by the Tax Court or another trial court. Recall that the Tax Court is generally considered to have more technical expertise than other trial courts.

**Example 3** On a very technical question, your research turns up an applicable Tax Court decision that provides favorable support for the position your client wants to take. You also find a district court decision on substantially identical facts but with opposite results.

**Discussion: If the two cases are identical in all other respects, the Tax Court decision is the higher authority. Similarly, a regular decision of the U.S. Tax Court generally carries more weight than a memorandum decision.**

Other factors to be considered in determining the level of authority of a court decision include whether the decision is unanimous or split and the jurisdictional issues regarding the taxpayer's residence, discussed earlier. All the factors can be determined by actually reading the case.

The most important factor determining the relative importance or weight accorded a court decision is how other courts have viewed the decision. Using a citator is crucial for determining how the opinion stacks up with other decisions on the same issue. A strong decision would be one with a long history of favorable evaluation by other courts.

## 16-4e Step 4: Reach Conclusions, Make Recommendations, and Communicate the Results

The final research step is both objective and subjective. You must reach objective conclusions about each primary authority and how it applies to the facts and issues under consideration. In reporting to the client, you must include all your conclusions, whether they result in a favorable outcome for the taxpayer or not. These objective conclusions state what you believe is the current state of the law.

From these conclusions, you must subjectively determine which of the often-conflicting interpretations is the correct one to recommend. Your recommendation should include a research memorandum that encompasses a statement of the relevant facts, the tax issues considered, the conclusions and recommendations reached for each issue, and the authorities, reasoning, and analysis used to arrive at each conclusion and recommendation. Always provide citations to supporting primary authorities.

The research memorandum provides the basis for a separate letter to the taxpayer, which, although containing basically the same information, is less detailed. The importance of the research memorandum and letter cannot be over-emphasized. All your research will be wasted if you do not communicate the results effectively.

# 16-5 COMPREHENSIVE RESEARCH EXAMPLE

## 16-5a Step 1: Establish the Facts and Determine the Issues

LO 9 Apply the tax research process to a comprehensive problem.

Sam, a surgeon, and his wife, Sara, own and rent out a vacation home. During the year, they use the home 20 days and rent it out for 40 days. Rental income for the year is $4,000. Total expenses are as follows:

| | |
|---|---|
| Interest and taxes | $4,200 |
| Utilities and maintenance | 1,500 |
| Depreciation | 6,000 |

Sam has asked for assistance in determining the tax treatment of these expenditures.

## 16-5b Step 2: Locate the Relevant Authorities

Using any of the tax services leads to Sec. 280A, "Disallowance of Certain Expenses in Connection with Business Use of Home, Rental of Vacation Homes, Etc." A review of the editorial discussion and annotations indicates that Prop. Reg. Sec. 1.280A-3 and *Bolton v. Commissioner*, 694 F.2d 556, 51 A.F.T.R.2d 83-305, 83-20 USTC ¶9699 (9th Cir., 1982), affirming 77 T.C. 104 (1981), may also be applicable.

## 16-5c Step 3: Assess the Importance of the Authorities

Completion of this step requires review of each authority identified to determine its applicability. Always examine the relevant Code section first. If questions remain unanswered, you must look to the administrative and judicial interpretations to see if they provide definitive answers or at least some direction.

### The Code

Exhibit 16-7 provides the relevant portions of Sec. 280A. The general rule of Sec. 280A(a) limits a taxpayer's business deductions for expenses incurred for a dwelling unit if that unit was used as a personal residence during the taxable year. Under Sec. 280A(d)(1), the general rule of Sec. 280A(a) applies if the taxpayer's personal use of the dwelling unit exceeds the greater of 14 days or 10 percent of the number of days the unit is rented. Because Sam and Sara's personal use of the vacation home exceeds both 14 days and 10 percent of the rental days, the general limitation applies.

Sec. 280A(b) provides that nonbusiness expenditures otherwise deductible (e.g., taxes, interest, and casualty losses) are not subject to the general limitation in Sec. 280A(a). Sec. 280A(c)(3) provides another exception to the general limitation by allowing a deduction for "any item attributable to rental of the unit" (e.g., utilities, maintenance, and depreciation). The latter so-called maintenance expenditures, however, must first be allocated to the rental use under the rules of Sec. 280A(e)(1) and then are limited under the rules of Sec. 280A(c)(5).

Sec. 280A(e)(1) requires that the maintenance expenditures attributable to the rental use be allocated using the following formula:

$$\frac{\text{Number of days in the tax year the unit is rented}}{\text{Total number of days in the tax year the unit is used}}$$

All maintenance expenditures are multiplied by this ratio to arrive at a tentative deduction figure. Applying the formula to the facts for Sam and Sara results in the following calculation:

$$\frac{40(\text{days rented})}{60(\text{days used})} \times 66.67\% \times \$7{,}500 = \$5{,}000$$

In other words, of the total maintenance expenditures of $7,500, the maximum amount allocable to the rental activity that may be deducted is $5,000.

Sec. 280A(c)(5) may further limit deductions for maintenance expenditures. It provides that all expenses (interest, taxes, casualty losses, and maintenance expenditures) allocable to the rental activity cannot exceed the gross rental income. Further, it requires that deductions

Exhibit 16-7

## Code Section 280A

Sec. 280A Disallowance of **Certain Expenses** in Connection with Business Use of Home, Rental of Vacation Homes, etc.

(a) **General Rule.** Except as otherwise provided in this section, in the case of a taxpayer who is an individual or an S corporation, no deduction otherwise allowable under this chapter shall be allowed with respect to the use of a dwelling unit which is used by the taxpayer during the taxable years as a residence.

(b) **Exception for interest, taxes, casualty losses, etc.** Subsection (a) shall not apply to any deduction allowable to the taxpayer without regard to its connection with his trade or business (or with his income-producing activity).

(c) **Exceptions for certain business or rental use; limitation on deductions for such use.**

....

(3) **Rental use.** Subsection (a) shall not apply to any item which is attributable to the rental of the dwelling unit or portion thereof (determined after the application of subsection (e)).

....

(5) **Limitation on deductions.** In the case of a use described in paragraph (1), (2), or (4), and in the case of a use described in paragraph (3) where the dwelling unit is used by the taxpayer during the taxable year as a residence, the deductions allowed under this chapter for the taxable year by reason of being attributed to such use shall not exceed the excess of—

(A) the gross income derived from such use for the taxable year, over

(B) the sum of—

(i) the deductions allocable to such use which are allowable under this chapter for the taxable year whether or not such unit (or portion thereof) was so used, and

(ii) the deductions allocable to the trade or business (or rental activity) in which such use occurs (but which are not allocable to such use) for such taxable year....

(d) **Expenses attributable to rental.**

(1) **In general.** In any case where a taxpayer who is an individual or an S corporation uses a dwelling unit for personal purposes on any day during the taxable year (whether or not he is treated under this section as using such unit as a residence), the amount deductible under this chapter with respect to expenses attributable to the rental of the unit (or portion thereof) for the taxable year shall not exceed an amount which bears the same relationship to such expenses as the number of days during each year that the unit (or portion thereof) is rented at a fair rental bears to the total number of days during such year that the unit (or portion thereof) is used.

(2) **Exception for deductions otherwise allowable.** This subsection shall not apply with respect to deductions which would be allowable under this chapter for the taxable year whether or not such unit (or portion thereof) was rented.

allowed (e.g., interest, taxes, and casualty losses), whether the unit was used as a rental or not, be allocated to the rental activity and to the amount otherwise allowable as itemized deductions. Any maintenance expenditures are then allowable to the extent that gross rental income exceeds the interest, taxes, and casualty losses allocable to the rental use. Although Sec. 280A(e) does provide the rules for allocating the maintenance expenditures, it provides no guidance for allocating the interest, taxes, and casualty losses. As the editorial commentary in the tax service noted, this has been an area of dispute, with the proposed regulations suggesting one method and the court in *Bolton* suggesting another allocation method.

### Regulations

Prop. Reg. Sec. 1.280A-3(c)(1) requires that interest and taxes be allocated in the same fashion as maintenance expenditures under Sec. 280A(e)(1). For Sam and Sara, a tentative conclusion is that the allocation used should be 40:60 (as suggested in the proposed regulation), which would yield the following calculations:

| | Total | Rental Use | Itemized Deduction | Not Deductible |
|---|---|---|---|---|
| Gross rental income | $ 4,000 | $ 4,000 | — | — |
| Interest & taxes | (4,200) | (2,800) | $1,400 | |
| Excess | | $ 1,200 | | |
| Maintenance | (7,500) | (1,200) | | $6,300 |
| Total | | $ -0- | $1,400 | $6,300 |

### Court Decision

In *Bolton*, the U.S. Court of Appeals for the Ninth Circuit affirmed a decision of the U.S. Tax Court which held that the interpretation provided in the proposed regulation was inconsistent with the statute, its history, and the legislative purpose behind Sec. 280A. The courts held that interest and taxes, unlike maintenance expenditures, are expenses that continue or accrue on a daily basis throughout the year. Accordingly, they should be allocated according to a ratio of days rented to total days in the year.

For Sam and Sara, a tentative conclusion using an allocation of 40:60 for the maintenance expenditures and 40:365 for interest and taxes, as suggested in *Bolton*, would be as follows:

| | Total | Rental Use | Itemized Deduction | Not Deductible |
|---|---|---|---|---|
| Gross rental income | $ 4,000 | $ 4,000 | — | — |
| Interest & taxes | (4,200) | (460) | $3,740 | |
| Excess | | $ 3,540 | | |
| Maintenance | (7,500) | (3,540) | | $3,960 |
| Total | | $ -0- | $3,740 | $3,960 |

It should be noted that the proposed regulations were initially issued on August 7, 1980, and amended on July 21, 1983. The ninth circuit's decision in *Bolton* was rendered on December 2, 1982, which was before the last revision to the proposed regulations. The citator provides the information that the IRS has not issued an acquiescence or nonacquiescence to the unfavorable *Bolton* decision, that the ninth circuit's decision has been cited in numerous Tax Court regular and memorandum decisions, and that its decision has been followed by the tenth circuit in *Edith McKinney v. Comm.*, 732 F.2d 416, 52 A.F.T.R.2d 83-6281, 83-2 USTC ¶9655 (10th Cir., 1983).

### 16-5d Step 4: Reach Conclusions, Make Recommendations, and Communicate the Results

The conclusion reached by the court in *Bolton* is much more favorable for Sara and Sam than the position taken by the proposed regulations. The Tax Court's allocation formula results in a smaller allocation of interest and taxes to the rental unit, an increase in itemized deductions, and a decrease in taxable income for the current year.

A recommendation to Sara and Sam to follow the allocation formula in *Bolton* should be accompanied by some words of caution. The proposed regulations that were struck down have not been amended to reflect the Tax Court and ninth circuit decisions. The failure to amend the proposed regulations could be a signal that the IRS will continue to litigate similar cases in the hope of receiving a favorable decision in another circuit. You should prepare a research memorandum and letter to Sara and Sam that reflects these findings and conclusions.

## 16-6 RESEARCH MEMORANDUM

The research results should be written in memorandum form and placed in a file for the client. The client file provides a record of the work performed. The memorandum is the basis for the letter that is prepared and sent to the client. The below sample memorandum follows the standard format used by tax practitioners.

SAMPLE RESEARCH MEMORANDUM

### 16-6a Facts

Sam, a surgeon, and his wife, Sara, own and rent out a vacation home. During the year, they use the home 20 days and rent it out for 40 days. Rental income for the year is $4,000. Total expenses are as follows:

| | |
|---|---|
| Interest and taxes | $4,200 |
| Utilities and maintenance | 1,500 |
| Depreciation | 6,000 |

## 16-6b Issues

How should the rental expenses be deducted?

## 16-6c Conclusions

The rental expenses should be allocated and deducted as follows:

| | Total | | Rental Use | Itemized Deduction | Not Deductible |
|---|---|---|---|---|---|
| Gross rental income | $ 4,000 | | $ 4,000 | | |
| Interest & taxes | (4,200) | (40/365) | (460) | $3,740 | |
| Excess | | | $ 3,540 | | |
| Maintenance | (7,500) | (40/60) | (3,540) | | $3,960 |
| Total | | | $ -0- | $3,740 | $3,960 |

## 16-6d Reasoning

The general rule of Sec. 280A applies if the personal use of a dwelling exceeds the greater of 14 days or 10 percent of the number of days the unit is rented. Expenses allocable to the rental activity cannot exceed the gross rental income [Sec. 280A(c)(5)]. Sec. 280A(c)(3) provides that expenses attributable to rental of the unit must first be allocated to the rental use using the following formula: Number of days in the tax year the unit is rented/Total number of days in the tax year the unit is used, or 40/60 in this case. Deductions allowed whether the unit was used as a rental must be allocated to the rental activity before the otherwise allocable expenses. Prop. Reg. Sec. 1.280A-3(c)(1) requires that interest and taxes be allocated using the same formula. However, the allocation shown above for interest and taxes (40/365) is supported by the holding in the case of *Bolton v. Commissioner*, 694 F.2d 556, 51 A.F.T.R.2d83-305, 83-20 USTC ¶9699 (9th Cir., 1982), affirming 77 T.C. 104 (1981). The Tax Court and the ninth circuit held that the allocation in Prop. Reg. Sec. 1.280A-3(c)(1) was inconsistent with the statute, its history, and the legislative purpose behind Sec. 280A. The courts held that interest and taxes, unlike maintenance expenditures, are expenses that continue or accrue on a daily basis throughout the year. Accordingly, they should be allocated according to a ratio of days rented to total days in the year.

Since the IRS has not acquiesced in *Bolton*, the taxpayers should be warned that this allocation may be challenged. However, the *Bolton* decision has been cited in numerous Tax Court regular and memorandum decisions, and has been followed by the tenth circuit in *Edith McKinney v. Commissioner*, 732 F.2d 416, 52 A.F.T.R.2d 83-6281, 83-2 USTC §9655 (10th Cir., 1983).

# CHAPTER SUMMARY

Tax research is the process by which the primary tax law authorities are located, evaluated, and applied to a specific factual situation. The different types of primary authorities are related to the three principal functions of government: legislative, administrative, and judicial. Legislative authorities include the Constitution, treaties, the Internal Revenue Code of 1986, and the committee reports issued by Congress as new tax laws are enacted. Administrative authorities consist of Treasury regulations, revenue rulings, revenue procedures, and other miscellaneous pronouncements issued by the Internal Revenue Service. Judicial authorities include decisions by the various trial and appellate courts in tax-related matters.

Secondary authorities are all other publications that help in locating, evaluating, and applying the primary authorities to the specific factual situation under consideration. They consist primarily of tax services; citators, tax journals, and tax newsletters; and computer systems that allow searches of tax databases.

A systematic procedure must be followed to locate, evaluate, and apply the primary authorities to a specific factual situation. The steps involved in this process are to establish the facts and identify the issues, locate the relevant authorities, evaluate and apply the authorities to the facts, reach conclusions and make recommendations, and communicate the results to interested parties.

# KEY TERMS

acquiescence (p. 16-10)
actions on decision (AOD) (p. 16-11)
citator (p. 16-17)
cited case (p. 16-17)
citing case (p. 16-17)
computer-assisted tax research (CATR) (p. 16-16)
*Cumulative Bulletin* (C.B.) (p. 16-14)
*Federal Reporter*, second or third series (F.2d or F.3d) (p. 16-15)
*Federal Supplement* (F. Supp.) (p. 16-15)
*Federal Tax Citator* (p. 16-17)
final regulations (p. 16-9)
general counsel's memoranda (GCM) (p. 16-11)
*Internal Revenue Bulletin* (I.R.B.) (p. 16-14)
interpretive regulation (p. 16-9)
legislative regulation (p. 16-9)
letter ruling (p. 16-11)
nonacquiescence (p. 16-10)
primary authorities (p. 16-3)
private letter ruling (LTR) (p. 16-10)
proposed regulation (p. 16-9)
reporter (p. 16-14)
*Reports of the United States Tax Court* (T.C.) (p. 16-14)
revenue procedure (p. 16-10)
revenue ruling (p. 16-10)
secondary authorities (p. 16-3)
*Supreme Court Reports* (S. Ct.) (p. 16-15)
Tax Court memorandum decision (p. 16-12)
Tax Court regular decision (p. 16-12)
tax service (p. 16-16)
technical advice memorandum (TAM) (p. 16-11)
technical memoranda (TM) (p. 16-11)
temporary regulation (p. 16-9)
trial court (p. 16-11)
*United States Reports* (U.S.) (p. 16-15)
U.S. Courts of Appeals (p. 16-12)
U.S. Court of Appeals for the Federal Circuit (p. 16-12)
U.S. Court of Federal Claims (p. 16-12)
U.S. District Court (p. 16-11)
U.S. Supreme Court. (p. 16-12)
U.S. Tax Court. (p. 16-12)

# PRIMARY TAX LAW SOURCES

[1]See Secs. 8001–8023 for information on the organization, membership, powers, and other matters relating to the Joint Committee on Taxation.

[2]Sec. 894—Requires application of the Internal Revenue Code to give due regard to any treaty obligations of the United States.

[3]Sec. 7801—Specifies the powers and the duties of the secretary of the Treasury.

[4]Sec. 7802—Establishes the position of commissioner of the Internal Revenue Service, whose duties are to be prescribed by the secretary of the Treasury.

[5]Sec. 7805—Authorizes the secretary of the Treasury to issue the rules and regulations necessary for the enforcement of the income tax law.

[6]Mayo Foundation for Medical and Educational Research v. United States, 562 U.S. 44 (2011)

[7]Cumulative List of Actions Relating to Court Decisions, 1994-1 CB 1—Indicates that the IRS will issue acquiescence and nonacquiescence on decisions of courts other than regular Tax Court decisions.

[8]The abbreviations given here are those commonly used in citing various tax materials. However, some of these abbreviations are different from those specified by *The Bluebook, A Uniform System of Citation* (the lawyer's bible) and do not appear in the list of abbreviations used by the *Cumulative Bulletin*, to which the *Bluebook* defers on tax matters. Thus, tax researchers occasionally may encounter cites to Tech. Adv. Mem. instead of TAM, to Tech. Mem. instead of TM, and to PLR instead of LTR.

[9]See Secs. 7401–7434 for organization, jurisdiction, and other procedural matters relating to the Tax Court. Similar matters for district court cases involving tax-related issues are covered in Sections 7401–7434.

[10]Golsen v. Commissioner of Internal Revenue, 54 T.C. 742 (1970)

# DISCUSSION QUESTIONS

1. **LO1** Differentiate primary tax law authorities and secondary tax law authorities.
2. **LO2** Briefly describe the three categories of primary authorities and the types of authorities within each category.
3. **LO5** Name the types of secondary authorities.
4. **LO2** On what grounds have tax protesters challenged the income tax?
5. **LO2** The Internal Revenue Code is just one part of the *U.S. Code*. Explain.
6. **LO2** Name the subdivisions of the Internal Revenue Code.
7. **LO2** What would be the general nature of Sec. 612? Sec. 6601?
8. **LO2** How many chapters are within Subtitle A?
9. **LO2** What are some things to look out for when reading the Code?
10. **LO2** Give examples of how the Code is sometimes used to achieve economic and social objectives.
11. **LO2** Briefly describe the process by which a new tax law is passed.
12. **LO2** What three reports are issued as part of the legislative process?
13. **LO2** How are the Joint Conference Committee and the Joint Committee on Taxation different?
14. **LO3** What is a Treasury regulation? Is it binding on the courts?

15. **LO3** Differentiate an interpretive regulation and a legislative regulation.
16. **LO3** Differentiate a proposed regulation and a temporary regulation.
17. **LO3** What are revenue rulings? revenue procedures?
18. **LO3** How are a revenue ruling and a Treasury regulation different? a revenue ruling and a private letter ruling?
19. **LO3** What does it mean when the IRS issues an acquiescence or nonacquiescence?
20. **LO3** What impact would an IRS announcement of nonacquiescence to a court decision have on a taxpayer in a similar situation?
21. **LO2** Name the other types of pronouncements issued by the IRS, and briefly describe their content.
22. **LO3** What are the three trial courts? Which is most important?
23. **LO3** What is meant by the *Golsen* rule?
24. **LO3** Do district courts have to follow the decisions of all circuit courts?
25. **LO3** What does it mean when the Supreme Court issues a writ of certiorari?
26. **LO3** Assume that the Supreme Court interprets a certain Code section in a manner that members of Congress believe is contrary to what they meant when they enacted that part of the Code. What (if anything) can Congress do?
27. **LO4** Interpret the following citations:
    a. SENATE FINANCE COMMITTEE, S. REP. No. 2, 97th Cong., 2d Sess. (April 15, 1982).
    b. LTR 8101067.
    c. Rev. Proc. 78-172, 1978-2 C.B. 22.
    d. *Lacy v. Comm.*, 344 F.2d 123, 89-1 USTC ¶1221, 43 A.F.T.R. 89-2233 (9th Cir., 1989).
28. **LO4** Provide the correct citations for the following:
    a. The fifteenth revenue procedure issued in 1993 and found on page 12 of the third *Internal Revenue Bulletin* issued in 1993.
    b. Subsection (a) of the first temporary income tax regulation interpreting Section 63.
    c. An acquiescence issued by the IRS on page 1 of volume 1 of the 1992 *Cumulative Bulletin* related to *Chasteen v. Comm.*, which was reported on page 132 of volume 77 of *Reports of the United States Tax Court* in 1991.
29. **LO5** Why do some court decisions have two or three different citations?
30. **LO5** Describe the two major categories of tax services.
31. **LO5** When can a researcher rely on an editorial opinion expressed in the tax services?
32. **LO5** Differentiate a cited case and a citing case.
33. **LO5** What is meant by the history of a cited case?
34. **LO5** Assume that you have found an excellent article in *Tax Notes* that provides a favorable interpretation of Sec. 469. Can you rely on that article as authority for your position? In general, what role do tax periodicals and newsletters play in tax research?
35. **LO6** What are some advantages of CATR?
36. **LO6** Which CATR services are available at your university?

## PROBLEMS

37. **LO6** Use any print or CATR service or the Internet to find a Code section(s) on the following income topics. For each item, indicate the Code section number(s) and full title of the relevant Code section(s).
    a. Discharge of indebtedness
    b. Exclusion for employees' educational expenses
    c. Prizes
38. **LO6** Use any print or CATR service or the Internet to find a Code section(s) on the following deduction topics. For each item, indicate the Code section number(s) and full title of the relevant Code section(s).
    a. Charitable contributions
    b. Dividends-received deduction for corporations
    c. Medical expenses
39. **LO6** Use any print or CATR service or the Internet to find a Code section(s) on the following loss topics. For each item, indicate the Code section number(s) and full title of the relevant Code section(s).
    a. Bad debts
    b. Net operating loss deduction
    c. Passive activity losses

40. **LO6** Use any print or CATR service or the Internet to find a Code section(s) on the following property and cost recovery topics. For each item, indicate the Code section number(s) and full title of the relevant Code section(s).
   a. Basis of player contracts on sale of a franchise
   b. Capital gains and losses for security dealers
   c. Percentage depletion

41. **LO6** Use any print or CATR service or the Internet to find a Code section(s) on the following general tax concepts topics. For each item, indicate the Code section number(s) and the full title of the relevant Code section(s).
   a. Income tax rates for individuals
   b. Losses between related taxpayers
   c. Withholding of income tax on wages

42. **LO6** Use any print or CATR service or the Internet to find the name of a 1995 Supreme Court decision involving the taxability of a settlement received as compensation for age discrimination. Find the name of the case, a standard legal citation, and the date that the Court issued its decision.

43. **LO6** Use any print or CATR service or the Internet to find the Revenue Ruling or Revenue Procedure that provides instructions on requesting a letter ruling. Indicate the number of the Revenue Ruling or Revenue Procedure and the IRS reference.

44. **LO6** Use any print or CATR service to find the following information about the Tax Cuts and Jobs Act of 2017:
   a. The public law number and enactment date
   b. A reference to the full text of the act
   c. A secondary authority that discusses the act

45. **LO7** What is the distinction between tax compliance and tax planning?

46. **LO8** Briefly describe the steps involved in tax research.

# RESEARCH CASES

## Income Cases

47. Gary is an internal auditor for Bodine Information Systems (BIF). In 2018, BIF opened a large production plant in Las Vegas, Nevada. Subsequently, Gary has had to spend several months each year at the Las Vegas facility. Gary has always fancied himself a proficient blackjack player. During his trips to Las Vegas, he stays at a hotel on the Strip and spends a considerable amount of his off-duty time gambling.

In February 2019, Gary applies for and receives a $20,000 line of credit at the hotel to be used for gambling. The line of credit lets him receive gambling chips in exchange for signing markers, which are negotiable drafts payable to the hotel and drawn on Gary's personal bank account. The hotel's practice is to hold the markers for 60 days, at which time Gary pays them with a personal check.

By the beginning of 2020, Gary is gambling heavily at the hotel. He requests and receives an increase in his credit limit to $100,000. Gary continues to lose heavily, and through accounting oversights by the hotel, his debt rises to $325,000 by October 2020. The checks that Gary writes to cover the markers are returned for insufficient funds, and the hotel immediately cut off his credit. The hotel subsequently files suit in state court, seeking repayment of the $325,000 owed on the markers.

In early 2021, Gary negotiates an agreement with the hotel in which he will settle the debt for four monthly payments of $25,000 ($100,000). Gary pays the $100,000 per the terms of the agreement. He seeks your advice as to the tax consequences of the settlement with the hotel. That is, does he have to include in his gross income the amount of the debt he didn't have to repay?

48. Adrian is a salesperson who represents several wholesale companies. On January 2, 2021, she receives by mail a commission check from Ace Distributors in the amount of $10,000 and dated December 30, 2020. Adrian is concerned about the year in which the $10,000 is taxable. Although the check is dated 2020, she contends that it would have been unreasonable for her to drive the 50 miles to the Ace offices on a holiday to collect the check. Further, Adrian maintains that even if she had made the trip on a holiday to collect the check, by the time she returned home, her bank would have closed and she could not have received credit for the check until after the first of the year. Adrian would like you to determine whether she should include the $10,000 on her 2020 or 2021 tax return.

49. Hawaii law requires the state to deposit part of its annual pineapple income in the Hawaiian Long-lasting Fund. All income from the fund is deposited in the state's general fund. The fund's general manager is permitted to use the funds to buy only certain income-producing assets, such as government and corporate obligations, preferred and common stock of U.S. corporations, and equity interests in partnerships and other entities that invest in real estate. Each year, part of the fund's income is transferred to a dividend fund that distributes the dividends to native Hawaiians.

At issue is whether such payments constitute income to native Hawaiians and, if so, what type of income is being received—is income generated from the distributions either investment income or passive activity income?

50. After Maria and Tatsuo divorced 15 years ago, their two minor children continue to live with Maria. Pursuant to their divorce decree, Tatsuo pays Maria $1,000 per month in child support and $1,800 per month in alimony. The divorce decree specifies that in the event of a court-ordered increase in child support, the alimony payment amount will decrease by the amount of the child support increase. That is, Tatsuo's total monthly payment cannot exceed $2,800. Determine how much gross income Maria has from the payments received from Tatsuo.

51. Lorissa owes Waterbury State Bank $200,000. During the current year, she is unable to make the required payments on the loan and negotiates the following terms to extinguish the debt. Lorissa transfers to Waterbury ownership of investment property with a value of $90,000 and a basis of $55,000, and common stock with a value of $50,000 and a basis of $70,000. Lorissa also pays Waterbury $5,000 cash, and Waterbury forgives the remaining amount of debt. Before the agreement, Lorissa's assets are $290,000, and her liabilities are $440,000.

Read and analyze the following authorities and determine how much gross income Lorissa has from the extinguishment of the debt:

Sec. 108.
Reg. Sec. 1.61-12.
Reg. Sec. 1.1001-2.
*Julian S. Danenberg*, 73 T.C. 370 (1979).
*James J. Gehl*, 50 F.3d 12 (8th Cir., 1995) affg., 102 T.C. 784 (1994).

Communication Skills

52. Henry invests $50,000 in an entity called Forward Investments on January 20, 2020. Under the terms of the investment agreement, the $50,000 is considered a loan that Forward will use to invest in derivative contracts. Henry is to receive 2 percent of the amount Forward earns each month from his investment plus 10 percent simple interest on funds left invested for a full year. Henry can withdraw part or all of his investment at any time on 10 days' notice to Forward.

During 2019, Henry receives quarterly statements of earnings on his investment in Forward. As of December 31, 2020, the statements indicate that Henry has earned $9,600. In January 2021, Henry hears a rumor that Forward Investments is not a legitimate investment broker. On January 26, 2021, Henry withdraws his investment, receiving $60,050 (the $50,000 original investment plus $10,050 in earnings). In late February, he learns that Forward Investments is a pyramid scheme through which early investors were paid earnings out of capital contributions by later investors. The U.S. Securities and Exchange Commission files suit against Forward in March 2021.

Henry wants to know the taxability of the amounts he received from Forward. He thinks that he never really earned any income from his investment because he was paid out of later investors' capital contributions. Write Henry a letter explaining the income tax effects of the payments he received from Forward Investments.

53. Sam is an executive with a U.S. corporation. During the current year, he is working in another country. His employer provides a corporation-owned residence for Sam that is located three miles from his office. The residence is far above the standard he was accustomed to in the United States. However, the employer feels that it is important for Sam to live in luxurious surroundings because of the business image it conveys. Sam is expected to entertain customers and conduct business in the home as is customary in that country, where people are thought to be very status-conscious. The home contains an office that Sam uses in the evenings to transact business over the phone with customers in different time zones. The fair rental value of the home is $48,000. Does Sam have any income from this housing arrangement?

54. Rick and Maria had been married for 20 years before their divorce in 2020. At that time, they made the usual property settlement: Maria got the house, the van, and the cat; Rick got the mortgage, the Ford, and the dog. Other property was divided equally except as described below. Communication Skills

At the time of their divorce, Maria had instituted a number of lawsuits against various fast-food chains for infringement of her patent on an automated burrito-stuffing machine. Maria had developed the machine in the early '90s and patented it under her name. At that time, her efforts to license the machine to fast-food outlets were unsuccessful. Five years ago, she observed a similar machine in Tucker's Tacos, a fast-food Mexican restaurant, and instituted her first claim against that chain. Subsequent research revealed that several other chains had stolen her idea without compensating her, and she sued them for patent infringement.

As part of the divorce decree, 20 percent of any net proceeds (1 percent for each year of marriage) that Maria ultimately receives from the lawsuits is to be paid to Rick. During the current year, Maria settles the initial suit with Tucker's Tacos for $200,000. The proceeds are placed into an escrow account from which the costs of litigation are paid. Rick receives a check for $30,000 from the escrow agent for his share of the net proceeds. Maria receives the balance from the account. The remaining lawsuits are still being litigated.

Rick would like to know if he must include the $30,000 in his gross income. Write Rick a letter explaining the tax treatment of the $30,000 he received from the escrow account.

## Deduction Cases

55. Mason owns Brickman, Inc., which specializes in laying brick patios, terraces, and walkways. Mason bids on a contract with State University to build several large terraces as well as the walkways adjoining the terraces. Although he is the low bidder, Mason is approached by Don, purchasing agent for State University, who lets Mason know that to secure the contract, Mason must make a cash payment to a firm that is building a swimming pool for Don. Mason makes the required payment and secures the contract. Later, Don demands, and Mason makes, a payment to a rancher for the purchase of a horse for Don's children. The payments made by Mason are not illegal under state law. Mason seeks your advice as to the deductibility of these payments.

Read and analyze the following authorities, and determine whether Mason can deduct the payments he made to Don:

Sec. 162.
*Raymond Bertolini Trucking v. Comm.*, 736 F.2d 1120 (6th Cir., 1984).
*Car-Ron Asphalt Paving Co. Inc. v. Comm.*, 758 F.2d 1132 (6th Cir., 1985).

56. Jefferson is a grade school teacher whose annual income from teaching is $30,000. He has always enjoyed bowling, and his local pro urged him to turn professional. He subsequently begins working for the pro as an unpaid assistant and enters an apprenticeship program with the Professional Bowlers' Association of America (PBA). As an apprentice, he accumulates credits toward becoming a member of the PBA by taking approved classes, working as an assistant pro, and competing in pro tournaments. Jefferson expects to be approved as a full member of the PBA next year.

    Although Jefferson continues to teach full-time, he goes to the bowling alley each day after school and practices after fulfilling his duties as an unpaid assistant. During the summer, he spends 12 to 15 hours each day at the bowling alley. In addition, he participates in as many PBA tournaments as he can work into his schedule.

    Jefferson has come to you for advice on the deductibility of the expenses he has incurred in his bowling career. Since deciding to turn pro, he has won money in tournaments every year. However, his expenses have exceeded his earnings by $5,000 to $10,000 per year.

57. Seaweed Salvagers is a corporation engaged in producing foodstuffs from seaweed. Seaweed's primary salvaging plant is located in California. Because salvaging technology hasn't changed through the years, Seaweed's primary salvaging equipment was purchased in the early 1970s. At that time, the primary insulation material used in the machines was asbestos. In 1986, the Occupational Safety and Health Administration (OSHA) lowered the standard for concentrations of allowable airborne asbestos fibers in the workplace. In addition, California requires employers to monitor airborne concentration levels to ensure that they do not exceed permissible exposure levels.

    To comply with these requirements and to provide its workers with a safe workplace, Seaweed institutes an asbestos abatement program. After careful study, Seaweed determines that the major asbestos problem occurs during ordinary repairs and maintenance of the equipment. Initially, Seaweed institutes a program of continuous monitoring and encapsulation during repair and maintenance periods. However, Seaweed finds that this is inadequate because (a) it does not ensure that all parts of the plant are in compliance, (b) repairs and maintenance costs are increasing dramatically, and (c) the extra down time during maintenance and repairs reduces production to a level that is financially unprofitable.

    During the current year, Seaweed begins removing the asbestos insulation from the machinery and replacing it with an alternative, environmentally friendly insulation material. The new insulation material is about 15 percent less efficient than the asbestos material and results in no energy or other cost savings. The cost of replacing the insulation in one machine is about $13,000. The annual repair and maintenance cost of one machine averages $45,000. Each machine has an estimated fair market value of $600,000.

    Seaweed believes that it should be able to expense the cost of removing the asbestos insulation and replacing it with the alternative insulation. Read and analyze the following authorities, and determine whether Seaweed can deduct the asbestos removal costs:

    Sec. 263.
    Reg. Sec. 1.162-4.
    Reg. Sec. 1.263(a)-1.
    *Indopco Inc. v. Comm.*, 112 S. Ct. 1038 (1992).
    LTR 9240004.
    Rev. Rul. 94-38.

58. Georgia and June are active volunteers in their local church. Georgia serves as an usher one Sunday morning a month. June sings in the church choir every Sunday morning and attends choir practice each Wednesday evening. Based on the distance from their home to church, June drives 500 miles a year to attend choir

practice and sing on Sunday. Georgia leaves home by herself to arrive at church early on the mornings she serves as an usher and put 120 miles on her car this year on these trips. June paid $1,000 for singing lessons to improve her voice so that she might be chosen to sing a solo at church. Are any of these expenses related to serving as an usher or singing in the church choir deductible by Georgia or June?

59. Grace, the minister of the local United Methodist Church, has some tax questions regarding her employment status. This is her first year as a United Methodist minister after having served as a Baptist preacher for 20 years. She wonders if the conversion affects her tax situation in any way. For instance, she questions whether she is an employee for income tax purposes. She also asks if she can deduct the out-of-pocket costs related to her work, such as books, travel expenses, and computer equipment. Write a memo to Grace explaining her tax status and the deductibility of her job-related expenses. Communication Skills

60. Warren is chief executive of a major corporation and is very concerned about his premature balding. He contacts a hair transplant specialist and wants to have surgery performed this year. Write a memo advising Warren whether the hair transplant surgery would be deductible. Communication Skills

61. Rosemary attends classes provided by her church. She makes payments to the church that are required to attend the classes. She plans to deduct the payments as charitable contributions to her church. Can Rosemary deduct the payments as charitable contributions?

62. Jon purchases a farm for $2,200,000. The previous owners had planted parallel rows of bushes and trees on the land when they acquired it to block the wind from the part of the farm that was planted with crops. The trees and bushes have never produced salable timber or any fruit, nuts, or other products that could be sold. Can a portion of the cost of the land be allocated to the trees and bushes and be depreciated?

63. Larry is a professional gambler, specializing in dog racing. He spends 50 to 60 hours per week studying racing forms and placing bets at the track. During the current year, Larry has winnings of $240,000 on $380,000 of bets placed. He has no other business income. His wife, Jane, is employed as a university professor and earns $55,000 annually. They also have $15,000 in income from investments. Because Larry devotes all his time to his dog-racing activities, he feels that he should be able to deduct the loss he incurred in his "business" against their other income.

    Read and analyze the following authorities to determine the deduction Larry is allowed for his dog-racing losses:

    Sec. 162.
    Sec. 165.
    *Commissioner v. Groetzinger*, 480 U.S. 23 (1987).
    *Pete C. Valenti*, 68 TCM 838 (1994).

64. Francine is a self-employed marketing consultant based in Fort Worth, Texas. During the year, she travels to various cities in the United States to meet prospective clients and make presentations at seminars.

    Francine can substantially reduce her airfare expense if she stays in a particular city on a Saturday night. For example, if she flies to Chicago on Thursday, does marketing business on Thursday and Friday, and returns on Saturday morning, her round-trip airfare will be $850. If she stays through Saturday night and returns early on Sunday morning, the airfare drops to $350 and she pays $150 for an additional night in a hotel and incurs $50 of additional meal costs. This saves $500 in airfare (reduced from $850 to $350), at an additional cost of only $200. If she stays over Saturday night, she can either stay in the hotel and do administrative work on her laptop computer or visit friends in the Chicago area.

    Francine wants to know how much of the additional hotel and meal costs she can deduct if she stays over on Saturday night. She would also like to know if the deductibility of these expenses depends on what she does on Saturday in Chicago.

65. Harvey is employed by the U.S. Customs Service. Early in the year, he accepts a position in the London office. In addition to a raise in his pay grade, the terms of the London assignment let Harvey collect a monthly living quarters allowance (LQA) for rent and utility expenses. The LQA is exempt from tax under Section 912(1)(c).

    Upon arriving in London, Harvey and his spouse are unable to find suitable quarters to rent. They subsequently purchase a flat for $160,000. During the current year, they pay $10,000 in mortgage interest on the loan used to purchase the flat and $1,300 in property taxes on the flat. The total LQA Harvey receives for the year is $11,000.

    Harvey was talking to a military attaché in the office and was surprised to hear that military personnel are allowed to deduct the interest and taxes they pay on their homes even though they receive an LQA comparable to that received by Harvey. He would like to know whether the same treatment is available for his mortgage interest and property taxes.

## Loss Cases

66. Kimberly is a developer of apartment complexes. Two years ago, she formed Deckside Apartments, a partnership, and initiates development of the Deckside Apartments complex. The Staten Investment Fund agrees to finance the development at an annual interest rate of 10 percent, secured by a mortgage on the property. However, state law limits the annual interest rate for noncorporate borrowers to 8 percent. To avoid this state usury law, Kimberly incorporates Hump Day, Inc., under state law. Kimberly is the only shareholder of Hump Day, Inc. The next day, Deckside Apartments and Hump Day, Inc., enter into a written agreement under which the corporation holds title to the apartments solely for the purpose of obtaining financing. Hump Day cannot convey, assign, or encumber the property without the permission of Deckside, has no obligation to maintain the property, assumes no liability regarding the financing, and is held harmless from any liability it might sustain as the agent for Deckside.

    Staten Investment Fund agrees to provide the financing to Hump Day, Inc., as the corporate nominee of Deckside, provided that Kimberly personally guarantees the note. Upon completion of the apartments, Kimberly, through Hump Day, Inc., obtains the permanent financing from Staten and pays off the short-term construction loans that she had obtained to build the apartments. An apartment manager is hired to oversee the operation of the apartments. All rents collected are deposited to and expenses paid from an account opened by the partnership.

    During the current year, the apartments generate substantial operating losses. Kimberly seeks your advice as to the proper treatment of these losses.

Communication Skills

67. Fingeland's Forest Choppers is a corporation engaged in the production of timber and lumber. Two years ago, Fingeland's reforested a clear-cut area by planting nursery-grown seedlings. Last year, a severe drought kills 80 percent of the seedlings, forcing Fingeland's to replant the entire area in the current year. The loss is not covered by insurance. Fingeland's had capitalized the cost of preparing the site for reforestation and the seedling planting costs in a deferred reforestation account two years ago.

    Fingeland's would like to know whether it can deduct as a casualty loss the costs it incurred to replant the clear-cut area in the current year.

    Read and analyze the following authorities, and determine whether Fingeland's can deduct the costs as a casualty loss, and if so, in what year the loss is deductible.

    Sec. 165.
    Sec. 611.
    Reg. Sec. 1.611-3.
    Rev. Rul. 81-2.
    Rev. Rul. 87-59.
    Rev. Rul. 90-61.

Write a memorandum to your supervisor explaining your conclusions on Fingeland's deduction of the costs of replanting the clear-cut area in the current year.

68. Mae and Ahnjong are equal owners of Denson, Inc., an S corporation. Denson owns 5,000 shares of stock in Cowboy Country. Denson paid $300,000 for the Cowboy Country stock, which is qualified small business stock. During the current year, Denson sells 4,000 shares of Cowboy Country for $100,000. Denson's accountant is preparing the current-year tax return and is unsure of the reporting of the stock sale to Mae and Ahnjong.

Read and analyze the following authorities and determine how the sale of the stock should be reported to Mae and Ahnjong:

Sec. 1244.
Sec. 1363.
Reg. Sec. 1.1244(a)-1.
*Virgil D. Rath*, 101 T.C. 196 (1994).

## Entity Cases

69. Evelyn is the president and sole shareholder of Ephron Corporation. Ephron is an accrual basis taxpayer and uses a calendar year. Evelyn is a cash basis, calendar-year taxpayer.

During the second half of 2020, Ephron recorded several million dollars of sales to customers with cash payment expected in the first half of 2021. To reduce the taxable income at the corporate level, Ephron accrued a $200,000 bonus to Evelyn on December 15, 2020. As of December 15, 2020, the corporation does not have cash on hand to pay the bonus but expected to receive cash from customers in March or April 2021.

Evelyn was considering the following alternatives for the corporation's payment of the bonus:

- Have the corporation immediately borrow more on its commercial line of credit and pay the bonus by December 31, 2020.
- Wait for the cash flow from customers and pay the bonus around March 1, 2021.
- Wait to pay the bonus until around April 15, 2021.

Read and analyze the following authorities and determine when the corporation is allowed to deduct the bonus for each of the three payment alternatives:

Sec. 267.
Reg. Sec. 1.267(a)-1.

70. The Lopez family has owned several large apartment buildings for many years. They organized Lopez Properties, Inc., to own and manage the properties. The corporation is an accrual basis taxpayer and uses a calendar year. All shares of Lopez Properties are owned by Frank, Susan, and their mother, Ida. Frank and Susan are president and chief financial officer of the corporation, respectively.

Lopez Properties expects to have the following items of income and expense during the current year:

| | |
|---|---|
| Rental revenue | $1,200,000 |
| Maintenance expenses | 150,000 |
| Depreciation | 250,000 |
| Real estate taxes | 400,000 |
| Officers' salaries | 200,000 |

Read and analyze Sections 541 through 547 and determine if Lopez Properties has a problem with the personal holding company (PHC) tax. If it does, estimate the amount of PHC tax and suggest alternatives for reducing or eliminating the PHC problem.

Communication Skills

71. Omega Investments, Inc., was formed in 2003 by 10 unrelated individual investors. It operates a chain of electronics stores. The corporation suffered losses in its early years but has become profitable in recent years.

The corporation elected S corporation status in 2003. Over the years, the original shareholders have gifted shares to their children and transferred them to trusts for their grandchildren. At the end of last year, there were 70 shareholders. Additional gifts made in the current year have increased the number of shareholders to 90.

The company needs more cash and would like to sell additional shares. Write a memo advising the investors of the tax implications of issuing additional shares of stock.

72. Fernando has been an attorney in the legal department of Mega Manufacturing, Inc., for the past 15 years. As part of Mega's restructuring plan, he will lose his job as an employee of Mega, but he will continue contracting with Mega to work on specific engagements as a self-employed attorney.

Fernando is concerned about protecting his retirement assets. He has $200,000 vested in Mega's qualified retirement plan. Mega made the contributions to the retirement plan as part of its defined contribution plan. When Fernando leaves the company, he can request that his funds be withdrawn and paid to him in cash or to the administrator of a designated qualified retirement program. Fernando wants to continue saving for his retirement when he becomes self-employed.

What are the tax consequences of the distribution from the Mega retirement plan?

## Property Cases

73. Dagwood has come to you with a pressing problem. In November 2010, he purchased an office building that he has rented out to various businesses. On May 2 of the current year, a fire swept through the building, totally destroying it. To make matters worse, his lifelong accountant was trapped in the building and perished in the fire (along with all of Dagwood's income tax records). The following is all the information Dagwood has available about the building:

Dagwood is sure that he purchased the building in November 2010, because he has a property tax statement indicating that the land was revalued at $30,000 and the building at $300,000 for property tax purposes at that time. The date is further supported by a canceled check dated November 28, 2010, for $550,000, payable to the company from which he had purchased the property. Although he doesn't have the tax records to support any deductions on the property, he's confident that his former accountant took the maximum deductions allowable on the property as it had always produced a loss for income tax purposes.

He recently received a check for $400,000 from his insurance company for the destruction of the building. In the interim, Dagwood has been obtaining estimates of the cost of putting another office building on the property. However, his analysis of the construction costs, combined with the potential rental income generated by the building, indicates that putting another office building on the property would not be profitable in either the short or the long term. He has received an offer to sell the land for $84,000. If he does sell the land, he is considering purchasing an upscale apartment building in another part of town.

Before he proceeds with the sale of the land and the purchase of the apartment building, he needs to know the tax effects of the fire and the sale of the land. Dagwood is afraid that he may have a big tax bill to pay and won't be able to afford the apartment building after he settles up with the IRS.

Read and analyze the following authorities and determine how much gain or loss Dagwood will have to recognize from the fire if he purchases the apartment building:

Sec. 1033.
Rev. Rul. 64-237.
Rev. Rul. 59-361.
*Henry G. Masser*, 30 T.C. 741 (1958).

74. Dale's son is a senior in high school and is planning to go away to college next year. Dale would like to buy a house near the campus and rent it to his son. He comes to you for advice on the tax ramifications of this arrangement. What advice can you give him on setting up a rental arrangement with his son?

75. Marjorie is a software systems engineer for Hacker Corporation. In November 2018, she inherited two parcels of land in Brower Township from her grandfather. Her grandfather's estate valued the parcels, which are adjacent to each other and total 25 acres, at $11,000. Marjorie thought the parcels were worth more than $11,000, so she asked the estate's appraiser why the parcels weren't valued higher. The appraiser told her that the zoning on the land allows only one residence every two acres, which severely diminishes the resale value.

Communication Skills

In 2019, Marjorie applied to Brower Township for a change of zoning. The Brower Township Board of Supervisors denied her application in November 2019. Marjorie filed a constitutional challenge to Brower Township's zoning ordinance in 2020. The board of supervisors denied her constitutional challenge. Marjorie filed an appeal of the denial in Brower County District Court on September 25, 2020. On October 5, 2020, the Brower Township Board of Supervisors began consideration of a new zoning ordinance. Under the ordinance, Marjorie's land would be rezoned to a designation that would allow three residences per acre. At this point, Marjorie withdrew her court appeal, pending the outcome of the new zoning ordinance. On January 10, 2021, the new zoning ordinance was adopted. Marjorie estimated that the value of the land increased to at least $21,000 as a result of the rezoning.

Marjorie incurred $14,000 in attorney's fees and other costs in challenging the zoning ordinance. She paid $3,500 of the expenditures in 2020 and $10,500 in 2021. She would like to know the proper income tax treatment of these expenses. Can Marjorie deduct the costs of challenging the zoning ordinance? Write a memorandum explaining the deductibility of the costs of challenging the zoning ordinance.

76. Rachel lives in a downtown apartment in Gotham City. She has three years remaining on her apartment lease when her landlord, Blaylock Company, approaches her about moving out. Blaylock wants to demolish the apartment building and build an office tower in its place.

Rachel hires a lawyer who negotiates a lease termination settlement with Blaylock over the leasehold rights. After intense negotiations, Blaylock agrees to pay $100,000 in cash and the $25,000 in legal fees related to the negotiation and to provide Rachel with a similar apartment rent-free for three years. Rachel requests that Blaylock issue no checks directly to her. Instead, Blaylock is to pay her lawyer the $25,000 billed and issue a check for $100,000 to her brother, who lives in Mexico.

Rachel believes that none of these transactions will have any effect on her taxable income because the checks are not issued to her. Furthermore, because she did not own the apartment building, she did not realize a gain from the sale of the property.

Does the settlement result in any taxable income or deductions for Rachel?

## Accounting Methods/Procedure Cases

77. Mr. and Mrs. Lucky have been married for 25 years. Last year, they won $200,000 at a casino. They knew that this would put them in the highest tax bracket for the year. To avoid this, they went to Mexico on December 28 and obtained a divorce. They continued to live together and plan to file separate returns using the single filing status. They remarry in February. What is their correct filing status?

78. The Kona Rural Electric Co-op (KREC) is an accrual basis public utility. All new customers are required to pay a deposit equal to three times the customer's estimated monthly bill or $100, whichever is greater. The purpose of the deposit is to ensure

that timely payment is made on accounts. The funds so received are not segregated from other KREC funds and are used in the ordinary course of business. Interest at the rate of 5 percent is paid annually on the deposits. Customers may elect to receive a check for the interest or may accept the payment as a credit on their monthly bill.

KREC's policy is to refund the deposit when a customer discontinues service or has made timely monthly payments for 8 consecutive months or for 9 of 12 consecutive months. When deposits are refunded, interest is paid on the deposit through the date of the refund. KREC's experience with the deposit requirement is that 80 percent of all deposits are returned within one year of receipt. Approximately 5 percent of all deposits are ultimately used to satisfy delinquent customer accounts.

KREC would like to know whether the deposits should be included in income when they are received or deferred until they are used to satisfy customer accounts.

79. Al is in the state penitentiary after being convicted of a series of crimes. He still corresponds with his girlfriend to ask for money, and this year, she has sent him a total of $1,200. Al's only other income is the $1,000 he has been paid for making license plates. Is Al eligible for the earned income credit?

80. Tomiko owns the copyright to several classic Motown songs. In 2019, he became aware that Tinseltown Records was selling several of his songs without his permission. He sues Tinseltown seeking $1,000,000 in damages. In 2021, the court awards Tomiko $500,000 in compensatory damages, $50,000 in prejudgment interest, postjudgment interest to the date of payment, and court costs. Tinseltown is aware that Tomiko is likely to appeal the judgment and offers to settle for $600,000 with no payment of postjudgment interest or court costs. On the advice of his attorney, Tomiko rejects the settlement offer.

On December 29, 2021, Tomiko receives a check for $600,000 from Tinseltown. An accompanying letter notes that the payment is in full settlement of the order of the court. Tomiko believes that if he cashes the check, he will forfeit his right to appeal the judgment, the postjudgment interest, and court costs. Accordingly, he immediately returns the check to Tinseltown via overnight mail, stating in a letter that his appeal rights are not exhausted and he is returning the check until such time as the issue is settled. Tinseltown remails the check on December 31, 2021. Included with the check is a letter advising Tomiko that Tinseltown intends to deduct the $600,000 in 2021 and that the funds are available for his unrestricted use. On January 15, 2021, Tomiko files an appeal seeking an increase in the damage award. The next day, he deposits Tinseltown's check into his business account. On June 5, 2021, the appeals court rejects Tomiko's appeal for higher damages. Tomiko is a cash basis taxpayer. In what year should he include the $600,000 in income?

Read the following authorities, and determine the proper year for Tomiko to include the $600,000 in income:

Sec. 451.
Reg. Sec. 1.451-2.
*Walter I. Bones*, 4 T.C. 415 (1944).
*Fromson v. Comm.*, 32 Fed.Cl. 1, 74 A.F.T.R.2d, 5642 (Cl. Ct., 1994), 94-2 USTC ¶50,425.

Communication Skills

81. Ernie's Farm and Garden Implement Store sells, repairs, and services farm and garden equipment. In 2020, the state attorney general began to investigate customers' complaints that Ernie's was adding a delivery and handling fee to each product—fees that are illegal under state law. In 2021, Ernie's entered into a consent judgment under which it was to make restitution of every delivery and handling fee charged to customers after April 1, 2019. The judgment also required Ernie's to give the attorney general's office a list of every customer entitled to restitution and to issue a coupon in the name of each customer.

The coupons offered each customer the option of a $50 discount on the purchase of any part or service or $90 toward the purchase of any new or used equipment. If not satisfied with the coupon offer, the customer could redeem the coupon for $40 in cash. Ernie's mailed out 1,860 coupons in April and May 2021. As of December 31, 2021, 835 coupons had been redeemed as follows: 405 for cash refunds, 390 for $50 discounts for parts and services, and 40 for $90 discounts on equipment purchases.

The controller of Ernie's is not certain that the company can deduct the amounts it gave customers for refunds or discounts in 2021 and has asked your firm for advice. Your supervisor has assigned you to determine Ernie's 2021 deduction. Write a memorandum to your supervisor explaining Ernie's 2021 deduction for the coupons.

82. Lydia and Andre are divorcing this year. Because they are contesting the terms of the settlement, they will not file a joint return for the current year. Lydia receives a Form 1099-INT from Andre's accountant and a letter stating that Lydia should include 50 percent of the $6,200 interest on their savings account in her taxable income. Andre's Social Security number is listed on the account (Lydia's is not), and the Form 1099-INT was issued in his name, although they own the account as joint tenants with the right of survivorship. Under applicable state law, both spouses have an equal right to jointly held property. Lydia doesn't think that she should be taxed on this income because the account is in Andre's name and he was issued the Form 1099-INT. Lydia has come to you for advice. Write a letter to Lydia explaining who is taxed on the $6,200 in interest. Communication Skills

# Tax Return Problem

APPENDIX

# A

iStock.com/davidf

## INTRODUCTION

The information below will allow you to prepare the 2020 federal tax return for Bill and Joyce Schnappauf. The information is provided in three phases, which correspond to the three major components of computing income tax—gross income, deductions and losses, and property transactions. If your instructor assigns these problems, at the end of each major segment (i.e., Chapters 4, 8, and 12), you should complete the appropriate portions of the forms indicated. If you are not using a tax software package, you should not complete the second page of Form 1040 until you have completed Chapter 12.

Completing the tax return problem will help you understand the reporting procedures for the information in each major segment of the text. In addition, it will aid you in reviewing the major topics discussed in the book; it serves as an overview of the course.

## THE SCHNAPPAUF FAMILY

In 2020, Bill and Joyce Schnappauf live in Wakefield, R.I. Bill is 53, and Joyce is 51. Bill is a district sales manager for USC Equipment Corporation, a Rhode Island firm that manufactures and distributes gaming equipment. Joyce is a self-employed author of children's books. The Schnappaufs have three children, Will, 21, Dan, 19, and Tom, 16. In February 2021, the Schnappaufs provide the following basic information for preparing their 2020 federal income tax return:

1. The Schnappaufs use the cash method of accounting and file their return on a calendar-year basis.
2. Unless otherwise stated, assume that the Schnappaufs want to minimize the current year's tax liability. That is, they would like to defer income when possible and take the largest deductions possible, a practice they have followed in the past.
3. Joyce's Social Security number is 371-42-5207.
4. Bill's Social Security number is 150-52-0546.
5. Will's Social Security number is 372-46-2611.
6. Dan's Social Security number is 377-42-3411.
7. Tom's Social Security number is 375-49-6511.
8. The Schnappaufs do not have any foreign bank accounts or foreign trusts.
9. Their address is 27 Northup Street, Wakefield, R.I. (02879).
10. The Schnappaufs do not wish to contribute to the presidential election campaign.

## PHASE I—CHAPTERS 1–4

The first phase of the tax return problem is designed to introduce you to some of the tax forms and the supporting documentation (Forms W-2, 1099-INT, etc.) needed to complete a basic tax return. The first four chapters focus on the income aspects of individual taxation. Accordingly, this phase of the tax return focuses on the basic income concepts.

1. Bill's W-2 is provided (Exhibit A-1). The 2020 W-2 includes his salary ($98,000), bonus ($61,000), and income from group-term life insurance coverage in excess of $50,000 ($132.48), and is reduced by his 7 percent contribution ($6,860) to USC's qualified pension plan. The company matches Bill's contribution to the plan.
2. The Schnappaufs receive two 1099-INTs for interest (Exhibits A-2 and A-3), two 1099-DIVs for dividends (Exhibits A-4 and A-5), and a combined interest and dividend statement (Exhibit A-6).
3. Joyce and her brother, Bob, are co-owners of, and active participants in, a furniture-restoration business. Joyce owns 30 percent, and Bob owns 70 percent of the business. The business was formed as an S corporation in 2012. During 2020, the company pays $5,000 in dividends. The basis of Joyce's stock is $33,000.

4. The Schnappaufs receive a 2019 federal income tax refund of $818 on May 12, 2020. On May 15, 2020, they receive their income tax refund from the state of Rhode Island. In January 2021, the state mails the Schnappaufs a Form 1099-G (Exhibit A-7). Their total itemized deductions in 2019 were $30,161.
5. During 2020, Joyce is the lucky ninety-third caller to a local radio station and wins $300 in cash and a Tablet. Despite repeated calls to the radio station, she has not received a Form 1099—MISC. In announcing the prize, the radio station host said that the manufacturer's suggested retail price for the Tablet is $720. However, Joyce has a catalog from Supersonic Electronics that advertises the Tablet for $595.
6. The Schnappaufs receive a Form W-2G (Exhibit A-8) for their winnings at the Yardley Casino in Connecticut.
7. On June 26, 2020, Bill receives a check for $15,480 from the United Insurance Corporation. Though he was unaware of it, he was the designated beneficiary of an insurance policy on the life of his uncle. The policy had a maturity value of $15,100, and the letter from the company stated that his uncle had paid premiums on the policy of $3,620 (Exhibit A-9).
8. Joyce is active in the school PTO. During the year, she receives an award for outstanding service to the organization. She receives a plaque and two $125 gift certificates that were donated to the PTO by local merchants.
9. To complete phase I, you will need Form 1040, Schedule B, and Schedule D.

INSTRUCTIONS: If you are using tax software to prepare the tax return or are not completing phases II and III of the problem, ignore the instructions that follow. If you are preparing the return manually, you cannot complete some of the forms used in phase I until you receive additional information provided in phase II or phase III. Therefore, as a general rule, you should only post the information to the appropriate form and not compute totals for that form. The following specific instructions will assist you in preparing Part I of the return.

a. The only form that can be totaled is Schedule B.
b. Only post the appropriate information to Schedule D. Do not total any columns. More information is provided in phase III of the tax return problem.
c. Do not calculate total income or adjusted gross income on page 1 of Form 1040.
d. Post the appropriate information on page 2 of Form 1040, but do not total this page, compute the federal tax liability, or determine the refund or balance due.

PREPARATION AID: Tax forms and instructions can be downloaded from the IRS's home page (www.irs.treas.gov). You can also download IRS Publication 17, which is a useful guide in preparing the tax return.

## PHASE II—CHAPTERS 5–8

This is the second phase of the tax return problem you began at the end of Chapter 4. This phase of the tax return incorporates the material from Chapters 5 through 8 by providing you with information concerning the Schnappaufs' deductions for 2020. They provide you with the following information.

1. Joyce writes children's books for a variety of publishers. She has been self-employed since 2012. As a freelance writer, Joyce incurs costs associated with preparing a manuscript for which she does not yet have a contract. During the year, Joyce makes four business trips, each 3 days long, to meet with various publishers. For shorter trips that are closer to home, she either drives or takes the train and returns the same day. On December 10, 2020, Joyce receives an advance (see below) on her next book. Under the contract, Joyce is scheduled to begin work on the book on February 1, 2021, and must have it completed by November 30, 2021. The Schnappaufs' home has two telephones. Joyce has a separate phone number for her business. The information on Joyce's business is listed below.

| | |
|---|---|
| Royalties (Exhibits A-10 to A-12) | |
| Publisher's advance | $4,000 |
| Office supplies | 170 |
| Train tickets | 535 |
| Airfare (4 trips) | 1,670 |
| Lodging (12 nights) | 2,240 |
| Meals (12 days) | 610 |
| Telephone ($28 monthly fee per phone line) | 672 |
| Internet provider | 570 |
| Cell phone, including business calls | 913 |
| Business-related postage | 87 |
| Printing/copying | 162 |
| Legal fees | 2,000 |
| Interest on auto | 254 |

2. On January 2, 2020, Joyce purchases a new car to use in her business. The car, a Volster, costs $15,200. Joyce pays $2,200 in cash and finances the balance through the dealer. She uses the car 45 percent of the time for business and drives a total of 10,800 miles during 2020. The total expenses for the 10,800 miles driven are: repairs and maintenance, $240; insurance, $920; and gasoline, $1,960. The correct depreciation expense for 2020 is $684 ($15,200 × 45% × 10%).
3. Joyce's office is located in a separate room in the house and occupies 375 square feet. The total square footage of the house is 2,500. The Schnappaufs purchased the home on July 7, 2006, for $70,000. The local practice is to allocate 10 percent of the purchase price to land. The depreciation percentage for the office is 0.02564. When Joyce started her business on January 1, 2012, the fair market value of the house was $108,000. The total household expenses for 2020 are as follows:

| | |
|---|---|
| Heat | $2,170 |
| Insurance | 1,480 |
| Electricity | 740 |
| Repairs to kitchen | 3,100 |
| Cleaning | 1,560 |

4. Bill and Joyce each contribute the maximum to their respective IRA accounts in 2020. The IRA account is Joyce's only retirement vehicle. Bill's basis in his IRA before the current year's contribution is $26,000, and Joyce's basis is $36,000. The fair market value of Bill's IRA on 12/31/20 is $41,720, and the fair market value of Joyce's IRA is $57,100. In addition, Bill and Joyce contributed $2,000 to a Coverdell Education Savings Account for Thomas.
5. The Schnappaufs incur the following medical expenses (before considering the $700 reimbursement they receive from their health insurance policy):

| | |
|---|---|
| Medical premiums | $3,800 |
| Doctors | 1,200 |
| Chiropractor | 650 |
| Dentist | 1,900 |
| Vet fees (family dog Sandy) | 345 |
| Prescription drugs | 340 |
| Over-the-counter drugs (aspirin, cough syrup) | 175 |

In addition, Bill purchases an Exsoaligner machine for $700. The machine was recommended by the chiropractor to help strengthen Bill's back muscles.

6. The Schnappaufs pay the following property taxes:

| | |
|---|---|
| Wakefield house | $11,200 |
| Family car used by Bill (ad valorem) | 480 |
| Joyce's car (ad valorem) | 520 |

7. The Schnappaufs receive two Form 1099s for the cost of interest on bank loans. They also pay interest on their personal credit cards.

| | |
|---|---|
| Jefferson Trust 1098 (Exhibit A-13—Wakefield house) | |
| Jefferson Trust 1098 (Exhibit A-14—Home equity) | |
| Dempsey's Department Store revolving account | $191 |
| Brooks' Bargain Basement revolving account | 67 |
| Jefferson Trust bank card | 212 |

The proceeds from the home equity loan were used to renovate their kitchen.

8. Bill and Joyce make cash charitable contributions to the United Fund Campaign ($5,700), Adelade University ($2,510), Tremon University ($1,900), and Christ the King Church in Kingston, R.I. ($8,100). The Schnappaufs have documentation to verify their cash contributions. They also donate property to the Salvation Army on July 15, 2020:

| Property | FMV | Original Cost | Date Acquired |
|---|---|---|---|
| Antique table | $410 | $225 | 1/4/08 |
| Dishwasher | 130 | 700 | 5/6/12 |
| Sofa bed | 90 | 800 | 13/14/14 |
| Men's suits (2) | 140 | 540 | Various |

The Salvation Army acknowledges that these amounts represent the fair market value of the donated items.

9. The Schnappaufs incur $3,450 in gambling losses.

10. Because Joyce is self-employed, they make federal estimated tax payments of $210 per quarter on April 15, 2020, June 15, 2020, September 15, 2020, and January 15, 2021. They also make estimated payments of $150 per quarter to the state of Rhode Island on April 15, 2020, June 15, 2020, September 15, 2020, and December 31, 2020.

11. Bill and Joyce paid $7,400 in tuition, $840 for books, and $9,300 for room and board for Will, a junior, to attend Springbrook State University. They also paid $16,410 in tuition, $950 in books, and $10,100 in room and board for Dan, a freshman at Prescott College.

12. Other information:
    a. Joyce's business is named Queensbridge Books, and her employer I.D. number is 05-3456345.
    b. The Salvation Army's address is 15 High Street, Wakefield, R.I. 02879.
    c. To complete phase II, you will need the following additional forms: Schedule A, Schedule C, Schedule SE, and Forms 4562, 4684, 8283, 8606, 8829, and 8863.

INSTRUCTIONS: If you are using tax software to prepare the tax return or are not completing phase III of the problem, ignore the instructions that follow.

As in phase I, there are forms in phase II that cannot be completed without additional information which is provided in phase III. Therefore, as a general rule, you should only post the information to the appropriate form and not compute totals for that form. The following specific instructions will assist you in preparing Part II of the return.

a. The only form that can be completed at the end of phase II is Form 8283.
b. Do not calculate total income or adjusted gross income on page 1 of Form 1040.
c. Post the appropriate information on page 2 of Form 1040, but do not total this page, compute the federal tax liability, or determine the refund or balance due.
d. Do not calculate the total itemized deductions on Schedule A.
e. Do not total Joyce's expenses on Schedule C.
f. Do not compute Joyce's self-employment tax on Schedule SE.

g. Do not complete the summary section of Form 4562.
h. On Form 8829, complete Part I, and only post the appropriate indirect expenses. Do not calculate the allowable depreciation or the allowable home office deduction.

## PHASE III—CHAPTERS 9–12

This is the third and final phase of the Schnappauf family's tax return. This phase incorporates the material in Chapters 9, 10, 11, and 12 requires you to analyze the various types of property transactions discussed in those chapters.

1. On February 11, 2020, Bill inherits his father's summer home. The house, located in South Lake Tahoe, Nevada, has a fair market value of $550,000 at the date of his father's death. His parents had purchased the house in 1981 for $140,000 and made $122,000 worth of capital improvements to it. Twenty percent of the total value of the property is attributable to the land. Because Bill and Joyce ultimately would like to use the property as a vacation home, they decide to rent it out. Bill actively participates in the management of the property. The property is first advertised for rent on March 1, 2020, but is not rented until April 15, 2020. Bill provides the following income and expense information for the Lake Tahoe rental property:

| | |
|---|---|
| Rent | $21,000 |
| Repairs | 6,250 |
| Management fee | 4,800 |
| Property taxes | 15,100 |
| Insurance | 3,500 |

In addition, Bill buys a new stove for $1,800 and a new refrigerator for $1,450 on March 20, 2020.

2. The Schnappaufs receive Form 1099-B (Exhibit A-15) from Pebble Beach Investors for the sale of several securities. The details on the securities sales are provided below. The selling price listed is net of brokerage commissions and represents the amount the Schnappaufs actually receive from the sale.

| Stock | Date Acquired | Date Sold | Sale Price | Purchase Price |
|---|---|---|---|---|
| 150 shares Pfizer Corporation | 5/12/97 | 8/15/20 | $ 6,000 | $ * |
| 300 shares Texas Instruments | 7/30/02 | 10/25/20 | 17,100 | ** |
| 50 shares Alcoa | 6/10/14 | 10/23/20 | 525 | 1,800 |
| 25 shares Luminent | 4/28/20 | 9/4/20 | 900 | 2,700 |
| 60 shares Textron | 9/11/20 | 10/27/20 | 10,410 | 9,100 |
| 300 shares Hasbro | 1/7/09 | 12/20/20 | 6,125 | 3,150 |

*When Joyce graduated from college on May 12, 1997, her father gave her 150 shares of Pfizer Corporation stock that he had acquired on October 27, 1989, for $1,300. At the date of the gift, the fair market value of the stock was $1,800. In January 2006, Pfizer Corporation stock split 2 for 1.

**The Schnappaufs acquired 500 shares of preferred stock in Texas Instruments for $7,810. Shortly after the purchase, they received a nontaxable 10 percent stock dividend.

3. On May 18, 2020, Joyce purchases a computer system for $2,700. She also buys a color printer/copier/fax machine for $450. All the equipment is used exclusively in her business.
4. On June 12, 2020, Joyce sells her old computer system for $300 and her printer for $75. She had acquired the computer system and printer on February 18, 2017, for $2,800 and $425, respectively. When the Schnappaufs prepared their 2017 tax return, they elected to expense the computer and printer using Section 179. The computer system and the printer were used exclusively in her business.

5. Joyce receives a Schedule K-1 (Exhibit A-16) for her interest in the furniture-restoration business.
6. Other information:
   a. The rental property in Lake Tahoe is located at 100 Paraiso Drive, South Lake Tahoe (88197).
7. The Shnappauf's Qualifed Business Income from Queensbridge Books is $6,967 and $7,125 from B & F. These amounts should appear as QBI on Line 1 of Form 8995.

INSTRUCTIONS: To complete phase III, you need the following additional forms: Schedule E and Forms 4562 and 8582. You now have all the information necessary to complete the schedules that you did not finish in phases I and II.

*Exhibit A-1*

| 22222 | a Employee's social security number 150-52-0546 | OMB No. 1545-0008 | |
|---|---|---|---|
| b Employer identification number (EIN) 05-7652473 | | 1 Wages, tips, other compensation $152,272.48 | 2 Federal income tax withheld $13,871.00 |
| c Employer's name, address, and ZIP code<br>USC Equipment Corp.<br>18 Perry Rd.<br>Warwick, RI 02806 | | 3 Social security wages $137,700.00 | 4 Social security tax withheld $8,537.40 |
| | | 5 Medicare wages and tips $152,272.48 | 6 Medicare tax withheld $2,207.95 |
| | | 7 Social security tips | 8 Allocated tips |
| d Control number | | 9 | 10 Dependent care benefits |
| e Employee's first name and initial / Last name / Suff.<br>Bill Schnappauf<br>27 Northrup St.<br>Wakefield, RI 02879 | | 11 Nonqualified plans | 12a Code C \| $132.48 |
| | | 13 Statutory employee ☐ Retirement plan ☒ Third-party sick pay ☐ | 12b Code D \| $6,860.00 |
| | | 14 Other | 12c Code |
| f Employee's address and ZIP code | | | 12d Code |

| 15 State | Employer's state ID number | 16 State wages, tips, etc. | 17 State income tax | 18 Local wages, tips, etc. | 19 Local income tax | 20 Locality name |
|---|---|---|---|---|---|---|
| RI | 05-R7652473 | $152,272.48 | $5,577.18 | | | |
| | | | | | | |

Form **W-2** **Wage and Tax Statement** 2020

Department of the Treasury—Internal Revenue Service

**Copy 1—For State, City, or Local Tax Department**

*Exhibit A-2*

☐ CORRECTED (if checked)

| PAYER'S name, street address, city or town, state or province, country, ZIP or foreign postal code, and telephone no. | | Payer's RTN (optional) | OMB No. 1545-0112 | | Interest Income |
|---|---|---|---|---|---|
| Wakefield Savings Bank<br>565 Main St.<br>Wakefield, RI 02879 | | 1 Interest income<br>$ 615.00 | 2020<br>Form 1099-INT | | |
| | | 2 Early withdrawal penalty<br>$ | | | Copy B<br>For Recipient |
| PAYER'S TIN<br>05-2217118 | RECIPIENT'S TIN<br>150-52-0546 | 3 Interest on U.S. Savings Bonds and Treas. obligations<br>$ | | | |
| RECIPIENT'S name<br>Bil & Joyce Schnappauf | | 4 Federal income tax withheld<br>$ | 5 Investment expenses<br>$ | | This is important tax information and is being furnished to the IRS. If you are required to file a return, a negligence penalty or other sanction may be imposed on you if this income is taxable and the IRS determines that it has not been reported. |
| Street address (including apt. no.)<br>27 Northrup St. | | 6 Foreign tax paid<br>$ | 7 Foreign country or U.S. possession | | |
| City or town, state or province, country, and ZIP or foreign postal code<br>Wakefield, RI 02879 | | 8 Tax-exempt interest<br>$ | 9 Specified private activity bond interest<br>$ | | |
| | | 10 Market discount<br>$ | 11 Bond premium<br>$ | | |
| | FATCA filing requirement ☐ | 12 Bond premium on Treasury obligations<br>$ | 13 Bond premium on tax-exempt bond<br>$ | | |
| Account number (see instructions)<br>120356 | | 14 Tax-exempt and tax credit bond CUSIP no. | 15 State | 16 State identification no. | 17 State tax withheld<br>$<br>$ |

Form **1099-INT** (keep for your records) www.irs.gov/Form1099INT Department of the Treasury - Internal Revenue Service

## Exhibit A-3

☐ CORRECTED (if checked)

| PAYER'S name, street address, city or town, state or province, country, ZIP or foreign postal code, and telephone no. | | Payer's RTN (optional) | OMB No. 1545-0112 | Interest Income |
|---|---|---|---|---|
| Hawthorn Savings Bank<br>11 Vespa Plaza<br>Boston, MA 02211 | | 1 Interest income<br>$ 417.00 | 2020<br>Form 1099-INT | |
| | | 2 Early withdrawal penalty<br>$ | | Copy B<br>For Recipient |
| PAYER'S TIN<br>05-8173693 | RECIPIENT'S TIN<br>371-42-5207 | 3 Interest on U.S. Savings Bonds and Treas. obligations<br>$ | | |
| RECIPIENT'S name<br>Joyce Schnappauf | | 4 Federal income tax withheld<br>$ | 5 Investment expenses<br>$ | This is important tax information and is being furnished to the IRS. If you are required to file a return, a negligence penalty or other sanction may be imposed on you if this income is taxable and the IRS determines that it has not been reported. |
| Street address (including apt. no.)<br>27 Northrup St. | | 6 Foreign tax paid<br>$ | 7 Foreign country or U.S. possession | |
| City or town, state or province, country, and ZIP or foreign postal code<br>Wakefield, RI 02879 | | 8 Tax-exempt interest<br>$ | 9 Specified private activity bond interest<br>$ | |
| | | 10 Market discount<br>$ | 11 Bond premium<br>$ | |
| | FATCA filing requirement ☐ | 12 Bond premium on Treasury obligations<br>$ | 13 Bond premium on tax-exempt bond<br>$ | |
| Account number (see instructions)<br>471938 | | 14 Tax-exempt and tax credit bond CUSIP no. | 15 State / 16 State identification no. | 17 State tax withheld<br>$<br>$ |

Form **1099-INT** (keep for your records) www.irs.gov/Form1099INT Department of the Treasury - Internal Revenue Service

## Exhibit A-4

☐ VOID ☐ CORRECTED

| PAYER'S name, street address, city or town, state or province, country, ZIP or foreign postal code, and telephone no. | | 1a Total ordinary dividends | OMB No. 1545-0110 | Dividends and Distributions |
|---|---|---|---|---|
| Collingwood Capital Fund<br>100 American Avenue<br>Providence, RI 02902 | | $ 176.00 | 2020 | |
| | | 1b Qualified dividends<br>$ 176.00 | Form 1099-DIV | |
| | | 2a Total capital gain distr.<br>$ 105.00 | 2b Unrecap. Sec. 1250 gain<br>$ | Copy 1<br>For State Tax Department |
| PAYER'S TIN<br>05-1473191 | RECIPIENT'S TIN<br>371-42-5207 | 2c Section 1202 gain<br>$ | 2d Collectibles (28%) gain<br>$ | |
| RECIPIENT'S name<br>Joyce Schnappauf | | 3 Nondividend distributions<br>$ | 4 Federal income tax withheld<br>$ 47.20 | |
| Street address (including apt. no.)<br>27 Northrup St. | | 5 Section 199A dividends<br>$ | 6 Investment expenses<br>$ | |
| | | 7 Foreign tax paid<br>$ | 8 Foreign country or U.S. possession | |
| City or town, state or province, country, and ZIP or foreign postal code<br>Wakefield, RI 02879 | | 9 Cash liquidation distributions<br>$ | 10 Noncash liquidation distributions<br>$ | |
| | FATCA filing requirement ☐ | 11 Exempt-interest dividends<br>$ | 12 Specified private activity bond interest dividends<br>$ | |
| Account number (see instructions) | | 13 State / 14 State identification no. | 15 State tax withheld<br>$<br>$ | |

Form **1099-DIV** www.irs.gov/Form1099DIV Department of the Treasury - Internal Revenue Service

## Exhibit A-5

☐ VOID ☐ CORRECTED

| PAYER'S name, street address, city or town, state or province, country, ZIP or foreign postal code, and telephone no. | 1a Total ordinary dividends | OMB No. 1545-0110 | |
|---|---|---|---|
| Coca-Cola Corporation<br>125 Beltway Blvd.<br>Atlanta, GA 30313 | $ 1,372.00 | 2020 | Dividends and Distributions |
| | 1b Qualified dividends<br>$ 1,372.00 | Form 1099-DIV | |
| | 2a Total capital gain distr.<br>$ | 2b Unrecap. Sec. 1250 gain<br>$ | Copy 1<br>For State Tax Department |
| PAYER'S TIN: 05-6179147 / RECIPIENT'S TIN: 150-52-0546 | 2c Section 1202 gain<br>$ | 2d Collectibles (28%) gain<br>$ | |
| RECIPIENT'S name<br>Bill Schnappauf | 3 Nondividend distributions<br>$ | 4 Federal income tax withheld<br>$ | |
| Street address (including apt. no.)<br>27 Northrup St. | 5 Section 199A dividends<br>$ | 6 Investment expenses<br>$ | |
| | 7 Foreign tax paid<br>$ | 8 Foreign country or U.S. possession | |
| City or town, state or province, country, and ZIP or foreign postal code<br>Wakefield, RI 02879 | 9 Cash liquidation distributions<br>$ | 10 Noncash liquidation distributions<br>$ | |
| FATCA filing requirement ☐ | 11 Exempt-interest dividends<br>$ | 12 Specified private activity bond interest dividends<br>$ | |
| Account number (see instructions) | 13 State / 14 State identification no. | 15 State tax withheld<br>$<br>$ | |

Form **1099-DIV** www.irs.gov/Form1099DIV Department of the Treasury - Internal Revenue Service

## Exhibit A-6

**Pebble Beach Investors**
175 Norman Way
Monterey, CA 95436

**Forms 1099 for 2020**

**This is important tax information and is being furnished to the Internal Revenue Service. We are required to report, on Forms 1099, all dividends, interest, royalties and proceeds on sales collected on your behalf. A negligence penalty will be imposed if this income is taxable and the Internal Revenue Service determines that it has not been reported.**

**1099-DIV Dividends**

This section reports dividends and distributions earned on investments and any taxes withheld or paid. All dividends are qualified dividend income.

| Entity | Description | Amount | Federal Tax Withheld |
|---|---|---|---|
| Pfizer Corporation | Gross dividends | $210 | $0 |
| Apple | Gross dividends | $391 | $0 |

**1099-INT Interest**

This section reports interest earned on investments and any taxes withheld or paid.

| Entity | Description | Amount | Federal Tax Withheld |
|---|---|---|---|
| New Jersey Economic Development Bonds | Gross interest | $ 457 | $ 0 |
| New York City Municipal Bonds | Gross interest | $1,208 | $ 0 |
| Ford Motor Bonds | Gross interest | $ 717 | $144 |

## Exhibit A-7

☐ VOID ☐ CORRECTED

| PAYER'S name, street address, city or town, state or province, country, ZIP or foreign postal code, and telephone no. | | 1 Unemployment compensation | OMB No. 1545-0120 | **Certain Government Payments** |
|---|---|---|---|---|
| State of Rhode Island<br>Taxation Office<br>One Capitol Hill<br>Providence, RI 02908 | | $<br>2 State or local income tax refunds, credits, or offsets<br>$ 818.00 | **2020**<br>Form **1099-G** | |
| PAYER'S TIN<br>05-0000199 | RECIPIENT'S TIN<br>150-52-0546 | 3 Box 2 amount is for tax year<br>2019 | 4 Federal income tax withheld<br>$ | **Copy 1** |
| RECIPIENT'S name<br>Bill & Joyce Schnappauf | | 5 RTAA payments<br>$ | 6 Taxable grants<br>$ | **For State Tax Department** |
| Street address (including apt. no.)<br>27 Nothrup St. | | 7 Agriculture payments<br>$ | 8 Check if box 2 is trade or business income ▶ ☐ | |
| City or town, state or province, country, and ZIP or foreign postal code<br>Wakefield, RI 02879 | | 9 Market gain<br>$ | | |
| Account number (see instructions) | | 10a State | 10b State identification no. | 11 State income tax withheld<br>$<br>$ |

Form **1099-G** www.irs.gov/Form1099G Department of the Treasury - Internal Revenue Service

## Exhibit A-8

3232 ☐ VOID ☐ CORRECTED

| PAYER'S name, street address, city or town, province or state, country, and ZIP or foreign postal code | | 1 Reportable winnings | 2 Date won | OMB No. 1545-0238 |
|---|---|---|---|---|
| Yardly Casino<br>423 Higgins Drive<br>Groton, CT 03657 | | $ 6,200.00 | 0612/2020 | **2020**<br>**Form W-2G** |
| | | 3 Type of wager<br>Blackjack | 4 Federal income tax withheld<br>$ | **Certain Gambling Winnings** |
| | | 5 Transaction | 6 Race | |
| | | 7 Winnings from identical wagers<br>$ | 8 Cashier | |
| PAYER'S federal identification number<br>05-4568231 | PAYER'S telephone number<br>210-423-6531 | 9 Winner's taxpayer identification no.<br>150-52-0546 | 10 Window | For Privacy Act and Paperwork Reduction Act Notice, see the **2020 General Instructions for Certain Information Returns.** |
| WINNER'S name<br>Bill Schnappauf | | 11 First I.D. | 12 Second I.D. | |
| Street address (including apt. no.)<br>27 Northrup st. | | 13 State/Payer's state identification no. | 14 State winnings<br>$ | |
| City or town, province or state, country, and ZIP or foreign postal code<br>Wakefield, RI 02879 | | 15 State income tax withheld<br>$ | 16 Local winnings<br>$ | **File with Form 1096** |
| | | 17 Local income tax withheld<br>$ | 18 Name of locality | **Copy A**<br>**For Internal Revenue Service Center** |

Under penalties of perjury, I declare that, to the best of my knowledge and belief, the name, address, and taxpayer identification number that I have furnished correctly identify me as the recipient of this payment and any payments from identical wagers, and that no other person is entitled to any part of these payments.

**Signature ▶** **Date ▶**

Form **W-2G** Cat. No. 10138V www.irs.gov/FormW2G Department of the Treasury - Internal Revenue Service

**Do Not Cut or Separate Forms on This Page – Do Not Cut or Separate Forms on This Page**

*Exhibit A-9*

June 15, 2020

United Insurance Corporation
150 Hird Highway
Essedon, Connecticut 06457

Re: Policy # SB 6996782

Dear Mr. Schnappauf:

Enclosed please find a check for $15,480. The enclosed check consists of the face value of the insurance policy ($15,100) plus the accrued interest from the date of your uncle's death. The interest income of $380 is calculated beginning 15 days after the death (December 17, 2019) through the payment date of June 15, 2020. The premiums paid on this policy total $3,620. A portion of the payment you receive may be taxable. We suggest you contact your tax advisor to determine the appropriate tax treatment of the payment.

If you have any questions concerning the payment, please feel free to contact me at (203) 591-4359.

Sincerely,

Kathy Sorento
Policy Manager

------------------------------------SUBSTITUTE 1099-INT----------------------------------

Exhibit A-10

☐ VOID ☐ CORRECTED

PAYER'S name, street address, city or town, state or province, country, ZIP or foreign postal code, and telephone no.

West Publishing
457 German Way
St. Paul, MN 54678

1 Rents
$

2 Royalties
$ 5,170.00

OMB No. 1545-0115

2020

Form 1099-MISC

**Miscellaneous Income**

3 Other income
$

4 Federal income tax withheld
$

**Copy 1**
**For State Tax Department**

PAYER'S TIN
05-1919431

RECIPIENT'S TIN
371-42-5207

5 Fishing boat proceeds
$

6 Medical and health care payments
$

RECIPIENT'S name
Joyce Schnappauf

7 Payer made direct sales of $5,000 or more of consumer products to a buyer (recipient) for resale ☐

8 Substitute payments in lieu of dividends or interest
$

Street address (including apt. no.)
27 Northrup St.

9 Crop insurance proceeds
$

10 Gross proceeds paid to an attorney
$

City or town, state or province, country, and ZIP or foreign postal code
Wakefield, RI 02879

11

12 Section 409A deferrals
$

Account number (see instructions)

FATCA filing requirement ☐

13 Excess golden parachute payments
$

14 Nonqualified deferred compensation
$

| 15 State tax withheld | 16 State/Payer's state no. | 17 State income |
|---|---|---|
| $ | | $ |
| $ | | $ |

Form **1099-MISC** www.irs.gov/Form1099MISC Department of the Treasury - Internal Revenue Service

## Exhibit A-11

☐ VOID ☐ CORRECTED

PAYER'S name, street address, city or town, state or province, country, ZIP or foreign postal code, and telephone no.

**Mountain Publishing**
**480 Payton Lane**
**Dallas, TX 72194**

1 Rents $

2 Royalties $ 6,250.00

OMB No. 1545-0115

**2020**

Form **1099-MISC**

**Miscellaneous Income**

3 Other income $

4 Federal income tax withheld $

**Copy 1**
**For State Tax Department**

PAYER'S TIN: 05-9765421

RECIPIENT'S TIN: 371-42-5207

5 Fishing boat proceeds $

6 Medical and health care payments $

RECIPIENT'S name

**Joyce Schnappauf**

7 Payer made direct sales of $5,000 or more of consumer products to a buyer (recipient) for resale ☐

8 Substitute payments in lieu of dividends or interest $

Street address (including apt. no.)

**27 Northrup St.**

9 Crop insurance proceeds $

10 Gross proceeds paid to an attorney $

City or town, state or province, country, and ZIP or foreign postal code

**Wakefield, RI 02879**

11

12 Section 409A deferrals $

Account number (see instructions)

FATCA filing requirement ☐

13 Excess golden parachute payments $

14 Nonqualified deferred compensation $

15 State tax withheld $ $

16 State/Payer's state no.

17 State income $ $

Form **1099-MISC** www.irs.gov/Form1099MISC Department of the Treasury - Internal Revenue Service

*Exhibit A-12*

☐ VOID ☐ CORRECTED

| | | | |
|---|---|---|---|
| PAYER'S name, street address, city or town, state or province, country, ZIP or foreign postal code, and telephone no.<br>**Head Start Books**<br>**647 Fifth Avenue**<br>**New York, NY 11140** | **1** Rents<br>$<br>**2** Royalties<br>$ 11,200.00 | OMB No. 1545-0115<br>**2020**<br>Form **1099-MISC** | **Miscellaneous Income** |
| | **3** Other income<br>$ | **4** Federal income tax withheld<br>$ | **Copy 1**<br>**For State Tax Department** |
| PAYER'S TIN: 05-1719274 / RECIPIENT'S TIN: 371-42-5207 | **5** Fishing boat proceeds<br>$ | **6** Medical and health care payments<br>$ | |
| RECIPIENT'S name<br>**Joyce Schnappauf** | **7** Payer made direct sales of $5,000 or more of consumer products to a buyer (recipient) for resale ☐ | **8** Substitute payments in lieu of dividends or interest<br>$ | |
| Street address (including apt. no.)<br>**27 Northrup St.** | **9** Crop insurance proceeds<br>$ | **10** Gross proceeds paid to an attorney<br>$ | |
| City or town, state or province, country, and ZIP or foreign postal code<br>**Wakefield, RI 02879** | **11** | **12** Section 409A deferrals<br>$ | |
| Account number (see instructions) / FATCA filing requirement ☐ | **13** Excess golden parachute payments<br>$ | **14** Nonqualified deferred compensation<br>$ | |
| | **15** State tax withheld<br>$<br>$ | **16** State/Payer's state no. | **17** State income<br>$<br>$ |

Form **1099-MISC** www.irs.gov/Form1099MISC Department of the Treasury - Internal Revenue Service

## Exhibit A-13

☐ CORRECTED (if checked)

| | | | |
|---|---|---|---|
| RECIPIENT'S/LENDER'S name, street address, city or town, state or province, country, ZIP or foreign postal code, and telephone no.<br><br>**Jefferson Trust**<br>**50 Presidential Avenue**<br>**Falmouth, RI 02458** | | ***Caution:** The amount shown may not be fully deductible by you. Limits based on the loan amount and the cost and value of the secured property may apply. Also, you may only deduct interest to the extent it was incurred by you, actually paid by you, and not reimbursed by another person. | OMB No. 1545-1380<br>**2020**<br>Form **1098**<br><br>**Mortgage Interest Statement** |
| | | **1** Mortgage interest received from payer(s)/borrower(s)*<br>$ 8,140.00 | **Copy B For Payer/ Borrower** |
| RECIPIENT'S/LENDER'S TIN<br>**05-6771794** | PAYER'S/BORROWER'S TIN<br>**150-52-0546** | **2** Outstanding mortgage principal<br>$ | **3** Mortgage origination date |
| | | **4** Refund of overpaid interest<br>$ | **5** Mortgage insurance premiums<br>$ |
| PAYER'S/BORROWER'S name<br>**Bil & Joyce Schnappauf** | | **6** Points paid on purchase of principal residence<br>$ | |
| Street address (including apt. no.)<br>**27 Northrup St.** | | **7** ☐ If address of property securing mortgage is the same as PAYER'S/BORROWER'S address, the box is checked, or the address or description is entered in box 8. | |
| City or town, state or province, country, and ZIP or foreign postal code<br>**Wakefield, RI 02879** | | **8** Address or description of property securing mortgage (see instructions) | |
| **9** Number of properties securing the mortgage | **10** Other | | **11** Mortgage acquisition date |
| Account number (see instructions) | | | |

The information in boxes 1 through 9 and 11 is important tax information and is being furnished to the IRS. If you are required to file a return, a negligence penalty or other sanction may be imposed on you if the IRS determines that an underpayment of tax results because you overstated a deduction for this mortgage interest or for these points, reported in boxes 1 and 6; or because you didn't report the refund of interest (box 4); or because you claimed a nondeductible item.

Form **1098** (Keep for your records) www.irs.gov/Form1098 Department of the Treasury - Internal Revenue Service

*Exhibit A-14*

☐ CORRECTED (if checked)

| RECIPIENT'S/LENDER'S name, street address, city or town, state or province, country, ZIP or foreign postal code, and telephone no.<br><br>Jefferson Trust<br>50 Presidential Avenue<br>Falmouth, RI 02458 | | *Caution: The amount shown may not be fully deductible by you. Limits based on the loan amount and the cost and value of the secured property may apply. Also, you may only deduct interest to the extent it was incurred by you, actually paid by you, and not reimbursed by another person. | OMB No. 1545-1380<br>2020<br>Form 1098 | **Mortgage Interest Statement** |
|---|---|---|---|---|
| | | 1 Mortgage interest received from payer(s)/borrower(s)*<br>$ 5,100.00 | | **Copy B For Payer/ Borrower** |
| RECIPIENT'S/LENDER'S TIN<br>05-6771794 | PAYER'S/BORROWER'S TIN<br>150-52-0546 | 2 Outstanding mortgage principal<br>$ | 3 Mortgage origination date | The information in boxes 1 through 9 and 11 is important tax information and is being furnished to the IRS. If you are required to file a return, a negligence penalty or other sanction may be imposed on you if the IRS determines that an underpayment of tax results because you overstated a deduction for this mortgage interest or for these points, reported in boxes 1 and 6; or because you didn't report the refund of interest (box 4); or because you claimed a nondeductible item. |
| PAYER'S/BORROWER'S name<br><br>Bil & Joyce Schnappauf | | 4 Refund of overpaid interest<br>$ | 5 Mortgage insurance premiums<br>$ | |
| | | 6 Points paid on purchase of principal residence<br>$ | | |
| Street address (including apt. no.)<br><br>27 Northrup St. | | 7 ☐ If address of property securing mortgage is the same as PAYER'S/BORROWER'S address, the box is checked, or the address or description is entered in box 8. | | |
| City or town, state or province, country, and ZIP or foreign postal code<br><br>Wakefield, RI 02879 | | 8 Address or description of property securing mortgage (see instructions) | | |
| 9 Number of properties securing the mortgage | 10 Other | | | |
| Account number (see instructions) | | | | 11 Mortgage acquisition date |

Form **1098** (Keep for your records) www.irs.gov/Form1098 Department of the Treasury - Internal Revenue Service

## Exhibit A-15

☐ VOID ☐ CORRECTED

| | | | |
|---|---|---|---|
| PAYER'S name, street address, city or town, state or province, country, ZIP or foreign postal code, and telephone no.<br>Pebble Beach Investors<br>175 Norman Way<br>Monterey, CA 95436 | Applicable checkbox on Form 8949 | OMB No. 1545-0715<br>2020<br>Form 1099-B | Proceeds From Broker and Barter Exchange Transactions |
| | 1a Description of property (Example: 100 sh. XYZ Co.) | | |
| | 1b Date acquired | 1c Date sold or disposed | |
| PAYER'S TIN 05-6795137 / RECIPIENT'S TIN 371-42-5207 | 1d Proceeds $ 41,060.00 | 1e Cost or other basis $ | Copy 1 For State Tax Department |
| | 1f Accrued market discount $ | 1g Wash sale loss disallowed $ | |
| RECIPIENT'S name<br>Joyce Schnappauf | 2 Short-term gain or loss ☐ Long-term gain or loss ☐ Ordinary ☐ | 3 If checked, proceeds from: Collectibles ☐ QOF ☐ | |
| Street address (including apt. no.)<br>27 Northrup St. | 4 Federal income tax withheld $ | 5 If checked, noncovered security ☐ | |
| City or town, state or province, country, and ZIP or foreign postal code<br>Wakefield, RI 02879 | 6 Reported to IRS: Gross proceeds ☐ Net proceeds ☐ | 7 If checked, loss is not allowed based on amount in 1d ☐ | |
| Account number (see instructions) | 8 Profit or (loss) realized in 2020 on closed contracts $ | 9 Unrealized profit or (loss) on open contracts—12/31/2019 $ | |
| CUSIP number / FATCA filing requirement ☐ | 10 Unrealized profit or (loss) on open contracts—12/31/2020 $ | 11 Aggregate profit or (loss) on contracts $ | |
| 14 State name / 15 State identification no. / 16 State tax withheld $ $ | 12 If checked, basis reported to IRS ☐ | 13 Bartering $ | |

Form 1099-B www.irs.gov/Form1099B Department of the Treasury - Internal Revenue Service

Exhibit A-16

671120

☐ Final K-1 ☐ Amended K-1 OMB No. 1545-0123

**Schedule K-1 (Form 1120-S)** **2020**
Department of the Treasury
Internal Revenue Service

For calendar year 2020, or tax year

beginning / / 2020 ending / /

## Shareholder's Share of Income, Deductions, Credits, etc.

▶ See separate instructions.

### Part I Information About the Corporation

**A** Corporation's employer identification number
05-7652473

**B** Corporation's name, address, city, state, and ZIP code
B & F Antique Restoration
13 Weathervane Road
Wakefield, RI 02879

**C** IRS Center where corporation filed return
Andover, MA 05501

### Part II Information About the Shareholder

**D** Shareholder's identifying number
371-42-5207

**E** Shareholder's name, address, city, state, and ZIP code
Joyce Schnappauf
27 Northrup Street
Wakefield, RI 02879

**F** Current year allocation percentage . . . 30 %

**G** Shareholder's number of shares
Beginning of tax year . . . . . . ______
End of tax year . . . . . . . . ______

**H** Loans from shareholder
Beginning of tax year . . . . . . $ ______
End of tax year . . . . . . . . $ ______

For IRS Use Only

### Part III Shareholder's Share of Current Year Income, Deductions, Credits, and Other Items

| Line | Item | Amount | Line | Item | Amount |
|---|---|---|---|---|---|
| 1 | Ordinary business income (loss) | 7,125.00 | 13 | Credits | |
| 2 | Net rental real estate income (loss) | | | | |
| 3 | Other net rental income (loss) | | | | |
| 4 | Interest income | | | | |
| 5a | Ordinary dividends | | | | |
| 5b | Qualified dividends | | 14 | Foreign transactions | |
| 6 | Royalties | | | | |
| 7 | Net short-term capital gain (loss) | | | | |
| 8a | Net long-term capital gain (loss) | | | | |
| 8b | Collectibles (28%) gain (loss) | | | | |
| 8c | Unrecaptured section 1250 gain | | | | |
| 9 | Net section 1231 gain (loss) | | | | |
| 10 | Other income (loss) | | 15 | Alternative minimum tax (AMT) items | |
| 11 | Section 179 deduction | 620.00 | 16 | Items affecting shareholder basis | |
| | | | d | | 1,500.00 |
| 12 | Other deductions | | | | |
| a | | 310.00 | | | |
| | | | 17 | Other information | |
| | | | V* | | STMT |

18 ☐ More than one activity for at-risk purposes*
19 ☐ More than one activity for passive activity purposes*

* See attached statement for additional information.

# Tax Rate Schedules and Tax Tables

APPENDIX B

Thinglass/Shutterstock.com; Anton Starikov/Shutterstock.com

# 2021 INDIVIDUAL TAX RATE SCHEDULES

Table B-1

## Single Taxpayers

| If Taxable Income Is Over | But Not Over | The Tax Is | of the Amount Over |
|---|---|---|---|
| $ 0 | 9,950 | ....... 10% | $ 0 |
| 9,950 | 40,525 | $ 995.00 + 12% | 9,950 |
| 40,525 | 86,375 | 4,664.00 + 22% | 40,525 |
| 86,375 | 164,925 | 14,751.00 + 24% | 86,375 |
| 164,925 | 209,425 | 33,603.00 + 32% | 164,925 |
| 209,425 | 523,600 | 47,843.00 + 35% | 209,425 |
| 523,600 | ....... | 157,804.25 + 37% | 523,600 |

Table B-2

## Married Taxpayers Filing Jointly and Surviving Spouse

| If Taxable Income Is Over | But Not Over | The Tax Is | of the Amount Over |
|---|---|---|---|
| $ 0 | 19,900 | ....... 10% | $ 0 |
| 19,900 | 81,050 | $ 1,990.00 + 12% | 19,900 |
| 81,050 | 172,750 | 9,328.00 + 22% | 81,050 |
| 172,750 | 329,850 | 29,502.00 + 24% | 172,750 |
| 329,850 | 418,850 | 67,260.00 + 32% | 329,850 |
| 418,850 | 628,300 | 95,686.00 + 35% | 418,850 |
| 628,300 | | 168,993.50 + 37% | 628,300 |

Table B-3

## Head of Household

| If Taxable Income Is Over | But Not Over | The Tax Is | of the Amount Over |
|---|---|---|---|
| $ 0 | 14,200 | ....... 10% | $ 0 |
| 14,200 | 54,200 | $ 1,420.00 + 12% | 14,200 |
| 54,200 | 86,350 | 6,220.00 + 22% | 54,200 |
| 86,350 | 164,900 | 13,293.00 + 24% | 86,350 |
| 164,900 | 209,400 | 32,145.00 + 32% | 164,900 |
| 209,400 | 523,600 | 46,385.00 + 35% | 209,400 |
| 523,600 | | 156,355.00 + 37% | 523,600 |

Table B-4

## Married Taxpayers, Filing Separately

| If Taxable Income Is Over | But Not Over | The Tax Is | of the Amount Over |
|---|---|---|---|
| $ 0 | 9,950 | ....... 10% | $ 0 |
| 9,950 | 40,525 | $ 995.00 + 12% | 9,950 |
| 40,525 | 86,375 | 4664.00 + 22% | 40,525 |
| 86,375 | 164,925 | 14,751.00 + 24% | 86,375 |
| 164,925 | 209,425 | 33,603.00 + 32% | 164,925 |
| 209,425 | 314,150 | 47,843.00 + 35% | 209,425 |
| 314,150 | | 84,496.75 + 37% | 314,150 |

# 2021 CORPORATE TAX RATE SCHEDULE

*Table B-5*

All corporate taxable income is taxed at a flat 21 percent rate.

# 2020 INDIVIDUAL TAX TABLE

## 2020 Tax Table

CAUTION

*See the instructions for line 16 to see if you must use the Tax Table below to figure your tax.*

**Example.** Mr. and Mrs. Brown are filing a joint return. Their taxable income on Form 1040, line 15, is $25,300. First, they find the $25,300–25,350 taxable income line. Next, they find the column for married filing jointly and read down the column. The amount shown where the taxable income line and filing status column meet is $2,644. This is the tax amount they should enter in the entry space on Form 1040, line 16.

**Sample Table**

| At Least | But Less Than | Single | Married filing jointly* | Married filing sepa-rately | Head of a house-hold |
|---|---|---|---|---|---|
| | | Your tax is— | | | |
| **25,200** | **25,250** | 2,830 | 2,632 | 2,830 | 2,745 |
| **25,250** | **25,300** | 2,836 | 2,638 | 2,836 | 2,751 |
| **25,300** | **25,350** | 2,842 | (2,644) | 2,842 | 2,757 |
| **25,350** | **25,400** | 2,848 | 2,650 | 2,848 | 2,763 |

Extract of tax table to illustrate example.

| If line 15 (taxable income) is— | | And you are— | | | |
|---|---|---|---|---|---|
| At least | But less than | Single | Married filing jointly* | Married filing sepa-rately | Head of a house-hold |
| | | Your tax is— | | | |
| 0 | 5 | 0 | 0 | 0 | 0 |
| 5 | 15 | 1 | 1 | 1 | 1 |
| 15 | 25 | 2 | 2 | 2 | 2 |
| 25 | 50 | 4 | 4 | 4 | 4 |
| 50 | 75 | 6 | 6 | 6 | 6 |
| 75 | 100 | 9 | 9 | 9 | 9 |
| 100 | 125 | 11 | 11 | 11 | 11 |
| 125 | 150 | 14 | 14 | 14 | 14 |
| 150 | 175 | 16 | 16 | 16 | 16 |
| 175 | 200 | 19 | 19 | 19 | 19 |
| 200 | 225 | 21 | 21 | 21 | 21 |
| 225 | 250 | 24 | 24 | 24 | 24 |
| 250 | 275 | 26 | 26 | 26 | 26 |
| 275 | 300 | 29 | 29 | 29 | 29 |
| 300 | 325 | 31 | 31 | 31 | 31 |
| 325 | 350 | 34 | 34 | 34 | 34 |
| 350 | 375 | 36 | 36 | 36 | 36 |
| 375 | 400 | 39 | 39 | 39 | 39 |
| 400 | 425 | 41 | 41 | 41 | 41 |
| 425 | 450 | 44 | 44 | 44 | 44 |
| 450 | 475 | 46 | 46 | 46 | 46 |
| 475 | 500 | 49 | 49 | 49 | 49 |
| 500 | 525 | 51 | 51 | 51 | 51 |
| 525 | 550 | 54 | 54 | 54 | 54 |
| 550 | 575 | 56 | 56 | 56 | 56 |
| 575 | 600 | 59 | 59 | 59 | 59 |
| 600 | 625 | 61 | 61 | 61 | 61 |
| 625 | 650 | 64 | 64 | 64 | 64 |
| 650 | 675 | 66 | 66 | 66 | 66 |
| 675 | 700 | 69 | 69 | 69 | 69 |
| 700 | 725 | 71 | 71 | 71 | 71 |
| 725 | 750 | 74 | 74 | 74 | 74 |
| 750 | 775 | 76 | 76 | 76 | 76 |
| 775 | 800 | 79 | 79 | 79 | 79 |
| 800 | 825 | 81 | 81 | 81 | 81 |
| 825 | 850 | 84 | 84 | 84 | 84 |
| 850 | 875 | 86 | 86 | 86 | 86 |
| 875 | 900 | 89 | 89 | 89 | 89 |
| 900 | 925 | 91 | 91 | 91 | 91 |
| 925 | 950 | 94 | 94 | 94 | 94 |
| 950 | 975 | 96 | 96 | 96 | 96 |
| 975 | 1,000 | 99 | 99 | 99 | 99 |

| If line 15 (taxable income) is— | | And you are— | | | |
|---|---|---|---|---|---|
| At least | But less than | Single | Married filing jointly* | Married filing sepa-rately | Head of a house-hold |
| | | Your tax is— | | | |
| **1,000** | | | | | |
| 1,000 | 1,025 | 101 | 101 | 101 | 101 |
| 1,025 | 1,050 | 104 | 104 | 104 | 104 |
| 1,050 | 1,075 | 106 | 106 | 106 | 106 |
| 1,075 | 1,100 | 109 | 109 | 109 | 109 |
| 1,100 | 1,125 | 111 | 111 | 111 | 111 |
| 1,125 | 1,150 | 114 | 114 | 114 | 114 |
| 1,150 | 1,175 | 116 | 116 | 116 | 116 |
| 1,175 | 1,200 | 119 | 119 | 119 | 119 |
| 1,200 | 1,225 | 121 | 121 | 121 | 121 |
| 1,225 | 1,250 | 124 | 124 | 124 | 124 |
| 1,250 | 1,275 | 126 | 126 | 126 | 126 |
| 1,275 | 1,300 | 129 | 129 | 129 | 129 |
| 1,300 | 1,325 | 131 | 131 | 131 | 131 |
| 1,325 | 1,350 | 134 | 134 | 134 | 134 |
| 1,350 | 1,375 | 136 | 136 | 136 | 136 |
| 1,375 | 1,400 | 139 | 139 | 139 | 139 |
| 1,400 | 1,425 | 141 | 141 | 141 | 141 |
| 1,425 | 1,450 | 144 | 144 | 144 | 144 |
| 1,450 | 1,475 | 146 | 146 | 146 | 146 |
| 1,475 | 1,500 | 149 | 149 | 149 | 149 |
| 1,500 | 1,525 | 151 | 151 | 151 | 151 |
| 1,525 | 1,550 | 154 | 154 | 154 | 154 |
| 1,550 | 1,575 | 156 | 156 | 156 | 156 |
| 1,575 | 1,600 | 159 | 159 | 159 | 159 |
| 1,600 | 1,625 | 161 | 161 | 161 | 161 |
| 1,625 | 1,650 | 164 | 164 | 164 | 164 |
| 1,650 | 1,675 | 166 | 166 | 166 | 166 |
| 1,675 | 1,700 | 169 | 169 | 169 | 169 |
| 1,700 | 1,725 | 171 | 171 | 171 | 171 |
| 1,725 | 1,750 | 174 | 174 | 174 | 174 |
| 1,750 | 1,775 | 176 | 176 | 176 | 176 |
| 1,775 | 1,800 | 179 | 179 | 179 | 179 |
| 1,800 | 1,825 | 181 | 181 | 181 | 181 |
| 1,825 | 1,850 | 184 | 184 | 184 | 184 |
| 1,850 | 1,875 | 186 | 186 | 186 | 186 |
| 1,875 | 1,900 | 189 | 189 | 189 | 189 |
| 1,900 | 1,925 | 191 | 191 | 191 | 191 |
| 1,925 | 1,950 | 194 | 194 | 194 | 194 |
| 1,950 | 1,975 | 196 | 196 | 196 | 196 |
| 1,975 | 2,000 | 199 | 199 | 199 | 199 |

| If line 15 (taxable income) is— | | And you are— | | | |
|---|---|---|---|---|---|
| At least | But less than | Single | Married filing jointly* | Married filing sepa-rately | Head of a house-hold |
| | | Your tax is— | | | |
| **2,000** | | | | | |
| 2,000 | 2,025 | 201 | 201 | 201 | 201 |
| 2,025 | 2,050 | 204 | 204 | 204 | 204 |
| 2,050 | 2,075 | 206 | 206 | 206 | 206 |
| 2,075 | 2,100 | 209 | 209 | 209 | 209 |
| 2,100 | 2,125 | 211 | 211 | 211 | 211 |
| 2,125 | 2,150 | 214 | 214 | 214 | 214 |
| 2,150 | 2,175 | 216 | 216 | 216 | 216 |
| 2,175 | 2,200 | 219 | 219 | 219 | 219 |
| 2,200 | 2,225 | 221 | 221 | 221 | 221 |
| 2,225 | 2,250 | 224 | 224 | 224 | 224 |
| 2,250 | 2,275 | 226 | 226 | 226 | 226 |
| 2,275 | 2,300 | 229 | 229 | 229 | 229 |
| 2,300 | 2,325 | 231 | 231 | 231 | 231 |
| 2,325 | 2,350 | 234 | 234 | 234 | 234 |
| 2,350 | 2,375 | 236 | 236 | 236 | 236 |
| 2,375 | 2,400 | 239 | 239 | 239 | 239 |
| 2,400 | 2,425 | 241 | 241 | 241 | 241 |
| 2,425 | 2,450 | 244 | 244 | 244 | 244 |
| 2,450 | 2,475 | 246 | 246 | 246 | 246 |
| 2,475 | 2,500 | 249 | 249 | 249 | 249 |
| 2,500 | 2,525 | 251 | 251 | 251 | 251 |
| 2,525 | 2,550 | 254 | 254 | 254 | 254 |
| 2,550 | 2,575 | 256 | 256 | 256 | 256 |
| 2,575 | 2,600 | 259 | 259 | 259 | 259 |
| 2,600 | 2,625 | 261 | 261 | 261 | 261 |
| 2,625 | 2,650 | 264 | 264 | 264 | 264 |
| 2,650 | 2,675 | 266 | 266 | 266 | 266 |
| 2,675 | 2,700 | 269 | 269 | 269 | 269 |
| 2,700 | 2,725 | 271 | 271 | 271 | 271 |
| 2,725 | 2,750 | 274 | 274 | 274 | 274 |
| 2,750 | 2,775 | 276 | 276 | 276 | 276 |
| 2,775 | 2,800 | 279 | 279 | 279 | 279 |
| 2,800 | 2,825 | 281 | 281 | 281 | 281 |
| 2,825 | 2,850 | 284 | 284 | 284 | 284 |
| 2,850 | 2,875 | 286 | 286 | 286 | 286 |
| 2,875 | 2,900 | 289 | 289 | 289 | 289 |
| 2,900 | 2,925 | 291 | 291 | 291 | 291 |
| 2,925 | 2,950 | 294 | 294 | 294 | 294 |
| 2,950 | 2,975 | 296 | 296 | 296 | 296 |
| 2,975 | 3,000 | 299 | 299 | 299 | 299 |

*This column must also be used by a qualifying widow(er).

*(Continued)*

## 2020 Tax Table — *Continued*

| If line 15 (taxable income) is— | | And you are— | | | |
|---|---|---|---|---|---|
| At least | But less than | Single | Married filing jointly* | Married filing separately | Head of a household |
| | | Your tax is— | | | |
| **3,000** | | | | | |
| 3,000 | 3,050 | 303 | 303 | 303 | 303 |
| 3,050 | 3,100 | 308 | 308 | 308 | 308 |
| 3,100 | 3,150 | 313 | 313 | 313 | 313 |
| 3,150 | 3,200 | 318 | 318 | 318 | 318 |
| 3,200 | 3,250 | 323 | 323 | 323 | 323 |
| 3,250 | 3,300 | 328 | 328 | 328 | 328 |
| 3,300 | 3,350 | 333 | 333 | 333 | 333 |
| 3,350 | 3,400 | 338 | 338 | 338 | 338 |
| 3,400 | 3,450 | 343 | 343 | 343 | 343 |
| 3,450 | 3,500 | 348 | 348 | 348 | 348 |
| 3,500 | 3,550 | 353 | 353 | 353 | 353 |
| 3,550 | 3,600 | 358 | 358 | 358 | 358 |
| 3,600 | 3,650 | 363 | 363 | 363 | 363 |
| 3,650 | 3,700 | 368 | 368 | 368 | 368 |
| 3,700 | 3,750 | 373 | 373 | 373 | 373 |
| 3,750 | 3,800 | 378 | 378 | 378 | 378 |
| 3,800 | 3,850 | 383 | 383 | 383 | 383 |
| 3,850 | 3,900 | 388 | 388 | 388 | 388 |
| 3,900 | 3,950 | 393 | 393 | 393 | 393 |
| 3,950 | 4,000 | 398 | 398 | 398 | 398 |
| **4,000** | | | | | |
| 4,000 | 4,050 | 403 | 403 | 403 | 403 |
| 4,050 | 4,100 | 408 | 408 | 408 | 408 |
| 4,100 | 4,150 | 413 | 413 | 413 | 413 |
| 4,150 | 4,200 | 418 | 418 | 418 | 418 |
| 4,200 | 4,250 | 423 | 423 | 423 | 423 |
| 4,250 | 4,300 | 428 | 428 | 428 | 428 |
| 4,300 | 4,350 | 433 | 433 | 433 | 433 |
| 4,350 | 4,400 | 438 | 438 | 438 | 438 |
| 4,400 | 4,450 | 443 | 443 | 443 | 443 |
| 4,450 | 4,500 | 448 | 448 | 448 | 448 |
| 4,500 | 4,550 | 453 | 453 | 453 | 453 |
| 4,550 | 4,600 | 458 | 458 | 458 | 458 |
| 4,600 | 4,650 | 463 | 463 | 463 | 463 |
| 4,650 | 4,700 | 468 | 468 | 468 | 468 |
| 4,700 | 4,750 | 473 | 473 | 473 | 473 |
| 4,750 | 4,800 | 478 | 478 | 478 | 478 |
| 4,800 | 4,850 | 483 | 483 | 483 | 483 |
| 4,850 | 4,900 | 488 | 488 | 488 | 488 |
| 4,900 | 4,950 | 493 | 493 | 493 | 493 |
| 4,950 | 5,000 | 498 | 498 | 498 | 498 |
| **5,000** | | | | | |
| 5,000 | 5,050 | 503 | 503 | 503 | 503 |
| 5,050 | 5,100 | 508 | 508 | 508 | 508 |
| 5,100 | 5,150 | 513 | 513 | 513 | 513 |
| 5,150 | 5,200 | 518 | 518 | 518 | 518 |
| 5,200 | 5,250 | 523 | 523 | 523 | 523 |
| 5,250 | 5,300 | 528 | 528 | 528 | 528 |
| 5,300 | 5,350 | 533 | 533 | 533 | 533 |
| 5,350 | 5,400 | 538 | 538 | 538 | 538 |
| 5,400 | 5,450 | 543 | 543 | 543 | 543 |
| 5,450 | 5,500 | 548 | 548 | 548 | 548 |
| 5,500 | 5,550 | 553 | 553 | 553 | 553 |
| 5,550 | 5,600 | 558 | 558 | 558 | 558 |
| 5,600 | 5,650 | 563 | 563 | 563 | 563 |
| 5,650 | 5,700 | 568 | 568 | 568 | 568 |
| 5,700 | 5,750 | 573 | 573 | 573 | 573 |
| 5,750 | 5,800 | 578 | 578 | 578 | 578 |
| 5,800 | 5,850 | 583 | 583 | 583 | 583 |
| 5,850 | 5,900 | 588 | 588 | 588 | 588 |
| 5,900 | 5,950 | 593 | 593 | 593 | 593 |
| 5,950 | 6,000 | 598 | 598 | 598 | 598 |

| If line 15 (taxable income) is— | | And you are— | | | |
|---|---|---|---|---|---|
| At least | But less than | Single | Married filing jointly* | Married filing separately | Head of a household |
| | | Your tax is— | | | |
| **6,000** | | | | | |
| 6,000 | 6,050 | 603 | 603 | 603 | 603 |
| 6,050 | 6,100 | 608 | 608 | 608 | 608 |
| 6,100 | 6,150 | 613 | 613 | 613 | 613 |
| 6,150 | 6,200 | 618 | 618 | 618 | 618 |
| 6,200 | 6,250 | 623 | 623 | 623 | 623 |
| 6,250 | 6,300 | 628 | 628 | 628 | 628 |
| 6,300 | 6,350 | 633 | 633 | 633 | 633 |
| 6,350 | 6,400 | 638 | 638 | 638 | 638 |
| 6,400 | 6,450 | 643 | 643 | 643 | 643 |
| 6,450 | 6,500 | 648 | 648 | 648 | 648 |
| 6,500 | 6,550 | 653 | 653 | 653 | 653 |
| 6,550 | 6,600 | 658 | 658 | 658 | 658 |
| 6,600 | 6,650 | 663 | 663 | 663 | 663 |
| 6,650 | 6,700 | 668 | 668 | 668 | 668 |
| 6,700 | 6,750 | 673 | 673 | 673 | 673 |
| 6,750 | 6,800 | 678 | 678 | 678 | 678 |
| 6,800 | 6,850 | 683 | 683 | 683 | 683 |
| 6,850 | 6,900 | 688 | 688 | 688 | 688 |
| 6,900 | 6,950 | 693 | 693 | 693 | 693 |
| 6,950 | 7,000 | 698 | 698 | 698 | 698 |
| **7,000** | | | | | |
| 7,000 | 7,050 | 703 | 703 | 703 | 703 |
| 7,050 | 7,100 | 708 | 708 | 708 | 708 |
| 7,100 | 7,150 | 713 | 713 | 713 | 713 |
| 7,150 | 7,200 | 718 | 718 | 718 | 718 |
| 7,200 | 7,250 | 723 | 723 | 723 | 723 |
| 7,250 | 7,300 | 728 | 728 | 728 | 728 |
| 7,300 | 7,350 | 733 | 733 | 733 | 733 |
| 7,350 | 7,400 | 738 | 738 | 738 | 738 |
| 7,400 | 7,450 | 743 | 743 | 743 | 743 |
| 7,450 | 7,500 | 748 | 748 | 748 | 748 |
| 7,500 | 7,550 | 753 | 753 | 753 | 753 |
| 7,550 | 7,600 | 758 | 758 | 758 | 758 |
| 7,600 | 7,650 | 763 | 763 | 763 | 763 |
| 7,650 | 7,700 | 768 | 768 | 768 | 768 |
| 7,700 | 7,750 | 773 | 773 | 773 | 773 |
| 7,750 | 7,800 | 778 | 778 | 778 | 778 |
| 7,800 | 7,850 | 783 | 783 | 783 | 783 |
| 7,850 | 7,900 | 788 | 788 | 788 | 788 |
| 7,900 | 7,950 | 793 | 793 | 793 | 793 |
| 7,950 | 8,000 | 798 | 798 | 798 | 798 |
| **8,000** | | | | | |
| 8,000 | 8,050 | 803 | 803 | 803 | 803 |
| 8,050 | 8,100 | 808 | 808 | 808 | 808 |
| 8,100 | 8,150 | 813 | 813 | 813 | 813 |
| 8,150 | 8,200 | 818 | 818 | 818 | 818 |
| 8,200 | 8,250 | 823 | 823 | 823 | 823 |
| 8,250 | 8,300 | 828 | 828 | 828 | 828 |
| 8,300 | 8,350 | 833 | 833 | 833 | 833 |
| 8,350 | 8,400 | 838 | 838 | 838 | 838 |
| 8,400 | 8,450 | 843 | 843 | 843 | 843 |
| 8,450 | 8,500 | 848 | 848 | 848 | 848 |
| 8,500 | 8,550 | 853 | 853 | 853 | 853 |
| 8,550 | 8,600 | 858 | 858 | 858 | 858 |
| 8,600 | 8,650 | 863 | 863 | 863 | 863 |
| 8,650 | 8,700 | 868 | 868 | 868 | 868 |
| 8,700 | 8,750 | 873 | 873 | 873 | 873 |
| 8,750 | 8,800 | 878 | 878 | 878 | 878 |
| 8,800 | 8,850 | 883 | 883 | 883 | 883 |
| 8,850 | 8,900 | 888 | 888 | 888 | 888 |
| 8,900 | 8,950 | 893 | 893 | 893 | 893 |
| 8,950 | 9,000 | 898 | 898 | 898 | 898 |

| If line 15 (taxable income) is— | | And you are— | | | |
|---|---|---|---|---|---|
| At least | But less than | Single | Married filing jointly* | Married filing separately | Head of a household |
| | | Your tax is— | | | |
| **9,000** | | | | | |
| 9,000 | 9,050 | 903 | 903 | 903 | 903 |
| 9,050 | 9,100 | 908 | 908 | 908 | 908 |
| 9,100 | 9,150 | 913 | 913 | 913 | 913 |
| 9,150 | 9,200 | 918 | 918 | 918 | 918 |
| 9,200 | 9,250 | 923 | 923 | 923 | 923 |
| 9,250 | 9,300 | 928 | 928 | 928 | 928 |
| 9,300 | 9,350 | 933 | 933 | 933 | 933 |
| 9,350 | 9,400 | 938 | 938 | 938 | 938 |
| 9,400 | 9,450 | 943 | 943 | 943 | 943 |
| 9,450 | 9,500 | 948 | 948 | 948 | 948 |
| 9,500 | 9,550 | 953 | 953 | 953 | 953 |
| 9,550 | 9,600 | 958 | 958 | 958 | 958 |
| 9,600 | 9,650 | 963 | 963 | 963 | 963 |
| 9,650 | 9,700 | 968 | 968 | 968 | 968 |
| 9,700 | 9,750 | 973 | 973 | 973 | 973 |
| 9,750 | 9,800 | 978 | 978 | 978 | 978 |
| 9,800 | 9,850 | 983 | 983 | 983 | 983 |
| 9,850 | 9,900 | 988 | 988 | 988 | 988 |
| 9,900 | 9,950 | 994 | 993 | 994 | 993 |
| 9,950 | 10,000 | 1,000 | 998 | 1,000 | 998 |
| **10,000** | | | | | |
| 10,000 | 10,050 | 1,006 | 1,003 | 1,006 | 1,003 |
| 10,050 | 10,100 | 1,012 | 1,008 | 1,012 | 1,008 |
| 10,100 | 10,150 | 1,018 | 1,013 | 1,018 | 1,013 |
| 10,150 | 10,200 | 1,024 | 1,018 | 1,024 | 1,018 |
| 10,200 | 10,250 | 1,030 | 1,023 | 1,030 | 1,023 |
| 10,250 | 10,300 | 1,036 | 1,028 | 1,036 | 1,028 |
| 10,300 | 10,350 | 1,042 | 1,033 | 1,042 | 1,033 |
| 10,350 | 10,400 | 1,048 | 1,038 | 1,048 | 1,038 |
| 10,400 | 10,450 | 1,054 | 1,043 | 1,054 | 1,043 |
| 10,450 | 10,500 | 1,060 | 1,048 | 1,060 | 1,048 |
| 10,500 | 10,550 | 1,066 | 1,053 | 1,066 | 1,053 |
| 10,550 | 10,600 | 1,072 | 1,058 | 1,072 | 1,058 |
| 10,600 | 10,650 | 1,078 | 1,063 | 1,078 | 1,063 |
| 10,650 | 10,700 | 1,084 | 1,068 | 1,084 | 1,068 |
| 10,700 | 10,750 | 1,090 | 1,073 | 1,090 | 1,073 |
| 10,750 | 10,800 | 1,096 | 1,078 | 1,096 | 1,078 |
| 10,800 | 10,850 | 1,102 | 1,083 | 1,102 | 1,083 |
| 10,850 | 10,900 | 1,108 | 1,088 | 1,108 | 1,088 |
| 10,900 | 10,950 | 1,114 | 1,093 | 1,114 | 1,093 |
| 10,950 | 11,000 | 1,120 | 1,098 | 1,120 | 1,098 |
| **11,000** | | | | | |
| 11,000 | 11,050 | 1,126 | 1,103 | 1,126 | 1,103 |
| 11,050 | 11,100 | 1,132 | 1,108 | 1,132 | 1,108 |
| 11,100 | 11,150 | 1,138 | 1,113 | 1,138 | 1,113 |
| 11,150 | 11,200 | 1,144 | 1,118 | 1,144 | 1,118 |
| 11,200 | 11,250 | 1,150 | 1,123 | 1,150 | 1,123 |
| 11,250 | 11,300 | 1,156 | 1,128 | 1,156 | 1,128 |
| 11,300 | 11,350 | 1,162 | 1,133 | 1,162 | 1,133 |
| 11,350 | 11,400 | 1,168 | 1,138 | 1,168 | 1,138 |
| 11,400 | 11,450 | 1,174 | 1,143 | 1,174 | 1,143 |
| 11,450 | 11,500 | 1,180 | 1,148 | 1,180 | 1,148 |
| 11,500 | 11,550 | 1,186 | 1,153 | 1,186 | 1,153 |
| 11,550 | 11,600 | 1,192 | 1,158 | 1,192 | 1,158 |
| 11,600 | 11,650 | 1,198 | 1,163 | 1,198 | 1,163 |
| 11,650 | 11,700 | 1,204 | 1,168 | 1,204 | 1,168 |
| 11,700 | 11,750 | 1,210 | 1,173 | 1,210 | 1,173 |
| 11,750 | 11,800 | 1,216 | 1,178 | 1,216 | 1,178 |
| 11,800 | 11,850 | 1,222 | 1,183 | 1,222 | 1,183 |
| 11,850 | 11,900 | 1,228 | 1,188 | 1,228 | 1,188 |
| 11,900 | 11,950 | 1,234 | 1,193 | 1,234 | 1,193 |
| 11,950 | 12,000 | 1,240 | 1,198 | 1,240 | 1,198 |

*(Continued)*

*This column must also be used by a qualifying widow(er).

## 2020 Tax Table — *Continued*

| If line 15 (taxable income) is— At least | But less than | Single | Married filing jointly* | Married filing separately | Head of a household |
|---|---|---|---|---|---|
| **12,000** | | | | | |
| 12,000 | 12,050 | 1,246 | 1,203 | 1,246 | 1,203 |
| 12,050 | 12,100 | 1,252 | 1,208 | 1,252 | 1,208 |
| 12,100 | 12,150 | 1,258 | 1,213 | 1,258 | 1,213 |
| 12,150 | 12,200 | 1,264 | 1,218 | 1,264 | 1,218 |
| 12,200 | 12,250 | 1,270 | 1,223 | 1,270 | 1,223 |
| 12,250 | 12,300 | 1,276 | 1,228 | 1,276 | 1,228 |
| 12,300 | 12,350 | 1,282 | 1,233 | 1,282 | 1,233 |
| 12,350 | 12,400 | 1,288 | 1,238 | 1,288 | 1,238 |
| 12,400 | 12,450 | 1,294 | 1,243 | 1,294 | 1,243 |
| 12,450 | 12,500 | 1,300 | 1,248 | 1,300 | 1,248 |
| 12,500 | 12,550 | 1,306 | 1,253 | 1,306 | 1,253 |
| 12,550 | 12,600 | 1,312 | 1,258 | 1,312 | 1,258 |
| 12,600 | 12,650 | 1,318 | 1,263 | 1,318 | 1,263 |
| 12,650 | 12,700 | 1,324 | 1,268 | 1,324 | 1,268 |
| 12,700 | 12,750 | 1,330 | 1,273 | 1,330 | 1,273 |
| 12,750 | 12,800 | 1,336 | 1,278 | 1,336 | 1,278 |
| 12,800 | 12,850 | 1,342 | 1,283 | 1,342 | 1,283 |
| 12,850 | 12,900 | 1,348 | 1,288 | 1,348 | 1,288 |
| 12,900 | 12,950 | 1,354 | 1,293 | 1,354 | 1,293 |
| 12,950 | 13,000 | 1,360 | 1,298 | 1,360 | 1,298 |
| **13,000** | | | | | |
| 13,000 | 13,050 | 1,366 | 1,303 | 1,366 | 1,303 |
| 13,050 | 13,100 | 1,372 | 1,308 | 1,372 | 1,308 |
| 13,100 | 13,150 | 1,378 | 1,313 | 1,378 | 1,313 |
| 13,150 | 13,200 | 1,384 | 1,318 | 1,384 | 1,318 |
| 13,200 | 13,250 | 1,390 | 1,323 | 1,390 | 1,323 |
| 13,250 | 13,300 | 1,396 | 1,328 | 1,396 | 1,328 |
| 13,300 | 13,350 | 1,402 | 1,333 | 1,402 | 1,333 |
| 13,350 | 13,400 | 1,408 | 1,338 | 1,408 | 1,338 |
| 13,400 | 13,450 | 1,414 | 1,343 | 1,414 | 1,343 |
| 13,450 | 13,500 | 1,420 | 1,348 | 1,420 | 1,348 |
| 13,500 | 13,550 | 1,426 | 1,353 | 1,426 | 1,353 |
| 13,550 | 13,600 | 1,432 | 1,358 | 1,432 | 1,358 |
| 13,600 | 13,650 | 1,438 | 1,363 | 1,438 | 1,363 |
| 13,650 | 13,700 | 1,444 | 1,368 | 1,444 | 1,368 |
| 13,700 | 13,750 | 1,450 | 1,373 | 1,450 | 1,373 |
| 13,750 | 13,800 | 1,456 | 1,378 | 1,456 | 1,378 |
| 13,800 | 13,850 | 1,462 | 1,383 | 1,462 | 1,383 |
| 13,850 | 13,900 | 1,468 | 1,388 | 1,468 | 1,388 |
| 13,900 | 13,950 | 1,474 | 1,393 | 1,474 | 1,393 |
| 13,950 | 14,000 | 1,480 | 1,398 | 1,480 | 1,398 |
| **14,000** | | | | | |
| 14,000 | 14,050 | 1,486 | 1,403 | 1,486 | 1,403 |
| 14,050 | 14,100 | 1,492 | 1,408 | 1,492 | 1,408 |
| 14,100 | 14,150 | 1,498 | 1,413 | 1,498 | 1,413 |
| 14,150 | 14,200 | 1,504 | 1,418 | 1,504 | 1,419 |
| 14,200 | 14,250 | 1,510 | 1,423 | 1,510 | 1,425 |
| 14,250 | 14,300 | 1,516 | 1,428 | 1,516 | 1,431 |
| 14,300 | 14,350 | 1,522 | 1,433 | 1,522 | 1,437 |
| 14,350 | 14,400 | 1,528 | 1,438 | 1,528 | 1,443 |
| 14,400 | 14,450 | 1,534 | 1,443 | 1,534 | 1,449 |
| 14,450 | 14,500 | 1,540 | 1,448 | 1,540 | 1,455 |
| 14,500 | 14,550 | 1,546 | 1,453 | 1,546 | 1,461 |
| 14,550 | 14,600 | 1,552 | 1,458 | 1,552 | 1,467 |
| 14,600 | 14,650 | 1,558 | 1,463 | 1,558 | 1,473 |
| 14,650 | 14,700 | 1,564 | 1,468 | 1,564 | 1,479 |
| 14,700 | 14,750 | 1,570 | 1,473 | 1,570 | 1,485 |
| 14,750 | 14,800 | 1,576 | 1,478 | 1,576 | 1,491 |
| 14,800 | 14,850 | 1,582 | 1,483 | 1,582 | 1,497 |
| 14,850 | 14,900 | 1,588 | 1,488 | 1,588 | 1,503 |
| 14,900 | 14,950 | 1,594 | 1,493 | 1,594 | 1,509 |
| 14,950 | 15,000 | 1,600 | 1,498 | 1,600 | 1,515 |
| **15,000** | | | | | |
| 15,000 | 15,050 | 1,606 | 1,503 | 1,606 | 1,521 |
| 15,050 | 15,100 | 1,612 | 1,508 | 1,612 | 1,527 |
| 15,100 | 15,150 | 1,618 | 1,513 | 1,618 | 1,533 |
| 15,150 | 15,200 | 1,624 | 1,518 | 1,624 | 1,539 |
| 15,200 | 15,250 | 1,630 | 1,523 | 1,630 | 1,545 |
| 15,250 | 15,300 | 1,636 | 1,528 | 1,636 | 1,551 |
| 15,300 | 15,350 | 1,642 | 1,533 | 1,642 | 1,557 |
| 15,350 | 15,400 | 1,648 | 1,538 | 1,648 | 1,563 |
| 15,400 | 15,450 | 1,654 | 1,543 | 1,654 | 1,569 |
| 15,450 | 15,500 | 1,660 | 1,548 | 1,660 | 1,575 |
| 15,500 | 15,550 | 1,666 | 1,553 | 1,666 | 1,581 |
| 15,550 | 15,600 | 1,672 | 1,558 | 1,672 | 1,587 |
| 15,600 | 15,650 | 1,678 | 1,563 | 1,678 | 1,593 |
| 15,650 | 15,700 | 1,684 | 1,568 | 1,684 | 1,599 |
| 15,700 | 15,750 | 1,690 | 1,573 | 1,690 | 1,605 |
| 15,750 | 15,800 | 1,696 | 1,578 | 1,696 | 1,611 |
| 15,800 | 15,850 | 1,702 | 1,583 | 1,702 | 1,617 |
| 15,850 | 15,900 | 1,708 | 1,588 | 1,708 | 1,623 |
| 15,900 | 15,950 | 1,714 | 1,593 | 1,714 | 1,629 |
| 15,950 | 16,000 | 1,720 | 1,598 | 1,720 | 1,635 |
| **16,000** | | | | | |
| 16,000 | 16,050 | 1,726 | 1,603 | 1,726 | 1,641 |
| 16,050 | 16,100 | 1,732 | 1,608 | 1,732 | 1,647 |
| 16,100 | 16,150 | 1,738 | 1,613 | 1,738 | 1,653 |
| 16,150 | 16,200 | 1,744 | 1,618 | 1,744 | 1,659 |
| 16,200 | 16,250 | 1,750 | 1,623 | 1,750 | 1,665 |
| 16,250 | 16,300 | 1,756 | 1,628 | 1,756 | 1,671 |
| 16,300 | 16,350 | 1,762 | 1,633 | 1,762 | 1,677 |
| 16,350 | 16,400 | 1,768 | 1,638 | 1,768 | 1,683 |
| 16,400 | 16,450 | 1,774 | 1,643 | 1,774 | 1,689 |
| 16,450 | 16,500 | 1,780 | 1,648 | 1,780 | 1,695 |
| 16,500 | 16,550 | 1,786 | 1,653 | 1,786 | 1,701 |
| 16,550 | 16,600 | 1,792 | 1,658 | 1,792 | 1,707 |
| 16,600 | 16,650 | 1,798 | 1,663 | 1,798 | 1,713 |
| 16,650 | 16,700 | 1,804 | 1,668 | 1,804 | 1,719 |
| 16,700 | 16,750 | 1,810 | 1,673 | 1,810 | 1,725 |
| 16,750 | 16,800 | 1,816 | 1,678 | 1,816 | 1,731 |
| 16,800 | 16,850 | 1,822 | 1,683 | 1,822 | 1,737 |
| 16,850 | 16,900 | 1,828 | 1,688 | 1,828 | 1,743 |
| 16,900 | 16,950 | 1,834 | 1,693 | 1,834 | 1,749 |
| 16,950 | 17,000 | 1,840 | 1,698 | 1,840 | 1,755 |
| **17,000** | | | | | |
| 17,000 | 17,050 | 1,846 | 1,703 | 1,846 | 1,761 |
| 17,050 | 17,100 | 1,852 | 1,708 | 1,852 | 1,767 |
| 17,100 | 17,150 | 1,858 | 1,713 | 1,858 | 1,773 |
| 17,150 | 17,200 | 1,864 | 1,718 | 1,864 | 1,779 |
| 17,200 | 17,250 | 1,870 | 1,723 | 1,870 | 1,785 |
| 17,250 | 17,300 | 1,876 | 1,728 | 1,876 | 1,791 |
| 17,300 | 17,350 | 1,882 | 1,733 | 1,882 | 1,797 |
| 17,350 | 17,400 | 1,888 | 1,738 | 1,888 | 1,803 |
| 17,400 | 17,450 | 1,894 | 1,743 | 1,894 | 1,809 |
| 17,450 | 17,500 | 1,900 | 1,748 | 1,900 | 1,815 |
| 17,500 | 17,550 | 1,906 | 1,753 | 1,906 | 1,821 |
| 17,550 | 17,600 | 1,912 | 1,758 | 1,912 | 1,827 |
| 17,600 | 17,650 | 1,918 | 1,763 | 1,918 | 1,833 |
| 17,650 | 17,700 | 1,924 | 1,768 | 1,924 | 1,839 |
| 17,700 | 17,750 | 1,930 | 1,773 | 1,930 | 1,845 |
| 17,750 | 17,800 | 1,936 | 1,778 | 1,936 | 1,851 |
| 17,800 | 17,850 | 1,942 | 1,783 | 1,942 | 1,857 |
| 17,850 | 17,900 | 1,948 | 1,788 | 1,948 | 1,863 |
| 17,900 | 17,950 | 1,954 | 1,793 | 1,954 | 1,869 |
| 17,950 | 18,000 | 1,960 | 1,798 | 1,960 | 1,875 |
| **18,000** | | | | | |
| 18,000 | 18,050 | 1,966 | 1,803 | 1,966 | 1,881 |
| 18,050 | 18,100 | 1,972 | 1,808 | 1,972 | 1,887 |
| 18,100 | 18,150 | 1,978 | 1,813 | 1,978 | 1,893 |
| 18,150 | 18,200 | 1,984 | 1,818 | 1,984 | 1,899 |
| 18,200 | 18,250 | 1,990 | 1,823 | 1,990 | 1,905 |
| 18,250 | 18,300 | 1,996 | 1,828 | 1,996 | 1,911 |
| 18,300 | 18,350 | 2,002 | 1,833 | 2,002 | 1,917 |
| 18,350 | 18,400 | 2,008 | 1,838 | 2,008 | 1,923 |
| 18,400 | 18,450 | 2,014 | 1,843 | 2,014 | 1,929 |
| 18,450 | 18,500 | 2,020 | 1,848 | 2,020 | 1,935 |
| 18,500 | 18,550 | 2,026 | 1,853 | 2,026 | 1,941 |
| 18,550 | 18,600 | 2,032 | 1,858 | 2,032 | 1,947 |
| 18,600 | 18,650 | 2,038 | 1,863 | 2,038 | 1,953 |
| 18,650 | 18,700 | 2,044 | 1,868 | 2,044 | 1,959 |
| 18,700 | 18,750 | 2,050 | 1,873 | 2,050 | 1,965 |
| 18,750 | 18,800 | 2,056 | 1,878 | 2,056 | 1,971 |
| 18,800 | 18,850 | 2,062 | 1,883 | 2,062 | 1,977 |
| 18,850 | 18,900 | 2,068 | 1,888 | 2,068 | 1,983 |
| 18,900 | 18,950 | 2,074 | 1,893 | 2,074 | 1,989 |
| 18,950 | 19,000 | 2,080 | 1,898 | 2,080 | 1,995 |
| **19,000** | | | | | |
| 19,000 | 19,050 | 2,086 | 1,903 | 2,086 | 2,001 |
| 19,050 | 19,100 | 2,092 | 1,908 | 2,092 | 2,007 |
| 19,100 | 19,150 | 2,098 | 1,913 | 2,098 | 2,013 |
| 19,150 | 19,200 | 2,104 | 1,918 | 2,104 | 2,019 |
| 19,200 | 19,250 | 2,110 | 1,923 | 2,110 | 2,025 |
| 19,250 | 19,300 | 2,116 | 1,928 | 2,116 | 2,031 |
| 19,300 | 19,350 | 2,122 | 1,933 | 2,122 | 2,037 |
| 19,350 | 19,400 | 2,128 | 1,938 | 2,128 | 2,043 |
| 19,400 | 19,450 | 2,134 | 1,943 | 2,134 | 2,049 |
| 19,450 | 19,500 | 2,140 | 1,948 | 2,140 | 2,055 |
| 19,500 | 19,550 | 2,146 | 1,953 | 2,146 | 2,061 |
| 19,550 | 19,600 | 2,152 | 1,958 | 2,152 | 2,067 |
| 19,600 | 19,650 | 2,158 | 1,963 | 2,158 | 2,073 |
| 19,650 | 19,700 | 2,164 | 1,968 | 2,164 | 2,079 |
| 19,700 | 19,750 | 2,170 | 1,973 | 2,170 | 2,085 |
| 19,750 | 19,800 | 2,176 | 1,978 | 2,176 | 2,091 |
| 19,800 | 19,850 | 2,182 | 1,984 | 2,182 | 2,097 |
| 19,850 | 19,900 | 2,188 | 1,990 | 2,188 | 2,103 |
| 19,900 | 19,950 | 2,194 | 1,996 | 2,194 | 2,109 |
| 19,950 | 20,000 | 2,200 | 2,002 | 2,200 | 2,115 |
| **20,000** | | | | | |
| 20,000 | 20,050 | 2,206 | 2,008 | 2,206 | 2,121 |
| 20,050 | 20,100 | 2,212 | 2,014 | 2,212 | 2,127 |
| 20,100 | 20,150 | 2,218 | 2,020 | 2,218 | 2,133 |
| 20,150 | 20,200 | 2,224 | 2,026 | 2,224 | 2,139 |
| 20,200 | 20,250 | 2,230 | 2,032 | 2,230 | 2,145 |
| 20,250 | 20,300 | 2,236 | 2,038 | 2,236 | 2,151 |
| 20,300 | 20,350 | 2,242 | 2,044 | 2,242 | 2,157 |
| 20,350 | 20,400 | 2,248 | 2,050 | 2,248 | 2,163 |
| 20,400 | 20,450 | 2,254 | 2,056 | 2,254 | 2,169 |
| 20,450 | 20,500 | 2,260 | 2,062 | 2,260 | 2,175 |
| 20,500 | 20,550 | 2,266 | 2,068 | 2,266 | 2,181 |
| 20,550 | 20,600 | 2,272 | 2,074 | 2,272 | 2,187 |
| 20,600 | 20,650 | 2,278 | 2,080 | 2,278 | 2,193 |
| 20,650 | 20,700 | 2,284 | 2,086 | 2,284 | 2,199 |
| 20,700 | 20,750 | 2,290 | 2,092 | 2,290 | 2,205 |
| 20,750 | 20,800 | 2,296 | 2,098 | 2,296 | 2,211 |
| 20,800 | 20,850 | 2,302 | 2,104 | 2,302 | 2,217 |
| 20,850 | 20,900 | 2,308 | 2,110 | 2,308 | 2,223 |
| 20,900 | 20,950 | 2,314 | 2,116 | 2,314 | 2,229 |
| 20,950 | 21,000 | 2,320 | 2,122 | 2,320 | 2,235 |

Your tax is— (values in the Single through Head of a household columns)

*(Continued)*

*This column must also be used by a qualifying widow(er).

## 2020 Tax Table — *Continued*

| If line 15 (taxable income) is— At least | But less than | And you are— Single | Married filing jointly* | Married filing sepa-rately | Head of a house-hold |
|---|---|---|---|---|---|
| | | Your tax is— | | | |
| **21,000** | | | | | |
| 21,000 | 21,050 | 2,326 | 2,128 | 2,326 | 2,241 |
| 21,050 | 21,100 | 2,332 | 2,134 | 2,332 | 2,247 |
| 21,100 | 21,150 | 2,338 | 2,140 | 2,338 | 2,253 |
| 21,150 | 21,200 | 2,344 | 2,146 | 2,344 | 2,259 |
| 21,200 | 21,250 | 2,350 | 2,152 | 2,350 | 2,265 |
| 21,250 | 21,300 | 2,356 | 2,158 | 2,356 | 2,271 |
| 21,300 | 21,350 | 2,362 | 2,164 | 2,362 | 2,277 |
| 21,350 | 21,400 | 2,368 | 2,170 | 2,368 | 2,283 |
| 21,400 | 21,450 | 2,374 | 2,176 | 2,374 | 2,289 |
| 21,450 | 21,500 | 2,380 | 2,182 | 2,380 | 2,295 |
| 21,500 | 21,550 | 2,386 | 2,188 | 2,386 | 2,301 |
| 21,550 | 21,600 | 2,392 | 2,194 | 2,392 | 2,307 |
| 21,600 | 21,650 | 2,398 | 2,200 | 2,398 | 2,313 |
| 21,650 | 21,700 | 2,404 | 2,206 | 2,404 | 2,319 |
| 21,700 | 21,750 | 2,410 | 2,212 | 2,410 | 2,325 |
| 21,750 | 21,800 | 2,416 | 2,218 | 2,416 | 2,331 |
| 21,800 | 21,850 | 2,422 | 2,224 | 2,422 | 2,337 |
| 21,850 | 21,900 | 2,428 | 2,230 | 2,428 | 2,343 |
| 21,900 | 21,950 | 2,434 | 2,236 | 2,434 | 2,349 |
| 21,950 | 22,000 | 2,440 | 2,242 | 2,440 | 2,355 |
| **22,000** | | | | | |
| 22,000 | 22,050 | 2,446 | 2,248 | 2,446 | 2,361 |
| 22,050 | 22,100 | 2,452 | 2,254 | 2,452 | 2,367 |
| 22,100 | 22,150 | 2,458 | 2,260 | 2,458 | 2,373 |
| 22,150 | 22,200 | 2,464 | 2,266 | 2,464 | 2,379 |
| 22,200 | 22,250 | 2,470 | 2,272 | 2,470 | 2,385 |
| 22,250 | 22,300 | 2,476 | 2,278 | 2,476 | 2,391 |
| 22,300 | 22,350 | 2,482 | 2,284 | 2,482 | 2,397 |
| 22,350 | 22,400 | 2,488 | 2,290 | 2,488 | 2,403 |
| 22,400 | 22,450 | 2,494 | 2,296 | 2,494 | 2,409 |
| 22,450 | 22,500 | 2,500 | 2,302 | 2,500 | 2,415 |
| 22,500 | 22,550 | 2,506 | 2,308 | 2,506 | 2,421 |
| 22,550 | 22,600 | 2,512 | 2,314 | 2,512 | 2,427 |
| 22,600 | 22,650 | 2,518 | 2,320 | 2,518 | 2,433 |
| 22,650 | 22,700 | 2,524 | 2,326 | 2,524 | 2,439 |
| 22,700 | 22,750 | 2,530 | 2,332 | 2,530 | 2,445 |
| 22,750 | 22,800 | 2,536 | 2,338 | 2,536 | 2,451 |
| 22,800 | 22,850 | 2,542 | 2,344 | 2,542 | 2,457 |
| 22,850 | 22,900 | 2,548 | 2,350 | 2,548 | 2,463 |
| 22,900 | 22,950 | 2,554 | 2,356 | 2,554 | 2,469 |
| 22,950 | 23,000 | 2,560 | 2,362 | 2,560 | 2,475 |
| **23,000** | | | | | |
| 23,000 | 23,050 | 2,566 | 2,368 | 2,566 | 2,481 |
| 23,050 | 23,100 | 2,572 | 2,374 | 2,572 | 2,487 |
| 23,100 | 23,150 | 2,578 | 2,380 | 2,578 | 2,493 |
| 23,150 | 23,200 | 2,584 | 2,386 | 2,584 | 2,499 |
| 23,200 | 23,250 | 2,590 | 2,392 | 2,590 | 2,505 |
| 23,250 | 23,300 | 2,596 | 2,398 | 2,596 | 2,511 |
| 23,300 | 23,350 | 2,602 | 2,404 | 2,602 | 2,517 |
| 23,350 | 23,400 | 2,608 | 2,410 | 2,608 | 2,523 |
| 23,400 | 23,450 | 2,614 | 2,416 | 2,614 | 2,529 |
| 23,450 | 23,500 | 2,620 | 2,422 | 2,620 | 2,535 |
| 23,500 | 23,550 | 2,626 | 2,428 | 2,626 | 2,541 |
| 23,550 | 23,600 | 2,632 | 2,434 | 2,632 | 2,547 |
| 23,600 | 23,650 | 2,638 | 2,440 | 2,638 | 2,553 |
| 23,650 | 23,700 | 2,644 | 2,446 | 2,644 | 2,559 |
| 23,700 | 23,750 | 2,650 | 2,452 | 2,650 | 2,565 |
| 23,750 | 23,800 | 2,656 | 2,458 | 2,656 | 2,571 |
| 23,800 | 23,850 | 2,662 | 2,464 | 2,662 | 2,577 |
| 23,850 | 23,900 | 2,668 | 2,470 | 2,668 | 2,583 |
| 23,900 | 23,950 | 2,674 | 2,476 | 2,674 | 2,589 |
| 23,950 | 24,000 | 2,680 | 2,482 | 2,680 | 2,595 |
| **24,000** | | | | | |
| 24,000 | 24,050 | 2,686 | 2,488 | 2,686 | 2,601 |
| 24,050 | 24,100 | 2,692 | 2,494 | 2,692 | 2,607 |
| 24,100 | 24,150 | 2,698 | 2,500 | 2,698 | 2,613 |
| 24,150 | 24,200 | 2,704 | 2,506 | 2,704 | 2,619 |
| 24,200 | 24,250 | 2,710 | 2,512 | 2,710 | 2,625 |
| 24,250 | 24,300 | 2,716 | 2,518 | 2,716 | 2,631 |
| 24,300 | 24,350 | 2,722 | 2,524 | 2,722 | 2,637 |
| 24,350 | 24,400 | 2,728 | 2,530 | 2,728 | 2,643 |
| 24,400 | 24,450 | 2,734 | 2,536 | 2,734 | 2,649 |
| 24,450 | 24,500 | 2,740 | 2,542 | 2,740 | 2,655 |
| 24,500 | 24,550 | 2,746 | 2,548 | 2,746 | 2,661 |
| 24,550 | 24,600 | 2,752 | 2,554 | 2,752 | 2,667 |
| 24,600 | 24,650 | 2,758 | 2,560 | 2,758 | 2,673 |
| 24,650 | 24,700 | 2,764 | 2,566 | 2,764 | 2,679 |
| 24,700 | 24,750 | 2,770 | 2,572 | 2,770 | 2,685 |
| 24,750 | 24,800 | 2,776 | 2,578 | 2,776 | 2,691 |
| 24,800 | 24,850 | 2,782 | 2,584 | 2,782 | 2,697 |
| 24,850 | 24,900 | 2,788 | 2,590 | 2,788 | 2,703 |
| 24,900 | 24,950 | 2,794 | 2,596 | 2,794 | 2,709 |
| 24,950 | 25,000 | 2,800 | 2,602 | 2,800 | 2,715 |
| **25,000** | | | | | |
| 25,000 | 25,050 | 2,806 | 2,608 | 2,806 | 2,721 |
| 25,050 | 25,100 | 2,812 | 2,614 | 2,812 | 2,727 |
| 25,100 | 25,150 | 2,818 | 2,620 | 2,818 | 2,733 |
| 25,150 | 25,200 | 2,824 | 2,626 | 2,824 | 2,739 |
| 25,200 | 25,250 | 2,830 | 2,632 | 2,830 | 2,745 |
| 25,250 | 25,300 | 2,836 | 2,638 | 2,836 | 2,751 |
| 25,300 | 25,350 | 2,842 | 2,644 | 2,842 | 2,757 |
| 25,350 | 25,400 | 2,848 | 2,650 | 2,848 | 2,763 |
| 25,400 | 25,450 | 2,854 | 2,656 | 2,854 | 2,769 |
| 25,450 | 25,500 | 2,860 | 2,662 | 2,860 | 2,775 |
| 25,500 | 25,550 | 2,866 | 2,668 | 2,866 | 2,781 |
| 25,550 | 25,600 | 2,872 | 2,674 | 2,872 | 2,787 |
| 25,600 | 25,650 | 2,878 | 2,680 | 2,878 | 2,793 |
| 25,650 | 25,700 | 2,884 | 2,686 | 2,884 | 2,799 |
| 25,700 | 25,750 | 2,890 | 2,692 | 2,890 | 2,805 |
| 25,750 | 25,800 | 2,896 | 2,698 | 2,896 | 2,811 |
| 25,800 | 25,850 | 2,902 | 2,704 | 2,902 | 2,817 |
| 25,850 | 25,900 | 2,908 | 2,710 | 2,908 | 2,823 |
| 25,900 | 25,950 | 2,914 | 2,716 | 2,914 | 2,829 |
| 25,950 | 26,000 | 2,920 | 2,722 | 2,920 | 2,835 |
| **26,000** | | | | | |
| 26,000 | 26,050 | 2,926 | 2,728 | 2,926 | 2,841 |
| 26,050 | 26,100 | 2,932 | 2,734 | 2,932 | 2,847 |
| 26,100 | 26,150 | 2,938 | 2,740 | 2,938 | 2,853 |
| 26,150 | 26,200 | 2,944 | 2,746 | 2,944 | 2,859 |
| 26,200 | 26,250 | 2,950 | 2,752 | 2,950 | 2,865 |
| 26,250 | 26,300 | 2,956 | 2,758 | 2,956 | 2,871 |
| 26,300 | 26,350 | 2,962 | 2,764 | 2,962 | 2,877 |
| 26,350 | 26,400 | 2,968 | 2,770 | 2,968 | 2,883 |
| 26,400 | 26,450 | 2,974 | 2,776 | 2,974 | 2,889 |
| 26,450 | 26,500 | 2,980 | 2,782 | 2,980 | 2,895 |
| 26,500 | 26,550 | 2,986 | 2,788 | 2,986 | 2,901 |
| 26,550 | 26,600 | 2,992 | 2,794 | 2,992 | 2,907 |
| 26,600 | 26,650 | 2,998 | 2,800 | 2,998 | 2,913 |
| 26,650 | 26,700 | 3,004 | 2,806 | 3,004 | 2,919 |
| 26,700 | 26,750 | 3,010 | 2,812 | 3,010 | 2,925 |
| 26,750 | 26,800 | 3,016 | 2,818 | 3,016 | 2,931 |
| 26,800 | 26,850 | 3,022 | 2,824 | 3,022 | 2,937 |
| 26,850 | 26,900 | 3,028 | 2,830 | 3,028 | 2,943 |
| 26,900 | 26,950 | 3,034 | 2,836 | 3,034 | 2,949 |
| 26,950 | 27,000 | 3,040 | 2,842 | 3,040 | 2,955 |
| **27,000** | | | | | |
| 27,000 | 27,050 | 3,046 | 2,848 | 3,046 | 2,961 |
| 27,050 | 27,100 | 3,052 | 2,854 | 3,052 | 2,967 |
| 27,100 | 27,150 | 3,058 | 2,860 | 3,058 | 2,973 |
| 27,150 | 27,200 | 3,064 | 2,866 | 3,064 | 2,979 |
| 27,200 | 27,250 | 3,070 | 2,872 | 3,070 | 2,985 |
| 27,250 | 27,300 | 3,076 | 2,878 | 3,076 | 2,991 |
| 27,300 | 27,350 | 3,082 | 2,884 | 3,082 | 2,997 |
| 27,350 | 27,400 | 3,088 | 2,890 | 3,088 | 3,003 |
| 27,400 | 27,450 | 3,094 | 2,896 | 3,094 | 3,009 |
| 27,450 | 27,500 | 3,100 | 2,902 | 3,100 | 3,015 |
| 27,500 | 27,550 | 3,106 | 2,908 | 3,106 | 3,021 |
| 27,550 | 27,600 | 3,112 | 2,914 | 3,112 | 3,027 |
| 27,600 | 27,650 | 3,118 | 2,920 | 3,118 | 3,033 |
| 27,650 | 27,700 | 3,124 | 2,926 | 3,124 | 3,039 |
| 27,700 | 27,750 | 3,130 | 2,932 | 3,130 | 3,045 |
| 27,750 | 27,800 | 3,136 | 2,938 | 3,136 | 3,051 |
| 27,800 | 27,850 | 3,142 | 2,944 | 3,142 | 3,057 |
| 27,850 | 27,900 | 3,148 | 2,950 | 3,148 | 3,063 |
| 27,900 | 27,950 | 3,154 | 2,956 | 3,154 | 3,069 |
| 27,950 | 28,000 | 3,160 | 2,962 | 3,160 | 3,075 |
| **28,000** | | | | | |
| 28,000 | 28,050 | 3,166 | 2,968 | 3,166 | 3,081 |
| 28,050 | 28,100 | 3,172 | 2,974 | 3,172 | 3,087 |
| 28,100 | 28,150 | 3,178 | 2,980 | 3,178 | 3,093 |
| 28,150 | 28,200 | 3,184 | 2,986 | 3,184 | 3,099 |
| 28,200 | 28,250 | 3,190 | 2,992 | 3,190 | 3,105 |
| 28,250 | 28,300 | 3,196 | 2,998 | 3,196 | 3,111 |
| 28,300 | 28,350 | 3,202 | 3,004 | 3,202 | 3,117 |
| 28,350 | 28,400 | 3,208 | 3,010 | 3,208 | 3,123 |
| 28,400 | 28,450 | 3,214 | 3,016 | 3,214 | 3,129 |
| 28,450 | 28,500 | 3,220 | 3,022 | 3,220 | 3,135 |
| 28,500 | 28,550 | 3,226 | 3,028 | 3,226 | 3,141 |
| 28,550 | 28,600 | 3,232 | 3,034 | 3,232 | 3,147 |
| 28,600 | 28,650 | 3,238 | 3,040 | 3,238 | 3,153 |
| 28,650 | 28,700 | 3,244 | 3,046 | 3,244 | 3,159 |
| 28,700 | 28,750 | 3,250 | 3,052 | 3,250 | 3,165 |
| 28,750 | 28,800 | 3,256 | 3,058 | 3,256 | 3,171 |
| 28,800 | 28,850 | 3,262 | 3,064 | 3,262 | 3,177 |
| 28,850 | 28,900 | 3,268 | 3,070 | 3,268 | 3,183 |
| 28,900 | 28,950 | 3,274 | 3,076 | 3,274 | 3,189 |
| 28,950 | 29,000 | 3,280 | 3,082 | 3,280 | 3,195 |
| **29,000** | | | | | |
| 29,000 | 29,050 | 3,286 | 3,088 | 3,286 | 3,201 |
| 29,050 | 29,100 | 3,292 | 3,094 | 3,292 | 3,207 |
| 29,100 | 29,150 | 3,298 | 3,100 | 3,298 | 3,213 |
| 29,150 | 29,200 | 3,304 | 3,106 | 3,304 | 3,219 |
| 29,200 | 29,250 | 3,310 | 3,112 | 3,310 | 3,225 |
| 29,250 | 29,300 | 3,316 | 3,118 | 3,316 | 3,231 |
| 29,300 | 29,350 | 3,322 | 3,124 | 3,322 | 3,237 |
| 29,350 | 29,400 | 3,328 | 3,130 | 3,328 | 3,243 |
| 29,400 | 29,450 | 3,334 | 3,136 | 3,334 | 3,249 |
| 29,450 | 29,500 | 3,340 | 3,142 | 3,340 | 3,255 |
| 29,500 | 29,550 | 3,346 | 3,148 | 3,346 | 3,261 |
| 29,550 | 29,600 | 3,352 | 3,154 | 3,352 | 3,267 |
| 29,600 | 29,650 | 3,358 | 3,160 | 3,358 | 3,273 |
| 29,650 | 29,700 | 3,364 | 3,166 | 3,364 | 3,279 |
| 29,700 | 29,750 | 3,370 | 3,172 | 3,370 | 3,285 |
| 29,750 | 29,800 | 3,376 | 3,178 | 3,376 | 3,291 |
| 29,800 | 29,850 | 3,382 | 3,184 | 3,382 | 3,297 |
| 29,850 | 29,900 | 3,388 | 3,190 | 3,388 | 3,303 |
| 29,900 | 29,950 | 3,394 | 3,196 | 3,394 | 3,309 |
| 29,950 | 30,000 | 3,400 | 3,202 | 3,400 | 3,315 |

*This column must also be used by a qualifying widow(er).

*(Continued)*

## 2020 Tax Table — *Continued*

| If line 15 (taxable income) is— | | And you are— | | | |
|---|---|---|---|---|---|
| At least | But less than | Single | Married filing jointly* | Married filing sepa-rately | Head of a house-hold |
| | | Your tax is— | | | |
| **30,000** | | | | | |
| 30,000 | 30,050 | 3,406 | 3,208 | 3,406 | 3,321 |
| 30,050 | 30,100 | 3,412 | 3,214 | 3,412 | 3,327 |
| 30,100 | 30,150 | 3,418 | 3,220 | 3,418 | 3,333 |
| 30,150 | 30,200 | 3,424 | 3,226 | 3,424 | 3,339 |
| 30,200 | 30,250 | 3,430 | 3,232 | 3,430 | 3,345 |
| 30,250 | 30,300 | 3,436 | 3,238 | 3,436 | 3,351 |
| 30,300 | 30,350 | 3,442 | 3,244 | 3,442 | 3,357 |
| 30,350 | 30,400 | 3,448 | 3,250 | 3,448 | 3,363 |
| 30,400 | 30,450 | 3,454 | 3,256 | 3,454 | 3,369 |
| 30,450 | 30,500 | 3,460 | 3,262 | 3,460 | 3,375 |
| 30,500 | 30,550 | 3,466 | 3,268 | 3,466 | 3,381 |
| 30,550 | 30,600 | 3,472 | 3,274 | 3,472 | 3,387 |
| 30,600 | 30,650 | 3,478 | 3,280 | 3,478 | 3,393 |
| 30,650 | 30,700 | 3,484 | 3,286 | 3,484 | 3,399 |
| 30,700 | 30,750 | 3,490 | 3,292 | 3,490 | 3,405 |
| 30,750 | 30,800 | 3,496 | 3,298 | 3,496 | 3,411 |
| 30,800 | 30,850 | 3,502 | 3,304 | 3,502 | 3,417 |
| 30,850 | 30,900 | 3,508 | 3,310 | 3,508 | 3,423 |
| 30,900 | 30,950 | 3,514 | 3,316 | 3,514 | 3,429 |
| 30,950 | 31,000 | 3,520 | 3,322 | 3,520 | 3,435 |
| **31,000** | | | | | |
| 31,000 | 31,050 | 3,526 | 3,328 | 3,526 | 3,441 |
| 31,050 | 31,100 | 3,532 | 3,334 | 3,532 | 3,447 |
| 31,100 | 31,150 | 3,538 | 3,340 | 3,538 | 3,453 |
| 31,150 | 31,200 | 3,544 | 3,346 | 3,544 | 3,459 |
| 31,200 | 31,250 | 3,550 | 3,352 | 3,550 | 3,465 |
| 31,250 | 31,300 | 3,556 | 3,358 | 3,556 | 3,471 |
| 31,300 | 31,350 | 3,562 | 3,364 | 3,562 | 3,477 |
| 31,350 | 31,400 | 3,568 | 3,370 | 3,568 | 3,483 |
| 31,400 | 31,450 | 3,574 | 3,376 | 3,574 | 3,489 |
| 31,450 | 31,500 | 3,580 | 3,382 | 3,580 | 3,495 |
| 31,500 | 31,550 | 3,586 | 3,388 | 3,586 | 3,501 |
| 31,550 | 31,600 | 3,592 | 3,394 | 3,592 | 3,507 |
| 31,600 | 31,650 | 3,598 | 3,400 | 3,598 | 3,513 |
| 31,650 | 31,700 | 3,604 | 3,406 | 3,604 | 3,519 |
| 31,700 | 31,750 | 3,610 | 3,412 | 3,610 | 3,525 |
| 31,750 | 31,800 | 3,616 | 3,418 | 3,616 | 3,531 |
| 31,800 | 31,850 | 3,622 | 3,424 | 3,622 | 3,537 |
| 31,850 | 31,900 | 3,628 | 3,430 | 3,628 | 3,543 |
| 31,900 | 31,950 | 3,634 | 3,436 | 3,634 | 3,549 |
| 31,950 | 32,000 | 3,640 | 3,442 | 3,640 | 3,555 |
| **32,000** | | | | | |
| 32,000 | 32,050 | 3,646 | 3,448 | 3,646 | 3,561 |
| 32,050 | 32,100 | 3,652 | 3,454 | 3,652 | 3,567 |
| 32,100 | 32,150 | 3,658 | 3,460 | 3,658 | 3,573 |
| 32,150 | 32,200 | 3,664 | 3,466 | 3,664 | 3,579 |
| 32,200 | 32,250 | 3,670 | 3,472 | 3,670 | 3,585 |
| 32,250 | 32,300 | 3,676 | 3,478 | 3,676 | 3,591 |
| 32,300 | 32,350 | 3,682 | 3,484 | 3,682 | 3,597 |
| 32,350 | 32,400 | 3,688 | 3,490 | 3,688 | 3,603 |
| 32,400 | 32,450 | 3,694 | 3,496 | 3,694 | 3,609 |
| 32,450 | 32,500 | 3,700 | 3,502 | 3,700 | 3,615 |
| 32,500 | 32,550 | 3,706 | 3,508 | 3,706 | 3,621 |
| 32,550 | 32,600 | 3,712 | 3,514 | 3,712 | 3,627 |
| 32,600 | 32,650 | 3,718 | 3,520 | 3,718 | 3,633 |
| 32,650 | 32,700 | 3,724 | 3,526 | 3,724 | 3,639 |
| 32,700 | 32,750 | 3,730 | 3,532 | 3,730 | 3,645 |
| 32,750 | 32,800 | 3,736 | 3,538 | 3,736 | 3,651 |
| 32,800 | 32,850 | 3,742 | 3,544 | 3,742 | 3,657 |
| 32,850 | 32,900 | 3,748 | 3,550 | 3,748 | 3,663 |
| 32,900 | 32,950 | 3,754 | 3,556 | 3,754 | 3,669 |
| 32,950 | 33,000 | 3,760 | 3,562 | 3,760 | 3,675 |
| **33,000** | | | | | |
| 33,000 | 33,050 | 3,766 | 3,568 | 3,766 | 3,681 |
| 33,050 | 33,100 | 3,772 | 3,574 | 3,772 | 3,687 |
| 33,100 | 33,150 | 3,778 | 3,580 | 3,778 | 3,693 |
| 33,150 | 33,200 | 3,784 | 3,586 | 3,784 | 3,699 |
| 33,200 | 33,250 | 3,790 | 3,592 | 3,790 | 3,705 |
| 33,250 | 33,300 | 3,796 | 3,598 | 3,796 | 3,711 |
| 33,300 | 33,350 | 3,802 | 3,604 | 3,802 | 3,717 |
| 33,350 | 33,400 | 3,808 | 3,610 | 3,808 | 3,723 |
| 33,400 | 33,450 | 3,814 | 3,616 | 3,814 | 3,729 |
| 33,450 | 33,500 | 3,820 | 3,622 | 3,820 | 3,735 |
| 33,500 | 33,550 | 3,826 | 3,628 | 3,826 | 3,741 |
| 33,550 | 33,600 | 3,832 | 3,634 | 3,832 | 3,747 |
| 33,600 | 33,650 | 3,838 | 3,640 | 3,838 | 3,753 |
| 33,650 | 33,700 | 3,844 | 3,646 | 3,844 | 3,759 |
| 33,700 | 33,750 | 3,850 | 3,652 | 3,850 | 3,765 |
| 33,750 | 33,800 | 3,856 | 3,658 | 3,856 | 3,771 |
| 33,800 | 33,850 | 3,862 | 3,664 | 3,862 | 3,777 |
| 33,850 | 33,900 | 3,868 | 3,670 | 3,868 | 3,783 |
| 33,900 | 33,950 | 3,874 | 3,676 | 3,874 | 3,789 |
| 33,950 | 34,000 | 3,880 | 3,682 | 3,880 | 3,795 |
| **34,000** | | | | | |
| 34,000 | 34,050 | 3,886 | 3,688 | 3,886 | 3,801 |
| 34,050 | 34,100 | 3,892 | 3,694 | 3,892 | 3,807 |
| 34,100 | 34,150 | 3,898 | 3,700 | 3,898 | 3,813 |
| 34,150 | 34,200 | 3,904 | 3,706 | 3,904 | 3,819 |
| 34,200 | 34,250 | 3,910 | 3,712 | 3,910 | 3,825 |
| 34,250 | 34,300 | 3,916 | 3,718 | 3,916 | 3,831 |
| 34,300 | 34,350 | 3,922 | 3,724 | 3,922 | 3,837 |
| 34,350 | 34,400 | 3,928 | 3,730 | 3,928 | 3,843 |
| 34,400 | 34,450 | 3,934 | 3,736 | 3,934 | 3,849 |
| 34,450 | 34,500 | 3,940 | 3,742 | 3,940 | 3,855 |
| 34,500 | 34,550 | 3,946 | 3,748 | 3,946 | 3,861 |
| 34,550 | 34,600 | 3,952 | 3,754 | 3,952 | 3,867 |
| 34,600 | 34,650 | 3,958 | 3,760 | 3,958 | 3,873 |
| 34,650 | 34,700 | 3,964 | 3,766 | 3,964 | 3,879 |
| 34,700 | 34,750 | 3,970 | 3,772 | 3,970 | 3,885 |
| 34,750 | 34,800 | 3,976 | 3,778 | 3,976 | 3,891 |
| 34,800 | 34,850 | 3,982 | 3,784 | 3,982 | 3,897 |
| 34,850 | 34,900 | 3,988 | 3,790 | 3,988 | 3,903 |
| 34,900 | 34,950 | 3,994 | 3,796 | 3,994 | 3,909 |
| 34,950 | 35,000 | 4,000 | 3,802 | 4,000 | 3,915 |
| **35,000** | | | | | |
| 35,000 | 35,050 | 4,006 | 3,808 | 4,006 | 3,921 |
| 35,050 | 35,100 | 4,012 | 3,814 | 4,012 | 3,927 |
| 35,100 | 35,150 | 4,018 | 3,820 | 4,018 | 3,933 |
| 35,150 | 35,200 | 4,024 | 3,826 | 4,024 | 3,939 |
| 35,200 | 35,250 | 4,030 | 3,832 | 4,030 | 3,945 |
| 35,250 | 35,300 | 4,036 | 3,838 | 4,036 | 3,951 |
| 35,300 | 35,350 | 4,042 | 3,844 | 4,042 | 3,957 |
| 35,350 | 35,400 | 4,048 | 3,850 | 4,048 | 3,963 |
| 35,400 | 35,450 | 4,054 | 3,856 | 4,054 | 3,969 |
| 35,450 | 35,500 | 4,060 | 3,862 | 4,060 | 3,975 |
| 35,500 | 35,550 | 4,066 | 3,868 | 4,066 | 3,981 |
| 35,550 | 35,600 | 4,072 | 3,874 | 4,072 | 3,987 |
| 35,600 | 35,650 | 4,078 | 3,880 | 4,078 | 3,993 |
| 35,650 | 35,700 | 4,084 | 3,886 | 4,084 | 3,999 |
| 35,700 | 35,750 | 4,090 | 3,892 | 4,090 | 4,005 |
| 35,750 | 35,800 | 4,096 | 3,898 | 4,096 | 4,011 |
| 35,800 | 35,850 | 4,102 | 3,904 | 4,102 | 4,017 |
| 35,850 | 35,900 | 4,108 | 3,910 | 4,108 | 4,023 |
| 35,900 | 35,950 | 4,114 | 3,916 | 4,114 | 4,029 |
| 35,950 | 36,000 | 4,120 | 3,922 | 4,120 | 4,035 |
| **36,000** | | | | | |
| 36,000 | 36,050 | 4,126 | 3,928 | 4,126 | 4,041 |
| 36,050 | 36,100 | 4,132 | 3,934 | 4,132 | 4,047 |
| 36,100 | 36,150 | 4,138 | 3,940 | 4,138 | 4,053 |
| 36,150 | 36,200 | 4,144 | 3,946 | 4,144 | 4,059 |
| 36,200 | 36,250 | 4,150 | 3,952 | 4,150 | 4,065 |
| 36,250 | 36,300 | 4,156 | 3,958 | 4,156 | 4,071 |
| 36,300 | 36,350 | 4,162 | 3,964 | 4,162 | 4,077 |
| 36,350 | 36,400 | 4,168 | 3,970 | 4,168 | 4,083 |
| 36,400 | 36,450 | 4,174 | 3,976 | 4,174 | 4,089 |
| 36,450 | 36,500 | 4,180 | 3,982 | 4,180 | 4,095 |
| 36,500 | 36,550 | 4,186 | 3,988 | 4,186 | 4,101 |
| 36,550 | 36,600 | 4,192 | 3,994 | 4,192 | 4,107 |
| 36,600 | 36,650 | 4,198 | 4,000 | 4,198 | 4,113 |
| 36,650 | 36,700 | 4,204 | 4,006 | 4,204 | 4,119 |
| 36,700 | 36,750 | 4,210 | 4,012 | 4,210 | 4,125 |
| 36,750 | 36,800 | 4,216 | 4,018 | 4,216 | 4,131 |
| 36,800 | 36,850 | 4,222 | 4,024 | 4,222 | 4,137 |
| 36,850 | 36,900 | 4,228 | 4,030 | 4,228 | 4,143 |
| 36,900 | 36,950 | 4,234 | 4,036 | 4,234 | 4,149 |
| 36,950 | 37,000 | 4,240 | 4,042 | 4,240 | 4,155 |
| **37,000** | | | | | |
| 37,000 | 37,050 | 4,246 | 4,048 | 4,246 | 4,161 |
| 37,050 | 37,100 | 4,252 | 4,054 | 4,252 | 4,167 |
| 37,100 | 37,150 | 4,258 | 4,060 | 4,258 | 4,173 |
| 37,150 | 37,200 | 4,264 | 4,066 | 4,264 | 4,179 |
| 37,200 | 37,250 | 4,270 | 4,072 | 4,270 | 4,185 |
| 37,250 | 37,300 | 4,276 | 4,078 | 4,276 | 4,191 |
| 37,300 | 37,350 | 4,282 | 4,084 | 4,282 | 4,197 |
| 37,350 | 37,400 | 4,288 | 4,090 | 4,288 | 4,203 |
| 37,400 | 37,450 | 4,294 | 4,096 | 4,294 | 4,209 |
| 37,450 | 37,500 | 4,300 | 4,102 | 4,300 | 4,215 |
| 37,500 | 37,550 | 4,306 | 4,108 | 4,306 | 4,221 |
| 37,550 | 37,600 | 4,312 | 4,114 | 4,312 | 4,227 |
| 37,600 | 37,650 | 4,318 | 4,120 | 4,318 | 4,233 |
| 37,650 | 37,700 | 4,324 | 4,126 | 4,324 | 4,239 |
| 37,700 | 37,750 | 4,330 | 4,132 | 4,330 | 4,245 |
| 37,750 | 37,800 | 4,336 | 4,138 | 4,336 | 4,251 |
| 37,800 | 37,850 | 4,342 | 4,144 | 4,342 | 4,257 |
| 37,850 | 37,900 | 4,348 | 4,150 | 4,348 | 4,263 |
| 37,900 | 37,950 | 4,354 | 4,156 | 4,354 | 4,269 |
| 37,950 | 38,000 | 4,360 | 4,162 | 4,360 | 4,275 |
| **38,000** | | | | | |
| 38,000 | 38,050 | 4,366 | 4,168 | 4,366 | 4,281 |
| 38,050 | 38,100 | 4,372 | 4,174 | 4,372 | 4,287 |
| 38,100 | 38,150 | 4,378 | 4,180 | 4,378 | 4,293 |
| 38,150 | 38,200 | 4,384 | 4,186 | 4,384 | 4,299 |
| 38,200 | 38,250 | 4,390 | 4,192 | 4,390 | 4,305 |
| 38,250 | 38,300 | 4,396 | 4,198 | 4,396 | 4,311 |
| 38,300 | 38,350 | 4,402 | 4,204 | 4,402 | 4,317 |
| 38,350 | 38,400 | 4,408 | 4,210 | 4,408 | 4,323 |
| 38,400 | 38,450 | 4,414 | 4,216 | 4,414 | 4,329 |
| 38,450 | 38,500 | 4,420 | 4,222 | 4,420 | 4,335 |
| 38,500 | 38,550 | 4,426 | 4,228 | 4,426 | 4,341 |
| 38,550 | 38,600 | 4,432 | 4,234 | 4,432 | 4,347 |
| 38,600 | 38,650 | 4,438 | 4,240 | 4,438 | 4,353 |
| 38,650 | 38,700 | 4,444 | 4,246 | 4,444 | 4,359 |
| 38,700 | 38,750 | 4,450 | 4,252 | 4,450 | 4,365 |
| 38,750 | 38,800 | 4,456 | 4,258 | 4,456 | 4,371 |
| 38,800 | 38,850 | 4,462 | 4,264 | 4,462 | 4,377 |
| 38,850 | 38,900 | 4,468 | 4,270 | 4,468 | 4,383 |
| 38,900 | 38,950 | 4,474 | 4,276 | 4,474 | 4,389 |
| 38,950 | 39,000 | 4,480 | 4,282 | 4,480 | 4,395 |

*(Continued)*

*This column must also be used by a qualifying widow(er).

## 2020 Tax Table — *Continued*

| If line 15 (taxable income) is— At least | But less than | And you are— Single | Married filing jointly* | Married filing separately | Head of a household |
|---|---|---|---|---|---|
| | | Your tax is— | | | |
| **39,000** | | | | | |
| 39,000 | 39,050 | 4,486 | 4,288 | 4,486 | 4,401 |
| 39,050 | 39,100 | 4,492 | 4,294 | 4,492 | 4,407 |
| 39,100 | 39,150 | 4,498 | 4,300 | 4,498 | 4,413 |
| 39,150 | 39,200 | 4,504 | 4,306 | 4,504 | 4,419 |
| 39,200 | 39,250 | 4,510 | 4,312 | 4,510 | 4,425 |
| 39,250 | 39,300 | 4,516 | 4,318 | 4,516 | 4,431 |
| 39,300 | 39,350 | 4,522 | 4,324 | 4,522 | 4,437 |
| 39,350 | 39,400 | 4,528 | 4,330 | 4,528 | 4,443 |
| 39,400 | 39,450 | 4,534 | 4,336 | 4,534 | 4,449 |
| 39,450 | 39,500 | 4,540 | 4,342 | 4,540 | 4,455 |
| 39,500 | 39,550 | 4,546 | 4,348 | 4,546 | 4,461 |
| 39,550 | 39,600 | 4,552 | 4,354 | 4,552 | 4,467 |
| 39,600 | 39,650 | 4,558 | 4,360 | 4,558 | 4,473 |
| 39,650 | 39,700 | 4,564 | 4,366 | 4,564 | 4,479 |
| 39,700 | 39,750 | 4,570 | 4,372 | 4,570 | 4,485 |
| 39,750 | 39,800 | 4,576 | 4,378 | 4,576 | 4,491 |
| 39,800 | 39,850 | 4,582 | 4,384 | 4,582 | 4,497 |
| 39,850 | 39,900 | 4,588 | 4,390 | 4,588 | 4,503 |
| 39,900 | 39,950 | 4,594 | 4,396 | 4,594 | 4,509 |
| 39,950 | 40,000 | 4,600 | 4,402 | 4,600 | 4,515 |
| **40,000** | | | | | |
| 40,000 | 40,050 | 4,606 | 4,408 | 4,606 | 4,521 |
| 40,050 | 40,100 | 4,612 | 4,414 | 4,612 | 4,527 |
| 40,100 | 40,150 | 4,618 | 4,420 | 4,618 | 4,533 |
| 40,150 | 40,200 | 4,629 | 4,426 | 4,629 | 4,539 |
| 40,200 | 40,250 | 4,640 | 4,432 | 4,640 | 4,545 |
| 40,250 | 40,300 | 4,651 | 4,438 | 4,651 | 4,551 |
| 40,300 | 40,350 | 4,662 | 4,444 | 4,662 | 4,557 |
| 40,350 | 40,400 | 4,673 | 4,450 | 4,673 | 4,563 |
| 40,400 | 40,450 | 4,684 | 4,456 | 4,684 | 4,569 |
| 40,450 | 40,500 | 4,695 | 4,462 | 4,695 | 4,575 |
| 40,500 | 40,550 | 4,706 | 4,468 | 4,706 | 4,581 |
| 40,550 | 40,600 | 4,717 | 4,474 | 4,717 | 4,587 |
| 40,600 | 40,650 | 4,728 | 4,480 | 4,728 | 4,593 |
| 40,650 | 40,700 | 4,739 | 4,486 | 4,739 | 4,599 |
| 40,700 | 40,750 | 4,750 | 4,492 | 4,750 | 4,605 |
| 40,750 | 40,800 | 4,761 | 4,498 | 4,761 | 4,611 |
| 40,800 | 40,850 | 4,772 | 4,504 | 4,772 | 4,617 |
| 40,850 | 40,900 | 4,783 | 4,510 | 4,783 | 4,623 |
| 40,900 | 40,950 | 4,794 | 4,516 | 4,794 | 4,629 |
| 40,950 | 41,000 | 4,805 | 4,522 | 4,805 | 4,635 |
| **41,000** | | | | | |
| 41,000 | 41,050 | 4,816 | 4,528 | 4,816 | 4,641 |
| 41,050 | 41,100 | 4,827 | 4,534 | 4,827 | 4,647 |
| 41,100 | 41,150 | 4,838 | 4,540 | 4,838 | 4,653 |
| 41,150 | 41,200 | 4,849 | 4,546 | 4,849 | 4,659 |
| 41,200 | 41,250 | 4,860 | 4,552 | 4,860 | 4,665 |
| 41,250 | 41,300 | 4,871 | 4,558 | 4,871 | 4,671 |
| 41,300 | 41,350 | 4,882 | 4,564 | 4,882 | 4,677 |
| 41,350 | 41,400 | 4,893 | 4,570 | 4,893 | 4,683 |
| 41,400 | 41,450 | 4,904 | 4,576 | 4,904 | 4,689 |
| 41,450 | 41,500 | 4,915 | 4,582 | 4,915 | 4,695 |
| 41,500 | 41,550 | 4,926 | 4,588 | 4,926 | 4,701 |
| 41,550 | 41,600 | 4,937 | 4,594 | 4,937 | 4,707 |
| 41,600 | 41,650 | 4,948 | 4,600 | 4,948 | 4,713 |
| 41,650 | 41,700 | 4,959 | 4,606 | 4,959 | 4,719 |
| 41,700 | 41,750 | 4,970 | 4,612 | 4,970 | 4,725 |
| 41,750 | 41,800 | 4,981 | 4,618 | 4,981 | 4,731 |
| 41,800 | 41,850 | 4,992 | 4,624 | 4,992 | 4,737 |
| 41,850 | 41,900 | 5,003 | 4,630 | 5,003 | 4,743 |
| 41,900 | 41,950 | 5,014 | 4,636 | 5,014 | 4,749 |
| 41,950 | 42,000 | 5,025 | 4,642 | 5,025 | 4,755 |
| **42,000** | | | | | |
| 42,000 | 42,050 | 5,036 | 4,648 | 5,036 | 4,761 |
| 42,050 | 42,100 | 5,047 | 4,654 | 5,047 | 4,767 |
| 42,100 | 42,150 | 5,058 | 4,660 | 5,058 | 4,773 |
| 42,150 | 42,200 | 5,069 | 4,666 | 5,069 | 4,779 |
| 42,200 | 42,250 | 5,080 | 4,672 | 5,080 | 4,785 |
| 42,250 | 42,300 | 5,091 | 4,678 | 5,091 | 4,791 |
| 42,300 | 42,350 | 5,102 | 4,684 | 5,102 | 4,797 |
| 42,350 | 42,400 | 5,113 | 4,690 | 5,113 | 4,803 |
| 42,400 | 42,450 | 5,124 | 4,696 | 5,124 | 4,809 |
| 42,450 | 42,500 | 5,135 | 4,702 | 5,135 | 4,815 |
| 42,500 | 42,550 | 5,146 | 4,708 | 5,146 | 4,821 |
| 42,550 | 42,600 | 5,157 | 4,714 | 5,157 | 4,827 |
| 42,600 | 42,650 | 5,168 | 4,720 | 5,168 | 4,833 |
| 42,650 | 42,700 | 5,179 | 4,726 | 5,179 | 4,839 |
| 42,700 | 42,750 | 5,190 | 4,732 | 5,190 | 4,845 |
| 42,750 | 42,800 | 5,201 | 4,738 | 5,201 | 4,851 |
| 42,800 | 42,850 | 5,212 | 4,744 | 5,212 | 4,857 |
| 42,850 | 42,900 | 5,223 | 4,750 | 5,223 | 4,863 |
| 42,900 | 42,950 | 5,234 | 4,756 | 5,234 | 4,869 |
| 42,950 | 43,000 | 5,245 | 4,762 | 5,245 | 4,875 |
| **43,000** | | | | | |
| 43,000 | 43,050 | 5,256 | 4,768 | 5,256 | 4,881 |
| 43,050 | 43,100 | 5,267 | 4,774 | 5,267 | 4,887 |
| 43,100 | 43,150 | 5,278 | 4,780 | 5,278 | 4,893 |
| 43,150 | 43,200 | 5,289 | 4,786 | 5,289 | 4,899 |
| 43,200 | 43,250 | 5,300 | 4,792 | 5,300 | 4,905 |
| 43,250 | 43,300 | 5,311 | 4,798 | 5,311 | 4,911 |
| 43,300 | 43,350 | 5,322 | 4,804 | 5,322 | 4,917 |
| 43,350 | 43,400 | 5,333 | 4,810 | 5,333 | 4,923 |
| 43,400 | 43,450 | 5,344 | 4,816 | 5,344 | 4,929 |
| 43,450 | 43,500 | 5,355 | 4,822 | 5,355 | 4,935 |
| 43,500 | 43,550 | 5,366 | 4,828 | 5,366 | 4,941 |
| 43,550 | 43,600 | 5,377 | 4,834 | 5,377 | 4,947 |
| 43,600 | 43,650 | 5,388 | 4,840 | 5,388 | 4,953 |
| 43,650 | 43,700 | 5,399 | 4,846 | 5,399 | 4,959 |
| 43,700 | 43,750 | 5,410 | 4,852 | 5,410 | 4,965 |
| 43,750 | 43,800 | 5,421 | 4,858 | 5,421 | 4,971 |
| 43,800 | 43,850 | 5,432 | 4,864 | 5,432 | 4,977 |
| 43,850 | 43,900 | 5,443 | 4,870 | 5,443 | 4,983 |
| 43,900 | 43,950 | 5,454 | 4,876 | 5,454 | 4,989 |
| 43,950 | 44,000 | 5,465 | 4,882 | 5,465 | 4,995 |
| **44,000** | | | | | |
| 44,000 | 44,050 | 5,476 | 4,888 | 5,476 | 5,001 |
| 44,050 | 44,100 | 5,487 | 4,894 | 5,487 | 5,007 |
| 44,100 | 44,150 | 5,498 | 4,900 | 5,498 | 5,013 |
| 44,150 | 44,200 | 5,509 | 4,906 | 5,509 | 5,019 |
| 44,200 | 44,250 | 5,520 | 4,912 | 5,520 | 5,025 |
| 44,250 | 44,300 | 5,531 | 4,918 | 5,531 | 5,031 |
| 44,300 | 44,350 | 5,542 | 4,924 | 5,542 | 5,037 |
| 44,350 | 44,400 | 5,553 | 4,930 | 5,553 | 5,043 |
| 44,400 | 44,450 | 5,564 | 4,936 | 5,564 | 5,049 |
| 44,450 | 44,500 | 5,575 | 4,942 | 5,575 | 5,055 |
| 44,500 | 44,550 | 5,586 | 4,948 | 5,586 | 5,061 |
| 44,550 | 44,600 | 5,597 | 4,954 | 5,597 | 5,067 |
| 44,600 | 44,650 | 5,608 | 4,960 | 5,608 | 5,073 |
| 44,650 | 44,700 | 5,619 | 4,966 | 5,619 | 5,079 |
| 44,700 | 44,750 | 5,630 | 4,972 | 5,630 | 5,085 |
| 44,750 | 44,800 | 5,641 | 4,978 | 5,641 | 5,091 |
| 44,800 | 44,850 | 5,652 | 4,984 | 5,652 | 5,097 |
| 44,850 | 44,900 | 5,663 | 4,990 | 5,663 | 5,103 |
| 44,900 | 44,950 | 5,674 | 4,996 | 5,674 | 5,109 |
| 44,950 | 45,000 | 5,685 | 5,002 | 5,685 | 5,115 |
| **45,000** | | | | | |
| 45,000 | 45,050 | 5,696 | 5,008 | 5,696 | 5,121 |
| 45,050 | 45,100 | 5,707 | 5,014 | 5,707 | 5,127 |
| 45,100 | 45,150 | 5,718 | 5,020 | 5,718 | 5,133 |
| 45,150 | 45,200 | 5,729 | 5,026 | 5,729 | 5,139 |
| 45,200 | 45,250 | 5,740 | 5,032 | 5,740 | 5,145 |
| 45,250 | 45,300 | 5,751 | 5,038 | 5,751 | 5,151 |
| 45,300 | 45,350 | 5,762 | 5,044 | 5,762 | 5,157 |
| 45,350 | 45,400 | 5,773 | 5,050 | 5,773 | 5,163 |
| 45,400 | 45,450 | 5,784 | 5,056 | 5,784 | 5,169 |
| 45,450 | 45,500 | 5,795 | 5,062 | 5,795 | 5,175 |
| 45,500 | 45,550 | 5,806 | 5,068 | 5,806 | 5,181 |
| 45,550 | 45,600 | 5,817 | 5,074 | 5,817 | 5,187 |
| 45,600 | 45,650 | 5,828 | 5,080 | 5,828 | 5,193 |
| 45,650 | 45,700 | 5,839 | 5,086 | 5,839 | 5,199 |
| 45,700 | 45,750 | 5,850 | 5,092 | 5,850 | 5,205 |
| 45,750 | 45,800 | 5,861 | 5,098 | 5,861 | 5,211 |
| 45,800 | 45,850 | 5,872 | 5,104 | 5,872 | 5,217 |
| 45,850 | 45,900 | 5,883 | 5,110 | 5,883 | 5,223 |
| 45,900 | 45,950 | 5,894 | 5,116 | 5,894 | 5,229 |
| 45,950 | 46,000 | 5,905 | 5,122 | 5,905 | 5,235 |
| **46,000** | | | | | |
| 46,000 | 46,050 | 5,916 | 5,128 | 5,916 | 5,241 |
| 46,050 | 46,100 | 5,927 | 5,134 | 5,927 | 5,247 |
| 46,100 | 46,150 | 5,938 | 5,140 | 5,938 | 5,253 |
| 46,150 | 46,200 | 5,949 | 5,146 | 5,949 | 5,259 |
| 46,200 | 46,250 | 5,960 | 5,152 | 5,960 | 5,265 |
| 46,250 | 46,300 | 5,971 | 5,158 | 5,971 | 5,271 |
| 46,300 | 46,350 | 5,982 | 5,164 | 5,982 | 5,277 |
| 46,350 | 46,400 | 5,993 | 5,170 | 5,993 | 5,283 |
| 46,400 | 46,450 | 6,004 | 5,176 | 6,004 | 5,289 |
| 46,450 | 46,500 | 6,015 | 5,182 | 6,015 | 5,295 |
| 46,500 | 46,550 | 6,026 | 5,188 | 6,026 | 5,301 |
| 46,550 | 46,600 | 6,037 | 5,194 | 6,037 | 5,307 |
| 46,600 | 46,650 | 6,048 | 5,200 | 6,048 | 5,313 |
| 46,650 | 46,700 | 6,059 | 5,206 | 6,059 | 5,319 |
| 46,700 | 46,750 | 6,070 | 5,212 | 6,070 | 5,325 |
| 46,750 | 46,800 | 6,081 | 5,218 | 6,081 | 5,331 |
| 46,800 | 46,850 | 6,092 | 5,224 | 6,092 | 5,337 |
| 46,850 | 46,900 | 6,103 | 5,230 | 6,103 | 5,343 |
| 46,900 | 46,950 | 6,114 | 5,236 | 6,114 | 5,349 |
| 46,950 | 47,000 | 6,125 | 5,242 | 6,125 | 5,355 |
| **47,000** | | | | | |
| 47,000 | 47,050 | 6,136 | 5,248 | 6,136 | 5,361 |
| 47,050 | 47,100 | 6,147 | 5,254 | 6,147 | 5,367 |
| 47,100 | 47,150 | 6,158 | 5,260 | 6,158 | 5,373 |
| 47,150 | 47,200 | 6,169 | 5,266 | 6,169 | 5,379 |
| 47,200 | 47,250 | 6,180 | 5,272 | 6,180 | 5,385 |
| 47,250 | 47,300 | 6,191 | 5,278 | 6,191 | 5,391 |
| 47,300 | 47,350 | 6,202 | 5,284 | 6,202 | 5,397 |
| 47,350 | 47,400 | 6,213 | 5,290 | 6,213 | 5,403 |
| 47,400 | 47,450 | 6,224 | 5,296 | 6,224 | 5,409 |
| 47,450 | 47,500 | 6,235 | 5,302 | 6,235 | 5,415 |
| 47,500 | 47,550 | 6,246 | 5,308 | 6,246 | 5,421 |
| 47,550 | 47,600 | 6,257 | 5,314 | 6,257 | 5,427 |
| 47,600 | 47,650 | 6,268 | 5,320 | 6,268 | 5,433 |
| 47,650 | 47,700 | 6,279 | 5,326 | 6,279 | 5,439 |
| 47,700 | 47,750 | 6,290 | 5,332 | 6,290 | 5,445 |
| 47,750 | 47,800 | 6,301 | 5,338 | 6,301 | 5,451 |
| 47,800 | 47,850 | 6,312 | 5,344 | 6,312 | 5,457 |
| 47,850 | 47,900 | 6,323 | 5,350 | 6,323 | 5,463 |
| 47,900 | 47,950 | 6,334 | 5,356 | 6,334 | 5,469 |
| 47,950 | 48,000 | 6,345 | 5,362 | 6,345 | 5,475 |

*(Continued)*

*This column must also be used by a qualifying widow(er).

**2020 Tax Table** — *Continued*

| If line 15 (taxable income) is— At least | But less than | And you are— Single | Married filing jointly* | Married filing separately | Head of a household |
|---|---|---|---|---|---|
| | | Your tax is— | | | |
| **48,000** | | | | | |
| 48,000 | 48,050 | 6,356 | 5,368 | 6,356 | 5,481 |
| 48,050 | 48,100 | 6,367 | 5,374 | 6,367 | 5,487 |
| 48,100 | 48,150 | 6,378 | 5,380 | 6,378 | 5,493 |
| 48,150 | 48,200 | 6,389 | 5,386 | 6,389 | 5,499 |
| 48,200 | 48,250 | 6,400 | 5,392 | 6,400 | 5,505 |
| 48,250 | 48,300 | 6,411 | 5,398 | 6,411 | 5,511 |
| 48,300 | 48,350 | 6,422 | 5,404 | 6,422 | 5,517 |
| 48,350 | 48,400 | 6,433 | 5,410 | 6,433 | 5,523 |
| 48,400 | 48,450 | 6,444 | 5,416 | 6,444 | 5,529 |
| 48,450 | 48,500 | 6,455 | 5,422 | 6,455 | 5,535 |
| 48,500 | 48,550 | 6,466 | 5,428 | 6,466 | 5,541 |
| 48,550 | 48,600 | 6,477 | 5,434 | 6,477 | 5,547 |
| 48,600 | 48,650 | 6,488 | 5,440 | 6,488 | 5,553 |
| 48,650 | 48,700 | 6,499 | 5,446 | 6,499 | 5,559 |
| 48,700 | 48,750 | 6,510 | 5,452 | 6,510 | 5,565 |
| 48,750 | 48,800 | 6,521 | 5,458 | 6,521 | 5,571 |
| 48,800 | 48,850 | 6,532 | 5,464 | 6,532 | 5,577 |
| 48,850 | 48,900 | 6,543 | 5,470 | 6,543 | 5,583 |
| 48,900 | 48,950 | 6,554 | 5,476 | 6,554 | 5,589 |
| 48,950 | 49,000 | 6,565 | 5,482 | 6,565 | 5,595 |
| **49,000** | | | | | |
| 49,000 | 49,050 | 6,576 | 5,488 | 6,576 | 5,601 |
| 49,050 | 49,100 | 6,587 | 5,494 | 6,587 | 5,607 |
| 49,100 | 49,150 | 6,598 | 5,500 | 6,598 | 5,613 |
| 49,150 | 49,200 | 6,609 | 5,506 | 6,609 | 5,619 |
| 49,200 | 49,250 | 6,620 | 5,512 | 6,620 | 5,625 |
| 49,250 | 49,300 | 6,631 | 5,518 | 6,631 | 5,631 |
| 49,300 | 49,350 | 6,642 | 5,524 | 6,642 | 5,637 |
| 49,350 | 49,400 | 6,653 | 5,530 | 6,653 | 5,643 |
| 49,400 | 49,450 | 6,664 | 5,536 | 6,664 | 5,649 |
| 49,450 | 49,500 | 6,675 | 5,542 | 6,675 | 5,655 |
| 49,500 | 49,550 | 6,686 | 5,548 | 6,686 | 5,661 |
| 49,550 | 49,600 | 6,697 | 5,554 | 6,697 | 5,667 |
| 49,600 | 49,650 | 6,708 | 5,560 | 6,708 | 5,673 |
| 49,650 | 49,700 | 6,719 | 5,566 | 6,719 | 5,679 |
| 49,700 | 49,750 | 6,730 | 5,572 | 6,730 | 5,685 |
| 49,750 | 49,800 | 6,741 | 5,578 | 6,741 | 5,691 |
| 49,800 | 49,850 | 6,752 | 5,584 | 6,752 | 5,697 |
| 49,850 | 49,900 | 6,763 | 5,590 | 6,763 | 5,703 |
| 49,900 | 49,950 | 6,774 | 5,596 | 6,774 | 5,709 |
| 49,950 | 50,000 | 6,785 | 5,602 | 6,785 | 5,715 |
| **50,000** | | | | | |
| 50,000 | 50,050 | 6,796 | 5,608 | 6,796 | 5,721 |
| 50,050 | 50,100 | 6,807 | 5,614 | 6,807 | 5,727 |
| 50,100 | 50,150 | 6,818 | 5,620 | 6,818 | 5,733 |
| 50,150 | 50,200 | 6,829 | 5,626 | 6,829 | 5,739 |
| 50,200 | 50,250 | 6,840 | 5,632 | 6,840 | 5,745 |
| 50,250 | 50,300 | 6,851 | 5,638 | 6,851 | 5,751 |
| 50,300 | 50,350 | 6,862 | 5,644 | 6,862 | 5,757 |
| 50,350 | 50,400 | 6,873 | 5,650 | 6,873 | 5,763 |
| 50,400 | 50,450 | 6,884 | 5,656 | 6,884 | 5,769 |
| 50,450 | 50,500 | 6,895 | 5,662 | 6,895 | 5,775 |
| 50,500 | 50,550 | 6,906 | 5,668 | 6,906 | 5,781 |
| 50,550 | 50,600 | 6,917 | 5,674 | 6,917 | 5,787 |
| 50,600 | 50,650 | 6,928 | 5,680 | 6,928 | 5,793 |
| 50,650 | 50,700 | 6,939 | 5,686 | 6,939 | 5,799 |
| 50,700 | 50,750 | 6,950 | 5,692 | 6,950 | 5,805 |
| 50,750 | 50,800 | 6,961 | 5,698 | 6,961 | 5,811 |
| 50,800 | 50,850 | 6,972 | 5,704 | 6,972 | 5,817 |
| 50,850 | 50,900 | 6,983 | 5,710 | 6,983 | 5,823 |
| 50,900 | 50,950 | 6,994 | 5,716 | 6,994 | 5,829 |
| 50,950 | 51,000 | 7,005 | 5,722 | 7,005 | 5,835 |

| If line 15 (taxable income) is— At least | But less than | And you are— Single | Married filing jointly* | Married filing separately | Head of a household |
|---|---|---|---|---|---|
| | | Your tax is— | | | |
| **51,000** | | | | | |
| 51,000 | 51,050 | 7,016 | 5,728 | 7,016 | 5,841 |
| 51,050 | 51,100 | 7,027 | 5,734 | 7,027 | 5,847 |
| 51,100 | 51,150 | 7,038 | 5,740 | 7,038 | 5,853 |
| 51,150 | 51,200 | 7,049 | 5,746 | 7,049 | 5,859 |
| 51,200 | 51,250 | 7,060 | 5,752 | 7,060 | 5,865 |
| 51,250 | 51,300 | 7,071 | 5,758 | 7,071 | 5,871 |
| 51,300 | 51,350 | 7,082 | 5,764 | 7,082 | 5,877 |
| 51,350 | 51,400 | 7,093 | 5,770 | 7,093 | 5,883 |
| 51,400 | 51,450 | 7,104 | 5,776 | 7,104 | 5,889 |
| 51,450 | 51,500 | 7,115 | 5,782 | 7,115 | 5,895 |
| 51,500 | 51,550 | 7,126 | 5,788 | 7,126 | 5,901 |
| 51,550 | 51,600 | 7,137 | 5,794 | 7,137 | 5,907 |
| 51,600 | 51,650 | 7,148 | 5,800 | 7,148 | 5,913 |
| 51,650 | 51,700 | 7,159 | 5,806 | 7,159 | 5,919 |
| 51,700 | 51,750 | 7,170 | 5,812 | 7,170 | 5,925 |
| 51,750 | 51,800 | 7,181 | 5,818 | 7,181 | 5,931 |
| 51,800 | 51,850 | 7,192 | 5,824 | 7,192 | 5,937 |
| 51,850 | 51,900 | 7,203 | 5,830 | 7,203 | 5,943 |
| 51,900 | 51,950 | 7,214 | 5,836 | 7,214 | 5,949 |
| 51,950 | 52,000 | 7,225 | 5,842 | 7,225 | 5,955 |
| **52,000** | | | | | |
| 52,000 | 52,050 | 7,236 | 5,848 | 7,236 | 5,961 |
| 52,050 | 52,100 | 7,247 | 5,854 | 7,247 | 5,967 |
| 52,100 | 52,150 | 7,258 | 5,860 | 7,258 | 5,973 |
| 52,150 | 52,200 | 7,269 | 5,866 | 7,269 | 5,979 |
| 52,200 | 52,250 | 7,280 | 5,872 | 7,280 | 5,985 |
| 52,250 | 52,300 | 7,291 | 5,878 | 7,291 | 5,991 |
| 52,300 | 52,350 | 7,302 | 5,884 | 7,302 | 5,997 |
| 52,350 | 52,400 | 7,313 | 5,890 | 7,313 | 6,003 |
| 52,400 | 52,450 | 7,324 | 5,896 | 7,324 | 6,009 |
| 52,450 | 52,500 | 7,335 | 5,902 | 7,335 | 6,015 |
| 52,500 | 52,550 | 7,346 | 5,908 | 7,346 | 6,021 |
| 52,550 | 52,600 | 7,357 | 5,914 | 7,357 | 6,027 |
| 52,600 | 52,650 | 7,368 | 5,920 | 7,368 | 6,033 |
| 52,650 | 52,700 | 7,379 | 5,926 | 7,379 | 6,039 |
| 52,700 | 52,750 | 7,390 | 5,932 | 7,390 | 6,045 |
| 52,750 | 52,800 | 7,401 | 5,938 | 7,401 | 6,051 |
| 52,800 | 52,850 | 7,412 | 5,944 | 7,412 | 6,057 |
| 52,850 | 52,900 | 7,423 | 5,950 | 7,423 | 6,063 |
| 52,900 | 52,950 | 7,434 | 5,956 | 7,434 | 6,069 |
| 52,950 | 53,000 | 7,445 | 5,962 | 7,445 | 6,075 |
| **53,000** | | | | | |
| 53,000 | 53,050 | 7,456 | 5,968 | 7,456 | 6,081 |
| 53,050 | 53,100 | 7,467 | 5,974 | 7,467 | 6,087 |
| 53,100 | 53,150 | 7,478 | 5,980 | 7,478 | 6,093 |
| 53,150 | 53,200 | 7,489 | 5,986 | 7,489 | 6,099 |
| 53,200 | 53,250 | 7,500 | 5,992 | 7,500 | 6,105 |
| 53,250 | 53,300 | 7,511 | 5,998 | 7,511 | 6,111 |
| 53,300 | 53,350 | 7,522 | 6,004 | 7,522 | 6,117 |
| 53,350 | 53,400 | 7,533 | 6,010 | 7,533 | 6,123 |
| 53,400 | 53,450 | 7,544 | 6,016 | 7,544 | 6,129 |
| 53,450 | 53,500 | 7,555 | 6,022 | 7,555 | 6,135 |
| 53,500 | 53,550 | 7,566 | 6,028 | 7,566 | 6,141 |
| 53,550 | 53,600 | 7,577 | 6,034 | 7,577 | 6,147 |
| 53,600 | 53,650 | 7,588 | 6,040 | 7,588 | 6,153 |
| 53,650 | 53,700 | 7,599 | 6,046 | 7,599 | 6,159 |
| 53,700 | 53,750 | 7,610 | 6,052 | 7,610 | 6,168 |
| 53,750 | 53,800 | 7,621 | 6,058 | 7,621 | 6,179 |
| 53,800 | 53,850 | 7,632 | 6,064 | 7,632 | 6,190 |
| 53,850 | 53,900 | 7,643 | 6,070 | 7,643 | 6,201 |
| 53,900 | 53,950 | 7,654 | 6,076 | 7,654 | 6,212 |
| 53,950 | 54,000 | 7,665 | 6,082 | 7,665 | 6,223 |

| If line 15 (taxable income) is— At least | But less than | And you are— Single | Married filing jointly* | Married filing separately | Head of a household |
|---|---|---|---|---|---|
| | | Your tax is— | | | |
| **54,000** | | | | | |
| 54,000 | 54,050 | 7,676 | 6,088 | 7,676 | 6,234 |
| 54,050 | 54,100 | 7,687 | 6,094 | 7,687 | 6,245 |
| 54,100 | 54,150 | 7,698 | 6,100 | 7,698 | 6,256 |
| 54,150 | 54,200 | 7,709 | 6,106 | 7,709 | 6,267 |
| 54,200 | 54,250 | 7,720 | 6,112 | 7,720 | 6,278 |
| 54,250 | 54,300 | 7,731 | 6,118 | 7,731 | 6,289 |
| 54,300 | 54,350 | 7,742 | 6,124 | 7,742 | 6,300 |
| 54,350 | 54,400 | 7,753 | 6,130 | 7,753 | 6,311 |
| 54,400 | 54,450 | 7,764 | 6,136 | 7,764 | 6,322 |
| 54,450 | 54,500 | 7,775 | 6,142 | 7,775 | 6,333 |
| 54,500 | 54,550 | 7,786 | 6,148 | 7,786 | 6,344 |
| 54,550 | 54,600 | 7,797 | 6,154 | 7,797 | 6,355 |
| 54,600 | 54,650 | 7,808 | 6,160 | 7,808 | 6,366 |
| 54,650 | 54,700 | 7,819 | 6,166 | 7,819 | 6,377 |
| 54,700 | 54,750 | 7,830 | 6,172 | 7,830 | 6,388 |
| 54,750 | 54,800 | 7,841 | 6,178 | 7,841 | 6,399 |
| 54,800 | 54,850 | 7,852 | 6,184 | 7,852 | 6,410 |
| 54,850 | 54,900 | 7,863 | 6,190 | 7,863 | 6,421 |
| 54,900 | 54,950 | 7,874 | 6,196 | 7,874 | 6,432 |
| 54,950 | 55,000 | 7,885 | 6,202 | 7,885 | 6,443 |
| **55,000** | | | | | |
| 55,000 | 55,050 | 7,896 | 6,208 | 7,896 | 6,454 |
| 55,050 | 55,100 | 7,907 | 6,214 | 7,907 | 6,465 |
| 55,100 | 55,150 | 7,918 | 6,220 | 7,918 | 6,476 |
| 55,150 | 55,200 | 7,929 | 6,226 | 7,929 | 6,487 |
| 55,200 | 55,250 | 7,940 | 6,232 | 7,940 | 6,498 |
| 55,250 | 55,300 | 7,951 | 6,238 | 7,951 | 6,509 |
| 55,300 | 55,350 | 7,962 | 6,244 | 7,962 | 6,520 |
| 55,350 | 55,400 | 7,973 | 6,250 | 7,973 | 6,531 |
| 55,400 | 55,450 | 7,984 | 6,256 | 7,984 | 6,542 |
| 55,450 | 55,500 | 7,995 | 6,262 | 7,995 | 6,553 |
| 55,500 | 55,550 | 8,006 | 6,268 | 8,006 | 6,564 |
| 55,550 | 55,600 | 8,017 | 6,274 | 8,017 | 6,575 |
| 55,600 | 55,650 | 8,028 | 6,280 | 8,028 | 6,586 |
| 55,650 | 55,700 | 8,039 | 6,286 | 8,039 | 6,597 |
| 55,700 | 55,750 | 8,050 | 6,292 | 8,050 | 6,608 |
| 55,750 | 55,800 | 8,061 | 6,298 | 8,061 | 6,619 |
| 55,800 | 55,850 | 8,072 | 6,304 | 8,072 | 6,630 |
| 55,850 | 55,900 | 8,083 | 6,310 | 8,083 | 6,641 |
| 55,900 | 55,950 | 8,094 | 6,316 | 8,094 | 6,652 |
| 55,950 | 56,000 | 8,105 | 6,322 | 8,105 | 6,663 |
| **56,000** | | | | | |
| 56,000 | 56,050 | 8,116 | 6,328 | 8,116 | 6,674 |
| 56,050 | 56,100 | 8,127 | 6,334 | 8,127 | 6,685 |
| 56,100 | 56,150 | 8,138 | 6,340 | 8,138 | 6,696 |
| 56,150 | 56,200 | 8,149 | 6,346 | 8,149 | 6,707 |
| 56,200 | 56,250 | 8,160 | 6,352 | 8,160 | 6,718 |
| 56,250 | 56,300 | 8,171 | 6,358 | 8,171 | 6,729 |
| 56,300 | 56,350 | 8,182 | 6,364 | 8,182 | 6,740 |
| 56,350 | 56,400 | 8,193 | 6,370 | 8,193 | 6,751 |
| 56,400 | 56,450 | 8,204 | 6,376 | 8,204 | 6,762 |
| 56,450 | 56,500 | 8,215 | 6,382 | 8,215 | 6,773 |
| 56,500 | 56,550 | 8,226 | 6,388 | 8,226 | 6,784 |
| 56,550 | 56,600 | 8,237 | 6,394 | 8,237 | 6,795 |
| 56,600 | 56,650 | 8,248 | 6,400 | 8,248 | 6,806 |
| 56,650 | 56,700 | 8,259 | 6,406 | 8,259 | 6,817 |
| 56,700 | 56,750 | 8,270 | 6,412 | 8,270 | 6,828 |
| 56,750 | 56,800 | 8,281 | 6,418 | 8,281 | 6,839 |
| 56,800 | 56,850 | 8,292 | 6,424 | 8,292 | 6,850 |
| 56,850 | 56,900 | 8,303 | 6,430 | 8,303 | 6,861 |
| 56,900 | 56,950 | 8,314 | 6,436 | 8,314 | 6,872 |
| 56,950 | 57,000 | 8,325 | 6,442 | 8,325 | 6,883 |

*(Continued)*

*This column must also be used by a qualifying widow(er).

## 2020 Tax Table — *Continued*

If line 15 (taxable income) is— / And you are— / Your tax is—

### 57,000

| At least | But less than | Single | Married filing jointly* | Married filing separately | Head of a household |
|---|---|---|---|---|---|
| 57,000 | 57,050 | 8,336 | 6,448 | 8,336 | 6,894 |
| 57,050 | 57,100 | 8,347 | 6,454 | 8,347 | 6,905 |
| 57,100 | 57,150 | 8,358 | 6,460 | 8,358 | 6,916 |
| 57,150 | 57,200 | 8,369 | 6,466 | 8,369 | 6,927 |
| 57,200 | 57,250 | 8,380 | 6,472 | 8,380 | 6,938 |
| 57,250 | 57,300 | 8,391 | 6,478 | 8,391 | 6,949 |
| 57,300 | 57,350 | 8,402 | 6,484 | 8,402 | 6,960 |
| 57,350 | 57,400 | 8,413 | 6,490 | 8,413 | 6,971 |
| 57,400 | 57,450 | 8,424 | 6,496 | 8,424 | 6,982 |
| 57,450 | 57,500 | 8,435 | 6,502 | 8,435 | 6,993 |
| 57,500 | 57,550 | 8,446 | 6,508 | 8,446 | 7,004 |
| 57,550 | 57,600 | 8,457 | 6,514 | 8,457 | 7,015 |
| 57,600 | 57,650 | 8,468 | 6,520 | 8,468 | 7,026 |
| 57,650 | 57,700 | 8,479 | 6,526 | 8,479 | 7,037 |
| 57,700 | 57,750 | 8,490 | 6,532 | 8,490 | 7,048 |
| 57,750 | 57,800 | 8,501 | 6,538 | 8,501 | 7,059 |
| 57,800 | 57,850 | 8,512 | 6,544 | 8,512 | 7,070 |
| 57,850 | 57,900 | 8,523 | 6,550 | 8,523 | 7,081 |
| 57,900 | 57,950 | 8,534 | 6,556 | 8,534 | 7,092 |
| 57,950 | 58,000 | 8,545 | 6,562 | 8,545 | 7,103 |

### 58,000

| At least | But less than | Single | Married filing jointly* | Married filing separately | Head of a household |
|---|---|---|---|---|---|
| 58,000 | 58,050 | 8,556 | 6,568 | 8,556 | 7,114 |
| 58,050 | 58,100 | 8,567 | 6,574 | 8,567 | 7,125 |
| 58,100 | 58,150 | 8,578 | 6,580 | 8,578 | 7,136 |
| 58,150 | 58,200 | 8,589 | 6,586 | 8,589 | 7,147 |
| 58,200 | 58,250 | 8,600 | 6,592 | 8,600 | 7,158 |
| 58,250 | 58,300 | 8,611 | 6,598 | 8,611 | 7,169 |
| 58,300 | 58,350 | 8,622 | 6,604 | 8,622 | 7,180 |
| 58,350 | 58,400 | 8,633 | 6,610 | 8,633 | 7,191 |
| 58,400 | 58,450 | 8,644 | 6,616 | 8,644 | 7,202 |
| 58,450 | 58,500 | 8,655 | 6,622 | 8,655 | 7,213 |
| 58,500 | 58,550 | 8,666 | 6,628 | 8,666 | 7,224 |
| 58,550 | 58,600 | 8,677 | 6,634 | 8,677 | 7,235 |
| 58,600 | 58,650 | 8,688 | 6,640 | 8,688 | 7,246 |
| 58,650 | 58,700 | 8,699 | 6,646 | 8,699 | 7,257 |
| 58,700 | 58,750 | 8,710 | 6,652 | 8,710 | 7,268 |
| 58,750 | 58,800 | 8,721 | 6,658 | 8,721 | 7,279 |
| 58,800 | 58,850 | 8,732 | 6,664 | 8,732 | 7,290 |
| 58,850 | 58,900 | 8,743 | 6,670 | 8,743 | 7,301 |
| 58,900 | 58,950 | 8,754 | 6,676 | 8,754 | 7,312 |
| 58,950 | 59,000 | 8,765 | 6,682 | 8,765 | 7,323 |

### 59,000

| At least | But less than | Single | Married filing jointly* | Married filing separately | Head of a household |
|---|---|---|---|---|---|
| 59,000 | 59,050 | 8,776 | 6,688 | 8,776 | 7,334 |
| 59,050 | 59,100 | 8,787 | 6,694 | 8,787 | 7,345 |
| 59,100 | 59,150 | 8,798 | 6,700 | 8,798 | 7,356 |
| 59,150 | 59,200 | 8,809 | 6,706 | 8,809 | 7,367 |
| 59,200 | 59,250 | 8,820 | 6,712 | 8,820 | 7,378 |
| 59,250 | 59,300 | 8,831 | 6,718 | 8,831 | 7,389 |
| 59,300 | 59,350 | 8,842 | 6,724 | 8,842 | 7,400 |
| 59,350 | 59,400 | 8,853 | 6,730 | 8,853 | 7,411 |
| 59,400 | 59,450 | 8,864 | 6,736 | 8,864 | 7,422 |
| 59,450 | 59,500 | 8,875 | 6,742 | 8,875 | 7,433 |
| 59,500 | 59,550 | 8,886 | 6,748 | 8,886 | 7,444 |
| 59,550 | 59,600 | 8,897 | 6,754 | 8,897 | 7,455 |
| 59,600 | 59,650 | 8,908 | 6,760 | 8,908 | 7,466 |
| 59,650 | 59,700 | 8,919 | 6,766 | 8,919 | 7,477 |
| 59,700 | 59,750 | 8,930 | 6,772 | 8,930 | 7,488 |
| 59,750 | 59,800 | 8,941 | 6,778 | 8,941 | 7,499 |
| 59,800 | 59,850 | 8,952 | 6,784 | 8,952 | 7,510 |
| 59,850 | 59,900 | 8,963 | 6,790 | 8,963 | 7,521 |
| 59,900 | 59,950 | 8,974 | 6,796 | 8,974 | 7,532 |
| 59,950 | 60,000 | 8,985 | 6,802 | 8,985 | 7,543 |

### 60,000

| At least | But less than | Single | Married filing jointly* | Married filing separately | Head of a household |
|---|---|---|---|---|---|
| 60,000 | 60,050 | 8,996 | 6,808 | 8,996 | 7,554 |
| 60,050 | 60,100 | 9,007 | 6,814 | 9,007 | 7,565 |
| 60,100 | 60,150 | 9,018 | 6,820 | 9,018 | 7,576 |
| 60,150 | 60,200 | 9,029 | 6,826 | 9,029 | 7,587 |
| 60,200 | 60,250 | 9,040 | 6,832 | 9,040 | 7,598 |
| 60,250 | 60,300 | 9,051 | 6,838 | 9,051 | 7,609 |
| 60,300 | 60,350 | 9,062 | 6,844 | 9,062 | 7,620 |
| 60,350 | 60,400 | 9,073 | 6,850 | 9,073 | 7,631 |
| 60,400 | 60,450 | 9,084 | 6,856 | 9,084 | 7,642 |
| 60,450 | 60,500 | 9,095 | 6,862 | 9,095 | 7,653 |
| 60,500 | 60,550 | 9,106 | 6,868 | 9,106 | 7,664 |
| 60,550 | 60,600 | 9,117 | 6,874 | 9,117 | 7,675 |
| 60,600 | 60,650 | 9,128 | 6,880 | 9,128 | 7,686 |
| 60,650 | 60,700 | 9,139 | 6,886 | 9,139 | 7,697 |
| 60,700 | 60,750 | 9,150 | 6,892 | 9,150 | 7,708 |
| 60,750 | 60,800 | 9,161 | 6,898 | 9,161 | 7,719 |
| 60,800 | 60,850 | 9,172 | 6,904 | 9,172 | 7,730 |
| 60,850 | 60,900 | 9,183 | 6,910 | 9,183 | 7,741 |
| 60,900 | 60,950 | 9,194 | 6,916 | 9,194 | 7,752 |
| 60,950 | 61,000 | 9,205 | 6,922 | 9,205 | 7,763 |

### 61,000

| At least | But less than | Single | Married filing jointly* | Married filing separately | Head of a household |
|---|---|---|---|---|---|
| 61,000 | 61,050 | 9,216 | 6,928 | 9,216 | 7,774 |
| 61,050 | 61,100 | 9,227 | 6,934 | 9,227 | 7,785 |
| 61,100 | 61,150 | 9,238 | 6,940 | 9,238 | 7,796 |
| 61,150 | 61,200 | 9,249 | 6,946 | 9,249 | 7,807 |
| 61,200 | 61,250 | 9,260 | 6,952 | 9,260 | 7,818 |
| 61,250 | 61,300 | 9,271 | 6,958 | 9,271 | 7,829 |
| 61,300 | 61,350 | 9,282 | 6,964 | 9,282 | 7,840 |
| 61,350 | 61,400 | 9,293 | 6,970 | 9,293 | 7,851 |
| 61,400 | 61,450 | 9,304 | 6,976 | 9,304 | 7,862 |
| 61,450 | 61,500 | 9,315 | 6,982 | 9,315 | 7,873 |
| 61,500 | 61,550 | 9,326 | 6,988 | 9,326 | 7,884 |
| 61,550 | 61,600 | 9,337 | 6,994 | 9,337 | 7,895 |
| 61,600 | 61,650 | 9,348 | 7,000 | 9,348 | 7,906 |
| 61,650 | 61,700 | 9,359 | 7,006 | 9,359 | 7,917 |
| 61,700 | 61,750 | 9,370 | 7,012 | 9,370 | 7,928 |
| 61,750 | 61,800 | 9,381 | 7,018 | 9,381 | 7,939 |
| 61,800 | 61,850 | 9,392 | 7,024 | 9,392 | 7,950 |
| 61,850 | 61,900 | 9,403 | 7,030 | 9,403 | 7,961 |
| 61,900 | 61,950 | 9,414 | 7,036 | 9,414 | 7,972 |
| 61,950 | 62,000 | 9,425 | 7,042 | 9,425 | 7,983 |

### 62,000

| At least | But less than | Single | Married filing jointly* | Married filing separately | Head of a household |
|---|---|---|---|---|---|
| 62,000 | 62,050 | 9,436 | 7,048 | 9,436 | 7,994 |
| 62,050 | 62,100 | 9,447 | 7,054 | 9,447 | 8,005 |
| 62,100 | 62,150 | 9,458 | 7,060 | 9,458 | 8,016 |
| 62,150 | 62,200 | 9,469 | 7,066 | 9,469 | 8,027 |
| 62,200 | 62,250 | 9,480 | 7,072 | 9,480 | 8,038 |
| 62,250 | 62,300 | 9,491 | 7,078 | 9,491 | 8,049 |
| 62,300 | 62,350 | 9,502 | 7,084 | 9,502 | 8,060 |
| 62,350 | 62,400 | 9,513 | 7,090 | 9,513 | 8,071 |
| 62,400 | 62,450 | 9,524 | 7,096 | 9,524 | 8,082 |
| 62,450 | 62,500 | 9,535 | 7,102 | 9,535 | 8,093 |
| 62,500 | 62,550 | 9,546 | 7,108 | 9,546 | 8,104 |
| 62,550 | 62,600 | 9,557 | 7,114 | 9,557 | 8,115 |
| 62,600 | 62,650 | 9,568 | 7,120 | 9,568 | 8,126 |
| 62,650 | 62,700 | 9,579 | 7,126 | 9,579 | 8,137 |
| 62,700 | 62,750 | 9,590 | 7,132 | 9,590 | 8,148 |
| 62,750 | 62,800 | 9,601 | 7,138 | 9,601 | 8,159 |
| 62,800 | 62,850 | 9,612 | 7,144 | 9,612 | 8,170 |
| 62,850 | 62,900 | 9,623 | 7,150 | 9,623 | 8,181 |
| 62,900 | 62,950 | 9,634 | 7,156 | 9,634 | 8,192 |
| 62,950 | 63,000 | 9,645 | 7,162 | 9,645 | 8,203 |

### 63,000

| At least | But less than | Single | Married filing jointly* | Married filing separately | Head of a household |
|---|---|---|---|---|---|
| 63,000 | 63,050 | 9,656 | 7,168 | 9,656 | 8,214 |
| 63,050 | 63,100 | 9,667 | 7,174 | 9,667 | 8,225 |
| 63,100 | 63,150 | 9,678 | 7,180 | 9,678 | 8,236 |
| 63,150 | 63,200 | 9,689 | 7,186 | 9,689 | 8,247 |
| 63,200 | 63,250 | 9,700 | 7,192 | 9,700 | 8,258 |
| 63,250 | 63,300 | 9,711 | 7,198 | 9,711 | 8,269 |
| 63,300 | 63,350 | 9,722 | 7,204 | 9,722 | 8,280 |
| 63,350 | 63,400 | 9,733 | 7,210 | 9,733 | 8,291 |
| 63,400 | 63,450 | 9,744 | 7,216 | 9,744 | 8,302 |
| 63,450 | 63,500 | 9,755 | 7,222 | 9,755 | 8,313 |
| 63,500 | 63,550 | 9,766 | 7,228 | 9,766 | 8,324 |
| 63,550 | 63,600 | 9,777 | 7,234 | 9,777 | 8,335 |
| 63,600 | 63,650 | 9,788 | 7,240 | 9,788 | 8,346 |
| 63,650 | 63,700 | 9,799 | 7,246 | 9,799 | 8,357 |
| 63,700 | 63,750 | 9,810 | 7,252 | 9,810 | 8,368 |
| 63,750 | 63,800 | 9,821 | 7,258 | 9,821 | 8,379 |
| 63,800 | 63,850 | 9,832 | 7,264 | 9,832 | 8,390 |
| 63,850 | 63,900 | 9,843 | 7,270 | 9,843 | 8,401 |
| 63,900 | 63,950 | 9,854 | 7,276 | 9,854 | 8,412 |
| 63,950 | 64,000 | 9,865 | 7,282 | 9,865 | 8,423 |

### 64,000

| At least | But less than | Single | Married filing jointly* | Married filing separately | Head of a household |
|---|---|---|---|---|---|
| 64,000 | 64,050 | 9,876 | 7,288 | 9,876 | 8,434 |
| 64,050 | 64,100 | 9,887 | 7,294 | 9,887 | 8,445 |
| 64,100 | 64,150 | 9,898 | 7,300 | 9,898 | 8,456 |
| 64,150 | 64,200 | 9,909 | 7,306 | 9,909 | 8,467 |
| 64,200 | 64,250 | 9,920 | 7,312 | 9,920 | 8,478 |
| 64,250 | 64,300 | 9,931 | 7,318 | 9,931 | 8,489 |
| 64,300 | 64,350 | 9,942 | 7,324 | 9,942 | 8,500 |
| 64,350 | 64,400 | 9,953 | 7,330 | 9,953 | 8,511 |
| 64,400 | 64,450 | 9,964 | 7,336 | 9,964 | 8,522 |
| 64,450 | 64,500 | 9,975 | 7,342 | 9,975 | 8,533 |
| 64,500 | 64,550 | 9,986 | 7,348 | 9,986 | 8,544 |
| 64,550 | 64,600 | 9,997 | 7,354 | 9,997 | 8,555 |
| 64,600 | 64,650 | 10,008 | 7,360 | 10,008 | 8,566 |
| 64,650 | 64,700 | 10,019 | 7,366 | 10,019 | 8,577 |
| 64,700 | 64,750 | 10,030 | 7,372 | 10,030 | 8,588 |
| 64,750 | 64,800 | 10,041 | 7,378 | 10,041 | 8,599 |
| 64,800 | 64,850 | 10,052 | 7,384 | 10,052 | 8,610 |
| 64,850 | 64,900 | 10,063 | 7,390 | 10,063 | 8,621 |
| 64,900 | 64,950 | 10,074 | 7,396 | 10,074 | 8,632 |
| 64,950 | 65,000 | 10,085 | 7,402 | 10,085 | 8,643 |

### 65,000

| At least | But less than | Single | Married filing jointly* | Married filing separately | Head of a household |
|---|---|---|---|---|---|
| 65,000 | 65,050 | 10,096 | 7,408 | 10,096 | 8,654 |
| 65,050 | 65,100 | 10,107 | 7,414 | 10,107 | 8,665 |
| 65,100 | 65,150 | 10,118 | 7,420 | 10,118 | 8,676 |
| 65,150 | 65,200 | 10,129 | 7,426 | 10,129 | 8,687 |
| 65,200 | 65,250 | 10,140 | 7,432 | 10,140 | 8,698 |
| 65,250 | 65,300 | 10,151 | 7,438 | 10,151 | 8,709 |
| 65,300 | 65,350 | 10,162 | 7,444 | 10,162 | 8,720 |
| 65,350 | 65,400 | 10,173 | 7,450 | 10,173 | 8,731 |
| 65,400 | 65,450 | 10,184 | 7,456 | 10,184 | 8,742 |
| 65,450 | 65,500 | 10,195 | 7,462 | 10,195 | 8,753 |
| 65,500 | 65,550 | 10,206 | 7,468 | 10,206 | 8,764 |
| 65,550 | 65,600 | 10,217 | 7,474 | 10,217 | 8,775 |
| 65,600 | 65,650 | 10,228 | 7,480 | 10,228 | 8,786 |
| 65,650 | 65,700 | 10,239 | 7,486 | 10,239 | 8,797 |
| 65,700 | 65,750 | 10,250 | 7,492 | 10,250 | 8,808 |
| 65,750 | 65,800 | 10,261 | 7,498 | 10,261 | 8,819 |
| 65,800 | 65,850 | 10,272 | 7,504 | 10,272 | 8,830 |
| 65,850 | 65,900 | 10,283 | 7,510 | 10,283 | 8,841 |
| 65,900 | 65,950 | 10,294 | 7,516 | 10,294 | 8,852 |
| 65,950 | 66,000 | 10,305 | 7,522 | 10,305 | 8,863 |

*(Continued)*

*This column must also be used by a qualifying widow(er).

## 2020 Tax Table — *Continued*

| If line 15 (taxable income) is— | | And you are— | | | |
|---|---|---|---|---|---|
| At least | But less than | Single | Married filing jointly* | Married filing sepa-rately | Head of a house-hold |
| | | Your tax is— | | | |
| **66,000** | | | | | |
| 66,000 | 66,050 | 10,316 | 7,528 | 10,316 | 8,874 |
| 66,050 | 66,100 | 10,327 | 7,534 | 10,327 | 8,885 |
| 66,100 | 66,150 | 10,338 | 7,540 | 10,338 | 8,896 |
| 66,150 | 66,200 | 10,349 | 7,546 | 10,349 | 8,907 |
| 66,200 | 66,250 | 10,360 | 7,552 | 10,360 | 8,918 |
| 66,250 | 66,300 | 10,371 | 7,558 | 10,371 | 8,929 |
| 66,300 | 66,350 | 10,382 | 7,564 | 10,382 | 8,940 |
| 66,350 | 66,400 | 10,393 | 7,570 | 10,393 | 8,951 |
| 66,400 | 66,450 | 10,404 | 7,576 | 10,404 | 8,962 |
| 66,450 | 66,500 | 10,415 | 7,582 | 10,415 | 8,973 |
| 66,500 | 66,550 | 10,426 | 7,588 | 10,426 | 8,984 |
| 66,550 | 66,600 | 10,437 | 7,594 | 10,437 | 8,995 |
| 66,600 | 66,650 | 10,448 | 7,600 | 10,448 | 9,006 |
| 66,650 | 66,700 | 10,459 | 7,606 | 10,459 | 9,017 |
| 66,700 | 66,750 | 10,470 | 7,612 | 10,470 | 9,028 |
| 66,750 | 66,800 | 10,481 | 7,618 | 10,481 | 9,039 |
| 66,800 | 66,850 | 10,492 | 7,624 | 10,492 | 9,050 |
| 66,850 | 66,900 | 10,503 | 7,630 | 10,503 | 9,061 |
| 66,900 | 66,950 | 10,514 | 7,636 | 10,514 | 9,072 |
| 66,950 | 67,000 | 10,525 | 7,642 | 10,525 | 9,083 |
| **67,000** | | | | | |
| 67,000 | 67,050 | 10,536 | 7,648 | 10,536 | 9,094 |
| 67,050 | 67,100 | 10,547 | 7,654 | 10,547 | 9,105 |
| 67,100 | 67,150 | 10,558 | 7,660 | 10,558 | 9,116 |
| 67,150 | 67,200 | 10,569 | 7,666 | 10,569 | 9,127 |
| 67,200 | 67,250 | 10,580 | 7,672 | 10,580 | 9,138 |
| 67,250 | 67,300 | 10,591 | 7,678 | 10,591 | 9,149 |
| 67,300 | 67,350 | 10,602 | 7,684 | 10,602 | 9,160 |
| 67,350 | 67,400 | 10,613 | 7,690 | 10,613 | 9,171 |
| 67,400 | 67,450 | 10,624 | 7,696 | 10,624 | 9,182 |
| 67,450 | 67,500 | 10,635 | 7,702 | 10,635 | 9,193 |
| 67,500 | 67,550 | 10,646 | 7,708 | 10,646 | 9,204 |
| 67,550 | 67,600 | 10,657 | 7,714 | 10,657 | 9,215 |
| 67,600 | 67,650 | 10,668 | 7,720 | 10,668 | 9,226 |
| 67,650 | 67,700 | 10,679 | 7,726 | 10,679 | 9,237 |
| 67,700 | 67,750 | 10,690 | 7,732 | 10,690 | 9,248 |
| 67,750 | 67,800 | 10,701 | 7,738 | 10,701 | 9,259 |
| 67,800 | 67,850 | 10,712 | 7,744 | 10,712 | 9,270 |
| 67,850 | 67,900 | 10,723 | 7,750 | 10,723 | 9,281 |
| 67,900 | 67,950 | 10,734 | 7,756 | 10,734 | 9,292 |
| 67,950 | 68,000 | 10,745 | 7,762 | 10,745 | 9,303 |
| **68,000** | | | | | |
| 68,000 | 68,050 | 10,756 | 7,768 | 10,756 | 9,314 |
| 68,050 | 68,100 | 10,767 | 7,774 | 10,767 | 9,325 |
| 68,100 | 68,150 | 10,778 | 7,780 | 10,778 | 9,336 |
| 68,150 | 68,200 | 10,789 | 7,786 | 10,789 | 9,347 |
| 68,200 | 68,250 | 10,800 | 7,792 | 10,800 | 9,358 |
| 68,250 | 68,300 | 10,811 | 7,798 | 10,811 | 9,369 |
| 68,300 | 68,350 | 10,822 | 7,804 | 10,822 | 9,380 |
| 68,350 | 68,400 | 10,833 | 7,810 | 10,833 | 9,391 |
| 68,400 | 68,450 | 10,844 | 7,816 | 10,844 | 9,402 |
| 68,450 | 68,500 | 10,855 | 7,822 | 10,855 | 9,413 |
| 68,500 | 68,550 | 10,866 | 7,828 | 10,866 | 9,424 |
| 68,550 | 68,600 | 10,877 | 7,834 | 10,877 | 9,435 |
| 68,600 | 68,650 | 10,888 | 7,840 | 10,888 | 9,446 |
| 68,650 | 68,700 | 10,899 | 7,846 | 10,899 | 9,457 |
| 68,700 | 68,750 | 10,910 | 7,852 | 10,910 | 9,468 |
| 68,750 | 68,800 | 10,921 | 7,858 | 10,921 | 9,479 |
| 68,800 | 68,850 | 10,932 | 7,864 | 10,932 | 9,490 |
| 68,850 | 68,900 | 10,943 | 7,870 | 10,943 | 9,501 |
| 68,900 | 68,950 | 10,954 | 7,876 | 10,954 | 9,512 |
| 68,950 | 69,000 | 10,965 | 7,882 | 10,965 | 9,523 |

| If line 15 (taxable income) is— | | And you are— | | | |
|---|---|---|---|---|---|
| At least | But less than | Single | Married filing jointly* | Married filing sepa-rately | Head of a house-hold |
| | | Your tax is— | | | |
| **69,000** | | | | | |
| 69,000 | 69,050 | 10,976 | 7,888 | 10,976 | 9,534 |
| 69,050 | 69,100 | 10,987 | 7,894 | 10,987 | 9,545 |
| 69,100 | 69,150 | 10,998 | 7,900 | 10,998 | 9,556 |
| 69,150 | 69,200 | 11,009 | 7,906 | 11,009 | 9,567 |
| 69,200 | 69,250 | 11,020 | 7,912 | 11,020 | 9,578 |
| 69,250 | 69,300 | 11,031 | 7,918 | 11,031 | 9,589 |
| 69,300 | 69,350 | 11,042 | 7,924 | 11,042 | 9,600 |
| 69,350 | 69,400 | 11,053 | 7,930 | 11,053 | 9,611 |
| 69,400 | 69,450 | 11,064 | 7,936 | 11,064 | 9,622 |
| 69,450 | 69,500 | 11,075 | 7,942 | 11,075 | 9,633 |
| 69,500 | 69,550 | 11,086 | 7,948 | 11,086 | 9,644 |
| 69,550 | 69,600 | 11,097 | 7,954 | 11,097 | 9,655 |
| 69,600 | 69,650 | 11,108 | 7,960 | 11,108 | 9,666 |
| 69,650 | 69,700 | 11,119 | 7,966 | 11,119 | 9,677 |
| 69,700 | 69,750 | 11,130 | 7,972 | 11,130 | 9,688 |
| 69,750 | 69,800 | 11,141 | 7,978 | 11,141 | 9,699 |
| 69,800 | 69,850 | 11,152 | 7,984 | 11,152 | 9,710 |
| 69,850 | 69,900 | 11,163 | 7,990 | 11,163 | 9,721 |
| 69,900 | 69,950 | 11,174 | 7,996 | 11,174 | 9,732 |
| 69,950 | 70,000 | 11,185 | 8,002 | 11,185 | 9,743 |
| **70,000** | | | | | |
| 70,000 | 70,050 | 11,196 | 8,008 | 11,196 | 9,754 |
| 70,050 | 70,100 | 11,207 | 8,014 | 11,207 | 9,765 |
| 70,100 | 70,150 | 11,218 | 8,020 | 11,218 | 9,776 |
| 70,150 | 70,200 | 11,229 | 8,026 | 11,229 | 9,787 |
| 70,200 | 70,250 | 11,240 | 8,032 | 11,240 | 9,798 |
| 70,250 | 70,300 | 11,251 | 8,038 | 11,251 | 9,809 |
| 70,300 | 70,350 | 11,262 | 8,044 | 11,262 | 9,820 |
| 70,350 | 70,400 | 11,273 | 8,050 | 11,273 | 9,831 |
| 70,400 | 70,450 | 11,284 | 8,056 | 11,284 | 9,842 |
| 70,450 | 70,500 | 11,295 | 8,062 | 11,295 | 9,853 |
| 70,500 | 70,550 | 11,306 | 8,068 | 11,306 | 9,864 |
| 70,550 | 70,600 | 11,317 | 8,074 | 11,317 | 9,875 |
| 70,600 | 70,650 | 11,328 | 8,080 | 11,328 | 9,886 |
| 70,650 | 70,700 | 11,339 | 8,086 | 11,339 | 9,897 |
| 70,700 | 70,750 | 11,350 | 8,092 | 11,350 | 9,908 |
| 70,750 | 70,800 | 11,361 | 8,098 | 11,361 | 9,919 |
| 70,800 | 70,850 | 11,372 | 8,104 | 11,372 | 9,930 |
| 70,850 | 70,900 | 11,383 | 8,110 | 11,383 | 9,941 |
| 70,900 | 70,950 | 11,394 | 8,116 | 11,394 | 9,952 |
| 70,950 | 71,000 | 11,405 | 8,122 | 11,405 | 9,963 |
| **71,000** | | | | | |
| 71,000 | 71,050 | 11,416 | 8,128 | 11,416 | 9,974 |
| 71,050 | 71,100 | 11,427 | 8,134 | 11,427 | 9,985 |
| 71,100 | 71,150 | 11,438 | 8,140 | 11,438 | 9,996 |
| 71,150 | 71,200 | 11,449 | 8,146 | 11,449 | 10,007 |
| 71,200 | 71,250 | 11,460 | 8,152 | 11,460 | 10,018 |
| 71,250 | 71,300 | 11,471 | 8,158 | 11,471 | 10,029 |
| 71,300 | 71,350 | 11,482 | 8,164 | 11,482 | 10,040 |
| 71,350 | 71,400 | 11,493 | 8,170 | 11,493 | 10,051 |
| 71,400 | 71,450 | 11,504 | 8,176 | 11,504 | 10,062 |
| 71,450 | 71,500 | 11,515 | 8,182 | 11,515 | 10,073 |
| 71,500 | 71,550 | 11,526 | 8,188 | 11,526 | 10,084 |
| 71,550 | 71,600 | 11,537 | 8,194 | 11,537 | 10,095 |
| 71,600 | 71,650 | 11,548 | 8,200 | 11,548 | 10,106 |
| 71,650 | 71,700 | 11,559 | 8,206 | 11,559 | 10,117 |
| 71,700 | 71,750 | 11,570 | 8,212 | 11,570 | 10,128 |
| 71,750 | 71,800 | 11,581 | 8,218 | 11,581 | 10,139 |
| 71,800 | 71,850 | 11,592 | 8,224 | 11,592 | 10,150 |
| 71,850 | 71,900 | 11,603 | 8,230 | 11,603 | 10,161 |
| 71,900 | 71,950 | 11,614 | 8,236 | 11,614 | 10,172 |
| 71,950 | 72,000 | 11,625 | 8,242 | 11,625 | 10,183 |

| If line 15 (taxable income) is— | | And you are— | | | |
|---|---|---|---|---|---|
| At least | But less than | Single | Married filing jointly* | Married filing sepa-rately | Head of a house-hold |
| | | Your tax is— | | | |
| **72,000** | | | | | |
| 72,000 | 72,050 | 11,636 | 8,248 | 11,636 | 10,194 |
| 72,050 | 72,100 | 11,647 | 8,254 | 11,647 | 10,205 |
| 72,100 | 72,150 | 11,658 | 8,260 | 11,658 | 10,216 |
| 72,150 | 72,200 | 11,669 | 8,266 | 11,669 | 10,227 |
| 72,200 | 72,250 | 11,680 | 8,272 | 11,680 | 10,238 |
| 72,250 | 72,300 | 11,691 | 8,278 | 11,691 | 10,249 |
| 72,300 | 72,350 | 11,702 | 8,284 | 11,702 | 10,260 |
| 72,350 | 72,400 | 11,713 | 8,290 | 11,713 | 10,271 |
| 72,400 | 72,450 | 11,724 | 8,296 | 11,724 | 10,282 |
| 72,450 | 72,500 | 11,735 | 8,302 | 11,735 | 10,293 |
| 72,500 | 72,550 | 11,746 | 8,308 | 11,746 | 10,304 |
| 72,550 | 72,600 | 11,757 | 8,314 | 11,757 | 10,315 |
| 72,600 | 72,650 | 11,768 | 8,320 | 11,768 | 10,326 |
| 72,650 | 72,700 | 11,779 | 8,326 | 11,779 | 10,337 |
| 72,700 | 72,750 | 11,790 | 8,332 | 11,790 | 10,348 |
| 72,750 | 72,800 | 11,801 | 8,338 | 11,801 | 10,359 |
| 72,800 | 72,850 | 11,812 | 8,344 | 11,812 | 10,370 |
| 72,850 | 72,900 | 11,823 | 8,350 | 11,823 | 10,381 |
| 72,900 | 72,950 | 11,834 | 8,356 | 11,834 | 10,392 |
| 72,950 | 73,000 | 11,845 | 8,362 | 11,845 | 10,403 |
| **73,000** | | | | | |
| 73,000 | 73,050 | 11,856 | 8,368 | 11,856 | 10,414 |
| 73,050 | 73,100 | 11,867 | 8,374 | 11,867 | 10,425 |
| 73,100 | 73,150 | 11,878 | 8,380 | 11,878 | 10,436 |
| 73,150 | 73,200 | 11,889 | 8,386 | 11,889 | 10,447 |
| 73,200 | 73,250 | 11,900 | 8,392 | 11,900 | 10,458 |
| 73,250 | 73,300 | 11,911 | 8,398 | 11,911 | 10,469 |
| 73,300 | 73,350 | 11,922 | 8,404 | 11,922 | 10,480 |
| 73,350 | 73,400 | 11,933 | 8,410 | 11,933 | 10,491 |
| 73,400 | 73,450 | 11,944 | 8,416 | 11,944 | 10,502 |
| 73,450 | 73,500 | 11,955 | 8,422 | 11,955 | 10,513 |
| 73,500 | 73,550 | 11,966 | 8,428 | 11,966 | 10,524 |
| 73,550 | 73,600 | 11,977 | 8,434 | 11,977 | 10,535 |
| 73,600 | 73,650 | 11,988 | 8,440 | 11,988 | 10,546 |
| 73,650 | 73,700 | 11,999 | 8,446 | 11,999 | 10,557 |
| 73,700 | 73,750 | 12,010 | 8,452 | 12,010 | 10,568 |
| 73,750 | 73,800 | 12,021 | 8,458 | 12,021 | 10,579 |
| 73,800 | 73,850 | 12,032 | 8,464 | 12,032 | 10,590 |
| 73,850 | 73,900 | 12,043 | 8,470 | 12,043 | 10,601 |
| 73,900 | 73,950 | 12,054 | 8,476 | 12,054 | 10,612 |
| 73,950 | 74,000 | 12,065 | 8,482 | 12,065 | 10,623 |
| **74,000** | | | | | |
| 74,000 | 74,050 | 12,076 | 8,488 | 12,076 | 10,634 |
| 74,050 | 74,100 | 12,087 | 8,494 | 12,087 | 10,645 |
| 74,100 | 74,150 | 12,098 | 8,500 | 12,098 | 10,656 |
| 74,150 | 74,200 | 12,109 | 8,506 | 12,109 | 10,667 |
| 74,200 | 74,250 | 12,120 | 8,512 | 12,120 | 10,678 |
| 74,250 | 74,300 | 12,131 | 8,518 | 12,131 | 10,689 |
| 74,300 | 74,350 | 12,142 | 8,524 | 12,142 | 10,700 |
| 74,350 | 74,400 | 12,153 | 8,530 | 12,153 | 10,711 |
| 74,400 | 74,450 | 12,164 | 8,536 | 12,164 | 10,722 |
| 74,450 | 74,500 | 12,175 | 8,542 | 12,175 | 10,733 |
| 74,500 | 74,550 | 12,186 | 8,548 | 12,186 | 10,744 |
| 74,550 | 74,600 | 12,197 | 8,554 | 12,197 | 10,755 |
| 74,600 | 74,650 | 12,208 | 8,560 | 12,208 | 10,766 |
| 74,650 | 74,700 | 12,219 | 8,566 | 12,219 | 10,777 |
| 74,700 | 74,750 | 12,230 | 8,572 | 12,230 | 10,788 |
| 74,750 | 74,800 | 12,241 | 8,578 | 12,241 | 10,799 |
| 74,800 | 74,850 | 12,252 | 8,584 | 12,252 | 10,810 |
| 74,850 | 74,900 | 12,263 | 8,590 | 12,263 | 10,821 |
| 74,900 | 74,950 | 12,274 | 8,596 | 12,274 | 10,832 |
| 74,950 | 75,000 | 12,285 | 8,602 | 12,285 | 10,843 |

*(Continued)*

*This column must also be used by a qualifying widow(er).

## 2020 Tax Table — *Continued*

| If line 15 (taxable income) is— At least | But less than | And you are— Single | Married filing jointly* | Married filing sepa-rately | Head of a house-hold |
|---|---|---|---|---|---|
| | | Your tax is— | | | |
| **75,000** | | | | | |
| **75,000** | **75,050** | 12,296 | 8,608 | 12,296 | 10,854 |
| **75,050** | **75,100** | 12,307 | 8,614 | 12,307 | 10,865 |
| **75,100** | **75,150** | 12,318 | 8,620 | 12,318 | 10,876 |
| **75,150** | **75,200** | 12,329 | 8,626 | 12,329 | 10,887 |
| **75,200** | **75,250** | 12,340 | 8,632 | 12,340 | 10,898 |
| **75,250** | **75,300** | 12,351 | 8,638 | 12,351 | 10,909 |
| **75,300** | **75,350** | 12,362 | 8,644 | 12,362 | 10,920 |
| **75,350** | **75,400** | 12,373 | 8,650 | 12,373 | 10,931 |
| **75,400** | **75,450** | 12,384 | 8,656 | 12,384 | 10,942 |
| **75,450** | **75,500** | 12,395 | 8,662 | 12,395 | 10,953 |
| **75,500** | **75,550** | 12,406 | 8,668 | 12,406 | 10,964 |
| **75,550** | **75,600** | 12,417 | 8,674 | 12,417 | 10,975 |
| **75,600** | **75,650** | 12,428 | 8,680 | 12,428 | 10,986 |
| **75,650** | **75,700** | 12,439 | 8,686 | 12,439 | 10,997 |
| **75,700** | **75,750** | 12,450 | 8,692 | 12,450 | 11,008 |
| **75,750** | **75,800** | 12,461 | 8,698 | 12,461 | 11,019 |
| **75,800** | **75,850** | 12,472 | 8,704 | 12,472 | 11,030 |
| **75,850** | **75,900** | 12,483 | 8,710 | 12,483 | 11,041 |
| **75,900** | **75,950** | 12,494 | 8,716 | 12,494 | 11,052 |
| **75,950** | **76,000** | 12,505 | 8,722 | 12,505 | 11,063 |
| **76,000** | | | | | |
| **76,000** | **76,050** | 12,516 | 8,728 | 12,516 | 11,074 |
| **76,050** | **76,100** | 12,527 | 8,734 | 12,527 | 11,085 |
| **76,100** | **76,150** | 12,538 | 8,740 | 12,538 | 11,096 |
| **76,150** | **76,200** | 12,549 | 8,746 | 12,549 | 11,107 |
| **76,200** | **76,250** | 12,560 | 8,752 | 12,560 | 11,118 |
| **76,250** | **76,300** | 12,571 | 8,758 | 12,571 | 11,129 |
| **76,300** | **76,350** | 12,582 | 8,764 | 12,582 | 11,140 |
| **76,350** | **76,400** | 12,593 | 8,770 | 12,593 | 11,151 |
| **76,400** | **76,450** | 12,604 | 8,776 | 12,604 | 11,162 |
| **76,450** | **76,500** | 12,615 | 8,782 | 12,615 | 11,173 |
| **76,500** | **76,550** | 12,626 | 8,788 | 12,626 | 11,184 |
| **76,550** | **76,600** | 12,637 | 8,794 | 12,637 | 11,195 |
| **76,600** | **76,650** | 12,648 | 8,800 | 12,648 | 11,206 |
| **76,650** | **76,700** | 12,659 | 8,806 | 12,659 | 11,217 |
| **76,700** | **76,750** | 12,670 | 8,812 | 12,670 | 11,228 |
| **76,750** | **76,800** | 12,681 | 8,818 | 12,681 | 11,239 |
| **76,800** | **76,850** | 12,692 | 8,824 | 12,692 | 11,250 |
| **76,850** | **76,900** | 12,703 | 8,830 | 12,703 | 11,261 |
| **76,900** | **76,950** | 12,714 | 8,836 | 12,714 | 11,272 |
| **76,950** | **77,000** | 12,725 | 8,842 | 12,725 | 11,283 |
| **77,000** | | | | | |
| **77,000** | **77,050** | 12,736 | 8,848 | 12,736 | 11,294 |
| **77,050** | **77,100** | 12,747 | 8,854 | 12,747 | 11,305 |
| **77,100** | **77,150** | 12,758 | 8,860 | 12,758 | 11,316 |
| **77,150** | **77,200** | 12,769 | 8,866 | 12,769 | 11,327 |
| **77,200** | **77,250** | 12,780 | 8,872 | 12,780 | 11,338 |
| **77,250** | **77,300** | 12,791 | 8,878 | 12,791 | 11,349 |
| **77,300** | **77,350** | 12,802 | 8,884 | 12,802 | 11,360 |
| **77,350** | **77,400** | 12,813 | 8,890 | 12,813 | 11,371 |
| **77,400** | **77,450** | 12,824 | 8,896 | 12,824 | 11,382 |
| **77,450** | **77,500** | 12,835 | 8,902 | 12,835 | 11,393 |
| **77,500** | **77,550** | 12,846 | 8,908 | 12,846 | 11,404 |
| **77,550** | **77,600** | 12,857 | 8,914 | 12,857 | 11,415 |
| **77,600** | **77,650** | 12,868 | 8,920 | 12,868 | 11,426 |
| **77,650** | **77,700** | 12,879 | 8,926 | 12,879 | 11,437 |
| **77,700** | **77,750** | 12,890 | 8,932 | 12,890 | 11,448 |
| **77,750** | **77,800** | 12,901 | 8,938 | 12,901 | 11,459 |
| **77,800** | **77,850** | 12,912 | 8,944 | 12,912 | 11,470 |
| **77,850** | **77,900** | 12,923 | 8,950 | 12,923 | 11,481 |
| **77,900** | **77,950** | 12,934 | 8,956 | 12,934 | 11,492 |
| **77,950** | **78,000** | 12,945 | 8,962 | 12,945 | 11,503 |
| **78,000** | | | | | |
| **78,000** | **78,050** | 12,956 | 8,968 | 12,956 | 11,514 |
| **78,050** | **78,100** | 12,967 | 8,974 | 12,967 | 11,525 |
| **78,100** | **78,150** | 12,978 | 8,980 | 12,978 | 11,536 |
| **78,150** | **78,200** | 12,989 | 8,986 | 12,989 | 11,547 |
| **78,200** | **78,250** | 13,000 | 8,992 | 13,000 | 11,558 |
| **78,250** | **78,300** | 13,011 | 8,998 | 13,011 | 11,569 |
| **78,300** | **78,350** | 13,022 | 9,004 | 13,022 | 11,580 |
| **78,350** | **78,400** | 13,033 | 9,010 | 13,033 | 11,591 |
| **78,400** | **78,450** | 13,044 | 9,016 | 13,044 | 11,602 |
| **78,450** | **78,500** | 13,055 | 9,022 | 13,055 | 11,613 |
| **78,500** | **78,550** | 13,066 | 9,028 | 13,066 | 11,624 |
| **78,550** | **78,600** | 13,077 | 9,034 | 13,077 | 11,635 |
| **78,600** | **78,650** | 13,088 | 9,040 | 13,088 | 11,646 |
| **78,650** | **78,700** | 13,099 | 9,046 | 13,099 | 11,657 |
| **78,700** | **78,750** | 13,110 | 9,052 | 13,110 | 11,668 |
| **78,750** | **78,800** | 13,121 | 9,058 | 13,121 | 11,679 |
| **78,800** | **78,850** | 13,132 | 9,064 | 13,132 | 11,690 |
| **78,850** | **78,900** | 13,143 | 9,070 | 13,143 | 11,701 |
| **78,900** | **78,950** | 13,154 | 9,076 | 13,154 | 11,712 |
| **78,950** | **79,000** | 13,165 | 9,082 | 13,165 | 11,723 |
| **79,000** | | | | | |
| **79,000** | **79,050** | 13,176 | 9,088 | 13,176 | 11,734 |
| **79,050** | **79,100** | 13,187 | 9,094 | 13,187 | 11,745 |
| **79,100** | **79,150** | 13,198 | 9,100 | 13,198 | 11,756 |
| **79,150** | **79,200** | 13,209 | 9,106 | 13,209 | 11,767 |
| **79,200** | **79,250** | 13,220 | 9,112 | 13,220 | 11,778 |
| **79,250** | **79,300** | 13,231 | 9,118 | 13,231 | 11,789 |
| **79,300** | **79,350** | 13,242 | 9,124 | 13,242 | 11,800 |
| **79,350** | **79,400** | 13,253 | 9,130 | 13,253 | 11,811 |
| **79,400** | **79,450** | 13,264 | 9,136 | 13,264 | 11,822 |
| **79,450** | **79,500** | 13,275 | 9,142 | 13,275 | 11,833 |
| **79,500** | **79,550** | 13,286 | 9,148 | 13,286 | 11,844 |
| **79,550** | **79,600** | 13,297 | 9,154 | 13,297 | 11,855 |
| **79,600** | **79,650** | 13,308 | 9,160 | 13,308 | 11,866 |
| **79,650** | **79,700** | 13,319 | 9,166 | 13,319 | 11,877 |
| **79,700** | **79,750** | 13,330 | 9,172 | 13,330 | 11,888 |
| **79,750** | **79,800** | 13,341 | 9,178 | 13,341 | 11,899 |
| **79,800** | **79,850** | 13,352 | 9,184 | 13,352 | 11,910 |
| **79,850** | **79,900** | 13,363 | 9,190 | 13,363 | 11,921 |
| **79,900** | **79,950** | 13,374 | 9,196 | 13,374 | 11,932 |
| **79,950** | **80,000** | 13,385 | 9,202 | 13,385 | 11,943 |
| **80,000** | | | | | |
| **80,000** | **80,050** | 13,396 | 9,208 | 13,396 | 11,954 |
| **80,050** | **80,100** | 13,407 | 9,214 | 13,407 | 11,965 |
| **80,100** | **80,150** | 13,418 | 9,220 | 13,418 | 11,976 |
| **80,150** | **80,200** | 13,429 | 9,226 | 13,429 | 11,987 |
| **80,200** | **80,250** | 13,440 | 9,232 | 13,440 | 11,998 |
| **80,250** | **80,300** | 13,451 | 9,241 | 13,451 | 12,009 |
| **80,300** | **80,350** | 13,462 | 9,252 | 13,462 | 12,020 |
| **80,350** | **80,400** | 13,473 | 9,263 | 13,473 | 12,031 |
| **80,400** | **80,450** | 13,484 | 9,274 | 13,484 | 12,042 |
| **80,450** | **80,500** | 13,495 | 9,285 | 13,495 | 12,053 |
| **80,500** | **80,550** | 13,506 | 9,296 | 13,506 | 12,064 |
| **80,550** | **80,600** | 13,517 | 9,307 | 13,517 | 12,075 |
| **80,600** | **80,650** | 13,528 | 9,318 | 13,528 | 12,086 |
| **80,650** | **80,700** | 13,539 | 9,329 | 13,539 | 12,097 |
| **80,700** | **80,750** | 13,550 | 9,340 | 13,550 | 12,108 |
| **80,750** | **80,800** | 13,561 | 9,351 | 13,561 | 12,119 |
| **80,800** | **80,850** | 13,572 | 9,362 | 13,572 | 12,130 |
| **80,850** | **80,900** | 13,583 | 9,373 | 13,583 | 12,141 |
| **80,900** | **80,950** | 13,594 | 9,384 | 13,594 | 12,152 |
| **80,950** | **81,000** | 13,605 | 9,395 | 13,605 | 12,163 |
| **81,000** | | | | | |
| **81,000** | **81,050** | 13,616 | 9,406 | 13,616 | 12,174 |
| **81,050** | **81,100** | 13,627 | 9,417 | 13,627 | 12,185 |
| **81,100** | **81,150** | 13,638 | 9,428 | 13,638 | 12,196 |
| **81,150** | **81,200** | 13,649 | 9,439 | 13,649 | 12,207 |
| **81,200** | **81,250** | 13,660 | 9,450 | 13,660 | 12,218 |
| **81,250** | **81,300** | 13,671 | 9,461 | 13,671 | 12,229 |
| **81,300** | **81,350** | 13,682 | 9,472 | 13,682 | 12,240 |
| **81,350** | **81,400** | 13,693 | 9,483 | 13,693 | 12,251 |
| **81,400** | **81,450** | 13,704 | 9,494 | 13,704 | 12,262 |
| **81,450** | **81,500** | 13,715 | 9,505 | 13,715 | 12,273 |
| **81,500** | **81,550** | 13,726 | 9,516 | 13,726 | 12,284 |
| **81,550** | **81,600** | 13,737 | 9,527 | 13,737 | 12,295 |
| **81,600** | **81,650** | 13,748 | 9,538 | 13,748 | 12,306 |
| **81,650** | **81,700** | 13,759 | 9,549 | 13,759 | 12,317 |
| **81,700** | **81,750** | 13,770 | 9,560 | 13,770 | 12,328 |
| **81,750** | **81,800** | 13,781 | 9,571 | 13,781 | 12,339 |
| **81,800** | **81,850** | 13,792 | 9,582 | 13,792 | 12,350 |
| **81,850** | **81,900** | 13,803 | 9,593 | 13,803 | 12,361 |
| **81,900** | **81,950** | 13,814 | 9,604 | 13,814 | 12,372 |
| **81,950** | **82,000** | 13,825 | 9,615 | 13,825 | 12,383 |
| **82,000** | | | | | |
| **82,000** | **82,050** | 13,836 | 9,626 | 13,836 | 12,394 |
| **82,050** | **82,100** | 13,847 | 9,637 | 13,847 | 12,405 |
| **82,100** | **82,150** | 13,858 | 9,648 | 13,858 | 12,416 |
| **82,150** | **82,200** | 13,869 | 9,659 | 13,869 | 12,427 |
| **82,200** | **82,250** | 13,880 | 9,670 | 13,880 | 12,438 |
| **82,250** | **82,300** | 13,891 | 9,681 | 13,891 | 12,449 |
| **82,300** | **82,350** | 13,902 | 9,692 | 13,902 | 12,460 |
| **82,350** | **82,400** | 13,913 | 9,703 | 13,913 | 12,471 |
| **82,400** | **82,450** | 13,924 | 9,714 | 13,924 | 12,482 |
| **82,450** | **82,500** | 13,935 | 9,725 | 13,935 | 12,493 |
| **82,500** | **82,550** | 13,946 | 9,736 | 13,946 | 12,504 |
| **82,550** | **82,600** | 13,957 | 9,747 | 13,957 | 12,515 |
| **82,600** | **82,650** | 13,968 | 9,758 | 13,968 | 12,526 |
| **82,650** | **82,700** | 13,979 | 9,769 | 13,979 | 12,537 |
| **82,700** | **82,750** | 13,990 | 9,780 | 13,990 | 12,548 |
| **82,750** | **82,800** | 14,001 | 9,791 | 14,001 | 12,559 |
| **82,800** | **82,850** | 14,012 | 9,802 | 14,012 | 12,570 |
| **82,850** | **82,900** | 14,023 | 9,813 | 14,023 | 12,581 |
| **82,900** | **82,950** | 14,034 | 9,824 | 14,034 | 12,592 |
| **82,950** | **83,000** | 14,045 | 9,835 | 14,045 | 12,603 |
| **83,000** | | | | | |
| **83,000** | **83,050** | 14,056 | 9,846 | 14,056 | 12,614 |
| **83,050** | **83,100** | 14,067 | 9,857 | 14,067 | 12,625 |
| **83,100** | **83,150** | 14,078 | 9,868 | 14,078 | 12,636 |
| **83,150** | **83,200** | 14,089 | 9,879 | 14,089 | 12,647 |
| **83,200** | **83,250** | 14,100 | 9,890 | 14,100 | 12,658 |
| **83,250** | **83,300** | 14,111 | 9,901 | 14,111 | 12,669 |
| **83,300** | **83,350** | 14,122 | 9,912 | 14,122 | 12,680 |
| **83,350** | **83,400** | 14,133 | 9,923 | 14,133 | 12,691 |
| **83,400** | **83,450** | 14,144 | 9,934 | 14,144 | 12,702 |
| **83,450** | **83,500** | 14,155 | 9,945 | 14,155 | 12,713 |
| **83,500** | **83,550** | 14,166 | 9,956 | 14,166 | 12,724 |
| **83,550** | **83,600** | 14,177 | 9,967 | 14,177 | 12,735 |
| **83,600** | **83,650** | 14,188 | 9,978 | 14,188 | 12,746 |
| **83,650** | **83,700** | 14,199 | 9,989 | 14,199 | 12,757 |
| **83,700** | **83,750** | 14,210 | 10,000 | 14,210 | 12,768 |
| **83,750** | **83,800** | 14,221 | 10,011 | 14,221 | 12,779 |
| **83,800** | **83,850** | 14,232 | 10,022 | 14,232 | 12,790 |
| **83,850** | **83,900** | 14,243 | 10,033 | 14,243 | 12,801 |
| **83,900** | **83,950** | 14,254 | 10,044 | 14,254 | 12,812 |
| **83,950** | **84,000** | 14,265 | 10,055 | 14,265 | 12,823 |

*(Continued)*

*This column must also be used by a qualifying widow(er).

## 2020 Tax Table — *Continued*

| If line 15 (taxable income) is— At least | But less than | Single | Married filing jointly* | Married filing separately | Head of a household |
|---|---|---|---|---|---|
| | | Your tax is— | | | |
| **84,000** | | | | | |
| 84,000 | 84,050 | 14,276 | 10,066 | 14,276 | 12,834 |
| 84,050 | 84,100 | 14,287 | 10,077 | 14,287 | 12,845 |
| 84,100 | 84,150 | 14,298 | 10,088 | 14,298 | 12,856 |
| 84,150 | 84,200 | 14,309 | 10,099 | 14,309 | 12,867 |
| 84,200 | 84,250 | 14,320 | 10,110 | 14,320 | 12,878 |
| 84,250 | 84,300 | 14,331 | 10,121 | 14,331 | 12,889 |
| 84,300 | 84,350 | 14,342 | 10,132 | 14,342 | 12,900 |
| 84,350 | 84,400 | 14,353 | 10,143 | 14,353 | 12,911 |
| 84,400 | 84,450 | 14,364 | 10,154 | 14,364 | 12,922 |
| 84,450 | 84,500 | 14,375 | 10,165 | 14,375 | 12,933 |
| 84,500 | 84,550 | 14,386 | 10,176 | 14,386 | 12,944 |
| 84,550 | 84,600 | 14,397 | 10,187 | 14,397 | 12,955 |
| 84,600 | 84,650 | 14,408 | 10,198 | 14,408 | 12,966 |
| 84,650 | 84,700 | 14,419 | 10,209 | 14,419 | 12,977 |
| 84,700 | 84,750 | 14,430 | 10,220 | 14,430 | 12,988 |
| 84,750 | 84,800 | 14,441 | 10,231 | 14,441 | 12,999 |
| 84,800 | 84,850 | 14,452 | 10,242 | 14,452 | 13,010 |
| 84,850 | 84,900 | 14,463 | 10,253 | 14,463 | 13,021 |
| 84,900 | 84,950 | 14,474 | 10,264 | 14,474 | 13,032 |
| 84,950 | 85,000 | 14,485 | 10,275 | 14,485 | 13,043 |
| **85,000** | | | | | |
| 85,000 | 85,050 | 14,496 | 10,286 | 14,496 | 13,054 |
| 85,050 | 85,100 | 14,507 | 10,297 | 14,507 | 13,065 |
| 85,100 | 85,150 | 14,518 | 10,308 | 14,518 | 13,076 |
| 85,150 | 85,200 | 14,529 | 10,319 | 14,529 | 13,087 |
| 85,200 | 85,250 | 14,540 | 10,330 | 14,540 | 13,098 |
| 85,250 | 85,300 | 14,551 | 10,341 | 14,551 | 13,109 |
| 85,300 | 85,350 | 14,562 | 10,352 | 14,562 | 13,120 |
| 85,350 | 85,400 | 14,573 | 10,363 | 14,573 | 13,131 |
| 85,400 | 85,450 | 14,584 | 10,374 | 14,584 | 13,142 |
| 85,450 | 85,500 | 14,595 | 10,385 | 14,595 | 13,153 |
| 85,500 | 85,550 | 14,606 | 10,396 | 14,606 | 13,164 |
| 85,550 | 85,600 | 14,618 | 10,407 | 14,618 | 13,176 |
| 85,600 | 85,650 | 14,630 | 10,418 | 14,630 | 13,188 |
| 85,650 | 85,700 | 14,642 | 10,429 | 14,642 | 13,200 |
| 85,700 | 85,750 | 14,654 | 10,440 | 14,654 | 13,212 |
| 85,750 | 85,800 | 14,666 | 10,451 | 14,666 | 13,224 |
| 85,800 | 85,850 | 14,678 | 10,462 | 14,678 | 13,236 |
| 85,850 | 85,900 | 14,690 | 10,473 | 14,690 | 13,248 |
| 85,900 | 85,950 | 14,702 | 10,484 | 14,702 | 13,260 |
| 85,950 | 86,000 | 14,714 | 10,495 | 14,714 | 13,272 |
| **86,000** | | | | | |
| 86,000 | 86,050 | 14,726 | 10,506 | 14,726 | 13,284 |
| 86,050 | 86,100 | 14,738 | 10,517 | 14,738 | 13,296 |
| 86,100 | 86,150 | 14,750 | 10,528 | 14,750 | 13,308 |
| 86,150 | 86,200 | 14,762 | 10,539 | 14,762 | 13,320 |
| 86,200 | 86,250 | 14,774 | 10,550 | 14,774 | 13,332 |
| 86,250 | 86,300 | 14,786 | 10,561 | 14,786 | 13,344 |
| 86,300 | 86,350 | 14,798 | 10,572 | 14,798 | 13,356 |
| 86,350 | 86,400 | 14,810 | 10,583 | 14,810 | 13,368 |
| 86,400 | 86,450 | 14,822 | 10,594 | 14,822 | 13,380 |
| 86,450 | 86,500 | 14,834 | 10,605 | 14,834 | 13,392 |
| 86,500 | 86,550 | 14,846 | 10,616 | 14,846 | 13,404 |
| 86,550 | 86,600 | 14,858 | 10,627 | 14,858 | 13,416 |
| 86,600 | 86,650 | 14,870 | 10,638 | 14,870 | 13,428 |
| 86,650 | 86,700 | 14,882 | 10,649 | 14,882 | 13,440 |
| 86,700 | 86,750 | 14,894 | 10,660 | 14,894 | 13,452 |
| 86,750 | 86,800 | 14,906 | 10,671 | 14,906 | 13,464 |
| 86,800 | 86,850 | 14,918 | 10,682 | 14,918 | 13,476 |
| 86,850 | 86,900 | 14,930 | 10,693 | 14,930 | 13,488 |
| 86,900 | 86,950 | 14,942 | 10,704 | 14,942 | 13,500 |
| 86,950 | 87,000 | 14,954 | 10,715 | 14,954 | 13,512 |

| If line 15 (taxable income) is— At least | But less than | Single | Married filing jointly* | Married filing separately | Head of a household |
|---|---|---|---|---|---|
| | | Your tax is— | | | |
| **87,000** | | | | | |
| 87,000 | 87,050 | 14,966 | 10,726 | 14,966 | 13,524 |
| 87,050 | 87,100 | 14,978 | 10,737 | 14,978 | 13,536 |
| 87,100 | 87,150 | 14,990 | 10,748 | 14,990 | 13,548 |
| 87,150 | 87,200 | 15,002 | 10,759 | 15,002 | 13,560 |
| 87,200 | 87,250 | 15,014 | 10,770 | 15,014 | 13,572 |
| 87,250 | 87,300 | 15,026 | 10,781 | 15,026 | 13,584 |
| 87,300 | 87,350 | 15,038 | 10,792 | 15,038 | 13,596 |
| 87,350 | 87,400 | 15,050 | 10,803 | 15,050 | 13,608 |
| 87,400 | 87,450 | 15,062 | 10,814 | 15,062 | 13,620 |
| 87,450 | 87,500 | 15,074 | 10,825 | 15,074 | 13,632 |
| 87,500 | 87,550 | 15,086 | 10,836 | 15,086 | 13,644 |
| 87,550 | 87,600 | 15,098 | 10,847 | 15,098 | 13,656 |
| 87,600 | 87,650 | 15,110 | 10,858 | 15,110 | 13,668 |
| 87,650 | 87,700 | 15,122 | 10,869 | 15,122 | 13,680 |
| 87,700 | 87,750 | 15,134 | 10,880 | 15,134 | 13,692 |
| 87,750 | 87,800 | 15,146 | 10,891 | 15,146 | 13,704 |
| 87,800 | 87,850 | 15,158 | 10,902 | 15,158 | 13,716 |
| 87,850 | 87,900 | 15,170 | 10,913 | 15,170 | 13,728 |
| 87,900 | 87,950 | 15,182 | 10,924 | 15,182 | 13,740 |
| 87,950 | 88,000 | 15,194 | 10,935 | 15,194 | 13,752 |
| **88,000** | | | | | |
| 88,000 | 88,050 | 15,206 | 10,946 | 15,206 | 13,764 |
| 88,050 | 88,100 | 15,218 | 10,957 | 15,218 | 13,776 |
| 88,100 | 88,150 | 15,230 | 10,968 | 15,230 | 13,788 |
| 88,150 | 88,200 | 15,242 | 10,979 | 15,242 | 13,800 |
| 88,200 | 88,250 | 15,254 | 10,990 | 15,254 | 13,812 |
| 88,250 | 88,300 | 15,266 | 11,001 | 15,266 | 13,824 |
| 88,300 | 88,350 | 15,278 | 11,012 | 15,278 | 13,836 |
| 88,350 | 88,400 | 15,290 | 11,023 | 15,290 | 13,848 |
| 88,400 | 88,450 | 15,302 | 11,034 | 15,302 | 13,860 |
| 88,450 | 88,500 | 15,314 | 11,045 | 15,314 | 13,872 |
| 88,500 | 88,550 | 15,326 | 11,056 | 15,326 | 13,884 |
| 88,550 | 88,600 | 15,338 | 11,067 | 15,338 | 13,896 |
| 88,600 | 88,650 | 15,350 | 11,078 | 15,350 | 13,908 |
| 88,650 | 88,700 | 15,362 | 11,089 | 15,362 | 13,920 |
| 88,700 | 88,750 | 15,374 | 11,100 | 15,374 | 13,932 |
| 88,750 | 88,800 | 15,386 | 11,111 | 15,386 | 13,944 |
| 88,800 | 88,850 | 15,398 | 11,122 | 15,398 | 13,956 |
| 88,850 | 88,900 | 15,410 | 11,133 | 15,410 | 13,968 |
| 88,900 | 88,950 | 15,422 | 11,144 | 15,422 | 13,980 |
| 88,950 | 89,000 | 15,434 | 11,155 | 15,434 | 13,992 |
| **89,000** | | | | | |
| 89,000 | 89,050 | 15,446 | 11,166 | 15,446 | 14,004 |
| 89,050 | 89,100 | 15,458 | 11,177 | 15,458 | 14,016 |
| 89,100 | 89,150 | 15,470 | 11,188 | 15,470 | 14,028 |
| 89,150 | 89,200 | 15,482 | 11,199 | 15,482 | 14,040 |
| 89,200 | 89,250 | 15,494 | 11,210 | 15,494 | 14,052 |
| 89,250 | 89,300 | 15,506 | 11,221 | 15,506 | 14,064 |
| 89,300 | 89,350 | 15,518 | 11,232 | 15,518 | 14,076 |
| 89,350 | 89,400 | 15,530 | 11,243 | 15,530 | 14,088 |
| 89,400 | 89,450 | 15,542 | 11,254 | 15,542 | 14,100 |
| 89,450 | 89,500 | 15,554 | 11,265 | 15,554 | 14,112 |
| 89,500 | 89,550 | 15,566 | 11,276 | 15,566 | 14,124 |
| 89,550 | 89,600 | 15,578 | 11,287 | 15,578 | 14,136 |
| 89,600 | 89,650 | 15,590 | 11,298 | 15,590 | 14,148 |
| 89,650 | 89,700 | 15,602 | 11,309 | 15,602 | 14,160 |
| 89,700 | 89,750 | 15,614 | 11,320 | 15,614 | 14,172 |
| 89,750 | 89,800 | 15,626 | 11,331 | 15,626 | 14,184 |
| 89,800 | 89,850 | 15,638 | 11,342 | 15,638 | 14,196 |
| 89,850 | 89,900 | 15,650 | 11,353 | 15,650 | 14,208 |
| 89,900 | 89,950 | 15,662 | 11,364 | 15,662 | 14,220 |
| 89,950 | 90,000 | 15,674 | 11,375 | 15,674 | 14,232 |

| If line 15 (taxable income) is— At least | But less than | Single | Married filing jointly* | Married filing separately | Head of a household |
|---|---|---|---|---|---|
| | | Your tax is— | | | |
| **90,000** | | | | | |
| 90,000 | 90,050 | 15,686 | 11,386 | 15,686 | 14,244 |
| 90,050 | 90,100 | 15,698 | 11,397 | 15,698 | 14,256 |
| 90,100 | 90,150 | 15,710 | 11,408 | 15,710 | 14,268 |
| 90,150 | 90,200 | 15,722 | 11,419 | 15,722 | 14,280 |
| 90,200 | 90,250 | 15,734 | 11,430 | 15,734 | 14,292 |
| 90,250 | 90,300 | 15,746 | 11,441 | 15,746 | 14,304 |
| 90,300 | 90,350 | 15,758 | 11,452 | 15,758 | 14,316 |
| 90,350 | 90,400 | 15,770 | 11,463 | 15,770 | 14,328 |
| 90,400 | 90,450 | 15,782 | 11,474 | 15,782 | 14,340 |
| 90,450 | 90,500 | 15,794 | 11,485 | 15,794 | 14,352 |
| 90,500 | 90,550 | 15,806 | 11,496 | 15,806 | 14,364 |
| 90,550 | 90,600 | 15,818 | 11,507 | 15,818 | 14,376 |
| 90,600 | 90,650 | 15,830 | 11,518 | 15,830 | 14,388 |
| 90,650 | 90,700 | 15,842 | 11,529 | 15,842 | 14,400 |
| 90,700 | 90,750 | 15,854 | 11,540 | 15,854 | 14,412 |
| 90,750 | 90,800 | 15,866 | 11,551 | 15,866 | 14,424 |
| 90,800 | 90,850 | 15,878 | 11,562 | 15,878 | 14,436 |
| 90,850 | 90,900 | 15,890 | 11,573 | 15,890 | 14,448 |
| 90,900 | 90,950 | 15,902 | 11,584 | 15,902 | 14,460 |
| 90,950 | 91,000 | 15,914 | 11,595 | 15,914 | 14,472 |
| **91,000** | | | | | |
| 91,000 | 91,050 | 15,926 | 11,606 | 15,926 | 14,484 |
| 91,050 | 91,100 | 15,938 | 11,617 | 15,938 | 14,496 |
| 91,100 | 91,150 | 15,950 | 11,628 | 15,950 | 14,508 |
| 91,150 | 91,200 | 15,962 | 11,639 | 15,962 | 14,520 |
| 91,200 | 91,250 | 15,974 | 11,650 | 15,974 | 14,532 |
| 91,250 | 91,300 | 15,986 | 11,661 | 15,986 | 14,544 |
| 91,300 | 91,350 | 15,998 | 11,672 | 15,998 | 14,556 |
| 91,350 | 91,400 | 16,010 | 11,683 | 16,010 | 14,568 |
| 91,400 | 91,450 | 16,022 | 11,694 | 16,022 | 14,580 |
| 91,450 | 91,500 | 16,034 | 11,705 | 16,034 | 14,592 |
| 91,500 | 91,550 | 16,046 | 11,716 | 16,046 | 14,604 |
| 91,550 | 91,600 | 16,058 | 11,727 | 16,058 | 14,616 |
| 91,600 | 91,650 | 16,070 | 11,738 | 16,070 | 14,628 |
| 91,650 | 91,700 | 16,082 | 11,749 | 16,082 | 14,640 |
| 91,700 | 91,750 | 16,094 | 11,760 | 16,094 | 14,652 |
| 91,750 | 91,800 | 16,106 | 11,771 | 16,106 | 14,664 |
| 91,800 | 91,850 | 16,118 | 11,782 | 16,118 | 14,676 |
| 91,850 | 91,900 | 16,130 | 11,793 | 16,130 | 14,688 |
| 91,900 | 91,950 | 16,142 | 11,804 | 16,142 | 14,700 |
| 91,950 | 92,000 | 16,154 | 11,815 | 16,154 | 14,712 |
| **92,000** | | | | | |
| 92,000 | 92,050 | 16,166 | 11,826 | 16,166 | 14,724 |
| 92,050 | 92,100 | 16,178 | 11,837 | 16,178 | 14,736 |
| 92,100 | 92,150 | 16,190 | 11,848 | 16,190 | 14,748 |
| 92,150 | 92,200 | 16,202 | 11,859 | 16,202 | 14,760 |
| 92,200 | 92,250 | 16,214 | 11,870 | 16,214 | 14,772 |
| 92,250 | 92,300 | 16,226 | 11,881 | 16,226 | 14,784 |
| 92,300 | 92,350 | 16,238 | 11,892 | 16,238 | 14,796 |
| 92,350 | 92,400 | 16,250 | 11,903 | 16,250 | 14,808 |
| 92,400 | 92,450 | 16,262 | 11,914 | 16,262 | 14,820 |
| 92,450 | 92,500 | 16,274 | 11,925 | 16,274 | 14,832 |
| 92,500 | 92,550 | 16,286 | 11,936 | 16,286 | 14,844 |
| 92,550 | 92,600 | 16,298 | 11,947 | 16,298 | 14,856 |
| 92,600 | 92,650 | 16,310 | 11,958 | 16,310 | 14,868 |
| 92,650 | 92,700 | 16,322 | 11,969 | 16,322 | 14,880 |
| 92,700 | 92,750 | 16,334 | 11,980 | 16,334 | 14,892 |
| 92,750 | 92,800 | 16,346 | 11,991 | 16,346 | 14,904 |
| 92,800 | 92,850 | 16,358 | 12,002 | 16,358 | 14,916 |
| 92,850 | 92,900 | 16,370 | 12,013 | 16,370 | 14,928 |
| 92,900 | 92,950 | 16,382 | 12,024 | 16,382 | 14,940 |
| 92,950 | 93,000 | 16,394 | 12,035 | 16,394 | 14,952 |

*(Continued)*

*This column must also be used by a qualifying widow(er).

## 2020 Tax Table — *Continued*

| If line 15 (taxable income) is— | | And you are— | | | |
|---|---|---|---|---|---|
| At least | But less than | Single | Married filing jointly* | Married filing separately | Head of a household |
| | | Your tax is— | | | |
| **93,000** | | | | | |
| 93,000 | 93,050 | 16,406 | 12,046 | 16,406 | 14,964 |
| 93,050 | 93,100 | 16,418 | 12,057 | 16,418 | 14,976 |
| 93,100 | 93,150 | 16,430 | 12,068 | 16,430 | 14,988 |
| 93,150 | 93,200 | 16,442 | 12,079 | 16,442 | 15,000 |
| 93,200 | 93,250 | 16,454 | 12,090 | 16,454 | 15,012 |
| 93,250 | 93,300 | 16,466 | 12,101 | 16,466 | 15,024 |
| 93,300 | 93,350 | 16,478 | 12,112 | 16,478 | 15,036 |
| 93,350 | 93,400 | 16,490 | 12,123 | 16,490 | 15,048 |
| 93,400 | 93,450 | 16,502 | 12,134 | 16,502 | 15,060 |
| 93,450 | 93,500 | 16,514 | 12,145 | 16,514 | 15,072 |
| 93,500 | 93,550 | 16,526 | 12,156 | 16,526 | 15,084 |
| 93,550 | 93,600 | 16,538 | 12,167 | 16,538 | 15,096 |
| 93,600 | 93,650 | 16,550 | 12,178 | 16,550 | 15,108 |
| 93,650 | 93,700 | 16,562 | 12,189 | 16,562 | 15,120 |
| 93,700 | 93,750 | 16,574 | 12,200 | 16,574 | 15,132 |
| 93,750 | 93,800 | 16,586 | 12,211 | 16,586 | 15,144 |
| 93,800 | 93,850 | 16,598 | 12,222 | 16,598 | 15,156 |
| 93,850 | 93,900 | 16,610 | 12,233 | 16,610 | 15,168 |
| 93,900 | 93,950 | 16,622 | 12,244 | 16,622 | 15,180 |
| 93,950 | 94,000 | 16,634 | 12,255 | 16,634 | 15,192 |
| **94,000** | | | | | |
| 94,000 | 94,050 | 16,646 | 12,266 | 16,646 | 15,204 |
| 94,050 | 94,100 | 16,658 | 12,277 | 16,658 | 15,216 |
| 94,100 | 94,150 | 16,670 | 12,288 | 16,670 | 15,228 |
| 94,150 | 94,200 | 16,682 | 12,299 | 16,682 | 15,240 |
| 94,200 | 94,250 | 16,694 | 12,310 | 16,694 | 15,252 |
| 94,250 | 94,300 | 16,706 | 12,321 | 16,706 | 15,264 |
| 94,300 | 94,350 | 16,718 | 12,332 | 16,718 | 15,276 |
| 94,350 | 94,400 | 16,730 | 12,343 | 16,730 | 15,288 |
| 94,400 | 94,450 | 16,742 | 12,354 | 16,742 | 15,300 |
| 94,450 | 94,500 | 16,754 | 12,365 | 16,754 | 15,312 |
| 94,500 | 94,550 | 16,766 | 12,376 | 16,766 | 15,324 |
| 94,550 | 94,600 | 16,778 | 12,387 | 16,778 | 15,336 |
| 94,600 | 94,650 | 16,790 | 12,398 | 16,790 | 15,348 |
| 94,650 | 94,700 | 16,802 | 12,409 | 16,802 | 15,360 |
| 94,700 | 94,750 | 16,814 | 12,420 | 16,814 | 15,372 |
| 94,750 | 94,800 | 16,826 | 12,431 | 16,826 | 15,384 |
| 94,800 | 94,850 | 16,838 | 12,442 | 16,838 | 15,396 |
| 94,850 | 94,900 | 16,850 | 12,453 | 16,850 | 15,408 |
| 94,900 | 94,950 | 16,862 | 12,464 | 16,862 | 15,420 |
| 94,950 | 95,000 | 16,874 | 12,475 | 16,874 | 15,432 |
| **95,000** | | | | | |
| 95,000 | 95,050 | 16,886 | 12,486 | 16,886 | 15,444 |
| 95,050 | 95,100 | 16,898 | 12,497 | 16,898 | 15,456 |
| 95,100 | 95,150 | 16,910 | 12,508 | 16,910 | 15,468 |
| 95,150 | 95,200 | 16,922 | 12,519 | 16,922 | 15,480 |
| 95,200 | 95,250 | 16,934 | 12,530 | 16,934 | 15,492 |
| 95,250 | 95,300 | 16,946 | 12,541 | 16,946 | 15,504 |
| 95,300 | 95,350 | 16,958 | 12,552 | 16,958 | 15,516 |
| 95,350 | 95,400 | 16,970 | 12,563 | 16,970 | 15,528 |
| 95,400 | 95,450 | 16,982 | 12,574 | 16,982 | 15,540 |
| 95,450 | 95,500 | 16,994 | 12,585 | 16,994 | 15,552 |
| 95,500 | 95,550 | 17,006 | 12,596 | 17,006 | 15,564 |
| 95,550 | 95,600 | 17,018 | 12,607 | 17,018 | 15,576 |
| 95,600 | 95,650 | 17,030 | 12,618 | 17,030 | 15,588 |
| 95,650 | 95,700 | 17,042 | 12,629 | 17,042 | 15,600 |
| 95,700 | 95,750 | 17,054 | 12,640 | 17,054 | 15,612 |
| 95,750 | 95,800 | 17,066 | 12,651 | 17,066 | 15,624 |
| 95,800 | 95,850 | 17,078 | 12,662 | 17,078 | 15,636 |
| 95,850 | 95,900 | 17,090 | 12,673 | 17,090 | 15,648 |
| 95,900 | 95,950 | 17,102 | 12,684 | 17,102 | 15,660 |
| 95,950 | 96,000 | 17,114 | 12,695 | 17,114 | 15,672 |
| **96,000** | | | | | |
| 96,000 | 96,050 | 17,126 | 12,706 | 17,126 | 15,684 |
| 96,050 | 96,100 | 17,138 | 12,717 | 17,138 | 15,696 |
| 96,100 | 96,150 | 17,150 | 12,728 | 17,150 | 15,708 |
| 96,150 | 96,200 | 17,162 | 12,739 | 17,162 | 15,720 |
| 96,200 | 96,250 | 17,174 | 12,750 | 17,174 | 15,732 |
| 96,250 | 96,300 | 17,186 | 12,761 | 17,186 | 15,744 |
| 96,300 | 96,350 | 17,198 | 12,772 | 17,198 | 15,756 |
| 96,350 | 96,400 | 17,210 | 12,783 | 17,210 | 15,768 |
| 96,400 | 96,450 | 17,222 | 12,794 | 17,222 | 15,780 |
| 96,450 | 96,500 | 17,234 | 12,805 | 17,234 | 15,792 |
| 96,500 | 96,550 | 17,246 | 12,816 | 17,246 | 15,804 |
| 96,550 | 96,600 | 17,258 | 12,827 | 17,258 | 15,816 |
| 96,600 | 96,650 | 17,270 | 12,838 | 17,270 | 15,828 |
| 96,650 | 96,700 | 17,282 | 12,849 | 17,282 | 15,840 |
| 96,700 | 96,750 | 17,294 | 12,860 | 17,294 | 15,852 |
| 96,750 | 96,800 | 17,306 | 12,871 | 17,306 | 15,864 |
| 96,800 | 96,850 | 17,318 | 12,882 | 17,318 | 15,876 |
| 96,850 | 96,900 | 17,330 | 12,893 | 17,330 | 15,888 |
| 96,900 | 96,950 | 17,342 | 12,904 | 17,342 | 15,900 |
| 96,950 | 97,000 | 17,354 | 12,915 | 17,354 | 15,912 |
| **97,000** | | | | | |
| 97,000 | 97,050 | 17,366 | 12,926 | 17,366 | 15,924 |
| 97,050 | 97,100 | 17,378 | 12,937 | 17,378 | 15,936 |
| 97,100 | 97,150 | 17,390 | 12,948 | 17,390 | 15,948 |
| 97,150 | 97,200 | 17,402 | 12,959 | 17,402 | 15,960 |
| 97,200 | 97,250 | 17,414 | 12,970 | 17,414 | 15,972 |
| 97,250 | 97,300 | 17,426 | 12,981 | 17,426 | 15,984 |
| 97,300 | 97,350 | 17,438 | 12,992 | 17,438 | 15,996 |
| 97,350 | 97,400 | 17,450 | 13,003 | 17,450 | 16,008 |
| 97,400 | 97,450 | 17,462 | 13,014 | 17,462 | 16,020 |
| 97,450 | 97,500 | 17,474 | 13,025 | 17,474 | 16,032 |
| 97,500 | 97,550 | 17,486 | 13,036 | 17,486 | 16,044 |
| 97,550 | 97,600 | 17,498 | 13,047 | 17,498 | 16,056 |
| 97,600 | 97,650 | 17,510 | 13,058 | 17,510 | 16,068 |
| 97,650 | 97,700 | 17,522 | 13,069 | 17,522 | 16,080 |
| 97,700 | 97,750 | 17,534 | 13,080 | 17,534 | 16,092 |
| 97,750 | 97,800 | 17,546 | 13,091 | 17,546 | 16,104 |
| 97,800 | 97,850 | 17,558 | 13,102 | 17,558 | 16,116 |
| 97,850 | 97,900 | 17,570 | 13,113 | 17,570 | 16,128 |
| 97,900 | 97,950 | 17,582 | 13,124 | 17,582 | 16,140 |
| 97,950 | 98,000 | 17,594 | 13,135 | 17,594 | 16,152 |
| **98,000** | | | | | |
| 98,000 | 98,050 | 17,606 | 13,146 | 17,606 | 16,164 |
| 98,050 | 98,100 | 17,618 | 13,157 | 17,618 | 16,176 |
| 98,100 | 98,150 | 17,630 | 13,168 | 17,630 | 16,188 |
| 98,150 | 98,200 | 17,642 | 13,179 | 17,642 | 16,200 |
| 98,200 | 98,250 | 17,654 | 13,190 | 17,654 | 16,212 |
| 98,250 | 98,300 | 17,666 | 13,201 | 17,666 | 16,224 |
| 98,300 | 98,350 | 17,678 | 13,212 | 17,678 | 16,236 |
| 98,350 | 98,400 | 17,690 | 13,223 | 17,690 | 16,248 |
| 98,400 | 98,450 | 17,702 | 13,234 | 17,702 | 16,260 |
| 98,450 | 98,500 | 17,714 | 13,245 | 17,714 | 16,272 |
| 98,500 | 98,550 | 17,726 | 13,256 | 17,726 | 16,284 |
| 98,550 | 98,600 | 17,738 | 13,267 | 17,738 | 16,296 |
| 98,600 | 98,650 | 17,750 | 13,278 | 17,750 | 16,308 |
| 98,650 | 98,700 | 17,762 | 13,289 | 17,762 | 16,320 |
| 98,700 | 98,750 | 17,774 | 13,300 | 17,774 | 16,332 |
| 98,750 | 98,800 | 17,786 | 13,311 | 17,786 | 16,344 |
| 98,800 | 98,850 | 17,798 | 13,322 | 17,798 | 16,356 |
| 98,850 | 98,900 | 17,810 | 13,333 | 17,810 | 16,368 |
| 98,900 | 98,950 | 17,822 | 13,344 | 17,822 | 16,380 |
| 98,950 | 99,000 | 17,834 | 13,355 | 17,834 | 16,392 |
| **99,000** | | | | | |
| 99,000 | 99,050 | 17,846 | 13,366 | 17,846 | 16,404 |
| 99,050 | 99,100 | 17,858 | 13,377 | 17,858 | 16,416 |
| 99,100 | 99,150 | 17,870 | 13,388 | 17,870 | 16,428 |
| 99,150 | 99,200 | 17,882 | 13,399 | 17,882 | 16,440 |
| 99,200 | 99,250 | 17,894 | 13,410 | 17,894 | 16,452 |
| 99,250 | 99,300 | 17,906 | 13,421 | 17,906 | 16,464 |
| 99,300 | 99,350 | 17,918 | 13,432 | 17,918 | 16,476 |
| 99,350 | 99,400 | 17,930 | 13,443 | 17,930 | 16,488 |
| 99,400 | 99,450 | 17,942 | 13,454 | 17,942 | 16,500 |
| 99,450 | 99,500 | 17,954 | 13,465 | 17,954 | 16,512 |
| 99,500 | 99,550 | 17,966 | 13,476 | 17,966 | 16,524 |
| 99,550 | 99,600 | 17,978 | 13,487 | 17,978 | 16,536 |
| 99,600 | 99,650 | 17,990 | 13,498 | 17,990 | 16,548 |
| 99,650 | 99,700 | 18,002 | 13,509 | 18,002 | 16,560 |
| 99,700 | 99,750 | 18,014 | 13,520 | 18,014 | 16,572 |
| 99,750 | 99,800 | 18,026 | 13,531 | 18,026 | 16,584 |
| 99,800 | 99,850 | 18,038 | 13,542 | 18,038 | 16,596 |
| 99,850 | 99,900 | 18,050 | 13,553 | 18,050 | 16,608 |
| 99,900 | 99,950 | 18,062 | 13,564 | 18,062 | 16,620 |
| 99,950 | 100,000 | 18,074 | 13,575 | 18,074 | 16,632 |

**$100,000 or over**
use the Tax Computation Worksheet

*This column must also be used by a qualifying widow(er).

APPENDIX C

# Tax Forms

Coprid/Shutterstock.com; iStockphoto.com/Mike Clarke

Form **1040** Department of the Treasury—Internal Revenue Service (99)
**U.S. Individual Income Tax Return** **2020** OMB No. 1545-0074 IRS Use Only—Do not write or staple in this space.

**Filing Status** Check only one box. ☐ Single ☐ Married filing jointly ☐ Married filing separately (MFS) ☐ Head of household (HOH) ☐ Qualifying widow(er) (QW)

If you checked the MFS box, enter the name of your spouse. If you checked the HOH or QW box, enter the child's name if the qualifying person is a child but not your dependent ▶

| Your first name and middle initial | Last name | | | **Your social security number** |
|---|---|---|---|---|
| If joint return, spouse's first name and middle initial | Last name | | | **Spouse's social security number** |
| Home address (number and street). If you have a P.O. box, see instructions. | | | Apt. no. | **Presidential Election Campaign** Check here if you, or your spouse if filing jointly, want $3 to go to this fund. Checking a box below will not change your tax or refund. ☐ **You** ☐ **Spouse** |
| City, town, or post office. If you have a foreign address, also complete spaces below. | | State | ZIP code | |
| Foreign country name | Foreign province/state/county | | Foreign postal code | |

At any time during 2020, did you receive, sell, send, exchange, or otherwise acquire any financial interest in any virtual currency? ☐ **Yes** ☐ **No**

**Standard Deduction** **Someone can claim:** ☐ You as a dependent ☐ Your spouse as a dependent
☐ Spouse itemizes on a separate return or you were a dual-status alien

**Age/Blindness** **You:** ☐ Were born before January 2, 1956 ☐ Are blind **Spouse:** ☐ Was born before January 2, 1956 ☐ Is blind

**Dependents** (see instructions):
If more than four dependents, see instructions and check here ▶ ☐

| **(1)** First name | Last name | **(2)** Social security number | **(3)** Relationship to you | **(4)** ✔ if qualifies for (see instructions): Child tax credit | Credit for other dependents |
|---|---|---|---|---|---|
| | | | | ☐ | ☐ |
| | | | | ☐ | ☐ |
| | | | | ☐ | ☐ |
| | | | | ☐ | ☐ |

Attach Sch. B if required.

**Standard Deduction for—**
- Single or Married filing separately, $12,400
- Married filing jointly or Qualifying widow(er), $24,800
- Head of household, $18,650
- If you checked any box under *Standard Deduction*, see instructions.

| | | | | | | |
|---|---|---|---|---|---|---|
| 1 | Wages, salaries, tips, etc. Attach Form(s) W-2 | | | | 1 | |
| 2a | Tax-exempt interest | 2a | | **b** Taxable interest | 2b | |
| 3a | Qualified dividends | 3a | | **b** Ordinary dividends | 3b | |
| 4a | IRA distributions | 4a | | **b** Taxable amount | 4b | |
| 5a | Pensions and annuities | 5a | | **b** Taxable amount | 5b | |
| 6a | Social security benefits | 6a | | **b** Taxable amount | 6b | |
| 7 | Capital gain or (loss). Attach Schedule D if required. If not required, check here ▶ ☐ | | | | 7 | |
| 8 | Other income from Schedule 1, line 9 | | | | 8 | |
| 9 | Add lines 1, 2b, 3b, 4b, 5b, 6b, 7, and 8. This is your **total income** ▶ | | | | 9 | |
| 10 | Adjustments to income: | | | | | |
| a | From Schedule 1, line 22 | | | 10a | | |
| b | Charitable contributions if you take the standard deduction. See instructions | | | 10b | | |
| c | Add lines 10a and 10b. These are your **total adjustments to income** ▶ | | | | 10c | |
| 11 | Subtract line 10c from line 9. This is your **adjusted gross income** ▶ | | | | 11 | |
| 12 | **Standard deduction or itemized deductions** (from Schedule A) | | | | 12 | |
| 13 | Qualified business income deduction. Attach Form 8995 or Form 8995-A | | | | 13 | |
| 14 | Add lines 12 and 13 | | | | 14 | |
| 15 | **Taxable income.** Subtract line 14 from line 11. If zero or less, enter -0- | | | | 15 | |

**For Disclosure, Privacy Act, and Paperwork Reduction Act Notice, see separate instructions.** Cat. No. 11320B Form **1040** (2020)

Form 1040 (2020) Page **2**

| | | | | |
|---|---|---|---|---|
| 16 | **Tax** (see instructions). Check if any from Form(s): 1 ☐ 8814 2 ☐ 4972 3 ☐ ______ | | | 16 |
| 17 | Amount from Schedule 2, line 3 | | | 17 |
| 18 | Add lines 16 and 17 | | | 18 |
| 19 | Child tax credit or credit for other dependents | | | 19 |
| 20 | Amount from Schedule 3, line 7 | | | 20 |
| 21 | Add lines 19 and 20 | | | 21 |
| 22 | Subtract line 21 from line 18. If zero or less, enter -0- | | | 22 |
| 23 | Other taxes, including self-employment tax, from Schedule 2, line 10 | | | 23 |
| 24 | Add lines 22 and 23. This is your **total tax** ▶ | | | 24 |
| 25 | Federal income tax withheld from: | | | |
| a | Form(s) W-2 | 25a | | |
| b | Form(s) 1099 | 25b | | |
| c | Other forms (see instructions) | 25c | | |
| d | Add lines 25a through 25c | | | 25d |
| 26 | 2020 estimated tax payments and amount applied from 2019 return | | | 26 |
| 27 | Earned income credit (EIC) | 27 | | |
| 28 | Additional child tax credit. Attach Schedule 8812 | 28 | | |
| 29 | American opportunity credit from Form 8863, line 8 | 29 | | |
| 30 | Recovery rebate credit. See instructions | 30 | | |
| 31 | Amount from Schedule 3, line 13 | 31 | | |
| 32 | Add lines 27 through 31. These are your **total other payments and refundable credits** ▶ | | | 32 |
| 33 | Add lines 25d, 26, and 32. These are your **total payments** ▶ | | | 33 |

• If you have a qualifying child, attach Sch. EIC.
• If you have nontaxable combat pay, see instructions.

**Refund**

Direct deposit? See instructions.

| | | |
|---|---|---|
| 34 | If line 33 is more than line 24, subtract line 24 from line 33. This is the amount you **overpaid** | 34 |
| 35a | Amount of line 34 you want **refunded to you.** If Form 8888 is attached, check here ▶ ☐ | 35a |
| ▶ b | Routing number ▶ **c** Type: ☐ Checking ☐ Savings | |
| ▶ d | Account number | |
| 36 | Amount of line 34 you want **applied to your 2021 estimated tax** ▶ 36 | |

**Amount You Owe**

For details on how to pay, see instructions.

| | | |
|---|---|---|
| 37 | Subtract line 33 from line 24. This is the **amount you owe now** ▶ | 37 |
| | **Note:** Schedule H and Schedule SE filers, line 37 may not represent all of the taxes you owe for 2020. See Schedule 3, line 12e, and its instructions for details. | |
| 38 | Estimated tax penalty (see instructions) ▶ 38 | |

**Third Party Designee**

Do you want to allow another person to discuss this return with the IRS? See instructions ▶ ☐ **Yes.** Complete below. ☐ **No**

Designee's name ▶ Phone no. ▶ Personal identification number (PIN) ▶

**Sign Here**

Under penalties of perjury, I declare that I have examined this return and accompanying schedules and statements, and to the best of my knowledge and belief, they are true, correct, and complete. Declaration of preparer (other than taxpayer) is based on all information of which preparer has any knowledge.

Joint return? See instructions. Keep a copy for your records.

| Your signature | Date | Your occupation | If the IRS sent you an Identity Protection PIN, enter it here (see inst.) ▶ |
|---|---|---|---|
| Spouse's signature. If a joint return, **both** must sign. | Date | Spouse's occupation | If the IRS sent your spouse an Identity Protection PIN, enter it here (see inst.) ▶ |
| Phone no. | Email address | | |

**Paid Preparer Use Only**

| Preparer's name | Preparer's signature | Date | PTIN | Check if: ☐ Self-employed |
|---|---|---|---|---|
| Firm's name ▶ | | | Phone no. | |
| Firm's address ▶ | | | Firm's EIN ▶ | |

Go to *www.irs.gov/Form1040* for instructions and the latest information. Form **1040** (2020)

| SCHEDULE A (Form 1040) Department of the Treasury Internal Revenue Service (99) | **Itemized Deductions** ▶ Go to *www.irs.gov/ScheduleA* for instructions and the latest information. ▶ Attach to Form 1040 or 1040-SR. **Caution:** If you are claiming a net qualified disaster loss on Form 4684, see the instructions for line 16. | OMB No. 1545-0074 2020 Attachment Sequence No. **07** |
|---|---|---|

Name(s) shown on Form 1040 or 1040-SR | **Your social security number**

| Section | Line | Description | Box | Amount | Box | Amount |
|---|---|---|---|---|---|---|
| **Medical and Dental Expenses** | | **Caution:** Do not include expenses reimbursed or paid by others. | | | | |
| | 1 | Medical and dental expenses (see instructions) | 1 | | | |
| | 2 | Enter amount from Form 1040 or 1040-SR, line 11 [2] | | | | |
| | 3 | Multiply line 2 by 7.5% (0.075) | 3 | | | |
| | 4 | Subtract line 3 from line 1. If line 3 is more than line 1, enter -0- | | | 4 | |
| **Taxes You Paid** | 5 | State and local taxes. | | | | |
| | a | State and local income taxes or general sales taxes. You may include either income taxes or general sales taxes on line 5a, but not both. If you elect to include general sales taxes instead of income taxes, check this box ▶ ☐ | 5a | | | |
| | b | State and local real estate taxes (see instructions) | 5b | | | |
| | c | State and local personal property taxes | 5c | | | |
| | d | Add lines 5a through 5c | 5d | | | |
| | e | Enter the smaller of line 5d or $10,000 ($5,000 if married filing separately) | 5e | | | |
| | 6 | Other taxes. List type and amount ▶ | 6 | | | |
| | 7 | Add lines 5e and 6 | | | 7 | |
| **Interest You Paid** **Caution:** Your mortgage interest deduction may be limited (see instructions). | 8 | Home mortgage interest and points. If you didn't use all of your home mortgage loan(s) to buy, build, or improve your home, see instructions and check this box ▶ ☐ | | | | |
| | a | Home mortgage interest and points reported to you on Form 1098. See instructions if limited | 8a | | | |
| | b | Home mortgage interest not reported to you on Form 1098. See instructions if limited. If paid to the person from whom you bought the home, see instructions and show that person's name, identifying no., and address ▶ | 8b | | | |
| | c | Points not reported to you on Form 1098. See instructions for special rules | 8c | | | |
| | d | Mortgage insurance premiums (see instructions) | 8d | | | |
| | e | Add lines 8a through 8d | 8e | | | |
| | 9 | Investment interest. Attach Form 4952 if required. See instructions | 9 | | | |
| | 10 | Add lines 8e and 9 | | | 10 | |
| **Gifts to Charity** **Caution:** If you made a gift and got a benefit for it, see instructions. | 11 | Gifts by cash or check. If you made any gift of $250 or more, see instructions | 11 | | | |
| | 12 | Other than by cash or check. If you made any gift of $250 or more, see instructions. You **must** attach Form 8283 if over $500 | 12 | | | |
| | 13 | Carryover from prior year | 13 | | | |
| | 14 | Add lines 11 through 13 | | | 14 | |
| **Casualty and Theft Losses** | 15 | Casualty and theft loss(es) from a federally declared disaster (other than net qualified disaster losses). Attach Form 4684 and enter the amount from line 18 of that form. See instructions | | | 15 | |
| **Other Itemized Deductions** | 16 | Other—from list in instructions. List type and amount ▶ | | | 16 | |
| **Total Itemized Deductions** | 17 | Add the amounts in the far right column for lines 4 through 16. Also, enter this amount on Form 1040 or 1040-SR, line 12 | | | 17 | |
| | 18 | If you elect to itemize deductions even though they are less than your standard deduction, check this box ▶ ☐ | | | | |

**SCHEDULE B (Form 1040)**

Department of the Treasury Internal Revenue Service (99)

# Interest and Ordinary Dividends

▶ Go to *www.irs.gov/ScheduleB* for instructions and the latest information.
▶ Attach to Form 1040 or 1040-SR.

OMB No. 1545-0074 | 2020 | Attachment Sequence No. 08

Name(s) shown on return | Your social security number

## Part I Interest

(See instructions and the instructions for Forms 1040 and 1040-SR, line 2b.)

**Note:** If you received a Form 1099-INT, Form 1099-OID, or substitute statement from a brokerage firm, list the firm's name as the payer and enter the total interest shown on that form.

| | | | Amount |
|---|---|---|---|
| 1 | List name of payer. If any interest is from a seller-financed mortgage and the buyer used the property as a personal residence, see the instructions and list this interest first. Also, show that buyer's social security number and address ▶ | 1 | |
| 2 | Add the amounts on line 1 | 2 | |
| 3 | Excludable interest on series EE and I U.S. savings bonds issued after 1989. Attach Form 8815 | 3 | |
| 4 | Subtract line 3 from line 2. Enter the result here and on Form 1040 or 1040-SR, line 2b ▶ | 4 | |

**Note:** If line 4 is over $1,500, you must complete Part III.

## Part II Ordinary Dividends

(See instructions and the instructions for Forms 1040 and 1040-SR, line 3b.)

**Note:** If you received a Form 1099-DIV or substitute statement from a brokerage firm, list the firm's name as the payer and enter the ordinary dividends shown on that form.

| | | | Amount |
|---|---|---|---|
| 5 | List name of payer ▶ | 5 | |
| 6 | Add the amounts on line 5. Enter the total here and on Form 1040 or 1040-SR, line 3b ▶ | 6 | |

**Note:** If line 6 is over $1,500, you must complete Part III.

## Part III Foreign Accounts and Trusts

**Caution:** If required, failure to file FinCEN Form 114 may result in substantial penalties. See instructions.

| | You must complete this part if you **(a)** had over $1,500 of taxable interest or ordinary dividends; **(b)** had a foreign account; or **(c)** received a distribution from, or were a grantor of, or a transferor to, a foreign trust. | Yes | No |
|---|---|---|---|
| 7a | At any time during 2020, did you have a financial interest in or signature authority over a financial account (such as a bank account, securities account, or brokerage account) located in a foreign country? See instructions | | |
| | If "Yes," are you required to file FinCEN Form 114, Report of Foreign Bank and Financial Accounts (FBAR), to report that financial interest or signature authority? See FinCEN Form 114 and its instructions for filing requirements and exceptions to those requirements | | |
| b | If you are required to file FinCEN Form 114, enter the name of the foreign country where the financial account is located ▶ | | |
| 8 | During 2020, did you receive a distribution from, or were you the grantor of, or transferor to, a foreign trust? If "Yes," you may have to file Form 3520. See instructions | | |

**SCHEDULE C (Form 1040)**

Department of the Treasury Internal Revenue Service (99)

# Profit or Loss From Business

(Sole Proprietorship)

► Go to *www.irs.gov/ScheduleC* for instructions and the latest information.

► Attach to Form 1040, 1040-SR, 1040-NR, or 1041; partnerships generally must file Form 1065.

OMB No. 1545-0074

**2020**

Attachment Sequence No. **09**

Name of proprietor | **Social security number (SSN)**

**A** Principal business or profession, including product or service (see instructions) | **B Enter code from instructions** ►

**C** Business name. If no separate business name, leave blank. | **D Employer ID number (EIN)** (see instr.)

**E** Business address (including suite or room no.) ►

City, town or post office, state, and ZIP code

**F** Accounting method: **(1)** ☐ Cash **(2)** ☐ Accrual **(3)** ☐ Other (specify) ►

**G** Did you "materially participate" in the operation of this business during 2020? If "No," see instructions for limit on losses . ☐ **Yes** ☐ **No**

**H** If you started or acquired this business during 2020, check here . . . . ► ☐

**I** Did you make any payments in 2020 that would require you to file Form(s) 1099? See instructions . . . ☐ **Yes** ☐ **No**

**J** If "Yes," did you or will you file required Form(s) 1099? . . . ☐ **Yes** ☐ **No**

## Part I Income

| | | | |
|---|---|---|---|
| 1 | Gross receipts or sales. See instructions for line 1 and check the box if this income was reported to you on Form W-2 and the "Statutory employee" box on that form was checked . . . ► ☐ | 1 | |
| 2 | Returns and allowances . . . | 2 | |
| 3 | Subtract line 2 from line 1 . . . | 3 | |
| 4 | Cost of goods sold (from line 42) . . . | 4 | |
| 5 | **Gross profit.** Subtract line 4 from line 3 . . . | 5 | |
| 6 | Other income, including federal and state gasoline or fuel tax credit or refund (see instructions) . . . | 6 | |
| 7 | **Gross income.** Add lines 5 and 6 . . . ► | 7 | |

## Part II Expenses. Enter expenses for business use of your home **only** on line 30.

| | | | | | | | |
|---|---|---|---|---|---|---|---|
| 8 | Advertising . . . . . | 8 | | 18 | Office expense (see instructions) | 18 | |
| 9 | Car and truck expenses (see instructions) . . . . . | 9 | | 19 | Pension and profit-sharing plans | 19 | |
| | | | | 20 | Rent or lease (see instructions): | | |
| 10 | Commissions and fees . | 10 | | a | Vehicles, machinery, and equipment | 20a | |
| 11 | Contract labor (see instructions) | 11 | | b | Other business property . . . | 20b | |
| 12 | Depletion . . . . . | 12 | | 21 | Repairs and maintenance . . . | 21 | |
| 13 | Depreciation and section 179 expense deduction (not included in Part III) (see instructions) . . . . . | 13 | | 22 | Supplies (not included in Part III) . | 22 | |
| | | | | 23 | Taxes and licenses . . . . . | 23 | |
| | | | | 24 | Travel and meals: | | |
| 14 | Employee benefit programs (other than on line 19) . . | 14 | | a | Travel . . . . . . . . | 24a | |
| 15 | Insurance (other than health) | 15 | | b | Deductible meals (see instructions) . . . . . . | 24b | |
| 16 | Interest (see instructions): | | | 25 | Utilities . . . . . . . . | 25 | |
| a | Mortgage (paid to banks, etc.) | 16a | | 26 | Wages (less employment credits) . | 26 | |
| b | Other . . . . . . | 16b | | 27a | Other expenses (from line 48) . . | 27a | |
| 17 | Legal and professional services | 17 | | b | **Reserved for future use** . . . | 27b | |

| | | | |
|---|---|---|---|
| 28 | **Total expenses** before expenses for business use of home. Add lines 8 through 27a . . . ► | 28 | |
| 29 | Tentative profit or (loss). Subtract line 28 from line 7 . . . | 29 | |
| 30 | Expenses for business use of your home. Do not report these expenses elsewhere. Attach Form 8829 unless using the simplified method. See instructions.<br>**Simplified method filers only:** Enter the total square footage of (a) your home: ________<br>and (b) the part of your home used for business: ________ . Use the Simplified Method Worksheet in the instructions to figure the amount to enter on line 30 . . . | 30 | |
| 31 | **Net profit or (loss).** Subtract line 30 from line 29.<br>• If a profit, enter on both **Schedule 1 (Form 1040), line 3,** and on **Schedule SE, line 2.** (If you checked the box on line 1, see instructions). Estates and trusts, enter on **Form 1041, line 3.**<br>• If a loss, you **must** go to line 32. | 31 | |
| 32 | If you have a loss, check the box that describes your investment in this activity. See instructions.<br>• If you checked 32a, enter the loss on both **Schedule 1 (Form 1040), line 3,** and on **Schedule SE, line 2.** (If you checked the box on line 1, see the line 31 instructions). Estates and trusts, enter on **Form 1041, line 3.**<br>• If you checked 32b, you **must** attach **Form 6198.** Your loss may be limited. | 32a ☐ All investment is at risk.<br>32b ☐ Some investment is not at risk. | |

**For Paperwork Reduction Act Notice, see the separate instructions.** Cat. No. 11334P **Schedule C (Form 1040) 2020**

**Part III** **Cost of Goods Sold** (see instructions)

33 Method(s) used to value closing inventory: a ☐ Cost b ☐ Lower of cost or market c ☐ Other (attach explanation)

34 Was there any change in determining quantities, costs, or valuations between opening and closing inventory? If "Yes," attach explanation . . . ☐ Yes ☐ No

| | | | |
|---|---|---|---|
| 35 | Inventory at beginning of year. If different from last year's closing inventory, attach explanation | 35 | |
| 36 | Purchases less cost of items withdrawn for personal use | 36 | |
| 37 | Cost of labor. Do not include any amounts paid to yourself | 37 | |
| 38 | Materials and supplies | 38 | |
| 39 | Other costs | 39 | |
| 40 | Add lines 35 through 39 | 40 | |
| 41 | Inventory at end of year | 41 | |
| 42 | **Cost of goods sold.** Subtract line 41 from line 40. Enter the result here and on line 4 | 42 | |

**Part IV** **Information on Your Vehicle.** Complete this part **only** if you are claiming car or truck expenses on line 9 and are not required to file Form 4562 for this business. See the instructions for line 13 to find out if you must file Form 4562.

43 When did you place your vehicle in service for business purposes? (month/day/year) ▶ / /

44 Of the total number of miles you drove your vehicle during 2020, enter the number of miles you used your vehicle for:

a Business ____________ b Commuting (see instructions) ____________ c Other ____________

45 Was your vehicle available for personal use during off-duty hours? . . . ☐ Yes ☐ No

46 Do you (or your spouse) have another vehicle available for personal use?. . . ☐ Yes ☐ No

47a Do you have evidence to support your deduction? . . . ☐ Yes ☐ No

b If "Yes," is the evidence written? . . . ☐ Yes ☐ No

**Part V** **Other Expenses.** List below business expenses not included on lines 8–26 or line 30.

| | |
|---|---|
| | |
| | |
| | |
| | |
| | |
| | |
| | |
| | |
| | |
| **48 Total other expenses.** Enter here and on line 27a | 48 |

**SCHEDULE D**
**(Form 1040)**

Department of the Treasury
Internal Revenue Service (99)

# Capital Gains and Losses

▶ Attach to Form 1040, 1040-SR, or 1040-NR.
▶ Go to *www.irs.gov/ScheduleD* for instructions and the latest information.
▶ Use Form 8949 to list your transactions for lines 1b, 2, 3, 8b, 9, and 10.

OMB No. 1545-0074
**2020**
Attachment Sequence No. **12**

Name(s) shown on return | **Your social security number**

Did you dispose of any investment(s) in a qualified opportunity fund during the tax year? ☐ **Yes** ☐ **No**
If "Yes," attach Form 8949 and see its instructions for additional requirements for reporting your gain or loss.

## Part I Short-Term Capital Gains and Losses—Generally Assets Held One Year or Less (see instructions)

| See instructions for how to figure the amounts to enter on the lines below. This form may be easier to complete if you round off cents to whole dollars. | **(d)** Proceeds (sales price) | **(e)** Cost (or other basis) | **(g)** Adjustments to gain or loss from Form(s) 8949, Part I, line 2, column (g) | **(h) Gain or (loss)** Subtract column (e) from column (d) and combine the result with column (g) |
|---|---|---|---|---|
| **1a** Totals for all short-term transactions reported on Form 1099-B for which basis was reported to the IRS and for which you have no adjustments (see instructions). However, if you choose to report all these transactions on Form 8949, leave this line blank and go to line 1b . | | | | |
| **1b** Totals for all transactions reported on Form(s) 8949 with **Box A** checked . . . . . . . . . . . . . . | | | | |
| **2** Totals for all transactions reported on Form(s) 8949 with **Box B** checked . . . . . . . . . . . . . . | | | | |
| **3** Totals for all transactions reported on Form(s) 8949 with **Box C** checked . . . . . . . . . . . . . . | | | | |

| | | |
|---|---|---|
| **4** Short-term gain from Form 6252 and short-term gain or (loss) from Forms 4684, 6781, and 8824 . . | **4** | |
| **5** Net short-term gain or (loss) from partnerships, S corporations, estates, and trusts from Schedule(s) K-1 . . . . . . . . . . . . . . . . . . . . . . . . . . . | **5** | |
| **6** Short-term capital loss carryover. Enter the amount, if any, from line 8 of your **Capital Loss Carryover Worksheet** in the instructions . . . . . . . . . . . . . . . . . . | **6** | ( ) |
| **7** **Net short-term capital gain or (loss).** Combine lines 1a through 6 in column (h). If you have any long-term capital gains or losses, go to Part II below. Otherwise, go to Part III on the back . . . . . . . | **7** | |

## Part II Long-Term Capital Gains and Losses—Generally Assets Held More Than One Year (see instructions)

| See instructions for how to figure the amounts to enter on the lines below. This form may be easier to complete if you round off cents to whole dollars. | **(d)** Proceeds (sales price) | **(e)** Cost (or other basis) | **(g)** Adjustments to gain or loss from Form(s) 8949, Part II, line 2, column (g) | **(h) Gain or (loss)** Subtract column (e) from column (d) and combine the result with column (g) |
|---|---|---|---|---|
| **8a** Totals for all long-term transactions reported on Form 1099-B for which basis was reported to the IRS and for which you have no adjustments (see instructions). However, if you choose to report all these transactions on Form 8949, leave this line blank and go to line 8b . | | | | |
| **8b** Totals for all transactions reported on Form(s) 8949 with **Box D** checked . . . . . . . . . . . . . . | | | | |
| **9** Totals for all transactions reported on Form(s) 8949 with **Box E** checked . . . . . . . . . . . . . . | | | | |
| **10** Totals for all transactions reported on Form(s) 8949 with **Box F** checked. . . . . . . . . . . . . . | | | | |

| | | |
|---|---|---|
| **11** Gain from Form 4797, Part I; long-term gain from Forms 2439 and 6252; and long-term gain or (loss) from Forms 4684, 6781, and 8824 . . . . . . . . . . . . . . . . . . . . . | **11** | |
| **12** Net long-term gain or (loss) from partnerships, S corporations, estates, and trusts from Schedule(s) K-1 | **12** | |
| **13** Capital gain distributions. See the instructions . . . . . . . . . . . . . . . . . . | **13** | |
| **14** Long-term capital loss carryover. Enter the amount, if any, from line 13 of your **Capital Loss Carryover Worksheet** in the instructions . . . . . . . . . . . . . . . . . . . . . | **14** | ( ) |
| **15** **Net long-term capital gain or (loss).** Combine lines 8a through 14 in column (h). Then, go to Part III on the back . . . . . . . . . . . . . . . . . . . . . . . . . . . | **15** | |

**For Paperwork Reduction Act Notice, see your tax return instructions.** Cat. No. 11338H **Schedule D (Form 1040) 2020**

**Part III** **Summary**

| | | | |
|---|---|---|---|
| **16** | Combine lines 7 and 15 and enter the result . . . . . . . . . . . . . . . . . . . . | **16** | |
| | • If line 16 is a **gain,** enter the amount from line 16 on Form 1040, 1040-SR, or 1040-NR, line 7. Then, go to line 17 below.<br>• If line 16 is a **loss,** skip lines 17 through 20 below. Then, go to line 21. Also be sure to complete line 22.<br>• If line 16 is **zero,** skip lines 17 through 21 below and enter -0- on Form 1040, 1040-SR, or 1040-NR, line 7. Then, go to line 22. | | |
| **17** | Are lines 15 and 16 **both** gains?<br>☐ **Yes.** Go to line 18.<br>☐ **No.** Skip lines 18 through 21, and go to line 22. | | |
| **18** | If you are required to complete the **28% Rate Gain Worksheet** (see instructions), enter the amount, if any, from line 7 of that worksheet . . . . . . . . . . . . . . . . . . ▶ | **18** | |
| **19** | If you are required to complete the **Unrecaptured Section 1250 Gain Worksheet** (see instructions), enter the amount, if any, from line 18 of that worksheet . . . . . . . . . . ▶ | **19** | |
| **20** | Are lines 18 and 19 both zero or blank and are you not filing Form 4952?<br>☐ **Yes.** Complete the **Qualified Dividends and Capital Gain Tax Worksheet** in the instructions for Forms 1040 and 1040-SR, line 16. **Don't** complete lines 21 and 22 below.<br>☐ **No.** Complete the **Schedule D Tax Worksheet** in the instructions. **Don't** complete lines 21 and 22 below. | | |
| **21** | If line 16 is a loss, enter here and on Form 1040, 1040-SR, or 1040-NR, line 7, the **smaller** of:<br>• The loss on line 16; or<br>• ($3,000), or if married filing separately, ($1,500) } . . . . . . . . . . . . . . . . | **21** | ( ) |
| | **Note:** When figuring which amount is smaller, treat both amounts as positive numbers. | | |
| **22** | Do you have qualified dividends on Form 1040, 1040-SR, or 1040-NR, line 3a?<br>☐ **Yes.** Complete the **Qualified Dividends and Capital Gain Tax Worksheet** in the instructions for Forms 1040 and 1040-SR, line 16.<br>☐ **No.** Complete the rest of Form 1040, 1040-SR, or 1040-NR. | | |

**SCHEDULE E** (Form 1040)

Department of the Treasury Internal Revenue Service (99)

# Supplemental Income and Loss

**(From rental real estate, royalties, partnerships, S corporations, estates, trusts, REMICs, etc.)**

**▶ Attach to Form 1040, 1040-SR, 1040-NR, or 1041.**

**▶ Go to *www.irs.gov/ScheduleE* for instructions and the latest information.**

OMB No. 1545-0074

**2020**

Attachment Sequence No. **13**

Name(s) shown on return | **Your social security number**

**Part I** **Income or Loss From Rental Real Estate and Royalties** **Note:** If you are in the business of renting personal property, use **Schedule C.** See instructions. If you are an individual, report farm rental income or loss from **Form 4835** on page 2, line 40.

**A** Did you make any payments in 2020 that would require you to file Form(s) 1099? See instructions . . . . . ☐ **Yes** ☐ **No**

**B** If "Yes," did you or will you file required Form(s) 1099? . . . . . ☐ **Yes** ☐ **No**

| **1a** | Physical address of each property (street, city, state, ZIP code) |
|---|---|
| **A** | |
| **B** | |
| **C** | |

| **1b** | Type of Property (from list below) | **2** For each rental real estate property listed above, report the number of fair rental and personal use days. Check the **QJV** box only if you meet the requirements to file as a qualified joint venture. See instructions. | | **Fair Rental Days** | **Personal Use Days** | **QJV** |
|---|---|---|---|---|---|---|
| **A** | | | **A** | | | ☐ |
| **B** | | | **B** | | | ☐ |
| **C** | | | **C** | | | ☐ |

**Type of Property:**

1 Single Family Residence 3 Vacation/Short-Term Rental 5 Land 7 Self-Rental
2 Multi-Family Residence 4 Commercial 6 Royalties 8 Other (describe)

| **Income:** | **Properties:** | | **A** | **B** | **C** |
|---|---|---|---|---|---|
| **3** | Rents received . . . . . | **3** | | | |
| **4** | Royalties received . . . . . | **4** | | | |
| **Expenses:** | | | | | |
| **5** | Advertising . . . . . | **5** | | | |
| **6** | Auto and travel (see instructions) . . . | **6** | | | |
| **7** | Cleaning and maintenance . . . | **7** | | | |
| **8** | Commissions. . . . . | **8** | | | |
| **9** | Insurance . . . . . | **9** | | | |
| **10** | Legal and other professional fees . . . | **10** | | | |
| **11** | Management fees . . . . . | **11** | | | |
| **12** | Mortgage interest paid to banks, etc. (see instructions) | **12** | | | |
| **13** | Other interest. . . . . | **13** | | | |
| **14** | Repairs. . . . . | **14** | | | |
| **15** | Supplies . . . . . | **15** | | | |
| **16** | Taxes . . . . . | **16** | | | |
| **17** | Utilities. . . . . | **17** | | | |
| **18** | Depreciation expense or depletion . . . | **18** | | | |
| **19** | Other (list) ▶ | **19** | | | |
| **20** | Total expenses. Add lines 5 through 19 . . . | **20** | | | |
| **21** | Subtract line 20 from line 3 (rents) and/or 4 (royalties). If result is a (loss), see instructions to find out if you must file **Form 6198** . . . . . | **21** | | | |
| **22** | Deductible rental real estate loss after limitation, if any, on **Form 8582** (see instructions) . . . | **22** | ( ) | ( ) | ( ) |

| | | | |
|---|---|---|---|
| **23a** | Total of all amounts reported on line 3 for all rental properties . . . . | **23a** | |
| **b** | Total of all amounts reported on line 4 for all royalty properties . . . . | **23b** | |
| **c** | Total of all amounts reported on line 12 for all properties . . . . | **23c** | |
| **d** | Total of all amounts reported on line 18 for all properties . . . . | **23d** | |
| **e** | Total of all amounts reported on line 20 for all properties . . . . | **23e** | |

| | | | |
|---|---|---|---|
| **24** | **Income.** Add positive amounts shown on line 21. **Do not** include any losses . . . . . | **24** | |
| **25** | **Losses.** Add royalty losses from line 21 and rental real estate losses from line 22. Enter total losses here . | **25** | ( ) |
| **26** | **Total rental real estate and royalty income or (loss).** Combine lines 24 and 25. Enter the result here. If Parts II, III, IV, and line 40 on page 2 do not apply to you, also enter this amount on Schedule 1 (Form 1040), line 5. Otherwise, include this amount in the total on line 41 on page 2 . | **26** | |

**For Paperwork Reduction Act Notice, see the separate instructions.** Cat. No. 11344L **Schedule E (Form 1040) 2020**

Schedule E (Form 1040) 2020 Attachment Sequence No. **13** Page **2**

| Name(s) shown on return. Do not enter name and social security number if shown on other side. | **Your social security number** |
|---|---|
| | |

**Caution:** The IRS compares amounts reported on your tax return with amounts shown on Schedule(s) K-1.

## Part II Income or Loss From Partnerships and S Corporations

**Note:** If you report a loss, receive a distribution, dispose of stock, or receive a loan repayment from an S corporation, you **must** check the box in column **(e)** on line 28 and attach the required basis computation. If you report a loss from an at-risk activity for which **any** amount is **not** at risk, you **must** check the box in column **(f)** on line 28 and attach **Form 6198.** See instructions.

27 Are you reporting any loss not allowed in a prior year due to the at-risk or basis limitations, a prior year unallowed loss from a passive activity (if that loss was not reported on Form 8582), or unreimbursed partnership expenses? If you answered "Yes," see instructions before completing this section . . . ☐ **Yes** ☐ **No**

| 28 | **(a)** Name | **(b)** Enter **P** for partnership; **S** for S corporation | **(c)** Check if foreign partnership | **(d)** Employer identification number | **(e)** Check if basis computation is required | **(f)** Check if any amount is not at risk |
|---|---|---|---|---|---|---|
| A | | | ☐ | | ☐ | ☐ |
| B | | | ☐ | | ☐ | ☐ |
| C | | | ☐ | | ☐ | ☐ |
| D | | | ☐ | | ☐ | ☐ |

| | **Passive Income and Loss** | | **Nonpassive Income and Loss** | | |
|---|---|---|---|---|---|
| | **(g)** Passive loss allowed (attach **Form 8582** if required) | **(h)** Passive income from **Schedule K-1** | **(i)** Nonpassive loss allowed (see **Schedule K-1**) | **(j)** Section 179 expense deduction from **Form 4562** | **(k)** Nonpassive income from **Schedule K-1** |
| A | | | | | |
| B | | | | | |
| C | | | | | |
| D | | | | | |
| 29a Totals | | | | | |
| b Totals | | | | | |

| | | | |
|---|---|---|---|
| 30 | Add columns (h) and (k) of line 29a. . . . | 30 | |
| 31 | Add columns (g), (i), and (j) of line 29b. . . . | 31 | ( ) |
| 32 | **Total partnership and S corporation income or (loss).** Combine lines 30 and 31 . . . . | 32 | |

## Part III Income or Loss From Estates and Trusts

| 33 | **(a)** Name | **(b)** Employer identification number |
|---|---|---|
| A | | |
| B | | |

| | **Passive Income and Loss** | | **Nonpassive Income and Loss** | |
|---|---|---|---|---|
| | **(c)** Passive deduction or loss allowed (attach **Form 8582** if required) | **(d)** Passive income from **Schedule K-1** | **(e)** Deduction or loss from **Schedule K-1** | **(f)** Other income from **Schedule K-1** |
| A | | | | |
| B | | | | |
| 34a Totals | | | | |
| b Totals | | | | |

| | | | |
|---|---|---|---|
| 35 | Add columns (d) and (f) of line 34a . . . | 35 | |
| 36 | Add columns (c) and (e) of line 34b . . . | 36 | ( ) |
| 37 | **Total estate and trust income or (loss).** Combine lines 35 and 36 . . . | 37 | |

## Part IV Income or Loss From Real Estate Mortgage Investment Conduits (REMICs)—Residual Holder

| 38 | **(a)** Name | **(b)** Employer identification number | **(c)** Excess inclusion from **Schedules Q,** line 2c (see instructions) | **(d)** Taxable income (net loss) from **Schedules Q,** line 1b | **(e)** Income from **Schedules Q,** line 3b |
|---|---|---|---|---|---|
| | | | | | |

| | | | |
|---|---|---|---|
| 39 | Combine columns (d) and (e) only. Enter the result here and include in the total on line 41 below | 39 | |

## Part V Summary

| | | | |
|---|---|---|---|
| 40 | Net farm rental income or (loss) from **Form 4835.** Also, complete line 42 below . . . | 40 | |
| 41 | **Total income or (loss).** Combine lines 26, 32, 37, 39, and 40. Enter the result here and on Schedule 1 (Form 1040), line 5 ▶ | 41 | |
| 42 | **Reconciliation of farming and fishing income.** Enter your **gross** farming and fishing income reported on Form 4835, line 7; Schedule K-1 (Form 1065), box 14, code B; Schedule K-1 (Form 1120-S), box 17, code AD; and Schedule K-1 (Form 1041), box 14, code F. See instructions . . | 42 | |
| 43 | **Reconciliation for real estate professionals.** If you were a real estate professional (see instructions), enter the net income or (loss) you reported anywhere on Form 1040, Form 1040-SR, or Form 1040-NR from all rental real estate activities in which you materially participated under the passive activity loss rules . . . | 43 | |

**SCHEDULE SE (Form 1040)**

Department of the Treasury Internal Revenue Service (99)

# Self-Employment Tax

▶ Go to *www.irs.gov/ScheduleSE* for instructions and the latest information.
▶ Attach to Form 1040, 1040-SR, or 1040-NR.

OMB No. 1545-0074
**2020**
Attachment Sequence No. **17**

Name of person with self-employment income (as shown on Form 1040, 1040-SR, or 1040-NR) | Social security number of person with **self-employment** income ▶

## Part I Self-Employment Tax

**Note:** If your only income subject to self-employment tax is **church employee income,** see instructions for how to report your income and the definition of church employee income.

**A** If you are a minister, member of a religious order, or Christian Science practitioner **and** you filed Form 4361, but you had $400 or more of **other** net earnings from self-employment, check here and continue with Part I . . . . . . . . ▶ ☐

Skip lines 1a and 1b if you use the farm optional method in Part II. See instructions.

| | | | |
|---|---|---|---|
| **1a** | Net farm profit or (loss) from Schedule F, line 34, and farm partnerships, Schedule K-1 (Form 1065), box 14, code A | **1a** | |
| **b** | If you received social security retirement or disability benefits, enter the amount of Conservation Reserve Program payments included on Schedule F, line 4b, or listed on Schedule K-1 (Form 1065), box 20, code AH | **1b** | ( ) |

Skip line 2 if you use the nonfarm optional method in Part II. See instructions.

| | | | | | |
|---|---|---|---|---|---|
| **2** | Net profit or (loss) from Schedule C, line 31; and Schedule K-1 (Form 1065), box 14, code A (other than farming). See instructions for other income to report or if you are a minister or member of a religious order | | | **2** | |
| **3** | Combine lines 1a, 1b, and 2 | | | **3** | |
| **4a** | If line 3 is more than zero, multiply line 3 by 92.35% (0.9235). Otherwise, enter amount from line 3 | | | **4a** | |
| | **Note:** If line 4a is less than $400 due to Conservation Reserve Program payments on line 1b, see instructions. | | | | |
| **b** | If you elect one or both of the optional methods, enter the total of lines 15 and 17 here | | | **4b** | |
| **c** | Combine lines 4a and 4b. If less than $400, **stop;** you don't owe self-employment tax. **Exception:** If less than $400 and you had **church employee income,** enter -0- and continue ▶ | | | **4c** | |
| **5a** | Enter your **church employee income** from Form W-2. See instructions for definition of church employee income | **5a** | | | |
| **b** | Multiply line 5a by 92.35% (0.9235). If less than $100, enter -0- | | | **5b** | |
| **6** | Add lines 4c and 5b | | | **6** | |
| **7** | Maximum amount of combined wages and self-employment earnings subject to social security tax or the 6.2% portion of the 7.65% railroad retirement (tier 1) tax for 2020 | | | **7** | 137,700 |
| **8a** | Total social security wages and tips (total of boxes 3 and 7 on Form(s) W-2) and railroad retirement (tier 1) compensation. If $137,700 or more, skip lines 8b through 10, and go to line 11 | **8a** | | | |
| **b** | Unreported tips subject to social security tax from Form 4137, line 10 | **8b** | | | |
| **c** | Wages subject to social security tax from Form 8919, line 10 | **8c** | | | |
| **d** | Add lines 8a, 8b, and 8c | | | **8d** | |
| **9** | Subtract line 8d from line 7. If zero or less, enter -0- here and on line 10 and go to line 11 ▶ | | | **9** | |
| **10** | Multiply the **smaller** of line 6 or line 9 by 12.4% (0.124) | | | **10** | |
| **11** | Multiply line 6 by 2.9% (0.029) | | | **11** | |
| **12** | **Self-employment tax.** Add lines 10 and 11. Enter here and on **Schedule 2 (Form 1040), line 4** | | | **12** | |
| **13** | **Deduction for one-half of self-employment tax.** Multiply line 12 by 50% (0.50). Enter here and on **Schedule 1 (Form 1040), line 14** | **13** | | | |

## Part II Optional Methods To Figure Net Earnings (see instructions)

**Farm Optional Method.** You may use this method **only** if **(a)** your gross farm income[1] wasn't more than $8,460, **or (b)** your net farm profits[2] were less than $6,107.

| | | | |
|---|---|---|---|
| **14** | Maximum income for optional methods | **14** | 5,640 |
| **15** | Enter the **smaller** of: two-thirds (2/3) of gross farm income[1] (not less than zero) **or** $5,640. Also, include this amount on line 4b above | **15** | |

**Nonfarm Optional Method.** You may use this method **only** if **(a)** your net nonfarm profits[3] were less than $6,107 and also less than 72.189% of your gross nonfarm income,[4] **and (b)** you had net earnings from self-employment of at least $400 in 2 of the prior 3 years. **Caution:** You may use this method no more than five times.

| | | | |
|---|---|---|---|
| **16** | Subtract line 15 from line 14 | **16** | |
| **17** | Enter the **smaller** of: two-thirds (2/3) of gross nonfarm income[4] (not less than zero) **or** the amount on line 16. Also, include this amount on line 4b above | **17** | |

[1] From Sch. F, line 9; and Sch. K-1 (Form 1065), box 14, code B.
[2] From Sch. F, line 34; and Sch. K-1 (Form 1065), box 14, code A—minus the amount you would have entered on line 1b had you not used the optional method.
[3] From Sch. C, line 31; and Sch. K-1 (Form 1065), box 14, code A.
[4] From Sch. C, line 7; and Sch. K-1 (Form 1065), box 14, code C.

**For Paperwork Reduction Act Notice, see your tax return instructions.** Cat. No. 11358Z **Schedule SE (Form 1040) 2020**

Schedule SE (Form 1040) 2020 Attachment Sequence No. **17** Page **2**

## Part III Maximum Deferral of Self-Employment Tax Payments

If line 4c is zero, skip lines 18 through 20, and enter -0- on line 21.

| | | | |
|---|---|---|---|
| 18 | Enter the portion of line 3 that can be attributed to March 27, 2020, through December 31, 2020 . . | 18 | |
| 19 | If line 18 is more than zero, multiply line 18 by 92.35% (0.9235); otherwise, enter the amount from line 18 | 19 | |
| 20 | Enter the portion of lines 15 and 17 that can be attributed to March 27, 2020, through December 31, 2020 . . . . . | 20 | |
| 21 | Combine lines 19 and 20 . . . . . | 21 | |

If line 5b is zero, skip line 22 and enter -0- on line 23.

| | | | |
|---|---|---|---|
| 22 | Enter the portion of line 5a that can be attributed to March 27, 2020, through December 31, 2020 . . | 22 | |
| 23 | Multiply line 22 by 92.35% (0.9235) . . . . . | 23 | |
| 24 | Add lines 21 and 23 . . . . . | 24 | |
| 25 | Enter the smaller of line 9 or line 24 . . . . . | 25 | |
| 26 | Multiply line 25 by 6.2% (0.062). Enter here and see the instructions for line 12e of Schedule 3 (Form 1040) . . . . . | 26 | |

**Schedule SE (Form 1040) 2020**

Form **1065**

Department of the Treasury
Internal Revenue Service

# U.S. Return of Partnership Income

For calendar year 2020, or tax year beginning ____________, 2020, ending ____________, 20____.

▶ Go to *www.irs.gov/Form1065* for instructions and the latest information.

OMB No. 1545-0123

**2020**

| | | | |
|---|---|---|---|
| A Principal business activity | Type or Print | Name of partnership | D Employer identification number |
| B Principal product or service | | Number, street, and room or suite no. If a P.O. box, see instructions. | E Date business started |
| C Business code number | | City or town, state or province, country, and ZIP or foreign postal code | F Total assets (see instructions) $ |

**G** Check applicable boxes: **(1)** ☐ Initial return **(2)** ☐ Final return **(3)** ☐ Name change **(4)** ☐ Address change **(5)** ☐ Amended return

**H** Check accounting method: **(1)** ☐ Cash **(2)** ☐ Accrual **(3)** ☐ Other (specify) ▶

**I** Number of Schedules K-1. Attach one for each person who was a partner at any time during the tax year ▶

**J** Check if Schedules C and M-3 are attached . . . ▶ ☐

**K** Check if partnership: **(1)** ☐ Aggregated activities for section 465 at-risk purposes **(2)** ☐ Grouped activities for section 469 passive activity purposes

**Caution:** Include **only** trade or business income and expenses on lines 1a through 22 below. See instructions for more information.

|  |  |  | | |
|---|---|---|---|---|
| Income | 1a | Gross receipts or sales | 1a | |
| | b | Returns and allowances | 1b | |
| | c | Balance. Subtract line 1b from line 1a | 1c | |
| | 2 | Cost of goods sold (attach Form 1125-A) | 2 | |
| | 3 | Gross profit. Subtract line 2 from line 1c | 3 | |
| | 4 | Ordinary income (loss) from other partnerships, estates, and trusts (attach statement) | 4 | |
| | 5 | Net farm profit (loss) (attach Schedule F (Form 1040)) | 5 | |
| | 6 | Net gain (loss) from Form 4797, Part II, line 17 (attach Form 4797) | 6 | |
| | 7 | Other income (loss) (attach statement) | 7 | |
| | 8 | **Total income (loss).** Combine lines 3 through 7 | 8 | |
| Deductions (see instructions for limitations) | 9 | Salaries and wages (other than to partners) (less employment credits) | 9 | |
| | 10 | Guaranteed payments to partners | 10 | |
| | 11 | Repairs and maintenance | 11 | |
| | 12 | Bad debts | 12 | |
| | 13 | Rent | 13 | |
| | 14 | Taxes and licenses | 14 | |
| | 15 | Interest (see instructions) | 15 | |
| | 16a | Depreciation (if required, attach Form 4562) | 16a | |
| | b | Less depreciation reported on Form 1125-A and elsewhere on return | 16b | 16c |
| | 17 | Depletion **(Do not deduct oil and gas depletion.)** | 17 | |
| | 18 | Retirement plans, etc. | 18 | |
| | 19 | Employee benefit programs | 19 | |
| | 20 | Other deductions (attach statement) | 20 | |
| | 21 | **Total deductions.** Add the amounts shown in the far right column for lines 9 through 20 | 21 | |
| | 22 | **Ordinary business income (loss).** Subtract line 21 from line 8 | 22 | |
| Tax and Payment | 23 | Interest due under the look-back method—completed long-term contracts (attach Form 8697) | 23 | |
| | 24 | Interest due under the look-back method—income forecast method (attach Form 8866) | 24 | |
| | 25 | BBA AAR imputed underpayment (see instructions) | 25 | |
| | 26 | Other taxes (see instructions) | 26 | |
| | 27 | **Total balance due.** Add lines 23 through 26 | 27 | |
| | 28 | Payment (see instructions) | 28 | |
| | 29 | **Amount owed.** If line 28 is smaller than line 27, enter amount owed | 29 | |
| | 30 | **Overpayment.** If line 28 is larger than line 27, enter overpayment | 30 | |

**Sign Here**

Under penalties of perjury, I declare that I have examined this return, including accompanying schedules and statements, and to the best of my knowledge and belief, it is true, correct, and complete. Declaration of preparer (other than partner or limited liability company member) is based on all information of which preparer has any knowledge.

▶ Signature of partner or limited liability company member ▶ Date

May the IRS discuss this return with the preparer shown below? See instructions. ☐ **Yes** ☐ **No**

**Paid Preparer Use Only**

| Print/Type preparer's name | Preparer's signature | Date | Check ☐ if self-employed | PTIN |
|---|---|---|---|---|
| Firm's name ▶ | | | Firm's EIN ▶ | |
| Firm's address ▶ | | | Phone no. | |

Form 1065 (2020) Page **2**

**Schedule B Other Information**

| | | Yes | No |
|---|---|---|---|
| **1** | What type of entity is filing this return? Check the applicable box: | | |
| **a** | ☐ Domestic general partnership **b** ☐ Domestic limited partnership | | |
| **c** | ☐ Domestic limited liability company **d** ☐ Domestic limited liability partnership | | |
| **e** | ☐ Foreign partnership **f** ☐ Other ▶ | | |
| **2** | At the end of the tax year: | | |
| **a** | Did any foreign or domestic corporation, partnership (including any entity treated as a partnership), trust, or tax-exempt organization, or any foreign government own, directly or indirectly, an interest of 50% or more in the profit, loss, or capital of the partnership? For rules of constructive ownership, see instructions. If "Yes," attach Schedule B-1, Information on Partners Owning 50% or More of the Partnership . . . . . . . . . . . | | |
| **b** | Did any individual or estate own, directly or indirectly, an interest of 50% or more in the profit, loss, or capital of the partnership? For rules of constructive ownership, see instructions. If "Yes," attach Schedule B-1, Information on Partners Owning 50% or More of the Partnership . . . . . . . . . . . . . . . . . | | |
| **3** | At the end of the tax year, did the partnership: | | |
| **a** | Own directly 20% or more, or own, directly or indirectly, 50% or more of the total voting power of all classes of stock entitled to vote of any foreign or domestic corporation? For rules of constructive ownership, see instructions. If "Yes," complete (i) through (iv) below . . . . . . . . . . . . . . . . . . . . . . | | |

| **(i)** Name of Corporation | **(ii)** Employer Identification Number (if any) | **(iii)** Country of Incorporation | **(iv)** Percentage Owned in Voting Stock |
|---|---|---|---|
| | | | |
| | | | |
| | | | |
| | | | |

| | | Yes | No |
|---|---|---|---|
| **b** | Own directly an interest of 20% or more, or own, directly or indirectly, an interest of 50% or more in the profit, loss, or capital in any foreign or domestic partnership (including an entity treated as a partnership) or in the beneficial interest of a trust? For rules of constructive ownership, see instructions. If "Yes," complete (i) through (v) below . . | | |

| **(i)** Name of Entity | **(ii)** Employer Identification Number (if any) | **(iii)** Type of Entity | **(iv)** Country of Organization | **(v)** Maximum Percentage Owned in Profit, Loss, or Capital |
|---|---|---|---|---|
| | | | | |
| | | | | |
| | | | | |
| | | | | |

| | | Yes | No |
|---|---|---|---|
| **4** | Does the partnership satisfy **all four** of the following conditions? | | |
| **a** | The partnership's total receipts for the tax year were less than $250,000. | | |
| **b** | The partnership's total assets at the end of the tax year were less than $1 million. | | |
| **c** | Schedules K-1 are filed with the return and furnished to the partners on or before the due date (including extensions) for the partnership return. | | |
| **d** | The partnership is not filing and is not required to file Schedule M-3 . . . . . . . . . . . . . . <br>If "Yes," the partnership is not required to complete Schedules L, M-1, and M-2; item F on page 1 of Form 1065; or item L on Schedule K-1. | | |
| **5** | Is this partnership a publicly traded partnership, as defined in section 469(k)(2)? . . . . . . . . . . . | | |
| **6** | During the tax year, did the partnership have any debt that was canceled, was forgiven, or had the terms modified so as to reduce the principal amount of the debt? . . . . . . . . . . . . . . . . . . . . . | | |
| **7** | Has this partnership filed, or is it required to file, Form 8918, Material Advisor Disclosure Statement, to provide information on any reportable transaction? . . . . . . . . . . . . . . . . . . . . . . . | | |
| **8** | At any time during calendar year 2020, did the partnership have an interest in or a signature or other authority over a financial account in a foreign country (such as a bank account, securities account, or other financial account)? See instructions for exceptions and filing requirements for FinCEN Form 114, Report of Foreign Bank and Financial Accounts (FBAR). If "Yes," enter the name of the foreign country ▶ | | |
| **9** | At any time during the tax year, did the partnership receive a distribution from, or was it the grantor of, or transferor to, a foreign trust? If "Yes," the partnership may have to file Form 3520, Annual Return To Report Transactions With Foreign Trusts and Receipt of Certain Foreign Gifts. See instructions . . . . . . | | |
| **10a** | Is the partnership making, or had it previously made (and not revoked), a section 754 election? . . . . <br>See instructions for details regarding a section 754 election. | | |
| **b** | Did the partnership make for this tax year an optional basis adjustment under section 743(b) or 734(b)? If "Yes," attach a statement showing the computation and allocation of the basis adjustment. See instructions . . . . | | |

Form 1065 (2020) Page 3

**Schedule B Other Information** *(continued)*

| | | Yes | No |
|---|---|---|---|
| c | Is the partnership required to adjust the basis of partnership assets under section 743(b) or 734(b) because of a substantial built-in loss (as defined under section 743(d)) or substantial basis reduction (as defined under section 734(d))? If "Yes," attach a statement showing the computation and allocation of the basis adjustment. See instructions | | |
| 11 | Check this box if, during the current or prior tax year, the partnership distributed any property received in a like-kind exchange or contributed such property to another entity (other than disregarded entities wholly owned by the partnership throughout the tax year) . . . ▶ ☐ | | |
| 12 | At any time during the tax year, did the partnership distribute to any partner a tenancy-in-common or other undivided interest in partnership property? . . . | | |
| 13 | If the partnership is required to file Form 8858, Information Return of U.S. Persons With Respect To Foreign Disregarded Entities (FDEs) and Foreign Branches (FBs), enter the number of Forms 8858 attached. See instructions . . . ▶ | | |
| 14 | Does the partnership have any foreign partners? If "Yes," enter the number of Forms 8805, Foreign Partner's Information Statement of Section 1446 Withholding Tax, filed for this partnership . . . ▶ | | |
| 15 | Enter the number of Forms 8865, Return of U.S. Persons With Respect to Certain Foreign Partnerships, attached to this return . . . ▶ | | |
| 16a | Did you make any payments in 2020 that would require you to file Form(s) 1099? See instructions . . . | | |
| b | If "Yes," did you or will you file required Form(s) 1099? . . . | | |
| 17 | Enter the number of Forms 5471, Information Return of U.S. Persons With Respect To Certain Foreign Corporations, attached to this return . . . ▶ | | |
| 18 | Enter the number of partners that are foreign governments under section 892 . . . ▶ | | |
| 19 | During the partnership's tax year, did the partnership make any payments that would require it to file Form 1042 and 1042-S under chapter 3 (sections 1441 through 1464) or chapter 4 (sections 1471 through 1474)? . . . | | |
| 20 | Was the partnership a specified domestic entity required to file Form 8938 for the tax year? See the Instructions for Form 8938 | | |
| 21 | Is the partnership a section 721(c) partnership, as defined in Regulations section 1.721(c)-1(b)(14)? . . . | | |
| 22 | During the tax year, did the partnership pay or accrue any interest or royalty for which one or more partners are not allowed a deduction under section 267A? See instructions . . .<br>If "Yes," enter the total amount of the disallowed deductions . . . ▶ $ | | |
| 23 | Did the partnership have an election under section 163(j) for any real property trade or business or any farming business in effect during the tax year? See instructions . . . | | |
| 24 | Does the partnership satisfy one or more of the following? See instructions . . . | | |
| a | The partnership owns a pass-through entity with current, or prior year carryover, excess business interest expense. | | |
| b | The partnership's aggregate average annual gross receipts (determined under section 448(c)) for the 3 tax years preceding the current tax year are more than $26 million and the partnership has business interest. | | |
| c | The partnership is a tax shelter (see instructions) and the partnership has business interest expense.<br>If "Yes" to any, complete and attach Form 8990. | | |
| 25 | Is the partnership electing out of the centralized partnership audit regime under section 6221(b)? See instructions.<br>If "Yes," the partnership must complete Schedule B-2 (Form 1065). Enter the total from Schedule B-2, Part III, line 3 . . . ▶<br>If "No," complete Designation of Partnership Representative below. | | |

**Designation of Partnership Representative** (see instructions)

Enter below the information for the partnership representative (PR) for the tax year covered by this return.

Name of PR ▶

| U.S. address of PR ▶ | | U.S. phone number of PR ▶ | |
|---|---|---|---|

If the PR is an entity, name of the designated individual for the PR ▶

| U.S. address of designated individual ▶ | | U.S. phone number of designated individual ▶ | |
|---|---|---|---|

| | | Yes | No |
|---|---|---|---|
| 26 | Is the partnership attaching Form 8996 to certify as a Qualified Opportunity Fund? . . .<br>If "Yes," enter the amount from Form 8996, line 16 . . . ▶ $ | | |
| 27 | Enter the number of foreign partners subject to section 864(c)(8) as a result of transferring all or a portion of an interest in the partnership or of receiving a distribution from the partnership . . . ▶ | | |
| 28 | At any time during the tax year, were there any transfers between the partnership and its partners subject to the disclosure requirements of Regulations section 1.707-8? . . . | | |
| 29 | Since December 22, 2017, did a foreign corporation directly or indirectly acquire substantially all of the properties constituting a trade or business of your partnership, and was the ownership percentage (by vote or value) for purposes of section 7874 greater than 50% (for example, the partners held more than 50% of the stock of the foreign corporation)? If "Yes," list the ownership percentage by vote and by value. See instructions.<br>Percentage: By Vote By Value | | |

Form 1065 (2020) Page **4**

**Schedule K Partners' Distributive Share Items**

| Section | Line | Item | | Total amount |
|---|---|---|---|---|
| Income (Loss) | 1 | Ordinary business income (loss) (page 1, line 22) | | 1 |
| | 2 | Net rental real estate income (loss) (attach Form 8825) | | 2 |
| | 3a | Other gross rental income (loss) | 3a | |
| | b | Expenses from other rental activities (attach statement) | 3b | |
| | c | Other net rental income (loss). Subtract line 3b from line 3a | | 3c |
| | 4 | Guaranteed payments: **a** Services 4a **b** Capital 4b | | |
| | | **c** Total. Add lines 4a and 4b | | 4c |
| | 5 | Interest income | | 5 |
| | 6 | Dividends and dividend equivalents: **a** Ordinary dividends | | 6a |
| | | **b** Qualified dividends 6b **c** Dividend equivalents 6c | | |
| | 7 | Royalties | | 7 |
| | 8 | Net short-term capital gain (loss) (attach Schedule D (Form 1065)) | | 8 |
| | 9a | Net long-term capital gain (loss) (attach Schedule D (Form 1065)) | | 9a |
| | b | Collectibles (28%) gain (loss) | 9b | |
| | c | Unrecaptured section 1250 gain (attach statement) | 9c | |
| | 10 | Net section 1231 gain (loss) (attach Form 4797) | | 10 |
| | 11 | Other income (loss) (see instructions) Type ▶ | | 11 |
| Deductions | 12 | Section 179 deduction (attach Form 4562) | | 12 |
| | 13a | Contributions | | 13a |
| | b | Investment interest expense | | 13b |
| | c | Section 59(e)(2) expenditures: **(1)** Type ▶ **(2)** Amount ▶ | | 13c(2) |
| | d | Other deductions (see instructions) Type ▶ | | 13d |
| Self-Employment | 14a | Net earnings (loss) from self-employment | | 14a |
| | b | Gross farming or fishing income | | 14b |
| | c | Gross nonfarm income | | 14c |
| Credits | 15a | Low-income housing credit (section 42(j)(5)) | | 15a |
| | b | Low-income housing credit (other) | | 15b |
| | c | Qualified rehabilitation expenditures (rental real estate) (attach Form 3468, if applicable) | | 15c |
| | d | Other rental real estate credits (see instructions) Type ▶ | | 15d |
| | e | Other rental credits (see instructions) Type ▶ | | 15e |
| | f | Other credits (see instructions) Type ▶ | | 15f |
| Foreign Transactions | 16a | Name of country or U.S. possession ▶ | | |
| | b | Gross income from all sources | | 16b |
| | c | Gross income sourced at partner level | | 16c |
| | | Foreign gross income sourced at partnership level | | |
| | d | Reserved for future use ▶ **e** Foreign branch category ▶ | | 16e |
| | f | Passive category ▶ **g** General category ▶ **h** Other (attach statement) ▶ | | 16h |
| | | Deductions allocated and apportioned at partner level | | |
| | i | Interest expense ▶ **j** Other ▶ | | 16j |
| | | Deductions allocated and apportioned at partnership level to foreign source income | | |
| | k | Reserved for future use ▶ **l** Foreign branch category ▶ | | 16l |
| | m | Passive category ▶ **n** General category ▶ **o** Other (attach statement) ▶ | | 16o |
| | p | Total foreign taxes (check one): ▶ Paid ☐ Accrued ☐ | | 16p |
| | q | Reduction in taxes available for credit (attach statement) | | 16q |
| | r | Other foreign tax information (attach statement) | | |
| Alternative Minimum Tax (AMT) Items | 17a | Post-1986 depreciation adjustment | | 17a |
| | b | Adjusted gain or loss | | 17b |
| | c | Depletion (other than oil and gas) | | 17c |
| | d | Oil, gas, and geothermal properties—gross income | | 17d |
| | e | Oil, gas, and geothermal properties—deductions | | 17e |
| | f | Other AMT items (attach statement) | | 17f |
| Other Information | 18a | Tax-exempt interest income | | 18a |
| | b | Other tax-exempt income | | 18b |
| | c | Nondeductible expenses | | 18c |
| | 19a | Distributions of cash and marketable securities | | 19a |
| | b | Distributions of other property | | 19b |
| | 20a | Investment income | | 20a |
| | b | Investment expenses | | 20b |
| | c | Other items and amounts (attach statement) | | |

Form 1065 (2020) Page **5**

**Analysis of Net Income (Loss)**

| | | | | | | | |
|---|---|---|---|---|---|---|---|
| 1 | Net income (loss). Combine Schedule K, lines 1 through 11. From the result, subtract the sum of Schedule K, lines 12 through 13d, and 16p | | | | | 1 | |
| 2 | Analysis by partner type: | **(i)** Corporate | **(ii)** Individual (active) | **(iii)** Individual (passive) | **(iv)** Partnership | **(v)** Exempt Organization | **(vi)** Nominee/Other |
| a | General partners | | | | | | |
| b | Limited partners | | | | | | |

**Schedule L** **Balance Sheets per Books**

| | | Beginning of tax year | | End of tax year | |
|---|---|---|---|---|---|
| | **Assets** | **(a)** | **(b)** | **(c)** | **(d)** |
| 1 | Cash | | | | |
| 2a | Trade notes and accounts receivable | | | | |
| b | Less allowance for bad debts | | | | |
| 3 | Inventories | | | | |
| 4 | U.S. government obligations | | | | |
| 5 | Tax-exempt securities | | | | |
| 6 | Other current assets (attach statement) | | | | |
| 7a | Loans to partners (or persons related to partners) | | | | |
| b | Mortgage and real estate loans | | | | |
| 8 | Other investments (attach statement) | | | | |
| 9a | Buildings and other depreciable assets | | | | |
| b | Less accumulated depreciation | | | | |
| 10a | Depletable assets | | | | |
| b | Less accumulated depletion | | | | |
| 11 | Land (net of any amortization) | | | | |
| 12a | Intangible assets (amortizable only) | | | | |
| b | Less accumulated amortization | | | | |
| 13 | Other assets (attach statement) | | | | |
| 14 | Total assets | | | | |
| | **Liabilities and Capital** | | | | |
| 15 | Accounts payable | | | | |
| 16 | Mortgages, notes, bonds payable in less than 1 year | | | | |
| 17 | Other current liabilities (attach statement) | | | | |
| 18 | All nonrecourse loans | | | | |
| 19a | Loans from partners (or persons related to partners) | | | | |
| b | Mortgages, notes, bonds payable in 1 year or more | | | | |
| 20 | Other liabilities (attach statement) | | | | |
| 21 | Partners' capital accounts | | | | |
| 22 | Total liabilities and capital | | | | |

**Schedule M-1** **Reconciliation of Income (Loss) per Books With Income (Loss) per Return**

**Note:** The partnership may be required to file Schedule M-3. See instructions.

| | | | | | |
|---|---|---|---|---|---|
| 1 | Net income (loss) per books | | 6 | Income recorded on books this year not included on Schedule K, lines 1 through 11 (itemize): | |
| 2 | Income included on Schedule K, lines 1, 2, 3c, 5, 6a, 7, 8, 9a, 10, and 11, not recorded on books this year (itemize): ______ | | a | Tax-exempt interest $ ______ | |
| 3 | Guaranteed payments (other than health insurance) | | 7 | Deductions included on Schedule K, lines 1 through 13d, and 16p, not charged against book income this year (itemize): | |
| 4 | Expenses recorded on books this year not included on Schedule K, lines 1 through 13d, and 16p (itemize): | | a | Depreciation $ ______ | |
| a | Depreciation $ ______ | | 8 | Add lines 6 and 7 | |
| b | Travel and entertainment $ ______ | | 9 | Income (loss) (Analysis of Net Income (Loss), line 1). Subtract line 8 from line 5 | |
| 5 | Add lines 1 through 4 | | | | |

**Schedule M-2** **Analysis of Partners' Capital Accounts**

| | | | | | |
|---|---|---|---|---|---|
| 1 | Balance at beginning of year | | 6 | Distributions: **a** Cash | |
| 2 | Capital contributed: **a** Cash | | | **b** Property | |
| | **b** Property | | 7 | Other decreases (itemize): ______ | |
| 3 | Net income (loss) per books | | | | |
| 4 | Other increases (itemize): ______ | | 8 | Add lines 6 and 7 | |
| 5 | Add lines 1 through 4 | | 9 | Balance at end of year. Subtract line 8 from line 5 | |

651119

☐ Final K-1 ☐ Amended K-1 OMB No. 1545-0123

**Schedule K-1 (Form 1065)** **2020**

Department of the Treasury
Internal Revenue Service

For calendar year 2020, or tax year

beginning / / 2020 ending / /

# Partner's Share of Income, Deductions, Credits, etc.

▶ See separate instructions.

## Part I Information About the Partnership

**A** Partnership's employer identification number

**B** Partnership's name, address, city, state, and ZIP code

**C** IRS Center where partnership filed return ▶

**D** ☐ Check if this is a publicly traded partnership (PTP)

## Part II Information About the Partner

**E** Partner's SSN or TIN (Do not use TIN of a disregarded entity. See instructions.)

**F** Name, address, city, state, and ZIP code for partner entered in E. See instructions.

**G** ☐ General partner or LLC member-manager ☐ Limited partner or other LLC member

**H1** ☐ Domestic partner ☐ Foreign partner

**H2** ☐ If the partner is a disregarded entity (DE), enter the partner's:

TIN ________ Name ________

**I1** What type of entity is this partner? ________

**I2** If this partner is a retirement plan (IRA/SEP/Keogh/etc.), check here ☐

**J** Partner's share of profit, loss, and capital (see instructions):

| | Beginning | Ending |
|---|---|---|
| Profit | % | % |
| Loss | % | % |
| Capital | % | % |

Check if decrease is due to sale or exchange of partnership interest . . ☐

**K** Partner's share of liabilities:

| | Beginning | Ending |
|---|---|---|
| Nonrecourse . . | $ | $ |
| Qualified nonrecourse financing . . . | $ | $ |
| Recourse . . . | $ | $ |

☐ Check this box if Item K includes liability amounts from lower tier partnerships.

**L** **Partner's Capital Account Analysis**

| | |
|---|---|
| **Beginning capital account** . . . . | $ |
| Capital contributed during the year . . | $ |
| Current year net income (loss) . . . | $ |
| Other increase (decrease) (attach explanation) | $ |
| Withdrawals & distributions . . . . | $ ( ) |
| **Ending capital account** . . . . . | $ |

**M** Did the partner contribute property with a built-in gain or loss?

☐ Yes ☐ No If "Yes," attach statement. See instructions.

**N** **Partner's Share of Net Unrecognized Section 704(c) Gain or (Loss)**

| | |
|---|---|
| Beginning . . . . . . . . . | $ |
| Ending . . . . . . . . . . | $ |

## Part III Partner's Share of Current Year Income, Deductions, Credits, and Other Items

| | | | |
|---|---|---|---|
| 1 | Ordinary business income (loss) | 15 | Credits |
| 2 | Net rental real estate income (loss) | | |
| 3 | Other net rental income (loss) | 16 | Foreign transactions |
| 4a | Guaranteed payments for services | | |
| 4b | Guaranteed payments for capital | | |
| 4c | Total guaranteed payments | | |
| 5 | Interest income | | |
| 6a | Ordinary dividends | | |
| 6b | Qualified dividends | | |
| 6c | Dividend equivalents | 17 | Alternative minimum tax (AMT) items |
| 7 | Royalties | | |
| 8 | Net short-term capital gain (loss) | | |
| 9a | Net long-term capital gain (loss) | 18 | Tax-exempt income and nondeductible expenses |
| 9b | Collectibles (28%) gain (loss) | | |
| 9c | Unrecaptured section 1250 gain | | |
| 10 | Net section 1231 gain (loss) | 19 | Distributions |
| 11 | Other income (loss) | | |
| | | 20 | Other information |
| 12 | Section 179 deduction | | |
| 13 | Other deductions | | |
| 14 | Self-employment earnings (loss) | | |

**21** ☐ More than one activity for at-risk purposes*

**22** ☐ More than one activity for passive activity purposes*

*See attached statement for additional information.

For IRS Use Only

Form **1120**
Department of the Treasury
Internal Revenue Service

# U.S. Corporation Income Tax Return

For calendar year 2020 or tax year beginning ________, 2020, ending ________, 20 ____

▶ Go to *www.irs.gov/Form1120* for instructions and the latest information.

OMB No. 1545-0123

**2020**

| A Check if: | TYPE OR PRINT | | B Employer identification number |
|---|---|---|---|
| 1a Consolidated return (attach Form 851) ☐ | | Name | |
| b Life/nonlife consolidated return ☐ | | Number, street, and room or suite no. If a P.O. box, see instructions. | C Date incorporated |
| 2 Personal holding co. (attach Sch. PH) ☐ | | City or town, state or province, country, and ZIP or foreign postal code | D Total assets (see instructions) $ |
| 3 Personal service corp. (see instructions) ☐ | | | |
| 4 Schedule M-3 attached ☐ | | E Check if: (1) ☐ Initial return (2) ☐ Final return (3) ☐ Name change (4) ☐ Address change | |

**Income**

| Line | Description | | | Line | Amount |
|---|---|---|---|---|---|
| 1a | Gross receipts or sales | 1a | | | |
| b | Returns and allowances | 1b | | | |
| c | Balance. Subtract line 1b from line 1a | | | 1c | |
| 2 | Cost of goods sold (attach Form 1125-A) | | | 2 | |
| 3 | Gross profit. Subtract line 2 from line 1c | | | 3 | |
| 4 | Dividends and inclusions (Schedule C, line 23) | | | 4 | |
| 5 | Interest | | | 5 | |
| 6 | Gross rents | | | 6 | |
| 7 | Gross royalties | | | 7 | |
| 8 | Capital gain net income (attach Schedule D (Form 1120)) | | | 8 | |
| 9 | Net gain or (loss) from Form 4797, Part II, line 17 (attach Form 4797) | | | 9 | |
| 10 | Other income (see instructions—attach statement) | | | 10 | |
| 11 | **Total income.** Add lines 3 through 10 ▶ | | | 11 | |

**Deductions (See instructions for limitations on deductions.)**

| Line | Description | | | Line | Amount |
|---|---|---|---|---|---|
| 12 | Compensation of officers (see instructions—attach Form 1125-E) ▶ | | | 12 | |
| 13 | Salaries and wages (less employment credits) | | | 13 | |
| 14 | Repairs and maintenance | | | 14 | |
| 15 | Bad debts | | | 15 | |
| 16 | Rents | | | 16 | |
| 17 | Taxes and licenses | | | 17 | |
| 18 | Interest (see instructions) | | | 18 | |
| 19 | Charitable contributions | | | 19 | |
| 20 | Depreciation from Form 4562 not claimed on Form 1125-A or elsewhere on return (attach Form 4562) | | | 20 | |
| 21 | Depletion | | | 21 | |
| 22 | Advertising | | | 22 | |
| 23 | Pension, profit-sharing, etc., plans | | | 23 | |
| 24 | Employee benefit programs | | | 24 | |
| 25 | Reserved for future use | | | 25 | |
| 26 | Other deductions (attach statement) | | | 26 | |
| 27 | **Total deductions.** Add lines 12 through 26 ▶ | | | 27 | |
| 28 | Taxable income before net operating loss deduction and special deductions. Subtract line 27 from line 11 | | | 28 | |
| 29a | Net operating loss deduction (see instructions) | 29a | | | |
| b | Special deductions (Schedule C, line 24) | 29b | | | |
| c | Add lines 29a and 29b | | | 29c | |

**Tax, Refundable Credits, and Payments**

| Line | Description | Line | Amount |
|---|---|---|---|
| 30 | **Taxable income.** Subtract line 29c from line 28. See instructions | 30 | |
| 31 | Total tax (Schedule J, Part I, line 11) | 31 | |
| 32 | 2020 net 965 tax liability paid (Schedule J, Part II, line 12) | 32 | |
| 33 | Total payments, credits, and section 965 net tax liability (Schedule J, Part III, line 23) | 33 | |
| 34 | Estimated tax penalty. See instructions. Check if Form 2220 is attached ▶ ☐ | 34 | |
| 35 | **Amount owed.** If line 33 is smaller than the total of lines 31, 32, and 34, enter amount owed | 35 | |
| 36 | **Overpayment.** If line 33 is larger than the total of lines 31, 32, and 34, enter amount overpaid | 36 | |
| 37 | Enter amount from line 36 you want: **Credited to 2021 estimated tax** ▶ **Refunded** ▶ | 37 | |

**Sign Here**

Under penalties of perjury, I declare that I have examined this return, including accompanying schedules and statements, and to the best of my knowledge and belief, it is true, correct, and complete. Declaration of preparer (other than taxpayer) is based on all information of which preparer has any knowledge.

▶ Signature of officer | Date | ▶ Title

May the IRS discuss this return with the preparer shown below? See instructions. ☐ **Yes** ☐ **No**

**Paid Preparer Use Only**

| Print/Type preparer's name | Preparer's signature | Date | Check ☐ if self-employed | PTIN |
|---|---|---|---|---|
| Firm's name ▶ | | | Firm's EIN ▶ | |
| Firm's address ▶ | | | Phone no. | |

Form 1120 (2020) Page **2**

| **Schedule C** **Dividends, Inclusions, and Special Deductions** (see instructions) | **(a)** Dividends and inclusions | **(b)** % | **(c)** Special deductions **(a)** × **(b)** |
|---|---|---|---|
| **1** Dividends from less-than-20%-owned domestic corporations (other than debt-financed stock) | | 50 | |
| **2** Dividends from 20%-or-more-owned domestic corporations (other than debt-financed stock) | | 65 | |
| **3** Dividends on certain debt-financed stock of domestic and foreign corporations | | See instructions | |
| **4** Dividends on certain preferred stock of less-than-20%-owned public utilities | | 23.3 | |
| **5** Dividends on certain preferred stock of 20%-or-more-owned public utilities | | 26.7 | |
| **6** Dividends from less-than-20%-owned foreign corporations and certain FSCs | | 50 | |
| **7** Dividends from 20%-or-more-owned foreign corporations and certain FSCs | | 65 | |
| **8** Dividends from wholly owned foreign subsidiaries | | 100 | |
| **9** **Subtotal.** Add lines 1 through 8. See instructions for limitations | | See instructions | |
| **10** Dividends from domestic corporations received by a small business investment company operating under the Small Business Investment Act of 1958 | | 100 | |
| **11** Dividends from affiliated group members | | 100 | |
| **12** Dividends from certain FSCs | | 100 | |
| **13** Foreign-source portion of dividends received from a specified 10%-owned foreign corporation (excluding hybrid dividends) (see instructions) | | 100 | |
| **14** Dividends from foreign corporations not included on line 3, 6, 7, 8, 11, 12, or 13 (including any hybrid dividends) | | | |
| **15** Section 965(a) inclusion | | See instructions | |
| **16a** Subpart F inclusions derived from the sale by a controlled foreign corporation (CFC) of the stock of a lower-tier foreign corporation treated as a dividend (attach Form(s) 5471) (see instructions) | | 100 | |
| **b** Subpart F inclusions derived from hybrid dividends of tiered corporations (attach Form(s) 5471) (see instructions) | | | |
| **c** Other inclusions from CFCs under subpart F not included on line 15, 16a, 16b, or 17 (attach Form(s) 5471) (see instructions) | | | |
| **17** Global Intangible Low-Taxed Income (GILTI) (attach Form(s) 5471 and Form 8992) | | | |
| **18** Gross-up for foreign taxes deemed paid | | | |
| **19** IC-DISC and former DISC dividends not included on line 1, 2, or 3 | | | |
| **20** Other dividends | | | |
| **21** Deduction for dividends paid on certain preferred stock of public utilities | | | |
| **22** Section 250 deduction (attach Form 8993) | | | |
| **23** **Total dividends and inclusions.** Add column (a), lines 9 through 20. Enter here and on page 1, line 4 | | | |
| **24** **Total special deductions.** Add column (c), lines 9 through 22. Enter here and on page 1, line 29b | | | |

Form **1120** (2020)

Form 1120 (2020) Page **3**

## Schedule J Tax Computation and Payment (see instructions)

### Part I—Tax Computation

| | | | | | |
|---|---|---|---|---|---|
| 1 | Check if the corporation is a member of a controlled group (attach Schedule O (Form 1120)). See instructions ▶ ☐ | | | | |
| 2 | Income tax. See instructions | | | 2 | |
| 3 | Base erosion minimum tax amount (attach Form 8991) | | | 3 | |
| 4 | Add lines 2 and 3 | | | 4 | |
| 5a | Foreign tax credit (attach Form 1118) | 5a | | | |
| b | Credit from Form 8834 (see instructions) | 5b | | | |
| c | General business credit (attach Form 3800) | 5c | | | |
| d | Credit for prior year minimum tax (attach Form 8827) | 5d | | | |
| e | Bond credits from Form 8912 | 5e | | | |
| 6 | **Total credits.** Add lines 5a through 5e | | | 6 | |
| 7 | Subtract line 6 from line 4 | | | 7 | |
| 8 | Personal holding company tax (attach Schedule PH (Form 1120)) | | | 8 | |
| 9a | Recapture of investment credit (attach Form 4255) | 9a | | | |
| b | Recapture of low-income housing credit (attach Form 8611) | 9b | | | |
| c | Interest due under the look-back method—completed long-term contracts (attach Form 8697) | 9c | | | |
| d | Interest due under the look-back method—income forecast method (attach Form 8866) | 9d | | | |
| e | Alternative tax on qualifying shipping activities (attach Form 8902) | 9e | | | |
| f | Interest/tax due under Section 453A(c) and/or Section 453(l) | 9f | | | |
| g | Other (see instructions—attach statement) | 9g | | | |
| 10 | **Total.** Add lines 9a through 9g | | | 10 | |
| 11 | **Total tax.** Add lines 7, 8, and 10. Enter here and on page 1, line 31 | | | 11 | |

### Part II—Section 965 Payments (see instructions)

| | | | |
|---|---|---|---|
| 12 | 2020 net 965 tax liability paid from Form 965-B, Part II, column (k), line 4. Enter here and on page 1, line 32 | 12 | |

### Part III—Payments, Refundable Credits, and Section 965 Net Tax Liability

| | | | | | |
|---|---|---|---|---|---|
| 13 | 2019 overpayment credited to 2020 | | | 13 | |
| 14 | 2020 estimated tax payments | | | 14 | |
| 15 | 2020 refund applied for on Form 4466 | | | 15 | ( ) |
| 16 | Combine lines 13, 14, and 15 | | | 16 | |
| 17 | Tax deposited with Form 7004 | | | 17 | |
| 18 | Withholding (see instructions) | | | 18 | |
| 19 | **Total payments.** Add lines 16, 17, and 18 | | | 19 | |
| 20 | Refundable credits from: | | | | |
| a | Form 2439 | 20a | | | |
| b | Form 4136 | 20b | | | |
| c | Reserved for future use | 20c | | | |
| d | Other (attach statement—see instructions) | 20d | | | |
| 21 | **Total credits.** Add lines 20a through 20d | | | 21 | |
| 22 | 2020 net 965 tax liability from Form 965-B, Part I, column (d), line 4. See instructions | | | 22 | |
| 23 | **Total payments, credits, and section 965 net tax liability.** Add lines 19, 21, and 22. Enter here and on page 1, line 33 | | | 23 | |

Form **1120** (2020)

Form 1120 (2020) Page **4**

## Schedule K Other Information (see instructions)

| | | Yes | No |
|---|---|---|---|
| 1 | Check accounting method: **a** ☐ Cash **b** ☐ Accrual **c** ☐ Other (specify) ▶ | | |
| 2 | See the instructions and enter the: | | |
| a | Business activity code no. ▶ | | |
| b | Business activity ▶ | | |
| c | Product or service ▶ | | |
| 3 | Is the corporation a subsidiary in an affiliated group or a parent–subsidiary controlled group? If "Yes," enter name and EIN of the parent corporation ▶ | | |
| 4 | At the end of the tax year: | | |
| a | Did any foreign or domestic corporation, partnership (including any entity treated as a partnership), trust, or tax-exempt organization own directly 20% or more, or own, directly or indirectly, 50% or more of the total voting power of all classes of the corporation's stock entitled to vote? If "Yes," complete Part I of Schedule G (Form 1120) (attach Schedule G) | | |
| b | Did any individual or estate own directly 20% or more, or own, directly or indirectly, 50% or more of the total voting power of all classes of the corporation's stock entitled to vote? If "Yes," complete Part II of Schedule G (Form 1120) (attach Schedule G) | | |
| 5 | At the end of the tax year, did the corporation: | | |
| a | Own directly 20% or more, or own, directly or indirectly, 50% or more of the total voting power of all classes of stock entitled to vote of any foreign or domestic corporation not included on **Form 851,** Affiliations Schedule? For rules of constructive ownership, see instructions. If "Yes," complete (i) through (iv) below. | | |

| **(i)** Name of Corporation | **(ii)** Employer Identification Number (if any) | **(iii)** Country of Incorporation | **(iv)** Percentage Owned in Voting Stock |
|---|---|---|---|
| | | | |
| | | | |
| | | | |

| | | Yes | No |
|---|---|---|---|
| b | Own directly an interest of 20% or more, or own, directly or indirectly, an interest of 50% or more in any foreign or domestic partnership (including an entity treated as a partnership) or in the beneficial interest of a trust? For rules of constructive ownership, see instructions. If "Yes," complete (i) through (iv) below. | | |

| **(i)** Name of Entity | **(ii)** Employer Identification Number (if any) | **(iii)** Country of Organization | **(iv)** Maximum Percentage Owned in Profit, Loss, or Capital |
|---|---|---|---|
| | | | |
| | | | |
| | | | |

| | | Yes | No |
|---|---|---|---|
| 6 | During this tax year, did the corporation pay dividends (other than stock dividends and distributions in exchange for stock) in excess of the corporation's current and accumulated earnings and profits? See sections 301 and 316<br>If "Yes," file **Form 5452,** Corporate Report of Nondividend Distributions. See the instructions for Form 5452.<br>If this is a consolidated return, answer here for the parent corporation and on Form 851 for each subsidiary. | | |
| 7 | At any time during the tax year, did one foreign person own, directly or indirectly, at least 25% of the total voting power of all classes of the corporation's stock entitled to vote or at least 25% of the total value of all classes of the corporation's stock?<br>For rules of attribution, see section 318. If "Yes," enter:<br>**(a)** Percentage owned ▶ ______ and **(b)** Owner's country ▶<br>**(c)** The corporation may have to file **Form 5472,** Information Return of a 25% Foreign-Owned U.S. Corporation or a Foreign Corporation Engaged in a U.S. Trade or Business. Enter the number of Forms 5472 attached ▶ | | |
| 8 | Check this box if the corporation issued publicly offered debt instruments with original issue discount ▶ ☐<br>If checked, the corporation may have to file **Form 8281,** Information Return for Publicly Offered Original Issue Discount Instruments. | | |
| 9 | Enter the amount of tax-exempt interest received or accrued during the tax year ▶ $ | | |
| 10 | Enter the number of shareholders at the end of the tax year (if 100 or fewer) ▶ | | |
| 11 | If the corporation has an NOL for the tax year and is electing to forego the carryback period, check here (see instructions) ▶ ☐<br>If the corporation is filing a consolidated return, the statement required by Regulations section 1.1502-21(b)(3) must be attached or the election will not be valid. | | |
| 12 | Enter the available NOL carryover from prior tax years (do not reduce it by any deduction reported on page 1, line 29a.) ▶ $ | | |

Form 1120 (2020) Page **5**

**Schedule K** **Other Information** *(continued from page 4)*

| | | Yes | No |
|---|---|---|---|
| 13 | Are the corporation's total receipts (page 1, line 1a, plus lines 4 through 10) for the tax year **and** its total assets at the end of the tax year less than $250,000? | | |
| | If "Yes," the corporation is not required to complete Schedules L, M-1, and M-2. Instead, enter the total amount of cash distributions and the book value of property distributions (other than cash) made during the tax year ▶ $ | | |
| 14 | Is the corporation required to file Schedule UTP (Form 1120), Uncertain Tax Position Statement? See instructions | | |
| | If "Yes," complete and attach Schedule UTP. | | |
| 15a | Did the corporation make any payments in 2020 that would require it to file Form(s) 1099? | | |
| b | If "Yes," did or will the corporation file required Form(s) 1099? | | |
| 16 | During this tax year, did the corporation have an 80%-or-more change in ownership, including a change due to redemption of its own stock? | | |
| 17 | During or subsequent to this tax year, but before the filing of this return, did the corporation dispose of more than 65% (by value) of its assets in a taxable, non-taxable, or tax deferred transaction? | | |
| 18 | Did the corporation receive assets in a section 351 transfer in which any of the transferred assets had a fair market basis or fair market value of more than $1 million? | | |
| 19 | During the corporation's tax year, did the corporation make any payments that would require it to file Forms 1042 and 1042-S under chapter 3 (sections 1441 through 1464) or chapter 4 (sections 1471 through 1474) of the Code? | | |
| 20 | Is the corporation operating on a cooperative basis? | | |
| 21 | During the tax year, did the corporation pay or accrue any interest or royalty for which the deduction is not allowed under section 267A? See instructions | | |
| | If "Yes," enter the total amount of the disallowed deductions ▶ $ | | |
| 22 | Does the corporation have gross receipts of at least $500 million in any of the 3 preceding tax years? (See sections 59A(e)(2) and (3)) | | |
| | If "Yes," complete and attach Form 8991. | | |
| 23 | Did the corporation have an election under section 163(j) for any real property trade or business or any farming business in effect during the tax year? See instructions | | |
| 24 | Does the corporation satisfy one or more of the following? See instructions | | |
| a | The corporation owns a pass-through entity with current, or prior year carryover, excess business interest expense. | | |
| b | The corporation's aggregate average annual gross receipts (determined under section 448(c)) for the 3 tax years preceding the current tax year are more than $26 million and the corporation has business interest expense. | | |
| c | The corporation is a tax shelter and the corporation has business interest expense. | | |
| | If "Yes," complete and attach Form 8990. | | |
| 25 | Is the corporation attaching Form 8996 to certify as a Qualified Opportunity Fund? | | |
| | If "Yes," enter amount from Form 8996, line 15 ▶ $ | | |
| 26 | Since December 22, 2017, did a foreign corporation directly or indirectly acquire substantially all of the properties held directly or indirectly by the corporation, and was the ownership percentage (by vote or value) for purposes of section 7874 greater than 50% (for example, the shareholders held more than 50% of the stock of the foreign corporation)? If "Yes," list the ownership percentage by vote and by value. See instructions | | |
| | Percentage: By Vote By Value | | |

Form **1120** (2020)

Form 1120 (2020) Page 6

**Schedule L** **Balance Sheets per Books**

| Assets | Beginning of tax year (a) | (b) | End of tax year (c) | (d) |
|---|---|---|---|---|
| 1 Cash | | | | |
| 2a Trade notes and accounts receivable | | | | |
| b Less allowance for bad debts | ( ) | | ( ) | |
| 3 Inventories | | | | |
| 4 U.S. government obligations | | | | |
| 5 Tax-exempt securities (see instructions) | | | | |
| 6 Other current assets (attach statement) | | | | |
| 7 Loans to shareholders | | | | |
| 8 Mortgage and real estate loans | | | | |
| 9 Other investments (attach statement) | | | | |
| 10a Buildings and other depreciable assets | | | | |
| b Less accumulated depreciation | ( ) | | ( ) | |
| 11a Depletable assets | | | | |
| b Less accumulated depletion | ( ) | | ( ) | |
| 12 Land (net of any amortization) | | | | |
| 13a Intangible assets (amortizable only) | | | | |
| b Less accumulated amortization | ( ) | | ( ) | |
| 14 Other assets (attach statement) | | | | |
| 15 Total assets | | | | |
| **Liabilities and Shareholders' Equity** | | | | |
| 16 Accounts payable | | | | |
| 17 Mortgages, notes, bonds payable in less than 1 year | | | | |
| 18 Other current liabilities (attach statement) | | | | |
| 19 Loans from shareholders | | | | |
| 20 Mortgages, notes, bonds payable in 1 year or more | | | | |
| 21 Other liabilities (attach statement) | | | | |
| 22 Capital stock: **a** Preferred stock | | | | |
| **b** Common stock | | | | |
| 23 Additional paid-in capital | | | | |
| 24 Retained earnings—Appropriated (attach statement) | | | | |
| 25 Retained earnings—Unappropriated | | | | |
| 26 Adjustments to shareholders' equity (attach statement) | | | | |
| 27 Less cost of treasury stock | | ( ) | | ( ) |
| 28 Total liabilities and shareholders' equity | | | | |

**Schedule M-1** **Reconciliation of Income (Loss) per Books With Income per Return**

**Note:** The corporation may be required to file Schedule M-3. See instructions.

| | | | |
|---|---|---|---|
| 1 Net income (loss) per books | | 7 Income recorded on books this year not included on this return (itemize): | |
| 2 Federal income tax per books | | Tax-exempt interest $ | |
| 3 Excess of capital losses over capital gains | | | |
| 4 Income subject to tax not recorded on books this year (itemize): | | | |
| 5 Expenses recorded on books this year not deducted on this return (itemize): | | 8 Deductions on this return not charged against book income this year (itemize): | |
| a Depreciation $ | | a Depreciation $ | |
| b Charitable contributions $ | | b Charitable contributions $ | |
| c Travel and entertainment $ | | | |
| | | 9 Add lines 7 and 8 | |
| 6 Add lines 1 through 5 | | 10 Income (page 1, line 28)—line 6 less line 9 | |

**Schedule M-2** **Analysis of Unappropriated Retained Earnings per Books (Schedule L, Line 25)**

| | | | |
|---|---|---|---|
| 1 Balance at beginning of year | | 5 Distributions: **a** Cash | |
| 2 Net income (loss) per books | | **b** Stock | |
| 3 Other increases (itemize): | | **c** Property | |
| | | 6 Other decreases (itemize): | |
| | | 7 Add lines 5 and 6 | |
| 4 Add lines 1, 2, and 3 | | 8 Balance at end of year (line 4 less line 7) | |

Form **1120** (2020)

Form **1120-S**

Department of the Treasury
Internal Revenue Service

# U.S. Income Tax Return for an S Corporation

▶ **Do not file this form unless the corporation has filed or is attaching Form 2553 to elect to be an S corporation.**
▶ **Go to *www.irs.gov/Form1120S* for instructions and the latest information.**

OMB No. 1545-0123

**2020**

For calendar year 2020 or tax year beginning , 2020, ending , 20

| | TYPE OR PRINT | |
|---|---|---|
| **A** S election effective date | Name | **D Employer identification number** |
| **B** Business activity code number (see instructions) | Number, street, and room or suite no. If a P.O. box, see instructions. | **E** Date incorporated |
| **C** Check if Sch. M-3 attached ☐ | City or town, state or province, country, and ZIP or foreign postal code | **F** Total assets (see instructions) $ |

**G** Is the corporation electing to be an S corporation beginning with this tax year? ☐ Yes ☐ No If "Yes," attach Form 2553 if not already filed

**H** Check if: **(1)** ☐ Final return **(2)** ☐ Name change **(3)** ☐ Address change **(4)** ☐ Amended return **(5)** ☐ S election termination or revocation

**I** Enter the number of shareholders who were shareholders during any part of the tax year . . . . . . . . ▶

**J** Check if corporation: **(1)** ☐ Aggregated activities for section 465 at-risk purposes **(2)** ☐ Grouped activities for section 469 passive activity purposes

**Caution:** Include **only** trade or business income and expenses on lines 1a through 21. See the instructions for more information.

|  |  |  | | |
|---|---|---|---|---|
| Income | 1a | Gross receipts or sales | 1a | |
| | b | Returns and allowances | 1b | |
| | c | Balance. Subtract line 1b from line 1a | | 1c |
| | 2 | Cost of goods sold (attach Form 1125-A) | | 2 |
| | 3 | Gross profit. Subtract line 2 from line 1c | | 3 |
| | 4 | Net gain (loss) from Form 4797, line 17 (attach Form 4797) | | 4 |
| | 5 | Other income (loss) (see instructions—attach statement) | | 5 |
| | 6 | **Total income (loss).** Add lines 3 through 5 ▶ | | 6 |
| Deductions (see instructions for limitations) | 7 | Compensation of officers (see instructions—attach Form 1125-E) | | 7 |
| | 8 | Salaries and wages (less employment credits) | | 8 |
| | 9 | Repairs and maintenance | | 9 |
| | 10 | Bad debts | | 10 |
| | 11 | Rents | | 11 |
| | 12 | Taxes and licenses | | 12 |
| | 13 | Interest (see instructions) | | 13 |
| | 14 | Depreciation not claimed on Form 1125-A or elsewhere on return (attach Form 4562) | | 14 |
| | 15 | Depletion **(Do not deduct oil and gas depletion.)** | | 15 |
| | 16 | Advertising | | 16 |
| | 17 | Pension, profit-sharing, etc., plans | | 17 |
| | 18 | Employee benefit programs | | 18 |
| | 19 | Other deductions (attach statement) | | 19 |
| | 20 | **Total deductions.** Add lines 7 through 19 ▶ | | 20 |
| | 21 | **Ordinary business income (loss).** Subtract line 20 from line 6 | | 21 |
| Tax and Payments | 22a | Excess net passive income or LIFO recapture tax (see instructions) | 22a | |
| | b | Tax from Schedule D (Form 1120-S) | 22b | |
| | c | Add lines 22a and 22b (see instructions for additional taxes) | | 22c |
| | 23a | 2020 estimated tax payments and 2019 overpayment credited to 2020 | 23a | |
| | b | Tax deposited with Form 7004 | 23b | |
| | c | Credit for federal tax paid on fuels (attach Form 4136) | 23c | |
| | d | Reserved for future use | 23d | |
| | e | Add lines 23a through 23d | | 23e |
| | 24 | Estimated tax penalty (see instructions). Check if Form 2220 is attached ▶ ☐ | | 24 |
| | 25 | **Amount owed.** If line 23e is smaller than the total of lines 22c and 24, enter amount owed | | 25 |
| | 26 | **Overpayment.** If line 23e is larger than the total of lines 22c and 24, enter amount overpaid | | 26 |
| | 27 | Enter amount from line 26: **Credited to 2021 estimated tax ▶** **Refunded ▶** | | 27 |

**Sign Here**

Under penalties of perjury, I declare that I have examined this return, including accompanying schedules and statements, and to the best of my knowledge and belief, it is true, correct, and complete. Declaration of preparer (other than taxpayer) is based on all information of which preparer has any knowledge.

▶ Signature of officer | Date | ▶ Title

May the IRS discuss this return with the preparer shown below? See instructions. ☐ Yes ☐ No

| **Paid Preparer Use Only** | Print/Type preparer's name | Preparer's signature | Date | Check ☐ if self-employed | PTIN |
|---|---|---|---|---|---|
| | Firm's name ▶ | | | Firm's EIN ▶ | |
| | Firm's address ▶ | | | Phone no. | |

## Schedule B Other Information (see instructions)

| | | Yes | No |
|---|---|---|---|
| 1 | Check accounting method: a ☐ Cash b ☐ Accrual c ☐ Other (specify) ▶ | | |
| 2 | See the instructions and enter the: a Business activity ▶ b Product or service ▶ | | |
| 3 | At any time during the tax year, was any shareholder of the corporation a disregarded entity, a trust, an estate, or a nominee or similar person? If "Yes," attach Schedule B-1, Information on Certain Shareholders of an S Corporation . . | | |
| 4 | At the end of the tax year, did the corporation: | | |
| a | Own directly 20% or more, or own, directly or indirectly, 50% or more of the total stock issued and outstanding of any foreign or domestic corporation? For rules of constructive ownership, see instructions. If "Yes," complete (i) through (v) below . . . | | |

| **(i)** Name of Corporation | **(ii)** Employer Identification Number (if any) | **(iii)** Country of Incorporation | **(iv)** Percentage of Stock Owned | **(v)** If Percentage in (iv) Is 100%, Enter the Date (if any) a Qualified Subchapter S Subsidiary Election Was Made |
|---|---|---|---|---|
| | | | | |
| | | | | |
| | | | | |
| | | | | |

| | | Yes | No |
|---|---|---|---|
| b | Own directly an interest of 20% or more, or own, directly or indirectly, an interest of 50% or more in the profit, loss, or capital in any foreign or domestic partnership (including an entity treated as a partnership) or in the beneficial interest of a trust? For rules of constructive ownership, see instructions. If "Yes," complete (i) through (v) below . . . | | |

| **(i)** Name of Entity | **(ii)** Employer Identification Number (if any) | **(iii)** Type of Entity | **(iv)** Country of Organization | **(v)** Maximum Percentage Owned in Profit, Loss, or Capital |
|---|---|---|---|---|
| | | | | |
| | | | | |
| | | | | |
| | | | | |

| | | Yes | No |
|---|---|---|---|
| 5a | At the end of the tax year, did the corporation have any outstanding shares of restricted stock? . . . If "Yes," complete lines (i) and (ii) below. | | |
| | **(i)** Total shares of restricted stock . . . ▶ | | |
| | **(ii)** Total shares of non-restricted stock . . . ▶ | | |
| b | At the end of the tax year, did the corporation have any outstanding stock options, warrants, or similar instruments? . If "Yes," complete lines (i) and (ii) below. | | |
| | **(i)** Total shares of stock outstanding at the end of the tax year ▶ | | |
| | **(ii)** Total shares of stock outstanding if all instruments were executed ▶ | | |
| 6 | Has this corporation filed, or is it required to file, **Form 8918,** Material Advisor Disclosure Statement, to provide information on any reportable transaction? . . . | | |
| 7 | Check this box if the corporation issued publicly offered debt instruments with original issue discount . . . ▶ ☐ If checked, the corporation may have to file **Form 8281,** Information Return for Publicly Offered Original Issue Discount Instruments. | | |
| 8 | If the corporation **(a)** was a C corporation before it elected to be an S corporation **or** the corporation acquired an asset with a basis determined by reference to the basis of the asset (or the basis of any other property) in the hands of a C corporation, **and** **(b)** has net unrealized built-in gain in excess of the net recognized built-in gain from prior years, enter the net unrealized built-in gain reduced by net recognized built-in gain from prior years. See instructions . . . ▶ $ | | |
| 9 | Did the corporation have an election under section 163(j) for any real property trade or business or any farming business in effect during the tax year? See instructions . . . | | |
| 10 | Does the corporation satisfy one or more of the following? See instructions . . . | | |
| a | The corporation owns a pass-through entity with current, or prior year carryover, excess business interest expense. | | |
| b | The corporation's aggregate average annual gross receipts (determined under section 448(c)) for the 3 tax years preceding the current tax year are more than $26 million and the corporation has business interest expense. | | |
| c | The corporation is a tax shelter and the corporation has business interest expense. If "Yes," complete and attach Form 8990. | | |
| 11 | Does the corporation satisfy **both** of the following conditions? . . . | | |
| a | The corporation's total receipts (see instructions) for the tax year were less than $250,000. | | |
| b | The corporation's total assets at the end of the tax year were less than $250,000. If "Yes," the corporation is not required to complete Schedules L and M-1. | | |

Form 1120-S (2020) Page **3**

| **Schedule B** | **Other Information** (see instructions) *(continued)* | Yes | No |
|---|---|---|---|
| 12 | During the tax year, did the corporation have any non-shareholder debt that was canceled, was forgiven, or had the terms modified so as to reduce the principal amount of the debt? | | |
| | If "Yes," enter the amount of principal reduction ▶ $ | | |
| 13 | During the tax year, was a qualified subchapter S subsidiary election terminated or revoked? If "Yes," see instructions | | |
| 14a | Did the corporation make any payments in 2020 that would require it to file Form(s) 1099? | | |
| b | If "Yes," did the corporation file or will it file required Form(s) 1099? | | |
| 15 | Is the corporation attaching Form 8996 to certify as a Qualified Opportunity Fund? | | |
| | If "Yes," enter the amount from Form 8996, line 15 ▶ $ | | |

| **Schedule K** | | **Shareholders' Pro Rata Share Items** | | | **Total amount** |
|---|---|---|---|---|---|
| Income (Loss) | 1 | Ordinary business income (loss) (page 1, line 21) | | 1 | |
| | 2 | Net rental real estate income (loss) (attach Form 8825) | | 2 | |
| | 3a | Other gross rental income (loss) | 3a | | |
| | b | Expenses from other rental activities (attach statement) | 3b | | |
| | c | Other net rental income (loss). Subtract line 3b from line 3a | | 3c | |
| | 4 | Interest income | | 4 | |
| | 5 | Dividends: **a** Ordinary dividends | | 5a | |
| | | **b** Qualified dividends | 5b | | |
| | 6 | Royalties | | 6 | |
| | 7 | Net short-term capital gain (loss) (attach Schedule D (Form 1120-S)) | | 7 | |
| | 8a | Net long-term capital gain (loss) (attach Schedule D (Form 1120-S)) | | 8a | |
| | b | Collectibles (28%) gain (loss) | 8b | | |
| | c | Unrecaptured section 1250 gain (attach statement) | 8c | | |
| | 9 | Net section 1231 gain (loss) (attach Form 4797) | | 9 | |
| | 10 | Other income (loss) (see instructions) Type ▶ | | 10 | |
| Deductions | 11 | Section 179 deduction (attach Form 4562) | | 11 | |
| | 12a | Charitable contributions | | 12a | |
| | b | Investment interest expense | | 12b | |
| | c | Section 59(e)(2) expenditures Type ▶ | | 12c | |
| | d | Other deductions (see instructions) Type ▶ | | 12d | |
| Credits | 13a | Low-income housing credit (section 42(j)(5)) | | 13a | |
| | b | Low-income housing credit (other) | | 13b | |
| | c | Qualified rehabilitation expenditures (rental real estate) (attach Form 3468, if applicable) | | 13c | |
| | d | Other rental real estate credits (see instructions) Type ▶ | | 13d | |
| | e | Other rental credits (see instructions) Type ▶ | | 13e | |
| | f | Biofuel producer credit (attach Form 6478) | | 13f | |
| | g | Other credits (see instructions) Type ▶ | | 13g | |
| Foreign Transactions | 14a | Name of country or U.S. possession ▶ | | | |
| | b | Gross income from all sources | | 14b | |
| | c | Gross income sourced at shareholder level | | 14c | |
| | | Foreign gross income sourced at corporate level | | | |
| | d | Reserved for future use | | 14d | |
| | e | Foreign branch category | | 14e | |
| | f | Passive category | | 14f | |
| | g | General category | | 14g | |
| | h | Other (attach statement) | | 14h | |
| | | Deductions allocated and apportioned at shareholder level | | | |
| | i | Interest expense | | 14i | |
| | j | Other | | 14j | |
| | | Deductions allocated and apportioned at corporate level to foreign source income | | | |
| | k | Reserved for future use | | 14k | |
| | l | Foreign branch category | | 14l | |
| | m | Passive category | | 14m | |
| | n | General category | | 14n | |
| | o | Other (attach statement) | | 14o | |
| | | Other information | | | |
| | p | Total foreign taxes (check one): ☐ Paid ☐ Accrued ▶ | | 14p | |
| | q | Reduction in taxes available for credit (attach statement) | | 14q | |
| | r | Other foreign tax information (attach statement) | | | |

Form **1120-S** (2020)

Form 1120-S (2020) Page **4**

**Schedule K** **Shareholders' Pro Rata Share Items** *(continued)*

| | | | | Total amount |
|---|---|---|---|---|
| Alternative Minimum Tax (AMT) Items | 15a | Post-1986 depreciation adjustment | 15a | |
| | b | Adjusted gain or loss | 15b | |
| | c | Depletion (other than oil and gas) | 15c | |
| | d | Oil, gas, and geothermal properties—gross income | 15d | |
| | e | Oil, gas, and geothermal properties—deductions | 15e | |
| | f | Other AMT items (attach statement) | 15f | |
| Items Affecting Shareholder Basis | 16a | Tax-exempt interest income | 16a | |
| | b | Other tax-exempt income | 16b | |
| | c | Nondeductible expenses | 16c | |
| | d | Distributions (attach statement if required) (see instructions) | 16d | |
| | e | Repayment of loans from shareholders | 16e | |
| Other Information | 17a | Investment income | 17a | |
| | b | Investment expenses | 17b | |
| | c | Dividend distributions paid from accumulated earnings and profits | 17c | |
| | d | Other items and amounts (attach statement) | | |
| Recon-ciliation | 18 | **Income (loss) reconciliation.** Combine the amounts on lines 1 through 10 in the far right column. From the result, subtract the sum of the amounts on lines 11 through 12d and 14p | 18 | |

**Schedule L** **Balance Sheets per Books**

| | Beginning of tax year | | End of tax year | |
|---|---|---|---|---|
| **Assets** | **(a)** | **(b)** | **(c)** | **(d)** |
| 1 Cash | | | | |
| 2a Trade notes and accounts receivable | | | | |
| b Less allowance for bad debts | ( ) | | ( ) | |
| 3 Inventories | | | | |
| 4 U.S. government obligations | | | | |
| 5 Tax-exempt securities (see instructions) | | | | |
| 6 Other current assets (attach statement) | | | | |
| 7 Loans to shareholders | | | | |
| 8 Mortgage and real estate loans | | | | |
| 9 Other investments (attach statement) | | | | |
| 10a Buildings and other depreciable assets | | | | |
| b Less accumulated depreciation | ( ) | | ( ) | |
| 11a Depletable assets | | | | |
| b Less accumulated depletion | ( ) | | ( ) | |
| 12 Land (net of any amortization) | | | | |
| 13a Intangible assets (amortizable only) | | | | |
| b Less accumulated amortization | ( ) | | ( ) | |
| 14 Other assets (attach statement) | | | | |
| 15 Total assets | | | | |
| **Liabilities and Shareholders' Equity** | | | | |
| 16 Accounts payable | | | | |
| 17 Mortgages, notes, bonds payable in less than 1 year | | | | |
| 18 Other current liabilities (attach statement) | | | | |
| 19 Loans from shareholders | | | | |
| 20 Mortgages, notes, bonds payable in 1 year or more | | | | |
| 21 Other liabilities (attach statement) | | | | |
| 22 Capital stock | | | | |
| 23 Additional paid-in capital | | | | |
| 24 Retained earnings | | | | |
| 25 Adjustments to shareholders' equity (attach statement) | | | | |
| 26 Less cost of treasury stock | | ( ) | | ( ) |
| 27 Total liabilities and shareholders' equity | | | | |

Form 1120-S (2020) Page **5**

**Schedule M-1** **Reconciliation of Income (Loss) per Books With Income (Loss) per Return**

**Note:** The corporation may be required to file Schedule M-3. See instructions.

| | | | | | |
|---|---|---|---|---|---|
| 1 | Net income (loss) per books . . . . | | 5 | Income recorded on books this year not included on Schedule K, lines 1 through 10 (itemize): | |
| 2 | Income included on Schedule K, lines 1, 2, 3c, 4, 5a, 6, 7, 8a, 9, and 10, not recorded on books this year (itemize) ________________ | | a | Tax-exempt interest $ ________________ | |
| 3 | Expenses recorded on books this year not included on Schedule K, lines 1 through 12 and 14p (itemize): | | 6 | Deductions included on Schedule K, lines 1 through 12 and 14p, not charged against book income this year (itemize): | |
| a | Depreciation $ ________________ | | a | Depreciation $ ________________ | |
| b | Travel and entertainment $ ________________ | | 7 | Add lines 5 and 6 . . . . . . . | |
| 4 | Add lines 1 through 3 . . . . . . | | 8 | Income (loss) (Schedule K, line 18). Subtract line 7 from line 4 . . . . | |

**Schedule M-2** **Analysis of Accumulated Adjustments Account, Shareholders' Undistributed Taxable Income Previously Taxed, Accumulated Earnings and Profits, and Other Adjustments Account** (see instructions)

| | | **(a)** Accumulated adjustments account | **(b)** Shareholders' undistributed taxable income previously taxed | **(c)** Accumulated earnings and profits | **(d)** Other adjustments account |
|---|---|---|---|---|---|
| 1 | Balance at beginning of tax year . . . . . . | | | | |
| 2 | Ordinary income from page 1, line 21 . . . | | | | |
| 3 | Other additions . . . . . . . . . . . . | | | | |
| 4 | Loss from page 1, line 21 . . . . . . . | ( ) | | | |
| 5 | Other reductions . . . . . . . . . . . | ( ) | | | ( ) |
| 6 | Combine lines 1 through 5 . . . . . . . . | | | | |
| 7 | Distributions . . . . . . . . . . . . . | | | | |
| 8 | Balance at end of tax year. Subtract line 7 from line 6 . . . . . . . . . . . . . | | | | |

Form **1120-S** (2020)

671120

☐ Final K-1 ☐ Amended K-1 OMB No. 1545-0123

**Schedule K-1 (Form 1120-S)** **2020**

Department of the Treasury
Internal Revenue Service

For calendar year 2020, or tax year

beginning / / 2020 ending / /

# Shareholder's Share of Income, Deductions, Credits, etc.

▶ See separate instructions.

## Part I Information About the Corporation

**A** Corporation's employer identification number

**B** Corporation's name, address, city, state, and ZIP code

**C** IRS Center where corporation filed return

## Part II Information About the Shareholder

**D** Shareholder's identifying number

**E** Shareholder's name, address, city, state, and ZIP code

**F** Current year allocation percentage . . . ______ %

**G** Shareholder's number of shares
Beginning of tax year . . . . . ______
End of tax year . . . . . . . . ______

**H** Loans from shareholder
Beginning of tax year . . . . . . $ ______
End of tax year . . . . . . . . $ ______

For IRS Use Only

## Part III Shareholder's Share of Current Year Income, Deductions, Credits, and Other Items

| | | | |
|---|---|---|---|
| 1 | Ordinary business income (loss) | 13 | Credits |
| 2 | Net rental real estate income (loss) | | |
| 3 | Other net rental income (loss) | | |
| 4 | Interest income | | |
| 5a | Ordinary dividends | | |
| 5b | Qualified dividends | 14 | Foreign transactions |
| 6 | Royalties | | |
| 7 | Net short-term capital gain (loss) | | |
| 8a | Net long-term capital gain (loss) | | |
| 8b | Collectibles (28%) gain (loss) | | |
| 8c | Unrecaptured section 1250 gain | | |
| 9 | Net section 1231 gain (loss) | | |
| 10 | Other income (loss) | 15 | Alternative minimum tax (AMT) items |
| 11 | Section 179 deduction | 16 | Items affecting shareholder basis |
| 12 | Other deductions | | |
| | | 17 | Other information |

18 ☐ More than one activity for at-risk purposes*

19 ☐ More than one activity for passive activity purposes*

*See attached statement for additional information.

Form **2106**

Department of the Treasury
Internal Revenue Service (99)

# Employee Business Expenses

**(for use only by Armed Forces reservists, qualified performing artists, fee-basis state or local government officials, and employees with impairment-related work expenses)**

**▶ Attach to Form 1040, 1040-SR, or 1040-NR.**

**▶ Go to *www.irs.gov/Form2106* for instructions and the latest information.**

OMB No. 1545-0074

**2020**

Attachment Sequence No. **129**

| Your name | Occupation in which you incurred expenses | **Social security number** |
|---|---|---|
| | | |

## Part I Employee Business Expenses and Reimbursements

| **Step 1 Enter Your Expenses** | | **Column A** Other Than Meals | **Column B** Meals |
|---|---|---|---|
| **1** Vehicle expense from line 22 or line 29. (Rural mail carriers: See instructions.) | 1 | | |
| **2** Parking fees, tolls, and transportation, including train, bus, etc., that **didn't** involve overnight travel or commuting to and from work | 2 | | |
| **3** Travel expense while away from home overnight, including lodging, airplane, car rental, etc. **Don't** include meals | 3 | | |
| **4** Business expenses not included on lines 1 through 3. **Don't** include meals | 4 | | |
| **5** Meals expenses (see instructions) | 5 | | |
| **6** **Total expenses.** In Column A, add lines 1 through 4 and enter the result. In Column B, enter the amount from line 5 | 6 | | |

**Note:** If you weren't reimbursed for any expenses in Step 1, skip line 7 and enter the amount from line 6 on line 8.

### Step 2 Enter Reimbursements Received From Your Employer for Expenses Listed in Step 1

| | | | |
|---|---|---|---|
| **7** Enter reimbursements received from your employer that **weren't** reported to you in box 1 of Form W-2. Include any reimbursements reported under code "L" in box 12 of your Form W-2 (see instructions) | 7 | | |

### Step 3 Figure Expenses To Deduct

| | | | |
|---|---|---|---|
| **8** Subtract line 7 from line 6. If zero or less, enter -0-. However, if line 7 is greater than line 6 in Column A, report the excess as income on Form 1040 or 1040-SR, line 1 (or on Form 1040-NR, line 1a) | 8 | | |
| **Note:** If **both columns** of line 8 are zero, you can't deduct employee business expenses. Stop here and attach Form 2106 to your return. | | | |
| **9** In Column A, enter the amount from line 8. In Column B, multiply line 8 by 50% (0.50) | 9 | | |
| **10** Add the amounts on line 9 of both columns and enter the total here. Also, enter the total on Schedule 1 (Form 1040), line 11. Employees with impairment-related work expenses, see the instructions for rules on where to enter the total on your return ▶ | 10 | | |

**For Paperwork Reduction Act Notice, see your tax return instructions.** Cat. No. 11700N Form **2106** (2020)

Form 2106 (2020) Page **2**

**Part II** **Vehicle Expenses**

| **Section A—General Information** (You must complete this section if you are claiming vehicle expenses.) | | **(a)** Vehicle 1 | **(b)** Vehicle 2 |
|---|---|---|---|
| **11** Enter the date the vehicle was placed in service | 11 | / / | / / |
| **12** Total miles the vehicle was driven during 2020 | 12 | miles | miles |
| **13** Business miles included on line 12 | 13 | miles | miles |
| **14** Percent of business use. Divide line 13 by line 12 | 14 | % | % |
| **15** Average daily roundtrip commuting distance | 15 | miles | miles |
| **16** Commuting miles included on line 12 | 16 | miles | miles |
| **17** Other miles. Add lines 13 and 16 and subtract the total from line 12 | 17 | miles | miles |

**18** Was your vehicle available for personal use during off-duty hours? ☐ **Yes** ☐ **No**

**19** Do you (or your spouse) have another vehicle available for personal use? ☐ **Yes** ☐ **No**

**20** Do you have evidence to support your deduction? ☐ **Yes** ☐ **No**

**21** If "Yes," is the evidence written? ☐ **Yes** ☐ **No**

**Section B—Standard Mileage Rate** (See the instructions for Part II to find out whether to complete this section or Section C.)

| **22** Multiply line 13 by 57.5¢ (0.575). Enter the result here and on line 1 | 22 | |
|---|---|---|

**Section C—Actual Expenses**

| | | **(a)** Vehicle 1 | | **(b)** Vehicle 2 | |
|---|---|---|---|---|---|
| **23** Gasoline, oil, repairs, vehicle insurance, etc. | 23 | | | | |
| **24a** Vehicle rentals | 24a | | | | |
| **b** Inclusion amount (see instructions) | 24b | | | | |
| **c** Subtract line 24b from line 24a | 24c | | | | |
| **25** Value of employer-provided vehicle (applies only if 100% of annual lease value was included on Form W-2—see instructions) | 25 | | | | |
| **26** Add lines 23, 24c, and 25 | 26 | | | | |
| **27** Multiply line 26 by the percentage on line 14 | 27 | | | | |
| **28** Depreciation (see instructions) | 28 | | | | |
| **29** Add lines 27 and 28. Enter total here and on line 1 | 29 | | | | |

**Section D—Depreciation of Vehicles** (Use this section only if you owned the vehicle and are completing Section C for the vehicle.)

| | | **(a)** Vehicle 1 | | **(b)** Vehicle 2 | |
|---|---|---|---|---|---|
| **30** Enter cost or other basis (see instructions) | 30 | | | | |
| **31** Enter section 179 deduction and special allowance (see instructions) | 31 | | | | |
| **32** Multiply line 30 by line 14 (see instructions if you claimed the section 179 deduction or special allowance) | 32 | | | | |
| **33** Enter depreciation method and percentage (see instructions) | 33 | | | | |
| **34** Multiply line 32 by the percentage on line 33 (see instructions) | 34 | | | | |
| **35** Add lines 31 and 34 | 35 | | | | |
| **36** Enter the applicable limit explained in the line 36 instructions | 36 | | | | |
| **37** Multiply line 36 by the percentage on line 14 | 37 | | | | |
| **38** Enter the **smaller** of line 35 or line 37. If you skipped lines 36 and 37, enter the amount from line 35. Also enter this amount on line 28 above | 38 | | | | |

Form **2106** (2020)

Form **2441**

Department of the Treasury
Internal Revenue Service (99)

# Child and Dependent Care Expenses

▶ Attach to Form 1040, 1040-SR, or 1040-NR.

▶ Go to *www.irs.gov/Form2441* for instructions and the latest information.

1040 / 1040-SR / 1040-NR ← 2441

OMB No. 1545-0074

**2020**

Attachment Sequence No. **21**

Name(s) shown on return | **Your social security number**

You cannot claim a credit for child and dependent care expenses if your filing status is married filing separately unless you meet the requirements listed in the instructions under "Married Persons Filing Separately." If you meet these requirements, check this box. ☐

**Part I** **Persons or Organizations Who Provided the Care—**You **must** complete this part.
(If you have more than two care providers, see the instructions.)

| 1 (a) Care provider's name | (b) Address (number, street, apt. no., city, state, and ZIP code) | (c) Identifying number (SSN or EIN) | (d) Amount paid (see instructions) |
|---|---|---|---|
| | | | |
| | | | |

Did you receive **dependent care benefits?**
**No** ——▶ Complete only Part II below.
**Yes** ——▶ Complete Part III on the back next.

**Caution:** If the care was provided in your home, you may owe employment taxes. For details, see the instructions for Schedule 2 (Form 1040), line 7a.

**Part II** **Credit for Child and Dependent Care Expenses**

**2** Information about your **qualifying person(s).** If you have more than two qualifying persons, see the instructions.

| (a) Qualifying person's name First | Last | (b) Qualifying person's social security number | **(c) Qualified expenses** you incurred and paid in 2020 for the person listed in column (a) |
|---|---|---|---|
| | | | |
| | | | |

**3** Add the amounts in column (c) of line 2. **Don't** enter more than $3,000 for one qualifying person or $6,000 for two or more persons. If you completed Part III, enter the amount from line 31 . . . **3**

**4** Enter your **earned income.** See instructions . . . **4**

**5** If married filing jointly, enter your spouse's earned income (if you or your spouse was a student or was disabled, see the instructions); **all others**, enter the amount from line 4 . . . **5**

**6** Enter the **smallest** of line 3, 4, or 5 . . . **6**

**7** Enter the amount from Form 1040, 1040-SR, or 1040-NR, line 11 . **7**

**8** Enter on line 8 the decimal amount shown below that applies to the amount on line 7.

| If line 7 is: Over | But not over | Decimal amount is | If line 7 is: Over | But not over | Decimal amount is |
|---|---|---|---|---|---|
| $0 | 15,000 | .35 | $29,000 | 31,000 | .27 |
| 15,000 | 17,000 | .34 | 31,000 | 33,000 | .26 |
| 17,000 | 19,000 | .33 | 33,000 | 35,000 | .25 |
| 19,000 | 21,000 | .32 | 35,000 | 37,000 | .24 |
| 21,000 | 23,000 | .31 | 37,000 | 39,000 | .23 |
| 23,000 | 25,000 | .30 | 39,000 | 41,000 | .22 |
| 25,000 | 27,000 | .29 | 41,000 | 43,000 | .21 |
| 27,000 | 29,000 | .28 | 43,000 | No limit | .20 |

**8** X .

**9** Multiply line 6 by the decimal amount on line 8. If you paid 2019 expenses in 2020, see the instructions . . . **9**

**10** Tax liability limit. Enter the amount from the Credit Limit Worksheet in the instructions . . . **10**

**11** **Credit for child and dependent care expenses.** Enter the **smaller** of line 9 or line 10 here and on Schedule 3 (Form 1040), line 2 . . . **11**

**For Paperwork Reduction Act Notice, see your tax return instructions.** Cat. No. 11862M Form **2441** (2020)

Form 2441 (2020) Page **2**

## Part III Dependent Care Benefits

| | | | |
|---|---|---|---|
| **12** Enter the total amount of **dependent care benefits** you received in 2020. Amounts you received as an employee should be shown in box 10 of your Form(s) W-2. **Don't** include amounts reported as wages in box 1 of Form(s) W-2. If you were self-employed or a partner, include amounts you received under a dependent care assistance program from your sole proprietorship or partnership | | 12 | |
| **13** Enter the amount, if any, you carried over from 2019 and used in 2020 during the grace period. See instructions | | 13 | |
| **14** Enter the amount, if any, you forfeited or carried forward to 2021. See instructions | | 14 | ( ) |
| **15** Combine lines 12 through 14. See instructions | | 15 | |
| **16** Enter the total amount of **qualified expenses** incurred in 2020 for the care of the **qualifying person(s)** | 16 | | |
| **17** Enter the **smaller** of line 15 or 16 | 17 | | |
| **18** Enter your **earned income.** See instructions | 18 | | |
| **19** Enter the amount shown below that applies to you.<br>• If married filing jointly, enter your spouse's earned income (if you or your spouse was a student or was disabled, see the instructions for line 5).<br>• If married filing separately, see instructions.<br>• All others, enter the amount from line 18. | 19 | | |
| **20** Enter the **smallest** of line 17, 18, or 19 | 20 | | |
| **21** Enter $5,000 ($2,500 if married filing separately **and** you were required to enter your spouse's earned income on line 19) | 21 | | |
| **22** Is any amount on line 12 from your sole proprietorship or partnership?<br>☐ **No.** Enter -0-.<br>☐ **Yes.** Enter the amount here | | 22 | |
| **23** Subtract line 22 from line 15 | 23 | | |
| **24** **Deductible benefits.** Enter the **smallest** of line 20, 21, or 22. Also, include this amount on the appropriate line(s) of your return. See instructions | | 24 | |
| **25** **Excluded benefits.** If you checked "No" on line 22, enter the smaller of line 20 or 21. Otherwise, subtract line 24 from the smaller of line 20 or line 21. If zero or less, enter -0- | | 25 | |
| **26** **Taxable benefits.** Subtract line 25 from line 23. If zero or less, enter -0-. Also, include this amount on Form 1040 or 1040-SR, line 1; or Form 1040-NR, line 1a. On the dotted line next to Form 1040 or 1040-SR, line 1; or Form 1040-NR, line 1a, enter "DCB" | | 26 | |

To claim the child and dependent care credit, complete lines 27 through 31 below.

| | | |
|---|---|---|
| **27** Enter $3,000 ($6,000 if two or more qualifying persons) | 27 | |
| **28** Add lines 24 and 25 | 28 | |
| **29** Subtract line 28 from line 27. If zero or less, **stop.** You can't take the credit. **Exception.** If you paid 2019 expenses in 2020, see the instructions for line 9 | 29 | |
| **30** Complete line 2 on the front of this form. **Don't** include in column (c) any benefits shown on line 28 above. Then, add the amounts in column (c) and enter the total here | 30 | |
| **31** Enter the **smaller** of line 29 or 30. Also, enter this amount on line 3 on the front of this form and complete lines 4 through 11 | 31 | |

Form **4562**

Department of the Treasury
Internal Revenue Service (99)

# Depreciation and Amortization

**(Including Information on Listed Property)**

▶ Attach to your tax return.

▶ Go to *www.irs.gov/Form4562* for instructions and the latest information.

OMB No. 1545-0172

**2020**

Attachment Sequence No. **179**

| Name(s) shown on return | Business or activity to which this form relates | Identifying number |
|---|---|---|
| | | |

## Part I Election To Expense Certain Property Under Section 179

**Note:** If you have any listed property, complete Part V before you complete Part I.

| | | | |
|---|---|---|---|
| 1 | Maximum amount (see instructions) | 1 | |
| 2 | Total cost of section 179 property placed in service (see instructions) | 2 | |
| 3 | Threshold cost of section 179 property before reduction in limitation (see instructions) | 3 | |
| 4 | Reduction in limitation. Subtract line 3 from line 2. If zero or less, enter -0- | 4 | |
| 5 | Dollar limitation for tax year. Subtract line 4 from line 1. If zero or less, enter -0-. If married filing separately, see instructions | 5 | |

| 6 | (a) Description of property | (b) Cost (business use only) | (c) Elected cost |
|---|---|---|---|
| | | | |
| | | | |

| | | | |
|---|---|---|---|
| 7 | Listed property. Enter the amount from line 29 | 7 | |
| 8 | Total elected cost of section 179 property. Add amounts in column (c), lines 6 and 7 | 8 | |
| 9 | Tentative deduction. Enter the **smaller** of line 5 or line 8 | 9 | |
| 10 | Carryover of disallowed deduction from line 13 of your 2019 Form 4562 | 10 | |
| 11 | Business income limitation. Enter the smaller of business income (not less than zero) or line 5. See instructions | 11 | |
| 12 | Section 179 expense deduction. Add lines 9 and 10, but don't enter more than line 11 | 12 | |
| 13 | Carryover of disallowed deduction to 2021. Add lines 9 and 10, less line 12 ▶ | 13 | |

**Note:** Don't use Part II or Part III below for listed property. Instead, use Part V.

## Part II Special Depreciation Allowance and Other Depreciation (Don't include listed property. See instructions.)

| | | | |
|---|---|---|---|
| 14 | Special depreciation allowance for qualified property (other than listed property) placed in service during the tax year. See instructions | 14 | |
| 15 | Property subject to section 168(f)(1) election | 15 | |
| 16 | Other depreciation (including ACRS) | 16 | |

## Part III MACRS Depreciation (Don't include listed property. See instructions.)

**Section A**

| | | | |
|---|---|---|---|
| 17 | MACRS deductions for assets placed in service in tax years beginning before 2020 | 17 | |
| 18 | If you are electing to group any assets placed in service during the tax year into one or more general asset accounts, check here ▶ ☐ | | |

**Section B—Assets Placed in Service During 2020 Tax Year Using the General Depreciation System**

| (a) Classification of property | (b) Month and year placed in service | (c) Basis for depreciation (business/investment use only—see instructions) | (d) Recovery period | (e) Convention | (f) Method | (g) Depreciation deduction |
|---|---|---|---|---|---|---|
| 19a 3-year property | | | | | | |
| b 5-year property | | | | | | |
| c 7-year property | | | | | | |
| d 10-year property | | | | | | |
| e 15-year property | | | | | | |
| f 20-year property | | | | | | |
| g 25-year property | | | 25 yrs. | | S/L | |
| h Residential rental | | | 27.5 yrs. | MM | S/L | |
| property | | | 27.5 yrs. | MM | S/L | |
| i Nonresidential real | | | 39 yrs. | MM | S/L | |
| property | | | | MM | S/L | |

**Section C—Assets Placed in Service During 2020 Tax Year Using the Alternative Depreciation System**

| (a) Classification of property | (b) Month and year placed in service | (c) Basis for depreciation | (d) Recovery period | (e) Convention | (f) Method | (g) Depreciation deduction |
|---|---|---|---|---|---|---|
| 20a Class life | | | | | S/L | |
| b 12-year | | | 12 yrs. | | S/L | |
| c 30-year | | | 30 yrs. | MM | S/L | |
| d 40-year | | | 40 yrs. | MM | S/L | |

## Part IV Summary (See instructions.)

| | | | |
|---|---|---|---|
| 21 | Listed property. Enter amount from line 28 | 21 | |
| 22 | **Total.** Add amounts from line 12, lines 14 through 17, lines 19 and 20 in column (g), and line 21. Enter here and on the appropriate lines of your return. Partnerships and S corporations—see instructions | 22 | |
| 23 | For assets shown above and placed in service during the current year, enter the portion of the basis attributable to section 263A costs | 23 | |

Form 4562 (2020) Page **2**

**Part V** **Listed Property** (Include automobiles, certain other vehicles, certain aircraft, and property used for entertainment, recreation, or amusement.)

**Note:** For any vehicle for which you are using the standard mileage rate or deducting lease expense, complete **only** 24a, 24b, columns (a) through (c) of Section A, all of Section B, and Section C if applicable.

**Section A—Depreciation and Other Information (Caution:** See the instructions for limits for passenger automobiles.**)**

**24a** Do you have evidence to support the business/investment use claimed? ☐ **Yes** ☐ **No** **24b** If "Yes," is the evidence written? ☐ **Yes** ☐ **No**

| **(a)** Type of property (list vehicles first) | **(b)** Date placed in service | **(c)** Business/ investment use percentage | **(d)** Cost or other basis | **(e)** Basis for depreciation (business/investment use only) | **(f)** Recovery period | **(g)** Method/ Convention | **(h)** Depreciation deduction | **(i)** Elected section 179 cost |
|---|---|---|---|---|---|---|---|---|
| **25** Special depreciation allowance for qualified listed property placed in service during the tax year and used more than 50% in a qualified business use. See instructions . | | | | | | **25** | | |
| **26** Property used more than 50% in a qualified business use: | | | | | | | | |
| | | % | | | | | | |
| | | % | | | | | | |
| | | % | | | | | | |
| **27** Property used 50% or less in a qualified business use: | | | | | | | | |
| | | % | | | | S/L – | | |
| | | % | | | | S/L – | | |
| | | % | | | | S/L – | | |
| **28** Add amounts in column (h), lines 25 through 27. Enter here and on line 21, page 1 . | | | | | | **28** | | |
| **29** Add amounts in column (i), line 26. Enter here and on line 7, page 1 . . . . . . . . . . . . . . | | | | | | | **29** | |

**Section B—Information on Use of Vehicles**

Complete this section for vehicles used by a sole proprietor, partner, or other "more than 5% owner," or related person. If you provided vehicles to your employees, first answer the questions in Section C to see if you meet an exception to completing this section for those vehicles.

| | **(a)** Vehicle 1 | | **(b)** Vehicle 2 | | **(c)** Vehicle 3 | | **(d)** Vehicle 4 | | **(e)** Vehicle 5 | | **(f)** Vehicle 6 | |
|---|---|---|---|---|---|---|---|---|---|---|---|---|
| **30** Total business/investment miles driven during the year (**don't** include commuting miles) . | | | | | | | | | | | | |
| **31** Total commuting miles driven during the year | | | | | | | | | | | | |
| **32** Total other personal (noncommuting) miles driven . . . . . . . . . | | | | | | | | | | | | |
| **33** Total miles driven during the year. Add lines 30 through 32 . . . . . . . | | | | | | | | | | | | |
| | **Yes** | **No** | **Yes** | **No** | **Yes** | **No** | **Yes** | **No** | **Yes** | **No** | **Yes** | **No** |
| **34** Was the vehicle available for personal use during off-duty hours? . . . . . | | | | | | | | | | | | |
| **35** Was the vehicle used primarily by a more than 5% owner or related person? . . | | | | | | | | | | | | |
| **36** Is another vehicle available for personal use? | | | | | | | | | | | | |

**Section C—Questions for Employers Who Provide Vehicles for Use by Their Employees**

Answer these questions to determine if you meet an exception to completing Section B for vehicles used by employees who **aren't** more than 5% owners or related persons. See instructions.

| | **Yes** | **No** |
|---|---|---|
| **37** Do you maintain a written policy statement that prohibits all personal use of vehicles, including commuting, by your employees? . . . . . . . . . . . . . . . . . . . . . . . . . | | |
| **38** Do you maintain a written policy statement that prohibits personal use of vehicles, except commuting, by your employees? See the instructions for vehicles used by corporate officers, directors, or 1% or more owners . . | | |
| **39** Do you treat all use of vehicles by employees as personal use? . . . . . . . . . . . . . | | |
| **40** Do you provide more than five vehicles to your employees, obtain information from your employees about the use of the vehicles, and retain the information received? . . . . . . . . . . . . . . | | |
| **41** Do you meet the requirements concerning qualified automobile demonstration use? See instructions. . . . . | | |

**Note:** If your answer to 37, 38, 39, 40, or 41 is "Yes," don't complete Section B for the covered vehicles.

**Part VI** **Amortization**

| **(a)** Description of costs | **(b)** Date amortization begins | **(c)** Amortizable amount | **(d)** Code section | **(e)** Amortization period or percentage | **(f)** Amortization for this year |
|---|---|---|---|---|---|
| **42** Amortization of costs that begins during your 2020 tax year (see instructions): | | | | | |
| | | | | | |
| | | | | | |
| **43** Amortization of costs that began before your 2020 tax year . . . . . . . . . . . . | | | | **43** | |
| **44** **Total.** Add amounts in column (f). See the instructions for where to report . . . . . . . . | | | | **44** | |

Form **4562** (2020)

Form **4797**

Department of the Treasury
Internal Revenue Service

# Sales of Business Property

**(Also Involuntary Conversions and Recapture Amounts Under Sections 179 and 280F(b)(2))**

▶ Attach to your tax return.

▶ Go to *www.irs.gov/Form4797* for instructions and the latest information.

OMB No. 1545-0184

2020

Attachment Sequence No. 27

| Name(s) shown on return | Identifying number |
|---|---|
| | |

| | | | |
|---|---|---|---|
| 1 | Enter the gross proceeds from sales or exchanges reported to you for 2020 on Form(s) 1099-B or 1099-S (or substitute statement) that you are including on line 2, 10, or 20. See instructions . . . . . . . . . . . . | 1 | |

## Part I Sales or Exchanges of Property Used in a Trade or Business and Involuntary Conversions From Other Than Casualty or Theft—Most Property Held More Than 1 Year (see instructions)

| 2 (a) Description of property | (b) Date acquired (mo., day, yr.) | (c) Date sold (mo., day, yr.) | (d) Gross sales price | (e) Depreciation allowed or allowable since acquisition | (f) Cost or other basis, plus improvements and expense of sale | (g) Gain or (loss) Subtract (f) from the sum of (d) and (e) |
|---|---|---|---|---|---|---|
| | | | | | | |
| | | | | | | |
| | | | | | | |
| | | | | | | |

| | | | |
|---|---|---|---|
| 3 | Gain, if any, from Form 4684, line 39 . . . . . . . . . . . . | 3 | |
| 4 | Section 1231 gain from installment sales from Form 6252, line 26 or 37 . . . . . . . . . . | 4 | |
| 5 | Section 1231 gain or (loss) from like-kind exchanges from Form 8824 . . . . . . . . . . | 5 | |
| 6 | Gain, if any, from line 32, from other than casualty or theft . . . . . . . . . . | 6 | |
| 7 | Combine lines 2 through 6. Enter the gain or (loss) here and on the appropriate line as follows . . . . . . . | 7 | |
| | **Partnerships and S corporations.** Report the gain or (loss) following the instructions for Form 1065, Schedule K, line 10, or Form 1120-S, Schedule K, line 9. Skip lines 8, 9, 11, and 12 below.<br><br>**Individuals, partners, S corporation shareholders, and all others.** If line 7 is zero or a loss, enter the amount from line 7 on line 11 below and skip lines 8 and 9. If line 7 is a gain and you didn't have any prior year section 1231 losses, or they were recaptured in an earlier year, enter the gain from line 7 as a long-term capital gain on the Schedule D filed with your return and skip lines 8, 9, 11, and 12 below. | | |
| 8 | Nonrecaptured net section 1231 losses from prior years. See instructions . . . . . . . . . . . | 8 | |
| 9 | Subtract line 8 from line 7. If zero or less, enter -0-. If line 9 is zero, enter the gain from line 7 on line 12 below. If line 9 is more than zero, enter the amount from line 8 on line 12 below and enter the gain from line 9 as a long-term capital gain on the Schedule D filed with your return. See instructions . . . . . . . . . . | 9 | |

## Part II Ordinary Gains and Losses (see instructions)

10 Ordinary gains and losses not included on lines 11 through 16 (include property held 1 year or less):

| | | | | | | |
|---|---|---|---|---|---|---|
| | | | | | | |
| | | | | | | |
| | | | | | | |
| | | | | | | |

| | | | |
|---|---|---|---|
| 11 | Loss, if any, from line 7 . . . . . . . . . . . . | 11 | ( ) |
| 12 | Gain, if any, from line 7 or amount from line 8, if applicable . . . . . . . . . . | 12 | |
| 13 | Gain, if any, from line 31 . . . . . . . . . . . . | 13 | |
| 14 | Net gain or (loss) from Form 4684, lines 31 and 38a . . . . . . . . . . | 14 | |
| 15 | Ordinary gain from installment sales from Form 6252, line 25 or 36 . . . . . . . . . | 15 | |
| 16 | Ordinary gain or (loss) from like-kind exchanges from Form 8824 . . . . . . . . . | 16 | |
| 17 | Combine lines 10 through 16 . . . . . . . . . . . . | 17 | |
| 18 | For all except individual returns, enter the amount from line 17 on the appropriate line of your return and skip lines a and b below. For individual returns, complete lines a and b below. | | |
| a | If the loss on line 11 includes a loss from Form 4684, line 35, column (b)(ii), enter that part of the loss here. Enter the loss from income-producing property on Schedule A (Form 1040), line 16. (Do not include any loss on property used as an employee.) Identify as from "Form 4797, line 18a." See instructions . . . . . . . . . . | 18a | |
| b | Redetermine the gain or (loss) on line 17 excluding the loss, if any, on line 18a. Enter here and on Schedule 1 (Form 1040), Part I, line 4 . . . . . . . . . . . . | 18b | |

Form 4797 (2020) Page **2**

## Part III Gain From Disposition of Property Under Sections 1245, 1250, 1252, 1254, and 1255 (see instructions)

| 19 **(a)** Description of section 1245, 1250, 1252, 1254, or 1255 property: | **(b)** Date acquired (mo., day, yr.) | **(c)** Date sold (mo., day, yr.) |
|---|---|---|
| A | | |
| B | | |
| C | | |
| D | | |

| **These columns relate to the properties on lines 19A through 19D.** ▶ | | **Property A** | **Property B** | **Property C** | **Property D** |
|---|---|---|---|---|---|
| 20 Gross sales price (**Note:** *See line 1 before completing.*) | 20 | | | | |
| 21 Cost or other basis plus expense of sale | 21 | | | | |
| 22 Depreciation (or depletion) allowed or allowable | 22 | | | | |
| 23 Adjusted basis. Subtract line 22 from line 21 | 23 | | | | |
| 24 Total gain. Subtract line 23 from line 20 | 24 | | | | |
| 25 **If section 1245 property:** | | | | | |
| a Depreciation allowed or allowable from line 22 | 25a | | | | |
| b Enter the **smaller** of line 24 or 25a | 25b | | | | |
| 26 **If section 1250 property:** If straight line depreciation was used, enter -0- on line 26g, except for a corporation subject to section 291. | | | | | |
| a Additional depreciation after 1975. See instructions | 26a | | | | |
| b Applicable percentage multiplied by the **smaller** of line 24 or line 26a. See instructions | 26b | | | | |
| c Subtract line 26a from line 24. If residential rental property **or** line 24 isn't more than line 26a, skip lines 26d and 26e | 26c | | | | |
| d Additional depreciation after 1969 and before 1976 | 26d | | | | |
| e Enter the **smaller** of line 26c or 26d | 26e | | | | |
| f Section 291 amount (corporations only) | 26f | | | | |
| g Add lines 26b, 26e, and 26f | 26g | | | | |
| 27 **If section 1252 property:** Skip this section if you didn't dispose of farmland or if this form is being completed for a partnership. | | | | | |
| a Soil, water, and land clearing expenses | 27a | | | | |
| b Line 27a multiplied by applicable percentage. See instructions | 27b | | | | |
| c Enter the **smaller** of line 24 or 27b | 27c | | | | |
| 28 **If section 1254 property:** | | | | | |
| a Intangible drilling and development costs, expenditures for development of mines and other natural deposits, mining exploration costs, and depletion. See instructions | 28a | | | | |
| b Enter the **smaller** of line 24 or 28a | 28b | | | | |
| 29 **If section 1255 property:** | | | | | |
| a Applicable percentage of payments excluded from income under section 126. See instructions | 29a | | | | |
| b Enter the **smaller** of line 24 or 29a. See instructions | 29b | | | | |

**Summary of Part III Gains.** Complete property columns A through D through line 29b before going to line 30.

| | | |
|---|---|---|
| 30 Total gains for all properties. Add property columns A through D, line 24 | 30 | |
| 31 Add property columns A through D, lines 25b, 26g, 27c, 28b, and 29b. Enter here and on line 13 | 31 | |
| 32 Subtract line 31 from line 30. Enter the portion from casualty or theft on Form 4684, line 33. Enter the portion from other than casualty or theft on Form 4797, line 6 | 32 | |

## Part IV Recapture Amounts Under Sections 179 and 280F(b)(2) When Business Use Drops to 50% or Less (see instructions)

| | | **(a) Section 179** | **(b) Section 280F(b)(2)** |
|---|---|---|---|
| 33 Section 179 expense deduction or depreciation allowable in prior years | 33 | | |
| 34 Recomputed depreciation. See instructions | 34 | | |
| 35 Recapture amount. Subtract line 34 from line 33. See the instructions for where to report | 35 | | |

Form **8863**

Department of the Treasury
Internal Revenue Service (99)

# Education Credits
## (American Opportunity and Lifetime Learning Credits)

▶ Attach to Form 1040 or 1040-SR.

▶ Go to *www.irs.gov/Form8863* for instructions and the latest information.

OMB No. 1545-0074

**2020**

Attachment Sequence No. **50**

| Name(s) shown on return | Your social security number |
|---|---|
| | |

**CAUTION** *Complete a separate Part III on page 2 for each student for whom you're claiming either credit before you complete Parts I and II.*

## Part I Refundable American Opportunity Credit

| | | | | | |
|---|---|---|---|---|---|
| 1 | After completing Part III for each student, enter the total of all amounts from all Parts III, line 30 . . | | | 1 | |
| 2 | Enter: $180,000 if married filing jointly; $90,000 if single, head of household, or qualifying widow(er) . . . . . . . . . . . . . . . . . . . . | 2 | | | |
| 3 | Enter the amount from Form 1040 or 1040-SR, line 11. If you're filing Form 2555 or 4563, or you're excluding income from Puerto Rico, see Pub. 970 for the amount to enter . . . . . . . . . . . . . . . . . . . . | 3 | | | |
| 4 | Subtract line 3 from line 2. If zero or less, **stop**; you can't take any education credit . . . . . . . . . . . . . . . . . . . . . . . . . . | 4 | | | |
| 5 | Enter: $20,000 if married filing jointly; $10,000 if single, head of household, or qualifying widow(er) . . . . . . . . . . . . . . . . . . . . | 5 | | | |
| 6 | If line 4 is:<br>• Equal to or more than line 5, enter 1.000 on line 6 . . . . . . . . . . . . . . .<br>• Less than line 5, divide line 4 by line 5. Enter the result as a decimal (rounded to at least three places) . . . . . . . . . . . . . . . . . . . . | | | 6 | . |
| 7 | Multiply line 1 by line 6. **Caution:** If you were under age 24 at the end of the year **and** meet the conditions described in the instructions, you **can't** take the refundable American opportunity credit; skip line 8, enter the amount from line 7 on line 9, and check this box . . . . . . . . ▶ ☐ | | | 7 | |
| 8 | **Refundable American opportunity credit.** Multiply line 7 by 40% (0.40). Enter the amount here and on Form 1040 or 1040-SR, line 29. Then go to line 9 below. . . . . . . . . . . . . . . | | | 8 | |

## Part II Nonrefundable Education Credits

| | | | | | |
|---|---|---|---|---|---|
| 9 | Subtract line 8 from line 7. Enter here and on line 2 of the Credit Limit Worksheet (see instructions) . | | | 9 | |
| 10 | After completing Part III for each student, enter the total of all amounts from all Parts III, line 31. If zero, skip lines 11 through 17, enter -0- on line 18, and go to line 19 . . . . . . . . . . . | | | 10 | |
| 11 | Enter the smaller of line 10 or $10,000 . . . . . . . . . . . . . . . . . . . . . . . | | | 11 | |
| 12 | Multiply line 11 by 20% (0.20) . . . . . . . . . . . . . . . . . . . . . . . . . . . | | | 12 | |
| 13 | Enter: $138,000 if married filing jointly; $69,000 if single, head of household, or qualifying widow(er) . . . . . . . . . . . . . . . . . . . . | 13 | | | |
| 14 | Enter the amount from Form 1040 or 1040-SR, line 11. If you're filing Form 2555 or 4563, or you're excluding income from Puerto Rico, see Pub. 970 for the amount to enter . . . . . . . . . . . . . . . . . . . . | 14 | | | |
| 15 | Subtract line 14 from line 13. If zero or less, skip lines 16 and 17, enter -0- on line 18, and go to line 19 . . . . . . . . . . . . . . . . . . | 15 | | | |
| 16 | Enter: $20,000 if married filing jointly; $10,000 if single, head of household, or qualifying widow(er) . . . . . . . . . . . . . . . . . . . . | 16 | | | |
| 17 | If line 15 is:<br>• Equal to or more than line 16, enter 1.000 on line 17 and go to line 18<br>• Less than line 16, divide line 15 by line 16. Enter the result as a decimal (rounded to at least three places) . . . . . . . . . . . . . . . . . . . . . . . . . . . . | | | 17 | . |
| 18 | Multiply line 12 by line 17. Enter here and on line 1 of the Credit Limit Worksheet (see instructions) ▶ | | | 18 | |
| 19 | **Nonrefundable education credits.** Enter the amount from line 7 of the Credit Limit Worksheet (see instructions) here and on Schedule 3 (Form 1040), line 3 . . . . . . . . . . . . . . . | | | 19 | |

Form 8863 (2020) Page **2**

Name(s) shown on return | **Your social security number**

**CAUTION** ***Complete Part III for each student for whom you're claiming either the American opportunity credit or lifetime learning credit. Use additional copies of page 2 as needed for each student.***

**Part III** **Student and Educational Institution Information.** See instructions.

**20** Student name (as shown on page 1 of your tax return)

**21** Student social security number (as shown on page 1 of your tax return)

**22** Educational institution information (see instructions)

| **a.** Name of first educational institution | **b.** Name of second educational institution (if any) |
|---|---|
| **(1)** Address. Number and street (or P.O. box). City, town or post office, state, and ZIP code. If a foreign address, see instructions. | **(1)** Address. Number and street (or P.O. box). City, town or post office, state, and ZIP code. If a foreign address, see instructions. |
| **(2)** Did the student receive Form 1098-T from this institution for 2020? ☐ Yes ☐ No | **(2)** Did the student receive Form 1098-T from this institution for 2020? ☐ Yes ☐ No |
| **(3)** Did the student receive Form 1098-T from this institution for 2019 with box 7 checked? ☐ Yes ☐ No | **(3)** Did the student receive Form 1098-T from this institution for 2019 with box 7 checked? ☐ Yes ☐ No |
| **(4)** Enter the institution's employer identification number (EIN) if you're claiming the American opportunity credit or if you checked "Yes" in **(2)** or **(3).** You can get the EIN from Form 1098-T or from the institution. __ __ – __ __ __ __ __ __ __ | **(4)** Enter the institution's employer identification number (EIN) if you're claiming the American opportunity credit or if you checked "Yes" in **(2)** or **(3).** You can get the EIN from Form 1098-T or from the institution. __ __ – __ __ __ __ __ __ __ |

| | | | |
|---|---|---|---|
| **23** | Has the Hope Scholarship Credit or American opportunity credit been claimed for this student for any 4 tax years before 2020? | ☐ Yes — **Stop!** Go to line 31 for this student. | ☐ No — Go to line 24. |
| **24** | Was the student enrolled at least half-time for at least one academic period that began or is treated as having begun in 2020 at an eligible educational institution in a program leading towards a postsecondary degree, certificate, or other recognized postsecondary educational credential? See instructions. | ☐ Yes — Go to line 25. | ☐ No — **Stop!** Go to line 31 for this student. |
| **25** | Did the student complete the first 4 years of postsecondary education before 2020? See instructions. | ☐ Yes — **Stop!** Go to line 31 for this student. | ☐ No — Go to line 26. |
| **26** | Was the student convicted, before the end of 2020, of a felony for possession or distribution of a controlled substance? | ☐ Yes — **Stop!** Go to line 31 for this student. | ☐ No — Complete lines 27 through 30 for this student. |

**CAUTION** *You* ***can't*** *take the American opportunity credit and the lifetime learning credit for the* ***same student*** *in the same year. If you complete lines 27 through 30 for this student, don't complete line 31.*

**American Opportunity Credit**

| | | | |
|---|---|---|---|
| **27** | Adjusted qualified education expenses (see instructions). **Don't enter more than $4,000** . . . . . | **27** | |
| **28** | Subtract $2,000 from line 27. If zero or less, enter -0- . . . . . . . . . . . . . . . . . | **28** | |
| **29** | Multiply line 28 by 25% (0.25) . . . . . . . . . . . . . . . . . . . . . . . | **29** | |
| **30** | If line 28 is zero, enter the amount from line 27. Otherwise, add $2,000 to the amount on line 29 and enter the result. Skip line 31. Include the total of all amounts from all Parts III, line 30, on Part I, line 1 . | **30** | |

**Lifetime Learning Credit**

| | | | |
|---|---|---|---|
| **31** | Adjusted qualified education expenses (see instructions). Include the total of all amounts from all Parts III, line 31, on Part II, line 10 . . . . . . . . . . . . . . . . . . . . | **31** | |

Form **8863** (2020)

Form **8917**
(Rev. January 2020)
Department of the Treasury
Internal Revenue Service

# Tuition and Fees Deduction

▶ **Attach to Form 1040 or 1040-SR.**
▶ **Go to *www.irs.gov/Form8917* for the latest information.**

OMB No. 1545-0074
Attachment Sequence No. **60**

Name(s) shown on return | **Your social security number**

**CAUTION** *Use this form for qualified tuition and fees paid in 2018, 2019, or 2020, and later years if legislation extends the deduction (see instructions). File a separate Form 8917 for each year after 2017 for which you qualify to take the deduction.*

*You **can't** take both an education credit from Form 8863 and the tuition and fees deduction from this form for the **same student** for the same tax year.*

***Before you begin:***

✔ To see if you qualify for this deduction, see *Who Can Take the Deduction* in the instructions below.

✔ If you file Form 1040 or 1040-SR, figure any write-in adjustments.

- For 2018: Figure any write-in adjustments to be entered on the dotted line next to Schedule 1 (Form 1040), line 36.
- For 2019: Figure any write-in adjustments to be entered on the dotted line next to Schedule 1 (Form 1040 or 1040-SR), line 22.
- For 2020 and later years: Figure any write-in adjustments for Schedule 1 (Form 1040 or 1040-SR); see the Instructions for Forms 1040 and 1040-SR.

| 1 | **(a)** Student's name (as shown on page 1 of your tax return) First name | Last name | **(b)** Student's social security number (as shown on page 1 of your tax return) | **(c)** Adjusted qualified expenses (see instructions) |
|---|---|---|---|---|
| | | | | |
| | | | | |
| | | | | |

| | | | |
|---|---|---|---|
| **2** | Add the amounts on line 1, column (c), and enter the total . . . . . . . . . . . . . | **2** | |
| **3** | Enter the amount from your **"total income"** line of Form 1040 or 1040-SR . . . . . . . . . . . . . . . . . . . . **3** | | |
| **4** | • For 2018: Enter the total of the amounts on your 2018 Schedule 1 (Form 1040), lines 23 through 33, plus any write-in adjustments you entered on the dotted line next to Schedule 1 (Form 1040), line 36.<br>• For 2019 and 2020: Enter the total of the amounts on your 2019 Schedule 1 (Form 1040 or 1040-SR), lines 10 through 20, plus any write-in adjustments you entered on the dotted line next to Schedule 1 (Form 1040 or 1040-SR), line 22.<br>• For later years: See *www.irs.gov/Form8917* to find out if the line references above for 2019 have changed . . . . . . . . . **4** | | |
| **5** | Subtract line 4 from line 3.* If the result is more than $80,000 ($160,000 if married filing jointly), **stop**; you can't take the deduction for tuition and fees . . . . . . . . . . . . . . . . .<br>* If you're filing Form 2555, 2555-EZ, or 4563, or you're excluding income from Puerto Rico, see *Effect of the Amount of Your Income on the Amount of Your Deduction* in Pub. 970 to figure the amount to enter on line 5. | **5** | |
| **6** | **Tuition and fees deduction.** Is the amount on line 5 more than $65,000 ($130,000 if married filing jointly)?<br>☐ **Yes.** Enter the smaller of line 2, or $2,000.<br>☐ **No.** Enter the smaller of line 2, or $4,000. . . . . . . . . . . . . . . . .<br>**Also enter** this amount on line 21 of the 2019 and 2020 Schedule 1 (Form 1040 or 1040-SR), or line 34 of the 2018 Schedule 1 (Form 1040). See *www.irs.gov/Form8917* to find out if the line references above for 2019 have changed. | **6** | |

## General Instructions

Section references are to the Internal Revenue Code unless otherwise noted.

## What's New

**Deduction extended.** The tuition and fees deduction is extended for qualified tuition and fees paid in calendar years 2018, 2019, and 2020. Don't claim the deduction for expenses paid after 2020 unless the credit is extended again. Use Form 8917 (Rev. January 2020) and these instructions for years after 2017, unless a newer revision is issued indicating it is succeeding this revision.

**Periodic updating.** Form 8917 will no longer be updated annually. Instead, it will only be updated when necessary. For previous years, use the applicable Form 8917 for that year.

***Example 1.*** Use the 2017 Form 8917 for your 2017 qualified tuition and fees expenses deduction on your 2017 original or amended return.

**Form 1040-SR.** Form 1040-SR is a new form for 2019 and later years, with larger print and available for taxpayers 65 years or older. Although it's often mentioned with Form 1040 on Form 8917 and in these instructions, it isn't available for 2018.

## Future Developments

For the latest information about developments related to Form 8917 and its instructions, such as legislation enacted after they were published, go to *www.irs.gov/Form8917*.

## Reminders

**Form 1098-T requirement.** To be eligible to claim the tuition and fees deduction, American opportunity credit, or the lifetime earning credit, the law requires a taxpayer (or a dependent) to have received a Form 1098-T from an eligible educational institution.

However, a taxpayer may claim one of these education benefits if the student doesn't receive a Form 1098-T because the student's educational institution isn't required to send a Form 1098-T to the student under existing rules (for example, if the student is a nonresident alien, has qualified education expenses paid entirely with scholarships, or has qualified education expenses paid under a formal billing arrangement). If a student's educational institution isn't required to provide a Form 1098-T to the student, a taxpayer may claim one of these education benefits without a Form 1098-T if the taxpayer otherwise qualifies, can demonstrate that the taxpayer (or a dependent) was enrolled at an eligible educational institution, and can substantiate the payment of qualified tuition and related expenses.

## Purpose of Form

Use Form 8917 (Rev. January 2020) to figure and take the deduction for tuition and fees expenses **paid in calendar years 2018, 2019, and 2020, and later years if the deduction is extended.**

This deduction is based on adjusted qualified education expenses paid to an eligible educational institution (postsecondary). See *Qualified Education Expenses*, later, for more information.

**TIP** *You may be able to take the American opportunity credit or lifetime learning credit for your education expenses instead of the tuition and fees deduction. See Form 8863, Education Credits, and Pub. 970, Tax Benefits for Education, for more information about these credits.*

## Who Can Take the Deduction

You may be able to take the deduction if you, your spouse, or a dependent you claim on your tax return was a student enrolled at or attending an eligible educational institution. The deduction is based on the amount of qualified education expenses you paid for the student in the current year for academic periods beginning in the current year or beginning in the first 3 months of the following year.

Generally, in order to claim the deduction for education expenses for a dependent, you must have paid the expenses in the current year and must claim the student as a dependent on your current year tax return (the "Dependents" line of Form 1040 or 1040-SR). For additional information, see Pub. 970.

You **can't** claim the tuition and fees deduction if any of the following apply.

- Your filing status is married filing separately.
- Another person can claim an exemption for you as a dependent on his or her tax return. You can't take the deduction even if the other person doesn't actually claim that exemption.
- Your modified adjusted gross income (MAGI), as figured on line 5, is more than $80,000 ($160,000 if filing a joint return).
- You were a nonresident alien for any part of the year and didn't elect to be treated as a resident alien for tax purposes. More information on nonresident aliens can be found in Pub. 519, U.S. Tax Guide for Aliens.

You **can't** claim a tuition and fees deduction for any student if you or anyone else claims an American opportunity or lifetime learning credit (Form 8863) in the current year for expenses of the student for whom the qualified education expenses were paid. However, a state tax credit won't disqualify you from claiming a tuition and fees deduction.

## Qualified Education Expenses

Generally, qualified education expenses are amounts paid in the current year for tuition and fees required for the student's enrollment or attendance at an eligible educational institution. Required fees include amounts for books, supplies, and equipment used in a course of study if required to be paid to the institution as a condition of enrollment or attendance. It doesn't matter whether the expenses were paid in cash, by check, by credit or debit card, or with borrowed funds.

Qualified education expenses include nonacademic fees, such as student activity fees, athletic fees, or other expenses unrelated to the academic course of instruction, **only if** the fee must be paid to the institution as a condition of enrollment or attendance. However, fees for personal expenses (described below) are never qualified education expenses.

Qualified education expenses **don't** include amounts paid for the following.

- Personal expenses. This means room and board, insurance, medical expenses (including student health fees), transportation, and other similar personal, living, or family expenses.
- Any course or other education involving sports, games, or hobbies, or any noncredit course, unless such course or other education is part of the student's degree program or helps the student acquire or improve job skills.

Qualified education expenses don't include any expenses for which you take any other deduction, such as on Schedule A (Form 1040 or 1040-SR) or Schedule C (Form 1040 or 1040-SR).

You may receive Form 1098-T, Tuition Statement, from the institution reporting either payments received in the current year or amounts billed in the current year. However, the amounts may be different from the amount you paid (or are treated as having paid). In completing Form 8917, use only the amounts you actually paid (plus any amounts you're treated as having paid) in the current year (reduced, as necessary, as described in *Adjusted Qualified Education Expenses,* later). See Pub. 970 for more information on Form 1098-T.

Qualified education expenses paid directly to the institution by someone other than you or the student are treated as paid to the student and then paid by the student to the institution.

## Academic Period

An academic period is any quarter, semester, trimester, or any other period of study as reasonably determined by an eligible educational institution. If an eligible educational institution uses credit hours or clock hours and doesn't have academic terms, each payment period may be treated as an academic period.

## Prepaid Expenses

Qualified education expenses paid in the current year for an academic period that begins in the first 3 months of the following year can be used in figuring the tuition and fees deduction for the current year only.

***Example 2.*** Qualified education expenses paid in 2018 for an academic period that begins in the first 3 months of 2019 can be used in figuring the tuition and fees deduction for 2018 only. See *Academic Period,* earlier.

***Example 3.*** If you pay $2,000 in December 2019 for qualified tuition for the 2020 winter quarter that begins in January 2020, you can use that $2,000 in figuring the tuition and fees deduction for 2019 only (if you meet all the other requirements).

CAUTION *You can't use any amount you paid in the previous or future year to figure the qualified education expenses you use to figure your current year tuition and fees deduction.*

***Example 4.*** *You can't use any amount you paid in 2017 or 2019 to figure the qualified deduction expenses you use to figure your 2018 tuition and fees deduction.*

## Adjusted Qualified Education Expenses

For each student, reduce the qualified education expenses paid by or on behalf of that student under the following rules. The result is the amount of adjusted qualified education expenses for each student.

**Tax-free educational assistance.** For tax-free educational assistance received in the current year, reduce the qualified educational expenses for each academic period by the amount of tax-free educational assistance allocable to that academic period. See *Academic Period,* earlier.

Tax-free educational assistance includes:

1. The tax-free part of any scholarship or fellowship grant (including Pell grants);

2. The tax-free part of any employer-provided educational assistance;

3. Veterans' educational assistance; and

4. Any other educational assistance that is excludable from gross income (tax free), other than as a gift, bequest, devise, or inheritance.

TIP *You may be able to increase the combined value of your tuition and fees deduction and certain educational assistance if the student includes some or all of the educational assistance in income in the year it is received. For details, see Pub. 970.*

Generally, any scholarship or fellowship grant is treated as tax-free educational assistance. However, a scholarship or fellowship grant isn't treated as tax-free educational assistance to the extent the student includes it in gross income (the student may or may not be required to file a tax return) for the year the scholarship or fellowship grant is received and either:

- The scholarship or fellowship grant (or any part of it) **must** be applied (by its terms) to expenses (such as room and board) other than qualified education expenses as defined in *Qualified education expenses* in Pub. 970; or
- The scholarship or fellowship grant (or any part of it) **may** be applied (by its terms) to expenses (such as room and board) other than qualified education expenses as defined in *Qualified education expenses* in Pub. 970.

**Tax-free educational assistance treated as a refund.** Some tax-free educational assistance received after the current year may be treated as a refund of qualified education expenses paid in the current year. This tax-free educational assistance is any tax-free educational assistance received by you or anyone else after the current year for qualified education expenses paid on behalf of a student in the current year (or attributable to enrollment at an eligible educational institution during the current year).

If this tax-free educational assistance is received after the current year but before you file your current year income tax return, see *Refunds received after the current year but before your income tax return is filed,* later. If this tax-free educational assistance is received after the current year and after you file your current year income tax return, see *Refunds received after the current year and after your income tax return is filed,* later.

**Refunds.** A refund of qualified education expenses may reduce adjusted qualified education expenses for the tax year or may require you to include some or all of the refund in your gross income for the year the refund is received. See Pub. 970 for more information. Some tax-free educational assistance received after the current year may be treated as a refund. See *Tax-free educational assistance treated as a refund,* earlier.

***Refunds received in the current year.*** For each student, figure the adjusted qualified education expenses for the current year by adding all the qualified education expenses paid in the current year and subtracting any refunds of those expenses received from the eligible educational institution during the current year.

***Refunds received after the current year but before your income tax return is filed.*** If anyone receives a refund after the current year of qualified education expenses you paid on behalf of a student in the current year and the refund is received before you file your current year income tax return, reduce the amount of qualified education expenses for the current year by the amount of the refund.

***Refunds received after the current year and after your income tax return is filed.*** If anyone receives a refund after the current year of qualified education expenses you paid on behalf of a student in the current year and the refund is received after you file your current year income tax return, you may need to include some or all of the refund in your gross income for the year the refund is received. See Pub. 970 for more information.

**Coordination with Coverdell education savings accounts and qualified tuition programs.** Reduce your qualified education expenses by any qualified education expenses used to figure the exclusion from gross income of (a) interest received under an education savings bond program, or (b) any distribution from a Coverdell education savings account or qualified tuition program (QTP). For a QTP, this applies only to the amount of tax-free earnings that were distributed, not to the recovery of contributions to the program.

## Eligible Educational Institution

An eligible educational institution is generally any accredited public, nonprofit, or proprietary (private) college, university, vocational school, or other postsecondary institution. Also, the institution must be eligible to participate in a student aid program administered by the Department of Education. Virtually all accredited postsecondary institutions meet this definition.

An eligible educational institution also includes certain educational institutions located outside the United States that are eligible to participate in a student aid program administered by the Department of Education.

**TIP** *The educational institution should be able to tell you if it is an eligible institution.*

## Additional Information

See Pub. 970 for more information about the tuition and fees deduction.

## Specific Instructions

### Line 1

Complete columns (a) through (c) on line 1 for each student for whom you elect to take the tuition and fees deduction.

**Note:** If you have more than three students who qualify for the tuition and fees deduction, enter "See attached" next to line 1 and attach a statement with the required information for each additional student. Include the amounts from line 1, column (c), for all students in the total you enter on line 2.

### Column (c)

For each student, enter the amount of adjusted qualified education expenses. The expenses must have been paid for the student in the current year for academic periods beginning in the current year but before April 1 of the following year.

Form **8829**

Department of the Treasury
Internal Revenue Service (99)

# Expenses for Business Use of Your Home

► File only with Schedule C (Form 1040). Use a separate Form 8829 for each home you used for business during the year.

► Go to *www.irs.gov/Form8829* for instructions and the latest information.

OMB No. 1545-0074

**2020**

Attachment Sequence No. **176**

Name(s) of proprietor(s) | Your social security number

## Part I Part of Your Home Used for Business

| | | | |
|---|---|---|---|
| 1 | Area used regularly and exclusively for business, regularly for daycare, or for storage of inventory or product samples (see instructions) | 1 | |
| 2 | Total area of home | 2 | |
| 3 | Divide line 1 by line 2. Enter the result as a percentage | 3 | % |
| | **For daycare facilities not used exclusively for business, go to line 4. All others, go to line 7.** | | |
| 4 | Multiply days used for daycare during year by hours used per day — 4 ___ hr. | | |
| 5 | If you started or stopped using your home for daycare during the year, see instructions; otherwise, enter 8,784 — 5 ___ hr. | | |
| 6 | Divide line 4 by line 5. Enter the result as a decimal amount — 6 ___ . | | |
| 7 | Business percentage. For daycare facilities not used exclusively for business, multiply line 6 by line 3 (enter the result as a percentage). All others, enter the amount from line 3 ► | 7 | % |

## Part II Figure Your Allowable Deduction

| | | | (a) Direct expenses | (b) Indirect expenses | | |
|---|---|---|---|---|---|---|
| 8 | Enter the amount from Schedule C, line 29, **plus** any gain derived from the business use of your home, **minus** any loss from the trade or business not derived from the business use of your home. See instructions. | | | | 8 | |
| | See instructions for columns (a) and (b) before completing lines 9–22. | | | | | |
| 9 | Casualty losses (see instructions) | 9 | | | | |
| 10 | Deductible mortgage interest (see instructions) | 10 | | | | |
| 11 | Real estate taxes (see instructions) | 11 | | | | |
| 12 | Add lines 9, 10, and 11 | 12 | | | | |
| 13 | Multiply line 12, column (b), by line 7 | | 13 | | | |
| 14 | Add line 12, column (a), and line 13 | | | | 14 | |
| 15 | Subtract line 14 from line 8. If zero or less, enter -0- | | | | 15 | |
| 16 | Excess mortgage interest (see instructions) | 16 | | | | |
| 17 | Excess real estate taxes (see instructions) | 17 | | | | |
| 18 | Insurance | 18 | | | | |
| 19 | Rent | 19 | | | | |
| 20 | Repairs and maintenance | 20 | | | | |
| 21 | Utilities | 21 | | | | |
| 22 | Other expenses (see instructions) | 22 | | | | |
| 23 | Add lines 16 through 22 | 23 | | | | |
| 24 | Multiply line 23, column (b), by line 7 | | 24 | | | |
| 25 | Carryover of prior year operating expenses (see instructions) | | 25 | | | |
| 26 | Add line 23, column (a), line 24, and line 25 | | | | 26 | |
| 27 | Allowable operating expenses. Enter the **smaller** of line 15 or line 26 | | | | 27 | |
| 28 | Limit on excess casualty losses and depreciation. Subtract line 27 from line 15 | | | | 28 | |
| 29 | Excess casualty losses (see instructions) | | 29 | | | |
| 30 | Depreciation of your home from line 42 below | | 30 | | | |
| 31 | Carryover of prior year excess casualty losses and depreciation (see instructions) | | 31 | | | |
| 32 | Add lines 29 through 31 | | | | 32 | |
| 33 | Allowable excess casualty losses and depreciation. Enter the **smaller** of line 28 or line 32 | | | | 33 | |
| 34 | Add lines 14, 27, and 33 | | | | 34 | |
| 35 | Casualty loss portion, if any, from lines 14 and 33. Carry amount to **Form 4684.** See instructions | | | | 35 | |
| 36 | **Allowable expenses for business use of your home.** Subtract line 35 from line 34. Enter here and on Schedule C, line 30. If your home was used for more than one business, see instructions. ► | | | | 36 | |

## Part III Depreciation of Your Home

| | | | |
|---|---|---|---|
| 37 | Enter the **smaller** of your home's adjusted basis or its fair market value. See instructions | 37 | |
| 38 | Value of land included on line 37 | 38 | |
| 39 | Basis of building. Subtract line 38 from line 37 | 39 | |
| 40 | Business basis of building. Multiply line 39 by line 7 | 40 | |
| 41 | Depreciation percentage (see instructions) | 41 | % |
| 42 | Depreciation allowable (see instructions). Multiply line 40 by line 41. Enter here and on line 30 above | 42 | |

## Part IV Carryover of Unallowed Expenses to 2021

| | | | |
|---|---|---|---|
| 43 | Operating expenses. Subtract line 27 from line 26. If less than zero, enter -0- | 43 | |
| 44 | Excess casualty losses and depreciation. Subtract line 33 from line 32. If less than zero, enter -0- | 44 | |

**For Paperwork Reduction Act Notice, see your tax return instructions.** Cat. No. 13232M Form **8829** (2020)

# How to Decode the Code

APPENDIX

D

Coprid/Shutterstock.com; iStockphoto.com/David Freund

# HOW TO DECODE THE CODE

The federal income tax is based on a system of rules and regulations that determine the treatment of various items of income and expense. This system has been developed around general concepts that guide us in its application to various types of transactions. The four major groupings are as follows:

- general concepts
- accounting concepts
- income concepts
- deduction concepts

Once you understand this small number of unifying concepts, you can apply them to almost every aspect of the system.

## Income Tax Concepts with Related Constructs and Doctrines

### General Concepts

**Ability to Pay** A tax should be based on the amount that the taxpayer can afford to pay, relative to other taxpayers (p. 2-2).
- Income, exclusions, deductions, losses, tax credits
- Progressive rate structure

**Administrative Convenience** Those items for which the cost of compliance would exceed the revenue generated are not taxed (p. 2-3).
- Standard deduction

**Arm's-Length Transaction** A transaction in which all parties have bargained in good faith and for their individual benefit, not for the benefit of the transaction group (p. 2-4).
- Related party
- Constructive ownership

**Pay as You Go** A tax should be collected as close as possible to the time in which the income is earned (p. 2-5).
- Withholding
- Estimated tax payments

### Accounting Concepts

**Entity** All items of income, deduction, and so on are traced to the tax unit responsible for the item (p. 2-6).
- Taxable/Conduit
- Assignment of income

**Annual Accounting Period** All entities must report the results of their operations on an annual basis (the tax year). Each tax year stands on its own, apart from other tax years (p. 2-9).
- Accounting method
- Tax benefit rule
- Substance over form

### Income Concepts

**All-Inclusive Income** All income received is taxable unless a specific provision in the tax law either excludes the income from taxation or defers its recognition to a future tax year (p. 2-12).

**Legislative Grace** Any tax relief provided is the result of a specific act of Congress that must be strictly applied and interpreted. All income received is taxable unless a specific provision in the tax law excludes the income from taxation. Deductions must be approached with the philosophy that nothing is deductible unless a provision in the tax law allows the deduction (p. 2-12).
- Capital asset
- Capital gains and losses

**Capital Recovery** No income is realized until the taxpayer receives more than the amount invested to produce the income. The amount invested in an asset represents the maximum amount recoverable (p. 2-13).
- Basis

**Realization** No income or loss is recognized until it has been realized. A realization involves a change in the form and/or substance of a taxpayer's property rights that results from an arm's-length transaction (p. 2-14).
- Claim of right
- Constructive receipt

**Wherewithal to Pay** Income is recognized in the period in which the taxpayer has the means to pay the tax on the income (p. 2-16).

### Deduction Concepts

**Legislative Grace** Any tax relief provided is the result of a specific act of Congress that must be strictly applied and interpreted. All income received is taxable unless a specific provision in the tax law excludes the income from taxation. Deductions must be approached with the philosophy that nothing is deductible unless a provision in the tax law allows the deduction (p. 2-12).

**Business Purpose** To be deductible, an expenditure or a loss must have a business or other economic purpose that exceeds any tax avoidance motive. The primary motive for the transaction must be to make a profit (p. 2-18).

**Capital Recovery** No income is realized until the taxpayer receives more than the amount invested to produce the income. The amount invested in an asset represents the maximum amount recoverable (p. 2-13).
- Basis
- Capital expenditure

# 2021 Tax Rate Schedules

## Single Taxpayers

| If Taxable Income Is Over | But Not Over | The Tax Is | of the Amount Over |
|---|---|---|---|
| $ 0 | 9,950 | ....... 10% | $ 0 |
| 9,950 | 40,525 | $ 995.00 + 12% | 9,950 |
| 40,525 | 86,375 | 4,664.00 + 22% | 40,525 |
| 86,375 | 164,925 | 14,751.00 + 24% | 86,375 |
| 164,925 | 209,425 | 33,603.00 + 32% | 164,925 |
| 209,425 | 523,600 | 47,843.00 + 35% | 209,425 |
| 523,600 | ....... | 157,804.25 + 37% | 523,600 |

## Married Taxpayers Filing Jointly and Surviving Spouse

| If Taxable Income Is Over | But Not Over | The Tax Is | of the Amount Over |
|---|---|---|---|
| $ 0 | 19,900 | ....... 10% | $ 0 |
| 19,900 | 81,050 | $ 1,990.00 + 12% | 19,900 |
| 81,050 | 172,750 | 9,328.00 + 22% | 81,050 |
| 172,750 | 329,850 | 29,502.00 + 24% | 172,750 |
| 329,850 | 418,850 | 67,260.00 + 32% | 329,850 |
| 418,850 | 628,300 | 95,686.00 + 35% | 418,850 |
| 628,300 | | 168,993.50 + 37% | 628,300 |

## Head of Household

| If Taxable Income Is Over | But Not Over | The Tax Is | of the Amount Over |
|---|---|---|---|
| $ 0 | 14,200 | ....... 10% | $ 0 |
| 14,200 | 54,200 | $ 1,420.00 + 12% | 14,200 |
| 54,200 | 86,350 | 6,220.00 + 22% | 54,200 |
| 86,350 | 164,900 | 13,293.00 + 24% | 86,350 |
| 164,900 | 209,400 | 32,145.00 + 32% | 164,900 |
| 209,400 | 523,600 | 46,385.00 + 35% | 209,400 |
| 523,600 | | 156,355.00 + 37% | 523,600 |

## Married Taxpayers, Filing Separately

| If Taxable Income Is Over | But Not Over | The Tax Is | of the Amount Over |
|---|---|---|---|
| $ 0 | 9,950 | ....... 10% | $ 0 |
| 9,950 | 40,525 | $ 995.00 + 12% | 9,950 |
| 40,525 | 86,375 | 4664.00 + 22% | 40,525 |
| 86,375 | 164,925 | 14,751.00 + 24% | 86,375 |
| 164,925 | 209,425 | 33,603.00 + 32% | 164,925 |
| 209,425 | 314,150 | 47,843.00 + 35% | 209,425 |
| 314,150 | | 84,496.75 + 37% | 314,150 |

## Corporate Tax Rate Schedule

All corporate taxable income is taxed at a flat 21% rate.

## Social Security Tax Rates

OASDI – 6.20% on up to $142,800 of salaries and wages
MHI – 1.45% on all salaries and wages

## Individual Income Tax Formula

| | |
|---|---|
| Income (broadly conceived) | $XX,XXX |
| Less: Exclusions | (X,XXX) |
| Gross income | $XX,XXX |
| Less: Deductions for adjusted gross income | (X,XXX) |
| Adjusted gross income | $XX,XXX |
| Less: Deductions from adjusted gross income— | |
| The greater of— | |
| The total itemized deductions or standard deduction | (X,XXX) |
| Taxable income | $XX,XXX |

## Basic Standard Deduction Amounts

| Filing Status | Standard Deduction Amount 2021 |
|---|---|
| Single | $12,550 |
| Married, filing jointly | 25,100 |
| Surviving spouse | 25,100 |
| Head of household | 18,800 |
| Married, filing separately | 12,550 |

## Amount of Each Additional Standard Deduction for Age and Blindness

| Filing Status | Standard Deduction Amount 2021 |
|---|---|
| Single | $1,700 |
| Married, filing jointly | 1,350 |
| Surviving spouse | 1,350 |
| Head of household | 1,700 |
| Married, filing separately | 1,350 |

## Present Value Tables

**Present Value of a Single Payment**

| Year | 5% | 6% | 7% | 8% | 9% | 10% | 12% |
|---|---|---|---|---|---|---|---|
| 1 | 0.952 | 0.943 | 0.935 | 0.926 | 0.917 | 0.909 | 0.893 |
| 2 | 0.907 | 0.890 | 0.873 | 0.857 | 0.842 | 0.826 | 0.797 |
| 3 | 0.864 | 0.840 | 0.816 | 0.794 | 0.772 | 0.751 | 0.712 |
| 4 | 0.823 | 0.792 | 0.793 | 0.735 | 0.708 | 0.683 | 0.636 |
| 5 | 0.784 | 0.747 | 0.713 | 0.681 | 0.650 | 0.621 | 0.567 |
| 6 | 0.746 | 0.705 | 0.666 | 0.630 | 0.596 | 0.564 | 0.507 |
| 7 | 0.711 | 0.665 | 0.623 | 0.583 | 0.547 | 0.513 | 0.452 |
| 8 | 0.677 | 0.627 | 0.582 | 0.540 | 0.502 | 0.467 | 0.404 |
| 9 | 0.645 | 0.592 | 0.544 | 0.500 | 0.460 | 0.424 | 0.361 |
| 10 | 0.614 | 0.558 | 0.508 | 0.463 | 0.422 | 0.386 | 0.322 |

## Future Value of an Ordinary Annuity of $1 per Period

| Period (n) | 4% | 5% | 6% | 7% | 8% | 9% | 10% | 12% |
|---|---|---|---|---|---|---|---|---|
| 1 | 1.00000 | 1.00000 | 1.00000 | 1.00000 | 1.00000 | 1.00000 | 1.00000 | 1.00000 |
| 5 | 5.41632 | 5.52563 | 5.63709 | 5.75074 | 5.86660 | 5.98471 | 6.10510 | 6.35285 |
| 10 | 12.00611 | 12.57789 | 13.18079 | 13.81645 | 14.48656 | 15.19293 | 15.93742 | 17.54874 |
| 15 | 20.02359 | 21.57856 | 23.27597 | 25.12902 | 27.15211 | 29.36092 | 31.77248 | 37.27971 |
| 20 | 29.77808 | 33.06595 | 36.78559 | 40.99549 | 45.76196 | 51.16012 | 57.27500 | 72.05244 |
| 25 | 41.64591 | 47.72710 | 54.86451 | 63.24904 | 73.10594 | 84.70090 | 98.34706 | 133.33387 |
| 30 | 56.08494 | 66.43885 | 79.05819 | 94.46079 | 113.28321 | 136.30754 | 164.49402 | 241.33268 |
| 35 | 73.6522 | 90.32031 | 111.43478 | 138.2368 | 172.31680 | 215.71076 | 271.02437 | 431.66350 |
| 40 | 95.02552 | 120.79977 | 154.76197 | 199.6351 | 259.05652 | 337.88245 | 442.59256 | 767.09142 |

# GLOSSARY

The numbers in parentheses at the end of each definition refer to the chapters in which each term is discussed.

## A

**Abandoned spouse** - A related relief provision lets an abandoned spouse file as a head of household. A married person is treated as an abandoned spouse if a dependent child lives in the taxpayer's home for more than half the year and the taxpayer's spouse does not live in the home at any time during the last half of the year. The benefit provided by this provision is that a married taxpayer is considered unmarried for the entire year and is allowed to file as head of household. See *filing status.* (8)

**Ability-to-pay concept** - A tax should be based on the amount that the taxpayer can afford to pay, relative to other taxpayers. (2)

**Accelerated Cost Recovery System (ACRS)** - Applies to tangible property placed in service after 1980 and before 1987. ACRS was enacted to encourage investment that would lead to economic expansion by accelerating the capital recovery taxpayers received from depreciating property. (10)

**Accountable plan** - See *employer reimbursement plan.* (6)

**Accounting method** - The taxpayer must select an accounting method to determine the year(s) in which taxable transactions are to be reported. The two basic allowable methods are the *cash basis of accounting* and the *accrual basis of accounting.* Taxpayers using the cash basis are taxed on income as it is received and take deductions as they are paid. In contrast, accrual basis taxpayers report their income as it is earned and take deductions as they are incurred, without regard to the actual receipt or payment of cash. (2, 5)

**Accrual basis of accounting** - See *accounting method.* (2)

**Acquiescence** - A pronouncement by the IRS that it will follow the decision of a court case to the extent that the decision favored the taxpayer. (16)

**Acquisition debt** - See *qualified home mortgage interest.* (8)

**Actions on Decisions (AOD)** - A statement from the Chief Counsel's Office indicating whether an adverse court opinion should be appealed. (16)

**Active income** - Income from a trade or business in which the taxpayer materially participates. This category includes wages and salaries, as well as income from a trade or business in which the taxpayer materially participates. Working interest in oil and gas deposits and certain low-income housing projects are always considered active income. Such activities may produce losses that are not subject to the passive loss rules. (7)

**Active investor** - See *securities dealer.* (5)

**Active participant** - See *active participation exception.* (7, 15)

**Active participation exception** - *Active participants* in rental real estate may use passive activity losses amounting to as much as $25,000 per year to offset portfolio and active sources of income. An active participant must own at least a 10% interest in the activity and have significant and bonafide involvement in the activity, a standard less stringent than that for material participation. The $25,000 annual deduction amount is phased out when the individual's AGI exceeds $100,000. (7)

**Active trader** - See *securities dealer.* (5)

**Actual cost method** - See *auto expense.* (6)

**Ad valorem taxes** - Taxes that are based on the value of the property being taxed (e.g., property taxes). However, most property taxes are not based on the true fair market value of the property. Rather, the *assessed value* of the property is used to determine the tax. The assessed value of property is typically 50 to 75% of the estimated market value of the property. (1)

**Adjusted basis** - The original basis, plus or minus changes in the amount of unrecovered investment. It roughly corresponds to the book-value concept studied in financial accounting. At any point in time, the remaining capital investment to be recovered is represented by an asset's adjusted basis. An asset's adjusted basis may never be less than zero. (2, 9, 10)

**Adjusted Gross Income (AGI)** - Deductions of individuals are broken into two classes—deductions for AGI and deductions from AGI. This difference in deductions results in an intermediate income number called the AGI. It is used to provide limitations on the deductions from AGI of an individual taxpayer. *Deductions for adjusted gross income* include trade or business expenses, rental and royalty expenses, capital losses, and certain other expenditures that the tax law specifically allows. Once the allowable amount of an expenditure has been determined, it is not subject to further reduction based on the income of the taxpayer. (1, 5, 8)

**Adjusted net capital gain** - The net long-term gain from the capital gain and loss netting procedure minus the 28% rate gain plus eligible dividend income. The 28% rate gain is equal to the sum of the net collectibles gain, and gain on qualified small business stock reduced by net short-term capital losses and any long-term capital loss carryovers from previous years. If the 28% rate gain is negative, the remaining loss is netted against unrecaptured Section 1250 gains. Any remaining loss is netted against the adjusted net capital gain. The adjusted net capital gain is taxed at 15% (0% if the taxpayer is in the 10% or 15% marginal tax rate bracket, 20% if the taxpayer is in the 37% marginal tax rate bracket). (3, 11)

**Administrative convenience concept** - Items may be omitted from the tax base whenever the cost of compliance would exceed the revenue generated. The cost is generally the time and effort for taxpayers to accumulate the information necessary to implement the concept as well as the cost to the government of ensuring compliance. (2)

**Age test** - See *qualifying child.* (8)

**Alimony** - In a divorce situation, one spouse often makes payments to a former spouse. The payments may be to provide for the support of children (called *child support payments*), they may be simply a sharing of income between the two parties (called *alimony*), or they may constitute a division of marital property (*property settlement*). (3)

**All-events test** - An accrual basis taxpayer may deduct expenses in the year in which two tests are met: the all-events and economic performance tests. The all-events test is met when all events have occurred that determine that a liability exists and the amount of the liability can be determined with reasonable accuracy. The *economic performance test* requires economic performance to have occurred with regard to the liability. Economic performance occurs when services or property are provided to the taxpayer or when the taxpayer uses property. (5)

**All-inclusive income concept** - All income received is taxable unless some specific provision can be found in the tax law that excludes the item in question from taxation or defers its recognition to a future tax year. The tax law always starts with the proposition that anything of value received is taxable. (2)

**Alternate valuation date** - See *inherited property.* (9)

**Alternative Depreciation System (ADS)** - The ADS system must be used to calculate depreciation deductions for purposes of the alternative minimum tax. ADS depreciation is generally computed using the straight-line method over a specified longer alternative recovery period. An election to use ADS for regular tax purposes is made on a class-by-class, year-by-year basis for property other than real estate. For real estate, the ADS is elected on a property-by-property basis in the year of acquisition. (10)

**Alternative Minimum Tax (AMT)** - An alternative calculation of the tax liability that results in the minimum amount of tax that the taxpayer must pay. The AMT is a separate, parallel tax system. Within this system, many preference items allowed in the calculation of the regular tax liability are either not allowed or the amount of tax relief provided is greatly diminished. (15)

**Alternative minimum tax adjustment** - Accounts for the effect of items that must be determined using either alternative calculations or alternative methods for AMT purposes. In general, the use of the AMT calculation or method results in either accelerating income items or deferring deduction items. The net effect of either is a higher taxable income in the initial period(s) of difference. However, most adjustment items are not disallowed for AMT purposes; they are merely spread out (in the case of deductions) or accelerated (in the case of income items). The difference in the two calculations is temporary, not permanent. (15)

**Alternative minimum tax rate** - A tax rate of either 26% or 28% applies to the taxpayer's AMTI. (15)

**Alternative Minimum Taxable Income (AMTI)** - The tax base used to calculate the alternative minimum tax. AMTI is calculated by making modifications to regular taxable income for prescribed adjustment and preference items. (15)

**American Opportunity Tax Credit (AOTC)** - The American Opportunity Tax Credit (AOTC) allows the taxpayer a 100% tax credit on the first $2,000 of qualifying higher education expenses and a 25% credit on the next $2,000 of qualifying expenses. Only tuition, fees, and course materials paid on behalf of the taxpayer, the taxpayer's spouse, or a dependent of the taxpayer are qualified higher education expenses. The AOTC can only be claimed for the first four years of undergraduate study and is phased out ratably for married taxpayers with adjusted gross incomes between $160,000 and $180,000 and for all other taxpayers when adjusted gross income is between $80,000 and $90,000. (8)

**Amortization** - Amortization is a tax accounting method used to recover the investment in assets. This provides a reasonable allocation of bases to the annual accounting periods benefited by the use of the assets. Intangible property with definite useful lives, such as patents, copyrights, goodwill, or agreements not to compete, may be amortized. (10)

**Amount realized** - Capital is recovered at disposition by offsetting the adjusted basis at the date of disposition with the amount realized from the *property disposition.* The amount realized from a disposition is the amount received from the disposition (generally the sales price of the property), less the expenses incurred to make the disposition. If the amount is greater than the adjusted basis, the taxpayer has a *realized gain* on the disposition. If the amount realized is less than the adjusted basis, capital investment is not fully recovered, resulting in a *realized loss.* (9, 11)

**AMT minimum tax credit** - A problem can arise if accelerated income is taxed first under the AMT and later, when the timing difference reverses, for regular tax purposes. To avoid double taxation of reversal items, Congress enacted a minimum tax credit that can only be used to reduce the regular tax liability in later years when the regular tax exceeds the alternative minimum tax. The credit is calculated each year in which the AMT applies. (15)

**Annual accounting period concept** - All entities must report the results of their operations on an annual basis (the tax year). Each tax year stands on its own, apart from other tax years. (2)

**Annual loss** - See *loss.* (1, 7)

**Annuity** - An annuity is a string of payments received over equal time periods for a determinable period. The general formula for determining the amount of each payment that is a return of capital and therefore excluded from income is called the *annuity exclusion ratio.* The formula is the cost of the contract divided by the number of payments expected from the contract. The number of payments expected from the contract is based on a standard set of expected payments for a single taxpayer and a separate table of expected payments when the annuity will continue to be paid to a survivor after the death of the taxpayer. (3)

**Annuity exclusion ratio** - See *annuity.* (3)

**Arm's-length transaction concept** - All parties to the transaction have bargained in good faith and for their individual benefit, not for the benefit of the transaction group. Transactions not made at arm's length are generally given no tax effect or are not given the intended tax effect. (2)

**Assessments for local benefits** - Real estate taxes that are related to assessments for local benefits, such as sidewalks, streets, sewers, and other improvements, and are not deductible. The tax imposed for local benefits is deemed to increase the value of the taxpayer's property and is considered a capital expenditure. The tax is added to the improved asset's basis, which may be recoverable through depreciation, amortization, or upon its disposition. (6)

**Assignment-of-income doctrine** - The tax entity that owns the income produced is responsible for the tax on the income, regardless of which entity actually receives the income. Merely directing payment of income (assigning income) that has been earned by one entity to another, although legal, does not relieve the owner of the income from paying tax. (2)

**At-risk rules** - Taxpayers cannot deduct losses in excess of the amount they have at risk in an activity. The at-risk amount is equal to cash or other assets that have been contributed to the activity. In addition, any debts of the activity that the taxpayer would have to pay if the activity could not are also considered at risk. Thus, the amount at risk in an activity is the maximum amount of personal funds (assets) that could be lost if the activity failed. The amount at risk is also adjusted for the taxpayer's share of the income (loss) from the activity and reduced by withdrawals from the activity. Any current period losses that are not deductible because they exceed the taxpayer's at-risk amount are carried forward and are deductible when the taxpayer has enough at risk to allow the deduction. (7, 14)

**Auto expense** - A taxpayer can choose one of two methods of computing a deduction for using an auto for business purposes, the standard mileage rate method or the actual cost method. Using the *standard mileage rate method*, a taxpayer deducts a certain amount for each business mile the car was driven during the tax year. The standard mileage rate is designed to be an estimate of the cost of operating the car. Because these costs change over time, the standard rate is set each year to reflect changes in the cost of operating a car (57.5 cents per mile for 2020). In addition to the standard mileage rate, the taxpayer can deduct direct out-of-pocket expenses unrelated to the operating costs of the car that are incurred while attending to business. Using the *actual cost method*, a taxpayer can deduct depreciation, gas and oil, repairs, insurance, interest, license, and other expenses of driving the car. If the car is used for both business and personal purposes, the expenses must be allocated according to the miles driven for each purpose. (6)

**Average tax rate** - The average rate of tax on each dollar of income that is taxable. The total federal income tax divided by taxable income (tax base). See also *proportional rate structure*. (1)

## B

**Bargain purchase** - A true bargain purchase is taxable to the buyer. Such a purchase occurs when the difference between the purchase price and the fair market value represents an effort by the seller to confer an economic advantage to the buyer. Bargain purchases are typically found in employer/employee purchases and related party transactions. (3, 9)

**Basis** - The amount of unrecovered investment in an asset. As amounts are expended and/or recovered relative to an asset over time, the basis is adjusted in consideration of such changes. See *adjusted basis*. (2)

**Below market-rate loan** - A loan made between related parties at an interest rate lower than the market rate for similar loans. (3)

**Boot** - When properties of different values are exchanged, the party with the property of lower value must equalize the value being exchanged by transferring cash, securities, services, assumptions of debt, or other property not of like kind. This nonqualifying property is called *boot*. (12)

**Business bad debt** - To be deductible, a bad debt must be related to a transaction that has a business purpose. If the bad debt arose from a transaction in the taxpayer's trade or business, the bad debt is allowed as a business deduction; otherwise, the bad debt is considered a nonbusiness bad debt. A *nonbusiness bad debt* cannot be deducted if the debt was voluntarily forgiven or the forgiveness of the debt was intended as a gift. Nonbusiness bad debts are deducted as a short-term capital loss, using the specific charge-off method. See *specific charge-off method*. (6)

**Business casualty loss** - See *casualty*. (7)

**Business expense** - Expenses that are either profit motivated or related to a business purpose. (5)

**Business gifts** - A taxpayer can deduct up to $25 per year per donee for gifts to business customers. Gifts are not subject to the 50% limitation that applies to meals and entertainment expenses. To apply the $25 limitation, direct and indirect gifts given to a person must be counted. An indirect gift is one made to a related party, such as a taxpayer's spouse or child. (6)

**Business purpose concept** - To be deductible, an expenditure or a loss must have a business or other economic purpose that exceeds any tax avoidance motive. The primary motive for the transaction must be to make a profit. Two general types of expense deductions in the tax law embody the profit motive requirement: expenses incurred in a trade or business and those related to the production of income (investment activity). These are commonly referred to as *trade or business expenses* and *investment expenses*. (2)

**Business purpose tax year** - See *natural business year*. (13)

## C

**Cafeteria plan** - A menu of tax-free benefits that is offered at the employer's cost. Each employee is allowed to choose a certain dollar amount of benefits from the menu or may choose to take the cash cost of the benefit. Employees who choose the tax-free benefits are not taxed on the value of the benefit; however, those who elect to receive cash are taxed on the amount of cash received. The employer must make the benefits of the plan available to all employees on a nondiscriminatory basis. (4)

**Capital asset** - Any asset that is *not* a receivable, inventory, real or depreciable property used in a trade or business, and certain intangible assets, such as copyrights. Common capital assets of individuals include stocks, bonds, and personal use assets. (2, 3, 7, 11)

**Capital expenditure** - Taxpayers cannot deduct capital expenditures in total in the period in which they are paid. The main characteristic of a capital expenditure is that its usefulness extends substantially beyond the end of the tax year in which the expenditure is made. (2, 5)

**Capital gains (loss)** - The difference between the sales price of a capital asset and the adjusted basis of that asset. See *adjusted net capital gain* and *net capital loss.* (2, 6)

**Capital recovery concept** - No income is realized until the taxpayer receives more than the amount invested to produce the income. The amount invested in an asset represents the maximum amount recoverable. (2)

**Carryback** - See *net operating loss.* (7)

**Carryforward** - See *net operating loss.* (7)

**Carryover basis** - Indicates that all or part of an asset's basis transfers from one owner to another or from one asset to another. Transactions resulting in carryover basis are subject to special rules for determining holding period—an adding on of the holding period of the prior asset or of a prior owner. (9)

**Cash basis of accounting** - See *accounting method.* (2)

**Cash-equivalent approach** - Income does not have to be received in cash to be recognized. The receipt of anything with a fair market value triggers recognition of income. (3)

**Casualty** - The result of some sudden, unexpected, and/or unusual event (i.e., fire, storms, earthquakes, and accidents). Thefts are treated as casualties. Actual physical damage to property must occur. When a business property is fully destroyed (or stolen), the measure of the *business casualty loss* for fully destroyed property is the property's basis. If the insurance proceeds received from a casualty exceed the adjusted basis of the property, the result would be a *casualty gain*, which is subject to a special election under which a casualty gain may be deferred. When a casualty occurs and property is not totally destroyed, an estimate must be made of the amount lost as a result of the casualty. In this case, a *casualty loss* is equal to the lower of the decline in the value of the property or the adjusted basis of the property. (7)

**Casualty gain (loss)** - See *casualty* and *involuntary conversion.* (7)

**Centralized management** - See *corporation.* (13)

**Certainty** - One of Adam Smith's maxims which indicates that a taxpayer should know when and how a tax is to be paid. (1)

**Charitable contributions** - Individuals are allowed an itemized deduction for donations to *charitable organizations*—those organized for religious, charitable, educational, scientific, or literary purposes. The deductible amount of charitable contributions has three major limitations. The overall amount of the deduction cannot exceed 60% of the taxpayer's AGI. Contributions of ordinary income property are limited to the lesser of the property's adjusted basis or its fair market value. Contributions of capital gain property that are deducted at fair market value cannot exceed 30% of AGI. But a taxpayer who is willing to give up the deduction related to the property's appreciation (i.e., use the adjusted basis as the deductible amount) is not subject to the 30% limit. Any contributions in excess of the limitations are carried forward for deduction for five years. (14)

**Charitable organizations** - See *charitable contribution.* (8)

**Child care cost credit** - A tax credit designed to provide incentive for employers to provide child care for their employees, either on the workplace premises or in a qualified facility. The credit is the sum of 25% of the qualified child care expenses the employer incurs plus 10% of qualified child care resources and referral expenditures associated with providing such services. (15)

**Child credit** - A taxpayer can claim a $2,000 tax credit for each qualifying child under 17 years of age. The definition of a qualifying child is similar to the definition of a child for dependency purposes with two minor exceptions. First, the child must be under age 17 at the end of the tax year. Second, a dependent child must be a U.S. citizen or a resident of the United States. (8)

**Child support payments** - See *alimony.* (3)

**Child- and dependent-care credit** - Taxpayers who incur expenses for child and dependent care that enable them to be employed are eligible for a nonrefundable credit based on the amount of their expenses and their earned income level. The taxpayer must incur employment-related expenses for the care of qualified individuals. A qualifying individual includes any dependent under the age of 13 or a dependent or a spouse of the taxpayer who is mentally or physically incapacitated. The expenditures qualifying for the credit cannot exceed the earned income of the taxpayer. (8)

**Citators** - Primarily used to determine both the history of a judicial decision and how that decision has been criticized, approved, or otherwise commented upon in other court decisions. The most common citators are RIA's *Federal Tax Citator* and Commerce Clearing House's two-volume set, which is included in its tax service. (16)

**Cited case** - Citators refer to the case being evaluated as the *cited case*, and any cases discussing that case are called the *citing cases.* Cited cases are listed alphabetically, followed by the citing cases and rulings. (16)

**Citing cases** - See *cited case.* (16)

**Citizen or residency test** - See *qualifying child; qualifying relative.* (8)

**Claim-of-right doctrine** - A realization occurs whenever an amount is received without restriction as to its disposition. An item is received without restriction when the receiver has no definitive obligation to repay the amount received. (2)

**Class life** - Both ACRS and MACRS require that assets be categorized in classes. The class life of an asset determines its cost-recovery period. In general, assets have longer class lives under MACRS than the same assets under ACRS. (10)

**Closely held corporation** - For passive loss purposes, a corporation is closely held if five or fewer shareholders own 50% or more of the stock in the corporation during the last half of the tax year. Closely held corporations are allowed to use net passive losses to offset activity income of the business. However, they cannot use passive losses to offset portfolio income. (7, 14)

**Collectibles gain (loss)** - Gains and losses from sales of collectibles that are held for more than 12 months. Collectibles include works of art, rugs, antiques, metals, gems, stamps, coins, and alcoholic beverages. A net collectibles gain is taxed at a maximum rate of 28%. (3)

**Compensatory damage payments** - Monetary compensation paid to a party in litigation for the loss sustained by the party. (4)

**Computer-Assisted Tax Research (CATR)** - Secondary source of tax information in which the computer is used to access a large database containing the full text of virtually all primary and secondary authorities. The major CATR systems are LEXIS and WESTLAW. (16)

**Concept** - A broad principle that provides guidance on the income tax treatment of transactions. (2)

**Conduit entity** - A nontaxable reporting entity, the tax attributes of which (income, deductions, losses, credits) flow through to its owner(s) for tax purposes. (2, 5, 9)

**Construct** - A mechanism that has been developed to implement a concept. (2)

**Constructive ownership rules** - These rules are related to the related party provisions. Some individuals might attempt to reduce their direct ownership in a corporation or a partnership by distributing ownership among family members, other corporations, or partnerships that they control. This effort is stymied by the constructive ownership rules, which state the relationships within which an individual is deemed to indirectly own an interest actually owned by another person or entity. (2)

**Constructive receipt doctrine** - Cash basis taxpayers are deemed to be in receipt of income when it is credited to their accounts or otherwise made unconditionally available to them. Physical possession of income is not required for it to be taxed. (2)

**Continuity of life** - See *corporation.* (13)

**Contributory pension plan** - A pension plan that requires the employee to make a contribution to the plan. The required contribution is usually a percentage (i.e., 50% or 100%) of the employer's contribution or a percentage (i.e., 3% or 5%) of the employee's salary. (15)

**Controlled Foreign Corporation (CFC)** - A controlled foreign corporation is a corporation with operations abroad that is a controlled subsidiary of a U.S. corporation. A CFC is any foreign corporation that is more than 10% owned by U.S. shareholders. (15)

**Convenience** - One of Adam Smith's maxims which indicates that a tax should be levied at the time that it is most convenient for the taxpayer to pay the tax. (1)

**Corporate depreciation recapture** - Corporations must recapture as ordinary income 20% of the difference between the amount that would be ordinary income if the property were classified as Section 1245 property and the amount that would be ordinary income if the property were classified as Section 1250 property. (14)

**Corporate distribution** - A corporate distribution can be in the form of cash or property. The tax treatment of a corporate distribution to a shareholder depends on the type of the distribution (i.e., liquidating or nonliquidating). A nonliquidating distribution is taxable if the amount distributed (referred to as a *dividend*) comes from the corporation's current and/or accumulated earnings. If the amount of the distribution exceeds both current and accumulated earnings and profits, the capital recovery concept dictates that the distribution is a tax-free return of capital to the shareholders. If a shareholder receives a distribution in excess of the basis of the stock (excess capital recovery), the shareholder recognizes a capital gain. With a liquidating distribution, the shareholder recognizes either a capital gain or loss depending on whether the distribution is greater than or less than the shareholder's basis in the stock. (14)

**Corporation** - An artificial entity created under the auspices of state law. As a separate legal entity, a corporation can enter into contracts in its name, own property, be sued for malfeasance, and is required to pay income tax based on its taxable income. Corporations provide limited liability to its owners such that the owner's liability extends only to the amount invested in the entity. The characteristics of free transferability of ownership, continuity of life, *limited liability*, and the characteristic of *centralized management* lend themselves to raising large amounts of money from many sources. *Free transferability of ownership interest* means that a corporate shareholder may sell or buy shares at any time without restriction. *Continuity of life* ensures that the business will not cease to exist, regardless of which shareholders trade their stock. The biggest disadvantage of a corporation is the double taxation of dividends. See *double taxation.* (13)

**Correspondence examinations** - A type of IRS exam consisting of letters sent between the IRS and a taxpayer. (1)

**Cost depletion** - One of the two methods used to compute depletion of natural resources. The cost depletion computation allocates the unrecovered basis over the number of mineral units of the natural resource (useful life of the resource) to which the investment relates. Because an estimate of the remaining recoverable units at the end of each year is used to make the computation, the cost depletion per unit will probably change each tax year. See also *percentage depletion (statutory depletion).* (10)

**Coverdell Education Savings Account (CESA)** - A taxpayer can make a nondeductible contribution of up to $2,000 to a Coverdell Education Savings Account for the benefit of an individual who is not 18 years of age. The total annual contribution to an individual's Education Savings Account is limited to $2,000. The amount an individual can contribute to a Coverdell Education Savings Account is phased out ratably for married taxpayers filing a joint return with adjusted gross income between $190,000 and $220,000 and for all other taxpayers with adjusted gross income between $95,000 and $110,000. The income earned on the assets accumulates tax-free and is never taxed to the beneficiary if the income is used to pay qualified education expenses of the beneficiary. (6)

***Cumulative Bulletin (C.B.)*** - An official publication of the IRS, consolidating material that first was published in the *Internal Revenue Bulletin* in a hard-cover volume (usually semiannual). (16)

# D

**De minimis fringe benefits** - Those items that are too small to permit a reasonable accounting (i.e., free coffee in break room, employee parties, and small holiday gifts). The exclusion is based on administrative convenience. (4)

**Death benefit payments** - A payment made to a deceased employee's beneficiaries. Death benefit payments are taxable. (3)

**Deductions** - Amounts that the tax law specifically allows as subtractions from gross income. (1, 5)

**Deductions for adjusted gross income** - See *adjusted gross income.* (1, 5, 6)

**Deductions from adjusted gross income** - Certain personal expenditures and other specified nonpersonal expenditures are allowed to be deducted by individuals as deductions from AGI. These deductions are commonly referred to as *itemized deductions.* (1, 5, 8)

**Deferral** - An item that does not affect the current period's taxable income but will affect taxable income in some future tax year. (1)

**Deferral method** - Accrual basis taxpayers are allowed to defer prepaid income from advance payments received from services, the sale of goods, the use of intellectual property, the occupancy of space or the use of property if the occupancy or use is ancillary to the provision of services (e.g., advance receipts for hotel rooms), guaranty or warranty contracts ancillary to the preceding items, subscriptions, and membership in an organization. The taxpayer must include the advance payment in gross income in the year of receipt to the extent the advance payment is included in gross receipts for financial accounting purposes. The remaining income from advance payment must be included in gross income in the next tax year (regardless of when it is included for financial accounting purposes). (3)

**Deferred (third-party) exchange** - Allows a transaction to be structured as an exchange when the two parties to an exchange do not have property that they want to exchange directly. The property to be exchanged must be identified within 45 days of the date of the first property transfer. In addition, the exchange must be completed within 180 days of the first property transfer. (12)

**Defined benefit plan** - A pension plan that bases retirement benefits on the number of years an employee has worked and the employee's annual salary. (15)

**Defined contribution plan** - A pension plan in which an employee's pension benefits are based on the total contributions (made by both the employee and employer) to the plan, along with the gains and losses (net of expenses) earned by the assets in the plan. (15)

**Dependent** - To qualify as a dependent, an individual must be either a *qualifying child* or a *qualifying relative* of the taxpayer. (8)

**Depletion** - A tax accounting method used to recover the investment in assets, such as oil or coal, that waste away through extraction. This provides a reasonable allocation of bases to the annual accounting periods benefited by the use of the assets. (10)

**Depreciable basis** - The amount of basis that is subject to depreciation and is the amount used to determine the annual depreciation deduction. The depreciable basis does not change during the asset's tax life unless additional capital expenditures are made in regard to the asset. (10)

**Depreciation** - A tax accounting method used to recover investment in long-lived assets. This provides a reasonable allocation of bases to the annual accounting periods benefited by the use of the assets. Tangible property, used in a trade or business or held for the purpose of investment, with definite useful lives, such as buildings and office equipment, are subject to depreciation. (10)

**Depreciation conventions** - MACRS uses conventions to allocate depreciation to the first and last years. MACRS uses the mid-year, mid-quarter, and mid-month conventions to allocate depreciation in the first and last year of an asset's life. The *mid-year convention* assumes that all property is placed in service and disposed of in the middle of the year. The *mid-quarter convention* assumes that all property is placed in service and disposed of in the middle of the quarter year of acquisition and disposition. The *mid-month convention* is based on the number of months in service, but the months of acquisition and disposition are counted only as half months. (10)

**Depreciation recapture** - Depreciation recapture rules reclassify gains from depreciation as ordinary income. Recapture can be considered as giving back the ordinary deduction that created the gain. Only the gain in excess of the recapture amount is accorded capital gain or Section 1231 treatment. The depreciation recapture rules apply only to gains caused by depreciation; losses are not subject to recapture. (11)

**Direct construction costs** - Costs that are actually incurred to physically construct an asset. Examples of direct costs include materials, labor, supplies, and payments to subcontractors. See *indirect construction costs.* (9)

**Disability payments** - Amounts received as disability payments (sick pay or wage-continuation plans) from an employer-provided health and accident plan are included in gross income. However, the same payments made from a plan purchased by the individual taxpayer are excluded from gross income. (4)

**Discharge of indebtedness** - If a lender forgives all or a portion of the debt of the borrower, the borrower realizes an increase in wealth from the reduction of the liability. The borrower who is relieved of a debt has obtained a claim of right to the amount of debt forgiven. The increase in wealth is generally taxable to the borrower. The tax law provides an exception to the general rule of taxability of a discharge of indebtedness when the borrower is insolvent (liabilities exceed assets), both before and after the forgiveness of the debt, and for discharges of qualified principal residence indebtedness. (4)

**Discriminant Function System (DIF)** - A computer program used by the IRS to select individual tax returns for audit. (1)

**Dividend** - See *corporate distribution* and *stock dividend.* (14)

**Dividends-Received Deduction (DRD)** - Because of the double taxation effect, if one corporation is a shareholder in another corporation, triple taxation results. The dividends-received deduction generally provides only partial relief from triple taxation. The actual amount of the DRD depends upon the percentage of ownership the recipient shareholder holds in the distributing corporation. See also *double taxation.* (14)

**Doctrine** - A construct that has been developed by the courts. (2)

**Document perfection program** - A process whereby the IRS checks virtually all tax returns for mathematical, tax calculation, and clerical errors. (1)

**Dominant motive** - An expense frequently is incurred for both business and personal reasons. To be deductible, the expense must bear a proximate relationship to the income-producing activity. In addition, the primary or dominant motivation for incurring the expense must be the business purpose. (5)

**Donated inventory** - Inventory that a corporation gives to a qualified charity is allowed a deduction greater than the *basis* of the property. (14)

**Double taxation** - Obtaining cash distributions is generally the ultimate objective of corporate owners. Cash is distributed to shareholders via dividends. Dividends are payments of already-taxed earnings of corporations. When shareholders receive dividends, taxation occurs again. The double taxation effect results because the corporation is recognized as a separate taxpaying entity. See also *dividends-received deduction.* (13)

## E

**Early withdrawal** - The withdrawal of assets from a taxpayer's qualified pension plan before the taxpayer reaches age 59½. The penalty for early withdrawal does not apply if the distribution is due to death or disability, or is used to cover medical expenses that exceed 10% of adjusted gross income. In addition, the penalty does not apply if an individual who is at least 55 years old elects to retire early. (15)

**Earned income** - Income derived from labor. The most common forms of earned income are wages, salaries, tips, bonuses, and commissions; income from the active conduct of a trade or business; income from the rendering of services; and income from the performance of illegal activities. (3)

**Earned Income Credit (EIC)** - Provides tax relief to low-income taxpayers. The credit is refundable (paid even if no tax is due). The amount of the credit is dependent on the taxpayer's earned income and phases out after income reaches a predetermined level. Married taxpayers are required to file a joint return to take the EIC. (8)

**Economic performance test** - See *all-events test.* (5)

**Economy** - One of Adam Smith's maxims which indicates that a tax should have minimum compliance and administrative costs. (1)

**Education expense** - A taxpayer may deduct education expenses if it meets either of the following requirements: The education is a requirement—either by law or the taxpayer's employer—for the taxpayer's continued employment, or the education maintains or improves the skills required in the taxpayer's trade or business. (6)

**Educational assistance program** - Up to $5,250 in payments made by an employer to an employee for such costs as tuition and books are excludable if the payments are made from a nondiscriminatory educational assistance program. (4)

**Effective tax rate** - The total federal income tax divided by the taxpayer's economic income (the tax base plus nontaxable income). (1)

**Eligible dividends** - Dividends from a domestic corporation or qualifying foreign corporation are taxed at the long term capital gain rate. (3)

**Employee discount** - To exclude employee discounts from taxation, the discount must be made available to all employees on a nondiscriminatory basis and the goods and/or services provided must be in the same line of business. The excludable discount on goods is limited to the gross profit percentage on the goods purchased. Excludable service discounts are limited to 20%. (4)

**Employer reimbursement plan** - An employer reimbursement plan is an *accountable plan* if employees are required to file an adequate accounting (documentation) of their expenses with their employer and to return excess reimbursements to the employer. If reimbursement equals actual expenses (any excess reimbursement is returned to the employer), the employee does not report the reimbursement. If reimbursement is less than actual expenses, the reimbursement must be included in the employee's gross income and the portion of the expenses reimbursed is deductible for AGI. If the reimbursement is greater than actual expenses, the employee must include the excess reimbursement in gross income. If an employer reimbursement plan is *nonaccountable*, the employee must include the reimbursement (if any) in gross income. No deductions for AGI are allowed. (6)

**Employer's athletic facility** - The value of the use of an employer's athletic facility may be excluded from taxation, provided that the facility is on the employer's premises and substantially all use of the facility is by employees and their families. (4)

**Employer-provided lodging** - For a taxpayer to exclude from taxable income the value of employer-provided lodging, the lodging must be on the employer's premises and must be for the convenience of the employer. In addition, the lodging must be a condition of employment—the employee has no choice but to live in the employer-provided housing. (4)

**Entity concept** - All items of income, deductions, and so on are traced to the tax unit responsible for the item. (2)

**Equality** - One of Adam Smith's maxims which indicates that a tax should be based on the taxpayer's ability to pay the tax. (1)

**Estate tax** - A tax that is paid on the fair market value of the assets of a deceased taxpayer. The tax is paid by the executor of the estate from the assets of the estate. (1)

**Excess contribution** - A contribution made to a qualified pension plan, IRA, Roth IRA, Keogh plan, SEP, or SIMPLE in excess of the maximum allowable contribution. Excess contributions are subject to a 10% penalty. (15)

**Exclusions** - Increases in a taxpayer's wealth and recoveries of the taxpayer's capital investment that Congress has decided should not be subject to income tax. Thus, income exclusions are not counted as gross income. Common income exclusions include inheritances, gifts, and interest on certain municipal bonds. (1)

**Expense** - A current period expenditure that is incurred in order to earn income. Deductions for expenses are limited to those incurred in a trade or business, in an income-producing activity (investment activity), and for certain specifically allowed personal expenses of individuals. (1)

## F

**Family entity** - A tax-planning technique that combines the aspects of the progressive tax rate schedule with the use of the owner's children or relatives to minimize the overall family tax liability. With a family entity, the owner's children or relatives become owners (partners) in the business. Because the income from a family entity flows through to each owner, the net income from the business is taxed at the owner's marginal tax rate. (14)

**Federal reporter, second or third series (F.2d or F.3d)** - *Federal Reporter*, 2d or 3d series. (16)

**Federal supplement (F. Supp.)** - *Federal Supplement.* (16)

**Federal Tax Citator** - Research Institute of America's research source used to determine the history of a judicial decision. (16)

**Field examinations** - A type of IRS exam held at the client's headquarters or other client-office location. (1)

**Filing requirements** - Individuals are generally required to file a return when their gross income exceeds their standard deduction amount. (8)

**Filing status** - All taxpayers must take deductions and pay taxes based on their filing status. Filing status indicates whether a taxpayer is married or unmarried. Married taxpayers may file jointly or separately. To qualify for *married, filing jointly* the taxpayers must be legally married on the last day of the tax year. In the case of a death of a spouse, a *surviving spouse* who has at least one dependent child or stepchild living at home may use the joint return tax rates to compute the tax for the two years after the year the spouse dies. Filing *married, filing separately* is primarily used when a husband and wife cannot agree to file together and are not divorced or legally separated by year end. A *single* taxpayer is a person who is not married on the last day of the tax year and who does not have any dependents to support. To qualify as a *head of household*, an unmarried taxpayer must maintain a home that is the principal residence for more than half of the year for a *qualifying child* or a *qualifying relative.* The taxpayer's parents do not have to live in the taxpayer's home if they meet the dependency tests. The benefit of filing as a head of household is extended to an abandoned spouse. A married person is treated as an *abandoned spouse* if a dependent child lives in the taxpayer's home for more than half of the year and the taxpayer's spouse does not live in the home at any time during the last half of the year. (8)

**Final regulations** - The Treasury Department's official explanation of a related provision in the Internal Revenue Code. Also called a *Treasury regulation.* (16)

**Fiscal year** - A period of 12 months ending on the last day of any month other than December, or a 52- to 53-week taxable year. The 52- to 53-week fiscal year ends on the same day of the week each year. The year must end either the last time a particular day occurs during the month or the day that occurs closest to the end of a particular month. (13)

**Flexible benefits plan** - The employee has an annual amount withheld from his or her salary that is used to pay medical expenses or child-care expenses. Amounts paid into the account by the employee are not included in the employee's gross income, thus the term *salary reduction plan.* These plans allow employees to pay for medical costs and child care with before-tax dollars rather than after-tax dollars. (4)

**Foreign-earned income** - To provide relief from double taxation for U.S. citizens working in foreign countries, the tax law allows individuals two options. First, taxpayers may include the foreign earned income in their taxable income, calculate the U.S. tax on the income, and take a tax credit for any foreign taxes paid. The amount of the allowable *foreign tax credit* is the lesser of the actual foreign taxes paid or the U.S. tax that would have been paid on the foreign earned income. Under the second option, individuals may exclude up to $107,600 in foreign earned income for each full year they work in a foreign country. An individual must be either a bona fide resident of the foreign country or must be present in the foreign country for 330 days in any 12 consecutive months to obtain the foreign earned income exclusion. (4)

## G

**Gain** - The difference between the selling price of an asset and its basis; the result of disposing of the asset. Gains result in income. (1)

**General Business Credit (GBC)** - Limits the amount of tax credits that can be used to reduce an individual's or a corporation's tax liability. The general business credit is limited to a taxpayer's net regular tax liability minus the greater of (1) the taxpayer's tentative alternative minimum tax, or (2) 25% of the taxpayer's net regular tax liability in excess of $25,000. A taxpayer's net regular tax liability is defined as a taxpayer's regular tax liability minus certain credits (e.g., child-care credit, foreign tax credit). (15)

**General Counsel's Memoranda (GCM)** - General counsel's memorandum. (16)

**Gift** - A gift in the statutory sense proceeds from a detached and disinterested generosity that originates from affection, respect, admiration, charity, or like impulses. What controls is the intention with which payment, however voluntary, has been made. A gift is a transfer of property from a donor to a donee that is not a profit-motivated arm's-length transaction. Neither the donor nor the donee recognizes any income or pays income tax on the transfer of gift property. A *gift tax* may be imposed on the donor for the fair market value of the gift at the date of transfer. (4, 7, 9)

**Gift taxes** - See *gift.* (1)

**Goodwill** - In the purchase of a business, goodwill represents the difference between the purchase price and fair market value of the net assets acquired. If purchased after August 9, 1993, goodwill is amortized over 15 years. (9)

**Gross income** - Gross income is income broadly defined, minus income items that are excluded from taxation. Items of gross income are included in the computation of taxable income. Generally, gross income is the starting point for reporting income items on a tax return. (1)

**Gross income test** - See *qualifying relative.* (8)

**Gross sales price** - The price agreed upon by the seller and buyer in a transaction. (11)

**Group term life insurance** - Premiums paid by an employer on the first $50,000 face amount of group term life insurance are excluded from taxation. The exclusion is available only for term insurance that is provided to a group of employees on a nondiscriminatory basis. (4)

**Guaranteed payment** - See *partnership.* (13)

## H

**Head of household** - See *filing status.* (8)

**Health and accident insurance** - Premiums paid by an employer to purchase health and accident insurance coverage for employees (and their dependents) are excluded from the employee's income. (4)

**Health Savings Accounts (HSAs)** - A savings account used to pay medical expenses with pre-tax income. Earnings on an HSA are not taxed. Distributions from an HSA that are used to pay medical expenses are excluded from gross income. To be eligible to establish an HSA, an individual must be covered by a high-deductible health insurance plan. Contributions to an HSA can be made by an employer or the individual establishing the account. Contributions by an employer are excluded from the employee's gross income. Contributions by an individual are deductible for adjusted gross income. (4)

**Hobby** - A taxpayer may engage in an income-earning activity primarily for personal reasons, such as recreation and personal enjoyment, which disqualify it as a trade or business or an investment activity; profitability is a secondary concern. Such an activity is classified as a hobby because it lacks a business purpose. A taxpayer's allowable hobby expenses cannot exceed the gross income from the hobby. Expenses in excess of hobby income are referred to as *hobby losses*, which are not deductible. (5)

**Hobby losses** - See *hobby.* (5)

**Holding period** - The length of time an asset is owned. An asset's holding period normally begins on the day after it is acquired and ends on the day of its disposition. (3, 11)

**Home equity debt** - See *qualified home mortgage interest.* (8)

**Home office deduction** - Taxpayers who operate a trade or business out of their home can claim a deduction for expenses related to its business use. To claim a deduction, strict tests must be satisfied. The exclusive use test states that a specific part of the home must be used exclusively for carrying on a trade or business. The home office area must also be regularly used as the principal place to conduct a trade or business belonging to the taxpayer, or as a place to meet or deal with patients, clients, or customers in the normal course of the trade or business. Employee use must be for the convenience of the employer and required as a condition of employment before any deductions for a home office may be taken. The home office deduction is limited to the income earned from the home office activity after deducting all other business expenses that are unrelated to the use of the home office. (5)

**Horizontal equity** - Exists when two similarly situated taxpayers are taxed the same. (1)

**Hybrid method of accounting** - Allows the taxpayer to account for sales of merchandise and the related cost of goods sold on the accrual basis and to use the cash basis for all other items of income and expense; a mixture of the accrual and cash methods. (3)

## I

**Improvements by a lessee** - A property owner does not have income when a lessee makes improvements to the owner's property or when such improvements revert to the property owner at the termination of the lease. This allows the property owner to defer the gain in value that results from the improvements until the property is sold, at which time the owner will have the wherewithal to pay the tax on the increased value. (4)

**Imputed income** - The three most common forms of imputed income subject to tax are below market-rate loans, payment of expenses by others, and bargain purchases. Most imputed income is not taxed. (3)

**Incentive Stock Option (ISO)** - A stock option that receives favorable tax treatment. A taxpayer is not taxed when the ISO is granted or when the individual exercises it. Rather, upon the sale of the stock, the taxpayer is allowed capital gain treatment on the difference between the sales price of the stock and the price paid for the option (i.e., exercise price). However, this difference is a tax preference item in computing an individual's alternative minimum tax liability. (15)

**Incidence of taxation** - Refers to the entity that is responsible for the payment of tax on the income generated by an entity. Owners of conduit entities pay tax on their share of the entity's income. A corporation pays tax on its taxable income; shareholders are taxed on dividends received from the corporation. (13)

**Indirect construction costs** - General costs of a business not directly related to a construction project but that support the project. Examples include interest on funds to finance the construction, taxes, general administrative costs, and depreciation on equipment used in the project. See also *direct construction costs.* (9)

**Individual Retirement Account (IRA)** - All taxpayers are allowed to contribute up to $6,000 per year of their earned income to an IRA. A husband and wife who both have earned sources of income may each contribute up to the $6,000 limit to separate IRA accounts. An IRA can also be established for a nonworking spouse. However, the total amount paid into the two IRAs cannot exceed $12,000, and no one account can receive more than $6,000. If an individual and spouse are not covered by an employer-sponsored retirement plan, all allowable contributions made to the plan are deductible for adjusted gross income. The IRA deduction is reduced if one taxpayer is covered by an employer-provided retirement plan. (6, 15)

**Information-matching program** - The process whereby the IRS matches information from W-2 and Form 1099s to the amounts reported on a taxpayer's return. (1)

**Inheritance** - The value of property received by inheritance is excluded from taxation. Property held in an estate is subject to the estate tax. Thus, the income tax exclusion for inheritances avoids a double taxation of the property of a deceased taxpayer. (4)

**Inherited property** - Property passing from a dead person to an heir. The general rule for determining the initial basis is the fair market value of the property on the date of death, called the *primary valuation date.* The executor of the estate may elect to use the *alternative valuation date,* which is six months after the date of death. If assets are distributed before the six-month valuation date and the alternative valuation date has been elected, the asset's basis is the fair market value on the date it is distributed. (9)

**Initial basis** - Represents the taxpayer's total investment in an asset on its acquisition date. It is equal to the purchase price of the asset plus any cost incurred to get the asset ready for its intended use (i.e., commissions, legal fees, surveys). (9)

**Installment sale** - Occurs whenever property is sold and at least one payment is received in the tax year subsequent to the year of sale. Taxpayers who are not dealers in the particular type of property must recognize income from the casual sale of property by using the installment method, unless they elect to recognize the entire gain in the year of the sale. The installment method is based on the wherewithal-to-pay concept and recognizes income proportionally as the selling price is received. (3)

**Intangible property** - Property that lacks any physical characteristics and exists only because of economic rights the property possesses. (9, 10)

***Internal Revenue Bulletin* (I.R.B.)** - An official weekly publication of the IRS that includes announcements, Treasury regulations, revenue rulings, revenue procedures, and other information that is of interest to a tax researcher. (16)

**Internal Revenue Code of 1986** - The current statutory source of federal income tax law. (1)

**Interpretive regulation** - Issued under the general authority given to the Treasury Department to provide official interpretations of Internal Revenue Code provisions. (16)

**Investment expenses** - See *business purpose concept.* (5)

**Investment-related losses** - A loss on the sale or other disposition of an investment asset. (7)

**Involuntary conversion** - Occurs when a gain or loss is realized from a transaction that occurs against the taxpayer's will (beyond the control of the taxpayer). Involuntary conversions result when property is destroyed or damaged in a casualty or theft, when a government unit condemns property under its power of eminent domain, or when a foreign government seizes or nationalizes property. Losses on involuntary conversions of business or investment property are always recognized in full. When an involuntary conversion results in a *casualty gain,* the taxpayer may elect to defer the gain if a qualified replacement property is purchased. (12)

**IRS appeals division** - The branch of the IRS that hears administrative appeals following an audit. (1)

**Itemized deduction** - See *deductions from adjusted gross income.* (1, 5)

## J

**Joint return test** - See *qualifying relative.* (8)

## L

**Legal fees** - Fees paid for legal advice are deductible if incurred for a Business Purpose. (6)

**Legislative grace concept** - Any tax relief provided to taxpayers is the result of specific acts of Congress that must be strictly applied and interpreted. All income received is taxable unless a specific provision can be found in the tax law that excludes the income from taxation. Deductions must be approached with the philosophy that nothing is deductible unless a provision in the tax law allows the deduction. (2)

**Legislative regulation** - Issued when Congress specifically delegates authority to the Treasury Department to write specific rules for a designated Code section. Legislative regulations carry a higher level of authority than interpretative regulations. (16)

**Letter rulings** - Private letter rulings and technical advice memoranda are generically referred to as *letter rulings* and, although they are not officially published by the government, they are unofficially made available to the public by many private publishers, such as Commerce Clearing House and Research Institute of America. (16)

**Life insurance proceeds** - Payments from life insurance that are paid upon the death of the insured are generally excluded from income tax, although life insurance proceeds may be included in the dead person's gross estate, which is subject to estate tax. Life insurance proceeds are excluded even if the payments are received in installments, although any earnings included in the installment payments are taxable. (4)

**Lifetime Learning Tax Credit (LLTC)** - The Lifetime Learning Tax Credit (LLTC) provides a 20% credit for up to \$10,000 of qualified higher education expenses. The LLTC is limited to a maximum of \$2,000 (\$10,000 × 20%), regardless of the number of qualifying individuals incurring higher education expenses. The LLTC can be claimed for expenses incurred each year for undergraduate or graduate courses at colleges and universities. To qualify, the individual must be at least a halftime student in a degree program or certificate program. The credit can also be claimed for an individual enrolled in a course(s) that helps the individual acquire or improve his or her job skills. Only tuition and fees paid on behalf of the taxpayer, the taxpayer's spouse, or a dependent of the taxpayer are qualified higher education expenses. The LLTC is phased out ratably for married taxpayers with adjusted gross incomes between \$118,000 and \$138,000 and for all other taxpayers when adjusted gross income is between \$59,000 and \$69,000. (8)

**Like-kind exchange rules** - The exchange of like-kind property. The tax law requires the deferral of the recognition of gain or loss until the property is disposed of, providing cash (or other assets) with which to pay the tax. A gain on a like-kind exchange is recognized to the extent of any boot received (but never more than the realized gain on the exchange). Losses on like-kind exchanges are never recognized, even when boot is received. Nonrecognition of gains and losses on exchanges of like-kind property is mandatory. See also *boot.* (12)

**Like-kind property** - The like-kind exchange rules require that the property being transferred in an exchange be real property used in a trade or business or held as an investment. The property must be of like kind in the taxpayer's hands, not the prior owner's. Real property may be exchanged for any other real property in a like-kind exchange. (12)

**Limited liability** - See *corporation.* (13)

**Limited Liability Company (LLC)** - Combines the corporate characteristic of limited liability with the conduit tax treatment of partnerships. While corporations are created by filing articles of incorporation, LLCs file articles of organization. The entity generally must have two or more members, have an objective to carry on a business, and establish a specific method for dividing the profits and losses from the business. (13)

**Limited Liability Partnership (LLP)** - A general partnership with the added characteristic of limited liability for owners. An LLP permits the usual partnership conduit tax treatment but limits the liabilities of its owners (partners). (13)

**Limited partnership** - A partnership in which at least one partner's liability is limited to the amount of her or his investment in the partnership. This attribute provides a measure of protection for the limited partners' personal assets. To obtain the limited liability attribute, limited partners give up any right to participate in the management of the business. Management is left to at least one general partner whose liability is not limited and who is responsible for the ongoing activities of the business. (7, 13)

**Liquidating distribution** - A distribution of cash or property to the owners of an entity made upon the termination and liquidation of the entity. (14)

**Listed property** - Listed property includes the following categories of property: passenger autos; other property used for transportation such as trucks, trains, buses, or boats; property of a type that is generally used for purposes of entertainment, recreation, or amusement; any computer or peripheral equipment; any cellular telephone or similar communications equipment. The *listed property rules* require taxpayers to substantiate the extent of an asset's business use. If listed property is not used predominantly in a trade or business, the business use portion of the asset must be depreciated using the Alternative Depreciation System (ADS). If more than 50% of an asset's total use for each year of its tax life is related to the taxpayer's trade or business, the asset is treated the same as any other business asset. (10)

**Listed property rules** - See *listed property.* (10)

**Lobbying expenses** - Expenditures made by an individual or business in connection with influencing federal or state legislation is generally not deductible. (5)

**Long-term capital gain (loss)** - A gain (loss) on the sale of a capital asset that is held for more than 12 months. (3)

**Lookback recapture rule** - See *Section 1231 netting procedure.* (11)

**Loss** - Occurs when an asset is disposed of for a selling price that is less than its basis. Such a loss is referred to as a *transaction loss* and represents a loss of capital invested in the asset. An *annual loss* results from an excess of allowable deductions for a tax year over the reported income for the year. (1)

**Loss-of-income damages** - See *compensatory damage payments.* (4)

## M

**Majority-interest tax year** - A partnership is required to use the same tax year as those partners holding a majority interest (more than 50%) in partnership profits and capital. (13)

**Marginal tax rate** - The rate of tax that will be paid on the next dollar of income or the rate of tax that will be saved by the next dollar of deduction. Used in tax planning to determine the effect of reporting additional income or deductions during a tax year. See also *proportional rate structure.* (1)

**Married, filing jointly (separetely)** - See *filing status.* (8)

**Material participant** - See *material participation.* (7)

**Material participation** - Requires that the taxpayer be involved in the operations of the activity on a regular, continuous, and substantial basis. The basic test for material participation is that the individual (including the individual's spouse) participates in the activity for more than 500 hours per year. Six other tests qualify a taxpayer as a material participant based on lower levels of participation. See *passive activity* and *real estate professional exception.* (7)

**Meals provided by the employer** - The value of meals provided an employee free of charge may be excluded from the employee's income if the meals are provided on the employer's business premises and the provision of the meals is for the convenience of the employer. Cash meal allowances are generally taxable because they are not meals provided by the employer. (4)

**Medical expenses** - Individuals are allowed an itemized deduction for their unreimbursed medical costs. To be deductible, medical expenses must be incurred for the diagnosis, cure, mitigation, treatment, or prevention of disease, or they must be incurred for the purpose of affecting a structure or function of the body. Unreimbursed medical costs are only deductible to the extent they exceed 7.5% of AGI. (8)

**Mid-month convention** - See *depreciation convention.* (10)

**Mid-quarter convention** - See *depreciation convention.* (10)

**Mid-year convention** - See *depreciation convention.* (10)

**Minor child** - Congress in 1986 enacted provisions that are designed to eliminate the tax rate advantage that could have been gained under prior law through shifting of unearned forms of income from parents to a minor child. The basic thrust is to tax the net unearned income of a child who has not attained the age of 18 or a full-time student under the age of 24 (minor child) at the parents' marginal rate. (8)

**Mixed-use asset** - See *mixed-use property.* (5)

**Mixed-use expenditures** - Expenses that are incurred for both profit and personal reasons. These expenditures must be allocated between business and personal use and deducted according to the rules for each use. (5)

**Mixed-use property** - A single property may be used in more than one use category. Proper accounting for mixed-use property requires a reasonable allocation of costs between the uses of the property. Also called *mixed-use asset.* (9)

**Modified Accelerated Cost Recovery System (MACRS)** - Applies to tangible property placed in service after 1986.

Congress specified longer recovery periods for depreciable assets that would result in depreciation slower than allowed by ACRS. (10)

**Money purchase plan** - A *defined contribution plan* that requires the company and the employee (if it is a contributory plan) to contribute a fixed percentage of the employee's salary to the pension plan. (15)

**Multiple asset purchase** - When more than one asset is bought for a single price, the cost must be allocated to the individual assets in proportion to their fair market value on the date purchased. An appraisal of the individual assets usually provides a reasonable basis for allocating the purchase price. The buyer and seller can agree, at arm's length, on an allocation of the purchase price. The cost of real estate can also be allocated according to the values assessed for property tax purposes. (9)

**Municipal bond interest** - The tax law provides an exclusion for interest earned on bonds issued by state and local governments (cities, counties, state agencies such as turnpike authorities) of the United States as well as those of U.S. possessions (Guam, Puerto Rico). (4)

# N

**Natural business year** - The annual accounting period encompassing all related income and expenses. An S corporation must generally use a calendar year. However, an alternate year can be used under the *ownership tax year* or the business purpose tax year exceptions. To qualify, an S corporation must have peak and off-peak business periods. The natural business year is the end of the peak business period. An annual accounting period qualifies as a *business purpose tax year* if the gross receipts from sales or services for the final two months of the current year and each of the two preceding years equals or exceeds 25% of the gross receipts for the entire 12-month period. (13)

**Necessary expense** - To be deductible, an expense must be necessary—a reasonable and prudent businessperson would incur the expense in a similar situation. The expense need not be essential to the continued existence of the income-producing activity. (5)

**Net capital loss** - An excess of capital losses over capital gains for a tax year. Individuals are allowed to deduct up to $3,000 of net capital losses as a deduction for adjusted gross income. Any loss in excess of $3,000 is carried forward to the next tax year. (3, 7)

**Net collectibles gains** - An excess of *collectibles gains* over *collectibles losses.* Net collectibles gains are taxed at a maximum rate of 28%. (3, 11)

**Net Operating Loss (NOL)** - An annual loss incurred in a trade or business in which the taxpayer materially participates. It results from an excess of allowable deductions over income for the accounting period. For a taxable entity (i.e., individuals and corporations). With the adoption of the 2017 TCJA, a taxpayer is no longer allowed to carryback an NOL and can only carry forward the loss. While the losses can now be carried forward indefinitely, the new law only allows a taxpayer to offset 80% of the current years' taxable income with the carryforward loss. The new NOL rules are effective for tax years beginning after December 31, 2018, and apply to all corporations except real estate investment trusts and property and casualty companies. (7)

**Net short-term capital gain** - The excess of capital gains over capital losses on assets that have been held for one year or less. (3)

**No-additional-cost services** - A service given to an employee by an employer free of charge. For a no additional cost service to be excluded from taxation, the service must be made available to employees on a nondiscriminatory basis and must also be in the same line of business in which the employee works. (4)

**Non-support test** - See *qualifying child.* (8)

**Nonaccountable plan** - See *employee reimbursement plan.* (6)

**Nonacquiescence** - An announcement by the IRS that it will not follow a court decision that was adverse to the government. (16)

**Nonbusiness bad debts** - See *business bad debt.* (6)

**Noncontributory pension plan** - A pension plan that does not require the employee to make contributions to the plan. However, most of these plans allow the employee to make contributions to the plan. (15)

**Nonliquidating distribution** - A distribution of cash or property made to the owners of a continuing entity. (14)

**Nonqualified pension plan** - A pension plan that does not allow either the employee's or the employer's contribution to the plan to be tax deferred. In addition, the income earned on these contributions is subject to tax. (15)

**Nonqualified Stock Option (NQSO)** - A stock option that allows the employee to acquire the employer's stock at a specified price beginning on a specified date. The tax consequences to the employee depend on whether the stock option has a readily ascertainable fair market value. If it does, the employee recognizes as income an amount equal to the fair market value of the option at the date of grant. If it does not, the employee recognizes income equal to the difference between the fair market value of the stock at the date of exercise and the exercise price. The employer is entitled to a corresponding deduction at the time the employee recognizes income. (15)

**Nonrecognition transactions** - A transaction that is not given current effect. The initial realization is considered part of a continuing investment process. Under the substance-over-form doctrine, the new property acquired in the transaction (i.e., like-kind exchanges and involuntary conversions) is viewed as a continuation of the original investment in the asset. Also, the taxpayer lacks the wherewithal to pay the tax on the realized gain because the amount realized on the transaction is reinvested in the replacement asset. For total deferral of gain, any amounts realized from the disposition must be fully reinvested in a replacement asset. (12)

**Nonrecourse debt** - A liability that is secured only by the underlying property; the borrower is not personally liable for the debt. (7, 13)

**Nonresident alien** - An individual who is a resident of another country and is not a citizen or resident of the United States. (15)

# O

**Office examinations** - A type of IRS exam held at a local IRS office. (1)

**One-year rule for prepaid expenses** - A cash basis taxpayer may deduct prepaid expenses in the year paid if the prepayment does not create an asset that extends substantially beyond the end of the year of payment. The courts have held that a prepayment of an expense that will be used up before the end of the tax year following the year of prepayment can be deducted when paid. The taxpayer must show that the payment is required by the creditor and that the payment does not distort income. Prepaid taxes are deductible in the year paid, even if the prepayment results in a refund in a later year. Prepaid interest is not generally deductible under the one-year rule. (5)

**Ordinary expense** - To be deductible, an expenditure must qualify as an ordinary expense. The expense must be of a kind commonly incurred in the particular income-earning activity. The expense may be said to be customary or usual for the activity. The expenditure must also be assignable to the current accounting period. (5)

**Ordinary income** - Recurring income earned by a taxpayer for a tax year; the type of income that people and businesses expect to earn. Ordinary income typically includes business profits, rent from property, interest on investments, and wages. Ordinary income receives no special treatment under the tax laws. (1)

**Organizational costs** - Because a corporation is a legal entity formed under state law, various expenditures (i.e., legal services, accounting services, and fees paid to the state of incorporation) must be incurred to accomplish the corporate creation. Most of the expenses benefit future periods of the corporation's life. A corporation may elect to deduct up to $5,000 of qualified organizational costs. Any remaining costs are amortized over a period of 180 months. If the election to amortize these expenses is not made on the tax return for the first taxable year, the costs are not deductible until the corporation ceases business and liquidates. (13)

**Original Issue Discount (OID) securities** - A debt instrument for which the interest is paid upon maturity of the debt rather than throughout the term of the debt. (3)

**Ownership tax year** - The tax year of more than 50% of the owners of an S corporation. (13)

# P

**Partnership** - A general partnership is characterized as follows for tax purposes: a partner's liability is not limited; the life of the partnership depends on the life of the partner(s); all partners share in the partnership management; partnership interests are not freely transferable. Although partnerships are considered conduits for the purpose of income taxation, they are treated as separate entities under local law. Partnerships can transact business and own property in their own names, separate from the partners. (13)

**Partnership debt** - Initial basis in a partnership begins with a person's contribution of assets or services in exchange for a capital interest. Basis is increased by a partner's share of partnership liabilities. Partnership debt assumed by a partner and the partner's share of partnership debt are deemed to be additional cash contributions by the partner to the partnership. Decreases in partnership debt are deemed cash distributions to the partner and reduce the partner's basis in the partnership. (13)

**Partnership distribution** - A partner's receipt of a cash or property distribution from a partnership is generally tax free. No gain is recognized (capital recovery concept) until after the basis in the capital investment is recovered. Any excess of cash (or the basis of property) over the basis in a partner's interest is a recognizable gain for the partner who receives it. (14)

**Passenger automobile limitation** - The annual amount of deductible depreciation for a passenger automobile is first limited by its business percentage. This amount is further limited by an annual maximum depreciation deduction. (10)

**Passive activity** - The conduct of any trade or business in which the taxpayer does not materially participate. Limited partnership interests are always passive. Rental activities are generally passive unless the real estate professional exception applies. Working interests in oil and gas deposits and certain low-income housing projects are always active and not subject to the passive loss rules. See *real estate professional exception.* (7)

**Passive Activity Loss (PAL) rules** - The purpose of the passive activity rules is to deny current loss deductions for tax shelter activities. The general rule is that passive losses may only be deducted to the extent of passive income, not against income from portfolio or active income. Any passive activity loss that is not deductible in the current year is suspended. A *suspended loss* is not permanently disallowed but is carried forward and may be deducted against passive income in subsequent years. Deductions of suspended losses are allowed when passive activities are disposed of by sale and because of death. Gifts of passive activities do not result in deduction of suspended losses from the activity. (7)

**Pay-as-you-go concept** - A tax should be collected as close as possible to the time in which the income is earned. (1, 2)

**Percentage depletion** - One of two methods used to compute depletion of natural resources. Percentage depletion is calculated by multiplying gross income from the sale of the natural resource by a statutory percentage. The statutory percentage is the depletion rate specified by the tax law. The maximum allowable percentage depletion deduction for the tax year is 50% of the taxable income from the natural resource before subtracting the depletion deduction. See also *cost depletion.* (10)

**Percentage-of-completed-contract method** - For taxpayers who meet the $26 million gross receipts test and enter into a contract after December 31, 2019, for the construction or improvement of real property are not required to use the percentage of completion method if the work will be completed within two years after date construction begins. Otherwise, long-term construction contracts must be accounted for by using the percentage-of-completed contract method. Income is recognized according to the amount of work completed on the contract each year. The work completed must be based on costs incurred during the year in relation to the estimated total costs of the project. (3)

**Personal casualty losses** - The only personal use loss that the tax law allows as a deduction (itemized) is for losses from casualty incurred in a federal disaster area. Personal casualty losses are always measured as the lower of the decline in the value of the property or the basis of the property. The amount of loss must be reduced by any insurance proceeds received. Personal use casualty losses are also reduced by a $100 *statutory floor* amount per occurrence. An *annual personal casualty loss limitation* is imposed that limits total personal casualty loss deductions for the year to the extent that they exceed 10% of the taxpayer's adjusted gross income. The loss increases the taxpayers' itemized deductions or their standard deduction. (7)

**Personal expense** - Expenses that are personal in nature and are neither trade or business expenses nor production of income expenses. (2)

**Personal physical injury** - See *compensatory damage payments.* (4)

**Personal property** - Any tangible property that is not real property. Personal property includes machines, equipment, furniture, computers, and autos. (1, 9)

**Personal use property** - Any property that is used by the taxpayer for purely personal purposes. *Personal use* applies to personal property, real property, and intangible property. (9)

**Points** - Points are prepaid interest amounts that are required to acquire financing. They are expressed as a percentage of the value of the loan and paid at loan acquisition. They represent prepaid interest, which usually is capitalized and amortized over the term of the loan. In the year the points are paid, the tax law allows a deduction for points paid to acquire an initial mortgage on a taxpayer's principal residence. Points paid to refinance an existing mortgage must be capitalized and amortized as interest expense over the term of the loan. (8)

**Portfolio income** - Consists of unearned income from dividends, interest, royalties, annuities, and other assets held as investments. In portfolio activities, the investor only receives income from the activity and does not share in the expenses related to the activity. Any losses on portfolio income generally occur at the point of sale of the asset producing the income. (7)

**Primary authorities** - The legislative, administrative, and/or judicial sources. The legislative authorities include the Constitution, tax treaties, and law enacted by Congress. The administrative authorities are the official interpretations of the law prepared by the Treasury Department and the Internal Revenue Service. Decisions by the various trial and appellate courts represent the judicial authorities. (16)

**Primary valuation date** - See *inherited property.* (9)

**Principal partner tax year** - When the majority interest partners do not have the same tax year, the partnership must use the tax year of its principal partners. Principal partners are partners with at least a 5% interest. (13)

**Principal residence** - The place where the taxpayer lives most of the time. A taxpayer can have only one principal residence at a time. A principal residence can be a house, mobile home, cooperative apartment, condominium, or a houseboat. (12)

**Principal residence test** - See *qualifying child.* (8)

**Private Letter Ruling (LTR)** - Issued by the National Office of the IRS in response to specific questions raised by taxpayers and typically deal with prospective transactions. An LTR applies only to the taxpayer requesting the ruling and does not bind the IRS to take the same position when dealing with a different taxpayer. (16)

**Production-of-income expenses** - Expenses that related to either investment activities or related to the determination, collection, or payment of taxes. (2, 5)

**Profit-sharing plan** - A *defined contribution plan* that does not require a fixed annual contribution. The plan must specify a formula for allocating the contributions among each of the plan's participants, and a separate account must be maintained for each employee. (15)

**Progressive rate structure** - A tax in which the average tax rate increases as the tax base increases. The marginal tax rate will be higher than the average tax rate as the tax base increases. The average tax rate, the marginal tax rate, and total tax all increase with increases in the tax base. (1)

**Property** - Any long-lived asset that is owned by a taxpayer. The terms *asset* and *property* are used interchangeably to mean anything owned or possessed by a taxpayer. Property is classified by both its use and its type for tax purposes. The use of property determines whether deductions are allowed for current-year expenditures made in relation to the property and for capital recovery deductions for depreciation, depletion, or amortization. To take any deductions relating to property, there must be a business purpose (used in a trade or business or held for the production of income) for the property. All property is either tangible or intangible property. The type of property does not change from taxpayer to taxpayer. (9)

**Property disposition** - See *amount realized.* (9)

**Property settlement** - See *alimony.* (3)

**Proportional rate structure** - A tax for which the average tax rate remains the same as the tax base increases (also referred to as a *flat tax*). The marginal tax rate and the average tax rate are the same at all levels of the tax base. As the tax base increases, the total tax paid will increase at a constant rate. Examples include sales taxes, real estate and personal property taxes, and certain excise taxes, such as the tax on gasoline. (1)

**Proposed regulations** - Issued to let the public know what the IRS believes is the proper interpretation of a related Code provision and to provide an opportunity for the public to comment before a regulation is issued in final form. (16)

**Protest letter** - A written response by the taxpayer to the IRS agent's findings at the end of an audit. (1)

**Punitive damages** - See *damage payments.* (4)

## Q

**Qualified Business Income (QBI)** - The deduction is based on the taxpayer's Qualified Business Income (QBI), which is defined as the net income from the pass-through business after all business deductions and before any salaries to S corporation owners, and guaranteed payments allocated to partners in a partnership. Regardless of the type of pass-through business in which a taxpayer is engaged, when the taxpayer's taxable income is less than $163,300 (if single) or $326,600 (if married) the calculation of the QBI deduction is straightforward. The taxpayer's QBI deduction is the lesser of (1) 20% of their QBI or (2) 20% of their taxable income not including capital gains but before the QBI deduction. (6)

**Qualified education loan** - A loan used to pay tuition, fees, room and board, and other necessary higher education expenses of the taxpayer, the taxpayer's spouse, or a dependent of the taxpayer. The interest paid on the loan is a deduction for adjusted gross income. The maximum amount of interest that can be deducted is $2,500. (6)

**Qualified home mortgage interest** - Only interest on debt that is secured by the taxpayer's principal residence and one other residence is deductible. Qualified home mortgage interest includes both acquisition debt and home equity debt. *Acquisition debt* is any debt incurred to acquire, construct, or substantially improve a qualified residence of the taxpayer. *Home equity debt* is any debt that is secured by a personal residence and is used to improve the residence. Interest paid on up to $750,000 of acquisition debt is deductible. Interest on debt in excess of $750,000 is considered personal interest and is not deductible. (8)

**Qualified pension plan** - Payments made by an employer to an employee's account in a qualified pension plan are not taxable in the period in which the payments are made. The tax on such payments is deferred until the employee actually withdraws the payments from the plan. Earnings on amounts paid into such plans are not taxed until they are withdrawn by the employee. (4, 15)

**Qualified retirement planning services** - Employees can exclude the value of qualified retirement planning services provided by an employer. To be excluded, the services must consist of retirement planning advice or information provided to employees and their spouses by an employer who maintains a qualified employee retirement plan, and must be available on substantially the same terms to all members of the group who normally receive information and education about the plan. (4)

**Qualified small business stock** - Stock originally issued after February 17, 2009, by a corporation that did not have assets in excess of $50 million after September 27, 2010, and before the stock issuance. The stock must be purchased at its original issuance. If the stock is held for more than five years, 75% of the gain on the sale of the stock is excluded from income. If the stock is acquired after September 27, 2010, the exclusion is increased to 100%. The remaining gain is taxed at a maximum rate of 28%. (11)

**Qualifying child** - A child must meet five tests to be a qualifying child. The *relationship test* requires the child to be the taxpayer's son, daughter, stepson, stepdaughter, eligible foster child, or descendant of such a child, or a brother, sister, stepbrother, stepsister, or any decedent of any such relative. The *age test* requires the child to be under the age of 19 (under 24 if a full-time student). The *citizen* or *residency* test requires the child to be a citizen or resident of the United States, or a resident of Canada or Mexico. The *principal residence test* requires the child to have the same principal residence as the taxpayer for more than half of the year. The *non-support test* requires that the child must not have provided more than half of his or her own support. (8)

**Qualifying relative** - A qualifying relative must meet five tests. The *gross income test* requires the gross income of the individual to be less than $4,300 in 2020. The *support test* requires that the taxpayer treating the individual as a dependent provide more than one-half the support of the relative. The *relationship or member of household test* requires the dependent to be either a relative or a member of the taxpayer's household for the entire year. The *citizen or residency test* requires a dependent to be a citizen or resident of the United States, or a resident of Canada or Mexico. Under the *joint return test*, a dependent may not file a joint return with his or her spouse unless they would not be required to a file a tax return but file a return solely for the purpose of obtaining a refund. (8)

## R

**Real estate** - See *real property*. (9)

**Real estate professional exception** - Rental activities of taxpayers meeting this exception are not passive activities. To qualify for this exception, the taxpayer must materially participate in the rental activity, more than 50% of the taxpayer's total personal service time must be devoted to real property trades or businesses in which the taxpayer materially participates, and more than 750 hours of personal service time must be performed in real property trades or businesses in which the taxpayer materially participates. (7)

**Real property** - In general, real property is land and any structures that are permanently attached to land, such as buildings. (1, 9)

**Real property trade or business** - A trade or business involving the development, redevelopment, construction, acquisition, conversion, rental operation, management, leasing, or brokerage of real property. (7)

**Realization concept** - No income or loss is recognized for tax purposes (is included in taxable income) until it has been realized by the taxpayer. In most cases, a realization occurs when an arm's-length transaction takes place. A realization involves a change in the form and/or the substance of a taxpayer's property rights that results from an arm's-length transaction. (2)

**Realized gain (loss)** - See *amount realized*. (9)

**Reasonable compensation** - Employee compensation is subject to two basic tests for deductibility. First, payments must be for services actually performed by the employee. Second, the total payment for services of the employee must be reasonable in amount. When the compensation paid to an employee is found to be excessive, only a reasonable salary deduction is allowed. Whether compensation paid an employee is reasonable is decided by considering several factors, including (1) the employee's duties, responsibilities, and pay history; (2) the volume and complexity of the business; (3) the time required to do the work; (4) the ability and accomplishments of the employee; (5) the general cost of living and the company pay policy; (6) the relationship of the compensation, the gross and the net income of the business, and dividends paid to shareholders. Reasonable compensation issues generally arise in connection with related parties. (6)

**Reasonable expenses** - To be deductible, an expense must be reasonable in amount. The reasonableness test most often becomes an issue in transactions involving related parties. (5)

**Recognized gain (loss)** - To recognize a gain or loss means to include the amount of the gain or loss in the current year's taxable income calculation. (11)

**Recourse debt** - A loan for which the debtor remains liable until the debt is repaid. If the borrower defaults on the loan, the lender may obtain a judgment against the borrower who must make up the amount of the default. See *partnership debt.* (13)

**Refundable tax credit** - The taxpayer is entitled to a refund of any excess credit. This is a form of negative income tax. The taxpayer not only pays no tax but receives a payment from the government that is based on the taxpayer's income. (8)

**Regressive rate structure** - A tax in which the average tax rate decreases as the tax base increases. The marginal tax rate will be less than the average tax rate as the tax base increases. Although the average tax rate and the marginal tax rate both decrease as the tax base increases, the total tax paid will increase. (1)

**Rehabilitation tax credits** - To provide incentive for businesses to rehabilitate older buildings, rehabilitation expenditures incurred on a certified historic structure are granted a 20% tax credit. The basis of the building or structure must be reduced by the amount of credit taken. To retain the full benefit of the tax credit, the property must be held for five full years. (15)

**Related party** - Family members and corporations that are owned by family members are considered related parties, as are certain other relationships between entities in which the power to control the substance of a transaction is evidenced through majority ownership. (5, 6, 7)

**Related party provisions** - A series of tax law provisions defining relationships that are not deemed to transact at Arms-length. See *Arms-length transaction concept.* (2)

**Relationship test** - See *qualifying relative.* (8)

**Relationship, or member of household, test** - See *qualifying relative.* (8)

**Rental activity** - A payment received primarily for the use of tangible property. Rental activities are generally considered passive activities, unless the real estate exception applies. Rental activities that also provide significant services (i.e., hotel rooms, car rentals, hospital rooms, and golf course fees) are exempt from the passive loss rules as long as the owner(s) of such activities meet the material participation standard. The most common forms of passive activity rentals involve the rental of real property (i.e., apartment buildings, rental houses, office building rentals, warehouse rentals, factory rentals). (7)

**Repair-and-maintenance expense** - Expenditures on an asset that do not appreciably extend the asset's useful life or materially add to its value. (5)

**Replacement** - Expenditures on an asset that appreciably extend the asset's useful life. (5)

**Reporter** - A series of books published by the federal government or by a private publishing company that provides the full text of court decisions. Different reporters are cited for each court that renders a decision. (16)

**Reports of the United States Tax Court (T.C.)** - The official government reporter for regular decisions of the U.S. Tax Court. (16)

**Required Minimum Distribution (RMD)** - The amount required to be withdrawn in a specific year from qualified pension plans, Keoghs, and IRAs by taxpayers who reach age $70\frac{1}{2}$ in that year. (15)

**Research and Experimental (R&E) tax credit** - Encourages research and development of new technologies and processes. The incremental credit is equal to 20% of the qualified research expenditures in the current year in excess of the base amount. The basic research credit is equal to 20% of qualified expenditures for research that is intended to advance scientific knowledge without a specific commercial objective. The payments must be made in cash under written agreement, and the research must be performed or controlled by a university, college, or other nonprofit scientific research organization. (15)

**Resident alien** - An individual who is not a citizen of the United States but has established a legal residence in the United States. (15)

**Revenue procedures** - Issued to explain internal IRS administrative practices and procedures. (16)

**Revenue rulings** - Interpretation by the IRS of the Code and regulations as they apply to specific factual situations. A revenue ruling represents official policy of the IRS. (16)

**Roth IRA** - Taxpayers are allowed to make a $6,000 nondeductible contribution to a Roth IRA. Total contributions made to all IRA accounts cannot exceed $6,000 per taxpayer. For an unmarried taxpayer, the amount that can be contributed to a Roth IRA is phased out ratably when adjusted gross income exceeds $124,000. No contribution is allowed when adjusted gross income exceeds $139,000. For married taxpayers, the amount of the contribution is phased out when adjusted gross income exceeds $196,000 and is fully phased out when adjusted gross income exceeds $206,000. The major advantage of a Roth IRA over a conventional nondeductible IRA is that qualified distributions from a Roth IRA, including the income earned on the IRA assets, are not included in the taxpayer's gross income. (6, 15)

## S

**S corporation** - A corporation that elects to be taxed as a conduit entity. An S corporation retains the nontax characteristics of a corporation, while allowing the income of the corporation to be taxed to the shareholders. See *corporation.* (13)

**Salary reduction plan** - See *flexible benefits plan.* (4)

**Savings bonds** - Savings bonds issued by the U.S. government. (3)

**Savings Incentive Match Plan for Employees (SIMPLE)** - A retirement plan designed to encourage small businesses (fewer than 100 employees) to establish a qualified pension plan. An employer can choose to establish either a SIMPLE-IRA or a SIMPLE-401(k). Under either a SIMPLE-IRA or a SIMPLE-401(k), eligible employees can choose to have a percentage of their salary, up to a maximum of $13,500, contributed to the plan. The employer's contribution must be made using one of the following funding formulas. (1) Match an employee's contribution up to a maximum of 3% of the employee's compensation. In a SIMPLE-IRA, the employer can elect to match a lower percentage but no less than 1% of each employee's compensation. Within a five-year period, the employer can twice elect to contribute less than 3% of each employee's compensation. (2) Contribute 2% of an employee's compensation. Under this option employees do not have to contribute to the plan but can elect to make a contribution. The employer's contribution of 2% of an employee's compensation is mandatory, even if the employee does not contribute. (15)

**Scholarship** - A college student who is a candidate for a degree may exclude the value of the scholarship, provided that the award does not require the student to perform any future services such as teaching, grading papers, or tutoring. The scholarship must be gratuitous in nature and not merely a form of compensation for past, present, or future services. The amount of the exclusion is limited to the direct costs of the student's college education. Direct costs consist of the student's tuition, fees, books, supplies, and other equipment required in the course of instruction. Amounts received in excess of the direct costs of the education are taxable. (4)

**Secondary authorities** - Serves primarily as a tool in locating the relevant primary authority and a source for better understanding, interpretation, and application of primary authorities. Secondary authorities include all statements, pronouncements, explanations, or interpretations of the law that are not primary and consist chiefly of tax services, citators, computer software systems that research tax databases, and tax journals and newsletters. (16)

**Section 1231 gain (loss)** - Results from the sale or other disposition of a Section 1231 property. (11)

**Section 1231 netting procedure** - Tax treatments accorded Section 1231 assets apply to the net gain or loss on all Section 1231 transactions occurring during a tax year. The Section 1231 netting procedure nets together all casualty (theft) gains and losses on Section 1231 assets to produce a single net casualty gain or loss for the year. If the result is a loss, all casualty gains and losses for the year are considered ordinary losses. If the result of the netting is a gain, the net casualty gain is netted together with all other Section 1231 gains and losses occurring during the year. If the result is a loss, all gains and losses for the year are considered ordinary. When the result is a gain, another netting must take place (*lookback recapture rule*). This nets the current year net Section 1231 gain against any Section 1231 ordinary loss deductions taken in the previous five years. (11)

**Section 1231 property** - Property held for more than twelve months that is used in a trade or business; timber, coal, and domestic iron ore; livestock that is held for more than one year and horses that are held for more than two years; and unharvested crops. (11)

**Section 1245 property** - All depreciable tangible personal property is Section 1245 property (i.e., autos, trucks, equipment, machinery, computers, patents, copyrights, leaseholds, and livestock). Certain real property depreciated using ACRS is classified as Section 1245 property. (11)

**Section 1245 recapture rule** - Section 1245 assets are subject to a full recapture of all depreciation taken as ordinary income. No capital gain or Section 1231 treatment results from the sale of a Section 1245 asset unless it is sold for more than its original cost. (11)

**Section 1250 property** - In general, depreciable real property is Section 1250 property (i.e., office buildings, apartment buildings, warehouses, factory buildings, and low-income housing). However, certain real property depreciated using ACRS is also classified as Section 1245 property. (11)

**Section 1250 recapture rule** - Under Section 1250, only gains that are attributable to excess depreciation are recaptured as ordinary income. *Excess depreciation* is defined as the total depreciation taken to date, less the allowable straight-line depreciation on the asset. (11)

**Section 179** - Under this provision, taxpayers are allowed to expense up to $1,040,000 (2020) of the cost of tangible personal property used in a trade or business. Amounts expensed under this provision reduce the depreciable basis of the property. The amount of the annual deduction limit is reduced when purchases of qualifying property exceed $2,590,000 in 2020. In addition, the deductible amount cannot exceed the taxable income from the active conduct of all the taxpayer's trade or business activities. (10)

**Securities dealer** - A person who transacts in securities may be an active investor, an active trader, or a dealer in securities. Unlike active traders and dealers, active investors are not considered to be in a trade or business. A securities dealer purchases a security expecting to realize a profit from selling it to a customer for a fee or commission. An *active investor* is a person who continuously, regularly, and extensively manages his or her own portfolio with a view toward long-term appreciation in the portfolio's value and not short-term profit. An active investor's expenses are deductible only as miscellaneous itemized deductions. An *active trader* earns a livelihood buying and selling securities for personal profit. The active trader's expenses are deductible for adjusted gross income. (5)

**Self-employment tax** - Self-employed individuals pay a Social Security tax equal to the sum of the employer's and employee's payments (15.3%). Because employees are not taxed on the Social Security contribution made on their behalf by their employers, self-employed taxpayers are allowed to deduct one-half of their self-employment tax as a business expense to equalize the tax treatments of employees and the self-employed. (1, 6, 13)

**Self-insured medical plan** - A plan established by a company that chooses to self-insure by making payments to a fund that is used to pay employees' medical expenses. The payments are excluded from employees' income. However, if a self-insured medical plan discriminates in favor of highly compensated employees, the amounts paid for medical expenses of a highly compensated employee covered by the plan are included in the individual's taxable income. (4)

**Short-term capital gain (loss)** - A gain (loss) on the sale on a capital asset that is held for 12 months or less. (3)

**Simplified Employee Pension Plan (SEP)** - A pension plan that can be established by any organizational form. The major advantage of a SEP is that it is administratively more convenient and economical than other qualified pension plans. Contributions to the plan are made to an IRA owned by the employee. A SEP must cover all employees who (1) are at least

21 years of age, (2) have performed services for the business during the year and at least three of the previous five years, and (3) have received at least $600 (2020) in compensation. (15)

**Single** - See *filing status.* (8)

**Small business stock** - The tax law provides an exception to the $3,000 annual capital loss deduction limitation on losses incurred on qualifying small business stock. This allows an individual taxpayer to deduct up to $50,000 in losses on small business stock per year or $100,000 for a married couple filing a joint return. The stock must be purchased directly from the corporation at original issue. The corporation must satisfy several other requirements, the most important of which is that the contributed capital of the corporation at the time the stock is issued must be less than $1,000,000. See *qualified small business stock.* (7)

**Social security taxes** - Under the Federal Insurance Contribution Act (FICA), a tax is levied on wages and salaries earned. Social Security taxes are matched by employers. Employees are not taxed on the Social Security contribution made on their behalf by their employers. In 2020, a tax of 6.2% is levied on the first $137,700 of wages for Old Age, Survivors, and Disability Insurance (OASDI). A tax of 1.45% on all wages and salaries pays for Medical Health Insurance (MHI). (1)

**Sole proprietorship** - A business that is owned by one person. A sole proprietorship is not an entity separate and apart from its owner. The owner of the business is responsible for the payment of tax on the income of a sole proprietorship. (13)

**Special audit programs** - A method of audit selection that involves a combination of computer and manual selection based on a set of standards. (1)

**Specific charge-off method** - Bad debts are deductible when the taxpayer determines that a particular debt is no longer collectible. *Business bad debts* are deductible in the accounting period in which the facts known to the taxpayer indicate that the account is fully or partially uncollectible. *Nonbusiness bad debts* are not deductible until the accounting period in which the actual amount of worthlessness of the debt is known to the taxpayer. (6)

**Split basis rule for gifts** - If the fair market of the gift property at the date of the gift is less than the donor's basis, the property has one basis for determining gains and a separate basis for determining losses on dispositions (split basis). The basis for determining gains is the donor's adjusted basis. The basis for determining losses is the fair market value on the date of the gift. This effectively eliminates the transfer of unrealized losses from one taxpayer to another by gift. (9)

**Split basis rules for business property** - When property held for personal use is changed to property held for a business purpose, the split basis rules apply. If the fair market value of personal use property is more than its adjusted basis on the date business use begins, the asset's adjusted basis is used to compute depreciation and gain or loss on its disposition. If the fair market value of personal use property is less than its adjusted basis on the date it is changed to a business use, the initial basis for gain is the property's adjusted basis on the conversion date and the initial basis for loss and depreciation is the property's fair market value on the conversion date. If the property is later sold for an amount that falls between the adjusted basis for gain and the adjusted basis for loss, the adjusted basis for the sale is the sales price. (9)

**Standard deduction** - An amount that Congress allows all taxpayers to deduct, regardless of their actual qualifying itemized deductions. Thus, taxpayers itemize their deductions only if their total allowable itemized deductions exceed the standard deduction. (1, 8)

**Standard mileage rate method** - See *auto expense.* (6)

**Start-up costs** - Start-up costs are related to investigating and creating a new active trade or business. Start-up costs are the expenses incurred before the new business begins its activities. Start-up costs include surveys and analyses of markets, facilities, and labor force; travel to develop the business and locate potential customers and suppliers; advertising the new business; salaries to train employees; salaries for executives and consultants; and various other expenses such as legal and accounting fees. (5, 13)

**Statute of limitations** - The time period within which the IRS or the taxpayer must assert that a tax return is not correct. The general statute of limitations period is three years from the due date of the return. Several exceptions extend the statute of limitations beyond the general 3-year period. (1)

**Statutory floor** - See *personal casualty loss.* (7)

**Stock dividend** - A dividend in cash or other property distributed to a shareholder generally is taxable as income to the shareholders. Also, the distributing corporation may not take a deduction for the amount of dividends distributed for tax purposes. But the receipt of a stock dividend does not constitute a realization of income. The value of a shareholder's interest does not change; it is merely spread over more ownership units. However, if the recipient of the stock dividend has the option to receive cash in lieu of stock, the dividend is taxed as if the cash option had been selected. In this case, the shares of the stock are deemed to have a cash equivalent and thus are taxable. (4, 9)

**Stock option** - A right to buy a share of stock at a fixed price (referred to as the exercise price) within a specified period of time. (15)

**Subpart F income** - Income of a controlled foreign corporation that is taxed to the parent when it is earned rather than when it is paid as a dividend. Subpart F income includes interest, dividends, royalties, insurance income, and foreign base company income. (15)

**Substance-over-form doctrine** - Transactions are to be taxed according to their true intention rather than some form that may have been contrived. (2)

**Substantial risk of forfeiture** - Exists when an employee is required to meet certain conditions or requirements before being eligible to receive a stock option. (15)

**Substantiation requirements** - Entertainment, auto, travel, and gift expenses are subject to strict documentation requirements. The tax law requires the taxpayer to keep records that show the amount of the expense; the time and place of travel or entertainment or date and description of a gift; the business purpose of the travel, entertainment, or gift; and the business relationship to the person entertained or receiving the gift. Failure to keep the records necessary to substantiate an expense can result in loss of the deduction. (6)

**Support test** - See *dependent.* (8)

**Supreme Court Reports (S.Ct.)** - West Publishing's reporter for decisions of the U.S. Supreme Court. (16)

**Surviving spouse** - See *filing status.* (8)

**Suspended loss** - See *passive activity loss rules.* (7)

## T

**Tangible property** - Any property that has a physical existence (form, shape, and substance). (9)

**Tax avoidance** - The use of legal methods allowed by the tax law to minimize a tax liability. Tax avoidance generally involves planning an intended transaction to obtain a specific tax treatment. (1)

**Tax base** - The value that is subject to tax. See also *proportional rate structure.* (1)

**Tax benefit rule** - Any deduction taken in a prior year that is recovered in a subsequent year is reported as income in the year it is recovered, to the extent that a tax benefit is received from the deduction. The tax benefit received is the amount by which taxable income was actually reduced by the deduction recovered. (2)

**Tax court memorandum decisions** - All decisions that are not Tax Court regular decisions. They are published by Research Institute of America (RIA) in *T.C. Memorandum Decisions* (T.C. Memo) and by Commerce Clearing House (CCH) under the title *Tax Court Memorandum Decisions* (TCM). (16)

**Tax court regular decisions** - Presumed to have value as precedents or involve issues that have not previously been considered. Regular decisions are generally regarded as having stronger authority than memorandum decisions. Published by the government in a reporter called *Reports of the United States Tax Court* (T.C.). (16)

**Tax credit** - A direct reduction in the income tax liability. In effect, tax credits are treated like tax prepayments. (1, 8, 15)

**Tax evasion** - Occurs when a taxpayer uses fraudulent methods or deceptive behavior to hide the actual tax liability. Tax evasion usually involves three elements: a willfulness on the part of the taxpayer, an underpayment of tax, and an affirmative act by the taxpayer to evade the tax. (1)

**Tax home** - See *travel expenses.* (6)

**Tax services** - A type of secondary authority that principally serves as a tool in locating the primary authorities related to various factual circumstances. One category of tax services consists of very limited editorial discussion and numerous brief interpretations and citations to the primary authorities other than the Code and regulations, which are provided in full text [e.g., *Standard Federal Tax Reporter* (CCH) and *United States Tax Reporter* (RIA)]. The other category of tax services contains extensive editorial discussion and interpretation of the law with citations to the primary authorities provided in footnotes [e.g., *Federal Tax Coordinator Second* (RIA), *Tax Management Portfolios* (Bureau of National Affairs), and *Mertens Law of Federal Income Taxation* (Callaghan and Co.)]. (16)

**Tax shelter** - Any investment activity that is designed to minimize the effect of the income tax on wealth accumulation. The term is generally applied to investments that produce significant tax losses as a result of the allowable deductions associated with the investment. The losses are then used to offset (shelter) taxable income from other income sources. Eventually, the taxpayer investing in such a shelter will have to pay a tax on the investment when it is sold. However, the deduction of losses from the shelter in tax years prior to the payment of tax on the gain presents a time value of money savings opportunity. (7)

**Tax treaty** - An agreement between two countries that explains how a citizen or corporation of one country is taxed when working or conducting business in the other country. The primary objective of a tax treaty is to prevent income from being taxed in both countries (i.e., double taxation). Tax treaties also promote cooperation among taxing countries in complying with the tax laws of the treaty nations. (15)

**Taxable entity** - Entities that are liable for the payment of tax. The four entities responsible for the payment of income tax are individuals, regular (or C) corporations, estates, and some trusts. (2)

**Taxable income** - The tax base for the federal income tax. The difference between the total income of a taxpayer and the deductions allowed that taxpayer. (1)

**Taxable year** - The period for which an entity reports its taxable income. (13)

**Taxes** - Itemized deductions are allowed for amounts paid in for state and local income taxes, real estate taxes, and other personal property taxes. State sales taxes may be deducted in lieu of state income taxes. To be deductible, personal property taxes must be ad valorem (based on the value of the property being taxed). (8)

**Taxpayer Compliance Measurement Program (TCMP)** - An IRS program that randomly selects returns from every income level and are then subjected to a comprehensive audit. The results are then used to refine the *Discriminant Function System (DIF).* (1)

**Technical Advice Memorandum (TAM)** - A private letter ruling on a completed transaction. A TAM is a request for assistance by the local office of the IRS and typically arises during an ongoing audit. The TAM is issued by the National Office of the IRS and is not binding on the IRS. (16)

**Technical Memoranda (TM)** - Memoranda issued by the Treasury Department to explain Treasury Regulations. (16)

**Temporary regulations** - Issued to provide taxpayers with guidance until a final regulation is issued. All temporary regulations must be issued as proposed regulations; the regulation expires if not amended or issued as a final regulation within three years. (16)

**Theft** - Similar to a casualty in that it must be sudden and unexpected. A theft may occur as a result of a robbery, larceny, or an embezzlement. The damage caused by a theft is that the entire property is lost. A theft is treated as property fully destroyed (all value lost). (7)

**Theft loss** - See *theft.* (7)

**Trade or business expenses** - See *business purpose concept.* (2, 5)

**Trade or business loss** - A general category that pertains to a *transaction loss.* These losses are treated as ordinary losses in the period they are incurred and deducted without limit against income from the trade or business. For an individual, a trade or business loss is deductible as a deduction for AGI. An exception to this rule is for losses on exchanges of business property that must be deferred to a future period. (7)

**Transaction loss** - Results from a single disposition of property. The loss must be categorized by the activity producing the loss to determine its deductibility: trade or business losses, investment-related losses, and personal use losses. In general, transaction losses must have a business purpose to be deductible. See *loss.* (1, 7)

**Transfer pricing** - Methods that set the sales price for goods and services between related entities. Requiring the use of prescribed transfer pricing methods minimizes tax avoidance that may occur because of the related parties' ability to control the timing, amount, and location of the exchange price. (15)

**Transferability of ownership interest** - See *corporation.* (13)

**Travel expenses** - A taxpayer can deduct travel expenses (i.e., transportation, lodging, 50% of the cost of meals, and incidental expenses—telephone calls, laundry, etc.) incurred while pursuing a business purpose. For an expense to qualify as travel, the taxpayer must be away from her or his tax home overnight. A *tax home* is the general area where the taxpayer conducts her or his principal business activity. Overnight is substantially longer than a normal workday and can be less than 24 hours. The taxpayer cannot deduct any of the transportation costs if the purpose of the trip is primarily personal. If more than 50% of the total time is related to personal activities, the primary purpose will be deemed to be personal. (6)

**Treasury regulations** - The Treasury Department's official explanation of a related provision in the Internal Revenue Code. Also called a *final regulation.* (1)

**Trial courts** - Courts of original jurisdiction that are used to initiate litigation. Taxpayers willing to pay the tax in dispute and then sue for a refund have the option of taking their case to a *U.S. District Court* or the *U.S. Court of Federal Claims.* In order to have a jury trial, taxpayers must file in district court. Taxpayers may choose not to pay the additional tax and file a petition in *U.S. Tax Court* for relief. (16)

## U

**U.S. Court of Appeals for the Federal Circuit** - An appellate court that reviews decisions of the U.S. Court of Federal Claims. (16)

**U.S. Court of Federal Claims** - A trial-level court in which the taxpayer typically sues the government for a refund of overpaid tax liability, although it also hears certain nontax claims against the federal government. Its decisions must be appealed to the U.S. Court of Appeals for the Federal Circuit in Washington, D.C. See *trial courts.* (16)

**U.S. Courts of Appeals** - Federal appellate courts that hear appeals from U.S. Tax Court, U.S. District Court, and U.S. Court of Federal Claims. The courts are organized as 12 geographic circuits, each of which hears appeals from taxpayers living within its geographic area. The U.S. Court of Appeals for the Federal Circuit hears all appeals from the U.S. Court of Federal Claims. (16)

**U.S. District Court** - The trial-level federal court that hears cases only from taxpayers who live within the specific geographic area over which the court presides. (16)

**U.S. Supreme Court** - The ultimate appellate court of the United States. The Court limits its review of tax cases to those of major importance or to those in which the decisions of the circuit courts conflict. (16)

**U.S. Tax Court** - Often referred to as the "poor person's court" because taxpayers in dispute with the IRS may choose not to pay additional tax and file a petition for relief in Tax Court, which specializes in tax matters. (16)

**Unearned income** - Unearned income constitutes a return on an investment and does not require any labor by the owner of the investment in order to produce the income. The most common forms of unearned income are interest income, dividend income, income from rental and royalty-producing activities, income from annuities, income from conduit entities, and gains from the sale of investments producing any of the five forms of unearned income. (3)

**Unified donative-transfers credit** - A lifetime credit that taxpayers may use to reduce gift and estate taxes. The credit is equivalent to being able to exclude $11.58 million in property from the estate and gift tax over the lifetime of the taxpayer. (1)

**United States Reports (U.S.)** - The U.S. government's official reporter for decisions of the U.S. Supreme Court. (16)

**Unrecaptured section 1250 gain** - The amount of gain on the sale of a Section 1250 property (not otherwise treated as ordinary income) that would be ordinary income if the property were Section 1245 property. Unrecaptured Section 1250 gains are taxed at a maximum rate of 25%. The amount of unrecaptured Section 1250 gain taxed at 25% cannot exceed the net Section 1231 gain for the year. (11)

## V

**Vacation home** - A taxpayer who owns a vacation home that is used for family vacations and rented to unrelated persons during the remainder of the year is subject to special rules. The use of the vacation home for more than a minimal length of time as rental property and as a personal vacation home (i.e., personal use is more than 14 days) results in the deduction for expenses being limited to the amount of the rental income. Vacation home expenses in excess of current income can be carried forward for use in a later year. (5)

**Vertical equity** - Exists when taxpayers with different situations are taxed differently but fairly in relation to each taxpayer's ability to pay the tax. (1)

## W

**Wash sale** - Occurs when a security is sold at a loss and is replaced within 30 days before or after the sales date with a substantially identical security. A loss from a wash sale is deferred until the taxpayer's interest in the replacement stock is disposed of in a taxable transaction. The wash sale rule applies on a first-in, first-out basis only to the extent the loss stock is replaced. As a result, a loss on shares of stock not replaced is deductible. The wash sale provisions do not apply to dispositions at a gain, to securities that are sold at a loss but not replaced, or to dealers in securities. (7, 9)

**Wherewithal-to-pay concept** - Income is recognized in the period in which the taxpayer has the means to pay the tax on the income. (2)

**Workers' compensation** - Payments from a state workers' compensation fund are excluded from taxation. These payments are made to workers who become unable to work as a result of a work-related injury. (4)

**Working interest in an oil and gas deposit** - An outright ownership interest held by the operator of the property. A working interest has unlimited liability for all debts of the operation and is responsible for the costs of operating the property. A working interest in an oil and gas deposit is always considered an active business for purposes of the passive activity rules. (7)

**Working-condition fringe benefit** - Any item provided to an employee that would have been deductible by the employee as an employee business expense if the employee had paid for the item. This class of fringe benefits includes dues to professional organizations, professional journals, and uniforms. Free parking is specifically included as a working-condition fringe benefit. (4)

**Worthless securities** - When a security becomes worthless, a technical disposition does not take place. However, the tax law gives recognition to the loss of investment suffered by the taxpayer in such situations by allowing a realization of the loss on the last day of the tax year in which the security is determined to be worthless. The loss realized is the basis of the worthless security. Using the last day of the tax year as the date of realization determines the holding period of the security. (11)

# INDEX

Page numbers followed by "t" refer to Tables and Exhibits and those followed by "f" refer to Figures.

## A

## D

## F



## G



## H



## I

## J



## K



## L



## M

## N



## O



## P

## Present Value Tables

**Present Value of a Single Payment**

| Year | 5% | 6% | 7% | 8% | 9% | 10% | 12% |
|---|---|---|---|---|---|---|---|
| 1 | 0.952 | 0.943 | 0.935 | 0.926 | 0.917 | 0.909 | 0.893 |
| 2 | 0.907 | 0.890 | 0.873 | 0.857 | 0.842 | 0.826 | 0.797 |
| 3 | 0.864 | 0.840 | 0.816 | 0.794 | 0.772 | 0.751 | 0.712 |
| 4 | 0.823 | 0.792 | 0.793 | 0.735 | 0.708 | 0.683 | 0.636 |
| 5 | 0.784 | 0.747 | 0.713 | 0.681 | 0.650 | 0.621 | 0.567 |
| 6 | 0.746 | 0.705 | 0.666 | 0.630 | 0.596 | 0.564 | 0.507 |
| 7 | 0.711 | 0.665 | 0.623 | 0.583 | 0.547 | 0.513 | 0.452 |
| 8 | 0.677 | 0.627 | 0.582 | 0.540 | 0.502 | 0.467 | 0.404 |
| 9 | 0.645 | 0.592 | 0.544 | 0.500 | 0.460 | 0.424 | 0.361 |
| 10 | 0.614 | 0.558 | 0.508 | 0.463 | 0.422 | 0.386 | 0.322 |

## Future Value of an Ordinary Annuity of $1 per Period

| Period (n) | 4% | 5% | 6% | 7% | 8% | 9% | 10% |
|---|---|---|---|---|---|---|---|
| 1 | 1.00000 | 1.00000 | 1.00000 | 1.00000 | 1.00000 | 1.00000 | 1.00000 |
| 5 | 5.41632 | 5.52563 | 5.63709 | 5.75074 | 5.86660 | 5.98471 | 6.10510 |
| 10 | 12.00611 | 12.57789 | 13.18079 | 13.81645 | 14.48656 | 15.19293 | 15.93742 |
| 15 | 20.02359 | 21.57856 | 23.27597 | 25.12902 | 27.15211 | 29.36092 | 31.77248 |
| 20 | 29.77808 | 33.06595 | 36.78559 | 40.99549 | 45.76196 | 51.16012 | 57.27500 |
| 25 | 41.64591 | 47.72710 | 54.86451 | 63.24904 | 73.10594 | 84.70090 | 98.34706 |
| 30 | 56.08494 | 66.43885 | 79.05819 | 94.46079 | 113.28321 | 136.30754 | 164.49402 |
| 35 | 73.6522 | 90.32031 | 111.43478 | 138.2368 | 172.31680 | 215.71076 | 271.02437 |
| 40 | 95.02552 | 120.79977 | 154.76197 | 199.6351 | 259.05652 | 337.88245 | 442.59256 |